MANAGEMENT:
THE NEW WORKPLACE

7e

Richard L. Daft
Vanderbilt University

Dorothy Marcic
Vanderbilt University

MANAGEMENT: THE NEW WORKPLACE

7e

Richard L. Daft
Vanderbilt University

Dorothy Marcic
Vanderbilt University

SOUTH-WESTERN
CENGAGE Learning

Australia • Brazil • Japan • Korea • Mexico • Singapore • Spain • United Kingdom • United States

SOUTH-WESTERN
CENGAGE Learning™

Management: The New Workplace
Seventh Edition

Richard L. Daft, Dorothy Marcic

Vice President of Editorial, Business:
Jack W. Calhoun

Editor-in-Chief: Melissa S. Acuña

Executive Editor: Scott Person

Developmental Editor: Erin Guendelsberger

Marketing Manager: Clint Kernen

Sr. Marketing Communications Manager:
Jim Overly

Sr. Editorial Assistant: Ruth Belanger

Content Project Manager: Holly Henjum

Media Editor: Rob Ellington

Sr. Buyer, Manufacturing: Sandee Milewski

Permission Account Manager, Image:
Deanna Ettinger

Permission Account Manager, Text: Margaret
Chamberlain-Gaston

Production Service/Compositor: MPS Limited,
A Macmillan Company

Sr. Art Director: Tippy McIntosh

Cover Designer: Patti Hudepohl

B/W image: iStockphoto

Color Image: Shutterstock images/
Gail Johnson

For product information and technology assistance, contact us at
Cengage Learning Customer & Sales Support, 1-800-354-9706

For permission to use material from this text or product,
submit all requests online at **www.cengage.com/permissions**
Further permissions questions can be emailed to
permissionrequest@cengage.com

Library of Congress Control Number: 2009941731

International Student Edition ISBN 13: 978-0-538-46927-2
International Student Edition ISBN 10: 0-538-46927-7

Cengage Learning International Offices

Asia
cengageasia.com
tel: (65) 6410 1200

Australia/New Zealand
cengage.com.au
tel: (61) 3 9685 4111

Brazil
cengage.com.br
tel: (011) 3665 9900

India
cengage.co.in
tel: (91) 11 30484837/38

Latin America
cengage.com.mx
tel: +52 (55) 1500 6000

UK/Europe/Middle East/Africa
cengage.co.uk
tel: (44) 207 067 2500

Represented in Canada by Nelson Education, Ltd.
nelson.com
tel: (416) 752 9100/(800) 668 0671

For product information: **www.cengage.com/international**
Visit your local office: **www.cengage.com/global**
Visit our corporate website: **www.cengage.com**

Availability of resources may differ by region. Check with your local Cengage Learning representative for details

Printed in China by China Translation & Printing Serivces Limited
1 2 3 4 5 6 7 13 12 11 10

In memory of Danny Seals (1948–2009)
whose songs soothe many a soul.
"Love is the Answer."

Preface

MANAGING FOR INNOVATION IN A CHANGING WORLD

In recent years, organizations have been buffeted by massive and far-reaching social, technological, and economic changes. Any manager who still believed in the myth of stability was rocked out of complacency when, one after another, large financial institutions in the United States began to fail. Business schools, as well as managers and businesses, were scrambling to keep up with the fast-changing story and evaluate its impact. This edition of *Management: The New Workplace* addresses themes and issues that are directly relevant to the current, fast-shifting business environment. We revised *Management: The New Workplace* with a goal of helping current and future managers find innovative solutions to the problems that plague today's organizations—whether they are everyday challenges or once-in-a-lifetime crises. The world in which most students will work as managers is undergoing a tremendous upheaval. Ethical turmoil, the need for crisis management skills, e-business, rapidly changing technologies, globalization, outsourcing, global virtual teams, knowledge management, global supply chains, the Wall Street meltdown, and other changes place demands on managers that go beyond the techniques and ideas traditionally taught in management courses. Managing today requires the full breadth of management skills and capabilities. This text provides comprehensive coverage of both traditional management skills and the new competencies needed in a turbulent environment characterized by economic turmoil, political confusion, and general uncertainty.

In the traditional world of work, management was to control and limit people, enforce rules and regulations, seek stability and efficiency, design a top-down hierarchy, and achieve bottom-line results. To spur innovation and achieve high performance, however, managers need different skills to engage workers' hearts and minds as well as take advantage of their physical labor. The new workplace asks that managers focus on leading change, harnessing people's creativity and enthusiasm, finding shared visions and values, and sharing information and power. Teamwork, collaboration, participation, and learning are guiding principles that help managers and employees maneuver the difficult terrain of today's turbulent business environment. Managers focus on developing, not controlling, people to adapt to new technologies and extraordinary environmental shifts, and thus achieve high performance and total corporate effectiveness.

Our vision for the seventh edition of *Management: The New Workplace* is to present the newest management ideas for turbulent times in a way that is interesting and valuable to students while retaining the best of traditional management thinking. To achieve this vision, we have included the most recent management concepts and research and have shown the contemporary application of management ideas in organizations. A chapter feature for new managers, called the New Manager's Self-Test, gives students a sense of what will be expected when they become managers. The combination of established scholarship, new ideas, and real-life applications gives students a taste of the energy, challenge, and adventure inherent in the dynamic field of management. We have worked with the South-Western/Cengage Learning staff to provide a textbook better than any other at capturing the excitement of organizational management.

Availability of resources may differ by region. Check with your local Cengage Learning representative for details.

We revised *Management: The New Workplace* to provide a book of utmost quality that will create in students both respect for the changing field of management and confidence that they can understand and master it. The textual portion of this book has been enhanced through the engaging, easy-to-understand writing style and the many in-text examples, boxed items, and short exercises that make the concepts come alive for students. The graphic component has been enhanced with several new exhibits and a new set of photo essays that illustrate specific management concepts. The well-chosen photographs provide vivid illustrations and intimate glimpses of management scenes, events, and people. The photos are combined with brief essays that explain how a specific management concept looks and feels. Both the textual and graphic portions of the textbook help students grasp the often abstract and distant world of management.

FOCUS ON INNOVATION: NEW TO THE SEVENTH EDITION

The seventh edition of *Management: The New Workplace* is especially focused on the future of management education by identifying and describing emerging ideas and examples of innovative organizations and by providing enhanced learning opportunities for students.

LEARNING OPPORTUNITIES

The seventh edition has taken a leap forward in pedagogical features to help students understand their own management capabilities and learn what it is like to manage in an organization today. New Manager's Self-Tests in each chapter provide opportunities for students to understand their management abilities. These short feedback questionnaires give students insight into how they would function in the real world of management. End-of-chapter questions have been carefully revised to encourage critical thinking and application of chapter concepts. End-of-text cases and ethical dilemmas help students sharpen their diagnostic skills for management problem solving.

CHAPTER CONTENT

Within each chapter, many topics have been added or expanded to address the current issues managers face. At the same time, chapter text has been tightened and sharpened to provide greater focus on the key topics that count for management today.

Chapter 1 includes a section on making the leap from being an individual contributor in the organization to becoming a new manager and getting work done primarily through others. The chapter introduces the skills and competencies needed to manage organizations effectively, including issues such as managing diversity, coping with globalization, and managing crises. In addition, the chapter discusses today's emphasis within organizations on innovation as a response to a rapidly changing environment. This chapter also covers the historical development of management and organizations and examines new management thinking for turbulent times.

Chapter 2 contains an updated look at current issues related to the environment and corporate culture, including a new section on issues related to the natural environment and managers' response to environmental advocates. The chapter also illustrates how managers shape a high-performance culture as an innovative response to a shifting environment.

Chapter 3 takes a look at the growing power of China and India in today's global business environment and what this means for managers around the world. The chapter discusses the need for *cultural intelligence*, and a new section looks at understanding communication differences as an important aspect of learning to manage internationally or work with people from different cultures. In addition, the complex issues surrounding globalization are discussed, including a consideration of the current globalization backlash. A new section on human resources points out the need for evaluating whether people are suitable for foreign assignments.

Chapter 4 makes the business case for incorporating ethical values in the organization. The chapter includes a new discussion of the *bottom-of-the-pyramid* business concept and how managers are successfully applying this new thinking. The chapter also has an expanded discussion of ethical challenges managers face today, including responses to recent financial scandals. It considers global ethical issues, as well, including a discussion of corruption rankings of various countries.

Chapter 5 provides a more focused discussion of the overall planning process and a new discussion of using strategy maps for aligning goals. This chapter also takes a close look at crisis planning and how to use scenarios. The chapter's section on planning for high performance has been enhanced by a new discussion of intelligence teams and an expanded look at using performance dashboards to help managers plan in a fast-changing environment. This chapter also covers the basics of formulating and implementing strategy. It looks at new trends in strategy, including the dynamic capabilities approach and partnership strategies.

Chapter 6 gives an overview of managerial decision making with an expanded discussion of how conflicting interests among managers can create uncertainty regarding decisions. A new section on why managers often make bad decisions looks at the biases that can cloud judgment, and also included is a new section on innovative group decision making and the dangers of groupthink. This chapter continues to cover recent trends in information technology and e-business. The discussion of information technology has been updated to include the trend toward user-generated content through wikis, blogs, and social networking. The chapter explores how these new technologies are being applied within organizations along with traditional information systems. The chapter also discusses e-commerce strategies, the use of business intelligence software, and knowledge management.

Chapter 7 discusses basic principles of organizing and describes both traditional and contemporary organizational structures in detail. The chapter includes a discussion of organic versus mechanistic structures and when each is more effective. Chapter 7 also provides a description of the virtual network organization form.

Chapter 8 includes a more focused discussion of the critical role of managing change and innovation today. The chapter includes a new discussion of the ambidextrous approach for both creating and using innovations and has expanded material on exploration and creativity, the importance of internal and external cooperation, and the growing trend toward open innovation.

Chapter 9 includes an expanded discussion of the strategic role of HRM in building human capital. The chapter has new sections on coaching and mentoring and the trend toward part-time and contingent employment. New ways of doing background checks on applicants, such as checking their pages on social networks, are discussed, and the chapter also looks at the changing social contract between employers and employees. Chapter 9 has been revised and updated to reflect the most recent thinking on organizational diversity issues. The chapter looks at how diversity is changing the domestic and global workforce and includes a new section on the traditional versus inclusive models for managing diversity. This chapter also contains new coverage of the dividends of diversity; an expanded discussion of prejudice, discrimination, and stereotypes; and a new look at the difference between stereotyping and valuing cultural differences.

Chapter 10 provides an overview of financial and quality control, including Six Sigma, ISO certification, and a new application of the balanced scorecard, which views employee learning and growth as the foundation of high performance. The discussion of hierarchical versus decentralized control has been updated and expanded. The chapter also addresses current concerns about corporate governance.

Chapter 11 continues its solid coverage of the basics of organizational behavior, including personality, values and attitudes, perception, emotional intelligence, learning and problem-solving styles, and stress management. Many exercises and questionnaires throughout this chapter enhance students' understanding of organizational behavior topics and their own personalities and attitudes.

Availability of resources may differ by region. Check with your local Cengage Learning representative for details.

ix

Chapter 12 has been enriched with a discussion of followership. The chapter emphasizes that good leaders and good followers share common characteristics. Good leadership can make a difference, often through subtle, everyday actions. The discussion of power and influence has been expanded to include the sources of power that are available to followers as well as leaders. The discussions of charismatic, transformational, and interactive leadership have all been revised and refocused.

Chapter 13 covers the foundations of motivation and also incorporates recent thinking about motivational tools for today, including an expanded treatment of employee engagement. The chapter looks at new motivational ideas such as the importance of helping employees achieve work-life balance, incorporating fun and learning into the workplace, giving people a chance to fully participate, and helping people find meaning in their work.

Chapter 14 begins with a discussion of how managers facilitate strategic conversations by using communication to direct everyone's attention to the vision, values, and goals of the organization. The chapter explores the foundations of good communication and includes a new section on gender differences in communication, an enriched discussion of dialogue, and a refocused look at the importance of effective written communication in today's technologically connected workplace, including the use of new forms of manager communication such as blogs.

Chapter 15 includes a new section on the dilemma of teams, acknowledging that teams are sometimes ineffective and looking at the reasons for this, including such problems as free riders, lack of trust among team members, and so forth. The chapter then looks at how to make teams effective, including a significantly revised discussion of what makes an effective team leader. The chapter covers the types of teams and includes a new look at effectively using technology in virtual teams. The chapter also includes a section on managing conflict, including the use of negotiation.

In addition to the topics listed above, this text integrates coverage of the Internet and new technology into the various topics covered in each and every chapter.

ORGANIZATION

The chapter sequence in *Management: The New Workplace* is organized around the management functions of planning, organizing, leading, and controlling. These four functions effectively encompass both management research and characteristics of the manager's job.

Part One introduces the world of management, including the nature of management, issues related to today's chaotic environment, the learning organization, historical perspectives on management, and the technology-driven workplace.

Part Two examines the environments of management and organizations. This section includes material on the business environment and corporate culture, the global environment, ethics and social responsibility, and the natural environment.

Part Three presents chapters on planning, including organizational goal setting and planning, strategy formulation and implementation, and the decision-making process.

Part Four focuses on organizing processes. These chapters describe dimensions of structural design, the design alternatives managers can use to achieve strategic objectives, structural designs for promoting innovation and change, the design and use of the human resource function, and the ways managing diverse employees are significant to the organizing function.

Part Five describes the controlling function of management, including basic principles of total quality management and the design of control systems.

Part Six is devoted to leadership. The section begins with a chapter on organizational behavior, providing grounding in understanding people in organizations. This foundation paves the way for subsequent discussion of leadership, motivation of employees, communication, and team management.

Availability of resources may differ by region. Check with your local Cengage Learning representative for details.

xi

INNOVATIVE FEATURES

A major goal of this book is to offer better ways of using the textbook medium to convey management knowledge to the reader. To this end, the book includes several innovative features that draw students in and help them contemplate, absorb, and comprehend management concepts. South-Western has brought together a team of experts to create and coordinate color photographs, video cases, beautiful artwork, and supplemental materials for the best management textbook and package on the market.

Chapter Outline and Learning Outcomes. Each chapter begins with a clear statement of its learning outcomes and an outline of its contents. These devices provide an overview of what is to come and can also be used by students to guide their study and test their understanding and retention of important points.

New Manager's Questions. The text portion of each chapter begins with three questions faced by organization managers. The questions pertain to the topics of the chapter and will heighten students' interest in chapter concepts. In the part of the text relevant to that question, the answer will be given, so that students can compare the "correct" answer to the ones they gave at the beginning of the chapter.

Take Action. At strategic places through the chapter, students are invited to Take Action to apply a particular concept or think about how they would apply it as a practicing manager. This call to action further engages students in the chapter content. Some of the Take Action features also refer students to the associated New Manager's Self-Test, or direct students from the chapter content to relevant end-of-chapter materials, such as a self learning exercise or an ethical dilemma.

New Manager's Self-Test. A New Manager's Self-Test in each chapter of the text provides opportunities for self-assessment as a way for students to experience management issues in a personal way. The change from individual performer to new manager is dramatic, and these self-tests provide insight into what to expect and how students might perform in the world of the new manager.

Concept Connection Photo Essays. A key feature of the book is the use of photographs accompanied by detailed photo essay captions that enhance learning. Each caption highlights and illustrates one or more specific concepts from the text to reinforce student understanding of the concepts. Although the photos are beautiful to look at, they also convey the vividness, immediacy, and concreteness of management events in today's business world.

Contemporary Examples. Every chapter of the text contains several written examples of management incidents. They are placed at strategic points in the chapter and are designed to illustrate the application of concepts to specific companies. These in-text examples—indicated by an icon in the margin—include well-known U.S. and international companies such as Toyota, Facebook, UPS, LG Electronics, Google, Unilever,

Availability of resources may differ by region. Check with your local Cengage Learning representative for details.

Siemens, and eBay, as well as less-well-known companies such as Red 5 Studios, Strida, Genmab AS, and ValueDance, and not-for-profit organizations such as the U.S. Federal Bureau of Investigation (FBI). These examples put students in touch with the real world of organizations so that they can appreciate the value of management concepts.

Spotlight on... Boxes. These features address a specific topic straight from the field of management that is of special interest to students. They may describe a contemporary topic or problem that is relevant to chapter content, or they may contain a diagnostic question-naire or a special example of how managers handle a problem. The boxes heighten student interest in the subject matter and provide an auxiliary view of management issues not typically available in textbooks.

Benchmarking Boxes. Each chapter contains a box that highlights some effective and productive technique or system developed by an outstanding manager or company.

Business Blooper. While most of the book gives students insights into effective management behavior, forgetting common mistakes can be a real loss. Therefore, each chapter describes ineffective decisions or behaviors which have led to disastrous outcomes in companies.

Video Cases. At the end of the text is a video case section that illustrates the concepts presented in the text. The videos enhance class discussion, because students can see the direct application of the management theories they have learned. Companies discussed in the video package include Recycline, Flight 001, and Numi Organic Teas. Each video case explores the issues covered in the video, allowing students to synthesize the material they've just viewed. The video cases culminate with several questions that can be used to launch classroom discussion or as homework.

Exhibits. Several exhibits have been added or revised in the seventh edition to enhance student understanding. Many aspects of management are research based, and some concepts tend to be abstract and theoretical. The many exhibits throughout this book enhance students' awareness and understanding of these concepts. These exhibits consolidate key points, indicate relationships among concepts, and visually illustrate concepts. They also make effective use of color to enhance their imagery and appeal.

Glossaries. Learning the management vocabulary is essential to understanding contemporary management. This process is facilitated in three ways. First, key concepts are bold-faced and completely defined where they first appear in the text. Second, brief definitions are set out in the margin for easy review and follow-up. Third, a glossary summarizing all key terms and definitions appears at the end of the book for handy reference.

Chapter Summary and Discussion Questions. Each chapter closes with a summary of the essential points that students should retain. The discussion questions are a complementary learning tool that will enable students to check their understanding of key issues, to think beyond basic concepts, and to determine areas that require further study. The summary and discussion questions help students discriminate between main and supporting points and provide mechanisms for self-teaching.

End of Chapter Application Opportunities. End-of-chapter exercises called Self Learning, Group Learning, Action Learning, and Ethical Dilemma provide opportunities for content application. Students can take self-tests, providing an opportunity to experience management issues in a personal way. These exercises take the form of questionnaires, scenarios, and activities, and many also provide an opportunity for students to work in teams. The exercises are tied into the chapters through the Take Action feature that refers students to the end-of-chapter exercises at the appropriate point in the chapter content.

Case for Critical Analysis. Also appearing at the end of the text is a collection of cases that are brief but substantive and provide an opportunity for student analysis and class discussion. Some of these cases are about companies whose names students will recognize; others are based on real management events but the identities of companies and managers have been disguised. These cases allow students to sharpen their diagnostic skills for management problem solving.

Availability of resources may differ by region. Check with your local Cengage Learning representative for details.

SUPPLEMENTARY MATERIALS

Instructor's Manual. Designed to provide support for instructors new to the course, as well as innovative materials for experienced professors, the Instructor's Manual includes Chapter Outlines, annotated learning objectives, Lecture Notes, and sample Lecture Outlines. Additionally, the Instructor's Manual includes answers and teaching notes to end-of-chapter materials. This manual was prepared by David A. Foote, Middle Tennessee State University.

Test Bank. Scrutinized for accuracy, the Test Bank includes more than 2,000 true/false, multiple-choice, short-answer, and essay questions. Page references are indicated for every question, as are designations of either factual or application so that instructors can provide a balanced set of questions for student exams. A level of difficulty is also assigned to each question. All questions are tagged based on AACSB guidelines. This test bank was prepared by Amit Shah, Frostburg State University.

ExamView. Available on the Web site, ExamView contains all of the questions in the Test Bank. This program is an easy-to-use test creation software compatible with Microsoft Windows. Instructors can add or edit questions, instructions, and answers, and select questions (randomly or numerically) by previewing them on the screen. Instructors can also create and administer quizzes online, whether over the Internet, a local area network (LAN), or a wide area network (WAN).

PowerPoint Lecture Presentation. Available on the Web site, the PowerPoint Lecture Presentation enables instructors to customize their own multimedia classroom presentation. Containing an average of 27 slides per chapter, the package includes figures and tables from the text, as well as outside materials to supplement chapter concepts. Material is organized by chapter and can be modified or expanded for individual classroom use. PowerPoint slides are also easily printed to create customized Transparency Masters. The PowerPoint slides were prepared by Kimberly Hurns, Washtenaw Community College.

Video Package. The video package for *Management: The New Workplace*, seventh edition, contains two options: On the Job videos and BizFlix videos. *On the Job* videos use real-world companies to illustrate management concepts as outlined in the text. Focusing on both small and large business, the videos give students an inside perspective on the situations and issues that corporations face. *BizFlix* are film clips taken from popular Hollywood movies such as *Failure to Launch, Rendition,* and *Friday Night Lights,* and integrated into the seventh edition of Daft/Marcic. Clips are supported by short cases and discussion questions at the end of the text.

Web Site (www.cengage.com/international). Discover a rich array of online teaching and learning management resources that you won't find anywhere else. Resources include interactive learning tools, links to critical management Web sites, and password-protected teaching resources available for download.

Premium Student Web Site (www.cengage.com/login). Give your students access to additional study aides for your management course. With this optional package, students gain access to the Daft/Marcic premium Web site. There your students will find interactive quizzes, flashcards, PowerPoint slides, learning games, and more to reinforce chapter concepts. Add the seventh edition of *Management: The New Workplace* to your bookshelf at www.cengage.com/login and access the Daft/Marcic Premium Web site to learn more.

Availability of resources may differ by region. Check with your local Cengage Learning representative for details.

ACKNOWLEDGMENTS

RLD. A gratifying experience for me was working with the team of dedicated professionals at South-Western who were committed to the vision of producing the best management text ever. I am grateful to Scott Person, executive editor, whose enthusiasm, creative ideas, assistance, and vision kept this book's spirit alive. Erin Guendelsberger, developmental editor, provided superb project coordination and offered excellent ideas and suggestions to help the team meet a demanding and sometimes arduous schedule. Clint Kernen, marketing manager, provided keen market knowledge and innovative ideas for instructional support. Holly Henjum, senior content project manager, cheerfully and expertly guided me through the production process. Tippy McIntosh contributed her graphic arts skills to create a visually dynamic design. Ruth Belanger, editorial assistant, and Julia Tucker, marketing coordinator, skillfully pitched in to help keep the project on track. In addition, BJ Parker, Copyshop, USA, contributed the Continuing Case.

Here at Vanderbilt I want to extend special appreciation to my assistant, Barbara Haselton. Barbara provided excellent support and assistance on a variety of projects that gave me time to write. I also want to acknowledge an intellectual debt to my colleagues: Bruce Barry, Ray Friedman, Neta Moye, Rich Oliver, David Owens, Ranga Ramanujam, Bart Victor, and Tim Vogus. Thanks also to Deans Jim Bradford and Bill Christie, who have supported my writing projects and maintained a positive scholarly atmosphere in the school. I'd like to pay special tribute to my longtime editorial associate, Pat Lane.

Finally, I want to acknowledge the love and contributions of my wife, Dorothy Marcic. Dorothy has been very supportive during this revision as we share our lives together. I also want to acknowledge the love and support from my five daughters—Danielle, Amy, Roxanne, Solange, and Elizabeth—who make my life special during our precious time together. Thanks also to B. J. and Kaitlyn and Kaci and Matthew for their warmth and smiles that brighten my life, especially during our days together skiing and on the beach.

R.L.D.

DM. There have been numerous people who have given time and support on this project, including my assistants, Allison Greer and Thomas Higgins. Friends and colleagues who gave invaluable support include Georgia Sauer, Jane Faily, Lynn Lobban, Gail Phanuf, Peter Neamann, Victoria Marsick, Bob and Debby Rosenfeld, Nick Ritchie, Karen Streets-Anderson, Kathy Diaz, Andi Seals, Adrienne Corn, Mark and Maxine Rossman, Adrienne Wing-Roush, Rich Oliver, Hillary Chapman, Mehr Mansuri, Annie Deardorff, Michael Heitzler, and Shidan Majidi. How can one do such a project without family love and support? My sister, Janet Mittelsteadt, is a true friend; my cousins Marilyn Nowak (a bright light), Michael Shoemaker (the genealogist who has helped me find my own roots), and Katherine Runde (who is so precious); my Aunt Babe, who is forever a link to the past. There is no way to imagine my life without my three beautiful daughters—Roxanne, Solange, and Elizabeth—who have taught me more than all my degrees combined. And, finally, my husband and partner, Dick Daft, whose collaboration on this book indicates one aspect of our unity and connection.

D.M.

Another group of people who made a major contribution to this textbook are the management experts who provided advice, reviews, answers to questions, and suggestions for changes, insertions, and clarifications. We want to thank each of these colleagues for their valuable feedback and suggestions on the seventh edition:

Larry Aaronson
Community College of Baltimore County

David Alexander
Christian Brothers University

Reginald L Audibert
California State University—Long Beach

Burrell A. Brown
California University of Pennsylvania

Paula Buchanan
Jacksonville State University

Diane Caggiano
Fitchburg State College

Bruce Charnov
Hofstra University

Paul Coakley
The Community College of Baltimore County

Gloria Cockerell
Collin College

Jack Cox
Amberton University

Paul Ewell
Bridgewater College

Mary M. Fanning
College of Notre Dame of Maryland

Merideth Ferguson
Baylor University

Karen Fritz
Bridgewater College

Wayne Gawlik
Joliet Junior College

Yezdi H. Godiwalla
University of Wisconsin—Whitewater

James Halloran
Wesleyan College

Stephen R. Hiatt
Catawba College

Betty Hoge
Bridgewater College

Jody Jones
Oklahoma Christian University

David Kaiser
University of Minnesota

Jerry Kinard
Western Carolina University

Sal Kukalis
California State University—Long Beach

Joyce LeMay
Bethel University

Michael A. Mazzocco
University of Illinois

Wade McCutcheon
East Texas Baptist College

Tom Miller
Concordia University

W J Mitchell
Bladen Community College

John Okpara
Bloomsburg University

Lori A. Peterson
Augsburg College

Michael Provitera
Barry University

Abe Qastin
Lakeland College

David Ransom
Hocking College

Holly Caldwell Ratwani
Bridgewater College

Terry L. Riddle
*Central Virginia
Community College*

Peter Straus
Chico State

Thomas Sy
*California State
University—Long Beach*

Kevin A. Van Dewark
Humphreys College

Donna Waldron
*Manchester Community
College*

Noemy Watchel
Kean University

Peter Wachtel
Kean University

Nancy Zimmerman
*Community College
of Baltimore County,
Catonsville*

We would also like to
continue to acknowledge
those reviewers who have
contributed comments,
suggestions, and feedback
on previous editions:
David C. Adams
Manhattanville College

Erin M. Alexander
*University of Houston–Clear
Lake*

Hal Babson
*Columbus State Community
College*

Reuel Barksdale
*Columbus State Community
College*

Gloria Bemben
*Finger Lakes Community
College*

Pat Bernson
County College of Morris

Art Bethke
*Northeast Louisiana
University*

Thomas Butte
Humboldt State University

Peter Bycio
Xavier University, Ohio

Diane Caggiano
Fitchburg State College

Douglas E. Cathon
St. Augustine's College

Jim Ciminskie
*Bay de Noc Community
College*

Dan Connaughton
University of Florida

Bruce Conwers
Kaskaskia College

Byron L. David
*The City College of
New York*

Richard De Luca
William Paterson University

Robert DeDominic
Montana Tech

Linn Van Dyne
Michigan State University

John C. Edwards
East Carolina University

Mary Ann Edwards
College of Mount St. Joseph

Janice M. Feldbauer
Austin Community College

Daryl Fortin
Upper Iowa University

Michael P. Gagnon
*New Hampshire Community
Technical College*

Richard H. Gayor
Antelope Valley College

Dan Geeding
Xavier University, Ohio

James Genseal
Joliet Junior College

Peter Gibson
Becker College

Carol R. Graham
Western Kentucky University

Gary Greene
Manatee Community College

Ken Harris
Indiana University Southeast

Paul Hayes
*Coastal Carolina Community
College*

Dennis Heaton
*Maharishi University
of Management, Iowa*

Jeffrey D. Hines
Davenport College

Bob Hoerber
Westminster College

Don Schreiber
Baylor University

Kilmon Shin
Ferris State University

Daniel G. Spencer
University of Kansas

Gary Spokes
Pace University

M. Sprencz
David N. Meyers College

Shanths Srinivas
California State Polytechnic University, Pomona

Jeffrey Stauffer
Ventura College

William A. Stower
Seton Hall University

Mary Studer
Southwestern Michigan College

Bruce C. Walker
Northeast Louisiana University

Mark Weber
University of Minnesota

Emilia S. Westney
Texas Tech University

Stan Williamson
Northeast Louisiana University

Alla L. Wilson
University of Wisconsin–Green Bay

Ignatius Yacomb
Loma Linda University

Imad Jim Zbib
Ramapo College of New Jersey

Vic Zimmerman
Pima Community College

James Swenson
Moorhead State University, Minnesota

Irwin Talbot
St. Peter's College

Andrew Timothy
Lourdes College

Frank G. Titlow
St. Petersburg Junior College

John Todd
University of Arkansas

Philip Varca
University of Wyoming

Dennis L. Varin
Southern Oregon University

Gina Vega
Merrimack College

George S. Vozikis
University of Tulsa

Bruce C. Walker
Northeast Louisiana University

Mark Weber
University of Minnesota

Emilia S. Westney
Texas Tech University

Stan Williamson
Northeast Louisiana University

Alla L. Wilson
University of Wisconsin–Green Bay

Ignatius Yacomb
Loma Linda University

Imad Jim Zbib
Ramapo College of New Jersey

Vic Zimmerman
Pima Community College

Richard L. Daft, PhD, is the Brownlee O. Currey, Jr., Professor of Management in the Owen Graduate School of Management at Vanderbilt University. Professor Daft specializes in the study of organization theory and leadership. Dr. Daft is a fellow of the Academy of Management and has served on the editorial boards of *Academy of Management Journal, Administrative Science Quarterly,* and *Journal of Management Education.* He was the associate editor-in-chief of *Organization Science* and served for three years as associate editor of *Administrative Science Quarterly.*

Professor Daft has authored or co-authored 12 books, including *Organization Theory and Design* (South-Western, 2007), *The Leadership Experience* (South-Western, 2008), and *What to Study: Generating and Developing Research Questions* (Sage, 1982). He published *Fusion Leadership: Unlocking the Subtle Forces That Change People and Organizations* (Berrett-Koehler, 2000, with Robert Lengel). He has also authored dozens of scholarly articles, papers, and chapters. His work has been published in *Administrative Science Quarterly, Academy of Management Journal, Academy of Management Review, Strategic Management Journal, Journal of Management, Accounting Organizations and Society, Management Science, MIS Quarterly, California Management Review,* and *Organizational Behavior Teaching Review.* Professor Daft is currently working on a new book, *The Executive and the Elephant.* He also is an active teacher and consultant. He has taught management, leadership, organizational change, organizational theory, and organizational behavior.

Professor Daft served as associate dean, produced for-profit theatrical productions, and helped manage a start-up enterprise. He has been involved in management development and consulting for many companies and government organizations, including the American Banking Association, Bridgestone, Bell Canada, the National Transportation Research Board, Nortel, TVA, Pratt & Whitney, State Farm Insurance, Tenneco, the United States Air Force, the United States Army, J. C. Bradford & Co., Central Parking System, Entergy Sales and Service, Bristol-Myers Squibb, First American National Bank, and the Vanderbilt University Medical Center.

Dorothy Marcic, EdD, MPH, is a former faculty member at Vanderbilt University. Dr. Marcic is also a former Fulbright Scholar at the University of Economics in Prague and the Czech Management Center, where she taught courses and did research in leadership, organizational behavior, and cross-cultural management. She teaches courses at the Monterrey Institute of International Studies and the University of Economics, in Prague, and has taught courses or given presentations at the Helsinki School of Economics, Slovenia Management Center, College of Trade in Bulgaria, City University of Slovakia, Landegg Institute in Switzerland, the Swedish Management Association, Technion University in Israel, and the London School of Economics. Other international work includes projects at the Autonomous University in Guadalajara, Mexico, and a training program for the World Health Organization in Guatemala. She has served on the boards of the Organizational Teaching Society, the Health Administration Section of the American Public Health Association, and the Journal of Applied Business Research.

Dr. Marcic has authored 12 books, including *Organizational Behavior: Experiences and Cases* (South-Western Publishing, 6th edition, 2001), *Management International* (West Publishing, 1984), *Women and Men in Organizations* (George Washington University,

1984), and *Managing with the Wisdom of Love: Uncovering Virtue in People and Organizations* (Jossey-Bass, 1997), which was rated one of the top 10 business books of 1997 by *Management General*. In addition, she has had dozens of articles printed in such publications as *Journal of Management Development, International Quarterly of Community Health Education, Psychological Reports,* and *Executive Development*. She has recently been exploring how to use the arts in the teaching of leadership and has a new book, *RESPECT: Women and Popular Music* (Texere, 2002), which serves as the basis for the musical theater production *Respect: A Musical Journey of Women*.

Professor Marcic has conducted hundreds of seminars on various business topics and consulted for executives at AT&T Bell Labs; the governor and cabinet of North Dakota; the U.S. Air Force; Slovak Management Association; Eurotel; Czech Ministry of Finance; the Cattaraugus Center; USAA Insurance; State Farm Insurance; and the Salt River–Pima Indian Tribe in Arizona.

Brief Contents

Contents

PART 3 Planning   130

PART 4 Organizing   208

PART 6 Leading 344

Chapter 15

Leading Teams 470

MANAGEMENT: THE NEW WORKPLACE

7e

Richard L. Daft
Vanderbilt University

Dorothy Marcic
Vanderbilt University

1 PART ONE

Introduction

The digital revolution is enabling people to consume movies, music, books, and TV shows from their computer screens in the most remote places. Yet the brave new world of digital entertainment, with its anywhere access and unlimited programming options, is as treacherous as it is exciting. Today's wired consumers face a range of digital dangers from computer viruses and spam to identity theft.

Take *Harry Potter and the Half-Blood Prince*, for example. In addition to shattering box office records, the 2009 Warner Brothers film sparked an unexpected wave of cybercrime across the Web. In one widely reported incident, Potter fans searching online to watch the boy wizard's big-screen adventure unknowingly downloaded malicious software (malware) that stole credit card numbers and banking information. The so-called Harry Potter Virus infected thousands of computers worldwide.

But the perils of the digital age are not limited to the world of entertainment. The banking community is plagued by sensational cyberheists, and even the Pentagon's computers have been compromised by acts of cyberterrorism.

With so many dangers lurking in the shadows, managers at digital entertainment companies must demonstrate an ability to anticipate problems before they happen and respond quickly when crises hit.

1 Chapter One

Innovation for Turbulent Times

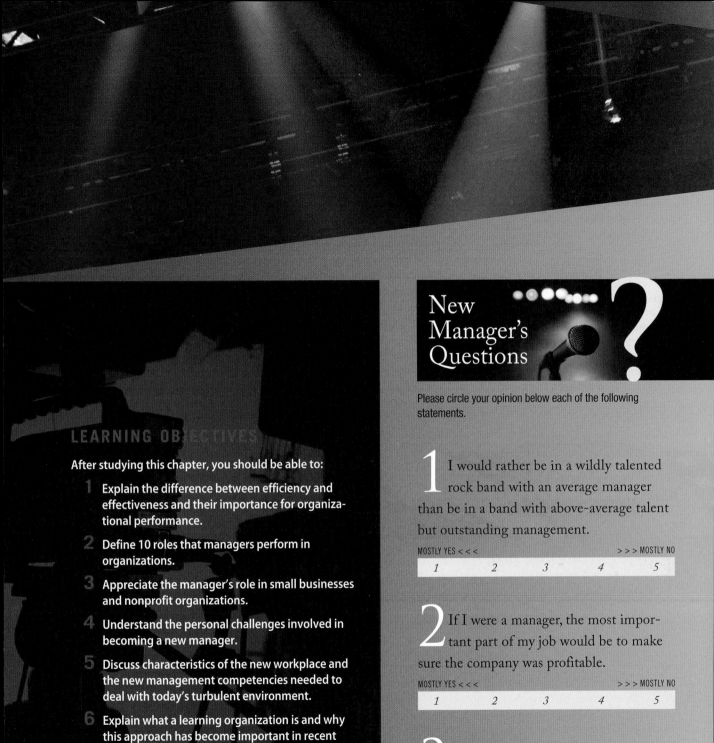

After studying this chapter, you should be able to:

1. Explain the difference between efficiency and effectiveness and their importance for organizational performance.

2. Define 10 roles that managers perform in organizations.

3. Appreciate the manager's role in small businesses and nonprofit organizations.

4. Understand the personal challenges involved in becoming a new manager.

5. Discuss characteristics of the new workplace and the new management competencies needed to deal with today's turbulent environment.

6. Explain what a learning organization is and why this approach has become important in recent years.

7. Understand how historical forces influence the practice of management.

8. Identify and explain major developments in the history of management thought.

9. Describe the major components of the classical and humanistic management perspectives.

10. Explain the concept of total quality management.

New Manager's Questions

Please circle your opinion below each of the following statements.

1 I would rather be in a wildly talented rock band with an average manager than be in a band with above-average talent but outstanding management.

MOSTLY YES < < <　　　　　　　　　　> > > MOSTLY NO

| 1 | 2 | 3 | 4 | 5 |

2 If I were a manager, the most important part of my job would be to make sure the company was profitable.

MOSTLY YES < < <　　　　　　　　　　> > > MOSTLY NO

| 1 | 2 | 3 | 4 | 5 |

3 As a new manager, I would do everything possible to remove all signs of bureaucracy in my organization.

MOSTLY YES < < <　　　　　　　　　　> > > MOSTLY NO

| 1 | 2 | 3 | 4 | 5 |

Many new managers expect to have power, to be in control, and to be personally responsible for departmental outcomes. A big surprise for many people when they first step into a management role is that they are much less in control of things than they expected. Managers are dependent on subordinates more than vice-versa because they are evaluated on the work of other people rather than on their own work. In a world of rapid change, unexpected events, and uncertainty, organizations need managers who can build networks and pull people together toward common goals.

The nature of management is to motivate and coordinate others to cope with diverse and far-reaching challenges. For example, Bruce Moeller, chief executive officer (CEO) of DriveCam, begins his work day by walking around visiting managers in operations, marketing, sales, engineering, finance, and so forth. Those managers, in turn, walk around talking with their direct reports, and on down the line. Moeller believes continual, free-flowing communication keeps everyone "on the same page" and helps employees meet goals at DriveCam, a company that sells and installs video recorders that monitor the behavior of commercial drivers.[1] Western-swing band Asleep at the Wheel is around today because the leader learned to be a good manager, as you'll see in the Benchmarking feature below.

Become a better manager of yourself now: meet deadlines, balance needs of different courses, and manage a positive relationship with your professors.

In the past, many managers did exercise tight control over employees. But the field of management is undergoing a revolution that asks managers to do more with less, to engage whole employees, to see change rather than stability as natural, and to inspire vision

BENCH-MARKING

Asleep at the Wheel

Ray Benson's nine Grammy awards didn't help him keep his band, Asleep at the Wheel, in good financial condition. His creativity and musical abilities weren't enough, he realized. That was the insight and motivation that allowed him to upgrade and transform the band a mere 37 years after it formed.

The Wheel (as it's called by the fans) had its first hit in 1975 with a country song, and it opened for big acts such as Tammy Wynette. Famous people saw the band, *Rolling Stone Magazine* wrote an article, and band members thought the success would continue. So, like other music stars, Benson spent a lot of money not only on himself but also on the band, which grew to 12 members. "I grossed $1 million and was in debt. Something wasn't right." Still, Benson bought a recording studio and got big names such as Willie Nelson to record there. Then disco came and they went. It was dismal.

The bottom came in 2001 when Benson's practice of co-mingling his money with the band's caused big problems when he divorced his wife, who was also the band's business manager. Searching for a new manager led to Peter Schwartz, whose decade-long experience in a Cajun band was almost as important as his Harvard master's of business administration (MBA). "It shocked me that a traditional business education would

address issues important to me in running a band," he noted. That's when he left the band for Harvard.

Schwartz's first tasks were to return Asleep at the Wheel to an ensemble band, its core mission, and to exploit its niche appeal. He now uses "straight MBA stuff" with Benson's creativity. "My job is to guide him in what ideas are going to stick," said Schwartz. "How big is the audience? Is there money in it? In the music business, there really isn't that rigor."

Owning the studio has helped cut production costs and allowed the band to create its own label and finally earn well-deserved royalties, even though sales are less than before. "There are 150,000 people who are passionate enough to spend $100 a year on The Wheel. The Internet allows us to capture that," said Schwartz. Schwartz and Benson teamed up to mount a theatrical version of the band and got sponsors to underwrite grants of $700,000. In 2009, the band released the long-awaited album *Willie and the Wheel* and toured with Willie Nelson with great success. All ticket sales go to the band. Benson's finally making decent money. And it only took 37 years and MBA skills.

SOURCES: Anthony Violanti, "Asleep at the Wheel Will Make Sure You Stay Awake," *Ocala Star-Banner*, Mar. 19, 2009; J. Freedom du Lac, "Back from Ridiculous, Willie Offers a Swing Sublime," *Washington Post*, Feb. 3, 2009, p. C01; Roy Furchgott, "The Band Struts Again, Under an MBA Baton," *New York Times*, May 16, 2007, p. H6.

1 I would rather be in a wildly talented rock band with an average manager than be in a band with above-average talent but outstanding management.

ANSWER: It is better to have a stellar management team, as both U2 and Asleep at the Wheel found out.

and cultural values that allow people to create a truly collaborative and productive workplace. In today's work environment, managers rely less on command and control and more on coordination and communication. This approach differs significantly from a traditional mind-set that emphasizes tight top-down control, employee separation and specialization, and management by impersonal measurement and analysis.

This textbook introduces and explains the process of management and the changing ways of thinking about the world that are critical for managers. By reviewing the actions of some successful and not-so-successful managers, you will learn the fundamentals of management. By the end of this chapter, you will already recognize some of the skills managers use to keep organizations on track, and you will begin to understand how managers can achieve astonishing results through people. By the end of this book, you will understand fundamental management skills for planning, organizing, leading, and controlling a department or entire organization.

Why Innovation Matters

The theme of this text is innovation. To gain or keep a competitive edge, managers have renewed their emphasis on innovation, shifting away from a relentless focus on controlling costs and toward investing in the future. In a survey of nearly 1,000 executives in North America, Europe, South America, and Asia, 86 percent agreed that "innovation is more important than cost reduction for long-term success."[2]

Why does innovation matter? Innovations in products, services, management systems, production processes, corporate values, and other aspects of the organization are what keeps companies growing, changing, and thriving. Without innovation, no company can survive over the long run. The growing clout and expertise of companies in developing countries, particularly China and India, have many Western managers worried. In a hypercompetitive global environment, companies must innovate more—and more quickly—than ever. Throughout this text, we will spotlight various companies that reflect that new innovation is imperative. In addition, Chapter 8 discusses innovation and change in detail. First, let's begin our adventure into the world of management by learning some basics about what it means to be a manager.

The Definition of Management

Every day, managers solve difficult problems, turn organizations around, and achieve astonishing performances. To be successful, every organization needs good managers.

What characteristic do all good managers have in common? They get things done through their organizations. Managers are the *executive function* of the organization, responsible for building and coordinating an entire system rather than performing specific tasks. In other words, rather than doing all the work themselves, good managers create the systems and conditions that enable others to perform those tasks. As a boy, Walmart

© PETER ANDREW BOSCH/THE MIAMI HERALD

A business may develop from a founder's talent, but good management and vision can take it to the next level. Tattoo artists Ami James (left) and Chris Núñez started the business Miami Ink, which is the namesake of the TLC/Discovery reality television program, which finished its fourth and final season in 2008. The partners pitched the concept for the show with a friend and turned their business into the most well-known tattoo design studio in the United States. Planning for life after reality TV, James and Núñez created another Miami tattoo studio, Love Hate Tattoo, because TLC/Discovery owned the rights to the name "Miami Ink" when the series ended.

·········> CONCEPT CONNECTION <··········

As a leader, expect the best from people; you are more likely to get it.

As a new manager, remember that management means getting things done through other people. You can't do it all yourself. As a manager, your job is to create the environment and conditions that engage other people in goal accomplishment.

management
The attainment of organizational goals in an effective and efficient manner through planning, organizing, leading, and controlling organizational resources.

founder Sam Walton made $4,000 a year at his paper route. How? Walton had a natural talent for management, and he created a system whereby he hired and coordinated others to help deliver papers rather than simply delivering what he could on his own.[3]

By creating the right systems and environment, managers ensure that the department or organization will survive and thrive beyond the tenure of any specific supervisor or manager. Consider that Jack Welch was CEO of General Electric (GE) through 20 amazingly successful years, but the leadership transition to Jeff Immelt in 2001 was as smooth as silk, and GE has stayed at or near the top of lists such as *Fortune* magazine's "Most Admired Companies," the *Financial Times* "most respected" survey, and *Barron's* most admired companies. People who have studied GE aren't surprised. The company has thrived for more than a century because managers created the right environment and systems. In the late 1800s, CEO Charles Coffin emphasized that GE's most important product was not lightbulbs or transformers, but *managerial talent*. Managers at GE spend a huge amount of time on human-resources issues—recruiting, training, appraising, mentoring, and developing leadership talent for the future.[4]

Recognizing the role and importance of other people is a key aspect of good management. Early 20th-century management scholar Mary Parker Follett defined management as "the art of getting things done through people."[5]

More recently, noted management theorist Peter Drucker stated that the job of managers is to give direction to their organizations, provide leadership, and decide how to use organizational resources to accomplish goals.[6] Getting things done through people and other resources and providing leadership and direction are what managers do. These activities apply not only to top executives such as Eric Schmidt of Google and Indra Nooyi of PepsiCo but also to the manager of a restaurant in your home town, the leader of an airport security team, a supervisor of an accounting department, and a director of sales and marketing. Thus, our definition of management is as follows:

> **Management** is the attainment of organizational goals in an effective and efficient manner through planning, organizing, leading, and controlling organizational resources.

This definition holds two important ideas: (1) the four functions of planning, organizing, leading, and controlling; and (2) the attainment of organizational goals in an effective and efficient manner. Let's first take a look at the four primary management functions. Later in the chapter, we'll discuss organizational effectiveness and efficiency, as well as the multitude of skills managers use to successfully perform their jobs.

Exhibit 1.1 illustrates the process of how managers use resources to attain organizational goals through the functions of planning, organizing, leading, and controlling. Although some management theorists identify additional management functions such as staffing, communicating, and decision making, those additional functions will be discussed as subsets of the four primary functions in Exhibit 1.1. Chapters of this book are devoted to the multiple activities and skills associated with each function, as well as to the environment, global competitiveness, and ethics, which influence how managers perform these functions.

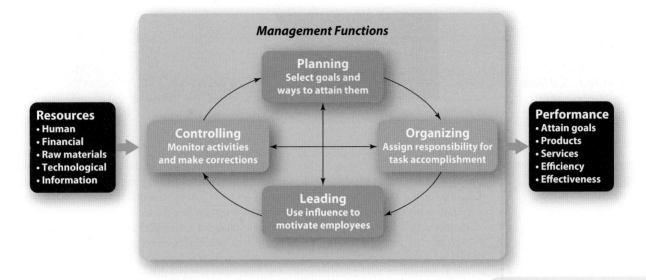

Management Functions

Planning
Select goals and
ways to attain them

Resources
• Human
• Financial
• Raw materials
• Technological
• Information

Controlling
Monitor activities
and make corrections

Organizing
Assign responsibility for
task accomplishment

Leading
Use influence to
motivate employees

Performance
• Attain goals
• Products
• Services
• Efficiency
• Effectiveness

EXHIBIT 1.1
The Process of
Management

Organizational Performance

The other part of our definition of management is the attainment of organizational goals in an efficient and effective manner. Management is so important because organizations are so important. In an industrialized society where complex technologies dominate, organizations bring together knowledge, people, and raw materials to perform tasks no individual could do alone. Without organizations, how could technology be provided that enables us to share information around the world in an instant? How could electricity be produced from huge dams and nuclear power plants? And how could thousands of video games, compact discs, and DVDs be made available for our entertainment? Organizations pervade our society, and managers are responsible for seeing that resources are used wisely to attain organizational goals.

Our formal definition of an **organization** is a social entity that is goal directed and deliberately structured. *Social entity* means being made up of two or more people. *Goal directed* means designed to achieve some outcome such as make a profit (Walmart), win pay increases for members (AFL-CIO), meet spiritual needs (United Methodist Church), or provide social satisfaction (college sorority). *Deliberately structured* means that tasks are divided, and responsibility for their performance is assigned to organization members. This definition applies to all organizations, including both profit and nonprofit. Small, offbeat, and nonprofit organizations are more numerous than large, visible corporations—and just as important to society.

Based on our definition of management, the manager's responsibility is to coordinate resources in an effective and efficient manner to accomplish the organization's goals. Organizational **effectiveness** is the degree to which the organization achieves a *stated goal*, or succeeds in accomplishing what it tries to do. Organizational effectiveness means providing a product or service that customers value. Organizational **efficiency** refers to the amount of resources used to achieve an organizational goal. It is based on how much money and how many raw materials and people are necessary for producing a given volume of output. Efficiency can be calculated as the amount of resources used to produce a product or service.

Efficiency and effectiveness can both be high in the same organization. Managers at retailer Target, for instance, continually look for ways to increase efficiency while also meeting the company's quality and customer satisfaction goals.

*Always remember
how important the
organization or group is
to get things done.*

organization
A social entity that is goal
directed and deliberately
structured.

effectiveness
The degree to which the
organization achieves a
stated goal.

efficiency
The use of minimal
resources—raw materials,
money, and people—to
produce a desired volume of
output.

EXHIBIT 1.2

Relationship of Conceptual, Human, and Technical Skills to Management

- - - - - - - - - - -

Conceptual Skills   Human Skills   Technical Skills

TARGET

Expect more, pay less. An astonishing 97 percent of Americans recognize Target's red-and-white bull's-eye brand, and almost as many are familiar with the slogan. "Sometimes we focus a little bit more on the 'pay less,' sometimes on the 'expect more,' but the guardrails are there," says Gregg Steinhafel, who took over as CEO of the trendy retailer in May 2008.

Target's slogan not only offers a promise to customers but also reflects the company's emphasis on both effectiveness and efficiency. Target has an elite, secret team called the "creative cabinet" that is made up of outsiders of various ages, interests, and nationalities who provide ideas and insights that keep the company on the cutting edge of consumer trends and give their input regarding managers' strategic initiatives. Innovation, design, and quality are key goals, and managers focus on providing a fun store experience and a unique, exciting product line. At the same time, they keep a close eye on costs and operating efficiencies to keep prices low. "I talk a lot about gross margin rate and the key drivers to improve our metrics and performance," Steinhafel says. In its SuperTarget centers, the retailer is able to consistently underprice supermarkets on groceries by about 10 percent to 15 percent, and it comes very close to Walmart's rock-bottom prices.

As the economy slows, Target, like other retailers, has found the need to adjust worker hours and look for other efficiencies, which has drawn unfavorable attention from worker advocacy groups. Managers have to walk a fine line to continue to meet their goals for both efficiency and effectiveness.[7]

All managers have to pay attention to costs, but severe cost cutting to improve efficiency can sometimes hurt organizational effectiveness. The ultimate responsibility of managers is to achieve high **performance**, which is the attainment of organizational goals by using resources in an efficient *and* effective manner.

MANAGEMENT SKILLS

A manager's job is complex and multidimensional and, as we shall see throughout this book, requires a range of skills. Although some management theorists propose a long list of skills, the necessary skills for managing a department or an organization can be summarized in three categories: conceptual, human, and technical.[8] As illustrated in Exhibit 1.2, the application of these skills changes as managers move up in the organization. Although the degree of each skill necessary at different levels of an organization may vary, all managers must possess skills in each of these important areas to perform effectively.

Management Types

Managers use conceptual, human, and technical skills to perform the four management functions of planning, organizing, leading, and controlling in all organizations—large and small, manufacturing and service, profit and nonprofit, traditional and Internet-based. But not all managers' jobs are the same. Managers are responsible for different departments, work at different levels in the hierarchy, and meet different requirements for achieving high performance. Twenty-five-year-old Daniel Wheeler is a first-line manager in his first

performance
The organization's ability to attain its goals by using resources in an efficient and effective manner.

management job at Del Monte Foods, where he is directly involved in promoting products, approving packaging sleeves, and organizing sampling events.[9] Kevin Kurtz is a middle manager at Lucasfilm, where he works with employees to develop marketing campaigns for some of the entertainment company's hottest films.[10] Domenic Antonellis is CEO of the New England Confectionary Co. (Necco), the company that makes those tiny pastel candy hearts stamped with phrases such as "Be Mine" and "Kiss Me."[11] All three are managers and must contribute to planning, organizing, leading, and controlling their organizations—but in different amounts and ways.

WHEN SKILLS FAIL

Everyone has flaws and weaknesses, and these shortcomings become most apparent under conditions of rapid change and uncertainty.[12] Therefore, during turbulent times, managers really have to stay on their toes and apply all their skills and competencies in a way that benefits the organization and its stakeholders—employees, customers, investors, the community, and so forth. In recent years, numerous highly publicized examples showed us what happens when managers fail to effectively and ethically apply their skills to meet the demands of an uncertain, rapidly changing world. Companies such as Enron, Tyco, and WorldCom were flying high in the 1990s but came crashing down under the weight of financial scandals. Others, such as Rubbermaid and Kmart, are struggling because of years of management missteps.

Although corporate greed and deceit grab the headlines, many more companies falter or fail less spectacularly.

Managers fail to listen to customers, misinterpret signals from the marketplace, or can't build a cohesive team and execute a strategic plan. Over the past several years, many CEOs, including Bob Nardelli at Home Depot, Carly Fiorina at Hewlett-Packard, and Michael Eisner at Disney have been ousted due to their failure to implement their strategic plans or to keep stakeholders happy.

Recent examinations of struggling organizations and executives offer a glimpse into the mistakes managers often make in a turbulent environment.[13] One of the biggest blunders is managers' failure to comprehend and adapt to the rapid pace of change in the world around them. A related problem is top managers who create a climate of fear in the organization so that people are afraid to tell the truth and strive primarily to avoid the boss's wrath. Thus, bad news gets hidden and important signals from the marketplace are missed. People stop thinking creatively, avoid responsibility, and may even slide into unethical behavior if it keeps them on the boss's good side.[14]

Other critical management missteps include poor communication and interpersonal skills, failing to listen, treating employees as instruments to be used, failing to clarify direction and performance expectations, suppressing dissenting viewpoints, and being unable to build a management team characterized by mutual trust and respect.[15] Bob Nardelli was forced out at Home Depot largely because he was unable to build trust and cohesiveness among his board and management team, and his brusque and unfeeling style alienated executives and rank and file workers alike. Using expletives for emphasis at one meeting soon after his arrival as CEO, Nardelli reportedly said, "You guys don't know how to run a . . . business." At the annual meeting where shareholder advocates were protesting Nardelli's extravagant pay package, the CEO limited shareholder questions to one minute, sealing his image as a callous executive unwilling to listen and compromise. He tried to redeem himself by going on a "listening tour," but the damage had been done.[16] Contrast Nardelli's approach with that of Jim McNerney, who spent his first six months as CEO of Boeing talking with employees around the company to understand Boeing's strengths and challenges and emphasizing the need for cooperation and teamwork.[17]

Complete the Self Learning on page 36 that pertains to management skills. Reflect on the strength of your preferences among the three skills and the implications for you as a manager.

To be a better manager, learn to listen and treat people with respect.

MAKING THE LEAP: BECOMING A NEW MANAGER

Many people who are promoted into a management position have little idea what the job actually entails and receive little training about how to handle their new role. It's no wonder that, among managers, first-line supervisors tend to experience the most job burnout and attrition.[18]

Organizations often promote the star performers—those who demonstrate individual expertise in their area of responsibility and have an ability to work well with others—both to reward the individual and to build new talent into the managerial ranks. But making the shift from individual contributor to manager is often tricky. Dianne Baker, an expert nurse who was promoted to supervisor of an outpatient cardiac rehabilitation center, quickly found herself overwhelmed by the challenge of supervising former peers, keeping up with paperwork, and understanding financial and operational issues.[19] Baker's experience is duplicated every day as new managers struggle with the transition to their new jobs. Harvard professor Linda Hill followed a group of 19 managers over the first year of their managerial careers and found that one key to success is to recognize that becoming a manager involves more than learning a new set of skills. Rather, becoming a manager means a profound transformation in the way people think of themselves, called *personal identity*, which includes letting go of deeply held attitudes and habits and learning new ways of thinking.[20] Exhibit 1.3 outlines the transformation from individual performer to manager.

Recall our earlier discussion of the role of manager as the executive function of the organization, the person who builds systems rather than doing specific tasks. The individual performer is a specialist and a "doer." His or her mind is conditioned to think in terms of performing specific tasks and activities as expertly as possible. The manager, on the other hand, has to be a generalist and learn to coordinate a broad range of activities. Whereas the individual performer strongly identifies with his or her specific tasks, the manager has to identify with the broader organization and industry.

In addition, the individual performer gets things done mostly through his or her own efforts and develops the habit of relying on himself or herself, rather than on others. The manager, though, gets things done through other people. Indeed, one of the most common mistakes new managers make is wanting to do all the work themselves rather than delegating to others and developing others' abilities.[21] Lisa Drakeman made this mistake when she moved from teaching religion to being CEO of a biotechnology startup.

EXHIBIT 1.3

Making the Leap from Individual Performer to Manager

– – – – – – – – –

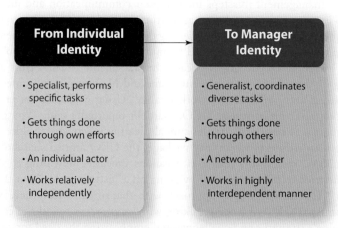

From Individual Identity	**To Manager Identity**
• Specialist, performs specific tasks	• Generalist, coordinates diverse tasks
• Gets things done through own efforts	• Gets things done through others
• An individual actor	• A network builder
• Works relatively independently	• Works in highly interdependent manner

SOURCE: Based on Exhibit 1.1, "Transformation of Identity," in Linda A. Hill, *Becoming a Manager: Mastery of a New Identity*, 2nd ed. (Boston: Harvard Business School Press, 2003): 6. Copyright © 2003 by the Harvard Business School Publishing Corporation; all rights reserved.

Manager Achievement Test

Rate each of the following items based on your orientation toward personal achievement. Read each item and check either Mostly True or Mostly False as you feel right now.

	MOSTLY TRUE	MOSTLY FALSE
1. I enjoy the feeling I get from mastering a new skill.	_____	_____
2. Working alone is typically better than working in a group.	_____	_____
3. I like the feeling I get from winning.	_____	_____
4. I like to develop my skills to a high level.	_____	_____
5. I rarely depend on anyone else to get things done.	_____	_____
6. I am frequently the most valuable contributor to a team.	_____	_____
7. I like competitive situations.	_____	_____
8. To get ahead, it is important to be viewed as a winner.	_____	_____

SCORING AND INTERPRETATION: Give yourself one point for each Mostly True answer. In this case, a *low score* is better. A high score means a focus on personal achievement separate from others, which is ideal for a specialist or individual contributor. However, a manager is a generalist who gets things done through others. A desire to be a winner may put you in competition with your people rather than helping you focus on developing their skills. As a manager, you will not succeed as a lone achiever who does not facilitate and coordinate others. If you checked three or fewer items as Mostly True, then your basic orientation is good. If you scored six or higher, your focus is on being an individual winner. You will want to shift your perspective to become an excellent manager.

LISA DRAKEMAN, GENMAB AS

Lisa Drakeman was teaching religion at Princeton when her husband asked her to help out at Medarex, a new biotechnology company he founded to develop antibody-based medicines for cancer, inflammation, and infectious disease. Drakeman began performing various tasks part-time, but soon found herself heading up a spinoff company, Genmab AS of Denmark.

One of the toughest things Drakeman had to learn was to stop doing everything herself. In the beginning, she attended every meeting, interviewed every job candidate, and read every draft of clinical trial designs. She soon realized that she couldn't master every detail and that trying to do so would stall the company's growth. Although it was hard to step back, Drakeman eventually made the transition from doing individual tasks to performing the executive function. She established clear procedures and began delegating the details of products and clinical trials to others. Rather than interviewing job candidates herself, she set up human-resource systems to enable others to interview, hire, and train employees. By developing from individual performer to manager, Drakeman helped Genmab grow from 25 employees to around 200 within a few years.[22]

Another problem for many new managers is that they expect to have greater freedom to do what they think is best for the organization. In reality, though, managers find themselves hemmed in by interdependencies. Being a successful manager means thinking in terms of building teams and networks, as well as becoming a motivator and organizer within

Try to make a personal transformation from individual performer to manager, accomplishing work by engaging and coordinating other people. Look back at your results on the questionnaire at the beginning of this chapter to see how your priorities align with the demands placed on a manager.

a highly interdependent system of people and work. Although the distinctions may sound simple in the abstract, they are anything but. In essence, becoming a manager means becoming a new person and viewing oneself in a completely new way.

Many new managers have to make the transformation in a "trial by fire," learning on the job as they go, but organizations are beginning to be more responsive to the need for new manager training. The cost to organizations of losing good employees who can't make the transition is greater than the cost of providing training to help new managers cope, learn, and grow. In addition, some of today's organizations are using great care in selecting people for managerial positions, including ensuring that each candidate understands what management involves and really wants to be a manager. A career as a manager can be highly rewarding, but it can also be stressful and frustrating. The Spotlight on Skills further examines some of the challenges new managers face. After reading this feature, can you answer "Yes" to the question "Do I really want to be a manager?"

DO YOU REALLY WANT TO BE A MANAGER?

Is management for you? Becoming a manager is considered by most people to be a positive, forward-looking career move. Indeed, life as a manager offers appealing aspects. However, it also holds many challenges, and not every person will be happy and fulfilled in a management position. Here are some of the issues would-be managers should consider before deciding they want to pursue a management career:

1. **The increased workload.** It isn't unusual for managers to work 70 to 80 hours per week, and some work even longer hours. A manager's job always starts before a shift and ends hours after the shift is over. When Ray Sarnacki was promoted to manager at an aerospace company, he found himself frustrated by the incessant travel, endless paperwork, and crowded meeting schedule. He eventually left the job and found happiness in a position earning about one-fifth of his peak managerial salary.

2. **The challenge of supervising former peers.** This issue can be one of the toughest for new managers. They frequently struggle to find the right approach, with some trying too hard to remain "one of the gang," and others asserting their authority too harshly. In almost all cases, the transition from a peer-to-peer relationship to a manager-to-subordinate one is challenging and stressful.

3. **The headache of responsibility for other people.** A lot of people get into management because they like the idea of having power, but the reality is that many managers feel overwhelmed by the responsibility of hiring, supervising, and disciplining others. New managers are often astonished at the amount of time it takes to handle "people problems." Kelly Cannell, who quit her job as a manager, puts it this way: "What's the big deal [about managing people]? The big deal is that people are human. . . . To be a good manager, you have to mentor them, listen to their problems, counsel them, and at the end of the day you still have your own work on your plate. . . . Don't take the responsibility lightly, because no matter what you think, managing people is not easy."

4. **Being caught in the middle.** Except for those in the top echelons, managers find themselves acting as a backstop, caught between upper management and the workforce. Even when managers disagree with the decisions of top executives, they are responsible for implementing them.[23]

For some people, the frustrations of management aren't worth it. For others, management is a fulfilling and satisfying career choice and the emotional rewards can be great. One key to being happy as a manager may be carefully evaluating whether you can answer yes to the question, "Do I really want to be a manager?"

SPOTLIGHT ON
SKILLS

Are You Ready to Be a Manager?[24]

Welcome to the world of management. Are you ready for it? This questionnaire will help you see whether your priorities align with the demands placed on today's managers. Rate each of the following items based on what you think is the appropriate emphasis for that task to your success as a new manager of a department. Your task is to rate the top four priority items as "High Priority" and the other four as "Low Priority." In other words, for each entry you will have four items rated high and four rated low.

	MOSTLY TRUE	MOSTLY FALSE
1. Spend 50 percent or more of your time in the care and feeding of people.	_____	_____
2. Make sure people understand that you are in control of the department.	_____	_____
3. Use lunches to meet and network with peers in other departments.	_____	_____
4. Implement the changes you believe will improve department performance.	_____	_____
5. Spend as much time as possible talking with and listening to subordinates.	_____	_____
6. Make sure jobs get out on time.	_____	_____
7. Reach out to your boss to discuss his expectations for you and your department.	_____	_____
8. Make sure you set clear expectations and policies for your department.	_____	_____

SCORING AND INTERPRETATION: All eight items in the list may be important, but the odd-numbered items are considered more important than the even-numbered items for long-term success as a manager. If you checked three or four of the odd-numbered items, then consider yourself ready for a management position. A successful new manager discovers that a lot of time has to be spent in the care and feeding of people, including direct reports and colleagues. People who fail in new management jobs often do so because they have poor working relationships or they misjudge management philosophy or cultural values. Developing good relationships in all directions is typically more important than holding on to old work skills or emphasizing control and task outcomes. Successful outcomes typically will occur when relationships are solid. After a year or so in a managerial role, successful people learn that more than half their time is spent networking and building relationships.

MANAGER ACTIVITIES

Most new managers are unprepared for the variety of activities managers routinely perform. One of the most interesting findings about managerial activities is how busy managers are and how hectic the average workday can be.

Adventures in Multitasking. Managerial activity is characterized by variety, fragmentation, and brevity.[25] The widespread and voluminous nature of a manager's involvements leaves little time for quiet reflection. The average time spent on any one activity is less than nine minutes.

Managers shift gears quickly. Significant crises are interspersed with trivial events in no predictable sequence. Every manager's job, while in most cases not as potentially dangerous, is similar in its diversity and fragmentation to that of U.S. Marine Corps officers managing the reconstruction efforts in Iraq. Consider the diverse events in a typical day for Capt. Sean Miller in Fallujah, Iraq:[26]

- Begins the day meeting with tribal sheiks and local officials to decide which projects to finance.

- Drives to a command center to check the status of a job that a contractor has left unfinished.

- Walks to a nearby school to discuss awards for students who recite passages from the Koran.

- Is interrupted by a handful of people who have come with questions or demands: One asks about a relative he says had been detained several years ago, another pushes a contract for review into Miller's hands, a third is seeking work, and so on.

- Finally returns to the discussion of student awards.

- Agrees to a tour of the school, where a contractor explains his request for a $50,000 generator that Miller thinks can be obtained for $8,000.

- Checks the recently cleaned grounds at another school and finds that papers and other trash once again litter the area.

- Notices a man running a pipe from his roof and warns him against running his sewage to the school.

- Calms and directs his marines, who grow skittish as children, some in their upper teens, rush from the school building.

- Stops by a café to hear young men's complaints that they are asked to pay bribes to get a job on the police force.

- Near sunset, takes photos of a still-damaged cemetery door that contractors have been paid to repair.

Notice how much of your day is spent multitasking—talking on your cell phone while instant messaging or completing an assignment while twittering.

Life on Speed Dial. The manager performs a great deal of work at an unrelenting pace.[27] A manager' work is fast paced and requires great energy. The managers observed by Henry Mintzberg processed 36 pieces of mail each day, attended eight meetings, and took a tour through the building or plant. As soon as a manager's daily calendar is set, unexpected disturbances erupt. New meetings are required. During time away from the office, executives catch up on work-related reading, paperwork, phone calls, and e-mail. Technology, such as e-mail, instant messaging, cell phones, and laptops, intensifies the pace. For example, Brett Yormark of the New Jersey Nets typically responds to about 60 messages before he even shaves and dresses for the day.[28]

Students often long to be done with school and enter the "real world" of work. A few years later, they pine for the days when their classes were done at noon and they had time to hang out.

The fast pace of a manager's job is illustrated by Heather Coin, a Cheesecake Factory manager. "I really try to keep the plates spinning," Coin says, comparing her management job to a circus act. "If I see a plate slowing down, I go and give it a spin and move on." She arrives at work about 9:30 A.M. and checks the financials for how the restaurant performed the day before. Next comes a staff meeting and various personnel duties. Before and after the lunch shift, she's pitching in with whatever needs to be done—making salads in the kitchen, expediting the food, busing the tables, or talking with guests. After lunch, from 3 to 4:30 P.M., Heather takes care of administrative duties, paperwork, or meetings with upper management, media, or community organizations. At 4:30, she holds a shift-change meeting to ensure a smooth transition from the day crew to the night crew. Throughout the day, Heather also

Category	Role	Activity
Informational	Monitor	Seek and receive information, scan periodicals and reports, maintain personal contacts.
	Disseminator	Forward information to other organization members; send memos and reports, make phone calls.
	Spokesperson	Transmit information to outsiders through speeches, reports, memos.
Interpersonal	Figurehead	Perform ceremonial and symbolic duties such as greeting visitors, signing legal documents.
	Leader	Direct and motivate subordinates; train, counsel, and communicate with subordinates.
	Liaison	Maintain information links both inside and outside organization; use e-mail, phone calls, meetings.
Decisional	Entrepreneur	Initiate improvement projects; identify new ideas, delegate idea responsibility to others.
	Disturbance handler	Take corrective action during disputes or crises; resolve conflicts among subordinates; adapt to environmental crises.
	Resource allocator	Decide who gets resources; schedule, budget, set priorities.
	Negotiator	Represent department during negotiation of union contracts, sales, purchases, budgets; represent departmental interests.

EXHIBIT 1.4
Ten Manager Roles
‐ ‐ ‐ ‐ ‐ ‐ ‐ ‐ ‐ ‐

SOURCES: Adapted from Henry Mintzberg, *The Nature of Managerial Work* (New York: Harper & Row, 1973): 92–93; and Henry Mintzberg, "Managerial Work: Analysis from Observation," *Management Science* 18 (1971): B97–B110.

mentors staff members, which she considers the most rewarding part of her job. After the evening rush, she usually heads for home about 10 P.M., the end of another 12.5-hour day.[29]

MANAGER ROLES

Mintzberg's observations and subsequent research indicate that diverse manager activities can be organized into 10 roles.[30] Each **role** is a set of expectations for a manager's behavior. Exhibit 1.4 provides examples of each of the roles. These roles are divided into three conceptual categories: informational (managing by information), interpersonal (managing through people), and decisional (managing through action). Each role represents activities that managers undertake to ultimately accomplish the functions of planning, organizing, leading, and controlling.

Although it is necessary to separate the components of the manager's job to understand the different roles and activities of a manager, it is important to remember that the real job of management cannot be practiced as a set of independent parts; all the roles interact in the real world of management. As Mintzberg says, "The manager who only communicates or only conceives never gets anything done, while the manager who only 'does' ends up doing it all alone."[31]

TAKE ACTION

Don't make the mistake of always "doing" as a manager—you also need to plan and think.

role
A set of expectations for one's behavior.

Managing in Small Businesses and Nonprofit Organizations

Small businesses are growing in importance. Hundreds of small businesses are opened every month, but the environment for small businesses today is highly complicated. Small companies sometimes have difficulty developing the managerial dexterity needed to survive in a turbulent environment. One survey on trends and future developments in small businesses found that nearly half of respondents saw inadequate management skills as a threat to their companies, as compared to less than 25 percent of larger organizations.[32] Appendix A provides detailed information about managing in small businesses and entrepreneurial startups.

One interesting finding is that managers in small businesses tend to emphasize roles that are different from those of managers in large corporations. Managers in small companies often see their most important role as that of spokesperson because they must promote the small, growing company to the outside world. The entrepreneur role is also critical in small businesses because managers have to be innovative and help their organizations develop new ideas to remain competitive. Small-business managers tend to rate lower on the leader and information-processing roles compared with their counterparts in large corporations.

Nonprofit organizations also represent a major application of management talent. Organizations such as the Salvation Army, Nature Conservancy, Greater Chicago Food Depository, Girl Scouts, and Cleveland Orchestra all require excellent management. The functions of planning, organizing, leading, and controlling apply to nonprofits just as they do to business organizations, and managers in nonprofit organizations use similar skills and perform similar activities. The primary difference is that managers in businesses direct their activities toward earning money for the company, whereas managers in nonprofits direct their efforts toward generating some kind of social impact. The unique characteristics and needs of nonprofit organizations created by this distinction present unique challenges for managers.[33]

As a nonprofit manager, you must remember to balance the mission with efficient use of resources.

Financial resources for nonprofit organizations typically come from government appropriations, grants, and donations rather than from the sale of products or services to customers. In businesses, managers focus on improving the organization's products and services to increase sales revenues. In nonprofits, however, services are typically provided to nonpaying clients, and a major problem for many organizations is securing a steady stream of funds to continue operating. Nonprofit managers, committed to serving clients with limited resources, must focus on keeping organizational costs as low as possible.[34] Donors generally want their money to go directly to helping clients rather than for overhead costs. If nonprofit managers can't demonstrate a highly efficient use of resources, then they might have a hard time securing additional donations or government appropriations. Although the Sarbanes-Oxley Act (the 2002 corporate governance reform law) doesn't apply to nonprofits, for example, many are adopting its guidelines, striving for greater transparency and accountability to boost credibility with constituents and be more competitive when seeking funding.[35]

In addition, because nonprofit organizations do not have a conventional *bottom line*, managers often struggle with the question of what constitutes results and effectiveness. It is easy to measure dollars and cents, but the metrics of success in nonprofits are much more ambiguous. Managers have to measure intangibles such as "improve public health," "make a difference in the lives of the disenfranchised," or "increase appreciation for the arts." This intangible nature also makes it more difficult to gauge the performance of employees and managers. An added complication is that managers often depend on volunteers and donors who cannot be supervised and controlled in the same way a business manager deals with employees.

The roles defined by Mintzberg also apply to nonprofit managers, but these may differ somewhat. We might expect managers in nonprofit organizations to place more emphasis on the roles of spokesperson (to "sell" the organization to donors and the public), leader (to build a mission-driven community of employees and volunteers), and resource allocator (to distribute government resources or grant funds that are often assigned top down).

Managers in all organizations—large corporations, small businesses, and nonprofit organizations—carefully integrate and adjust the management functions and roles to meet challenges within their own circumstances and keep their organizations healthy.

Management and the New Workplace

Rapid environmental shifts, such as changes in technology, globalization, and shifting social values, are causing fundamental transformations that have a dramatic impact on the manager's job. These transformations are reflected in the transition to a new workplace, as illustrated in Exhibit 1.5.

NEW WORKPLACE CHARACTERISTICS

The primary characteristic of the new workplace is the *digitization* of business, which has radically altered the nature of work, employees, and the workplace itself.[36] The *old workplace* is characterized by routine, specialized tasks, and standardized control procedures. Employees typically perform their jobs in one specific company facility, such as an automobile factory located in Detroit or an insurance agency located in Des Moines. Individuals concentrate on doing their own specific tasks, and managers are cautious about sharing knowledge and information across boundaries. The organization is coordinated and controlled through the vertical hierarchy, with decision-making authority residing with upper-level managers.

In the *new workplace*, by contrast, work is free-flowing and *flexible*. Structures are flatter, and lower-level employees make decisions based on widespread information and are guided by the organization's mission and values.[37] *Empowered employees* are expected to seize opportunities and solve problems as they emerge. Knowledge is widely shared, and people throughout the company keep in touch with a broad range of colleagues via advanced technology. The valued worker is one who learns quickly, shares knowledge, and is comfortable with risk, change, and ambiguity. People expect to work on a variety of projects and jobs throughout their careers rather than staying in one field or with one company.

Consider how fast and far information moves on such platforms as YouTube and Facebook to get an idea of information transfer in the workplace.

	The New Workplace	The Old Workplace
Characteristics		
Technology	Digital	Mechanical
Work	Flexible, virtual	Structured, localized
Workforce	Empowered; diverse	Loyal employees; homogeneous
Management Competencies		
Leadership	Empowering	Autocratic
Doing Work	By teams	By individuals
Relationships	Collaboration	Conflict, competition

EXHIBIT 1.5

The Transition to a New Workplace

The new workplace is organized around *networks* rather than rigid hierarchies, and work is often *virtual*, with managers having to supervise and coordinate people who never actually "come to work" in the traditional sense.[38] Flexible hours, telecommuting, and virtual teams are increasingly popular ways of working that require new skills from managers. Using virtual teams allows organizations to tap the best people for a particular job, no matter where they are located. Teams may include outside contractors, suppliers, customers, competitors, and interim managers. **Interim managers** are managers who are not affiliated with a specific organization but work on a project-by-project basis or provide expertise to organizations in a specific area.[39] This approach enables a company to benefit from a specialist's skills without making a long-term commitment, and it provides flexibility for managers who like the challenge, variety, and learning that comes from working in a wide range of organizations.

Technology also enables companies to shift significant chunks of what were once considered core functions to outsiders via *outsourcing, joint ventures,* and other complex *alliances.* U.S. companies have been sending manufacturing work to other countries for years to cut costs. Now, high-level knowledge work is also being outsourced to countries such as India, Malaysia, and South Africa.[40]

NEW MANAGEMENT COMPETENCIES

In the face of these transitions, managers must rethink their approach to organizing, directing, and motivating employees. Today's best managers give up their command-and-control mind-set to focus on coaching and providing guidance, creating organizations that are fast, flexible, innovative, and relationship oriented.

Instead of "management-by-keeping-tabs," managers employ an *empowering leadership* style.[41] When people are working at scattered locations, managers can't continually monitor behavior. In addition, they are sometimes coordinating the work of people who aren't under their direct control such as those in partner organizations. They have to set clear expectations; guide people toward goal accomplishment through vision, values, and regular communication; and develop a level of trust in employees' commitment to getting the job done.

Success in the new workplace depends on the strength and quality of *collaborative relationships.* New ways of working emphasize collaboration across functions and hierarchical levels as well as with other companies. *Team-building skills* are crucial. Instead of managing a department of employees, many managers act as team leaders of ever-shifting, temporary projects. When a manager at IBM needs to staff a project, he or she gives a list of skills needed to the human-resources department, which provides a pool of people who are qualified. The manager then puts together the best combination of people for the project, which often means pulling people from many different locations. IBM estimates that about 40 percent of its employees participate in virtual teams.[42]

The shift to a new way of managing isn't easy for traditional managers who are accustomed to being "in charge," making all the decisions, and knowing where their subordinates are and what they're doing at every moment. Even many new managers have a hard time with today's flexible work environment. Managers of departments participating

Whenever you make a mistake or something doesn't work out right, get in the habit of asking yourself what could you have done differently to make it better.

Read the "Ethical Dilemma" on page 38 that pertains to managing in the new workplace. Think about what you would do and why to begin understanding how you will solve thorny management problems.

interim manager
A manager who is not affiliated with a specific organization but works on a project-by-project basis or provides expertise to organizations in a specific area.

Assess Your Answer

2 If I were a manager, the most important part of my job would be to make sure the company was profitable.

ANSWER: Today's manager's need to pay attention not only to profits but also to the needs of customers and employees.

in Best Buys' Results-Only Work Environment program, which allows employees to work anywhere, anytime as long as they complete assignments and meet goals, find it difficult to keep themselves from checking to see who's logged onto the company network.[43]

Turbulent Times: Managing Crises and Unexpected Events

Many managers may dream of working in an organization and a world where life seems relatively calm, orderly, and predictable, but their reality is one of increasing turbulence and disorder. Today's managers and organizations face various levels of crisis every day—everything from the loss of computer data, to charges of racial discrimination, to a factory fire, to workplace violence. However, these organizational crises are compounded by crises on a more global level. Consider a few of the major events that affected U.S. companies within the last few years: the global financial meltdown, the ruination of Lehman Brothers, the lawlessness with subprime mortgages, the conning by Bernie Madoff, the scandal of executive bonuses, the collapse of the stock market, the destruction of the space shuttle *Columbia* and the ensuing investigation that revealed serious cultural and management problems at NASA, Hurricane Katrina's devastating impact on every organization in New Orleans and the Gulf Coast and numerous companies that do business with them, the removal of spinach from supermarkets because of *E. coli*, and continuing terrorist threats against the United States and its allies. No wonder so many companies hire experts to manage crises. Even Paris Hilton's family hired a crisis manager after she was arrested and sent to jail.[44] These and other events brought the uncertainty and turbulence of today's world clearly to the forefront of everyone's mind and have made crisis management a critical skill for every manager.

Dealing with the unexpected has always been part of the manager's job, but our world has become so fast, interconnected, and complex that unexpected events happen more frequently and often with greater and more painful consequences. All of the new management skills and competencies we discussed are important to managers in such an environment. In addition, crisis management places further demands on today's managers. Some of the most recent thinking on crisis management suggests the importance of five leadership skills.[45]

1. Stay calm.
2. Be visible.
3. Put people before business.
4. Tell the truth.
5. Know when to get back to business.

STAY CALM

A leader's emotions are contagious, so leaders have to stay calm, focused, and optimistic about the future. Perhaps the most important part of a manager's job in a crisis situation is to absorb people's fears and uncertainties. Although they acknowledge the difficulties, they remain rock steady and hopeful, which gives comfort, inspiration, and hope to others.

BE VISIBLE

When people's worlds become ambiguous and frightening, they need to feel that someone is in control. After Hurricane Katrina hit New Orleans, Scott Cowen, president of Tulane University, stayed on campus until he was sure everyone was evacuated and everything

BUSINESS BLOOPER

Thomas the Tank Engine

When Thomas the Tank Engine was recalled by the company RC2 because of lead paint issues, it wasn't the first recall. The Oakbrook, Illinois company had issued previous recalls on other toys as a result of lead paint. And Thomas was only one of 74 toy recalls in 2007, igniting fear in parents. But RC2 didn't handle the disaster well and hasn't yet managed being in the spotlight. Crisis management experts tell companies to be as truthful as possible right away in the midst of a scandal and to be aggressively forthright in supplying information. RC2 was very quiet in the first week. Executives did not return repeated phone calls from the news media. The worst part was when a reporter went to the manufacturing plant in China and was forcibly detained for nine hours.

SOURCES: Diane C Lade, "Playing with Fire: Toy Safety," *South Florida Sun-Sentinel*, Nov. 26, 2008, p. D1; David Barbaroza and Louise Story, "Train Wreck," *New York Times*, June 19, 2007, C1, C4.

that could possibly be done to control the damage was in place.[46] Crisis is a time when leadership cannot be delegated. When Russian president Vladimir Putin continued his holiday after the sinking of the submarine *Kursk* in August 2000, his reputation diminished worldwide.[47]

Even more changes and challenges are on the horizon for organizations and managers. It's an exciting time to be entering the field of management. Throughout this book, you will learn much more about the new workplace, about the new and dynamic roles managers are playing in the 21st century, and about how you can be an effective manager in a complex, ever-changing world.

THE LEARNING ORGANIZATION

One of the toughest challenges for managers today is to get people focused on adaptive change to meet the demands of an uncertain and rapidly changing environment. Few problems today come with ready-made solutions, and they require that people throughout the company think in new ways and learn new values and attitudes.[48] These needs demand a new approach to management and a new kind of organization.

Facebook represents that new organization and has provided chaotic challenges for its founder and CEO, Mark Zuckerberg, as described in the Spotlight on Skills box.

Managers began thinking about the concept of the learning organization after the publication of Peter Senge's book, *The Fifth Discipline: The Art and Practice of Learning Organizations*.[49] Senge described the kind of changes managers needed to undergo to help their organizations adapt to an increasingly chaotic world. These ideas gradually evolved to describe characteristics of the organization itself. The **learning organization** can be defined as one in which everyone is engaged in identifying and solving problems, which enables the organization to continuously experiment, change, and improve, thus increasing its capacity to grow, learn, and achieve its purpose.

The essential idea is problem solving, in contrast to the traditional organization designed for efficiency. In the learning organization, all employees look for problems such as understanding special customer needs. Employees also solve problems, which means putting things together in unique ways to meet a customer's needs. Today's best managers know that sustained competitive advantage can come only by developing the learning capacity of everyone in the organization.

To foster learning, share information and talk often to people in other units.

learning organization
An organization in which everyone is engaged in identifying and solving problems, enabling the organization to continuously experiment, improve, and increase its capability.

Facebook

Mark Zuckerberg, Facebook's 24-year-old CEO, is possibly the world's youngest billionaire. Not bad for a guy who had legal actions taken against him for defacing a rental house in Palo Alto and recently traded flip-flops and disheveled clothes at business meetings for the more grown-up shirt and tie. As a Harvard student, Zuckerberg was chastised for computer hacking, and then in his linoleum-floored dorm room he got the idea to let fellow students create online personal Web pages or "profiles." After graduation, he and some friends moved to Palo Alto, where he managed to get funding for the site, aimed first at college students only. He would work from late morning to middle of the night and was so socially uncomfortable that people thought he was stiff. But that didn't stop the company's growth, which surged in 2006, after anyone with an e-mail address could join.

Several of Facebook's new initiatives, such as Beacon—which alerted friends when someone made a purchase outside of Facebook—caused huge backlash and accusations of privacy invasion. Zuckerman, who previously announced in a speech that "young people are just smarter," realized he needed some management maturity and hired veterans from Google, YouTube, and AOL Instant Messaging, as well as engaging high-profile mentors from the *Washington Post* and Silicon Valley, whining to one of them, "Is being a CEO always this hard?" Zuckerberg worries that the fast-paced, communicative culture of Facebook will change as it grows—adding 1 million members daily—and seeks advice from his mentors and "elders" at the company. Still, he has held onto the CEO reins longer than most young entrepreneurs, but some think the wunderkind is in over his head trying to figure out profits from Facebook's scale and popularity while avoiding the leveling off that beset MySpace. What's a shy, code-writing guy doing in the executive office? Sure, he's passionate about the company, but so were many people about AOL once upon a time. Zuckerberg has to figure out ways to stay on top.

Despite Zuckerberg's missteps and lack of experience, Facebook continues to grow, garnering sales of about $325 million in 2008, though its expenses are higher. It now has more users than there are people in Brazil. Microsoft recently invested $240 million for a 1.6-percent stake. Will Zuckerberg become the next Bill Gates, or will his venture follow in the footsteps of the once stellar and now-defunct Netscape? Check on the newsfeeds to see.

SOURCES: Brad Stone, "Is Facebook Growing Up Too Fast?" *New York Times,* Mar. 29, 2009, BU1, BU6–7; Jessi Hempel, "How Facebook Is Taking Over Our Lives," *Fortune* (Mar. 2, 2009) 159(4): 48.

MANAGING THE TECHNOLOGY-DRIVEN WORKPLACE

The shift to the learning organization goes hand in hand with the current transition to a technology-driven workplace. Today, many employees perform much of their work on computers and may work in virtual teams, connected electronically to colleagues around the world. Even in factories that produce physical goods, machines have taken over much of the routine and uniform work, freeing workers to use more of their minds and abilities. Moreover, companies are using technology to keep in touch with customers and collaborate with other organizations on an unprecedented scale.

Over the history of management, many fashions and fads have appeared. Critics argue that new techniques may not represent permanent solutions. Other people feel that managers adopt new techniques for continuous improvement in a fast-changing world.

In 1993, Bain and Company started a large research project to interview and survey thousands of corporate executives about the 25 most popular management tools and techniques. The list for 2007 and their usage rates are below. How many tools do you know? For more information on specific tools, visit the Bain Web site: www.bain.com/management_tools/home.asp.

Fashion. Over the last decade, tools such as *activity-based management, one-to-one marketing, scenario planning,* and *virtual teams* have dropped out of the top 25. *Business process reengineering*

CONTEMPORARY MANAGEMENT TOOLS

has been mercurial, with 69 percent usage in 1995, dropping to 38 percent in 2000, before increasing again to 69 percent in 2007.

Global. North American executives are more likely to look outward, using *strategic alliances* and *collaborative innovation* more than companies in other parts of the world. European executives are big users of *customer segmentation*. Latin American executives use the fewest number of tools. Asia-Pacific executives report higher use of newer tools such as *consumer ethnography* and *corporate blogs*.[50]

Source: Darrell Rigby and Barbara Bilodeau, "Bain's Global 2007 Management Tools and Trends Survey, *Strategy & Leadership 35*, no. 5 (2007): 9–16. Copyright 2007 by Emerald Group Publishing Limited. Reproduced with permission of Emerald Group Publishing Limited in the format Textbook via Copyright Clearance Center.

Recent challenges such as a tough economy and rocky stock market, environmental and organizational crises, lingering anxieties over war and terrorism, and the public suspicion and skepticism resulting from corporate scandals have left today's executives searching for any management tool—new or old—that can help them get the most out of limited resources. This search for guidance is reflected in a proliferation of books, scholarly articles, and conferences dedicated to examining management fashions and trends.[51] Exhibit 1.6 illustrates the evolution of significant management perspectives over time, most of which will be examined in the remainder of this chapter. The timeline reflects the dominant time period for each approach, but elements of each are still used in today's organizations.

Classical Perspective

The practice of management can be traced to 3000 B.C. and the first government organizations developed by the Sumerians and Egyptians, but the formal study of management is relatively recent.[52] The early study of management as we know it today began with what is now called the **classical perspective**.

The classical perspective on management emerged during the 19th and early 20th centuries. The factory system that began to appear in the 1800s posed challenges that earlier organizations had not encountered. Problems arose in tooling the plants, organizing managerial structure, training employees (many of them non–English-speaking immigrants), scheduling complex manufacturing operations, and dealing with increased labor dissatisfaction and resulting strikes.

classical perspective
A management perspective that emerged during the nineteenth and early 20th centuries that emphasized a rational, scientific approach to the study of management and sought to make organizations efficient operating machines.

EXHIBIT 1.6
Management Perspectives over Time

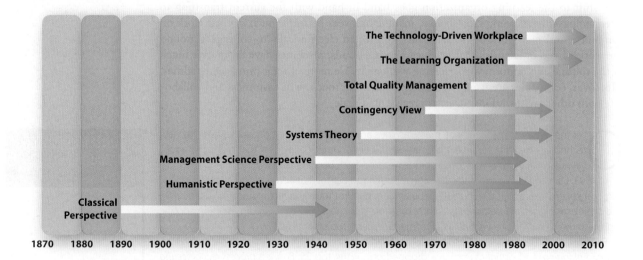

The Technology-Driven Workplace

The Learning Organization

Total Quality Management

Contingency View

Systems Theory

Management Science Perspective

Humanistic Perspective

Classical Perspective

1870   1880   1890   1900   1910   1920   1930   1940   1950   1960   1970   1980   1980   2000   2010

These myriad new problems and the development of large, complex organizations demanded a new approach to coordination and control, and a "new sub-species of economic man—the salaried manager"[53] was born. Between 1880 and 1920, the number of professional managers in the United States grew from 161,000 to more than 1 million.[54] These professional managers began developing and testing solutions to the mounting challenges of organizing, coordinating, and controlling large numbers of people and increasing worker productivity. Thus began the evolution of modern management with the classical perspective.

This perspective contains three subfields, each with a slightly different emphasis: scientific management, bureaucratic organizations, and administrative principles.[55]

SCIENTIFIC MANAGEMENT

Scientific management emphasizes scientifically determined jobs and management practices as the way to improve efficiency and labor productivity. In the late 1800s, a young engineer, Frederick Winslow Taylor (1856–1915), proposed that workers "could be retooled like machines, their physical and mental gears recalibrated for better productivity."[56] Taylor insisted that improving productivity meant that management itself would have to change and, further, that the manner of change could be determined only by scientific study; hence, the label **scientific management** emerged. Taylor suggested that decisions based on rules of thumb and tradition be replaced with precise procedures developed after careful study of individual situations.[57]

Taylor's philosophy is encapsulated in his statement, "In the past the man has been first. In the future, the system must be first."[58] The scientific management approach is illustrated by the unloading of iron from rail cars and reloading finished steel for the Bethlehem Steel plant in 1898.

Taylor calculated that with correct movements, tools, and sequencing, each man was capable of loading 47.5 tons per day instead of the typical 12.5 tons. He also worked out an incentive system that paid each man $1.85 a day for meeting the new standard, an increase from the previous rate of $1.15. Productivity at Bethlehem Steel shot up overnight.

Although he was known as the *father of scientific management*, Taylor was not alone in this area. Henry Gantt, an associate of Taylor's, developed the *Gantt chart*—a bar graph that measures planned and completed work along each stage of production by time elapsed. Two other important pioneers in this area were the husband-and-wife team of Frank B. and Lillian M. Gilbreth. Frank B. Gilbreth (1868–1924) pioneered *time and motion study* and arrived at many of his management techniques independently of Taylor. He stressed efficiency and was known for his quest for the one best way to do work. Although Gilbreth is known for his early work with bricklayers, his work had great impact on medical surgery by drastically reducing the time patients spent on the operating table. Surgeons were able to save countless lives through the application

Lillian M. Gilbreth (1878–1972) and Frank B. Gilbreth (1868–1924). This husband-and-wife team contributed to the principles of scientific management. His development of time and motion studies and her work in industrial psychology pioneered many of today's management and human-resource techniques.

············> **CONCEPT CONNECTION** <··········

scientific management
A subfield of the classical management perspective that emphasized scientifically determined changes in management practices as the solution to improving labor productivity.

Automaker Henry Ford made extensive use of Frederick Taylor's scientific management techniques, as illustrated by this assembly of an automobile at a Ford plant circa 1930. Ford replaced workers with machines for heavy lifting and moving autos from one worker to the next. This reduced worker hours and improved efficiency and productivity. Under this system, a Ford vehicle rolled off the assembly line every 10 seconds.

············> **CONCEPT CONNECTION** <··········

EXHIBIT 1.7

Characteristics
of Scientific
Management

GENERAL APPROACH

- Developed standard method for performing each job.
- Selected workers with appropriate abilities for each job.
- Trained workers in standard method.
- Supported workers by planning their work and eliminating interruptions.
- Provided wage incentives to workers for increased output.

CONTRIBUTIONS

- Demonstrated the importance of compensation for performance.
- Initiated the careful study of tasks and jobs.
- Demonstrated the importance of personnel selection and training.

CRITICISMS

- Did no appreciate the social context of work and higher needs of workers.
- Did not acknowledge variance among individuals.
- Tended to regard workers as uniformed and ignored their ideas and suggestions.

of time and motion study. Lillian M. Gilbreth (1878–1972) was more interested in the human aspect of work. When her husband died at the age of 56, she had 12 children ages 2 to 19. The undaunted "first lady of management" went right on with her work. She presented a paper in place of her late husband, continued their seminars and consulting, lectured, and eventually became a professor at Purdue University.[59] She pioneered in the field of industrial psychology and made substantial contributions to human-resource management.

Exhibit 1.7 shows the basic ideas of scientific management. To use this approach, managers should develop standard methods for doing each job, select workers with the appropriate abilities, train workers in the standard methods, support workers and eliminate interruptions, and provide wage incentives.

The ideas of scientific management that began with Taylor dramatically increased productivity across all industries, and they are still important today. A recent *Harvard Business Review* article discussing innovations that shaped modern management puts scientific management at the top of its list of 12 influential innovations. Indeed, the ideas of creating a system for maximum efficiency and organizing work for maximum productivity are deeply embedded in our organizations.[60]

However, because scientific management ignored the social context and workers' needs, it led to increased conflict and sometimes violent clashes between managers and employees. Under this system, workers often felt exploited—a sharp contrast from the harmony and cooperation that Taylor and his followers had envisioned.

BUREAUCRATIC ORGANIZATIONS

A systematic approach developed in Europe that looked at the organization as a whole is the **bureaucratic organizations** approach, a subfield within the classical perspective. Max Weber (1864–1920), a German theorist, introduced most of the concepts on bureaucratic organizations.[61]

bureaucratic organizations
A subfield of the classical management perspective that emphasized management on an impersonal, rational basis through such elements as clearly defined authority and responsibility, formal record keeping, and separation of management and ownership.

During the late 1800s, many European organizations were managed on a personal, family-like basis. Employees were loyal to a single individual rather than to the organization or its mission. The dysfunctional consequence of this management practice was that resources were used to realize individual desires rather than organizational goals. Employees in effect owned the organization and used resources for their own gain rather than to serve customers. Weber envisioned organizations that would be managed on an impersonal, rational basis. This form of organization was called a *bureaucracy*.

Weber believed that an organization based on rational authority would be more efficient and adaptable to change because continuity is related to formal structure and positions rather than to a particular person, who may leave or die. To Weber, rationality in organizations meant employee selection and advancement based not on whom you know, but rather on competence and technical qualifications, which are assessed by examination or according to training and experience. The organization relies on rules and written records for continuity. In addition, rules and procedures are impersonal and applied uniformly to all employees. A clear division of labor arises from distinct definitions of authority and responsibility, legitimized as official duties. Positions are organized in a hierarchy, with each position under the authority of a higher one. The manager depends not on his or her personality for successfully giving orders but on the legal power invested in the managerial position.

The term *bureaucracy* has taken on a negative meaning in today's organizations and is associated with endless rules and red tape. We have all been frustrated by waiting in long lines or following seemingly silly procedures. However, rules and other bureaucratic procedures provide a standard way of dealing with employees. Everyone gets equal treatment, and everyone knows what the rules are. This foundation enables many organizations to become extremely efficient. Consider United Parcel Service (UPS), sometimes called *Big Brown*.

UNITED PARCEL SERVICE (UPS)

UPS specializes in the delivery of small packages, delivering more than 13 million every business day. In addition, UPS is gaining market share in air service, logistics, and global information services. Why has UPS been so successful? One important factor is the concept of bureaucracy. UPS is bound up in rules and regulations. It teaches drivers an astounding 340 steps for how to correctly deliver a package—such as how to load the truck, how to fasten their seat belts, how to walk, and how to carry their keys. Specific safety rules apply to drivers, loaders, clerks, and managers. Strict dress codes are enforced—clean uniforms (called *browns*) every day, black or brown polished shoes with nonslip soles, no beards, no hair below the collar, and so on. Supervisors conduct three-minute inspections of drivers each day. The company also has rules specifying cleanliness standards for buildings, trucks, and other properties. No eating or drinking is permitted at employee desks. Every manager is given bound copies of policy books and is expected to use them.

UPS has a well-defined division of labor. Each plant consists of specialized drivers, loaders, clerks, washers, sorters, and maintenance personnel. UPS thrives on written records, and the company has been a leader in using new technology to enhance reliability and efficiency. Drivers use a computerized clipboard to track everything from miles per gallon to data on parcel delivery. All drivers have daily worksheets that specify performance goals and work output.

Technical qualification is the criterion for hiring and promotion. The UPS policy book says the leader is expected to have the knowledge and capacity to justify the position of leadership. Favoritism is forbidden. The bureaucratic model works just fine at UPS, "the tightest ship in the shipping business."[62]

3 As a new manager, I would do everything possible to remove all signs of bureaucracy in my organization.

ANSWER: Some aspects of bureaucracy, such as treating everyone fairly and developing rules, can actually be a positive contribution to a company's well-being.

Assess
Your
Answer

ADMINISTRATIVE PRINCIPLES

Another major subfield within the classical perspective is known as the **administrative principles** approach. Whereas scientific management focused on the productivity of the individual worker, the administrative principles approach focused on the total organization. The contributors to this approach included Henri Fayol, Mary Parker Follett, and Chester I. Barnard.

Henri Fayol (1841–1925) was a French mining engineer who worked his way up to become head of a major mining group known as Comambault. Comambault survives today as part of Le Creusot-Loire, the largest mining and metallurgical group in central France. In his later years, Fayol wrote down his concepts on administration, based largely on his own management experiences.[63]

In his most significant work, *General and Industrial Management*, Fayol discussed 14 general principles of management, several of which are part of management philosophy today. For example:

- **Unity of command.** Each subordinate receives orders from one—and only one—superior.

- **Division of work.** Managerial work and technical work are amenable to specialization to produce more and better work with the same amount of effort.

- **Unity of direction.** Similar activities in an organization should be grouped together under one manager.

- **Scalar chain.** A chain of authority extends from the top to the bottom of the organization and should include every employee.

Fayol felt that these principles could be applied in any organizational setting. He also identified five basic functions or elements of management: *planning, organizing, commanding, coordinating,* and *controlling.* These functions underlie much of the general approach to today's management theory.

Mary Parker Follett (1868–1933) was trained in philosophy and political science at what today is Radcliffe College. She applied herself in many fields, including social psychology and management. She wrote of the importance of common superordinate goals for reducing conflict in organizations.[64] Her work was popular with businesspeople of her day but was often overlooked by management scholars.[65] Follett's ideas served as a contrast to scientific management and are reemerging as applicable for modern managers who deal with rapid changes in today's global environment. Her approach to leadership stressed the importance of people rather than engineering techniques. She offered the pithy admonition "Don't hug your blueprints" and analyzed the dynamics of management–organization interactions. Follett addressed issues that are timely today such as ethics, power, and how to lead in a way that encourages employees to give their best. The concepts of *empowerment*, facilitating rather than controlling employees and allowing employees to act depending on the authority of the situation opened new areas for theoretical study by Chester Barnard and others.[66]

Chester I. Barnard (1886–1961) studied economics at Harvard but failed to receive a degree because he lacked a course in laboratory science. He went to work in the statistical department of AT&T and in 1927 became president of New Jersey Bell. One of Barnard's significant contributions was the concept of the informal organization. The *informal organization* occurs in all formal organizations and includes cliques and naturally occurring social groupings. Barnard argued that

administrative principles
A subfield of the classical management perspective that focuses on the total organization rather than the individual worker, delineating the management functions of planning, organizing, commanding, coordinating, and controlling.

FROM NATIONAL ARCHIVES

This 1914 photograph shows the initiation of a new arrival at a Nebraska planting camp. This initiation was not part of the formal rules and illustrates the significance of the informal organization described by Barnard. Social values and behaviors were powerful forces that could help or hurt the planting organization, depending on how they were managed.

·····> CONCEPT CONNECTION <·····

organizations are not machines and stressed that informal relationships are powerful forces that can help the organization if properly managed. Another significant contribution was the *acceptance theory of authority*, which states that people have free will and can choose whether to follow management orders. People typically follow orders because they perceive positive benefit to themselves, but they do have a choice. Managers should treat employees properly because their acceptance of authority may be critical to organization success in important situations.[67]

The overall classical perspective as an approach to management was very powerful and gave companies fundamental new skills for establishing high productivity and effective treatment of employees. Indeed, the United States surged ahead of the world in management techniques, and other countries, especially Japan, borrowed heavily from American ideas.

Humanistic Perspective

Mary Parker Follett and Chester Barnard were early advocates of a more **humanistic perspective** on management that emphasized the importance of understanding human behaviors, needs, and attitudes in the workplace as well as social interactions and group processes.[68] We will discuss three subfields based on the humanistic perspective: the human-relations movement, the human-resources perspective, and the behavioral sciences approach.

HUMAN-RELATIONS MOVEMENT

The **human-relations movement** was based on the idea that truly effective control comes from within the individual worker rather than from strict, authoritarian control.[69] This school of thought recognized and directly responded to social pressures for enlightened treatment of employees. The early work on industrial psychology and personnel selection received little attention because of the prominence of scientific management. Then a series of studies at a Chicago electric company, which came to be known as the **Hawthorne studies**, changed all that.

Beginning about 1895, a struggle developed between manufacturers of gas and electric lighting fixtures for control of the residential and industrial markets.[70] By 1909, electric lighting had begun to win, but the increasingly efficient electric fixtures used less total power. The electric companies began a campaign to convince industrial users that they needed more light to get more productivity. When advertising did not work, the industry began using experimental tests to demonstrate its argument. Managers were skeptical about the results, so the Committee on Industrial Lighting (CIL) was set up to run the tests. To further add to the tests' credibility, Thomas Edison was made honorary chairman of the CIL. In one test location—the Hawthorne plant of the Western Electric Company—some interesting events occurred.

The major part of this work involved four experimental and three control groups. In all, five different tests were conducted. These pointed to the importance of factors *other* than illumination in affecting productivity. To more carefully examine these factors, numerous other experiments were conducted.[71] The results of the most famous study, the first Relay Assembly Test Room (RATR) experiment, were extremely controversial. Under the guidance of two Harvard professors, Elton Mayo and Fritz Roethlisberger, the RATR studies lasted a number of years, starting in 1924, and involved 24 separate experimental periods. So many factors were changed and so many unforeseen factors uncontrolled that scholars disagree on the factors that truly contributed to the general increase in performance over that time period. Most early interpretations, however, agreed on one thing: Money was not

humanistic perspective
A management perspective that emerged in 1930 and emphasized understanding human behavior, needs, and attitudes in the workplace.

human-relations movement
A movement in management thinking and practice that emphasizes satisfaction of employees' basic needs as the key to increased worker productivity.

Hawthorne studies
A series of experiments on worker productivity begun in 1924 at the Hawthorne plant of Western Electric Company in Illinois; attributed employees' increased output to managers' better treatment of them during the study.

the cause of the increased output.[72] It was believed that the factor that best explained increased output was *human relations*. Employees performed better when managers treated them in a positive manner. Recent reanalyses of the experiments have revealed that a number of factors were different for the workers involved, and some suggest that money may well have been the single most important factor.[73] An interview with one of the original participants revealed that just getting into the experimental group had meant a huge increase in income.[74]

These new data clearly show that money mattered a great deal at Hawthorne. In addition, worker productivity increased partly as a result of the increased feelings of importance and group pride employees felt by virtue of being selected for this important project.[75] One unintended contribution of the experiments was a rethinking of field research practices. Researchers and scholars realized that the researcher can influence the outcome of an experiment by being too closely involved with research subjects. This phenomenon has come to be known as the *Hawthorne effect* in research methodology. Subjects behaved differently because of the active participation of researchers in the Hawthorne experiments.[76]

From a historical perspective, whether the studies were academically sound is of less importance than the fact that they stimulated an increased interest in looking at employees as more than extensions of production machinery. The interpretation that employees' output increased when managers treated them in a positive manner started a revolution in worker treatment for improving organizational productivity. Despite flawed methodology or inaccurate conclusions, the findings provided the impetus for the human-relations movement. This approach shaped management theory and practice for far more than a quarter-century, and the belief that human relations is the best approach for increasing productivity persists today.

Before reading on, take the New Manager's Self-Test on page 32. This test will give you feedback about how your personal manager frame of reference relates to human-resource and other perspectives described in this chapter.

HUMAN-RESOURCES PERSPECTIVE

The human-relations movement initially espoused a *dairy farm* view of management—contented cows give more milk, so satisfied workers will give more work. Gradually, views with deeper content began to emerge. The **human-resources perspective** maintained an interest in worker participation and considerate leadership but shifted the emphasis to consider the daily tasks that people perform. The human-resources perspective combines prescriptions for design of job tasks with theories of motivation.[77] In the human-resources view, jobs should be designed so that tasks are not perceived as dehumanizing or demeaning but instead allow workers to use their full potential. Two of the best known contributors to the human-resources perspective were Abraham Maslow and Douglas McGregor.

Abraham Maslow (1908–1970), a practicing psychologist, observed that his patients' problems usually stemmed from an inability to satisfy their needs. Thus, he generalized his work and suggested a hierarchy of needs. Maslow's hierarchy started with physiological needs and progressed to safety, belongingness, esteem, and, finally, self-actualization needs. Chapter 13 discusses his ideas in more detail.

Douglas McGregor (1906–1964) had become frustrated with the early simplistic human-relations notions while president of Antioch College in Ohio. He challenged both the classical perspective and the early human-relations assumptions about human behavior. Based on his experiences as a manager and consultant, his training as a psychologist, and the work of Maslow, McGregor formulated his Theory X and Theory Y, which are explained in Exhibit 1.8.[78] McGregor believed that the classical perspective was based on Theory X assumptions about workers. He also felt that a slightly modified version of Theory X fit early human-relations ideas. In other words, human-relations ideas did not go

human-resources perspective
A management perspective that suggests jobs should be designed to meet higher-level needs by allowing workers to use their full potential.

ASSUMPTIONS OF THEORY X

- The average human being has an inherent dislike of work and will avoid it if possible.
- Because of the human characteristic of dislike for work, most people must be coerced, controlled, directed, or threatened with punishment to get them to put forth adequate effort toward the achievement of organizational objectives.
- The average human being prefers to be directed, wishes to avoid responsibility, has relatively little ambition, and wants security above all.

ASSUMPTIONS OF THEORY Y

- The expenditure of physical and mental effort in work is as natural as play or rest. The average human being does not inherently dislike work.
- External control and the threat of punishment are not the only means for bringing about effort toward organizational objectives. A person will exercise self-direction and self-control in the service of objectives to which he or she is committed.
- The average human being learns, under proper conditions, not only to accept but to seek responsibility.
- The capacity to exercise a relatively high degree of imagination, ingenuity, and creativity in the solution of organizational problems is widely, not narrowly, distributed in the population.
- Under the conditions of modern industrial life, the intellectual potentialities of the average human being are only partially utilized.

EXHIBIT 1.8

Theory X and Theory Y

- - - - - - - - - - -

SOURCE: Douglas McGregor, *The Human Side of Enterprise* (New York: McGraw-Hill, 1960), pp. 33–48.

far enough. McGregor proposed Theory Y as a more realistic view of workers for guiding management thinking.

The point of Theory Y is that organizations can take advantage of the imagination and intellect of all their employees. Employees will exercise self-control and will contribute to organizational goals when given the opportunity. A few companies today still use Theory X management, but many are using Theory Y techniques. Consider how hearing-aid maker Oticon applies Theory Y assumptions to tap into employee creativity and mind power.

OTICON

Oticon, a Danish company that made the world's first digital hearing aid, was once a typical hierarchical organization with a rather stodgy culture. That all changed in the early 1990s when chief executive Lars Kolind turned everything on its head by throwing out the old structures and controls.

Kolind believed workers would be more creative, more productive, and more satisfied if they had fewer controls and limitations. Suddenly, employees were free to work on any project and join any team they chose. There was no hierarchy, no organization charts, no titles, and few rules. Permanent desks were done away with in favor of filing cabinets on wheels that people pushed from project to project. Kolind called it "the spaghetti organization" because the company held together without a fixed structure. Ideas began bubbling up and turning into hot new products, such as a hearing aid that required less adjustment. Productivity increased, and sales and profits soared.

Some of the old structures were reinstated as the company grew larger and after Kolind left the company. For example, everyone now reports to a direct supervisor, and people no longer have complete freedom to choose projects. New top leaders believe some structure is helpful as long as workers aren't constrained and burdened by tight controls. The Theory Y spirit survives at Oticon, helping to keep the company an innovation leader.[79]

NEW MANAGER'S SELF-TEST

Evolution of Style

This questionnaire asks you to describe yourself. For each item, give the number "4" to the phrase that best describes you, "3" to the item that is next best, and on down to "1" for the item that is least like you.

1. My strongest skills are:

_____ a. analytical skills

_____ b. interpersonal skills

_____ c. political skills

_____ d. flair for drama

- -

2. The best way to describe me is:

_____ a. technical expert

_____ b. good listener

_____ c. skilled negotiator

_____ d. inspirational leader

- -

3. What has helped me the most to be successful is my ability to:

_____ a. make good decisions

_____ b. coach and develop people

_____ c. build strong alliances and a power base

_____ d. inspire and excite others

- -

4. What people are most likely to notice about me is my:

_____ a. attention to detail

_____ b. concern for people

_____ c. ability to succeed in the face of conflict and opposition

_____ d. charisma

- -

5. My most important leadership trait is:

_____ a. clear, logical thinking

_____ b. caring and support for others

_____ c. toughness and aggressiveness

_____ d. imagination and creativity

- -

6. I am best described as:

_____ a. an analyst

_____ b. a humanist

_____ c. a politician

_____ d. a visionary

- -

SCORING AND INTERPRETATION: New managers typically view their world through one or more mental frames of reference. (1) The *structural frame* of reference sees the organization as a machine that can be economically efficient and that provides a manager with formal authority to achieve goals. This manager frame became strong during the era of scientific management and bureaucratic administration. (2) The *human-resource frame* sees the organization as people, with manager emphasis given to support, empowerment, and belonging. This manager frame gained importance with the rise of the humanistic perspective. (3) The *political frame* sees the organization as a competition for resources to achieve goals, with manager emphasis on negotiation and hallway coalition building. This frame reflects the need within systems theory to have all parts working together. (4) The *symbolic frame* of reference sees the organization as theater—a place to achieve dreams—with manager emphasis on symbols, vision, culture, and inspiration. This manager frame is important for learning organizations.

Which frame reflects your way of viewing the world? *The first two frames of reference—structural and human resource—are more important for new managers.* These two frames usually are mastered first. As new managers gain experience and move up the organization, they should acquire political skills and also learn to use symbols for communication. It is important for new managers not to be stuck for years in one way of viewing the organization because their progress may be limited. Many new managers evolve through and master each of the four frames as they become more skilled and experienced.

A higher score represents your way of viewing the organization and will influence your management style. Compute your scores as follows:

ST = 1a + 2a + 3a + 4a + 5a + 6a = _____

HR = 1b + 2b + 3b + 4b + 5b + 6b = _____

PL = 1c + 2c + 3c + 4c + 5c + 6c = _____

SY = 1d + 2d + 3d + 4d + 5d + 6d = _____

SOURCE: Roy G. Williams and Terrence E. Deal, *When Opposites Dance: Balancing the Manage and Leader Within* (Palo Alto, CA: Davies-Black, 2003), pp. 24–28. Reprinted with permission.

BEHAVIORAL SCIENCES APPROACH

The **behavioral sciences approach** uses scientific methods and draws from sociology, psychology, anthropology, economics, and other disciplines to develop theories about human behavior and interaction in an organizational setting. This approach can be seen in practically every organization. When IBM conducts research to determine the best set of tests, interviews, and employee profiles to use when selecting new employees, it is using behavioral science techniques. When Best Buy electronics stores train new managers in the techniques of employee motivation, most of the theories and findings are rooted in behavioral science research.

One specific set of management techniques based in the behavioral sciences approach is *organization development* (OD). In the 1970s, organization development evolved as a separate field that applied the behavioral sciences to improve the organization's health and effectiveness through its ability to cope with change, improve internal relationships, and increase problem-solving capabilities.[80] The techniques and concepts of organization development have since been broadened and expanded to address the increasing complexity of organizations and the environment, and OD is still a vital approach for managers. OD will be discussed in detail in Chapter 8. Other concepts that grew out of the behavioral sciences approach include matrix organizations, self-managed teams, ideas about corporate culture, and management by wandering around. Indeed, the behavioral sciences approach has influenced the majority of tools, techniques, and approaches that managers have applied to organizations since the 1970s.

All the remaining chapters of this book contain research findings and management applications that can be attributed to the behavioral sciences approach.

Management Science Perspective

World War II caused many management changes. The massive and complicated problems associated with modern global warfare presented managerial decision makers with the need for more sophisticated tools than ever before. The **management science perspective** emerged to address those problems. This view is distinguished for its application of mathematics, statistics, and other quantitative techniques to management decision making and problem solving.

TOTAL QUALITY MANAGEMENT

The theme of quality is another concept that permeates current management thinking. The quality movement is strongly associated with Japanese companies, but these ideas emerged partly as a result of American influence after World War II. The ideas of W. Edwards Deming, known as the "father of the quality movement," were initially scoffed at in the United States, but the Japanese embraced his theories and modified them to help rebuild their industries into world powers.[81] Japanese companies achieved a significant departure from the American model by gradually shifting from an inspection-oriented approach to quality control toward an approach emphasizing employee involvement in the prevention of quality problems.[82]

During the 1980s and into the 1990s, **total quality management (TQM)**, which focuses on managing the total organization to deliver quality to customers, moved to the forefront in helping U.S. managers deal with global competition. The approach infuses quality values throughout every activity within a company, with frontline workers intimately involved in the process. Four significant elements of quality management are employee involvement, focus on the customer, benchmarking, and continuous improvement.

behavioral sciences approach
A subfield of the humanistic management perspective that applies social science in an organizational context and draws from economics, psychology, sociology, and other disciplines.

management science perspective
A management perspective that emerged during World War II and applied mathematics, statistics, and other quantitative techniques to managerial problems.

total quality management (TQM)
A concept that focuses on managing the total organization to deliver quality to customers. Four significant elements of TQM are employee involvement, focus on the customer, benchmarking, and continuous improvement.

© COURTESY OF HYUNDAI

The inclusion of Hyundai Motor Company's Elantra SE and Santa Fe in the 2008 top 10 autos by *Consumer Reports* shows how commitment to total quality management can improve a company's products and market position. When Hyundai entered the U.S. market in 1999, its autos got low-quality ratings from consumers. First, managers increased the quality team from 100 to 865 people and held quality seminars to train employees. They also benchmarked products, using vehicle lifts and high-intensity spotlights to compare against competing brands. Committing to continuous improvement, Hyundai delayed several new models to resolve problems. Within five years Hyundai earned quality ratings comparable to Honda and just behind Toyota.

> CONCEPT CONNECTION <

Employee involvement means that achieving quality requires companywide participation in quality control. All employees are *focused on the customer*; companies find out what customers want and try to meet their needs and expectations. *Benchmarking* refers to a process whereby companies find out how others do something better than they do and then try to imitate or improve on it. *Continuous improvement* is the implementation of small, incremental improvements in all areas of the organization on an ongoing basis. TQM is not a quick fix, but companies such as General Electric, Texas Instruments, Procter & Gamble, and DuPont achieved astonishing results in efficiency, quality, and customer satisfaction through total quality management.[83] TQM is still an important part of today's organizations, and managers consider benchmarking in particular to be a highly effective and satisfying management technique.[84]

Some of today's companies pursue highly ambitious quality goals to demonstrate their commitment to improving quality. For example, *Six Sigma*, popularized by Motorola and General Electric, specifies a goal of no more than 3.4 defects per million parts. However, the term also refers to a broad quality control approach that emphasizes a disciplined and relentless pursuit of higher quality and lower costs. TQM will be discussed in detail in Chapter 10.

All of the ideas and approaches discussed in the latter part of this chapter go into the mix that makes up modern management. A recent book on management thinking indicates dozens of ideas and techniques in current use that can trace their roots to these historical perspectives.[85] In addition, innovative concepts continue to emerge to address management challenges in today's turbulent world. Organizations experiment with new ways of managing that more adequately respond to the demands of today's environment and customers. Two recent innovations in management include the shift to a learning organization and managing the technology-driven workplace.

Summary

This chapter introduced the topic of management and defined the types of roles and activities managers perform. Managers are responsible for attaining organizational goals in an efficient and effective manner through the four management functions of planning, organizing, leading, and controlling. Managers are the executive function of the organization. Rather than performing specific tasks, they are responsible for creating systems and conditions that enable others to achieve high performance.

To perform the four functions, managers need three types of skills—conceptual, human, and technical. Conceptual skills are more important at top levels of the organization, human skills are important at all levels, and technical skills are most important for first-line managers.

A manager's job varies depending on whether one is a top manager, middle manager, or first-line manager. A manager's job may also differ across the organization to include project managers and interim managers as well as functional managers (including line managers and staff managers) and general managers.

Becoming a manager requires a shift in thinking. New managers often struggle with the challenges of coordinating a broad range of people and activities, delegating to and developing others, and relating to former peers in a new way.

Managers' activities are associated with 10 roles: the informational roles of monitor, disseminator, and spokesperson; the interpersonal roles of figurehead, leader, and liaison; and the decisional roles of entrepreneur, disturbance handler, resource allocator, and negotiator.

Rapid and dramatic change in recent years has caused significant shifts in the workplace and the manager's job. Rather than managing by command and control, managers of today and tomorrow use an empowering leadership style that focuses on vision, values, and communication. Team-building skills are crucial. Instead of just directing tasks, managers focus on building relationships, which may include customers, partners, and suppliers.

An understanding of the evolution of management helps current and future managers appreciate where we are now and continue to progress toward better management. Elements of various historical approaches go into the mix that makes up modern management.

Three major perspectives on management evolved since the late 1800s: the classical perspective, the humanistic perspective, and the management science perspective. Each perspective encompasses several specialized subfields that provided important ideas still relevant in organizations today.

The shift to a learning organization goes hand in hand with the transition to a technology-driven workplace. Important new management approaches include supply-chain management, customer-relationship management, and outsourcing. These approaches require managers to think in new ways about the role of employees, customers, and partners. Today's best managers value employees for their ability to think, build relationships, and share knowledge, which is quite different from the scientific management perspective of a century ago.

Discussion Questions

1. How do you feel about having a manager's responsibility in today's world characterized by uncertainty, ambiguity, and sudden changes or threats from the environment? Describe some skills and qualities that are important to managers under these conditions.

2. Assume you are a project manager at a biotechnology company, working with managers from research, production, and marketing on a major product modification. You notice that every memo you receive from the marketing manager has been copied to senior management. At every company function, she spends time talking to the big shots. You are also aware that sometimes when you and the other project members are slaving away over the project, she is playing golf with senior managers. What is your evaluation of her behavior? As project manager, what do you do?

3. Jeff Immelt of GE said that the most valuable thing he learned in business school was that "there are 24 hours in a day, and you can use all of them." Do you agree or disagree? What are some of the advantages to this approach to being a manager? What are some of the drawbacks?

4. Why do some organizations seem to have a new CEO every year or two, whereas others have top leaders who stay with the company for many years (e.g., Jack Welch's 20 years as CEO at General Electric)? What factors about the manager or about the company might account for this difference?

5. You are a bright, hard-working, entry-level manager who fully intends to rise up through the ranks. Your performance evaluation gives you high marks for your technical skills but low marks when it comes to people skills. Do you think people skills can be learned, or do you need to rethink your career path? If people skills can be learned, how would you go about it?

6. If managerial work is characterized by variety, fragmentation, and brevity, how do managers perform basic management functions such as planning, which would seem to require reflection and analysis?

7. A college professor told her students, "The purpose of a management course is to teach students about management, not to teach them to be managers." Do you agree or disagree with this statement? Discuss.

8. Based on your experience at work or school, describe some ways in which the principles of scientific management and bureaucracy are still used in organizations. Do you believe these characteristics will ever cease to be a part of organizational life? Discuss.

9. Why can an event such as the Hawthorne studies be a major turning point in the history of management even if the idea is later shown to be in error? Discuss.

10. As organizations become more technology driven, which do you think will become more important—the management of the human element of the organization or the management of technology? Discuss.

11. In the Bain survey of management tools, corporate blogs were used in 30 percent of companies and also have the highest projected growth rates among managers. What might explain this? Do you think corporate blogs will ever become as popular as customer-relationship management systems?

Self Learning

Management Aptitude Questionnaire

Rate each of the following questions according to the following scale:

① I am never like this.

② I am rarely like this.

③ I am sometimes like this.

④ I am often like this.

⑤ I am always like this.

1. When I have a number of tasks or homework to do, I set priorities and organize the work around deadlines.
   1 2 3 4 5

2. Most people would describe me as a good listener.
   1 2 3 4 5

3. When I am deciding on a particular course of action for myself (such as hobbies to pursue, languages to study, which job to take, special projects to be involved in), I typically consider the long-term (three years or more) implications of what I would choose to do.
   1 2 3 4 5

4. I prefer technical or quantitative courses rather than those involving literature, psychology, or sociology.
   1 2 3 4 5

5. When I have a serious disagreement with someone, I hang in there and talk it out until it is completely resolved.
   1 2 3 4 5

6. When I have a project or assignment, I really get into the details rather than the "big picture" issues.
   1 2 3 4 5

7. I would rather sit in front of my computer than spend a lot of time with people.
   1 2 3 4 5

8. I try to include others in activities or discussions.
   1 2 3 4 5

9. When I take a course, I relate what I am learning to other courses I took or concepts I learned elsewhere.
   1 2 3 4 5

10. When somebody makes a mistake, I want to correct the person and let her or him know the proper answer or approach.
    1 2 3 4 5

11. I think it is better to be efficient with my time when talking with someone, rather than worry about the other person's needs, so that I can get on with my real work.
    1 2 3 4 5

12. I know my long-term vision of career, family, and other activities and have thought it over carefully.
    1 2 3 4 5

13. When solving problems, I would much rather analyze some data or statistics than meet with a group of people.
    1 2 3 4 5

14. When I am working on a group project and someone doesn't pull a fair share of the load, I am more likely to complain to my friends rather than confront the slacker.
    1 2 3 4 5

15. Talking about ideas or concepts can get me really enthused or excited.
    1 2 3 4 5

16. The type of management course for which this book is used is really a waste of time.
    1 2 3 4 5

17. I think it is better to be polite and not to hurt people's feelings.
    1 2 3 4 5

18. Data or things interest me more than people.
    1 2 3 4 5

Scoring and Interpretation

Subtract your scores for questions 6, 10, 14, and 17 from the number 6 and then add the total points for the following sections:

1, 3, 6, 9, 12, 15   Conceptual skills total score _____

2, 5, 8, 10, 14, 17   Human skills total score _____

4, 7, 11, 13, 16, 18   Technical skills total score _____

These skills are three abilities needed to be a good manager. Ideally, a manager should be strong (though not necessarily equal) in all three. Anyone noticeably weaker in any of the skills should take courses and read to build up that skill. For further background on the three skills, please refer to the explanation in "Management Skills" on page 10.

Group Learning

A. The Absolute Worst Manager

1. By yourself, think of two managers you have had—the best and the worst. Write down a few sentences to describe each.

   The best manager I ever had was . . .

   The worst manager I ever had was . . .

2. Divide into groups of five to seven members. Share your experiences. Each group should choose a couple of examples to share with the whole group. Complete the table below as a group.

	management principles followed or broken	skills evident or missing	lessons to be learned	advice you would give managers
The best managers				
The worst managers				

3. What are the common problems managers have?

4. Prepare a list of "words of wisdom" you would give as a presentation to a group of managers. What are some basic principles they should use to be effective?

SOURCE: This exercise was contributed by Dorothy Marcic. ©2001 Dorothy Marcic. Do not reprint without permission.

Action Learning

1. Make plans to interview two different managers, a younger one and an older one, and preferably in two different professions.

2. Ask them questions such as:
   a. How did you get to your current job? What was your career path?
   b. What did you want to be when you were younger?
   c. What do you find most satisfying about your work? Most frustrating?
   d. What were the biggest surprises after you chose this career?
   e. What were and are the biggest obstacles to you moving ahead in your career?
   f. What is a typical workday?
   g. What advice would you give to college students who want to go into this profession?

3. Write a short paper (two to three pages) that compares the two people you interviewed. What were their similarities? Differences? Did age make a difference? If they were different genders, did that make a difference? What insights did you gain?

4. Your instructor may ask you to form small groups and discuss your findings. Be prepared to share with them the whole class.

Ethical Dilemma

Can Management Afford to Look the Other Way?

Harry Rull had been with Shellington Pharmaceuticals for 30 years. After a tour of duty in the various plants and seven years overseas, Harry was back at headquarters, looking forward to his new role as vice president of U.S. marketing.

Two weeks into his new job, Harry received some unsettling news about one of the managers under his supervision. Over casual lunch conversation, the director of human resources mentioned that Harry should expect a phone call about Roger Jacobs, manager of new product development. Jacobs had a history of being "pretty horrible" to his subordinates, she said, and one disgruntled employee asked to speak to someone in senior management. After lunch, Harry did some follow-up work. Jacobs' performance reviews had been stellar, but his personnel file also contained a large number of notes documenting charges of Jacobs' mistreatment of subordinates. The complaints ranged from "inappropriate and derogatory remarks" to subsequently dropped charges of sexual harassment. What was more disturbing was that the amount as well as the severity of complaints had increased with each of Jacobs' 10 years with Shellington.

When Harry questioned the company president about the issue, he was told, "Yeah, he's had some problems, but you can't just replace someone with an eye for new products.

You're a bottom-line guy; you understand why we let these things slide." Not sure how to handle the situation, Harry met briefly with Jacobs and reminded him to "keep the team's morale up." Just after the meeting, Sally Barton from human resources called to let him know that the problem she'd mentioned over lunch had been worked out. However, she warned, another employee had now come forward demanding that her complaints be addressed by senior management.

What Would You Do?

1. Ignore the problem. Jacobs' contributions to new product development are too valuable to risk losing him, and the problems over the past 10 years have always worked themselves out anyway. No sense starting something that could make you look bad.

2. Launch a full-scale investigation of employee complaints about Jacobs and make him aware that the documented history over the past 10 years has put him on thin ice.

3. Meet with Jacobs and the employee to try to resolve the current issue, then start working with Sally Barton and other senior managers to develop stronger policies regarding sexual harassment and treatment of employees, including clear-cut procedures for handling complaints.

SOURCE: Based on Doug Wallace, "A Talent for Mismanagement: What Would You Do?" *Business Ethics* 2 (Nov.–Dec. 1992): 3–4.

2 PART TWO
The Environment

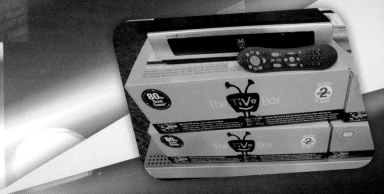

AP Photo/Paul Sakuma; Alex Segre/Alamy; filonmar/istockphoto.com

mazon.com has a reputation for innovation and good corporate citizenship. In little more than a decade, the Seattle-based company has grown from a small Web-based bookseller to a global merchandiser of movies, music, video games, and more. In addition, the company's good rapport with the public has been bolstered by important philanthropic efforts such as its worldwide disaster-relief program and sponsorship of literary organizations.

But a recent momentary lapse of judgment has raised questions about Amazon's ethical and social responsibilities in the age of digital media. In 2009, users of the company's Kindle wireless reading device discovered that Amazon managers snooped through their virtual bookshelves and deleted copies of *1984* and *Animal Farm*—famous George Orwell books depicting bleak worlds dominated by invasive government and bureaucratic control. To pacify an angry public, founder

and chief executive officer (CEO) Jeff Bezos apologized for the company's intrusive erasure of customer downloads, explaining that a third-party publisher had posted the e-books to Amazon's online store without proper authorization.

Despite the mea culpa, the irony of Amazon's Orwellian move was not lost on the general public, and the incident underscored an important management principle: ethical leadership and decision making are critical to maintaining stakeholder trust

2 Chapter Two

The Environment and Corporate Culture

New Manager's Questions

Please circle your opinion below each of the following statements.

1 I think sales companies should be allowed to send out large catalogs because it can increase revenues.

MOSTLY YES < < <   > > > MOSTLY NO

1	2	3	4	5

2 I like my job to have a good deal of stability.

MOSTLY YES < < <   > > > MOSTLY NO

1	2	3	4	5

3 When I get a new job, the managers should accept me for who I am and let me be myself.

MOSTLY YES < < <   > > > MOSTLY NO

1	2	3	4	5

In an organization in a highly uncertain environment, everything seems to be changing. In that case, an important quality for a new manager is *mindfulness,* which includes the qualities of being open-minded and an independent thinker. In a stable environment, a manager with a closed mind may perform okay because much work can be done in the same old way. In an uncertain environment, even a new manager needs to facilitate new thinking, new ideas, and new ways of working. A high score on the preceding items suggests higher mindfulness and a better fit with an uncertain environment.

The environments in which businesses operate are increasingly dynamic, requiring managers to be ready to react and respond to even subtle environmental shifts. Mattel was shaken when it learned that a Chinese subcontractor used lead paint while manufacturing its toys. Because of the potential health hazard, Mattel recalled nearly 850,000 of its most popular toys—months before its holiday selling season. The recall not only frightened consumers but also sparked a global debate about the safety of Chinese-made products. Mattel's managers moved swiftly to reassure nervous parents of the company's high safety standards in its Chinese factories. In addition, CEO Robert Eckert explained the recall to consumers on the company's Web site and announced steps Mattel was taking to prevent further recalls.[1]

Mattel's prompt response, teamed with its long-standing history of successful manufacturing in China, led many independent analysts and watchdog groups to say that it may be the best role model for how to operate prudently in China. "Mattel realized very early that they were always going to be in the crosshairs of sensitivities about child labor and product safety, and they knew they had to play it straight. Mattel was in China before China was cool, and they learned to do business there in a good way," says M. Eric Johnson, a Dartmouth management professor.[2]

As a manager, read and follow news to keep up on coming changes.

Environmental surprises, like the one Mattel faced in China, leave some managers unable to adapt their companies to new competition, shifting consumer interests, or new technologies. The study of management traditionally focused on factors within the organization—a closed-systems view—such as leading, motivating, and controlling employees. The classical, behavioral, and management science schools described in Chapter 1 looked at internal aspects of organizations over which managers have direct control. These views are accurate but incomplete. To be effective, managers must monitor and respond to the environment—an open-systems view. The events that have the greatest impact on an organization typically originate in the external environment. In addition, globalization and worldwide societal turbulence affect companies in new ways, making the international environment of growing concern to managers everywhere.

This chapter explores in detail components of the external environment and how they affect the organization. The chapter also examines a major part of the organization's internal environment—corporate culture. Corporate culture is shaped by the external environment and is an important part of the context within which managers do their jobs. One impact of the environment is that as parents become more educated, they have higher demands for educational toys, a situation one company is exploiting, as noted in this chapter's Benchmarking box.

The External Environment

organizational environment
All elements existing outside the organization's boundaries that have the potential to affect the organization.

general environment
The layer of the external environment that affects the organization indirectly.

The tremendous and far-reaching changes occurring in today's world can be understood by defining and examining components of the external environment. The external **organizational environment** includes all elements existing outside the boundary of the organization that have the potential to affect the organization.[3] The environment includes competitors, resources, technology, and economic conditions that influence the organization. It does not include those events so far removed from the organization that their impact is not perceived.

The organization's external environment can be further conceptualized as having two layers: general and task environments, as illustrated in Exhibit 2.1.[4] The **general environment**

BENCH-MARKING

LeapFrog

Talk about asking for trouble. The U.S. toy industry is dominated by giants: Mattel, Hasbro, Fisher Price, and Little Tykes, among others. With so many failed startups in recent years (anyone remember Purple Moon?), it would be foolish for a new company to introduce a toy that would compete with the big guys, wouldn't it? Not to mention that educational toys don't usually make money. Luckily, Mike Wood and Jim Marggraff at LeapFrog didn't know that. When high-paid law partner Wood got frustrated looking for materials to teach his 3 year-old to read, he started building an electronic toy that would help children make sounds that corresponded to letters of the alphabet. Clumsy prototype in hand, he got an order for 40,000 units from Toys "R" Us. That was enough for him to bid the law firm goodbye, raise $800,000 from friends and family, and start his own company, LeapFrog. After a series of follow-up toys, Wood took $40 million for a majority stake in his company to Knowledge Universe, owned by Michael Milken (former junk-bond king of the 1980s) and others.

That's when Jim Marggraff entered the picture. He had left a lucrative job at Cisco Systems to launch his innovative globe, which had an interactive pen-like pointer. When Marggraff's pointer was paired with Wood's unit, Leap-Pad was born—a paper book placed on top of a pad that looks like an Etch A Sketch. When a kid touches pen to paper, the book "talks" the word selected.

Still there were all those big toy companies to worry about. Few companies lived to tell about it. In a market dominated by GameBoy, Pokemon, and now Wii, the odds were against LeapFrog. Still, its $49.99 LeapPad became the best-selling plaything in 2000, outdoing even the red-hot Razor scooter. Good things just kept happening. Revenues have been strong—more than $350 million—despite the weak economy. With Walmart and Toys "R" Us its biggest customers, LeapFrog is trying to increase sales to schools and they're already in 100,000 classrooms, not to mention in six languages and 35 countries.

LeapFrog's newest product—Leapster2—is a learning game for preschoolers and is selling above expectations. Another newbie, Tag Reading System, won Educational Toy of the Year. Several years ago, LeapFrog introduced a talking-pen computer that has character-recognition software. The $99 Fly allows teens and tweens to draw a piano and then play it by tapping their fingers on the screen, or to translate words from English to Spanish. Its design includes elements of a calculator, notepad, and alarm clock. With this new product, LeapFrog is growing with its customers, allowing them to keep buying their products as they get older. Now they can Fly.

SOURCES: "LeapFrog Reaffirms 2009 Outlook," *PR Newswire*, Mar. 26, 2009, p. 1; Jim Milliott, "LeapFrog IPO Looks to Raise $150 Million," *Publisher's Weekly*, May 6, 2002, 13; and Edward C. Baig, "Will Pen Be Mightier than Other Toys?" *USA Today*, Jan. 18, 2005, p. B3.

is the outer layer that is widely dispersed and affects organizations indirectly. It includes social, economic, legal–political, international, natural, and technological factors that influence all organizations about equally. Increases in the inflation rate or the percentage of dual-career couples in the workforce are part of the organization's general environment. These events do not directly change day-to-day operations, but they do affect all organizations eventually. The **task environment** is closer to the organization and includes the sectors that conduct day-to-day transactions with the organization and directly influence its basic operations and performance. It is generally considered to include competitors, suppliers, customers, and the labor market.

The organization also has an **internal environment**, which includes the elements within the organization's boundaries. The internal environment is composed of current employees, management, and especially corporate culture, which defines employee behavior in the internal environment and how well the organization will adapt to the external environment.

Exhibit 2.1 illustrates the relationship among the general, task, and internal environments. As an open system, the organization draws resources from the external environment and releases goods and services back to it. We will now discuss the two layers of the external environment in more detail. Then we will discuss corporate culture, the key element in the internal environment. Other aspects of the internal environment, such as structure and technology, will be covered in later chapters of this book.

task environment
The layer of the external environment that directly influences the organization's operations and performance.

internal environment
The environment that includes the elements within the organization's boundaries.

EXHIBIT 2.1

Location of the Organization's General, Task, and Internal Environments

As preparation for a career as a manager, when you will probably have to deal with employees and customers from different cultures, seek out foreign students and spend time with them and learn to get along with people who are different from you.

General Environment

Technological

Natural

International

Task Environment

Customers

Internal Environment

Employees   Culture

Labor Market

Competitors

Management

Suppliers

Legal/Political

Sociocultural

Economics

GENERAL ENVIRONMENT

The general environment represents the outer layer of the environment. These dimensions influence the organization over time but often are not involved in day-to-day transactions with it. The dimensions of the general environment include international, technological, sociocultural, economic, legal–political, and natural.

International. The **international dimension** of the external environment represents events originating in foreign countries as well as opportunities for U.S. companies in other countries. Note in Exhibit 2.1 that the international dimension represents a context that influences all other aspects of the external environment. The international environment provides new competitors, customers, and suppliers and shapes social, technological, and economic trends as well.

Today, every company has to compete on a global basis. High-quality, low-priced automobiles from Japan and Korea have permanently changed the American automobile industry. In cell phones and handhelds, U.S.-based companies face stiff competition from Korea's Samsung, Finland's Nokia, and Taiwan's High Tech Computer Corporation. For many U.S. companies, such as Google, domestic markets have become saturated, and the only potential for growth lies overseas. Google's mission is to reach even the most far-flung corners of the globe by providing search results in more than 35 languages and a translation feature for users regardless of their native tongue.[5]

The most dramatic change in the international environment in recent years is the shift of economic power to China and India. Together, these countries have the population, brain-power, and dynamism to transform the global economy of the 21st century. If things continue on the current track, some analysts predict that India will overtake Germany as the

international dimension
Portion of the external environment that represents events originating in foreign countries as well as opportunities for U.S. companies in other countries.

technological dimension
The dimension of the general environment that includes scientific and technological advancements in the industry and society at large.

world's third-largest economy within three decades, and China will overtake the United States as number one by midcentury. In China, per capita income has tripled in a generation, and leaders are building the infrastructure for decades of expansion, as reflected in the country's hunger for raw materials. In 2005, China represented roughly 47 percent of the global cement consumption, 30 percent of coal, and 26 percent of crude steel. No one can predict the future with complete accuracy, but it is clear that however things in India and China shake out, U.S. and other Western firms have no choice but to pay attention.

The global environment represents a complex, ever-changing, and uneven playing field compared with the domestic environment. Managers who are used to thinking only about the domestic environment must learn new rules to remain competitive. When operating globally, managers have to consider legal, political, sociocultural, and economic factors not only in their home countries but also in other countries. Global managers working in China, for example, recognize that their competitive success begins with their ability to build personal relationships and emotional bonds with their Chinese contacts. The Spotlight on Skills box on page 48 offers tips for creating successful business relationships in China.

© BEN MARGOT/ASSOCIATED PRESS

"The big idea behind fair trade is that you can actually make globalization work for the poor," says Paul Rice, founder and CEO of TransFair USA. TransFair is the only U.S. organization authorized to grant the fair trade logo to products made from a growing list of crops for which farmers in developing countries have been paid a fair price such as coffee, cocoa, and sugar. The Oakland, California-based nonprofit is influencing the international dimension of today's business environment by helping increase the sales of fair trade products around the world. Rice says adhering to TransFair standards is just good business as the global environment grows increasingly important.

········> **CONCEPT CONNECTION** <········

Technological. The **technological dimension** includes scientific and technological advancements in a specific industry as well as in society at large. In recent years, this dimension created massive changes for organizations in all industries. Twenty years ago, many organizations didn't even use desktop computers. Today, computer networks, Internet access, handheld devices, videoconferencing capabilities, cell phones, and laptops are the minimum tools for doing business.

A new generation of handhelds allows users to check their corporate e-mail, daily calendars, business contacts, and even customer orders from any location with a wireless network. Cell phones can now switch seamlessly between cellular networks and corporate WiFi connections. Some companies hand out wireless key fobs with continually updated security codes that enable employees to log onto their corporate networks and securely view data or write e-mails from any PC with a broadband connection.[6]

Other technological advances will affect organizations and managers. The decoding of the human genome could lead to revolutionary medical advances. Cloning technology and stem cell research are raising both scientific and ethical concerns. Because of microchip innovations, Motorola can now make the MotoFone F3 affordable to the world's poor, opening up vast economic opportunities for entrepreneurs in developing countries.[7] Nanotechnology, which refers to manipulating matter at its tiniest scale, is moving from the research lab to the marketplace. Some 1,200 nanotechnology start-ups have emerged around the world, and smart managers at established organizations such as 3M, Dow Chemical, Samsung, NASA, Intel, Johnson & Johnson, and IBM are investing research dollars in this technological breakthrough.[8]

Sociocultural. The **sociocultural dimension** of the general environment represents the demographic characteristics as well as the norms, customs, and values of the general

The new generation is more technologically savvy than any other before it. But even greater technological innovations will come down the line. Make it your business to stay on top of the new technologies, no matter what age you are.

sociocultural dimension
The dimension of the general environment representing the demographic characteristics, norms, customs, and values of the population within which the organization operates.

SPOTLIGHT ON SKILLS

Creating *Guanxi* in China

With its low labor costs and huge potential market, China is luring thousands of U.S. companies in search of growth opportunities. Yet Usha C. V. Haley of the University of New Haven recently found that only one-third of multinationals doing business in China have actually turned a profit. One reason Western businesses fall short of expectations, experts agree, is that they fail to grasp the centuries-old concept of *guanxi* that lies at the heart of Chinese culture.

At its simplest level, guanxi is a supportive, mutually beneficial connection between two people. Eventually, those personal relationships are linked together into a network, and it is through these networks that business gets done. Anyone considering doing business in China should keep in mind the following basic rules:

- **Business is always personal.** It is impossible to translate "Don't take it so personally—it's only business" into Chinese. Western managers tend to believe that if they conclude a successful transaction, a good business relationship will follow. The development of a personal relationship is an added bonus but not really necessary when it comes to getting things done. In the Chinese business world, however, a personal relationship must be in place before managers even consider entering a business transaction. Western managers doing business in China should cultivate personal relationships—both during and outside of business hours. Accept any and all social invitations—for drinks, a meal, or even a potentially embarrassing visit to a karaoke bar.
- **Don't skip the small talk.** Getting right down to business and bypassing the small talk during a meeting might feel like an efficient use of time to an American manager. To the

Chinese, however, this approach neglects the all-important work of forging an emotional bond. Be aware that the real purpose of your initial meetings with potential business partners is to begin building a relationship, so keep your patience if the deal you are planning to discuss never even comes up.

- **Remember that relationships are not short-term.** The work of establishing and nurturing guanxi relationships in China is never done. Western managers must put aside their usual focus on short-term results and recognize that it takes a long time for foreigners to be accepted into a guanxi network. Foreign companies often must prove their trustworthiness and reliability over time. For example, firms that weathered the political instability that culminated in the 1989 student protests in Tiananmen Square found it much easier to do business afterward.
- **Make contact frequently.** Some experts recommend hiring ethnic Chinese staff members and then letting them do the heavy lifting of relationship building. Others emphasize that Westerners themselves should put plenty of time and energy into forging links with Chinese contacts; those efforts will pay off because the contacts can smooth the way by tapping into their own guanxi networks. Whatever the strategy, contact should be frequent and personal. In addition, be sure to keep careful track of the contacts you make. In China, any and all relationships are bound to be important at some point in time.

SOURCES: Michelle Dammon Loyalka, "Doing Business in China," *BusinessWeek Online* (Jan. 6, 2006) (www.businessweek.com/smallbiz/); Los Angeles Chinese Learning Center, "Chinese Business Culture" (http://chinese-school.netfirms.com/guanxi.html); and Beijing British Embassy, "Golden Hints for Doing Business in China" (http://chinese-school.netfirms.com/goldenhints.html).

A steady stream of immigrants will keep coming into North America, making it more and more diverse. Try to learn more about them.

population. Important sociocultural characteristics are geographical distribution and population density, age, and education levels. Today's demographic profiles are the foundation of tomorrow's workforce and consumers. Forecasters see increased globalization of both consumer markets and the labor supply, with increasing diversity both within organizations and consumer markets.[9] Consider the following key demographic trends in the United States:

1. The United States is experiencing the largest influx of immigrants in more than a century. The Hispanic population is expected to grow to 102.6 million, an increase of 188 percent since 2000, and it will make up about a quarter of the U.S. population by 2050. In this same time period, non-Hispanic whites will make up only about 50 percent of the population, down from 74 percent in 1995 and 69 percent in 2004.[10]

2. Members of Generation Y are flooding the workplace. To replace the 64 million skilled workers who will start retiring by the end of this decade, companies will be poised to

attract Gen Y workers if they offer competitive salaries, flat hierarchies, support networks, work-life balance, challenging work, and feedback on performance.[11]

3. The fastest-growing type of living arrangement is single-father households, which rose 62 percent in 10 years, even though two-parent and single-mother households are still much more numerous.[12]

Demographic trends affect organizations in other countries just as powerfully. Japan, Italy, and Germany are all faced with aging workforces and customer bases due to years of declining birth rates. In both Italy and Japan, the proportion of people over the age of 65 reached 20 percent in 2006.[13]

Economic. The **economic dimension** represents the general economic health of the country or region in which the organization operates. Consumer purchasing power, the unemployment rate, and interest rates are part of an organization's economic environment. Because organizations today are operating in a global environment, the economic dimension has become exceedingly complex and creates enormous uncertainty for managers. The economies of countries are more closely tied together now. For example, the economic recession and the decline of consumer confidence in the United States in the early 2000s affected economies and organizations around the world. Similarly, economic problems in Asia and Europe had a tremendous impact on companies and the stock market in the United States.

One significant recent trend in the economic environment is the frequency of mergers and acquisitions. Citibank and Travelers merged to form Citigroup, IBM purchased Pricewaterhouse Coopers Consulting, and Cingular acquired AT&T Wireless. In the toy industry, the three largest toy makers—Hasbro, Mattel, and Tyco—gobbled up at least a dozen smaller competitors within a few years. At the same time, however, a tremendous vitality is evident in the small-business sector of the economy. Entrepreneurial start-ups are a significant aspect of today's U.S. economy and will be discussed in Appendix A.

economic dimension
The dimension of the general environment representing the overall economic health of the country or region in which the organization operates.

Legal–Political. The **legal–political dimension** includes government regulations at the local, state, and federal levels, as well as political activities designed to influence company behavior. The U.S. political system encourages capitalism, and the government tries not to overregulate business, though this approach is being questioned, considering the worldwide economic collapse. Even before changes, though, government laws have specified rules of the game. The federal government influences organizations through the Occupational Safety and Health Administration, Environmental Protection Agency, fair trade practices, libel statutes allowing lawsuits against business, consumer-protection legislation, product-safety requirements, import and export restrictions, and information and labeling

legal–political dimension
The dimension of the general environment that includes federal, state, and local government regulations and political activities designed to influence company behavior.

BUSINESS BLOOPER

AIG Bonuses

Despite being one of the companies at the heart of the global financial collapse, and after receiving more than $170 billion in taxpayer bailout money (and now 80 percent owned by the U.S. government), American International Group (AIG) gave out $160 million in bonuses to executives. After a public and congressional outcry, three-fourths of the top earners agreed to return the bonuses. But some of them went to people outside the United States who were evidently not shamed into giving back anything. AIG leaders were not tuned into the American public's seething rage toward what seemed like excessive extras going to the already wealthy, especially when so many are losing jobs and homes.

SOURCE: Edmund Andrews, "AIG Planning Huge Bonuses," *New York Times*, Mar. 14, 2009, p. A1; and Michael Kazin, "The Outrage Factor," *Newsweek*, Mar. 30, 2009, p. 22.

1 I think sales companies should be allowed to send out large catalogs because it can increase revenues.

ANSWER: Modern companies need to be mindful of environmental costs from the excessive use of paper.

pressure groups
Interest groups that work within the legal–political framework to influence companies to behave in socially responsible ways.

natural dimension
The dimension of the general environment that includes all elements that occur naturally on Earth, including plants, animals, rocks, and natural resources such as air, water, and climate.

requirements. Many organizations also have to contend with government and legal issues in other countries. The European Union (EU) adopted environmental and consumer-protection rules that are costing American companies hundreds of millions of dollars a year. Companies such as Hewlett-Packard, Ford Motor Company, and General Electric have to pick up the bill for recycling the products they sell in the EU, for example.[14]

Managers must also recognize a variety of **pressure groups** that work within the legal–political framework to influence companies to behave in socially responsible ways. WakeUp Walmart, a union-backed campaign group, drums up public awareness of Walmart's business practices to force the retailer to improve worker's wages and health-care benefits. The group's campaign director hopes smaller companies will then follow suit.[15] Other activists have boldly petitioned Home Depot, which introduced the Eco Option brand for its environmentally friendly products, to stop advertising on Fox News, whose hosts and commentators dismiss global warming as ludicrous.[16]

© SUZY POLING

High-school buddies Eric Ryan (left) and Adam Lowry make environmentally friendly products look good. Their company, Method, produces nontoxic cleaning products with a concern for the natural environment and packages them in designer-style bottles. Lowry, a chemical engineer, and Ryan, with an advertising background, founded Method in 2000, and sales grew to nearly $100 million in 2007.

Natural. In response to pressure from environmental advocates, organizations have become increasingly sensitive to Earth's diminishing natural resources and the environmental impact of their products. As a result, the natural dimension of the external environment is growing in importance. The **natural dimension** includes all elements that occur naturally on Earth, including plants, animals, rocks, and natural resources such as air, water, and climate.

The natural dimension is different from other sectors of the general environment because it has no voice of its own. Influence on managers to meet needs in the natural environment may come from other sectors such as government regulation, consumer concerns, bad press in the news media, competitors' actions, and even employees.[17] For example, environmental groups advocate various action and policy goals that include reduction and cleanup of human-made pollution, development of renewable energy resources, and sustainable use of scarce resources such as water, land, and air. More recently, there has been a strong concern about climate change, especially global warming, which is caused by greenhouse gases, most notably carbon dioxide.

Concern about the environment has prompted companies to take these actions:

- **Eliminate nonbiodegradable plastic bags from the environment.** Whole Foods will stop offering disposable, plastic grocery bags in all 270 stores, replacing them with recyclable bags. This changemeans roughly 100 million plastic bags will be kept out of the environment in the first eight months of the new program.[18]

- **Improve the efficiency of plants and factories.** Nissan's Sunderland factory in the United Kingdom will use eight wind turbines to generate 6 percent of the plant's energy requirements, cutting carbon dioxide emissions by 4,000 tons per year. Toyota recycles 100,000 tons of wastewater a year in its reverse osmosis facility in its Burnaston (United Kingdom) plant.[19]

- **Invest in cleaner technologies.** General Electric, which once polluted the Hudson River with polychlorinated biphenyls as it manufactured transformers, now promises that it will invest $1.5 billion annually in researching cleaner forms of technology by 2010, up from $700 million in 2004.[20]

TASK ENVIRONMENT

As described earlier, the task environment includes those sectors that have a direct working relationship with the organization, among them customers, competitors, suppliers, and the labor market.

Customers. Those people and organizations in the environment that acquire goods or services from the organization are **customers**. As recipients of the organization's output, customers are important because they determine the organization's success. Patients are the customers of hospitals, students the customers of schools, and travelers the customers of airlines. Many companies are searching for ways to reach the coveted teen and youth market by tying marketing messages into online social networks such as MySpace and Facebook. With high school and college students representing a $375-billion consumer spending market, it's serious business for managers at companies such as Target, Apple, Coca-Cola, and Disney. Apple sponsors an Apple-lovers group on Facebook, giving away iPod Shuffles in weekly contests. Target has sponsored a group on MySpace that features a 15-year-old professional snowboarder wearing a Target logo on his helmet.[21]

Customers today have greater power because of the Internet, which presents threats as well as opportunities for managers. Today's customers can directly affect the organization's reputation and sales, for example, through gripe sites such as UNTIED.com, where United Airlines employees and disgruntled fliers rail against the air carrier. "In this new information environment," says Kyle Shannon, CEO of e-commerce consultancy Agency.com, "you've got to assume everyone knows everything."[22]

Competitors. Specific competitive issues characterize each industry. Other organizations in the same industry or type of business that provide goods or services to the same set of customers are referred to as **competitors**. The recording industry differs from the steel industry and the pharmaceutical industry.

Competitive wars are being waged worldwide in all industries. Market leader MySpace keeps a close eye on Facebook's growing popularity. Both are battling it out for market leadership and advertising market share.[23] Netflix and Blockbuster use innovative pricing and distribution to win the loyalty of online movie customers. Internet jeweler Blue Nile clashes with Tiffany's, Zale's, and Kay's in a contest for leadership in the diamond ring market. Using its low overhead and strong purchasing power, Blue Nile sells diamond rings for 35 percent below most bricks-and-mortar stores.[24]

Suppliers. **Suppliers** provide the raw materials the organization uses to produce its output. A steel mill requires iron ore, machines, and financial resources. A small, private university may use hundreds of suppliers for paper, pencils, cafeteria food, computers, trucks, fuel, electricity, and textbooks. Companies from toolmakers to construction firms and auto manufacturers were hurt earlier in this decade by an unanticipated jump in the price of steel from suppliers. Just as they were starting to see an upturn in their business, the cost of raw materials jumped 30 percent in a two-month period.[25] Consider also that China now produces more than 85 percent of the vitamin C used by companies in the United States. An

customers
People and organizations in the environment that acquire goods or services from the organization.

competitors
Other organizations in the same industry or type of business that provide goods or services to the same set of customers.

suppliers
People and organizations that provide the raw materials the organization uses to produce its output.

labor market
The people available for hire by the organization.

agreement among China's four largest producers led to an increase in the price of vitamin C from $3 a kilogram to as high as $9 a kilogram.[26]

Many companies are using fewer suppliers and trying to build good relationships with them so that they will receive high-quality parts and materials at lower prices. The relationship between manufacturers and suppliers has traditionally been an adversarial one, but managers are finding that cooperation is the key to saving money, maintaining quality, and speeding products to market.

Labor Market.   The **labor market** represents people in the environment who can be hired to work for the organization. Every organization needs a supply of trained, qualified personnel. Unions, employee associations, and the availability of certain classes of employees can influence the organization's labor market. Labor-market forces affecting organizations right now include: (1) the growing need for computer-literate knowledge workers; (2) the need for continuous investment in human resources through recruitment, education, and training to meet the competitive demands of the borderless world; and (3) the effects of international trading blocs, automation, outsourcing, and shifting facility locations on labor dislocations, creating unused labor pools in some areas and labor shortages in others.

Changes in these various sectors of the general and task environments can create tremendous challenges, especially for organizations operating in complex, rapidly changing industries. Nortel Networks, a Canadian company with multiple U.S. offices, is an example of an organization operating in a highly complex environment.

NORTEL NETWORKS

Nortel Networks is a global company that connects people to the information they need through advanced communication technologies. With customers in more than 150 countries, Nortel designs and installs new networks and upgrades, and it supports and manages existing systems.[27] Nortel's complex external environment, illustrated in Exhibit 2.2, directly influences its operations and performance. The Canadian-based company began in 1895 as a manufacturer of telephones and has reinvented itself many times to keep up with changes in the environment. In the late 1990s, the company transformed itself into a major player in wireless technology and equipment for connecting businesses and individuals to the Internet. In 1997, the company was about to be run over by rivals such as Cisco Systems that were focused on Internet gear. Then-CEO John Roth knew he needed to do something bold to respond to changes in the technological environment. A name change to Nortel Networks symbolized and reinforced the company's new goal of providing unified network solutions to customers worldwide.

Today, Nortel's purpose is clear—to create a high-performance 21st-century communications company that leverages innovative technology and simplifies the complicated, hyperconnected world.[28] To achieve this goal, Nortel adapts and responds to the uncertainty of the external environment. One response to the competitive environment was to spend billions to acquire data and voice networking companies, including Bay Networks (which makes Internet and data equipment), Cambrian Systems (a hot maker of optical technology), Periphonics (maker of voice-response systems), and Clarify (customer-relationship management software). These companies brought Nortel top-notch technology, helping the company snatch customers away from rivals Cisco and Lucent Technologies. In addition, even during rough economic times, Nortel kept spending nearly 20 percent of its revenues on research and development to keep pace with changing technology.

Internationally, Nortel has made impressive inroads in Taiwan, China, Brazil, Mexico, Colombia, Japan, and Sweden, among other countries. China's Ministry of Railways selected mobile communications railway technologies from Nortel to provide a secure, wireless network for trains traveling as fast as 350 km/hr.[29] It also won customers by recognizing the continuing need for traditional equipment and offering hybrid gear that combines old telephone technology with new Internet features, allowing companies to transition from the old to the new. Bold new technologies for Nortel include fourth-generation broadband wireless, Carrier Ethernet, optical, next-generation services and applications, and secure networking.[30] Nortel is considered a leader in wireless gear and won contracts from Verizon Communications and Orange SA, a unit of France Telecom, to supply equipment that sends phone calls as packets of digital data like that used over the Internet. Nortel also capitalizes on strategic alliances by teaming with Microsoft, Dell, and IBM.[31]

EXHIBIT 2.2

The External
Environment of Nortel
- - - - - - - - - - -

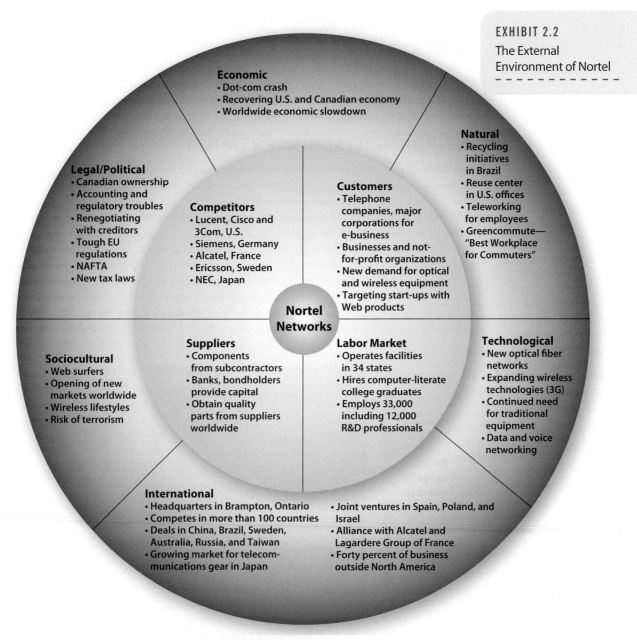

Economic
- Dot-com crash
- Recovering U.S. and Canadian economy
- Worldwide economic slowdown

Natural
- Recycling initiatives in Brazil
- Reuse center in U.S. offices
- Teleworking for employees
- Greencommute—"Best Workplace for Commuters"

Legal/Political
- Canadian ownership
- Accounting and regulatory troubles
- Renegotiating with creditors
- Tough EU regulations
- NAFTA
- New tax laws

Competitors
- Lucent, Cisco and 3Com, U.S.
- Siemens, Germany
- Alcatel, France
- Ericsson, Sweden
- NEC, Japan

Customers
- Telephone companies, major corporations for e-business
- Businesses and not-for-profit organizations
- New demand for optical and wireless equipment
- Targeting start-ups with Web products

Nortel Networks

Sociocultural
- Web surfers
- Opening of new markets worldwide
- Wireless lifestyles
- Risk of terrorism

Suppliers
- Components from subcontractors
- Banks, bondholders provide capital
- Obtain quality parts from suppliers worldwide

Labor Market
- Operates facilities in 34 states
- Hires computer-literate college graduates
- Employs 33,000 including 12,000 R&D professionals

Technological
- New optical fiber networks
- Expanding wireless technologies (3G)
- Continued need for traditional equipment
- Data and voice networking

International
- Headquarters in Brampton, Ontario
- Competes in more than 100 countries
- Deals in China, Brazil, Sweden, Australia, Russia, and Taiwan
- Growing market for telecommunications gear in Japan
- Joint ventures in Spain, Poland, and Israel
- Alliance with Alcatel and Lagardere Group of France
- Forty percent of business outside North America

SOURCES: "Chinese Ministry of Railways Chooses Nortel Mobile Network," *M2Presswire*, Business and Company Resource Center database, (accessed Jan. 29, 2008); Nortel Web site (www.nortel.com) (accessed Feb. 5, 2008); W. C. Symonds, J. B. Levine, N. Gross, and P. Coy, "High-Tech Star: Northern Telecom Is Challenging Even AT&T," *BusinessWeek* (July 27, 1992): 54–58; I. Austen, "Hooked on the Net," *Canadian Business* (June 26–July 10, 1998): 95–103; J. Weber with A. Reinhardt and P. Burrows, "Racing Ahead at Nortel," *BusinessWeek* (Nov. 8, 1999): 93–99; "Nortel's Waffling Continues: First Job Cuts, Then Product Lines, and Now the CEO," *Telephony* (May 21, 2001): 12; and M. Heinzl, "Nortel's Profits of 499 Million Exceeds Forecast," *Wall Street Journal*, Jan. 30, 2004.

Companies moving in an Internet-speed environment risk a hard landing, and when the demand for Internet equipment slumped in the early 2000s, Nortel's business was devastated. The company cut more than two-thirds of its workforce and closed dozens of plants and offices. An accounting scandal that led to fraud investigations and senior executive dismissals made things even worse. At one point, Nortel's stock was trading for less than a dollar. By early 2006, however, positive changes in the economic environment, along with a savvy new CEO, put Nortel back on an uphill swing. Bright spots for the company in 2007 included improved earnings, a boost in orders, and improved profitability. But then the economic downturn amplified all of Nortel's problems. Despite valiant efforts, Nortel went into bankruptcy in 2009 and ultimately sold off all its assets.[33]

The Organization–Environment Relationship

Why do organizations care so much about factors in the external environment? The reason is that the environment creates uncertainty for organization managers, and they must respond by designing the organization to adapt to the environment.

ENVIRONMENTAL UNCERTAINTY

Organizations must manage environmental uncertainty to be effective. *Uncertainty* means that managers do not have sufficient information about environmental factors to understand and predict environmental needs and changes.[34]

As indicated in Exhibit 2.3, environmental characteristics that influence uncertainty are the number of factors that affect the organization and the extent to which those factors change. A large multinational such as Nortel Networks has thousands of factors in the external environment creating uncertainty for managers. When external factors change rapidly, the organization experiences high uncertainty; examples are telecommunications and aerospace firms, computer and electronics companies, and e-commerce organizations that sell products and services over the Internet. Companies have to make an effort to adapt to the rapid changes in the environment. When an organization deals with only a few external factors and these factors

EXHIBIT 2.3

The External Environment and Uncertainty

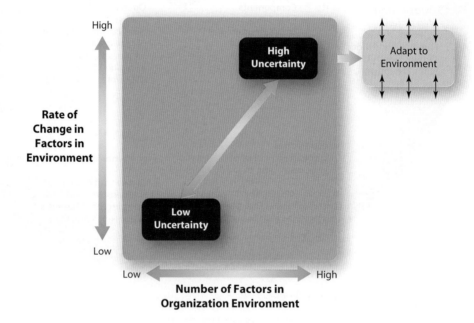

2 I like my job to have a good deal of stability.

ANSWER: With each passing year, the environment for organizations gets more unpredictable, which results in jobs being increasingly less predictable. Even so, some industries or sectors are not as unstable as others. When looking for a job, be honest with yourself about how much stability you need and then make that one of the considerations when evaluating different positions.

Are You Fit for Managerial Uncertainty?[35]

Do you approach uncertainty with an open mind? Think back to how you thought or behaved during a time of uncertainty when you were in a formal or informal leadership position. Please answer whether each of the following items as Mostly True or Mostly False in that circumstance.

	MOSTLY TRUE	MOSTLY FALSE
1. Enjoyed hearing about new ideas even when working toward a deadline.	_____	_____
2. Welcomed unusual viewpoints of others even if we were working under pressure.	_____	_____
3. Made it a point to attend industry trade shows and company events.	_____	_____
4. Specifically encouraged others to express opposing ideas and arguments.	_____	_____
5. Asked "dumb" questions.	_____	_____
6. Always offered comments on the meaning of data or issues.	_____	_____
7. Expressed a controversial opinion to bosses and peers.	_____	_____
8. Suggested ways of improving my and others' ways of doing things.	_____	_____

SCORING AND INTERPRETATION: Give yourself one point for each item you marked as Mostly True. If you scored less than 5 you might want to start your career as a manager in a stable rather than unstable environment. A score of 5 or above suggests a higher level of mindfulness and a better fit for a new manager in an organization with an uncertain environment.

are relatively stable, such as those affecting soft-drink bottlers or food processors, managers experience low uncertainty and can devote less attention to external issues.

ADAPTING TO THE ENVIRONMENT

If an organization faces increased uncertainty with respect to competition, customers, suppliers, or government regulations, managers can use several strategies to adapt to these changes, including boundary-spanning roles, interorganizational partnerships, and mergers or joint ventures.

People in departments such as marketing and purchasing span the boundary to work with customers and suppliers, both face to face and through market research. Some organizations are staying in touch with customers through the Internet, such as by monitoring gripe sites, communicating with customers on company Web sites, and contracting with market-research firms that use the Web to monitor rapidly changing marketplace trends.[36] Another recent approach to boundary spanning is the use of *business intelligence*, which results from using sophisticated software to search through large amounts of internal and external data to spot patterns, trends, and relationships that might be significant. For example, Verizon Wireless uses business intelligence software to actively monitor customer interactions and fix problems almost immediately.[37]

EXHIBIT 2.4
The Shift to a Partnership Paradigm

From Adversarial Orientation ⟶	To Partnership Orientation
• Suspicion, competition, arm's length	• Trust, value added to both sides
• Price, efficiency, own profits	• Equity, fair dealing, everyone profits
• Information and feedback limited	• E-business links to share information and conduct digital transactions
• Lawsuits to resolve conflict	• Close coordination; virtual teams and people onsite
• Minimal involvement and up-front investment	• Involvement in partner's product design and production
• Short-term contracts	• Long-term contracts
• Contracts limit the relationship	• Business assistance goes beyond the contract

Read the Ethical Dilemma on page 70 that pertains to competitive intelligence. Do you have the courage to risk your job by challenging the boss's inappropriate use of confidential information?

Boundary spanning is an increasingly important task in organizations because environmental shifts can happen so quickly in today's world. Managers need good information about their competitors, customers, and other elements of the environment to make good decisions. Thus, the most successful companies involve everyone in boundary-spanning activities.

Managers in partnering organizations are also shifting from an adversarial orientation to a partnership orientation. The new paradigm, shown in Exhibit 2.4, is based on trust and the ability of partners to work out equitable solutions to conflicts so that everyone profits from the relationship. Managers work to reduce costs and add value to both sides rather than trying to get all the benefits for their own company. The new model is also characterized by a high level of information sharing, including e-business links for automatic ordering, payments, and other transactions. In addition, person-to-person interaction provides corrective feedback and solves problems. People from other companies may be on-site or participate in virtual teams to enable close coordination. Partners are frequently involved in one another's product design and production, and they are committed for the long term. It is not unusual for business partners to help one another, even outside of what is specified in the contract.[38]

A step beyond strategic partnerships is for companies to become involved in mergers or joint ventures to reduce environmental uncertainty. A **merger** occurs when two or more organizations combine to become one. For example, Wells Fargo merged with Norwest Corporation to form the nation's fourth-largest banking corporation.

A **joint venture** involves a strategic alliance or program by two or more organizations. A joint venture typically occurs when a project is too complex, expensive, or uncertain for one firm to handle alone. Oprah Winfrey's Harpo Inc. formed a joint venture with Hearst Magazines to launch *O, The Oprah Magazine*.[39] Despite her popularity and success with her television show, Winfrey recognized the complexity and uncertainty involved in starting a new magazine. The combined resources and management talents of the partners contributed to the most successful start-up ever in the magazine publishing industry.

The Internal Environment: Corporate Culture

merger
The combining of two or more organizations into one.

joint venture
A strategic alliance or program by two or more organizations.

The internal environment within which managers work includes corporate culture, production technology, organization structure, and physical facilities. Of these, corporate culture surfaces as extremely important to competitive advantage. The internal culture must fit the needs of the external environment and company strategy. When this fit occurs, highly committed employees create a high-performance organization that is tough to beat.[40]

Most people don't think about culture; it's just "how we do things around here" or "the way things are here." However, managers have to think about culture because it typically plays a significant role in organizational success. The concept of culture has been of growing concern to managers since the 1980s as turbulence in the external environment has grown, often requiring new values and attitudes. Organizational culture has been defined and studied in many and varied ways. For the purposes of this chapter, we define **culture** as the set of key values, beliefs, understandings, and norms shared by members of an organization.[41] The concept of culture helps managers understand the hidden, complex aspects of organizational life. Culture is a pattern of shared values and assumptions about how things are done within the organization. This pattern is learned by members as they cope with external and internal problems and taught to new members as the correct way to perceive, think, and feel. One type of organization is an online forum or discussion group, which also develops its own culture. The Spotlight on Ethics box below gives some rules for avoiding negative interactions.

Culture can be analyzed at three levels, as illustrated in Exhibit 2.5, with each level becoming less obvious.[42] At the surface level are visible artifacts, which include such things as manner of dress, patterns of behavior, physical symbols, organizational ceremonies, and office layout. Visible artifacts are all the things one can see, hear, and observe by watching members of the organization. At a deeper level are the expressed values and beliefs, which are not observable but can be discerned from how people explain and justify what they do. Members of the organization hold these values at a conscious level. They can be interpreted from the stories, language, and symbols organization members use to represent them.

Some values become so deeply embedded in a culture that members are no longer consciously aware of them. These basic, underlying assumptions and beliefs are the essence of culture and subconsciously guide behavior and decisions. In some organizations, a basic

culture
The set of key values, beliefs, understandings, and norms that members of an organization share.

SPOTLIGHT ON ETHICS

Netiquette to Avoid Flaming

1. Know your group. Before you post, find out the purpose of the group and the purpose of the listserv. If there is a page online where you can read about this, the better. Look also for frequently asked questions (FAQs); you may find your concerns addressed here.

2. Don't crosspost your bloggings (particularly if they are longer than two paragraphs). People generally don't like to be the inadvertent recipients of your dissertations.

3. Make sure your postings are relevant to that particular forum. If you are new to the list, do not lecture others on correct thinking; you may be more ignorant than you think.

4. Don't demand documentation or proof for someone's ideas. You may politely inquire about where those concepts came from, but remember to ask sincerely. If you can't be humble when asking, don't do it.

5. Don't post advertisements, even if you think a lot of the members would benefit from this wonderful and amazing

whatever it is. People get enough unwanted ads without you adding your own.

6. If you are responding to one person, send that person a private e-mail.

7. Don't threaten or insult, no matter how self-righteous you feel. Avoid psychoanalyzing members or attributing negative motives.

8. If you are flamed, don't respond back in kind; it only increases the hostility and will bring others in to "defend" the person you attacked.

9. Remember, even though you probably haven't met most of the members, they are still human beings with feelings. Just because their faces are unseen and you know little if anything about them, this is no reason to vent your own stored-up anger. Be a decent person on the list and a good citizen to the group.

EXHIBIT 2.5
Levels of Corporate
Culture

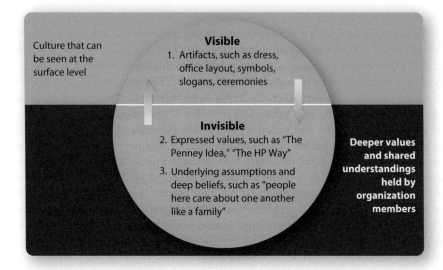

Culture that can be seen at the surface level

Visible
1. Artifacts, such as dress, office layout, symbols, slogans, ceremonies

Invisible
2. Expressed values, such as "The Penney Idea," "The HP Way"
3. Underlying assumptions and deep beliefs, such as "people here care about one another like a family"

Deeper values and shared understandings held by organization members

assumption might be that people are essentially lazy and will shirk their duties whenever possible; thus, employees are closely supervised and given little freedom, and colleagues are frequently suspicious of one another. More enlightened organizations operate on the basic assumption that people want to do a good job; in these organizations, employees are given more freedom and responsibility, and colleagues trust one another and work cooperatively.

The fundamental values that characterize an organization's culture can be understood through the visible manifestations of symbols, stories, heroes, slogans, and ceremonies.

SYMBOLS

A **symbol** is an object, act, or event that conveys meaning to others. Symbols can be considered a rich, nonverbal language that vibrantly conveys the organization's important values concerning how people relate to one another and interact with the environment.[43] For example, managers at a New York-based start-up that provides Internet solutions to local television broadcasters wanted a way to symbolize the company's unofficial mantra of "drilling down to solve problems." They bought a dented old drill for $2 and dubbed it "The Team Drill." Each month, the drill is presented to a different employee in recognition of exceptional work, and the employee personalizes the drill in some way before passing it on to the next winner.[44]

symbol
An object, act, or event that conveys meaning to others.

story
A narrative based on true events and repeated frequently and shared among organizational employees.

STORIES

A **story** is a narrative based on true events and is repeated frequently and shared among organizational employees. Stories paint pictures that help symbolize the firm's vision and values and help employees personalize and absorb them.[45] A frequently told story at UPS concerns an employee who, without authorization, ordered an extra Boeing 737 to ensure

Assess Your Answer

3 When I get a new job, the managers should accept me for who I am and let me be myself.

ANSWER: Each organization has its own culture, its own assumptions and expectations of behavior. To succeed, you should spend time observing the culture and try to adapt to it, that is, without giving up any of your own core values.

timely delivery of a load of Christmas packages that had been left behind in the holiday rush. As the story goes, rather than punishing the worker, UPS rewarded his initiative. By telling this story, UPS workers communicate that the company stands behind its commitment to worker autonomy and customer service.[46] A story of Toyota's founder Kiichiro Toyoda, described in the following example, illustrates his commitment to the "Toyota Way," a set of values that serve as the foundation of Toyota's success.

TOYOTA

Toyota Motor Corporation, an automotive powerhouse, is the most profitable automaker in the world. Known for award-winning reliability and quality, Toyota leads the industry in manufacturing and customer service. At a time when GM and Ford are closing plants, Toyota is holding on, much better off than other car makers. It had an operating loss in 2009, the first time in seven years. Toyota is also a leader and innovator in hybrid technology. Toyota offers six Toyota and Lexus hybrid vehicles in the United States, where it has sold more than 500,000 hybrids, surpassing the rest of the industry combined.[47]

What makes this company so successful? For Toyota, the answer is a strong corporate culture based on "The Toyota Way." A popular story of Toyota's founder Kiichiro Toyoda demonstrates his commitment to the culture during the early days of the company's history. Toyoda visited a plant and found a worker scratching his head and muttering about how his grinding machine would not run. Toyoda rolled up his sleeves and thrust his hands into the machine's oil pan. He came up with two handfuls of sludge and threw them to the floor. "How can you expect to do your job without getting your hands dirty," he exclaimed. This was the origin of one of the key elements of Toyota's culture: *genchi genbutsu,* meaning "go and see." To Toyota employees, this means go and seek out facts and information that help you make good decisions—even if it means rolling up your sleeves and getting dirty.[48]

SOURCE: Hans Greimel, "As Losses Mount, Toyota Cuts Costs," *Automotive News* (Feb. 9, 2009): 25.

HEROES

A **hero** is a figure who exemplifies the deeds, character, and attributes of a strong culture. Heroes are role models for employees to follow. Sometimes heroes are real, such as the female security supervisor who once challenged IBM's chairman because he wasn't carrying the appropriate clearance identification to enter a security area.[49] Heroes show how to do the right thing in the organization. Companies with strong cultures take advantage of achievements to define heroes who uphold key values.

At 3M Corporation, top managers keep alive the image of heroes who developed projects that were killed by top management. One hero was a vice president who was fired earlier in his career for persisting with a new product even after his boss had told him, "That's a stupid idea. Stop!" After the worker was fired, he would not leave. He stayed in an unused office, working without a salary on the new product idea. Eventually he was rehired, the idea succeeded, and he was promoted to vice president. The lesson of this hero as a major element in 3M's culture is to persist at what you believe in.[50]

SLOGANS

A **slogan** is a phrase or sentence that succinctly expresses a key corporate value. Many companies use a slogan or saying to convey special meaning to employees. The Ritz-Carlton adopted the slogan, "Ladies and gentlemen taking care of ladies and gentlemen" to demonstrate its cultural commitment to take care of both employees and customers. "We're in the service business, and service comes only from people. Our promise is to take care of them, and provide a happy place for them to work," said General Manager Mark DeCocinis, who manages the Portman Hotel in Shanghai, recipient of the "Best Employer in Asia" for three consecutive years.[51] Cultural values can also be discerned in written public statements

hero
A figure who exemplifies the deeds, character, and attributes of a strong corporate culture.

slogan
A phrase or sentence that succinctly expresses a key corporate value.

What are the slogans on your campus? List as many as you can. What does that tell you about what the culture values?

To understand culture, ask yourself: What is the culture of most of your courses? Is the culture serious, playful, angry? Does it require you to behave in a certain way to your instructors? To other students?

As a new manager, pay attention to culture. Recognize the ways in which cultural values can help or hurt your department's performance. Consciously shape adaptive values through the use of symbols, stories, heroes, ceremonies, and slogans.

Complete the Self Learning exercise on page 68 that pertains to adaptive cultures. How would you shape adaptive values in a company for which you worked?

ceremony
A planned activity at a special event that is conducted for the benefit of an audience.

such as corporate mission statements or other formal statements that express the core values of the organization. The mission statement for Hallmark Cards, for example, emphasizes values of excellence, ethical and moral conduct in all relationships, business innovation, and corporate social responsibility.[52]

CEREMONIES

A **ceremony** is a planned activity at a special event that is conducted for the benefit of an audience. Managers hold ceremonies to provide dramatic examples of company values. Ceremonies are special occasions that reinforce valued accomplishments, create a bond among people by allowing them to share an important event, and anoint and celebrate heroes.[53] In a ceremony to mark its 20th anniversary, Southwest Airlines rolled out a specialty plane it created called the "Lone Star One" that was designed like the Texas state flag to signify the company's start in Texas. Later, when the NBA chose Southwest Airlines as the league's official airline, Southwest launched another specialty plane, the "Slam Dunk One," designed in blue and orange with a large basketball painted toward the front of the plane. Today, 10 specialty planes celebrate significant milestones in Southwest's history and demonstrate key cultural values.[54]

In summary, organizational culture represents the values, norms, understandings, and basic assumptions that employees share, and these values are signified by symbols, stories, heroes, slogans, and ceremonies. Managers help define important symbols, stories, and heroes to shape the culture.

Environment and Culture

A big influence on internal corporate culture is the external environment. Cultures can vary widely across organizations; however, organizations within the same industry often reveal similar cultural characteristics because they are operating in similar environments.[55] The internal culture should embody what it takes to succeed in the environment. If the external environment requires extraordinary customer service, the culture should encourage good service; if it calls for careful technical decision making, cultural values should reinforce managerial decision making.

ADAPTIVE CULTURES

Research at Harvard on 207 U.S. firms illustrated the critical relationship between corporate culture and the external environment. The study found that a strong corporate culture alone did not ensure business success unless the culture encouraged healthy adaptation to the external environment. As illustrated in Exhibit 2.6, adaptive corporate cultures have different values and behavior from unadaptive corporate cultures. In adaptive cultures, managers are concerned about customers and those internal people and processes that bring about useful change. In the unadaptive corporate cultures, managers are concerned about themselves, and their values tend to discourage risk taking and change. Thus, a strong culture alone is not enough, because an unhealthy culture may encourage the organization to march resolutely in the wrong direction. Healthy cultures help companies adapt to the environment.[56]

TYPES OF CULTURES

In considering what cultural values are important for the organization, managers consider the external environment as well as the company's strategy and goals. Studies suggest that the right fit between culture, strategy, and the environment is associated with four categories

	Adaptive Corporate Cultures	Unadaptive Corporate Cultures
Visible Behavior	Managers pay close attention to all their constituencies, especially customers, and initiate change when needed to serve their legitimate interests, even if it entails taking some risks.	Managers tend to behave somewhat insularly, politically, and bureaucratically. As a result, they do not change their strategies quickly to adjust to or take advantage of changes in their business environments.
Expressed Values	Managers care deeply about customers, stockholders, and employees. They also strongly value people and processes that can create useful change (e.g., leadership initiatives up and down the management hierarchy).	Managers care mainly about themselves, their immediate work group, or some product (or technology) associated with that work group. They value the orderly and risk-reducing management process much more highly than leadership initiatives.

SOURCE: Adapted with the permission of The Free Press, a division of Simon & Schuster Adult Publishing Group, from *Corporate Culture and Performance* by John P. Kotter and James L. Heskett. Copyright © 1992 by Kotter Associates, Inc. and James L. Heskett. All rights reserved.

EXHIBIT 2.6
Environmentally Adaptive Versus Unadaptive Corporate Cultures

or types of culture, as illustrated in Exhibit 2.7. These categories are based on two dimensions: (1) the extent to which the external environment requires flexibility or stability and (2) the extent to which a company's strategic focus is internal or external. The four categories associated with these differences are adaptability, achievement, involvement, and consistency.[57]

The **adaptability culture** emerges in an environment that requires fast response and high-risk decision making. Managers encourage values that support the company's ability to rapidly detect, interpret, and translate signals from the environment into new behavior responses. Employees have autonomy to make decisions and act freely to meet new needs, and responsiveness to customers is highly valued. Managers also actively create change by encouraging and rewarding creativity, experimentation, and risk taking. Lush Cosmetics, a fast-growing maker of shampoos, lotions, and bath products made from fresh ingredients such as mangoes and avocados, provides a good example of an adaptability culture.

adaptability culture
A culture characterized by values that support the company's ability to interpret and translate signals from the environment into new behavior responses.

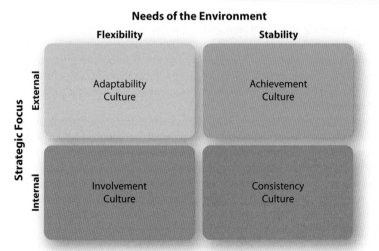

Needs of the Environment

EXHIBIT 2.7
Four Types of Corporate Cultures

SOURCES: Based on D. R. Denison and A. K. Mishra, "Toward a Theory of Organizational Culture and Effectiveness," *Organization Science,* 6(2) (Mar.–Apr. 1995): 204–223; R. Hooijberg and F. Petrock, "On Cultural Change: Using the Competing Values Framework to Help Leaders Execute a Transformational Strategy," *Human Resource Management* 32(1) (1993): 29–50; and R. E. Quinn, *Beyond Rational Management: Mastering the Paradoxes and Competing Demands of High Performance* (San Francisco: Jossey-Bass, 1988).

© MISTY KEASLER

John Zapp, general manager of a group of dealerships in Oklahoma City, realized his Buick-Pontiac-GMC and Dodge-Chrysler-Jeep outlets were losing sales to neighboring Toyota and Honda shops. To maximize sells on the current floor traffic, Zapp reconfigured his inventory to focus on selling preowned vehicles, which increased profit per auto. The key to keeping the preowned vehicles moving off the lot is the company's achievement culture. Zapp sets high goals and gives cash incentives to salespeople who move the preowned inventory faster.

》 CONCEPT CONNECTION 《

TAKE ACTION

Are your courses concerned more with the adaptability, achievement, or involvement cultures? What about your student clubs?

A guiding motto at the company is "We reserve the right to make mistakes." Founder and CEO Mark Constantine is passionately devoted to change and encourages employees to break boundaries, experiment, and take risks. The company kills off one-third of its product line every year to offer new and offbeat products.[58] Other companies in the cosmetics industry, as well as those involved in electronics, e-commerce, and fashion, often use an adaptability culture because they must move quickly to respond to rapid changes in the environment.

The **achievement culture** is suited to organizations concerned with serving specific customers in the external environment but without the intense need for flexibility and rapid change. This results-oriented culture values competitiveness, aggressiveness, personal initiative, and willingness to work long and hard to achieve results. An emphasis on winning and achieving specific ambitious goals is the glue that holds the organization together.[59] Siebel Systems, which sells complex software systems, thrives on an achievement culture. Professionalism and aggressiveness are core values. Employees are forbidden to eat at their desks or to decorate with more than one or two personal photographs. People who succeed at Siebel are focused, competitive, and driven to win. Those who perform and meet stringent goals are handsomely rewarded; those who don't are fired.[60]

The **involvement culture** emphasizes an internal focus on the involvement and participation of employees to adapt rapidly to changing needs from the environment. This culture places high value on meeting the needs of employees, and the organization may be characterized by a caring, family-like atmosphere. Managers emphasize values such as cooperation, consideration of both employees and customers, and avoiding status differences. Consider the involvement culture at Valero, which is partly responsible for helping the company become the top oil refinery in the United States.

VALERO

When Hurricane Katrina hit New Orleans in late August 2005, companies throughout the region set their disaster plans into action. But few matched the heroic efforts put forth by employees at Valero's St. Charles oil refinery. Just eight days after the storm, the St. Charles facility was up and running, while a competitor's plant across the road was weeks away from getting back online. During the same time period, St. Charles's disaster crew managed to locate every one of the plant's 570 employees.

Part of the credit goes to Valero's family-like, let's-get-it-done-together culture, which has given Valero a distinctive edge during an era of cutthroat global competition in the oil industry. As CEO Bill Greehey transformed Valero, once primarily a natural-gas-pipeline company, into the nation's largest oil refinery business, he also instilled a culture where people care about one another and the company. Many of the refineries Valero bought were old and run-down. After buying a refinery, Greehey's first steps would be to assure people their jobs were secure, bring in new safety equipment, and promise employees that if they worked hard he would put them first before shareholders and customers. Employees held up their end of the bargain, and so did Greehey.

Putting employees first has engendered amazing loyalty and dedication. When Greehey visited the St. Charles facility after Katrina, he was surprised to be greeted at a giant tent with a standing ovation. Even in the aftermath of a hurricane, employees had held to their tradition of throwing a plant-wide barbecue lunch whenever Greehey visits a plant. "Right now morale is so high in this refinery you can't get at it with a space shuttle," an electrical superintendent at St. Charles said. "Valero has been giving away gas, chain saws, putting up trailers for the employees. They've kept every employee paid. Other refineries shut down and stopped paying. What else can you ask?"[61]

Some managers might think putting employees ahead of customers and shareholders is nice but not very good for business. But at Valero, a strong involvement culture based on putting employees first has paid off in terms of high employee performance and rising market share, profits, and shareholder value.

The final category of culture, the **consistency culture**, uses an internal focus and a consistency orientation for a stable environment. Following the rules and being thrifty are valued, and the culture supports and rewards a methodical, rational, orderly way of doing things. In today's fast-changing world, few companies operate in a stable environment, and most managers are shifting toward cultures that are more flexible and in tune with changes in the environment. However, one thriving company, Pacific Edge Software, successfully implemented elements of a consistency culture, ensuring that all its projects are on time and on budget. The husband-and-wife team of Lisa Hjorten and Scott Fuller implanted a culture of order, discipline, and control from the moment they founded the company. The emphasis on order and focus means employees can generally go home by 6 P.M. rather than work all night to finish important projects. Hjorten insists that the company's culture isn't rigid or uptight, just *careful*. Although sometimes being careful means being slow, so far Pacific Edge has managed to keep pace with the demands of the external environment.[62]

Each of these four categories of culture can be successful. In addition, organizations usually have values that fall into more than one category. The relative emphasis on various cultural values depends on the needs of the environment and the organization's focus. Managers are responsible for instilling the cultural values the organization needs to be successful in its environment.

Shaping Corporate Culture for Innovative Response

Research conducted by a Stanford University professor indicates that the one factor that increases a company's value the most is people and how they are treated.[63] In addition, surveys found that CEOs cite organizational culture as their most important mechanism for attracting, motivating, and retaining talented employees, a capability they consider the single best predictor of overall organizational excellence.[64] In a survey of Canadian senior executives, fully 82 percent believe a direct correlation exists between culture and financial performance.[65]

Corporate culture plays a key role in creating an organizational climate that enables learning and innovative responses to threats from the external environment, challenging new opportunities, or organizational crises. However, managers realize they can't focus all their effort on values; they also need a commitment to solid business performance.

MANAGING THE HIGH-PERFORMANCE CULTURE

Companies that succeed in a turbulent world are those that pay careful attention to both cultural values *and* business performance. Cultural values can energize and motivate employees by appealing to higher ideals and unifying people around shared goals. In addition, values boost performance by shaping and guiding employee behavior so that everyone's actions are aligned with strategic priorities.[66] Exhibit 2.8 illustrates four organizational outcomes based on the relative attention managers pay to cultural values and business performance.[67] A company in quadrant A pays little attention to either values or business

TAKE ACTION

Would you rather work in an organization with an adaptability, achievement, involvement, or consistency culture? Complete the New Manager's Self Test on page 64 to get an idea of what type of culture you would be most comfortable working in.

achievement culture
A results-oriented culture that values competitiveness, personal initiative, and achievement.

involvement culture
A culture that places high value on meeting the needs of employees and values cooperation and equality.

consistency culture
A culture that values and rewards a methodical, rational, orderly way of doing things.

NEW MANAGER'S SELF-TEST

Culture Preference

The fit between a new manager and organization culture can determine success and satisfaction. To understand your culture preference, rank order the items below from 1 to 8 based on the strength of your preference (1 = strongest preference).

1. The organization is very personal, much like an extended family.

2. The organization is dynamic and changing, where people take risks.

3. The organization is achievement oriented, with the focus on competition and getting jobs done.

4. The organization is stable and structured and has clarity and established procedures.

5. Management style is characterized by teamwork and participation.

6. Management style is characterized by innovation and risk taking.

7. Management style is characterized by high performance demands and achievement.

8. Management style is characterized by security and predictability.

'SCORING AND INTERPRETATION: Each question pertains to one of the four types of culture in Exhibit 2.7. To compute your preference for each type of culture, add the scores for each set of two questions as follows:

    Involvement culture—total for questions 1, 4: _____

    Adaptability culture—total for questions 2, 6: _____

    Achievement culture—total for questions 3, 7: _____

    Consistency culture—total for questions 4, 8: _____

A lower score means a stronger culture preference. You will likely be more comfortable and more effective as a new manager in a corporate culture that is compatible with your personal preferences. A higher score means the culture would not fit your expectations, and you would have to change your style and preference to be comfortable. Review the text discussion of the four culture types. Do your cultural preference scores seem correct to you? Can you think of companies that fit your culture preference?

SOURCE: Adapted from Kim S. Cameron and Robert D. Quinn, *Diagnosing and Changing Organizational Culture* (Reading, MA: Addison-Wesley, 1999).

results and is unlikely to survive for long. Managers in quadrant B organizations are highly focused on creating a strong cohesive culture, but they don't tie organizational values directly to goals and desired business results. When cultural values aren't connected to business performance, they aren't likely to benefit the organization during hard times. The corporate culture at Lego headquarters in Billund, Denmark, nearly doomed the toymaker in the 1990s when sales plummeted as children turned away from traditional toys to video games. Imagination and creativity, not business performance, were what guided Lego. The attitude among employees was, "We're doing great stuff for kids—don't bother us with financial goals." New leader Jorgen Vig Knudstorp upended the corporate culture with a

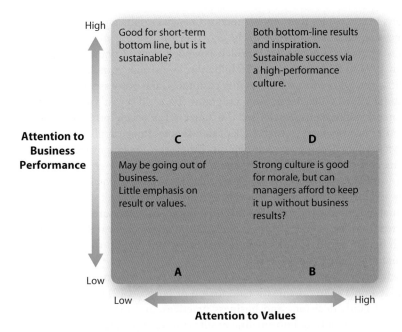

| | High | Good for short-term bottom line, but is it sustainable? | Both bottom-line results and inspiration. Sustainable success via a high-performance culture. | | EXHIBIT 2.8 Combining Culture and Performance |

Attention to Business Performance

High — Good for short-term bottom line, but is it sustainable? — Both bottom-line results and inspiration. Sustainable success via a high-performance culture.

C **D**

May be going out of business. Little emphasis on result or values. — Strong culture is good for morale, but can managers afford to keep it up without business results?

Low — **A** **B**

Low ← → High

Attention to Values

SOURCE: Adapted from Jeff Rosenthal and Mary Ann Masarech, "High-Performance Cultures: How Values Can Drive Business Results," *Journal of Organizational Excellence* (Spring 2003): 3–18.

new employee motto: "I am here to make money for the company." The shift to bottom-line results appears to be making a difference, although Lego still has a long way to go.[68]

Quadrant C represents organizations that are focused primarily on bottom-line results and pay little attention to organizational values.

This approach may be profitable in the short run, but the success is difficult to sustain over the long term because the "glue" that holds the organization together—that is, shared cultural values—is missing. Think about the numerous get-rich-quick goals of dot-com entrepreneurs. Thousands of companies that sprang up in the late 1990s were aimed primarily at fast growth and quick profits, with little effort to build a solid organization based on long-term mission and values. When the crash came, these companies failed. Those that survived were typically companies with strong cultural values that helped them weather the storm. For example, both eBay and Amazon.com managers paid careful attention to organizational culture, as did smaller e-commerce companies such as Canada's Mediagrif Interactive Technologies, an online business-to-business brokerage that allows businesses to meet online and trade their goods.[69]

Finally, companies in quadrant D put high emphasis on both culture and solid business performance as drivers of organizational success. Managers in these organizations align values with the company's day-to-day operations—hiring practices, performance management, budgeting, criteria for promotions and rewards, and so forth. A 2004 study of corporate values by Booz Allen Hamilton and the Aspen Institute found that

What do you think of quadrant C courses where cutthroat competition to make grades is the top priority? And where the teacher doesn't care about the students, only how well they do on assignments and tests?

© GETTY IMAGES

The idea for this vertical fashion show at Rockefeller Center, where an acrobatic rappelling troupe walked down the side of a building, was born in Target's high-performance culture. Target has quarterly big idea internal contests in which departments compete for additional budget allocations awarded for innovative ideas. The fun, creative competition encourages a sense of employee ownership and reinforces shared values. Tapping into employee talent helps Target meet its mission of providing customers with more for less.

CONCEPT CONNECTION

managers in companies that report superior financial results typically put a high emphasis on values and link them directly to the way they run the organization.[70] A good example is the fast-growing Umpqua Bank, which expanded from 11 branches and $140 million in assets in 1994 to 92 branches and $5 billion in assets nine years later. At Umpqua, every element of the culture focuses on serving customers, and every aspect of operations reflects the cultural values. Consider training programs. To avoid the "it's not my job" attitude that infects many banks, managers devised the "universal associate" program, which trains every bank staffer in every task, so that a teller can take a mortgage application and a loan officer can process your checking account deposit. Employees are empowered to make their own decisions about how to satisfy customers, and branches have free rein to devise unique ways to coddle the clientele in their particular location. Umpqua also carefully measures and rewards the cultural values it wants to maintain. The bank's executive vice president of cultural enhancement devised a software program that measures how cultural values are connected to performance, which the bank calls *return on quality* (ROQ). The ROQ scores for each branch and department are posted every month, and they serve as the basis for determining incentives and rewards.[71]

Quadrant D organizations represent the **high-performance culture**, a culture that (1) is based on a solid organizational mission or purpose, (2) embodies shared adaptive values that guide decisions and business practices, and (3) encourages individual employee ownership of both bottom-line results and the organization's cultural backbone.[72]

One of the most important things managers do is create and influence organizational culture to meet strategic goals because culture has a significant impact on performance. In *Corporate Culture and Performance*, Kotter and Heskett provided evidence that companies that intentionally managed cultural values outperformed similar companies that did not. Recent research validated that some elements of corporate culture are positively correlated with higher financial performance.[73] A good example is Caterpillar Inc. Caterpillar developed a cultural assessment process to measure and manage how effectively the culture contributes to organizational effectiveness. The assessment gave top executives hard data documenting millions of dollars in savings attributed directly to cultural factors.[74]

CULTURAL LEADERSHIP

A primary way in which managers shape cultural norms and values to build a high-performance culture is through *cultural leadership*. Managers must *overcommunicate* to ensure that employees understand the new culture values, and they signal these values in actions as well as words.

A **cultural leader** defines and uses signals and symbols to influence corporate culture. Cultural leaders influence culture in two key areas:

1. **The cultural leader articulates a vision for the organizational culture that employees can believe in.** The leader defines and communicates central values that employees believe in and will rally around. Values are tied to a clear and compelling mission or core purpose.

2. **The cultural leader heeds the day-to-day activities that reinforce the cultural vision.** The leader makes sure that work procedures and reward systems match and reinforce the values. Actions speak louder than words, so cultural leaders "walk their talk."[75]

Managers widely communicate the cultural values through words and actions. Values statements that aren't reinforced by management behavior are meaningless or even harmful for employees and the organization. Whole Foods founder and CEO John Mackey wants his managers to place more value on creating "a better person, company, and world" than on pursuing personal financial gain. To demonstrate his personal commitment to this belief,

Have you had a course in which all students worked really hard because they respected the teacher, who is a smart and approachable person with high standards?

Even as a new manager, you can manage for high performance by creating an adaptive culture and tying cultural values to the accomplishment of business results. Act as a cultural leader by communicating the desired values and outcomes and then modeling them in your daily behavior and decisions.

high-performance culture
A culture based on a solid organizational mission or purpose that uses shared adaptive values to guide decisions and business practices and to encourage individual employee ownership of both bottom-line results and the organization's cultural backbone.

cultural leader
A manager who uses signals and symbols to influence corporate culture.

he asked the board of directors to donate all his future stock options to the company's two foundations, the Animal Compassion Foundation and the Whole Planet Foundation.[76]

Cultural leaders also uphold their commitment to values during difficult times or crises, as illustrated by the example of Bill Greehey at Valero earlier in this chapter. On *Fortune* magazine's list of the 100 best companies to work for, Valero zoomed from number 23 to number 3 based on its treatment of employees following the devastating 2005 hurricanes. Despite the costs, Valero kept people on the payroll throughout the crisis, set up special booths to feed volunteers, and donated $1 million to the American Red Cross for hurricane relief efforts.[77] Upholding the cultural values helps organizations weather a crisis and come out stronger on the other side. Creating and maintaining a high-performance culture is not easy in today's turbulent environment and changing workplace, but through their words—and particularly their actions—cultural leaders let everyone in the organization know what really counts.

Summary

The organizational environment includes all elements existing outside the organization's boundaries that have the potential to affect the organization. Events in the external environment are considered important influences on organizational behavior and performance. The external environment consists of two layers: the task environment and the general environment. The task environment includes customers, competitors, suppliers, and the labor market. The general environment includes technological, sociocultural, economic, legal–political, international, and natural dimensions. Management techniques for helping the organization adapt to the environment include boundary-spanning roles, interorganizational partnerships, and mergers and joint ventures.

The organization also has an internal environment, which includes the elements within the organization's boundaries. A major internal element that helps organizations adapt to the environment is culture. Corporate culture is an important part of the internal organizational environment and includes the key values, beliefs, understandings, and norms that organization members share. Organizational activities that illustrate corporate culture include symbols, stories, heroes, slogans,

and ceremonies. For the organization to be effective, corporate culture should be aligned with organizational strategy and the needs of the external environment.

Four types of culture are adaptability, achievement, involvement, and consistency. Strong cultures are effective when they enable an organization to meet strategic goals and adapt to changes in the external environment.

Culture is important because it can have a significant impact on organizational performance. Managers emphasize both values and business results to create a high-performance culture, enabling the organization to achieve solid business performance through the actions of motivated employees who are aligned with the mission and goals of the company.

Managers create and sustain adaptive high-performance cultures through cultural leadership. They define and articulate important values that are tied to a clear and compelling mission, and they widely communicate and uphold the values through their words and particularly their actions. Work procedures, budgeting, decision making, reward systems, and other day-to-day activities are aligned with the cultural values.

Discussion Questions

1. How can you prepare yourself to become an effective manager in an increasingly uncertain and global business environment?

2. Would the task environment for a cellular phone company contain the same elements as that for a government welfare agency? Discuss.

3. What do you think are the most important forces in the external environment creating uncertainty for organizations today? Do the forces you identified typically arise in the task environment or in the general environment?

4. Contemporary best-selling management books often argue that customers are the most important element in the external environment. Do you agree? In what company situations might this statement be untrue?

5. Why do you think many managers are surprised by environmental changes and unable to help their organizations adapt? Can a manager ever be prepared for an

environmental change as dramatic as that experienced by airlines in the United States following the September 11, 2001, terrorist attacks in New York and Washington?

6. Why are interorganizational partnerships so important for today's companies? What elements in the current environment might contribute to either an increase or a decrease in interorganizational collaboration? Discuss.

7. Many companies are "going green" or adopting environmentally friendly business strategies. Clorox, for example, now offers an eco-friendly household cleaner called Green Works. How do companies benefit from going green?

8. Why are symbols important to a corporate culture? Do stories, heroes, slogans, and ceremonies have symbolic value? Discuss.

9. Both China and India are rising economic powers. How might your approach to doing business with Communist China be different from your approach to doing business with India, the world's most populous democracy? In which country would you expect to encounter the most rules? The most bureaucracy?

10. General Electric is famous for firing the lowest-performing 10 percent of its managers each year. With its strict no-layoff policy, Valero Energy believes people need to feel secure in their jobs to perform their best. Yet both are high-performing companies. How do you account for the success of such opposite philosophies?

Self Learning

Think of a specific full-time job you have held. Please answer the following questions according to your perception of the *managers above you* in that job. Circle a number on the 1–5 scale based on the extent to which you agree with each statement about the managers above you: 5 MOSTLY YES; 4 Agree; 3 Neither agree nor disagree; 2 Disagree; 1 MOSTLY NO.

1. Good ideas got serious consideration from management above me.
   1 2 3 4 5

2. Management above me was interested in ideas and suggestions from people at my level in the organization.
   1 2 3 4 5

3. When suggestions were made to management above me, they received fair evaluation.
   1 2 3 4 5

4. Management did not expect me to challenge or change the status quo.
   1 2 3 4 5

5. Management specifically encouraged me to bring about improvements in my workplace.
   1 2 3 4 5

6. Management above me took action on recommendations made from people at my level.
   1 2 3 4 5

7. Management rewarded me for correcting problems.
   1 2 3 4 5

8. Management clearly expected me to improve work unit procedures and practices.
   1 2 3 4 5

9. I felt free to make recommendations to management above me to change existing practices.
   1 2 3 4 5

10. Good ideas did not get communicated upward because management above me was not very approachable.
    1 2 3 4 5

Scoring and Interpretation

To compute your score: Subtract each of your scores for questions 4 and 10 from 6. Using your adjusted scores, add the numbers for all 10 questions to give you the total score. Divide that number by 10 to get your average score: _____.

An adaptive culture is shaped by the values and actions of top and middle managers. When managers actively encourage and welcome change initiatives from below, the organization will be infused with values for change. These 10 questions measure your management's openness to change. A typical average score for management openness to change is about 3. If your average score was 4 or higher, you worked in an organization that expressed strong cultural values of adaptation. If your average score was 2 or below, the culture was probably nonadaptive.

Thinking about your job, is the level of management openness to change correct for the organization? Why? Compare your scores to those of another student and take turns describing what it was like working for the managers above your jobs. Do you sense a relationship between job satisfaction and your management's openness to change? What specific management characteristics and corporate values explain the openness scores in the two jobs?

SOURCES: S. J. Ashford, N. P. Rothbard, S. K. Piderit, and J. E. Dutton, "Out on a Limb: The Role of Context and Impression Management in Issue Selling," *Administrative Science Quarterly* 43 (1998): 23–57; and E. W. Morrison and C. C. Phelps, "Taking Charge at Work: Extrarole Efforts to Initiate Workplace Change," *Academy of Management Journal* 42 (1999): 403–419.

Group Learning

Organizational Graffiti

Needed:

   (a) 2 × 2 Post-it Notes™ or blank sheets of paper (optional)

   (b) Colored sticky dots (optional)

1. Each person creates a graffito on the Post-it or paper. The topics should relate to the following questions (your instructor may choose di fferent questions) (5 to 10 minutes): (a) What are the norms of behavior in most of your courses? (b) What types of norms would you prefer instead?

2. All notes are stuck up on a large board (or pages are taped on the blackboard) (5 min.).

3. The whole group works together to organize graffiti into theme categories, reducing the number of categories without sacrificing substance (5–10 min.).

4. Each grouping is given a title by the group (5–10 min.).

5. Each person is given three sticky dots, which are used to "vote" for most important title. If sticky dots are not used or not available, each person puts three check marks by titles. Someone can use all of his or her marks or dots on one title if desired (5 min.).

6. The top two titles are discussed as action plans (10–20 min.). What does the group plan to do? Who will do it? When? How? How will the group know how well it is doing? What is the first step? How can this information benefit the whole school or department?

7. Final discussion (5–10 min.). What did you learn about cultures and norms? How can it be helpful to make the implicit explicit?

Optional method: Small groups develop their own group graffiti and present it to entire class.

SOURCE: Adapted from Christopher Taylor, "Organizational Graffiti: A Different Approach to Uncovering Issues," *Journal of Management Education*, 23(3) (June 1999), 290–296. Copyright © 1999, OBTS Teaching Society for Management Educators.

Action Learning

Answer the following questions yourself:

1. How do you spend a typical day? Weekend?

2. What kind of music do you listen to? How do you listen to it? How many favorite groups do you have? Name some.

3. How much time do you spend on the phone or online each day?

4. What do you expect to do when you are 25 years old (or 35, 45, etc. if you are older)?

5. When (if ever) do you expect to marry and have kids?

6. What is dating like now?

7. Do your parents support you? If so, how much does it cost them roughly for a year, including things such as tuition, room, and board?

8. How old do you expect to be before your parents don't support you at all financially other than occasional birthday or holiday gifts?

9. Do you work while going to school? How much and what type?

10. If you've had several jobs, describe the differences between them.

11. How do you spend your disposable income?

12. How often do you travel? To where? Who pays?

After you've answered these, go to your parents or two other similarly aged adults (male and female) and ask them these questions.

Ask them to think back to when they were about your age and respond in terms of their lives back then.

13. How did you spend a typical day? Weekend?

14. What kind of music did you listen to? How did you listen to it? How many favorite groups did you have? Name some.

15. How much time did you spend on the phone each day?

16. What did you expect to do when you were 25 years old (or 35, 45, etc. if you were older)?

17. When did you get married and have kids?

18. What was dating like back then?

19. How long did your parents support you? If they did so during college, how much did it cost them roughly for a year, including things such as tuition, room, and board?

20. At what age did your parents stop supporting you financially other than occasional birthday or holiday gifts?

21. Did you work while going to school (high school or college)? How much and what type?

22. What's the difference between the jobs you had back then and now? Is your work life more or less predictable?

23. How did you spend your disposable income?

24. How often did you travel? To where? Who paid?

Write a short paper that describes the differences between your world and that of your parents at that age. What were the biggest differences?

Your instructor may ask you to participate in a class discussion about this.

Ethical Dilemma

Competitive Intelligence Predicament

Miquel Vasquez was proud of his job as a new product manager for a biotechnology start-up, and he loved the high stakes and tough decisions that went along with the job. But as he sat in his den after a long day, he was troubled, struggling over what had happened earlier that day and the information he now possessed.

Just before lunch, Miquel's boss had handed him a stack of private strategic documents from their closest competitor. It was a competitive intelligence gold mine—product plans, pricing strategies, partnership agreements, and other documents, most clearly marked "proprietary and confidential." When Miquel asked where the documents came from, his boss told him with a touch of pride that he had taken them right off the competing firm's server. "I got into a private section of their intranet and downloaded everything that looked interesting," he said. Later, realizing Miquel was suspicious, the boss would say only that he had obtained "electronic access" via a colleague and had not personally broken any passwords. Maybe not, Miquel thought to himself, but this situation wouldn't pass the *60 Minutes* test. If word of this acquisition of a competitor's confidential data ever got out to the press, the company's reputation would be ruined.

Miquel didn't feel good about using these materials. He spent the afternoon searching for answers to his dilemma, but found no clear company policies or regulations that offered any guidance. His sense of fair play told him that to use the information was unethical, if not downright illegal. What bothered him even more was the knowledge that this kind of thing might happen again. Using this confidential information would certainly give him and his company a competitive advantage, but Miquel wasn't sure he wanted to work for a firm that would stoop to such tactics.

What Would You Do?

1. Go ahead and use the documents to the company's benefit, but make clear to your boss that you don't want him passing confidential information to you in the future. If he threatens to fire you, threaten to leak the news to the press.

2. Confront your boss privately and let him know you're uncomfortable with how the documents were obtained and what possession of them says about the company's culture. In addition to the question of the legality of using the information, point out that it is a public relations nightmare waiting to happen.

3. Talk to the company's legal counsel and contact the Society of Competitive Intelligence Professionals for guidance. Then, with their opinions and facts to back you up, go to your boss.

SOURCE: Adapted from Kent Weber, "Gold Mine or Fool's Gold?" *Business Ethics* (Jan.–Feb. 2001): 18.

3 Chapter Three

Managing in a Global Environment

LEARNING OBJECTIVES

After studying this chapter, you should be able to:

1 Describe the emerging borderless world and some issues of particular concern for today's managers.

2 Describe market-entry strategies that businesses use to develop foreign markets.

3 Define international management and explain how it differs from the management of domestic business operations.

4 Indicate how dissimilarities in the economic, sociocultural, and legal–political environments throughout the world can affect business operations.

5 Describe how regional trading alliances are re-shaping the international business environment.

6 Describe the characteristics of a multinational corporation.

7 Explain cultural intelligence and why it is necessary for managers working in foreign countries.

New Manager's Questions

Please circle your opinion below each of the following statements.

1 I have no desire to live abroad, or to work overseas, even for a short while.

MOSTLY YES < < <   > > > MOSTLY NO

1	2	3	4	5

2 I would never want to be part of a business operation in a place with political instability.

MOSTLY YES < < <   > > > MOSTLY NO

1	2	3	4	5

3 I really admire cultures that are high achieving.

MOSTLY YES < < <   > > > MOSTLY NO

1	2	3	4	5

Do you think if you stay in your hometown as a manager you won't have to interact with people from other cultures? Think again. Many people who grew up in small towns with little diversity fail to appreciate the importance of cross-cultural skills. Yet in today's world, every manager needs to think globally. Rapid advances in technology and communications have made the international dimension an increasingly important part of the external environment discussed in Chapter 2. The future of our businesses and our societies is being shaped by global rather than local relationships.

A global mind-set and international experience are fast becoming prerequisites for managerial success. Many organizations based in the United States, including Walmart, FedEx, Starbucks, and Nike, have learned that the greatest potential for growth lies overseas. In addition, the demand for raw materials such as steel, aluminum, cement, and copper has slowed in the United States but is booming in countries such as China, India, and Brazil.[1] For online companies, too, going global is a key to growth. The number of residential Internet subscribers in China is growing significantly faster than that of the United States. Western Europe and Japan together account for a huge share of the world's e-commerce revenue.[2]

The environment for today's organizations has become extremely competitive and highly complex. Less-developed countries are challenging mature countries in a number of industries. China is the world's largest maker of consumer electronics and is rapidly and expertly moving into biotechnology, computer manufacturing, and semiconductors. At least 19 advanced new semiconductor plants are in or nearing operation in China.[3] The pace of innovation in India is startling in industries as diverse as precision manufacturing, health care, and pharmaceuticals, and some observers see the beginnings of hypercompetitive multinationals in that country.[4]

This chapter introduces basic concepts about the global environment and international management. First, we consider the difficulty managers have operating in an increasingly borderless world. We then touch on various types of strategies and techniques for entering foreign markets and address the economic, legal–political, and sociocultural challenges companies encounter within the global business environment. The chapter also describes multinational corporations, looks at the impact of trade agreements, and considers the globalization backlash. The final section of the chapter talks about some of the challenges managers face when working cross-culturally.

A Borderless World

A manager's reality is that isolation from international forces is no longer possible. Consider that the FBI now ranks cybercrime as one of its top priorities because electronic boundaries between countries are virtually nonexistent. This openness has many positive aspects, but it also means hackers in one nation can steal secrets from companies in another or unleash viruses, worms, or other rogue programs to destroy the computer systems of corporations and governments around the world. The FBI has more than 150 agents in some 56 international offices, including Iraq and China, up from about a dozen offices in the early 1990s.[5]

Business has also become a unified, global field as trade barriers fall, communication becomes faster and cheaper, and consumer tastes in everything from clothing to cellular phones converge. Thomas Middelhoff of Germany's Bertelsmann AG, which purchased U.S. publisher Random House, put it this way: "There are no German and American companies. There are only

Today's companies compete in a borderless world. Procter & Gamble's sales in Southeast Asia make up a rapidly growing percentage of the company's worldwide sales. These shoppers are purchasing Procter & Gamble's diaper products, Pampers, in Malaysia.

·····▷ CONCEPT CONNECTION ◁······

NEW MANAGER'S SELF-TEST

Are You Ready to Work Internationally?[8]

Are you ready to negotiate a sales contract with someone from another country? Companies large and small deal on a global basis. To what extent are you guilty of the behaviors below? Please answer each item as Mostly True or Mostly False for you.

	MOSTLY TRUE	MOSTLY FALSE
1. Impatient? Do you have a short attention span? Do you want to keep moving to the next topic?	_____	_____
2. A poor listener? Are you uncomfortable with silence? Does your mind think about what you want to say next?	_____	_____
3. Argumentative? Do you enjoy arguing for its own sake?	_____	_____
4. Unfamiliar with cultural specifics in other countries? Do you have limited experience in other countries?	_____	_____
5. Short-term oriented? Do you place more emphasis on the short term than on the long term in your thinking and planning?	_____	_____
6. "All business"? Do you think that it is a waste of time getting to know someone personally before discussing business?	_____	_____
7. Legalistic to win your point? Do you hold others to an agreement regardless of changing circumstances?	_____	_____
8. Thinking "win–lose" when negotiating? Do you usually try to win a negotiation at the other's expense?	_____	_____

SCORING AND INTERPRETATION: American managers often display cross-cultural ignorance during business negotiations compared to counterparts in other countries. American habits can be disturbing; these include emphasizing areas of disagreement over agreement, spending little time understanding the views and interests of the other side, and adopting an adversarial attitude. Americans often like to leave a negotiation thinking they won, which can be embarrassing to the other side. For this quiz, a low score shows better international presence. If you answered "Mostly True" to three or fewer questions, then consider yourself ready to assist with an international negotiation. If you scored six or more "Mostly True" responses, it is time to learn more about other national cultures before participating in international business deals. Try to develop greater focus on other people's needs and an appreciation for different viewpoints. Be open to compromise and develop empathy for people who are different from you.

successful and unsuccessful companies."[6] The difficulties and risks of a borderless world are matched by benefits and opportunities.

Today, even small companies can locate different parts of the organization wherever it makes the most business sense. Virtual connections enable close, rapid coordination among people working in different parts of the world, so it is no longer necessary to keep everything in one place. Organizations can go wherever they want to find the lowest costs or the best brainpower. Many companies outsource certain functions to contractors in other countries as easily as if the contractor were located right next door. For example, Excel Foundry and Machine in Pekin, Illinois, makes parts for machinery used in heavy construction and

	1. Domestic	2. International	3. Multinational	4. Global
Strategic Orientation	Domestically oriented	Export-oriented, multidomestic	Multinational	Global
Stage of Development	Initial foreign involvement	Competitive positioning	Explosion of international operations	Global
Cultural Sensitivity	Of little importance	Very important	Somewhat important	Critically important
Manager Assumptions	"One best way"	"Many good ways"	"The least-cost way"	"Many good ways"

SOURCE: Based on Nancy J. Adler, *International Dimensions of Organizational Behavior*, 4th ed. (Cincinnati: South-Western, 2002): 8–9.

EXHIBIT 3.1
Four Stages of Globalization

As a new manager, learn to "think globally." Take an interest in international people and issues. Expand your thinking by reading and networking broadly.

mining operations. President Doug Parsons uses a strategy of outsourcing the easily duplicated parts to contractors in China so that Excel can focus more money and energy on making specialty products and innovating for the future.[7]

A borderless world means consumers can no longer tell from which country they're buying. U.S.-based Ford Motor Company owns Sweden's Volvo, while the iconic American beer Miller is owned by a South African company. Toyota is a Japanese corporation, but it has manufactured more than 10 million vehicles in North American factories. The technology behind Intel's Centrino wireless components was born in a lab in Haifa, Israel, and Chinese researchers designed the microprocessors that control the pitch of the blade on General Electric's giant wind turbines.[9]

For managers who think globally, the whole world is a source of ideas, resources, information, employees, and customers. Managers can move their companies into the international arena on a variety of levels. The process of globalization typically passes through four distinct stages as illustrated in Exhibit 3.1.

Today, the number of global or stateless corporations is increasing and the awareness of national borders decreasing; this is reflected in the frequency of foreign participation at the top management levels. Consider what's happening in the corner office of corporate America, where 14 of the *Fortune* 100 companies are now run by foreign-born chief executive officers (CEOs). Citigroup tapped India-born Vikram S. Pandit as its CEO. Alcoa's top leader was born in Morocco, and Dow Chemical is headed by a native Australian.[10]

The trend is seen in other countries as well. Wales-born Howard Stringer was named Sony's first non-Japanese CEO in 2004, and Nancy McKinstry is the first American to head Dutch publisher Wolters Kluwer.[11] Increasingly, managers at lower levels are also expected to know a second or third language and have international experience.

Getting Started Internationally

market-entry strategy
An organizational strategy for entering a foreign market.

Organizations have a couple of ways to become involved internationally. One is to seek cheaper sources of materials or labor offshore, which is called *offshoring* or *global outsourcing*. Another is to develop markets for finished products outside their home countries, which may include exporting, licensing, and direct investing. These **market-entry strategies**

Assess Your Answer

1 I have no desire to live abroad, or to work overseas, even for a short while.

ANSWER: To advance in their careers, young managers should strongly consider international assignments.

SPOTLIGHT ON SKILLS

Cross-Cultural Communication

American managers are often at a disadvantage when doing business overseas. Part of this is the lack of foreign language skills, as well as inexperience in dealing with other cultures and living conditions that Americans find less than ideal. Consequently, many mistakes are made—mistakes that could easily be avoided. Studies show that when managers are prepared and trained for cross-cultural interactions, their productivity increases by 30 percent.

The manager's attitude is perhaps the most important factor in success. Those who go abroad with a sense of "wonder" about the new culture are better off than those with a judgmental view of "If it is different, then my culture must be better." Seeing differences as new and interesting is more productive than being critical. One way is to begin to *appreciate* rather than *evaluate* cultural differences. Such evaluations lead to an "us versus them" approach, which never sits well with the locals. One of the keys to cultural adaptation is open-mindedness, being able to respect other points of view.

Though every culture has its own way of communicating, here are some basic principles to follow in international business relations:

1. Always show respect and listen carefully. Don't be in a hurry to finish the "business." Many other cultures value the social component of these interactions.
2. Try to gain an appreciation for the differences between Geert Hofstede's "masculine" and feminine" cultures. (We explore Hofstede's theories in more detail later in this chapter.) American masculine business behaviors include high achievement, acquisition of material goods, and efficiency whereas other, more feminine cultures value relationships, leisure time with family, and developing a sense of community. Don't mistake this more feminine approach with lack of motivation. Similarly, cultures that value "being and inner spiritual development" rather than compulsive "doing" are not necessarily inferior.
3. Try hard not to feel your way is the best. This can come across as arrogance and rubs salt in the deep wounds of some lesser-developed countries.
4. Emphasize points of agreement.
5. When there are disagreements, check on the perceived definitions of words. Often there may be a huge or subtle shade of meaning that is causing the problem. You may actually both be trying to say the same thing.
6. Save face and "give" face as well, for this can be a way of showing honor to others.

7. Don't go alone. Take someone who knows the culture or language better than you. If you are conversing in English and others "know" the language, you might be surprised how much they miss. Often taking an excellent translator along is a good investment.
8. Don't assume the other country sees leadership the same as you do. In many other cultures, *empowerment* seems more like anarchy and the result of an ineffectual manager.
9. Don't lose your temper.
10. Don't embarrass anyone in front of others. Even if you meant it as a "joke," it likely won't be taken that way.
11. Avoid forming cliques and try to interact with the locals as much as possible. Americans often tend to hang together in packs or tribes, which is not welcoming to the locals.
12. Be aware that most Asian countries are *high-context cultures* based on a complicated system of relationships and moral codes (some of which might not seem "moral" to you) whereas American culture is *low context*, meaning people are more direct and rely on legal codes.
13. Leave the common American task-oriented, fast-paced style at home. Effective transfer of skills to other cultures requires a patient nonjudgmentalism. Hasty criticisms of the foreigner's ideas only serve to shut that person down and close the door to meaningful interactions.
14. Some countries such as Israel, however, are even more fast paced, and people become impatient with Americans' small talk.
15. Also be sensitive to the difference between the North American low-context culture—where employees are encouraged to be self-reliant—and high-context cultures (much of Asia, Africa, South America), where workers expect warmly supportive relationships with their American supervisors and co-workers.
16. If you travel to the increasingly visited out-of-the-way locations, learn to tolerate unpredictability and go without what you might consider basic amenities. Avoid complaining to business clients about poor phone service, lack of hot water (or any water, for that matter), erratic electricity, or unsavory food. Just remember: You are a guest and should act with the grace that goes along with that role.

SOURCE: "Competency of Intercultural Management," *Jakarta Post,* Mar. 11, 2009, p. 17; "Improved Cross-Cultural Communication Increases Global Sourcing, Productivity, Accenture Study Finds," *Business Wire,* July 12, 2006, p. 1.

EXHIBIT 3.2

Strategies
for Entering
International Markets

- - - - - - - - - - -

exporting
An entry strategy in which
the organization maintains its
production facilities within its
home country and transfers
its products for sale in
foreign countries.

countertrade
The barter of products for
other products rather than
their sale for currency.

global outsourcing
Engaging in the international
division of labor so as to
obtain the cheapest sources
of labor and supplies
regardless of country; also
called *offshoring*.

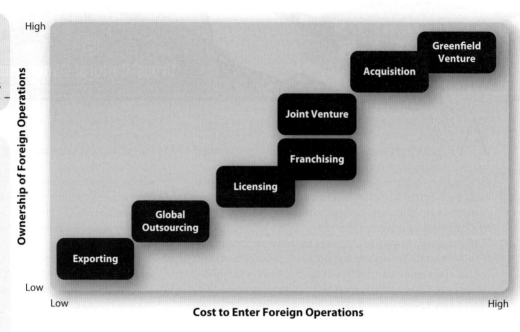

Christopher Norman Chocolates found that
perfection-obsessed Japanese customers appreciate the difference between the New York
company's hand-painted chocolates and French
and Belgium chocolates. Joe Guiliano (left) and
John Down, partners in the high-end specialty
chocolate company, first exported the chocolates
through a Japanese distributor with experience
in this niche market. Later they moved to a
licensing agreement, with the distributor making
the confections in a facility near Tokyo.

represent alternative ways to sell products and services in foreign markets. Most firms begin
with exporting and work up to direct investment. Exhibit 3.2 shows the strategies companies can use to enter foreign markets. One company that maximizes the use of advantages in
different countries is Hong Kong–based Li & Fung, described in this chapter's Benchmarking box.

EXPORTING

With **exporting**, the corporation maintains its production facilities within
the home nation and transfers its products for sale in foreign countries.[12]
Exporting enables a company to market its products in other countries at
modest resource cost and with limited risk. Exporting does entail numerous
problems based on physical distances, government regulations, foreign currencies, and cultural differences, but it is less expensive than committing the
firm's own capital to building plants in host countries. A form of exporting
to less-developed countries is called **countertrade**, which is the barter of
products for products rather than the sale of products for currency. Many
less-developed countries have products to exchange but have no foreign
currency. An estimated 20 percent of world trade is countertrade.

OUTSOURCING

Global outsourcing, also called *offshoring*, means engaging in the international division of labor so that work activities can be done in countries
with the cheapest sources of labor and supplies. Millions of low-level jobs
such as textile manufacturing, call-center operations, and credit-card processing have been outsourced to low-wage countries in recent years. The
Internet and plunging telecommunications costs are enabling companies to
outsource more and higher-level work as well. Netgear, a company based in
Santa Clara, California, makes networking equipment that is designed and
marketed in the United States, engineered in Taiwan, and manufactured in

BENCH-MARKING

Li & Fung

If you buy a shirt at Guess or The Limited, chances are it was outsourced through Li & Fung in Hong Kong. Run by Harvard graduates and Hong Kong natives William and Victor Fung, Li & Fung has no machines, no factories, and no fabrics. The Fungs only deal in information. They work with 7,500 suppliers in 38 countries, taking orders from companies such as Ambercrombie & Fitch, Disney, Levi Strauss, Timberland, Liz Claiborne, and American Eagle Outfitters. "There are no secrets to manufacturing," says Managing Director William. "A shirt is a shirt." Instead, they build on proprietary information, such as how to make that shirt faster or more efficiently.

When an order comes in, the Fungs use personalized Web sites to fine-tune the specifications with the customer. Taking that information and feeding it into their own intranet, they are able to find the best supplier of raw materials and the best factories to make assembly. An order for pants from an American brand ended up this way: Fabric was woven in China because China could do dark green dyes. Fasteners were done in Hong Kong and Korea because they were more durable. These were then shipped to Guatemala for sewing. "For simple things like pants with four seams, Guatemala is great," says division manager Ada Liu. With Guatemala's close proximity to the United States, only a few days are needed for the finished product to be ready for delivery. If production problems occur in Guatemala, then Li & Fung can tap into its extensive database to find another place for manufacturing. As the order progresses, customers can make last-minute changes through the company's Web site.

As recently as 10 years ago, when the company was run by phone and fax, Li & Fung would get an order for 50,000 cargo pants and have them delivered five months later; today it takes only a few weeks. Now, with customers able to get online and making adjustments to the color or cut right before those are done, there are fewer mistakes and fewer unhappy customers. Because this new system has increased productivity, quality and pricing have brought Li & Fung a compound annual growth of 23 percent, with 2010 revenues expected at $20 billion.

Until a few years ago, stores changed their clothes four times a year for each season. In this new economy, some of them rotate their clothes every week. It makes the name of the store Express take on a new meaning.

SOURCES: Paul Betts et al., "Hong Kong Trade Sourcing Group Has a Makeover," *Financial Times*, Mar. 26, 2009, p. 19; and "Li & Fung Ltd.," *Wall Street Journal Asia*, June 18, 2007, p. 9.

China, helping the small company take advantage of the efficiencies it can gain in three different countries.[13]

The most recent trend is outsourcing core processes, which Joe McGrath, CEO of Unisys, refers to as the "natural next phase of the offshoring movement."[14] After the Sarbanes-Oxley Act went into effect, Unisys had a hard time finding enough internal auditors in the United States, so managers outsourced their core auditing practice to China. Large pharmaceutical companies farm out much of their early-stage chemistry research to cheaper labs in China and India.[15] Many organizations are even outsourcing aspects of innovation. One survey found that 65 percent of companies reported that part of their research and development (R&D) takes place overseas. Both Microsoft and General Electric have research centers in China, and IBM has established an R&D center in India.[16]

Take out several items of clothing and look at the labels (or get in a group and have everyone read the label on the top back of the shirt in front of them). Look for "Made in . . . ." labels. How many countries are there?

FRANCHISING

Franchising occurs when a franchisee buys a complete package of materials and services, including equipment, products, product ingredients, trademark and trade name rights, managerial advice, and a standardized operating system, as well as the name and systems of the franchisor. With *licensing*, on the other hand, a licensee generally keeps its own company name, autonomy, and operating systems. The fast-food chains are some of the best-known franchisors. The story is often told of the Japanese child visiting Los Angeles who excitedly pointed out to his parents, "They have McDonald's in America."

franchising
A form of licensing in which an organization provides its foreign franchisees with a complete package of materials and services.

CHINA INC.

Many companies today are going straight to China or India as a first step into international business. Business in both countries is booming, and U.S. and European companies are taking advantage of opportunities for all of the tactics we've discussed in this section: exporting, outsourcing, licensing, and direct investment. Foreign companies are investing more in business in China than they are spending anywhere else in the world.[17] In addition, multinationals based in the United States and Europe manufacture more and more products in China using design, software, and services from India. This trend prompted one business writer to coin the term *Chindia* to reflect the combined power of the two countries in the international dimension.[18]

Outsourcing is perhaps the most widespread approach to international involvement in China and India. China manufactures an ever-growing percentage of the industrial and consumer products sold in the United States—and in other countries as well. China produces more clothes, shoes, toys, television sets, DVD players, and cell phones than any other country. U.S. furniture and cabinetmakers have also shifted much of their production to that country in recent years, and manufacturers in China are moving into higher-ticket items such as automobiles, computers, and airplane parts.

China can manufacture almost any product at a much lower cost than Western manufacturers. Despite the advantages, however, companies are finding that operating smoothly in China isn't automatic. Mattel learned the hard way after having to recall millions of Chinese-made toys tainted with lead paint, as mentioned in Chapter 2, hurting the company financially and damaging its reputation. If a company such as Mattel that has been operating in China since the late 1950s can run into trouble, think of the uncertainty newcomers must face.[19]

India, for its part, is a rising power in software design, services, and precision engineering. Nearly 50 percent of microchip engineering for Conexant Systems is done in India.[20] The California company makes the intricate brains behind Internet access for home computers and satellite-connection set-top boxes for televisions. Google sees India as the perfect place for finding the next set of ideas to keep the company on the cutting edge in global information services.

Google didn't go to India for cheap labor. It went there for technological talent. When the company wanted to open a new R&D center, it chose Basngalore, partly because many of the Indian engineers working at Google's California headquarters wanted to return home and participate in India's growth. Managers knew Google would have a hard time finding the technological brainpower the company needed in the United States alone. The company also has a larger facility in Hyderabad and two smaller offices in Mumbai and Delhi.

In addition to its hopes for India as a hotbed of innovation, Google also sees India as a vast potential market. The country's online advertising industry is miniscule today but projected to grow rapidly. Managers also believe that people in India are perfectly suited to help Google develop products for emerging markets where billions of people aren't yet on the Internet. "The fact that they come from this culture, the fact that they've seen the population of the world that's not on the Internet . . . puts them in a fairly unique position to transcend both worlds and be creative about emerging-world products," says Prasad Ram who heads the Bangalore research center.

For one thing, Indian engineers know that developing markets have different priorities. For most people in developed countries such as the United States, Internet use is about lifestyle, but for those in developing nations such as India and China, it's about *livelihood*. They want to know how the Internet can help them generate income, improve their communities, and further their own and the country's economic development. That entrepreneurial spirit is a perfect fit for Google, where the guiding philosophy is to take risks and be aggressive in finding new applications to serve new markets.[21]

Google isn't the first U.S. company to see India as a major source of technological talent. Yahoo employs about 900 engineers at a research center in India, and IBM has become the country's largest foreign employer with more than 50,000 people employed there.

The International Business Environment

International management is the management of business operations conducted in more than one country. The fundamental tasks of business management—including the financing, production, and distribution of products and services—do not change in any substantive way when a firm is transacting business across international borders. The basic management functions of planning, organizing, leading, and controlling are the same whether a company operates domestically or internationally. However, managers will experience greater difficulties and risks when performing these management functions on an international scale. Consider the following blunders:

- When U.S. chicken entrepreneur Frank Purdue translated a successful advertising slogan into Spanish, "It takes a tough man to make a tender chicken" came out as "It takes a virile man to make a chicken affectionate. "[22]

- It took McDonald's more than a year to figure out that Hindus in India do not eat beef. The company's sales took off only after McDonald's started making burgers sold in India out of lamb.[23]

- In Africa, the labels on bottles and cans show pictures of the contents so illiterate shoppers can know what they're buying. When a baby-food company showed a picture of an infant on its label, the product didn't sell very well.[24]

- United Airlines discovered that even colors can doom a product. The airline handed out white carnations when it started flying from Hong Kong, only to discover that such flowers represent death and bad luck to many Asians.[25]

Some of these examples might seem humorous, but there's nothing funny about them to managers trying to operate in a highly competitive global environment. What should managers of emerging global companies look for to avoid obvious international mistakes? When they are comparing one country with another, the economic, legal–political, and sociocultural sectors present the greatest difficulties. Key factors to understand in the international environment are summarized in Exhibit 3.3.

international management
The management of business operations conducted in more than one country.

EXHIBIT 3.3
Key Factors in the International Environment

Economic
- Economic development
- Infrastructure
- Resource and product markets
- Per capita income
- Exchange rates
- Economic conditions

Legal-Political
- Political risk
- Government takeovers
- Tariffs, quotas, taxes
- Terrorism, political instability
- Laws, regulations

Organization

Sociocultural
- Social values, beliefs
- Language
- Religion (objects, taboos, holidays)
- Kinship patterns
- Formal education, literacy
- Time orientation

BUSINESS BLOOPER

Aeroflot

Two recent incidents on Russia's Aeroflot Airlines suggest that the airline lacks management oversight. The pilot of a jet taking off from London was chatting with passengers when they noticed his speech was slurred. On another flight, a passenger got tired of the sloppy service he was receiving from two flight attendants, who had sampled from the liquor tray and were way over the legal limit. After more frustration dealing with the intoxicated attendants, the passenger asked if there was a sober employee who would be able to serve him. Their response suggests a need for customer service training: They beat up the passenger.

SOURCE: Lisa Monforton, "Flying High? You'll Be Grounded," *Vancouver Sun*, Mar. 21, 2009, p. G10; and Adam Horowitz, Mark Athitakis, Mark Lasswell, and Owen Thomas, "101 Dumbest Moments in Business," *Business 2.0* (Jan.–Feb. 2005): 103–112.

The Economic Environment

The economic environment represents the economic conditions in the country where the international organization operates. This part of the environment includes such factors as economic development, resource and product markets, and exchange rates, each of which is discussed in the following sections. In addition, factors such as inflation, interest rates, and economic growth are also part of the international economic environment.

ECONOMIC DEVELOPMENT

If one day you can go to a developing country and get outside of the foreigners' living area to see how average people live, you will be astounded at how people manage to survive on so little.

Economic development differs widely among the countries and regions of the world. Countries can be categorized as either *developing* or *developed*. Developing countries are referred to as *less-developed countries (LDCs)*. The criterion traditionally used to classify countries as developed or developing is *per capita income*, which is the income generated by the nation's production of goods and services divided by total population. The developing countries have low per capita incomes. Most LDCs are located in Asia, Africa, and South America. Developed countries are generally located in North America, Europe, and Japan. Most international business firms are headquartered in the wealthier, economically advanced countries, but smart managers are investing heavily in Asia, Eastern Europe, Latin America, and Africa.[26] These companies face risks and challenges today, but they stand to reap huge benefits in the future.

Each year, the World Economic Forum analyzes data to gauge how companies are doing in the economic development race. The Forum then releases its *Global Competitiveness Report*, which tallies 113 factors that contribute to an economy's competitiveness.[27] The report considers both hard data and perceptions of business leaders around the world and considers government policies, institutions, market size, the sophistication of financial markets, and other factors that drive productivity and thus enable sustained economic growth. Exhibit 3.4 shows the top 10 countries in the overall ranking along with several other countries for comparison. Note that highly developed countries rank higher in the competitiveness index. One important factor in gauging competitiveness is a country's **infrastructure**—that is, the physical facilities such as highways, airports, utilities, and telephone lines that support economic activities.

infrastructure
A country's physical facilities that support economic activities.

Country	Overall Ranking
United States	1
Switzerland	2
Denmark	3
Sweden	4
Germany	5
Finland	6
Singapore	7
Japan	8
United Kingdom	9
Netherlands	10
South Korea	11
Chile	26
Kuwait	30
China	34
Lithuania	38
South Africa	44
India	48

EXHIBIT 3.4
World Economic Forum Global Competitiveness Index 2007–2008

SOURCE: The *Global Competitiveness Report 2007–08*, World Economic Forum (www.gcr.weforum.org) (accessed April 30, 2008).

RESOURCE AND PRODUCT MARKETS

When operating in another country, company managers must evaluate the market demand for their products. If market demand is high, then managers may choose to export products to that country. To develop plants, however, resource markets for providing needed raw materials and labor must also be available. For example, the greatest challenge for McDonald's, which sells Big Macs on every continent except Antarctica, is to obtain supplies of everything from potatoes to hamburger buns to plastic straws. At McDonald's in Cracow, the burgers come from a Polish plant, partly owned by Chicago-based OSI Industries; the onions come from Fresno, California; the buns come from a production and distribution center near Moscow; and the potatoes come from a plant in Aldrup, Germany.[28]

EXCHANGE RATES

The *exchange rate* is the rate at which one country's currency is exchanged for another country's. Volatility in exchange rates is a major concern for companies doing business internationally.[29] Changes in the exchange rate can have major implications for the profitability of international operations that exchange millions of dollars into other currencies every day.[30] For example, assume that the U.S. dollar is exchanged for 0.8 euros. If the dollar increases in value to 0.9 euros, U.S. goods will be more expensive in France because it will take more euros to buy a dollar's worth of U.S. goods. It will be more difficult to export U.S. goods to France, and profits will be slim. If the dollar drops to a value of 0.7 euros, by contrast, U.S. goods will be cheaper in France and can be exported at a profit.

When you travel overseas, never buy foreign money on the streets. In many places this is illegal and you can end up in jail, or you might end up with counterfeit money. Use regular banks, legal money changers, or ATMs.

The Legal–Political Environment

When they go international, businesses must deal with unfamiliar political systems as well as with more government supervision and regulation. Government officials and the general public often view foreign companies as outsiders or even intruders and are suspicious of their effects on economic independence and political sovereignty.

Political risk is defined as the risk of lost assets, earning power, or managerial control due to politically based events or actions by host governments.[31] One example is a new government effort in Russia to tighten financial monitoring. Critics charge that tax authorities demand confidential client information without a legal basis and vary their interpretation of Russian law as it pleases them. PricewaterhouseCoopers has had its Moscow offices raided and was ordered to pay $15 million in back taxes that the firm said it didn't owe.[32] Political risk also includes government takeovers of property and acts of violence directed against a firm's properties or employees. In Mexico, for example, business executives and their families are prime targets for gangs of kidnappers, many of which are reportedly led by state and local police. Estimates are that big companies in Mexico typically spend between 5 percent and 15 percent of their annual budgets on security,[33] and organizations in other countries face similar security issues.

Some companies buy political risk insurance, and risk management has emerged as a critical element of management strategy for multinational organizations.[34] To reduce uncertainty, companies sometimes rely on the *Index of Economic Freedom*, which ranks countries according to the impact political intervention has on business decisions, and the *Corruption Perception Index*, which assesses 91 countries according to the level of perceived corruption in government and public administration.[35]

Another frequently cited problem for international companies is **political instability**, which includes riots, revolutions, civil disorders, and frequent changes in government. In recent decades, civil wars and large-scale violence occurred in Ukraine, Indonesia, Thailand, Sri Lanka (Ceylon), and Myanmar (Burma). China is highly vulnerable to periods of widespread public unrest due to the shifting political climate. The Middle East remains an area of extreme instability as the United States pursues a difficult and protracted reconstruction following the Iraqi war. U.S. firms or companies linked to the United States often are subject to major threats in countries characterized by political instability.

Differing laws and regulations also make doing business a true challenge for international firms. Host governments have myriad laws concerning libel statutes, consumer protection, information and labeling, employment and safety, and wages. International companies must learn these rules and regulations and abide by them. In addition, the Internet increases the impact of foreign laws on U.S. companies because it expands the potential for doing business on a global basis. First Net Card, started in 1999 to provide credit for online transactions to anyone in the world, found the complication of dealing with international credit and banking laws mind-boggling. After two years and a mountain of legal research, the company was licensed to provide credit only in the United States, Canada, and Britain.[36]

political risk
A company's risk of loss of assets, earning power, or managerial control due to politically based events or actions by host governments.

political instability
Events such as riots, revolutions, or government upheavals that affect the operations of an international company.

© JOHN & LISA MERRILL/CORBIS

Despite the political risk, political instability, and local laws and regulations of countries such as Morocco, the Coca-Cola Company earns about 80 percent of its profits from markets outside North America. The soft-drink company suffered in global markets after complaints of tainted products from Belgium bottling plants. Managers are busily trying to rebuild relationships because of the importance of international sales.

········> CONCEPT CONNECTION <········

2 I would never want to be part of a business operation in a place with political instability.

ANSWER: Though doing business in countries with political instability is risky, it can offer some of the highest financial returns.

The Sociocultural Environment

A nation's culture includes the shared knowledge, beliefs, and values, as well as the common modes of behavior and ways of thinking among members of a society. Cultural factors can be more perplexing than political and economic factors when working or living in a foreign country.

SOCIAL VALUES

Many U.S. managers fail to realize that the values and behaviors that typically govern how business is done in the United States don't translate to the rest of the world. One way managers can get a handle on local cultures is to understand differences in social values.

Hofstede's Value Dimensions. In research that included 116,000 IBM employees in 40 countries, Geert Hofstede identified four dimensions of national value systems that influence organizational and employee working relationships.[37] Examples of how countries rate on the four dimensions are shown in Exhibit 3.5.

1. *Power distance.* High **power distance** means that people accept inequality in power among institutions, organizations, and people. Low power distance means that people expect equality in power. Countries that value high power distance include Malaysia, the Philippines, and Panama. Countries that value low power distance include Denmark, Austria, and Israel.

2. *Uncertainty avoidance.* High **uncertainty avoidance** means that members of a society feel uncomfortable with uncertainty and ambiguity and thus support beliefs that promise

power distance
The degree to which people accept inequality in power among institutions, organizations, and people.

uncertainty avoidance
A value characterized by people's intolerance for uncertainty and ambiguity and resulting support for beliefs that promise certainty and conformity.

Country	Power Distance[a]	Uncertainty Avoidance[b]	Individualism[c]	Masculinity[d]
Australia	7	7	2	5
Costa Rica	8 (tie)	2 (tie)	10	9
France	3	2 (tie)	4	7
West Germany	8 (tie)	5	5	3
India	2	9	6	6
Japan	5	1	7	1
Mexico	1	4	8	2
Sweden	10	10	3	10
Thailand	4	6	9	8
United States	6	8	1	4

a_1 = highest power distance
10 = lowest power distance
c_1 = highest individualism
10 = lowest individualism

b_1 = highest uncertainty avoidance
10 = lowest uncertainty avoidance
d_1 = highest masculinity
10 = lowest masculinity

EXHIBIT 3.5
Rank Orderings of 10 Countries along Four Dimensions of National Value Systems

SOURCES: Dorothy Marcic, *Organizational Behavior and Cases*, 4th ed. (St. Paul, MN: West, 1995). Based on two books by Geert Hofstede: *Culture's Consequences* (London: Sage Publications, 1984) and *Cultures and Organizations: Software of the Mind* (New York: McGraw-Hill, 1991).

certainty and conformity. Low uncertainty avoidance means that people have high tolerance for the unstructured, the unclear, and the unpredictable. High uncertainty avoidance countries include Greece, Portugal, and Uruguay. Among countries with low uncertainty avoidance values are Singapore and Jamaica.

3. *Individualism and collectivism.* Individualism reflects a value for a loosely knit social framework in which individuals are expected to take care of themselves. Collectivism means a preference for a tightly knit social framework in which individuals look after one another and organizations protect their members' interests. Countries with individualist values include the United States, Canada, Great Britain, and Australia. Countries with collectivist values include Guatemala, Ecuador, and China.

4. *Masculinity and femininity.* Masculinity stands for preference for achievement, heroism, assertiveness, work centrality (with resultant high stress), and material success. Femininity reflects the values of relationships, cooperation, group decision making, and quality of life. Among the societies with strong masculine values are Japan, Austria, Mexico, and Germany. Countries with feminine values include Sweden, Norway, Denmark, and France. Both men and women subscribe to the dominant value in masculine and feminine cultures.

Hofstede and his colleagues later identified a fifth dimension: long-term versus short-term orientation. The **long-term orientation**, found in China and other Asian countries, includes a greater concern for the future and highly values thrift and perseverance. A **short-term orientation**, found in Russia and West African nations, is more concerned with the past and the present and places a high value on tradition and meeting social obligations.[38] Researchers continue to explore and expand on Hofstede's findings. For example, in the last 25 years, more than 1,400 articles and numerous books have been published on individualism and collectivism alone.[39]

GLOBE Project Value Dimensions. Recent research by the Global Leadership and Organizational Behavior Effectiveness (GLOBE) Project extends Hofstede's assessment and offers a broader understanding for today's managers. The GLOBE Project used data collected from 18,000 managers in 62 countries to identify 9 dimensions that explain cultural differences, including those identified by Hofstede.[40]

1. *Assertiveness.* A high value on assertiveness means a society encourages toughness, assertiveness, and competitiveness. Low assertiveness means that people value tenderness and concern for others over being competitive.

2. *Future orientation.* Similar to Hofstede's time orientation, this dimension refers to the extent to which a society encourages and rewards planning for the future over short-term results and quick gratification.

3. *Uncertainty avoidance.* As with Hofstede's study, this dimension gauges the degree to which members of a society feel uncomfortable with uncertainty and ambiguity.

4. *Gender differentiation.* This dimension refers to the extent to which a society maximizes gender-role differences. In countries with low gender differentiation such as Denmark, women typically have a higher status and stronger role in decision making. Countries with high gender differentiation accord men higher social, political, and economic status.

5. *Power distance.* This dimension is the same as Hofstede's and refers to the degree to which people expect and accept equality or inequality in relationships and institutions.

6. *Societal collectivism.* This term defines the degree to which practices in institutions such as schools, businesses, and other social organizations encourage a tightly knit collectivist society in which people are an important part of a group or a highly individualistic society.

To understand, consider that Americans are much more individualistic than Asian and Middle Eastern countries. In those places, the person's identity is closely tied to his or her extended family and many obligations result—coupled with deep ties of love. And people are always helping one another, with a strong streak of reciprocity.

Remember that people from some Asian and Middle Eastern countries have more obligations with their families, while Americans have fewer family obligations but more workplace obligations. It all evens out.

individualism
A preference for a loosely knit social framework in which individuals are expected to take care of themselves.

collectivism
A preference for a tightly knit social framework in which individuals look after one another and organizations protect their members' interests.

long-term orientation
A greater concern for the future and high value on thrift and perseverance.

short-term orientation
A concern with the past and present and a high value on meeting social obligations.

3 I really admire cultures that are high achieving.

ANSWER: Cultures that value relationships rather than material success usually have stronger families and community lives. Neither orientation is better; they are just different.

7. *Individual collectivism.* Rather than looking at how societal organizations favor individualism versus collectivism, this dimension looks at the degree to which individuals take pride in being members of a family, close circle of friends, team, or organization.

8. *Performance orientation.* A society with a high performance orientation places high emphasis on performance and rewards people for performance improvements and excellence. A low performance orientation means people pay less attention to performance and more attention to loyalty, belonging, and background.

9. *Humane orientation.* The final dimension refers to the degree to which a society encourages and rewards people for being fair, altruistic, generous, and caring. A country high on humane orientation places high value on helping others and being kind. A country low on this orientation expects people to take care of themselves. Self-enhancement and gratification are of high importance.

TAKE ACTION

Read the Ethical Dilemma on page 102 that pertains to social and cultural differences.

Exhibit 3.6 gives examples of how some countries rank on several of the GLOBE dimensions. These dimensions give managers an added tool for identifying and managing cultural differences. Although Hofstede's dimensions are still valid, the GLOBE research provides a more comprehensive view of cultural similarities and differences.

Social values greatly influence organizational functioning and management styles. Consider the difficulty that managers encountered when implementing self-directed work teams in Mexico. As shown in Exhibit 3.5, Mexico is characterized by very high power distance and a relatively low tolerance for uncertainty, characteristics that often conflict with the American concept of teamwork, which emphasizes shared power and authority, with team members working on a variety of problems without formal guidelines, rules, and

Dimension	Low	Medium	High
Assertiveness	Sweden Switzerland Japan	Egypt Iceland France	Spain United States Germany (former East)
Future Orientation	Russia Italy Kuwait	Slovenia Australia India	Denmark Canada Singapore
Gender Differentiation	Sweden Denmark Poland	Italy Brazil Netherlands	South Korea Egypt China
Performance Orientation	Russia Greece Venezuela	Israel England Japan	United States Taiwan Hong Kong
Humane Orientation	Germany France Singapore	New Zealand Sweden United States	Indonesia Egypt Iceland

EXHIBIT 3.6

Examples of Country Rankings on Selected GLOBE Value Dimensions

SOURCE: Mansour Javidan and Robert J. House, "Cultural Acumen for the Global Manager: Lessons from Project GLOBE," *Organizational Dynamics* 29(4) (2001): 289–305. Copyright © 2001, Elsevier Science, Inc. All rights reserved.

SPOTLIGHT ON SKILLS

How Well Do You Play the Culture Game?

How good are you at understanding cross-cultural differences in communication and etiquette? For fun, see how many of the following questions you can answer correctly. The answers appear at the end.

1. You want to do business with a Greek company, but the representative insists on examining every detail of your proposal for several hours. This time-consuming detail means that the Greek representative:
   a. doesn't trust the accuracy of your proposal.
   b. is being polite and really doesn't want to go ahead with the deal.
   c. is signaling you to consider a more reasonable offer but doesn't want to ask directly.
   d. is uncomfortable with detailed proposals and would prefer a simple handshake.
   e. is showing good manners and respect to you and your proposal.

2. Male guests in many Latin American countries often give their visitors an *abrazzo* when greeting them. An *abrazzo* is:
   a. a light kiss on the nose.
   b. a special gift, usually wine or food.
   c. clapping hands in the air as the visitor approaches.
   d. a strong embrace or kiss with hand on shoulder.
   e. a firm two-handed handshake lasting almost one minute.

3. Japanese clients visit you at your office for a major meeting. Where should the top Japanese official be seated?
   a. Closest to the door
   b. As close to the middle of the room as possible
   c. Anywhere in the room; seating location isn't important to Japanese businesspeople
   d. Somewhere away from the door with a piece of artwork behind him or her
   e. Always beside rather than facing the host

4. One of the most universal gestures is:
   a. A pat on the back (congratulations)
   b. A smile (happiness or politeness)
   c. Scratching your chin (thinking)
   d. Closing your eyes (boredom)
   e. Arm up, shaking back and forth (waving)

5. While visiting a German client, you compliment the client's beautiful pen set. What will probably happen?
   a. The client will insist very strongly that you take it.
   b. The client will tell you where to buy such a pen set at a good price.
   c. The client will accept the compliment and get on with business.

d. The client will probably get upset that you aren't paying attention to the business at hand.
   e. The client will totally ignore the comment.

6. Managers from which country are least likely to tolerate someone being five minutes late for an appointment?
   a. United States   b. Australia
   c. Brazil   d. Sweden
   e. Saudi Arabia

7. In which one of the following countries are office arrangements not usually an indicator of the person's status?
   a. United Kingdom   b. Germany
   c. Saudi Arabia   d. China
   e. United States

8. In many Asian cultures, a direct order such as "Get me the Amex report" is most likely to be given by:
   a. senior management to most subordinates.
   b. a junior employee to a peer.
   c. senior management only to very junior employees.
   d. junior employees to outsiders.
   e. None of the above

9. In the United States, scratching one's head usually means that the person is confused or skeptical. In Russia, it means:
   a. "You're crazy!"
   b. "I am listening carefully."
   c. "I want to get to know you better."
   d. "I'm confused or skeptical."
   e. None of the above

10. A polite way to give your business card to a Japanese businessperson is:
   a. casually and after several hours of getting to know the person.
   b. when first meeting and by presenting your card with both hands.
   c. at the very end of the first meeting.
   d. casually during the meeting and with the information down to show humility.
   e. never; it is considered rude in Japan to give business cards.

SOURCES: Steven L. McShane and Mary Ann Von Glinow, *Organizational Behavior: Emerging Realities for the Workplace Revolution*, 3rd ed. (New York: McGraw-Hill/Irwin, 2004); "Cross-Cultural Communication Game," developed by Steven L. McShane, based on material in R. Axtell, *Gestures: The Do's and Taboos of Body Language Around the World* (New York: Wiley, 1991); R. Mead, *Cross-Cultural Management Communication* (Chichester, UK: Wiley, 1990), Chapter 7; and J. V. Thill and C. L. Bovée, *Excellence in Business Communication* (New York: McGraw-Hill, 1995), Chapter 17.

Answers
1. e; 2. d; 3. d; 4. b; 5. c; 6. d; 7. c; 8. c; 9. d; 10. b

structure. Many workers in Mexico, as well as in France and Mediterranean countries, expect organizations to be hierarchical. In Russia, people are good at working in groups and like competing as a team rather than on an individual basis. Organizations in Germany and other central European countries typically strive to be impersonal, well-oiled machines. Effective management styles differ in each country, depending on cultural characteristics.[41]

COMMUNICATION DIFFERENCES

People from some cultures tend to pay more attention to the social context (social setting, nonverbal behavior, social status) of their verbal communication than Americans do. For example, American managers working in China have discovered that social context is considerably more important in that culture, and they need to learn to suppress their impatience and devote the time necessary to establish personal and social relationships.

Exhibit 3.7 indicates how the emphasis on social context varies among countries. In a **high-context culture**, people are sensitive to circumstances surrounding social exchanges. People use communication primarily to build personal social relationships. Meaning is derived from context (setting, status, and nonverbal behavior) more than from explicit words, relationships and trust are more important than business, and the welfare and harmony of the group are valued. In a **low-context culture**, people use communication primarily to exchange facts and information, meaning is derived primarily from words, business transactions are more important than building relationships and trust, and individual welfare and achievement are more important than the group.[42]

To understand how differences in cultural context affect communications, consider the expression, "The squeaky wheel gets the oil." It means that the loudest person will get the most attention, and attention is assumed to be favorable. Equivalent sayings in China and Japan are "Quacking ducks get shot," and "The nail that sticks up gets hammered down," respectively. Standing out as an individual in these cultures clearly merits unfavorable attention.

High-context cultures include Asian and Arab countries. Low-context cultures tend to be North American and Northern European. Even within North America, cultural subgroups vary in the extent to which context counts, explaining why differences among groups can hinder successful communication. White females, Native Americans, and African Americans all tend to prefer higher context communication more than white males do. A high-context interaction requires more time because a relationship has to be developed, and trust and friendship must be established. Furthermore, most male managers and most people doing the hiring in organizations are from low-context cultures, which conflicts with people entering the organization from a background in a higher context culture.

As a new manager, you must remember that understanding national culture is as important as paying attention to economic and political matters when working in or with a foreign country.

Refer back to your score on the New Manager's Self-Test on page 75. It will give you some insight into whether you lean toward low-context or high-context communications.

high-context culture
A culture in which communication is used to enhance personal relationships.

low-context culture
A culture in which communication is used to exchange facts and information.

High
Context ↑
Chinese
Korean
Japanese
Vietnamese
Arab
Greek
Spanish
Italian
English
North American
Scandinavian
Low
Context ↓
Swiss
German

EXHIBIT 3.7
High-Context and Low-Context Cultures

SOURCE: Edward T. Hall, *Beyond Culture* (Garden City, NY: Anchor Press/Doubleday, 1976); and J. Kennedy and A. Everest, "Put Diversity in Context," *Personnel Journal* (Sept. 1991): 50–54.

OTHER CULTURAL CHARACTERISTICS

Start watching more foreign movies and notice how people interact, what values are important to the characters, and what outcomes are desired. Watching foreign movies from a variety of countries will help you manage cross-cultural situations.

Other cultural characteristics that influence international organizations are language, religion, social organization, education, and attitudes. Some countries such as India are characterized by *linguistic pluralism*, meaning that several languages exist there. Other countries rely heavily on spoken versus written language. Religion includes sacred objects, philosophical attitudes toward life, taboos, and rituals. Social organization includes such matters as status systems, kinship and families, social institutions, and opportunities for social mobility. Education influences the literacy level, the availability of qualified employees, and the predominance of primary or secondary degrees.

Attitudes toward achievement, work, and people can all affect organizational productivity. For example, one study found that the prevalent American attitude that treats employees as a resource to be used (an *instrumental* attitude toward people) can be a strong impediment to business success in countries where people are valued as an end in themselves rather than as a means to an end (a *humanistic* attitude). U.S. companies sometimes use instrumental human-resource policies that conflict with local humanistic values.[43]

Ethnocentrism, which refers to a natural tendency of people to regard their own culture as superior and to downgrade or dismiss other cultural values, can be found in all countries. Strong ethnocentric attitudes within a country make it difficult for foreign firms to operate there. American managers are regularly accused of an ethnocentric attitude that assumes the American way is the best way. Take the quiz in this section's New Manager's Self Test (page 96) to see how much you know about cross-cultural communication and etiquette.

As business grows increasingly global, U.S. managers are learning that cultural differences cannot be ignored if international operations are to succeed. South Korean appliance maker LG Electronics rules in emerging markets because of managers' attention to cultural factors.

LG ELECTRONICS

Two decades ago, managers at South Korea's LG Electronics decided to solve a longtime problem for homemakers: how to keep the kimchi from stinking up the fridge. Kimchi, a fermented cabbage dish seasoned with garlic and chili, is served with most meals in Korea. Kimchi leftovers in the refrigerator inevitably taint other foods and leave a pungent odor that lingers for weeks. LG built a refrigerator with a special compartment to isolate the smelly kimchi, and it quickly became a must-have in Korean homes.

LG managers realized that their understanding of Korean culture led to an amazingly successful new product. So, they reasoned, why not apply that concept to designing products for other markets? LG doesn't just build a standard appliance and expect the whole world to love it. Instead, it taps into local idiosyncrasies in key markets by opening in-country research, manufacturing, and marketing facilities, enabling the company to "speak to consumers individually," as one manager put it. The approach led to products such as the kebab microwave in Iran, which includes a microwave-safe skewer rack and a preset for reheating shish kebabs, and the karaoke phone in Russia that can be programmed with the top 100 Russian songs, whose lyrics scroll across the screen when they're played. The phone was an instant hit in a country where people like to entertain at home during the long winters.

In India, LG has introduced a number of successful products such as refrigerators with larger vegetable- and water-storage compartments, surge-resistant power supplies, and brightly colored finishes that reflect local preferences. Microwaves are designed with a dark interior to hide masala stains. After learning that many Indians use their televisions to listen to music, LG came out with a model featuring an ultra sound system. These efforts made LG the unprecedented leader in appliance sales in India, with market share in some categories nearly twice that of the competition.[44]

ethnocentrism
A cultural attitude marked by the tendency to regard one's own culture as superior to others.

By making an effort to learn about local tastes and preferences, LG has become the appliance maker to beat in emerging global markets. Managers have now turned their attention to China, where LG is building extensive in-country facilities and learning all it can about local cultural preferences in the world's biggest consumer market.

International Trade Alliances

One of the most visible changes in the international business environment in recent years has been the development of regional trading alliances and international trade agreements. These developments are significantly shaping global trade.

GATT AND THE WORLD TRADE ORGANIZATION

The General Agreement on Tariffs and Trade (GATT), signed by 23 nations in 1947, started as a set of rules to ensure nondiscrimination, clear procedures, the negotiation of disputes, and the participation of lesser-developed countries in international trade.[45] GATT sponsored eight rounds of international trade negotiations aimed at reducing trade restrictions. The 1986 to 1994 Uruguay Round (the first to be named for a developing country) involved 125 countries and cut more tariffs than ever before. In addition to lowering tariffs, 30 percent from the previous level, the Uruguay Round boldly moved the world closer to global free trade by calling for the establishment of the World Trade Organization (WTO).

The WTO represents the maturation of GATT into a permanent global institution that can monitor international trade and has legal authority to arbitrate disputes on some 400 trade issues. As of July 2007, 151 countries, including China, were members of the WTO. As a permanent membership organization, the WTO is bringing greater trade liberalization in goods, information, technological developments, and services; stronger enforcement of rules and regulations; and greater power to resolve disputes among trading partners.

EUROPEAN UNION

An alliance begun in 1957 to improve economic and social conditions among its members, the European Economic Community has evolved into the 27-nation European Union (EU) illustrated in Exhibit 3.8. The biggest expansion came in 2004, when the EU welcomed 10 new members from southern and eastern Europe.[46]

The goal of the EU is to create a powerful single market system for Europe's millions of consumers, allowing people, goods, and services to move freely. The increased competition and economies of scale within Europe enable companies to grow large and efficient, becoming more competitive in the United States and other world markets. Some observers fear that the EU will become a trade barrier, creating a *fortress Europe* that will be difficult to penetrate by companies in other nations.

Another aspect of significance to countries operating globally is the introduction of the euro. Sixteen member states of the EU have adopted the **euro**, a single European currency that replaced national currencies in Austria, Belgium, Cyprus, Finland, France, Germany, Greece, Ireland, Italy, Luxembourg, Malta, the Netherlands, Portugal, Slovakia, Slovenia, and Spain. Several other countries are using the euro under formal agreements, although they haven't yet met all the conditions to officially adopt the single currency.[47] The implications of a single European currency are enormous, within as well as outside Europe. Because it potentially replaces as many as 27 European domestic currencies, the euro will affect legal contracts, financial management, sales and marketing tactics, manufacturing, distribution, payroll, pensions, training, taxes, and information-management systems. Every corporation that does business in or with EU countries will feel the impact.[48]

NORTH AMERICAN FREE TRADE AGREEMENT (NAFTA)

The North American Free Trade Agreement (NAFTA), which went into effect on January 1, 1994, merged the United States, Canada, and Mexico into the world's largest trading bloc with more than 421 million consumers. Intended to spur growth and investment, increase

euro
TA single European currency that replaced the currencies of 15 European nations.

EXHIBIT 3.8
The Nations of the
European Union

exports, and expand jobs in all three nations, NAFTA broke down tariffs and trade re-strictions over a 15-year-period in a number of key areas. Thus, by 2008, virtually all U.S. industrial exports into Canada and Mexico were duty-free.

Over the first decade of NAFTA, U.S. trade with Mexico increased more than three-fold while trade with Canada also rose dramatically.[49] Significantly, NAFTA spurred the entry of small businesses into the global arena. Jeff Victor, general manager of Treatment Products, Ltd., which makes car cleaners and waxes, credits NAFTA for his surging export volume. Prior to the pact, Mexican tariffs as high as 20 percent made it impossible for the Chicago-based company to expand its presence south of the border.[50]

However, opinions over the benefits of NAFTA appear to be as divided as they were when talks began, with some people calling it a spectacular success and others referring to it as a dismal failure.[51] Although NAFTA has not lived up to its grand expectations, experts stress that it increased trade, investment, and income and continues to enable companies in all three countries to compete more effectively with rival Asian and European firms.[52]

The Globalization Backlash

As the world becomes increasingly interconnected, a backlash over globalization is occurring. In a *Fortune* magazine poll, 68 percent of Americans say other countries benefit the most from free trade. The sentiment is reflected in other countries such as Germany, France, even India. "For some reason, everyone thinks they are the loser," said former U.S. trade representative Mickey Kantor.[53]

In the United States, the primary concern is the loss of jobs as companies expand their offshoring activities by exporting more and more work overseas. Consider, for example, that Boeing uses aeronautical specialists in Russia to design luggage bins and wing parts for planes. They make about $650 a month; a counterpart in the United States would be making $6,000.[54] The transfer of jobs such as making shoes, clothing, and toys began two decades ago. Today, services and knowledge work are rapidly moving to developing countries. An analyst at Forrester Research Inc. predicts that at least 3.3 million mostly white-collar jobs and $136 billion in wages will shift from the United States to low-wage countries by 2015.[55] Many American shoppers say they'd be willing to pay higher

Protesters shout slogans during a demonstration against the World Trade Organization outside a hotel in Jakarta, Indonesia, February 2007. Hundreds of activists held a demonstration to protest the visit of WTO Director General Pascal Lamy and to urge the Indonesian government to not waiver on its stance favoring product exemptions. With increased globalization has come a globalization backlash, with most groups thinking other groups and countries benefit more from international trade.

⋯⋯⋯▷ CONCEPT CONNECTION ◁⋯⋯⋯

prices to keep down foreign competition. President Barack Obama tapped into strong sentiments when he declared, "People don't want a cheaper T-shirt if they're losing a job in the process."[56]

Business leaders, meanwhile, insist that economic benefits flow back to the U.S. economy in the form of lower prices, expanded markets, and increased profits that can fund innovation.[57] Some American companies are clearly benefiting from free trade. When Kalexsyn, a small chemistry research company in Kalamazoo, Michigan, couldn't get contracts with major U.S. pharmaceutical companies that were sending work to India and China, the owners found that European companies were eager to outsource chemical research to the United States.[58] U.S. exports grew 12 percent in 2006, based partly on the need for equipment and supplies for building infrastructure in place such as China, Brazil, and India.[59] United Technologies, which makes Pratt & Whitney engines, Sikorsky helicopters, and Otis elevators, has seen both its revenues and its stock price surge.[60] Yet the antiglobalization fervor is just getting hotter—and is not likely to dissipate anytime soon. In the end, it is not whether globalization is good or bad, but how business and government managers can work together to ensure that the advantages of a global world are fully and fairly shared.

Managing in a Global Environment

New managers who want their careers to move forward recognize the importance of global experience.[61] But working in a foreign country can present tremendous personal and organizational challenges. A clue to the complexity of working internationally comes from a study of the factors that contribute to global manager failures. Based on extensive interviews with global managers, researchers found that personal traits, the specific cultural context, or management mistakes made by the organization could all contribute to failure in an international assignment.[62]

Before reading the next section, find out your cultural intelligence (CQ) by answering the questions in the New Manager's Self-Test on page 96. As a new manager, begin soon to develop cultural intelligence so you can work effectively with people from other countries.

DEVELOPING CULTURAL INTELLIGENCE

Managers will be most successful in foreign assignments if they are culturally flexible and able to adapt easily to new situations and ways of doing things. In other words, managers working internationally need cultural intelligence. **Cultural intelligence (CQ)** refers to a person's ability to use reasoning and observation skills to interpret unfamiliar gestures and situations and devise appropriate behavioral responses.[63]

It is important for a manager working in a foreign country to study the language and learn as much as possible about local norms, customs, beliefs, and taboos. However, that information alone cannot prepare the manager for every conceivable situation. Developing a high level of CQ enables a person to interpret unfamiliar situations and adapt quickly. Rather than a list of global "dos and don'ts," CQ is a practical learning approach that enables a person to ferret out clues to a culture's shared understandings and respond to new situations in culturally appropriate ways. Consider what Pat McGovern does whenever he travels to a foreign country. McGovern is the founder and CEO of IDG, a technology publishing and research firm in Massachusetts that owns magazines such as *CIO* and *Computerworld*. IDG operates in 85 countries and gets 80 percent of its profits from outside the United States. When McGovern goes to a country for the first time, he spends the weekend just wandering around observing people. By watching how people in a foreign country behave, McGovern says he gets a sense of the culture—how fast people walk, how much they gesture, what they wear, how they treat one another.[64] McGovern believes you can be in sync anywhere if you pay attention.

Cultural intelligence includes three components that work together: cognitive, emotional, and physical.[65] The cognitive component involves a person's observational and learning skills and the ability to pick up on clues to understanding. The emotional aspect concerns one's self-confidence and self-motivation. A manager has to believe in his or her ability to understand and assimilate into a different culture. Difficulties and setbacks are triggers to work harder, not a cause to give up. Working in a foreign environment is stressful, and most managers in foreign assignments face a period of homesickness, loneliness, and culture shock from being suddenly immersed in a culture with completely different languages, foods, values, beliefs, and ways of doing things. *Culture shock* refers to the frustration and anxiety that result from constantly being subjected to strange and unfamiliar cues about what to do and how to do it. A person with high CQ is able to move quickly through this initial period of culture shock.

The third component of CQ, the physical, refers to a person's ability to shift his or her speech patterns, expressions, and body language to be in tune with people from a different culture. Most managers aren't equally strong in all three areas, but maximizing cultural intelligence requires that they draw on all three facets. In a sense, CQ requires that the head, heart, and body work in concert.

High CQ also requires that a manager be open and receptive to new ideas and approaches. One study found that people who adapt to global management most easily are those who have grown up learning how to understand, empathize, and work with others who are different from themselves. For example, Singaporeans consistently hear English and Chinese spoken side by side. The Dutch have to learn English, German, and French, as well as Dutch, to interact and trade with their economically dominant neighbors. English Canadians must not only be well-versed in American culture and politics but also be able to consider the views and ideas of French Canadians, who, in turn, must learn to think like North Americans, members of a global French community, Canadians, and Quebecois.[66] People in the United States who have grown up without this kind of language and cultural diversity typically have more difficulties with foreign assignments, but willing managers from any country can learn to open their minds and appreciate other viewpoints.

MANAGING CROSS-CULTURALLY

Which two of the following three items go together: a panda, a banana, and a monkey? If you said a monkey and a banana, you answered like a majority of Asians; if you said a panda

How many of your friends are a different ethnicity than you, come from other countries, practice other religions, or are from a different socioeconomic class? How prepared are you to work with them?

cultural intelligence (CQ)
A person's ability to use reasoning and observation skills to interpret unfamiliar gestures and situations and devise appropriate behavioral responses.

and a monkey, you answered like a majority of people in Western Europe and the United States. Where Westerners see distinct categories (animals), Asians see relationships (monkeys eat bananas).[67] Although this test is not definitive, it serves to illustrate an important fact for managers. The cultural differences in how people think and see the world affect working relationships. To be effective on an international level, managers need to interpret the culture of the country and organization in which they are working and develop the sensitivity required to avoid making costly cultural blunders.[68]

In addition to developing cultural intelligence, managers can prepare for foreign assignments by understanding how the country differs in terms of the Hofstede and GLOBE social values discussed earlier in this chapter. These values greatly influence how a manager should interact with subordinates and colleagues in the new assignment. For example, the United States scores extremely high on individualism, and a U.S. manager working in a country such as Japan, which scores high on collectivism, will have to modify his or her approach to leading and controlling to be successful. The following examples are broad generalizations, but they give some clues to how expatriate managers can be more successful. Expatriates are employees who live and work in a country other than their own.

Human Resources. Not every manager will thrive in an international assignment, and careful screening, selection, and training of employees to serve overseas increase the potential for corporate global success. Human-resource managers consider global skills in the selection process. In addition, expatriates receive cross-cultural training that develops language skills and provides cultural and historical orientation.[69] Equally important is honest self-analysis by overseas candidates and their families. Before seeking or accepting an assignment in another country, a candidate should ask him- or herself such questions as the following:

- Can you initiate social contacts in a foreign culture?

- Can you adjust well to different environments and changes in personal comfort or quality of living such as the lack of television, limited hot water, varied cuisine, and national phone strikes?

- Can you manage your future reentry into the job market by networking and maintaining contacts in your home country?[70]

Employees working overseas must adjust to all of these conditions. In addition, managers going global often find that their management styles need adjustment to succeed in a country other than their native ones.

When you return from an extended time abroad, you experience reverse culture shock, *which means adapting back to your own culture, which is often more difficult than going away.*

Leading. In relationship-oriented societies that rank high on collectivism such as those in Asia, the Arab world, and Latin America, leaders typically use a warm, personalized approach with employees. One of the greatest difficulties U.S. leaders encounter in doing business in China, for example, is failing to recognize that to the Chinese any relationship is a personal relationship.[71] Managers are expected to have periodic social visits with workers, inquiring about morale and health. Leaders should be especially careful about how and in what context they criticize others. To Asians, Africans, Arabs, and Latin Americans, the loss of self-respect brings dishonor to themselves and their families. The principle of *saving face* is highly important in some cultures.

Complete the Self Learning exercise on page 98, which pertains to your global management potential. How well do your knowledge and preferences reflect a global perspective?

Decision Making. In the United States, midlevel managers may discuss a problem and give the boss a recommendation. On the other hand, managers in Iran, which reflects South Asian cultural values, expect the boss to make a decision and issue specific instructions.[72] In Mexico, employees often don't understand participatory decision making. Mexico ranks extremely high on power distance, and many workers expect managers to exercise their power in making decisions and issuing orders. American managers working in Mexico have been advised to rarely explain a decision because workers may perceive this as a sign of weakness.[73] In contrast, managers in many Arab and African nations are expected to use consultative decision making in the extreme.

expatriates
Employees who live and work in a country other than their own.

NEW MANAGER'S SELF-TEST

Are You Culturally Intelligent?

The job of a manager demands a lot, and before long your activities will include situations that will test your knowledge and capacity for dealing with people from other national cultures. Are you ready? To find out, think about your experiences in other countries or with people from other countries. To what extent does each of the following statements characterize your behavior? Please answer each of the following items as Mostly True or Mostly False for you.

	MOSTLY TRUE	MOSTLY FALSE
1. I plan how I'm going to relate to people from a different culture before I meet them.	_____	_____
2. I understand the religious beliefs of other cultures.	_____	_____
3. I understand the rules for nonverbal behavior in other cultures.	_____	_____
4. I seek out opportunities to interact with people from different cultures.	_____	_____
5. I can handle the stresses of living in a different culture with relative ease.	_____	_____
6. I am confident that I can befriend locals in a culture that is unfamiliar to me.	_____	_____
7. I change my speech style (e.g., accent, tone) when a cross-cultural interaction requires it.	_____	_____
8. I alter my facial expressions and gestures as needed to facilitate a cross-culture interaction.	_____	_____
9. I am quick to change the way I behave when a cross-culture encounter seems to require it.	_____	_____

SCORING AND INTERPRETATION: Each question pertains to some aspect of cultural intelligence. Questions 1–3 pertain to the head (*cognitive CQ* subscale), questions 4–6 to the heart (*emotional CQ* subscale), and questions 7–9 to behavior (*physical CQ* subscale). If you have sufficient international experience and CQ to have answered "Mostly True" to two of three questions for each subscale or six of nine for all the questions, then consider yourself at a high level of CQ for a new manager. If you scored one or fewer "Mostly True" on each subscale or three or fewer for all nine questions, it is time to learn more about other national cultures. Hone your observational skills and learn to pick up on clues about how people from a different country respond to various situations.

SOURCES: Based on P. Christopher Earley and Elaine Mosakowski, "Cultural Intelligence," *Harvard Business Review* (October 2004): 139–146; and Soon Ang, Lynn Van Dyne, Christine Koh, K. Yee Ng, Klaus J. Templer, Cheryl Tay, and N. Anand Chandrasekar, "Cultural Intelligence: Its Measurement and Effects on Cultural Judgment and Decision Making, Cultural Adaptation and Task Performance," *Management and Organization Review* 3 (2007): 335–371.

Motivating. Motivation must fit the incentives within the culture. Recent data from Towers Perrin give some insight into what motivates people in different countries based on what potential employees say they want most from the company. In the United States, competitive base pay is considered most important, whereas prospective employees in Brazil look for career opportunities. In China, people want chances to learn, and employees in Spain put work-life balance at the top of their list.[74] Another study also found that intrinsic factors such as challenge, recognition, and the work itself are less effective in countries that value high power distance. It may be that workers in these cultures perceive manager recognition and support as manipulative and therefore demotivating.[75] A high value for collectivism in Japan means that employees are motivated in groups. An individual bonus for a high performer would be considered humiliating, but a reward for the team could be highly motivating. Managers in Latin America, Africa, and the Middle East can improve motivation by showing respect for employees as individuals with needs and interests outside of work.[76]

Controlling. When things go wrong, managers in foreign countries often are unable to get rid of employees who do not work out. Consider the following research finding: When asked what to do about an employee whose work had been subpar for 1 year after 15 years of exemplary performance, 75 percent of Americans and Canadians said fire her; only 20 percent of Singaporeans and Koreans chose that solution.[77] In Europe, Mexico, and Indonesia, as well, to hire and fire based on performance seems unnaturally brutal. In addition, workers in some countries are protected by strong labor laws and union rules.

Managers also have to learn not to control the wrong things. A Sears manager in Hong Kong insisted that employees come to work on time instead of 15 minutes late. The employees did exactly as they were told, but they also left on time instead of working into the evening as they had previously. A lot of work was left unfinished. The manager eventually told the employees to go back to their old ways. His attempt at control had a negative effect.

Don't get frustrated with people in high power-distance countries if they don't take initiative or want to make decisions. Just realize their culture is different. They don't have to be like you. Remember the saying, "When in Rome, do as the Romans."

As a means of learning across borders, here is a poem that addresses cultural differences.

An Asian View of Cultural Difference

Eastern Perspective	**Western Perspective**
We live in time.	You live in space.
We are always at rest.	You are always on the move.
We are passive.	You are aggressive.
We like to contemplate.	You like to act.
We accept the world as it is.	You try to change the world according to your blueprint.
We live in peace with nature.	You try to impose your will in her.
Religion is our first love.	Technology is your passion.
We delight to think about the meaning of life.	You delight in physics.
We believe in freedom of silence.	You believe in freedom of speech.
We lapse into meditation.	You strive for articulation.
We marry first, then love.	You love first, then marry.
Our marriage is the beginning of a love affair.	Your marriage is the happy end of a romance.
It is an indissoluble bond.	It is a contract.
Our love is mute.	Your love is vocal.
We try to conceal it from the world.	You delight in showing it to others.
Self-denial is the secret to our survival.	Self-assertiveness is the key to your success.
We are taught from the cradle to want less and less.	You are urged every day to want more and more.
We glorify austerity and renunciation.	You emphasize gracious living and enjoyment.
In the sunset years of life we renounce the world and prepare for the hereafter.	You retire to enjoy the fruits of your labor.

SOURCE: Dr. Mai Van Trang, Indochinese Materials Center

Summary

Successful companies are expanding their business overseas and successfully competing with foreign companies on their home turf. International markets provide many opportunities but are also fraught with difficulty.

Major alternatives for entering foreign markets are outsourcing, exporting, and franchising through joint ventures or wholly owned subsidiaries.

Business in the global arena involves special risks and difficulties because of complicated economic, legal–political, and sociocultural forces. Moreover, the global environment changes rapidly, as illustrated by the emergence of the World Trade Organization, the European Union, and the North American Free Trade Agreement.

The expansion of free-trade policies has sparked a globalization backlash among people who fear losing their jobs and economic security.

Managers and companies doing business internationally face many challenges and must develop a high level of cultural intelligence (CQ) to be successful. CQ, which involves a cognitive component (head), an emotional component (heart), and a physical component (body), helps managers interpret unfamiliar situations and devise culturally appropriate responses.

Social and cultural values differ widely across cultures and influence appropriate patterns of leadership, decision making, motivation, and managerial control.

Discussion Questions

1. What specifically would the experience of living and working in another country contribute to your skills and effectiveness as a manager in your own country?

2. What might be some long-term ramifications of the war in Iraq for U.S. managers and companies operating internationally?

3. What do you think is your strongest component of cultural intelligence? Your weakest? How would you go about shoring up your weaknesses?

4. What steps could a company take to avoid making product design and marketing mistakes when introducing new products into India? How would you go about hiring a plant manager for a facility you are planning to build in India?

5. What opportunities are available to you and your classmates to increase your cultural intelligence and your ability to function in another country?

6. Should a multinational corporation operate as a tightly integrated, worldwide business system, or would it be more effective to let each national subsidiary operate autonomously?

7. How might the globalization backlash affect you as a future manager or the company for which you work?

8. Two U.S. companies are competing to take over a large factory in the Czech Republic. One delegation tours the facility and asks questions about how the plant might be run more efficiently. The other delegation focuses on ways to improve working conditions and produce a better product. Which delegation do you think is more likely to succeed with the plant? Why? What information would you want to collect to decide whether to acquire the plant for your company?

9. Which style of communicating do you think would be most beneficial to the long-term success of a U.S. company operating internationally: high-context or low-context communications? Why?

10. How might the social value of low versus high power distance influence how you would lead and motivate employees? What about the value of low- versus high-performance orientation?

Self Learning

Rate Your Global Management Potential

A global environment requires that managers learn to deal effectively with people and ideas from a variety of cultures. How well prepared are you to be a global manager? Read the following statements and circle the number on the response scale that most closely reflects how well the statement describes you.

Good Description 10 9 8 7 6 5 4 3 2 1 Poor Description

1. I reach out to people from different cultures.
   10 9 8 7 6 5 4 3 2 1

2. I frequently attend seminars and lectures about other cultures or international topics.
   10 9 8 7 6 5 4 3 2 1

3. I believe female expatriates can be equally as effective as male expatriates.
   10   9   8   7   6   5   4   3   2   1

4. I have a basic knowledge about several countries in addition to my native country.
   10   9   8   7   6   5   4   3   2   1

5. I have good listening and empathy skills.
   10   9   8   7   6   5   4   3   2   1

6. I have spent more than two weeks traveling or working in another country.
   10   9   8   7   6   5   4   3   2   1

7. I easily adapt to the different work ethics of students from other cultures when we are involved in a team project.
   10   9   8   7   6   5   4   3   2   1

8. I can speak a foreign language.
   10   9   8   7   6   5   4   3   2   1

9. I know which countries tend to cluster into similar sociocultural and economic groupings.
   10   9   8   7   6   5   4   3   2   1

10. I feel capable of assessing different cultures on the basis of power distance, uncertainty avoidance, individualism, and masculinity.
    10   9   8   7   6   5   4   3   2   1

    Total Score: _____

Scoring and Interpretation

Add up the total points for the ten questions. If you scored 81–100 points, you have a great capacity for developing good global management skills. A score of 61–80 points indicates that you have potential but may lack skills in certain areas, such as language or foreign experience. A score of 60 or less means you need to do some serious work to improve your potential for global management. Regardless of your total score, go back over each item and make a plan of action to increase scores of less than five on any question.

SOURCE: Based in part on "How Well Do You Exhibit Good Intercultural Management Skills?" in John W. Newstrom and Keith Davis, *Organizational Behavior: Human Behavior at Work* (Boston: McGraw-Hill Irwin, 2002): 415–416.

Group Learning

Test Your Global IQ

A. Complete the test below on your own. Do *not* look up the answers.

B. In class, the instructor will divide you into groups of three to four students and ask you to come up with group scores on the same test.

C. Only after you've answered all of the following questions as a group can you look up the correct answers.

D. How well did your group do? Did it do better than the individuals?

E. After hearing how other groups in your class did, how would you rate your group in terms of global IQ?

How aware are you of the rest of the planet? If you will be working internationally, the better you know about the world, the more successful you are likely to be.

1. Which six countries make up more than half of the world's population?

   1.   4.
   2.   5.
   3.   6.

2. Which six most commonly spoken first languages account for one-third of the total world population?

   1.   4.
   2.   5.
   3.   6.

3. How many living languages are there in the world (that is, languages that are still spoken)?

   a. 683
   b. 2,600
   c. 6,800

4. How many sovereign nations were there in 2005?

   a. 303
   b. 203
   c. 103

5. The proportion of people in the world age 60 and older will increase ____ percent by 2050.

6. The number of people who have immigrated from poorer countries to developed ones has been _____ million per year in recent years.

7. Between 1970 and 2000, the number of people in the world suffering from malnutrition

   a. declined.
   b. remained about the same.
   c. increased.

8. In 2007, the world spent approximately $14.1 trillion on health care. How much did the world spend on armies and military weapons and systems?

   a. $100 billion
   b. $1.2 trillion
   c. $17 trillion

9. What percentage of the world's expenditures on the military was spent by the United States?

10. The United States spends the most per person on health care than any other nation, about $6,000. Where does the United States rank in terms of life expectancy? _____

11. According to the United Nations (UN), France has the best health-care system in the world, costing $3,900 per person. What did the UN rank the United States in terms of total health care system?

    a. 27th   b. 37th

12. According to the United Nations, what percentage of the world's work (paid and unpaid) is done by women?

    a. 1/3
    b. 1/2
    c. 2/3
    d. 3/4

13. Women make up _____ percent of the world's illiterates.

14. In some African countries, _____ percent of women have suffered female genital mutilation.

15. According to the United Nations, what percentage of the world's income is earned by women?

    a. 1/10
    b. 3/10
    c. 5/10
    d. 7/10

16. The nations of Africa, Asia, Latin America, and the Middle East—often referred to as the *third world*—contain about 78 percent of the world's population. What percentage of the world's monetary income do they possess?

    a. 10
    b. 20
    c. 30
    d. 40

17. Americans constitute approximately 5 percent of the world's population. What percentage of the world's resources do Americans consume?

    a. 15
    b. 25
    c. 35
    d. 45

18. Which city has the worst air pollution—New York, Mexico City, or Moscow?

19. The total output of the world economy was $6.3 trillion in 1950. What was it in 2008?

20. The number of host computers on the Internet grew by _____ percent from 1990 to 2008.

21. In 2007, 33 million people worldwide were infected with HIV or had AIDS. Which three countries have the highest rage of HIV infection? Which two countries had the greatest decrease of cases?

22. The world's urban population will grow from 2.86 billion to _____ billion in 2030.

23. The average amount of water used per day by a person living in Ethiopia, Eritrea, Djibouti, Gambia, Somalia, Mali, Mozambique, Tanzania, or Uganda is the same as someone in a developed country

    a. making a pot of tea (1 liter).
    b. cleaning his or her teeth with the tap water running (10 liters).
    c. filling up a dishwasher (65 liters).
    d. taking a bath (200 liters).

24. Sixty-five million girls do not go to school. What's the main reason behind their exclusion from education?

    a. Girls are less intelligent than boys.
    b. In many countries it's illegal for girls to go to school.
    c. Poverty takes a greater toll on girls.
    d. Girls drop out earlier to get married and have babies.

25. Which country gives least aid as a proportion of gross domestic production?

    a. the United States
    b. Saudi Arabia
    c. Japan
    d. Switzerland

26. Imagine the world's population is represented by 100 people. Fill in the blanks below to indicate what percentage of people would be the following:

    _____ would be Asian.
    _____ would be nonwhite.
    _____ would be non-Christian.
    _____ would live in substandard housing.
    _____ would be illiterate.
    _____ would have a college education.
    _____ would own a computer.

27. True or false: In the developed world, the population is aging, meaning there are fewer young people for each retiring adult. In developing countries, on the other hand, there are relatively more young people. _____

28. Russia controls what percentage of the world's energy supply?

    a. 15
    b. 25
    c. 40

29. Which country is the United States' biggest trading partner?

    a. Canada
    b. China
    c. Mexico

30. In Asia, how many city dwellers will be added by 2030?

    a. 600 million

    b. 850 million

    c. 1 billion

31. Which city will have the greatest population in 20 years?

    a. Los Angeles

    b. Mumbai

    c. Tokyo

32. Each year, how much money do Mexican immigrants send back to Mexico to family members?

    a. $900 million

    b. $9 billion

    c. $20 billion

SOURCES: *State of the World: Into a Warming World* (Washington, DC: Worldwatch Institute, 2009); United Nations Web site, 2009; "What's Your Global IQ?" *Newsweek*, July 2–July 9, 2007: 36–37; *World Economic and Social Survey 2007: Development in an Aging World* (E/2007/50/Rev.1) (New York: United Nations, 2007); "State of the World Quiz," BBC News *This World*, Feb. 2, 2005.

Action Learning

Global Economy Scavenger Hunt

To get a perspective on the pervasiveness of the global economy, you will be asked to find a number of things and bring them back to class.

1. Divide into teams of four to six class members each.

2. Each team is to bring items to a future class from the list below.

3. On the day in class, each team will give a short, two-minute presentation on the items that were the most difficult to find or the most interesting, as well as answer the questions at the end of the exercise.

4. How many countries did your team get items from? How many for the entire class?

List for Scavenger Hunt

1. Brochures of annual reports of four multinational corporations.

2. Evidence from three local businesses to show they do business internationally.

3. The name of a local retail store that sells only products "Made in America."

4. Ten toys or games that originated in other countries.

5. Five toys or games that had components from one country and were assembled in another or somehow developed in more than one country.

6. Food items from 25 different countries.

7. Articles of clothing from 15 different countries.

8. List of books sold in your town by authors from 12 different countries. Where were the books published? Who translated them?

9. List of twelve films in the past five years that starred someone from another country.

10. List of five films in the past five years that had multinational crews and locations. Include at least one that was coproduced by two or more countries.

11. Descriptions of interviews from five foreigners (not from your team or the class) in which they are asked six things they like about the United States and six things they don't like.

12. A list of eight places where a language other than English is displayed (on a bulletin board, poster, etc.).

13. Two maps of the world drawn before 1900.

14. Five items in your town that were manufactured in another country but were not made in that country six years ago.

Questions for Discussion

1. What did you learn about the reach of global manufacturing from this assignment?

2. Based on your hunt and research, which industries seem to be the most global? Which are the least global?

3. Which countries were represented more often? Which least often?

4. What did you learn about the United States and its position in the world?

SOURCE: Adapted from Jan Drum, Steve Hughes, and George Otere, "Global Scavenger Hunt," in *Global Winners* (Yarmouth, ME: Intercultural Press, 1994): 21–23.

Ethical Dilemma

AH Biotech

Dr. Abraham Hassan knew he couldn't put off the decision any longer. AH Biotech—the company started by this psychiatrist turned entrepreneur and based in Bound Brook, New Jersey—had developed a novel drug that seemed to promise long-term relief from panic attacks. If approved by the federal Food and Drug Administration, it would be the company's first product. It was now time for large-scale clinical trials. But where should AH Biotech conduct those tests?

David Berger, who headed up research and development, was certain he already knew the answer to that question: Albania. "Look, doing these trials in Albania will be quicker, easier, and a lot cheaper than doing them in the States," he pointed out. "What's not to like?"

Dr. Hassan had to concede Berger's arguments were sound. If they did trials in the United States, AH Biotech would spend considerable time and money advertising for patients and then finding physicians who'd be willing to serve as clinical trial investigators. Rounding up U.S. doctors prepared to take on that job was getting increasingly difficult. They just didn't want to take time out of their busy practices to do the testing, not to mention all the record keeping such a study entailed.

Albania was an entirely different story. It was one of the poorest Eastern European countries, if not *the* poorest, with a just barely functioning health-care system. Albanian physicians and patients would practically arrive at AH Biotech's doorstep asking to take part. Physicians there could earn much better money as clinical investigators for a U.S. company than they could actually practicing medicine, and patients saw signing up as test subjects as their best chance for receiving any treatment at all, let alone cutting-edge Western medicine. All of these factors meant that the company could count on realizing at least a 25-percent savings, maybe more, by running the tests overseas.

What's not to like? As the Egyptian-born CEO of a start-up biotech company with investors and employees hoping for its first marketable drug, there was absolutely nothing for

Dr. Hassan not to like. It was when he thought like a U.S.-trained physician that he felt qualms. If he used U.S. test subjects, he knew they'd likely continue to receive the drug until it was approved. At that point, most would have insurance that covered most of the cost of their prescriptions. But he already knew it wasn't going to make any sense to market the drug in a poor country such as Albania; when the study was over, he'd have to cut off treatment. Sure, he conceded, panic attacks weren't usually fatal. But he knew how debilitating these sudden bouts of feeling completely terrified were: the pounding heart, chest pain, choking sensation, and nausea. The severity and unpredictability of these attacks often made a normal life all but impossible. How could he offer people dramatic relief and then snatch it away?

What Would You Do?

1. Do the clinical trials in Albania. You'll be able to bring the drug to market faster and cheaper, which will be good for AH Biotech's employees and investors and good for the millions of people who suffer from anxiety attacks.

2. Do the clinical trials in the United States. Even though it will certainly be more expensive and time consuming, you'll feel as if you're living up to the part of the Hippocratic oath that instructed you to "prescribe regimens for the good of my patients according to my ability and my judgment and never do harm to anyone."

3. Do the clinical trials in Albania. If the drug is approved, use part of the profits to set up a compassionate use program in Albania, even though setting up a distribution system and training doctors to administer the drug, monitor patients for adverse effects, and track results will entail considerable expense.

SOURCES: Based on Gina Kolata, "Companies Facing Ethical Issue as Drugs Are Tested Overseas," *New York Times*, March 5, 2004, p. A1; and Julie Schmit, "Costs, Regulations Move More Drug Tests Outside USA," *USA Today*, June 16, 2005, p. B1.

4 Chapter Four

Managerial Ethics and Corporate Social Responsibility

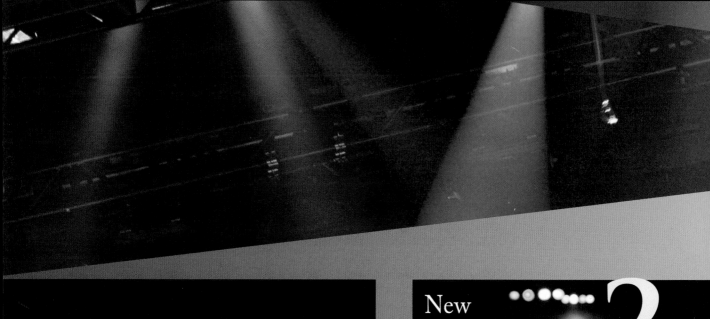

LEARNING OBJECTIVES

After studying this chapter, you should be able to:

1 Define ethics and explain how ethical behavior relates to behavior governed by law and free choice.

2 Explain the utilitarian, individualism, moral-rights, and justice approaches for evaluating ethical behavior.

3 Describe the factors that shape a manager's ethical decision making.

4 Identify important stakeholders for an organization and discuss how managers balance the interests of various stakeholders.

5 Explain the bottom-of-the-pyramid concept and some of the innovative strategies companies are using.

6 Explain the philosophy of sustainability and why organizations are embracing it.

7 Define corporate social responsibility and how to evaluate it using economic, legal, ethical, and discretionary criteria.

8 Discuss how ethical organizations are created through ethical leadership and organizational structures and systems.

New Manager's Questions

Please circle your opinion below each of the following statements.

1 If an action is legal, then it is also ethical.

MOSTLY YES < < <   > > > MOSTLY NO

| 1 | 2 | 3 | 4 | 5 |

2 It's wrong to be a snitch or a tattler, even if it is about telling on your company when it is doing something illegal or immoral.

MOSTLY YES < < <   > > > MOSTLY NO

| 1 | 2 | 3 | 4 | 5 |

3 It's not the manager's job to solve problems in the outside world.

MOSTLY YES < < <   > > > MOSTLY NO

| 1 | 2 | 3 | 4 | 5 |

WorldCom is one of many examples of widespread moral lapses and corporate financial scandals that have brought the topic of ethics to the forefront. The pervasiveness of ethical lapses in the early 2000s was astounding. Once-respected firms such as Enron, Arthur Andersen, Tyco, and HealthSouth became synonymous with greed, deceit, and financial chicanery. No wonder a public poll found that 79 percent of respondents in the United States believe questionable business practices are widespread. Fewer than one-third said they think most chief executive officers (CEOs) are honest.[1] The sentiment is echoed in other countries as well. Recent investigations of dozens of top executives in Germany for tax evasion, bribery, and other forms of corruption have destroyed the high level of public trust business leaders there once enjoyed, with just 15 percent of respondents now saying business leaders are trustworthy.[2]

This chapter expands on the ideas about environment, corporate culture, and the international environment discussed in Chapters 2 and 3. We first focus on the topic of ethical values, which builds on the idea of corporate culture. We examine fundamental approaches that can help managers think through difficult ethical issues, and we look at factors that influence how managers make ethical choices. Understanding these ideas will help you build a solid foundation on which to base future decision making. We also examine organizational relationships to the external environment as reflected in corporate social responsibility. The final section of the chapter describes how managers build an ethical organization using codes of ethics and other organizational policies, structures, and systems.

What Is Managerial Ethics?

Ethics is difficult to define in a precise way. In a general sense, **ethics** is the code of moral principles and values that governs the behaviors of a person or group with respect to what is right or wrong. Ethics sets standards as to what is good or bad in conduct and decision making.[3] An ethical issue is present in a situation when the actions of a person or organization may harm or benefit others.[4] Yet ethical issues can sometimes be exceedingly complex. People in organizations may hold widely divergent views about the most ethically appropriate or inappropriate actions related to a situation.[5] Managers often face situations in which it is difficult to determine what is right. In addition, they might be torn between their misgivings and their sense of duty to their bosses and the organization. Sometimes, managers want to take a stand but don't have the backbone to go against others, bring unfavorable attention to themselves, or risk their jobs.

Ethics can be more clearly understood when compared with behaviors governed by law and by free choice. Exhibit 4.1 illustrates that human behavior falls into three categories. The first is codified law in which values and standards are written into the legal system and are enforceable in the courts. In this area, lawmakers set rules that people and corporations must follow in a certain way, such as obtaining licenses for cars or paying corporate taxes. The courts alleged that executives at companies such as WorldCom and Enron broke the law, for example, by manipulating financial results using off-balance-sheet partnerships to improperly create income and hide debt.[6] The domain of free choice is at the opposite end of the scale and pertains to behavior about which the law has no say and for which an individual or organization enjoys complete freedom. A manager's choice of where to eat lunch and a music company's choice of the number of CDs to release are examples of free choice.

ethics
The code of moral principles and values that governs the behaviors of a person or group with respect to what is right or wrong.

EXHIBIT 4.1
Three Domains of Human Action

| Domain of Codified Law (Legal Standard) | Domain of Ethics (Social Standard) | Domain of Free Choice (Personal Standard) |

Amount of Explicit Control

High ← → Low

1 If an action is legal, then it is also ethical.

ANSWER: Actions can be legal and yet highly unethical, although behaviors are often both legal and ethical.

Between these domains lies the area of ethics. This domain has no specific laws, yet it does have standards of conduct based on shared principles and values about moral conduct that guide an individual or company. Executives at Enron, for example, did not break any specific laws by encouraging employees to buy more shares of stock even when they believed the company was in financial trouble and the price of the shares was likely to decline. However, this behavior was a clear violation of the executives' ethical responsibilities to employees.[7] These managers were acting based on their own interests rather than their duties to employees and other stakeholders.

Try to do the right thing, the ethical thing, rather than just follow "the law."

Many companies and individuals get into trouble with the simplified view that choices are governed by either law or free choice. This view leads people to mistakenly assume that if it's not illegal then it must be ethical—as if there were no third domain.[8] A better option is to recognize the domain of ethics and accept moral values as a powerful force for good that can regulate behaviors both inside and outside organizations. As described in the Business Blooper below, Michael Phelps and Chris Brown got into trouble because they did not understand that their free choices violated important norms.

Ethical Dilemmas: What Would You Do?

Ethics is always about making decisions, and some issues are difficult to resolve. Because ethical standards are not codified, disagreements and dilemmas about proper behavior often occur. An **ethical dilemma** arises in a situation concerning right or wrong when values are in conflict.[9] Right and wrong cannot be clearly identified.

The individual who must make an ethical choice in an organization is the *moral agent*.[10] Here are some dilemmas that a manager in an organization might face. Think about how you would handle them.

ethical dilemma
A situation that arises when all alternative choices or behaviors are deemed undesirable because of potentially negative consequences, making it difficult to distinguish right from wrong.

1. Your company requires a terrorist watch list that screens all new customers and takes approximately 24 hours from the time an order is placed. You can close a lucrative deal with

BUSINESS BLOOPER

Michael Phelps and Chris Brown

Because he had won 14 Olympic medals, eight in Beijing alone, in 2008 Michael Phelps was named one of America's Most Fascinating People by *TV Guide*, and was awarded millions of dollars in endorsement deals. Maybe he forgot that being a celebrity means your behavior is watched closely, because in January 2009 a photo of him smoking marijuana from a bong appeared everywhere. As a consequence, Phelps started losing lucrative endorsement deals, such as the one he had with cereal maker Kellogg, which stated that Phelps' drug use was "not consistent" with the company's image. He almost got dropped by Subway, which removed links to him from the company Web site; after Phelps's public apology, the fast-food company decided to keep him onboard.

Also, Chris Brown, who had made big money singing the praises of Doublemint gum, was dropped by the Wm. Wrigley Jr. Company after he was arrested and charged with making criminal threats against singer Rihanna.

SOURCE: Charisse Jones, "Scandals Tarnish Star Endorsements," *USA Today*, Feb. 23, 2009, p. 5B.

Protective Life Corporation shows its commitment to ethics through its corporate strategy: "Offer great products at highly competitive prices and provide the kind of attentive service we'd hope to get from others." Treating others the way you want to be treated is one approach to making ethically responsible decisions and handling ethical dilemmas. However, insurance companies often have to rely on a utilitarian approach to ethical decision making that considers how to provide the greatest good to the greatest number of policyholders.

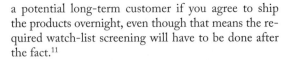

a potential long-term customer if you agree to ship the products overnight, even though that means the required watch-list screening will have to be done after the fact.[11]

2. As a sales manager for a major pharmaceuticals company, you've been asked to promote a new drug that costs $2,500 per dose. You've read the reports saying the drug is only 1 percent more effective than an alternate drug that costs less than $625 per dose. The VP of sales wants you to aggressively promote the $2,500-per-dose drug. He reminds you that if you don't do so, lives could be lost that might have been saved with that 1-percent increase in drug effectiveness.

3. Your company is hoping to build a new overseas manufacturing plant. You could save about $5 million by not installing standard pollution-control equipment that is required in the United States. The plant will employ many local workers in a poor country where jobs are scarce. Your research shows that pollutants from the factory could potentially damage the local fishing industry. Yet building the factory with the pollution-control equipment will likely make the plant too expensive to build.[12]

4. You have been collaborating with a fellow manager on an important project. One afternoon, you walk into his office a bit earlier than scheduled and see sexually explicit images on his computer monitor. The company has a zero-tolerance sexual-harassment policy as well as strict guidelines regarding personal use of the Internet. However, your colleague was in his own office and not bothering anyone else.[13]

These kinds of dilemmas and issues fall squarely in the domain of ethics. How would you handle each of the above situations? Now consider the following hypothetical dilemma, which scientists are using to study human morality.[14]

- A runaway trolley is heading down the tracks toward five unsuspecting people. You're standing near a switch that will divert the trolley onto a siding, but there is a single worker on the siding who cannot be warned in time to escape and will almost certainly be killed. Would you throw the switch?

- What if the worker is standing on a bridge over the tracks and you have to push him off the bridge to stop the trolley with his body in order to save the five unsuspecting people? (Assume his body is large enough to stop the trolley and yours is not.) Would you push the man, even though he would almost certainly be killed?

These dilemmas show how complex questions of ethics and morality can sometimes be. In *Time* magazine's readers' poll, 97 percent of respondents said they could throw the switch (which would almost certainly lead to the death of the worker), but only 42 percent said they could actually push the man to his death.[15]

Criteria for Ethical Decision Making

Most ethical dilemmas involve a conflict between the needs of the part and the needs of the whole: the individual versus the organization or the organization versus society as a whole. For example, should a company perform surveillance on managers' nonworkplace

conduct, which might benefit the organization as a whole but reduce the individu...
of employees? Or should products that fail to meet tough Food and Drug Adm...
standards be exported to other countries where government standards are lowe...
the company but potentially harming world citizens? Sometimes ethical deci...
conflict between two groups. For example, should the potential for local he...
resulting from a company's effluents take precedence over the jobs it create...
leading employer?

Managers faced with these kinds of tough ethical choices often benefit f...
strategy—one based on norms and values—to guide their decision making...
ics uses several approaches to describe values for guiding ethical decision mak...
these approaches that are relevant to managers are the utilitarian approach, individualism
approach, moral-rights approach, and justice approach.[16]

110

Go back to
on ethic...
page 10...
First ...
de...

UTILITARIAN APPROACH

The **utilitarian approach**, espoused by the 19th-century philosophers Jeremy Bentham
and John Stuart Mill, holds that moral behavior produces the greatest good for the greatest number. Under this approach, a decision maker is expected to consider the effect of
each decision alternative on all parties and select the one that optimizes the benefits for
the greatest number of people. In the trolley dilemma above, for instance, the utilitarian
approach would hold that it would be moral to push one person to his death in order to
save five. In organizations, because actual computations can be complex, simplifying them
is considered appropriate. For example, a simple economic frame of reference could be
used by calculating dollar costs and dollar benefits. The utilitarian ethic is cited as the basis
for the recent trend among companies to monitor employee use of the Internet and police
personal habits such as alcohol and tobacco consumption because such behavior affects the
entire workplace.[17]

INDIVIDUALISM APPROACH

The **individualism approach** contends that acts are moral when they promote the individual's best long-term interests. Individual self-direction is paramount, and external
forces that restrict self-direction should be severely limited.[18] Individuals calculate the
best long-term advantage to themselves as a measure of a decision's goodness. The action
that is intended to produce a greater ratio of good to bad for the individual compared with
other alternatives is the right one to perform. In theory, with everyone pursuing self-
direction, the greater good is ultimately served because people learn to accommodate each
other in their own long-term interest. Individualism is believed to lead to honesty and
integrity because that works best in the long run; lying and cheating for immediate self-
interest just causes business associates to lie and cheat in return. Thus, individualism
ultimately leads to behavior toward others that fits standards of behavior people want
toward themselves.[19]

One value of understanding this approach is to recognize short-term variations if they
are proposed. People might argue for short-term self-interest based on individualism, but
that misses the point. Because individualism is easily misinterpreted to support immediate
self-gain, it is not popular in the highly organized and group-oriented society of today.
This approach is closest to the domain of free choice described in Exhibit 4.1.

MORAL-RIGHTS APPROACH

The **moral-rights approach** asserts that human beings have fundamental rights and lib-
erties that cannot be taken away by an individual's decision. Thus, an ethically correct decision is one that best maintains the rights of those affected by it.

*Make decisions that
benefit others, not just
yourself.*

**utilitarian
approach**
The ethical concept that
moral behaviors produce the
greatest good for the greatest
number.

**individualism
approach**
The ethical concept that acts
are moral when they promote
an individual's best long-term
interests.

**moral-rights
approach**
The ethical concept that moral
decisions are those that best
maintain the rights of those
people affected by them.

Six moral rights should be considered during decision making:

1. *The right of free consent.* Individuals are to be treated only as they knowingly and freely consent to be treated.

2. *The right to privacy.* Individuals can choose to do as they please away from work and have control of information about their private life.

3. *The right of freedom of conscience.* Individuals may refrain from carrying out any order that violates their moral or religious norms.

4. *The right of free speech.* Individuals may criticize truthfully the ethics or legality of actions of others.

5. *The right to due process.* Individuals have a right to an impartial hearing and fair treatment.

6. *The right to life and safety.* Individuals have a right to live without endangerment or violation of their health and safety.

To make ethical decisions, managers need to avoid interfering with the fundamental rights of others. Performing experimental treatments on unconscious trauma patients, for example, might be construed to violate the right to free consent. A decision to monitor employees' nonwork activities violates the right to privacy. Sexual harassment is unethical because it violates the right to freedom of conscience. The right of free speech would support whistle-blowers who call attention to illegal or inappropriate actions within a company.

JUSTICE APPROACH

The **justice approach** holds that moral decisions must be based on standards of equity, fairness, and impartiality. Three types of justice are of concern to managers: distributive, procedural, and compensatory. **Distributive justice** requires that different treatment of people not be based on arbitrary characteristics. Individuals who are similar in ways that are relevant to a decision should be treated similarly. Thus, men and women should not receive different salaries if they are performing the same job. However, people who differ in a substantive way, such as job skills or job responsibility, can be treated differently in proportion to the differences in skills or responsibility among them. This difference should have a clear relationship to organizational goals and tasks.

Procedural justice requires that rules be administered fairly. Rules should be clearly stated and consistently and impartially enforced.

Compensatory justice argues that individuals should be compensated for the cost of their injuries by the party responsible. Moreover, individuals should not be held responsible for matters over which they have no control.

The justice approach is closest to the thinking underlying the domain of law in Exhibit 4.1 because it assumes that justice is applied through rules and regulations. This theory does not require complex calculations such as those demanded by a utilitarian approach, nor does it justify self-interest as the individualism approach does. Managers are expected to define attributes on which different treatment of employees is acceptable. Questions such as how minority workers should be compensated for past discrimination are extremely difficult. However, this approach justifies the ethical behavior of efforts to correct past wrongs, play fair under the rules, and insist on job-relevant differences as the basis for different levels of pay or promotion opportunities. Most of the laws guiding human-resource management (Chapter 9) are based on the justice approach.

Understanding these various approaches is only a first step. Managers still have to consider how to apply them. The approaches offer general principles that managers can recognize as useful in making ethical decisions.

the section
dilemmas on
and select two.
apply the utilitarian
approach to reach a
cision in each situation,
and then apply the
moral-rights approach.
Did you reach the same
or different conclusions?
As a new manager, do
you think one approach
is generally better for
managers to use?

Take time to make decisions so that you treat others fairly and with justice.

justice approach
The ethical concept that moral decisions must be based on standards of equity, fairness, and impartiality.

distributive justice
The concept that different treatment of people should not be based on arbitrary characteristics. In the case of substantive differences, people should be treated differently in proportion to the differences among them.

procedural justice
The concept that rules should be clearly stated and consistently and impartially enforced.

compensatory justice
The concept that individuals should be compensated for the cost of their injuries by the party responsible and also that individuals should not be held responsible for matters over which they have no control.

A Manager's Ethical Choices

A number of factors influence a manager's ability to make ethical decisions. Individuals bring specific personality and behavioral traits to the job. Personal needs, family influence, and religious background all shape a manager's value system. Specific personality characteristics, such as ego strength, self-confidence, and a strong sense of independence, may enable managers to make ethical choices despite personal risks.

One important personal trait is the stage of moral development.[20] A simplified version of one model of personal moral development is shown in Exhibit 4.2.

At the *preconventional level*, individuals are concerned with external rewards and punishments and obey authority to avoid detrimental personal consequences. In an organizational context, this level may be associated with managers who use an autocratic or coercive leadership style with employees who are oriented toward dependable accomplishment of specific tasks.

At level two, called the *conventional level*, people learn to conform to the expectations of good behavior as defined by colleagues, family, friends, and society. Meeting social and interpersonal obligations is important. Work-group collaboration is the preferred way to accomplish organizational goals, and managers use a leadership style that encourages interpersonal relationships and cooperation.

At the *postconventional* or *principled* level, individuals are guided by an internal set of values based on universal principles of justice and right and will even disobey rules or laws that violate these principles. Internal values become more important than the expectations of significant others. This chapter's Benchmarking box gives some tips for how postconventional managers can effectively challenge their superiors concerning questionable ethical matters. One example of the postconventional or principled approach comes from World War II. When the USS *Indianapolis* sank after being torpedoed, one Navy pilot disobeyed orders and risked his life to save men who were being picked off by sharks. The pilot was operating from the highest level of moral development in attempting the rescue despite a direct order from superiors. When managers operate from this highest level of development, they use transformative or servant leadership, focusing on the needs of followers and encouraging others to think for themselves and to engage in higher levels of moral reasoning. Employees are empowered and given opportunities for constructive participation in governance of the organization.

Listen to your conscience and take moral actions; independently investigate where the truth lies and what is the right thing to do.

EXHIBIT 4.2

Three Levels of Personal Moral Development

Level 3: Postconventional

Follows self-chosen principles of justice and right. Aware that people hold different values and seeks creative solutions to ethical dilemmas. Balances concern for individual with concern for common good.

Level 2: Conventional

Lives up to expectations of others. Fulfills duties and obligations of social system. Upholds laws.

Level 1: Preconventional

Follows rules to avoid punishment. Acts in own interest. Obedience for its own sake.

	Level 1: Preconventional	Level 2: Conventional	Level 3: Postconventional
Leadership Style:	Autocratic/coercive	Guiding/encouraging, team oriented	Transforming, or servant leadership
Employee Behavior:	Task accomplishment	Work group collaboration	Empowered employees, full participation

SOURCE: Based on L. Kohlberg, "Moral Stages and Moralization: The Cognitive-Developmental Approach," in T. Lickona (Ed.), *Moral Development and Behavior: Theory, Research, and Social Issues* (New York: Holt, Rinehart, and Winston, 1976): 31–53; and Jill W. Graham, "Leadership, Moral Development and Citizenship Behavior," *Business Ethics Quarterly* 5(1) (Jan. 1995): 43–54.

2 It's wrong to be a snitch or a tattler, even if it is about telling on your company when it is doing something illegal or immoral.

ANSWER: It takes courage and often a higher level of ethical development to go against strong authority in a company and report illegal behavior. Rather than calling people who take such steps *whistle-blowers*, a term that has a negative connotation, why not call them *conscience seekers*?

TAKE ACTION

As a new manager, strive for a high level of personal moral development. You can test your development by completing the New Manager's Self Test on page 114.

The great majority of managers operate at level two, meaning their ethical thought and behavior is greatly influenced by their superiors, colleagues, and other significant people in the organization or industry. A few have not advanced beyond level one. Only about 20 percent of American adults reach the level-three postconventional stage of moral development. People at level three are able to act in an independent, ethical manner regardless of expectations from others inside or outside the organization. Managers at level three of moral development will make ethical decisions whatever the organizational consequences for them.

Globalization makes ethical issues even more complicated for today's managers.[21] For example, although tolerance for bribery is waning, bribes are still considered a normal part of doing business in many foreign countries. Transparency International, an international organization that monitors corruption, publishes an annual report ranking 30 leading exporting countries based on the propensity of international businesses to offer bribes. Exhibit 4.3 shows the results of the organization's most recent available report. Emerging

EXHIBIT 4.3

The Transparency International Bribe Payers Index

Rank		Score	Rank		Score
1	Switzerland	7.81	16	Portugal	6.47
2	Sweden	7.62	17	Mexico	6.45
3	Australia	7.59	18	Hong Kong	6.01
4	Austria	7.50	18(tie)	Israel	6.01
5	Canada	7.46	20	Italy	5.94
6	United Kingdom	7.39	21	South Korea	5.83
7	Germany	7.34	22	Saudi Arabia	5.75
8	Netherlands	7.28	23	Brazil	5.65
9	Belgium	7.22	24	South Africa	5.61
9(tie)	United States	7.22	25	Malaysia	5.59
11	Japan	7.10	26	Taiwan	5.41
12	Singapore	6.78	27	Turkey	5.23
13	Spain	6.63	28	Russia	5.16
14	UAE	6.62	29	China	4.94
15	France	6.50	30	India	4.62

SOURCE: Adapted from "Transparency International Bribe Payers Index 2006." Copyright 2006 Transparency International: The Global Coalition Against Corruption. Used with permission. For more information, visit http://www.transparency.org.

How to Challenge the Boss on Ethical Issues

Many of today's top executives put a renewed emphasis on ethics in light of serious ethical lapses that tarnished the reputations and hurt the performance of previously respected and successful companies. Yet keeping an organization in ethical line is an ongoing challenge, and it requires that people at all levels be willing to stand up for what they think is right. Challenging the boss or other senior leaders on potentially unethical behaviors is particularly unnerving for most people. Here are some tips for talking to the boss about an ethically questionable decision or action. Following these guidelines can increase the odds that you'll be heard and that your opinions will be seriously considered.

- *Do your research.* Marshal any facts and figures that support your position on the issue at hand and develop an alternative policy or course of action that you can suggest at the appropriate time. Prepare succinct answers to any questions you anticipate being asked about your plan.
- *Begin the meeting by giving your boss the floor.* Make sure you really do understand what the decision or policy is and the reasons behind it. Ask open-ended questions and listen actively, showing through both your responses and your body language that you're seriously listening and trying to understand the other person's position. In particular, seek out information about what the senior manager sees as the decision or policy's benefits as well as any potential downsides. It'll give you information you can use later to highlight how your plan can produce similar benefits while avoiding the potential disadvantages.
- *Pay attention to your word choice and demeanor.* No matter how strongly you feel about the matter, don't rant and rave about it. You're more likely to be heard if you remain calm, objective, and professional. Try to disagree without making it

personal. Avoid phrases such as "You're wrong," "You can't," "You should," and "How could you?" to prevent triggering the other person's automatic defense mechanisms.
- *Take care how you suggest your alternative solution.* You can introduce your plan with phrases such as "Here's another way to look at this" or "What would you think about . . . ?" Check for your superior's reactions both by explicitly asking for feedback and being sensitive to body language clues. Point out the potential negative consequences of implementing decisions that might be construed as unethical by customers, shareholders, suppliers, or the public.
- *Be patient. Don't demand a resolution on the spot.* During your conversation, you may realize that your plan needs some work, or your boss might just need time to digest the information and opinions you've presented. It's often a good idea to ask for a follow-up meeting.

If the decision or action being considered is clearly unethical or potentially illegal, and this meeting doesn't provide a quick resolution, you might need to take your concerns to higher levels or even blow the whistle to someone outside the organization who can make sure the organization stays in line. However, most managers don't want to take actions that will harm the organization, its people, or the community. In many cases, questionable ethical issues can be resolved by open and honest communication. That, however, requires that people have the courage—and develop the skills—to confront their superiors in a calm and rational way.

SOURCES: Kevin Daley, "How to Disagree: Go Up Against Your Boss or a Senior Executive and Live to Tell the Tale," *T&D* (Apr. 2004); Diane Moore, "How to Disagree with Your Boss—and Keep Your Job," *Toronto Star*, Nov. 12, 2003; and "How to Disagree with Your Boss," *WikiHow* (http://wiki.ehow.com/Disagree-With-Your-Boss).

export powers rank the worst, with India showing the greatest propensity for bribery and China, which has become the world's fourth largest exporter, almost as bad. However, multinational firms in the United States, Japan, France, and Spain also reveal a relatively high propensity to pay bribes overseas.[22]

These are difficult issues for managers to resolve. Companies that don't oil the wheels of contract negotiations in foreign countries can put themselves at a competitive disadvantage, yet managers walk a fine line when doing deals overseas. Although U.S. laws allow certain types of payments, tough federal antibribery laws are also in place. Many companies, including Monsanto, Schering-Plough, and IBM, have gotten into trouble with the U.S. Securities and Exchange Commission (SEC) for using incentives to facilitate foreign deals.

NEW MANAGER'S SELF-TEST

Self and Others

Leaders differ in how they view human nature and the tactics they use to get things done through others. Answer the questions below based on how you view yourself and others. Think carefully about each question and be honest about what you feel inside. Please answer whether each item below is Mostly True or Mostly False for you.

	MOSTLY TRUE	MOSTLY FALSE
1. I prefer not to depend on anyone else to get things done.	_____	_____
2. I appreciate that I am a special person.	_____	_____
3. I help orient new people even though it is not required.	_____	_____
4. I like to be the center of attention.	_____	_____
5. I am always ready to lend a helping hand to those around me.	_____	_____
6. I tend to see my co-workers as competitors.	_____	_____
7. I am quick to see and point out others' mistakes.	_____	_____
8. I frequently interrupt someone to make my point.	_____	_____
9. I often have to admit that people around me are not very competent.	_____	_____

SCORING AND INTERPRETATION: This scale is about orientation toward self versus others. A high score suggests you could be ego-centered and may come across to others as something of a jerk. To compute your score, give yourself 1 point for each Mostly False answer to items 3 and 5 and 1 point for each Mostly True answer to items 1, 2, 4, 6, 7, 8, and 9. A score of 7 to 9 points suggests a self-oriented person who might take the *individualism approach* to the extreme or function at the *preconventional level* of moral development (Exhibit 4.2). A score of 4 to 6 points suggests a balance between self and others. A score from 0 to 3 points would indicate an "other" orientation associated with a *utilitarian* or *moral-rights approach* and *level-2 or level-3 moral development*, suggesting little likelihood of coming across as a jerk.

What Is Corporate Social Responsibility?

corporate social responsibility (CSR)
The obligation of organization management to make decisions and take actions that will enhance the welfare and interests of society as well as the organization.

Now let's turn to the issue of corporate social responsibility. In one sense, the concept of social responsibility, like ethics, is easy to understand: It means distinguishing right from wrong and doing right. It means being a good corporate citizen. The formal definition of **corporate social responsibility (CSR)** is management's obligation to make choices and take actions that will contribute to the welfare and interests of society as well as the organization.[23]

As straightforward as this definition seems, CSR can be a difficult concept to grasp because different people have different beliefs as to which actions improve society's welfare.[24] To make matters worse, social responsibility covers a range of issues, many of which are ambiguous with respect to right or wrong. If a bank deposits the money from a trust fund into a low-interest account for 90 days, from which it makes a substantial profit, is it being a responsible corporate citizen? How about two companies engaging in intense competition? Is it socially responsible for the stronger corporation to drive the weaker one into bankruptcy or a forced merger? Or consider companies such as Chiquita, Kmart, and Dana Corporation, all of which declared bankruptcy—which is perfectly legal—to avoid mounting financial obligations to suppliers, labor unions, or competitors. These examples contain moral, legal, and economic considerations that make socially responsible behavior hard to define.

ORGANIZATIONAL STAKEHOLDERS

One reason for the difficulty understanding and applying CSR is that managers must confront the question, "Responsibility to whom?" Recall from Chapter 2 that the organization's environment consists of several sectors in both the task and general environment. From a social responsibility perspective, enlightened organizations view the internal and external environment as a variety of stakeholders.

A **stakeholder** is any group within or outside the organization that has a stake in the organization's performance. Each stakeholder has a different criterion of responsiveness because it has a different interest in the organization.[25] For example, Walmart uses aggressive bargaining tactics with suppliers so that it is able to provide low prices for customers. Some stakeholders see this type of corporate behavior as responsible because it benefits customers and forces suppliers to be more efficient. Others, however, argue that the aggressive tactics are unethical and socially irresponsible because they force U.S. manufacturers to lay off workers, close factories, and outsource from low-wage countries. One supplier said clothing is being sold so cheaply at Walmart that many U.S. companies could not compete even if they paid their employees nothing.[26]

The organization's performance affects stakeholders, but stakeholders can also have a tremendous effect on the organization's performance and success. Consider the case of Monsanto, a leading competitor in the life sciences industry.

© AP IMAGES

The International Olympic Committee must respond to numerous stakeholders, including the 205 national Olympic committees that make up its membership, the countries and cities at which various Olympic events will be held, the business community that will cater to attendees, numerous sponsors, media organizations, the participating athletes, and an international public that has varying and conflicting interests. The symbolic running of the torch for the 2008 Olympics was plagued by protests over China's alleged human rights violations. In this photo, Ross Lahive protests as the torch passes through San Francisco.

> CONCEPT CONNECTION <

stakeholder
Any group within or outside the organization that has a stake in the organization's performance.

MONSANTO

Over the past decade or so, Monsanto has been transformed from a chemicals firm into a biotechnology company. The organization's vast array of stakeholders around the world includes customers, investors, suppliers, partners, health and agricultural organizations, regulatory agencies, research institutes, and governments.

Monsanto experienced some big problems in recent years because of its failure to satisfy various stakeholder groups. For example, the company's genetic seed business has been the target of controversy and protest. Small farmers were concerned about new dependencies that might arise for them from using the new seeds. European consumers rebelled against a perceived imposition of unlabeled, genetically modified food ingredients. Research institutes and other organizations took offense at what they perceived as Monsanto's arrogant approach to the new business. Activist groups accused the company of creating "Frankenstein foods." To make matters even worse, in seeking to sell genetically modified seeds in Indonesia, managers allegedly bribed government officials, which got Monsanto into hot water with the SEC.

In light of these stakeholder issues, CEO Hendrik Verfaillie offered an apology to some stakeholders at a *Farm Journal* conference in Washington, D.C., saying that Monsanto "was so blinded by its enthusiasm for this great new technology that it missed the concerns the technology raised for many people." Verfaillie also announced a five-part pledge that aims to restore positive stakeholder relationships. Each of the five commitments requires an ongoing dialogue between Monsanto managers and various stakeholder constituencies. The company paid $1.5 million to settle the SEC charges and is voluntarily cooperating with regulatory investigators. Monsanto managers understand the importance of effectively managing critical stakeholder relationships.[27]

Exhibit 4.4 illustrates important stakeholders for Monsanto. Most organizations are similarly influenced by a variety of stakeholder groups. Investors and shareholders, employees, customers, and suppliers are considered primary stakeholders, without whom the organization cannot survive. Investors, shareholders, and suppliers' interests are served by managerial efficiency—that is, use of resources to achieve profits. Employees expect work satisfaction, pay, and good supervision. Customers are concerned with decisions about the quality, safety, and availability of goods and services. When any primary stakeholder group becomes seriously dissatisfied, the organization's viability is threatened.[28]

Other important stakeholders are the government and the community, which have become increasingly important in recent years. Most corporations exist only under the proper charter and licenses and operate within the limits of safety laws, environmental protection requirements, antitrust regulations, antibribery legislation, and other laws and regulations in the government sector. The community includes local government, the natural and physical environments, and the quality of life provided for residents. Special-interest

EXHIBIT 4.4

Major Stakeholders Relevant to Monsanto Company

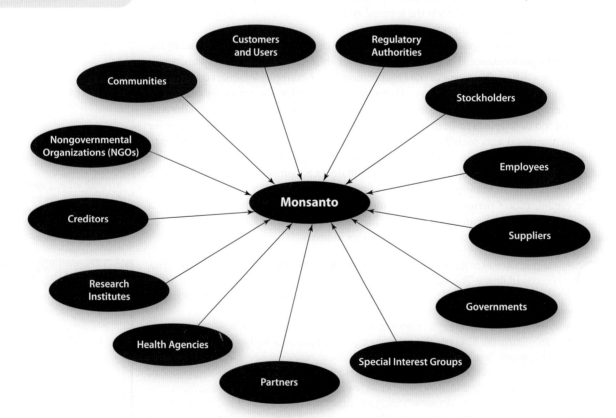

SOURCES: Based on information in D. Wheeler, B. Colbert, and R. E. Freeman, "Focusing on Value: Reconciling Corporate Social Responsibility, Sustainability, and a Stakeholder Approach in a Networked World," *Journal of General Management* 28(3) (Spring 2003): 1–28; and J. E. Post, L. E. Preston, and S. Sachs, "Managing the Extended Enterprise: The New Stakeholder View," *California Management Review* 45(1) (Fall 2002): 6–28.

groups, still another stakeholder, may include trade associations, political action committees, professional associations, and consumerists. Socially responsible organizations consider the effects of their actions on all stakeholder groups. Some large businesses with the resources needed to serve developing countries are extending their field of stakeholders by serving the *bottom of the pyramid*.

THE BOTTOM OF THE PYRAMID

The **bottom-of-the-pyramid (BOP) concept**, sometimes called *base of the pyramid*, proposes that corporations can alleviate poverty and other social ills, as well as make significant profits, by selling to the world's poorest people. The term *bottom of the pyramid* refers to the more than 4 billion people who make up the lowest level of the world's economic "pyramid" as defined by per capita income. These people earn less than $1,500 (U.S.) a year, with about one-fourth of them earning less than a dollar a day.[29] Traditionally, these people haven't been served by most large businesses because products and services are too expensive, inaccessible, and not suited to their needs. A number of leading companies are changing that by adopting BOP business models geared to serving the poorest of the world's consumers.

The BOP motive is twofold. Of course, companies are in business with a goal to make money, and managers see a vast untapped market in emerging economies. However, another goal is to play a pivotal role in addressing global poverty and other problems such as environmental destruction, social decay, and political instability in the developing world. Although the BOP concept has gained significant attention only recently, the basic idea is nothing new. Here's an example of a company that has been practicing bottom-of-the-pyramid activities for more than a hundred years.

> **bottom-of-the-pyramid (BOP) concept**
> The idea that large corporations can both alleviate social problems and make a profit by selling goods and services to the world's poorest people.

UNILEVER AND HINDUSTAN LEVER

The World Health Organization estimates that diarrhea-related illnesses kill more than 1.8 million people a year. One way to prevent the spread of these diseases is better hand washing, and marketing managers for Lifebuoy soap are trying to make sure people know that fact.

British soap maker Lever Brothers (now the global organization Unilever) introduced Lifebuoy to India more than a century ago, promoting it as the enemy of dirt and disease. The basic approach today is the same. Several years ago, the company's India subsidiary, Hindustan Lever Limited, introduced a campaign called *Swasthya Chetna* ("Glowing Health"), sending Lifebuoy teams into rural villages with a "glo-germ kit" to show people that even clean-looking hands can carry dangerous germs—and that soap-washed hands don't.

Sales of Lifebuoy have risen sharply since the campaign, aided by the introduction of a smaller-size bar that costs five rupees (about 12 cents). Just as important, says Hindustan Lever's chairman Harish Manwani, the campaign has reached around 80 million of the rural poor with education about how to prevent needless deaths.[30]

Marketing manager Punit Misra, who oversees the Lifebuoy brand, emphasizes that "profitable responsibility" is essential for companies to have a true impact on solving the world's problems. "If it's not really self-sustaining, somewhere along the line it will drop

3 It's not the manager's job to solve problems in the outside world.

Assess Your Answer

ANSWER: A company is a "citizen" of the country in which it resides, as well as a citizen of the world. And just as ordinary citizens need to be concerned about issues regarding the environment, or community-harming problems such as extreme poverty, companies need to be aware and take actions that are decent and yet reasonable.

off," Misra says.[31] Other proponents of bottom-of-the pyramid thinking agree that BOP works because it ties social responsibility directly into the heart of the company. Businesses contribute to lasting change when the profit motive goes hand in hand with the desire to make a contribution to humankind.

The Ethic of Sustainability

Corporations involved in bottom-of-the-pyramid activities, as well as a number of other companies around the world, are also embracing a revolutionary idea called *sustainability* or *sustainable development*. **Sustainability** refers to economic development that generates wealth and meets the needs of the current generation while saving the environment so future generations can meet their needs as well.[32] With a philosophy of sustainability, managers weave environmental and social concerns into every strategic decision, revise policies and procedures to support sustainability efforts, and measure their progress toward sustainability goals. One of the most ardent, and perhaps unlikely, advocates of sustainability is a carpet manufacturer.

INTERFACE

For Ray Anderson, who founded the carpet-tile company Interface, the approach to the environment used to be "to follow the law." Then he started reading about environmental issues and had an epiphany: "I was running a company that was plundering the Earth," Anderson says.

How things have changed since then. Anderson challenged Interface to become a "restorative enterprise," an operation that does no harm to the biosphere and takes nothing from Earth than cannot be recycled or quickly regenerated.

Since 1994, Interface's use of fossil fuels is down 45 percent, with net greenhouse-gas production down 60 percent. The company's global operations use only one-third the water they formerly used. Interface's contributions to garbage landfills have been cut by 80 percent. One key to the company's success, Anderson says, is a comprehensive approach that incorporates sustainability into every aspect of the business. Rather than going green by tacking on this or that environmental program, managers looked at and revised the whole system.[33]

Ray Anderson's mission is a lot easier than it used to be. Even companies that have typically paid little attention to the green movement are grappling with issues related to sustainability, partly because of the growing clout of environmentalists. Surveys show that American consumers find nonprofit green groups more credible than businesses, for example.[34] Another study found that master's of business administration students would forgo an average of $13,700 in compensation to work for a company that had a good reputation for environmental sustainability.[35] Even Walmart is paying attention. The company teamed up with Conservation International to help develop ways to cut energy consumption, switch to renewable power, and sell millions of energy-efficient fluorescent bulbs.[36] Sustainability argues that organizations can find innovative ways to create wealth at the same time they are preserving natural resources. General Mills used to pay to have oat hulls from its cereal production process hauled to the landfill. Now customers compete to buy the company's solid waste to be burned as fuel. GM earns more money from recycling than it once spent on disposal.[37]

Do your part to recycle both at work and at home; drive a fuel-efficient vehicle.

Evaluating Corporate Social Responsibility

A model for evaluating corporate social performance is presented in Exhibit 4.5. The model indicates that total corporate social responsibility can be subdivided into four primary criteria: economic, legal, ethical, and discretionary responsibilities.[38] These four criteria fit together to form the whole of a company's social responsiveness.

sustainability
Economic development that generates wealth and meets the needs of the current population while preserving the environment for the needs of future generations.

Discretionary Responsibility
Contribute to the community; be a good corporate citizen.

Ethical Responsibility
Be ethical. Do what is right. Avoid harm.

Legal Responsibility
Obey the law.

Economic Responsibility
Be profitable.

Total Corporate Social Responsibility

SOURCES: Based on Archie B. Carroll, "A Three-Dimensional Conceptual Model of Corporate Performance," *Academy of Management Review* 4 (1979): 499; A. B. Carroll, "The Pyramid of Corporate Social Responsibility: Toward the Moral Management of Corporate Stakeholders," *Business Horizons* 34 (July–Aug. 1991): 42; and Mark S. Schwartz and Archie B. Carroll, "Corporate Social Responsibility: A Three-Domain Approach," *Business Ethics Quarterly* 13(4) (2003): 503–530.

EXHIBIT 4.5
Criteria of Corporate Social Performance

economic and ethical responsibilities
Required activities that concern financial well-being of the organization and the legal and moral decisions.

The first criterion of social responsibility is *economic responsibility*. The business institution is, above all, the basic economic unit of society. Its responsibility is to produce the goods and services that society wants and to maximize profits for its owners and shareholders. Economic responsibility carried to the extreme is called the *profit-maximizing view* and was advocated by Nobel Prize-winning economist Milton Friedman. This view argues that the corporation should be operated on a profit-oriented basis, with its sole mission to increase its profits as long as it stays within the rules of the game.[39] The purely profit-maximizing view is no longer considered an adequate criterion of performance in Canada, the United States, and Europe. This approach means that economic gain is the only social responsibility and can lead companies into trouble.

Legal responsibility defines what society deems as important with respect to appropriate corporate behavior.[40] In other words, businesses are expected to fulfill their economic goals within the framework of legal requirements imposed by local town councils, state legislatures, and federal regulatory agencies.

© GETTY IMAGES

The fall of financial services icon Bear Sterns grabbed the headlines, but numerous mortgage companies were declaring bankruptcy at the same time. When we look for those who failed to meet their **economic and ethical responsibilities** in the mortgage industry meltdown, we can find plenty of blame to go around. Some mortgage brokers and companies had lenient lending policies and offered exotic mortgage types that borrowers did not fully understand. Some home buyers and real-estate investors overextended their purchasing. Some financial institutions bundled mortgages into investment securities and sold those to other institutions. The resulting large number of foreclosed mortgages left empty houses, failed companies, and devastated families that will negatively affect some communities for years.

> CONCEPT CONNECTION <

Examples of illegal acts by corporations include committing corporate fraud, intentionally selling defective goods, performing unnecessary repairs or procedures, deliberately misleading consumers, and billing clients for work not done. Organizations that knowingly break the law are poor performers in this category. For example, Dow Chemical was fined $2 million for violating an agreement to halt false safety claims about its pesticide products. Prudential Insurance also came under fire for misleading consumers about variable life insurance policies.[41]

Ethical responsibility includes behaviors that are not necessarily codified into law and may not serve the corporation's direct economic interests. As described earlier in this chapter, to be *ethical*, organization decision makers should act with equity, fairness, and impartiality; respect the rights of individuals; and provide different treatment of individuals only when relevant to the organization's goals and tasks.[42] *Unethical* behavior occurs when decisions enable an individual or company to gain at the expense of other people or society as a whole. Consider what's happening in the student loan industry, which has come under close scrutiny after an investigation found that Student Loan Xpress paid financial aid directors at three universities a total of $160,000 in consulting fees, personal tuition reimbursement, and other payments as a way of getting placed on the universities' lists of preferred lenders. Investigators are seeking to determine whether lenders are being recommended to students because of the hidden payments officials are receiving rather than the fact that they offer the best lending terms to students.[43]

Discretionary responsibility is purely voluntary and is guided by a company's desire to make social contributions not mandated by economics, law, or ethics. Discretionary activities include generous philanthropic contributions that offer no payback to the company and are not expected. For example, General Mills spends more than 5 percent of pretax profits on social responsibility initiatives and charitable giving.[44] Another good illustration of discretionary behavior occurred when Emigrant Savings deposited $1,000 into the accounts of nearly 1,000 customers living in areas hit hardest by Hurricane Katrina.[45] Discretionary responsibility is the highest criterion of social responsibility because it goes beyond societal expectations to contribute to the community's welfare.

Managing Company Ethics and Social Responsibility

An expert on the topic of ethics said, "Management is responsible for creating and sustaining conditions in which people are likely to behave themselves."[46] Exhibit 4.6 illustrates ways in which managers create and support an ethical organization. One of the most important steps managers can take is to practice ethical leadership. **Ethical leadership** means that managers are honest and trustworthy, fair in their dealings with employees and customers, and behave ethically in both their personal and professional lives. Managers and first-line supervisors are important role models for ethical behavior, and they strongly influence the ethical climate in the organization by adhering to high ethical standards in their own behavior and decisions. Moreover, managers are proactive in influencing employees to embody and reflect ethical values.[47]

Managers can also implement organizational mechanisms to help employees and the company stay on an ethical footing. Some of the primary ones are codes of ethics, ethical structures, and measures to protect whistle-blowers.

CODE OF ETHICS

A **code of ethics** is a formal statement of the company's values concerning ethics and social issues; it communicates to employees what the company stands for. Codes of ethics

Read the Ethical Dilemma on page 128 that pertains to legal and ethical responsibilities. How important is it to you to protect the natural environment?

Remember that your company needs not only to make a profit but also to be a good citizen, follow the law, and be moral.

discretionary responsibility
Organizational responsibility that is voluntary and guided by the organization's desire to make social contributions not mandated by economics, law, or ethics.

ethical leadership
Providing strategy and being a role model for the organization to make legal and moral choices and to be a good citizen of the community.

code of ethics
A formal statement of the organization's values regarding ethics and social issues.

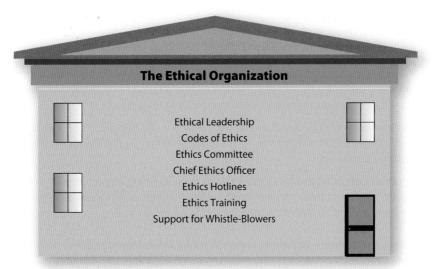

The Ethical Organization

Ethical Leadership
Codes of Ethics
Ethics Committee
Chief Ethics Officer
Ethics Hotlines
Ethics Training
Support for Whistle-Blowers

SOURCE: Adapted from Linda Klebe Treviño, Laura Pincus Hartman, and Michael Brown, "Moral Person and Moral Manager," *California Management Review* 42(4) (Summer 2000): 128–142.

tend to exist in two types: principle-based statements and policy-based statements. *Principle-based statements* are designed to affect corporate culture; they define fundamental values and contain general language about company responsibilities, quality of products, and treatment of employees. General statements of principle are often called *corporate credos*. One good example is Johnson & Johnson's "The Credo."

Policy-based statements generally outline the procedures to be used in specific ethical situations. These situations include marketing practices, conflicts of interest, observance of laws, proprietary information, political gifts, and equal opportunities. Examples of policy-based statements are Boeing's "Business Conduct Guidelines," Chemical Bank's "Code of Ethics," GTE's "Code of Business Ethics" and "Anti-Trust and Conflict of Interest Guidelines," and Norton's "Norton Policy on Business Ethics."[48]

Codes of ethics state the values or behaviors expected and those that will not be tolerated. A survey of *Fortune* 1,000 companies found that 98 percent address issues of ethics and business conduct in formal corporate documents, and 78 percent of those have separate codes of ethics that are widely distributed.[49] When top management supports and enforces these codes, including rewards for compliance and discipline for violation, ethics codes can boost a company's ethical climate.[50] The code of ethics for the *Milwaukee Journal Sentinel* gives employees some guidelines for dealing with ethical questions.

Do an Internet search for Johnson & Johnson's Credo, which is available in 36 languages. For more than 60 years, the Credo has guided Johnson & Johnson's managers in making decisions that honor the company's responsibilities to employees, customers, the community, and stockholders.

MILWAUKEE JOURNAL SENTINEL

In recent years, charges of plagiarism and other ethical violations cast a spotlight on newspaper publishers and other media outlets. Executives at Journal Communications, the parent company of the *Milwaukee Journal Sentinel,* hope the company's clear and comprehensive code of ethics will reinforce the public's trust as well as prevent misconduct. This excerpt from the opening sections of the code outlines some broad provisions defining what the company stands for:

Journal Communications and its subsidiaries operate in a complex and changing society. The actions of the company's employees, officers and directors clearly affect other members of that society. Therefore, every employee has an obligation to conduct the day-to-day business of the company in conformity with the highest ethical standards and in accordance with the various laws and regulations that govern modern business operations. . . .

Journal Communications' ethical standards embrace not only the letter of the law, but also the spirit of the law. To that end, we must apply plain old-fashioned honesty and decency to every aspect of our job. We must never sacrifice ethics for expedience. Broadly put, we should treat others fairly and with respect.

If faced with an ethical question, we should ask:

- Is this action legal?
- Does it comply with company policies and/or good business conduct?
- Is it something I would not want my supervisors, fellow employees, subordinates or family to know about?
- Is it something I would not want the general public to know about?

We must not condone illegal or unethical behavior . . . by failing to report it, regardless of an employee's level of authority. . . . The company will protect us if we bring unethical activity to its attention.

The *Journal*'s code of ethics also includes statements concerning respect for people, respect for the company, conflicts of interest, unfair competition, relationships with customers, suppliers, and news sources, confidential information, and accepting gifts and favors.[51]

By giving people some guidelines for confronting ethical questions and promising protection from recriminations for people who report wrongdoing, the *Journal*'s code of ethics gives all employees the responsibility and the right to maintain the organization's ethical climate.

ETHICAL STRUCTURES

Complete the Self Learning exercise on page 127 that pertains to ethical work environments. With what level of ethical climate are you most comfortable? As a manager, how might you improve the ethical climate of a department for which you are responsible?

Ethical structures represent the various systems, positions, and programs a company can undertake to implement ethical behavior. One of the newest positions in organizations is the *chief accounting officer*, a response to widespread financial wrongdoing in recent years. These high-level executives handle reporting and compliance, ensure due diligence, and work with outside auditors.[52] An **ethics committee** is a group of executives appointed to oversee company ethics. The committee provides rulings on questionable ethical issues and assumes responsibility for disciplining wrongdoers. Motorola's Ethics Compliance Committee, for instance, is charged with interpreting, clarifying, and communicating the company's code of ethics and with adjudicating suspected code violations.

Many companies set up ethics offices with full-time staff to ensure that ethical standards are an integral part of company operations. These offices are headed by a **chief ethics officer**, a company executive who oversees all aspects of ethics and legal compliance, including establishing and broadly communicating standards, overseeing ethics training, dealing with exceptions or problems, and advising senior managers in the ethical and compliance aspects of decisions.[53] The title of *chief ethics officer* was almost unheard of a decade ago, but highly publicized ethical and legal problems in recent years sparked a growing demand for these ethics specialists. The Ethics and Compliance Officers Association, a trade group, reports that membership soared 70 percent—to more than 1,260 companies—in the five years following the collapse of Enron due to financial wrongdoing.[54] Most ethics offices also work as counseling centers to help employees resolve difficult ethical issues. A toll-free confidential *ethics hotline* allows employees to report questionable behavior as well as seek guidance concerning ethical dilemmas. Perhaps if there had been more ethics officers, the financial industry might not have had such a severe meltdown. And perhaps someone like Patrick Kuhse would not have been allowed to commit fraud as shown in the Spotlight on Ethics box.

Ethics training programs also help employees deal with ethical questions and translate the values stated in a code of ethics into everyday behavior.[55] Training programs are an important supplement to a written code of ethics. General Electric implemented a strong compliance and ethics training program for all 320,000 employees worldwide. Much of the training is conducted online, with employees able to test themselves on how

ethics committee
A group of executives assigned to oversee an organization's ethics by ruling on questionable issues and disciplining violators.

chief ethics officer
A company executive who oversees ethics and legal compliance.

⋯aining
; to help
⋯ith ethical
⋯lues.

SPOTLIGHT ON
ETHICS

Financial Scams: Prison

After spending four years in the federal penitentiary, Patrick Kuhse wants to warn college students that lapses in ethical behavior can be dangerous. His quest for money and a feeling of invincibility—common for young people, he says—were part of the reason he bribed a public official while working at a financial planning company. In order to avoid prosecution, he fled to Costa Rica, but soon realized he didn't want to live as an outlaw and turned himself in to the U.S. embassy.

Now Kuhse gives talks at universities whenever he can. Maybe he can help prevent others from making the same mistakes, and some people wish he'd have drummed some sense into Bernard Madoff and others. Kuhse says you do a little here, cut a little there, and pretty soon you see the world differently. Whether it is music sharing or plagiarizing, students make ethical decisions that shape their future mindsets. Unethical behavior looks more and more acceptable.

Sometimes you get a job, sign an ethics statement, and then your boss takes you into another room and says, "Now this is the way we really do this here." That's why Kuhse thinks college students need to learn the old adage: Money isn't everything.

Kuhse advises to surround yourself with mentors, people of integrity whom you trust. Your parents, your siblings, your spouse. Then listen to them. "I was relatively okay," he says, "until I stopped listening to my mom and my wife." When he speaks to students, he looks intently and asks, "Anyone want to follow in my footsteps?" Before they can answer, he continues, "If you mess up, admit it and move forward."

SOURCES: "Successful Broker Turned International Fugitive to Lecture on Business Ethics," Targeted News Service, Apr. 7, 2009; and Ray Scherer, "Ex-Con Offers Firsthand Greed Lesson," *Knight-Ridder/Tribune Business News*, Nov. 30, 2006, p. 1.

---

they would handle thorny ethical issues. In addition, small group meetings give people a chance to ask questions and discuss ethical dilemmas or questionable actions. Every quarter, each of GE's business units reports to headquarters the percentage of division employees who completed training sessions and the percentage that have read and signed "Spirit and Letter," the company's ethics guide.[56] At McMurray Publishing Company in Phoenix, all employees attend a *weekly* meeting on workplace ethics, where they discuss how to handle ethical dilemmas and how to resolve conflicting values.[57]

WHISTLE-BLOWING

Employee disclosure of illegal, immoral, or illegitimate practices on the employer's part is called **whistle-blowing**.[58] No organization can rely exclusively on codes of conduct and ethical structures to prevent all unethical behavior. Holding organizations accountable depends to some degree on individuals who are willing to blow the whistle if they detect illegal, dangerous, or unethical activities. Whistle-blowers often report wrongdoing to outsiders such as regulatory agencies, senators, and newspaper reporters. Some firms have instituted innovative programs and confidential hotlines to encourage and support internal whistle-blowing. For this practice to be an effective ethical safeguard, however, companies must view whistle-blowing as a benefit to the company and make dedicated efforts to protect whistle-blowers.[59] PricewaterhouseCoopers conducted a global economic

whistle-blowing
The disclosure by an employee of illegal, immoral, or illegitimate practices by an organization.

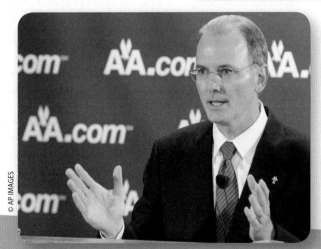

© AP IMAGES

When American Airlines and Southwest Airlines were allowed to continue flying planes that Federal Aviation Administration (FAA) inspectors thought needed repairs, some inspectors were allegedly threatened or punished to keep them quiet. The resulting whistle-blower complaints of the FAA inspectors faulted the cozy relationship between the FAA and the airline companies. Ultimately, the FAA grounded American and Southwest fleets of MD-80 airliners for mandated maintenance and repairs. American Airlines CEO Gerald Arpey said he believed that "the safety of our MD-80 fleet was never at issue."

········· **> CONCEPT CONNECTION <** ·········

Change the name from whistle-blower to conscience seeker and see how the behavior changes its meaning.

Complete the New Manager's Self Test on page 125 to give you insight into your own levels of courage.

Strive to be an ethical leader by adhering to high standards in your personal and professional behavior, codes of ethics, and ethics offices. Treasure whistle-blowers who have the courage to point out wrongdoing.

crime survey and reported that the two most effective investments in ethics programs are internal auditing and support of whistle-blowers.[60]

Without effective protection, whistle-blowers suffer. Whistle-blowing has become widespread, but it is still risky for employees, who can lose their jobs, be ostracized by co-workers, or be transferred to lower-level positions. Consider what happened when Linda Kimble reported that the car rental agency where she worked was pushing the sale of insurance to customers who already had coverage. Within a few weeks after making the complaint to top managers, Kimble was fired. The 2002 Sarbanes-Oxley Act provides some safety for whistle-blowers like Kimble. People fired for reporting wrongdoing can file a complaint under the law and are eligible for back pay, attorney's fees, and a chance to get their old job back, as Kimble did. The impact of the legislation is still unclear, but many whistle-blowers fear that they will suffer even more hostility if they return to the job after winning a case under Sarbanes-Oxley.[61]

Many managers still look on whistle-blowers as disgruntled employees who aren't good team players. Yet to maintain high ethical standards, organizations need people who are willing to point out wrongdoing. Managers can be trained to view whistle-blowing as a benefit rather than a threat, and systems can be set up to effectively protect employees who report illegal or unethical activities.

What does courage have to do with a chapter on ethics? Unfortunately, many managers slide into unethical or illegal behavior simply because they don't have the courage to stand up and do the right thing. Remember WorldCom? The small long-distance company became a dazzling star during the late 1990s telecommunications boom. Just as quickly, it all came crashing down as one executive after another was hauled away on conspiracy and securities fraud charges. For controller David Myers, it was one small step that put him on a slippery slope. When CEO Bernard Ebbers and chief financial officer (CFO) Scott Sullivan asked Myers to reclassify some expenses that would boost the company's earnings for the quarter, Myers admits that he "didn't think it was the right thing to do," but he didn't want to oppose his superiors. After that first mistake, Myers had to keep making—and asking his subordinates to make—increasingly irregular adjustments to try to get things back on track.[62]

THE BUSINESS CASE FOR ETHICS AND SOCIAL RESPONSIBILITY

Most managers now realize that paying attention to ethics and social responsibility is as important a business issue as paying attention to costs, profits, and growth. In the United States, varied stakeholders are increasingly pushing new reporting initiatives connected to the sustainability movement that emphasize the *triple bottom line* of economic, social, and environmental performance.

Naturally, the relationship of a corporation's ethics and social responsibility to its financial performance concerns both managers and management scholars and has generated a lively debate.[63] One concern of managers is whether good citizenship will hurt performance—after all, ethics programs and social responsibility cost money. A number of studies have been undertaken to determine whether heightened ethical and social responsiveness increases or decreases financial performance; their results have been varied but generally show a positive relationship between social responsibility and financial performance.[64] For example, a study of the financial performance of large U.S. corporations considered "best corporate citizens" found that they enjoy both superior reputations and superior financial performance.[65] Similarly, GovernanceMetrics International, an independent corporate governance ratings agency in New York, reports that the stocks of companies run on more selfless principles perform better than those run in a self-serving manner.[66] Although results from these studies are not proof, they do indicate that using resources for ethics and social responsibility does not hurt companies.[67] Moreover, one survey found that 70 percent of global CEOs believe corporate social responsibility is vital to their companies' profitability.[68]

Will You Be a Courageous Manager?

It probably won't happen right away, but soon enough in your duties as a new manager you will be confronted with a situation that will test the strength of your moral beliefs or your sense of justice. Are you ready? To find out, think about times when you were part of a student or work group. To what extent does each of the following statements characterize your behavior? Please answer each of the following items as Mostly True or Mostly False for you.

	MOSTLY TRUE	MOSTLY FALSE
1. I risked substantial personal loss to achieve the vision.	_____	_____
2. I took personal risks to defend my beliefs.	_____	_____
3. I would say no to inappropriate things even if I had a lot to lose.	_____	_____
4. My significant actions were linked to higher values.	_____	_____
5. I easily acted against the opinions and approval of others.	_____	_____
6. I quickly told people the truth as I saw it, even when it was negative.	_____	_____
7. I spoke out against group or organizational injustice.	_____	_____
8. I acted according to my conscience even if I would lose stature.	_____	_____

SCORING AND INTERPRETATION: Each of these questions pertains to some aspect of displaying courage in a group situation, which often reflects a person's level of moral development. Count the number of checks for Mostly True. If you scored five or more, congratulations! That behavior would enable you to become a courageous manager about moral issues. A score below four indicates that you may avoid difficult issues or have not been in situations that challenged your moral courage.

Study the specific questions for which you scored Mostly True and Mostly False to learn more about your specific strengths and weaknesses. Think about what influences your moral behavior and decisions, such as need for success or approval. Study the behavior of others you consider to be moral individuals. How might you increase your courage as a new manager?

Companies are also making an effort to measure the nonfinancial factors that create value. Researchers find, for example, that people prefer to work for companies that demonstrate a high level of ethics and social responsibility; thus, these organizations can attract and retain high-quality employees.[69] Customers pay attention, too. A study by Walker Research indicates that with price and quality being equal, two-thirds of customers say they would switch brands to do business with a company that is ethical and socially responsible.[70] Enlightened companies realize that integrity and trust are essential elements in sustaining successful and profitable business relationships with an increasingly connected web of employees, customers, suppliers, and partners. Although doing the right thing might not always be profitable in the short run, many managers believe it can provide a competitive advantage by developing a level of trust that money can't buy.

Summary

- Ethics is the code of moral principles that governs behavior with respect to what is right and wrong. An ethical issue is present in any situation when the actions of an individual or organization may harm or benefit others. Ethical decisions and behavior are typically guided by a value system. Four value-based systems that serve as criteria for ethical decision making are the utilitarian, individualism, moral-rights, and justice approaches.

- For an individual manager, the ability to make ethical choices depends partly on whether the person is at a preconventional, conventional, or postconventional level of moral development.

- Corporate social responsibility concerns a company's values toward society. The model for evaluating social performance uses four criteria: economic, legal, ethical, and discretionary.

- The question of how an organization can be a good corporate citizen is complicated because organizations respond to many different stakeholders, including customers, employees, stockholders, and suppliers. Some organizations are extending their field of stakeholders through bottom-of-the-pyramid business activities.

- One social issue of growing concern is responsibility to the natural environment. The philosophy of sustainability emphasizes economic development that meets the needs of today while preserving resources for the future.

- Managers can help organizations be ethical and socially responsible by practicing ethical leadership and using mechanisms such as codes of ethics, ethics committees, chief ethics officers, training programs, and procedures to protect whistle-blowers. After years of scandal, many managers are recognizing that managing ethics and social responsibility is just as important as paying attention to costs, profits, and growth. Companies that are ethical and socially responsible perform as well as—and often better than—those that are not socially responsible.

Discussion Questions

1. Dr. Martin Luther King, Jr., said, "As long as there is poverty in the world, I can never be rich. . . . As long as diseases are rampant, I can never be healthy. . . . I can never be what I ought to be until you are what you ought to be." Discuss this quote with respect to the material in this chapter. Would this idea be true for corporations, too?

2. Environmentalists are trying to pass laws for oil spills that would remove all liability limits for the oil companies. This change would punish corporations financially. Is this approach the best way to influence companies to be socially responsible?

3. Imagine yourself in a situation of being encouraged by colleagues to inflate your expense account. What factors do you think would influence your choice? Explain.

4. Is it socially responsible for organizations to undertake political activity or join with others in a trade association to influence the government? Discuss.

5. Was it ethical during the 1990s for automobile manufacturers to attempt to accommodate an ever-increasing consumer appetite for SUVs with their low fuel efficiency? Was it good business?

6. A noted business executive said, "A company's first obligation is to be profitable. Unprofitable enterprises can't afford to be socially responsible." Do you agree? How does this idea relate to the bottom-of-the-pyramid concept?

7. Do you believe it is ethical for companies to compile portfolios of personal information about their Web-site visitors without informing them? What about organizations monitoring their employees' e-mail? Discuss.

8. Which do you think would be more effective for shaping long-term ethical behavior in an organization: a written code of ethics combined with ethics training or strong ethical leadership? Which would have more impact on you? Why?

9. Lincoln Electric considers customers and employees to be more important stakeholders than shareholders. Is it appropriate for management to define some stakeholders as more important than others? Should all stakeholders be considered equal?

10. Do you think bottom-of-the-pyramid business practices can really have a positive effect on poverty and social problems in the developing world? Discuss.

Ethical Work Climates

Think of an organization for which you were employed. Answer the following questions twice. The first time, circle the number that best describes the way things actually were. The second time, answer the questions based on your beliefs about the ideal level to meet the needs of both individuals and the organization.

Disagree 1 2 3 4 5 Agree

1. What was best for everyone in the company was the major consideration there.
   1 2 3 4 5

2. Our major concern was always what was best for the other person.
   1 2 3 4 5

3. People were expected to comply with the law and professional standards over and above other considerations.
   1 2 3 4 5

4. In the company, the first consideration was whether a decision violated any law.
   1 2 3 4 5

5. It was very important to follow the company's rules and procedures there.
   1 2 3 4 5

6. People in the company strictly obeyed the company policies.
   1 2 3 4 5

7. In the company, people were mostly out for themselves.
   1 2 3 4 5

8. People were expected to do anything to further the company's interests, regardless of the consequences.
   1 2 3 4 5

9. In the company, people were guided by their own personal ethics.
   1 2 3 4 5

10. Each person in the company decided for himself or herself what was right and wrong.
    1 2 3 4 5

Scoring and Interpretation

Subtract each of your scores for questions 7 and 8 from the number 6. Then total your score for all 10 questions: Actual = _____ . Ideal = _____. These questions measure the dimensions of an organization's ethical climate. Questions 1 and 2 measure caring for people, questions 3 and 4 measure lawfulness, questions 5 and 6 measure adherence to rules, questions 7 and 8 measure emphasis on financial and company performance, and questions 9 and 10 measure individual independence. A total score above 40 indicates a highly positive ethical climate. A score from 30 to 40 indicates above-average ethical climate. A score from 20 to 30 indicates a below-average ethical climate, and a score below 20 indicates a poor ethical climate. How far from your ideal score was the actual score for your organization? What does that difference mean to you?

Go back over the questions and think about changes that you could have made to improve the ethical climate in the organization. Discuss with other students what you could do as a manager to improve ethics in future companies for which you work.

SOURCE: Based on Bart Victor and John B. Cullen, "The Organizational Bases of Ethical Work Climates," *Administrative Science Quarterly* 33 (1988): 101–125.

Ethical Dilemmas

In groups of four to six students, discuss the following situations and recommend the most ethical responses, using theories from the text to support your decisions.

1. An employee, whose mother is very sick, starts slacking in her work, causing other employees to stay later to get all the tasks done. If you were her boss, what would you do?

2. You see a student cheating during an exam, a test for which you have studied several weeks. That student gets a higher grade than you. What do you do? Would you feel differently about it if he got a lower grade?

3. Your mother is an executive at a record company. Sales have declined in the last two years, mostly because of music piracy and illegal downloads. You see lots of students downloading songs illegally. You know this affects your mother's income, probably her job, and ultimately your inheritance. What do you do?

4. Your group has a difficult assignment, part of which is a paper. One student announces that a friend of his did

a similar paper at another university and is willing to let your group copy that paper. What do you do?

5. A friend of yours has found a way to sneak in to the local movie theater without paying and invites you along. What do you do?

6. Your boss, who has been very supportive in your career, has asked you to "fudge the figures just a little" in your company's current earnings report so the stockholders will be satisfied. He says this is only because of the current dire economic conditions and he is worried about the company going into bankruptcy. What do you do?

Questions to Ask

1. Does an unethical behavior seem more acceptable if there is a mitigating circumstance such as a sick relative or the threat of a company's demise? Support your answer with theories from the text. What would philosophers say about making ethical behavior dependent on environmental threats?

2. Why is it so easy to justify your own unethical behaviors and see others at fault? How can you start to see your own moral lapses?

3. Why should we care about unethical behavior?

Action Learning

1. Find six newspaper articles from the past six months relating to someone violating business ethics, corruption in business, or someone in an organization violating a law.

2. Summarize each article.

3. Are there similar themes?

4. Do the accused seem repentant or defensive?

5. From what you have read, what conditions led to the ethics or legal breach?

6. What would you do as a manager to prevent such behavior in your organization?

7. Your instructor may conduct a discussion on these issues.

Ethical Dilemma

Should We Go Beyond the Law?

Nathan Rosillo stared out his office window at the lazy curves and lush, green, flower-lined banks of the Dutch Valley River. He'd grown up near here, and he envisioned the day his children would enjoy the river as he had as a child. But now his own company might make that a risky proposition.

Nathan is a key product developer at ChemTech Corporation, an industry leader. Despite its competitive position, ChemTech experienced several quarters of dismal financial performance. Nathan and his team developed a new lubricant product that the company sees as the turning point in its declining fortunes. Top executives are thrilled that they can produce the new product at a significant cost savings because of recent changes in environmental regulations. Regulatory agencies loosened requirements on reducing and recycling wastes, which means ChemTech can now release waste directly into the Dutch Valley River.

Nathan is as eager as anyone to see ChemTech survive this economic downturn, but he doesn't think this route is the way to do it. He expressed his opposition regarding the waste dumping to both the plant manager and his direct supervisor, Martin Feldman. Martin has always supported Nathan, but this time was different. The plant manager, too, turned a deaf ear. "We're meeting government standards," he'd said. "It's up to them to protect the water. It's up to us to make a profit and stay in business."

Frustrated and confused, Nathan turned away from the window, his prime office view mocking his inability to protect the river he loved. He knew the manufacturing vice president was visiting the plant next week. Maybe if he talked with her, she would agree that the decision to dump waste materials in the river was ethically and socially irresponsible. But if she didn't, he would be skating on thin ice. His supervisor had already accused him of not being a team player. Maybe he should just be a passive bystander— after all, the company isn't breaking any laws.

What Would You Do?

1. Talk to the manufacturing vice president and emphasize the responsibility ChemTech has as an industry leader to set an example. Present her with a recommendation that ChemTech participate in voluntary pollution reduction as a marketing tool, positioning itself as the environmentally friendly choice.

2. Mind your own business and just do your job. The company isn't breaking any laws, and if ChemTech's economic situation doesn't improve, a lot of people will be thrown out of work.

3. Call the local environmental advocacy group and get it to stage a protest of the company.

SOURCE: Adapted from Janet Q. Evans, "What Do You Do: What If Polluting Is Legal?" *Business Ethics* (Fall 2002): 20.

3 PART THREE
Planning

Figuring out the rules of a dramatically new game in the digital age is a daunting challenge for the strategic managers of TV networks.

Until relatively recently, major networks broadcast a limited selection of programs, essentially dictating what viewers watched and when. Because commercials allowed advertisers to reach millions of people, they supported the programming. Digital technology has changed all that. Today's viewers watch shows on TVs, computers, or iPods. They can buy current episodes or old favorites from such online stores as Apple's iTunes. They can also use sophisticated new digital video recorders to replay shows originally broadcast from only moments to months ago. Digital technology shifts power from broadcasters to consumers. Those consumers want complete control, unlimited choice, and personalized content. And the revolution is by no means over. Many people predict that television and the Internet will soon converge.

Networks face fundamental questions as they formulate strategies in this fast-changing environment. What should programs look like? How can networks generate revenue? Who are their competitors? Should networks compete or form partnerships? What business are they in? One thing is certain: There will be no shortage of opportunities for network managers to hone their decision-making skills.

5 Chapter Five

Managerial Planning and Goal Setting

LEARNING OBJECTIVES

After studying this chapter, you should be able to:

1 Define goals and plans and explain the relationship between them.

2 Explain the concept of organizational mission and how it influences goal setting and planning.

3 Describe the types of goals an organization should have and how managers use strategy maps to align goals.

4 Define the characteristics of effective goals.

5 Describe the four essential steps in the management by objectives (MBO) process.

6 Describe and explain the importance of contingency planning, scenario building, and crisis planning in today's environment.

7 Summarize the guidelines for high-performance planning in a fast-changing environment.

8 Define the components of strategic management.

9 Describe the strategic planning process and SWOT analysis.

10 Describe business-level strategies, including Porter's competitive forces and strategies and partnership strategies.

11 Explain the major considerations in formulating functional strategies.

New Manager's Questions

Please circle your opinion below each of the following statements.

1 It is better to have a very flexible and loose plan so you can easily adapt as you go along.

MOSTLY YES < < <				> > > MOSTLY NO
1	2	3	4	5

2 It's a good idea to make the product or service available to as many customers as possible.

MOSTLY YES < < <				> > > MOSTLY NO
1	2	3	4	5

3 Top managers should get together and develop a plan and then announce it to employees.

MOSTLY YES < < <				> > > MOSTLY NO
1	2	3	4	5

Practice planning every day. Make a list of your goals for the day and for the week; eventually planning will become second nature. Take the New Manager's Self-Test on page 136 to assess your level of goal-setting behavior.

goal
A desired future state that an organization attempts to realize.

plan
A blueprint specifying the resource allocations, schedules, and other actions necessary for attaining goals.

planning
The act of determining the organization's goals and the means for achieving them.

One of the primary responsibilities of managers is to decide where the organization should go in the future and how to get it there. In some organizations, typically small ones, planning is informal. In others, managers follow a well-defined planning framework. The company establishes a basic mission and periodically develops formal goals and plans for carrying it out. Large organizations such as Royal Dutch/Shell, IBM, and United Way undertake a comprehensive planning exercise each year in which they review their missions, goals, and plans to meet environmental changes or the expectations of important stakeholders such as the community, owners, or customers.

Of the four management functions—planning, organizing, leading, and controlling—described in Chapter 1, planning is considered the most fundamental. Everything else stems from planning. Yet planning also is the most controversial management function. How do managers plan for the future in a constantly changing environment? The economic, political, and social turmoil of recent years has sparked a renewed interest in organizational planning, particularly planning for unexpected problems and events. Yet planning cannot read an uncertain future. Planning cannot tame a turbulent environment. A statement by General Colin Powell, former U.S. secretary of state, offers a warning for managers: "No battle plan survives contact with the enemy."[1] Does that mean it's useless to make plans? Of course not. No plan can be perfect, but without plans and goals, organizations and employees flounder. However, good managers understand that plans should grow and change to meet new conditions.

In this chapter, we explore the process of planning and consider how managers develop effective plans. Special attention is given to goal setting, for that is where planning starts. Then we discuss the various types of plans that managers use to help the organization achieve those goals. We also take a look at planning approaches that help managers deal with uncertainty such as contingency planning, scenario building, and crisis planning. Finally, we examine new approaches to planning that emphasize the involvement of employees and other stakeholders in strategic thinking and execution. This chapter will look at strategic planning in depth and examine a number of strategic options that managers can use in a competitive environment. In Chapter 6, we look at management decision making. Proper decision-making techniques are crucial to selecting the organization's goals, plans, and strategic options.

From its beginning as a seven-cow farm in New England to a $300-million organic yogurt business, Stonyfield Farm has incorporated environmental responsibility into its **organizational planning**. Today, every operational plan encompasses Stonyfield's goal of carbon-neutral operations. Chief Executive Officer (CEO) Gary Hirshberg believes that businesses can be more profitable and help save the planet at the same time.

© COURTESY OF STONYFIELD FARM

Overview of Goals and Plans

A **goal** is a desired future state that the organization attempts to realize.[2] Goals are important because organizations exist for a purpose, and goals define and state that purpose. A **plan** is a blueprint for goal achievement and specifies the necessary resource allocations, schedules, tasks, and other actions. Goals specify future ends; plans specify today's means. The concept of **planning** usually incorporates both ideas; it means determining the organization's goals and defining the means for achieving them.[3]

Exhibit 5.1 illustrates the levels of goals and plans in an organization. The planning process starts with a formal mission that defines the basic purpose of the organization, especially for external audiences. The mission is the basis for the strategic (company) level of goals and plans, which in turn shapes the tactical

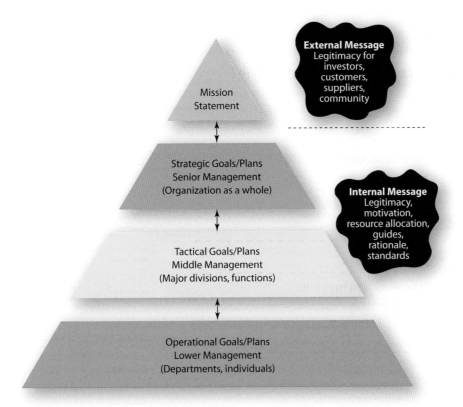

EXHIBIT 5.1
Levels of Goals and
Plans and Their
Importance

(divisional) level and the operational (departmental) level.[4] Top managers are typically responsible for establishing *strategic* goals and plans that reflect a commitment to both organizational efficiency and effectiveness. *Tactical* goals and plans are the responsibility of middle managers, such as the heads of major divisions or functional units. A division manager will formulate tactical plans that focus on the major actions the division must take to fulfill its part in the strategic plan set by top management. *Operational* plans identify the specific procedures or processes needed at lower levels of the organization such as individual departments and employees. Frontline managers and supervisors develop operational plans that focus on specific tasks and processes and that help meet tactical and strategic goals. Planning at each level supports the other levels.

PURPOSES OF GOALS AND PLANS

Uncertainty about the future and the complexity of today's environment overwhelm many managers and cause them to focus on operational issues and short-term results rather than long-term goals and plans. However, planning generally has a positive effect on a company's performance.[5] In addition to improving financial and operational performance, explicit goals and plans at each level illustrated in Exhibit 5.1 benefit organizations because they send important messages to both external and internal audiences:[6]

- *Legitimacy.* An organization's mission describes what the organization stands for and its reason for existence. It symbolizes legitimacy to external audiences such as investors, customers, suppliers, and the local community. The mission helps them look on the company in a favorable light. A strong mission also has an impact on employees, enabling them to become committed to the organization because they identify with its overall purpose and reason for existence.

- *Source of motivation and commitment.* Goals and plans enhance employees' motivation and commitment by reducing uncertainty and clarifying what they should accomplish. Lack of

NEW MANAGER'S SELF-TEST

Does Goal Setting Fit Your Management Style?

Are you a good planner? Do you set goals and identify ways to accomplish them? This questionnaire will help you understand how your work habits fit with making plans and setting goals. Answer the following questions as they apply to your work or study habits. Please indicate whether each item is Mostly True or Mostly False for you.

	MOSTLY TRUE	MOSTLY FALSE
1. I have clear, specific goals in several areas of my life.	_____	_____
2. I have a definite outcome in life I want to achieve.	_____	_____
3. I prefer general to specific goals.	_____	_____
4. I work better without specific deadlines.	_____	_____
5. I set aside time each day or week to plan my work.	_____	_____
6. I am clear about the measures that indicate when I have achieved a goal.	_____	_____
7. I work better when I set more challenging goals for myself.	_____	_____
8. I help other people clarify and define their goals.	_____	_____

SCORING AND INTERPRETATION: Give yourself 1 point for each item you marked as Mostly True except items 3 and 4. For items 3 and 4, give yourself 1 point for each one you marked Mostly False. A score of 5 or higher suggests a positive level of goal-setting behavior and good preparation for a new manager role in an organization. If you scored 4 or less, you might want to evaluate and begin to change your goal-setting behavior. An important part of a new manager's job is setting goals, measuring results, and reviewing progress for the department and subordinates.

These questions indicate the extent to which you have already adopted the disciplined use of goals in your life and work. But if you scored low, don't despair. Goal setting can be learned. Most organizations have goal-setting and review systems that new managers use. Not everyone thrives under a disciplined goal-setting system, but as a new manager, setting goals and assessing results are tools that will enhance your impact. Research indicates that setting clear, specific, and challenging goals in key areas will produce better performance.

Your goals will motivate you, so keep it up!

a clear goal can hamper motivation because people don't understand what they're working toward. Whereas a goal provides the "why" of an organization or subunit's existence, a plan tells the "how." A plan lets employees know what actions to undertake to achieve the goal.

- *Resource allocation.* Goals help managers decide where they need to allocate such resources as employees, money, and equipment. For example, DuPont has a goal of generating 25 percent of its revenues from renewable resources by 2010. This goal lets managers know they need to use resources to develop renewable and biodegradable materials, acquire businesses that produce products with renewable resources, and buy equipment that reduces waste, emissions, and energy usage.[7]

- *Guides to action.* Goals and plans provide a sense of direction. They focus attention on specific targets and direct employee efforts toward important outcomes. To see how goals can guide action, consider Guitar Center, one of the fastest-growing retailers in the United States. Managers give specific goals to sales teams at every Guitar Center store each morning, and employees do whatever they must, short of losing the company money, to meet the targets.

1 It is better to have a very flexible and loose plan so you can easily adapt as you go along.

ANSWER: Though flexibility is important, it is better to have clarity in your plans because it reduces anxiety in employees, who may be demotivated by what seems to them to be an ambiguous plan. One option might be to allow employees to develop the details of their own plans. This helps gain ownership of the process and still allows for clarity.

The fast-growing retailer's unwritten mantra of "Take the deal" means that salespeople are trained to take any profitable deal, even at razor-thin margins, to meet daily sales targets.[8]

- *Rationale for decisions.* Through goal setting and planning, managers clarify what the organization is trying to accomplish. They can make decisions to ensure that internal policies, roles, performance, structure, products, and expenditures will be made in accordance with desired outcomes. Decisions throughout the organization will be in alignment with the plan.

- *Standard of performance.* Because goals define desired outcomes for the organization, they also serve as performance criteria. They provide a standard of assessment. If an organization wishes to grow by 15 percent, and actual growth is 17 percent, then managers will have exceeded their prescribed standard.

THE ORGANIZATIONAL PLANNING PROCESS

The overall planning process, illustrated in Exhibit 5.2, prevents managers from thinking merely in terms of day-to-day activities. The process begins when managers develop

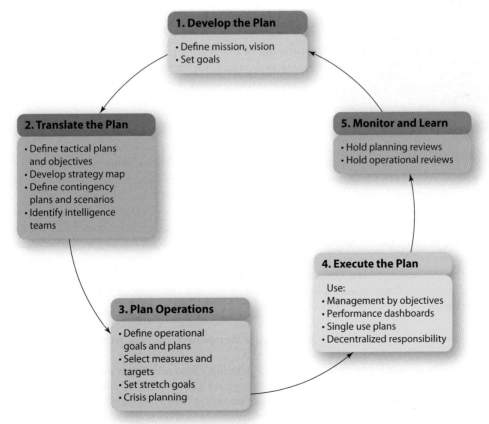

EXHIBIT 5.2
The Organizational
Planning Process

SOURCE: Based on Robert S. Kaplan and David P. Norton, "Mastering the Management System," *Harvard Business Review* (Jan, 2008): 63–77.

A candle-scented office in a cozy yellow house that feels like a retreat from the stresses of life: Does that sound like a trip to the dentist? It's part of what sets the Washington, D.C., practice of Dr. Lynn Locklear apart. Her mission, she says, is "to provide a level of services and dental care that significantly enhances the quality of your life." Dr. Locklear takes a holistic approach, viewing dental health as linked to a person's overall physical and emotional well-being. That philosophy helped Locklear's business boom and earned her recognition as the 2006 *Black Enterprise* "Business Innovator of the Year."

············> CONCEPT CONNECTION <············

Decide on your personal mission; what is your purpose in life?

mission
The organization's reason for existence.

mission statement
A broadly stated definition of the organization's basic business scope and operations that distinguish it from similar types of organizations.

the overall plan for the organization by clearly defining mission and strategic (company-level) goals. Second, they translate the plan into action, which includes defining tactical plans and objectives, developing a strategic map to align goals, formulating contingency and scenario plans, and identifying intelligence teams to analyze major competitive issues. Third, managers lay out the operational factors needed to achieve goals. This involves devising operational goals and plans, selecting the measures and targets that will be used to determine if things are on track, and identifying stretch goals and crisis plans that might need to be put into action. Tools for executing the plan include management by objectives, performance dashboards, single-use plans, and decentralized responsibility. Finally, managers periodically review plans to learn from results and shift plans as needed, starting a new planning cycle.

Goals in Organizations

Setting goals starts with top managers. The overall planning process begins with a mission statement and goals for the organization as a whole.

ORGANIZATIONAL MISSION

At the top of the goal hierarchy is the **mission**—the organization's reason for existence. The mission describes the organization's values, aspirations, and reason for being. A well-defined mission is the basis for development of all subsequent goals and plans. Without a clear mission, goals and plans may be developed haphazardly and not take the organization in the direction it needs to go.

The formal **mission statement** is a broadly stated definition of purpose that distinguishes the organization from others of a similar type. A well-designed mission statement can enhance employee motivation and organizational performance.[9] The content of a mission statement often focuses on the market and customers and identifies desired fields of endeavor. Some mission statements describe company characteristics such as corporate values, product quality, location of facilities, and attitude toward employees. The mission statement of Volvo Group is shown in Exhibit 5.3. Such short, straightforward mission statements describe basic business activities and purposes as well as the values that guide the company. Another example of this type of mission statement is that of State Farm Insurance:

State Farm's mission is to help people manage the risks of everyday life, recover from the unexpected, and realize their dreams.

We are people who make it our business to be like a good neighbor; who built a premier company by selling and keeping promises through our marketing partnership; who bring diverse talents and experiences to our work of serving the State Farm customer.

Our success is built on a foundation of shared values—quality service and relationships, mutual trust, integrity, and financial strength.[10]

VOLVO GROUP MISSION STATEMENT

By creating value for our customers, we create value for our shareholders.

We use our expertise to create transport-related products and services of superior quality, safety and environmental care for demanding customers in selected segments.

We work with energy, passion and respect for the individual.

SOURCE: AB Volvo. Reprinted with permission.

EXHIBIT 5.3
Mission Statement for Volvo Group

- - - - - - - - - - -

Because of mission statements such as those of Volvo Group and State Farm, employees as well as customers, suppliers, and stockholders know the company's stated purpose and values.

GOALS AND PLANS

Strategic goals, sometimes called *official goals*, are broad statements describing where the organization wants to be in the future. These goals pertain to the organization as a whole rather than to specific divisions or departments.

Strategic plans define the action steps by which the company intends to attain strategic goals. The strategic plan is the blueprint that defines the organizational activities and resource allocations—in the form of cash, personnel, space, and facilities—required for meeting these targets. Strategic planning tends to be long term and may define organizational action steps from two to five years in the future. The purpose of strategic plans is to turn organizational goals into realities within that time period. Consider the new strategic goals and plans at Borders, the number-two book retailer in the United States.

strategic goals
Broad statements of where the organization wants to be in the future; they pertain to the organization as a whole rather than to specific divisions or departments.

strategic plans
The action steps by which an organization intends to attain strategic goals.

From your mission statement, figure out how you will achieve it; that is your strategy.

> **BORDERS GROUP INC.**
>
> It's a tough environment for booksellers today. A sluggish book market, combined with competition from discounters, has put tremendous pressure on traditional book retailers to find the right approach to keep growing and thriving.
>
> Borders Group revolutionized bookselling in the 1990s by building huge superstores, and managers stayed with the strategic goals of building more bricks-and-mortar stores even after the Internet changed the rules of the game. A partnership with Amazon was the extent of Borders' online selling. Now managers are realizing that the bricks-and-mortar approach no longer works. Online book sales are soaring, while sales at U.S. bookstores have sagged. Recently named CEO George Jones announced a new strategic goal of making Borders a force in online bookselling.
>
> To achieve the goal, Borders ended its alliance with Amazon and is opening its own branded e-commerce site, giving Borders Rewards members the chance to earn benefits online, which they weren't able to do through Amazon. Managers are giving up on the idea of expanding the book superstore concept internationally and plan to sell off or franchise most of Borders's 73 overseas stores. The plan also calls for closing some of its U.S. stores, including nearly half of the smaller Waldenbooks outlets.[11]

The Borders CEO knows that achieving the goal "won't be a slam dunk," but he sees it as the best way to keep Borders relevant in the book retailing industry. The new strategic goals and plans, he believes, will revive the company by enabling Borders to provide greater benefits to customers and partner with a variety of companies for innovative projects.

After strategic goals are formulated, the next step is defining **tactical goals**, which are the results that major divisions and departments within the organization intend to achieve. These goals apply to middle management and describe what major subunits must do for the organization to achieve its overall goals.

Tactical plans are designed to help execute the major strategic plans and to accomplish a specific part of the company's strategy.[12] Tactical plans typically have a shorter time horizon than strategic plans—over the next year or so. The word *tactical* originally comes from the military. In a business or nonprofit organization, tactical plans define what major departments and organizational subunits will do to implement the organization's strategic plan. For example, the overall strategic plan of a large florist might involve becoming the number-one telephone and Internet-based purveyor of flowers, which requires high-volume sales during peak seasons such as Valentine's Day and Mother's Day. Human-resource managers will develop tactical plans to ensure that the company has the dedicated order takers and customer-service representatives it needs during these critical periods. Tactical plans might include cross-training employees so they can switch to different jobs as departmental needs change, allowing order takers to transfer to jobs at headquarters during off-peak times to prevent burnout, and using regular order takers to train and supervise temporary workers during peak seasons.[13] These actions help top managers implement their overall strategic plan. Normally, it is the middle manager's job to take the broad strategic plan and identify specific tactical plans.

The results expected from departments, work groups, and individuals are the **operational goals**. They are precise and measurable. "Process 150 sales applications each week," "Achieve 90 percent of deliveries on time," "Reduce overtime by 10 percent next month," and "Develop two new online courses in accounting" are examples of operational goals. Managers at the Internal Revenue Service set an operational goal of providing accurate responses to 85 percent of taxpayer questions.[14]

Operational plans are developed at the lower levels of the organization to specify action steps toward achieving operational goals and to support tactical plans. The operational plan is the department manager's tool for daily and weekly operations. Goals are stated in quantitative terms, and the department plan describes how goals will be achieved. Operational planning specifies plans for department managers, supervisors, and individual employees. Schedules are an important component of operational planning. Schedules define precise time frames for the completion of each operational goal required for the organization's tactical and strategic goals. Operational planning also must be coordinated with the budget because resources must be allocated for desired activities.

ALIGNING GOALS WITH STRATEGY MAPS

Effectively designed organizational goals are aligned; that is, they are consistent and mutually supportive so that the achievement of goals at low levels permits the attainment of high-level goals. Organizational performance is an outcome of how well these interdependent elements are aligned, so that individuals, teams, departments, and so forth are working in concert to attain specific goals that ultimately help the organization achieve high performance and fulfill its mission.[15]

Go to the Group Learning exercise on page 177; it pertains to developing action plans for accomplishing strategic goals.

tactical goals
Goals that define the outcomes that major divisions and departments must achieve for the organization to reach its overall goals.

tactical plans
Plans designed to help execute major strategic plans and to accomplish a specific part of the company's strategy.

operational goals
Specific, measurable results expected from departments, work groups, and individuals within the organization.

operational plans
Plans developed at the organization's lower levels that specify action steps toward achieving operational goals and that support tactical planning activities.

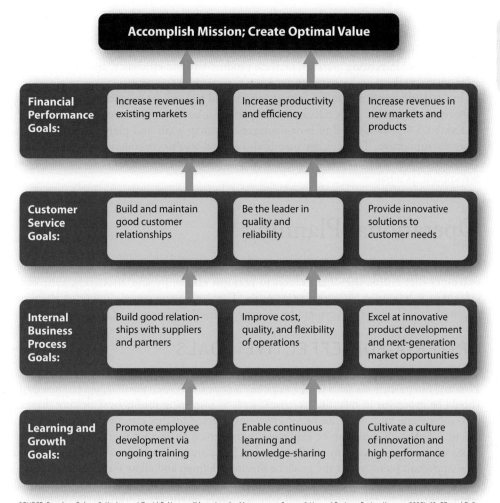

SOURCE: Based on Robert S. Kaplan and David P. Norton, "Mastering the Management System," *Harvard Business Review* (January 2008): 63–77; and R. S. Kaplan and D. P. Norton, "Having Trouble with Your Strategy? Then Map It," *Harvard Business Review* (September–October 2000): 167–176.

EXHIBIT 5.4
A Strategy Map for
Aligning Goals

An increasingly popular technique for achieving *goal alignment* is the strategy map. A **strategy map** is a visual representation of the key drivers of an organization's success and shows how specific goals and plans in each area are linked.[16] The strategy map provides a powerful way for managers to see the cause-and-effect relationships among goals and plans. The simplified strategy map in Exhibit 5.4 illustrates four key areas that contribute to a firm's long-term success—learning and growth, internal processes, customer service, and financial performance—and how the various goals and plans in each area link to the other areas. The idea is that learning and growth goals serve as a foundation to help achieve goals for excellent internal business processes. Meeting business process goals, in turn, enables the organization to meet goals for customer service and satisfaction, which helps the organization achieve its financial goals and optimize its value to all stakeholders.

In the strategy map shown in Exhibit 5.4, the organization has learning and growth goals that include developing employees, enabling continuous learning and knowledge sharing, and building a culture of innovation. Achieving these will help the organization build internal business processes that promote good relationships with suppliers and partners, improve the quality and flexibility of operations, and excel at developing innovative products and services. Accomplishing internal process goals, in turn, enables the

strategy map
A visual representation of the key drivers of an organization's success that shows the cause-and-effect relationships among goals and plans.

organization to maintain strong relationships with customers, be a leader in quality and reliability, and provide innovation solutions to emerging customer needs. At the top of the strategy map, the accomplishment of these lower-level goals helps the organization increase revenues in existing markets, increase productivity and efficiency, and grow through selling new products and services and serving new markets segments.

In a real-life organization, the strategy map would typically be more complex and would state concrete, specific goals relevant to the particular business. However, the generic map in Exhibit 5.4 gives an idea of how managers can map goals and plans so that they are mutually supportive. The strategy map is also a good way to communicate goals, because everyone in the organization can see what part they play in helping the organization accomplish its mission.

Operational Planning

Managers use operational goals to direct employees and resources toward achieving specific outcomes that enable the organization to perform efficiently and effectively. One consideration is how to establish effective goals. Then managers use a number of planning approaches, including management by objectives, single-use plans, and standing plans.

CRITERIA FOR EFFECTIVE GOALS

Make your goals measurable so that you can know when you achieve them.

Research has identified certain factors, listed in Exhibit 5.5, that characterize effective goals. First and foremost, goals need to be *specific and measurable*. When possible, operational goals should be expressed in quantitative terms, such as increasing profits by 2 percent, having zero incomplete sales order forms, or increasing average teacher effectiveness ratings from 3.5 to 3.7. Not all goals can be expressed in numerical terms, but vague goals have little motivating power for employees. By necessity, goals are qualitative as well as quantitative. The important point is that the goals be precisely defined and allow for measurable progress. Effective goals also have a *defined time period* that specifies the date on which goal attainment will be measured. School administrators might set a deadline for improving teacher-effectiveness ratings, for instance, at the end of the 2009 school term. When a goal involves a two- to three-year time horizon, setting specific dates for achieving parts of it is a good way to keep people on track toward the goal.

As a new manager, establish goals that are specific, measurable, and challenging but realistic. Reward people when they meet goals.

Goals should *cover key result areas*. Goals cannot be set for every aspect of employee behavior or organizational performance; if they were, their sheer number would render them meaningless. Instead, managers establish goals based on the idea of *choice and clarity*. A few carefully chosen, clear, and direct goals can more powerfully focus organizational attention, energy, and resources.[17] Managers should set goals that are *challenging but realistic*. When goals are unrealistic, they set employees up for failure and lead to a decrease in employee morale. However, if goals are too easy, employees may not feel motivated. Goals should also be *linked to rewards*. The ultimate impact of goals depends on the extent to which

EXHIBIT 5.5
Characteristics of Effective Goal Setting
- - - - - - - - - -

GOAL CHARACTERISTICS

- Specific and measurable
- Defined time period
- Cover key result areas
- Challenging but realistic
- Linked to rewards

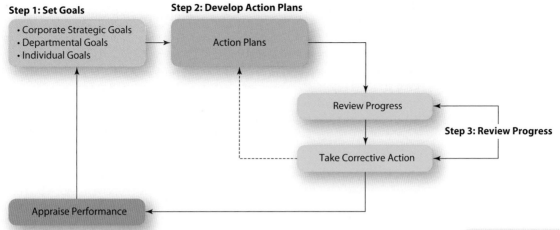

Step 1: Set Goals

- Corporate Strategic Goals
- Departmental Goals
- Individual Goals

Step 2: Develop Action Plans

Action Plans

Review Progress

Step 3: Review Progress

Take Corrective Action

Appraise Performance

Step 4: Appraise Overall Performance

EXHIBIT 5.6
Model of the MBO
Process

salary increases, promotions, and awards are based on goal achievement. Employees pay attention to what gets noticed and rewarded in the organization.[18]

MANAGEMENT BY OBJECTIVES

Described by famed management scholar Peter Drucker in his 1954 book, *The Practice of Management*, management by objectives has remained a popular and compelling method for defining goals and monitoring progress toward achieving them. **Management by objectives (MBO)** is a system whereby managers and employees define goals for every department, project, and person and use them to monitor subsequent performance.[19] A model of the essential steps of the MBO system is presented in Exhibit 5.6. Four major activities make MBO successful:[20]

1. *Set goals.* Setting goals involves employees at all levels and looks beyond day-to-day activities to answer the question "What are we trying to accomplish?" Managers heed the criteria of effective goals described in the previous section and make sure they assign responsibility for goal accomplishment. However, goals should be jointly derived. Mutual agreement between employee and supervisor creates the strongest commitment to achieving goals. In the case of teams, all team members may participate in setting goals.

2. *Develop action plans.* An *action plan* defines the course of action needed to achieve the stated goals. Action plans are made for both individuals and departments.

3. *Review progress.* A periodic progress review is important to ensure that action plans are working. These reviews can occur informally between managers and subordinates, where the organization may wish to conduct three-, six-, or nine-month reviews during the year. This periodic checkup allows managers and employees to see whether they are on target or whether corrective action is needed. Managers and employees should not be locked into predefined behavior and must be willing to take whatever steps are necessary to produce meaningful results. The point of MBO is to achieve goals. The action plan can be changed whenever goals are not being met.

4. *Appraise overall performance.* The final step in MBO is to carefully evaluate whether annual goals have been achieved for both individuals and departments. Success or failure to achieve goals can become part of the performance-appraisal system and the designation of salary increases and other rewards. The appraisal of departmental and overall corporate performance shapes goals for the next year. The MBO cycle repeats itself on an annual basis.

Periodically review your goals to see how you are doing and if you need to adjust them.

management by objectives (MBO)
A method of management whereby managers and employees define goals for every department, project, and person and use them to monitor subsequent performance.

EXHIBIT 5.7
MBO Benefits and Problems

Benefits of MBO	Problems with MBO
1. Manager and employee efforts are focused on activities that will lead to goal attainment.	1. Constant change prevents MBO from taking hold.
2. Performance can be improved at all company levels.	2. An environment of poor employer–employee relations reduces MBO effectiveness.
3. Employees are motivated.	3. Strategic goals may be displaced by operational goals.
4. Departmental and individual goals are aligned with company goals.	4. Mechanistic organizations and values that discourage participation can harm the MBO process.
	5. Too much paperwork saps MBO energy.

Many companies, including Intel, Tenneco, Black & Decker, and DuPont, have adopted MBO, and most managers think MBO is an effective management tool.[21] Managers believe they are better oriented toward goal achievement when MBO is used. In recent years, the U.S. Congress required that federal agencies use a type of MBO system to focus government employees on achieving specific outcomes.[22] Like any system, MBO achieves benefits when used properly but results in problems when used improperly. Benefits and problems are summarized in Exhibit 5.7.

The benefits of the MBO process can be many. Corporate goals are more likely to be achieved when they focus manager and employee efforts. Using a performance-measurement system such as MBO helps employees see how their jobs and performance contribute to the business, giving them a sense of ownership and commitment.[23] Performance is improved when employees are committed to attaining the goal, are motivated because they help decide what is expected, and are free to be resourceful. Goals at lower levels are aligned with and enable the attainment of goals at top management levels.

Problems with MBO occur when the company faces rapid change. The environment and internal activities must have some stability for performance to be measured and compared against goals. Setting new goals every few months allows no time for action plans and appraisal to take effect. Also, poor employer–employee relations reduce effectiveness because of an element of distrust that may be present between managers and workers. Sometimes goal "displacement" occurs if employees focus exclusively on their operational goals to the detriment of other teams or departments. Overemphasis on operational goals can harm the attainment of overall goals. Another problem arises in mechanistic organizations characterized by rigidly defined tasks and rules that may not be compatible with MBO's emphasis on mutual determination of goals by employee and supervisor. In addition, when participation is discouraged, employees will lack the training and values to jointly set goals with employers. Finally, if MBO becomes a process of filling out annual paperwork rather than energizing employees to achieve goals, it becomes an empty exercise. Once the paperwork is completed, employees forget about the goals, perhaps even resenting the paperwork in the first place.

SINGLE-USE AND STANDING PLANS

single-use plans
Plans that are developed to achieve a set of goals that are unlikely to be repeated in the future.

standing plans
Ongoing plans that are used to provide guidance for tasks performed repeatedly within the organization.

Single-use plans are developed to achieve a set of goals that are not likely to be repeated in the future. **Standing plans** are ongoing plans that provide guidance for tasks or situations that occur repeatedly within the organization. Exhibit 5.8 outlines the major types of single-use and standing plans. Single-use plans typically include both programs and projects. The primary standing plans are organizational policies, rules, and procedures. Standing plans generally pertain to such matters as employee illness, absences, smoking,

Single-Use Plans	Standing Plans	EXHIBIT 5.8 Major Types of Single-Use and Standing Plans

Program
• Plans for attaining a one-time organizational goal
• Major undertaking that may take several years to complete
• Large in scope; may be associated with several projects
  Examples: Building a new headquarters Converting all paper files to digital
 	
Project
• Also a set of plans for attaining a one-time goal
• Smaller in scope and complexity than a program; shorter in horizon
• Often one part of a larger program
  Examples: Renovating the office Setting up a company intranet
	Policy
	• Broad in scope—general guide to action
	• Based on organization's overall goals and strategic plan
	• Defines boundaries within which to make decisions
	  Examples: Sexual-harassment policies Internet and e-mail usage policies
	
	Rule
	• Narrow in scope
	• Describes how a specific action is to be performed
	• May apply to specific setting
	  Examples: No eating rule in areas of company where employees are visible to the public
	
	Procedure
	• Sometimes called a *standard operating procedure*
	• Defines a precise series of steps to attain certain goals
	  Examples: Procedures for issuing refunds Procedures for handling employee grievances	

discipline, hiring, and dismissal. Many companies are discovering a need to develop standing plans regarding the use of e-mail.

Top executives around the globe are discovering that casual e-mail messages can come back to haunt them—in court. The American Management Association surveyed 1,100 companies and found that 14 percent of them had been ordered to disclose e-mail messages. Eight brokerage firms were fined $8 million for not keeping and producing e-mail in accordance with Securities and Exchange Commission guidelines. Some companies have had to pay millions of dollars to settle sexual-harassment lawsuits arising from inappropriate e-mail.

As with any powerful tool, e-mail has the potential to be hazardous, backfiring not only on the employee but also on the organization. One study found that "potentially dangerous or nonproductive" messages account for fully 31 percent of all company e-mail. Experts say a formal written policy is the best way for companies to protect themselves, and they offer some tips for managers on developing effective policies governing the use of e-mail.

- *Make clear that all e-mail and its contents are the property of the company.* Many experts recommend warning employees that the company reserves the right to read any messages transmitted over its system. "Employees need to understand that a company can access employees' e-mail at any time without advance notice or consent," says lawyer Pam Reeves. This rule helps to discourage frivolous e-mails or those that might be considered crude and offensive.
- *Tie the policy to the company's sexual-harassment policy or other policies governing employee behavior on the job.* Starwood Hotel and Resorts ousted its CEO after an investigation uncovered e-mails that seemed to substantiate claims that he made sexual advances to female employees. In almost all sexual-harassment cases, judges have ruled that the use of e-mail is considered part of the workplace environment.

- *Establish clear guidelines on matters such as the use of e-mail for jokes and other nonwork-related communications, the sending of confidential messages, and how to handle junk e-mail.* At Prudential Insurance, for example, employees are prohibited from using company e-mail to share jokes, photographs, or any kind of nonbusiness information.
- *Establish guidelines for deleting or retaining messages.* Retention periods of 30 to 90 days for routine messages are typical. Most organizations also set up a centralized archive for retaining essential e-mail messages.
- *Consider having policies pop up on users' screens when they log on.* It is especially important to remind employees that e-mail belongs to the employer and may be monitored.

The field of computer forensics is booming, and even deleted e-mails can usually be tracked down. An effective policy is the best step companies can take to manage the potential risks of e-mail abuse.[24]

Planning for a Turbulent Environment

As increasing turbulence and uncertainty shake the business world, managers have turned to innovative planning approaches that help brace the organization for unexpected—even unimaginable—events. Three critical planning methods are contingency planning, building scenarios, and crisis planning.

CONTINGENCY PLANNING

If things don't work out as expected, try something different.

When organizations are operating in a highly uncertain environment or dealing with long time horizons, planning can sometimes seem like a waste of time. Indeed, inflexible plans may hinder rather than help an organization's performance in the face of rapid technological, social, economic, or other environmental change. In these cases, managers can develop multiple future alternatives to help them form more adaptive plans.

Contingency plans define company responses to be taken in the case of emergencies, setbacks, or unexpected conditions. To develop contingency plans, managers identify important factors in the environment such as possible economic downturns, declining markets, increases in cost of supplies, new technological developments, and safety accidents. Managers then forecast a range of alternative responses to the most likely high-impact contingencies, focusing on the worst case.[25] For example, if sales fall 20 percent and prices drop 8 percent, what will the company do? Managers can develop contingency plans that might include layoffs, emergency budgets, new sales efforts, or new markets. A real-life example comes from FedEx, which has to cope with some kind of unexpected disruption to its service somewhere in the world on a daily basis. In one recent year alone, managers activated contingency plans related to more than two dozen tropical storms, an air-traffic-controller strike in France, and a blackout in Los Angeles. The company also has contingency plans in place for events such as labor strikes, social upheavals in foreign countries, and incidents of terrorism.[26]

BUILDING SCENARIOS

An extension of contingency planning is a forecasting technique known as scenario building.[27] **Scenario building** involves looking at current trends and discontinuities and visualizing future possibilities. Rather than looking only at history and thinking about what has been, managers think about what *could be*. The events that cause the most damage to companies are those that no one even conceived of such as the collapse of the World Trade Center towers in New York due to terrorist attack. Managers can't predict the future, but they can rehearse a framework within which future events can be managed. With scenario building, a broad base of managers mentally rehearses different scenarios based

contingency plans
Plans that define company responses to specific situations such as emergencies, setbacks, and unexpected conditions.

scenario building
Looking at trends and discontinuities and imagining possible alternative futures to build a framework within which unexpected future events can be managed.

on anticipating varied changes that could affect the organization. Scenarios are like stories that offer alternative vivid pictures of what the future will be like and how managers will respond. Typically, two to five scenarios are developed for each set of factors, ranging from the most optimistic to the most pessimistic view.[28] Scenario building forces managers to mentally rehearse what they would do if their best-laid plans collapse.

Royal Dutch/Shell has long used scenario building to help managers navigate the instability and uncertainty of the oil industry. A classic example is the scenario Shell managers rehearsed in 1970 that focused on an imagined accident in Saudi Arabia that severed an oil pipeline, which in turn decreased supply. The market reacted by increasing oil prices, which allowed member nations of the Organization of the Petroleum Exporting Countries (OPEC) to pump less oil and make more money. This story caused managers to reexamine the standard assumptions about oil price and supply and imagine what would happen and how they would respond if OPEC increased prices. Nothing in the exercise told Shell managers to expect an embargo, but by rehearsing this scenario, they were much more prepared than the competition when OPEC announced its first oil embargo in October 1973. The company's speedy response to a massive shift in the environment enabled Shell to move in two years' from being the world's eighth largest oil company to number two.[29]

CRISIS PLANNING

Surveys of companies' use of management techniques reveal that the use of contingency and scenario planning surged after the September 11, 2001, terrorist attacks in the United States and has remained high ever since, reflecting a growing emphasis on managing uncertainty.[30] Some firms also engage in crisis planning to enable them to cope with unexpected events that are so sudden and devastating that they have the potential to destroy the organization if managers aren't prepared with a quick and appropriate response.

Crises have become integral features of organizations in today's world. Consider events such as the death of a 17-year-old girl due to a botched transplant at Duke University Hospital, deaths due to *E. coli* bacteria from Jack-in-the-Box hamburgers, the shooting rampage at Virginia Tech University, and the crash of the *Columbia* space shuttle. Although crises may vary, a carefully thought-out and coordinated plan can be used to respond to any disaster. In addition, crisis planning reduces the incidence of trouble, much like putting a good lock on a door reduces burglaries.[31] Exhibit 5.9 outlines two essential stages of crisis planning.[32]

- *Crisis Prevention.* The *crisis-prevention* stage involves activities managers undertake to try to prevent crises from occurring and to detect warning signs of potential crises. A critical part of the prevention stage is building open, trusting relationships with key stakeholders such as employees, customers, suppliers, governments, unions, and the community. By developing favorable relationships, managers can often prevent crises from happening

When planning, think through all the steps you need to take and all the possible outcomes that might happen. Then consider how you would react to the various outcomes.

As a new manager, you can learn scenario planning by visiting www.shell.com/ scenarios and also by using Google to search for "national intelligence agency scenarios" and finding links to scenario planning done by various organizations.

Crisis Planning
Prevention
• Build relationships.
• Detect signals from environment.
Preparation
• Designate crisis-management team and spokesperson.
• Create detailed crisis-management plan.
• Set up effective communications system.

EXHIBIT 5.9
Essential Stages of Crisis Planning
– – – – – – – – – –

SOURCE: Based on information in W. Timothy Coombs, *Ongoing Crisis Communication: Planning, Managing, and Responding* (Thousand Oaks, CA: Sage Publications, 1999).

Prevent crises through frequent communication, building trust, and careful planning.

and respond more effectively to those that cannot be avoided. For example, organizations that have open, trusting relationships with employees and unions may avoid crippling labor strikes. Coca-Cola suffered a major crisis in Europe because it failed to respond quickly to reports of "foul-smelling" Coke in Belgium. A former CEO observed that every problem the company has faced in recent years "can be traced to a singular cause: We neglected our relationships."[33]

- *Crisis Preparation.* The *crisis-preparation* stage includes all the detailed planning to handle a crisis when it occurs. Three steps in the preparation stage are: (1) designating a crisis-management team and spokesperson, (2) creating a detailed crisis-management plan, and (3) setting up an effective communications system. The crisis-management team, for example, is a cross-functional group of people who are designated to swing into action if a crisis occurs. The organization should also designate a spokesperson who will be the voice of the company during the crisis.[34] The crisis-management plan (CMP) is a detailed, written plan that specifies the steps to be taken, and by whom, if a crisis occurs. The CMP should include the steps for dealing with various types of crises, such as natural disasters like fires or earthquakes, normal accidents like economic crises or industrial accidents, and abnormal events such as product tampering or acts of terrorism.[35] A key point is that a crisis-management plan should be a living, changing document that is regularly reviewed, practiced, and updated as needed.

Planning for High Performance

The purpose of planning and goal setting is to help the organization achieve high performance. The process of planning is changing to be more in tune with today's environment and the shifting attitudes of employees. Traditionally, strategy and planning have been the domain of top managers. Today, however, managers involve people throughout the organization, which can spur higher performance because people understand the goals and plans and buy into them.

TRADITIONAL APPROACHES TO PLANNING

Traditionally, corporate planning has been done entirely by top executives, consulting firms, or, most commonly, central planning departments. **Central planning departments** are groups of planning specialists who report directly to the CEO or president. This approach was popular during the 1970s. Planning specialists were hired to gather data and develop detailed strategic plans for the corporation as a whole. This planning approach was top down because goals and plans were assigned to major divisions and departments from the planning department after approval by the president.

This approach worked well in many applications and is still popular with some companies. However, formal planning is increasingly being criticized as inappropriate for today's fast-paced environment. Central planning departments may be out of touch with the constantly changing realities faced by frontline managers and employees, which may leave people struggling to follow a plan that no longer fits the environment and customer needs. In addition, formal plans dictated by top managers and central planning departments can inhibit employee innovation and learning.

HIGH-PERFORMANCE APPROACHES TO PLANNING

A fresh approach to planning is to involve everyone in the organization and sometimes outside stakeholders as well in the planning process. The evolution to a new approach began with a shift to **decentralized planning**, which means that planning experts work with

central planning department
A group of planning specialists who develop plans for the organization as a whole and its major divisions and departments and typically report directly to the president or CEO.

decentralized planning
Managers of divisions or departments work with planning experts to develop their own goals and plans.

BUSINESS BLOOPER

Fox News, CNN, and Others

Apparently, Fox News is so hungry for its brand of news that it will spend a lot of energy to actually make the news. Although the movement was sparked by a rant from CNBC reporter Rick Santelli, who suggested a "tea party" to protest government bailouts of failed mortgages, Fox News quickly became the movement's leader, running 100 promos about its coverage of the so-called event. The network further sent out its big-name hosts to locations around the country and achieved the complicated task of covering events they appeared to be leading. Not to be outdone, CNN got on the bandwagon

of criticizing protestors, calling them "anti-government, anti-CNN." MSNBC wagged its fingers at the motives of those involved while spending inordinate amounts of airtime on the rallies. In olden times, cable news dispatched reporters to events and then showed footage on shows where screaming commentators sparred. Now they are evidently in a brave new world where the news desks are providing both the photos and the war.

SOURCE: David Carr, "Cable Wars Are Killing Objectivity," *New York Times*, Apr. 20, 2009, B1, B7.

managers in major divisions or departments to develop their own goals and plans. Managers throughout the company come up with their own creative solutions to problems and become more committed to following through on the plans. As the environment became even more volatile, top executives saw the benefits of pushing decentralized planning even further by having planning experts work directly with line managers and frontline employees to develop dynamic plans that meet fast-changing needs.

In a complex and competitive business environment, strategic thinking and execution become the expectation of every employee.[36] Planning comes alive when employees are involved in setting goals and determining the means to reach them. Here are some guidelines for planning in the new workplace. One wonders what type of planning, or even thinking, went into the changes happening in cable news, as described in the Business Blooper.

Set Stretch Goals for Excellence. Stretch goals are reasonable yet highly ambitious goals that are so clear, compelling, and imaginative that they fire up employees and engender excellence. Stretch goals are typically so far beyond the current levels that people have to be innovative to find ways to reach them. An extension of the stretch goal is the *big hairy audacious goal* or *BHAG*. The phrase was first proposed by James Collins and Jerry Porras in their 1996 article entitled "Building Your Company's Vision."[37] Since then, it has evolved to a term used to describe any goal that is so big, inspiring, and outside the prevailing paradigm that it hits people in the gut and shifts their thinking. At the same time, however, goals must be seen as achievable or employees will be discouraged and demotivated.[38]

Stretch goals and BHAGs have become extremely important because things move fast. A company that focuses on gradual, incremental improvements in products,

stretch goal
A reasonable yet highly ambitious and compelling goal that energizes people and inspires excellence.

© GARY VOLINSKY

Netflix is trying to meet a stretch goal of improving its Internet movie recommendation system ("People who liked this movie also rented . . . ") by 10 percent. In October 2006, the company invited the biggest math brains in the world to compete for a $1-million prize to reach that goal. In the first year, more than 2,500 teams from a dozen countries submitted entries. At the one-year anniversary, a team of AT&T researchers (Chris Volinsky, Yehuda Koren, and Bob Bell) won a $50,000 progress award for improving the system by 8.43 percent. Some people speculate that a 10-percent improvement is unobtainable. By May 2008, the team had reached a 9.15-percent improvement of the system.

Develop ambitious goals to get people enthused.

processes, or systems will get left behind. Managers can use these goals to compel employees to think in new ways that can lead to bold, innovative breakthroughs. Motorola used stretch goals to achieve *Six Sigma* quality, which has now become the standard for numerous companies. Managers first set a goal of a tenfold increase in quality over a two-year period. After this goal was met, they set a new stretch goal of a hundredfold improvement over a four-year period.[39]

Use Performance Dashboards. People need a way to see how plans are progressing and gauge their progress toward achieving goals. Companies began using *business performance dashboards* as a way for executives to keep track of key performance metrics such as sales in relation to targets, number of products on back order, or percentage of customer-service calls resolved within specified time periods. Today, dashboards are evolving into organization-wide systems that help align and track goals across the enterprise. Exhibit 5.10 shows a business performance dashboard from Celequest that can deliver real-time key performance metrics to any employee's desktop. The true power of dashboards comes from applying

EXHIBIT 5.10
Performance Dashboard for Planning

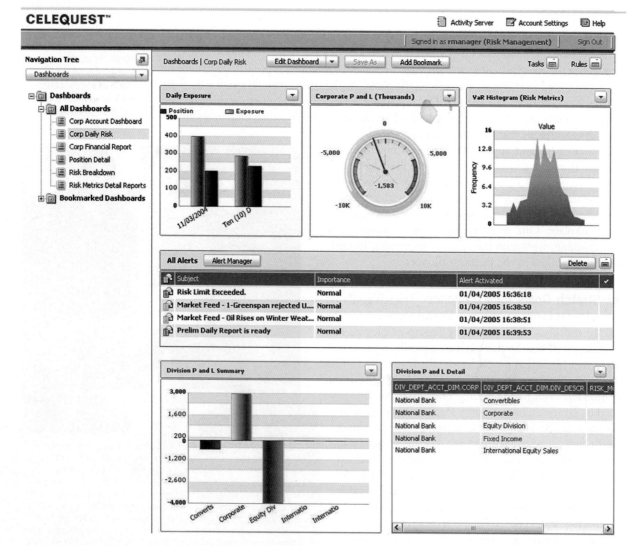

SOURCE: © Celequest/PRNewsFoto (Newscom).

them throughout the company, even on the factory floor, so that all employees can track progress toward goals, see when things are falling short, and find innovative ways to get back on course toward reaching the specified targets. At Emergency Medical Associates, a physician-owned medical group that manages emergency rooms for hospitals in New York and New Jersey, dashboards enable the staff to see when performance thresholds related to patient wait times, for example, aren't being met at various hospitals.[40] Some dashboard systems also incorporate software that lets users perform what-if scenarios to evaluate the impact of various alternatives for meeting goals.

Practice a new stretch goal every week. Find one right now.

As a new manager, involve others in planning and goal setting to enhance commitment and performance.
Make use of business performance dashboards.

Deploy Intelligence Teams. Anticipating and managing uncertainty and turbulence in the environment is a crucial part of planning, which means managers need good intelligence to make informed choices about goals and plans. A growing number of leading companies are using intelligence teams to manage this challenge. An **intelligence team** is a cross-functional group of managers and employees, usually led by a competitive intelligence professional, who work together to gain a deep understanding of a specific business issue with the aim of presenting insights, possibilities, and recommendations about goals and plans related to that issue.[41] Intelligence teams are useful when the organization confronts a major intelligence challenge. For example, consider a large financial services firm that learns that an even-larger rival is potentially moving to compete directly with one of its major profit-generating businesses. Top managers might form an intelligence team to identify when and how this might happen and how it might affect the organization. Intelligence teams can provide insights that enable managers to make more informed decisions about goals as well as devise contingency plans and scenarios related to major strategic issues. Disney has a goal of increasing viewership by boys ages 6 to 14, and it uses intelligent teams of anthropologists, as shown in the Benchmarking box.

intelligence team
A cross-functional group of managers and employees who work together to gain a deep understanding of a specific competitive issue and offer insight and recommendations for planning.

BENCH-MARKING
Disney XD

Winning over boys hasn't been easy for Disney since the days of *Davy Crockett*, especially since the company has hit it big with Hannah Montana. Kelly Pena is changing that by digging into teenage boys' minds, often by first digging through their dresser drawers. One of her big finds? A Black Sabbath T-shirt. "Wearing it makes me feel like I'm going to an R-rated movie," noted Dean, the shirt's 12-year-old owner. Pena's team of anthropologists is looking for more such nuggets to uncover insights into the world of uncommunicative boys ages 6 to 14.

Viewers to Disney's new XD cable channel, which took over from the Toon channel, can already see some of the results. Because the targeted viewers are more interested in a character's struggling to learn than in actually winning, the lead guy is Aaron Stone, mediocre basketball player. Generally speaking, media companies guard such endeavors and cover them in secrecy, but Disney is so proud of its "headquarters for boys," it is putting out the red carpet for anyone who wants to learn more. Why is this project so important? Boys in this age group spend

$50 billion worldwide. Disney hopes the XD channel will have similar success as *High School Musical*, spawning new shows and endless merchandising opportunities.

Pena knows she has to go beyond traditional media research. "You have to start with the kids themselves," she says. "Ratings show what boys are watching today, but they don't tell you what is missing in the marketplace." So far, she has learned boys think most entertainment aimed at them is "purposeless fun," while they yearn for "fun with a purpose." To find out how to incorporate these ideas into Disney XD, Pena looks on Dean's walls and bookshelves, watches him interact with his siblings, and notes every clue to his wants. One of her first big takeaways was that although Dean was trying to be nonchalant and grown-up in his answers, he still had stuffed animals on his bed and dinosaur sheets. After he answered several questions, he felt self-conscious. "Am I talking too much?" he asked. Not at all.

SOURCE: Brooks Barnes, "What Do Boys Want? She Digs into Minds and Closets to See," *New York Times*, Apr. 14, 2009, A1,14.

Thinking Strategically

The first part of this chapter provided an overview of the types of goals and plans that organizations use. In the second half, we will explore strategic management, which is one specific type of planning. First, we define the components of strategic management and discuss the purposes and levels of strategy. Then we examine several models of strategy formulation at the corporate and business levels. Finally, we discuss the tools managers use to execute their strategic plans.

What does it mean to "think strategically"? *Strategic thinking* means to take the long-term view and to see the big picture, including the organization and the competitive environment, and consider how they fit together. Strategic thinking is important for both businesses and nonprofit organizations. In for-profit firms, strategic planning typically pertains to competitive actions in the marketplace. In nonprofit organizations such as the Red Cross or the Salvation Army, strategic planning pertains to events in the external environment.

Research has shown that strategic thinking and planning positively affect a firm's performance and financial success.[42] Most managers are aware of the importance of strategic planning, as evidenced by a *McKinsey Quarterly* survey. Fifty-one percent of responding executives whose companies had no formal strategic planning process said they were dissatisfied with the company's development of strategy, compared to only 20 percent of those at companies that had a formal planning process.[43] CEOs at successful companies make strategic thinking and planning a top management priority. For an organization to succeed, the CEO must be actively involved in making the tough choices and trade-offs that define and support strategy.[44] However, senior executives at today's leading companies want middle- and low-level managers to think strategically as well. Understanding the strategy concept and the levels of strategy is an important start toward strategic thinking.

What Is Strategic Management?

strategic management
The set of decisions and actions used to formulate and implement strategies that will provide a competitively superior fit between the organization and its environment so as to achieve organizational goals.

strategy
The plan of action that prescribes resource allocation and other activities for dealing with the environment, achieving a competitive advantage, and attaining organizational goals.

competitive advantage
What sets the organization apart from others and provides it with a distinctive edge in the marketplace.

Strategic management refers to the set of decisions and actions used to formulate and execute strategies that will provide a competitively superior fit between the organization and its environment so as to achieve organizational goals.[45] Managers ask questions such as the following: What changes and trends are occurring in the competitive environment? Who are our competitors, and what are their strengths and weaknesses? Who are our customers? What products or services should we offer, and how can we offer them most efficiently? What does the future hold for our industry, and how can we change the rules of the game? Answers to these questions help managers make choices about how to position their organizations in the environment with respect to rival companies.[46] Superior organizational performance is not a matter of luck. It is determined by the choices that managers make.

PURPOSE OF STRATEGY

The first step in strategic management is to define an explicit **strategy**, which is the plan of action that describes resource allocation and activities for dealing with the environment, achieving a competitive advantage, and attaining the organization's goals. **Competitive advantage** refers to what sets the organization apart from others and provides it with a distinctive edge for meeting customer or client needs in the marketplace. The essence of formulating strategy is choosing how the organization will be different.[47] Managers make decisions about whether the company will perform different activities or will execute similar activities differently than its rivals do. Strategy necessarily changes over time to fit environmental conditions, but to remain competitive, companies develop strategies that focus on core competencies, develop synergy, and create value for customers.

Exploit Core Competence.

A company's **core competence** is something the organization does especially well in comparison to its competitors. A core competence represents a competitive advantage because the company acquires expertise that competitors do not have. A core competence may be in the area of superior research and development, expert technological know-how, process efficiency, or exceptional customer service.[48] At VF, a large apparel company that owns Vanity Fair, Nautica, Wrangler, and The North Face, strategy focuses on the company's core competencies of operational efficiency and merchandising know-how. When VF bought The North Face, for example, its distribution systems were so poor that stores were getting ski apparel at the end of winter and camping gear at the end of summer. The company's operating profit margin was minus 35 percent. Managers at VF revamped The North

COURTESY OF HAYES DIVERSIFIED TECHNOLOGIES

When the U.S. Marines needed rugged motorcycles, they looked to manufacturers of on- and off-road bikes. But most motorcycles run on gasoline, which is the wrong fuel for military purposes. Hayes Diversified Technologies had the competitive advantage. After 20 years of building adapted motorcycles for the Marines and the Army Special Forces, Hayes had developed a core competence in technology that addresses the fuel limitations faced by the military. Most military machines run on JB8 fuel, a formulation of diesel and kerosene. Hayes Diversified's new HDT M1030M1 motorcycle is designed for diesel service, so Hayes readily won the contract.

··> **CONCEPT CONNECTION** <·········

Face's sourcing, distribution, and financial systems and within five years doubled sales to $500 million and improved profit margins to a healthy 13 percent.[49] Gaylord Hotels, which has large hotel and conference centers in several states as well as the Opryland complex near Nashville, Tennessee, thrives based on a strategy of superior service for large group meetings.[50] Robinson Helicopter succeeds through superior technological know-how for building small, two-seater helicopters used for everything from police patrols in Los Angeles to herding cattle in Australia.[51] In each case, leaders identified what their company does especially well and built strategy around it.

Build Synergy.

When organizational parts interact to produce a joint effect that is greater than the sum of the parts acting alone, **synergy** occurs. The organization may attain a special advantage with respect to cost, market power, technology, or management skill. When properly managed, synergy can create additional value with existing resources, providing a big boost to the bottom line.[52] Synergy was the motivation for Pepsi to buy Frito-Lay for instance, and for News Corp. to buy MySpace.

Synergy can also be obtained by good relationships between organizations. For example, the Disney Channel invites magazines such as *J-14*, *Twist*, and *Popstar* to visit the set of shows like *Hannah Montana* and *High School Musical*, gives reporters access for interviews and photo shoots, and provides brief videos for the magazines to post on their Web sites. The synergy keeps preteen interest booming for both the television shows and the magazines.[53]

Deliver Value.

Delivering value to the customer is at the heart of strategy. Value can be defined as the combination of benefits received and costs paid. Managers help their companies create value by devising strategies that exploit core competencies and attain synergy. To compete with the rising clout of satellite television, for example, cable companies such as Time-Warner Cable and Comcast are offering *value packages* that offer a combination of

core competence
A business activity that an organization does particularly well in comparison to competitors.

synergy
The condition that exists when the organization's parts interact to produce a joint effect that is greater than the sum of the parts acting alone.

Always make sure the customer gets good value.

SAVE-A-LOT

basic cable, digital premium channels, video on demand, high-speed Internet, and digital phone service for a reduced cost.

Consider how Save-A-Lot has grown into one of the most successful grocery chains in the United States with a strategy based on exploiting core competencies, building synergy, and providing value to customers.

When most supermarket executives look at the inner city, they see peeling paint, low-income customers, rampant crime, and low profits. Save-A-Lot looks at the inner city and sees opportunity. Save-A-Lot was started in the late 1970s, when Bill Moran noticed that low-income and rural areas were poorly served by large supermarkets. Moran began opening small stores in low-rent areas and stocking them with a limited number of low-priced staples. Moran handwrote price signs and built crude shelves out of particle board. He made his own labels from low-quality paper, which suppliers then slapped on generic products.

Save-A-Lot has thrived ever since by using its core competency of cost efficiency, which enables the stores to sell goods at prices 40 percent lower than major supermarkets. Unlike the typical supermarket, which is about 45,000 square feet, Save-A-Lot stores use a compact 16,000-square-foot no-frills format, targets areas with dirt-cheap rent, and courts households earning less than $35,000 a year. Save-A-Lot stores don't have bakeries, pharmacies, or grocery baggers. Labor costs are kept ultra low. For example, whereas most grocery managers want employees to keep displays well stocked and tidy, Save-A-Lot managers tell employees to let the displays sell down before restocking.

Save-A-Lot has obtained synergy by developing good relationships with a few core suppliers. Most supermarkets charge manufacturers slotting fees to put their products on shelves, but not Save-A-Lot. In addition, the company doesn't ask suppliers to take back damaged goods. It just sticks up a handwritten "Oops" sign and marks prices even lower. Customers love it. Now, even branded food makers want a slice of the Save-A-Lot pie. Procter & Gamble (P&G), for example, developed a low-priced version of Folgers coffee, and the chain also sells low-priced brands of cheese from Kraft and cereal from General Mills.[54]

SOURCE: Janet Adamy, "Bare Essentials: To Find Growth, No-Frills Grocer Goes Where Other Chains Won't," [ital]Wall Street Journal[close ital] (August 30, 2005): A1, A8. Copyright [copyright symbol] 2005, Dow Jones & Company. Reproduced with permission of Dow Jones & Company, Inc. in the format Text via Copyright Clearance Center.

The Strategic Management Process

The overall strategic management process is illustrated in Exhibit 5.11. It begins when executives evaluate their current position with respect to mission, goals, and strategies. They then scan the organization's internal and external environments and identify strategic factors that might require change. Internal or external events might indicate a need to redefine the mission or goals or to formulate a new strategy at the corporate, business, or functional level. The final stage in the strategic management process is implementation of the new strategy. Producers for *American Idol* saw ratings were slipping not only for the show but also for network television in general and took steps to reduce the viewer erosion, as discussed in the Spotlight on Skills on the next page.

STRATEGY FORMULATION VERSUS EXECUTION

strategy formulation
The stage of strategic management that involves the planning and decision making that lead to the establishment of the organization's goals and of a specific strategic plan.

strategy execution
The stage of strategic management that involves the use of managerial and organizational tools to direct resources toward achieving strategic outcomes.

Strategy formulation includes the planning and decision making that lead to the establishment of the firm's goals and the development of a specific strategic plan.[55] **Strategy formulation** may include assessing the external environment and internal problems and integrating the results into goals and strategy. This process is in contrast to **strategy execution**, which is the use of managerial and organizational tools to direct resources toward accomplishing strategic results.[56] Strategy execution is the administration and implementation of the strategic plan. Managers may use persuasion, new equipment, changes in organization structure, or a revised reward system to ensure that employees and resources are used to make formulated strategy a reality.

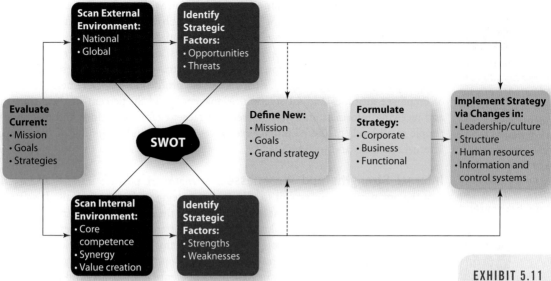

EXHIBIT 5.11
The Strategic
Management
Process
- - - - - - - - - -

SWOT ANALYSIS

Formulating strategy often begins with an assessment of the internal and external factors that will affect the organization's competitive situation. **SWOT analysis** includes a search for *strengths*, *weaknesses*, *opportunities*, and *threats* that affect organizational performance. External information about opportunities and threats may be obtained from a variety of sources including customers, government reports, professional journals, suppliers, bankers, friends in other organizations, consultants, or association meetings. Many firms

SWOT analysis
Analysis of the strengths,
weaknesses, opportunities,
and threats (SWOT) that affect
organizational performance.

SPOTLIGHT ON SKILLS

American Idol

How do you change a winning formula? Or, shall we say, winning but slipping. Though *American Idol* has been and still is the most popular network series (doing almost twice as good as the next best, *Dancing with the Stars*), its viewership has declined, dropping from 30 million viewers in its sixth season to 28 million in its seventh. At the beginning of season eight, producers decided to try another approach. Maybe all that shame and mortification is growing stale, they seemed to be thinking.

Hope is in and humiliation out—well, let's say, "diminished." *American Idol*'s eighth season featured strategic changes, including (1) a fourth judge, (2) a "wild card" round in which some contestants get a second chance, and (3) the embarrassment of fingernail-on-chalkboard singing reduced from four weeks to three. All this means less time on hopefuls making fools of themselves followed by Simon Cowell's insults. This trend actually began in 2007 after Cowell was widely criticized for disparaging a contestant who was revealed to have participated in Special Olympics. Later, officials at Special Olympics praised Cowell for giving the contestant another chance.

The result was fewer talentless hopefuls and reduced insults. But the show didn't give up completely on contestants living in fantasy worlds. So viewers hooked on the delusional participants can breathe a sigh of relief. Still, things change. New producer Ken Warwick, fresh off success on Britain's *Pop Idol*, doesn't expect that the show can remain the top success forever, especially since its audience is aging. And Paula Abdul's abrupt resignation in August 2009 left questions about the popularity of the ninth season. They've had a good run, nonetheless. Adds Warwick, "This wouldn't have been on the TV for eight years if it wasn't done right."

SOURCES: Edward Wyatt, "For 'Idol,' More Hope and Less Humiliation," *New York Times*, Jan. 13, 2009, p. C1; Michael Starr, "Paula Quits Idol," *New York Post*, Aug. 5, 2009, p. 3.

As a new manager, can you identify the core competence of your team or department and identify ways that it can contribute to the overall organization's strategy? Who are your team's or department's customers, and how can you deliver value?

When considering a strategy, look carefully at strengths, weaknesses, opportunities, and threats. Don't just jump into a course of action.

hire special scanning organizations to provide them with newspaper clippings, Internet research, and analyses of relevant domestic and global trends. In addition, many companies are hiring competitive intelligence professionals to scope out competitors, as we discussed in Chapter 2, and using intelligence teams, as described earlier in this chapter.

Executives acquire information about internal strengths and weaknesses from a variety of reports, including budgets, financial ratios, profit-and-loss statements, and surveys of employee attitudes and satisfaction. Managers spend 80 percent of their time giving and receiving information. Through frequent face-to-face discussions and meetings with people at all levels of the hierarchy, executives build an understanding of the company's internal strengths and weaknesses.

Internal Strengths and Weaknesses. *Strengths* are positive internal characteristics that the organization can exploit to achieve its strategic performance goals. *Weaknesses* are internal characteristics that might inhibit or restrict the organization's performance. Some examples of what executives evaluate to interpret strengths and weaknesses are given in Exhibit 5.12. The information sought typically pertains to specific functions such as marketing, finance, production, and research and development. Internal analysis also examines overall organization structure, management competence and quality, and human-resource characteristics. Based on their understanding of these areas, managers can determine their strengths or weaknesses compared with other companies.

External Opportunities and Threats. *Threats* are characteristics of the external environment that may prevent the organization from achieving its strategic goals. *Opportunities* are characteristics of the external environment that have the potential to help the organization achieve or exceed its strategic goals. Executives evaluate the external environment with information about the 10 sectors described in Chapter 2. The task environment sectors are the most relevant to strategic behavior and include the behavior of competitors, customers, suppliers, and the labor supply. The general environment contains those sectors that have an indirect influence on the organization but nevertheless must be understood and incorporated into strategic behavior. The general environment includes technological developments, the economy, legal–political and international events, natural resources, and sociocultural changes. Additional areas that might reveal opportunities or threats include pressure groups, interest groups, creditors, and potentially competitive industries.

EXHIBIT 5.12
Checklist for Analyzing Organizational Strengths and Weaknesses

Management and Organization	Marketing	Human Resources
Management quality	Distribution channels	Employee experience, education
Staff quality	Market share	Union status
Degree of centralization	Advertising efficiency	Turnover, absenteeism
Organization charts	Customer satisfaction	Work satisfaction
Planning, information, control systems	Product quality	Grievances
	Service reputation	
	Sales-force turnover	
Finance	**Production**	**Research and Development**
Profit margin	Plant location	Basic applied research
Debt–equity ratio	Machinery obsolescence	Laboratory capabilities
Inventory ratio	Purchasing system	Research programs
Return on investment	Quality control	New-product innovations
Credit rating	Productivity and efficiency	Technology innovations

Social networking company Facebook, which began as a site for college students, provides an example of how managers can use SWOT analysis in formulating an appropriate strategy.

Myspace had the lead in online social networking, but Facebook caught up (and then some) and is now getting all the attention. The start-up grew rapidly in the first four years after 23-year-old Mark Zuckerberg founded it while still a student at Harvard University. To keep Facebook growing, the young CEO made some strategic decisions that can be understood by looking at the company's strengths, weaknesses, opportunities, and threats.

Facebook's *strengths* include technological know-how and an aggressive and innovative culture. In addition, Facebook has a major partnership with Microsoft, which has invested $240 million, brokers banner ads for the company, and is developing tools that make it easy to create links between Windows applications and Facebook's network. In the time since Facebook expanded beyond students, membership has boomed, and Facebook is preferred over MySpace by older users and the Silicon Valley tech set. Work networks on Facebook are exploding. The primary *weakness* is a lack of management expertise to help the company meet the challenges of growing up.

The biggest *threat* to the company is that Facebook is still spending more cash than it is bringing in. In addition, Zuckerberg is gaining a reputation in the industry as an arrogant and standoffish manager, which could hurt Facebook's chances of successful partnerships. *Opportunities* abound to expand the company's operations internationally and to take advantage of Facebook's popularity to introduce features that can command higher Web advertising rates and bring in more revenue.

What does SWOT analysis suggest for Facebook? Zuckerberg is trying to capitalize on Facebook's popularity by making it a place for companies to provide services to members. For example, Prosper.com developed a Facebook application for its service that allows members to lend one another money at negotiated interest rates. Non-Internet companies such as Red Bull have also developed Facebook applications to reach Facebook's vast customer base. Companies that put applications on the Facebook Web site can experience a sort of viral popularity as word spreads among millions of members.

To implement the strategy, Zuckerberg is bringing in executives with more strategy experience than himself such as Chamath Palihapitiya, a former AOL manager, as vice president of product marketing and Sheryl Sandberg, formerly of Google, as chief operating officer. These managers have the traditional skills Facebook needs to execute the new strategy both in the United States and internationally.[57]

It's too soon to tell if Facebook's strategy is working.[58] Zuckerberg is continuing his efforts to build a more seasoned executive team to keep growing and avoid damaging mistakes as Facebook pursues its strategy.

Formulating Business-Level Strategy

Now we turn to strategy formulation within the strategic business unit in which the concern is how to compete. A popular and effective model for formulating strategy is Porter's competitive forces and strategies. Michael E. Porter studied a number of business organizations and proposed that business-level strategies are the result of five competitive forces in the company's environment.[59] More recently, Porter examined the impact of the Internet on business-level strategy.[60] New Web-based technology is influencing industries in both positive and negative ways, and understanding this impact is essential for managers to accurately analyze their competitive environments and design appropriate strategic actions.

Before reading further, you might also want to review your strategic strengths as determined by your responses to the questionnaire on page 165.

PORTER'S FIVE COMPETITIVE FORCES

Exhibit 5.13 illustrates the competitive forces that exist in a company's environment and indicates some ways in which Internet technology is affecting each area. These forces help determine a company's position vis-à-vis competitors in the industry environment.

1. *Potential new entrants.* Capital requirements and economies of scale are examples of two potential barriers to entry that can keep out new competitors. It is far more costly to

EXHIBIT 5.13
Porter's Five Forces
Affecting Industry
Competition

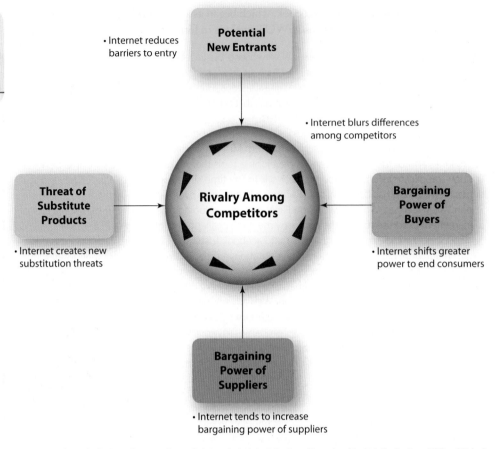

• Internet reduces
barriers to entry

**Potential
New Entrants**

• Internet blurs differences
among competitors

**Threat of
Substitute
Products**

**Rivalry Among
Competitors**

**Bargaining
Power of
Buyers**

• Internet creates new
substitution threats

• Internet shifts greater
power to end consumers

**Bargaining
Power of
Suppliers**

• Internet tends to increase
bargaining power of suppliers

SOURCE: Based on Michael E. Porter, *Competitive Strategy: Techniques for Analyzing Industries and Competitors* (New York: The Free Press, 1980); and Michael E. Porter, "Strategy and the Internet," *Harvard Business Review* (Mar. 2001): 63–78.

enter the automobile industry, for instance, than to start a specialized mail-order business. In general, Internet technology has made it much easier for new companies to enter an industry by curtailing the need for such organizational elements as an established sales force, physical assets such as buildings and machinery, and access to existing supplier and sales channels.

2. *Bargaining power of buyers.* Informed customers become empowered customers. The Internet provides easy access to a wide array of information about products, services, and competitors, thereby greatly increasing the bargaining power of end consumers. For example, a customer shopping for a car can gather extensive information about various options such as wholesale prices for new cars or average value for used vehicles, detailed specifications, repair records, and even whether a used car has ever been involved in an accident.

3. *Bargaining power of suppliers.* The concentration of suppliers and the availability of substitute suppliers are significant factors in determining supplier power. The sole supplier of engines to a manufacturer of small airplanes will have great power, for example. The impact of the Internet in this area can be both positive and negative; that is, procurement over the Web tends to give a company greater power over suppliers, but the Web also gives suppliers access to a greater number of customers, as well as the ability to reach end users. Overall, the Internet tends to raise the bargaining power of suppliers.

4. *Threat of substitute products.* The power of alternatives and substitutes for a company's product may be affected by changes in cost or in trends such as increased health consciousness that will deflect buyer loyalty. Companies in the sugar industry suffered from the growth of sugar substitutes; manufacturers of aerosol spray cans lost business

as environmentally conscious consumers chose other products. The Internet created a greater threat of new substitutes by enabling new approaches to meeting customer needs. For example, offers of low-cost airline tickets over the Internet hurt traditional travel agencies.

5. *Rivalry among competitors.* As illustrated in Exhibit 5.13, rivalry among competitors is influenced by the preceding four forces, as well as by cost and product differentiation. With the leveling force of the Internet and information technology, it has become more difficult for many companies to find ways to distinguish themselves from their competitors, which intensifies rivalry. Porter referred to the "advertising slugfest" when describing the scrambling and jockeying for position that occurs among fierce rivals within an industry. Nintendo and Sony are fighting for control of the video-game console industry, Netflix and Blockbuster are competing for the online mail-order movie rental business, and Pepsi and Coke are still battling it out in the cola wars.

As a new manager, examine the competitive forces that are affecting your organization.

COMPETITIVE STRATEGIES

In finding its competitive edge within these five forces, Porter suggests that a company can adopt one of three strategies: differentiation, cost leadership, or focus. The organizational characteristics typically associated with each strategy are summarized in Exhibit 5.14.

- *Differentiation.* The **differentiation** strategy involves an attempt to distinguish the firm's products or services from others in the industry. The organization may use creative advertising, distinctive product features, exceptional service, or new technology to achieve a product perceived as unique. Examples of products that have benefited from a differentiation strategy include Harley-Davidson motorcycles, Snapper lawn equipment, and GORE-TEX fabrics, all of which are perceived as distinctive in their markets. Service companies such as Starbucks, Whole Foods Market, and IKEA also use a differentiation strategy.

differentiation
A type of competitive strategy with which the organization seeks to distinguish its products or services from those of competitors.

Strategy	Organizational Characteristics
Differentiation	Acts in a flexible, loosely knit way, with strong coordination among departments
	Strong capability in basic rewards
	Creative flair; thinks "out of the box"
	Strong marketing abilities
	Rewards employee innovation
	Corporate reputation for quality or technological leadership
Cost Leadership	Strong central authority; tight cost controls
	Maintains standard operating procedures
	Easy-to-use manufacturing technologies
	Highly efficient procurement and distribution systems
	Close supervision, finite employee empowerment
Focus	Frequent, detailed control reports
	May use combination of above policies directed at particular strategic target
	Values and rewards flexibility and customer intimacy
	Measures cost of providing service and maintaining customer loyalty
	Pushes empowerment to employees with customer contact

EXHIBIT 5.14
Organizational Characteristics of Porter's Competitive Strategies

SOURCES: Based on Michael E. Porter, *Competitive Strategy: Techniques for Analyzing Industries and Competitors* (New York: The Free Press: 1980); Michael Treacy and Fred Wiersema, "How Market Leaders Keep Their Edge," *Fortune* (Feb. 6, 1995): 88–98; and Michael A. Hitt, R. Duane Ireland, and Robert E. Hoskisson, *Strategic Management* (St. Paul, MN: West, 1995): 100–113.

SPOTLIGHT ON SKILLS

Jack White and the White Stripes, Raconteurs, and The Dead Weather

Jack White never wanted to be like anyone else. As singer-guitarist of the White Stripes and the Raconteurs—not to mention his newest gig as drummer of The Dead Weather—he made sure that the image of the White Stripes (his first major-hit band) was unique and well planned, whether it involved musical arrangements or the band's black-white-red color scheme. With very few rock stars left, Jack White enters a room like the "real thing," along with the band's drummer, black-and-red-clad ex-wife Meg White. Most indie rock tastemaker's want bands that look like they do, but Jack White goes more for smoke and mirrors, the strategy that has caused detractors to relegate the White Stripes to the category of gimmickry. Jack believes his attention to the funky details is what makes the band successful. "Everything from your haircut to your clothes to the type of instrument you play to the melody of a song to the rhythm—they're all tricks to get people to pay attention," he said.

Having been ripped off by small record labels, the White Stripes don't mind being with a major record company. This doesn't mean they'll go mainstream, as most bands hope to do. The White Stripes are sticking to their indie roots. Their album *Icky Thump* is a more traditional sound for them. White said "there are songs on this album that could easily have been on our first," saying that the Beatles created a nearly impossible expectation of reinvention for rock groups. Fans want to hear some new and a lot of the familiar songs, says Jack.

As a young aspiring filmmaker, Jack changed to music but runs his operation much like a director would, creating a whole universe from casting to costumes to props. Almost everything the White Stripes do, then, is strategic and premeditated, not including the music. "Things happen song by song and by accident," he notes. "If you admit to the song that you are not in control, then some good things start to happen."

Now that he is also involved in the Raconteurs and The Dead Weather, fans are happy that he is still singing.

SOURCES: Ben Ratliff, "Jack White on the Drums? Don't Worry, He Still Sings," *New York Times*, Apr. 16, 2009, p. C1; and Alan Light, "Still True to the Red, White and Black," *New York Times*, June 10, 2007, p. 26.

TAKE ACTION

In order to succeed, try to really differentiate your product or have very competitive prices.

A differentiation strategy can reduce rivalry with competitors if buyers are loyal to a company's brand. Successful differentiation can also reduce the bargaining power of large buyers because other products are less attractive, which also helps the firm fight off threats of substitute products. In addition, differentiation erects entry barriers in the form of customer loyalty that a new entrant into the market would have difficulty overcoming, as shown in the strategy of Jack White and the White Stripes, which is described in the Spotlight on Skills box.

- *Cost leadership.* With a **cost leadership** strategy, the organization aggressively seeks efficient facilities, pursues cost reductions, and uses tight cost controls to produce products more efficiently than competitors. A low-cost position means that the company can undercut competitors' prices and still offer comparable quality and earn a reasonable profit. For example, Comfort Inn and Motel 6 are low-priced alternatives to Four Seasons and Marriott.

cost leadership
A type of competitive strategy with which the organization aggressively seeks efficient facilities, cuts costs, and employs tight cost controls to be more efficient than competitors.

Being a low-cost producer provides a successful strategy to defend against the five competitive forces in Exhibit 5.13. The most efficient, low-cost company is in the best position to succeed in a price war while still making a profit. Likewise, the low-cost producer is protected from powerful customers and suppliers because customers cannot find lower prices elsewhere and other buyers would have less slack for price negotiation with suppliers. If substitute products or potential new entrants occur, the low-cost producer is better positioned than higher-cost rivals to prevent loss of market share. The low price acts as a barrier against new entrants and substitute products.[61]

focus
A type of competitive strategy that emphasizes concentration on a specific regional market or buyer group.

- *Focus.* With a **focus** strategy, the organization concentrates on a specific regional market or buyer group. The company will use either a differentiation or a cost leadership approach, but only for a narrow target market. Save-A-Lot, described earlier, uses a focused cost leadership strategy, putting stores in low-income areas. Edward Jones

2 It's a good idea to make the product or service available to as many customers as possible.

ANSWER: Creating a target market is almost always more effective. If you try to sell to everybody, you might end up impacting no one. This is similar to light focused through a magnifying glass, which can create fire. Dissipated light, on the other hand, has little effect.

Investments, a St. Louis-based brokerage house, uses a focused differentiation strategy, building its business in rural and small town America and providing clients with conservative, long-term investment advice. Management scholar and consultant Peter Drucker once said the safety-first orientation means Edward Jones delivers a product "that no Wall Street house has ever sold before: peace of mind."[62]

Managers should think carefully about which strategy will provide their company with its competitive advantage. Gibson Guitar Corporation, famous in the music world for its innovative, high-quality products, found that switching to a low-cost strategy to compete against Japanese rivals such as Yamaha and Ibanez actually hurt the company. When managers realized people wanted Gibson products because of their reputation, not their price, they went back to a differentiation strategy and invested in new technology and marketing.[63] In his studies, Porter found that some businesses did not consciously adopt one of these three strategies and were stuck with no strategic advantage. Without a strategic advantage, businesses earned below-average profits compared with those that used differentiation, cost leadership, or focus strategies. Similarly, a five-year study of management practices in hundreds of businesses, referred to as the Evergreen Project, found that a clear strategic direction was a key factor that distinguished winners from losers.[64]

New Trends in Strategy

Organizations have been in a merger and acquisition frenzy in recent years. JPMorgan Chase and Bank One merged, AT&T bought Cingular Wireless, and Disney merged with ABC. Some companies still seek to gain or keep a competitive edge by acquiring new capabilities via mergers and acquisitions. Today, however, a decided shift has occurred toward enhancing the organization's existing capabilities as the primary means of growing and innovating. Another current trend is using strategic partnerships as an alternative to mergers and acquisitions.

INNOVATION FROM WITHIN

The strategic approach referred to as **dynamic capabilities** means that managers focus on leveraging and developing more from the firm's existing assets, capabilities, and core competencies in a way that will provide a sustained competitive advantage.[65] Learning, reallocation of existing assets, and internal innovation form the route to addressing new challenges in the competitive environment and meeting new customer needs. For example, General Electric, as described earlier, has acquired a number of other companies to enter a variety of diverse businesses. Today, though, the emphasis at GE is not on making deals but on stimulating and supporting internal innovation. Instead of spending billions to buy new businesses, CEO Jeff Immelt is investing in internal "Imagination Breakthrough" projects that will take GE into internally developed new lines of

dynamic capabilities
Leveraging and developing more from the firm's existing assets, capabilities, and core competencies in a way that will provide a sustained competitive advantage.

COURTESY OF IROBOT

The technology company iRobot is best known for the Roomba,—a petlike robotic vacuum shown here with a live animal pet. But iRobot also fulfils a more serious purpose of providing military robots that perform dangerous jobs such as clearing caves and sniffing out bombs. The company's dynamic capabilities approach included sending an engineer to Afghanistan for field testing and learning. For its consumer products, iRobot primarily uses internal interdisciplinary teams to incubate ideas. But partnerships feed iRobot's innovation machine, as well, such as when the company partnered with an explosives-sensor company to develop its bomb-sniffing bot.

⋯⋯⋯▷ CONCEPT CONNECTION ◁⋯⋯⋯

business, new geographic areas, and a new customer base. The idea is that getting growth out of existing businesses is cheaper and more effective than trying to buy it from outside.[66]

Another example of dynamic capabilities is IBM, which many analysts had written off as a has-been in the early 1990s. Since then, new top managers have steered the company through a remarkable transformation by capitalizing on IBM's core competence of expert technology by learning new ways to apply it to meet changing customer needs. By leveraging existing capabilities to provide solutions to major customer problems rather than just selling hardware, IBM has moved into businesses as diverse as life sciences, banking, and automotive.

STRATEGIC PARTNERSHIPS

Internal innovation doesn't mean companies always go it alone, however. Collaboration with other organizations, sometimes even with competitors, is an important part of how today's successful companies enter new areas of business. Consider P&G and Clorox. The companies are fierce rivals in cleaning products and water purification, but both profited by collaborating on a new plastic wrap. P&G researchers invented a wrap that seals tightly only where it is pressed, but P&G didn't have a plastic wrap category. Managers negotiated a strategic partnership with Clorox to market the wrap under the well-established Glad brand name, and Glad Press & Seal became one of the company's most popular products.[67]

The Internet is both driving and supporting the move toward partnership thinking. The ability to rapidly and smoothly conduct transactions, communicate information, exchange ideas, and collaborate on complex projects via the Internet means that companies such as Citigroup, Dow Chemical, and Herman Miller have been able to enter entirely new businesses by partnering in business areas that were previously unimaginable.[68]

Global Strategy

Many organizations operate globally and pursue a distinct strategy as the focus of global business. Senior executives try to formulate coherent strategies to provide synergy among worldwide operations for the purpose of fulfilling common goals. Yet managers face a strategic dilemma between the need for global integration and national responsiveness.

The various global strategies are shown in Exhibit 5.15. Recall from Chapter 3 that the first step toward a greater international presence is when companies begin exporting

SOURCES: Based on Michael A. Hitt, R. Duane Ireland, and Robert E. Hoskisson, *Strategic Management: Competitiveness and Globalization* (St. Paul, MN; West, 1995): 239; and Thomas M. Begley and David P. Boyd, "The Need for a Corporate Global Mindset," *MIT Sloan Management Review* (Winter 2003): 25–32.

EXHIBIT 5.15
Global Corporate
Strategies

domestically produced products to selected countries. The **export strategy** is shown in the lower left corner of the exhibit. Because the organization is domestically focused and has only a few exports, managers have little need to pay attention to issues of either local responsiveness or global integration. Organizations that pursue further international expansion must decide whether they want each global affiliate to act autonomously or whether activities should be standardized and centralized across countries. This choice leads managers to select a basic strategy alternative such as globalization versus multidomestic strategy. Some corporations may seek to achieve both global integration and national responsiveness by using a transnational strategy.

Strategy Execution

The final step in the strategic management process is strategy execution—how strategy is implemented or put into action. Many people argue that execution is the most important yet most difficult part of strategic management.[69] Indeed, many struggling companies may have file drawers full of winning strategies, but managers can't effectively execute them.[70]

No matter how brilliant the formulated strategy, the organization will not benefit if it is not skillfully executed. Strategy execution requires that all aspects of the organization be in congruence with the strategy and that every individual's efforts be coordinated toward

export strategy
Plans made to sell products
in foreign markets.

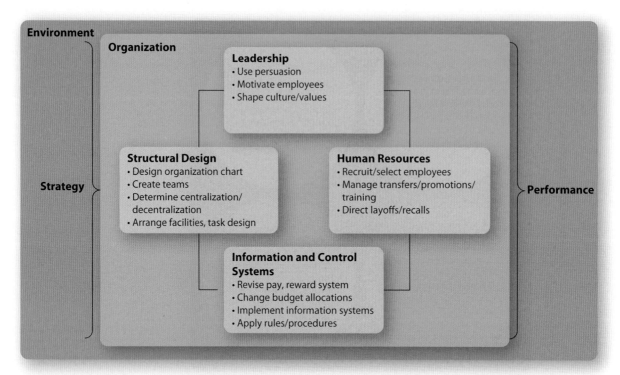

SOURCE: From Galbraith/Kazanjian. *Strategy Implementation*, 2E. © 1986 South-Western, a part of Cengage Learning. Reproduced by permission. www.cengage.comp/permissions

EXHIBIT 5.16
Tools for Putting
Strategy into Action

accomplishing strategic goals.[71] Strategy execution involves using several tools—parts of the firm that can be adjusted to put strategy into action—as illustrated in Exhibit 5.16. Once a new strategy is selected, it is implemented through changes in leadership, structure, information and control systems, and human resources.[72] Read the section "Tips for Effective Strategy Execution" on page 166 for more information.

- *Leadership.* The primary key to successful strategy execution is leadership. *Leadership* is the ability to influence people to adopt the new behaviors needed for putting the strategy into action. Leaders use persuasion, motivation techniques, and cultural values to support the new strategy. They might make speeches to employees, build coalitions of people who support the new strategic direction, and persuade middle managers to go along with their vision for the company. At IBM, for example, CEO Sam Palmisano used leadership to get people aligned with the strategy of getting IBM intimately involved in revamping and even running customers' business operations. To implement the new approach, he invested tons of money to teach managers at all levels how to lead rather than control their staffs. And he talked to people all over the company, appealing to their sense of pride and uniting them behind the new vision and strategy.[74]

(continues on p. 174)

Assess
Your
Answer

3 Top managers should get together and develop a plan and then announce it to employees.

ANSWER: It is much more effective to involve employees either in the development of goals or at least in meetings where there is a great deal of two-way communication. Engaging employees in meaningful discussions regarding the goals helps gain commitment and can greatly increase motivation.

What Is Your Strategy Strength?[73]

As a new manager, what are your strengths concerning strategy formulation and implementation? To find out, think about how *you handle challenges and issues* in your school or job. Then mark **a** or **b** for each of the following items, depending on which is more descriptive of your behavior. There are no right or wrong answers. Respond to each item as it best describes how you respond to work situations.

1. When keeping records, I tend to

_____ a. be careful about documentation.

_____ b. be haphazard about documentation.

2. If I run a group or a project, I

_____ a. have the general idea and let others figure out how to do the tasks.

_____ b. try to figure out specific goals, timelines, and expected outcomes.

3. My thinking style could be more accurately described as

_____ a. linear thinker, going from A to B to C.

_____ b. thinking like a grasshopper, hopping from one idea to another.

4. In my office or home things are

_____ a. here and there in various piles.

_____ b. laid out neatly or at least in reasonable order.

5. I take pride in developing

_____ a. ways to overcome a barrier to a solution.

_____ b. new hypotheses about the underlying cause of a problem.

6. I can best help strategy by encouraging

_____ a. openness to a wide range of assumptions and ideas.

_____ b. thoroughness when implementing new ideas.

7. One of my strengths is

_____ a. commitment to making things work.

_____ b. commitment to a dream for the future.

8. I am most effective when I emphasize

_____ a. inventing original solutions.

_____ b. making practical improvements.

SCORING AND INTERPRETATION: Managers have differing strengths and capabilities when it comes to formulating and implementing strategy. Here's how to determine yours. For *strategic formulator* strength, score 1 point for each **a** answer marked for questions 2, 4, 6, and 8, and for each **b** answer marked for questions 1, 3, 5, and 7. For *strategic implementer* strength, score 1 point for each **b** answer marked for questions 2, 4, 6, and 8, and for each **a** answer marked for questions 1, 3, 5, and 7. Which of your two scores is higher and by how much? The higher score indicates your strategy strength.

Formulator and implementer are two important ways new managers bring value to strategic management. New managers with implementer strengths tend to work within the situation and improve it by making it more efficient and reliable. Leaders with the formulator strength push toward out-of-the-box strategies and like to seek dramatic breakthroughs. Both styles are essential to strategic management. Strategic formulators often use their skills in creating whole new strategies, and strategic implementers often work with strategic improvements and implementation.

If the difference between your two scores is 2 or less, you have a balanced formulator–implementer style and work well in both arenas. If the difference is 4 or 5 points, then you have a moderately strong style and probably work best in the area of your strength. And if the difference is 7 or 8 points, then you have a distinctive strength and almost certainly would want to work in the area of your strength rather than in the opposite domain.

One survey found that only 57 percent of responding firms reported that managers successfully executed the new strategies they had devised. Strategy gives a company a competitive edge only if it is skillfully executed through the decisions and actions of frontline managers and employees. Here are a few clues for creating an environment and process conducive to effective strategy execution.

1. *Build commitment to the strategy.* People throughout the organization have to buy into the new strategy. Managers make a deliberate and concentrated effort to bring frontline employees into the loop so they understand the new direction and have a chance to participate in decisions about how it will be executed. When Saab managers wanted to shift their strategy, they met with frontline employees and dealers to explain the new direction and ask for suggestions and recommendations on how to put it into action. Clear, measurable goals and rewards that are tied to implementation efforts are also important for gaining commitment.

2. *Devise a clear execution plan.* Too often, managers put forth great effort to formulate a strategy and next to none in crafting a game plan for its execution. Without such a plan, managers and staff are likely to lose sight of the new strategy when they return to the everyday demands of their jobs. For successful execution, translate the strategy into a simple, streamlined plan that breaks the implementation process into a series of short-term actions with a timetable for each step. Make sure the plan spells out who is responsible for what part of the strategy execution, how success will be measured and tracked, and what resources will be required and how they will be allocated.

3. *Pay attention to culture.* Culture drives strategy, and without the appropriate cultural values, employees' behavior will be out of sync with the company's desired positioning in the marketplaces. For example, Air Canada's CEO made a sincere commitment to making the airline the country's customer-service leader. However, employee behavior didn't change because the old culture values supported doing things the way they had always been done.

4. *Take advantage of employees' knowledge and skills.* Managers need to get to know their employees on a personal basis so they understand how people can contribute to strategy execution. Most people want to be recognized and want to be valuable members of the organization. People throughout the organization have unused talents and skills that might be crucial for the success of a new strategy. In addition, managers can be sure people get training so they are capable of furthering the organization's new direction.

5. *Communicate, communicate, communicate.* Top managers have to continually communicate their firm commitment to the strategy through words and actions. In addition, managers have to keep tabs on how things are going, identify problems, and keep people informed about the organization's progress. Managers should break down barriers to effective communication across functional and hierarchical boundaries, often bringing customers into the communication loop as well. Information systems should provide accurate and timely information to the people who need it for decision making.

Executing strategy is a complex job that requires everyone in the company to be aligned with the new direction and working to make it happen. These tips, combined with the information in the text, can help managers meet the challenge of putting strategy into action.[75]

Use consensus and persuasion to build support for your strategy.

- *Structural Design.* Structural design pertains to managers' responsibilities, their degree of authority, and the consolidation of facilities, departments, and divisions. Structure also pertains to such matters as centralization versus decentralization and the design of job tasks. Trying to execute a strategy that conflicts with structural design, particularly in relation to managers' authority and responsibility, is a top obstacle to putting strategy into action effectively.[76] Many new strategies require making changes in organizational structure such as adding or changing positions, reorganizing into teams, redesigning jobs, and shifting managers' responsibility and accountability. At IBM, Palmisano dismantled the executive committee that previously presided over strategic initiatives and replaced it with committees made up of people from all over the company. In addition, the entire firm was reorganized into teams that work directly with customers. As the company moves into a new business such as insurance claims processing or supply-chain optimization, IBM assigns SWAT teams to work with a handful of initial clients to learn what customers want and deliver it fast. Practically every job in the giant corporation was redefined to support the new strategy.[77]

- *Information and Control Systems. Information and control systems* include reward systems, pay incentives, budgets for allocating resources, information-technology systems, and the organization's rules, policies, and procedures. Changes in these systems represent major tools for putting strategy into action.[78] For example, Pizza Hut has made excellent use of sophisticated information technology to support a differentiation strategy of continually innovating with new products. Data from point-of-sale customer transactions goes into a massive data warehouse. Managers can mine the data for competitive intelligence that enables them to predict trends as well as better manage targeted advertising and direct-mail campaigns.[79] Information technology can also be used to support a low-cost strategy such as what Walmart has done by accelerating checkout, managing inventory, and controlling distribution.[80]

- *Human Resources.* The organization's *human resources* are its employees. The human-resource function recruits, selects, trains, transfers, promotes, and lays off employees to achieve strategic goals. Longo Toyota of El Monte, California, recruits a highly diverse workforce to create a competitive advantage in selling cars and trucks. The staff speaks more than 30 languages and dialects, which gives Longo a lead because research shows that minorities prefer to buy a vehicle from someone who speaks their language and understands their culture.[81] Training employees is also important because it helps them understand the purpose and importance of a new strategy, overcome resistance, and develop the necessary skills and behaviors to implement the strategy. Southwest supports its low-cost strategy by cross-training employees to perform a variety of functions, minimizing turnover time of planes.[82]

Summary

This chapter discussed organizational planning, which involves defining goals and developing plans with which to achieve them.

An organization exists for a single, overriding purpose known as its *mission*—the basis for strategic goals and plans. Goals within the organization begin with strategic goals followed by tactical and operational goals. Plans are defined similarly, with strategic, tactical, and operational plans used to achieve the goals. Managers can use strategy maps to clearly align goals and communicate them throughout the organization.

Managers formulate goals that are specific and measurable, cover key result areas, are challenging but realistic, have a defined time period, and are linked to rewards.

The chapter described several types of operational plans, including management by objectives, single-use and standing plans, and contingency plans. Two extensions of contingency planning are scenario building and crisis planning. Scenarios are alternative vivid pictures of what the future might be like. They provide a framework for managers to cope with unexpected or unpredictable events. Crisis planning involves the stages of prevention and preparation.

In the past, planning was almost always done entirely by top managers, consultants, or central planning departments. During turbulent times, planning is decentralized and people throughout the organization are involved in establishing dynamic plans that can meet rapidly changing needs in the environment.

Some guidelines for high-performance planning in a turbulent environment include setting stretch goals for excellence, using performance dashboards, and organizing intelligence teams.

This chapter described important concepts of strategic management. Strategic management begins with an evaluation of the organization's current mission, goals, and strategy. This evaluation is followed by situation analysis (called SWOT analysis), which examines opportunities and threats in the external environment as well as strengths and weaknesses within the organization. Situation analysis leads to the formulation of explicit strategies, which indicate how the company intends to achieve a competitive advantage. Managers formulate strategies that focus on core competencies, develop synergy, and create value.

Even the most creative strategies have no value if they cannot be translated into action. Execution is the most important and most difficult part of strategy. Managers put strategy into action by aligning all parts of the organization to be in congruence with the new strategy. Four areas that managers focus on for strategy execution are leadership, structural design, information and control systems, and human resources.

Many organizations also pursue a separate global strategy. Managers can choose to use a globalization strategy, a multidomestic strategy, or a transnational strategy as the focus of global operations.

Discussion Questions

1. Write a brief mission statement for a local business with which you are familiar. How might having a clear, written mission statement benefit a small organization?

2. What strategic plans could be adopted by the college or university at which you are taking this management course to compete for students in the marketplace? Would these plans depend on the school's goals?

3. One of the benefits of a strategy map is that goals and how they are linked can be clearly communicated to everyone in the organization. Does a minimum-wage maintenance worker in a hospital really need to understand any goals beyond keeping the place clean? Discuss.

4. US Airways has more customer complaints due to late flights and mishandled baggage than any other major carrier. If you were an operations manager at US Airways, how might you use MBO to solve these problems? Could scenario planning be useful for airline managers who want planes to run on time? Discuss.

5. Why would an organization want to use an intelligence team? Discuss.

6. Some people say an organization could never be "prepared" for a disaster such as the massacre at Virginia Tech, which left 33 people dead. If so, then what's the point of crisis planning?

7. Come up with a BHAG for some aspect of your own life. How do you determine whether it makes sense to pursue a big hairy audacious goal?

8. FedEx acquired Kinko's based on the idea that its document delivery and office services would complement FedEx's package-delivery services as well as give the company greater presence in the small business market. Many college towns have a Kinko's store and FedEx services. Based on your experience as a customer of the two companies, can you see evidence of the synergy the deal makers hoped for?

9. Perform a SWOT analysis for the school or university you attend. Do you think university administrators consider the same factors when devising their strategy?

10. Game maker Electronic Arts (EA) was criticized as "trying to buy innovation" in its bid to acquire Take Two Interactive, known primarily for the game *Grand Theft Auto*. Does it make sense for EA to offer more than $2 billion to buy Take Two when creating a new video game costs only $20 million? Why would EA ignore internal innovation to choose an acquisition strategy?

Self Learning

Company Crime Wave

Senior managers in your organization are concerned about internal theft and have written a goal that reduces it by 20 percent in the first year. Your department has been assigned the task of writing an ethics policy that defines employee theft and prescribes penalties. Stealing goods is easily classified as theft, but other activities are more ambiguous. Before writing the policy, go through the following list and decide which behaviors should be defined as stealing and whether penalties should apply. Classify each item as an example of (1) theft, (2) acceptable behavior, or (3) in between with respect to written policy. Is it theft when an employee:

- gets paid for overtime not worked?

- takes a longer lunch or coffee break than authorized?

- punches a time card for another?

- comes in late or leaves early?

- fakes injury to receive workers' compensation?

- takes care of personal business on company time?

- occasionally uses company copying machines or makes long-distance telephone calls for personal purposes?

- takes a few stamps, pens, or other supplies for personal use?

- takes money from the petty cash drawer?

- uses company vehicles or tools for personal use but returns them?

- damages merchandise so a cohort can purchase it at a discount?

- accepts a gift from a supplier?

Now consider those items rated "in between." Do these items represent ethical issues as defined in Chapter 4? How should these items be handled in the company's written policy?

Your instructor may hold a class discussion. Be prepared to defend your answers.

Group Learning

Course Goal Setting

Consider goals for yourself regarding doing well in this course. What do you need to do in order to get a good grade? Goals should be according to the "Criteria for Effective Goals" in this chapter on page 142. In addition, you need a system to monitor your progress, such as the table below, which shows the types of goals you may choose to select for yourself.

1. Complete the following table on your own. Fill in each cell, writing down what you have done to achieve that goal. For example, under "Define vocabulary words,"

what would you need to remember those? Would you need to read them over six times, write them down on flash cards, or something else? List what you plan to do or did for each week. You can also add items of your own at the bottom of the table.

2. In groups of three to four students, compare your goals and what you need to do to achieve them.

3. How similar and different were the implementation strategies of group members? Which one seem most likely to be most effective?

Goals	Class Weeks			
	First Week (From Now)	Second Week	Third Week	Fourth Week
1. 100% attendance				
2. Class notes				
3. Read assigned chapters				
4. Outline chapters				
5. Define vocabulary words				
6. Answer end of chapter questions.				
7. Complete "Workbook" assignments				
8. Class participation				
9.				
10.				

Your instructor may ask you to turn in your monitor sheets at the end of the course.

SOURCE: Adapted from Nancy C. Morey, "Applying Goal Setting in the Classroom," *The Organizational Behavior Teaching Review*, 11(4) (1986–1987): 53–59. Copyright 1996 by Dorothy Marcic.

Action Learning

Developing Strategy for a Small Business

Instructions: In groups of four to six students, select a local business with which you (or group members) are familiar. Complete the following activities.

Activity 1: Perform a SWOT analysis for the business.
SWOT Analysis for _____ (name of company)

	Internal (Within Company)		External (Outside Company)
Positive	Strengths:		Opportunities:
Negative	Weaknesses:		Threats:

Activity 2: Write a statement of the business's current strategy.

Activity 3: Decide on a goal you would like the business to achieve in two years and write a statement of proposed strategy for achieving that goal.

Activity 4: Write a statement describing how the proposed strategy will be implemented.

Activity 5: What have you learned from this exercise?

Ethical Dilemma

Inspire Learning Corporation

When the idea first occurred to Marge Brygay, it seemed like such a win–win situation. Now she wasn't so sure.

Marge was a hardworking sales rep for Inspire Learning Corporation, a company intent on becoming the top educational software provider in five years. That newly adopted strategic goal translated into an ambitious million-dollar sales target for each of Inspire's sales reps. At the beginning of the fiscal year, her share of the sales department's operational goal seemed entirely reasonable to Marge. She believed in Inspire's products. The company had developed innovative, highly regarded math, language, science, and social studies programs for the K–12 market. What set the software apart was a foundation in truly cutting-edge research. Marge had seen for herself how Inspire programs could engage whole classrooms of normally unmotivated kids; the significant rise in test scores on those increasingly important standardized tests bore out her subjective impressions.

But now, just days before the end of the year, Marge's sales were $1,000 short of her million-dollar goal. The sale that would have put her comfortably over the top fell through because of last-minute cuts in one large school system's budget. At first, she was nearly overwhelmed with frustration, but then it occurred to her that if she contributed $1,000 to Central High, the inner-city high school in her territory probably most in need of what she had for sale, they could purchase the software and put her over the top.

Her scheme would certainly benefit Central High students. Achieving her sales goal would make Inspire happy, and it wouldn't do her any harm, either professionally or financially. Making the goal would earn her a $10,000 bonus check that would come in handy when the time came to write out that first tuition check for her oldest child, who had just been accepted to a well-known, private university.

Initially, it seemed like the perfect solution all the way around. The more she thought about it, however, the more it didn't quite sit well with her conscience. Time was running out. She needed to decide what to do.

What Would You Do?

1. Donate the $1,000 to Central High and consider the $10,000 bonus a good return on your gift.

2. Accept the fact you didn't quite make your sales goal this year. Figure out ways to work smarter next year to increase the odds of achieving your target.

3. Don't make the donation but investigate whether any other ways are available to help Central High raise the funds that would allow it to purchase the much-needed educational software.

SOURCE: Based on Shel Horowitz, "Should Mary Buy Her Own Bonus?" *Business Ethics* (Summer 2005): 34.

6 Chapter Six

Managerial Decision Making

CHAPTER OUTLINE

After studying this chapter, you should be able to:

1 Explain why decision making is an important component of good management.

2 Discuss the difference between programmed and nonprogrammed decisions and the decision characteristics of certainty and uncertainty.

3 Describe the ideal, rational model of decision making and the political model of decision making.

4 Explain the process by which managers actually make decisions in the real world.

5 Identify the six steps used in managerial decision making.

6 Describe four personal decision styles used by managers, and explain the biases that frequently cause managers to make bad decisions.

7 Identify and explain techniques for innovative group decision making.

8 Identify ways in which information technology has transformed the manager's job.

New Manager's Questions

Please circle your opinion below each of the following statements.

1 When a manager makes a well-reasoned decision, the next course of action is implementation.

MOSTLY YES < < <   > > > MOSTLY NO

1	2	3	4	5

2 It is almost always better to get full agreement from others when making a decision.

MOSTLY YES < < <   > > > MOSTLY NO

1	2	3	4	5

3 The increased technology in the workplace keeps people too disconnected from one another, making it harder to get their jobs done.

MOSTLY YES < < <   > > > MOSTLY NO

1	2	3	4	5

Managers often are referred to as *decision makers*, and every organization grows, prospers, or fails as a result of decisions by its managers. Many manager decisions are strategic, such as whether to build a new factory, move into a new line of business, or sell off a division. Yet managers also make decisions about every other aspect of an organization, including structure, control systems, responses to the environment, and human resources. Managers scout for problems, make decisions for solving them, and monitor the consequences to see whether additional decisions are required. Good decision making is a vital part of good management because decisions determine how the organization solves its problems, allocates resources, and accomplishes its goals.

The business world is full of evidence of both good and bad decisions. Apple, which seemed all but dead in the mid-1990s, became the world's most admired company in 2008 based on decisions made by chief executive officer (CEO) Steve Jobs and other top managers. No longer just a maker of computers, Apple is now in the music player business, the cell phone business, and the retailing business, among others. iTunes is now the second-largest seller of music behind Walmart.[1] Cadillac's sales made a comeback after managers ditched stuffy golf and yachting sponsorships and instead tied in with top Hollywood movies.[2] On the other hand, Maytag's decision to introduce the Neptune Drying Center was a complete flop. The new $1,200 product was hyped as a breakthrough in laundry, but the six-foot-tall Drying Center wouldn't fit into most people's existing laundry rooms. Or consider the decision of Timex managers to replace the classic tag line "It takes a licking and keeps on ticking" with the bland "Life is ticking." The desire to modernize their company's image led Timex managers to ditch one of the most recognizable advertising slogans in the world in favor of a lame and rather depressing new one.[3] Decision making is not easy. It must be done amid ever-changing factors, unclear information, and conflicting points of view.

Chapter 5 described strategic planning. This chapter explores the decision process that underlies strategic planning. Plans and strategies are arrived at through decision making; the better the decision making, the better the strategic planning. First, we examine decision characteristics. Then we look at decision-making models and the steps executives should take when making important decisions. The chapter also explores some biases that can cause managers to make bad decisions and some techniques for innovative group decision making. Later in the chapter we will explore the management of information technology and e-business. We begin by developing a basic understanding of information technology and the types of information systems frequently used in organizations. Then the chapter will look at the growing use of the Internet and e-business, including a discussion of fundamental e-business strategies, business-to-business marketplaces, use of information technology in business operations, and the importance of knowledge management.

Types of Decisions and Problems

A **decision** is a choice made from available alternatives. For example, an accounting manager's selection among Colin, Tasha, and Carlos for the position of junior auditor is a decision. Many people assume that making a choice is the major part of decision making, but it is only a part.

Decision making is the process of identifying problems and opportunities and then resolving them. Decision making involves effort both before and after the actual choice. Thus, the decision as to whether to select Colin, Tasha, or Carlos requires the accounting manager to ascertain whether a new junior auditor is needed, determine the availability of potential job candidates, interview candidates to acquire necessary information, select one candidate, and follow up with the socialization of the new employee into the organization to ensure the decision's success.

decision
A choice made from available alternatives.

decision making
The process of identifying problems and opportunities and then resolving them.

PROGRAMMED AND NONPROGRAMMED DECISIONS

Management decisions typically fall into one of two categories: programmed and nonprogrammed. **Programmed decisions** involve situations that have occurred often enough to enable decision rules to be developed and applied in the future.[4] Programmed decisions are made in response to recurring organizational problems. The decision to reorder paper and other office supplies when inventories drop to a certain level is a programmed decision. Other programmed decisions concern the types of skills required to fill certain jobs, the reorder point for manufacturing inventory, exception reporting for expenditures 10 percent or more over budget, and selection of freight routes for product deliveries. Once managers formulate decision rules, subordinates and others can make the decision, freeing managers for other tasks.

Nonprogrammed decisions are made in response to situations that are unique, poorly defined, and largely unstructured and that have important consequences for the organization. Many nonprogrammed decisions involve strategic planning because uncertainty is great and decisions are complex. Decisions to build a new factory, develop a new product or service, enter a new geographical market, or relocate headquarters to another city are all nonprogrammed decisions. One good example of a nonprogrammed decision is ExxonMobil's decision to form a consortium to drill for oil in Siberia. One of the largest foreign investments in Russia, the consortium committed $4.5 billion before pumping the first barrel and expects a total capital cost of more than $12 billion. The venture could produce 250,000 barrels a day, about 10 percent of ExxonMobil's global production. But if things go wrong, the oil giant will take a crippling hit. Orin Wolf entered into uncharted waters starting a new business on an unknown path, and he was therefore faced with many nonprogrammed decisions, as described in the Spotlight on Skills box on page 176.

FACING CERTAINTY AND UNCERTAINTY

One primary difference between programmed and nonprogrammed decisions relates to the degree of certainty or uncertainty that managers deal with in making the decision. In a perfect world, managers would have all the information necessary for making decisions. In reality, however, some things are unknowable; thus, some decisions will fail to solve the problem or attain the desired outcome. Managers try to obtain information about decision alternatives that will reduce decision uncertainty. Every decision situation can be organized on a scale according to the availability of information and the possibility of failure. The four positions on the scale are certainty, risk, uncertainty, and ambiguity, as illustrated in Exhibit 6.1. Whereas programmed decisions can be made in situations involving certainty,

If you have a decision to make that is repeated periodically, figure out how long the average time between decisions is and then enter a "to do" reminder in your calendar or personal digital assistant.

programmed decision
A decision made in response to a situation that has occurred often enough to enable decision rules to be developed and applied in the future.

nonprogrammed decision
A decision made in response to a situation that is unique, is poorly defined and largely unstructured, and has important consequences for the organization.

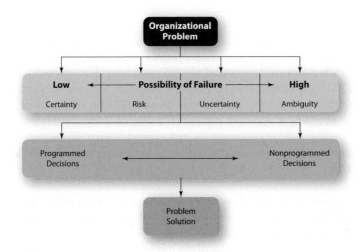

EXHIBIT 6.1

Conditions That Affect the Possibility of Decision Failure

SPOTLIGHT ON SKILLS

Off Broadway Booking, Inc.

Orin Wolf was a guy in his 20s who was trying to make a living in theater, first working in various jobs, and then moving up into management for some producers. He fell in love with selling tickets through alternative means. With one of his first shows, *Godfather Workout*, which was a one-man digest version of all the Godfather movies, he developed a partnership with Crunch Gym, which gave—you guessed it—"The Godfadda Workout." It didn't cost any money because Wolf and the gym did cross-promotion. He would also approach Macy's and organize promotional performances in its lobby and send bookmarks to every bookstore in the tri-state area (New York, New Jersey, and Connecticut). In such cases, he'd offer free tickets to employees.

After working for several years with producer Eric Krebs—often called the "father of off Broadway"—Wolf realized he wanted to use his talents and motivation to give some relief to the financially beleaguered off-Broadway community. But how? He went to Krebs and said, "I want to be a booking agency. And what if we are bold enough to call it 'Off Broadway Booking'?" Krebs was very supportive, helping Wolf secure two rounds of financing. The real work, though, was ahead. No one had ever started a business quite like this, which meant Wolf had to clear new ground and figure out how to become profitable. Wolf had to talk to a lot of people, theater owners, producers, and other bookers, trying to find a winning formula. During his countrywide travels, he discovered old vaudeville houses, built in the 1920s and 1930s, many of them now

designated as landmarks, that could not afford the big Broadway shows and weren't able to compete with the newer arenas where shows such as *Wicked* and *Jersey Boys* played. Maybe that was the route to take, connecting virtually abandoned houses with thirsty producers and audiences. Still, he needed someone who had an organization to get this off the ground.

Enter Will Prather, whose parents had built a dinner-theater company in several locations. Prather wanted to branch out and was intrigued with Wolf's idea. Their first show was a successful tour of *Beehive*, which was followed by *Footloose*. Finally, Wolf had a structure that worked. And it kept working through more tours, including *Wedding Singer*, and with more and more producers, to the point where Off Broadway Booking does about 200 contracts a year.

Though now in a decent office, Wolf started out alone, with one partner, working out of his office back in 2005. Since then, he's added several producing partners, including an attorney and an office manager. Economic downturn? Not a problem, says Wolf, as long as they continue to partner with creators and to provide quality. Part of Wolf's continued success no doubt is a result of his ability to make decisions under unusual circumstances. As Krebs remarked, "Orin is very, very smart and is extremely far-ranging in his thinking on where things can go. Plus he works harder than almost anyone else." A good combination.

SOURCES: Orin Wolf, personal communication, April 2009; Eric Krebs, personal communication, May 2009.

---

many situations that managers deal with every day involve at least some degree of uncertainty and require nonprogrammed decision making.

Certainty. Certainty means that all the information the decision maker needs is fully available.[5] Managers have information on operating conditions, resource costs or constraints, and each course of action and possible outcome. For example, if a company considers a $10,000 investment in new equipment that it knows for certain will yield $4,000 in cost savings per year over the next five years, then managers can calculate a before-tax rate of return of about 40 percent. If managers compare this investment with one that will yield only $3,000 per year in cost savings, then they can confidently select the 40-percent return. However, few decisions are certain in the real world. Most contain risk or uncertainty.

certainty
The situation in which all the information the decision maker needs is fully available.

risk
A situation in which a decision has clear-cut goals and good information is available but the future outcomes associated with each alternative are subject to chance.

Risk. Risk means that a decision has clear-cut goals and that good information is available, but the future outcomes associated with each alternative are subject to chance. However, enough information is available to allow the probability of a successful outcome for each alternative to be estimated.[6] Statistical analysis might be used to calculate the probabilities of success or failure. The measure of risk captures the possibility that future events will render the alternative unsuccessful. For example, to make restaurant location decisions, McDonald's can analyze potential customer demographics, traffic patterns, supply logistics, and the local competition and come up with reasonably good forecasts of how successful a restaurant will be in each possible location.[7]

Uncertainty. Uncertainty means that managers know which goals they wish to achieve, but information about alternatives and future events is incomplete. Factors that may affect a decision such as price, production costs, volume, or future interest rates are difficult to analyze and predict. Managers may have to make assumptions from which to forge the decision even though it will be wrong if the assumptions are incorrect. Former U.S. Treasury Secretary Robert Rubin defined uncertainty as a situation in which even a good decision might produce a bad outcome.[8] Managers face uncertainty every day. Many problems have no clear-cut solution, but managers rely on creativity, judgment, intuition, and experience to craft a response.

Former NBA Lakers player Magic Johnson is known as a sports star, but he's also a smart businessman. Johnson opened his first 12-screen cinema in south central Los Angeles while he was still a Lakers player. Despite the uncertainty involved in opening businesses in long-ignored urban communities, Johnson established Magic Johnson Enterprises to bring entertainment options and jobs to these areas. Today, the company owns or operates numerous Starbucks, AMC Magic Johnson Theater complexes, Burger Kings, T.G.I. Friday's, 24 Hour Fitness Magic Sport centers, and SodexhoMAGIC in underserved communities.

> CONCEPT CONNECTION <

Ambiguity and Conflict. Ambiguity is by far the most difficult decision situation. Ambiguity means that the goals to be achieved or the problem to be solved is unclear, alternatives are difficult to define, and information about outcomes is unavailable.[9] Ambiguity is what students would feel if an instructor created student groups, told each group to complete a project, but gave the groups no topic, direction, or guidelines whatsoever. In some situations, managers involved in a decision create ambiguity because they see things differently and disagree about what they want. Managers in different departments often have different priorities and goals for the decision, which can lead to conflicts over decision alternatives. For example, at Rockford Health Services, the decision about implementing a new self-service benefits system wasn't clear-cut. Human-resources (HR) managers wanted the system, which would allow employees to manage their own benefits and free up HR employees for more strategic activities, but the high cost of the software licenses conflicted with finance managers' goals of controlling costs. In addition, if HR got the new system, it meant managers in other departments might not get their projects approved.[10]

A highly ambiguous situation can create what is sometimes called a *wicked decision problem*. Wicked decisions are associated with conflicts over goals and decision alternatives, rapidly changing circumstances, fuzzy information, and unclear links among decision elements.[11] Sometimes managers will come up with a "solution" only to realize that they hadn't clearly defined the real problem to begin with.[12] Managers have a difficult time coming to grips with the issues and must conjure up reasonable scenarios in the absence of clear information.

As a new manager, develop decision rules for programmed decisions and let other people handle the decisions. Save your time and energy for coping with complex, nonprogrammed decisions.

Decision-Making Models

The approach managers use to make decisions usually falls into one of three types—the classical model, the administrative model, or the political model. The choice of model depends on the manager's personal preference, whether the decision is programmed or nonprogrammed, and the degree of uncertainty associated with the decision.

uncertainty
The situation that occurs when managers know which goals they wish to achieve, but information about alternatives and future events is incomplete.

ambiguity
A condition in which the goals to be achieved or the problem to be solved is unclear, alternatives are difficult to define, and information about outcomes is unavailable.

When faced with a difficult and ambiguous decision, develop a "worst-case scenario" for each of the possible choices to help you determine which course of action you want to do.

THE IDEAL, RATIONAL MODEL

The **classical model** of decision making is based on rational economic assumptions and manager beliefs about what ideal decision making should be. This model has arisen within the management literature because managers are expected to make decisions that are economically sensible and in the organization's best economic interests. The four assumptions underlying this model are as follows:

1. The decision maker operates to accomplish goals that are known and agreed on. Problems are precisely formulated and defined.

2. The decision maker strives for conditions of certainty and gathers complete information. All alternatives and the potential results of each are calculated.

3. Criteria for evaluating alternatives are known. The decision maker selects the alternative that will maximize the economic return to the organization.

4. The decision maker is rational and uses logic to assign values, order preferences, evaluate alternatives, and make the decision that will maximize the attainment of organizational goals.

classical model
A decision-making model based on the assumption that managers should make logical decisions that will be in the organization's best economic interests.

normative
An approach that defines how a decision maker should make decisions and provides guidelines for reaching an ideal outcome for the organization.

administrative model
A decision-making model that describes how managers actually make decisions in situations characterized by nonprogrammed decisions, uncertainty, and ambiguity.

The classical model of decision making is considered to be **normative**, which means it defines how a decision maker *should* make decisions. It does not describe how managers actually make decisions so much as it provides guidelines on how to reach an ideal outcome for the organization. The ideal, rational approach of the classical model is often unattainable by real people in real organizations, but the model has value because it helps decision makers be more rational and not rely entirely on personal preference in making decisions.

The classical model is most useful when applied to programmed decisions and to decisions characterized by certainty or risk because relevant information is available and probabilities can be calculated. For example, new analytical software programs automate many programmed decisions such as freezing the account of a customer who has failed to make payments, determining the cell phone service plan that is most appropriate for a particular customer, or sorting insurance claims so that cases are handled most efficiently.[13] Airlines use automated systems to optimize decisions about seat pricing, flight scheduling, and crew assignments. Retailers such as the Home Depot and Gap use software programs to analyze sales data and decide when, where, and how much to mark down prices. Many companies use systems that capture information about customers to help managers evaluate risks and make credit decisions.[14]

The growth of quantitative decision techniques that use computers has expanded the use of the classical approach. Quantitative techniques include such things as decision trees, payoff matrices, breakeven analysis, linear programming, forecasting, and operations research models. Southwest Airlines uses quantitative models to help retain its position as the industry's low-cost leader.

SOUTHWEST AIRLINES

Southwest's wacky, people-oriented culture has often been cited as a key factor in the company's success. But managers point out that keeping a hawk's eye on costs is just as much a part of the culture as silliness and fun.

One way managers keep a lid on costs is by applying technology to support decision making. Consider the use of a new breed of simulation software to help make decisions about the airline's freight operations. BiosGroup, a joint venture between Santa Fe Institute biologist Stuart Kauffman and the consulting firm Cap Gemini Ernst & Young, uses adaptive, agent-based computer modeling to help companies solve complex operations problems. For the Southwest project, the computer simulation model represented individual baggage handlers and other employees; the model was created to see how thousands of individual day-to-day decisions and interactions determined the behavior of the airline's overall freight operation.

A BiosGroup team spent many hours interviewing all the employees whose jobs related to freight handling. Then the team programmed the computer to simulate the people in the freight house who accepted a customer's package, those who figured out which flight the package should go on, those on the ramp who were loading the planes, and so forth. When the computer ran a simulation of a week's worth of freight operations, various aspects of operations were measured—such as how many times employees had to load and unload cargo or how often freight had to be stored overnight. The simulation indicated that, rather than unloading cargo from incoming flights and putting it on the next direct flight to its destination, Southwest would be better off to just let the freight take the long way around. Paradoxically, this approach turned out to usually get the freight to its destination faster and saved the time and cost of unloading and reloading.

Southwest managers lost no time in implementing the decision to change the freight-handling system. By applying technology to find a more efficient way of doing things, Southwest is saving an estimated $10 million over 5 years.[15]

HOW MANAGERS ACTUALLY MAKE DECISIONS

Another approach to decision making, called the **administrative model**, is considered to be **descriptive**, meaning that it describes how managers actually make decisions in complex situations rather than dictating how they *should* make decisions according to a theoretical ideal. The administrative model recognizes the human and environmental limitations that affect the degree to which managers can pursue a rational decision-making process. In difficult situations such as those characterized by nonprogrammed decisions, uncertainty, and ambiguity, managers are typically unable to make economically rational decisions even if they want to.[16]

Bounded Rationality and Satisficing. The administrative model of decision making is based on the work of Herbert A. Simon, who proposed two concepts that were instrumental in shaping the administrative model: bounded rationality and satisficing. **Bounded rationality** means that people have limits, or boundaries, on how rational they can be. The organization is incredibly complex, and managers have the time and ability to process only a limited amount of information with which to make decisions.[17] Because managers do not have the time or cognitive ability to process complete information about complex decisions, they must *satisfice*. **Satisficing** means that decision makers choose the first solution alternative that satisfies minimal decision criteria. Rather than pursuing all alternatives to identify the single solution that will maximize economic returns, managers will opt for the first solution that appears to solve the problem even if better solutions are presumed to exist. The decision maker cannot justify the time and expense of obtaining complete information.[18]

descriptive
An approach that describes how managers actually make decisions rather than how they should make decisions according to a theoretical ideal.

bounded rationality
The concept that people have the time and cognitive ability to process only a limited amount of information on which to base decisions.

satisficing
To choose the first solution alternative that satisfies minimal decision criteria, regardless of whether better solutions are presumed to exist.

BUSINESS BLOOPER

Northern Trust and Merrill Lynch

Consider the decision-making process taken here: After finance company Northern Trust of Chicago was given $1.5 billion in government bailout money, it proceeded to lay off 450 workers and then flew hundreds of clients and employees to Los Angeles, where they stayed in posh hotel rooms, dined on filet mignon, attended the PGA tournament and music concerts, and were given Tiffany swag bags. The PGA said "Northern No Trust" wrote one big and fat check to sponsor the event. A dinner at the Ritz Carlton cost $100,000, followed by a private concert by Chicago, and then the next day another expensive dinner with music by Earth, Wind & Fire and then a $50,000 trip to House of Blues. But maybe, just maybe, John Thain of Merrill Lynch outdid them by clandestinely shoving through $3.6 billion in bonuses at the very time his company was nearly insolvent and only saved from collapse by Bank of America and its $45-million bailout. It's good to know, though, where our tax dollars go.

SOURCE: Maureen Dowd, "I Ponied Up for Sheryl Crow?" *New York Times*, Feb. 25, 2009, p. A27..

Remember to choose the right decision approach. Use the classical model when problems are clear-cut, goals are agreed on, and clear information is available. For the classical model, use analytical procedures, including new software programs, to calculate the potential results of each alternative. When goals are vague or conflicting, decision time is limited, and information is unclear, use bounded rationality, satisficing, and intuition for decision making.

Managers sometimes generate alternatives for complex problems only until they find one they believe will work. For example, several years ago, then-CEO William Smithburg of Quaker attempted to thwart takeover attempts but had limited options. He satisficed with a quick decision to acquire Snapple, thinking he could use the debt acquired in the deal to discourage a takeover. The acquisition had the potential to solve the problem at hand; thus, Smithburg looked no further for possibly better alternatives.[19]

The administrative model relies on assumptions different from those of the classical model and focuses on organizational factors that influence individual decisions. According to the administrative model:

1. Decision goals often are vague, conflicting, and lack consensus among managers. Managers often are unaware of problems or opportunities that exist in the organization.

2. Rational procedures are not always used; when they are, they are confined to a simplistic view of the problem that does not capture the complexity of real organizational events.

3. Managers' searches for alternatives are limited because of human, information, and resource constraints.

4. Most managers settle for a satisficing rather than a maximizing solution, partly because they have limited information and partly because they have only vague criteria for what constitutes a maximizing solution.

Intuition. Another aspect of administrative decision making is intuition. **Intuition** represents a quick apprehension of a decision situation based on past experience but without conscious thought.[20] Intuitive decision making is not arbitrary or irrational because it is based on years of practice and hands-on experience that enable managers to quickly identify solutions without going through painstaking computations. In today's fast-paced business environment, intuition plays an increasingly important role in decision making. A survey of managers conducted by Christian and Timbers found that nearly half of executives say they rely more on intuition than on rational analysis to run their companies.[21]

Psychologists and neuroscientists have studied how people make good decisions using their intuition under extreme time pressure and uncertainty.[22] Good intuitive decision making is based on an ability to recognize patterns at lightning speed. When people have a depth of experience and knowledge in a particular area, the right decision often comes quickly and effortlessly as a recognition of information that has been largely forgotten by the conscious mind. For example, firefighters make decisions by recognizing what is typical or abnormal about a fire, based on their experiences. Similarly, in the business world, managers continuously perceive and process information that they may not consciously be aware of, and their base of knowledge and experience helps them make decisions that may be characterized by uncertainty and ambiguity. Some psychologists argue for intuition, as shown below.

intuition
The immediate comprehension of a decision situation based on past experience but without conscious thought.

WILDLAND FIREFIGHTERS

If you ever fall from a highway overpass onto the metal struts of a sign, just hope you get rescue workers who practice good decision making on the spot. In such a case, the wrong kind of rescue gear, even a seemingly good position for the victim, can spell disaster. Traditional thinking argues that the rescue worker should carefully consider the many options available. Unfortunately, these situations don't allow for the luxury of decision analysis. According to cognitive psychologist Gary Klein, only novices need to be burdened by the practice of evaluating every possible course of action. Experienced workers know the various consequences so well that they intuitively make the right choice.

Klein's best decision makers are wildland firefighters who work in the western United States as well as in Australia and New Zealand and are constantly putting out scorching fires. In doing so, they build a rich reservoir of experience from which to draw. Obsessive about learning from experience, they always do after-action reviews to see what could have been done better. As for leadership, the top people started at the bottom, so they know what it means to be in the midst of a killer fire. One fire commander claimed he had ESP. During a raging house fire, he ordered the hose team into the house, but the fire blazed on, baffling the commander with its persistence. Then his so-called sixth sense kicked in and he suddenly ordered everyone out of the house. Just as they vacated, the house collapsed. Rather than ESP, Klein says the commander's experience made him see that the fire was not matching his expectations. The fire was burning through the floor, so the sound was more quiet than usual and it was hotter than normal, indicating other more treacherous conditions. Similarly, air-traffic controllers shepherd 40-some planes at a time, each at a different altitude and each on a different route and at a different speed, and the controllers need to make quick, intuitive decisions. "Someone might ask, 'Why did you tell that guy to turn?'" says Memphis controller Peter Nesbitt, "and I might have to think about it for a moment." He gave the right directions but has to ponder why he did so.

What can companies learn from this? Decision making in times of uncertainty, risk, and time pressure requires experience, which allows the person to look for clues or patterns to help guide the course of action. Not all psychologists agree with Klein, but Malcolm Gladwell's book *Blink* says much the same thing. Basically, Klein and Gladwell would likely say that intuition is the ability to size up a situation quickly. Novices need the decision-making models, but real experience is the best teacher. [23]

However, intuitive decisions don't always work out, and managers should take care to apply intuition under the right circumstances and in the right way rather than considering it a magical way to make important decisions.[24] Managers may walk a fine line between two extremes: on the one hand, making arbitrary decisions without careful study; on the other hand, relying obsessively on rational analysis. One is not better than the other, and managers need to take a balanced approach by considering both rationality and intuition as important components of effective decision making.[25]

New managers typically use a different decision behavior than seasoned executives. The decision behavior of a successful CEO may be almost the opposite of a first-level supervisor. The difference is due partly to the types of decisions and partly to learning what works at each level. New managers often start out with a more directive, decisive, command-oriented behavior and gradually move toward more openness, acceptance of diverse viewpoints, and interactions with others as they move up the hierarchy.[26]

THE POLITICAL MODEL

The third model of decision making is useful for making nonprogrammed decisions when conditions are uncertain, information is limited, and there are manager conflicts about what goals to pursue or what course of action to take. Most organizational decisions involve many managers who are pursuing different goals, and they have to talk with one another to share information and reach an agreement. Managers often engage in coalition building when making complex organizational decisions. A **coalition** is an informal alliance among managers who support a specific goal. *Coalition building* is the process of forming alliances among managers. In other words, a manager who supports a specific alternative, such as increasing the corporation's growth by acquiring another company, talks informally to other executives and tries to persuade them to support the decision. Without a coalition, a powerful individual or group could derail the decision-making process. Coalition building gives several managers an opportunity to contribute to decision making, enhancing their commitment to the alternative that is ultimately adopted.[27]

The political model closely resembles the real environment in which most managers and decision makers operate. For example, interviews with CEOs in high-tech industries found that they strived to use some type of rational process in making decisions, but the way they actually decided things was through a complex interaction with other managers,

Do you tend to decide quickly or seek input from others when it comes to making an important decision? Complete the following New Manager's Self-Test on page 182 to find out your predominant approach.

Practice collaborating and developing alliances, because good ideas are not enough—you will need to build coalitions.

coalition
An informal alliance among managers who support a specific goal.

NEW MANAGER'S SELF-TEST

How Do You Make Decisions?

Most of us make decisions automatically and without realizing that people have diverse decision-making behaviors that they bring to management positions. Think back to how you make decisions in your personal, student, or work life, especially where other people are involved. Please answer whether each of the following items is Mostly True or Mostly False for you.

	MOSTLY TRUE	MOSTLY FALSE
1. I like to decide quickly and move on to the next thing.	_____	_____
2. I would use my authority to make the decision if certain I was right.	_____	_____
3. I appreciate decisiveness.	_____	_____
4. There is usually one correct solution to a problem.	_____	_____
5. I identify everyone who needs to be involved in the decision.	_____	_____
6. I explicitly seek conflicting perspectives.	_____	_____
7. I use discussion strategies to reach a solution.	_____	_____
8. I look for different meanings when faced with a great deal of data.	_____	_____
9. I take time to reason things through and use systematic logic.	_____	_____

SCORING AND INTERPRETATION: All nine items in the list reflect appropriate decision-making behavior, but items 1–4 are more typical of new managers. Items 5–8 are typical of successful senior manager decision making. Item 9 is considered part of good decision making at all levels. If you checked Mostly True for three or four of items 1–4 and 9, then consider yourself typical of a new manager. If you checked Mostly True for three or four of items 5–8 and 9, then you are using behavior consistent with top managers. If you checked a similar number of both sets of items, then your behavior is probably flexible and balanced.

subordinates, environmental factors, and organizational events.[28] Decisions are complex and involve many people, information is often ambiguous, and disagreement and conflict over problems and solutions are normal. The political model begins with four basic assumptions:

1. Organizations are made up of groups with diverse interests, goals, and values. Managers disagree about problem priorities and may not understand or share the goals and interests of other managers.

Assess Your Answer

1 When a manager makes a well-reasoned decision, the next course of action is implementation.

ANSWER: One of the most common mistakes is for a manager to move ahead on a course of action without getting support from colleagues and subordinates. It is usually necessary to build a coalition before implementation.

Classical Model	Administrative Model	Political Model
Clear-cut problem and goals	Vague problem and goals	Pluralistic; conflicting goals
Condition of certainty	Condition of uncertainty	Condition of uncertainty or ambiguity
Full information about alternatives and their outcomes	Limited information about alternatives and their outcomes	Inconsistent viewpoints; ambiguous information
Rational choice by individual for maximizing outcomes	Satisficing choice for resolving problem using intuition	Bargaining and discussion among coalition members

EXHIBIT 6.2

Characteristics of the Classical, Administrative, and Political Decision-Making Models

2. Information is ambiguous and incomplete. The attempt to be rational is limited by the complexity of many problems as well as by personal and organizational constraints.

3. Managers do not have the time, resources, or mental capacity to identify all dimensions of the problem and process all relevant information. Managers talk to each other and exchange viewpoints to gather information and reduce ambiguity.

4. Managers engage in the push and pull of debate to decide goals and discuss alternatives. Decisions are the result of bargaining and discussion among coalition members.

An example of the political model was when AOL chief executive Jonathan Miller built a coalition to support the development of a Yahoo-like free Web site. Opposition to offering AOL's rich content for free was strong, but Miller talked with other executives and formed a coalition that supported the move as the best way to rejuvenate the declining AOL in the shifting Internet service business. The decision proved to be a turning point, making AOL once more a relevant force on the Web and enticing tech titans such as Google and Microsoft as potential partners.[29]

The key dimensions of the classical, administrative, and political models are listed in Exhibit 6.2. Research into decision-making procedures found rational, classical procedures to be associated with high performance for organizations in stable environments. However, administrative and political decision-making procedures and intuition have been associated with high performance in unstable environments in which decisions must be made rapidly and under more difficult conditions.[30]

Decision-Making Steps

Whether a decision is programmed or nonprogrammed and regardless of managers' choice of the classical, administrative, or political model of decision making, six steps typically are associated with effective decision processes. These steps are summarized in Exhibit 6.3.

RECOGNITION OF DECISION REQUIREMENT

Managers confront a decision requirement in the form of either a problem or an opportunity. A **problem** occurs when organizational accomplishment is less than established goals. Some aspect of performance is unsatisfactory. An **opportunity** exists when managers see potential accomplishment that exceeds specified current goals. Managers see the possibility of enhancing performance beyond current levels.

Awareness of a problem or opportunity is the first step in the decision sequence and requires surveillance of the internal and external environment for issues that merit executive

As a new manager, use your political skills to reach a decision in the midst of disagreement about goals or problem solutions. Talk with other managers or employees and negotiate to gain support for the goal or solution you favor. Learn to compromise and to support others when appropriate.

Train your mind to analyze problems; in your own situation, practice diagnosing your own problems.

problem
A situation in which organizational accomplishments have failed to meet established goals.

opportunity
A situation in which managers see potential organizational accomplishments that exceed current goals.

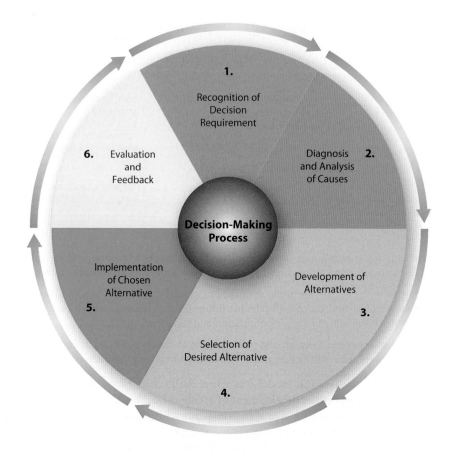

attention.[31] This process resembles the military concept of gathering intelligence. Managers scan the world around them to determine whether the organization is satisfactorily progressing toward its goals.

Some information comes from periodic financial reports, performance reports, and other sources that are designed to discover problems before they become too serious. Managers also take advantage of informal sources. They talk to other managers, gather opinions on how things are going, and seek advice on which problems should be tackled or which opportunities embraced.[32] Recognizing decision requirements is difficult because it often means integrating bits and pieces of information in novel ways. For example, the failure of U.S. intelligence leaders to recognize the imminent threat of al Qaeda prior to September 11, 2001, terrorist attacks has been attributed partly to the lack of systems that could help leaders put together myriad snippets of information that pointed to the problem.[33]

DIAGNOSIS AND ANALYSIS OF CAUSES

Once a problem or opportunity comes to a manager's attention, the understanding of the situation should be refined. **Diagnosis** is the step in the decision-making process in which managers analyze underlying causal factors associated with the decision situation.

Kepner and Tregoe, who conducted extensive studies of manager decision making, recommend that managers ask a series of questions to specify underlying causes, including the following:

- What is the state of disequilibrium affecting us?
- When did it occur?
- Where did it occur?

diagnosis
The step in the decision-making process in which managers analyze underlying causal factors associated with the decision situation.

- How did it occur?

- To whom did it occur?

- What is the urgency of the problem?

- What is the interconnectedness of events?

- What result came from which activity?[34]

Such questions help specify what actually happened and why. Managers at Avon are struggling to diagnose the underlying factors in the company's recent troubles. After six straight years of growing sales and earnings, revenues sagged, overhead spiked, and the stock price plummeted. CEO Andrea Jung and other top managers are examining the myriad problems facing Avon, tracing the pattern of the decline and looking at the interconnectedness of issues such as changing consumer interests, tight government regulations in developing countries, decreases in incentives for direct-sales representatives, handling manufacturing and marketing in each country independently, preventing the company from achieving economies of scale, and weak internal communications that allowed problems to go unnoticed.[35]

DEVELOPMENT OF ALTERNATIVES

The next stage is to generate possible alternative solutions that will respond to the needs of the situation and correct the underlying causes.

For a programmed decision, feasible alternatives are easy to identify and in fact usually are already available within the organization's rules and procedures. Nonprogrammed decisions, however, require developing new courses of action that will meet the company's needs. For decisions made under conditions of high uncertainty, managers may develop only one or two custom solutions that will satisfice for handling the problem. However, studies find that limiting the search for alternatives is a primary cause of decision failure in organizations.[36]

Always come up with several options to solve problems so that you can reasonably choose from among them.

Decision alternatives can be thought of as tools for reducing the difference between the organization's current and desired performance. For example, to improve sales at fast-food giant McDonald's, executives considered alternatives such as using mystery shoppers and unannounced inspections to improve quality and service, motivating demoralized franchisees to get them to invest in new equipment and programs, taking research and development out of the test kitchen and encouraging franchisees to help come up with successful new menu items, and closing some stores to avoid cannibalizing its own sales.[37]

SELECTION OF DESIRED ALTERNATIVE

Once feasible alternatives are developed, one must be selected. The decision choice is the selection of the most promising of several alternative courses of action. The best alternative is one in which the solution best fits the overall goals and values of the organization and achieves the desired results using the fewest resources.[38] The manager tries to select the choice with the least amount of risk and uncertainty. Because some risk is inherent for most nonprogrammed decisions, managers try to gauge prospects for success. They might rely on their intuition and experience to estimate whether a given course of action is likely to succeed. Basing choices on overall goals and values can also effectively guide managers' selection of alternatives. Recall from Chapter 2 that Valero Energy' decided to keep everyone on the payroll after Hurricane Katrina hit the Gulf Coast while other refineries shut down and laid off workers. For Valero managers, the choice was easy based on values of putting employees first. Valero's values-based decision making helped the company zoom from number 23 to number 3 on *Fortune* magazine's list of best companies to work for—and enabled Valero to get back to business weeks faster than competitors.[39]

EXHIBIT 6.4

Decision Alternatives
with Different Levels
of Risk

FOR EACH OF THE FOLLOWING DECISIONS, WHICH ALTERNATIVE WOULD YOU CHOOSE?

1. In the final seconds of a game with the college's traditional rival, the coach of a college football team may choose a play that has a 95-percent chance of producing a tie score or one with a 30-percent chance of leading to victory or to sure defeat if it fails.

2. The president of a Canadian company must decide whether to build a new plant within Canada that has a 90-percent chance of producing a modest return on investment or to build it in a foreign country with an unstable political history. The latter alternative has a 40-percent chance of failing, but the returns would be enormous if it succeeded.

3. A college senior with considerable acting talent must choose a career. She has the opportunity to go on to medical school and become a physician, a career in which she is 80 percent likely to succeed. She would rather be an actress but realizes that the opportunity for success is only 20 percent.

risk propensity
The willingness to undertake
risk with the opportunity of
gaining an increased payoff.

implementation
The step in the decision-
making process that
involves using managerial,
administrative, and
persuasive abilities to
translate the chosen
alternative into action.

Choosing among alternatives also depends on managers' personality factors and willingness to accept risk and uncertainty. **Risk propensity** is the willingness to undertake risk with the opportunity of gaining an increased payoff. The level of risk a manager is willing to accept will influence the analysis of cost and benefits to be derived from any decision. Consider the situations in Exhibit 6.4. In each situation, which alternative would you choose? A person with a low risk propensity would tend to take assured moderate returns by going for a tie score, building a domestic plant, or pursuing a career as a physician. A risk taker would go for the victory, build a plant in a foreign country, or embark on an acting career.

You need to secure payment from
a new customer seven time zones away.
Nervous?

UPS knows that many businesses have a low risk propensity when it comes to matters affecting their cash flow. The company's UPS Capital Insurance division reduces customers' risk of delayed payments through a variety of trade insurance policies. This advertisement for Exchange Collect promises peace of mind for companies dealing with international customers or suppliers. The service works like a secure international cash-on-delivery system, with UPS securing payment on behalf of the customer before delivering goods. For UPS customers, the results are improved cash flow and less risk.

IMPLEMENTATION OF CHOSEN ALTERNATIVE

The **implementation** stage involves the use of managerial, administrative, and persuasive abilities to ensure that the chosen alternative is carried out. This step is similar to the idea of strategy execution described in Chapter 5. The ultimate success of the chosen alternative depends on whether it can be translated into action.[40] Sometimes an alternative never becomes reality because managers lack the resources or energy needed to make things happen. Implementation may require discussion with people affected by the decision. Communication, motivation, and leadership skills must be used to see that the decision is carried out. When employees see that managers follow up on their decisions by tracking implementation success, they are more committed to positive action.[41]

EVALUATION AND FEEDBACK

In the evaluation stage of the decision process, decision makers gather information that tells them how well the decision was implemented and whether it was effective in achieving its goals. Feedback is important because decision making is a continuous, never-ending process.

·········▷ **CONCEPT CONNECTION** ◁·········

Decision making is not completed when a manager or board of directors votes yes or no. Feedback provides decision makers with information that can precipitate a new decision cycle. The decision may fail, thus generating a new analysis of the problem, evaluation of alternatives, and selection of a new alternative. Many big problems are solved by trying several alternatives in sequence, each providing modest improvement. Feedback is the part of monitoring that assesses whether a new decision needs to be made.

To illustrate the overall decision-making process, including evaluation and feedback, consider Tom's of Maine's decision to introduce a new deodorant.

When you make a decision, develop the mental discipline to carry it out.

TOM'S OF MAINE

Tom's of Maine, known for its all-natural personal hygiene products, saw an opportunity to expand its line with a new natural deodorant. However, the opportunity quickly became a problem when the deodorant worked only half of the time with half of the customers who used it, and its all-recyclable plastic dials were prone to breakage.

The problem of the failed deodorant led founder Tom Chappell and other managers to analyze and diagnose what went wrong. They finally determined that the company's product development process had run amok. The same group of merry product developers was responsible from conception to launch of the product. They were so attached to the product that they failed to test it properly or consider potential problems, becoming instead "a mutual admiration society." Managers considered several alternatives for solving the problem. The decision to publicly admit the problem and recall the deodorant was an easy one for Chappell, who runs his company on principles of fairness and honesty. The company not only apologized to its customers but also listened to their complaints and suggestions. Chappell himself helped answer calls and letters. Even though the recall cost the company $400,000 and led to a stream of negative publicity, it ultimately helped improve relationships with customers.

Evaluation and feedback also led Tom's of Maine to set up *acorn groups* from which it hopes mighty oaks of successful products will grow. Acorn groups are cross-departmental teams that will shepherd new products from beginning to end. The cross-functional teams are a mechanism for catching problems—and new opportunities—that ordinarily would be missed. They pass on their ideas and findings to senior managers and the product-development team.

Tom's was able to turn a problem into an opportunity, thanks to evaluation and feedback. The disaster not only ultimately helped the company solidify relationships with customers but also led to a formal mechanism for learning and sharing ideas—something the company did not have before.[42]

Tom's of Maine's decision illustrates all the decision steps, and the process ultimately ended in success. Strategic decisions always contain some risk, but feedback and follow-up decisions can help get companies back on track. By learning from their decision mistakes, managers can turn problems into opportunities.

Personal Decision Framework

If something you try fails, do an after-action review to evaluate what went wrong and what you would do differently next time.

Imagine you are a manager at Tom's of Maine, the Boeing Company, a local movie theater, or the public library. How would you go about making important decisions that might shape the future of your department or company? So far we have discussed a number of factors that affect how managers make decisions. For example, decisions may be programmed or nonprogrammed; situations are characterized by various levels of uncertainty; and managers may use the classical, administrative, or political model of decision making. In addition, the decision-making process follows six recognized steps, as shown in Exhibit 6.3.

However, not all managers go about making decisions in the same way. In fact, significant differences distinguish the ways in which individual managers may approach problems and make decisions concerning them. These differences can be explained by the concept of personal **decision styles**. Exhibit 6.5 illustrates the role of personal style in the decision-making process. Personal decision style refers to distinctions among people with respect to how they evaluate problems, generate alternatives, and make choices.

decision styles
Differences among people with respect to how they perceive problems and make decisions.

Situation	Personal Decision Style	Decision Choice
• Programmed/nonprogrammed • Classical, administrative, political • Decision steps	• Directive • Analytical • Conceptual • Behavioral	• Best solution to problem

SOURCES: Based on A. J. Rowe, J. D. Boulgaides, and M. R. McGrath, *Managerial Decision Making* (Chicago: Science Research Associates, 1984); and Alan J. Rowe and Richard O. Mason, *Managing with Style: A Guide to Understanding, Assessing, and Improving Your Decision Making* (San Francisco: Jossey-Bass, 1987).

EXHIBIT 6.5
Personal Decision Framework

Research has identified four major decision styles: directive, analytical, conceptual, and behavioral.[43]

1. The *directive style* is used by people who prefer simple, clear-cut solutions to problems. Managers who use this style often make decisions quickly because they do not like to deal with a lot of information and may consider only one or two alternatives. People who prefer the directive style generally are efficient and rational and prefer to rely on existing rules or procedures for making decisions.

2. Managers with an *analytical style* like to consider complex solutions based on as much data as they can gather. These individuals carefully consider alternatives and often base their decisions on objective, rational data from management control systems and other sources. They search for the best possible decision based on the information available.

Learn what your strengths are as a decision maker, then hire people who are good at the other types of decision making so that you will have a team that thinks about every option.

3. People who tend toward a *conceptual style* also like to consider a broad amount of information. However, they are more socially oriented than those with an analytical style and like to talk to others about the problem and possible alternatives for solving it. Managers using a conceptual style consider many broad alternatives, rely on information from both people and systems, and like to solve problems creatively.

4. The *behavioral style* is often the style adopted by managers having a deep concern for others as individuals. Managers using this style like to talk to people one on one and understand their feelings about the problem and the effect of a given decision on them. People with a behavioral style usually are concerned with the personal development of others and may make decisions that help others achieve their goals.

To learn more about how you rate on these four styles, go to the Self Learning exercise on page 204 that evaluates your personal decision style.

Many managers have a dominant decision style. One example is Jeff Zucker at NBC Entertainment. Zucker uses a primarily conceptual style, which makes him well suited to the television industry. He consults with dozens of programmers about possible new shows and likes to consider many broad alternatives before making decisions.[44] However, managers frequently use several different styles or a combination of styles in making the varied decisions they confront daily. A manager might use a directive style for deciding on which printing company to use for new business cards, yet shift to a more conceptual style when handling an interdepartmental conflict. The most effective managers are able to shift among styles as needed to meet the situation. Being aware of one's dominant decision style can help a manager avoid making critical mistakes when his or her usual style may be inappropriate to the problem at hand.

Why Do Managers Make Bad Decisions?

Managers are faced with a relentless demand for decisions, from solving minor problems to implementing major strategic changes. Even the best manager will make mistakes, but managers can increase their percentage of good decisions by understanding some of the factors that cause people to make bad ones. Most bad decisions are errors in judgment that originate in the human mind's limited capacity and in the natural biases managers display during decision making. Awareness of the following six biases can help managers make more enlightened choices:[45]

1. *Being influenced by initial impressions.* When considering decisions, the mind often gives disproportionate weight to the first information it receives. These initial impressions, statistics, or estimates act as an anchor to our subsequent thoughts and judgments. Anchors can be as simple as a random comment by a colleague or a statistic read in a newspaper. Past events and trends also act as anchors. For example, in business, managers frequently look at the previous year's sales when estimating sales for the coming year. Giving too much weight to the past can lead to poor forecasts and misguided decisions.

2. *Justifying past decisions.* Many managers fall into the trap of making choices that justify their past decisions, even if those decisions no longer seem valid. Consider managers who invest tremendous time and energy into improving the performance of a problem employee whom they now realize should never have been hired in the first place. Another example is when a manager continues to pour money into a failing project, hoping to turn things around. People don't like to make mistakes, so they continue to support a flawed decision in an effort to justify or correct the past.

3. *Seeing what you want to see.* People frequently look for information that supports their existing instinct or point of view and avoid information that contradicts it. This bias affects where managers look for information as well as how they interpret the information they find. People tend to give too much weight to supporting information and too little to information that conflicts with their established viewpoints. It is important for managers to be honest with themselves about their motives and to examine all the evidence with equal rigor. Having a devil's advocate is also a good way to avoid seeing only what you want to see.

4. *Perpetuating the status quo.* Managers may base decisions on what has worked in the past and fail to explore new options, dig for additional information, or investigate new technologies. For example, DuPont clung to its cash cow, nylon, despite growing evidence in the scientific community that a new product, polyester, was superior for tire cords. Celanese, a relatively small competitor, blew DuPont out of the water by exploiting this new evidence, quickly capturing 75 percent of the tire market.

5. *Being influenced by problem framing.* The decision response of a manager can be influenced by the mere wording of a problem. For example, consider a manager faced with a decision about salvaging the cargo of three barges that sank off the coast of Alaska. If managers are given the option of approving plan A, which has a 100-percent chance of saving the cargo of one of the three barges, worth $200,000; or plan B, which has a one-third chance of saving the cargo of all three barges, worth $600,000 and a two-thirds chance of saving nothing, then most managers choose option A. The same problem with a negative frame would give managers a choice of selecting plan C, which has a 100-percent chance of losing two of the three cargoes, worth $400,000; or plan D, which has a two-thirds chance of losing all three cargoes but a one-third chance of losing no cargo. With this framing, most managers choose option D. Because both problems are identical, the decision choice depends strictly on how the problem is framed.

6. *Overconfidence.* Most people overestimate their ability to predict uncertain outcomes. Before making a decision, managers have unrealistic expectations of their ability to understand the risk and make the right choice. Overconfidence is greatest when answering questions of moderate to extreme difficulty. For example, when people are asked to define quantities about which they have little direct knowledge ("What was Walmart's 2007 revenue?" "What was the market value of Google as of March 14, 2008?"), they overestimate their accuracy. Evidence of overconfidence is

As a new manager, be aware of biases that can cloud your judgment and lead to bad decisions. The Spotlight on Skills box on page 190 describes a new way of thinking about decision making that can help you avoid decision traps such as overconfidence, seeing only what you want to see, or justifying past decisions.

© copyright AP images

Facebook founder Mark Zuckerberg stepped into a hole when he decided to retrofit his site with a feature named Beacon. Beacon was designed to pass information about customer Web activity to participating vendors, providing a new source of revenue for Facebook. But when Beacon was implemented, Facebook was slammed with complaints about privacy intrusion and a lawsuit. What caused this poor decision? Based on the wild popularity of his social network site and his rapid rise in the business world, Zuckerberg was probably overly confident about how users would receive Beacon. Facebook management quickly decided to make it easier for customers to opt out of the service.

··········> **CONCEPT CONNECTION** <··

illustrated in cases in which subjects were so certain of an answer that they assigned odds of 1,000 to 1 of being correct but were actually correct only about 85 percent of the time. When uncertainty is high, managers may unrealistically expect that they can successfully predict outcomes and hence select the wrong alternative.

Innovative Group Decision Making

The ability to make fast, widely supported, high-quality decisions on a frequent basis is a critical skill in today's fast-moving organizations.[46] In many industries, the rate of competitive and technological change is so extreme that opportunities are fleeting, clear and complete information is seldom available, and the cost of a slow decision means lost business or even company failure. Do these factors mean managers should make the majority of decisions on their own? No. The rapid pace of the business environment calls for just the opposite—that is, for people throughout the organization to be involved in decision making and have the information, skills, and freedom they need to respond immediately to problems and questions.

SPOTLIGHT ON SKILLS

Evidence-Based Management

At a time when decision making is so important, many managers do not know how to make a good choice from among available alternatives. Using evidence-based decision making can help. Evidence-based decision making simply means a commitment to make more informed and intelligent decisions based on the best available facts and evidence. It means being aware of our biases and seeking and examining evidence with rigor. Managers practice evidence-based decision making by being careful and thoughtful rather than carelessly relying on assumptions, past experience, rules of thumb, or intuition

Here are some ideas for applying evidence-based decision making:

- *Demand Evidence.* Educate people throughout the organization to use data and facts as much as possible to inform their decisions. Many manager problems are uncertain, and hard facts and data aren't available, but by always asking for evidence, managers can avoid relying on faulty assumptions. Managers at one computer company kept blaming the marketing staff for the trouble the company had selling its products in retail stores. Then members of the senior team posed as mystery shoppers and tried to buy the company's computers. They kept encountering salesclerks who tried to dissuade them from purchasing the firm's products, citing the excessive price, clunky appearance, and poor customer service. Real-world observations told the team something that was very different from what it had assumed.

- *Practice the Five Whys.* One simple way to get people to think more broadly and deeply about problems rather than going with a superficial understanding and a first response is called the "Five Whys." For every problem, managers ask "Why?" not just once, but five times. The first *why* generally produces a superficial explanation for the problem, and each subsequent *why* probes deeper into the causes of the problem and potential solutions.

- *Do a Postmortem.* A technique many companies have adopted from the U.S. Army to encourage examination of the evidence and continuous learning is the after-action review. After implementation of any significant decision, managers evaluate what worked, what didn't, and how to do things better. Many problems are solved by trial and error. For example, postmortem reviews of decisions regarding attacks from roadside bombs in Iraq led soldiers to suggest implementation of an overall counterinsurgency strategy rather than relying so much on technology.

- *Balance Decisiveness and Humility.* The best decision makers have a healthy appreciation for what they don't know. They're always questioning and encouraging others to question their knowledge and assumptions. They foster a culture of inquiry, observation, and experimentation.

SOURCES: Based on Jeffrey Pfeffer and Robert I. Sutton, "Evidence-Based Management," *Harvard Business Review* (Jan. 2006): 62–74; Rosemary Stewart, *Evidence-Based Decision Making* (Abingdon, UK: Radcliffe Publishing, 2002); Joshua Klayman, Richard P. Larrick, and Chip Heath, "Organizational Repairs," *Across the Board* (Feb. 2000): 26–31; and Peter Eisler, Blake Morrison, and Tom Vanden Brook, "Strategy That's Making Iraq Safer Was Snubbed for Years," *USA Today*, December 19, 2007, p. A1.

Managers do make some decisions as individuals, but decision makers more often are part of a group. Indeed, major decisions in the business world rarely are made entirely by an individual.

START WITH BRAINSTORMING

Brainstorming uses a face-to-face interactive group to spontaneously suggest a wide range of alternatives for decision making. The keys to effective brainstorming are that people can build on one another's ideas; all ideas are acceptable, no matter how crazy they seem; and criticism and evaluation are not allowed. The goal is to generate as many ideas as possible. Brainstorming has been found to be highly effective for quickly generating a wide range of alternate solutions to a problem, but it does have some drawbacks. For one thing, people in a group often want to conform to what others are saying, a problem sometimes referred to as *groupthink*. Others may be concerned about pleasing the boss or impressing colleagues. In addition, many creative people simply have social inhibitions that limit their participation in a group session or make it difficult to come up with ideas in a group setting. In fact, one study found that when four people are asked to "brainstorm" individually, they typically come up with twice as many ideas as a group of four brainstorming together.

One recent approach, electronic brainstorming, takes advantage of the group approach while overcoming some disadvantages. **Electronic brainstorming**, sometimes called *brainwriting*, brings people together in an interactive group over a computer network.[47] One member writes an idea, another reads it and adds other ideas, and so on. Studies show that electronic brainstorming generates about 40 percent more ideas than individuals brainstorming alone, and 25 percent to 200 percent more ideas than regular brainstorming groups, depending on group size.[48] Why? Because the process is anonymous, the sky's the limit in terms of what people feel free to say. People can write down their ideas immediately, avoiding the possibility that a good idea might slip away while the person is waiting for a chance to speak in a face-to-face group. Social inhibitions and concerns are avoided, which typically allows for a broader range of participation. Another advantage is that electronic brainstorming can potentially be done with groups made up of employees from around the world, further increasing the diversity of alternatives.

ENGAGE IN RIGOROUS DEBATE

An important key to better decision making is to encourage a rigorous debate of the issue at hand.[49] Good managers recognize that constructive conflict based on divergent points of view can bring a problem into focus, clarify people's ideas, stimulate creative thinking, create a broader understanding of issues and alternatives, and improve decision quality.[50] Chuck Knight, the former CEO of Emerson Electric, always sparked heated debates during strategic planning meetings. Knight believed rigorous debate gave people a clearer picture of the competitive landscape and forced managers to look at all sides of an issue, helping them reach better decisions.[51]

Stimulating rigorous debate can be done in several ways. One way is by ensuring that the group is diverse in terms of age and gender, functional area of expertise, hierarchical level, and experience with the business. Some groups assign a **devil's advocate**, who has the role of challenging the assumptions and assertions made by the group.[52] The devil's advocate may force the group to rethink its approach to the problem and avoid reaching premature conclusions. Jeffrey McKeever, CEO of MicroAge, often plays the devil's advocate, changing his position in the middle of a debate to ensure that other executives don't just go along with his opinions.[53]

brainstorming
A technique that uses a face-to-face group to spontaneously suggest a broad range of alternatives for decision making.

electronic brainstorming
Bringing people together in an interactive group over a computer network to suggest alternatives; sometimes called *brainwriting*.

devil's advocate
A decision-making technique in which an individual is assigned the role of challenging the assumptions and assertions made by the group to prevent premature consensus.

Set up meetings in which you encourage diverse points of view.

Another approach is to have group members develop as many alternatives as they can as quickly as they can.[54] It allows the team to work with multiple alternatives and encourages people to advocate ideas they might not prefer simply to encourage debate. Still another way to encourage constructive conflict is to use a technique called **point–counterpoint**, which breaks a decision-making group into two subgroups and assigns them different, often competing responsibilities.[55] The groups then develop and exchange proposals and discuss and debate the various options until they arrive at a common set of understandings and recommendations.

AVOID GROUPTHINK

It is important for managers to remember that some disagreement and conflict is much healthier than blind agreement. Pressures for conformity exist in almost any group, and particularly when people in a group like one another they tend to avoid anything that might create disharmony. **Groupthink** refers to the tendency of people in groups to suppress contrary opinions.[56] When people slip into groupthink, the desire for harmony outweighs concerns over decision quality. Group members emphasize maintaining unity rather than realistically challenging problems and alternatives. People censor their personal opinions and are reluctant to criticize the opinions of others.

Author and scholar Jerry Harvey coined the related term *Abilene paradox* to illustrate the hidden pressures for conformity that can exist in groups.[57] Harvey tells the story of how members of his extended family sat sweltering on the porch in 104-degree heat in a small town about 50 miles from Abilene, Texas. When someone suggested driving to a café in Abilene, everyone went along with the idea, even though the car was not air conditioned. Everyone was miserable and returned home exhausted and irritable. Later, every person admitted that they hadn't wanted to make the trip and thought it was a ridiculous idea. They only went because they thought the others wanted to go.

point–counterpoint
A decision-making technique in which people are assigned to express competing points of view.

groupthink
The tendency of people in groups to suppress contrary opinions.

escalating commitment
Continuing to invest time and resources in a failing decision.

KNOW WHEN TO BAIL

In a fast-paced environment, good managers encourage risk taking and learning from mistakes, but they also aren't hesitant to pull the plug on something that isn't working. Research has found that managers and organizations often continue to invest time and money in a solution despite strong evidence that it is not appropriate. This tendency is referred to as **escalating commitment**. Managers might block or distort negative information because they don't want to be responsible for a bad decision, or they might simply refuse to accept that their solution is wrong. A recent study in Europe verified that even highly successful managers often miss or ignore warning signals because they become committed to a decision and believe if they persevere it will pay off.[58] As companies face increasing competition, complexity, and change, it is important that managers don't get so attached to their own ideas that they're unwilling to recognize when to move on. According to Stanford University professor Robert Sutton, the key to successful creative decision making is to "fail early, fail often, and pull the plug early."[59]

Assess Your Answer

2 It is almost always better to get full agreement from others when making a decision.

ANSWER: It is good to get buy-in from others on your team, but make sure you do so with brainstorming and debate and do not fall into groupthink.

Information Technology Has Transformed Management

Advanced information technology makes just-in-time inventory management work seamlessly, but it has also transformed management in many other ways. An organization's **information technology (IT)** consists of the hardware, software, telecommunications, database management, and other technologies it uses to store data and make them available in the form of information for organizational decision making. In general, information technology has positive implications for the practice of management.

BOUNDARIES DISSOLVE; COLLABORATION REIGNS

Walk into the video conference room at Infosys Technologies, a leader in India's outsourcing and software industry, and the first thing you'll see is a wall-sized flat-screen television. On that screen, Infosys can hold virtual meetings of the key players from its entire global supply chain for any project at any time of the day or night.[60]

Time, distance, and other boundaries between individuals, departments, and organizations are irrelevant in today's business world. Collaboration is what it's all about. Information technology can connect people around the world for the sharing and exchange of information and ideas. As Pulitzer Prize–winning columnist and writer Thomas L. Friedman puts it, "Wherever you look today . . . hierarchies are being flattened and value is being created less and less within vertical silos and more and more through horizontal collaboration within companies, between companies, and among individuals."[61]

KNOWLEDGE MANAGEMENT

Information technology plays a key role in managers' efforts to support and leverage organizational knowledge. **Knowledge management** refers to the efforts to systematically gather knowledge, organize it, make it widely available throughout the organization, and foster a culture of continuous learning and knowledge sharing.[62]

Knowledge is not the same thing as data or information, although it uses both. **Data** are simple, absolute facts and figures that may be of little use in and of themselves. A company might have data that show 30 percent of a particular product is sold to customers in Florida. To be useful to the organization, the data are processed into finished *information* by connecting them with other data—for example, 9 out of 10 of the products sold in Florida are bought by people over the age of 60. **Information** is data that have been linked with other data and converted into a useful context for specific use. **Knowledge** goes a step further; it is a conclusion drawn from the information after it is linked to other information and compared to what is already known. Knowledge, as opposed to information and data, always has a human factor. Books can contain information, but the information becomes knowledge only when a person absorbs it and puts it to use.[63]

IT systems facilitate knowledge management by enabling organizations to collect and store tremendous amounts of data, analyze that data so it can be transformed into information and knowledge, and share knowledge all across the enterprise. The most common organizational approach to knowledge management is sharing knowledge via information technology.[64] A variety of new software tools support collaboration and knowledge sharing through services such as Web conferencing, knowledge portals, content management, and the use of *wikis*. A **knowledge management portal** is a single, personalized point of access for employees to multiple sources of information on the corporate intranet. A **wiki** uses software to create a Web site that allows anyone with access to create, share, and edit content through a simple browser-based user interface. Organizations typically

information technology (IT)
The hardware, software, telecommunications, database management, and other technologies used to store, process, and distribute information.

knowledge management
The process of systematically gathering knowledge, making it widely available throughout the organization, and fostering a culture of learning.

data
Raw, unsummarized, and unanalyzed facts and figures.

information
Data that have been converted into a meaningful and useful context for the receiver.

knowledge
A conclusion drawn from information after it is linked to other information and compared to what is already known.

knowledge management portal
A single point of access for employees to multiple sources of information that provides personalized access on the corporate intranet.

wiki
A Web site that allows anyone with access, inside or outside the organization, to create, share, and edit content through a simple, browser-based user interface.

use a variety of IT systems to facilitate the collection, analysis, and sharing of information and knowledge.

Another IT application for knowledge management is the use of **business intelligence software** that analyzes data and extracts useful insights, patterns, and relationships that might be significant.[65] The application of business intelligence software at Cendant Hotel Group lets managers know immediately when a huge surge of interest in triple rooms in San Diego or Phoenix happens, enabling the company to add inventory or adjust offerings on its Web site. Similarly, managers in other firms can identify sets of products that particular market segments purchase, patterns of transactions that signal possible fraud, or patterns of product performance that may indicate defects.

MANAGEMENT INFORMATION SYSTEMS

A **management information system (MIS)** is a computer-based system that provides information and support for effective managerial decision making. The central elements of a management information system are illustrated in Exhibit 6.6.

An MIS typically supports the strategic decision-making needs of mid- and top-level management. However, as technology becomes more widely accessible, more employees are wired into networks, and organizations push decision making downward in the hierarchy, these kinds of systems are seeing use at all levels of the organization. For example, when a production supervisor needs to make a decision about production scheduling, he or she may need data on the anticipated number of orders in the coming month, inventory levels, and availability of computers and personnel. The MIS can provide these data. At Veterans Administration (VA) hospitals around the country, a sophisticated MIS called Vista enables people all across the organization to access complete patient information and provide better care. Once considered subpar in its performance and service, the VA has been transformed by technology into one of the highest-quality, most cost-effective medical providers in the United States.[66] Similarly, Mel Kiper Enterprises uses management information systems to keep its information current and competitive as shown in the Benchmarking box.

business intelligence software
Software that analyzes data from multiple sources and extracts useful insights, patterns, and relationships that might be significant.

management information system (MIS)
A computer-based system that provides information and support for effective managerial decision making.

EXHIBIT 6.6
Basic Elements of Management Information Systems

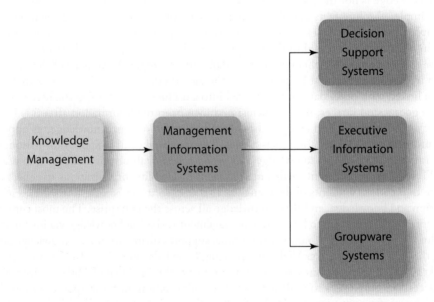

SOURCE: Adapted from Ralph M. Stair and George W. Reynolds, *Principles of Information Systems: A Managerial Approach*, 4th ed. (Cambridge, MA: Course Technology, 1999): 391.

BENCH-MARKING

Mel Kiper and the NFL Draft

Mel Kiper, Jr., may be a football draft genius and the person who pioneered the concept of a draft expert, but it is his wife, Kim Kiper, who has turned that talent into a successful family business. As a high-school student hoping to become a football scout, Mel gave reports to the Baltimore Colts' chief executive, Ernie Acorsi, who told him he should be selling the information. But it took until college, when Mel watched dozens of Baltimore Colts games on satellite dish in his family's back yard, for that idea to take hold. With an uncanny ability to spot talent, Mel was encouraged and helped by his father to start a college draft report service. Mel placed one ad in a football publication and got 130 orders. When his dad died, his mom took over the business side, working late into the night, copying customer information on individual cards and completing the accounting by hand.

After Mel and Kim got married (during football season, no less), Kim quit her job in pharmaceutical sales and worked with Mel, soon realizing they were in a crisis. "That was the beginning of the end," says Kim, because at that time, things were changing in draft publications. So she started by creating a computerized customer database and buying an automated postage machine, ultimately transforming Mel Kiper Enterprises into a sprawling home business. Their workday started at 8 A.M., with Mel spending hours on the phone (in the days before the Internet) getting team statistics, putting together radio spots at night to promote his draft guides, and then both of them working until 3 A.M. laying out the publications. From the beginning, he's provided the information and she runs the business. There's no overlap. Once a year, Mel spends two days on ESPN during draft picks with barely time for a bathroom break. Kim and their 14-year-old daughter say no one could live with the intense Mel from TV. "At home, he's so easy," says Kim. "Every time you see him on TV, he looks like he's going to bite someone's head off." But even at home, no one will watch games with him because he sits in his study changing channels in a crazy frenzy. Kim is a casual sports fan, but she prefers to lay out sports information to watching and following games. This suits Mel just fine. "You think I want a wife who knows football? That would drive me crazy."

SOURCE: Judy Battista, "A Mom-and-Pop Draft Empire," *New York Times,* Apr. 24, 2009, pp. B10, B14.

ENTERPRISE RESOURCE PLANNING SYSTEMS

Another key IT component for many companies is an approach to information management called *enterprise resource planning.* **Enterprise resource planning (ERP) systems** integrate and optimize all the various business processes across the entire firm.[67] A recent study by AMR Research indicates that the use of ERP continues to grow, with nearly half of the companies surveyed planning to spend more than $10 million on ERP activities. The study also showed an increase in the percentage of employees who are using ERP systems in organizations.[68]

An enterprise resource planning system can become the backbone of an organization's operations. It collects, processes, and provides information about an organization's entire enterprise, including orders, product design, production, purchasing, inventory, distribution, human resources, receipt of payments, and forecasting of future demand. Such a system links these areas of activity into a network, as illustrated in Exhibit 6.7.

When a salesperson takes an order, the ERP system checks to see how the order affects inventory levels, scheduling, human resources, purchasing, and distribution. The system replicates organizational processes in software, guides employees through the processes step by step, and automates as many of them as possible. For example, the software can automatically cut an accounts payable check as soon as a clerk confirms that goods have

enterprise resource planning (ERP) system
A networked information system that collects, processes, and provides information about an organization's entire enterprise from identification of customer needs and receipt of orders to distribution of products and receipt of payments.

Which Side of Your Brain Do You Use?[69]

The following questions ask you to describe your behavior. For each question, check the answer that best describes you.

1. I am usually running late for class or other appointments.

_____ a. Yes

_____ b. No

- -

2. When taking a test, I prefer:

_____ a. subjective questions (discussion or essay).

_____ b. objective questions (multiple choice).

- -

3. When making decisions, I typically:

_____ a. go with my gut—what feels right.

_____ b. carefully weigh each option.

- -

4. When solving a problem, I would more likely:

_____ a. take a walk, mull things over, and then discuss it with someone.

_____ b. write down alternatives, prioritize them, and then pick the best choice.

- -

5. I consider time spent daydreaming as:

_____ a. a viable tool for planning my future.

_____ b. a waste of time.

- -

6. To remember directions, I typically:

_____ a. visualize the information.

_____ b. make notes.

- -

7. My work style is mostly:

_____ a. to juggle several things at once.

_____ b. to concentrate on one task at a time until complete.

- -

8. My desk, work area, and laundry area are typically:

_____ a. cluttered.

_____ b. neat and organized.

- -

SCORING AND INTERPRETATION: People have two thinking processes—one visual and intuitive, which is often referred to as *right-brained thinking*; and the other verbal and analytical, referred to as *left-brained thinking*. The thinking process you prefer predisposes you to certain types of knowledge and information—visual charts and operations dashboards versus written reports, intuitive suggestions versus quantitative data—as effective input to your thinking and decision making.

Count the number of checked **a** and **b** items. Each **a** represents right-brain processing, and each **b** represents left-brain processing. If you scored 6 or higher on either, you have a distinct processing style. If you checked less than 6 for either, then you probably have a balanced style. New managers typically need left-brain processing to handle data and to justify decisions. At middle- and upper-management levels, right-brain processing enables visionary thinking and strategic insights.

been received in inventory, send an online purchase order immediately after a manager has authorized a purchase, or schedule production at the most appropriate plant after an order is received.[70] In addition, because the system integrates data about all aspects of operations, managers and employees at all levels can see how decisions and actions in one part of the organization affect other parts, using this information to make better decisions. Customers and suppliers are typically linked into the information exchange as well. When carefully implemented, ERP can cut costs, shorten cycle time, enhance productivity, and improve relationships with customers and suppliers.

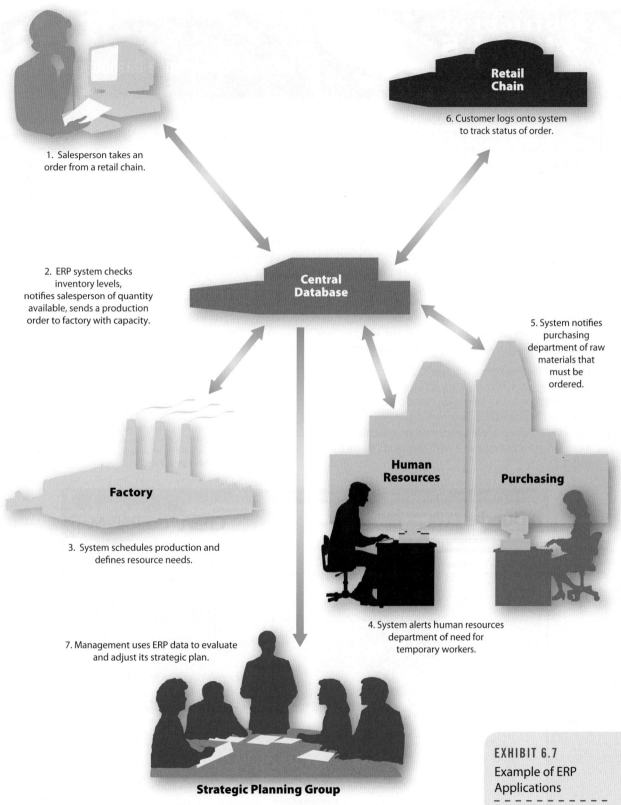

1. Salesperson takes an order from a retail chain.

2. ERP system checks inventory levels, notifies salesperson of quantity available, sends a production order to factory with capacity.

Central Database

Retail Chain

6. Customer logs onto system to track status of order.

5. System notifies purchasing department of raw materials that must be ordered.

Factory

Human Resources

Purchasing

3. System schedules production and defines resource needs.

4. System alerts human resources department of need for temporary workers.

7. Management uses ERP data to evaluate and adjust its strategic plan.

Strategic Planning Group

EXHIBIT 6.7
Example of ERP Applications

SOURCE: Adapted from Gail Edmondson, "Silicon Valley on the Rhine," *BusinessWeek* (Nov. 2, 1997): 162–166.

SPOTLIGHT ON SKILLS

Putting Performance Dashboards to Work

It's the first thing in the morning. You sit down at your computer, coffee cup in hand, and click on an icon. Attractively arrayed on the screen is current information organized under various headings—for example, "Calendar," "Tasks," "Key Performance Indicators," "Sales by Manager," and those always eye-catching "Alerts." Critical information about your business is presented in colorful tables, pie charts, graphs, and other visual displays. With just a glance, you're up to date on everything you need to know before you start your day. If you're puzzled by a particular figure or alarmed by an alert, you just click on the item and start "drilling down" into the data until you get a detailed picture of exactly what is going on. Welcome to the world of business performance dashboards.

As impressive as the technology is, it's the way organizations design and use dashboards that determines whether they turn out to be a boon or a distracting bane. Here are some tips.

- *Don't contribute to information overload.* Because dashboards collate information from many databases and programs, it's all too easy to construct a Web page that delivers too much information. To make dashboards useful, carefully choose what data will be tracked and what information will be displayed. Make sure it's what employees need to know to do their jobs better.

- *Let line managers and employees drive the development.* Always remember that designing a dashboard is primarily a strategic project, not a technical one. The IT department can help implement the dashboard, but it is the responsibility of managers to determine its content. One way to make sure people get the right information is to solicit input from end users during the design process.

- *Carefully assess who needs a dashboard.* At General Electric, business unit chiefs use dashboards, but CEO Jeffrey Immelt rarely does. Immelt doesn't want to get so mired in the details that he loses sight of the big picture. On the other hand, using dashboards to push information farther down into the organization can help employees at all levels see from day to day in concrete terms exactly how their actions contribute to an organization's success or failure in achieving its goals.

- *Don't forget the human touch.* Having all the latest facts and figures at your fingertips is certainly valuable, but it's only part of what managers need to know to run an effective organization. Getting out and talking to employees and customers is still just as important.

SOURCES: Spencer E. Ante, "Giving the Boss the Big Picture," *BusinessWeek* (Feb. 13, 2006): 48–51; Tad Leahy, "Warming Up to Performance Dashboards," *BusinessFinanceMag.com* (June 1, 2006) (http://businessfinancemag.com/article/warming-performance-dashboards-0601); Doug Bartholomew, "Gauging Success," *CFO-IT* (Summer 2005): 17–19;

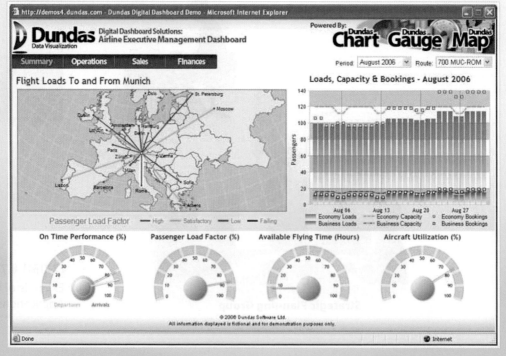

SOURCE: Dundas Data Visualization, www.dundas.com.

A New Generation of Information Technology

The force that is fueling growth on the Internet today isn't a bunch of dot-com startups, or even long-established companies making waves in the online world. Instead, power has shifted to the individual, with blogs, wikis, and social networking becoming the most explosive outbreaks in the world of information technology since the emergence of the World Wide Web.[71] A **blog** is a running Web log that allows an individual to post opinions and ideas about anything from the weather and dating relationships to a company's products, management, or business practices. An entire industry has sprung up to help managers navigate the world of blogs such as monitoring what is being said about the company, implementing damage-control strategies, and tracking what the majority of the world is thinking, minute by minute, to help the organization respond to emerging trends and opportunities.[72] In addition, managers at companies such as McDonald's, Marriott International, and even the once-secretive Boeing are posting blogs of their own to communicate with employees and customers and present the company's side of the story to the public.[73]

Companies are also tapping into the power of new IT applications as powerful collaboration tools within organizations, using group blogs, wikis, social networking, and peer-to-peer (P2P) file sharing. The simplicity and informality of blogs make them an easy and comfortable medium for people to communicate and share ideas, both with colleagues and outsiders. As described earlier, a wiki is similar to a blog and uses software to create a Web site that allows people to create, share, and edit content through a browser-based interface. Rather than simply sharing opinions and ideas as with a blog, wikis are free-form, allowing people to edit what they find on the site and add content.[74] The best-known example of a wiki is the online encyclopedia Wikipedia, where thousands of volunteer contributors have written, edited, and policed more than 9 million entries in more than a hundred languages.[75] Boeing and BMW both use wiki software to open much of their design work to partner organizations.

Social networking, also referred to as *social media* or *user-generated content*, is an extension of blogs and wikis.[76] Sites such as MySpace, Facebook, and Friendster provide an unprecedented peer-to-peer communication channel where people interact in an online community, share personal data and photos, produce and share all sorts of information and opinions, and unify activists and raise funds. Smart companies are finding ways to benefit from the phenomenon. Work networks on Facebook and MySpace are exploding, and some companies, including Dow Chemical, JPMorgan Chase, and Lockheed Martin, are starting their own in-house social networks as a way to facilitate information sharing.[77]

Peer-to-peer file sharing, such as that pioneered by Napster for sharing music online, enables personal computers (PCs) to communicate directly with one another over the Internet, bypassing central databases, servers, control points, and Web pages.[78] Peer-to-peer software lets any individual's computer "talk" directly to another PC without an intermediary, enhancing the opportunities for information sharing and collaboration. Peer-to-peer technology improves efficiency by eliminating the need for setting up and managing huge

Recognize that people need different MIS tools, depending on their work as well as how they like to process and use information.

blog
Web log that allows individuals to post opinions and ideas.

social networking
Online interaction in a community format where people share personal information and photos, produce and share all sorts of information and opinions, or unify activists and raise funds.

peer-to-peer file sharing
File sharing that allows PCs to communicate directly with one another over the Internet, bypassing central databases, servers, control points, and Web pages.

3 The increased technology in the workplace keeps people too disconnected from one another, making it harder to get their jobs done.

Assess Your Answer

ANSWER: Technology can actually bring people closer together if used properly, though not necessarily face to face. Communication can exist with more people, keeping a larger group in the loop. Because of the increased efficiencies, it can actually allow for more interaction time.

central storage systems. GlaxoSmithKline uses P2P technology to let its employees and researchers outside the company share their drug test data digitally and work collaboratively on new projects. Law firm Baker & McKenzie uses it to allow major clients to tap directly into its attorneys' files stored on computers worldwide.[79]

The Internet and E-Business

In recent years, most organizations have incorporated the Internet as part of their information-technology strategy.[80] Both business and nonprofit organizations quickly realized the potential of the Internet for expanding their operations globally, improving business processes, reaching new customers, and making the most of their resources. Exhibit 6.8 shows the popular iPod nano, one of the many products that Apple sells over the Internet and in retail stores.

Numerous organizations today are involved in some type of e-business. **E-business** can be defined as any business that takes place by digital processes over a computer network rather than in physical space. Most commonly today, it refers to electronic linkages over the Internet with customers, partners, suppliers, employees, or other key constituents. **E-commerce** is a more limited term that refers specifically to business exchanges or transactions that occur electronically.

Some organizations such as eBay, Amazon, Expedia, and Yahoo! would not exist without the Internet. However, most traditional, established organizations—including General Electric; the City of Madison, Wisconsin; Macy's; and the U.S. Postal Service—also make extensive use of the Internet, and we will focus on these types of organizations in the remainder of this section.

Exhibit 6.9 illustrates the key components of e-business for two organizations: a manufacturing company and a retail chain. First, each organization operates an **intranet**, an internal communications system that uses the technology and standards of the Internet but is accessible only to people within the company. The next component is a system that allows the separate companies to share data and information. An **extranet** is an external communications system that uses the Internet and is shared by two or more organizations. With an extranet, each organization moves certain data outside of its private intranet but makes the data available only to the other companies sharing the extranet. The final piece of the overall system is the Internet, which is accessible to the

e-business
Any business that takes place by digital processes over a computer network rather than in physical space.

e-commerce
Business exchanges or transactions that occur electronically.

intranet
An internal communications system that uses the technology and standards of the Internet but is accessible only to people within the organization.

extranet
An external communications system that uses the Internet and is shared by two or more organizations.

EXHIBIT 6.8
Apple Sells Products in Retail Stores and via the Internet
- - - - - - - - - -

© AP PHOTO/PAUL SAKUMA

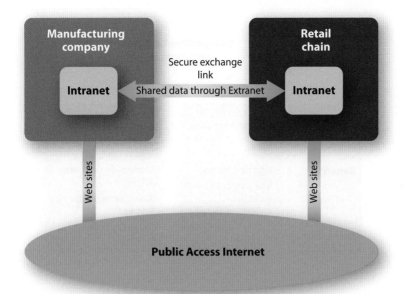

SOURCE: Based on Jim Turcotte, Bob Silveri, and Tom Jobson, "Are You Ready for the E-Supply Chain?" *APICS—The Performance Advantage* (Aug. 1998): 56–59.

EXHIBIT 6.9
The Key Components of E-Business for Two Traditional Organizations

general public. Organizations make some information available to the public through their Web sites, which may include products or services offered for sale.

The first step toward a successful e-business for an established firm is for managers to determine why they need such a business to begin with.[81] Failure to align the e-business initiative with corporate strategy can lead to e-business failure. Two basic strategic approaches for traditional organizations setting up an Internet operation are illustrated in Exhibit 6.10. Some companies embrace e-business primarily to expand into new markets and reach new customers. Others use e-business as a route to increased productivity and cost efficiency.

market expansion
A systematic attempt to increase sales through adding target groups.

E-BUSINESS STRATEGY: MARKET EXPANSION

An Internet division allows a company to establish direct links to customers and expand into new markets. The organization can provide access around the clock to a worldwide market. ESPN.com, for example, is the biggest Internet draw for sports, attracting a devoted audience of 18- to 34-year-old men, an audience that is less and less interested in traditional television. The site's ESPN360, a customizable high-speed service, offers supersharp video clips of everything from *SportsCenter* to poker tournaments, as well as behind-the-scenes coverage. To reach young viewers, other television networks, including Comedy Central, E. W. Scripps Networks (which owns HGTV and the Food Network), CBS Broadcasting, and NBC Universal, have also launched high-speed broadband channels to deliver short videos, pilots of new shows, or abbreviated and behind-the-scenes looks.[82] Retailers have also been big winners with a market-expansion strategy. JCPenney was one of the first traditional retailers to launch a Web site.

© BLAIR CORPORATI

Blair Corporation is a multichannel direct marketer of apparel and home merchandise for value-conscious customers. In 2003, Blair launched an Internet division aimed at **market expansion**. Using a variety of tools and techniques, including virtual catalogs, Blair.com added 170,000 new-to-file customers in its first year, with an average age nearly 15 years younger than its traditional core customers, "proof of the power of this new channel."

········➤ CONCEPT CONNECTION ◄········

EXHIBIT 6.10
Strategies for
Engaging Clicks with
Bricks

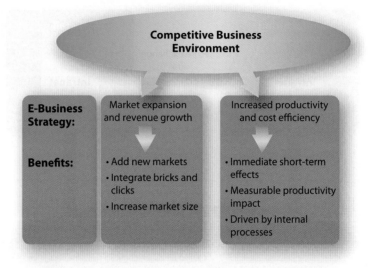

Competitive Business Environment

E-Business Strategy:	Market expansion and revenue growth	Increased productivity and cost efficiency
Benefits:	• Add new markets • Integrate bricks and clicks • Increase market size	• Immediate short-term effects • Measurable productivity impact • Driven by internal processes

JCPENNEY

Go to the ethical dilemma on page 206 that pertains to using the Internet for market expansion.

Not so long ago, the century-old JCPenney department store chain had so many troubles that some analysts predicted it wouldn't survive. Today, however, the retailer is thriving, thanks in part to its managers' mastery of e-business.

Penney was one of the first traditional retailers to launch a Web site, in 1994. Though that initial site sold only one product—Power Rangers—it gave the company invaluable experience for expansion once the Internet really took off. Today, Penney has one of the most productive online stores among mainstream retailers. The Web site has enabled the company to attract a younger customer base than those who typically shop at Penney's and find ways to lure them into bricks-and-mortar stores. Penney embraced the Internet wholeheartedly, encouraging cooperation between its Web site and stores from the beginning. It was the one of the first to allow customers to pick up and return items bought online at their local store, and it was the first to give online shoppers a way to check which clothes are in stock at local stores. It's no wonder Penney's ranks among the top five Web sites in terms of the number of paying customers it attracts.[83]

Like JCPenney, most retailers selling products online also now use their Web sites to drive more traffic into stores. Bloomingdale's tapped into the social-networking phenomenon by sponsoring a three-day event that allowed people to try on outfits in front of an interactive mirror that connected them to their friends via the Internet. Most other big retailers also now let online shoppers pick up purchases at the local store.

E-BUSINESS STRATEGY: INCREASING EFFICIENCY

With this approach, the e-business initiative is seen primarily as a way to improve the bottom line by increasing productivity and cutting costs. Automakers such as Toyota, General Motors, and Ford, for example, use e-business to reduce the cost of ordering and tracking parts and supplies and to implement just-in-time manufacturing. At Nibco, a manufacturer of piping products, 12 plants and distribution centers automatically share data on inventory and orders via the Internet, resulting in about 70 percent of orders being automated. The technology has helped Nibco trim its inventory by 13 percent as well as respond more quickly to changes in orders from customers.[85]

Several studies attest to real and significant gains in productivity from e-business.[86] Even the smallest companies can realize gains. Rather than purchasing parts from a local supplier at premium rates, a small firm can access a worldwide market and find the best price or negotiate better terms with the local supplier.[87] Service firms and government agencies can benefit, too. New York City became the first city to use the Internet to settle personal injury claims more efficiently. Using the city's Comptroller's Cybersettle Service, lawyers submit blind offers until a match is hit. If an agreement can't be reached, then the parties go back to face-to-face negotiations. The city saved $17 million in less than two years by settling 1,137 out of 7,000 claims online, and it reduced settlement times from four years to nine months.[88]

Summary

This chapter made several important points about the process of organizational decision making. The study of decision making is important because it describes how managers make successful strategic and operational decisions. Managers confront many types of decisions, including programmed and nonprogrammed, and these decisions differ according to the amount of risk, uncertainty, and ambiguity in the environment.

Three decision-making approaches were described: the classical model, which is an ideal, rational model of decision making; the administrative model, which is more descriptive of how managers actually make decisions; and the political model, which takes into consideration the discussion and coalition building that many decisions involve.

Decision making should involve six basic steps: problem recognition, diagnosis of causes, development of alternatives, choice of an alternative, implementation of the alternative, and feedback and evaluation. Another factor affecting decision making is the manager's personal decision style. The four major decision styles are directive, analytical, conceptual, and behavioral.

Being aware of common biases that cloud judgment can help managers avoid decision traps and make better choices. Biases to watch out for include being influenced by initial impressions, trying to correct or justify past flawed decisions, seeing only what you want to see, perpetuating the status quo, being influenced by problem framing, and being overconfident.

Many manager decisions are made as part of a group. In addition, involving lower-level employees in decision making contributes to individual and organizational learning. Managers can use the following guidelines to support innovative group decision making: start with brainstorming, engage in rigorous debate, avoid groupthink, and know when to bail. These techniques can improve the quality and effectiveness of decision making in an uncertain or fast-changing environment.

Managers rely on information technology for the efficient management and control of operations. Information technology and e-business have transformed management and contribute to enhanced collaboration and knowledge sharing. Sophisticated information-technology systems can gather huge amounts of data and transform them into useful information for decision makers. Management information systems that support operations and decision making include decision support systems, executive information systems, and collaborative work systems. An important IT solution for improving business operations is enterprise resource planning. Knowledge management is also an important application for new technology. Key technologies for knowledge management are business intelligence software and knowledge management portals on the corporate intranet.

Collaborative work systems allow groups of managers or employees to share information, collaborate electronically, and have access to computer-based support data for group decision making and problem solving. New IT tools, including blogs, wikis, social networking, and peer-to-peer file sharing, extend the power of the organization's collaborative systems.

Discussion Questions

1. You are a busy partner in a legal firm, and an experienced administrative assistant complains of continued headaches, drowsiness, dry throat, and occasional spells of fatigue and flu. She tells you she believes air quality in the building is bad and would like something to be done. How would you respond?

2. Why do you think decision making is considered a fundamental part of management effectiveness?

3. Explain the difference between risk and ambiguity. How might decision making differ for a risky versus an "ambiguous" situation?

4. Analyze three decisions you made over the past six months. Which of these were programmed and which were nonprogrammed? Which model—the classical, administrative, or political—best describes the approach you took to make each decision?

5. Can you think of a bad decision from your own school or work experience or from the recent business or political news that was made in an effort to correct or justify a past decision? As a new manager, how might you resist the urge to choose a decision alternative based on the idea that it might correct or validate a previous decision?

6. As a new, entry-level manager, how important is it for you to find ways to compensate for your relative lack of experience when trying to determine which alternative before you is most likely to succeed? What are some ways you can meet this challenge?

7. Do you think intuition is a valid approach to making decisions in an organization? Why or why not? How might intuition be combined with a rational decision approach?

8. What do you think is your dominant decision style? Is your style compatible with group techniques such as brainstorming and engaging in rigorous debate? Discuss.

9. How might the organizers of an upcoming Olympics use an extranet to get all the elements of the event up and running on schedule?

10. If you were a manager in charge of new product marketing, what are some ways you might harness the power of blogs and social-networking sites to help market your latest products?

11. The openness of wikis is both their strength and their weakness. As a business owner, why might you want to take advantage of this new technology? How might you guard against such potential problems as vulnerability to mistakes, pranks, self-serving posts, and cybervandalism?

Self Learning

What's Your Personal Decision Style?

Read each of the following questions and circle the answer that best describes you. Think about how you typically act in a work or school situation and mark the answer that first comes to mind. There are no right or wrong answers.

1. In performing my job or class work, I look for
   a. practical results.
   b. the best solution.
   c. creative approaches or ideas.
   d. good working conditions.

2. I enjoy jobs that
   a. are technical and well-defined.
   b. have a lot of variety.
   c. allow me to be independent and creative.
   d. involve working closely with others.

3. The people I most enjoy working with are
   a. energetic and ambitious.
   b. capable and organized.
   c. open to new ideas.
   d. agreeable and trusting.

4. When I have a problem, I usually
   a. rely on what has worked in the past.
   b. apply careful analysis.
   c. consider a variety of creative approaches.
   d. seek consensus with others.

5. I am especially good at
   a. remembering dates and facts.
   b. solving complex problems.
   c. seeing many possible solutions.
   d. getting along with others.

6. When I don't have much time, I
   a. make decisions and act quickly.
   b. follow established plans or priorities.
   c. take my time and refuse to be pressured.
   d. ask others for guidance and support.

7. In social situations, I generally
   a. talk to others.
   b. think about what's being discussed.
   c. observe.
   d. listen to the conversation.

8. Other people consider me
   a. aggressive.
   b. disciplined.
   c. creative.
   d. supportive.

9. What I dislike most is
   a. not being in control.
   b. doing boring work.
   c. following rules.
   d. being rejected by others.

10. The decisions I make are usually
   a. direct and practical.
   b. systematic or abstract.
   c. broad and flexible.
   d. sensitive to others' needs.

Scoring and Interpretation

These questions rate your personal decision style, as described in the text and listed in Exhibit 6.5.

Count the number of **a** answers. They provide your *directive* score.

Count the number of **b** answers for your *analytical* score.

The number of **c** answers is your *conceptual* score.

The number of **d** answers is your *behavioral* score.

What is your dominant decision style? Are you surprised, or does this result reflect the style you thought you used most often?

SOURCE: Adapted from Alan J. Rowe and Richard O. Mason, *Managing with Style: A Guide to Understanding, Assessing, and Improving Decision Making* (San Francisco: Jossey-Bass, 1987): 40–41.

Group Learning

An Ancient Tale

1. Read the introduction and case study and answer the questions.

2. In groups of three to four students discuss your answers.

3. Groups report to the whole class, and the instructor leads a discussion on the issues raised.

Introduction

To understand, analyze, and improve organizations, we must carefully think through the issue of who is responsible for what activities in different organizational settings. Often we hold responsible someone who has no control over the outcome, or we fail to teach or train someone who could make the vital difference.

To explore this issue, the following exercise could be conducted on either an individual or group basis. It provides an opportunity to see how different individuals assign responsibility for an event. It is also a good opportunity to discuss the concept of organizational boundaries (what is the organization, who is in or out, etc.)

Case Study

You should read the short story and respond quickly to the first three questions. Then take a little more time on questions 4 through 6. The results, criteria, and implications should then be discussed in groups.

Long ago in an ancient kingdom there lived a princess who was very young and very beautiful. The princess, recently married, lived in a large and luxurious castle with her husband, a powerful and wealthy lord. The young princess was not content, however, to sit and eat strawberries by herself while her husband took frequent and long journeys to neighboring kingdoms. She felt neglected and soon became quite unhappy. One day, while she was alone in the castle gardens, a handsome vagabond rode out of the forest bordering the castle. He spied the beautiful princess, quickly won her heart, and carried her away with him.

Following a day of dalliance, the young princess found herself ruthlessly abandoned by the vagabond. She then discovered that the only way back to the castle led through the bewitched forest of the wicked sorcerer. Fearing to venture into the forest alone, she sought out her kind and wise godfather. She explained her plight, begged forgiveness of the godfather, and asked his assistance in returning home before her husband returned. The godfather, however, surprised and shocked at her behavior, refused forgiveness and denied her any assistance. Discouraged but still determined, the princess disguised her identity and sought the help of the most noble of all the kingdom's knights. After hearing the sad story, the knight pledged his unfailing aid—for a modest fee. Alas, the princess had no money, and the knight rode away to save other damsels.

The beautiful princess had no one else from whom she might seek help and decided to brave the great peril alone. She followed the safest path she knew, but when she was almost through the forest, the wicked sorcerer spied her and caused her to be devoured by the fire-breathing dragon.

1. Who was inside the organization, and who was outside? Where were the boundaries?

2. Who is most responsible for the death of the beautiful princess?

3. Who is next most responsible? Least responsible?

4. What is your criterion for the above decisions?

5. What interventions would you suggest to prevent a recurrence?

6. What are the implications for *organizational development and change*?

Character	Most Responsible	Next Most Responsible	Least Responsible
Princess			
Husband			
Vagabond			
Godfather			
Knight			
Sorcerer			

Check one character in each column.

SOURCE: Adapted from J. B. Ritchie and Paul Thompson. Reprinted with permission from *Organization and People: Readings, Cases and Exercises in Organizational Behavior.* Copyright 1980 by West Publishing, pp. 68–70. All rights reserved, in Dorothy Marcic *Organizational Behavior: Experiences and Cases*, pp. 378-379.

Action Learning

1. Prior to class, interview four people (two students and two managers) on how they make decisions. Ask them:
   a. What types of decisions do you make every day? Only occasionally?
   b. What is the process you use to make a decision?
   c. Does the process change whether it is a minor everyday decision versus an important life decision?
   d. What do you do to learn from the outcomes of your decisions in terms of how to make decisions in the future?
   e. Give an example of a good decision and a poor one.

2. Come to class prepared to talk about your interviews.

3. Your instructor may divide you into groups to share your information.

4. What decision-making theories are relevant for the processes used by your interviewees?

5. What did you learn from this exercise that will help you make more effective decisions?

Ethical Dilemma

Manipulative or Not?

As head of the marketing department for Butter Crisp Snack Foods, 55-year-old Frank Bellows has been forced to learn a lot about the Internet in recent years. Although he initially resisted the new technology, Frank has gradually come to appreciate the potential of the Internet for serving existing customers and reaching potential new ones. In fact, he has been one of the biggest supporters of the company's increasing use of the Internet to stay in touch with customers.

However, something about this new plan just doesn't feel right. At this morning's meeting, Keith Deakins, Butter Crisp's CEO, announced that the company would soon be launching a Web site geared specifically to children. Although Deakins has the authority to approve the site on his own, he has asked all department heads to review the site and give their approval for its launch. He then turned the meeting over to the information-technology team that developed the new site, which will offer games and interactive educational activities. The team pointed out that although it will be clear that Butter Crisp is the sponsor of the site, the site will not include advertising of Butter Crisp products. So far, so good, Frank thinks. However, he knows that two of the young hotshot employees in his department have been helping to develop the site and that they provided a list of questions that children will be asked to answer online. Just to enter the Web site, for example, a user must provide his or her name, address, gender, e-mail address, and favorite TV show. In return, users receive "Crisp Cash," a form of virtual money that they can turn in for toys, games, Butter Crisp samples, and other prizes. After they enter the site, children can earn more Crisp Cash by providing other information about themselves and their families.

Frank watched the demonstration and agreed that the Web site does indeed have solid educational content. However, he is concerned about the tactics for gathering information from children when that information will almost certainly be used for marketing purposes. So far, it seems that the other department heads are solidly in favor of launching the Web site. Frank is wondering whether he can sign his approval with a clear conscience. He also knows that several groups, including the national PTA and the Center for Media Education, are calling for stricter governmental controls regarding collecting information from children via the Internet.

What Would You Do?

1. Stop worrying about it. There's nothing illegal about what Butter Crisp is proposing to do, and any personal information gathered will be closely guarded by the company. Children can't be harmed in any way by using the new Web site.

2. Begin talking with other managers and try to build a coalition in support of some stricter controls, such as requiring parental permission to enter areas of the site that offer Crisp Cash in exchange for personal information.

3. Contact the Center for Media Education and tell them you suspect Butter Crisp intends to use the Web site to conduct marketing research. The center might be able to apply pressure that would make it uncomfortable enough for Deakins to pull the plug on the new kid's Web site.

SOURCE: Based on Denise Gellene, "Big Firms Manipulating Kids on Web, Groups Say," *Los Angeles Times*, Mar. 29, 1996): A1, A20.

4 PART FOUR
Organizing

As the entertainment industry continues to move its programs, celebrities, and advertising dollars to the Internet, giant online networks have emerged to facilitate the shift and monetize hot trends.

Glam Media, Inc., publisher of the Glam.com fashion and lifestyle Web site, quickly joined the ranks of leading online media networks after its launch in 2003. The company's meteoric rise to the top-10 most trafficked online networks is a tribute to management's eye for recruiting top talent. Glam Media leadership teams are made up of technology, fashion, and publishing veterans from such prestigious companies as Elle, Harper's Bazaar, iVillage, Vogue, and IBM.

While millions of dollars from venture capitalists help Glam Media attract good talent, the organization's design and culture keep teams motivated and engaged. Like many young firms, Glam's organization is flat enough to enable employee empowerment, idea incubation, and rapid response to changing trends in the marketplace. A good example is Tinker.com, a recent Glam Media Lab venture that allows microbloggers to track popular conversation streams generated on Twitter. The Web app puts Glam Media in a position to unite advertisers with massive social networks—a lucrative idea for an emerging market.

In the world of entertainment, where change is the only constant, small learning organizations such as Glam Media have the flexibility needed to capitalize on new opportunities.

7 Chapter Seven

Designing Adaptive Organizations

LEARNING OBJECTIVES

After studying this chapter, you should be able to:

1 Discuss the fundamental characteristics of organizing, including such concepts as work specialization, chain of command, span of management, and centralization versus decentralization.

2 Describe functional and divisional approaches to structure.

3 Explain the matrix approach to structure and its application to both domestic and international organizations.

4 Describe the contemporary team and virtual network structures and why they are being adopted by organizations.

5 Explain why organizations need coordination across departments and hierarchical levels, and describe mechanisms for achieving coordination.

6 Identify how structure can be used to achieve an organization's strategic goals.

New Manager's Questions

Please circle your opinion below each of the following statements.

1 Managers should give employees the choice to work on whatever they want so that motivation stays high.

MOSTLY YES < < <   > > > MOSTLY NO

1	2	3	4	5

2 If people make mistakes on the job, they shouldn't be punished.

MOSTLY YES < < <   > > > MOSTLY NO

1	2	3	4	5

3 It is better for one person to be in charge of making decisions.

MOSTLY YES < < <   > > > MOSTLY NO

1	2	3	4	5

A manager's work is influenced by how the company is organized. New managers are typically more comfortable and more effective working in an organization system that is compatible with their leadership beliefs. Yet all organizations wrestle with the question of structural design, and reorganization often is necessary to reflect a new strategy, changing market conditions, or innovative technology. Good managers understand and learn to work within a variety of structural configurations.

In recent years, many companies have realigned departmental groupings, chains of command, and horizontal coordination mechanisms to attain new strategic goals. Managers at Nissan created cross-functional teams to enhance horizontal collaboration. Microsoft reorganized into three divisions, each focusing on a primary business line to increase flexibility in developing and delivering new products. Among former Chief Executive Officer (CEO) Robert Nardelli's plans for getting struggling automaker Chrysler back on track was a major reorganization that includes outsourcing some operations to developing countries.[1] Each of these organizations is using fundamental concepts of organizing.

Organizing is the deployment of organizational resources to achieve strategic goals. The deployment of resources is reflected in the organization's division of labor into specific departments and jobs, formal lines of authority, and mechanisms for coordinating diverse organization tasks.

Organizing is important because it follows from strategy—the topic of Part 3. Strategy defines *what* to do; organizing defines *how* to do it. Structure is a powerful tool for reaching strategic goals, and a strategy's success often is determined by its fit with organizational structure. Part 4 explains the variety of organizing principles and concepts used by managers. This chapter covers fundamental concepts that apply to all organizations and departments, including organizing the vertical structure and using mechanisms for horizontal coordination. Chapter 8 discusses how organizations can be structured to facilitate innovation and change. Chapter 9 considers how to use human resources to the best advantage within the organization's structure.

Successful artist Shepard Fairey has proven himself to be an effective manager too. Fairey runs his own marketing design firm, Studio Number One, a studio that designs unique graphics and logos used in untraditional advertising campaigns and on labels for clothing, soft drinks, and other products. Fairey manages a creative team of seven full-time employees and a handful of part-timers and interns. Even in a small organization such as this, organizing is a critical part of good management. Fairey has to be sure people are assigned and coordinated to do all the various jobs necessary to satisfy clients such as Express, Levi's, and Dr. Pepper and 7Up. The right organization structure enables Studio Number One to be "fast, deadline-sensitive, and responsive."

> CONCEPT CONNECTION <

Organizing the Vertical Structure

organizing
The deployment of organizational resources to achieve strategic goals.

organization structure
The framework in which the organization defines how tasks are divided, resources are deployed, and departments are coordinated.

The organizing process leads to the creation of organization structure, which defines how tasks are divided and resources deployed. **Organization structure** is defined as: (1) the set of formal tasks assigned to individuals and departments; (2) formal reporting relationships, including lines of authority, decision responsibility, number of hierarchical levels, and span of managers' control; and (3) the design of systems to ensure effective coordination of employees across departments.[2] Ensuring coordination across departments is just as critical as defining the departments to begin with. Without effective coordination systems, no structure is complete.

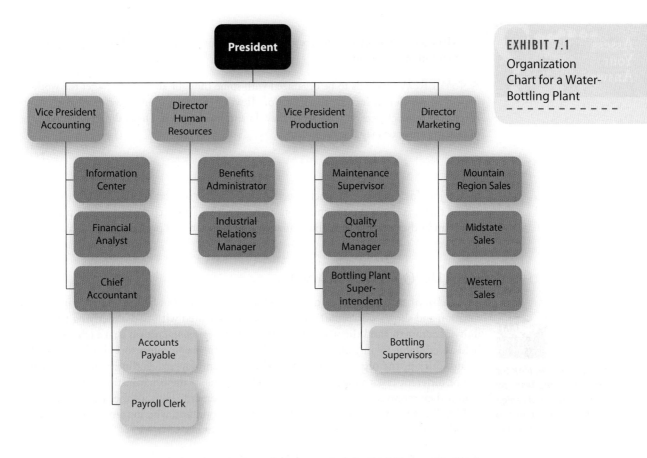

EXHIBIT 7.1
Organization Chart for a Water-Bottling Plant

The set of formal tasks and formal reporting relationships provides a framework for vertical control of the organization. The characteristics of vertical structure are portrayed in the **organization chart**, which is the visual representation of an organization's structure.

A sample organization chart for a water-bottling plant is illustrated in Exhibit 7.1. The plant has four major departments—accounting, human resources, production, and marketing. The organization chart delineates the chain of command, indicates departmental tasks and how they fit together, and provides order and logic for the organization. Every employee has an appointed task, line of authority, and decision responsibility. The following sections discuss several important features of vertical structure in more detail.

Make an organization chart of the place you work so that you can understand reporting relationships.

WORK SPECIALIZATION

Organizations perform a wide variety of tasks. A fundamental principle is that work can be performed more efficiently if employees are allowed to specialize.[3] **Work specialization,** sometimes called *division of labor*, is the degree to which organizational tasks are subdivided into separate jobs. Work specialization in Exhibit 7.1 is illustrated by the separation of production tasks into bottling, quality control, and maintenance. Employees within each department perform only the tasks relevant to their specialized function. When work specialization is extensive, employees specialize in a single task. Jobs tend to be small, but they can be performed efficiently. Work specialization is readily visible on an automobile assembly line where each employee performs the same task over and over again. It would not be efficient to have a single employee build the entire automobile or even perform a large number of unrelated jobs.

Despite the apparent advantages of specialization, many organizations are moving away from this principle. With too much specialization, employees are isolated and do only a single,

organization chart
The visual representation of an organization's structure.

work specialization
The degree to which organizational tasks are subdivided into individual jobs; also called *division of labor*.

1 Managers should give employees the choice to work on whatever they want so that motivation stays high.

ANSWER: Work needs to be organized with some thought about how to get the work done best, which may include specialization. It will help motivation, however, to give employees some choices in what work they do and how to do it. Depending on the type of task, this may or may not be possible.

boring job. In addition, too much specialization creates separation and hinders the coordination that is essential for organizations to be effective. Many companies are implementing teams and other mechanisms that enhance coordination and provide greater challenge for employees.

CHAIN OF COMMAND

As a manager, look for ways to group tasks by similar skills and assign competent people to each job.

The **chain of command** is an unbroken line of authority that links all persons in an organization and shows who reports to whom. It is associated with two underlying principles: unity of command and the scalar principle. *Unity of command* means that each employee is held accountable to only one supervisor. The *scalar principle* refers to a clearly defined line of authority in the organization that includes all employees. Authority and responsibility for different tasks should be distinct. All persons in the organization should know to whom they report as well as the successive management levels all the way to the top. In Exhibit 7.1, the payroll clerk reports to the chief accountant, who in turn reports to the vice president, who in turn reports to the company president.

Authority, Responsibility, and Delegation. The chain of command illustrates the authority structure of the organization. **Authority** is the formal and legitimate right of a manager to make decisions, issue orders, and allocate resources to achieve organizationally desired outcomes. Authority is distinguished by three characteristics:[5]

1. *Authority is vested in organizational positions, not people.* Managers have authority because of the positions they hold, and other people in the same positions would have the same authority.

2. *Authority is accepted by subordinates.* Although authority flows top-down through the organization's hierarchy, subordinates comply because they believe that managers have a legitimate right to issue orders. The *acceptance theory of authority* argues that a manager has authority only if subordinates choose to accept his or her commands. If subordinates refuse to obey because the order is outside their zone of acceptance, a manager's authority disappears.[6]

3. *Authority flows down the vertical hierarchy.* Positions at the top of the hierarchy are vested with more formal authority than positions at the bottom.

Responsibility is the flip side of the authority coin. **Responsibility** is the duty to perform the task or activity as assigned. Typically, managers are assigned authority commensurate with responsibility. When managers have responsibility for task outcomes but little authority, the job is possible but difficult. They rely on persuasion and luck. When managers have authority exceeding responsibility, then they may become tyrants, using authority toward frivolous outcomes.[7]

Accountability is the mechanism through which authority and responsibility are brought into alignment. **Accountability** means that the people with authority and responsibility

chain of command
An unbroken line of authority that links all individuals in the organization and specifies who reports to whom.

authority
The formal and legitimate right of a manager to make decisions, issue orders, and allocate resources to achieve organizationally desired outcomes.

responsibility
The duty to perform the task or activity an employee has been assigned.

accountability
The fact that the people with authority and responsibility are subject to reporting and justifying task outcomes to those above them in the chain of command.

NEW MANAGER'S SELF-TEST

What Are Your Leadership Beliefs?[4]

The fit between a new manager and the organization is often based on personal beliefs about the role of leaders. Things work best when organization design matches a new manager's beliefs about his or her leadership role. To understand your leadership beliefs, please answer each item below as Mostly True or Mostly False for you.

Think about the extent to which each statement reflects your beliefs about a leader's role in an organization. Mark as Mostly True the four statements that are *most* true for you, and mark as Mostly False the four that are *least* true for you.

	MOSTLY TRUE	MOSTLY FALSE
1. A leader should take charge of the group or organization.	_____	_____
2. The major tasks of a leader are to make and communicate decisions.	_____	_____
3. Group and organization members should be loyal to designated leaders.	_____	_____
4. The responsibility for taking risks lies with the leaders.	_____	_____
5. Leaders should foster member discussions about the future.	_____	_____
6. Successful leaders make everyone's learning their highest priority.	_____	_____
7. An organization needs to be always changing the way it does things to adapt to a changing world.	_____	_____
8. Everyone in an organization should be responsible for accomplishing organizational goals.	_____	_____

SCORING AND INTERPRETATION: Each question pertains to one of two subscales of *leadership beliefs.* Questions 1–4 reflect *position-based* leadership beliefs. This is the belief that the most competent and loyal people are placed in positions of leadership where they assume responsibility and authority for the group or organization. Questions 5–8 reflect *nonhierarchical* leadership beliefs. This belief is that the group or organization faces a complex system of adaptive challenges, and leaders see their job as facilitating the flow of information among members and their full engagement to respond to those challenges. The subscale for which you checked more items Mostly True may reveal your personal beliefs about position-based versus nonhierarchical leadership. Position-based beliefs typically work for managers in a traditional vertical hierarchy or mechanistic organization. Nonhierarchical beliefs typically work for managers engaged with horizontal organizing or organic organizations, such as managing teams, projects, and reengineering.

are subject to reporting and justifying task outcomes to those above them in the chain of command.[8] For organizations to function well, everyone needs to know what they are accountable for and accept the responsibility and authority for performing it. Accountability can be built into the organization structure. For example, at Whirlpool, incentive programs tailored to different hierarchical levels provide strict accountability. Performance of all managers is monitored, and bonus payments are tied to successful outcomes. Another example comes from Caterpillar Inc., which got hammered by new competition in the mid-1980s and reorganized to build in accountability.

Go to the Ethical Dilemma on page 242 that pertains to issues of authority, responsibility, and delegation.

2 If people make mistakes on the job, they shouldn't be punished.

ANSWER: *Punishment* is a strong word. When something goes wrong, there needs to be someone who is *accountable*. This actually prevents mistakes because people feel more responsible for success. Punishing and blaming are not often effective, but accountability done right is effective.

CATERPILLAR INC.

Caterpillar, which makes large construction equipment, engines, and power systems, had almost total control of its markets until the mid-1980s, when a combination of global recession and runaway inflation opened the door to a host of new competitors, including Japan's Komatsu. The company was losing $1 million a day seven days a week in the mid-1980s.

When George Schaefer took over as CEO, he and other top managers decided to undertake a major transformation to make sure Caterpillar wasn't caught flat-footed again. They started with structure. One major problem Schaefer saw was that the organization didn't have clear accountability. Schaefer pushed authority, responsibility, and accountability dramatically downward by reorganizing Caterpillar into several new business divisions that would be judged on divisional profitability. Business units could now design their own products, develop their own manufacturing processes, and set their own prices rather than getting permission or directives from headquarters. The division managers were strictly accountable for how they used their new decision-making authority. Each division was judged on profitability and return on assets (ROA), and any division that couldn't demonstrate 15 percent ROA was subject to elimination. The CEO held regular meetings with each division president and kept notes of what they said they would achieve. Then at the next meeting, he would review each manager's performance compared to his or her commitments. The compensation plan was also overhauled to base managers' bonuses on meeting divisional plan targets.

Previously, if things went wrong, division managers would blame headquarters. The clear accountability of the new structure forced people to find solutions to their problems rather than assign blame.[9]

Some top managers at Caterpillar had trouble letting go of authority in the new structure because they were used to calling all the shots, but the new structure was an important part of returning the company to profitability. Another important concept related to authority is delegation.[10] **Delegation** is the process managers use to transfer authority and responsibility to positions below them in the hierarchy. Most organizations today encourage managers to delegate authority to the lowest possible level to provide maximum flexibility to meet customer needs and adapt to the environment. However, as at Caterpillar, many managers find delegation difficult. When managers can't delegate, they undermine the role of their subordinates and prevent people from doing their jobs effectively. Techniques for effective delegation are discussed in the Spotlight on Skills box.

Line and Staff Authority. An important distinction in many organizations is between line authority and staff authority, reflecting whether managers work in line or staff departments in the organization's structure. *Line departments* perform tasks that reflect the organization's primary goal and mission. In a software company, line departments make and sell the product. In an Internet-based company, line departments would be those that develop and manage online offerings and sales. *Staff departments* include all those that provide specialized skills in support of line departments. Staff departments have an advisory relationship with line departments and typically include marketing, labor relations, research, accounting, and human resources.

Line authority means that people in management positions have formal authority to direct and control immediate subordinates. **Staff authority** is narrower and includes the

delegation
The process managers use to transfer authority and responsibility to positions below them in the hierarchy.

line authority
A form of authority in which individuals in management positions have the formal power to direct and control immediate subordinates.

staff authority
A form of authority granted to staff specialists in their area of expertise.

SPOTLIGHT ON SKILLS

How to Delegate

The attempt by top management to decentralize decision making often gets bogged down because middle managers are unable to delegate. Managers may cling tightly to their decision-making and task responsibilities. Failure to delegate occurs for a number of reasons: Managers are most comfortable making familiar decisions; they feel they will lose personal status by delegating tasks; they believe they can do a better job themselves; or they have an aversion to risk—they will not take a chance on delegating because performance responsibility ultimately rests with them.

Yet decentralization offers an organization many advantages. Decisions are made at the right level, lower-level employees are motivated, and employees have the opportunity to develop decision-making skills. Overcoming barriers to delegation in order to gain these advantages is a major challenge. The following approach can help each manager delegate more effectively:

1. Delegate the whole task. A manager should delegate an entire task to one person rather than dividing it among several people. This type of delegation gives the individual complete responsibility and increases his or her initiative while giving the manager some control over the results.

2. Select the right person. Not all employees have the same capabilities and degree of motivation. Managers must match talent to task if delegation is to be effective. They should identify subordinates who made independent decisions in the past and show a desire for more responsibility.

3. Ensure that authority equals responsibility. Merely assigning a task is not effective delegation. Managers often load subordinates with increased responsibility but do not extend their decision-making range. In addition to having responsibility for completing a task, the worker must be given the authority to make decisions about how best to do the job.

4. Give thorough instruction. Successful delegation includes information on what, when, why, where, who, and how. The subordinate must clearly understand the task and the expected results. It is a good idea to write down all provisions discussed, including required resources and when and how the results will be reported.

5. Maintain feedback. Feedback means keeping open lines of communication with the subordinate to answer questions and provide advice but without exerting too much control. Open lines of communication make it easier to trust subordinates. Feedback keeps the subordinate on the right track.

6. Evaluate and reward performance. Once the task is completed, the manager should evaluate results, not methods. When results do not meet expectations, the manager must assess the consequences. When they do meet expectations, the manager should reward employees for a job well done with praise, financial rewards when appropriate, and delegation of future assignments.

Are You a Positive Delegator?

Positive delegation is the way an organization implements decentralization. Do you help or hinder the decentralization process? If you answer yes to more than three of the following questions, then you may have a problem delegating:

*   I tend to be a perfectionist.
*   My boss expects me to know all the details of my job.
*   I don't have the time to explain clearly and concisely how a task should be accomplished.
*   I often end up doing tasks myself.
*   My subordinates typically are not as committed as I am.
*   I get upset when other people don't do the task right.
*   I really enjoy doing the details of my job to the best of my ability.
*   I like to be in control of task outcomes.

SOURCES: Thomas R. Horton, "Delegation and Team Building: No Solo Acts Please," *Management Review* (Sept. 1992): 58–61; Andrew E. Schwartz, "The Why, What, and to Whom of Delegation," *Management Solutions* (June 1987): 31–38; "Delegation," *Small Business Report* (June 1986): 38–43; and Russell Wild, "Clone Yourself," *Working Woman* (May 2000): 79–80.

right to advise, recommend, and counsel in the staff specialists' area of expertise. Staff authority is a communication relationship; staff specialists advise managers in technical areas. For example, the finance department of a manufacturing firm would have staff authority to coordinate with line departments about which accounting forms to use to facilitate equipment purchases and standardize payroll services.

SPAN OF MANAGEMENT

The **span of management** is the number of employees reporting to a supervisor. Sometimes called the *span of control*, this characteristic of structure determines how closely a supervisor can monitor subordinates. Traditional views of organization design recommended a span of management of about seven subordinates per manager. However, many lean organizations today have spans of management as high as 30, 40, and even higher. For example, at Consolidated Diesel's team-based engine-assembly plant, the span of management is 100.[11] Research over the past 40 or so years shows that span of management varies widely and that several factors influence the span.[12] Generally, when supervisors must be closely involved with subordinates, the span should be small; when supervisors need little involvement with subordinates, the span can be large. The following section describes the factors that are associated with less supervisor involvement and thus larger spans of control.

1. Work performed by subordinates is stable and routine.

2. Subordinates perform similar work tasks.

3. Subordinates are concentrated in a single location.

4. Subordinates are highly trained and need little direction in performing tasks.

5. Rules and procedures defining task activities are available.

6. Support systems and personnel are available for the manager.

7. Little time is required in nonsupervisory activities such as coordination with other departments or planning.

8. Managers' personal preferences and styles favor a large span.

The average span of control used in an organization determines whether the structure is tall or flat. A **tall structure** has an overall narrow span and more hierarchical levels. A **flat structure** has a wide span, is horizontally dispersed, and has fewer hierarchical levels.

Having too many hierarchical levels and narrow spans of control is a common structural problem for organizations. The result may be routine decisions that are made too high in the organization, which pulls higher-level executives away from important long-range strategic issues, and it limits the creativity and innovativeness of lower-level managers in solving problems.[13] The trend in recent years has been toward wider spans of control as a way to facilitate delegation.[14] Exhibit 7.2 illustrates how an international metals company was reorganized. The multilevel set of managers shown in panel a was replaced with ten operating managers and nine staff specialists reporting directly to the CEO, as shown in panel b. The CEO welcomed this wide span of 19 management subordinates because it fit his style, his management team was top quality and needed little supervision, and they were all located on the same floor of an office building.

CENTRALIZATION AND DECENTRALIZATION

Centralization and decentralization pertain to the hierarchical level at which decisions are made. **Centralization** means that decision authority is located near the top of the organization. With **decentralization**, decision authority is pushed downward to lower organization levels. Organizations may have to experiment to find the correct hierarchical level at which to make decisions. For example, most large school systems are highly centralized. However, a study by William Ouchi found that three large urban school systems that shifted to a decentralized structure—giving school principals and teachers more control over staffing, scheduling, and teaching methods and materials—performed better and more efficiently than centralized systems of similar size.[15]

span of management
The number of employees reporting to a supervisor; also called span of control.

tall structure
A management structure characterized by an overall narrow span of management and a relatively large number of hierarchical levels.

flat structure
A management structure characterized by an overall broad span of control and relatively few hierarchical levels.

centralization
The location of decision authority near top organizational levels.

decentralization
The location of decision authority near lower organizational levels.

a. Old, Tall Structure

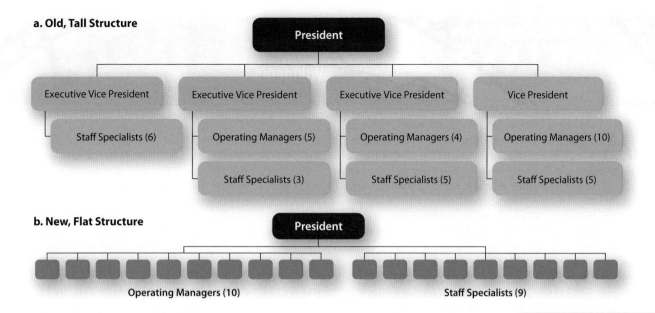

b. New, Flat Structure

EXHIBIT 7.2
Reorganization to Increase Span of Management for President of an International Metals Company
----

In the United States and Canada, the trend over the past 30 years has been toward greater decentralization of organizations. Decentralization is believed to relieve the burden on top managers, make greater use of employees' skills and abilities, ensure that decisions are made close to the action by well-informed people, and permit more rapid response to external changes. However, this trend does not mean that every organization should decentralize all decisions. Managers should diagnose the organizational situation and select the decision-making level that will best meet the organization's needs. Factors that typically influence centralization versus decentralization are as follows:

1. *Greater change and uncertainty in the environment are usually associated with decentralization.* A good example of how decentralization can help cope with rapid change and uncertainty occurred following Hurricane Katrina. Mississippi Power restored power in just 12 days thanks largely to a decentralized management system that empowered people at the electrical substations to make rapid on-the-spot decisions.[16] With the world rapidly changing, once could expect information management to be decentralized, as Wikipedia does, which is described in the Spotlight on Skills box on the next page.

2. *The amount of centralization or decentralization should fit the firm's strategy.* Top executives at New York City Transit are decentralizing the subway system to let managers of individual subway lines make almost every decision about what happens on the tracks, in the trains, and in the stations. Decentralization fits the strategy of responding faster and more directly to customer complaints or other problems. Previously, a request to fix a leak causing slippery conditions in a station could languish for years because the centralized system slowed decision making to a crawl.[17] Taking the opposite approach, Procter & Gamble recentralized some of its operations to take a more focused approach and leverage the giant company's capabilities across business units.[18]

3 It is better for one person to be in charge of making decisions.

ANSWER: It all depends. In a crisis, yes, one person is best, but under normal conditions, it is generally better if people have at least input or even become part of the actual decision-making team.

Assess Your Answer

At the height of the swine flu outbreak, related conversations on the Web spiked. Wikipedia had its entry updated 60 times in one hour, which caused the Centers for Disease Control and Prevention to keep their main Web site constantly current. In another example, not long after the news broke that six young men had been arrested for an alleged plot to blow up Fort Dix, Wikipedia contributor CltFn started at seven in the morning writing a "stub" (a placeholder) called "Fort Dix Terror Plot." A few minutes later, Gracenotes joined the process. Over the next several hours, a growing pack of contributors started adding to the story while in constant contact with another group of self-appointed editors. Soon Gracenotes (real name: Matthew Gruen) added and corrected the stub some 59 times until it was quite presentable and went onto the front page of Wikipedia. Around midnight, Gruen signed off, went to bed, and awoke the next morning to head off to junior high school.

Started in 2001, Wikipedia is a global online encyclopedia available in 250 languages, with 1.8 million articles in English alone. Depending on your bent, it is either one of the greatest inventions in information or the death knell of intellectual rigor.

The process by which Wikipedia gets its articles "right" is constant rewriting and editing in such an egalitarian fashion that it seems impossible that it could be accurate, especially about events unfolding in real time. To be sure, mistakes have been made, and people have "conned" the system. But they are usually found out and corrected very quickly.

Wikipedia's structure is the most decentralized imaginable, and with the chaotic system that has emerged, it is amazing that anything gets done. And yet it does through the efforts of thousands of motivated contributors. Founder and watcher Jimmy Wales isn't even sure who all these contributors are, but that fits with its decentralized culture. Wikipedians are passionately committed to weeding out the subjectivity in one another's writing and policing bias in others and, remarkably, in themselves. No one seems to know where they learned to do this. But one thing is certain: They are teaching it to each other.

SOURCE: "Swine Flu Spikes Frenzied Online Blog and Twitter Activity," *TB & Outbreaks Weekly*, May 12, 2009, p. 157; and Jonathan Dee, "All the News That Fit to Print Out," *New York Times Magazine*, July 1, 2007: 34–39.

3. *In times of crisis or risk of company failure, authority may be centralized at the top.* When Honda could not get agreement among divisions about new car models, President Nobuhiko Kawamoto made the decision himself.[19]

Departmentalization

Another fundamental characteristic of organization structure is **departmentalization**, which is the basis for grouping positions into departments and departments into the total organization. Managers make choices about how to use the chain of command to group people together to perform their work. Five approaches to structural design reflect different uses of the chain of command in departmentalization as illustrated in Exhibit 7.3. The functional, divisional, and matrix are traditional approaches that rely on the chain of command to define departmental groupings and reporting relationships along the hierarchy. Two innovative approaches are the use of teams and virtual networks, which have emerged to meet changing organizational needs in a turbulent global environment.

The basic difference among structures illustrated in Exhibit 7.3 is the way in which employees are departmentalized and to whom they report.[20] Each structural approach is described in detail in the following sections.

VERTICAL FUNCTIONAL APPROACH

What It Is. **Functional structure** is the grouping of positions into departments based on similar skills, expertise, work activities, and resource use. A functional structure can be

departmentaliza-tion
The basis on which individuals are grouped into departments and departments into the total organization.

functional structure
The grouping of positions into departments based on similar skills, expertise, and resource use.

1. Vertical Functional

Human Resources Manufacturing Accounting

2. Divisional

Product Division 1 Product Division 2

Human Resources Manufacturing Accounting Human Resources Manufacturing Accounting

3. Matrix

Human Resources Manufacturing Accounting

Product Division 1

Product Division 2

4. Team-Based

5. Virtual Network

Designer Manufacturer

Central Hub

Human Resources Agency Marketer

EXHIBIT 7.3
Five Approaches to Structural Design

Mary Berner started her job as chief executive of Reader's Digest Association by realigning its business units. She broke up the book and magazine units and reorganized them along consumer interests. This new divisional structure created ad-friendly clusters of consumer interests such as the new Food and Entertaining unit, which includes magazines *Every Day with Rachael Ray* and *Taste of Home* along with the Web site Allrecipes.com.

··········> CONCEPT CONNECTION <··········

When developing teams, try having people learn one another's jobs because it will give you more flexibility and keep workers more interested in their work.

divisional structure
An organization structure in which departments are grouped based on similar organizational outputs.

thought of as departmentalization by organizational resources because each type of functional activity—accounting, human resources, engineering, and manufacturing—represents specific resources for performing the organization's task. People, facilities, and other resources representing a common function are grouped into a single department. One example is Blue Bell Creameries, which relies on in-depth expertise in its various functional departments to produce high-quality ice creams for a limited regional market. The quality control department, for example, tests all incoming ingredients and ensures that only the best go into Blue Bell's ice cream. Quality inspectors also test outgoing products and, because of their years of experience, can detect the slightest deviation from expected quality. Blue Bell also has functional departments such as sales, production, maintenance, distribution, research and development, and finance.[21]

How It Works. Refer back to Exhibit 7.1 on page 213 for an example of a functional structure. The major departments under the president are groupings of similar expertise and resources such as accounting, human resources, production, and marketing. Each of the functional departments is concerned with the organization as a whole. The marketing department is responsible for all sales and marketing, for example, and the accounting department handles financial issues for the entire company.

The functional structure is a strong vertical design. Information flows up and down the vertical hierarchy, and the chain of command converges at the top of the organization. In a functional structure, people within a department communicate primarily with others in the same department to coordinate work and accomplish tasks or implement decisions that are passed down the hierarchy. Managers and employees are compatible because of similar training and expertise. Typically, rules and procedures govern the duties and responsibilities of each employee, and employees at lower hierarchical levels accept the right of those higher in the hierarchy to make decisions and issue orders.

DIVISIONAL APPROACH

What It Is. In contrast to the functional approach, in which people are grouped by common skills and resources, the **divisional structure** occurs when departments are grouped together based on similar organizational outputs. The divisional structure is sometimes called a *product structure*, *program structure*, or *self-contained unit structure*. Each of these terms means essentially the same thing: Diverse departments are brought together to produce a single organizational output, whether it is a product, a program, or service to a single customer.

Most large corporations have separate divisions that perform different tasks, use different technologies, or serve different customers. When a huge organization produces products for different markets, the divisional structure works because each division is an autonomous business. For example, United Technologies Corporation, which is among the 50 largest U.S. industrial firms, has numerous divisions, including Carrier (air conditioners and heating), Otis (elevators and escalators), Pratt & Whitney (aircraft engines), and Sikorsky (helicopters).[22]

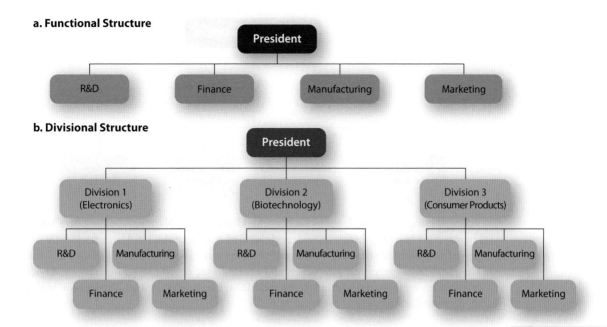

a. Functional Structure

President

R&D | Finance | Manufacturing | Marketing

b. Divisional Structure

President

Division 1 (Electronics) | Division 2 (Biotechnology) | Division 3 (Consumer Products)

R&D | Manufacturing | Finance | Marketing

How It Works. Functional and divisional structures are illustrated in Exhibit 7.4. In the divisional structure, divisions are created as self-contained units with separate functional departments for each division. For example, in Exhibit 7.4, each functional department resource needed to produce the product is assigned to each division. Whereas in a functional structure, all research-and-development (R&D) engineers are grouped together and work on all products, in a divisional structure separate R&D departments are created within each division. Each department is smaller and focuses on a single product line or customer segment. Departments are duplicated across product lines.

The primary difference between divisional and functional structures is that the chain of command from each function converges lower in the hierarchy. In a divisional structure, differences of opinion among research and development, marketing, manufacturing, and finance would be resolved at the divisional level rather than by the president. Thus, the divisional structure encourages decentralization. Decision making is pushed down at least one level in the hierarchy, freeing the president and other top managers for strategic planning.

Geographic- or Customer-Based Divisions. An alternative for assigning divisional responsibility is to group company activities by geographic region or customer group. For example, the Internal Revenue Service shifted to a structure focused on four distinct taxpayer (customer) groups: individuals, small businesses, corporations, and nonprofit or government agencies.[23] Top executives at Citigroup are considering reorganizing to a geographic structure to give the giant global corporation a more unified face to local customers.[24] A global geographic structure is illustrated in Exhibit 7.5 on page 224. In a geographic-based structure, all functions in a specific country or region report to the same division manager. The structure focuses company activities on local market conditions. Competitive advantage may come from the production or sale of a product or service adapted to a given country or region. Colgate-Palmolive Company is organized into regional divisions in North America, Europe, Latin America, East Asia, and the South Pacific.[25] The structure works for Colgate because personal care products often need to be tailored to cultural values and local customs.

EXHIBIT 7.4
Functional Versus Divisional Structures
- - - - - - - - - - - - - - - - -

EXHIBIT 7.5
Geographic-Based
Global Organization
Structure

Large nonprofit organizations such as the United Way, National Council of YMCAs, Habitat for Humanity International, and the Girl Scouts of the USA also frequently use a type of geographical structure with a central headquarters and semiautonomous local units. The national organization provides brand recognition, coordinates fund-raising services, and handles some shared administrative functions; day-to-day control and decision making are decentralized to local or regional units.[26]

MATRIX APPROACH

What It Is. The matrix approach combines aspects of both functional and divisional structures simultaneously in the same part of the organization. The matrix structure evolved as a way to improve horizontal coordination and information sharing.[27] One unique feature of the matrix is that it has dual lines of authority. In Exhibit 7.6, the functional hierarchy of authority runs vertically, and the divisional hierarchy of authority runs horizontally. The vertical structure provides traditional control within functional departments, and the horizontal structure provides coordination across departments. The matrix structure therefore supports a formal chain of command for both functional (vertical) and divisional (horizontal) relationships. As a result of this dual structure, some employees actually report to two supervisors simultaneously.

matrix approach
An organization structure that uses functional and divisional chains of command simultaneously in the same part of the organization.

EXHIBIT 7.6
Dual-Authority
Structure
in a Matrix
Organization

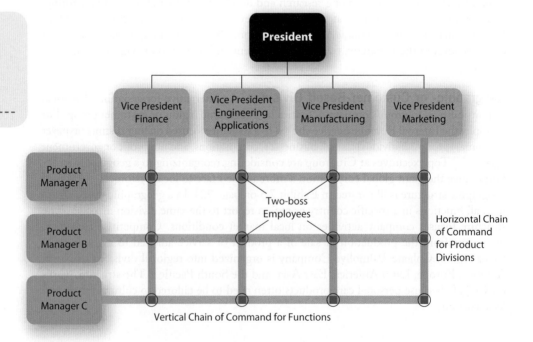

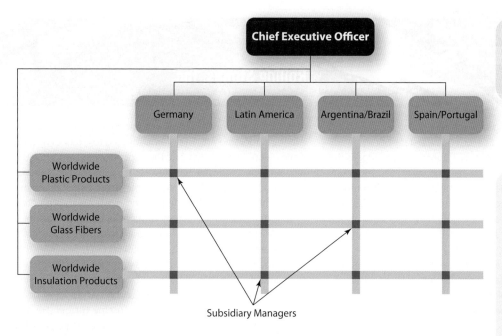

How It Works. The dual lines of authority make the matrix unique. To see how the matrix works, consider the global matrix structure in Exhibit 7.7. The two lines of authority are geographic and product. The geographic boss in Germany coordinates all subsidiaries in Germany, and the plastics products boss coordinates the manufacturing and sale of plastics products around the world. Managers of local subsidiary companies in Germany would report to two superiors, both the country boss and the product boss. The dual authority structure violates the unity-of-command concept described earlier in this chapter but is necessary to give equal emphasis to both functional and divisional lines of authority. Dual lines of authority can be confusing, but after managers learn to use this structure, the matrix provides excellent coordination simultaneously for each geographic region and each product line.

The success of the matrix structure depends on the abilities of people in key matrix roles. **Two-boss employees**, those who report to two supervisors simultaneously, must resolve conflicting demands from the matrix bosses. They must work with senior managers to reach joint decisions. They need excellent human relations skills with which to confront managers and resolve conflicts. The **matrix boss** is the product or functional boss responsible for one side of the matrix. The **top leader** is responsible for the entire matrix and oversees both the product and functional chains of command. His or her responsibility is to maintain a power balance between the two sides of the matrix. If disputes arise between them, the problem will be kicked upstairs to the top leader.[28]

TEAM APPROACH

What It Is. Probably the most widespread trend in departmentalization in recent years has been the implementation of team concepts. The vertical chain

two-boss employees
Employees who report to two supervisors simultaneously.

matrix boss
The product or functional boss, responsible for one side of the matrix.

top leader
The overseer of both the product and functional chains of command; responsible for the entire matrix.

cross-functional team
A group of employees from various functional departments that meet as a team to resolve mutual problems.

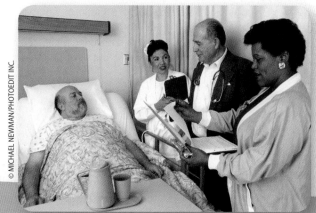

Hospitals and other health care providers face a great need for coordination because medical care needs to be integrated. For instance, collaborative care, like this **cross-functional team** of a nurse, doctor, and dietitian, helps patients with chronic illnesses require fewer emergency department visits. Rush University Medical Center in Chicago started its Virtual Integrated Practice (VIP) project to give physicians in private practice access to teams of physicians, dieticians, pharmacists, and social workers. VIP replicates the collaboration that can occur in a hospital setting by enabling members to share information via e-mail, phone, and fax.

© MICHAEL NEWMAN/PHOTOEDIT INC.

CONCEPT CONNECTION

SPOTLIGHT ON SKILLS

Rolling Stones, Inc.

Mick Jagger's persona is the foundation of the Rolling Stones, who jump like crazy guys on stage but are clearly the most successful music business group. Jagger's the one who inspires people to blow rent money on concert tickets and follow the band to the ends of the Earth. Since their rebirth in 1989, their revenues from tours, records, merchandise, and song rights have exceeded $1.5 billion. That's more than Bruce Springsteen, U2, Michael Jackson, or Britney Spears. After four decades of trial and error, they have learned how to maximize their assets. They are now a large business: global taxpayers with budgets, profit-and-loss statements, lawyers, accountants, bankers, and computer-technology issues. What separates them from any other band is that the Rolling Stones know what they are doing business-wise.

Some of their income is steady, but most is not. Revenue streams from touring are torrential when the band is on the road and they are nothing when the group is not touring. Record sales go up and down depending on whether a new album has been released. Music rights are the most predictable. To harness these assets, to make them interlock, the Stones have set up a unique business structure. The top four partners are not unlike the owners or principals in a blue-chip law firm or consulting practice. Overall management of the finances goes to Prince Rupert zu Lowenstein, the Stone's chief business advisor for three decades. Beyond that, the work falls to teams assigned specific parts of the business. Tour director Michael Cohl and business manager Joe Rascoff supervise a group of "companies" called Promotour, Promopub, Promotone, and Musidor, each with its own unique responsibilities. During tours, the whole company employs more than 350, but at other times only a few dozen people are working.

When the Stones started out, no one was making any money in rock and roll. They went from gig to gig not knowing if they would have lights or if their sound would work. Gradually, a touring industry has developed with traveling sound, stage, and lights. Mick was instrumental in professionalizing this part of the business, often negotiating himself with promoters in various cities. But once they brought in Canadian rock promoter Michael Cohl, the Stones learned to exploit all the financial potential. It started with the 1989 Steel Wheels Tour that Cohl organized himself, promising $40 million for 40 shows—unbelievable back then. He did this by cross-promoting, selling bus tours, sky boxes, TV and movie and merchandising deals, and getting corporate sponsors like Tommy Hilfiger. He also worked with the band to turn the stage into a theater, the first time anyone did this. By the end, Steel Wheels made $250 million. In recent years, the Stones have learned that doing smaller venues with fewer stadiums actually saves money. With stadiums, they had to have three stages and three crews. Now they have one stage and one crew. Less costs, more profits.

The Rolling Stones have come a long way since the 1960s, when they signed deals that made them no money—even if they were a hot group. Now they look hard at cost structures, revenue streams, and ways to reduce losses. At their age, no one knows how much longer they can tour. The music rights business can keep going on forever, but their bodies won't hold out for stage antics much longer. When that day arrives, it will be the end of one of the most successful enterprises in a crazy business.

SOURCE: Stephen Holden, "Only Rock 'n Roll, but They're Still at It," *New York Times*, Apr. 4, 2008, p. E12; and Guy Trebay, "Still Rocking His Own Look," *New York Times*, Nov. 23, 2006, G1.

---

of command is a powerful means of control, but passing all decisions up the hierarchy takes too long and keeps responsibility at the top. The team approach gives managers a way to delegate authority, push responsibility to lower levels, and be more flexible and responsive in the competitive global environment. Chapter 15 will discuss teams in detail. The Rolling Stones use the team-design approach for their business model, which is a prime reason the group is one of the world's most enduring entertainment organizations, as described in the Spotlight on Skills box.

How It Works. One approach to using teams in organizations is through *cross-functional teams*, which consist of employees from various functional departments who are responsible to meet as a team and resolve mutual problems. Team members typically still report to their functional departments, but they also report to the team, one member of whom may be the leader. Cross-functional teams are used to provide needed horizontal coordination to complement an existing divisional or functional structure. A frequent use of cross-functional teams is for change projects such as new product or service innovation.

The second approach is to use **permanent teams**, groups of employees who are organized in a way similar to a formal department. Each team brings together employees from all functional areas focused on a specific task or project, such as parts supply and logistics for an automobile plant. Emphasis is on horizontal communication and information sharing because representatives from all functions are coordinating their work and skills to complete a specific organizational task. Authority is pushed down to lower levels, and frontline employees are often given the freedom to make decisions and take action on their own. Team members may share or rotate team leadership. With a **team-based structure**, the entire organization is made up of horizontal teams that coordinate their work and work directly with customers to accomplish the organization's goals. At SEI, an investment services company, all work is distributed among 140 or so teams. Some are permanent, such as those that serve major customers or focus on specific markets, but many are designed to work on short-term projects or problems. Most desks are on wheels, and computer links called *pythons* drop from the ceiling in SEI's open office environment. As people change assignments, they unplug their pythons and move to new locations to work on the next project.[29]

THE VIRTUAL NETWORK APPROACH

What It Is. The most recent approach to departmentalization extends the idea of horizontal coordination and collaboration beyond the boundaries of the organization. In a variety of industries, vertically integrated, hierarchical organizations are giving way to loosely interconnected groups of companies with permeable boundaries.[30] *Outsourcing*, which means farming out certain activities such as manufacturing or credit processing, has become a significant trend. In addition, partnerships, alliances, and other complex collaborative forms are now a leading approach to accomplishing strategic goals. In the music industry, firms such as Vivendi Universal and Sony have formed networks of alliances with Internet service providers, digital retailers, software firms, and other companies to bring music to customers in new ways.[31] Some organizations take this networking approach to the extreme to create an innovative structure. The **virtual network structure** means that the firm subcontracts most of its major functions to separate companies and coordinates their activities from a small headquarters organization.[32] Indian telecom company Bharti Tele-Ventures Ltd., for example, outsources everything except marketing and customer management.[33]

Law firms are also doing more work online, as described in the Benchmarking feature on the next page.

How It Works. The organization may be viewed as a central hub surrounded by a network of outside specialists, as illustrated in Exhibit 7.8 (page 228). Rather than being housed under one roof, services such as accounting, design, manufacturing, and distribution are outsourced to separate organizations that are connected electronically to the central office.[34] Networked computer systems, collaborative software, and the Internet enable organizations to exchange data and information so rapidly and

permanent teams
A group of participants from several functions who are permanently assigned to solve ongoing problems of common interest.

team-based structure
Structure in which the entire organization is made up of horizontal teams that coordinate their activities and work directly with customers to accomplish the organization's goals.

virtual network structure
An organization structure that disaggregates major functions to separate companies that are brokered by a small headquarters organization.

© AP IMAGES

William Wang, founder of Vizio, Inc., produces a competitively priced plasma television using the virtual network approach. Wang keeps costs down by running a lean operation, outsourcing manufacturing, research and development, and technical support. Vizio plasma televisions are priced about 50 percent lower than most brands. "I would never imagine four or five years ago that Sony would look at us a competitor," says Wang.

>>>> CONCEPT CONNECTION <<<<

BENCH-MARKING

Virtual Law Firms

When Kevin Sharp finished his undergraduate business degree, he never thought he'd be an innovator in law practice organization structure. After finishing law school and working in a large firm for a number of years, he decided he wanted a different life, so he and a colleague started their own Nashville firm, Drescher & Sharp. A couple of years later, in late 2006, Sharp realized technology could help him create more efficiencies. Rather than having lots of attorneys in the office, with huge overhead costs, he thought a better idea was to create a virtual organization for many of the firm members. So he started hiring women who wanted to practice law part-time but still be home with their children and pets. Later on, other attorneys came on board who either just like working from home or were living too far away to commute. Sharp's timing couldn't have been better. When the economy tanked in late 2008, he already had a thriving virtual practice. What happened in dozens of other firms across the country was a bloodletting. No longer able to afford their heavy overhead, which was from highly paid young associates and extravagant office space, the firms were laying off lawyers by the hundreds. This did reduce their overhead, but it also cut back on their revenue, as the young attorneys were the ones doing most of the work. With Sharp's model, though, his overhead was low—and he was still getting a lot of work out of the attorneys in his practice. In recent years, attorney work is more and more done online. Gone are the days they have to rush to the courthouse to file papers. Now it's done with PDF files via e-mail. Therefore, being tied to an office nearby the courthouse is no longer an advantage.

In addition to the 11 lawyers in his firm, Sharp has five paralegals, some of whom work from home. Sharp communicates with his paralegal via Skype. Even though his paralegal lives in one of Nashville's exurbs and therefore is a local phone call away, using Skype allows her to remain "on" throughout the day. All Sharp has to do is click his telephone icon or send an instant message for the paralegal to respond on Skype. They are able to collaborate on documents and court filings online, and her commute time is eliminated.

Sharp estimates that he saves between 50 percent and 75 percent of typical overhead costs by having firm members virtual. He could cut more if all were strictly online, but some people just like to have an office to work in, so he offers them the space. What this new structure means is that Sharp can keep overhead low while increasing revenue. Will this structure catch on? Sharp has noticed an increase in this model, with more virtual firms starting. One owner gets 1,000 resumes a year from lawyers wanting to be in that virtual firm. It's an idea whose time has come.

SOURCE: Kevin Sharp, personal communication, May 2009.

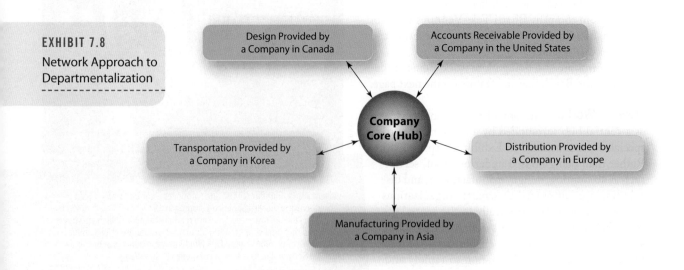

EXHIBIT 7.8

Network Approach to Departmentalization

Design Provided by a Company in Canada

Accounts Receivable Provided by a Company in the United States

Company Core (Hub)

Transportation Provided by a Company in Korea

Distribution Provided by a Company in Europe

Manufacturing Provided by a Company in Asia

smoothly that a loosely connected network of suppliers, manufacturers, assemblers, and distributors can look and act like one seamless company.

The idea behind networks is that a company can concentrate on what it does best and contract out other activities to companies with distinctive competence in those specific areas, which enables a company to do more with less.[35] Strida, a company based in Birmingham, England, provides an example of the virtual network approach.

STRIDA FOLDING BICYCLES

How do two people run an entire company that sells thousands of high-tech folding bicycles all over the world? Steedman Bass and Bill Bennet do it with a virtual network approach that outsources design, manufacturing, customer service, logistics, accounting, and just about everything else to other organizations.

Bass, an avid cyclist, got into the bicycle business when he and his partner Bennet bought the struggling British company Strida, which was having trouble making enough quality bicycles to meet even minimum orders. The partners soon realized why Strida was struggling. The design for the folding bicycle was a clever engineering idea, but it was a manufacturing nightmare. Bass and Bennet immediately turned over production engineering and new product development to an American bicycle designer, still with intentions of building the bikes at the Birmingham factory. However, a large order from Italy sent them looking for other options. Eventually, they transferred all manufacturing to Ming Cycle Company of Taiwan, which builds the bikes with parts sourced from parts manufacturers in Taiwan and mainland China.

Finally, the last piece of the puzzle was to contract with a company in Birmingham that would take over everything else from marketing to distribution. Bass and Bennet concentrate their energies on managing the partnerships that make the network function smoothly.[36]

With a network structure such as that used at Strida, it is difficult to answer the question "Where is the organization?" in traditional terms. The different organizational parts may be spread all over the world. They are drawn together contractually and coordinated electronically, creating a new form of organization. Much like building blocks, parts of the network can be added or taken away to meet changing needs.[37]

A similar approach to networking is called the **modular approach**. A manufacturing company uses outside suppliers to provide entire chunks of a product, which are then assembled into a final product by a handful of workers. The Canadian firm Bombardier's Continental business jet is made up of about a dozen huge modular components from all over the world: engine from the United States, nose and cockpit from Canada, fuselage from Northern Ireland, tail from Taiwan, wings from Japan, and so forth.[38] Automobile manufacturers are leaders in using the modular approach. The modular approach hands off responsibility for engineering and production of entire sections of an automobile, such as the chassis or interior, to outside suppliers. Suppliers design a module, making some of the parts themselves and subcontracting others. These modules are delivered right to the assembly line, where a handful of employees bolt them together into a finished vehicle.[39]

ADVANTAGES AND DISADVANTAGES OF EACH STRUCTURE

Each of these approaches to departmentalization—functional, divisional, matrix, team, and network—has strengths and weaknesses. The major advantages and disadvantages of each are listed in Exhibit 7.9 on page 230.

Functional Approach. Grouping employees by common task permits economies of scale and efficient resource use. For example, at American Airlines, all information-technology (IT) people work in the same large department. They have the expertise and skills to handle almost any IT problem for the organization. Large, functionally based

modular approach
The process by which a manufacturing company uses outside suppliers to provide large components of the product, which are then assembled into a final product by a few workers.

EXHIBIT 7.9

Structural
Advantages and
Disadvantages

Structural Approach	Advantages	Disadvantages
Functional	Efficient use of resources; economies of scale In-depth skill specialization and development Top manager direction and control	Poor communication across functional departments Slow response to external changes; lagging innovation Decisions concentrated at top of hierarchy, creating delay
Divisional	Fast response, flexibility in unstable environment Fosters concern for customer needs Excellent coordination across functional departments	Duplication of resources across divisions Less technical depth and specialization Poor coordination across divisions
Matrix	More efficient use of resources than single hierarchy Flexibility, adaptability to changing environment Interdisciplinary cooperation, expertise available to all divisions	Frustration and confusion from dual chain of command High conflict between two sides of the matrix Many meetings, more discussion than action
Team	Reduced barriers among departments, increased compromise Shorter response time, quicker decisions Better morale, enthusiasm from employee involvement	Dual loyalties and conflict Time and resources spent on meetings Unplanned decentralization
Virtual Network	Can draw on expertise worldwide Highly flexible and responsive Reduced overhead costs	Lack of control; weak boundaries Greater demands on managers Employee loyalty weakened

departments enhance the development of in-depth skills because people work on a variety of related problems and are associated with other experts within their own department. Because the chain of command converges at the top, the functional structure also provides a way to centralize decision making and provide unified direction from top managers. The primary disadvantages reflect barriers that exist across departments. Because people are separated into distinct departments, communication and coordination across functions are often poor, causing a slow response to environmental changes. Innovation and change require involvement of several departments. Another problem is that decisions involving more than one department may pile up at the top of the organization and be delayed.

Divisional Approach. By dividing employees and resources along divisional lines, the organization will be flexible and responsive to change because each unit is small and tuned in to its environment. By having employees working on a single product line, the concern for customers' needs is high. Coordination across functional departments is better because employees are grouped together in a single location and committed to one product line. Great coordination exists within divisions; however, coordination *across* divisions is often poor. Problems occurred at Hewlett-Packard, for example, when autonomous divisions went in opposite directions. The software produced in one division did not fit the hardware produced in another. Thus, the divisional structure was realigned to establish adequate coordination across divisions. Another major disadvantage is duplication of resources and the high cost of running separate divisions. Instead of a single research department in which all research people use a single facility, each division may have its own research facility. The organization loses efficiency and economies of scale. In addition, the small size of departments within each division may result in a lack of technical specialization, expertise, and training.

Matrix Approach. The matrix structure is controversial because of the dual chain of command. However, the matrix can be highly effective in a complex, rapidly changing environment in which the organization needs to be flexible and adaptable.[40] The conflict and frequent meetings generated by the matrix allow new issues to be raised and resolved. The matrix structure makes efficient use of human resources because specialists can be transferred from one division to another. The major problem is the confusion and frustration caused by the dual chain of command. Matrix bosses and two-boss employees have difficulty with the dual reporting relationships. The matrix structure also can generate high conflict because it pits divisional against functional goals in a domestic structure or product line versus country goals in a global structure. Rivalry between the two sides of the matrix can be exceedingly difficult for two-boss employees to manage. This problem leads to the third disadvantage: time lost to meetings and discussions devoted to resolving this conflict. Often the matrix structure leads to more discussion than action because different goals and points of view are being addressed. Managers may spend a great deal of time coordinating meetings and assignments, which takes time away from core work activities.[41]

As a new manager, understand the advantages and disadvantages of each approach to departmentalization. Recognize how each structure can provide benefits but might not be appropriate for every organization and situation.

Team Approach. The team concept breaks down barriers across departments and improves coordination and cooperation. Team members know one another's problems and compromise rather than blindly pursue their own goals. The team concept also enables the organization to more quickly adapt to customer requests and environmental changes and speeds decision making because decisions need not go to the top of the hierarchy for approval. Another big advantage is the morale boost. Employees are typically enthusiastic about their involvement in bigger projects rather than narrow departmental tasks. At video games company Ubisoft, for example, each studio is set up so that teams of employees and managers work collaboratively to develop new games. Employees don't make a lot of money, but they're motivated by the freedom they have to propose new ideas and put them into action.[42]

Yet the team approach has disadvantages as well. Employees may be enthusiastic about team participation, but they may also experience conflicts and dual loyalties. A cross-functional team may make different work demands on members than do their department managers, and members who participate in more than one team must resolve these conflicts. A large amount of time is devoted to meetings, thus increasing coordination time. Unless the organization truly needs teams to coordinate complex projects and adapt to the environment, it will lose production efficiency with them. Finally, the team approach may cause too much decentralization. Senior department managers who traditionally made decisions might feel left out when a team moves ahead on its own. Team members often do not see the big picture of the corporation and may make decisions that are good for their group but bad for the organization as a whole.

Virtual Network Approach. The biggest advantages to a virtual network approach are flexibility and competitiveness on a global scale. The extreme flexibility of a network approach is illustrated by today's "war on terrorism." Most experts agree that the insurgencies in Iraq, Pakistan, and Afghanistan are difficult to fight because they are far-flung collections of groups that share specific missions but are free to act on their own. "Attack any single part of it, and the rest carries on largely untouched," wrote one journalist after talking with U.S. and Iraqi officials. "It cannot be decapitated, because the insurgency, for the most part, has no head."[43] One response of the United States and its allies is to organize into networks to quickly change course, put new people in place as needed, and respond to situations and challenges as they emerge.[44]

Similarly, today's business organizations can benefit from a flexible network approach that lets them shift resources and respond quickly. A network organization can draw on resources and expertise worldwide to achieve the best quality and price and can sell its products and services worldwide. Flexibility comes from the ability to hire whatever services are needed and to change a few months later without constraints from owning plant, equipment, and facilities. The organization can continually redefine itself to fit new product and market opportunities. This structure is perhaps the leanest of all organization forms because little supervision is required. Large teams of staff specialists and administrators are not needed. A network organization may have only two or three levels of hierarchy compared with 10 or more in traditional organizations.[45]

One of the major disadvantages is lack of hands-on control. Managers do not have all operations under one roof and must rely on contracts, coordination, negotiation, and electronic linkages to hold things together. Each partner in the network necessarily acts in its own self-interest. The weak and ambiguous boundaries create higher uncertainty and greater demands on managers for defining shared goals, coordinating activities, managing relationships, and keeping people focused and motivated.[46] Finally, in this type of organization, employee loyalty can weaken. Employees might feel they can be replaced by contract services. A cohesive corporate culture is less likely to develop, and turnover tends to be higher because emotional commitment between organization and employee is weak.[47]

Organizing for Horizontal Coordination

One reason for the growing use of teams and networks is that many companies are recognizing the limits of traditional vertical organization structures in a fast-shifting environment. In general, the trend is toward breaking down barriers between departments, and many companies are moving toward horizontal structures based on work processes rather than departmental functions.[48] However, regardless of the type of structure, every organization needs mechanisms for horizontal integration and coordination. The structure of an organization is not complete without designing both the horizontal and vertical dimensions of structure.[49]

BUSINESS BLOOPER

Ticketmaster and Live Nation

If you think concert tickets are outrageous now, wait until the proposed merger of Ticketmaster and Live Nation goes through. And imagine the coordination it will require. Bruce Springsteen perhaps made the likelihood of the merger slightly more difficult when he posted an open letter to his fans charging Ticketmaster with a "clear conflict of interest when it directed fans to TicketsNow," a sister resell company that charges huge markups. "The abuse of our fans and our trust by Ticketmaster has me as furious as it has made many of you," noted Springsteen.

SOURCE: David Carr, "Big Music vs. Fans and Artists," *New York Times*, Feb. 9, 2009, p. B1.

THE NEED FOR COORDINATION

As organizations grow and evolve, two things happen. First, new positions and departments are added to deal with factors in the external environment or with new strategic needs. For example, in recent years, most colleges and universities established in-house legal departments to cope with increasing government regulations and a greater threat of lawsuits in today's society. Whereas small schools once relied on outside law firms, legal counsel is now considered crucial to the everyday operation of a college or university.[50] Many organizations establish IT departments to manage the proliferation of new information systems. As companies add positions and departments to meet changing needs, they grow more complex, with hundreds of positions and departments performing incredibly diverse activities.

Second, senior managers have to find a way to tie all these departments together. The formal chain of command and the supervision it provides is effective, but it is not enough. The organization needs systems to process information and enable communication among people in different departments and at different levels. **Coordination** refers to the quality of collaboration across departments. Without coordination, a company's left hand will not act in concert with the right hand, causing problems and conflicts. Coordination is required regardless of whether the organization has a functional, divisional, or team structure. Employees identify with their immediate department or team, taking its interest to heart, and they may not want to compromise with other units for the good of the organization as a whole.

The dangers of poor coordination are reflected in what Lee Iacocca said about Chrysler Corporation in the 1980s:

> What I found at Chrysler were 35 vice presidents, each with his own turf. . . . I couldn't believe, for example, that the guy running engineering departments wasn't in constant touch with his counterpart in manufacturing. But that's how it was. Everybody worked independently. I took one look at that system and I almost threw up. That's when I knew I was in really deep trouble.
>
> I'd call in a guy from engineering, and he'd stand there dumbfounded when I'd explain to him that we had a design problem or some other hitch in the engineering–manufacturing relationship. He might have the ability to invent a brilliant piece of engineering that would save us a lot of money. He might come up with a terrific new design. There was only one problem: He didn't know that the manufacturing people couldn't build it. Why? Because he had never talked to them about it. Nobody at Chrysler seemed to understand that interaction among the different functions in a company is absolutely critical. People in engineering and manufacturing almost have to be sleeping together. These guys weren't even flirting![51]

If one thing changed at Chrysler (now New Chrysler) in the years before Iacocca retired, it was improved coordination. Cooperation among engineering, marketing, and manufacturing enabled the rapid design and production of the popular PT Cruiser, for example.

The problem of coordination is amplified in the international arena because organizational units are differentiated not only by goals and work activities but also by geographical distance, time differences, cultural values, and perhaps language. How can managers ensure that needed coordination will take place in their company both domestically and globally? Coordination is the outcome of information and cooperation. Managers can design systems and structures to promote horizontal coordination. At Whirlpool, for example, managers decentralized operations to support a global strategy, giving more authority and responsibility to teams of designers and engineers in developing countries such as Brazil, and they established outsourcing relationships with manufacturers in China and India.[52] Exhibit 7.10 on page 234 illustrates the evolution of organizational structures, with a growing emphasis on horizontal coordination. Although the vertical functional

Remember that the more departments you have, the more time you need to devote to making sure the various departments talk to one another.

coordination
The quality of collaboration across departments.

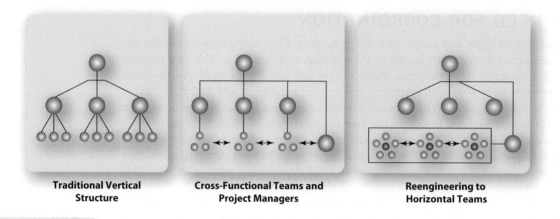

Traditional Vertical Structure

Cross-Functional Teams and Project Managers

Reengineering to Horizontal Teams

EXHIBIT 7.10

Evolution of Organization Structures

structure is effective in stable environments, it does not provide the horizontal coordination needed in times of rapid change. Innovations such as cross-functional teams, task forces, and project managers work within the vertical structure but provide a means to increase horizontal communication and cooperation. The next stage involves reengineering to structure the organization into teams working on horizontal processes. The vertical hierarchy is flattened, with perhaps only a few senior executives in traditional support functions such as finance and human resources.

TASK FORCES, TEAMS, AND PROJECT MANAGEMENT

A **task force** is a temporary team or committee designed to solve a short-term problem involving several departments.[53] Task force members represent their departments and share information that enables coordination. For example, the Shawmut National Corporation created a task force in human resources to consolidate all employment services into a single area. The task force looked at job banks, referral programs, employment procedures, and applicant tracking systems; found ways to perform these functions for all Shawmut's divisions in one human resource department; and then disbanded.[54] In addition to creating task forces, companies also set up *cross-functional teams*, as described earlier. A cross-functional team furthers horizontal coordination because participants from several departments meet regularly to solve ongoing problems of common interest.[55] This team is similar to a task force except that it works with ongoing rather than temporary problems and might exist for several years. Team members think in terms of working together for the good of the whole rather than just for their own department.

Companies also use project managers to increase coordination between functional departments. A **project manager** is a person who is responsible for coordinating the activities of several departments for the completion of a specific project.[56] Project managers are critical today because many organizations are continually reinventing themselves, creating flexible structures, and working on projects with an ever-changing assortment of people and organizations.[57] Project managers might work on several different projects at one time and might have to move in and out of new projects at a moment's notice.

The distinctive feature of the project manager position is that the person is not a member of one of the departments being coordinated. Project managers are located outside of the departments and have responsibility for coordinating several departments to achieve desired project outcomes. General Mills, Procter & Gamble, and General Foods all use product managers to coordinate their product lines. A manager is assigned to each line, such as Cheerios, Bisquick, and Hamburger Helper. Product managers set budget goals,

When you are doing a class group assignment and you are the leader, try using project management skills both with the other students and with the instructor.

task force
A temporary team or committee formed to solve a specific short-term problem involving several departments.

project manager
A person responsible for coordinating the activities of several departments on a full-time basis for the completion of a specific project.

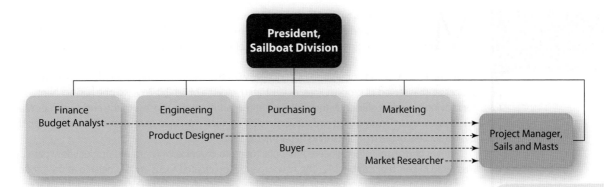

marketing targets, and strategies and obtain the cooperation from advertising, production, and sales personnel needed for implementing product strategy.

In some organizations, project managers are included on the organization chart, as illustrated in Exhibit 7.11. The project manager is drawn to one side of the chart to indicate authority over the project but not over the people assigned to it. Dashed lines to the project manager indicate responsibility for coordination and communication with assigned team members, but department managers retain line authority over functional employees. Project managers might also have titles such as product manager, integrator, program manager, or process owner. Project managers need excellent people skills. They use expertise and persuasion to achieve coordination among various departments, and their jobs involve getting people together, listening, building trust, confronting problems, and resolving conflicts and disputes in the best interest of the project and the organization.

Many organizations move to a stronger horizontal approach such as the use of permanent teams, project managers, or process owners after going through a redesign procedure called *reengineering*.

As a new manager, make sure to be a team or task force member who reaches out to facilitate horizontal coordination. Share information across departmental boundaries to improve horizontal communication and understanding.

REENGINEERING

Reengineering, which is also sometimes called *business process reengineering*, is the radical redesign of business processes to achieve dramatic improvements in cost, quality, service, and speed.[58] Because the focus of reengineering is on process rather than function, reengineering generally leads to a shift away from a strong vertical structure to one emphasizing stronger horizontal coordination and greater flexibility in responding to changes in the environment.

Reengineering changes the way managers think about how work is done in their organizations. Rather than focusing on narrow jobs structured into distinct, functional departments, they emphasize core processes that cut horizontally across the company and involve teams of employees working to provide value directly to customers.[59]

A **process** is an organized group of related tasks and activities that work together to transform inputs into outputs and create value. Common examples of processes include new product development, order fulfillment, and customer service.[60]

Reengineering frequently involves a shift to a horizontal team-based structure, as described earlier in this chapter. All the people who work on a particular process have easy access to one another so they can easily communicate and coordinate their efforts, share knowledge, and provide value to customers.[61] Consider how reengineering at Alcoa's Michigan Casting Center led to the formation of manufacturing teams that became the fundamental organizational unit.

reengineering
The radical redesign of business processes to achieve dramatic improvements in cost, quality, service, and speed; also called *business process reengineering*.

process
An organized group of related tasks and activities that work together to transform inputs into outputs and create value.

Michigan Casting Center (MCC) is now North America's largest supplier of aluminum steering knuckles for automotive suspension systems. However, in the mid-1990s, quality and delivery problems, combined with operational inefficiency and high turnover, almost put the company under.

At the time, MCC was organized by function, with the manufacturing function built around work processes that served all product lines, as illustrated in part a of Exhibit 7.12. No one had accountability for moving a product efficiently through the entire manufacturing process to the end customer. Managers operated in isolated silos and focused solely on their own area of responsibility rather than the overall success of the manufacturing department.

A team of managers reengineered manufacturing to organize work around product flow paths, as illustrated in part b of Exhibit 7.12. The new organization created focus and ownership at the product level by giving leaders responsibility and accountability across all work processes related to a specific product. Support staff members were assigned accountability for specific product lines, making them a part of the manufacturing teams as well. Cell leaders were empowered to solve problems and make decisions, leading to a deeper level of engagement, feeling of ownership, and sense of pride. Eventually, teams became capable of running the plant on their own, freeing managers to focus on strategic issues.

Operational efficiency, product quality, and delivery performance all improved dramatically under the reengineered system. For example, defective parts returned per million decreased from more than 6,000 to around 20 four years later. And by synchronizing internal activities, MCC was able to more effectively synchronize production with customers' requirements. Giving employees expanded jobs, clearer accountability, and more autonomy also led to greater job satisfaction and commitment. Voluntary turnover, which had been as high as 42 percent a year, decreased to around 4 percent.[62]

As illustrated by this example, reengineering can lead to stunning results. Like all business ideas, however, it has its drawbacks. Organizations often have difficulty realigning power relationships and management processes to support work redesign and thus may not reap the intended benefits of reengineering. According to some estimates, 70 percent of reengineering efforts fail to reach their intended goals.[63] Because reengineering is expensive, time consuming, and usually painful to implement, it seems best suited to companies that are facing serious competitive threats.

Structure Follows Strategy

As a potential new manager, check out your authority role models by completing the New Manager's Self Test on page 238.

As a manager, remember if your strategy changes, you need to revisit the structure to make sure it is appropriate.

Vertical hierarchies continue to thrive because they often provide important benefits for organizations, However, in today's environment, organizations with stronger horizontal designs typically perform better.[64] How do managers know whether to design a structure that emphasizes the formal, vertical hierarchy or one with an emphasis on horizontal communication and collaboration? The answer lies in the organization's strategic goals. The right structure is designed to fit the organization's strategy. A recent study demonstrated that business performance is strongly influenced by how well the company's structure is aligned with its strategic intent, so managers strive to pick strategies and structures that are congruent.[65]

In Chapter 5, we discussed several strategies that business firms can adopt. Two strategies proposed by Porter are differentiation and cost leadership.[66] With a differentiation strategy, the organization attempts to develop innovative products unique to the market. With a cost leadership strategy, the organization strives for internal efficiency.

Typically, strategic goals of cost efficiency occur in more stable environments while goals of innovation and flexibility occur in more uncertain environments. The terms *mechanistic* and *organic* can be used to explain structural responses to strategy and the environment.[67] Goals of efficiency and a stable environment are associated with a mechanistic system. This type of organization typically has a rigid, vertical, centralized structure, with most decisions made at the top. The organization is highly specialized and characterized by rules, procedures, and a clear hierarchy of authority. With goals of innovation and a rapidly changing

a. Traditional Manufacturing Structure

EXHIBIT 7.12

Reengineering Manufacturing at Michigan Casting Center

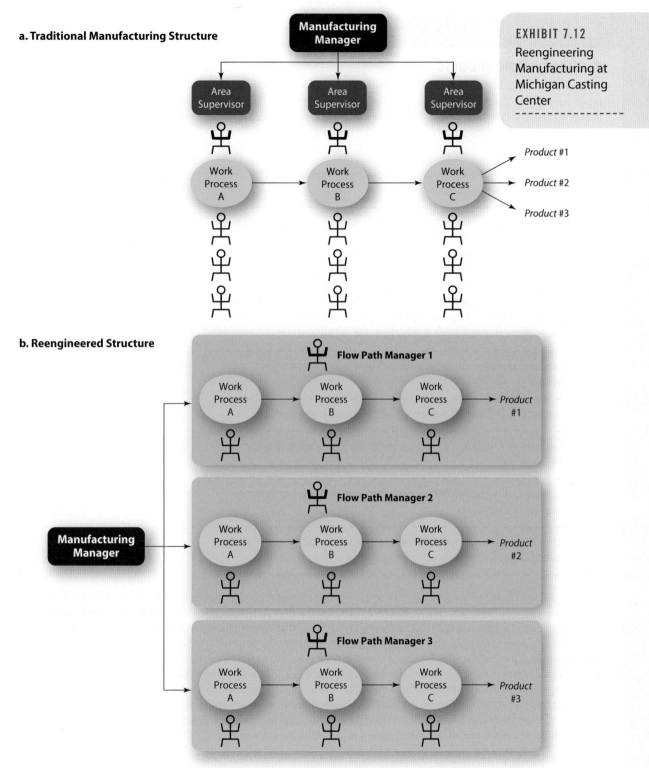

b. Reengineered Structure

SOURCES: Dan Groszkiewicz and Brent Warren, "Alcoa's Michigan Casting Center Runs the Business from the Bottom Up," *Journal of Organizational Excellence* (Spring 2006): 13–23. (Used with permission).

NEW MANAGER'S SELF-TEST

Authority Role Models

An organization's structure is based on authority. Expectations about authority for a new manager are often based on experiences in your first authority figures and role models—Mom and Dad. To understand your authority role models, please answer each of the following items as Mostly True or Mostly False for you. Think about each statement as it applies to the parent or parents who made primary decisions about raising you.

	MOSTLY TRUE	MOSTLY FALSE
1. My parent(s) believed that children should get their way in the family as often as the parents do.	_____	_____
2. When a family policy was established, my parent(s) discussed the reasoning behind it with the children.	_____	_____
3. My parent(s) believed it was for my own good if I was made to conform to what they thought was right.	_____	_____
4. My parent(s) felt the children should make up our own minds about what we wanted to do, even if they did not agree with us.	_____	_____
5. My parent(s) directed my activities through reasoning and discussion.	_____	_____
6. My parent(s) was clear about who was the boss in the family.	_____	_____
7. My parent(s) allowed me to decide most things for myself without a lot of direction.	_____	_____
8. My parent(s) took the children's opinions into consideration when making family decisions.	_____	_____
9. If I didn't meet parental rules and expectations, I could expect to be punished.	_____	_____

SCORING AND INTERPRETATION: Each question pertains to one of three subscales of parental authority. Questions 1, 4, and 7 reflect *permissive* parental authority; questions 2, 5, and 8 indicate *flexible* authority; and questions 3, 6, and 9 indicate *authoritarian* parental authority. The subscale for which you checked more items Mostly True may reveal personal expectations from your early role models that shape your comfort with authority as a new manager. *Authoritarian* expectations typically would fit in a traditional vertical structure with fixed rules and a clear hierarchy of authority (mechanistic organization characteristics). *Flexible* authority expectations typically would fit with horizontal organizing, such as managing teams, projects, and reengineering (organic organization characteristics). Because most organizations thrive on structure, *permissive* expectations may be insufficient to enforce accountability under any structure. How do you think your childhood role models affect your authority expectations? Remember, this questionnaire is just a guide because your current expectations about authority may not directly reflect your childhood experiences.

SOURCE: Adapted from John R. Buri, "Parental Authority Questionnaire," *Journal of Personality and Social Assessment* 57 (1991): 110–119.

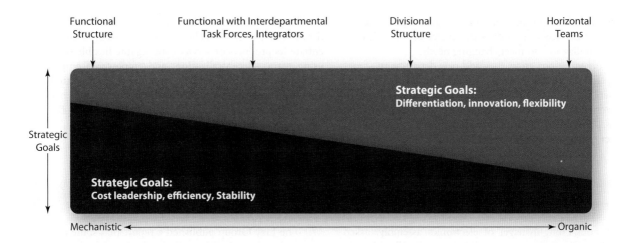

| Functional Structure | Functional with Interdepartmental Task Forces, Integrators | Divisional Structure | Horizontal Teams |

Strategic Goals:
Differentiation, innovation, flexibility

Strategic Goals

Strategic Goals:
Cost leadership, efficiency, Stability

Mechanistic ◄——————————————————————————————► Organic

EXHIBIT 7.13
Relationship of Structural Approach to Strategy and the Environment

environment, however, the organization tends to be much looser, free-flowing, and adaptive by using an organic system. The structure is more horizontal, and decision-making authority is decentralized. People at lower levels have more responsibility and authority for solving problems, enabling the organization to be more fluid and adaptable to changes.[68]

Exhibit 7.13 shows a simplified continuum that illustrates how different structural approaches are associated with strategy and the environment. The pure functional structure is appropriate for achieving internal efficiency goals in a stable environment. The vertical functional structure uses task specialization and a strict chain of command to gain efficient use of scarce resources, but it does not enable the organization to be flexible or innovative. In contrast, horizontal teams are appropriate when the primary goal is innovation and the organization needs flexibility to cope with an uncertain environment. Each team is small, is able to be responsive, and has the people and resources necessary for performing its task. The flexible horizontal structure enables organizations to differentiate themselves and respond quickly to the demands of a shifting environment but at the expense of efficient resource use.

Exhibit 7.13 also illustrates how other forms of structure represent intermediate steps on the organization's path to efficiency or innovation. The functional structure with cross-functional teams and project managers provides greater coordination and flexibility than the pure functional structure. The divisional structure promotes differentiation because each division can focus on specific products and customers, although divisions tend to be larger and less flexible than small teams. Exhibit 7.13 does not include all possible structures, but it illustrates how structures can be used to facilitate the organization's strategic goals.

Go to the Self Learning exercise on page 240 that pertains to organic versus mechanistic structure.

Summary

Fundamental characteristics of organization structure include work specialization, chain of command, authority and responsibility, span of management, and centralization and decentralization. These dimensions represent the vertical hierarchy and define how authority and responsibility are distributed.

Another major concept is departmentalization, which describes how organization employees are grouped. Three traditional approaches are functional, divisional, and matrix; contemporary approaches are team and virtual network structures. The functional approach groups employees by common skills and tasks. The opposite structure is divisional, which groups people by organizational output such that each division has a mix of functional skills and tasks. The matrix structure uses two chains of command simultaneously, and some employees have two bosses. The team approach uses permanent teams and cross-functional teams to achieve better coordination and employee commitment than is possible with a purely functional structure. The network approach means that a firm concentrates on what it does best and subcontracts other functions to separate organizations that are connected to the headquarters electronically.

Each organization form has advantages and disadvantages and can be used by managers to meet the needs of the competitive situation. In addition, managers adjust elements of the vertical structure, such as the degree of centralization or decentralization, to meet changing needs.

As organizations grow, they add new departments, functions, and hierarchical levels. A major problem for management is how to tie the whole organization together. Horizontal coordination mechanisms provide coordination across departments and include reengineering, task forces, project managers, and horizontal teams.

The correct structural approach is influenced by the firm's strategic goals. When a firm's strategy is to differentiate its products or services, an organic flexible structure using teams, decentralization, and empowered employees is appropriate. A mechanistic structure is appropriate for a low-cost strategy, which typically occurs in a stable environment. The structure needs to be looser and more flexible when environmental uncertainty is high.

Discussion Questions

1. Sandra Holt, manager of electronics assembly, asked Hector Cruz, her senior technician, to handle things in the department while she worked on the budget. Sandra needed peace and quiet for at least a week to complete her figures. After 10 days, Sandra discovered that Hector had hired a senior secretary, not realizing that Sandra had promised interviews to two other people. Evaluate Sandra's approach to delegation.

2. Many experts note that organizations have been making greater use of teams in recent years. What factors might account for this trend?

3. An organizational consultant was heard to say, "Some aspect of functional structure appears in every organization." Do you agree? Explain.

4. The divisional structure is often considered almost the opposite of a functional structure. Do you agree? Briefly explain the major differences in these two approaches to departmentalization.

5. Some people argue that the matrix structure should be adopted only as a last resort because the dual chains of command can create more problems than they solve. Discuss. Do you agree or disagree? Why?

6. What is the virtual network approach to structure? Is the use of authority and responsibility different compared with other forms of departmentalization? Explain.

7. The Hay Group published a report that some managers have personalities suited to horizontal relationships such as project management that achieve results with little formal authority. Other managers are more suited to operating roles with much formal authority in a vertical structure. In what type of structure—functional, matrix, team, or virtual network—do you believe your personality would best fit? Which structure would be the most challenging for you? Give your reasons.

8. Experts say that organizations are becoming increasingly decentralized, with authority, decision-making responsibility, and accountability being pushed farther down into the organization. How will this trend affect what will be asked of you as a new manager?

9. The chapter suggested that structure should be designed to fit strategy. Some theorists argue that strategy should be designed to fit the organization's structure. With which theory do you agree? Explain.

10. Carnival Cruise Lines provides pleasure cruises to the masses. Carnival has several ships and works on high volume and low price rather than offering luxury cruises. What would you predict about the organization structure of a Carnival Cruise ship compared with a company that had smaller ships for wealthy customers?

Self Learning

Organic Versus Mechanistic Organization Structure

Interview an employee at your university such as a department head or secretary. Have the employee answer the following 13 questions about his or her job and organizational conditions. Then answer the same set of questions for a job you have held.

Disagree Strongly 1 2 3 4 5 Agree Strongly

1. Your work would be considered routine.

   1 2 3 4 5

2. A clearly known way is established to do the major tasks you encounter.

   1 2 3 4 5

3. Your work has high variety and frequent exceptions.

   1 2 3 4 5

4. Communications from above consist of information and advice rather than instructions and directions.

   1 2 3 4 5

5. You have the support of peers and your supervisor to do your job well.

   1 2 3 4 5

6. You seldom exchange ideas or information with people doing other kinds of jobs.

   1 2 3 4 5

7. Decisions relevant to your work are made above you and passed down.

   1 2 3 4 5

8. People at your level frequently have to figure out for themselves what their jobs are for the day.

   1 2 3 4 5

9. Lines of authority are clear and precisely defined.

   1 2 3 4 5

10. Leadership tends to be democratic rather than autocratic in style.

    1 2 3 4 5

11. Job descriptions are written and up to date for each job.

    1 2 3 4 5

12. People understand each other's jobs and often do different tasks.

    1 2 3 4 5

13. A manual of policies and procedures is available to use when a problem arises.

    1 2 3 4 5

Scoring and Interpretation

To obtain the total score, subtract the scores for questions 1, 2, 6, 7, 9, 11, and 13 from the number 6 and total the adjusted scores.

Total Score, Employee: _____

Total Score, You: _____

Compare the total score for a place you have worked to the score of the university employee you interviewed. A total score of 52 or above suggests that you or the other respondent is working in an organic organization. The score reflects a loose, flexible structure that is often associated with uncertain environments and small-batch or service technology. People working in this structure feel empowered. Many organizations today are moving in the direction of flexible structures and empowerment.

A score of 26 or below suggests a mechanistic structure. This structure uses traditional control and functional specialization, which often occurs in a certain environment, a stable organization, and routine or mass-production technology. People in this structure may feel controlled and constrained.

Discuss the pros and cons of organic versus mechanistic structure. Does the structure of the employee you interviewed fit the nature of the organization's environment, strategic goals, and technology? How about the structure for your own workplace? How might you redesign the structure to make the work organization more effective?

Group Learning

Family Business

You are the parent of 10 children and have just used your inheritance to acquire a medium-sized pharmaceutical company. Last year's sales were down 18 percent from the previous year. In fact, the last three years have been real losers. You want to clean house of current managers over the next 10 years and bring your children into the business. Being a loving parent, you agree to send your children to college to educate each of them in one functional specialty. The 10 children are actually five sets of twins; the sets are exactly one year apart. The first set will begin college this fall, followed by the remaining sets the next four years. The big decision is which specialty each child should study. You want to have the most important functions taken over by your children as soon as possible, so you will ask the older children to study the most important areas.

Your task right now is to rank in order of priority the functions to which your children will be assigned and develop reasons for your ranking.

The 10 functions are:
   distribution
   manufacturing
   market research
   new-product development
   human resources
   product promotion
   quality assurance
   sales
   legal and governmental affairs
   office of the controller

1. Analyze your reasons for how functional priority relates to the company's environmental and strategic needs.

2. In groups of four to six students, rank the functions. Discuss the problem until group members agree on a single ranking.

3. How does the group's reasoning and ranking differ from your original thinking?

4. What did you learn about organization structure and design from this exercise?

Action Learning

You and Organization Structure

Background

Organization is a way of gaining some power against an unreliable environment. The environment provides the organization with inputs, which include raw materials, human resources, and financial resources. There is a service or product to produce that involves technology. The output goes to clients, a group that must be nurtured. The complexities of the environment and the technology determine the complexity of the organization.

To better understand the importance of organization structure in your life, do the following assignment in groups of four to six members.

Select one of the following situations to organize. Imagine you are the CEO and have to design the organization for maximum efficiency and effectiveness.

a. the registration process at your university or college;

b. a new fast-food franchise;

c. a sports rental in an ocean, ski, or snowboard resort area that rents snowboards, jet skis, and so on;

d. a bakery;

e. a social-networking company with a growing online customer base; and

f. a company that books rock entertainers, Broadway musicals, and indie techno bands.

After you have chosen an organization, complete the steps below.

Understanding the Organization

1. Write down the mission or purpose of the organization in a few sentences.

2. What are the specific things to be done to accomplish the mission?

3. Based on the specifics in question 2, develop an organization chart. Each position in the chart will perform a specific task or is responsible for a certain outcome.

4. Add duties to each job position in the chart. These will be the job descriptions.

5. How can you make sure people in each position will work together?

6. What level of skill and abilities is required at each position and level in order to hire the right persons?

7. Make a list of the decisions that would have to be made as you developed your organization.

8. Who is responsible for customer satisfaction? How will you know if customers' needs are met?

9. How will information flow within the organization?

10. After you have completed the preceding questions, go to the type of organization you designed. Spend some time there as a group and bring your results along. Discuss with your group each item, trying to determine if this organization is similar or different in structure to what you have proposed.

Your instructor may ask you to turn in a paper with your results or make a presentation to the class.

Adapted from "Organizing," in Donald D. White and H. William Vroman, *Action in Organizations*, 2nd ed. (Boston: Allyn & Bacon): 154.

Ethical Dilemma

A Matter of Delegation

Tom Harrington loved his job as an assistant quality control officer for Rockingham Toys. After six months of unemployment, he was anxious to make a good impression on his boss, Frank Golopolus. One of his new responsibilities was ensuring that new product lines met federal safety guidelines. Rockingham had made several manufacturing changes over the past year. Golopolus and the rest of the quality control team had been working 60-hour weeks to troubleshoot the new production process.

Harrington was aware of numerous changes in product-safety guidelines that he knew would affect the new Rockingham Toys. Golopolus was also aware of the guidelines, but he was taking no action to implement them. Harrington wasn't sure whether his boss expected him to implement the new procedures. The ultimate responsibility was his boss's, and Harrington was concerned about moving ahead on his own. To cover for his boss, he continued to avoid the questions he received from the factory floor, but he was beginning to wonder whether Rockingham would have time to make changes with the Christmas season rapidly approaching.

Harrington felt loyalty to Golopolus for giving him a job and didn't want to alienate him by interfering. However, he was beginning to worry what might happen if he didn't act.

Rockingham had a fine product-safety reputation and was rarely challenged on matters of quality. Should he question Golopolus about implementing the new safety guidelines?

What Would You Do?

1. Prepare a memo to Golopolus in which you summarize the new safety guidelines that affect the Rockingham product line and request his authorization for implementation.

2. Mind your own business. Golopolus hasn't said anything about the new guidelines, and you don't want to overstep your authority. You've been unemployed and need this job.

3. Send copies of the reports anonymously to the operations manager, who is Golopolus's boss.

SOURCE: Based on Doug Wallace, "The Man Who Knew Too Much," *Business Ethics* 2 (Mar.–Apr. 1993): 7–8.

8 Chapter Eight

Managing Change and Innovation

New Manager's Questions

Please circle your opinion below each of the following statements.

1 When a company makes a new product, the main concern after that is marketing it well.

MOSTLY YES < < <				> > > MOSTLY NO
1	2	3	4	5

2 The most important thing for a company to be innovative is to encourage lots of creative ideas.

MOSTLY YES < < <				> > > MOSTLY NO
1	2	3	4	5

3 Changing an organization is not as hard as people make out.

MOSTLY YES < < <				> > > MOSTLY NO
1	2	3	4	5

Glance through recent back issues of just about any business magazine and you will see them: *Wired* magazine's "Wired 40" list of the most innovative companies, *Fast Company*'s "Fast 50 World's Most Innovative Companies," and *BusinessWeek*'s "Twenty-Five Most Innovative Companies in the World." Everyone's talking about innovation and extolling the virtues of companies that do it right. Innovation is at the top of everyone's priority list today, but managing innovation and change has always been an important management capability. If organizations don't successfully change and innovate, they die. Consider that just 71 of the companies on *Fortune* magazine's first list of America's 500 largest corporations, compiled in 1955, survived the next half-century.[1]

Every organization sometimes faces the need to change swiftly and dramatically to cope with a changing environment. For example, Nokia is still the world's largest maker of cell phone handsets, but it lost its leading position in the United States by failing to match popular products like the Motorola Razr and Apple iPhone.[2] Samsung Electronics was becoming a brand associated with cheap, low-quality knockoffs until managers implemented new processes that transformed the company into a hotbed of innovation. "We cannot live without change," said Samsung Vice Chairman and Chief Executive Officer (CEO) Jong-Yong Yun. "The race for survival in this world is not to the strongest, but to the most adaptive."[3]

In this chapter, we look at how organizations can be designed to respond to the environment through internal change and development. First we look at two key aspects of change in organizations: introducing new products and technologies, and changing people and culture. Then we examine how managers implement change, including overcoming resistance.

Innovation and the Changing Workplace

To test your own ability to innovate, take the following New Manager's Self-Test.

In today's topsy-turvy world, managing change and innovation is taking center stage. Some observers of business trends suggest that the *knowledge economy* of the late 1900s and early 2000s is rapidly being transformed into the *creativity economy*. As more high-level knowledge work is outsourced to less-developed countries, companies in the United States, Europe, and Japan are evolving to the next level—generating economic value from creativity, imagination, and innovation.[4]

Sometimes, change and innovation are spurred by forces outside the organization such as when a powerful retailer such as Walmart demands annual price cuts or when a key supplier goes out of business. Many U.S. companies had to revise administrative procedures to comply with provisions of the Sarbanes-Oxley corporate governance reform law. In China, organizations feel pressure from the government to increase wages to help workers cope with rising food costs.[6] These outside forces compel managers to look for greater efficiencies in operations and other changes to keep their organizations profitable. Other times, managers within the company want to initiate major changes, such as forming employee-participation teams, introducing new products, or instituting new training systems, but they don't know how to make the changes successful. Organizations must embrace many types of change. Businesses must develop improved production technologies, create new products and services desired in the marketplace, implement new administrative systems, and upgrade employees' skills.

Today's successful companies are continually innovating. For example, Johnson & Johnson Pharmaceuticals uses biosimulation software from Entelos that compiles all known information about a disease such as diabetes or asthma and runs extensive virtual tests of new drug candidates. With a new-drug failure rate of 50 percent even at the last stage of clinical trials, the process helps scientists cut the time and expense of early testing and focus their efforts on the most promising prospects. Telephone companies are investing

NEW MANAGER'S SELF-TEST

Are You Innovative?[5]

Think about your current life. Indicate whether each item below is Mostly True or Mostly False for you.

	MOSTLY TRUE	MOSTLY FALSE
1. I am always seeking new ways to do things.	_____	_____
2. I consider myself creative and original in my thinking and behavior.	_____	_____
3. I rarely trust new gadgets until I see whether they work for people around me.	_____	_____
4. In a group or at work, I am often skeptical of new ideas.	_____	_____
5. I typically buy new foods, gear, and other innovations before other people.	_____	_____
6. I like to spend time trying out new things.	_____	_____
7. My behavior influences others to try new things.	_____	_____
8. Among my co-workers, I will be among the first to try out a new idea or method.	_____	_____

SCORING AND INTERPRETATION: *Personal innovativeness* reflects the awareness of the need to innovate and a readiness to try new things. Innovativeness is also thought of as the degree to which a person adopts innovations earlier than other people in the peer group. Innovativeness is considered a positive thing for people in many companies where individuals and organizations are faced with a constant need to change.

To compute your score on the personal innovativeness scale, add the number of Mostly True answers to items 1, 2, 5, 6, 7, 8 above and the Mostly False answers to items 3 and 4 for your score. A score of 6 to 8 indicates that you are very innovative and likely are one of the first people to adopt changes. A score of 4 to 5 would suggest that you are average or slightly above average in innovativeness compared to others. A score of 0 to 3 means that you may prefer the tried and true and hence are not excited about new ideas or innovations. As a new manager, a high score suggests you will emphasize innovation and change. A low score suggests you may prefer stability and established methods.

in technology to push deeper into the television and broadband markets. Automakers are perfecting fuel-cell power systems that could make today's internal combustion engine as obsolete as the steam locomotive.[7] Computer companies are developing computers that are smart enough to configure themselves, balance huge workloads, and know how to anticipate and fix problems before they happen.[8] Organizations that change successfully are both profitable and admired. Innovative companies such as Target and Procter & Gamble (P&G) have seen median profit margin growth of 3.4 percent a year since 1995, compared to only 0.4 percent for the median among Standard & Poor's Global 1200 companies.[9]

Organizational change is defined as the adoption of a new idea or behavior by an organization.[10] Many organizations struggle with changing successfully. In some cases, employees don't have the desire or motivation to come up with new ideas, or their ideas never get heard by managers who could put them into practice. In other cases, managers learn

organizational change
The adoption of a new idea or behavior by an organization.

1 When a company makes a new product, the main concern after that is marketing it well.

ANSWER: Marketing a product and marketing effectively are vital to success. But that is not all a company needs to worry about. If new and innovative products are not brought to market, the company is likely to gradually fail over time.

© AP IMAGES

Swimmer Michael Phelps, who scored a record-breaking eight gold medals at the Olympics in Beijing, wears the new Speedo LZR Racer one-piece suit. Olympic swimmers wearing the LZR Racer broke 25 world records. Speedo's "world's-fastest-swimsuit" innovation was developed with help from NASA scientists. The seams of the suit are ultrasonically sealed and wind-tunnel tested for surface drag. Each athlete gets a three-dimensional body scan to create a suit with core support in critical areas to make swimmers more streamlined. The $550 price was a good deal for Phelps. His sponsor Speedo gave him a $1 million bonus for his historic eight-medal win.

> CONCEPT CONNECTION <

about good ideas but have trouble getting cooperation from employees for implementation. Successful change requires that organizations be capable of both creating and implementing ideas, which means the organization must learn to be *ambidextrous*.[11]

An **ambidextrous approach** means incorporating structures and processes that are appropriate for both the creative impulse and for the systematic implementation of innovations. For example, a loose, flexible structure and greater employee freedom are excellent for the creation and initiation of ideas; however, these same conditions often make it difficult to implement a change because employees are less likely to comply. Or, as one scholar put it, companies "that are healthy enough to consider innovation are also hearty enough to resist change."[12] With an ambidextrous approach, managers encourage flexibility and freedom to innovate and propose new ideas with creative departments, venture teams, and other mechanisms we will discuss in this chapter, but they use a more rigid, centralized, and standardized approach for implementing innovations. In the following section, we discuss technology and product changes, which typically rely on new ideas that bubble up from lower levels of the organization.

Changing Things: New Products and Technologies

ambidextrous approach
Incorporating structures and processes that are appropriate for both the creative impulse and for the systematic implementation of innovations.

product change
A change in the organization's product or service outputs.

technology change
A change that pertains to the organization's production process.

Introducing new products and technologies is a vital area for innovation. A **product change** is a change in the organization's product or service outputs. Product and service innovation is the primary way in which organizations adapt to changes in markets, technology, and competition.[13] Examples of new products include Apple's iPhone 3G, Glad Force Flex trash bags, and the hydrogen-powered BMW Hydrogen 7. The introduction of *e-file*, which allows online filing of tax returns, by the U.S. Internal Revenue Service (IRS) is an example of a new service innovation. Product changes are related to changes in the technology of the organization. A **technology change** is a change in the organization's production process—how the organization does its work. Technology changes are designed to make the production of a product or service more efficient. The adoption of automatic mail sorting machines by the U.S. Postal Service is one example of a technology change.

Three critical innovation strategies for changing products and technologies are illustrated in Exhibit 8.1.[14] The first strategy, *exploration*, involves designing the organization to encourage creativity and the initiation of new ideas. The strategy of *cooperation*

Exploration	Cooperation	Entrepreneurship	
• Creativity • Experimentation • Idea incubators	• Horizontal coordination mechanisms • Customers, partners • Open innovation	• Idea champions • New venture teams • Skunkworks • New venture fund	**EXHIBIT 8.1** Three Innovative Strategies for New Products and Technologies

SOURCE: Based on Patrick Reinmoeller and Nicole van Baardwijk, "The Link Between Diversity and Resilience," *MIT Sloan Management Review* (Summer 2005): 61–65.

refers to creating conditions and systems to facilitate internal and external coordination and knowledge sharing. Finally, *entrepreneurship* means that managers put in place processes and structures to ensure that new ideas are carried forward for acceptance and implementation.

EXPLORATION

Exploration is the stage where ideas for new products and technologies are born. Managers design the organization for exploration by establishing conditions that encourage creativity and allow new ideas to spring forth. Creativity, which refers to the generation of novel ideas that might meet perceived needs or respond to opportunities for the organization, is the essential first step in innovation.[15] People noted for their creativity include Edwin Land, who invented the Polaroid camera, and Swiss engineer George de Mestral, who created Velcro after noticing the tiny hooks on the burrs caught on his wool socks. These people saw unique and creative opportunities in a familiar situation. Stanford University's Technology Ventures program recently sponsored a contest challenging people to come up with creative uses for everyday objects such as rubber bands. Ignacio Donoso Olive, a computer science student in Ecuador, connected bands to form an elastic hem around the mesh canopies that are hung over beds at night to combat malaria. The elastic band helps prevent the canopies, usually tucked under mattresses, from slipping loose and giving deadly entrance to mosquitoes.[16] Retail giant Zara became successful by continuously trying new business technologies as described in this chapter's Benchmarking box (page 250).

creativity
The generation of novel ideas that might meet perceived needs or offer opportunities for the organization.

Characteristics of highly creative people are illustrated in the left-hand column of Exhibit 8.2. Creative people often are known for originality, open-mindedness, curiosity, a focused approach to problem solving, persistence, a relaxed and playful attitude, and receptivity to new ideas.[17] Creativity can also be designed into organizations. Companies or departments within companies can be organized to be creative and initiate ideas for change. Most companies want more highly creative employees and often seek to hire creative individuals. However, the individual is only part of the story, and each of us has some potential for creativity. Managers are responsible for creating a work environment that allows creativity to flourish.[18]

The characteristics of creative organizations correspond to those of individuals, as illustrated in the right-hand column of Exhibit 8.2. Creative organizations are loosely structured. People

© ROBIN TWOMEY

Innovative companies such as Intuit want everyone to continually be coming up with new ideas. Founder Scott Cook and CEO Steve Bennett, shown here, encourage creativity during the exploration phase by embracing failure as readily as they do success. "I've had my share of really bad ideas," Cook admits. Yet failure can have hidden possibilities. Sticky notes, such as those shown here on Intuit's board, were invented at 3M Corporation based on a failed product—a not-very-sticky adhesive that resulted from a chemist's attempts to create a superglue. Post-it Notes became one of the best-selling office products ever.

>> CONCEPT CONNECTION <<

EXHIBIT 8.2
Characteristics of
Creative People and
Organizations

The Creative Individual	The Creative Organization or Department
1. Conceptual fluency Open-mindedness	**1.** Open channels of communication Contact with outside sources Overlapping territories; cross-pollination of ideas across disciplines Suggestion systems, brainstorming, freewheeling discussions
2. Originality	**2.** Assigning nonspecialists to problems Eccentricity allowed Hiring outside your comfort zone
3. Less authority Independence Self-confidence	**3.** Decentralization, loosely defined positions, loose control Acceptance of mistakes; rewarding risk taking People encouraged to challenge their bosses
4. Playfulness Undisciplined exploration Curiosity	**4.** Freedom to choose and pursue problems Not a tight ship; playful culture, doing the impractical Freedom to discuss ideas; long time horizon
5. Persistence Commitment Focused approach	**5.** Resources allocated to creative personnel and projects without immediate payoff Reward system encourages innovation Absolution of peripheral responsibilities

SOURCES: Based on Gary A. Steiner (Ed.), *The Creative Organization* (Chicago: University of Chicago Press, 1965): 16–18; Rosabeth Moss Kanter," The Middle Manager as Innovator," *Harvard Business Review* (July–Aug. 1982): 104–105; James Brian Quinn, "Managing Innovation: Controlled Chaos," *Harvard Business Review* (May–June 1985): 73–84; Robert I. Sutton, "The Weird Rules of Creativity," *Harvard Business Review* (Sept. 2001): 94–103; and Bridget Finn, "Playbook: Brainstorming for Better Brainstorming," *Business 2.0* (Apr. 2005), 109–114.

find themselves in a situation of ambiguity, assignments are vague, territories overlap, tasks are loosely defined, and much work is done through teams. Managers in creative companies embrace risk and experimentation. They involve employees in a varied range of projects so that people are not stuck in the rhythm of routine jobs, and they drive out the fear of making mistakes that can inhibit creative thinking.[19] Creative

BENCH-MARKING

Zara

In 2009, Gap lost its title as world's largest clothing retailer to Spanish company Zara, which is owned by Inditex. Since 2000, Zara has quadrupled in sales, largely due to its innovative business processes. Rather than taking the typical six months for clothing to go from drawing board to store rack, Zara does it in 15 to 30 days. And whereas the retail giants introduce a few thousand new product lines each year, Zara brings out 22,000. One reason the company can produce so much so quickly is its tight grip on every link in the supply chain. Such a "fast fashion" way of business has now become a model for other apparel chains such as Mango and TopShop. None of this happened overnight. Inditex's three decades in business have been spent perfecting its strategy, achieved by regularly breaking retailing rules. Instead of designers determining what comes next, at Zara store managers monitor daily what sells most, tracking everything from current sales to new clothing

customers ask for, and then they send that information to the company's 300 designers, who instantly style what is needed. And while most clothiers outsource production to low-cost Asian factories, Zara manufactures half its merchandise in factories in Spain, Portugal, and Morocco, with the most fashionable clothing made in-house and commodities such as T-shirts bought from Africa or Asia. Even though the European workers earn more, the company saves on time and shipping costs, making the process profitable. With such a system, the company can get new clothing into its European stores within 24 hours. Rivals think they can copy Zara a little, but business analyst Luca Solca voices caution. "The Inditex is an all-or-nothing proposition that has to be fully embraced to yield results," he said.

SOURCE: "Fashion Forward," *Foreign Policy*, Nov.–Dec. 2008, no. 169, p. 28; and Kerry Capell, "Zara Thrives by Breaking All the Rules," *BusinessWeek*, 20, 2008, p. 66.

2 The most important thing for a company to be innovative is to encourage lots of creative ideas.

ANSWER: Without stimulating new and even outlandish ideas, a company's capacity to innovate will be greatly reduced. Perhaps equally important, though, is organizing to sustain innovation. Without such a structure, most of the creative ideas will not come to fruition.

organizations have an internal culture of playfulness, freedom, challenge, and grassroots participation.[20]

To keep creativity alive at Google, managers let people spend 20 percent of their time working on any project they choose. People who interview for a job at the company are often asked, "If you could change the world using Google's resources, what would you build?" Google's managers instill a sense of creative fearlessness, which is part of the reason Google shows up at the top of numerous lists of most innovative companies.[21] Exhibit 8.3 shows the top 10 innovative companies from one recent list.

Another popular way to encourage new ideas within the organization is the **idea incubator**. An idea incubator provides a safe harbor where ideas from employees throughout the company can be developed without interference from company bureaucracy or politics.[22] Yahoo started an off-site incubator to speed up development of ideas and be more competitive with Google. Dubbed "Brickhouse" and located in a hip section of San Francisco, the idea incubator gets about 200 ideas submitted each month, and a panel sorts out the top 5 to 10. "The goal is to take the idea, develop it, and make sure it's seen by senior management quickly," says Salim Ismail, head of Brickhouse.[23]

COOPERATION

Another important aspect of innovation is providing mechanisms for both internal and external coordination. Ideas for product and technology innovations typically originate at lower levels of the organization and need to flow horizontally across departments. In addition, people and organizations outside the firm can be rich sources of innovative ideas. Lack of innovation

TAKE ACTION

As a new manager, inspire people to be more creative—give them opportunities to explore ideas outside their regular jobs and encourage experimentation, risk taking, and "crazy ideas." See mistakes as part of the learning process.

idea incubator
An in-house program that provides a safe harbor where ideas from employees throughout the organization can be developed without interference from company bureaucracy or politics.

Rank	Company	Headquarters	Most Known For
1	Apple	United States	New products
2	Google	United States	Customer experience
3	Toyota Motor Co.	Japan	Work processes
4	General Electric	United States	Work processes
5	Microsoft	United States	New products
6	Tata Group	India	New products
7	Nintendo	Japan	New products
8	Procter & Gamble	United States	Work processes
9	Sony	Japan	New products
10	Nokia	Finland	New products

EXHIBIT 8.3
The World's Most Innovative Companies

SOURCE: "The World's 50 Most Innovative Companies," *BusinessWeek* (Apr. 28, 2008), accessed at http://bwnt.businessweek.com/interactive_reports/innovative_companies on May 6, 2008.

BUSINESS BLOOPER

Banquet Pot Pies

In 2007, about 15,000 got sick from *Salmonella* bacteria after eating Banquet pot pies. ConAgra Foods, which sold more than 100 million of the 69 cents pies in 2008, tried to figure out which one of 25 ingredients was the culprit. After spot checking for pathogens and having no luck, the company finally gave up. Other food companies have admitted they don't even know where some of their ingredients come from. Makes you feel safe, right? Rather than risk being shut down, in 2009 ConAgra started putting the onus for killing the elusive pathogen on the consumer, telling them the pie needs to reach an internal temperature of 185 degrees, as measured by a food thermometer in several places. As if people who buy 69 cent pies will have a food thermometer in their utensil drawer.

SOURCE: Michael Moss, "For Frozen Entrees, 'Heat and 'Eat' Isn't Enough," *New York Times*, May 15, 2009, pp. A1, A3.

is widely recognized as one of the biggest problems facing today's businesses. Consider that 72 percent of top executives surveyed by *BusinessWeek* and the Boston Consulting Group reported that innovation is a top priority, yet almost half said they are dissatisfied with their results in that area.[24] Thus, many companies are undergoing a transformation in the way they find and use new ideas, focusing on improving both internal and external coordination. The company that manufactures Banquet pot pies is evidently hoping consumers will cooperate in order to prevent another *Salmonella* outbreak, as described in the Business Blooper box.

Internal Coordination. Successful innovation requires expertise from several departments simultaneously, and failed innovation is often the result of failed cooperation.[25] Consider the partner at a large accounting firm who was leading a team of 50 experts to develop new services. After a year of effort, they'd come up with few ideas, and the ones they had produced weren't successful. What went wrong? The leader had divided the team into three separate groups, so that researchers would come up with ideas, then hand them off to technical specialists, who in turn passed them along to marketers. Because the groups were working in isolation, much time and energy was spent on ideas that didn't meet technical specialists' criteria or that the marketers knew wouldn't work commercially.[26]

Companies that successfully innovate usually have the following characteristics:

1. People in marketing have a good understanding of customer needs.

2. Technical specialists are aware of recent technological developments and make effective use of new technology.

3. Members from key departments—research, manufacturing, and marketing—cooperate in the development of the new product or service.[27]

horizontal linkage model
An approach to product change that emphasizes shared development of innovations among several departments.

fast-cycle team
A multifunctional team that is provided with high levels of resources and empowerment to accomplish an accelerated product development project.

open innovation
Extending the search for and commercialization of new ideas beyond the boundaries of the organization.

One approach to successful innovation is called the **horizontal linkage model**, which is illustrated in the center circle of Exhibit 8.4.[28] The model shows that the research, manufacturing, and sales and marketing departments within an organization simultaneously contribute to new products and technologies. People from these departments meet frequently in teams and task forces to share ideas and solve problems. Research people inform marketing of new technical developments to learn whether they will be useful to customers. Marketing people pass customer complaints to research to use in the design of new products and to manufacturing people to develop new ideas for improving production speed and quality. Manufacturing informs other departments whether a product idea can be manufactured within cost limits.

The horizontal linkage model is increasingly important in today's high-pressure business environment that requires rapidly developing and commercializing products and services.

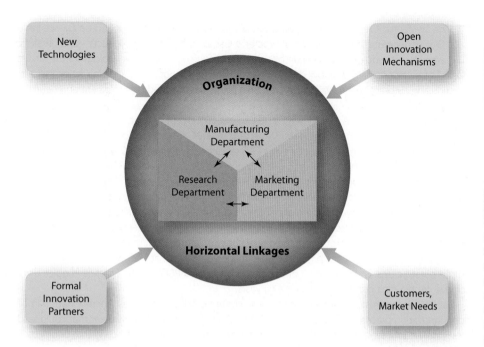

EXHIBIT 8.4
Coordination
Model for
Innovation

*Help people communicate
and cooperate
across organizational
boundaries. Implement
mechanisms that help
team members stay
in touch with what's
happening in other
departments and in the
marketplace.*

This kind of teamwork is similar to a rugby match in which players run together, passing the ball back and forth as they move downfield.[29] Speed is emerging as a pivotal strategic weapon in the global marketplace for a wide variety of industries.[30] Some companies use fast-cycle teams to deliver products and services faster than competitors, giving them a significant strategic advantage. A **fast-cycle team** is a multifunctional, and sometimes multinational, team that works under stringent timelines and is provided with high levels of resources and empowerment to accomplish an accelerated product development project.[31]

External Coordination. Exhibit 8.4 also illustrates that organizations look outside their boundaries to find and develop new ideas. Engineers and researchers stay aware of new technological developments. Marketing personnel pay attention to shifting market conditions and customer needs. Some organizations build formal strategic partnerships such as alliances and joint ventures to improve innovation success.

Today's most successful companies are including customers, strategic partners, suppliers, and other outsiders directly in the process of developing products and services. One of the hottest trends is *open innovation*.[32] In the past, most businesses generated their own ideas in-house and then developed, manufactured, marketed, and distributed them, a closed innovation approach. Today, however, forward-looking companies are trying a different method. **Open innovation** means extending the search for and commercialization of new ideas beyond the boundaries of the organization and even beyond the boundaries of the industry. In a survey conducted by IBM and *Industry Week* magazine, 40 percent of respondents said collaborating with customers and suppliers had the most significant impact on product development time to market.[33] Procter & Gamble, not so long ago a stodgy consumer products company, has become one of the country's hottest innovators and a role model for the open innovation process.

© JACOB SILBERBERG/LANDOV

Google cofounders Larry Page (left) and Sergey Brin take the stage during the September 2008 unveiling of the HTC G1 phone by T-Mobile, the first mobile phone to run on Google's Android software. Using an open innovation approach, Google issued a call for anyone to develop new software applications for its open-platform Android. The company's Developer Challenge will award a total of $10 million for the best new applications.

············> CONCEPT CONNECTION <············

The SwifferVac. Crest Spin Brush. Mr. Clean Magic Eraser. Valentino Rock 'n Rose Eau de Parfum. Olay Regenerist. These are some of Procter & Gamble's best-selling products—and all of them were developed in whole or in part by someone outside of P&G. The technology for the Mr. Clean Magic Eraser was originally developed by Germany's BASF for soundproofing and insulation in the construction and automotive industries. The Crest Spin Brush was invented by a small entrepreneurial firm in Cleveland.

Procter & Gamble CEO A. G. Lafley set a goal to get 50 percent of the company's innovation from outside the organization, up from about 35 percent in 2004 and only 10 percent in 2000. The company's top executives estimated that for every P&G researcher there were 200 scientists elsewhere who were just as good, so why not tap into that vast pool of creativity and talent? P&G developed a detailed, well-organized process for open innovation with its Connect and Develop strategy, which taps into networks of inventors, scientists, academics, partners, and suppliers to embrace the collective brains of the world. When P&G wanted to make snacks more fun by printing trivia questions, animal facts, jokes, and cartoon characters on its Pringles potato crisps, it drew up a technology brief defining the challenge and circulated it throughout the global network. It turned out that a small bakery in Bologna, Italy, had an ink-jet method for printing edible images on cakes that P&G was able to adapt for use on the potato crisps. The innovation of Pringles Prints helped P&G's North America Pringles division achieve double-digit growth for the next two years.

But P&G doesn't just look for extensions of its current product categories. An important part of its open innovation process is networking with external scientists in totally new areas that could lead to totally new businesses. For instance, who would have thought that the company that brings us Tide and Pampers could rival beauty titan Chanel in premium fragrance sales?[34]

In line with the new way of thinking we discussed in Chapter 1, which sees partnership and collaboration as more important than independence and competition, the boundaries between an organization and its environment are becoming porous, as illustrated by the P&G examples. Through open innovation, ideas flow back and forth among different people and companies that engage in partnerships, joint ventures, licensing agreements, and other alliances.

ENTREPRENEURSHIP

The third aspect of product and technology innovation is creating mechanisms to make sure new ideas are carried forward, accepted, and implemented. Managers can directly influence whether entrepreneurship flourishes in the organization by expressing support of entrepreneurial activities, giving employees a degree of autonomy, and rewarding learning and risk taking.[35] One important matter is fostering idea champions. The formal definition of an **idea champion** is a person who sees the need for and champions productive change within the organization.

Remember: Change does not occur by itself. Personal energy and effort are required to successfully promote a new idea. When Texas Instruments studied 50 of its new-product introductions, a surprising fact emerged: Without exception, every new product that failed lacked a zealous champion. In contrast, most of the new products that succeeded had a champion. Managers made an immediate decision: No new product would be approved unless someone championed it. Research confirms that successful new ideas are generally those that are backed by someone who believes in the idea wholeheartedly and is determined to convince others of its value.[36]

Sometimes management rejects a new idea, but champions are passionately committed to a new product or idea despite rejection by others. For example, Robert Vincent was fired twice by two different division managers at a semiconductor company. Both times, he convinced the president and chairman of the board to reinstate him to continue working on his idea for an airbag sensor that measures acceleration and deceleration. He couldn't get approval for research funding, so Vincent pushed to finish another project in half the time and used the savings to support the new product's development.[37]

Championing an idea successfully requires the roles in organizations illustrated in Exhibit 8.5. Sometimes a single person may play two or more of these roles, but successful

idea champion
A person who sees the need for and champions productive change within the organization.

Inventor	**Champion**	**Sponsor**	**Critic**
Develops and understands technical aspects of idea	Believes in idea	High-level manager who removes organizational barriers	Provides reality test
Does not know how to win support for the idea or make a business of it	Visualizes benefits	Approves and protects idea within organization	Looks for shortcomings
	Confronts organizational realities of cost, benefits		Defines hard-nosed criteria that idea must pass
	Obtains financial and political support		
	Overcomes obstacles		

SOURCES: Based on Harold L. Angle and Andrew H. Van de Ven, "Suggestions for Managing the Innovation Journey," in A. H. Van de Ven, H. L. Angle, and Marshall Scott Poole (Eds.), *Research in the Management of Innovation: The Minnesota Studies* (Cambridge, MA: Ballinger/Harper & Row, 1989); and Jay R. Galbraith, "Designing the Innovating Organization," *Organizational Dynamics* (Winter 1982): 5–25.

EXHIBIT 8.5
Four Roles in Organizational Change

- - - - - - - - - - -

As a new manager, have the courage to promote useful change. Are you an idea champion for changes or new ideas you believe in? To find out, complete the New Manager's Self-Test on page 256.

innovation in most companies involves an interplay of different people, each adopting one role. The *inventor* comes up with a new idea and understands its technical value but has neither the ability nor the interest to promote it for acceptance within the organization. The *champion* believes in the idea, confronts the organizational realities of costs and benefits, and gains the political and financial support needed to bring it to reality. The *sponsor* is a high-level manager who approves the idea, protects the idea, and removes major organizational barriers to acceptance. The *critic* counterbalances the zeal of the champion by challenging the concept and providing a reality test against hard-nosed criteria. The critic prevents people in the other roles from adopting a bad idea.[38]

Another way to facilitate entrepreneurship is through a **new-venture team**. A new-venture team is a unit separate from the rest of the organization that is responsible for developing and initiating a major innovation.[39] Whenever BMW Group begins developing a new car, the project's team members—from engineering, design, production, marketing, purchasing, and finance—are relocated to a separate Research and Innovation Center, where they work collaboratively to speed the new product to market.[40] New-venture teams give free rein to members' creativity because their separate facilities and location unleash people from the restrictions imposed by organizational rules and procedures. These teams typically are small, loosely structured, and flexible, reflecting the characteristics of creative organizations described in Exhibit 8.2.

One variation of a new-venture team is called a **skunkworks**.[41] A skunkworks is a separate small, informal, highly autonomous, and often secretive group that focuses on breakthrough ideas for the business. The original skunkworks, which still exists, was created by Lockheed Martin more than 50 years ago. The essence of a skunkworks is that highly talented people are given the time and freedom to let creativity reign.[42] The laser printer was invented by a Xerox researcher who was transferred to a skunkworks, the Xerox Palo Alto Research Center, after his ideas about using lasers were stifled within the company for being "too impractical and expensive."[43] Companies such as Cargill and IBM are launching entirely new businesses by using entrepreneurship groups similar to a skunkworks.[44] Good ideas that don't fit existing businesses are transferred for development to a separate formal organization called the Emerging Business Accelerator at Cargill and the Emerging Business Opportunities (EBO) program at IBM. One idea from IBM's EBO program—a digital media business to help manage video, audio, and still images—grew into a $1.7 billion business in only three years.[45]

A related idea is the **new-venture fund**, which provides resources from which individuals and groups can draw to develop new ideas, products, or businesses. At 3M, scientists can apply for Genesis Grants to work on innovative project ideas. The company awards anywhere from 12 to 20 of these grants each year, ranging from $50,000 to $100,000 each, for researchers to hire supplemental staff, acquire equipment, or fund whatever is needed to develop the new idea.[46] With these programs, the support and assistance of senior managers are often just as important as the funding.[47]

new-venture team
A unit separate from the mainstream of the organization that is responsible for developing and initiating innovations.

skunkworks
A separate, small, informal, highly autonomous, and often secretive group that focuses on breakthrough ideas for a business.

new-venture fund
A fund providing resources from which individuals and groups can draw to develop new ideas, products, or businesses.

NEW MANAGER'S SELF-TEST

Taking Charge of Change

As a new manager, do you have what it takes to be an idea champion? Will you initiate change? Think of a job you held for a period of time. Answer the following questions according to your behaviors and perspective on that job. Please answer whether each item is Mostly True or Mostly False for you.

	MOSTLY TRUE	MOSTLY FALSE
1. I often tried to adopt improved procedures for doing my job.	_____	_____
2. I felt a personal sense of responsibility to bring about change in my workplace.	_____	_____
3. I often tried to institute new work methods that were more effective for the company.	_____	_____
4. I often tried to change organizational rules or policies that were non-productive or counterproductive.	_____	_____
5. It was up to me to bring about improvement in my workplace.	_____	_____
6. I often made constructive suggestions for improving how things operated.	_____	_____
7. I often tried to implement new ideas for pressing organizational problems.	_____	_____
8. I often tried to introduce new structures, technologies, or approaches to improve efficiency.	_____	_____

SCORING AND INTERPRETATION: An important part of a new manager's job is to facilitate improvements through innovation and change. Will you be a champion for change? Your answers to the questions may indicate the extent to which you have a natural inclination toward taking charge of change. Not everyone thrives in a position of initiating change, but as a new manager, you will find that initiating change within the first six months will enhance your impact.

Give yourself 1 point for each item you marked as Mostly True. If you scored 4 or less, then you may not have been flexing your change muscles on the job. You may need to become more active at taking charge of change. Moreover, you may need to be in a more favorable change situation. Research indicates that jobs with open-minded management, where change is believed likely to succeed and be rewarded, increase a person's initiative. So the organization in which you are a new manager plus your own inclination will influence your initiation of change. A score of 5 or more suggests a positive level of previous change initiation behavior and solid preparation for a new manager role as an idea champion.

SOURCE: Based on Elizabeth W. Morrison and Corey C. Phelps, "Taking Charge at Work: Extrarole Efforts to Initiate Workplace Change," *Academy of Management Journal* 42 (1999): 403–419.

Changing People and Culture

people change
A change in the attitudes and behaviors of a few employees in the organization.

All successful changes involve changes in people and culture as well. Changes in people and culture pertain to how employees think—changes in mind-set. **People change** concerns just a few employees, such as sending a handful of middle managers to a training

3 Changing an organization is not as hard as people make out.

ANSWER: Organization change is very difficult—in fact, more difficult than most managers realize. If not done correctly, the department or unit will revert back to its old behaviors. Change that is lasting takes a long time—much longer than the short programs usually initiated.

course to improve their leadership skills. **Culture change** pertains to the organization as a whole, such as when the IRS shifted its basic mind-set from an organization focused on collection and compliance to one dedicated to informing, educating, and serving customers (taxpayers).[48] Large-scale culture change is not easy. Indeed, managers routinely report that changing people and culture is their most difficult job.[49] Two specific tools that can smooth the process are training and development programs and organization development.

Go to the Ethical Dilemma on page 268 that pertains to structural change.

TRAINING AND DEVELOPMENT

Training is one of the most frequently used approaches to changing people's mind-sets. A company might offer training programs to large blocks of employees on subjects such as teamwork, diversity, emotional intelligence, quality circles, communication skills, or participative management.

Successful companies want to provide training and development opportunities for everyone, but they might particularly emphasize training and development for managers with the idea that the behavior and attitudes of managers will influence people throughout the organization and lead to culture change. A number of Silicon Valley companies, including Intel, Advanced Micro Devices (AMD), and Sun Microsystems, regularly send managers to the Growth and Leadership Center, where they learn to use emotional intelligence to build better relationships. Nick Kepler, director of technology development at AMD, was surprised to learn how his emotionless approach to work was intimidating people and destroying the rapport needed to shift to a culture based on collaborative teamwork.[50]

ORGANIZATION DEVELOPMENT

Organization development (OD) is a planned, systematic process of change that uses behavioral science knowledge and techniques to improve an organization's health and effectiveness through its ability to adapt to the environment, improve internal relationships, and increase learning and problem-solving capabilities.[51] OD focuses on the human and social aspects of the organization and works to change attitudes and relationships among employees, helping to strengthen the organization's capacity for adaptation and renewal.[52]

OD can help managers address at least three types of current problems:[53]

1. *Mergers and acquisitions.* The disappointing financial results of many mergers and acquisitions are caused by the failure of executives to determine whether the administrative style and corporate culture of the two companies fit well together. Executives may concentrate on potential synergies in technology, products, marketing, and control systems but fail to recognize that two firms may have widely different values, beliefs, and practices. These differences create stress and anxiety for employees, and these negative emotions affect future performance. Cultural differences should be evaluated during the acquisition process, and OD experts can be used to smooth the integration of two firms.

2. *Organizational decline and revitalization.* Organizations that undergo a period of decline and revitalization experience a variety of problems, including a low level of trust, lack of

culture change
A major shift in the norms, values, attitudes, and mind-set of the entire organization.

organization development (OD)
The application of behavioral science techniques to improve an organization's health and effectiveness through its ability to cope with environmental changes, improve internal relationships, and increase learning and problem-solving capabilities.

innovation, high turnover, and high levels of conflict and stress. The period of transition requires opposite behaviors, including confronting stress, creating open communication, and fostering creative innovation to emerge with high levels of productivity. OD techniques can contribute greatly to cultural revitalization by managing conflicts, fostering commitment, and facilitating communication.

3. *Conflict management.* Conflict can occur at any time and place within a healthy organization. For example, a product team for the introduction of a new software package was formed at a computer company. Made up of strong-willed individuals, the team made little progress because members could not agree on project goals. At a manufacturing firm, salespeople promised delivery dates to customers that were in conflict with shop supervisor priorities for assembling customer orders. In a publishing company, two managers disliked each other intensely. They argued at meetings, lobbied politically against each other, and hurt the achievement of both departments. Organization development efforts can help resolve these kinds of conflicts, as well as conflicts that are related to growing diversity and the global nature of today's organizations.

Organization development can be used to solve the types of problems just described and many others. However, to be truly valuable to companies and employees, organization development practitioners go beyond looking at ways to settle specific problems. Instead, they become involved in broader issues that contribute to improving organizational life, such as encouraging a sense of community, pushing for an organizational climate of openness and trust, and making sure the company provides employees with opportunities for personal growth and development.[54]

OD Activities. OD consultants use a variety of specialized techniques to help meet OD goals. Three of the most popular and effective are the following:

1. *Team-building activities.* **Team building** enhances the cohesiveness and success of organizational groups and teams. For example, a series of OD exercises can be used with members of cross-departmental teams to help them learn to act and function as a team. An OD expert can work with team members to increase their communication skills, facilitate their ability to confront one another, and help them accept common goals.

2. *Survey-feedback activities.* **Survey feedback** begins with a questionnaire distributed to employees on values, climate, participation, leadership, and group cohesion within their organization. After the survey is completed, an OD consultant meets with groups of employees to provide feedback about their responses and the problems identified. Employees are engaged in problem solving based on the data.

3. *Large-group interventions.* In recent years, the need for bringing about fundamental organizational change in today's complex, fast-changing world prompted a growing interest in applications of OD techniques to large-group settings.[55] The **large-group intervention** approach brings together participants from all parts of the organization—often including key stakeholders from outside the organization as well—to discuss problems or opportunities and plan for change. A large-group intervention might involve 50 to 500 people and last several days. The idea is to include everyone who has a stake in the change, gather perspectives from all parts of the system, and enable people to create a collective future through sustained, guided dialogue.

Large-group interventions reflect a significant shift in the approach to organizational change from earlier OD concepts and approaches. Exhibit 8.6 lists the primary differences between the traditional OD model and the large-scale intervention model of organizational change.[56] In the newer approach, the focus is on the entire system, which takes into account the organization's interaction with its environment. The source of information for discussion is expanded to include customers, suppliers, community members, and even competitors, and this information is shared widely so that everyone has the same picture of the organization and its environment. The acceleration of change when the entire system is

team building
A type of OD intervention that enhances the cohesiveness of departments by helping members learn to function as a team.

survey feedback
A type of OD intervention in which questionnaires on organizational climate and other factors are distributed among employees and their results reported back to them by a change agent.

large-group intervention
An approach that brings together participants from all parts of the organization (and may include key outside stakeholders as well) to discuss problems or opportunities and plan for major change.

	Traditional Organization Development Model	Large-Group Intervention Model
Focus for action:	Specific problem or group	Entire system
Information Source:	Organization	Organization and environment
Distribution:	Limited	Widely shared
Time frame:	Gradual	Fast
Learning:	Individual, small group	Whole organization
Change process:	Incremental change	Rapid transformation

EXHIBIT 8.6
OD Approaches to Culture Change

SOURCE: Adapted from Barbara Benedict Bunker and Billie T. Alban, "Conclusion: What Makes Large Group Interventions Effective," *Journal of Applied Behavioral Science* 28(4) (Dec. 1992): 579–591.

TAKE ACTION

Implement training opportunities that can help people shift their attitudes, beliefs, and behaviors toward what is needed for team, department, and organization success.

involved can be remarkable. In addition, learning occurs across all parts of the organization simultaneously, rather than just by individuals or in small groups or business units. The result is that the large-group approach offers greater possibilities for fundamental, radical transformation of the entire culture, whereas the traditional approach creates incremental change in a few individuals or small groups at a time. General Electric's Work-Out Program provides an excellent example of the large-group intervention approach.

GENERAL ELECTRIC'S WORK-OUT

GE's Work-Out began in large-scale off-site meetings facilitated by a combination of top leaders, outside consultants, and human-resources specialists. In each business unit, the basic pattern was the same. Hourly and salaried workers came together from many different parts of the organization in an informal three-day meeting to discuss and solve problems. Gradually, the Work-Out events began to include external stakeholders such as suppliers and customers as well as employees. Today, Work-Out is not an event, but a process of how work is done and problems are solved at GE.

The format for Work-Out includes seven steps:

1. Choose a work process or problem for discussion.
2. Select an appropriate cross-functional team, including external stakeholders.
3. Assign a "champion" to follow through on recommendations.
4. Meet for several days and come up with recommendations to improve processes or solve problems.
5. Meet with leaders, who are asked to respond to recommendations on the spot.
6. Hold additional meetings as needed to implement the recommendations.
7. Start the process all over again with a new process or problem.

GE's Work-Out process forces a rapid analysis of ideas, the creation of solutions, and the development of a plan for implementation. Over time, this large-group process creates an organizational culture in which ideas are rapidly translated into action and positive business results.[57]

Large-group interventions represent a significant shift in the way leaders think about change and reflect an increasing awareness of the importance of dealing with the entire system, including external stakeholders, in any significant change effort.

OD Steps. Organization development experts acknowledge that changes in corporate culture and human behavior are tough to accomplish and require major effort. The theory underlying OD proposes three distinct stages for achieving behavioral and attitudinal change: (1) unfreezing, (2) changing, and (3) refreezing.[58]

The first stage, **unfreezing**, means that people throughout the organization are made aware of problems and the need for change. This stage creates the motivation for people

unfreezing
The stage of organization development in which participants are made aware of problems to increase their willingness to change their behavior.

to change their attitudes and behaviors. Unfreezing may begin when managers present information that shows discrepancies between desired behaviors or performance and the current state of affairs. In addition, managers need to establish a sense of urgency to unfreeze people and create an openness and willingness to change. The unfreezing stage is often associated with *diagnosis*, which uses an outside expert called a *change agent*. The **change agent** is an OD specialist who performs a systematic diagnosis of the organization and identifies work-related problems. He or she gathers and analyzes data through personal interviews, questionnaires, and observations of meetings. The diagnosis helps determine the extent of organizational problems and helps unfreeze managers by making them aware of problems in their behavior.

The second stage, **changing**, occurs when individuals experiment with new behavior and learn new skills to be used in the workplace. This process is sometimes known as *intervention*, during which the change agent implements a specific plan for training managers and employees. The changing stage might involve a number of specific steps.[59] For example, managers put together a coalition of people with the will and power to guide the change, create a vision for change that everyone can believe in, and widely communicate the vision and plans for change throughout the company. In addition, successful change involves using emotion as well as logic to persuade people and empowering employees to act on the plan and accomplish the desired changes.

The third stage, **refreezing**, occurs when individuals acquire new attitudes or values and are rewarded for them by the organization. The impact of new behaviors is evaluated and reinforced. The change agent supplies new data that show positive changes in performance. Managers may provide updated data to employees that demonstrate positive changes in individual and organizational performance. Top executives celebrate successes and reward positive behavioral changes. At this stage, changes are institutionalized in the organizational culture so that employees begin to view the changes as a normal, integral part of how the organization operates. Employees may also participate in refresher courses to maintain and reinforce the new behaviors.

Implementing Change

The final step to be managed in the change process is *implementation*. A new, creative idea will not benefit the organization until it is in place and being fully used. Executives at companies around the world are investing heavily in change and innovation projects, but many of them say they aren't very happy with their results.[60] One frustration for managers is that employees often seem to resist change for no apparent reason. To effectively manage the implementation process, managers should be aware of the reasons people resist change and use techniques to enlist employee cooperation. Major, corporate-wide changes can be particularly challenging, as discussed in Spotlight on Skills box on page 261.

NEED FOR CHANGE

Many people are not willing to change unless they perceive a problem or a crisis. However, many problems are subtle, so managers have to recognize and then make others aware of the need for change.[61]

One way in which managers sense a need for change is through the appearance of a **performance gap**—a disparity between existing and desired performance levels. They then try to create a sense of urgency so that others in the organization will recognize and understand the need for change (similar to the OD concept of *unfreezing*). Recall from Chapter 5 the discussion of SWOT analysis. Managers are responsible for monitoring threats and opportunities in the external environment as well as strengths and weaknesses

TAKE ACTION

Use organization development consultants and techniques such as team building, survey feedback, and large-group intervention for widespread change.

change agent
An OD specialist who contracts with an organization to facilitate change.

changing
The intervention stage of organization development in which individuals experiment with new workplace behavior.

refreezing
The reinforcement stage of organization development in which individuals acquire a desired new skill or attitude and are rewarded for it by the organization.

performance gap
A disparity between existing and desired performance levels.

Kara DioGuardia was brought in as the new judge in season eight of *American Idol* to shake things up. "People know all the moves now," says Idol blogger Rickey Yaneza. "They know what the judges will say." So a new judge will force viewers to react differently to the show and pay attention to the judges again. And not a moment too soon, considering the 2008 season had the lowest ratings for years, slipping 6 percent from the previous season. As this book went to press, Paula Abdul announced her resignation, and Ellen DeGeneres signed on as a new judge.

Introducing songwriter DioGuardia into the judge mix was new. After graduating from Duke University, DioGuardia moved to New York, hoping to become a rock star. But nothing worked. She was told her nose was too big, she was not black enough, she was not white enough, and so on. When her singing career went nowhere, she started writing. Even though a contract with MCA produced nothing, she kept at it until, after a few years, she was writing for Pink, Carrie Underwood, Hillary Duff, and even Paris Hilton, whose weak voice was helped by Dio-Guardia's strong lyrics and melody. Along the way, she started a publishing company, Arthouse Entertainment, which administers 15 other songwriters. She also spends a great deal of time on charity work with recovery program Phoenix House.

Idol's producers are hoping DioGuardia adds a much-needed spike in unpredictability. Even if it doesn't do well, she can take it. She's had failures before, such as the unsuccessful band Platinum Weird, whose demise she now credits with preparing her for the current gig. "I would never be prepared for this without having done that," she said.

SOURCE: Jon Caramanica, "Idols, You've Have to Pass Through Her," *New York Times*, Jan 11, 2009, pp. AR1, AR24; and Edward Wyatt, "'Idol' Will Now Search for a Fourth Judge," *New York Times*, Aug. 7, 2009, pp. C1, C12.

within the organization to determine whether change is needed. Big problems are easy to spot, but sensitive monitoring systems are needed to detect gradual changes that can fool managers into thinking their company is doing fine. An organization may be in greater danger when the environment changes slowly because managers may fail to trigger an organizational response. Because *American Idol*'s ratings have been dropping, producers saw the need for some changes, as shown in the Spotlight on Skills box.

RESISTANCE TO CHANGE

Getting others to understand the need for change is the first step in implementation. Yet most changes will encounter some degree of resistance. Idea champions often discover that other employees are unenthusiastic about their new ideas. Members of a new-venture group may be surprised when managers in the regular organization do not support or approve their innovations. Managers and employees not involved in an innovation often seem to prefer the status quo. People resist change for several reasons, and understanding them can help managers implement change more effectively.

Self-Interest. People typically resist a change they believe conflicts with their self-interests. A proposed change in job design, structure, or technology may lead to an increase in employees' workload, for example, or to a real or perceived loss of power, prestige, pay, or benefits. The fear of personal loss is perhaps the biggest obstacle to organizational change.[62] At Fabcon, which makes huge precast concrete wall panels for commercial buildings, employees resisted a new experimental automation process because it added to their workload and reduced their productivity. "They were already working long days; they want to go home, and they didn't want to spend time doing R&D," says Fabcon's CEO Michael Le Jeune.[63] Managers began working with the foremen to show them how the process could eventually save time and effort, and the change was eventually a success.

Lack of Understanding and Trust. Employees often distrust the intentions behind a change or do not understand the intended purpose of a change. If previous working relationships with an idea champion have been negative, then resistance may occur. One manager had a habit of initiating a change in the financial reporting system about every 12 months and then losing interest and not following through. After the third time, employees no longer went along with the change because they did not trust the manager's intention to follow through to their benefit.

Uncertainty. *Uncertainty* is the lack of information about future events. It represents a fear of the unknown. Uncertainty is especially threatening for employees who have a low tolerance for change and fear anything out of the ordinary. They do not know how a change will affect them and worry about whether they will be able to meet the demands of a new procedure or technology.[64] For example, union leaders at an American auto manufacturer resisted the introduction of employee-participation programs. They were uncertain about how the program would affect their status, so they opposed it at first.

Different Assessments and Goals. Another reason for resistance to change is that people who will be affected by an innovation may assess the situation differently from an idea champion or new-venture group. Critics frequently voice legitimate disagreements

SPOTLIGHT ON SKILLS

Making Change Stick

Employees are not always receptive to change. A combination of factors can lead to rejection of, or even outright rebellion against, management's "new and better ideas."

Consider what happened when managers at Lands' End Inc. of Dodgeville, Wisconsin, tried to implement a sweeping overhaul incorporating many of today's management trends—teams, 401(k) plans, peer reviews, and the elimination of guards and time clocks. Despite managers' best efforts, employees balked. They had liked the old family-like atmosphere and uncomplicated work environment, and they considered the new requirement for regular meetings a nuisance. "We spent so much time in meetings that we were getting away from the basic stuff of taking care of business," says one employee. Even a much-ballyhooed new mission statement seemed "pushy." One long-time employee complained, "We don't need anything hanging over our heads telling us to do something we're already doing."

Confusion and frustration reigned at Lands' End and was reflected in an earnings drop of 17 percent. Eventually, a new CEO initiated a return to the familiar "Lands' End way" of doing things. Teams were disbanded, and many of the once-promising initiatives were shelved as workers embraced what was familiar.

The inability of people to adapt to change is not new. Neither is the failure of management to sufficiently lay the groundwork to prepare employees for change. Harvard professor John P. Kotter established an eight-step plan for implementing change

that can provide a greater potential for successful transformation of a company:

1. Establish a sense of urgency through careful examination of the market and identification of opportunities and potential crises.
2. Form a powerful coalition of managers able to lead the change.
3. Create a vision to direct the change and the strategies for achieving that vision.
4. Communicate the vision throughout the organization.
5. Empower others to act on the vision by removing barriers, changing systems, and encouraging risk taking.
6. Plan for and celebrate visible, short-term performance improvements.
7. Consolidate improvements, reassess changes, and make necessary adjustments in the new programs.
8. Articulate the relationship between new behaviors and organizational success.

Major change efforts can be messy and full of surprises, but following these guidelines can break down resistance and mean the difference between success and failure.

SOURCES: Gregory A. Patterson, "Land's End Kicks Out Modern New Managers, Rejecting a Makeover," *Wall Street Journal*, Apr. 3, 1995, p. A1; and John P. Kotter, "Leading Changes: Why Transformation Efforts Fail," *Harvard Business Review* (Mar.–Apr. 1995): 59–67.

over the proposed benefits of a change. Managers in each department pursue different goals, and an innovation may detract from performance and goal achievement for some departments. For example, if marketing gets the new product it wants for customers, then the cost of manufacturing may increase, and the manufacturing superintendent will resist. Resistance may call attention to problems with the innovation. At a consumer products company in Racine, Wisconsin, middle managers resisted the introduction of a new employee program that turned out to be a bad idea. The managers truly believed that the program would do more harm than good.[65]

These reasons for resistance are legitimate in the eyes of employees affected by the change. The best procedure for managers is not to ignore resistance but to diagnose the reasons and design strategies to gain acceptance by users.[66] Strategies for overcoming resistance to change typically involve two approaches: the analysis of resistance through the force-field technique and the use of selective implementation tactics to overcome resistance.

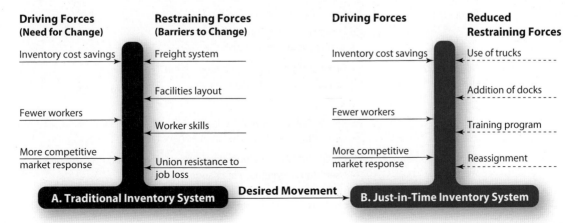

© PARADIGM LEARNING'S DISCOVERY MAP® ON IMPLEMENTING CHANGE AT MARATHON OIL

Marathon Oil Corporation took a creative approach to implementing change by using this Discovery Map to engage all 2,400 or so employees in the switch to using a new enterprise resource planning system. The ERP software system from SAP would impact all employees and operations at the international oil and gas production company and was seen as critical to the company's future competitiveness. Paradigm Learning, Inc., a Florida-based consulting firm, created the Discovery Map that visually communicates Marathon's change initiatives: its current reality and challenges, its vision for the future, and how to get there from here—with the new ERP system shown as the bridge.

················> CONCEPT CONNECTION <··········

FORCE-FIELD ANALYSIS

Force-field analysis grew from the work of Kurt Lewin, who proposed that change was a result of the competition between driving and restraining forces.[67] *Driving forces* can be thought of as problems or opportunities that provide motivation for change within the organization. *Restraining forces* are the various barriers to change, such as a lack of resources, resistance from middle managers, or inadequate employee skills. When a change is introduced, management should analyze both the forces that drive change (problems and opportunities) as well as the forces that resist it (barriers to change). By selectively removing forces that restrain change, the driving forces will be strong enough to enable implementation, as illustrated by the move from A to B in Exhibit 8.7. As barriers are reduced or removed, behavior will shift to incorporate the desired changes.

Just-in-time (JIT) inventory-control systems schedule materials to arrive at a company just as they are needed on the production line. In an Ohio manufacturing company, for example, management's analysis showed that the driving forces (opportunities) associated with the implementation of JIT were (1) the large cost savings from reduced inventories, (2) savings from needing fewer workers to handle the inventory, and (3) a quicker, more

force-field analysis
The process of determining which forces drive and which resist a proposed change.

EXHIBIT 8.7
Using Force-Field Analysis to Change from Traditional to Just-in-Time Inventory System

Driving Forces (Need for Change)	Restraining Forces (Barriers to Change)	Driving Forces	Reduced Restraining Forces
Inventory cost savings	Freight system	Inventory cost savings	Use of trucks
	Facilities layout		Addition of docks
Fewer workers	Worker skills	Fewer workers	Training program
More competitive market response	Union resistance to job loss	More competitive market response	Reassignment
A. Traditional Inventory System		**B. Just-in-Time Inventory System**	

Desired Movement

Recognize that people often have legitimate reasons for resisting change. Don't try to bulldoze a change through a wall of resistance. Use force-field analysis to evaluate driving and restraining. Try communication and education, participation, and negotiation to melt resistance.

competitive market response for the company. Restraining forces (barriers) discovered by managers were (1) a freight system that was too slow to deliver inventory on time, (2) a facility layout that emphasized inventory maintenance over new deliveries, (3) worker skills that were inappropriate for handling rapid inventory deployment, and (4) union resistance to loss of jobs. The driving forces were not sufficient to overcome the restraining forces.

To shift the behavior to JIT inventory control, managers attacked the barriers. An analysis of the freight system showed that delivery by truck provided the flexibility and quickness needed to schedule inventory arrival at a specific time each day. The problem with facility layout was met by adding four new loading docks. Inappropriate worker skills were attacked with a training program to instruct workers in both JIT methods and assembling products with uninspected parts. Union resistance was overcome by agreeing to reassign workers no longer needed for maintaining inventory to jobs in another plant. With the restraining forces reduced, the driving forces were sufficient to allow the JIT system to be implemented.

IMPLEMENTATION TACTICS

The other approach to managing implementation is to adopt specific tactics to overcome resistance. Researchers have studied various methods for dealing with resistance to change. The following five tactics, summarized in Exhibit 8.8, have proven successful.[68]

Communication and Education. *Communication* and *education* are used when solid information about the change is needed by users and others who may resist implementation. Education is especially important when the change involves new technical knowledge or users are unfamiliar with the idea. Canadian Airlines International spent a year and a half preparing and training employees before changing its entire reservations, airport, cargo, and financial systems as part of a new "service quality" strategy. Smooth implementation resulted from this intensive training and communications effort, which involved 50,000 tasks, 12,000 people, and 26 classrooms around the world.[69] Managers should also remember that implementing change requires speaking to people's hearts (touching their feelings) as well as to their minds (communicating facts). Emotion is a key component in persuading and influencing others. People are much more likely to change their behavior when they both understand the rational reasons for doing so and see a picture of change that influences their feelings.[70]

EXHIBIT 8.8

Tactics for Overcoming Resistance to Change

Approach	When to Use
Communication, education	• Change is technical. • Users need accurate information and analysis to understand change.
Participation	• Users need to feel involved. • Design requires information from others. • Users have power to resist.
Negotiation	• Group has power over implementation. • Group will lose out in the change.
Coercion	• A crisis exists. • Initiators clearly have power. • Other implementation techniques have failed.
Top management support	• Change involves multiple departments or reallocation of resources. • Users doubt legitimacy of change.

SOURCE: Based on J. P. Kotter and L. A. Schlesinger, "Choosing Strategies for Change," *Harvard Business Review* 57 (Mar.–Apr. 1979): 106–114.

Participation. *Participation* involves users and potential resisters in designing the change. This approach is time consuming, but it pays off because users understand and become committed to the change. At Learning Point Associates, which needed to change dramatically to meet new challenges, the change team drew up a comprehensive road map for transformation but had trouble getting the support of most managers. The managers argued that they hadn't been consulted about the plans and didn't feel compelled to participate in implementing them.[71] Research studies have shown that proactively engaging frontline employees in upfront planning and decision making about changes that affect their work results in much smoother implementation.[72] Participation also helps managers determine potential problems and understand the differences in perceptions of change among employees.

Negotiation. Negotiation is a more formal means of achieving cooperation. *Negotiation* uses formal bargaining to win acceptance and approval of a desired change. For example, if the marketing department fears losing power if a new management structure is implemented, then top managers may negotiate with marketing to reach a resolution. Companies that have strong unions frequently must formally negotiate change with the unions. The change may become part of the union contract to reflect the agreement of both parties.

Coercion. *Coercion* means that managers use formal power to force employees to change. Resisters are told to accept the change or lose rewards or even their jobs. In most cases, this approach should not be used because employees feel like victims, are angry at change managers, and may even sabotage the changes. However, coercion may be necessary in crisis situations when a rapid response is urgent. For example, a number of top managers at Coca-Cola had to be reassigned or let go after they refused to go along with a new CEO's changes for revitalizing the sluggish corporation.[73]

Top Management Support. The visible support of top management also helps overcome resistance to change. *Top management support* symbolizes to all employees that the change is important for the organization. One survey found that 80 percent of companies that are successful innovators have top executives who frequently reinforce the importance of innovation both verbally and symbolically.[74] Top management support is especially important when a change involves multiple departments or when resources are being reallocated among departments. Without top management support, changes can get bogged down in squabbling among departments. Moreover, when change agents fail to enlist the support of top executives, these leaders can inadvertently undercut the change project by issuing contradictory orders.

Managers can soften resistance and facilitate change and innovation by using smart techniques. At Remploy Ltd., needed changes were at first frightening and confusing to Remploy's workers, 90 percent of whom have some sort of disability. However, by communicating with employees, providing training, and closely involving them in the change process, managers were able to smoothly implement the new procedures and work methods. As machinist Helen Galloway put it, "Change is frightening, but because we all have a say, we feel more confident making those changes."[75]

Make sure to include top managers in your change projects. Build support at all levels.

Summary

Change is inevitable in organizations, and successful innovation is vital to the health of companies in all industries. This chapter discussed the techniques available for managing the change process. Two key aspects of change in organizations are changing products and technologies and changing people and culture.

Three essential innovation strategies for changing products and technologies are exploration, cooperation, and entrepreneurship. Exploration involves designing the organization to promote creativity, imagination, and idea generation. Cooperation requires mechanisms for internal coordination, such as horizontal linkages across departments, and mechanisms for connecting with external parties. One popular approach is open innovation, which extends the search for and commercialization of ideas beyond the boundaries of the organization. Entrepreneurship includes encouraging idea champions and establishing new-venture teams, skunkworks, and new-venture funds.

People and culture changes pertain to the skills, behaviors, and attitudes of employees. Training and organization development are important approaches to changing people's mind-sets and corporate culture. The OD process entails three steps: unfreezing (diagnosis of the problem), the actual change (intervention), and refreezing (reinforcement of new attitudes and behaviors). Popular OD techniques include team building, survey feedback, and large-group interventions.

Implementation of change first requires that people see a need for change. Managers should be prepared to encounter resistance. Some typical reasons for resistance include self-interest, lack of trust, uncertainty, and conflicting goals. Force-field analysis is one technique for diagnosing barriers, which often can be removed. Managers can also draw on the implementation tactics of communication, participation, negotiation, coercion, or top-management support.

Discussion Questions

1. Times of shared crisis—such as the September 11, 2001, terrorist attack on the World Trade Center and the Gulf Coast hurricanes in 2005—can induce many companies that have been bitter rivals to put their competitive spirit aside and focus on cooperation and courtesy. Do you believe this type of change will be a lasting one? Discuss.

2. A manager of an international chemical company said that few new products in her company were successful. What would you advise the manager to do to help increase the company's success rate?

3. As a manager, how would you deal with resistance to change when you suspect employees' fears of job loss are well founded?

4. How might businesses use the Internet to identify untapped customer needs through open innovation? What do you see as the major advantages and disadvantages of the open innovation approach?

5. If you were head of a police department in a midsized city, which technique do you think would be more effective for implementing changes in patrol officers' daily routines to stop more cars: communication and education, or proactively engaging them through participation?

6. Analyze the driving and restraining forces of a change you would like to make in your life. Do you believe understanding force-field analysis can help you more effectively implement a significant change in your own behavior?

7. Which role or roles—the inventor, champion, sponsor, or critic—would you most like to play in the innovation process? Why do you think idea champions are so essential to the initiation of change? Could they be equally important for implementation?

8. You are a manager, and you believe the expense reimbursement system for salespeople is far too slow, taking weeks instead of days. How would you go about convincing other managers that this problem needs to be addressed?

9. Do the underlying values of organization development differ from assumptions associated with other types of change? Discuss.

10. How do large-group interventions differ from OD techniques such as team building and survey feedback?

Self Learning

Innovation Climate

In order to examine differences in level of innovation encouragement in organizations, you will be asked to rate two different organizations. You may choose one in which you have worked or the university. The other should be someone else's workplace—a family member, friend, or acquaintance. Therefore, you will have to interview that person to answer the questions below. You should put your own answers in column A, your interviewee's answers in column B, and finally, what you think would be the "ideal" in column C.

Use the following scale of 1 to 5: 1 = don't agree at all to 5 = agree completely

Innovation Measures Item of Measure	Column A Your Organization	Column B Other Organization	Column C Your Ideal
1. Creativity is encouraged here.*			
2. People are allowed to solve the same problems in different ways.*			
3. I get free time to pursue creative ideas.#			
4. The organization publicly recognizes and also rewards those who are innovative.#			
5. Our organization is flexible and always open to change.*			

Below score items on the opposite scale: 1 = agree completely all through 5 = don't agree at all

6. The primary job of people here is to follow orders that come from the top.*			
7. The best way to get along here is to think and act like the others.*			
8. This place seems to be more concerned with the status quo than with change.*			
9. People are rewarded more if they don't rock the boat.#			
10. New ideas are great, but we don't have enough people or money to carry them out.#			

Note: * items indicate the organization's innovation climate
(pound sign) items show "resource support"

1. What comparisons about innovative climates can you make from these two organizations?

2. How might productivity differ when there is either a climate that supports innovation versus a climate that does not support innovation?

3. In which type of place would you rather work? Why?

SOURCE: Adapted from Susanne G. Scott and Reginald A. Bruce, "Determinants of Innovative Behavior: A Path Model of Individual Innovation in the Workplace," *Academy of Management Journal*, 37(3) (1994): 580–607.

Group Learning

ABS Crisis[76]

You are the internal OD consultant brought in by your company, ABS. There is an urgent problem that must be solved by the managers within a week. Because the company is near bankruptcy, your skills as a consultant are very important because you may be able to save the company. The situation is described below, and you must help facilitate the managers' efforts to reach a decision.

Case: In the last two years, the ABS Specialized Machinery Movers has suffered revenue losses because of increased competition and rising energy costs. ABS is known as a premier company in the industry that offers quality expertise and customer service. The company recently offered a low bid on a complex machinery-moving project. The company badly needed to generate revenue given its losses and offered the bid knowing that profit margins would be low unless drastic measures were taken. Upon winning the bid, the management set about to cut as many costs as possible in order to control costs on this low bid and increase the

profit margin. The ABS president believed that if this project did not produce profits, then the company would likely have to close.

One option is to cut labor costs by hiring illegal aliens. The project managers and supervisors for the job have years of experience and expertise; however, many of the laborers do not necessarily have to be highly skilled. The president and management are aware that it is unlawful to hire illegal immigrants, but they also know the laws regarding this issue are not enforced. They also are concerned that they may be putting unskilled workers at safety risk in this often hazardous line of work. The threat of losing the company remains of highest concern to the president and upper management.

Decisions must be made soon; the project's beginning date is only 25 days ahead.

After consulting with your colleagues, you feel the best course of action is to put the managers through a force-field analysis (see page 264). Create a chart like the one in Exhibit 8.7 (page 263).

1. On your own, fill in the driving and restraining forces of the ABS case.

2. In groups of four to six students, discuss these issues and come up with your group's driving and restraining forces.

3. Choose a spokesperson to present your results to the entire class.

SOURCE: By Jennie Carter Thomas and Harry N. Hollis, Belmont University. Used with permission.

Action Learning

1. Find two people to interview who have gone through an organization change in recent years.

2. Ask them the following questions:
   a. Describe the organization before the change: What was the work like? How did people get along with one another? Was the culture friendly? How did management treat employees?
   b. Who wanted the change? How was the decision made to bring about the change?
   c. Was an outside consultant brought in to help with the change? If not, who managed the change? How did the change process work? Was it effective?

   d. Describe the company after the change, using similar criteria from question 2a above.

3. Write a short paper describing the similarities and differences in the two situations.

4. What conclusions would you draw about organization change from what you learned in these two interviews?

5. Your instructor may ask you to discuss your findings in groups or as part of a class discussion.

Ethical Dilemma

Crowdsourcing

Last year, when Ai-Lan Nguyen told her friend Greg Barnwell that Off the Hook Tees, based in Asheville, North Carolina, was going to experiment with crowdsourcing, he warned her she wouldn't like the results. Now, as she was about to walk into a meeting called to decide whether to adopt this new business model, she was afraid her friend had been right.

Crowdsourcing uses the Internet to invite anyone, professionals and amateurs alike, to perform tasks such as product design that employees usually perform. In exchange, contributors receive recognition—but little or no pay. Ai-Lan, as vice president of operations for Off the Hook—a company specializing in witty T-shirts aimed at young adults—upheld the values of founder Chris Woodhouse, who like Ai-Lan was a graphic artist. Before he sold the company, the founder always insisted that T-shirts be well designed by top-notch graphic artists to make sure each screen print was a work of art. Those graphic artists reported to Ai-Lan.

During the past 18 months, Off the Hook's sales stagnated for the first time in its history. The crowdsourcing experiment was the latest in a series of attempts to jump-start sales growth. Last spring, Off the Hook issued its first open call for T-shirt designs and then posted the entries on the Web so people could vote for their favorites. The top five vote getters were handed over to the in-house designers, who tweaked the submissions until they met the company's usual quality standards.

When CEO Rob Taylor first announced the company's foray into crowdsourcing, Ai-Lan found herself reassuring the designers that their positions were not in jeopardy.

Now Ai-Lan was all but certain she would have to go back on her word. Not only had the crowdsourced tees sold well but also Rob had put a handful of winning designs directly into production, bypassing the design department altogether. Customers didn't notice the difference.

Ai-Lan concluded that Rob was ready to adopt some form of the Web-based crowdsourcing because it made T-shirt design more responsive to consumer desires. Practically speaking, it reduced the uncertainty that surrounded new designs, and it dramatically lowered costs. The people who won the competitions were delighted with the exposure it gave them.

However, when Ai-Lan looked at the crowdsourced shirts with her graphic artist's eye, she felt that the designs were competent but that none achieved the aesthetic standards attained by her in-house designers. Crowdsourcing essentially replaced training and expertise with public opinion. That made the artist in her uncomfortable.

More distressing, it was beginning to look as if Greg had been right when he'd told her that his working definition of crowdsourcing was "a billion amateurs want your job." It was easy to see that if Off the Hook adopted crowdsourcing, she would be handing out pink slips to most of her design people, long-time employees whose work she admired. "Sure, crowdsourcing costs the company less, but what about the human cost?" Greg asked.

What future course should Ai-Lan argue for at the meeting? And what personal decisions would she face if Off the Hook decided to put the crowd completely in charge when it came to T-shirt design?

What Would You Do?

1. Go to the meeting and argue for abandoning crowd-sourcing for now in favor of maintaining the artistic integrity and values that Off the Hook has always stood for.

2. Accept the reality that because Off the Hook's CEO Rob Taylor strongly favors crowdsourcing, it's a fait accompli. Be a team player and help work out the details of the new design approach. Prepare to lay off graphic designers as needed.

3. Accept the fact that converting Off the Hook to a crowdsourcing business model is inevitable, but because it violates your own personal values, start looking for a new job elsewhere.

SOURCE: Based on Paul Boutin, "Crowdsourcing: Consumers as Creators," *BusinessWeek Online* (July 13, 2006) (www.businessweek.com/innovate/content/jul2006/id20060713_755844.htm); Jeff Howe, "The Rise of Crowdsourcing," *Wired* (June 2006) (www.wired.com/wired/archive/14.06/crowds.html); and Jeff Howe, Crowdsourcing blog (www.crowdsourcing.com).

9

Chapter Nine

Managing Human Resources and Diversity

After studying this chapter, you should be able to:

1 Explain the strategic role of human-resource management.

2 Describe federal legislation and societal trends that influence human-resource management.

3 Explain what the changing social contract between organizations and employees means for workers and human-resource managers.

4 Describe the tools managers use to recruit and select employees, as well as how organizations develop an effective workforce through training and performance appraisal.

5 Explain how organizations maintain a workforce through the administration of wages and salaries, benefits, and terminations.

6 Understand the pervasive demographic changes occurring in the domestic and global marketplace and how corporations are responding.

7 Recognize the complex attitudes, opinions, and issues that employees bring to the workplace, including prejudice, discrimination, stereotypes, and ethnocentrism.

8 Recognize the factors that affect women's opportunities, including the glass ceiling, the opt-out trend, and the female advantage.

New Manager's Questions

Please circle your opinion below each of the following statements.

1 Managers need to have a prime focus on the bottom line—on the financial well-being of the company.

MOSTLY YES < < <				> > > MOSTLY NO
1	2	3	4	5

2 Hiring people to work for a company is about the economic contract between employer and employee.

MOSTLY YES < < <				> > > MOSTLY NO
1	2	3	4	5

3 The increasing numbers of foreign workers at U.S. companies need to spend a lot of attention learning the U.S. culture and adapting.

MOSTLY YES < < <				> > > MOSTLY NO
1	2	3	4	5

Hiring and keeping quality employees is one of the most urgent concerns for today's organizations.[1] Employees give a company its primary source of competitive advantage, so talent management is a top priority for smart managers. The term **human-resource management (HRM)** refers to the design and application of formal systems in an organization to ensure the effective and efficient use of human talent to accomplish organizational goals.[2] This system includes activities undertaken to attract, develop, and maintain an effective workforce. Managers have to find the right people, place them in positions where they can be most effective, and develop them so they contribute to company success.

Over the past decade, human-resource management has shed its old "personnel" image and gained recognition as a vital player in corporate strategy.[3] Increasingly, large corporations are outsourcing routine HR administrative activities, freeing HRM staff from time-consuming paperwork and enabling them to take on more strategic responsibilities. Human resources tops Gartner Inc.'s list of the most commonly outsourced business activities.[4]

All managers need to be skilled in the basics of human-resource management. Flatter organizations often require that managers throughout the organization play an active role in recruiting and selecting the right employees, developing effective training programs, or creating appropriate performance appraisal systems. HRM professionals act to guide and assist line managers in managing human resources to achieve the organization's strategic goals.

The Strategic Role of HRM Is to Drive Organizational Performance

Remember that employees are an important asset of the company.

How a company manages talent may be the single most important factor in sustained competitive success. Today's best human-resources departments not only support strategic objectives but also actively pursue an ongoing, integrated plan for furthering the organization's performance.[5] Research has found that effective human-resource management has a positive impact on strategic performance, including higher employee productivity and stronger financial results.[6]

THE STRATEGIC APPROACH

The strategic approach to human-resource management recognizes three key elements. First, all managers are involved in human-resource management. Second, employees are viewed as assets. Employees, not buildings and machinery, give a company its competitive edge. Third, human-resource management is a matching process, integrating the organization's strategy and goals with the correct approach to managing human capital.[7] In companies that take a strategic approach, HR managers are key players on the executive team and play a pivotal role in driving performance. At retailer Target, for example, the formal mission of the human-resources department is to "drive company performance by building a fast, fun, and friendly team committed to excellence." To fulfill the mission, HR managers are directly involved in building a culture that distinguishes Target from other retailers, finding the right people to fit the culture, then creating training programs, compensation, and other mechanisms to develop and retain quality employees.[8] Some current strategic issues of particular concern to managers include the following:

- The right people to become more competitive on a global basis.
- The right people for improving quality, innovation, and customer service.
- The right people to retain during mergers and acquisitions.
- The right people to apply new information technology for e-business.

All of these strategic decisions determine a company's need for skills and employees.

human-resource management (HRM)
Activities undertaken to attract, develop, and maintain an effective workforce within an organization.

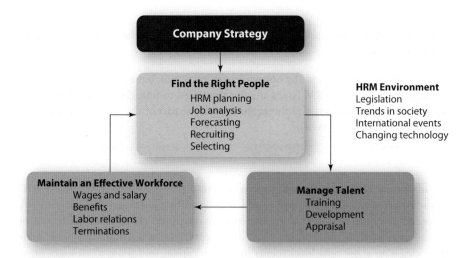

EXHIBIT 9.1
Strategic Human Resource Management

Company Strategy

Find the Right People
HRM planning
Job analysis
Forecasting
Recruiting
Selecting

HRM Environment
Legislation
Trends in society
International events
Changing technology

Maintain an Effective Workforce
Wages and salary
Benefits
Labor relations
Terminations

Manage Talent
Training
Development
Appraisal

This chapter examines the three primary goals of HRM as illustrated in Exhibit 9.1. HRM activities and goals do not take place inside a vacuum but within the context of issues and factors affecting the entire organization, such as globalization, changing technology, a growing need for rapid innovation, quick shifts in markets and the external environment, societal trends, government regulations, and changes in the organization's culture, structure, strategy, and goals.

The three broad HRM activities outlined in Exhibit 9.1 are to find the right people, manage talent so people achieve their potential, and maintain the workforce over the long term.[9] Achieving these goals requires skills in planning, recruiting, training, performance appraisal, wage and salary administration, benefit programs, and even termination.

TAKE ACTION

Don't hire someone just because they are available. Get the right person for your job.

human capital
The economic value of the knowledge, experience, skills, and capabilities of employees.

BUILDING HUMAN CAPITAL TO DRIVE PERFORMANCE

Today, more than ever, strategic decisions are related to human-resource considerations. In many companies, especially those that rely more on employee information, creativity, knowledge, and service rather than on production machinery, success depends on the ability to manage *human capital*.[10] **Human capital** refers to the economic value of the combined knowledge, experience, skills, and capabilities of employees.[11] To build human capital, HRM develops strategies for finding the best talent, enhancing their skills and knowledge with training programs and opportunities for personal and professional development, and providing compensation and benefits that support the sharing of knowledge and appropriately reward people for their contributions to the organization.

© DICK BLUME/SYRACUSE NEWSPAPERS/THE IMAGE WORKS

Lowe's 215,000 employees help customers with remodeling, building, and gardening ideas at its 1,575 stores. They cut lumber, blinds, pipe, and chains; thread pipes; assemble items; provide computer project design and landscape garden design; match paint colors; teach how-to clinics; and offer many other services. Managers know that providing superior customer service depends on human capital, so they invest in finding the best people and helping them develop and apply their combined knowledge, skills, experience, and talent.

> CONCEPT CONNECTION <

1 Managers need to have a prime focus on the bottom line—on the financial well-being of the company.

ANSWER: Paying attention to the bottom line is important, but managers must remember that people and HRM issues are directly related to financial success. Too often, managers only look at numbers and forget that people are part of the system and part of the success or failure of that system.

EXHIBIT 9.2

The Role and Value of Human-Capital Investments

The importance of human capital for business results is illustrated in Exhibit 9.2. The framework was developed by Accenture and used by software and services company SAP. SAP needed a way to evaluate and revise its human-capital processes to shift to a new strategy requiring stronger customer focus and greater individual employee accountability. The idea is to show how investments in human capital contribute to stronger organizational performance and better financial results. The framework begins at the bottom (level 4) by assessing internal processes such as workforce planning, career development, learning management, and so forth. Managers use these activities to increase human-capital capabilities (level 3), such as employee engagement or workforce adaptability. Enhanced capabilities, in turn, drive higher performance in key areas such as innovation or

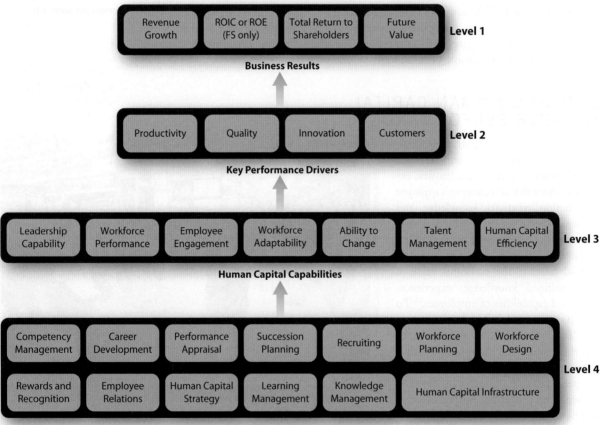

customer satisfaction (level 2). Finally, improvements in key performance areas lead to improved business results.[12]

GLOBALIZATION

An issue of significant concern for today's organizations is competing on a global basis, and the success of a company's global business strategies is closely tied to the effectiveness of the organization's global HR strategies.[13] A subfield known as **international human-resource management (IHRM)** specifically addresses the added complexity that results from coordinating and managing diverse people on a global scale.[14] Research in IHRM has revealed that, as the world becomes increasingly interconnected, some HR practices and trends are converging. However, IHRM managers need a high degree of cultural sensitivity and the ability to tailor and communicate policies and practices for different cultures.[15] What works in one country may not translate well to another.

As a new manager, recognize that human capital is the organization's most valuable asset; when hiring, look for the best people you can find and then treat them like gold, giving them opportunities to learn, grow, and develop new skills.

The Impact of Federal Legislation on HRM

A number of federal laws have been passed to ensure *equal employment opportunity* (EEO). Some of the most significant legislation and executive orders are summarized in Exhibit 9.3 (on the next page). The point of the laws is to stop discriminatory practices that are unfair to specific groups and to define enforcement agencies for these laws. EEO legislation attempts to balance the pay given to men and women; provide employment opportunities without regard to race, religion, national origin, and gender; ensure fair treatment for employees of all ages; and avoid discrimination against disabled individuals.

The Equal Employment Opportunity Commission (EEOC) created by the Civil Rights Act of 1964 initiates investigations in response to complaints concerning discrimination. The EEOC is the major agency involved with employment discrimination. **Discrimination** occurs when some applicants are hired or promoted based on criteria that are not job relevant; for example, refusing to hire a black applicant for a job he is qualified to fill or paying a woman a lower wage than a man for the same work are discriminatory acts. When discrimination is found, remedies include providing back pay and taking affirmative action. **Affirmative action** requires that an employer take positive steps to guarantee equal employment opportunities for people within protected groups. An affirmative action plan is a formal document that can be reviewed by employees and enforcement agencies. The goal of organizational affirmative action is to reduce or eliminate internal inequities among affected employee groups.

Failure to comply with equal employment opportunity legislation can result in substantial fines and penalties for employers. Suits for discriminatory practices can cover a broad range of employee complaints. One issue of growing concern is *sexual harassment*, which is also a violation of Title VII of the Civil Rights Act. The EEOC guidelines specify that behavior such as unwelcome advances, requests for sexual favors, and other verbal and physical conduct of a sexual nature becomes sexual harassment when submission to the conduct is tied to continued employment or advancement or when the behavior creates an intimidating, hostile, or offensive work environment.[16]

Exhibit 9.3 also lists the major federal laws related to compensation and benefits and health and safety issues. The scope of human-resource legislation is increasing at federal, state, and municipal levels. The working rights and conditions of women, minorities, older employees, and the disabled will likely receive increasing legislative attention in the future.

As a new manager, you may need to keep detailed records that document compliance with federal laws and regulations. Complete the New Manager's Self-Test (page 277) to see if you have a natural orientation toward systematic record keeping.

international human-resource management (IHRM)
A subfield of human-resource management that addresses the complexity that results from recruiting, selecting, developing, and maintaining a diverse workforce on a global scale.

discrimination
The hiring or promoting of applicants based on criteria that are not job relevant.

affirmative action
A policy that requires employers to take positive steps to guarantee equal employment opportunities for people within protected groups.

Federal Law	Year	Provisions
Equal Opportunity and Discrimination Laws		
Civil Rights Act	1991	Provides for possible compensatory and punitive damages plus traditional back pay for cases of intentional discrimination brought under title VII of the 1964 Civil Rights Act. Shifts the burden of proof to the employer.
Americans with Disabilities Act	1990	Prohibits discrimination against qualified individuals by employers on the basis of disability and demands that "reasonable accommodations" be provided for the disabled to allow performance of duties.
Vocational Rehabilitation Act	1973	Prohibits discrimination based on physical or mental disability and requires that employees be informed about affirmative action plans.
Age Discrimination in Employment Act (ADEA)	1967 (amended 1978, 1986)	Prohibits age discrimination and restricts mandatory retirement.
Civil Rights Act, Title VII	1964	Prohibits discrimination in employment on the basis of race, religion, color, sex, or national origin.
Compensation and Benefits Laws		
Health Insurance Portability Accountability Act (HIPPA)	1996	Allows employees to switch health insurance plans when changing jobs and get the new coverage regardless of preexisting health conditions; prohibits group plans from dropping a sick employee.
Family and Medical Leave Act	1993	Requires employers to provide as many as 12 weeks unpaid leave for childbirth, adoption, and family emergencies.
Equal Pay Act	1963	Prohibits sex differences in pay for substantially equal work.
Health and Safety Laws		
Consolidated Omnibus Budget Reconciliation Act (COBRA)	1985	Requires continued health insurance coverage (paid by employee) following termination.
Occupational Safety and Health Act (OSHA)	1970	Establishes mandatory safety and health standards in organizations.

EXHIBIT 9.3

Major Federal Laws Related to Human-Resource Management

The Changing Nature of Careers

Another current issue is the changing nature of careers and a shift in the relationship between employers and employees.

THE CHANGING SOCIAL CONTRACT

In the old social contract between organization and employee, the employee could contribute ability, education, loyalty, and commitment and expect in return that the company would provide wages and benefits, work, advancement, and training throughout the employee's working life. But volatile changes in the environment have disrupted this contract. Consider the following list found on a bulletin board at a company undergoing major restructuring:

- We can't promise you how long we'll be in business.

- We can't promise you that we won't be acquired.

- We can't promise that there'll be room for promotion.

- We can't promise that your job will exist when you reach retirement age.

- We can't promise that the money will be available for your pension.

- We can't expect your undying loyalty, and we aren't even sure we want it.[17]

Downsizing, outsourcing, rightsizing, and restructuring have led to the elimination of many positions in organizations. Employees who are left may feel little stability. The above list reflects a primarily negative view of the new employer–employee relationship, but there are positive aspects as well. Many people, particularly younger employees, like the expectation of responsibility and mobility embedded in the new social contract. Everyone is expected to be a self-motivated worker who is continuously acquiring new skills and demonstrating value to the organization.

Exhibit 9.4 lists some elements of the new social contract. The new contract is based on the concept of employability rather than lifetime employment. Individuals are responsible

Learn to be flexible and work with various people in different teams.

NEW MANAGER'S SELF-TEST

What Is Your HR Work Orientation?

As new manager, what is your orientation concerning day-to-day work issues? To find out, think about your preferences for the questions below. Circle **a** or **b** for each item, depending on which one is accurate for you. There are no right or wrong answers.

1. The work elements I prefer are

    _____ a. administrative.

    _____ b. conceptualizing.

2. The work elements I prefer are

    _____ a. creative.

    _____ b. organizing.

3. My mode of living is

    _____ a. conventional.

    _____ b. original.

4. Which is more important to you?

    _____ a. How something looks (form)

    _____ b. How well it works (function)

5. I like to work with

    _____ a. a practical person.

    _____ b. an idea person.

6. I am more

    _____ a. idealistic.

    _____ b. realistic.

7. For weekend activities, I prefer to

    _____ a. plan in advance.

    _____ b. be free to do what I want.

8. A daily work routine for me is

    _____ a. painful.

    _____ b. comfortable.

SCORING AND INTERPRETATION: The HR department typically is responsible for monitoring compliance with federal laws, and it provides detailed and specific employee procedures and records for an organization. Every new manager is involved in HR activities for his or her direct reports, which involves systematic record keeping, awareness of applicable laws, and follow through. For your HR work orientation, score 1 point for each **a** answer circled for questions 1, 3, 5, and 7 and 1 point for each **b** answer circled for questions 2, 4, 6, and 8.

New managers with a high score (7 or 8) for HR work orientation tend to be practical, organized, good at record keeping, and meet commitments on time. New managers with a low score (1 or 2) on HR work orientation tend to be more free spirited, creative, and conceptual. These managers tend to think out of the box and may dislike the organization, routine, and legal record keeping required for efficient HR management. If your score is midrange (3 to 6), you may do well with HR work if you put your mind to it, but HR may not be your area of greatest strength.

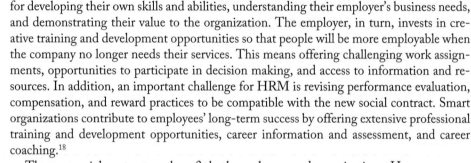

	New Contract	Old Contract
Employee	• Employability; personal responsibility • Partner in business improvement • Learning; skill development	• Job security • A cog in the machine • Knowing
Employer	• Creative development opportunities • Lateral career moves; incentive compensation • Challenging assignments • Information and resources; decision-making authority	• Standard training programs • Traditional compensation package • Routine jobs • Limited information

EXHIBIT 9.4

The Changing Social Contract

SOURCES: Based on Louisa Wah, "The New Workplace Paradox," *Management Review* (Jan. 1998): 7; and Douglas T. Hall and Jonathan E. Moss, "The New Protean Career Contract: Helping Organizations and Employees Adapt," *Organizational Dynamics* (Winter 1998): 22–37.

for developing their own skills and abilities, understanding their employer's business needs, and demonstrating their value to the organization. The employer, in turn, invests in creative training and development opportunities so that people will be more employable when the company no longer needs their services. This means offering challenging work assignments, opportunities to participate in decision making, and access to information and resources. In addition, an important challenge for HRM is revising performance evaluation, compensation, and reward practices to be compatible with the new social contract. Smart organizations contribute to employees' long-term success by offering extensive professional training and development opportunities, career information and assessment, and career coaching.[18]

The new social contract can benefit both employees and organizations. However, some companies take the new approach as an excuse to treat people as economic factors to be used when needed and then let go. This attitude hurts morale, employee commitment, and organizational performance. Studies in both the United States and China, for example, have found lower employee and firm performance and decreased commitment in companies where the interaction between employer and employee is treated as a contract like economic exchange rather than a genuine human and social relationship.[19]

Allow people to make genuine contributions of their talents to the organization and provide them with challenging work and opportunities to learn new skills.

INNOVATIONS IN HRM

The rapid change and uncertainty in today's business environment bring significant new challenges for human-resource management. Some important issues are becoming an employer of choice, addressing the needs of temporary employees and part-time workers, acknowledging growing employee demands for work–life balance, and humanely managing downsizing.

Assess Your Answer

2 Hiring people to work for a company is about the economic contract between employer and employee.

ANSWER: In addition to the economic contract is the equally important social contract. If people feel they are not appreciated and are seen as replaceable machine parts, then their motivation and loyalty will be diminished.

Becoming an Employer of Choice.

The old social contract may be broken for good, but today's best companies recognize the importance of treating people right and thinking for the long term rather than looking for quick fixes based on an economic exchange relationship with employees. An *employer of choice* is a company that is highly attractive to potential employees because of human-resources practices that focus not just on tangible benefits such as pay and profit sharing but also on intangibles (such as work–life balance, a trust-based work climate, and a healthy corporate culture) and that embraces a long-term view to solving immediate problems.[20] To engage people and spur high commitment and performance, an employer of choice chooses a carefully balanced set of HR strategies, policies, and practices that are tailored to the organization's own unique goals and needs.

As a manager, be mindful of your employee's need to achieve balance in their lives.

Using Temporary and Part-Time Employees.

Contingent workers are becoming a larger part of the workforce in both the United States and Europe. **Contingent workers** are people who work for an organization but not on a permanent or full-time basis. These include temporary placements, contracted professionals, leased employees, and part-time workers.[21] The temporary staffing industry doubled between 2002 and 2007 and is projected to grow into a $200 billion industry by 2010.[22] People in temporary jobs do everything from data entry, to project management, to becoming the interim chief executive officer (CEO). Although most temporary workers used to be in clerical and manufacturing positions, in recent years demand has grown for professionals, such as accountants and financial analysts, interim managers, information technology specialists, product managers, and even lawyers and health-care workers. A related trend is the use of *virtual teams*. Some are made up entirely of people who are hired on a project-by-project basis. Many companies depend on part-time or temporary employees to maintain flexibility.[23]

contingent workers
People who work for an organization, but not on a permanent or full-time basis, including temporary placements, contracted professionals, and leased employees.

contingent professionals
People, mostly retirees, who bring needed expertise.

telecommuting
Using computers and telecommunications equipment to perform work from home or another remote location.

Promoting Work–Life Balance.

Initiatives that enable employees to lead a balanced life are a critical part of many organizations' retention strategies. One approach is to let people work part of the time from home or another remote location. **Telecommuting** means using computers and telecommunications equipment to do work without going to an office. The most recent report from the Bureau of Labor Statistics shows that 30.7 million people in the United States worked from home at least one day a week in 2004. This includes more than 100,000 employees of the federal government, according to the Office of Personnel Management.[24] Other forms of *flexible scheduling* are also important in today's workplace, and 55 percent of HRM professionals surveyed say they are willing to negotiate flexible work arrangements with interviewees and new employees.[25]

In addition, many companies have implemented broad work–life balance initiatives, partly in response to the shift in expectations among young employees.[26] Generation Y workers are a fast-growing segment of the workforce. Typically, Gen Y employees work smart and work hard on the job, but they refuse to let work be their whole life. Unlike their parents, who placed a high priority on career, Gen Y workers expect the job to accommodate their personal lives.[27] Employers can learn from Tiger Woods that

The Federal Deposit Insurance Corporation is handling the increasing demand for its intervention in bank failures with contingent professionals, mostly retirees who bring the needed expertise. Gary Holloway, shown here, was recruited back after two years of retirement and now considers his office "on the road" as he travels to failing banks in his temporary job. An FDIC group swoops in like a SWAT team, sorts through a bank's troubled loans, sells assets, and reopens the bank under new ownership. Holloway brings to this task his experience with the FDIC during the 1980s savings and loan crisis, which resulted in 534 closings.

© ISAAC BREKKEN FOR THE NEW YORK TIMES/REDUX IMAGES

> CONCEPT CONNECTION <

BENCH-
MARKING

Tiger Woods

When the top golf player in the world says his greatest joy comes from fatherhood, people take notice. Though Tiger Woods' life may seem perfect, he suffers many of the same strains the average workaday parent does: how to give enough time and energy to your job while at the same time committing to the important vocation of child rearing. Until Woods had children in 2003, he could jet around the globe, first with his ever-present father (until his sad death in 2006) and also with his wife Elin, whom he married in 2002. Though young kids are relatively portable and can visit often, the grueling travel schedule of golf pros is not kind to little people. So Tiger spends a lot of time missing his children. Though his own father was doting, he was a retired Army officer and had no job responsibilities, so Tiger can't look to him completely as a role model. He also admires golfer Jack Nicklaus, who would fly home during tournaments to attend one of his five kids' sports matches or recitals. He was big on bedtime stories, but no diapers. True to his one-step-higher reputation, Tiger does diaper duty and pretty much anything else needed. Tiger's recent long hiatus following knee surgery allowed him a blissful time to bond with his 2-year-old daughter, Sam, as well as be around more after the birth of his infant son. Even with all the trophies and awards, Tiger values his family more than anything. As he says, "I couldn't be happier than where I am right now. Having the two kids is just unbelievable, how much fun we are all having, except the sleepless nights—that can be a little tough at times. But other than that it's just been incredible."

SOURCE: Karen Crouse, "All Eyes Are on Tiger Woods, the Father," *New York Times*, June 14, 2009, pp. SP1, SP6.

helping work–life balance creates happier, productive workers, as shown in this chapter's Benchmarking box.

Rightsizing the Organization. In some cases, organizations have more people than they need and have to let some employees go. **Rightsizing** refers to intentionally reducing the company's workforce to the point where the number of employees is deemed to be right for the company's current situation. Also called *downsizing*, planned reductions in the size of the workforce are a reality for many of today's companies. As the term *rightsizing* implies, the goal is to make the company stronger and more competitive by aligning the size of the workforce with the company's current needs. However, some researchers have found that massive cuts often fail to achieve the intended benefits and in some cases significantly harm the organization.[28] Unless HRM departments effectively and humanely manage the rightsizing process, layoffs can lead to decreased morale and performance. Managers can smooth the process by regularly communicating with employees and providing them with as much information as possible, providing assistance to workers who will lose their jobs, and using training and development to help address the emotional needs of remaining employees and enable them to cope with new or additional responsibilities.[29]

Finding the Right People

rightsizing
Intentionally reducing the company's workforce to the point where the number of employees is deemed to be right for the company's current situation.

Now let's turn to the three broad goals of HRM: finding, developing, and maintaining an effective workforce. The first step in finding the right people is human-resource planning in which managers or HRM professionals predict the need for new employees based on the types of vacancies that exist, as illustrated in Exhibit 9.5. The second step is to use recruiting procedures to communicate with potential applicants. The third step is to select from

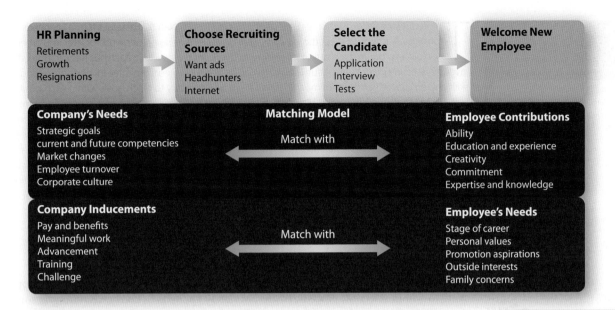

HR Planning	**Choose Recruiting Sources**	**Select the Candidate**	**Welcome New Employee**
Retirements Growth Resignations	Want ads Headhunters Internet	Application Interview Tests	

Company's Needs	**Matching Model**	**Employee Contributions**
Strategic goals current and future competencies Market changes Employee turnover Corporate culture	Match with ⟷	Ability Education and experience Creativity Commitment Expertise and knowledge

Company Inducements		**Employee's Needs**
Pay and benefits Meaningful work Advancement Training Challenge	Match with ⟷	Stage of career Personal values Promotion aspirations Outside interests Family concerns

EXHIBIT 9.5

Attracting an Effective Workforce

the applicants those persons believed to be the best potential contributors to the organization. Finally, the new employee is welcomed into the organization.

Underlying the organization's effort to attract employees is a matching model. With the **matching model**, the organization and the individual attempt to match the needs, interests, and values that they offer each other.[30] For example, a small software developer might require long hours from creative, technically skilled employees. In return, it can offer freedom from bureaucracy, tolerance of idiosyncrasies, and potentially high pay. A large manufacturer can offer employment security and stability, but it might have more rules and regulations and require greater skills for "getting approval from the higher-ups." The individual who would thrive working for the software developer might feel stymied and unhappy working for a large manufacturer. Both the company and the employee are interested in finding a good match.

HUMAN-RESOURCE PLANNING

Human-resource planning is the forecasting of human-resource needs and the projected matching of individuals with expected vacancies. Human-resource planning begins with several questions:

- What new technologies are emerging, and how will these affect the work system?

- What is the volume of the business likely to be in the next 5 to 10 years?

- What is the turnover rate, and how much, if any, is avoidable?

The responses to these questions are used to formulate specific questions pertaining to HR activities such as the following:

- What types of engineers will we need, and how many?

- How many administrative personnel will we need to support the additional engineers?

- Can we use temporary, part-time, or virtual workers to handle some tasks?[31]

By anticipating future human-resource needs, the organization can prepare itself to meet competitive challenges more effectively than organizations that react to problems only as they arise. One of the most successful applications of human-resource planning occurred at the Tennessee Valley Authority.

matching model
An employee selection approach in which the organization and the applicant attempt to match each other's needs, interests, and values.

human-resource planning
The forecasting of human-resource needs and the projected matching of individuals with expected job vacancies.

The Tennessee Valley Authority (TVA) created an eight-step plan that assesses future HR needs and formulates actions to meet those needs. Step one is laying the groundwork for later implementation of the program by creating planning and oversight teams within each business unit. Step two involves assessing processes and functions that can be benchmarked. Step three involves projecting the skills and employee numbers (demand data) that will be necessary to reach goals within each business unit. Once these numbers are in place, step four involves projecting the current employee numbers (supply data) over the planning horizon without new hires and taking into consideration the normal attrition of staff through death, retirement, resignation, and so forth. Comparison of the difference between supply and demand (step five) gives the future gap or surplus situation. This knowledge enables HR to develop strategies and operational plans (step six). Step seven involves communicating the action plan to employees. The final step is to periodically evaluate and update the plan as the organization's needs change. When TVA faces a demand for additional employees, this process enables the company to recruit workers with the skills needed to help meet organizational goals.[32]

RECRUITING

When recruiting, make sure you cast a wide net to get enough candidates to choose from.

recruiting
The activities or practices that define the desired characteristics of applicants for specific jobs.

job analysis
The systematic process of gathering and interpreting information about the essential duties, tasks, and responsibilities of a job.

job description
A concise summary of the specific tasks and responsibilities of a particular job.

job specification
An outline of the knowledge, skills, education, and physical abilities needed to adequately perform a job.

realistic job preview
A recruiting approach that gives applicants all pertinent and realistic information about the job and the organization.

Recruiting is defined as "activities or practices that define the characteristics of applicants to whom selection procedures are ultimately applied."[33] Today, recruiting is sometimes referred to as *talent acquisition* to reflect the importance of the human factor in the organization's success.[34] Even when unemployment rates are high, companies often have trouble finding people with the skills the organization needs. A survey by Manpower Inc. of 33,000 employers in 23 countries found that 40 percent reported having difficulty finding and hiring the desired talent.[35]

Although we frequently think of campus recruiting as a typical recruiting activity, many organizations use *internal recruiting*, or *promote-from-within* policies, to fill their high-level positions.[36] Internal recruiting has two major advantages: It is less costly than an external search, and it generates higher employee commitment, development, and satisfaction because it offers opportunities for career advancement to employees rather than outsiders. Frequently, however, *external recruiting*—recruiting newcomers from outside the organization—is advantageous. Applicants are provided by a variety of outside sources including advertising, state employment services, online recruiting services, private employment agencies (*headhunters*), job fairs, and employee referrals.

Assessing Organizational Needs. Basic building blocks of human-resource management include job analysis, job descriptions, and job specifications. **Job analysis** is a systematic process of gathering and interpreting information about the essential duties, tasks, and responsibilities of a job, as well as about the context within which the job is performed.[37] To perform job analysis, managers or specialists ask about work activities and work flow, the degree of supervision given and received in the job, knowledge and skills needed, performance standards, working conditions, and so forth. The manager then prepares a written **job description**, which is a clear and concise summary of the specific tasks, duties, and responsibilities; and **job specification**, which outlines the knowledge, skills, education, physical abilities, and other characteristics needed to adequately perform the job.

Job analysis helps organizations recruit the right kind of people and match them to appropriate jobs. For example, to enhance internal recruiting, Sara Lee Corporation identified 6 functional areas and 24 significant skills that it wants its finance executives to develop, as illustrated in Exhibit 9.6. Managers are tracked on their development and moved into other positions to help them acquire the needed skills.[38]

Realistic Job Previews. Job analysis also enhances recruiting effectiveness by enabling the creation of **realistic job previews**. A *realistic job preview* (RJP) gives applicants all

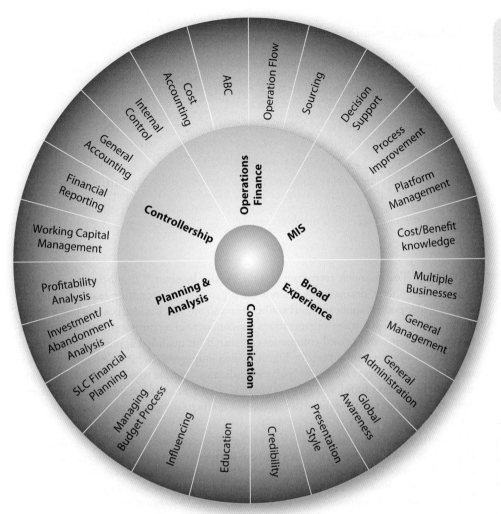

SOURCE: Victoria Griffith, "When Only Internal Expertise Will Do," *CFO* (Oct. 1998): 95–96, 102.

EXHIBIT 9.6
Sara Lee's Required
Skills for Finance
Executives
- - - - - - - - - - -

pertinent and realistic information—positive and negative—about the job and the organization.[39] RJPs contribute to greater employee satisfaction and lower turnover because they facilitate matching individuals, jobs, and organizations. Individuals have a better basis on which to determine their suitability to the organization and "self-select" into or out of positions based on full information.

Legal Considerations. Organizations must ensure that their recruiting practices conform to the law. As discussed earlier in this chapter, EEO laws stipulate that recruiting and hiring decisions cannot discriminate on the basis of race, national origin, religion, or gender. The Americans with Disabilities Act underscored the need for well-written job descriptions and specifications that accurately reflect the mental and physical dimensions of jobs so that people with disabilities will not be discriminated against. *Affirmative action* refers to the use of goals, timetables, or other methods in recruiting to promote the hiring, development, and retention of protected groups. Most large companies try to comply with affirmative action and EEO guidelines. Prudential Insurance Company's policy is presented in Exhibit 9.7. Prudential actively recruits employees and takes affirmative action steps to recruit individuals from all walks of life.

EXHIBIT 9.7
Prudential's
Corporate Recruiting
Policy

- - - - - - - - - -

An Equal Opportunity Employer

Prudential recruits, hires, trains, promotes, and compensates individuals without regard to race, color, religion or creed, age, sex, marital status, national origin, ancestry, liability for service in the armed forces of the United States, status as a special disabled veteran or veteran of the Vietnam era, or physical or mental handicap.

This is official company policy because: • we believe it is right
                                          • it makes good business sense
                                          • it is the law

We are also committed to an ongoing program of affirmative action in which members of under-represented groups are actively sought out and employed for opportunities in all parts and at all levels of the company. In employing people from all walks of life, Prudential gains access to the full experience of our diverse society.

E-Cruiting. Today, much recruiting is done via the Internet.[40] *E-cruiting*, or recruiting job applicants online, dramatically extends the organization's recruiting reach, offering access to a wider pool of applicants and saving time and money. Besides posting job openings on company Web sites, many organizations use commercial recruiting sites where job seekers can post their résumés and companies can search for qualified applicants. In addition, in industries where competition for highly skilled employees is stiff, new online services emerge to help managers search for "passive candidates," people who aren't looking for jobs but might be the best fit for a company's opening. Red 5 Studios Inc. took a highly creative approach to recruit passive candidates in the hot market for videogame producers.

**RED 5
STUDIOS INC.**

Several members of the team behind the popular online game *World of Warcraft* decided to start their own company, and Red 5 Studios was born. But the start-up quickly ran into a problem—how to attract good employees in an industry where competition for talent is stiff. The team decided to make a list of its "dream hires" and then set about recruiting those workers. They learned everything they could about each dream developer to personalize the pitch— searching on Google, playing the developer's games, tracking down the prospects' blogs and posts in industry forums, and so forth.

When the research was complete, Red 5 sent each prospect a package of boxes, nested like a Russian doll. In the final box was an iPod Shuffle engraved with the prospect's name and containing a recorded recruiting message from CEO Mark Kern. The recruiting strategy worked. Four months later, three of the passive candidates had joined Red 5 Studios, and another was considering making the move.[41]

Innovations in Recruiting. As the previous example shows, managers sometimes have to find innovative approaches to recruit the right people. Organizations look for ways to enhance their recruiting success. One highly effective method is getting referrals from current employees. Many organizations offer cash awards to employees who submit names of people who subsequently accept employment because referral by current employees is one of the cheapest and most reliable methods of external recruiting.[42] Companies also are increasingly searching among the membership of relevant trade groups such as at trade shows, meetings, and on the associations' Web sites. "All the good candidates seem to belong to a particular association and the ones who aren't as skilled usually don't," explains one recruiter.[43]

Some organizations also turn to nontraditional sources to find dedicated employees, particularly in a tight labor market. For example, when Walker Harris couldn't find workers for his ice company on the west side of Chicago, Harris Ice, he began hiring former prison inmates, many of whom have turned out to be reliable, loyal employees.[44] In Louisville, Kentucky, where the traditional labor force is shrinking, companies such as UPS, Allied

Van Lines, and General Electric are finding a source of hard-working employees among Asian, African, and Eastern European immigrants fleeing persecution.[45] Since 1998, Bank of America has hired and trained more than 3,000 former welfare recipients in positions that offer the potential for promotions and long-term careers. Numerous companies recruit older workers, who typically have lower turnover rates, especially for part-time jobs. The Home Depot offers "snowbird specials"—winter work in Florida and summers in Maine. Border's Bookstores entices retired teachers with book discounts and reading and discussion groups.[46] Recruiting on a global basis is on the rise as well. Public schools are recruiting teachers from overseas. High-tech companies are looking for qualified workers in foreign countries because they cannot find people with the right skills in the United States.[47]

SELECTING

The next step for managers is to select desired employees from the pool of recruited applicants. In the **selection** process, employers assess applicants' characteristics in an attempt to determine the "fit" between the job and applicant characteristics. Several selection devices are used for assessing applicant qualifications. The most frequently used are the application form, interview, employment test, and assessment center. Studies indicate that the greater the skill requirements and work demands of an open position, the greater the number and variety of selection tools the organization will use.[48] Human-resource professionals may use a combination of devices to get an idea of a candidate's potential performance. Selecting the right employees is important in many industries, including Hollywood, as described in the Spotlight on Skills box.

When selecting an employee, make sure you have enough means of seeing all sides of the person's personality and qualifications: Don't just look at the superficial criteria.

selection
The process of determining the skills, abilities, and other attributes a person needs to perform a particular job.

SPOTLIGHT ON SKILLS

Fast & Furious

Even Tinseltown has to worry about hiring the right people. Hollywood might tinker under the hood when producing movie sequels and sometimes uses different actors. After the original movie, *The Fast and the Furious*, was an unqualified hit in 2001, the first sequel featured Paul Walker, the only one of the original four stars. The third movie had none of the four. So when producer Neal H. Moritz announced the return of Vin Diesel and Walker, everyone was stunned. No one had ever successfully re-introduced original cast members after so long an absence. Even Diesel was surprised. "It's kind of tricky to revisit a character so long after the fact," he said. Eight years was a big gap.

None of this would have happened if the first movie hadn't been so popular. Adapted from a *Vibe* story about underground street races, Diesel and Walker starred in the $30 million film that went on to earn more than $207 million worldwide. Even without Diesel, the next movie, or first sequel, earned $237 million globally, while the second sequel, with no bankable actors, made $158 million.

No one expected the original movie to do very well, especially since it came out in the same summer as sequels to *Jurassic Park* and *The Mummy*. But when it opened as number

one, it became the sleeper of the summer, with cast, director, and producers part of a happy family. Director Rob Cohen called Walker to tell him how proud he was of the actor's work. But when Diesel turned down the sequel, it meant no work for the actresses who played Diesel's girlfriend and sister (Michelle Rodriguez and Jordana Brewster), and the team fell apart. When sequel number two was being planned, Diesel agreed to a short cameo with the option to produce the next film in the series. *Fast & Furious* offered Diesel and the other original stars a chance to regain professional success. All four had recently been in strings of less-than-blockbuster movies, so bringing them together could be a win for everyone—and also a big risk. Who would care about these characters after so many years? The story line had them returning as outsiders to an underground car world that had moved on from them.

The risk paid off. *Fast & Furious* became the highest-opening movie of 2009, bringing in $72.5 million in its first weekend and $152 million worldwide within seven weeks. So get the right people on the bus, or at least in the car.

SOURCES: Richard Verrier, "Theaters Cash in Amid Recession," *Journal-Gazette* [Fort Wayne, IN], May 24, 2009, p. H1; Davie Itzkoff, "What a Stunt! Can They Do It Again?" *New York Times*, Mar. 29, 2009, pp. AR11–AR12.

Application Form. The **application form** is used to collect information about the applicant's education, previous job experience, and other background characteristics. Research in the life insurance industry shows that biographical information inventories can validly predict future job success.[49]

One pitfall to be avoided is the inclusion of questions that are irrelevant to job success. In line with affirmative action, the application form should not ask questions that will create an adverse impact on protected groups unless the questions are clearly related to the job.[50] For example, employers should not ask whether the applicant rents or owns his or her own home because (1) an applicant's response might adversely affect his or her chances at the job, (2) minorities and women may be less likely to own a home, and (3) home ownership is probably unrelated to job performance. By contrast, the exam for certified public accountant (CPA) is relevant to job performance in a CPA firm; thus, it is appropriate to ask whether an applicant for employment has passed the CPA exam, even if only one-half of all female or minority applicants have done so versus 90 percent of male applicants.

Interview. The *interview* serves as a two-way communication channel that allows both the organization and the applicant to collect information that otherwise might be difficult to obtain. This selection technique is used in almost every job category in nearly every organization. It is another area where the organization can get into legal trouble if the interviewer asks questions that violate EEO guidelines. Exhibit 9.8 lists examples of appropriate and inappropriate interview questions.

application form
A device for collecting information about an applicant's education, previous job experience, and other background characteristics.

EXHIBIT 9.8

Employment Applications and Interviews: What Can You Ask?

Category	Okay to Ask	Inappropriate or Illegal to Ask
National origin	• The applicant's name • If applicant has ever worked under a different name	• The origin of applicant's name • Applicant's ancestry or ethnicity
Race	• Nothing	• Race or color of skin
Disabilities	• Whether applicant has any disabilities that might inhibit performance of job	• If applicant has any physical or mental defects • If applicant has ever filed workers' compensation claim
Age	• If applicant is 18 or older	• Applicant's age • When applicant graduated from high school
Religion	• Nothing	• Applicant's religious affiliation • What religious holidays applicant observes
Criminal record	• If applicant has ever been convicted of a crime	• If applicant has ever been arrested
Marital and family status	• Nothing	• Marital status, number of children or planned children • Child-care arrangements
Education and experience	• Where applicant went to school • Prior work experience	• When applicant graduated • Hobbies
Citizenship	• If applicant has a legal right to work in the United States	• If applicant is a citizen of another country

SOURCES: Based on "Appropriate and Inappropriate Interview Questions," in George Bohlander, Scott Snell, and Arthur Sherman, *Managing Human Resources*, 12th ed. (Cincinnati: South-Western, 2001): 207; and "Guidelines to Lawful and Unlawful Preemployment Inquiries," Appendix E in Robert L. Mathis and John H. Jackson, *Human Resource Management*, 2nd ed. (Cincinnati: South-Western, 2002): 189–190.

SPOTLIGHT ON SKILLS

What Makes a Good Interview Go Bad?

Have you ever had a job interview where everything seems to be going well but then takes a drastic turn for the worse? Understanding common blunders that tick off interviewers can make you more successful as both a job candidate and an interviewer. Here's one expert's list of the top seven:

1. *Not communicating enough.* People who won't talk drive interviewers crazy. These folks offer short answers to open-ended questions and don't follow up when the interviewer prods for more information.

2. *Not making eye contact.* Candidates who look around everywhere except at the interviewer provoke distrust. One expert advises extremely shy people to look at the interviewer's "third eye," just above and between the person's two eyes, to avoid this blunder.

3. *Talking too much.* Answering questions fully is important, but a candidate who babbles on and on puts most interviewers off.

4. *Using street slang or unprofessional language.* Street speak doesn't fit most corporate domains. In addition, saying *like*, *uh*, or *um* every other word quickly loses an interviewer's attention.

5. *Stretching the truth.* People want to present themselves in the best light, but many candidates go too far, embellishing their skills, hiding past job failures, or outright lying about educational qualifications. Interviewers can often sense this, which destroys trust.

6. *Making a fashion statement.* In most cases, people should wear traditional professional dress for an interview.

7. *Failing to effectively close.* Interviewers like a candidate who closes the interview by stating their interest or asking about the next step in the process, rather than just letting the interview fade away.

There are even more outlandish blunders that occasionally occur. Here are some of the unusual things that have happened during job interviews, based on surveys of vice presidents and human-resource directors at major U.S. corporations:

- The applicant announced she hadn't had lunch and proceeded to eat a hamburger and french fries in the interviewer's office.
- When asked if he had any questions about the job, the candidate answered, "Can I get an advance on my paycheck?"
- The applicant chewed bubble gum and constantly blew bubbles.
- The job candidate said the main thing he was looking for in a job was a quiet place where no one would bother him.
- The job applicant challenged the interviewer to arm wrestle.

SOURCES: Indira Dharchaudhuri, "Interviewers Pet Peeves," *Hindustan Times*, Feb. 24, 2004; and Martha H. Peak, "What Color Is Your Bumbershoot?" *Management Review* (October 1989): 63.

However, the interview is not generally a good predictor of job performance. One estimate is that conventional interviews have a 0.2 correlation with predicting a successful hire.[51] People can improve their chances of having a successful interview by understanding some common pet peeves that trigger a negative response from interviewers, as outlined in the Spotlight on Skills box above.

Today's managers are trying different approaches to overcome the limitations of the interview. Some put candidates through a series of interviews, each one conducted by a different person and each one probing a different aspect of the candidate. Others use *panel interviews* in which the candidate meets with several interviewers who take turns asking questions.[52] Some organizations also supplement traditional interviewing information with *computer-based interviews*. This type of interview typically requires a candidate to answer a series of multiple-choice questions tailored to the specific job.

The answers are compared to an ideal profile or to a profile developed on the basis of other candidates. Companies such as Pinkerton Security, Coopers & Lybrand, and Pic n' Pay Shoe Stores have found computer-based interviews to be valuable for searching out information regarding the applicant's honesty, work attitude, drug history, candor, dependability, and self-motivation.[53]

TAKE ACTION

Get the right people in the right jobs by assessing your team's needs, offering realistic job previews, and matching the needs and interests of the individual to those of the organization.

EXHIBIT 9.9

Try Your Hand at
Some Interview
Brain Teasers

How would you answer the following questions in a job interview?

1. How would you weigh a jet plane without using scales?
2. Why are manhole covers round?
3. How many golf balls can fit inside a standard school bus?
4. How much should you charge to wash all the windows in Seattle?
5. You're shrunk and trapped in a blender that will turn on in 60 seconds. What do you do?

Answers: There might be many solutions to these questions. Here are some that interviewers consider good answers:

1. Fly it onto an aircraft carrier or other ship big enough to hold it. Paint a mark on the hull of the ship showing the water level. Then remove the jet. The ship will rise in the water. Now load the ship with items of known weight (100 lb. bales of cotton, for instance) until it sinks to exactly the line you painted on the hull. The total weight of the items will equal the weight of the jet.
2. A square cover might fall into its hole. If you hold a square manhole cover vertically and turn it a little, it will fall easily into the hole. In contrast, a round cover with a slight recess in the center can never fall in, no matter how it is held.
3. About 500,000, assuming the bus is 50 balls high, 50 balls wide, and 200 balls long.
4. Assuming 10,000 city blocks, 600 windows per block, five minutes per window, and a rate of $20 per hour, about $10 million.
5. Use the measurement marks on the side of the container to climb out.

SOURCES: These questions are used at companies such as Microsoft, Google, and eBay. Reported in Michael Kaplan, "Job Interview Brainteasers," *Business 2.0* (Sept. 2007): 35–37; and William Poundstone, "Impossible Questions," *Across the Board* (Sept.–Oct. 2003): 44–48.

Employment Test. **Employment tests** may include intelligence tests, aptitude and ability tests, and personality inventories. Many companies today are particularly interested in personality inventories that measure such characteristics as openness to learning, initiative, responsibility, creativity, and emotional stability. Companies that put a premium on innovativeness and problem solving are also challenging applicants with *brain teasers*, having them ponder questions such as how many golf balls will fit inside a school bus. The answers aren't as important as how the applicant goes about solving the problem. See how you do answering the brain teasers in Exhibit 9.9.

Assessment Center. First developed by psychologists at AT&T, assessment centers are used to select individuals with high potential for managerial careers by such organizations as IBM, General Electric, and JCPenney.[54] **Assessment centers** present a series of managerial situations to groups of applicants over a two- or three-day period, for example. One technique is the *in-basket simulation*, which requires the applicant to play the role of a manager who must decide how to respond to 10 memos in his or her in basket within a two-hour period. Panels of two or three trained judges observe the applicant's decisions and assess the extent to which they reflect interpersonal, communication, and problem-solving skills. At a Michigan auto parts plant that makes a joint-venture engine from Daimler-Chrysler, Mitsubishi, and Hyundai, applicants for plant manager go through four-hour "day-in-the-life" simulations in which they have to juggle memos, phone calls, and employee or job problems.[55]

Some organizations now use this technique for hiring frontline workers as well. Mercury Communications in England uses an assessment center to select customer assistants. Applicants participate in simulated exercises with customers and in various other exercises designed to assess their listening skills, customer sensitivity, and ability to cope under pressure.[56]

Online Checks. One of the newest ways of gauging whether a candidate is right for the company is by seeing what the person has to say about him- or herself on social networking sites such as Facebook and MySpace. Recent college graduates looking for jobs have found

employment test
A written or computer-based test designed to measure a particular attribute such as intelligence or aptitude.

assessment center
A technique for selecting individuals with high managerial potential based on their performance on a series of simulated managerial tasks.

doors closed to them because of risqué or teasing photos or vivid comments about drinking, drug use, or sexual exploits. Recruiters from more than two dozen companies told career counselors at New York University, for example, that if an applicant's online presentation raises red flags, then the person isn't likely to even get an interview.[57] Companies today are not only interested in a candidate's educational and work qualifications but also in personal characteristics and values that fit with the organization's culture. One recruiter said the open admission of excessive drinking and so forth makes managers question the applicant's maturity and judgment. Sometimes an employer may have wished it could have seen an online video *before* hiring, rather than after, as described in this chapter's Business Blooper.

Managing Talent

Following selection, the next goal of HRM is to develop employees into an effective workforce. Key development activities include training and performance appraisal.

TRAINING AND DEVELOPMENT

Training and development represent a planned effort by an organization to help employees learn job-related skills and behaviors.[58] Organizations spent some $58.5 billion on training in 2007, with more than $16 billion of that spent on outside learning products and services. One of the fastest growing methods of training in today's organizations is the use of podcasting, which jumped from 5 percent in 2006 to 15 percent in 2007.[59]

On-the-Job Training. The most common method of training is on-the-job training. In **on-the-job training (OJT)**, an experienced employee is asked to take a new employee "under his or her wing" and show the newcomer how to perform job duties. OJT has many advantages, such as fewer out-of-pocket costs for training facilities, materials, or instructor fees and easy transfer of learning back to the job. When implemented well, OJT is considered the fastest and most effective means of facilitating learning in the workplace.[60] One type of on-the-job training involves moving people to various types of jobs within the organization, where they work with experienced employees to learn different tasks. This *cross-training* may place an employee in a new position for as short a time as a few hours or for as long as a year, enabling the employee to develop new skills and giving the organization greater flexibility.

Corporate Universities. Another popular approach to training and development is the corporate university. A **corporate university** is an in-house training and education facility

Remember that insufficient training is one reason many employees fail on the job.

on-the-job training (OJT)
A type of training in which an experienced employee "adopts" a new employee to teach him or her how to perform job duties.

corporate university
An in-house training and education facility that offers broad-based learning opportunities for employees.

"We don't do training," says Equifax Senior Vice President and chief learning officer Lynn Slavenski. "We do change." Slavenski oversaw the establishment of Equifax University for the consumer credit reporting company. What distinguishes a corporate university from most old-style training programs is that the courses—from classes teaching a specific technical skill to corporate-run MBA programs—are intentionally designed to foster the changes needed to achieve the organization's strategy.

········> **CONCEPT CONNECTION** <········

that offers broad-based learning opportunities for employees—and frequently for customers, suppliers, and strategic partners as well—throughout their careers.[61] One well-known corporate university is Hamburger University, McDonald's worldwide training center, which has been in existence for more than 40 years. Numerous other companies, including IBM, FedEx, General Electric, Intel, Harley-Davidson, and Capital One, pump millions of dollars into corporate universities to continually build human capital.[62] Employees at Caterpillar attend courses at Caterpillar University, which combines e-training, classroom sessions, and hands-on training activities. The U.S. Department of Defense runs Defense Acquisition University to provide ongoing training to 129,000 military and civilian workers in acquisitions, technology, and logistics.[63]

Promotion from Within. Another way to further employee development is through promotion from within, which helps companies retain and develop valuable people. Promotions provide more challenging assignments, prescribe new responsibilities, and help employees grow by expanding and developing their abilities. The Peebles Hydro Hotel in Scotland is passionate about promoting from within as a way to retain good people and give them opportunities for growth. A maid has been promoted to head housekeeper, a wine waitress to restaurant head, and a student worker to deputy manager. The hotel also provides constant training in all areas. These techniques, combined with a commitment to job flexibility, have helped the hotel retain high-quality workers at a time when others in the tourism and hospitality industry are suffering from a shortage of skilled labor. Staff members with 10, 15, or even 20 years of service aren't uncommon at Hydro.[64]

mentoring
When an experienced employee guides and supports a less-experienced employee.

coaching
A method of directing, instructing, and training a person with the goal of developing specific management skills.

performance appraisal
The process of observing and evaluating an employee's performance, recording the assessment, and providing feedback to the employee.

Mentoring and Coaching. For many management and professional jobs, traditional on-the-job training is supplemented or replaced by mentoring and coaching. With **mentoring**, an experienced employee guides and supports a newcomer or less-experienced employee. Mentors typically offer counsel regarding how to network and advance in the company in addition to guiding the employee in developing his or her skills and abilities. **Coaching** is a method of directing, instructing, and training a person with the goal to develop specific management skills. Coaching usually applies to higher-level managers who want to develop their personal competencies. For instance, a coach might observe a senior executive in action and provide feedback about how the executive can improve her interaction skills. Managers can also discuss difficult situations as they arise, with the coach helping them work through various alternative scenarios for dealing with the situations.[65]

PERFORMANCE APPRAISAL

Performance appraisal comprises the steps of observing and assessing employee performance, recording the assessment, and providing feedback to the employee. During performance appraisal, skillful managers give feedback and praise concerning the acceptable elements of the employee's performance. They also describe performance areas that need improvement. Employees can use this information to change their job performance. Unfortunately, only 3 in 10 employees in a recent survey believe their companies' performance-review system actually helps to improve performance, indicating a need for improved methods of appraisal and feedback.[66]

Generally, HRM professionals concentrate on two things to make performance appraisal a positive force in their organizations: (1) the accurate assessment of performance through the development and application of assessment systems such as rating scales and (2) training managers to effectively use the performance appraisal interview, so managers can provide feedback that will reinforce good performance and motivate employee development. Current thinking is that performance appraisal should be ongoing, not something that is done once a year as part of a consideration of raises.

Remember that more frequent feedback to employees is more effective than the once-a-year evaluation.

Assessing Performance Accurately. To obtain an accurate performance rating, managers acknowledge that jobs are multidimensional, so performance may be multidimensional as well. For example, a sports broadcaster might perform well on the job-knowledge dimension; that is, she or he might be able to report facts and figures about the players and describe which rule applies when there is a questionable play on the field. But the same broadcaster might not perform as well on another dimension such as communication. The person might be unable to express the information in a colorful way that interests the audience or might interrupt the other broadcasters. For performance to be rated accurately, the appraisal system should require the rater to assess each relevant performance dimension. A multidimensional form increases the usefulness of the performance appraisal and facilitates employee growth and development.

A recent trend in performance appraisal is called **360-degree feedback**, a process that uses multiple raters, including self-rating, as a way to increase awareness of strengths and weaknesses and guide employee development. Members of the appraisal group may include supervisors, co-workers, and customers, as well as the individual, thus providing appraisal of the employee from a variety of perspectives.[67]

One study found that 26 percent of companies used some type of multirater performance appraisal.[68]

Another alternative performance-evaluation method is the *performance-review ranking system*.[69] This method is increasingly coming under fire because it essentially evaluates employees by pitting them against one another. As most commonly used, a manager evaluates his or her direct reports relative to one another and categorizes each on a scale, such as A = outstanding performance (20 percent), B = high-middle performance (70 percent), or C = in need of improvement (10 percent). Some companies routinely fire those managers falling in the bottom 10 percent of the ranking. Proponents say the technique provides an effective way to assess performance and offer guidance for employee development. But critics of these systems, which are sometimes called *rank and yank*, argue that they are based on subjective judgments, produce skewed results, and discriminate against employees who are "different" from the mainstream. One study found that forced rankings that include firing the bottom 5 percent or 10 percent can lead to a dramatic improvement in organizational performance in the short term, but the benefits dissipate over several years as people become focused on competing with one another rather than improving the business.[70] Many companies are building more flexibility into the performance-review ranking system, and some are abandoning it altogether.[71]

Despite these concerns, the appropriate use of performance ranking has been useful for many companies, especially as a short-term way to improve performance. Consider how a variation of the system helps U.S. restaurant chain Applebee's retain quality workers in the high-turnover restaurant business.

360-degree feedback
A process that uses multiple raters, including self-rating, to appraise employee performance and guide development.

APPLEBEE'S
INTERNATIONAL
INC.

Most people working in fast-food and casual dining restaurants don't stay long. Turnover of hourly employees is a perpetual problem, averaging more than 200 percent a year in the casual dining sector for the past 30 years. Applebee's managers wanted to reduce their turnover rate, but they also wanted to focus their retention efforts on the best people.

A key aspect of the new retention strategy is the Applebee's performance management system. Twice a year, each hourly employee is rated on characteristics such as reliability, guest service, attitude, and teamwork. Managers then look at how each employee ranks with respect to all others in the restaurant, separating employees into the top 20 percent, the middle 60 percent, and the bottom 20 percent. Store managers are rewarded for retaining the top and middle performers.

The system is not the basis for firing low-ranking employees, but they usually leave soon enough anyway. Its value lies in helping managers focus their retention efforts on the more valuable employees. It's paying off. The turnover rate has dropped 50 percent since Applebee's began using the ranking system.[72]

stereotyping
Placing an employee into a class or category based on one or a few traits or characteristics.

halo effect
A type of rating error that occurs when an employee receives the same rating on all dimensions regardless of his or her performance on individual ones.

behaviorally anchored rating scale (BARS)
A rating technique that relates an employee's performance to specific job-related incidents.

Performance Evaluation Errors. Although we would like to believe that every manager assesses employees' performance in a careful and bias-free manner, researchers have identified several rating problems.[73] One of the most dangerous is **stereotyping**, which occurs when a rater places an employee into a class or category based on one or a few traits or characteristics—for example, stereotyping an older worker as slower and more difficult to train. Another rating error is the **halo effect** in which a manager gives an employee the same rating on all dimensions even if his or her performance is good on some dimensions and poor on others.

One approach to overcome performance evaluation errors is to use a behavior-based rating technique such as the behaviorally anchored rating scale. The **behaviorally anchored rating scale (BARS)** is developed from critical incidents pertaining to job performance. Each job performance scale is anchored with specific behavioral statements that describe varying degrees of performance. By relating employee performance to specific incidents, raters can more accurately evaluate an employee's performance.[74]

Exhibit 9.10 illustrates the BARS method for evaluating a production line supervisor. The production supervisor's job can be broken down into several dimensions such as equipment

EXHIBIT 9.10
Example of a Behaviorally Anchored Rating Scale

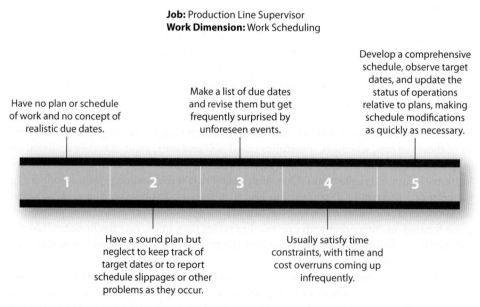

SOURCES: Based on J. P. Campbell, M. D. Dunnette, R. D. Arvey, and L. V. Hellervik, "The Development and Evaluation of Behaviorally Based Rating Scales," *Journal of Applied Psychology* 57 (1973): 15–22; and Francine Alexander, "Performance Appraisals," *Small Business Reports* (Mar. 1989): 20–29.

maintenance, employee training, and work scheduling. A behaviorally anchored rating scale should be developed for each dimension. The dimension in Exhibit 9.10 is work scheduling. Good performance is represented by a 4 or 5 on the scale and unacceptable performance as a 1 or 2. If a production supervisor's job has eight dimensions, then the total performance evaluation will be the sum of the scores for each of eight scales.

Maintaining an Effective Workforce

Now we turn to the topic of how managers and HRM professionals maintain a workforce that has been recruited and developed. Maintenance of the current workforce involves compensation, wage and salary systems, benefits, and occasional terminations.

COMPENSATION

The term **compensation** refers to: (1) all monetary payments and (2) all goods or commodities used in lieu of money to reward employees.[75] An organization's compensation structure includes wages or salaries and benefits such as health insurance, paid vacations, or employee fitness centers. Developing an effective compensation system is an important part of human-resource management because it helps to attract and retain talented workers. In addition, a company's compensation system has an impact on strategic performance.[76] Human-resource managers design the pay and benefits systems to fit company strategy and provide compensation equity.

Wage and Salary Systems. Ideally, management's strategy for the organization should be a critical determinant of the features and operations of the pay system.[77]

For example, managers may have the goal of maintaining or improving profitability or market share by stimulating employee performance. Thus, they should design and use a merit pay system rather than a system based on other criteria such as seniority.

The most common approach to employee compensation is *job-based pay*, which means linking compensation to the specific tasks an employee performs. However, these systems present several problems. For one thing, job-based pay may fail to reward the type of learning behavior needed for the organization to adapt and survive in today's environment. In addition, these systems reinforce organizational hierarchy and centralized decision making and control, which are inconsistent with the growing emphasis on employee participation and increased responsibility.[78]

Skill-based pay systems are becoming increasingly popular in both large and small companies, including Sherwin-Williams, Au Bon Pain, and Quaker Oats. Employees with higher skill levels receive higher pay than those with lower skill levels. At the Quaker Oats pet-food plant in Topeka, Kansas, for example, employees might start at something like $8.75 per hour but reach a top hourly rate of $14.50 when they master a series of skills.[79] Also called *competency-based pay*, skill-based pay systems encourage employees to develop their skills and competencies, thus making them more valuable to the organization as well as more employable if they leave their current jobs.

Compensation Equity. Whether the organization uses job-based pay or skill-based pay, good managers strive to maintain a sense of fairness and equity within the pay structure and thereby fortify employee morale. **Job evaluation** refers to the process of determining the value or worth of jobs within an organization through an examination of job content. Job-evaluation techniques enable managers to compare similar and dissimilar jobs and to determine internally equitable pay rates—that is, pay rates that employees believe are fair compared with those for other jobs in the organization.

Remember that jobs are multidimensional, and people need to be evaluated separately on each relevant dimension so they can be rewarded appropriately and improve their performance where needed.

As a manager, keep in mind that low pay often means higher turnover, which costs you more money.

compensation
Monetary payments (wages, salaries) and nonmonetary goods and commodities (benefits, vacations) used to reward employees.

job evaluation
The process of determining the value of jobs within an organization through an examination of job content.

Organizations also want to make sure their pay rates are fair compared to other companies. HRM managers may obtain **wage and salary surveys** that show what other organizations pay incumbents in jobs that match a sample of "key" jobs selected by the organization. These surveys are available from a number of sources, including the National Compensation Survey from the U.S. Bureau of Labor Statistics.

Pay for Performance. Many of today's organizations develop compensation plans based on a *pay-for-performance standard* to raise productivity and cut labor costs in a competitive global environment. **Pay for performance**, also called *incentive pay*, means tying at least part of compensation to employee effort and performance, whether it be through merit-based pay, bonuses, team incentives, or various gain-sharing or profit-sharing plans. Data show that, while growth in base wages is slowing in many industries, the use of pay-for-performance has steadily increased since the early 1990s, with approximately 70 percent of companies now offering some form of incentive pay.[80] With pay for performance, incentives are aligned with the behaviors needed to help the organization achieve its strategic goals. Employees have an incentive to make the company more efficient and profitable because no bonuses are paid if goals are not met.

BENEFITS

Consider skill-based pay systems and incentive pay to encourage high performers. If people have to be laid off or fired, do it humanely. Go to the Ethical Dilemma on page 312 that pertains to termination of employees for poor performance.

wage and salary surveys
Surveys that show what other organizations pay incumbents in jobs that match a sample of "key" jobs selected by the organization.

pay for performance
Incentive pay that ties at least part of compensation to employee effort and performance.

exit interview
An interview conducted with departing employees to determine the reasons for their termination.

The best human-resource managers know that a compensation package requires more than money. Although wage or salary is an important component, it is only a part. Equally important are the benefits offered by the organization. Benefits make up more than 40 percent of labor costs in the United States.[81]

Some benefits are required by law, such as Social Security, unemployment compensation, and workers' compensation. Other types of benefits, such as health insurance, vacations, and such things as on-site day-care or fitness centers are not required by law but are provided by organizations to maintain an effective workforce.

One reason benefits make up such a large portion of the compensation package is that health-care costs continue to increase. Many organizations are requiring that employees absorb a greater share of the cost of medical benefits, such as through higher co-payments and deductibles.

Computerization cuts the time and expense of administering benefits programs tremendously. At many companies, employees access their benefits package through an intranet, creating a "self-service" benefits administration.[82] This access also enables employees to change their benefits selections easily. Today's organizations realize that the "one-size-fits-all" benefits package is no longer appropriate, so they frequently offer *cafeteria-plan benefits packages* that allow employees to select the benefits of greatest value to them.[83] Other companies use surveys to determine which combination of fixed benefits is most desirable. The benefits packages provided by large companies attempt to meet the needs of all employees.

TERMINATION

Despite the best efforts of line managers and HRM professionals, the organization will lose employees. Some will retire, others will depart voluntarily for other jobs, and still others will be forced out through mergers and cutbacks or because of poor performance.

The value of termination for maintaining an effective workforce is twofold. First, employees who are poor performers can be dismissed. Productive employees often resent disruptive, low-performing employees who are allowed to stay with the company and receive pay and benefits comparable to theirs. Second, employers can use exit interviews as a valuable HR tool, regardless of whether the employee leaves voluntarily or is forced out. An **exit interview** is an interview conducted with departing employees to determine why they are leaving. Sixty-eight percent of companies surveyed by the Society for Human Resource Management say they either routinely or occasionally conduct formal exit interviews.[84] The value of the exit interview is to provide an inexpensive way to learn about pockets of dissatisfaction within the organization and hence find ways to reduce future turnover.[85] The oil-services giant Schlumberger includes an exit interview as part of a full-scale investigation of every departure, with the results posted online so managers all around the company can get insight into problems.[86] However, in many cases, employees who leave voluntarily are reluctant to air uncomfortable complaints or discuss their real reasons for leaving. Companies such as T-Mobile, Campbell Soup, and Conair found that having people complete an online exit questionnaire yields more open and honest information. When people have negative things to say about managers or the company, the online format is a chance to speak their mind without having to do it in a face-to-face meeting.[87]

For companies that experience downsizing through mergers or because of global competition or a shifting economy, large numbers of managers and workers are often terminated at the same time. In these cases, enlightened companies try to find a smooth transition for departing employees. By showing genuine concern in helping laid-off employees, a company communicates the value of human resources and helps maintain a positive corporate culture.

The Changing Workplace

Sweeping demographic changes in the U.S. population have transformed today's society, creating a cultural mosaic of diverse people. The nation's minority population, for example, is now 100.7 million, making about one in three U.S. residents a minority member. Roughly 32 million people speak Spanish at home, and nearly half of these people say they don't speak English very well, according to Census Bureau figures.[88] These demographic shifts, among others, are prompting companies in the United States and abroad to take notice because these trends open up new markets. To capitalize on those opportunities, organizations have recognized that their workplaces need to reflect the diversity in the marketplace. "Our country's consumer base is so varied," says Shelley Willingham-Hinton, president of the National Organization for Diversity in Sales and Marketing. "I can't think of how a company can succeed without having that kind of diversity with their employees."[89]

Forward-thinking organizations agree and are taking steps to attract and retain a workforce that reflects the cultural diversity of the population. They take seriously the fact that there is a link between the diversity of the workforce and financial success in the marketplace. To be successful, these organizations are hiring workers who share the same cultural background as the customers they are trying to reach. Avon, for example, turned around its inner-city markets by putting African American and Hispanic managers in charge of marketing to these populations.[90]

Today's organizations recognize that diversity is no longer just the right thing to do; it is a business imperative and perhaps the single most important factor of the 21st century for organization performance.[91] Companies that ignore diversity will have a hard time competing in a multicultural global environment. As Ted Childs, director of diversity at

3 The increasing numbers of foreign workers at U.S. companies need to spend a lot of attention learning the U.S. culture and adapting.

ANSWER: Though foreign-born workers do need to adapt, the companies must also learn to adjust to having people with various languages and practices in their workforces.

IBM, put it, "Diversity is the bridge between the workplace and the marketplace."[92] Global corporations Allstate, FedEx, IBM, Merrill Lynch, Verizon, and a number of others have been recognized as leaders in corporate diversity. They have made diversity a top priority and have taken steps toward creating a corporate culture that values equality and reflects today's multicultural consumer base.

In this last section of the chapter, we explore why demographic changes in the U.S. and global marketplaces have prompted corporations to place high value on creating a diverse workforce; it considers the advantages of a diverse workforce and the challenges in managing one. We look at the myriad complex issues that face managers and employees in a diverse workplace, including prejudice, stereotypes, discrimination, and ethnocentrism. Factors that specifically affect women—the glass ceiling, the opt-out trend, and the female advantage—are also considered.

When Brenda Thomson, the director of diversity and leadership education at the Las Vegas MGM Mirage, steps into one of the company's hotel lobbies, she closes her eyes and listens. "It's amazing all the different languages I can hear just standing in the lobbies of any of our hotels," she says. "Our guests come from all over the world, and it really makes us realize the importance of reflecting that diversity in our workplace."[93] The diversity Thomson sees in the lobbies of the MGM Mirage hotels is a small reflection of the cultural diversity seen in the larger domestic and global workplaces.

DIVERSITY IN THE UNITED STATES

Today's U.S. corporations reflect the country's image as a melting pot, but with a difference. In the past, the United States was a place where people of different national origins, ethnicities, races, and religions came together and blended to resemble one another. Opportunities for advancement were limited to those workers who easily fit into the mainstream of the larger culture. Some immigrants chose desperate measures to fit in, such as abandoning their native languages, changing their last names, and sacrificing their own unique cultures. In essence, everyone in workplace organizations was encouraged to share similar beliefs, values, and lifestyles despite differences in gender, race, and ethnicity.[94]

Now organizations recognize that everyone is not the same and that the differences people bring to the workplace are valuable.[95] Rather than expecting all employees to adopt similar attitudes and values, managers are learning that these differences enable their companies to compete globally and to tap into rich sources of new talent. Although diversity in North America has been a reality for some time, genuine efforts to accept and *manage* diverse people began only in recent years. Exhibit 9.11 lists some interesting milestones in the history of corporate diversity.

Diversity in corporate America has become a key topic, in part because of the vast changes occurring in today's workplace and consumer base. The average worker is older now, and many more women, people of color, and immigrants are seeking job and advancement opportunities. The following statistics illustrate some of the changes reshaping the workplace.

- *Aging workforce.* Baby boomers continue to affect the workplace as this massive group of workers progresses through its life stages. A baby boomer turns 60 every 7 seconds, continuously bumping up the average age of the workforce.[96] In 1986, the median age of the U.S. labor force was 35.4 years. It increased to 40.8 years in 2006 and will increase to 42.1 years in 2016.[97]

- *Growth in the numbers of Hispanic and Asian workers.* The greatest increase in employment will occur with Asians and Hispanics. In fact, the number of Hispanics in the workforce will increase by 6 million between 2006 and 2016, with 27 million Hispanics in the workforce by 2016.[98]

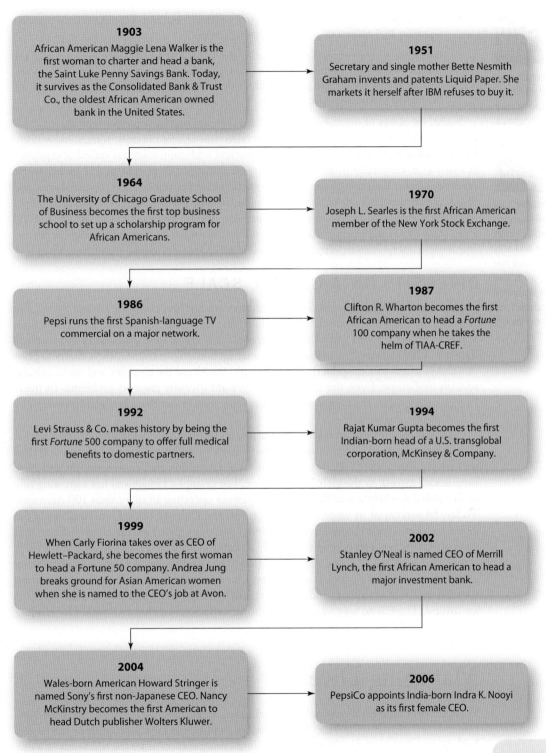

1903
African American Maggie Lena Walker is the first woman to charter and head a bank, the Saint Luke Penny Savings Bank. Today, it survives as the Consolidated Bank & Trust Co., the oldest African American owned bank in the United States.

1951
Secretary and single mother Bette Nesmith Graham invents and patents Liquid Paper. She markets it herself after IBM refuses to buy it.

1964
The University of Chicago Graduate School of Business becomes the first top business school to set up a scholarship program for African Americans.

1970
Joseph L. Searles is the first African American member of the New York Stock Exchange.

1986
Pepsi runs the first Spanish-language TV commercial on a major network.

1987
Clifton R. Wharton becomes the first African American to head a *Fortune* 100 company when he takes the helm of TIAA-CREF.

1992
Levi Strauss & Co. makes history by being the first *Fortune* 500 company to offer full medical benefits to domestic partners.

1994
Rajat Kumar Gupta becomes the first Indian-born head of a U.S. transglobal corporation, McKinsey & Company.

1999
When Carly Fiorina takes over as CEO of Hewlett–Packard, she becomes the first woman to head a Fortune 50 company. Andrea Jung breaks ground for Asian American women when she is named to the CEO's job at Avon.

2002
Stanley O'Neal is named CEO of Merrill Lynch, the first African American to head a major investment bank.

2004
Wales-born American Howard Stringer is named Sony's first non-Japanese CEO. Nancy McKinstry becomes the first American to head Dutch publisher Wolters Kluwer.

2006
PepsiCo appoints India-born Indra K. Nooyi as its first female CEO.

SOURCE: Adapted from "Spotlight on Diversity," special advertising section, *MBA Jungle* (Mar.–Apr. 2003): 58–61.

EXHIBIT 9.11

Some Milestones in the History of Corporate Diversity

As a manager, always notice the changing landscape of your customer demographics.

As a new manager, you will be challenged to create a workplace that is inclusive and bias free. Can you have the courage to take an active stand against prejudice and inappropriate, disrespectful behavior?

- *Minority purchasing power.* Hispanics, African Americans, and Asian Americans together represent $1.5 trillion in annual purchasing power.[99]

- *Growth in foreign–born population.* During the 1990s, the foreign-born population of the United States nearly doubled, and immigrants now number more than 37.5 million, meaning that almost one in eight people living in the United States was born in another country, the highest percentage since the 1920s.[100]

So far, the ability of organizations to manage diversity has not kept pace with these demographic trends, thus creating a number of significant challenges for minority workers and women. Progress for women and minorities in both pay and leadership roles has stalled or regressed at many U.S. corporations, as reflected in these statistics: 75 percent of 357 global senior executives report their companies have one or no minorities among their top executives, and 56 percent say they have one or no women among their top executives.[101] This inequality shapes perceptions about who can assume leadership roles. And the pay gap between white men and every other group still exists.[102] Corporations that truly value diversity will recognize pay inequality and discrimination in the workplace and make progress toward eliminating them.

DIVERSITY ON A GLOBAL SCALE

Implications of an increasingly diverse workforce are not limited to the United States. For example, the aging of the population is a global phenomenon. In addition, for organizations operating globally, social and cultural differences may create more difficulties and conflicts than any other sources. For instance, U.S. managers trying to transfer their diversity policies and practices to European divisions haven't considered the complex and social cultural systems in Europe. Even the meaning of the word *diversity* presents problems. In many European languages, the closest word implies separation rather than the inclusion sought by U.S. diversity programs.[103]

National cultures are intangible, pervasive, and difficult to comprehend. However, it is imperative that managers in organizations learn to understand local cultures and deal with them effectively.[104] Many companies have taken this challenge seriously and have experienced growth in the global marketplace. For example, Honeywell has a growing role in the global marketplace with 118,000 employees operating in more than 100 countries. Today, 54 percent of its employees work outside the United States. Honeywell made the global connection and incorporated diversity as part of its global strategies and believes that diversity provides the energy to fuel its high-performance culture and achieve sustainable competitive advantage.[105] The director of diversity at Kraft General Foods concurs. "Being global means that our customers are diverse. Our stockholders are diverse. The population which is available to us, our productivity, creativity, innovation, and people who supply us are diverse. There is no way we can run a business effectively without a deep understanding and accommodating all of these elements."[106]

Managing Diversity

Whether operating on a national or global scale, organizations recognize that their consumer base is changing, and they cannot prosper and succeed without a diverse workforce. Let's first explore the expanding definition of *diversity* and consider the dividends of cultivating a diverse workforce.

WHAT IS DIVERSITY?

diversity
All the ways in which employees differ.

Diversity is defined as all the ways in which people differ.[107] Diversity wasn't always defined this broadly. Decades ago, many companies defined diversity in terms of race, gender,

SPOTLIGHT ON SKILLS

A Guide for Expatriate Managers in America

Although each person is different, individuals from a specific country typically share certain values and attitudes. Managers planning to move to a foreign country can learn about these broad value patterns to help them adjust to working and living abroad. The following characteristics are often used to help foreign managers understand what Americans are like.

1. *Americans are informal.* They tend to treat everyone alike, even when individuals differ significantly in age or social status.
2. *Americans are direct and decisive.* To some foreigners, this behavior may seem abrupt or even rude. Typically, Americans don't "beat around the bush," which means they don't talk around things but get right to the point. They quickly define a problem and decide on the course of action they believe is most likely to get the desired results.
3. *Americans love facts.* They value statistics, data, and information in any form.
4. *Americans are competitive.* They like to keep score, whether at work or play. Americans like to win, and they don't tolerate failure well. Some foreigners might think Americans are aggressive or overbearing. For example, Americans are not at all shy about selling themselves. In fact, it's expected.
5. *Americans believe in work.* For many, commitment to work and career comes first. In general, Americans rarely take time off, even if a family member is ill. They don't believe in long vacations—even corporation presidents often take only two weeks, if that.

6. *Americans are independent and individualistic.* They place a high value on freedom and believe that people can control their own destinies.
7. *Americans are questioners.* They ask a lot of questions, even of someone they have just met. Some of these questions may seem pointless ("How ya doin'?") or personal ("What kind of work do you do?").
8. *Americans dislike silence.* They would rather talk about the weather than deal with silence in a conversation.
9. *Americans value punctuality.* They keep appointment calendars and live according to schedules and clocks.
10. *Americans pay close attention to appearances.* They take note of designer clothing and good grooming. They may, in fact, seem obsessed with bathing, eliminating body odors, and wearing clean clothes.

How many of these statements do you agree with? Discuss them with your friends and classmates, including people from different countries and members of different subcultural groups from the United States.

SOURCES: Winston Fletcher, "The American Way of Work," *Management Today* (Aug. 1, 2005): 46; "What Are Americans Like?" Exhibit 4-6 in Stephen P. Robbins and Mary Coulter, *Management*, 8th ed. (Upper Saddle River, NJ: Pearson Prentice Hall, 2005), as adapted from M. Ernest (Ed.), *Predeparture Orientation Handbook: For Foreign Students and Scholars Planning to Study in the United States* (Washington, DC: U.S. Information Agency, Bureau of Cultural Affairs, 1984): 103–105; Amanda Bennett, "American Culture Is Often a Puzzle for Foreign Managers in the U.S.," *Wall Street Journal*, Feb. 12, 1986, p. 1; "Don't Think Our Way's the Only Way," *Pryor Report* (Feb. 1988): 9; and B. Wattenberg, "The Attitudes Behind American Exceptionalism," *U.S. News and World Report* (Aug. 7, 1989): 25.

age, lifestyle, and disability. That focus helped create awareness, change mind-sets, and create new opportunities for many. Today, companies are embracing a more-inclusive definition of diversity that recognizes a spectrum of differences that influence how employees approach work, interact with each other, derive satisfaction from their work, and define who they are as people in the workplace.[108]

Exhibit 9.12 illustrates the difference between the traditional model and the inclusive model of diversity. The dimensions of diversity shown in the traditional model include inborn differences that are immediately observable and include race, gender, age, and physical ability. However, the inclusive model of diversity includes *all* of the ways in which employees differ, including aspects of diversity that can be acquired or changed throughout one's lifetime. These dimensions may have less impact than those included only in the traditional model but nevertheless affect a person's self-definition and worldview and the way the person is viewed by others. For example, the inclusive model of diversity recognizes people with different spiritual beliefs. As part of its diversity program, Target addresses issues of faith in its Minneapolis store. Muslim cashiers who object to ringing up pork

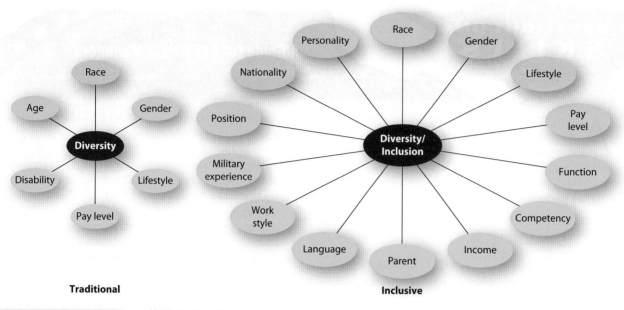

Traditional

Inclusive

SOURCE: Reproduced by permission. Anthony Oshiotse and Richard O'Leary, "Corning Creates an Inclusive Culture to Drive Technology Innovation and Performance," *Global Business and Organizational Excellence*, Wiley InterScience, March–April 2007, p. 12.

EXHIBIT 9.12

Traditional Versus Inclusive Models of Diversity

products due to religious beliefs are allowed to wear gloves, shift to other positions, or transfer to other stores.[109]

With 35 percent of its domestic workforce made up of African Americans, Hispanics, Asian Americans, and other minorities, UPS is widely recognized for its commitment to diversity. For the past seven consecutive years, a *Fortune* magazine survey has ranked UPS as one of the "50 Best Companies for Minorities." In addition, minorities hold 85 senior management positions, with African Americans filling 52 of those posts; 5 of the company's board of directors are African American.[110] Positive statistics such as these help UPS attract and retain a diverse workforce. UPS believes that the diversity reflected in its workforce is the key to its effectiveness.

Yet a diverse workforce poses unique challenges for managers at UPS and elsewhere. Employees with different backgrounds bring different opinions and ideas. Conflict, anxiety, and misunderstandings may increase. Embracing these differences and using them to improve company performance can be challenging. **Managing diversity**, a key management skill in today's global economy, means creating a climate in which the potential advantages of diversity for organizational or group performance are maximized while the potential disadvantages are minimized.[111]

Successful organizations seek a diverse and inclusive workforce. Indra Nooyi was named CEO of PepsiCo in 2006 after 12 years with the food and beverage giant, spending most of those years leading its global strategy. Both *Fortune* and *Forbes* magazines named the Indian-born executive one of the most powerful women in America. "I am not your normal, nondiverse CEO. I am everything that this company took forth in diversity and inclusion, and it has all come together with me," says Nooyi.

© AP IMAGES

> CONCEPT CONNECTION <

DIVIDENDS OF WORKPLACE DIVERSITY

Corporations that build strong, diverse organizations reap numerous dividends as described below.[112] The dividends of diversity include the following:

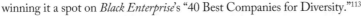

With roughly half of its 66,000 employees working outside the United States, it's not surprising that American Express is an acknowledged leader in managing global diversity. These East Indian staff members are shown in the company's Delhi offices. American Express developed a training module, "Valuing Diversity and Practicing Inclusion," for managers throughout the world, but executives let local facilitators customize the tool to fit their cultures. "We always allow them a period of time to be able to adapt, modify, and customize . . . so that it resonates well with employees," explains Henry Hernandez, vice president and chief diversity officer.

> CONCEPT CONNECTION

(photo credit: © RICHARD LORD/PHOTOEDIT INC.)

- *Better use of employee talent.* Companies with the best talent are the ones with the best competitive advantage. But attracting a diverse workforce is not enough; companies must also provide career opportunities and advancement for their minority and women employees if they wish to retain them.

- *Increased understanding of the marketplace.* The consumer market is becoming increasingly diverse. A diverse workforce is better able to anticipate and respond to changing consumer needs. Ford Motor Company realized it could reach its business objectives only if it created a workforce that reflected the multicultural face of the country. So it assembled a workforce made up of 25 percent minorities (18.4 percent are African American) to foster a culture of inclusion, winning it a spot on *Black Enterprise*'s "40 Best Companies for Diversity."[113]

- *Enhanced breadth of understanding in leadership positions.* Homogeneous top management teams tend to be myopic in their perspectives. According to Niall FitzGerald of Unilever, "It is important for any business operating in an increasingly complex and rapidly changing environment to deploy a broad range of talents. That provides a breadth of understanding of the world and environment and a fusion of the very best values and different perspectives which make up that world."[114]

- *Increased quality of team problem solving.* Teams with diverse backgrounds bring different perspectives to a discussion that result in more creative ideas and solutions.[115] Although 85 percent of Ernst & Young's senior leadership is still male, the company is taking steps to create a more diverse leadership team because it's better for business. "We know you get better solutions when you put a diverse team at the table. People come from different backgrounds and they have different frames of reference. When you put these people together, you get the best solution for our clients," says Billie Williamson, director of flexibility and gender equity strategy at Ernst & Young.[116]

- *Reduced costs associated with high turnover, absenteeism, and lawsuits.* Companies that foster a diverse workforce reduce turnover, absenteeism, and the risk of lawsuits. Because family responsibilities contribute to turnover and absenteeism, many companies now offer child-care and elder-care benefits, flexible work arrangements, telecommuting, and part-time employment to accommodate employee responsibilities at home. Discrimination lawsuits are also a costly side effect of a discriminatory work environment. A racial harassment suit against Lockheed Martin Corporation cost the company $2.5 million, the largest individual racial-discrimination payment obtained by the EEOC.[117]

These benefits of diversity are important for all organizations, but they are critical for agencies such as the Federal Bureau of Investigation (FBI) that are striving to keep communities safe in today's complex multicultural world. Not so long ago, if you were a woman

managing diversity
Creating a climate in which the potential advantages of diversity for organizational or group performance are maximized while the potential disadvantages are minimized.

or member of a minority group, you didn't stand a chance of becoming an FBI agent. Today, however, the agency's goal is to reflect the diversity of U.S. society.

FEDERAL BUREAU OF INVESTIGATION

How does the FBI gain credibility and obtain the information it needs to investigate and solve crimes? One way is by looking and thinking like the people in the communities where it seeks information. Each of the FBI's 56 field offices gets a report card on how well it has done in terms of making its offices reflective of the community. Each office is responsible for bringing minorities and women on board and providing them with advancement opportunities.

In addition, the FBI's national recruitment office was launched specifically to develop programs for recruiting women and minorities. One innovative initiative was the EdVenture Partners Collegiate Marketing Program, which worked with two historically African American universities. The program gave students college credit and funding to devise and implement a local marketing plan for the FBI. As a result of the program, the agency received 360 minority applications. "In many cases, the students' perceptions about the FBI were totally changed," says Gwen Hubbard, acting chief of the national recruitment office. "Initially, we were not viewed as an employer of choice by the diverse student populations." The EdVenture Partners program is being expanded to eight colleges and universities. Another initiative is a minority summer intern program that started with 21 full-time student interns and is being expanded to at least 40.

These programs on the national level, along with emphasis in the field offices on reflecting the local communities, ensure that the Federal Bureau of Investigation recruits diverse candidates. Today, the FBI has thousands of female and minority agents. Top leaders are also focusing on ways to make sure those people have full opportunity to move up the ranks so that there is diversity at leadership levels as well.[118]

Factors Shaping Personal Bias

To reap the benefits of diversity described above, organizations are seeking managers who will serve as catalysts in the workplace to reduce barriers and eliminate obstacles for disadvantaged people. *Managing diversity*, therefore, has become a sought-after management skill. To successfully manage a diverse workgroup and create a positive, productive environment for all employees, managers need to start with an understanding of the complex attitudes, opinions, and issues that already exist in the workplace or that employees bring into the workplace. These include several factors that shape personal bias: prejudice, discrimination, stereotypes, and ethnocentrism.

PREJUDICE, DISCRIMINATION, AND STEREOTYPES

Prejudice is the tendency to view people who are different as being deficient. If someone acts out their prejudicial attitudes toward people who are the targets of their prejudice, then **discrimination** has occurred.[119] Paying a woman less than a man for the same work is gender discrimination. Mistreating people because they have a different ethnicity is ethnic discrimination. Although blatant discrimination is not as widespread as in the past, bias in the workplace often shows up in subtle ways: a lack of choice assignments, the disregard by a subordinate of a minority manager's directions, or the ignoring of comments made by women and minorities at meetings. A survey by Korn Ferry International found that 59 percent of minority managers surveyed had observed a racially motivated double standard in the delegation of assignments.[120] Their perceptions are supported by a study that showed minority managers spend more time in the "bullpen" waiting for their chance and then have to prove themselves over and over again with each new assignment. Minority employees typically feel that they have to put in longer hours and extra effort

prejudice
The tendency to view people who are different as being deficient.

discrimination
When someone acts out their prejudicial attitudes toward people who are the targets of their prejudice.

to achieve the same status as their white colleagues. "It's not enough to be as good as the next person," says Bruce Gordon, president of Bell Atlantic's enterprise group. "We have to be better."[121]

A number of federal and state laws outlaw different types of discrimination, as discussed earlier in this chapter. These include the following:

- Title VII of the Civil Rights Act of 1964, which prohibits discrimination on the basis of race, color, religion, national origin, and sex.

- The Equal Pay Act of 1963, which prohibits employers from paying different wages to men and women who perform essentially the same work under similar working conditions.

- The Americans with Disabilities Act, which prohibits discrimination against persons with disabilities.

- The Age Discrimination in Employment Act, which prohibits discrimination against individuals who are age 40 or older.[122]

A major component of prejudice is **stereotyping**, or associating rigid, exaggerated, and irrational beliefs with a particular group of people.[123] To be successful managing diversity, managers need to eliminate harmful stereotypes from their thinking, shedding any biases that negatively affect the workplace. Managers can learn to *value differences*, which means they recognize cultural differences and see the differences with an appreciative attitude. To facilitate this attitude, managers can learn about cultural patterns and typical beliefs of groups to help understand why people act the way they do. It helps understand the difference between these two ways of thinking, most notably that stereotyping is a barrier to diversity but valuing cultural differences facilitates diversity. These two different ways of thinking are described as follow and illustrated in Exhibit 9.13.[124]

- *Stereotypes are often based on folklore, media portrayals, and other unreliable sources of information.* In contrast, legitimate cultural differences are backed up by systematic research of real differences.

- *Stereotypes contain negative connotations.* On the other hand, managers who value diversity view differences as potentially positive or neutral. For example, the observation that Asian males are typically less aggressive does not imply they are inferior or superior to white males—it simply means that there is a difference.

- *Stereotypes assume that all members of a group have the same characteristics.* Managers who value diversity recognize that individuals within a group of people may or may not share the same characteristics of the group.[125]

Remember that most discrimination is not overt, but rather unconscious. Even if you don't realize you are discriminating, you might still be.

To successfully manage diversity, you will need to shed stereotypes and judgmental attitudes while still appreciating the differences among people.

stereotyping
Associating a rigid, exaggerated, and irrational belief with a particular group of people.

Stereotyping	Valuing Cultural Differences
Is based on false assumptions, anecdotal evidence, or impressions without any direct experience with a group	Views are based on cultural differences verified by scientific research methods
Assigns negative traits to members of a group	Views cultural differences as positive or neutral
Assumes that all members of a group have the same characteristics	Does not assume that all individuals within a group have the same characteristics
Example: Suzuko Akoi is an Asian; therefore, she is not aggressive by white, male standards.	Example: As a group, Asians tend to be less aggressive than white, male Americans.

EXHIBIT 9.13

Difference Between Stereotyping and Valuing Cultural Differences

– – – – – – – – – –

SOURCE: Adapted from Taylor Cox, Jr., and Ruby L. Beale, *Developing Competency to Manage Diversity: Readings, Cases, and Activities* (San Francisco: Berrett-Koehler Publishers, 1997).

Managers not only should rid themselves of stereotypical thinking but also recognize the stereotype threat that may jeopardize the performance of at-risk employees. **Stereotype threat** describes the psychological experience of a person who, usually engaged in a task, is aware of a stereotype about his or her identity group that suggests that he or she will not perform well on that task.[126] Suppose you are a member of a minority group presenting complicated market research results to your management team and are anxious about making a good impression. Assume that some members of your audience have a negative stereotype about your identity group. As you ponder this, your anxiety skyrockets and your confidence is shaken. Understandably, your presentation suffers because you are distracted by worries and self-doubt as you invest energy in overcoming the stereotype. The feelings you are experiencing are called *stereotype threat*.

People most affected by stereotype threat are those we consider as disadvantaged in the workplace due to negative stereotypes—racial and ethnic minorities, members of lower socioeconomic classes, women, older people, gay and bisexual men and women, and people with disabilities. Although anxiety about performing a task may be normal, people with stereotype threat feel an extra scrutiny and worry that their failure will reflect not only on themselves as individuals but also on the larger group to which they belong. As Beyoncé Knowles said, "It's like you have something to prove, and you don't want to mess it up and be a negative reflection on black women."[127]

ETHNOCENTRISM

stereotype threat
A psychological experience of a person who, usually engaged in a task, is aware of a stereotype about his or her identify group that suggests he or she will not perform well on that task.

ethnocentrism
The belief that one's own group or subculture is inherently superior to other groups or cultures.

Valuing diversity by recognizing, welcoming, and cultivating differences among people so they can develop their unique talents and be effective organizational members is difficult to achieve. Ethnocentrism can be a roadblock to this type of thinking. **Ethnocentrism** is the belief that one's own group and subculture are inherently superior to other groups and cultures. Ethnocentrism makes it difficult to value diversity. Viewing one's own culture as the best culture is a natural tendency among most people. Moreover, the business world still tends to reflect the values, behaviors, and assumptions based on the experiences of a rather homogeneous, white, middle-class, male workforce. Indeed, most theories of management presume that workers share similar values, beliefs, motivations, and attitudes about work and life in general. These theories presume one set of behaviors best helps an organization to be productive and effective and therefore should be adopted by all employees.[128]

GOOGLE

Employees in Google's corporate headquarters come from all corners of the world, but they feel a little closer to home when they see familiar foods from their homelands on the cafeteria menu. With a goal of satisfying a diverse, ethnically varied palate, Google's first food guru and chef, Charlie Ayers, designed menus that reflected his eclectic tastes yet also met the needs of an increasingly diverse workforce. He created his own dishes, searched all types of restaurants for new recipes, and often got some of his best ideas from foreign-born employees. For example, a Filipino accountant offered a recipe for chicken *adobo*, a popular dish from her native country. Scattered around the Googleplex are cafes specializing in Southwestern, Italian, California-Mediterranean, and vegetarian cuisines. And because more and more Googlers originally hail from Asia, employees can find sushi at the Japanese-themed Pacific Café or Thai red curry beef at the East Meets West Café.

Google believes food can be a tool for supporting an inclusive workplace. The array of menu options gives people a chance to try new things and learn more about their co-workers. And Google knows that when people need a little comfort and familiarity, nothing takes the edge off of working in a foreign country like eating food that reminds you of home.[129]

Like Google, many of today's organizations are making conscious efforts to shift from a monoculture perspective to one of pluralism. Others, however, are still hindered by stereotypical thinking. Consider a recent report from the National Bureau of Economic Research titled "Are Greg and Emily More Employable than Lakisha and Jamal?" The report shows that employers often unconsciously discriminate against job applicants based solely on the Afrocentric names on their résumé. In interviews prior to the research, most human-resource managers surveyed said they expected only a small gap, and some expected to find a pattern of reverse discrimination. The results showed instead that white-sounding names got 50 percent more callbacks than black-sounding names, even when skills and experience were equal.[130] Discrimination's reach extends beyond U.S. borders. One study conducted in France revealed that a job candidate with a North African–sounding name had three times less chance than one with a French-sounding name to get an interview.[131]

Factors Affecting Women's Careers

Despite years of progress by women in the workforce, many women still find their career goals are unattainable or difficult to achieve. In addition, men as a group still have the benefit of higher wages and faster promotions. In the United States in 2005, for example, women employed full-time earned 81 cents for every dollar that men earned.[132] Both the glass ceiling and the decision to "opt out" of a high-pressure career have an impact on women's advancement opportunities and pay. Yet women are sometimes favored in leadership roles for demonstrating behaviors and attitudes that help them succeed in the workplace, a factor called "the female advantage."

GLASS CEILING

The **glass ceiling** is an invisible barrier that separates women from top management positions. They can look up through the ceiling and see top management, but prevailing attitudes and stereotypes present invisible obstacles to their own advancement. This barrier also impedes the career progress of minorities.

In addition, women and minorities are often excluded from informal manager networks and often don't get access to the type of general and line management experience that is required for moving to the top.[133] Research suggests the existence of *glass walls* that serve as invisible barriers to important lateral movement within the organization. Glass walls, like exclusion from manager networks, bar experience in areas such as line supervision that would enable women and minorities to advance vertically.[134]

Evidence that the glass ceiling persists is the distribution of women and minorities, who are clustered at the bottom levels of the corporate hierarchy. Among minority groups, women have made the biggest strides in recent years, but they still represent only 15.7 percent of corporate officers in America's 500 largest companies, up from 12.5 percent in 2000 and 8.7 percent in 1995.[135] In 2007, just seven companies, or 1 percent, among the *Fortune* 500 companies had female CEOs.[136] And both male and female African Americans and Hispanics hold only a small percentage of all management positions in the United States.[137]

Women and minorities also make less money. As shown in Exhibit 9.14 on the next page, African American men earn about 22 percent less, white women 24 percent less, and Hispanic men 37 percent less than white males. Minority women fare even worse, with African American women earning 35 percent less and Hispanic women 46 percent less than white males.[138]

Another sensitive issue related to the glass ceiling is homosexuals in the workplace. Many gay men and lesbians believe they will not be accepted as they are and risk losing their jobs or their chances for advancement. Gay employees of color are particularly hesitant to disclose their sexual orientation at work because by doing so they risk a double dose of discrimination.[139] Although some examples of openly gay corporate leaders can be found, such as David Geffen, co-founder of DreamWorks SKG, and Ford Vice Chairman Allan D. Gilmour, most managers still believe staying in the closet is the only way they

glass ceiling
Invisible barrier that separates women and minorities from top management positions.

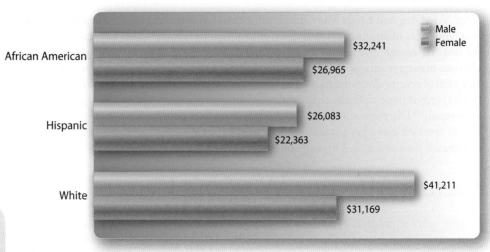

SOURCE: U.S. Census Bureau, "2006 Median Annual Earnings by Race and Sex," Current Population Survey, 2007, Annual Social and Economic Supplement (www.infoplease.com/us/census/median-earnings-by-race-2006.html).

EXHIBIT 9.14
The Wage Gap

– – – – – – – – – –

can succeed at work. Thus, gays and lesbians often fabricate heterosexual identities to keep their jobs or avoid running into the glass ceiling they see other employees encounter.

Establishing Mentor Relationships. The successful advancement of diverse group members means that organizations must find ways to eliminate the glass ceiling. One of the most successful structures to accomplish this goal is the mentoring relationship. A **mentor** is a higher-ranking organizational member who is committed to providing upward mobility and support to a protégé's professional career.[140] Mentoring provides minorities and women with direct training and inside information on the norms and expectations of the organization. A mentor also acts as a friend or counselor, enabling the employee to feel more confident and capable. Joseph Cleveland has made a point of helping young African Americans navigate the corporate maze in his career at General Electric and Lockheed Martin. For Pamela Blow-Mitchell, Cleveland's mentoring changed the course of her career and enabled her to seize opportunities she might otherwise have missed. "He kind of dunked down deep in the organization to initiate a conversation with someone that he saw potential in," said Mitchell. "At the time, I could not see the range of opportunities, but I trusted his advice."[141]

One researcher who studied the career progress of high-potential minorities found that those who advance the furthest all share one characteristic—a strong mentor or network of mentors who nurtured their professional development.[142] However, research also indicates that minorities, as well as women, are much less likely than men to develop mentoring relationships.[143] Women and minorities might not seek mentors because they feel that job competency should be enough to succeed, or they might feel uncomfortable seeking out a mentor when most of the senior executives are white males. Women might fear that initiating a mentoring relationship could be misunderstood as a romantic overture, whereas male mentors may think of women as mothers, wives, or sisters rather than as executive material. Cross-race mentoring relationships sometimes leave both parties uncomfortable, but the mentoring of minority employees must often be across race because of the low number of minorities in upper-level positions. The few minorities and women who have reached the upper ranks often are overwhelmed with mentoring requests from people like themselves, and they may feel uncomfortable in highly visible minority–minority or female–female mentoring relationships, which isolate them from the white male status quo.

Even as a new manager, you may have an opportunity to act as a mentor to a younger or less-experienced minority employee. Assist the employee in navigating the office politics and learning the unwritten rules about how things are done in the organization.

mentor
Higher-ranking organizational member who is committed to providing upward mobility and support to a protégé's professional career.

The solution is for organizations to overcome some of the barriers to mentor relationships between white males and minorities. When organizations can institutionalize the value of white males actively seeking women and minority protégés, they will benefit as women and minorities are steered into pivotal jobs and positions critical to advancement. Mentoring programs also are consistent with the Civil Rights Act of 1991, which requires the diversification of middle and upper management.

OPT-OUT TREND

Many women never hit the glass ceiling because they choose to get off the fast track long before it comes into view. In recent years, an ongoing discussion concerns something referred to as the *opt-out trend*. In a recent survey of nearly 2,500 women and 653 men, 37 percent of highly qualified women report that they voluntarily left the workforce at some point in their careers, compared to only 24 percent of similarly qualified men.[144]

Quite a debate rages over the reasons for the larger number of women who drop out of mainstream careers. Opt-out proponents say women are deciding that corporate success isn't worth the price in terms of reduced family and personal time, greater stress, and negative health effects.[145] For example, Marge Magner left her job as CEO of Citigroup's Consumer Group after suffering both the death of her mother and a personal life-changing accident in the same year. In evaluating her reasons, Magner said she realized that "life is about everything, not just the work."

One school of thought says women don't want corporate power and status in the same way that men do, and clawing one's way up the corporate ladder has become less appealing. Yet critics argue that this view is just another way to blame women themselves for the dearth of female managers at higher levels.[146] Vanessa Castagna, for example, left JCPenney after decades with the company not because she wanted more family or personal time but because she kept getting passed over for top jobs.[147] Although some women are voluntarily leaving the fast track, many more genuinely want to move up the corporate ladder but find their paths blocked. Fifty-five percent of executive women surveyed by Catalyst said they aspire to senior leadership levels.[148] In addition, a survey of 103 women voluntarily leaving executive jobs in *Fortune* 1000 companies found that corporate culture was cited as the number-one reason for leaving.[149] The greatest disadvantages of women leaders stem largely from prejudicial attitudes and a heavily male-oriented corporate culture.[150] Some years ago, when Procter & Gamble asked the female executives it considered "regretted losses" (that is, high performers the company wanted to retain) why they left their jobs, the most common answer was that they didn't feel valued by the company.[151]

THE FEMALE ADVANTAGE

Some people think women might actually be better managers, partly because of a more collaborative, less hierarchical, and more relationship-oriented approach that is in tune with today's global and multicultural environment.[152] As attitudes and values change with changing generations, the qualities women seem to naturally possess may lead to a gradual role reversal in organizations. For example, a stunning gender reversal is taking place in U.S. education, with girls taking over almost every leadership role from kindergarten to graduate school. In addition, women of all races and ethnic groups are outpacing men in earning bachelor's and master's degrees. In most higher education institutions, women make up 58 percent of enrolled students.[153] By 2010, according to the U.S. Department of Education, the girl–boy ratio should be 60 to 40.[154] Among 25- to 29-year-olds, 32 percent of women have college degrees, compared to 27 percent of men. Women are rapidly closing the MD and PhD gaps, and they make up about half of all U.S. law students, half

NEW MANAGER'S SELF-TEST

Are You Tuned into Gender Differences?

How much do you know about gender differences in behavior? Please answer whether each item below is True or False. Answer all questions before looking at the answers that follow the test.

	TRUE	FALSE
1. Men control the content of conversations, and they work harder to keep conversations going.	_____	_____
2. Women use less personal space than men.	_____	_____
3. A male speaker is listened to more carefully than a female speaker even when the two make identical presentations.	_____	_____
4. In the classroom, male students receive more reprimands and criticism.	_____	_____
5. Men are more likely to interrupt women than to interrupt other men.	_____	_____
6. Female managers communicate with more emotional openness and drama than male managers.	_____	_____
7. Women are more likely to answer questions not addressed to them.	_____	_____
8. In general, men smile more than women do.	_____	_____
9. Both male and female direct reports see female managers as better communicators than male managers.	_____	_____
10. In a classroom, teachers are more likely to give verbal praise to female students.	_____	_____

SCORING AND INTERPRETATION: Check your answers with the following key. If you scored 7 or more correctly, then consider yourself perceptive and observant about gender behavior. If you scored 3 or fewer, then you may want to tune in to the gender dynamics you are missing.

SOURCE: Myra Sadker and Joyce Kaser, *The Communications Gender Gap* (Washington, DC: Mid-Atlantic Center for Sex Equity, 1984).

Answers

1: False (men control content, women work harder); 2: True; 3: True; 4: True; 5: True; 6: False (managers of both sexes communicate about the same way); 7: False; 8: False (women smile more); 9: True; 10: False.

of all undergraduate business majors, and about 30 percent of MBA candidates. Overall, women's participation in both the labor force and civic affairs has steadily increased since the mid-1950s, while men's participation has slowly but steadily declined.[155]

According to James Gabarino, an author and professor of human development at Cornell University, women are "better able to deliver in terms of what modern society requires of people—paying attention, abiding by rules, being verbally competent, and dealing with interpersonal relationships in offices."[156] His observation is supported by the fact that female managers are typically rated higher by subordinates on interpersonal skills as well as on factors such as task behavior, communication, ability to motivate others, and goal accomplishment.[157] Recent research found a correlation between balanced gender composition in companies (that is, roughly equal male and female representation) and higher organizational performance. Moreover, a study by Catalyst indicates that organizations with the highest percentage of women in top management financially outperform, by about 35 percent, those with the lowest percentage of women in higher-level jobs.[158]

Summary

This chapter described how human-resource management plays a key strategic role in driving organizational performance through building human capital and enabling the company to be more competitive on a global basis.

The HR department must also implement procedures to reflect federal and state legislation and respond to changes in working relationships and career directions. The old social contract of the employee being loyal to the company and the company taking care of the employee until retirement no longer holds. Employees are responsible for managing their own careers.

The first goal of HRM is to attract an effective workforce through human-resource planning, recruiting, and employee selection. The second is to develop an effective workforce. Newcomers are introduced to the organization and to their jobs through orientation and training programs. Moreover, employees are evaluated through performance-appraisal programs. The third goal is to maintain an effective workforce through wage and salary systems, benefits packages, and termination procedures. In many organizations, information technology is being used to more effectively meet all three of these important HR goals.

The domestic and global marketplace is experiencing dramatic demographic changes, including an aging population and growing immigrant and minority populations. Savvy managers recognize that their workforces should reflect this cultural diversity.

Diversity is defined as all the ways in which employees differ. This definition has been broadened in recent years to be more inclusive and to recognize a broad spectrum of characteristics including age, religion, physical ability, race, ethnicity, sexual preference, and more. Because of the complexities of managing a diverse workforce, *managing diversity* is a key management skill today.

The dividends of diversity are numerous and include better use of employee talent, increased understanding of customers in the marketplace, enhanced breadth of understanding in leadership positions, increased quality of team problem solving, and reduced costs associated with high turnover, absenteeism, and lawsuits.

All employees bring to the workplace opinions and attitudes that affect their ability to treat people equally. Some of these issues include prejudice, discrimination, and stereotyping. The performance of minorities and other disadvantaged workers may be affected by a *stereotype threat*, a psychological reaction by employees that is triggered by worry and concern that others may doubt their abilities due to unfair stereotypes. Managers should be aware of the challenges minority employees face and be prepared to handle them, including issues related to ethnocentrism, the glass ceiling, the opt-out trend, and the female advantage.

Discussion Questions

1. Which selection criteria (personal interview, employment test, assessment center) do you think would be most valuable for predicting effective job performance for a manager in a record company? For one of your college professors? For a manager at a coffee shop such as Starbucks? Discuss.

2. Is it wise for managers to consider a candidate's MySpace or Facebook postings as grounds for rejection before even interviewing a promising candidate? Is it fair? Discuss.

3. If you are in charge of training and development, which training option or options—such as on-the job training, cross-training, classroom, podcasting, mentoring— would you be likely to choose for your company's sales staff? A customer service representative? An entry-level accountant?

4. If you were to draw up a telecommuting contract with an employee, what would it look like? Include considerations such as job description, compensation and benefits, performance measures, training, and grounds for dismissal.

5. How would you go about deciding whether to use a job-based, skills-based, or pay-for-performance compensation plan for employees in a T-shirt manufacturing plant? For waitstaff in a restaurant? For salespeople in an insurance company?

6. What purpose do exit interviews serve for maintaining an effective workforce?

7. Evaluate your own experiences so far with people from other backgrounds. How well do you think those experiences prepared you to understand the unique needs and dilemmas of a diverse workforce?

8. Describe employees who are most vulnerable to stereotype threat. Why is it important for managers to understand that some employees may experience stereotype threat?

9. What is the glass ceiling, and why do you think it has proven to be such a barrier to women and minorities?

10. You are a manager at an organization that has decided it needs a more diverse workforce. What steps or techniques will you use to accomplish this goal? What steps will you take to retain diverse employees once you have successfully recruited them?

Self Learning

How Tolerant Are You?

For each of the following questions, circle the answer that best describes you.

1. Most of your friends:

   a. are very similar to you.

   b. are very different from you and from each other.

   c. are like you in some respects but different in others.

2. When someone does something you disapprove of, you:

   a. break off the relationship.

   b. tell how you feel but keep in touch.

   c. tell yourself it matters little and behave as you always have.

3. Which virtue is most important to you?

   a. kindness

   b. objectivity

   c. obedience

4. When it comes to beliefs, you:

   a. do all you can to make others see things the same way you do.

   b. actively advance your point of view but stop short of argument.

   c. keep your feelings to yourself.

5. Would you hire a person who has had emotional problems?

   a. No

   b. Yes, provided the person shows evidence of complete recovery.

   c. Yes if the person is suitable for the job.

6. Do you voluntarily read material that supports views different from your own?

   a. never

   b. sometimes

   c. often

7. You react to old people with

   a. patience.

   b. annoyance.

   c. sometimes patience, sometimes annoyance.

8. Do you agree with the statement, "What is right and wrong depends on the time, place, and circumstance"?

   a. strongly agree

   b. agree to a point

   c. strongly disagree

9. Would you marry someone from a different race?

   a. yes

   b. no

   c. probably not

10. If someone in your family were homosexual, you would:

    a. view this as a problem and try to change the person to a heterosexual orientation.

    b. accept the person as a homosexual with no change in feelings or treatment.

    c. avoid or reject the person.

11. You react to little children with:

    a. patience.

    b. annoyance.

    c. sometimes patience, sometimes annoyance.

12. Other people's personal habits annoy you:
    a. often.
    b. not at all.
    c. only if extreme.

13. If you stay in a household run differently from yours (cleanliness, manners, meals, and other customs), you:
    a. adapt readily.
    b. quickly become uncomfortable and irritated.
    c. adjust for a while, but not for long.

14. Which statement do you agree with most?
    a. We should avoid judging others because no one can fully understand the motives of another person.
    b. People are responsible for their actions and have to accept the consequences.
    c. Both motives and actions are important when considering questions of right and wrong.

Scoring and Interpretation: Circle your score for each of the answers and total the scores:

1. a = 4; b = 0; c = 2
2. a = 4; b = 2; c = 0
3. a = 0; b = 2; c = 4
4. a = 4; b = 2; c = 0
5. a = 4; b = 2; c = 0
6. a = 4; b = 2; c = 0
7. a = 0; b = 4; c = 2
8. a = 0; b = 2; c = 4
9. a = 0; b = 4; c = 2
10. a = 2; b = 0; c = 4
11. a = 0; b = 4; c = 2
12. a = 4; b = 0; c = 2
13. a = 0; b = 4; c = 2
14. a = 0; b = 4; c = 2

Total Score

0–14: If you score 14 or below, you are a very tolerant person; dealing with diversity comes easily to you.

15–28: You are basically a tolerant person and others think of you as tolerant. In general, diversity presents few problems for you; you may be broad-minded in some areas and have less tolerant ideas in other areas of life such as attitudes toward older people or male–female social roles.

29–42: You are less tolerant than most people and should work on developing greater tolerance of people different from you. Your low tolerance level could affect your business or personal relationships.

43–56: You have a very low tolerance for diversity. The only people you are likely to respect are those with beliefs similar to your own. You reflect a level of intolerance that could cause difficulties in today's multicultural business environment.

Source: Adapted from the Tolerance Scale by Maria Heiselman, Naomi Miller, and Bob Schlorman, Northern Kentucky University, 1982. In George Manning, Kent Curtis, and Steve McMillen, *Building Community: The Human Side of Work* (Cincinnati: Thomson Executive Press, 1996): 272–277.

Group Learning

Hiring and Evaluating Using Core Competencies

1. Form groups of four to seven members. Develop a list of "core competencies" for the job of student in this course. (Or, alternately, you may choose a job in one of the group members' organizations). List the core competencies below.

   1.   5.
   2.   6.
   3.   7.
   4.   8.

2. Which of the above are the most important four?

   1.   3.
   2.   4.

3. What questions would you ask a potential employee or student in order to determine if that person could be successful in this class, based on the four most important core competencies? (interviewing)

   1.   3.
   2.   4.

4. What learning experiences would you develop to enhance those core competencies? (training and development)

   1.   3.
   2.   4.

5. How would you evaluate or measure the success of a student in this class based on the four core competencies? (performance evaluation)

   1.   3.
   2.   4.

Action Learning

Interview Questions

1. Meet with four to five people who have recently gone through job interviews. Ask them what questions they were asked and list those on a sheet of paper. Note whether questions were asked of more than one of these people—that is, how many people were asked that type of question? Find out which questions they found uncomfortable or invasive, and ask them how they responded to those questions.

2. Your instructor may ask you to form groups of three to five people. If so, come up with a composite list of questions. Refer to Exhibit 9.8 (page 286) to see which of the questions should not have been asked.

3. How did people answer difficult questions?

4. Be prepared to make a presentation to the entire class.

5. The instructor may lead a discussion about appropriate interview questions and how to respond to them.

Ethical Dilemma

A Conflict of Responsibilities

As director of human resources, Tess Danville was asked to negotiate a severance deal with Terry Winston, the Midwest regional sales manager for CynCom Systems. Winston's problems with drugs and alcohol had become severe enough to precipitate his dismissal. His customers were devoted to him, but top management was reluctant to continue gambling on his reliability. Lives depended on his work as the salesperson and installer of CynCom's respiratory diagnostic technology. Winston had been warned twice to clean up his act but had never succeeded. Only his unique blend of technical knowledge and high-powered sales ability had saved him before.

Now the vice president of sales asked Danville to offer Winston the option of resigning rather than being fired if he would sign a noncompete agreement and agree to go into rehabilitation. CynCom would also extend a guarantee of confidentiality on the abuse issue and a good work reference as thanks for the millions of dollars of business that Winston had brought to CynCom. Winston agreed to take the deal. After his departure, a series of near disasters was uncovered as a result of Winston's mismanagement. Some of his maneuvers to cover up his mistakes bordered on fraud.

Today, Danville received a message to call the human-resource director at a cardiopulmonary technology company to give a personal reference on Terry Winston. From the area code, she could see that he was not in violation of the noncompete agreement. She had also heard that Winston had completed a 30-day treatment program as promised. Danville knew she was expected to honor the confidentiality agreement, but she also knew that if his shady dealings had been discovered before his departure, he would have been fired without any agreement. Now she was being asked to give Winston a reference for another medical sales position.

What Would You Do?

1. Honor the agreement, trusting Winston's rehabilitation is complete on all levels and that he is now ready for a responsible position. Give a good recommendation.

2. Contact the vice president of sales and ask him to release you from the agreement or to give the reference himself. After all, he made the agreement. You don't want to lie.

3. Without mentioning specifics, give Winston such an unenthusiastic reference that you hope the other human-resources director can read between the lines and believe that Winston will be a poor choice.

PART FIVE

Controlling

5 PART FIVE

Controlling

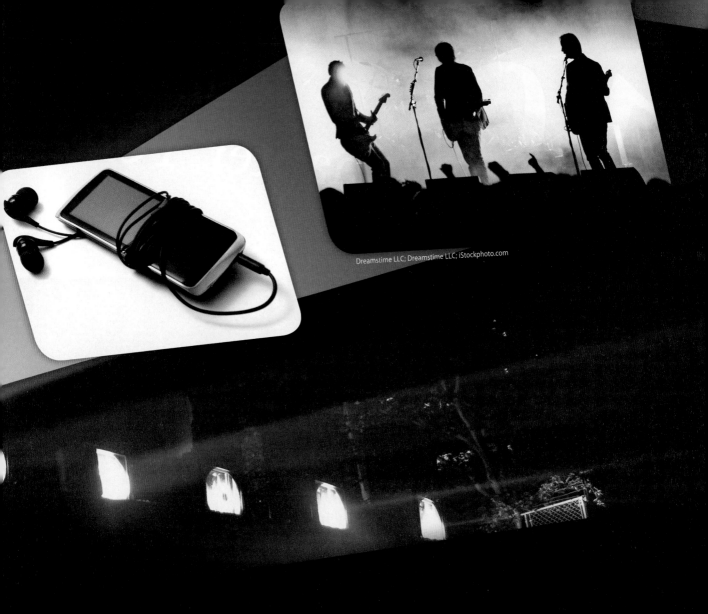

In the world of global business, delivering high quality products is a multiorganizational effort. Few companies know this better than Apple. The world's premier computer innovator used numerous business partners in the development of the iPod and iPhone, and the company's network of suppliers is now coordinating to create a tour de force in digital entertainment: a wireless multimedia tablet.

Approximately 10 inches in size, the gadget's lightweight digital touch screen delivers interactive movies, music, and e-book downloads from Apple's online product store. The all-in-one entertainment device promises to be the Holy Grail of entertainment media devices.

But making this dream tablet a reality has put enormous demands on Apple's supply chain management. The variety of external partners needed to create the product is astounding: Record companies, film studios, digital book publishers, computer components makers, lithium-ion battery producers, and telecommunications firms must coordinate tasks and production schedules to meet Apple's high manufacturing standards.

Fortunately, Apple instituted an end-to-end supply chain management process for the iPod and iPhone, and the test now is whether managers can deliver consistent quality as the company expands both its product horizons and manufacturing partners.

10

Chapter Ten

Managing Quality and Performance

LEARNING OBJECTIVES

After studying this chapter, you should be able to:

1 Define organizational control and explain why it is a key management function.

2 Explain the benefits of using the balanced scorecard to track performance and control of the organization.

3 Explain the four steps in the control process.

4 Discuss the use of financial statements, financial analysis, and budgeting as management controls.

5 Contrast the hierarchical and decentralized methods of control.

6 Identify the benefits of open-book management.

7 Describe the concept of total quality management and major TQM techniques such as quality circles, benchmarking, Six Sigma principles, reduced cycle time, and continuous improvement.

8 Identify current trends in quality and financial control, including ISO 9000, economic value–added and market value–added systems, activity-based costing, and corporate governance, and discuss their effects on organizations.

New Manager's Questions

Please circle your opinion below each of the following statements.

1 Controls are for bean counters.

STRONGLY AGREE < < <			> > > STRONGLY DISAGREE	
1	2	3	4	5

2 When there's a problem, a good manager finds who's at fault.

STRONGLY AGREE < < <			> > > STRONGLY DISAGREE	
1	2	3	4	5

3 Total quality management is just another fad.

STRONGLY AGREE < < <			> > > STRONGLY DISAGREE	
1	2	3	4	5

Control is an important issue that faces every manager in every organization, but new managers sometimes have a hard time finding the correct degree of control that will keep people productive without squelching their motivation and creativity. Managers face many control issues, including controlling work processes, regulating employee behavior, setting up basic systems for allocating financial resources, developing human resources, analyzing financial performance, and evaluating overall profitability. Another important aspect is quality control.

Consider the quality control challenge facing U.S. Army managers. Every week, dozens of war-battered Humvees from Iraq are shipped to a 36,000-acre army depot in Texarkana, Texas. The Red River Army Depot is one of the army's oldest and most important maintenance and storage bases. Faced with a shrinking defense budget, military experts had to find ways to repair the Humvees faster and with fewer personnel. They studied quality control processes used in the private sector and spearheaded the most ambitious business effort in the 231-year history of the U.S. Army: an attempt to adopt a quality control theory, Lean Six Sigma, across the entire service. "We need to free up resources so we can apply them to the operating side of the army. We need to equip our soldiers better and faster," says Mike Kirby, deputy undersecretary of the army for business transformation. The new quality control process includes a highly efficient assembly line where horns blare every 23 minutes to indicate station changes. The results are impressive: The facility now turns out 32 mission-ready Humvees a day, compared with three a week in 2004. And the new process has lowered the cost of repair for one vehicle from $89,000 to $48,000. Optimistic projections claim the Army could be saving billions of dollars each year in a decade.[1]

This chapter introduces basic mechanisms for controlling the organization. We begin by summarizing the objectives of the control process and the use of the balanced scorecard to measure performance. Then we discuss the four steps in the control process and methods for controlling financial performance, including the use of budgets and financial statements. The next sections examine the changing philosophy of control, today's approach to total quality management, and recent trends such as ISO certification, economic value-added and market value-added systems, activity-based costing, and corporate governance.

COURTESY OF HONEYWELL, INC.

A new philosophy about organizational control involves lower-level workers in management and control decisions. At the Honeywell Industrial Automation and Control facility in Phoenix, employees' quality control decisions cut defect rates by 70 percent, inventory by 46 percent, and customer lead times by an average of 75 percent.

> CONCEPT CONNECTION <

The Meaning of Control

It seemed like a perfect fit. In the chaotic aftermath of 2005's Hurricane Katrina, the American Red Cross needed private-sector help to respond to the hundreds of thousands of people seeking emergency aid. Staffing company Spherion Corporation had the expertise to hire and train temporary workers fast, and the company had a good track record working with the Red Cross. Yet Red Cross officials soon noticed something odd: An unusually large number of Katrina victim money orders, authorized by employees at the Spherion-staffed call center, were being cashed near the call center itself—in Bakersfield, California, far from the hurricane-ravaged area. A federal investigation found that some call-center employees were issuing money orders to fake hurricane victims and cashing the orders for themselves. Fortunately, the fraud was discovered quickly, but the weak control systems that allowed the scam to occur got both the Red Cross and Spherion into a public relations and political mess.[2]

A lack of control can have repercussions that damage an organization's health, hurt its reputation, and threaten

1 Controls are for bean counters.

ANSWER: Without adequate controls in an organization, chaos often occurs, so it is essential to have varying types of controls.

organizational control
The systematic process through which managers regulate organizational activities to make them consistent with expectations established in plans, targets, and standards of performance.

its future. One area in which many managers are implementing stronger controls is employee use of the Internet and e-mail, as described in the Spotlight on Skills box on page 320. To see what your attitude is towards control, complete the following New Manager's Self-Test.

Organizational control refers to the systematic process of regulating organizational activities to make them consistent with the expectations established in plans, targets, and standards of performance. In a classic article on the control function, Douglas S. Sherwin

NEW MANAGER'S SELF-TEST

What Is Your Attitude Toward Organizational Regulation and Control?[3]

Managers have to control people for organizations to survive, yet control should be the right amount and type. Companies are often less democratic than the society of which they are a part. Think honestly about your beliefs toward the regulation of other people and answer each item that follows as Mostly True or Mostly False.

	MOSTLY TRUE	MOSTLY FALSE
1. I believe people should be guided more by feelings and less by rules.	_____	_____
2. I think employees should be on time to work and to meetings.	_____	_____
3. I believe efficiency and speed are not as important as letting everyone have their say when making a decision.	_____	_____
4. I think employees should conform to company policies.	_____	_____
5. I let my significant other make the decision and have his or her way most of the time.	_____	_____
6. I like to tell other people what to do.	_____	_____
7. I am more patient with the least capable people.	_____	_____
8. I like to have things running "just so."	_____	_____

SCORING AND INTERPRETATION: Give yourself one point for each Mostly True answer to the odd-numbered questions and one point for each Mostly False answer to the even-numbered questions. A score of 6 or above suggests you prefer decentralized control for other people in organizations. A score of 3 or less suggests a preference for more control and bureaucracy in a company. Enthusiastic new managers may exercise too much of their new control and get a negative backlash. However, too little control may mean less accountability and productivity. The challenge for new managers is to strike the right balance for the job and people involved.

As a manager, always measure your goals and standards against the actual results.

summarizes the concept as follows: "The essence of control is action which adjusts operations to predetermined standards, and its basis is information in the hands of managers."[4] Thus, effectively controlling an organization requires information about performance standards and actual performance, as well as actions taken to correct any deviations from the standards. To effectively control an organization, managers need to decide what information is essential, how they will obtain that information, and how they can and should respond to it. Having the correct data is essential. Managers decide which standards, measurements, and metrics are needed to effectively monitor and control the organization and set up systems for obtaining that information. For example, an important metric for a pro football or basketball team might be the number of season tickets, which reduces the organization's dependence on more labor-intensive box-office sales.[5]

SPOTLIGHT ON SKILLS

Cyberslackers Beware: The Boss Is Watching

When employees have access to the Internet's vast resources, and the ability to communicate quickly via e-mail and instant messaging with anyone in the world, that's got to be good for productivity, right?

Not necessarily, as many organizations are discovering. Many companies are experiencing a growing problem with "cyberslackers," people who spend part of their workday sending personal e-mails, shopping, or downloading music and videos that hog available bandwidth and sometimes introduce viruses. In addition, it takes just a few bad apples engaging in harmful and possibly illegal activities, such as harassing other employees over the Web, to cause serious problems for their employers. So it's not surprising that the use of sophisticated software to both block employees' access to certain sites and monitor their Internet and e-mail use has grown exponentially.

A certain degree of vigilance is clearly warranted. However, enlightened managers strive for a balanced approach that protects the organization's interests while at the same time maintaining a positive, respectful work environment. Surveillance overkill can sometimes cost more than it saves, and it can also have a distinctly negative impact on employee morale. At the very least, employees may feel as though they're not being treated as trustworthy, responsible adults.

Here are some guidelines for creating an effective but fair "acceptable-use policy" for workplace Internet use.

- *Make sure employees understand that they have no legal right to privacy in the workplace.* The courts so far have upheld an organization's right to monitor any and all employee activities on computers purchased by an employer for work purposes.
- *Create a written Internet policy.* Make sure you clearly state what qualifies as a policy violation by giving clear, concrete

guidelines for acceptable use of e-mail, the Internet, and any other employer-provided hardware or software. For example, spell out the types of Web sites that are never to be visited while at work and what constitutes acceptable e-mail content. Are employees ever permitted to use the Web for personal use? If so, specify what they can do, for how long, and whether they need to confine their personal use to lunchtime or breaks. List the devices you'll be checking and tell them the filtering and monitoring procedures you have in place. Get employees to sign a statement saying they've read and understand the policy.

- *Describe the disciplinary process.* Give people a clear understanding of the consequences of violating the organization's Internet and electronic use policy. Make sure they know the organization will cooperate if a criminal investigation arises.
- *Review the policy at regular intervals.* You'll need to modify your guidelines as new technologies and devices appear.

Managers should remember that monitoring e-mail and Internet use doesn't have to be an all-or-nothing process. Some organizations use continuous surveillance; others only screen when they believe a problem exists, or they disseminate a policy and leave enforcement to the honor system. Look carefully at your workforce and the work it's doing, and assess your potential liability and security needs. Then come up with a policy and monitoring plan that makes sense for your organization.

SOURCES: Lorraine Cosgrove Ware, "People Watching," *CIO* (Aug. 15, 2005): 24; Art Lambert, "Technology in the Workplace: A Recipe for Legal Trouble," *Workforce.com* (Feb. 14, 2005) (www.workforce.com); Technical Resource Group, "Employee E-Mail and Internet Usage Monitoring: Issues and Concerns" (www.picktrg.com); Pui-Wing Tam, Erin White, Nick Wingfield, and Kris Maher, "Snooping E-Mail by Software Is Now a Workplace Norm," *Wall Street Journal*, Mar. 9, 2005; and Ann Sherman, "Firms Address Worries over Workplace Web Surfing," *Broward Daily Business Review* (May 17, 2006): 11.

CHOOSING STANDARDS AND MEASURES

Most organizations focus on measuring and controlling financial performance such as sales, revenue, and profit. Yet managers increasingly recognize the need to measure other intangible aspects of performance to manage the value-creating activities of the contemporary organization.[6] British Airways, for example, measures its performance in key areas of customer service because its strategy is to compete on superior service in an industry dominated by companies that compete on price. Underpinning this strategy is a belief that delivery of excellent service will result in higher levels of customer retention and profitability. Thus, British Airways measures and controls areas of customer service that have the greatest impact on a customer's service experience, including in-flight service, meal rating, baggage claim, and executive club membership.[7] Instead of relying only on financial measures to judge the company's performance, British Airways uses a number of different operational measures to track performance and control the organization.

Cousins Danny and Rock Klam measure success in terms of increased revenue, and Danny takes entrepreneurship classes to ensure that their donut and ice cream shops maintain high standards and lure more customers, as described in this chapter's Benchmarking box.

THE BALANCED SCORECARD

Like British Airways, many firms are now taking a more balanced perspective of company performance, integrating various dimensions of control that focus on markets and customers as well as employees and financials.[8] Organizations recognize that relying exclusively on financial measures can result in short-term, dysfunctional behavior. Nonfinancial measures provide a healthy supplement to the traditional financial measures, and companies are investing significant sums in developing more balanced measurement systems as a result.[9] The **balanced scorecard** is a comprehensive management-control system that balances traditional financial measures with operational measures relating to a company's critical success factors.[10]

> **balanced scorecard**
> A comprehensive management-control system that balances traditional financial measures with measures of customer service, internal business processes, and the organization's capacity for learning and growth.

BENCH-MARKING

Simply Splendid Donuts and Ice Cream

University of Houston senior Danny Klam decided he wanted to do his own internship while double majoring in entrepreneurship and marketing. So he opened three Simple Splendid Donuts and Ice Cream stores and usually gets up at 3 A.M. to open one of them. He started the first store with cousin Rock in 2004. There they offered chewy and fluffy treats and grew a large customer base fast, including a strong business clientele. Danny and Rock decided to start with a simple concept: donuts and ice cream. "Take the two worst things, health-wise, and combine them," says Danny. It started off so well, they added two more, with one including a drive-through and the other more of an office park model.

Taking courses in entreprenuership at the university's Entrepreneurship Center, Danny met Center Director Daniel Stepps,

a serial entrepreneur who had become somewhat of a mentor to Danny. Stepps can't speak more highly of Danny when he says that entrepreneurs are extremely market oriented, open-minded, and inquisitive, finding new ideas by reaching out to people while at the same time being coldly analytical and critical when looking at risk and feasibility. "Danny has those characteristics," says Stepps. And all this has paid off. In 2007, revenues were $650,000 and had grown to $1.2 million in 2009; they now have 12 employees. As for more expansion, Danny wants to wait until he graduates. "We can compete with Dunkin' Donuts," he says. As long has he can keep getting up in the middle of the night and going to work.

SOURCE: Zaneta Loh, "The Doughnut King of Texas," *Inc. Magazine*, Mar. 2009, p. 88.

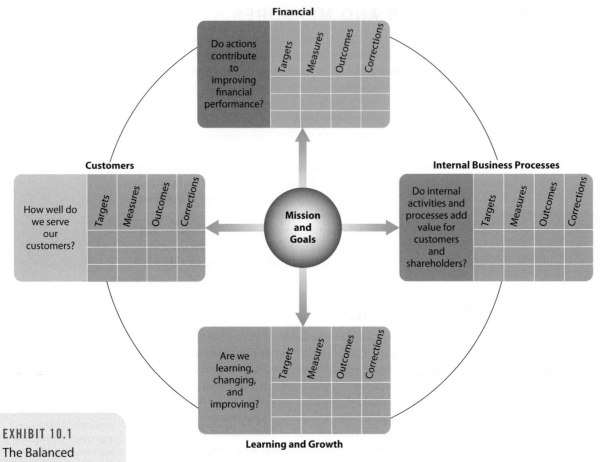

EXHIBIT 10.1
The Balanced
Scorecard

SOURCES: Based on Robert S. Kaplan and David P. Norton, "Using the Balanced Scorecard as a Strategic Management System," *Harvard Business Review* (Jan.–Feb. 1996): 75–85; and Chee W. Chow, Kamal M. Haddad, and James E. Williamson," Applying the Balanced Scorecard to Small Companies," *Management Accounting* 79(2) (Aug. 1997): 21–27.

A balanced scorecard contains four major perspectives, as illustrated in Exhibit 10.1: financial performance, customer service, internal business processes, and the organization's capacity for learning and growth.[11] Within these four areas, managers identify key performance metrics the organization will track. The *financial performance* perspective reflects a concern that the organization's activities contribute to improving short- and long-term financial performance. It includes traditional measures such as net income and return on investment. *Customer-service* indicators measure such things as how customers view the organization, as well as customer retention and satisfaction. *Business-process* indicators focus on production and operating statistics such as order fulfillment or cost per order. A good example of business process indicators comes from Facebook, one of the fastest-rising dot-coms in history. One of the internal activities it measures is the number of minutes visitors spend at its site. In March 2008, Facebook visitors spent a whopping 20 billion minutes at the site, compared to 6.4 billion minutes a year earlier. By measuring "minutes per visitor," Facebook is able to track its performance and adjust its strategy in response.[12]

The final component of the balanced scorecard looks at the organization's *potential for learning and growth*, focusing on how well resources and human capital are being managed for the company's future. Metrics may include such things as employee retention and the introduction of new products. The components of the scorecard are designed in an integrative manner, as illustrated in Exhibit 10.1.

Managers record, analyze, and discuss these various metrics to determine how well the organization is achieving its strategic goals. The balanced scorecard is an effective tool for managing and improving performance only if it is clearly linked to a well-defined organizational strategy and goals.[13] At its best, use of the scorecard cascades down from the top levels of the organization so that everyone becomes involved in thinking about and discussing strategy.[14] The scorecard has become the core management-control system for many organizations, including such well-known organizations as Bell Emergis (a division of Bell Canada), ExxonMobil, Cigna Insurance, Hilton Hotels Corporation, and even some units of the U.S. federal government.[15] As with all management systems, the balanced scorecard is not right for every organization in every situation. The simplicity of the system causes some managers to underestimate the time and commitment that is needed for the approach to become a truly useful management-control system. If managers implement the balanced scorecard using a *performance-measurement* orientation rather than a *performance-management* approach that links targets and measurements to corporate strategy, then use of the scorecard can actually hinder or even decrease organizational performance.[16]

Feedback-Control Model

All well-designed control systems involve the use of feedback to determine whether performance meets established standards. Managers need feedback, for example, in each of the four categories of the balanced scorecard. British Airways ties its use of the balanced scorecard to a feedback-control model. Scorecards are used as the agenda for monthly management meetings. Managers focus on the various elements of the scorecard to set targets, evaluate performance, and guide discussion about what further actions need to be taken.[17] In this section, we examine the key steps in the feedback-control model and then look at how the model applies to organizational budgeting.

Periodically review your own performance at school or on the job—that way you are using control mechanisms to improve your own performance.

STEPS OF FEEDBACK CONTROL

Managers set up control systems that consist of the four key steps illustrated in Exhibit 10.2: establish standards, measure performance, compare performance to standards, and make corrections as necessary.

Tamara Mellon understands the importance of saying "no" at the right times to avoid wasting company resources, as shown in the Spotlight on Skills box (on page 324).

EXHIBIT 10.2
Feedback-Control Model

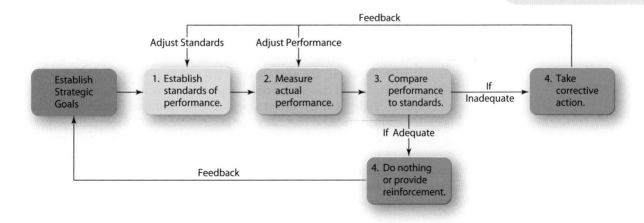

SPOTLIGHT ON SKILLS

Jimmy Choo Shoes

When Tamara Mellon was a little girl, she loved shoes—*really* loved them. On a trip with her kindergarten convent school, she begged a nun to buy her some cowboy boots. After college, she worked at British *Vogue*, and her boss soon realized Tamara had an obsession with extraordinarily stylish shoes. When she traveled to Nepal and needed to trek for miles, Tamara was nearly neurotic about which boot was best to wear. Her attention to detail on shoes, fashion layouts, and photographs was quite unusual.

She needed to find the perfect Greek sandal for a layout and found London's East End cobbler, Jimmy Choo, who had such clients as Princess Diana. After Tamara was promoted to *Vogue*'s accessories editor, she and Jimmy Choo worked closely together. When she decided to go out on her own, she saw an opportunity to be exploited: luxury shoes, which had no real competitor to Manolo Blahnik. Convincing her father to invest $250,000, she would run the company while Jimmy Choo and his fashion school-educated niece, Sandra Choi, would design and make the shoes. It was a typical start-up, working out of a basement, no computer. A larger problem surfaced. Though Jimmy Choo was a nice man and decent cobbler, he was incapable of designing a shoe line. Tamara and Choi had never done it either. But Tamara realized they had one thing Manolo Blahnik didn't have: a female chief executive officer (CEO). So they made

shoes that Tamara loved because she was the model customer: young, good-looking, style-conscious, and rich.

Tamara and her father had visions of opening 35 stores, but Jimmy Choo was nervous. He was, after all, a working man, with a family to support, and these wild speculative investments scared him. When Equinox Luxury Holdings offered to buy a controlling interest in Jimmy Choo, they took the $100 million, allowing Jimmy Choo himself to bow out with $25 million. The business grew further, and they expect to have 50 stores open worldwide within two years as the Asian market develops.

A careful businesswoman and manager, Tamara doesn't let her success keep her from making sound decisions, nor did she let her messy divorce from banking heir Matthew Mellon II in 2005 get in the way of company business. When a group of fragrance branders were trying to woo her and the company name, she pointedly asked them, "What went wrong with Patrick Cox?" (Cox is a shoe designer whose foray into fragrances was not successful.) That's the kind of thinking that has made her Britain's highest-profile female executive and gave her the ability to sell her company for $384 million in 2007. It's all about smart decision making and high-heeled courage.

SOURCES: Cheryl Lu-Lien Tan, "Taste—Bookshelf: Cobbler to the Stars," *Wall Street Journal Asia*, June 5, 2009, p. W15; Evgenia Peretz, "The Lady and the Heel," *Vanity Fair*, Aug. 2005, pp. 134–136 and 172–175.

Establish Standards of Performance. Within the organization's overall strategic plan, managers define goals for organizational departments in specific, operational terms that include a *standard of performance* against which to compare organizational activities. A standard of performance could include "reducing the reject rate from 15 to 3 percent," "increasing the corporation's return on investment to 7 percent," or "reducing the number of accidents to one per each 100,000 hours of labor." Managers should carefully assess what they will measure and how they will define it. In the auto industry, crash-test ratings provide a standard of performance established by the National Highway Traffic Safety Administration. When crash-test ratings are below standard, managers rethink design and manufacturing processes to improve crash-test results. Although Daimler's ultratiny Smart ForTwo car won a five-star rating for driver protection, it won just a three-star rating for passenger protection, indicating the need for improved passenger-safety features.[18]

Tracking such measures as customer service, employee involvement, or, for auto manufacturers, crash-test results, is an important supplement to traditional financial and operational performance measurement, but many companies have a hard time identifying and defining nonfinancial measurements.[19] To effectively evaluate and reward employees for the achievement of standards, managers need clear standards that reflect activities that contribute to the organization's overall strategy in a significant way. Standards should be defined clearly and precisely so employees know what they need to do and can determine whether their activities are on target.[20]

Measure Actual Performance. Most organizations prepare formal reports of quantitative performance measurements that managers review daily, weekly, or monthly. These measurements should be related to the standards set in the first step of the control process. For example, if sales growth is a target, the organization should have a means of gathering and reporting sales data. If the organization has identified appropriate measurements, regular review of these reports helps managers stay aware of whether the organization is doing what it should. Technology is aiding many organizations in measuring performance. For example, GPS tracking devices installed on government-issued vehicles are helping many communities reduce waste and abuse, in part by catching employees shopping, working out at the gym, or otherwise loafing while on the clock. Although some people claim this technology is intrusive, city officials claim that tracking the whereabouts of government employees has deterred abuses and saved taxpayers money. In Denver, 76 vehicles equipped with GPS units were driven 5,000 fewer miles than the unequipped fleet during the same period the year before, indicating the value of this type of quantitative measure.[21]

In most companies, managers do not rely exclusively on quantitative measures. They get out into the organization to see how things are going, especially for such goals as increasing employee participation and improving customer satisfaction. Managers have to observe for themselves whether employees are participating in decision making and have opportunities to add to and share their knowledge. Interaction with customers is necessary for managers to really understand whether activities are meeting customer needs.

Compare Performance to Standards. The third step in the control process is comparing actual activities to performance standards. When managers read computer reports or walk through the plant, they identify whether actual performance meets, exceeds, or falls short of standards. Typically, performance reports simplify such comparisons by placing the performance standards for the reporting period alongside the actual performance for the same period and by computing the variance—that is, the difference between each actual amount and the associated standard. To correct the problems that most require attention, managers focus on variances.

When performance deviates from a standard, managers must interpret the deviation. They are expected to dig beneath the surface and find the cause of the problem. If the sales goal is to increase the number of sales calls by 10 percent and a salesperson achieved an increase of 8 percent, then where did she fail to achieve her goal? Perhaps several businesses on her route closed, additional salespeople were assigned to her area by competitors, or she needs training in making

© Photodisc/Getty Images

Is it possible to make scientific discovery efficient? Managers at pharmaceuticals company Wyeth think so. They devised a streamlined research and development system driven by ambitious, quantifiable standards of performance. Managers routinely compare performance to standards and issue automated scorecards for each individual. Wyeth ties compensation to accomplishment of these all-or-nothing targets. "If the goal was to discover 12 drugs, 11 drugs are worth no points," says Wyeth Research President Robert Ruffolo, Jr., who oversaw the reengineering effort. So far, the approach has yielded impressive results. With no additional investment, Wyeth has seen the number of new drugs that emerge from the early discovery phase increase fourfold.

·········> **CONCEPT CONNECTION** <········

2 When there's a problem, a good manager finds who's at fault.

ANSWER: Comparing a standard to performance means the manager looks to find out why performance was low. But focusing on blaming a person is usually not productive and deflects attention away from analyzing the problem.

Assess Your Answer

To see if your team is functioning well, apply the feedback-control model, by defining clear standards of performance, measuring outcomes regularly, and taking corrective actions.

cold sales calls more effectively. Managers should take an inquiring approach to deviations to gain a broad understanding of factors that influence performance. Effective management control involves subjective judgment and employee discussions, as well as objective analysis of performance data.

Take Corrective Action. Managers also determine what changes, if any, are needed. In a traditional top-down approach to control, managers exercise their formal authority to make necessary changes. They may encourage employees to work harder, redesign the production process, or fire employees. In contrast, managers using a participative-control approach collaborate with employees to determine the corrective action necessary. As an example, Toyota's commitment to continuous improvement is reflected in its philosophy of "Problems First." In staff meetings, factory managers are asked to present their "problems first," triggering problem-solving sessions with managers that generate solutions. This approach reflects the company's commitment to seeking out better ways to manufacture cars. "Even with projects that had been a general success, we would ask, 'What didn't go well so we can make it better?'" says James Wiseman, vice president of corporate affairs for Toyota manufacturing in North America.[22]

As a manager, you must correct deficiencies; it's not enough to just measure.

Managers may wish to provide positive reinforcement when performance meets or exceeds standards. For example, they may reward a department that has exceeded its planned goals or congratulate employees for a job well done. Managers should not ignore high-performing departments at the expense of taking corrective actions elsewhere. The online auction company eBay provides a good illustration of the feedback-control model.

eBAY

When she was CEO of eBay, one of Meg Whitman's guiding rules was "If you can't measure it, you can't control it." Whitman has moved on to other pursuits, but eBay is still a company obsessed with performance measurement. Top managers personally monitor a slew of performance metrics, including standard measurements such as site visitors, new users, and time spent on the site, as well as the ratio of eBay's revenues to the value of goods traded.

Managers and employees throughout the company also monitor performance almost obsessively. Category managers, for example, have clear standards of performance for their auction categories (such as sports memorabilia, jewelry and watches, health and beauty, and fashion). They are constantly measuring, tweaking, and promoting their categories to meet or outperform the targets.

Top managers believe getting a firm grip on performance measurement is essential for a company to know where to spend money, where to assign more personnel, and which projects to promote or abandon. But performance measurement isn't just about numbers. At eBay, "it's all about the customer," and gauging customer (user) satisfaction requires a mix of methods such as surveys, monitoring eBay's discussion boards, and personal contact. Managers get their chance to really connect with users at the annual eBay Live conference. There they wander the convention hall floor talking with anyone and everyone about their eBay experiences.[23]

By defining standards, using a combination of measurement approaches, and comparing performance to standards, eBay managers are able to identify trouble spots and move quickly to take corrective action when and where it's needed.

APPLICATION TO BUDGETING

Go to the Self Learning exercise on pages 339–340 that pertains to budgetary control.

Budgetary control, one of the most commonly used methods of managerial control, is the process of setting targets for an organization's expenditures, monitoring results and comparing them to the budget, and making changes as needed. As a control device, budgets are reports that list planned and actual expenditures for cash, assets, raw materials, salaries, and other resources. In addition, budget reports usually list the variance between the budgeted and actual amounts for each item.

A budget is created for every division or department within an organization, no matter how small, as long as it performs a distinct project, program, or function. The fundamental unit of analysis for a budget control system is called a *responsibility center*. A **responsibility center** is defined as any organizational department or unit under the supervision of a single person who is responsible for its activity.[24] A three-person appliance sales office in Watertown, New York, is a responsibility center, as is a quality control department, a marketing department, and an entire refrigerator-manufacturing plant. The manager of each unit has budget responsibility. Top managers use budgets for the company as a whole, and middle managers traditionally focus on the budget performance of their department or division. Budgets that managers typically use include expense budgets, revenue budgets, cash budgets, and capital budgets.

Financial Control

In every organization, managers need to watch how well the organization is performing financially. Financial controls not only tell whether the organization is on sound financial footing but also can be useful indicators of other kinds of performance problems. For example, a sales decline may signal problems with products, customer service, or sales-force effectiveness.

FINANCIAL STATEMENTS

Financial statements provide the basic information used for financial control of an organization. Two major financial statements—the balance sheet and the income statement—are the starting points for financial control.

The **balance sheet** shows the firm's financial position with respect to assets and liabilities at a specific point in time. An example of a balance sheet is presented in Exhibit 10.3. The balance sheet provides three types of information: assets, liabilities, and owners' equity. *Assets* are what the company owns, and they include *current assets* (those that can be converted into cash in a short time period) and *fixed assets* (such as buildings and equipment that are long term in nature). *Liabilities* are the firm's debts, including both *current debt* (obligations that will be paid by the company in the near future) and *long-term debt* (obligations payable over a long period). *Owners' equity* is the difference between assets and liabilities and is the company's net worth in stock and retained earnings.

As a manager, regularly review your balance sheet.

responsibility center
An organizational unit under the supervision of a single person who is responsible for its activity.

balance sheet
A financial statement that shows the firm's financial position with respect to assets and liabilities at a specific point in time.

EXHIBIT 10.3
Balance Sheet
- - - - - - - - - - - -

New Creations Landscaping Consolidated Balance Sheet December 31, 2009					
Assets			**Liabilities and Owners' Equity**		
Current assets:			Current liabilities:		
Cash	$ 25,000		Accounts payable	$200,000	
Accounts receivable	75,000		Accrued expenses	20,000	
Inventory	500,000		Income taxes payable	30,000	
Total current assets		$ 600,000	Total current liabilities		$ 250,000
Fixed assets:			Long-term liabilities:		
Land	250,000		Mortgages payable	350,000	
Buildings and fixtures	1,000,000		Bonds outstanding	250,000	
Less depreciation	200,000		Total long-term liabilities		$ 600,000
Total fixed assets		1,050,000	Owners' equity:		
			Common stock	540,000	
			Retained earnings	260,000	
			Total owners' equity		800,000
Total assets		$1,650,000	Total liabilities and net worth		$1,650,000

EXHIBIT 10.4
Income Statement

New Creations Landscaping Income Statement For the Year Ended December 31, 2009		
Gross sales	$3,100,000	
Less sales returns	200,000	
Net sales		$2,900,000
Less expenses and cost of goods sold:	2,110,000	
Cost of goods sold	60,000	
Depreciation	200,000	
Sales expenses	90,000	
Administrative expenses		2,460,000
Operating profit		440,000
Other income		20,000
Gross income		460,000
Less interest expense	80,000	
Income before taxes		380,000
Less taxes	165,000	
Net income		$ 215,000

The **income statement**, sometimes called a *profit-and-loss statement* or *P&L* for short, summarizes the firm's financial performance for a given time interval, usually one year. A sample income statement is shown in Exhibit 10.4. Some organizations calculate the income statement at three-month intervals during the year to see whether they are on target for sales and profits. The income statement shows revenues coming into the organization from all sources and subtracts all expenses, including cost of goods sold, interest, taxes, and depreciation. The *bottom line* indicates the net income—profit or loss—for the given time period.

The owner of Aahs!, a specialty retailing chain in California, used the income statement to detect that sales and profits were dropping significantly during the summer months.[25] He immediately evaluated company activities and closed two money-losing stores. He also began a training program to teach employees how to increase sales and cut costs to improve net income. This use of the income statement follows the control model described in the previous section, beginning with setting targets, measuring actual performance, and then taking corrective action to improve performance to meet targets.

The Changing Philosophy of Control

Managers' approach to control is changing in many of today's organizations. In connection with the shift to employee participation and empowerment, many companies are adopting a *decentralized* rather than a *hierarchical* control process. Hierarchical control and decentralized control represent different philosophies of corporate culture, which was discussed in Chapter 2. Most organizations display some aspects of both hierarchical and decentralized control, but managers generally emphasize one or the other, depending on the organizational culture and their own beliefs about control.

HIERARCHICAL VERSUS DECENTRALIZED APPROACHES

Hierarchical control involves monitoring and influencing employee behavior through extensive use of rules, policies, hierarchy of authority, written documentation, reward systems,

income statement
A financial statement that summarizes the firm's financial performance for a given time interval; sometimes called a *profit-and-loss* statement.

hierarchical control
The use of rules, policies, hierarchy of authority, reward systems, and other formal devices to influence employee behavior and assess performance.

	Hierarchical Control	**Decentralized Control**
Basic Assumptions	People are incapable of self-discipline and cannot be trusted. They need to be monitored and controlled closely.	People work best when they are fully committed to the organization.
Actions	Uses detailed rules and procedures; formal control systems. Uses top-down authority, formal hierarchy, position power, quality control inspectors. Relies on task-related job descriptions. Emphasizes extrinsic rewards (pay, benefits, status). Features rigid organizational culture; distrust of cultural norms as means of control.	Features limited use of rules; relies on values, group and self-control, selection, and socialization. Relies on flexible authority, flat structure, expert power; everyone monitors quality. Relies on results-based job descriptions; emphasizes goals to be achieved. Emphasizes extrinsic and intrinsic rewards (meaningful work, opportunities for growth). Features adaptive culture; culture recognized as means for uniting individual, team, and organizational goals for overall control.
Consequences	Employees follow instructions and do *just* what they are told. Employees feel a sense of indifference toward work. Employee absenteeism and turnover is high.	Employees take initiative and seek responsibility. Employees are actively engaged and committed to their work. Employee turnover is low.

SOURCES: Based on Naresh Khatri, Alok Bavega, Suzanne A. Boren, and Abate Mammo, "Medical Errors and Quality of Care: From Control to Commitment," *California Management Review* 48(3) (Spring, 2006): 118; Richard E. Walton, "From Control to Commitment in the Workplace," *Harvard Business Review* (Mar.–Apr. 1985): 76–84; and Don Hellriegel, Susan E. Jackson, and John W. Slocum, Jr., *Management*, 8th ed. (Cincinnati: South-Western, 1999): 663.

EXHIBIT 10.5
Hierarchical and Decentralized Methods of Control

and other formal mechanisms.[26] In contrast, decentralized control relies on cultural values, traditions, shared beliefs, and trust to foster compliance with organizational goals. Managers operate on the assumption that employees are trustworthy and willing to perform effectively without extensive rules and close supervision.

Exhibit 10.5 contrasts the use of hierarchical and decentralized methods of control. Hierarchical methods define explicit rules, policies, and procedures for employee behavior. Control relies on centralized authority, the formal hierarchy, and close personal supervision. Responsibility for quality control rests with quality control inspectors and supervisors rather than with employees. Job descriptions generally are specific and task related, and managers define minimal standards for acceptable employee performance. In exchange for meeting the standards, individual employees are given extrinsic rewards such as wages, benefits, and possibly promotions up the hierarchy. Employees rarely participate in the control process, with any participation being formalized through mechanisms such as grievance procedures. With hierarchical control, the organizational culture is somewhat rigid, and managers do not consider culture a useful means of controlling employees and the organization. Technology often is used to control the flow and pace of work or to monitor employees, such as by measuring the number of minutes employees spend on phone calls or how many keystrokes they make at the computer.

Hierarchical control techniques can enhance organizational efficiency and effectiveness. Many employees appreciate a system that clarifies what is expected of them, and they may be motivated by challenging but achievable goals.[27] However, although many managers effectively use hierarchical control, too much control can backfire. Employees resent being watched too closely, and they may try to sabotage the control system. One veteran truck driver expressed his unhappiness with electronic monitoring to a *Wall Street Journal*

BUSINESS BLOOPER

Burger King Memphis

The same state that brought you Al Gore has now produced 12 Burger Kings in Memphis with huge outside signs declaring, "Global warming is baloney." To be more precise, it isn't actually BK, but its franchisee, Mirabile Investment Corporation (MIC) which owns 40 Tennessee BK's—that has the anti-science information directly above its "Drive-Through 24 hours" sign. After it was tipped off by a story in the *Memphis Flyer* local newspaper, BK International—wanting to maintain a positive image—demanded the signs be taken down. MIC refused. Said MIC's marketing VP John McNelis, "I would think (Burger King) would run from any form of controversy kinda like cockroaches when the lights get turned on.... Burger King can bluster all they want about what they can tell the franchisee to do, but we have free speech rights in this country, so I don't think there's any concerns." At least not for any cockroaches roaming around the restaurants or Graceland.

SOURCE: Leo Hickman, "'Global Warning is Baloney' Signs Put the Heat on Burger King," *Guardian International*, June 6, 2009, p. 20.

As a manager, determine whether you need organizational controls or whether your values and goals are enough to shape employee behavior.

What is your philosophy of control? Complete the New Manager's Self-Test on page 332 to get some feedback on your own approach to control.

As a manager, consider letting subordinates know what is going on and what is in the financial statements.

decentralized control
The use of organizational culture, group norms, and a focus on goals rather than on rules and procedures to foster compliance with organizational goals.

reporter investigating the use of devices that monitor truck locations. According to the driver, "It's getting worse and worse all the time. Pretty soon they'll want to put a chip in the drivers' ears and make them robots." He added that he occasionally escapes the relentless monitoring by parking under an overpass to take a needed nap out of range of the surveillance satellites.[28] Hierarchical control doesn't always work in franchise situations, as described in this chapter's Business Blooper.

Decentralized control is based on values and assumptions that are almost opposite to those of hierarchical control. Rules and procedures are used only when necessary. Managers rely instead on shared goals and values to control employee behavior. The organization places great emphasis on the selection and socialization of employees to ensure that workers have the appropriate values needed to influence behavior toward meeting company goals. No organization can control employees 100 percent of the time, and self-discipline and self-control are what keep workers performing their jobs up to standard. Empowerment of employees, effective socialization, and training all can contribute to internal standards that provide self-control.

With decentralized control, power is more dispersed and based on knowledge and experience as much as position. The organizational structure is flat and horizontal, as discussed in Chapter 7, with flexible authority and teams of workers solving problems and making improvements. Everyone is involved in quality control on an ongoing basis. Job descriptions generally are results based, with an emphasis more on the outcomes to be achieved than on the specific tasks to be performed. Managers use not only extrinsic rewards such as pay but also the intrinsic rewards of meaningful work and the opportunity to learn and grow. Technology is used to empower employees by giving them the information they need to make effective decisions, work together, and solve problems. People are rewarded for team and organizational success as well as for their individual performance, and the emphasis is on equity among employees. Employees participate in a wide range of areas, including setting goals, determining standards of performance, governing quality, and designing control systems.

With decentralized control, the culture is adaptive, and managers recognize the importance of organizational culture for uniting individual, team, and organizational goals for greater overall control. Ideally, with decentralized control, employees will pool their areas of expertise to arrive at procedures that are better than managers could come up with working alone.

OPEN-BOOK MANAGEMENT

One important aspect of decentralized control in many organizations is open-book management. An organization that promotes information sharing and teamwork admits employees throughout the organization into the loop of financial control and responsibility to encourage active participation and commitment to goals. **Open-book management** allows employees to see for themselves—through charts, computer printouts, meetings, and so forth—the financial condition of the company. Open-book management also shows the individual employee how his or her job fits into the big picture and affects the financial future of the organization. Finally, open-book management ties employee rewards to the company's overall success. With training in interpreting the financial data, employees can see the interdependence and importance of each function. If they are rewarded according to performance, they become motivated to take responsibility for their entire team or function rather than merely their individual jobs.[29] Cross-functional communication and cooperation are also enhanced.

© VITO PALMISANO

Honest Tea cofounder and CEO Seth Goldman (left) practices open-book management—sharing with employees information on sales, profit and loss, growth rate, expenses, salaries as a lump sum, stock price, and capitalization. Here Goldman tours Castle's Co-Packer, which produces and bottles organic brewed teas for his company, with *Beverage World* magazine editor Sarah Theodore (center) and Brian Dworkin of Castle's. When Coca-Cola bought 40 percent of Honest Tea, Goldman says, "we insisted on an arrangement that allowed all of our employees to invest alongside Coke in the transaction—there's no question that this structure has contributed to the passion and entrepreneurial spirit of our team."

······················> CONCEPT CONNECTION <········

The goal of open-book management is to get every employee thinking and acting like a business owner. To get employees to think like owners, management provides them with the same information owners have: what money is coming in and where it is going. Open-book management helps employees appreciate why efficiency is important to the organization's success as well as their own. Open-book management turns traditional control on its head. Development Counsellors International, a New York City public relations firm, found an innovative way to involve employees in the financial aspects of the organization.

open-book management
Sharing financial information and results with all employees in the organization.

W hen Andrew Levine took over as president of Development Counsellors International (DCI), the public relations firm founded by his father in 1960, he was eager to try open-book management. His first step was to add a financial segment to the monthly staff meeting, but employees just seemed bored. Most of them had no interest or skills in finance, statistics, and ratios.

Rather than providing standard training, Levine had an idea: Why not appoint a different staffer each month to be chief financial officer (CFO) for the day? That person would be required to figure out the financials and then present the financial reports at the monthly staff meeting. His first appointment was the receptionist, Sergio Barrios, who met with Levine and the company's CFO to go over the figures, look at any unusual increases or decreases in revenue or expenses, and talk about ideas to spark discussion. Levine was astounded by the reaction of staffers at the monthly meeting. Unlike Levine or another manager, Barrios was new to accounting and consequently explained things in a way that any layperson could understand. In addition, employees wanted to support Barrios as "one of their own," so they paid more attention and asked more questions.

At each monthly meeting, the CFO of the day goes through a breakdown of the company's sales and expenses, points out irregularities and trends in the numbers, takes questions from other staff members, and sparks discussion of current financial issues. At the end of the report, the person reveals the bottom line, indicating whether the company met its profit goal for the month. Each time DCI's accumulated profit hits another $100,000 increment during the course of the year, 30 percent of it is distributed to employees.[30]

DEVELOPMENT COUNSELLORS INTERNATIONAL

DCI has been profitable ever since Levine began the CFO-of-the-day program. In addition, employees are happier with their jobs, so turnover has decreased. Clients also

NEW MANAGER'S SELF-TEST

What Is Your Control Approach?

As a new manager, how will you control your work unit? What is your natural control approach? Please answer whether each of the following items is Mostly True or Mostly False for you.

	MOSTLY TRUE	MOSTLY FALSE
1. I find myself losing sight of long-term goals when there is a short-term crisis.	_____	_____
2. I prefer complex to simple problems and projects.	_____	_____
3. I am good at mapping out steps needed to complete a project.	_____	_____
4. I make most decisions without needing to know an overall plan.	_____	_____
5. I keep my personal books and papers in good order.	_____	_____
6. I prefer tasks that challenge my thinking ability.	_____	_____
7. I think about how my behavior relates to outcomes I desire.	_____	_____
8. I like to be part of a situation where results are measured and count for something.	_____	_____

SCORING AND INTERPRETATION: Control systems are designed and managed via a manager's "systems" thinking. Systems thinking considers how component parts of system interact to achieve desired goals. Systems thinking means seeing the world in an organized way and thinking about underlying cause-and-effect relationships. Give yourself 1 point for each Mostly True answer to items 2, 3, 5 to 8 and 1 point for each Mostly False answer to items 1 and 4. A score of 6 or above means that you appear to have a natural orientation toward systems thinking and control. You see the world in an organized way and focus on cause-and-effect relationships that produce outcomes. If you scored 3 or less, then you probably are not very focused on control issues and relationships. You may not have the time to understand complex relationships, or you may not be interested in it. As a new manager, you may have to put extra effort into understanding control relationships to produce the outcomes you and the organization desire.

Use open-book management to help employees think like owners.

tend to stick around longer because employees put more effort into building relationships. "Nobody wants to see a zero next to their client in the income column," Levine says.[31]

Managers in some countries have more trouble running an open-book company because prevailing attitudes and standards encourage confidentiality and even secrecy concerning financial results. Many businesspeople in countries such as China, Russia, and India, for example, are not accustomed to publicly disclosing financial details, which can present problems for multinational companies operating there.[32] Exhibit 10.6 lists a portion of a recent *Opacity Index*, which offers some indication of the degree to which various countries are open regarding economic matters. The higher the rating, the more opaque, or hidden, the economy of that country. In the partial index in Exhibit 10.6, Nigeria has the highest opacity rating at 57, and Finland the lowest at 9. The United States has an opacity rating of 23, a slight increase since the previous ratings. In countries with higher ratings, financial figures are typically closely guarded, and managers may be discouraged from sharing information with employees and the public. Globalization is beginning to have an impact

Country	2007–2008 Opacity Score	2005–2006 Score
Nigeria	57	60
Venezuela	48	50
Saudi Arabia	47	52
China	45	48
India	44	44
Indonesia	41	56
Russia	41	45
Mexico	37	43
Taiwan	34	33
South Korea	31	35
South Africa	26	32
Japan	25	26
United States	23	21
Canada	22	24
Germany	17	27
Ireland	16	25
Singapore	14	28
Hong Kong	12	19
Finland	9	17

EXHIBIT 10.6

International Opacity Index: Which Countries Have the Most Secretive Economies?

The higher the opacity score, the more secretive the national economy, meaning that prevailing attitudes and standards discourage openness regarding financial results and other data.

SOURCE: Data from Opacity Index 2007-2008, in Joel Kurtzman and Glenn Yago, *Opacity Index, 2007-2008: Measuring Global Business Risks* (Milken Insitute, April 2008), 3, Table 1. http://www.milkeninstitute.org/pdf/2008OpacityIndex.pdf.

on economic opacity in various countries by encouraging a convergence toward global accounting standards that support more accurate collection, recording, and reporting of financial information. Thus, most countries have improved their ratings over the past few years. Indonesia, Singapore, and Ireland all show significant decreases in opacity since the 2005–2006 ratings, for example.

Total Quality Management

Another popular approach based on a decentralized control philosophy is **total quality management (TQM)**, an organization-wide effort to infuse quality into every activity in a company through continuous improvement. Managing quality is a concern for every organization. The Yugo was the lowest-priced car on the market when it was introduced in the United States in 1985, yet four years later, the importer went bankrupt, largely as a

total quality management (TQM)
An organization-wide commitment to infusing quality into every activity through continuous improvement.

result of quality problems in both products and services.[33] In contrast, Toyota has steadily gained market share over the past several decades and has taken over General Motors as the world's top-selling automaker. The difference comes down to quality. Toyota is a model of what happens when a company makes a strong commitment to total quality management.

TQM became attractive to U.S. managers in the 1980s because it had been successfully implemented by such Japanese companies as Toyota, Canon, and Honda, which were gaining market share and an international reputation for high quality. The Japanese system was based on the work of such U.S. researchers and consultants as Deming, Juran, and Feigenbaum, whose ideas attracted U.S. executives after the methods were tested overseas.[34] The TQM philosophy focuses on teamwork, increasing customer satisfaction, and lowering costs. Organizations implement TQM by encouraging managers and employees to collaborate across functions and departments, as well as with customers and suppliers, to identify areas for improvement, no matter how small. Each quality improvement is a step toward perfection and meeting a goal of zero defects. Quality control becomes part of the day-to-day business of every employee rather than being assigned to specialized departments.

TQM TECHNIQUES

The implementation of total quality management involves the use of many techniques, including quality circles, benchmarking, Six Sigma principles, reduced cycle time, and continuous improvement.

Quality Circles. One technique for implementing the decentralized approach of TQM is to use quality circles. A **quality circle** is a group of 6 to 12 volunteer employees who meet regularly to discuss and solve problems affecting the quality of their work.[35] At a set time during the workweek, the members of the quality circle meet, identify problems, and try to find solutions. Circle members are free to collect data and take surveys. Many companies train people in team building, problem solving, and statistical quality control. The reason for using quality circles is to push decision making to an organization level at which recommendations can be made by the people who do the job and know it better than anyone else.

Benchmarking. Introduced by Xerox in 1979, benchmarking is now a major TQM component. **Benchmarking** is defined as "the continuous process of measuring products, services, and practices against the toughest competitors or those companies recognized as industry leaders to identify areas for improvement."[36] The key to successful benchmarking lies in analysis. Starting with its own mission statement, a company should honestly analyze its current procedures and determine areas for improvement. As a second step, a company carefully selects competitors worthy of copying. For example, Xerox studied the order-fulfillment techniques of L.L. Bean, the Freeport, Maine, mail-order firm, and learned ways to reduce warehouse costs by 10 percent. Companies can emulate internal processes and procedures of competitors but must take care to select companies whose methods are compatible. Once a strong, compatible program is found and analyzed, the benchmarking company can then devise a strategy for implementing a new program.

Six Sigma. Six Sigma quality principles were first introduced by Motorola in the 1980s and were later popularized by General Electric, where former CEO Jack Welch praised Six Sigma for quality and efficiency gains that saved the company billions of dollars. Based on the Greek letter *sigma*, which statisticians use to measure how far something deviates from perfection, **Six Sigma** is a highly ambitious quality standard that specifies a goal of no more than 3.4 defects per million parts. That essentially means being defect free 99.9997 percent of the time.[37] However, Six Sigma has deviated from its precise definition to become a generic term for a quality-control approach that takes nothing for granted and emphasizes

When starting a new venture or bringing change, go out and benchmark successful programs that are similar.

quality circle
A group of 6 to 12 volunteer employees who meet regularly to discuss and solve problems that affect the quality of their work.

benchmarking
The continuous process of measuring products, services, and practices against major competitors or industry leaders.

Six Sigma
A quality control approach that emphasizes a relentless pursuit of higher quality and lower costs.

a disciplined and relentless pursuit of higher quality and lower costs. The discipline is based on a five-step methodology referred to as *DMAIC* (define, measure, analyze, improve, and control, pronounced "deMay-ick" for short), which provides a structured way for organizations to approach and solve problems.[38]

Effectively implementing Six Sigma requires a major commitment from top management, because Six Sigma involves widespread change throughout the organization. Hundreds of organizations have adopted some form of Six Sigma program in recent years. Highly committed companies, including ITT Industries, Motorola, General Electric, Allied Signal, ABB Ltd., and the DuPont Company, send managers to weeks of training to become qualified as Six Sigma "black belts." These black belts lead projects aimed at improving targeted areas of the business.[39] Although originally applied to manufacturing, Six Sigma has evolved to a process used in all industries and affecting every aspect of company operations from human resources to customer service. Textron, whose products include Cessna jets and E-Z-Go golf carts, has trained nearly 10,000 in-house experts in Six Sigma and uses it in both its manufacturing and service sectors. Textron CEO Lewis Campbell offers proof that it's working. "Even though Cessna has been producing planes for 89 years and jets since 1972, they recently reduced by 17 percent the labor hours required to make their single-piston aircraft. That's a big number. They've taken the inspection time from 10 days to five. Textron financial used to take 320 hours each month collecting interest from customers. They've got that down to 56 hours."[40] Exhibit 10.7 lists some statistics that illustrate why Six Sigma is important for both manufacturing and service organizations.

The idea for "Unwind" events, such as this performance of traditional dance in the lobby of the Westin Kuala Lumpur in Malaysia, came from the staff of the Westin Chicago River North as a way to improve profitability and guest service. Unwind events are aimed at business travelers and designed to encourage guest interaction. Six Sigma specialists at each unit of Starwood Hotels & Resorts Worldwide facilitate the development of projects from the ideas of local staff. After rolling out a prototype, performance metrics are used to gauge the success or failure of the new projects. The Unwind program alone produced 120 new events, one for each Westin hotel.

COURTESY OF STARWOOD HOTELS & RESORTS WORLDWIDE; PHOTO PROVIDED BY BUSINESSWEEK

······▶ CONCEPT CONNECTION ◀········

Reduced Cycle Time. Cycle time has become a critical quality issue in today's fast-paced world. **Cycle time** refers to the steps taken to complete a company process, such as making an airline reservation, processing an online order, or opening a retirement fund. The simplification of work cycles, including dropping barriers between work steps and among departments and removing worthless steps in the process, enables a TQM program to succeed. Even if an organization decides not to use quality circles or other techniques, substantial improvement is possible by focusing on improved responsiveness and acceleration of activities into a shorter time. Reduction in cycle time improves overall company performance as well as quality.[41]

cycle time
The steps taken to complete a company process.

99 Percent Amounts to:	Six Sigma Amounts to:
117,000 pieces of lost first-class mail per hour	1 piece of lost first-class mail every two hours
800,000 mishandled personal checks each day	3 mishandled checks each day
23,087 defective computers shipped each month	8 defective computers shipped each month
7.2 hours per month without electricity	9 seconds per month without electricity

EXHIBIT 10.7

The Importance of Quality Improvement Programs

SOURCE: Based on data from *Statistical Abstract of the United States*, U.S. Postal Service, as reported in Tracy Mayor, "Six Sigma Comes to IT: Targeting Perfection," *CIO* (Dec. 1, 2003): 62–70.

L.L. Bean is a recognized leader in cycle time control. Workers once used flowcharts to track their movements, pinpoint wasted motions, and completely redesign the order-fulfillment process. Today, a computerized system breaks down an order based on the geographic area of the warehouse in which items are stored. Items are placed on conveyor belts, where electronic sensors re-sort the items for individual orders. After orders are packed, they are sent to a FedEx facility on-site. Improvements such as these have enabled L.L. Bean to process most orders within two hours after the order is received.[42]

Continuous Improvement. In North America, crash programs and designs have traditionally been the preferred method of innovation. Managers measure the expected benefits of a change and favor the ideas with the biggest payoffs. In contrast, Japanese companies have realized extraordinary success from making a series of mostly small improvements. This approach, called **continuous improvement** or *kaizen*, is the implementation of a large number of small, incremental improvements in all areas of the organization on an ongoing basis. In a successful TQM program, all employees learn that they are expected to contribute by initiating changes in their own job activities. The basic philosophy is that improving things a little bit at a time, all the time, has the highest probability of success. Innovations can start simple, and employees can build on their success in this unending process. Here's how one auto-parts plant benefits from a TQM and continuous-improvement philosophy.

DANA CORPORATION'S PERFECT CIRCLE PRODUCTS FRANKLIN STEEL PRODUCTS PLANT

The Dana Corporation's Perfect Circle Products Franklin Steel Products Plant in Franklin, Kentucky, manufactures as many as 3,500 different part numbers, primarily for automakers Ford, General Motors, and ChryslerGroup, as well as thousands of after-market products. In one recent year, the company churned out about 60 million oil-ring expanders, for example.

Despite the high-volume, high-mix environment, Dana Franklin has maintained a 99-percent on-time delivery rate to customers since 2001. For the first six months of 2004, customer complaints were zero per million products sold, and the customer reject rate was zero parts per million. The plant has been named one of *Industry Week* magazine's 10 best North American manufacturing facilities a record-setting six times. These results are amazing accomplishments for the plant's small workforce (just 44 production and management personnel), especially considering that some of the equipment they use is more than 50 years old. Yet the philosophy here is that with each unit produced, with each hour, with each day and each week, the plant gets just a little bit better. As plant manager Tim Parys says, "We've sort of adopted the Japanese philosophy in that the worst that the equipment ever runs is the day that you put it on the floor."

In addition to continuous improvement on the plant floor, typically two or three active Six Sigma initiatives are underway at any time in the plant. Almost everyone in the plant is a Six Sigma green belt or black belt. Dana Franklin holds regular four-day *kaizen* events in which team members selected from the entire workforce focus on eliminating wasteful materials, activities, and processes. Production technician Ronnie Steenbergen is convinced that *kaizen* works and can enable the factory to squeeze out even more improvements from its "old machines."[43]

Unfortunately, despite the effectiveness of the Franklin plant and the quality of its parts and service, production cutbacks by U.S. automakers, along with pressure from the automakers for ever-lower prices even as the cost of raw materials was skyrocketing, pushed parent company Dana into bankruptcy. The company is now struggling to restructure and survive in an increasingly tough industry.[44] Yet Dana remains committed to a strong continuous-improvement program. "As we pursue improved financial performance, we are taking aggressive actions to enhance our operational excellence. Chief among these are the establishment of shared, targeted metrics across all of our businesses; the implementation of the Dana Operating System, a coordinated approach to drive continuous improvement throughout our operations; and the review of our global manufacturing footprint to ensure

continuous improvement
The implementation of a large number of small, incremental improvements in all areas of the organization on an ongoing basis.

Positive Factors	Negative Factors
• Tasks make high skill demands on employees.	• Management expectations are unrealistically high.
• TQM serves to enrich jobs and motivate employees.	• Middle managers are dissatisfied about loss of authority.
• Problem-solving skills are improved for all employees.	• Workers are dissatisfied with other aspects of organizational life.
• Participation and teamwork are used to tackle significant problems.	• Union leaders are left out of QC discussions.
• Continuous improvement is a way of life.	• Managers wait for big, dramatic innovations.

EXHIBIT 10.8

Quality Program Success Factor

- - - - - - - - - -

that we are producing the right products in the right places to best serve the needs of our customers," said CEO Gary Convis.[45]

TQM SUCCESS FACTORS

Despite its promise, total quality management does not always work. A few firms have had disappointing results. In particular, Six Sigma principles might not be appropriate for all organizational problems, and some companies have expended tremendous energy and resources for little payoff.[46] Many contingency factors (listed in Exhibit 10.8) can influence the success of a TQM program. For example, quality circles are most beneficial when employees have challenging jobs; participation in a quality circle can contribute to productivity because it enables employees to pool their knowledge and solve interesting problems. TQM also tends to be most successful when it enriches jobs and improves employee motivation. In addition, when participating in the quality program improves workers' problem-solving skills, productivity is likely to increase. Finally, a quality program has the greatest chance of success in a corporate culture that values quality and stresses continuous improvement as a way of life, as at the Dana Franklin plant just described.

Trends in Quality and Financial Control

Many companies are responding to changing economic realities and global competition by reassessing organizational management and processes—including control mechanisms. Some of the major trends in quality and financial control include international quality standards, economic value–added and market value–added systems, activity-based costing, and increased corporate governance.

INTERNATIONAL QUALITY STANDARDS

One impetus for total quality management in the United States is the increasing significance of the global economy. Many countries have adopted a universal benchmark for

3 Total quality management is just another fad.

ANSWER: Total quality management has been implemented in many countries over the course of decades and has led to many organizational improvements, more efficiency, and lower costs for consumers.

Assess
Your
Answer

Be aware of current trends in control. Learn quality principles, new financial control systems, and open-book management and apply what works for your situation.

Remember—overcontrol can be just as bad as undercontrol. Find a balance between oversight and control on the one hand and mutual trust and respect on the other. Go to the Ethical Dilemma on page 341 that pertains to new workplace control issues.

ISO 9000 standards
A set of standards as outlined by the International Organization for Standardization that represent an international consensus of what constitutes effective quality management.

economic value-added (EVA)
A control system that measures performance in terms of after-tax profits minus the cost of capital invested in tangible assets.

quality management practices—ISO 9000 standards—which represent an international consensus of what constitutes effective quality management as outlined by the International Organization for Standardization.[47] Hundreds of thousands of organizations in 157 countries, including the United States, have been certified against ISO 9000 standards to demonstrate their commitment to quality. Europe continues to lead in the total number of certifications, but the greatest number of new certifications in recent years has been in the United States. One of the more interesting organizations to recently become ISO certified was the Phoenix, Arizona, Police Department's Records and Information Bureau. In today's environment, where the credibility of law-enforcement agencies has been called into question, the bureau wanted to make a clear statement about its commitment to quality and accuracy of information provided to law-enforcement personnel and the public.[48] ISO certification has become the recognized standard for evaluating and comparing companies on a global basis, and more U.S. companies are feeling the pressure to participate to remain competitive in international markets. In addition, many countries and companies require ISO certification before they will do business with an organization.

NEW FINANCIAL CONTROL SYSTEM

In addition to traditional financial tools, managers are using systems such as economic value–added to provide effective financial control.

Economic Value–Added (EVA). Hundreds of companies, including AT&T, Quaker Oats, the Coca-Cola Company, and Philips Petroleum Company, have set up **economic value–added (EVA)** measurement systems as a new way to gauge financial performance. EVA can be defined as a company's net (after-tax) operating profit minus the cost of capital invested in the company's tangible assets.[49] Measuring performance in terms of EVA is intended to capture all the things a company can do to add value from its activities, such as run the business more efficiently, satisfy customers, and reward shareholders. Each job, department, process, or project in the organization is measured by the value added. EVA can also help managers make more cost-effective decisions. At Boise Cascade, the vice president of information technology (IT) used EVA to measure the cost of replacing the company's existing storage devices against keeping the existing storage assets that had higher maintenance costs. Using EVA demonstrated that buying new storage devices would lower annual maintenance costs significantly and easily make up for the capital expenditure.[50]

Overcontrol of employees can be damaging to an organization as well. Managers might feel justified in monitoring e-mail and Internet use, as described earlier in this chapter, yet employees often resent and feel demeaned by close monitoring that limits their personal freedom and makes them feel as if they are constantly being watched. Excessive control of employees can lead to demotivation, low morale, lack of trust, and even hostility among workers. Managers have to find an appropriate balance, as well as develop and communicate clear policies regarding workplace monitoring. Although oversight and control are important, good organizations also depend on mutual trust and respect among managers and employees.

Summary

Organizational control is the systematic process through which managers regulate organizational activities to meet planned goals and standards of performance. Most organizations measure and control performance using financial measures. Increasingly, more organizations are measuring less-tangible aspects of performance.

The balanced scorecard is a comprehensive management-control system that balances traditional measures with operational measures relating to a company's critical success factors. The four major perspectives of the balanced scorecard are financial performance, customer service, internal business processes, and the organization's capacity for learning and growth.

The feedback-control model involves using feedback to determine whether performance meets established standards. Well-designed control systems include four key steps: establish standards, measure performance, compare performance to standards, and make corrections as necessary.

Budgetary control is one of the most commonly used forms of managerial control. Other financial controls include use of the balance sheet, income statement, and financial analysis of these documents.

The philosophy of controlling has shifted to reflect changes in leadership methods. Traditional hierarchical controls emphasize establishing rules and procedures, then monitoring employee behavior to make sure the rules and procedures are followed. With decentralized control, employees assume responsibility for monitoring their own performance.

Open-book management is used in decentralized organizations to share with all employees the financial condition of a company. Open-book management encourages active participation in achieving organizational goals, helps the employee understand how his or her job affects the financial success of the organization, and allows employees to see the interdependence and importance of each business function.

Total quality management is an organization-wide effort to infuse quality into every activity in a company through continuous improvement. Although based on the work of U.S. researchers and consultants, TQM was initially adopted and made popular by Japanese firms. TQM techniques include quality circles, benchmarking, Six Sigma, reduced cycle time, and continuous improvement.

Recent trends in control include the use of international quality standards, and economic value-added.

Discussion Questions

1. You're a manager who employs a participative-control approach. You've concluded that corrective action is necessary to improve customer satisfaction, but first you need to convince your employees that the problem exists. What kind of evidence do you think employees will find more compelling: quantitative measurements or anecdotes from your interactions with customers? Explain your answer.

2. Describe the advantages of using a balanced scorecard to measure and control organizational performance. Suppose you created a balanced scorecard for McDonald's. What specific customer-service measures would you include?

3. In bottom-up budgeting, lower-level managers anticipate their departments' resource needs and pass them up to top management for approval. Identify the advantages of bottom-up budgeting.

4. In the chapter example of eBay, CEO Meg Whitman is quoted as saying, "If you can't measure it, you can't control it." Do you agree with this statement? Provide examples from your school or business experience that support your argument.

5. Think of a class you've taken in the past. What standards of performance did your professor establish? How

was your actual performance measured? How was your performance compared to the standards? Do you think the standards and methods of measurement were fair? Were they appropriate to your assigned work? Why or why not?

6. Some critics argue that Six Sigma is a collection of superficial changes that often result in doing a superb job of building the wrong product or offering the wrong service. Do you agree or disagree? Explain.

7. What types of analysis can managers perform to help them diagnose a company's financial condition? How might a review of financial statements help managers diagnose other kinds of performance problems as well?

8. Why is benchmarking an important component of total quality management programs? Do you believe a company could have a successful TQM program without using benchmarking?

9. How might activity-based costing provide better financial control tools for managers of a company such as Kellogg that produces many different food products?

10. What is ISO certification? Why would a global company such as General Electric want ISO certification?

Self Learning

Is Your Budget in Control?

By the time you are in college, you are in charge of at least some of your own finances. How well you manage your personal budget may indicate how well you will manage

your company's budget on the job. Respond to the following statements to evaluate your own budgeting habits. If the statement doesn't apply directly to you, then respond the way you think you would behave in a similar situation.

	YES	NO
1. I spend all my money as soon as I get it.	_____	_____
2. At the beginning of each week (or month, or term), I write down all my fixed expenses.	_____	_____
3. I never seem to have any money left over at the end of the week (or month).	_____	_____
4. I pay all my expenses, but I never seem to have any money left over for fun.	_____	_____
5. I am not putting any money away in savings right now; I'll wait until after I graduate from college.	_____	_____
6. I can't pay all my bills.	_____	_____
7. I have a credit card, but I pay the balance in full each month.	_____	_____
8. I take cash advances on my credit card.	_____	_____
9. I know how much I can spend on eating out, movies, and other entertainment each week.	_____	_____
10. I pay cash for everything.	_____	_____
11. When I buy something, I look for value and determine the best buy.	_____	_____
12. I lend money to friends whenever they ask, even if it leaves me short of cash.	_____	_____
13. I never borrow money from friends.	_____	_____
14. I am putting aside money each month to save for something that I really need.	_____	_____

Scoring and Interpretation Yes responses to statements 2, 9, 10, 13, and 14 point to the most disciplined budgeting habits. Yes responses to 4, 5, 7, and 11 reveal adequate budgeting habits. Yes responses to 1, 3, 6, 8, and 12 indicate the poorest budgeting habits. If you have answered honestly, chances are you'll have a combination of all three. Look to see where you can improve your budgeting.

Group Learning

Making Rules

1. Assemble into groups of three to five members and discuss the following questions, either in or out of class, depending on the instructor's assignment.

2. As a group, develop a list of policies for the groups in your class. You will turn in the list of policies to your instructor.

3. Be prepared to defend your choices to the rest of the class.

As a way of figuring out what rules and policies make sense for your organization, you might start by deciding how your group would handle each of the following scenarios. Based on your discussion, you will be able to formulate a good working rule.

1. Your team agreed to meet at 1 P.M. Wednesday for two hours to work on the project. Jane doesn't show up until 1:20.

2. Your team divided up the tasks of the project and set up a meeting for each person to report on his or her

progress. When it's Fred's turn to present, he says that he didn't have time to complete his part.

3. When decisions need to be made during your team's meetings, Chris often says, "It doesn't matter what we do. Let's just hurry up and get it done and turn it in."

4. Your team members reported on the work each had been doing, but it was clear that Frank had not put much effort into his part.

5. The teams are given the next class period to work on their project. Sandy doesn't show up for class; she has all of your team's materials.

6. Phil frequently interrupts other team members during meetings.

7. Once Connie has an idea in her head, she won't listen to anyone else's opinions.

8. Bob takes over team meetings. Others rarely get a chance to talk.

9. Sarah is a popular student. It seems that other team members agree with what she says regardless of the quality of her idea.

10. Tom comes to all the team's meetings but rarely says anything.

11. During your meeting, Carolyn starts talking about things unrelated to the project, such as what's happening in other classes and upcoming parties.

12. Stan and Beth have very different opinions of how your team's work should progress. They seem to be at odds with each other most of the time. They argue during team meetings.

13. In your group, half the members are Asian, half are Caucasian. The Asian students don't say very much, and the Caucasian students dominate the group.

14. In your group, three members belong to the same sorority. They arrive and leave together, take breaks together, and spend time in the group talking about sorority activities.

After you've made your list of rules, discuss the following as a group:

1. Why are policies important?

2. What happens when there are no rules or policies?

3. Can you have too many policies?

Source: Developed by Karen Harlos, McGill University, karen.harlos@mcgill.ca

Action Learning

Schoolwork Standards

1. Interview four students who are not taking this course right now. Make sure two of them are top grade earners and two are about average. Tell the students you will keep their information confidential, that you will only be reporting results in a paper you will write, and that you will not divulge any names. And then stick to that promise.

2. Ask the students questions about how they study, how much they read, how they manage to work on and finish a project or paper, how they feel about grades, and so on.

3. Determine whether they use any of the control mechanisms described in this chapter such as feedback control.

4. Have they developed standards for their work? Do they compare the actual performance to the standard? What happens when the performance is less than expected—for example, when they don't get as high a grade?

5. Write a report for your instructor, comparing the top students to the others. Make sure you don't mention the students' names in your report; keep that information anonymous.

6. Your instructor may lead a class discussion on the findings. Again, do not mention anyone's names. It's fine, of course, if you want to talk about your own experiences as a student.

Ethical Dilemma

The Wages of Sin?

Chris Dykstra, responsible for loss prevention at Westwind Electronics, took a deep breath before he launched into making his case for the changes he was proposing in the company's shoplifting policy. He knew convincing Ross Chenoweth was going to be a hard sell. Ross, the president

and CEO, was the son of the founder of the local, still family-owned consumer electronics chain based in Phoenix, Arizona. He'd inherited not only the company but also his father's strict moral code.

"I think it's time to follow the lead of other stores," Chris began. He pointed out that most other retailers didn't bother calling the police and pressing charges unless the thief had shoplifted merchandise worth more than $50 to $100. In contrast, Westwind currently had the zero-tolerance policy toward theft that Ross's father had put in place when he started the business. Chris wanted to replace that policy with one that only prosecuted individuals between 18 and 65 who had stolen more than $20 worth of goods and had no previous history of theft at Westwind. In the case of first-time culprits under 18 or over 65, he argued for letting them off with a strict warning regardless of the value of their ill-gotten goods. Repeat offenders would be arrested.

"Frankly, the local police are getting pretty tired of having to come to our stores every time a teenager sticks a CD in his jacket pocket," Chris pointed out. "And besides, we just can't afford the costs associated with prosecuting everyone." Every time he pressed charges against a shoplifter who'd made off with a $10 item, Westwind lost money. The company had to engage a lawyer and pay employees overtime for their court appearances. In addition, Chris was looking at hiring more security guards to keep up with the workload. Westwind was already in a battle it was losing at the moment with the mass retailers who were competing all too successfully on price, so passing on the costs of its zero-tolerance policy to customers wasn't really an option. "Let's concentrate on catching dishonest employees and those organized theft rings. They're the ones who are really hurting us," Chris concluded.

There was a long pause after Chris finished his carefully prepared speech. Ross thought about his recently deceased father, both an astute businessman and a person for whom honesty was a key guiding principle. If he were sitting here today, he'd no doubt say that theft was theft, that setting a minimum was tantamount to saying that stealing was acceptable just as long as you don't steal too much. He looked at Chris. "You know, we've both got teenagers. Is this really a message you want to send out, especially to kids? You know as well as I do that there's nothing they like better than testing limits. It's almost an invitation to see if you can beat the system." But then Ross faltered as he found himself glancing at the latest financial figures on his desk—another in a string of quarterly losses. If Westwind went under, a lot of employees would be looking for another way to make a living. In his heart, he believed in his father's high moral standards, but he had to ask himself: Just how moral could Westwind afford to be?

What Would You Do?

1. Continue Westwind's zero-tolerance policy toward shoplifting. It's the right thing to do—and it will ultimately pay off in higher profitability because the chain's reputation for being tough on crime will reduce overall losses from theft.

2. Adopt Chris Dykstra's proposed changes and show more leniency to first-time offenders. It is a more cost-effective approach to the problem than the current policy, plus it stays close to his father's original intent.

3. Adopt Chris Dykstra's proposed changes with an even higher limit of $50 or $100, which is still less than the cost of prosecution. In addition, make sure the policy isn't publicized. That way you'll reduce costs even more and still benefit from your reputation for prosecuting all shoplifters.

Source: Based on Michael Barbaro, "Some Leeway for the Small Shoplifter," *New York Times*, July 13, 2006.

6 PART SIX
Leading

If there was ever an industry in need of transformational leadership, it's today's record business. Columbia Records believes it has such a leader in Rick Rubin, a veteran record producer and former disc jockey who was named co-chair of the Sony division in 2007.

Arguably the most visionary producer of the past 20 years, Rubin cofounded hip-hop record label Def Jam. Unlike many record company executives, however, he has no background in sound engineering, music, business, or law. His most important credential is that he's a passionate fan. Known for his unusually supportive, egalitarian leadership style, the bearded and shaggy-haired Rubin sees his role as nurturing creative people so they can do their best and create art.

Until recently, powerful record company executives decided what music got created. But now musicians are using computer software to produce their own high-quality recordings, and consumers are flocking to file-sharing sites and online stores. CD sales are dropping fast as listeners download singles and create their own CDs of personal favorites. So Rubin has his work cut out for him as he tries to help Columbia rethink its mission, strategy, and structure and come up with badly needed innovative products and technologies.

11

Chapter Eleven

Dynamics of Behavior in Organizations

LEARNING OBJECTIVES

After studying this chapter, you should be able to:

1 Define attitudes and explain their relationship to personality, perception, and behavior.

2 Discuss the importance of work-related attitudes.

3 Identify major personality traits and describe how personality can influence workplace attitudes and behaviors.

4 Define the four components of emotional intelligence and explain why they are important for today's managers.

5 Explain how people learn in general and in terms of individual learning styles.

6 Discuss the effects of stress and identify ways individuals and organizations can manage stress to improve employee health, satisfaction, and productivity.

New Manager's Questions

Please circle your opinion below each of the following statements.

1 Job satisfaction is about getting a good paycheck and liking the work you do.

STRONGLY AGREE < < <   > > > STRONGLY DISAGREE

1	2	3	4	5

2 Managers should be outgoing and agreeable.

STRONGLY AGREE < < <   > > > STRONGLY DISAGREE

1	2	3	4	5

3 As a manager, if one of your employees offends you, the best thing is to really let them have it, teach them a lesson.

STRONGLY AGREE < < <   > > > STRONGLY DISAGREE

1	2	3	4	5

Managers' attitudes, personality characteristics, values, and personal qualities such as self-confidence affect their behavior, including how they handle work situations and relate to others. These characteristics can profoundly affect the workplace and influence employee motivation, morale, and job performance. Equally important is a manager's' ability to understand others. Insight into why people behave the way they do is a part of good management.

People are an organization's most valuable resource—and the source of some of managers' most difficult problems. Individuals differ in many ways. Some are quiet and shy, while others are gregarious; some are perpetual optimists, while others tend to look at the negative side of things. People bring their individual differences to work each day, and these differences in attitudes, personality, and so forth influence how they interpret assignments, whether they like to be told what to do, how they handle challenges, and how they interact with others.

Three basic leadership skills are at the core of identifying and solving people problems: (1) diagnosing, or gaining insight into the situation a manager is trying to influence, (2) adapting individual behavior and resources to meet the needs of the situation, and (3) communicating in a way that others can understand and accept. Thus, managers need grounding in the principles of organizational behavior—that is, the ways individuals and groups tend to act in organizations. By increasing their knowledge of individual differences in the areas of attitudes, personality, perception, learning, and stress management, managers can understand and lead employees and colleagues through many workplace challenges. This chapter introduces basic principles of organizational behavior in each of these areas.

Organizational Behavior

No matter what job you have, strive to be a good corporate citizen, work hard, get along with others and try to be the kind of colleague others want to work with.

organizational behavior
An interdisciplinary field dedicated to the study of how individuals and groups tend to act in organizations.

organizational citizenship
Work behavior that goes beyond job requirements and contributes as needed to the organization's success.

Organizational behavior, commonly called OB, is an interdisciplinary field dedicated to the study of human attitudes, behavior, and performance in organizations. OB draws concepts from many disciplines, including psychology, sociology, cultural anthropology, industrial engineering, economics, ethics, and vocational counseling, as well as the discipline of management. The concepts and principles of organizational behavior are important to managers because in every organization human beings ultimately make the decisions that control how the organization acquires and uses resources. Those people may cooperate with, compete with, support, or undermine one another. Their beliefs and feelings about themselves, their co-workers, and the organization shape what they do and how well they do it. People can distract the organization from its strategy by engaging in conflict and misunderstandings, or they can pool their diverse talents and perspectives to accomplish much more as a group than they could ever do as individuals.

Organizational citizenship refers to the tendency of people to help one another and put in extra effort that goes beyond job requirements to contribute to the organization's success. An employee demonstrates organizational citizenship by being helpful to co-workers and customers, doing extra work when necessary, and looking for ways to improve products and procedures. These behaviors enhance the organization's performance and contribute to positive relationships both within the organization and with customers. Managers can encourage organizational citizenship by applying their knowledge of human behavior, such as selecting people with positive attitudes, managing different personalities, putting people in jobs where they can thrive, and enabling employees to cope with and learn from workplace challenges.[1]

Attitudes

Most students have probably heard the expression that someone "has an attitude problem," which means some consistent quality about the person affects his or her behavior in a negative way. An employee with an attitude problem might be hard to get along with, might constantly gripe and cause problems, and might persistently resist new ideas. We all seem to know intuitively what an attitude is, but we do not consciously think about how strongly attitudes affect our behavior. Defined formally, an **attitude** is an evaluation—either positive or negative—that predisposes a person to act in a certain way. Understanding employee attitudes is important to managers because attitudes determine how people perceive the work environment, interact with others, and behave on the job. Emerging research is revealing the importance of positive attitudes to both individual and organizational success. For example, studies have found that the characteristic most common to top executives is an optimistic attitude. People rise to the top because they have the ability to see opportunities where others see problems and can instill in others a sense of hope and possibility for the future.[2] Another positive attitude is self-confidence. To see how you rate, take the New Manager's Self-Test on page 350.

Managers strive to develop and reinforce positive attitudes among all employees because happy, positive people are healthier, more effective, and more productive.[3] Some companies, such as David's Bridal, the nation's largest bridal store chain, are applying scientific research to improve employee attitudes—and sales performance.

JetBlue founder David Neeleman illustrates the positive attitude and optimism that are common traits of successful leaders. Neeleman was shocked when the board of directors of JetBlue removed him as CEO after the highly reported stranding of 131,000 passengers during the 2007 Valentine's Day ice storm. At the time, Neeleman said he would never found another airline, but now he is launching a new low-cost carrier, Azul (the Portuguese word for blue) in Brazil. "Every time a door closes, another one opens up," Neeleman says. "And so I'm excited to be off to the country of my birth to start something new."

© ANDRE PENNER/AP IMAGES

> CONCEPT CONNECTION <

attitude
A cognitive and affective evaluation that predisposes a person to act in a certain way.

DAVID'S BRIDAL

Planning a wedding can be one of the most joyful experiences in a woman's life—and one of the most nerve-racking. The salespeople at David's Bridal, a 267-store chain owned by Federated Department Stores, bear the brunt of these intense emotions. For many salespeople, dealing with those emotions can be overwhelming and exhausting, translating into negative attitudes and impatience with already-stressed customers.

Managers turned to new research on happiness to help employees cope and develop more positive attitudes. In a pilot training program based on the work of psychologist Martin Seligman, salespeople were taught how to feel more cheerful with techniques such as "emotion regulation," "impulse control," and "learned optimism." These techniques enable salespeople to be more calm and centered with harried, indecisive brides-to-be, which helps customers stay calm and centered as well. The constructive behavior translates into better sales, meaning employees make better commissions, which in turn contributes to more positive attitudes toward the job.[4]

As this example shows, sometimes negative attitudes can result from characteristics of the job, such as a high stress level, but managers can find ways to help people have better attitudes. Managers should pay attention to negative attitudes because they can be both the result of underlying problems in the workplace as well as a contributor to forthcoming problems.[5]

If you find yourself having a negative reaction toward someone, try to look within yourself and see what it is inside of you that might be causing that attitude.

NEW MANAGER'S SELF-TEST

Are You Self-Confident?

Self-confidence is the foundation for many important behaviors of a new manager. To learn something about your level of self-confidence, answer the following questions. Please answer whether each item is Mostly True or Mostly False for you.

	MOSTLY TRUE	MOSTLY FALSE
1. I have lots of confidence in my decisions.	_____	_____
2. I would like to change some things about myself.	_____	_____
3. I am satisfied with my appearance and personality.	_____	_____
4. I would be nervous about meeting important people.	_____	_____
5. I come across as a positive person.	_____	_____
6. I sometimes think of myself as a failure.	_____	_____
7. I am able to do things as well as most people.	_____	_____
8. I find it difficult to believe nice things someone says about me.	_____	_____

SCORING AND INTERPRETATION: Many good things come from self-confidence. How self-confident are you? Give yourself 1 point for each odd-numbered item above marked as Mostly True and 1 point for each *even-numbered* item marked Mostly False. If you scored 3 or less, your self-confidence may not be very high. You might want to practice new behavior in problematic areas to develop greater confidence. A score of 6 or above suggests a high level of self-confidence and a solid foundation on which to begin your career as a new manager.

If a new manager lacks self-confidence, he or she is more likely to avoid difficult decisions and confrontations and may tend to overcontrol subordinates, which is called *micromanaging.* A lack of self-confidence also leads to less sharing of information and less time hiring and developing capable people. Self-confident managers, by contrast, can more easily delegate responsibility, take risks, give credit to others, confront problems, and assert themselves for the good of their team.

COMPONENTS OF ATTITUDES

One important step for managers is recognizing and understanding the *components* of attitudes, which is particularly important when attempting to change attitudes.

If you find yourself having a negative reaction toward someone, try to look within yourself and see what it is inside of you that might be causing that attitude.

Behavioral scientists consider attitudes to have three components: *cognitions* (thoughts), *affect* (feelings), and *behavior*.[6] The cognitive component of an attitude includes the beliefs, opinions, and information the person has about the object of the attitude, such as knowledge of what a job entails and opinions about personal abilities. The affective component is the person's emotions or feelings about the object of the attitude, such as enjoying or hating a job. The behavioral component of an attitude is the person's intention to behave toward the object of the attitude in a certain way. Exhibit 11.1 illustrates the three components of a positive attitude toward one's job. The cognitive element is the conscious thought "My job is interesting and challenging." The affective element is the feeling that "I love this job." These elements, in turn, are related to the behavioral component—an employee might arrive at work early because he or she is happy with the job.

Cognitive...thoughts...
"My job is interesting."

Affective...feelings...
"I love my job."

Behavioral...intention to act...
"I'm going to get to work early
with a smile on my face."

Attitude: Job Satisfaction

EXHIBIT 11.1
Components of an
Attitude

The emotional (affective) component is often the stronger factor in affecting behavior, so managers should be aware of situations that involve strong feelings. However, as a general rule, changing just one component—cognitions, affect, or behavior—can contribute to an overall change in attitude. Suppose a manager concludes that some employees have the attitude that the manager should make all the decisions affecting the department, but the manager prefers that employees assume more decision-making responsibility. To change the underlying attitude, the manager would consider whether to educate employees about the areas in which they can make good decisions (changing the cognitive component), build enthusiasm with pep talks about the satisfaction of employee empowerment (changing the affective component), or simply insist that employees make their own decisions (behavioral component) with the expectation that once they experience the advantages of decision-making authority, they will begin to like it.

HIGH-PERFORMANCE WORK ATTITUDES

The attitudes of most interest to managers are those related to work, especially attitudes that influence how well employees perform. Two attitudes that might relate to high performance are satisfaction with one's job and commitment to the organization.

Job Satisfaction. A positive attitude toward one's job is called **job satisfaction**. In general, people experience this attitude when their work matches their needs and interests, when working conditions and rewards (such as pay) are satisfactory, when they like their co-workers, and when they have positive relationships with supervisors. You can take the quiz in Exhibit 11.2 on page 352 to better understand some of the factors that contribute to job satisfaction.

Be mindful of your own attitude and how it affects people who work for you. A positive attitude can go a long way toward helping others feel good about themselves and their work responsibilities.

As a manager, make sure your employees have a reasonable workload and that they get enough help to organize their jobs.

job satisfaction
A positive attitude toward one's job.

Think of a job—either a current or previous job—that was important to you, and then answer the following questions with respect to how satisfied you were with that job. Please answer the six questions with a number 1–5 that reflects the extent of your satisfaction.

1 = Very dissatisfied   3 = Neutral   5 = Very satisfied
2 = Dissatisfied   4 = Satisfied

	1	2	3	4	5
1. Overall, how satisfied are you with your job?	1	2	3	4	5
2. How satisfied are you with the opportunities to learn new things?	1	2	3	4	5
3. How satisfied are you with your boss?	1	2	3	4	5
4. How satisfied are you with the people in your work group?	1	2	3	4	5
5. How satisfied are you with the amount of pay you receive?	1	2	3	4	5
6. How satisfied are you with the advancement you are making in the organization?	1	2	3	4	5

SCORING AND INTERPRETATION: Add up your responses to the six questions to obtain your total score: _____. The questions represent various aspects of satisfaction that an employee may experience on a job. If your score is 24 or above, then you probably feel satisfied with the job. If your score is 12 or below, then you probably do not feel satisfied. What is your level of performance in your job? Is your performance related to your level of satisfaction?

EXHIBIT 11.2
Rate Your Job Satisfaction

SOURCES: These questions were adapted from Daniel R. Denison, *Corporate Culture and Organizational Effectiveness* (New York: John Wiley, 1990); and John D. Cook, Susan J. Hepworth, Toby D. Wall, and Peter B. Warr, *The Experience of Work: A Compendium and Review of 249 Measures and Their Use* (San Diego, CA: Academic Press, 1981).

Many managers believe job satisfaction is important because they think satisfied employees will do better work. In fact, research shows that the link between satisfaction and performance is generally small and is influenced by other factors.[7] For example, the importance of satisfaction varies according to the amount of control the employee has; an employee doing routine tasks may produce about the same output no matter how he or she feels about the job. Managers of today's workers, however, often rely on job satisfaction to keep motivation and enthusiasm high. They can't afford to lose talented, highly skilled workers. Regrettably, a survey by International Survey Research found that Generation X employees (those born between 1961 and 1981), those who are carrying the weight of much of today's knowledge work, are the least satisfied of all demographic groups.[8]

Managers create the environment that determines whether employees have positive or negative attitudes toward their jobs.[9] A related attitude is organizational commitment.

Organizational Commitment. Organizational commitment refers to an employee's loyalty to and engagement with the organization. An employee with a high degree of organizational commitment is likely to say *we* when talking about the company. Such a person likes being a part of the organization and tries to contribute to its success. This attitude is illustrated by an incident at the A. W. Chesterton company, a manufacturer of mechanical seals and pumps. When two Chesterton pumps that supply water on the Navy aircraft carrier USS *John F. Kennedy* failed on a Saturday night just before the ship's scheduled departure, the team that produces the seals swung into action. Two members worked through the night to make new seals and deliver them for installation before the ship left port.[10]

organizational commitment
Loyalty to and heavy involvement in one's organization.

Assess Your Answer

1 Job satisfaction is about getting a good paycheck and liking the work you do.

ANSWER: Job satisfaction usually requires a number of things such as decent pay and liking the work itself, but it also means having a good boss, positive relationships with co-workers, and some control over the job itself and working conditions.

Most managers want to enjoy the benefits of loyal, committed employees, including low turnover and employee willingness to do more than the job's basic requirements. Results of a Towers Perrin-ISR survey of more than 360,000 employees from 41 companies around the world indicate that companies with highly committed employees perform better.[11] Alarmingly, another recent survey suggests that commitment levels around the world are relatively low. Only one-fifth of the respondents were categorized as fully engaged—that is, reflecting a high level of commitment. In the United States, the percentage classified as fully engaged was 29 percent, compared to 54 percent in Mexico, 37 in percent in Brazil, and 36 percent in India. Countries where employees reflect similar or lower levels of commitment than the United States include Canada at 23 percent, Spain at 19 percent, Germany at 17 percent, China at 16 percent, the United Kingdom at 14 percent, France at 12 percent, and Japan at only 3 percent.[12] Sometimes organizational commitment can lead to unethical behaviors, as described in this chapter's Business Blooper.

Trust in management decisions and integrity is one important component of organizational commitment.[13] Unfortunately, in recent years, many employees in the U.S. have lost that trust. Just 28 percent of people surveyed by *Fast Company* magazine said they think the chief executive officer (CEO) of their company has integrity. Another survey by Ajilon Professional Staffing found that only 29 percent of employees reported believing their boss cared about them and looked out for their interests.[14] Managers can promote stronger organizational commitment by being honest and trustworthy in their business dealings, keeping employees informed, giving them a say in decisions, providing the necessary training and other resources that enable them to succeed, treating them fairly, and offering rewards they value.

As a manager, if you want committed employees, make sure you are acting in a trustworthy fashion.

CONFLICTS AMONG ATTITUDES

Sometimes a person may discover that his or her attitudes conflict with one another or are not reflected in behavior. For example, a person's high level of organizational commitment might conflict with a commitment to family members. If employees routinely work evenings and weekends, then their long hours and dedication to the job might conflict with their belief that family ties are important. This conflict can create a state of **cognitive dissonance**, a psychological discomfort that occurs when individuals recognize

cognitive dissonance
A condition in which two attitudes or a behavior and an attitude conflict.

BUSINESS BLOOPER

Chevron and the Rain Forest

Chevron didn't like all the publicity surrounding the $27-billion lawsuit accusing the company of ruining the Ecuadorian rain forest. The upcoming expose and video report by *60 Minutes* were causing anxiety at the company. Rather than clean up the mess it allegedly made in Ecuador or try to pay for the damage, Chevron instead hired a former reporter to produce a look-alike so-called investigative-report video proclaiming the company's innocence—in fact, blaming an Ecuadorian company for the rain-forest damage. Chevron posted the video on its own site and on YouTube, and released a statement, claiming "We produced this video in response to a campaign waged by trial lawyers. They've turned to Hollywood

to tell a fictional story. We've turned to an award-winning, former journalist to tell a factual story." It seems Chevron considers *60 Minutes* to be "Hollywood." Amazon Watch representative Mitch Anderson said Chevron had resorted to "embarrassing public relations tactics" because the report done by credible news sources had not been framed the way the company wanted. But Chevron's efforts didn't go far. While the *60 Minutes* video was seen by 12 million people, Chevron's YouTube had only 2,000 viewers. If you consider the $27 billion size of the lawsuit, that's $13.5 million dollars per viewer on YouTube.

SOURCE: Brian Stelter, "When Chevron Hires Ex-Reporter to Investigate, Chevron Looks Good," *New York Times*, May 11, 2009, p. B5.

inconsistencies in their own attitudes and behaviors.[15] The theory of cognitive dissonance, developed by social psychologist Leon Festinger in the 1950s, says that people want to behave in accordance with their attitudes and usually will take corrective action to alleviate the dissonance and achieve balance.

In the case of working overtime, people who can control their hours might restructure responsibilities so that they have time for both work and family. In contrast, those employees who are unable to restructure workloads might develop an unfavorable attitude toward their employer, reducing their organizational commitment. They might resolve their dissonance by saying they would like to spend more time with their kids but their unreasonable employer demands that they work too many hours.

Perception

Always remember that your reactions to some incident will not necessarily be the same as others'.

Remember that other people will not always hear everything you say, especially if it is difficult information.

perception
The cognitive process people use to make sense out of the environment by selecting, organizing, and interpreting information.

perceptual selectivity
The process by which individuals screen and select the various stimuli that vie for their attention.

Another critical aspect of understanding behavior is perception. **Perception** is the cognitive process people use to make sense out of the environment by selecting, organizing, and interpreting information from the environment. Because of individual differences in attitudes, personality, values, interests, and so forth, people often "see" the same thing in different ways. A class that is boring to one student might be fascinating to another. One student might perceive an assignment to be challenging and stimulating, whereas another might find it a silly waste of time.

We can think of perception as a step-by-step process, as shown in Exhibit 11.3. First, we observe information (sensory data) from the environment through our senses: taste, smell, hearing, sight, and touch. Next, our mind screens the data and will select only the items we will process further. Third, we organize the selected data into meaningful patterns for interpretation and response. Most differences in perception among people at work are related to how they select and organize sensory data. You can experience differences in perceptual organization by looking at the visuals in Exhibit 11.4. What do you see in part **a** of Exhibit 11.4? Most people see this as a dog, but others see only a series of unrelated ink blots. Some people will see the figure in part **b** as a beautiful young woman while others will see an old one. Now look at part **c**. How many blocks do you see—six or seven? Some people have to turn the figure upside down before they can see seven blocks. These visuals illustrate how complex perception is. Changing people's perception can be complicated, as "The Rock" is finding out as described in the Spotlight on Skills box.

PERCEPTUAL SELECTIVITY

We are bombarded by so much sensory data that it is impossible to process it all. Thus, we tune in to some things and tune out others. **Perceptual selectivity** is the process by which individuals subconsciously screen and select the various objects and stimuli that vie for their attention.

People typically focus on stimuli that satisfy their needs and that are consistent with their attitudes, values, and personality. For example, employees who need positive feedback to feel good about themselves might pick up on positive statements made by a supervisor

EXHIBIT 11.3
The Perception Process

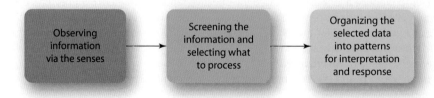

a. Do you see the dog?   **b.** Old Woman or young woman?   **c.** How many blocks?

EXHIBIT 11.4
Perception—What
Do You See?

but tune out most negative comments. A supervisor could use this understanding to tailor feedback in a positive way to help the employee improve work performance. The influence of needs on perception has been studied in laboratory experiments and found to have a strong impact on what people perceive.[16]

Characteristics of the stimuli themselves also affect perceptual selectivity. People tend to notice stimuli that stand out against other stimuli or that are more intense than surrounding stimuli. Examples would be a loud noise in a quiet room or a bright red dress at a party where most women are wearing basic black. People also tend to notice things that are familiar to them, such as a familiar voice in a crowd, as well as things that are new or different from their previous experiences. In addition, *primacy* and *recency* are important to perceptual

SPOTLIGHT ON
SKILLS

Dwayne Johnson: "The Rock"

How do you change the public's perception? Ask Dwayne Johnson, who is otherwise known as "the Rock." Johnson wants people to see him no longer as a meathead action star but as a family-friendly leading man in Hollywood's top tier. In order to achieve this goal, he's developed a careful strategy. First, he dropped his geological handle. He then went from he-man roles (*The Scorpion*) to family movies (*The Game Plan*) and even comedies (*Get Smart*). Finally, he's courting a wider audience, focusing on children, by appearing on the Nickelodeon network's Kids' Choice Awards and on *Hannah Montana*. He also served as the grand marshal at Disney World's Main Street Parade. To further sanitize his image, he flawlessly appeared at the Academy Awards to present a trophy.

Johnson's not the first action hero to try and cast a wider net. Arnold Schwarzenegger is considered the gold standard here. But others have failed miserably, such as Vin Diesel and Sylvester Stallone, who floundered when they strayed too far from their tough-guy roles.

Johnson, who is part African-American and part Samoan, grew up in poverty in Hawaii as part of a family of professional wrestlers. After several arrests as a teenager, he decided to make something of himself. He earned a criminology degree and played professional football for awhile, then finally went into the family business—wrestling—and became a big star. But as his World Wrestling Entertainment career peaked, he realized he was moving toward becoming a worn out slab of meat not unlike the character played by Mickey Rourke in *The Wrestler*. "That film rang really true," he says.

Johnson's star power in Disney's *The Game Plan* showed he can carry a movie—and this one earned $91 million in North America. And even if he can't sustain top billing in family movie land, his life is quite good. Paid millions for each movie, Johnson counts Will Smith as a friend, has an American Express Titanium card and a Louis Vuitton wallet, and owns a farm in Virginia. He does get teased by some of his former wrestling colleagues, especially because an upcoming role puts him as a tooth fairy. "There are definitely people who disagree with certain creative decisions you make. Pleasing everyone is pretty hard," he says.

SOURCE: Brooks Barnes, "Yep, He's Big," *New York Times*, March 8, 2009, pp. AR1, AR12.

selectivity. People pay relatively greater attention to sensory data that occur toward the beginning of an event or toward the end. Primacy supports the old truism that first impressions really do count, whether it be on a job interview, meeting a date's parents, or participating in a new social group. Recency reflects the reality that the last impression might be a lasting impression. For example, Malaysian Airlines discovered its value in building customer loyalty. A woman traveling with a nine-month-old might find the flight itself an exhausting blur, but one such traveler enthusiastically told people for years how Malaysian Airlines flight attendants helped her with baggage collection and ground transportation.[17]

perceptual distortions
Errors in perceptual judgment that arise from inaccuracies in any part of the perceptual process.

stereotyping
The tendency to assign an individual to a group or broad category and then attribute generalizations about the group to the individual.

halo effect
An overall impression of a person or situation based on one characteristic, either favorable or unfavorable.

projection
The tendency to see one's own personal traits in other people.

perceptual defense
The tendency of perceivers to protect themselves by disregarding ideas, objects, or people that are threatening to them.

attributions
Judgments about what caused a person's behavior—either characteristics of the person or of the situation.

PERCEPTUAL DISTORTIONS

Once people select the sensory data to be perceived, they begin grouping the data into recognizable patterns (perceptual organization). Of particular concern in the work environment are **perceptual distortions**, errors in perceptual judgment that arise from inaccuracies in any part of the perceptual process.

One common perceptual error is **stereotyping**, the tendency to assign an individual to a group or broad category (e.g., female, black, elderly; or male, white, disabled) and then to attribute widely held generalizations about the group to the individual. Thus, someone meets a new colleague, sees he is in a wheelchair, assigns him to the category "physically disabled," and attributes to this colleague generalizations she believes about people with disabilities, which may include a belief that he is less able than other co-workers. However, the person's inability to walk should not be seen as indicative of lesser abilities in other areas. Stereotyping prevents people from truly knowing those they classify in this way. In addition, negative stereotypes prevent talented people from advancing in an organization and fully contributing their talents to the organization's success.

The **halo effect** occurs when the perceiver develops an overall impression of a person or situation based on one characteristic, either favorable or unfavorable. In other words, a halo blinds the perceiver to other characteristics that should be used in generating a more complete assessment. The halo effect can play a significant role in performance appraisal, as we discussed in Chapter 9. For example, a person with an outstanding attendance record may be assessed as responsible, industrious, and highly productive; another person with less-than-average attendance may be assessed as a poor performer. Either assessment may be true, but it is the manager's job to be sure the assessment is based on complete information about all job-related characteristics and not just his or her preferences for good attendance.

Projection is the tendency of perceivers to see their own personal traits in other people; that is, they project their own needs, feelings, values, and attitudes into their judgment of others. A manager who is achievement oriented might assume that subordinates are as well. This assumption might cause the manager to restructure jobs to be less routine and more challenging, without regard for employees' actual satisfaction.

Perceptual defense is the tendency of perceivers to protect themselves against ideas, objects, or people that are threatening. People perceive things that are satisfying and pleasant but tend to disregard things that are disturbing and unpleasant. In essence, people develop blind spots in the perceptual process so that negative sensory data do not hurt them.

ATTRIBUTIONS

Among the judgments people make as part of the perceptual process are attributions. **Attributions** are judgments about what caused a person's behavior—something about the person or something about the situation. An *internal attribution* says characteristics of the person led to the behavior: "Susan missed the deadline because she's careless and lazy." An *external attribution* says something about the situation caused the person's behavior: "Susan missed the deadline because she couldn't get the information she needed in a timely manner." Attributions are important because they help people decide how to handle a situation. In the case of the missed deadline, a manager who blames it on the employee's personality will view Susan as the problem and might give her unfavorable performance reviews and less attention and support. In contrast, a manager who blames the behavior on the situation might try to prevent such situations in the future such as by improving horizontal communication mechanisms so people get the information they need in a timely way.

Social scientists have studied the attributions people make and identified three factors that influence whether an attribution will be external or internal.[18] These three factors are illustrated in Exhibit 11.5.

1. *Distinctiveness*: whether the behavior is unusual for that person (in contrast to a person displaying the same kind of behavior in many situations). If the behavior is distinctive, then the perceiver probably will make an *external* attribution.

2. *Consistency*: whether the person being observed has a history of behaving in the same way. People generally make *internal* attributions about consistent behavior.

3. *Consensus*: whether other people tend to respond to similar situations in the same way. A person who has observed others handle similar situations in the same way will likely make an *external* attribution; that is, it will seem that the situation produces the type of behavior observed.

In addition to these general rules, people tend to have biases that they apply when making attributions. When evaluating others, we tend to underestimate the influence of external factors and overestimate the influence of internal factors. This tendency is called the **fundamental attribution error**. Consider the case of someone being promoted to CEO. Employees, outsiders, and the media generally focus on the characteristics of the person that allowed him or her to achieve the promotion. In reality, however, the selection of that person might have been heavily influenced by external factors such as business conditions creating a need for someone with a strong financial or marketing background at that particular time.

Another bias that distorts attributions involves attributions we make about our own behavior. People tend to overestimate the contribution of internal factors to their successes and overestimate the contribution of external factors to their failures. This tendency, called

fundamental attribution error
The tendency to underestimate the influence of external factors on another's behavior and to overestimate the influence of internal factors.

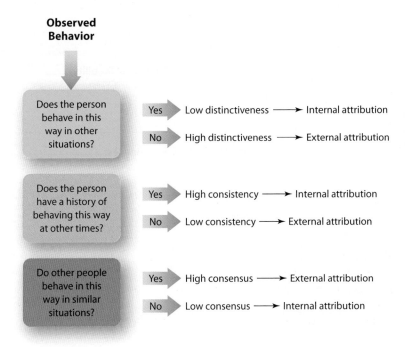

EXHIBIT 11.5
Factors Influencing Whether Attributions Are Internal or External

self-serving bias
The tendency to overestimate the contribution of internal factors to one's successes and the contribution of external factors to one's failures.

personality
The set of characteristics that underlie a relatively stable pattern of behavior in response to ideas, objects, or people in the environment.

Big Five personality factors
Dimensions that describe an individual's extroversion, agreeableness, conscientiousness, emotional stability, and openness to experience.

the **self-serving bias,** means people give themselves too much credit for what they do well and give external forces too much blame when they fail. Thus, if your manager says you don't communicate well enough, and you think your manager doesn't listen well enough, then the truth may actually lie somewhere in between.

Personality and Behavior

In recent years, many employers showed heightened interest in matching people's personalities to the needs of the job and the organization. An individual's **personality** is the set of characteristics that underlie a relatively stable pattern of behavior in response to ideas, objects, or people in the environment. Managers who appreciate the ways their employees' personalities differ have insight into what kinds of leadership behavior will be most influential.

PERSONALITY TRAITS

As the term is commonly used, people think of *personality* as traits, or the fairly consistent characteristics a person exhibits. Researchers investigated whether any traits stand up to scientific scrutiny. Although investigators examined thousands of traits over the years, their findings fit into five general dimensions that describe personality. These dimensions, often called the "Big Five" personality factors, are illustrated in Exhibit 11.6.[19] Each factor may contain a wide range of specific traits. The **Big Five personality factors** describe an individual's extroversion, agreeableness, conscientiousness, emotional stability, and openness to experience:

1. *Extroversion*—the degree to which a person is outgoing, sociable, assertive, and comfortable with interpersonal relationships.
2. *Agreeableness*—the degree to which a person is able to get along with others by being good-natured, likable, cooperative, forgiving, understanding, and trusting.

EXHIBIT 11.6

The Big Five
Personality Traits

– – – – – – – – – – –

Each individual's collection of personality traits is different; it is what makes us unique. But, although each *collection* of traits varies, we all share many common traits. The following phrases describe various traits and behaviors. Rate how accurately each statement describes you, based on a scale of 1 to 5, with 1 being very inaccurate and 5 very accurate. Describe yourself as you are now, not as you wish to be. There are no right or wrong answers.

1 2 3 4 5
Very Inaccurate   Very Accurate

Extroversion

I am usually the life of the party.	1	2	3	4	5
I feel comfortable around people.	1	2	3	4	5
I am talkative.	1	2	3	4	5

Agreeableness

I am kind and sympathetic.	1	2	3	4	5
I have a good word for everyone.	1	2	3	4	5
I never insult people.	1	2	3	4	5

Conscientiousness

I am systematic and efficient.	1	2	3	4	5
I pay attention to details.	1	2	3	4	5
I am always prepared for class.	1	2	3	4	5

Neuroticism (Low Emotional Stability)

I often feel critical of myself.	1	2	3	4	5
I often envy others.	1	2	3	4	5
I am temperamental.	1	2	3	4	5

Openness to New Experiences

I am imaginative.	1	2	3	4	5
I prefer to vote for liberal political candidates.	1	2	3	4	5
I really like art.	1	2	3	4	5

Which are your most prominent traits? For fun and discussion, compare your responses with those of classmates.

3. *Conscientiousness*—the degree to which a person is focused on a few goals, thus behaving in ways that are responsible, dependable, persistent, and achievement oriented.

4. *Emotional stability*—the degree to which a person is calm, enthusiastic, and self-confident, rather than tense, depressed, moody, or insecure.

5. *Openness to experience*—the degree to which a person has a broad range of interests and is imaginative, creative, artistically sensitive, and willing to consider new ideas.

As illustrated in the exhibit, these factors represent a continuum—that is, a person may have a low, moderate, or high degree of each quality. Answer the questions in Exhibit 11.6 to see where you fall on the Big Five scale for each factor. Having a moderate to high degree of each of the Big Five personality factors is considered desirable for a wide range of employees, but this isn't always a key to success. For example, having an outgoing, sociable personality (extroversion) is considered desirable for managers, but many successful top leaders, including Bill Gates, Charles Schwab, and Steven Spielberg,

Marriott carefully screens candidates for critical customer-service positions such as that of hotel concierge shown here. One important way managers determine whether people have the "right stuff" is through personality testing. During the application process, candidates answer a series of questions about their beliefs, attitudes, work habits, and how they might handle situations, enabling Marriott to identify people with interests and motivations that are compatible with company values. As managers reevaluate Marriott's mission and goals, the test also evolves. Some people fear personality tests have too much influence, determining not just who gets hired but who even gets an interview.

·············> CONCEPT CONNECTION <·······

are introverts, people who become drained by social encounters and need time alone to reflect and recharge their batteries. One study found that 4 in 10 top executives test out to be introverts.[20] Thus, the quality of extraversion is not as significant as is often presumed. Traits of agreeableness, on the other hand, seem to be particularly important in today's collaborative organizations. The days are over when a hard-driving manager can run roughshod over others to earn a promotion. Companies want managers who work smoothly with others and get help from lots of people inside and outside the organization. Executive search firm Korn/Ferry International examined data from millions of manager profiles since the early 2000s and found that the most successful executives today are team-oriented leaders who gather information and work collaboratively with many different people.[21]

Try to remember that the way you do things is not necessarily the only acceptable way; people with varying personality types may choose another way of operating.

One recent book argues that the secret to success in work and in life is *likability*. We all know we're more willing to do something for someone we like than for someone we don't, whether it is a teammate, a neighbor, a professor, or a supervisor. Managers can increase their likability by developing traits of agreeableness, including being friendly and cooperative, understanding other people in a genuine way, and striving to make people feel positive about themselves.[22]

Many companies, including JCPenney, DuPont, Toys "R" Us, and the Union Pacific Railroad, use personality testing to hire, evaluate, and promote employees. Surveys show that at least 30 percent of organizations use some kind of personality testing for hiring.[23] Entrepreneurial companies such as eHarmony are using sophisticated personality testing to match singles through online dating services.

2 Managers should be outgoing and agreeable.

ANSWER: Not all managers need to be outgoing, but getting along with others (agreeability) is essential.

Assess
Your
Answer

Online dating has grown into a half-billion dollar industry in just over 10 years. Personality tests are central to some of these organizations' strategies, and eHarmony is one of the most comprehensive at pursuing so-called serious daters, people who are searching for a lasting relationship.

The eHarmony compatibility matching system employs an exhaustive 436-question personality survey that is based on founder Neil Clark Warren's past professional experience and his company's research into long-lived marriages. Warren, who holds both divinity and clinical psychology degrees, believes the unions most likely to succeed are those between people who share at least 10 of the 29 personality traits that eHarmony measures.

Does the approach work? So far, the only company to track relationships it has helped create is eHarmony. Claiming to have helped bring about 16,000 marriages in 2005 alone, the company conducted an in-house study it says showed eHarmony couples enjoyed higher levels of marital satisfaction than those who had met through other channels.[24]

Despite growing use of personality tests, there is so far little hard evidence showing them to be valid predictors of job—or relationship—success.

EMOTIONAL INTELLIGENCE

In recent years, new insights into personality are emerging through research in the area of *emotional intelligence*. Emotional intelligence (EQ) includes four basic components:[25]

1. *Self-awareness*—the basis for all the other components; being aware of what you are feeling. People who are in touch with their feelings are better able to guide their own lives and actions. A high degree of self-awareness means you can accurately assess your own strengths and limitations and have a healthy sense of self-confidence.

2. *Self-management*—the ability to control disruptive or harmful emotions and balance one's moods so that worry, anxiety, fear, or anger do not cloud thinking and get in the way of what needs to be done. People who are skilled at self-management remain optimistic and hopeful despite setbacks and obstacles. This ability is crucial for pursuing long-term goals. MetLife found that applicants who failed the regular sales aptitude test but scored high on optimism made 21 percent more sales in their first year and 57 percent more in their second year than those who passed the sales test but scored high on pessimism.[26]

3. *Social awareness*—the ability to understand others and practice *empathy*, which means being able to put yourself in someone else's shoes, to recognize what others are feeling without them needing to tell you. People with social awareness are capable of understanding divergent points of view and interacting effectively with many different types of people.

4. *Relationship management*—the ability to connect to others, build positive relationships, respond to the emotions of others, and influence others. People with relationship-management skills know how to listen and communicate clearly, and they treat others with compassion and respect.

Studies show a positive relationship between job performance and high levels of emotional intelligence in a variety of jobs. Numerous organizations, including the U.S. Air Force and

Assess Your Answer

3 As a manager, if one of your employees offends you, the best thing is to really let them have it, teach them a lesson.

ANSWER: Having control of one's emotions and reactions is very important for today's managers. Rather than react in a mode of "showing them" or "getting back" at someone, a manager should carefully consider the best way to resolve an interpersonal problem. How can the problem be solved in a way that people will learn the most, in hopes of avoiding a similar problem in the future?

Canada Life, use EQ tests to measure such things as self-awareness, ability to empathize, and capacity to build positive relationships.[27] Altera Corporation uses "empathy coaches" to help its salespeople develop greater social awareness and see things from their customers' points of view.[28] EQ seems to be particularly important for jobs such as sales that require a high degree of social interaction. It's also critical for managers, who are responsible for influencing others and building positive attitudes and relationships in the organization. Managers with low emotional intelligence can undermine employee morale and harm the organization.

ATTITUDES AND BEHAVIORS INFLUENCED BY PERSONALITY

An individual's personality influences his or her work-related attitudes and behaviors. As a new manager, you will have to manage people with a wide variety of personality characteristics. This section's Spotlight on Skills (page 363) discusses how managers can cope with

Complete the New Manager's Self-Test below to assess your own level of emotional intelligence. You might also want to refer back to the questionnaire related to self-confidence at the beginning of this chapter. Self-confidence strongly influences a new manager's EQ.

NEW MANAGER'S SELF-TEST

What's Your EQ?

Understanding oneself and others is a major part of a new manager's job. To learn about your insights into yourself and others, answer each item below as Mostly True or Mostly False for you.

	MOSTLY TRUE	MOSTLY FALSE
1. I am aware of sensations and emotions within my body.	_____	_____
2. I am slow to react to others' slights or negative actions toward me.	_____	_____
3. I can tell my friends' moods from their behavior.	_____	_____
4. I am good at building consensus among others.	_____	_____
5. I have a good sense of why I have certain feelings.	_____	_____
6. I calm down right away if upset and am quick to forgive.	_____	_____
7. I often sense the impact of my words or behavior on others.	_____	_____
8. Other people are happier when I am around.	_____	_____

SCORING AND INTERPRETATION: The categories of emotional intelligence are below. Give yourself one point for each item marked Mostly True.

Self-Awareness: Items 1, 5
Self-Management: Items 2, 6
Social Awareness: Items 3, 7
Relationship Management: Items 4, 8

These are the four dimensions of EQ described in the text. If you scored 2 on a dimension, then you probably do well on it. If you scored 0 on a dimension, then you may want to work on that aspect of your EQ before becoming a manager. The important thing as a manager is to know and guide yourself, to understand the emotional state of others, and to guide your relationships in a positive direction.

the challenge of bridging personality differences. Four areas related to personality that are of particular interest to managers are locus of control, authoritarianism, Machiavellianism, and problem-solving styles.

Strive to take responsibility for your actions rather than always blaming others or the situation (external locus).

Locus of Control. People differ in terms of what they tend to accredit as the cause of their success or failure. Their **locus of control** defines whether they place the primary responsibility within themselves or on outside forces.[29] Some people believe that their own actions strongly influence what happens to them. They feel in control of their own fate. These individuals have a high *internal* locus of control. Other people believe that events in their lives occur because of chance, luck, or outside people and events. They feel more like pawns of their fate. These individuals have a high *external* locus of control.

As a manager, determining which candidates will have the best fit to the job is a real challenge and one done successfully by Teach for America, as shown in the Benchmarking box.

Research on locus of control shows real differences in behavior across a wide range of settings. People with an internal locus of control are easier to motivate because they believe the rewards are the result of their behavior. They are better able to handle complex information and problem solving, are more achievement oriented, and also more independent—and therefore more difficult to manage. By contrast, people with an external locus of control are harder to motivate, less involved in their jobs, and more likely to blame others when faced with a poor performance evaluation—but more compliant and conforming and, therefore, easier to manage.[30]

locus of control
The tendency to place the primary responsibility for one's success or failure either within oneself (internally) or on outside forces (externally).

BENCH-MARKING

Teach for America

Trying to hire the right graduates to send into high-risk inner-city schools is not child's play, but the Peace Corps–like program Teach for America (TFA) is doing a pretty good job. First off, it tries to convince top students to temporarily shelve their career goals and head toward one of the country's most troubled schools. During the application process, seniors who compete are subjected to hours of tests and interviews, all designed to measure their perseverance, organizational skills, and resilience—traits known to be critical because those hired get only five weeks of intense teacher training before they get thrust into the south Bronx or some other equally poor location. Founder Wendy Kopp doesn't soften the potential problems. "It can be really overwhelming and depressing," she cautions. "We all have bad days, and people who teach in Teach for American probably have more bad days than most."

It might sounds like a recipe for disaster, but Kopp has turned this 20-year-old nonprofit organization into a model for social change success. In 2008, 35,000 students, including 10 percent of Yale and Dartmouth' universities' senior classes, applied to TFA, and 4,100 were hired. This makes it one of the country's largest employers of college seniors. More would be hired, but the economy has put restraints in many school systems. The selection program is so effective that companies are now riding on its coattails. JPMorgan Chase found it was competing for the same top grads, so the company has formed a strategic recruiting alliance with TFA, staging joint events at colleges and offering job deferral, bonuses, and relocation costs. "We want employees who are committed to serving the community as well as to serving shareholders," said JPMorgan Chase's David Puth. Students are passing up higher-paying jobs to join Teach for America. Similarly, biotechnology company Amgen is partnering with the nonprofit, using it as a benchmark to redesign the bank's recruiting. Says VP Shannon McFayden, "We think TFA is the best college recruiting organization in the [United States]." Teach for America provides a five-week intensive course before school begins and asks for a two-year commitment. Even after those two years, two-thirds of alumni are still working in education, despite the fact they had other college majors. What do the new teachers think? Yale graduate David DeAngelis asked for a rural spot in Mississippi and is grateful for the experience. "You become part of the community almost immediately, part of the lives of students, of students' families," he said.

SOURCE: Thomas L. Friedman, "Swimming Without a Suit," *New York Times*, Apr. 22, 2009, p. A27; "More College Grads Joining Teach for America," *Gainesville Sun*, May 28, 2009; Patricia Sellers, "The Recruiter," *Fortune*, Nov. 27, 2006, pp. 87–90.

Bridging the Personality Gap

Personality differences among employees make the life of a new manager interesting—and sometimes exasperating. Consultant Deborah Hildebrand took a lighthearted look at this issue by comparing the manager to a ringmaster at the circus. Here are a few of the "performers" that managers encounter:

- *Lion Tamers.* These people are fiercely independent and like to be in control. They are willing to tackle the biggest, toughest projects but aren't typically good team players. The manager can give lion tamers some freedom, but make sure they understand who is ultimately in charge. Lion tamers crave recognition. Praising them for their accomplishments is a sure way to keep them motivated and prevent them from acting out to draw attention to themselves.
- *Clowns.* Everybody loves them, but clowns tend to goof off a little too much and disrupt the work of others. Keeping these people focused is the key to keeping them productive. A little micromanaging can be a good thing with a clown. It's also good to put clowns in jobs where socializing is a key to productivity and success.
- *Sideshow Performers.* These are the knife throwers, fire eaters, and sword swallowers. They have unique strengths and skills but tend to get overwhelmed with broad projects. These folks are expert team members because they like to combine their talents with others to make up a whole. Don't ask a sideshow performer to do a lion tamer's job.

This list is intended to be humorous, but in the real world of management, working with different personalities isn't always a laughing matter. Differences at work can create an innovative environment but also lead to stress, conflict, and bad feelings. Managers can learn to work more effectively with different personality types by following some simple tips.

1. *Understand your own personality and how you react to others.* Try to avoid judging people based on limited knowledge. Realize that everyone has many facets to his or her personality.
2. *Treat everyone with respect.* People like to be accepted and appreciated for who they are. Even if you find someone's personality grating, remain professional and keep your frustration and irritation to yourself.
3. *When leading a team or group, make sure everyone has an equal chance to participate.* Don't let the outgoing members dominate the scene.
4. *Remember that everyone wants to fit in.* No matter their personalities, people typically take on behavior patterns that are the norm for their environment. Managers can create norms that keep everyone focused on positive interactions and high performance.

SOURCES: Based on Deborah S. Hildebrand, "Managing Different Personalities," Suite101.com (June 25, 2007) (http://businessmanagement.suite101.com/article.cfm/managing_different_personalities); Jamie Walters and Sarah Fenson, "Building Rapport with Different Personalities," *Inc. com* (Mar. 2000) (www.inc.com/articles/2000/03/17713.html); Tim Millett, "Learning to Work with Different Personality Types" (http://ezinearticles.com/?Learning-To-Work-With-Different-Personality-Types&id=725606); and Carol Ritberter, "Understanding Personality: The Secret to Managing People" (www.dreammanifesto.com/understanding-personality-the-secret-of-managing-people.html) (accessed April 17, 2008).

Do you believe luck plays an important role in your life, or do you feel that you control your own fate? To find out more about your locus of control, read the instructions and complete the questionnaire in Exhibit 11.7 (on the next page).

Authoritarianism. **Authoritarianism** is the belief that power and status differences should exist within the organization.[31] Individuals high in authoritarianism tend to be concerned with power and toughness, obey recognized authority above them, stick to conventional values, critically judge others, and oppose the use of subjective feelings. The degree to which managers possess authoritarianism will influence how they wield and share power. The degree to which employees possess authoritarianism will influence how they react to their managers. If a manager and employees differ in their degree of authoritarianism, then the manager may have difficulty leading effectively. The trend toward empowerment and shifts in expectations among younger employees for more equitable relationships are contributing to a decline in strict authoritarianism in many organizations.

authoritarianism
The belief that power and status differences should exist within the organization.

Your Locus of Control

This questionnaire is designed to measure locus-of-control beliefs. Researchers using this questionnaire in a study of college students found a mean of 51.8 for men and 52.2 for women, with a standard deviation of 6 for each. The higher your score on this questionnaire, the more you tend to believe that you are generally responsible for what happens to you; in other words, higher scores are associated with *internal locus of control*. Low scores are associated with *external locus of control*. Scoring low indicates that you tend to believe that forces beyond your control—such as powerful other people, fate, or chance—are responsible for what happens to you.

For each of these 10 questions, indicate the extent to which you agree or disagree using the following scale:
1 = strongly disagree   4 = neither disagree nor agree   7 = strongly agree
2 = disagree   5 = slightly agree
3 = slightly disagree   6 = agree

1. When I get what I want, it is usually because I worked hard for it.	1 2 3 4 5 6 7
2. When I make plans, I am almost certain to make them work.	1 2 3 4 5 6 7
3. I prefer games involving some luck over games requiring pure skill.	1 2 3 4 5 6 7
4. I can learn almost anything if I set my mind to it.	1 2 3 4 5 6 7
5. My major accomplishments are entirely due to my hard work and ability.	1 2 3 4 5 6 7
6. I usually don't set goals because I have a hard time following through on them.	1 2 3 4 5 6 7
7. Competition discourages excellence.	1 2 3 4 5 6 7
8. Often people get ahead just by being lucky.	1 2 3 4 5 6 7
9. On any sort of exam or competition, I like to know how well I do relative to everyone else.	1 2 3 4 5 6 7
10. It's pointless to keep working on something that's too difficult for me.	1 2 3 4 5 6 7

SCORING AND INTERPRETATION: To determine your score, reverse the values you selected for questions 3, 6, 7, 8, and 10 (1 = 7, 2 = 6, 3 = 5, 4 = 4, 5 = 3, 6 = 2, 7 = 1). For example, if you strongly disagree with the statement in question 3, you would have given it a value of 1. Change this value to a 7. Reverse the scores in a similar manner for questions 6, 7, 8, and 10. Now add the point values for all 10 questions together. Your score: _____

SOURCES: Adapted from J. M. Burger, *Personality: Theory and Research* (Belmont, CA: Wadsworth, 1986): 400–401, cited in D. Hellriegel, J. W. Slocum, Jr., and R. W. Woodman, *Organizational Behavior*, 6th ed. (St. Paul, MN: West, 1992): 97–100. Original source: D. L. Paulhus, "Sphere-Specific Measures of Perceived Control," *Journal of Personality and Social Psychology*, 44, 1253–1265.

EXHIBIT 11.7

Measuring Locus of Control

Machiavellianism. Another personality dimension that is helpful in understanding work behavior is **Machiavellianism**, which is characterized by the acquisition of power and the manipulation of other people for purely personal gain. Machiavellianism is named after Niccolo Machiavelli, a 16th-century author who wrote *The Prince*, a book for noblemen of the day on how to acquire and use power.[32] Psychologists developed instruments to measure a person's Machiavellianism (Mach) orientation.[33] Research shows that high Machs are predisposed to being pragmatic, capable of lying to achieve personal goals, more likely to win in win–lose situations, and more likely to persuade than be persuaded.[34]

Different situations may require people who demonstrate one or the other type of behavior. In loosely structured situations, high Machs actively take control, while low Machs accept the direction given by others. Low Machs thrive in highly structured situations, while high Machs perform in a detached, disinterested way. High Machs are particularly good in jobs that require bargaining skills or that involve substantial rewards for winning.[35]

Problem-Solving Styles and the Myers–Briggs Type Indicator. Managers also need to realize that individuals solve problems and make decisions in different ways. One approach to understanding problem-solving styles grew out of the work of psychologist Carl Jung. Jung believed differences resulted from our preferences in how we go about gathering and evaluating information.[36] According to Jung, gathering information and evaluating information are separate activities. People gather information either by *sensation* or *intuition*, but not by both simultaneously. Sensation-type people would rather work with known facts and hard data and prefer routine and order in gathering information.

Machiavellianism

The tendency to direct much of one's behavior toward the acquisition of power and the manipulation of other people for personal gain.

Personal Style	Action Tendencies	Likely Occupations
Sensation–Thinking	• Emphasizes details, facts, certainty • Is a decisive, applied thinker • Focuses on short-term, realistic goals • Develops rules and regulations for judging performance	• Accounting • Production • Computer programming • Market research • Engineering
Intuitive–Thinking	• Prefers dealing with theoretical or technical problems • Is a creative, progressive, perceptive thinker • Focuses on possibilities using impersonal analysis • Is able to consider a number of options and problems simultaneously	• Systems design • Systems analysis • Law • Middle or top management • Teaching business or economics
Sensation–Feeling	• Shows concern for current, real-life human problems • Is pragmatic, analytical, methodical, and conscientious • Emphasizes detailed facts about people rather than tasks • Focuses on structuring organizations for the benefit of people	• Directing supervisor • Counseling • Negotiating • Selling • Interviewing
Intuitive–Feeling	• Avoids specifics • Is charismatic, participative, people oriented, and helpful • Focuses on general views, broad themes, and feelings • Decentralizes decision making, develops few rules and regulations	• Public relations • Advertising • Human resources • Politics • Customer service

Intuitive-type people would rather look for possibilities than work with facts, and they prefer solving new problems and using abstract concepts.

Evaluating information involves making judgments about the information a person has gathered. People evaluate information by *thinking* or *feeling*. These represent the extremes in orientation. Thinking-type individuals base their judgments on impersonal analysis, using reason and logic rather than personal values or emotional aspects of the situation. Feeling-type individuals base their judgments more on personal feelings such as harmony and tend to make decisions that result in approval from others.

According to Jung, only one of the four functions—sensation, intuition, thinking, or feeling—is dominant in an individual. However, the dominant function usually is backed up by one of the functions from the other set of paired opposites. Exhibit 11.8 shows the four problem-solving styles that result from these matchups, as well as occupations that people with each style tend to prefer.

Two additional sets of paired opposites that are not directly related to problem solving are *introversion–extroversion* and *judging–perceiving*. Introverts gain energy by focusing on personal thoughts and feelings, whereas extroverts gain energy from being around others and interacting with others. On the judging versus perceiving dimension, people with a judging preference like certainty and closure and tend to make decisions quickly based on available data. Perceiving people, on the other hand, enjoy ambiguity, dislike deadlines, and may change their minds several times as they gather large amounts of data and information to make decisions.

A widely used personality test that measures how people differ on all four of Jung's sets of paired opposites is the **Myers–Briggs Type Indicator (MBTI)**. The MBTI measures a person's preferences for introversion versus extroversion, sensation versus intuition, thinking versus feeling, and judging versus perceiving. The various combinations of these four preferences result in 16 unique personality types.

Each of the 16 different personality types can have positive and negative consequences for behavior. Based on the limited research that has been done, the two preferences that

EXHIBIT 11.8
Four Problem-
Solving Styles

- - - - - - - - - -

Go to the Self Learning exercise on page 373 that pertains to evaluating your Myers–Briggs personality type.

Myers–Briggs Type Indicator (MBTI)
Personality test that measures a person's preference for introversion versus extroversion, sensation versus intuition, thinking versus feeling, and judging versus perceiving.

seem to be most strongly associated with effective management in a variety of organizations and industries are thinking and judging.[37] However, people with other preferences can also be good managers. One advantage of understanding your natural preferences is to maximize your innate strengths and abilities. Dow Chemical manager Kurt Swogger believes the MBTI can help put people in the right jobs—where they will be happiest and make the strongest contribution to the organization.

DOW CHEMICAL

When Kurt Swogger arrived at Dow Chemical's plastics business in 1991, it took anywhere from 6 to 15 years to launch a new product—and the unit hadn't launched a single one for 3 years. Ten years later, a new product launch took just 2 to 4 years, and Swogger's research-and-development (R&D) team was launching hit after hit.

What changed? "The biggest obstacle to launching great new products was not having the right people in the right jobs," says Swogger. He began reassigning people based on his intuition and experience, distinguishing pure inventors from those who could add value later in the game and still others who were best at marketing the new products. Swogger says he was correct about 60 percent of the time. If someone didn't work out after six months, he'd put him or her in another assignment.

Seeking a better way to determine people's strengths, Swogger began using the Myers–Briggs Type Indicator (MBTI), predicting which types would be best suited to each stage of the product development and launch cycles. After administering the test to current and former Dow plastics employees, he found some startling results. In 1991, when Swogger came on board, the match between the right personality type and the right role was only 29 percent. By 2001, the rate had jumped to 93 percent. Swogger's next step was to administer the MBTI to new hires so he could immediately assign people to jobs that matched their natural thinking and problem-solving styles, leading to happier employees and higher organizational performance.[38]

Other organizations also use the MBTI, with 89 of the *Fortune* 100 companies recently reporting that they use the test in hiring and promotion decisions.[39] Putting the right people in the right jobs is a vital skill for managers, whether they do it based on intuition and experience or by using personality tests such as the MBTI.

PERSON–JOB FIT

person–job fit
The extent to which a person's ability and personality match the requirements of a job.

An important responsibility of managers is to try to match employee and job characteristics so that work is done by people who are well suited to do it. The extent to which a person's ability and personality match the requirements of a job is called **person–job fit**. When managers achieve person–job fit, employees are more likely to contribute and have higher levels of job satisfaction and commitment.[40] The importance of person–job fit became apparent during the dot-com heyday of the late 1990s. People who rushed to Internet companies in hopes of finding a new challenge—or making a quick buck—found themselves floundering in jobs for which they were unsuited. One manager recruited by a leading executive search firm lasted less than two hours at his new job. The search firm, a division of Russell Reynolds Associates, later developed a "Web factor" diagnostic to help determine whether people have the right

© LYNN DONALDSON, COURTESY PRINTINGFORLESS

Andrew Field, who owns a $25-million printing services company, PrintingForLess.com, uses dogs to help him create the person–environment fit when hiring new employees. The dog-friendly policy started at the company's inception when Field began bringing Jessie (far left), his border collie and black Labrador mix, to work on a daily basis. The idea caught on and now as many as 15 dogs frequent the office with their owners. Guided by rules such as owner accountability, a dog review board, and a dog-approval process, employees find the dogs are a great release for stress. Fields says that the dog policy helps him make good hires; candidates who respond favorably to the canine rule are likely to fit in with the office culture.

CONCEPT CONNECTION

personality for dot-com jobs, including such things as a tolerance for risk and uncertainty, an obsession with learning, and a willingness to do whatever needs doing, regardless of job title.[41]

A related concern is *person–environment fit*, which looks not only at whether the person and job are suited to one another but also at how well the individual will fit in the overall organizational environment. An employee who is by nature strongly authoritarian, for example, would have a hard time in an organization such as W. L. Gore and Associates, which has few rules, no hierarchy, no fixed or assigned authority, and no bosses. Many of today's organizations pay attention to person–environment fit from the beginning of the recruitment process. Texas Instruments' Web page includes an area called "Fit Check" that evaluates personality types anonymously and gives a prospective job candidate the chance to evaluate whether he or she would be a good match with the company.[42]

Learning

Years of schooling may condition many of us to think that learning is something students do in response to teachers in a classroom. With this view, in the managerial world of time deadlines and concrete action, learning seems remote—even irrelevant. However, successful managers need specific knowledge and skills as well as the ability to adapt to changes in the world around them. Managers have to learn. **Learning** is a change in behavior or performance that occurs as the result of experience. Two individuals who undergo similar experiences—for example, a business transfer to a foreign country—probably will differ in how they adapt their behaviors to (that is, learn from) the experience. In other words, each person learns in a different way.

THE LEARNING PROCESS

One model of the learning process, shown in Exhibit 11.9, depicts learning as a four-stage cycle.[43] First, a person encounters a concrete experience. This event is followed by thinking

learning
A change in behavior or performance that occurs as the result of experience.

EXHIBIT 11.9
The Experiential Learning Cycle

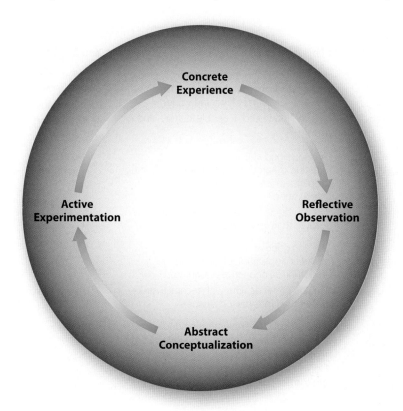

and reflective observation, which lead to abstract conceptualization and, in turn, to active experimentation. The results of the experimentation generate new experiences, and the cycle repeats. The arrows in the model indicate that this process is a recurring cycle. People continually test their conceptualizations and adapt them as a result of their personal reflections and observations about their experiences.

LEARNING STYLES

As a manager, remember that some employees learn by reading and learning concepts, while others need to "do" in order to learn.

Individuals develop personal learning styles that vary in terms of how much they emphasize each stage of the learning cycle. These differences occur because the learning process is directed by individual needs and goals. For example, an engineer might place greater emphasis on abstract concepts, while a salesperson might emphasize concrete experiences. Because of these preferences, personal learning styles typically have strong and weak points.

Questionnaires can assess a person's strong and weak points as a learner by measuring the relative emphasis the person places on each of the four learning stages shown in Exhibit 11.9: concrete experience, reflective observation, abstract conceptualization, and active experimentation. Some people have a tendency to overemphasize one stage of the learning process or to avoid some aspects of learning. Not many people have totally balanced profiles, but the key to effective learning is competence in each of the four stages when it is needed.

Researchers have identified four fundamental learning styles, outlined in Exhibit 11.10, labeled Diverger, Assimilator, Converger, and Accommodator. Each style combines elements of the four stages of the learning cycle.[44] The exhibit lists some questions that can help you understand your dominant learning abilities, and it identifies some occupations you might enjoy based on your dominant style. For example, people whose dominant style is Accommodator are often drawn to sales and marketing. Those with a primarily Diverger style might enjoy human-resource management.

EXHIBIT 11.10

What's Your Learning Style?

Learning Style Type	Dominant Learning Abilities	Is This Your Style?	You Might Be Good at
Diverger	• Concrete experience • Reflective observation	• Are you good at generating ideas, seeing a situation from multiple perspectives, and being aware of meaning and value? • Are you interested in people, culture, and the arts?	• Human-resource management • Counseling • Organization development specialist
Assimilator	• Abstract conceptualization • Reflective observation	• Are you good at inductive reasoning, creating theoretical models, and combining disparate observations into an integrated explanation? • Do you tend to be less concerned with people than ideas and abstract concepts?	• Research • Strategic planning
Converger	• Abstract conceptualization • Active experimentation	• Are you good at making decisions, the practical application of ideas, and hypothetical deductive reasoning? • Do you prefer dealing with technical tasks rather than interpersonal issues?	• Engineering
Accommodator	• Concrete experience • Active experimentation	• Are you good at implementing decisions, carrying out plans, and getting involved in new experiences? • Do you tend to be at ease with people but are sometimes seen as impatient or pushy?	• Marketing • Sales

Stress and Stress Management

Now let's turn our attention to a problem almost every manager will encounter at some time in his or her career: workplace stress. Formally defined, **stress** is an individual's physiological and emotional response to external stimuli that place physical or psychological demands on the individual and create uncertainty and lack of personal control when important outcomes are at stake.[45] These stimuli, called *stressors*, produce some combination of frustration (the inability to achieve a goal, such as the inability to meet a deadline because of inadequate resources) and anxiety (such as the fear of being disciplined for not meeting deadlines).

People's responses to stressors vary according to their personalities, the resources available to help them cope, and the context in which the stress occurs. When the level of stress is low relative to a person's coping resources, stress can be a positive force, stimulating desirable change and achievement. However, too much stress is associated with many negative consequences, including sleep disturbances, drug and alcohol abuse, headaches, ulcers, high blood pressure, and heart disease. People who are experiencing the ill effects of too much stress may become irritable or withdraw from interactions with their co-workers, take excess time off, and have more health problems. In the United States, an estimated 1 million people each day don't show up for work because of stress.[46] Similarly, a survey in the United Kingdom found that 68 percent of nonmanual workers and 42 percent of manual workers reported missing work because of stress-related illness.[47] Just as big a problem for organizations as absenteeism is *presenteeism*, which refers to people who go to work but are too stressed and distracted to be productive.[48] Clearly, too much stress is harmful to employees as well as to companies.

TYPE A AND TYPE B BEHAVIOR

Researchers observed that some people seem to be more vulnerable than others to the ill effects of stress. From studies of stress-related heart disease, they categorized people as having behavior patterns called Type A and Type B.[49] The **Type A behavior** pattern includes extreme competitiveness, impatience, aggressiveness, and devotion to work. In contrast, people with a **Type B behavior** pattern exhibit less of these behaviors. They consequently experience less conflict with other people and a more balanced, relaxed lifestyle. Type A people tend to experience more stress-related illness than Type B people.

Most Type A individuals are high-energy people and may seek positions of power and responsibility. By pacing themselves and learning control and intelligent use of their natural high-energy tendencies, Type A individuals can be powerful forces for innovation and leadership within their organizations. However, many Type A personalities cause stress-related problems for themselves and sometimes for those around them. Type B individuals typically live with less stress unless they are in high-stress situations. A number of factors can cause stress in the workplace, even for people who are not naturally prone to high stress.

CAUSES OF WORK STRESS

Workplace stress is skyrocketing worldwide. The World Congress on Health and Safety at Work presented studies suggesting that job-related stress may be as big a danger to the world's people as chemical and biological hazards.[50] The number of people in the United States who say they are overworked grew from 28 percent in 2001 to 44 percent in 2005, and one-third of Americans between the ages of 25 and 39 say they feel burned out by their jobs. Surveys in Canada consistently peg work as the top source of stress for people in that country. In India, growing numbers of young software professionals and call-center workers are falling prey to depression, anxiety, and other mental illnesses because of increasing

As a new manager, determine your natural learning style to understand how you approach problems, use your learning strengths, and better relate to people who have different styles. As you grow in your management responsibilities, strive for a balance among the four learning stages shown in Exhibit 11.9.

Go to the ethical dilemma on page 376 that pertains to organizational sources of stress.

If you are a Type A person with a high stress job, take a relaxing vacation; if you are a Type B with a low-key job, then you can do the seven-countries-in-five-days kind of trip.

stress
A physiological and emotional response to stimuli that place physical or psychological demands on an individual.

Type A behavior
Behavior pattern characterized by extreme competitiveness, impatience, aggressiveness, and devotion to work.

Type B behavior
Behavior pattern that lacks Type A characteristics and includes a more balanced, relaxed lifestyle.

workplace stress.[51] And in France, companies did some serious soul-searching after the notes of three engineers who committed suicide within five months implied that workplace stress was a major factor in their decision to end their lives.[52]

Most people have a general idea of what a stressful job is like: difficult, uncomfortable, exhausting, even frightening. Managers can better cope with their own stress and establish ways for the organization to help employees cope if they define the conditions that tend to produce work stress. One way to identify work stressors is to think about stress caused by the demands of job tasks and stress caused by interpersonal pressures and conflicts.

- *Task demands* are stressors arising from the tasks required of a person holding a particular job. Some kinds of decisions are inherently stressful: those made under time pressure, those that have serious consequences, and those that must be made with incomplete information. For example, emergency room doctors are under tremendous stress as a result of the task demands of their jobs. They regularly have to make quick decisions based on limited information that may determine whether a patient lives or dies. Almost all jobs, especially those of managers, have some level of stress associated with task demands. Task demands also sometimes cause stress because of **role ambiguity**, which means that people are unclear about what task behaviors are expected of them.

- *Interpersonal demands* are stressors associated with relationships in the organization. Although in some cases interpersonal relationships can alleviate stress, they also can be a source of stress when the group puts pressure on an individual or when conflicts arise between individuals. Managers can resolve many conflicts using techniques that will be discussed in Chapter 15. **Role conflict** occurs when an individual perceives incompatible demands from others. Managers often feel role conflict because the demands of their superiors conflict with those of the employees in their department. They may be expected to support employees and provide them with opportunities to experiment and be creative, while at the same time top executives are demanding a consistent level of output that leaves little time for creativity and experimentation.

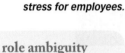

As a new manager, learn to recognize the conditions that cause stress in the workplace and then change what you can to alleviate unnecessary or excessive stress for employees.

role ambiguity
Uncertainty about what behaviors are expected of a person in a particular role.

role conflict
Incompatible demands of different roles.

INNOVATIVE RESPONSES TO STRESS MANAGEMENT

Organizations that want to challenge their employees and stay competitive will never be stress free, but healthy workplaces promote the physical and emotional well-being of their employees. Managers have direct control over many of the things that cause people stress, including their own behavior. Exhibit 11.11 lists some of the top things managers do to cause excessive and unnecessary stress.

EXHIBIT 11.11

How Managers Create Stress for Employees

Working for a bad boss is a major cause of workplace stress. Here are some things bad bosses do to create stress for their subordinates:

1. Impose unreasonable demands and overwhelming workloads.
2. Don't let people have a say in how they do their work.
3. Create perpetual doubt about how well employees are performing.
4. Refuse to get involved in conflicts between employees; let them work it out.
5. Fail to give people credit for their contributions and achievements.
6. Keep people guessing about what is expected of them.
7. Bully and harass people to keep them on their toes.
8. Don't allow people to form a community; tell them work isn't a social club.

SOURCES: Based on "Getting the Least From Your Staff," sidebar in Don Mills, "Running on High Octane or Burning Out Big Time?" *National Post* [Toronto], April 8, 2006; Donna Callea, "Workers Feeling the Burn; Employee Burnout a New Challenge to Productive, Morale, Experts Say," *News Journal*, March 27, 2006; and Joe Humphreys, "Stress Will Be Main Cause of Workplace Illness by 2020," *Irish Times*, July 27, 2005.

A variety of techniques can help individuals manage stress. Among the most basic strategies are those that help people stay healthy: exercising regularly, getting plenty of rest, and eating a healthful diet. Although individuals can pursue stress-management strategies on their own, today's enlightened companies support healthy habits to help people manage stress and be more productive. Stress costs businesses billions of dollars a year in absenteeism, lower productivity, staff turnover, accidents, and higher health insurance and workers' compensation costs.[53] Taking care of employees has become a business as well as an ethical priority. In Britain, employers are required to meet certain minimal conditions to manage workplace stress, such as ensuring that employees are not exposed to a poor physical work environment, have the necessary skills and training to meet their job requirements, and are given a chance to offer input into the way their work is done.[54]

Helping employees manage stress can be as simple as encouraging people to take regular breaks and vacations. Consider that more than a third of U.S. employees surveyed by the Families and Work Institute currently don't take their full allotment of vacation time.[55] Here are some proactive approaches managers are taking to combat the growing stress level in today's workplace:

© PETE CROUSER/SALO LLC

Many companies help employees manage stress by offering discounts to local gyms. At SALO, LLC, a financial staffing firm in Minneapolis, employees can exercise as they work. Here co-owners Amy Langer and John Folkstead walk as they meet. Langer and Folkstead experimented with a few treadmill desks to help get their employees and themselves moving more. The desks were such a hit with the staff that they installed 12 more stations. Employees report they have more energy and have lost weight since the treadmill desks were installed.

·········> CONCEPT CONNECTION <·········

- Some companies, including BellSouth, First Union, and Tribble Creative Group, have designated *quiet rooms* or meditation centers where employees can take short, calming breaks at any time they feel the need.[56] The time off is a valuable investment when it allows employees to approach their work with renewed energy and a fresh perspective.

- Wellness programs provide access to nutrition counseling and exercise facilities.

A worldwide study of wellness programs conducted by the Canadian government found that for each dollar spent, the company gets from $1.95 to $3.75 return payback from benefits.[57]

- Training programs and conferences can help people identify stress and teach them coping mechanisms. Training managers to recognize warning signs is critical.

- Manager intervention is a growing trend in enlightened companies. At Boston Consulting Group, for instance, the boss steps in if he or she sees someone working too hard or displaying signs of excessive stress. Mark Ostermann says, "It was a great feeling [to have the boss provide support]. I didn't have to complain to anyone. They were proactive in contacting me."[58]

- Broad work–life balance initiatives that may include flexible work options such as telecommuting and flexible hours, as well as benefits such as on-site day care or elder care, fitness centers, and personal services such as pickup and delivery of dry cleaning. *Daily flextime* is considered by many employees to be the most effective work–life practice, which means giving employees the freedom to vary their hours as needed, such as leaving early to take an elderly parent shopping or taking time off to attend a child's school play.[59]

TAKE ACTION

To avoid overstress, eat well, exercise, get enough sleep, and make sure you have a good emotional support system.

The study of organizational behavior reminds managers that employees are *human* resources with human needs. By acknowledging the personal aspects of employees' lives, these various initiatives communicate that managers and the organization care about employees. In addition, managers' attitudes make a tremendous difference in whether employees are stressed out and unhappy or relaxed, energetic, and productive.

Summary

The principles of organizational behavior describe how people as individuals and groups behave and affect the performance of the organization as a whole. Desirable work-related attitudes include job satisfaction and organizational commitment. Employees' and managers' attitudes can strongly influence employee motivation, performance, and productivity. Three components of attitudes are cognitions, emotions, and behavior.

Attitudes affect people's perceptions, and vice versa. Individuals often "see" things in different ways. The perceptual process includes perceptual selectivity and perceptual organization. Perceptual distortions such as stereotyping, the halo effect, projection, and perceptual defense are errors in judgment that can arise from inaccuracies in the perception process. Attributions are judgments that individuals make about whether a person's behavior was caused by internal or external factors.

Another area of interest is personality, the set of characteristics that underlie a relatively stable pattern of behavior. One way to think about personality is the Big Five personality traits of extroversion, agreeableness, conscientiousness, emotional stability, and openness to experience. Some important work-related attitudes and behaviors influenced by personality are locus of control, authoritarianism, Machiavellianism, and problem-solving styles. A widely used personality test is the Myers–Briggs Type Indicator. Managers want to find a good person–job fit by ensuring that a person's personality, attitudes, skills, abilities, and problem-solving styles match the requirements of the job and the organizational environment. New insight into personality has been gained through research in the area of emotional intelligence (EQ). Emotional intelligence includes the components of self-awareness, self-management, social awareness, and relationship management.

Even though people's personalities may be relatively stable, individuals can learn new behaviors. Learning refers to a change in behavior or performance that occurs as a result of experience. The learning process goes through a four-stage cycle, and individual learning styles differ. Four learning styles are Diverger, Assimilator, Converger, and Accommodator. Rapid changes in today's marketplace create a need for ongoing learning. They may also create greater stress for many of today's workers. The causes of work stress include task demands and interpersonal demands. Individuals and organizations can alleviate the negative effects of stress by engaging in a variety of techniques for stress management.

Discussion Questions

1. Why is it important for managers to have an understanding of organizational behavior? Do you think knowledge of OB might be more important at some managerial levels than at others? Discuss.

2. In what ways might the cognitive and affective components of attitude influence the behavior of employees who are faced with learning an entirely new set of computer-related skills to retain their jobs at a manufacturing facility?

3. The chapter suggests that optimism is an important characteristic for a manager, yet some employees complain that optimistic managers cause them significant stress because they expect their subordinates to meet unreasonable goals or expectations. How might an employee deal with a perpetually optimistic manager?

4. How might a manager be able to use an understanding of perceptual selectivity and perceptual organization to communicate more effectively with subordinates?

5. In the Big Five personality factors, extroversion is considered a "good" quality to have. Why might introversion be an equally positive quality?

6. Why do you think surveys show that Generation X employees experience the least job satisfaction of all demographic groups? Do you expect this finding to be true throughout their careers?

7. Which of the four components of emotional intelligence do you consider most important to an effective manager in today's world? Why?

8. How might understanding whether an employee has an internal or an external locus of control help a manager better communicate with, motivate, and lead the employee?

9. You are a manager, and you realize that one of your employees repeatedly teases co-workers born in another country, saying that they come from a backward country with pagan beliefs. How would you decide whether it's necessary to respond to the situation? If you decide to intervene, what would your response be?

10. Review Exhibit 11.10 (on page 368). Which learning style best characterizes you? How can you use this understanding to improve your learning ability? To improve your management skills?

11. Why do you think workplace stress is skyrocketing? Do you think it is a trend that will continue? Explain the reasons for your answer. Do you think it is the responsibility of managers and organizations to help employees manage stress? Why or why not?

Self Learning

Personality Assessment: Jung's Typology and the Myers-Briggs Type Indicator

For each of the following items, circle either **a** or **b**. In some cases, both **a** and **b** may apply to you. You should decide which is more like you, even if it is only slightly more true.

1. I would rather:
   a. solve a new and complicated problem.
   b. work on something that I have done before.

2. I like to:
   a. work alone in a quiet place.
   b. be where "the action" is.

3. I want a boss who:
   a. establishes and applies criteria in decisions.
   b. considers individual needs and makes exceptions.

4. When I work on a project, I:
   a. like to finish it and get some closure.
   b. often leave it open for possible change.

5. When making a decision, the most important considerations are:
   a. rational thoughts, ideas, and data.
   b. people's feelings and values.

6. On a project, I tend to:
   a. think it over and over before deciding how to proceed.
   b. start working on it right away, thinking about it as I go along.

7. When working on a project, I prefer to:
   a. maintain as much control as possible.
   b. explore various options.

8. In my work, I prefer to:
   a. work on several projects at a time, and learn as much as possible about each one.
   b. have one project that is challenging and keeps me busy.

9. I often:
   a. make lists and plans whenever I start something and may hate to seriously alter my plans.
   b. avoid plans and just let things progress as I work on them.

10. When discussing a problem with colleagues, it is easy for me:
    a. to see "the big picture."
    b. to grasp the specifics of the situation.

11. When the phone rings in my office or at home, I usually:
    a. consider it an interruption.
    b. don't mind answering it.

12. The word that describes me better is:
    a. analytical.
    b. empathetic.

13. When I am working on an assignment, I tend to:
    a. work steadily and consistently.
    b. work in bursts of energy with downtime in between.

14. When I listen to someone talk on a subject, I usually try to:
    a. relate it to my own experience and see whether it fits.
    b. assess and analyze the message.

15. When I come up with new ideas, I generally:
    a. "go for it."
    b. like to contemplate the ideas some more.

16. When working on a project, I prefer to:
    a. narrow the scope so it is clearly defined.
    b. broaden the scope to include related aspects.

17. When I read something, I usually:
    a. confine my thoughts to what is written there.
    b. read between the lines and relate the words to other ideas.

18. When I have to make a decision in a hurry, I often:
    a. feel uncomfortable and wish I had more information.
    b. am able to do so with available data.

19. In a meeting, I tend to:
    a. continue formulating my ideas as I talk about them.
    b. speak out only after I have carefully thought the issue through.

20. In work, I prefer spending a great deal of time on issues of:
    a. ideas.
    b. people.

21. In meetings, I am most often annoyed with people who:
    a. come up with many sketchy ideas.
    b. lengthen the meeting with many practical details.

22. I tend to be:
    a. a morning person.
    b. a night owl.

23. My style in preparing for a meeting is:

   a. to be willing to go in and be responsive.

   b. to be fully prepared and sketch an outline of the meeting.

24. In meetings, I would prefer for people to:

   a. display a fuller range of emotions.

   b. be more task oriented.

25. I would rather work for an organization where:

   a. my job was intellectually stimulating.

   b. I was committed to its goals and mission.

26. On weekends, I tend to:

   a. plan what I will do.

   b. just see what happens and decide as I go along.

27. I am more:

   a. outgoing.

   b. contemplative.

28. I would rather work for a boss who is:

   a. full of new ideas.

   b. practical.

In the following, choose the word in each pair that appeals to you more:

29. a. social   b. theoretical

30. a. ingenuity   b. practicality

31. a. organized   b. adaptable

32. a. active   b. concentration

Scoring and Interpretation Count one point for each of the following items that you circled in the inventory.

Score for I (Introversion)	Score for E (Extroversion)	Score for S (Sensing)	Score for N (Intuition)
2a	2b	1b	1a
6a	6b	10b	10a
11a	11b	13a	13b
15b	15a	16a	16b
19b	19a	17a	17b
22a	22b	21a	21b
27b	27a	28b	28a
32b	32a	30b	30a
Totals _____	_____	_____	_____

Circle the one with more points: I or E (If tied on I/E, don't count #11)

Circle the one with more points: S or N (If tied on S/N, don't count #16)

Score for T (Thinking)	Score for F (Feeling)	Score for J (Judging)	Score for P (Perceiving)
3a	3b	4a	4b
5a	5b	7a	7b
12a	12b	8b	8a
14b	14a	9a	9b
20a	20b	18b	18a
24b	24a	23b	23a
25a	25b	26a	26b
29b	29a	31a	31b
Totals _____	_____	_____	_____

Circle the one with more points: T or F (If tied on T/F, don't count #24)

Circle the one with more points: J or P (If tied on J/P, don't count #23)

Your Score Is: I or E _____ S or N _____ T or F _____ J or P _____

Your MBTI type is _____ (example: INTJ; ESFP; etc.)

Characteristics Frequently Associated with Each Myers–Briggs Type

Based on the work of psychologist Carl Jung, the Myers–Briggs Type Indicator (MBTI) is the most widely used personality assessment instrument in the world. The MBTI, which was described in the chapter text, identifies 16 different "types," shown with their dominant characteristics in the preceding chart. Remember that no one is a pure type, but each individual has preferences for introversion versus extroversion, sensing versus intuition, thinking versus feeling, and judging versus perceiving. Read the description of your type as determined by your scores in the survey. Do you believe the description fits your personality?

Source: From Dorothy Marcic, *Organizational Behavior*, 4th ed. © 1995 South-Western, Cengage Learning. Reproduced by permission. www.cengage.com/permissions.

Group Learning

Attributions

1. Divide into groups of two students each.
2. Person 1 reads only situation 1.
3. Person 2 reads only situation 2.
4. Each person individually circles the correct answer.
5. Each person in the pair then explains his or her own answer for the situation.
6. Do you understand why the answers might be different?
7. The instructor will then lead a discussion about fundamental attribution error.

Situation 1 You are the newly appointed manager of a bank branch with eight employees. During your second week on the job you notice that Chris, one of the tellers, has been late to work three days in a row. You don't know him well and can only guess the reasons for his tardiness, but you also noticed that he tends to return to work from his lunch break later than other tellers.

Based on the preceding information, what do you think is the most likely reason that Chris was late (circle one of the numbers):

1. He is not an organized and punctual person, and arriving on time is not very important to him.
2. He got caught in heavy traffic because of road construction or some other hazardous situation.

Situation 2 You are the newly appointed manager of a bank branch with eight employees. During your second week on the job you notice that Chris, one of the tellers, has been late to work three days in a row. You don't know him well and can only guess the reasons for this tardiness, but you also noticed that George, who lives near Chris, was late as well during these three days.

Based on the above, what do you think is the most likely reason that Chris was late (circle one of the numbers):

3. He is not an organized and punctual person, and arriving on time is not very important for him.
4. He got caught in heavy traffic because of road construction or some other hazardous situation that was beyond his control.

Developed by Jacob Eisenberg, University College Dublin, Ireland. Used with permission.

Action Learning

1. On your own, complete the following table below, making assessments of your family members according to the Myers–Briggs Type Indicator. Include some notes on why you have chosen each type for that particular person.
2. Talk over these assessments with at least one person in your family and try to listen to that other person's opinions, changing any of your own assessments as you think necessary.
3. In class in groups of three to four students, share your results and talk about why you think each person is a certain type and if you changed any assessments after the discussion with a family members. Also talk about how the combination of personality types has affected your family.
4. Your instructor may choose to have you write a paper on your assessments.

	Introvert or Extrovert?	Sensing or Intuition?	Thinking or Feeling?	Perceptive or Judging?
Mother				
Father				
Sibling				
Sibling				
Other				
Other				
Other				

Ethical Dilemma

SHOULD I FUDGE THE NUMBERS?

Sara MacIntosh recently joined MicroPhone, a large telecommunications company, to take over the implementation of a massive customer-service training project. The program was created by Kristin Cole, head of human resources and Sara's new boss. According to the grapevine, Kristin was hoping this project alone would give her the "star quality" she needed to earn a coveted promotion. Industry competition was heating up, and MicroPhone's strategy called for being the best at customer service, which meant having the most highly trained people in the industry, especially those who worked directly with customers. Kristin's new training program called for an average of one full week of intense customer-service training for each of 3,000 people at a price tag of about $40 million.

Kristin put together a team of overworked staffers to develop the training program, but now she needed someone well qualified and dedicated to manage and implement the project. Sara, with eight years of experience, a long list of accomplishments, and advanced degrees in finance and organizational behavior, seemed perfect for the job. However, during a thorough review of the proposal, Sara discovered some assumptions built into the formulas that raised red flags. She approached Dan Sotal, the team's coordinator, about her concerns, but the more Dan tried to explain how the financial projections were derived, the more Sara realized that Kristin's proposal was seriously flawed. No matter how she tried to work them out, the most that could be squeezed out of the $40 million budget was 20 hours of training per person, not the 40 hours everyone expected for such a high price tag.

Sara knew that, although the proposal had been largely developed before she came on board, it would bear her signature. As she carefully described the problems with the proposal to Kristin and outlined the potentially devastat-ing consequences, Kristin impatiently tapped her pencil. Finally, she stood up, leaned forward, and interrupted Sara, quietly saying, "Sara, make the numbers work so that it adds up to 40 hours and stays within the $40 million budget." Sara glanced up and replied, "I don't think it can be done unless we either change the number of employees who are to be trained or the cost figure . . ." Kristin's smile froze on her face and her eyes began to narrow as she again interrupted. "I don't think you understand what I'm saying. We have too much at stake here. *Make the previous numbers work.*" Stunned, Sara belatedly began to realize that Kristin was ordering her to fudge the numbers. She felt an anxiety attack coming on as she wondered what she should do.

What Would You Do?

1. Make the previous numbers work. Kristin and the entire team have put massive amounts of time into the project, and they all expect you to be a team player. You don't want to let them down. Besides, this project is a great opportunity for you in a highly visible position.

2. Stick to your principles and refuse to fudge the numbers. Tell Kristin you will work overtime to help develop an alternate proposal that stays within the budget by providing more training to employees who work directly with customers and fewer training hours for those who don't have direct customer contact.

3. Go to the team and tell team members what you've been asked to do. If they refuse to support you, then threaten to reveal the true numbers to the CEO and board members.

SOURCE: Adapted from Doug Wallace, "Fudge the Numbers or Leave," *Business Ethics* (May–June 1996): 58–59. Copyright 1996 by New Mountain Media LLC. Reproduced with permission of New Mountain Media LLC in the format Textbook via Copyright Clearance Center.

12

Chapter Twelve

Leadership

LEARNING OBJECTIVES

After studying this chapter, you should be able to:

1 Define leadership and explain its importance for organizations.

2 Describe how leadership is changing in today's organizations.

3 Identify personal characteristics associated with effective leaders.

4 Define task-oriented behavior and people-oriented behavior and explain how these categories are used to evaluate and adapt leadership style.

5 Describe Hersey and Blanchard's situational theory and its application to subordinate participation.

6 Discuss how leadership fits the organizational situation and how organizational characteristics can substitute for leadership behaviors.

7 Describe transformational leadership and when it should be used.

8 Explain how followership is related to effective leadership.

9 Identify sources of leader power and the tactics leaders use to influence others.

10 Explain servant leadership and moral leadership and their importance in contemporary organizations.

New Manager's Questions

Please circle your opinion below each of the following statements.

1 A strong, healthy ego helps a leader to be more effective and to take charge.

STRONGLY AGREE < < <   > > > STRONGLY DISAGREE

1	2	3	4	5

2 Good leaders are participative, engaged, and supportive.

STRONGLY AGREE < < <   > > > STRONGLY DISAGREE

1	2	3	4	5

3 Leaders should amass as much power as they can; it helps them get things done.

STRONGLY AGREE < < <   > > > STRONGLY DISAGREE

1	2	3	4	5

In the previous chapter, we explored differences in attitudes and personality that affect behavior. Some of the most important attitudes for the organization's success are those of its leaders because their attitudes and behaviors play a critical role in shaping employee attitudes such as their job satisfaction and organizational commitment. Yet there are as many variations among leaders as there are among other individuals, and many different styles of leadership can be effective.

Different leaders behave in different ways, depending on their individual differences as well as their followers' needs and the organizational situation. Consider the differing styles of Pat McGovern, founder and chair of IDG, a technology publishing and research firm that owns magazines such as *CIO*, *PC World*, and *Computerworld*; and Tom Siebel, chief executive officer (CEO) of software company Siebel Systems. McGovern treats employees to lunch at the Ritz on their 10th anniversary with IDG to tell them how important

NEW MANAGER'S SELF-TEST

What's Your Personal Style?

Ideas about effective leadership change over time. To understand your approach to leadership, think about your personal style toward others or toward a student group to which you belong and then answer each item below as Mostly True or Mostly False for you.

	MOSTLY TRUE	MOSTLY FALSE
1. I am a modest, unassuming person.	_____	_____
2. When a part of a group, I am more concerned about how the group does than how I do.	_____	_____
3. I prefer to lead with quiet modesty rather than personal assertiveness.	_____	_____
4. I feel personally responsible if the team does poorly.	_____	_____
5. I act with quiet determination.	_____	_____
6. I resolve to do whatever needs doing to produce the best result for the group.	_____	_____
7. I am proactive to help the group succeed.	_____	_____
8. I facilitate high standards for my group's performance.	_____	_____

SCORING AND INTERPRETATION: A recent view of leadership called level-five leadership says that the most successful leaders have two prominent qualities: humility and will. Give yourself 1 point for each item marked Mostly True.

Humility: Items 1, 2, 3, 4
Will: Items 5, 6, 7, 8

Humility means a quiet, modest, self-effacing manner. A humble person puts group or organizational success ahead of one's personal success. *Will* means a quiet but fierce resolve to stay the course to achieve the group's desired outcome and to help the group succeed. The traits of humility and will are opposite the traditional idea of leadership as loud and self-centered. If you scored 3 or 4 on either humility or will, then you are on track to level-five leadership, which says that ordinary people often make excellent leaders.

they are to the success of the company. He personally thanks almost every person in every business unit once a year, which takes about a month of his time. Managers provide him with a list of accomplishments for all their direct reports, which McGovern memorizes the night before his visit so he can congratulate people on specific accomplishments. In addition to appreciating and caring about employees, McGovern also shows that he believes in them by decentralizing decision making so that people have the autonomy to make their own decisions about how best to accomplish organizational goals. Tom Siebel, in contrast, is known as a disciplined and dispassionate manager who remains somewhat aloof from his employees and likes to maintain strict control over every aspect of the business. He enforces a dress code, sets tough goals and standards, and holds people strictly accountable. "We go to work to realize our professional ambitions, not to have a good time," Siebel says.[1] Both Siebel and McGovern have been successful as leaders, although their styles are quite different.

This chapter explores one of the most widely discussed and researched topics in management—leadership. Here we define leadership and explore how managers develop leadership qualities. We look at some important leadership approaches for contemporary organizations, as well as examine trait, behavioral, and contingency theories of leadership effectiveness, discuss charismatic and transformational leadership, explore the role of followership, and consider how leaders use power and influence to get things done. The final section of the chapter discusses servant leadership and moral leadership, two enduring approaches that have received renewed emphasis in recent years. Chapters 12 through 15 will look in detail at many of the functions of leadership, including employee motivation, communication, and encouraging teamwork.

Understand your own beliefs about leadership. Go to the Self Learning exercise on page 406 of this textbook to learn more about your beliefs and understanding.

The Nature of Leadership

Perhaps no topic is more important to organizational success than leadership. In most situations, a team, military unit, or volunteer organization is only as good as its leader. Consider the situation in Iraq as U.S. military advisors have worked to build Iraqi forces that can take over security duties without support from coalition troops. Many trainers say they encounter excellent individual soldiers and junior leaders but that many of the senior commanders

leadership
The ability to influence people toward the attainment of organizational goals.

are stuck in old authoritarian patterns that undermine their units. Whether an Iraqi unit succeeds or fails often comes down to one person—its commander—so advisors are putting emphasis on finding and strengthening good leaders.[2] Top leaders make a difference in business organizations as well. Baron Partners Fund picks stocks based largely on an evaluation of companies' senior executives because it believes top leaders who are smart, honorable, and treat their employees right typically lead their companies to greater financial success and greater shareholder returns.[3] The approach has proved successful, helping Baron's diversified stock fund consistently perform well.

Among all the ideas and writings about leadership, three aspects stand out—people, influence, and goals. Leadership occurs among people, involves the use of influence, and is used to attain goals.[4] *Influence* means that the relationship among people is not passive. Moreover, influence is designed to achieve some end or goal. Thus, **leadership** as defined here is the ability to influence people toward the attainment of

© ED ZURGA / AP IMAGES

CEO Matt Rubel moved Payless Shoes from bargain shopping to the frontlines of fashion. Under Rubel's leadership, Kansas-based Payless opened a design studio in Manhattan and partnered with young designers to offer exclusive designer shoes and handbags. He took the helm in 2005, and in 2006 Payless nearly doubled its earnings. Thanks to Rubel's makeover, Payless is luring fashion-conscious consumers who wouldn't have considered shopping there before. In 2007, *Footwear News* named Rubel its "Person of the Year."

·······> **CONCEPT CONNECTION** <·······

A new leader is emerging. He lives with his pet snail, Gary, in a pineapple at the bottom of the ocean and adores his fry-cook job at the Krusty Krab. He's the son of two round sea sponges, and he's a favorite television character of President Barack Obama. SpongeBob seems to get into trouble a lot. In fact, that is his gift. He hangs out with his starfish pal, Patrick, and his thrill-seeking friend Sandy Cheeks, a squirrel. SpongeBob has had some harrowing experiences and has learned important leadership skills:

1. Be resilient. Today it's all about the globalization and learning multicultural skills. When SpongeBob is marooned in a frightening abyss, he is forced to find his willpower and resources to learn a new dialect, find some chow, and maneuver his way back to Bikini Bottom. (Episode: "Rock Bottom.")

2. Recruit the finest. When he learns that his superhero friends and crime fighters Mermaidman and Barnacleboy have been relegated to a nursing home, SpongeBob convinces them to come out of retirement to fulfill their destinies: ward off evildoers from Goo Lagoon. (Episode: "Mermaidman and Barnacleman.")

3. No resting on laurels. SpongeBob is in a rut, but a good one. After becoming employee of the month 26 times straight, he feels himself at risk of losing the title. He compulsively strives to outcook, outclean, and outwork rival Squidward. "Having pride in your work," says SpongeBob, "is the only thing that makes it all worthwhile." (Episode: "Employee of the Month.")

4. Innovate and innovate. Good leaders are those that follow the rules, while great leaders change them. SpongeBob suggests multicolored "pretty parties," which are rejected by management. Undaunted, he sets out on his own, becoming a wild success. Showing cool business savvy, he sells his idea in the nick of time. (Episode: "Patty Hype.")

5. Recognize employees' limits. In order to cut costs, Mr. Krab, the ultimate miser, charges workers for such infractions as "existing" and "breathing." Squidward and SpongeBob complain and they are fired, causing them to "dismantle the establishment," an objective they take literally. (Episode: "Squid of Strike.")

SOURCES: Daniel Bubbeo, "Soakin' It All in 'SpongeBob SquarePants' Hits a Round Number with a Huge 10th Birthday Bash," *Newsday*, July 12, 2009, p. C 14; Lucas Conley, "Leadership Secrets of SpongeBob SquarePants," *Fast Company*, Sept 2004, p. 45.

goals. This definition captures the idea that leaders are involved with other people in the achievement of goals. Leadership is reciprocal, occurring *among* people.[5] Leadership is a "people" activity that is distinct from administrative paper shuffling or problem-solving activities. Role models for leadership can come from wide and varied sources, as shown in the Spotlight on Skills.

Contemporary Leadership

The concept of leadership evolves as the needs of organizations change. In other words, the environmental context in which leadership is practiced influences which approach might be most effective, as well as what kinds of leaders are most admired by society. The technology, economic conditions, labor conditions, and social and cultural mores of the times all play a role. A significant influence on leadership styles in recent years is the turbulence and uncertainty of the environment. Ethical and economic difficulties, corporate governance concerns, globalization, changes in technology, new ways of working, shifting employee expectations, and significant social transitions have contributed to a shift in how we think about and practice leadership.

Of particular interest for leadership in contemporary times is a *postheroic approach* that focuses on the subtle, unseen, and often unrewarded acts that good leaders perform every day rather than on the grand accomplishments of celebrated business heroes.[6] During the 1980s and 1990s, leadership became equated with larger-than-life personalities, strong egos, and personal ambitions. In contrast, the postheroic leader's major characteristic is humility.[7] **Humility** means being unpretentious and modest rather than arrogant and prideful. Humble leaders don't have to be in the center of things. They quietly build strong, enduring companies by developing and supporting others rather than touting their own abilities and accomplishments. The idea of the leader as a lone hero is deeply embedded in our culture, but the challenges of recent years have spurred leaders to take a more collaborative, integrated approach. A study by the Center for Creative Leadership found that more than 84 percent of business leaders surveyed agree that the definition of effective leadership has changed since the turn of the century, with many of them citing interdependence as a key to success.[8] Two approaches that are in tune with postheroic leadership for today's times are level-five leadership and interactive leadership.

LEVEL-FIVE LEADERSHIP

A study conducted by Jim Collins and his research associates identified the critical importance of what Collins calls *level-five leadership* in transforming companies from merely good to truly great organizations.[9] As described in his book *Good to Great: Why Some Companies Make the Leap . . . and Others Don't*, level-five leadership refers to the highest level in a hierarchy of manager capabilities, as illustrated in Exhibit 12.1.

A key characteristic of level-five leaders is an almost complete lack of ego coupled with a fierce resolve to do what is best for the organization. In contrast to the view of great leaders as larger-than-life personalities with strong egos and big ambitions, level-five leaders often seem shy and unpretentious. Although they accept full responsibility for mistakes, poor results, or failures, level-five leaders give credit for successes to other people. For example, Joseph F. Cullman III, former CEO of Philip Morris, staunchly refused to accept credit for the company's long-term success, citing his great colleagues, successors, and predecessors as the reason for the accomplishments. Another example is Darwin E. Smith. When he was promoted to CEO of Kimberly-Clark, Smith questioned whether the board really wanted to appoint him because he didn't believe he had the qualifications a CEO needed.

What did your score on the New Manager's Self-Test on page 380 say about your humility? Go to the Ethical Dilemma on page 407, which pertains to postheroic leadership for turbulent times.

humility
Being unpretentious and modest rather than arrogant and prideful.

EXHIBIT 12.1
Level-Five
Hierarchy

Level 5: Level 5 Executive
Builds enduring greatness through a paradoxical blend of personal humility and professional will.

Level 4: Effective Leader
Catalyzes commitment to and vigorous pursuit of a clear and compelling vision, stimulating higher performance standards.

Level 3: Competent Manager
Organizes people and resources toward the effective and efficient pursuit of predetermined objectives.

Level 2: Contributing Team Member
Contributes individual capabilities to the achievement of group objectives and works effectively with others in a group setting.

Level 1: Highly Capable Individual
Makes productive contributions through talent, knowledge, skills, and good work habits.

SOURCE: Jim Collins, *Good to Great: Why Some Companies Make the Leap . . . and Others Don't* (New York: HarperCollins, 2001), 20. Copyright © 2001 by Jim Collins. Reprinted with permission from Jim Collins.

Few people have ever heard of Darwin Smith, who led Kimberly-Clark from 1971 to 1991—and that's probably just the way he wanted it. Smith was somewhat shy and awkward in social situations, and he was never featured in splashy articles in *Fortune* magazine or the *Wall Street Journal*. Yet anyone who interpreted his appearance and demeanor as a sign of ineptness soon learned differently. Smith demonstrated an aggressive determination to revive Kimberly-Clark, which at the time was a stodgy old paper company that had seen years of falling stock prices. When he took over, the company's core business was in coated paper. Convinced that this approach doomed the company to mediocrity, Smith took the controversial step of selling the company's paper mills and investing all its resources in consumer products such as Kleenex and Huggies diapers.

Over his 20 years as CEO, Smith turned Kimberly-Clark into the leading consumer paper products company in the world, beating rivals Scott Paper and Procter & Gamble. The company generated cumulative stock returns that were 4.1 times greater than those of the general market. When asked about his exceptional performance after his retirement, Smith said simply, "I never stopped trying to become qualified for the job."[10]

As the example of Darwin Smith illustrates, despite their personal humility, level-five leaders have a strong will to do whatever it takes to produce great and lasting results for their organizations. They are extremely ambitious for their companies rather than for themselves. This goal becomes highly evident in the area of succession planning. Level-five leaders develop a solid corps of leaders throughout the organization so that when they leave the company can continue to thrive and grow even stronger. Egocentric leaders, by contrast, often set their successors up for failure because it will be a testament to their own greatness if the company doesn't perform well without them. Rather than building an organization around "a genius with a thousand helpers," level-five leaders want everyone to develop to their fullest potential.

INTERACTIVE LEADERSHIP

The focus on minimizing personal ambition and developing others is also a hallmark of interactive leadership. **Interactive leadership** means that the leader favors a consensual and collaborative process, and influence derives from relationships rather than position power and formal authority.[11] For example, Nancy Hawthorne, former chief financial officer at Continental Cablevision Inc., felt that her role as a leader was to delegate tasks and authority to others and to help them be more effective. "I was being traffic cop and coach and facilitator," Hawthorne says. "I was always into building a department that hummed."[12]

Interest in interactive leadership grew partly from observations about the differences in how women and men lead. Research indicates that women's style of leadership is typically different from most men's and is particularly suited to today's organizations.[13] Using data from actual performance evaluations, one study found that when rated by peers, subordinates, and bosses, female managers score significantly higher than men on abilities such as motivating others, fostering communication, and listening.[14] Another study of leaders and their followers in organizations including businesses, universities, and government agencies found that women typically score higher on social and emotional skills, which are crucial for interactive leadership.[15]

As a new manager, will your interpersonal style fit the contemporary leadership approaches described in the text? To find out, complete the following New Manager's Self Test.

interactive leadership
A leadership style characterized by values such as inclusion, collaboration, relationship building, and caring.

Assess Your Answer

1 A strong, healthy ego helps a leader to be more effective and to take charge.

ANSWER: Current research has shown that egoless leaders are actually the most effective and create the most productive and profitable companies.

However, men can be interactive leaders as well, as illustrated by the example of Pat McGovern of IDG earlier in the chapter. For McGovern, having personal contact with employees and letting them know they're appreciated is one of a leader's primary responsibilities. The characteristics associated with interactive leadership are emerging as valuable qualities for both male and female leaders in today's workplace. Values associated with interactive leadership include personal humility, inclusion, relationship building, and caring.

NEW MANAGER'S SELF-TEST

Interpersonal Patterns

The majority of a new manager's work is accomplished through interpersonal relationships. To understand your relationship pattern, consider the following 20 verbs. All of them describe some of the ways people feel and act from time to time. Think about your behavior in groups. How do you feel and act in groups? Check the five verbs that best describe your behavior in groups as you see it.

acquiesce	coordinate	lead
advise	criticize	oblige
agree	direct	relinquish
analyze	disapprove	resist
assist	evade	retreat
concede	initiate	withdraw
concur	judge	

SCORING AND INTERPRETATION: Two underlying patterns of interpersonal behavior are represented in the preceding list: *dominance* (authority or control) and *sociability* (intimacy or friendliness). Most individuals tend either to like to control things (high dominance) or to let others control things (low dominance). Similarly, most persons tend to be either warm and personal (high sociability) or somewhat distant and impersonal (low sociability). In the following diagram, circle the five verbs in the list that you used to describe yourself. The set of 10 verbs in either horizontal row (sociability dimension) or vertical column (dominance dimension) in which three or more are circled represents your tendency in interpersonal behavior.

	High Dominance	Low Dominance
High Sociability	advises	acquiesces
	coordinates	agrees
	directs	assists
	initiates	concurs
	leads	obliges
Low Sociability	analyzes	concedes
	criticizes	evades
	disapproves	relinquishes
	judges	retreats
	resists	withdraws

Your behavior pattern suggested in the diagram is a clue to your interpersonal style as a new manager. Which of the quadrants provides the best description of you? Is that the type of leader you aspire to become? Generally speaking, the high sociability and high dominance pattern reflects the type of leader to which many new managers aspire. How does your pattern correspond to the level-five and interactive leadership patterns described in the text?

SOURCE: From David W. Johnson and Frank P. Johnson, *Joining Together: Group Theory and Group Skills*, 8th ed. Published by Allyn and Bacon, Boston, MA. Copyright © 2003 by Pearson Education. Reproduced by permission of the publisher.

From Management to Leadership

Hundreds of books and articles have been written in recent years about the differences between management and leadership. Good management is essential in organizations, yet good managers also have to be leaders because distinctive qualities are associated with management and leadership that provide different strengths for the organization. As shown in Exhibit 12.2, management and leadership reflect two different sets of qualities and skills that frequently overlap within a single individual. A person might have more of one set of qualities than the other, but ideally a manager develops a balance of both manager and leader qualities.[16]

A primary distinction between management and leadership is that management promotes stability, order, and problem solving within the existing organizational structure and systems. This ensures that suppliers are paid, customers invoiced, products and services produced on time, and so forth. Leadership, on the other hand, promotes vision, creativity, and change. Leadership means questioning the status quo so that outdated, unproductive, or socially irresponsible norms can be replaced to meet new challenges. Consider the challenge Susan Decker faces as she runs the day-to-day business as the new president of Yahoo. Decker will need excellent management skills to improve financial results, oversee operational details, make tough decisions, and work with managers to execute Yahoo's strategy. She will also need consummate leadership abilities to create and inspire people with a vision that can help Yahoo emerge from under the shadow of search leader Google to find the key to recruiting and retaining top-notch talent and to rebuild the sagging morale inside the company.[17]

Leadership cannot replace management; it should be in addition to management. Good management is needed to help the organization meet current commitments, while good leadership is needed to move the organization into the future. Leadership's power comes from being built on the foundation of a well-managed organization.

To be a good manager, you must organize resources; to be a good leader, you must help others follow the vision.

traits
Distinguishing personal characteristics such as intelligence, values, and appearance.

EXHIBIT 12.2
Leader and Manager Qualities

- - - - - - - - - - -

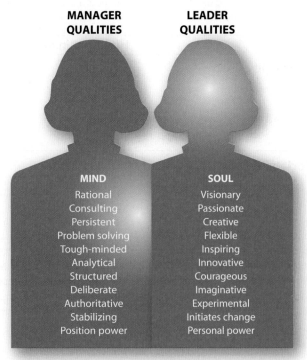

MANAGER QUALITIES

LEADER QUALITIES

MIND	SOUL
Rational	Visionary
Consulting	Passionate
Persistent	Creative
Problem solving	Flexible
Tough-minded	Inspiring
Analytical	Innovative
Structured	Courageous
Deliberate	Imaginative
Authoritative	Experimental
Stabilizing	Initiates change
Position power	Personal power

SOURCE: Based on Genevieve Capowski, "Anatomy of a Leader: Where Are the Leaders of Tomorrow?" *Management Review* (Mar. 1994): 12.

Leadership Traits

Early efforts to understand leadership success focused on the leader's traits. **Traits** are the distinguishing personal characteristics of a leader such as intelligence, honesty, self-confidence, and even appearance. The early research looked at leaders who had achieved a level of greatness, and hence it was referred to as the *great man* approach. The idea was relatively simple: Find out what made these people great and select future leaders who already exhibited the same traits or could be trained to develop them. Generally, early research found only a weak relationship between personal traits and leader success.[18]

In recent years, interest in examining leadership traits has reemerged. In addition to personality traits, the physical, social, and work-related characteristics of leaders have been studied.[19] Exhibit 12.3 summarizes the physical, social, and personal leadership characteristics that have received the greatest research support. However, these characteristics do not stand alone. The appropriateness of a trait or set of traits depends on the leadership situation. The same traits do not apply to every organization or situation. Further studies expand the understanding of leadership beyond the personal traits of the individual to focus on the dynamics of the relationship between leaders and followers.

Behavioral Approaches

The inability to define effective leadership based solely on traits led to an interest in looking at the behavior of leaders and how it might contribute to leadership success or failure. Two basic leadership behaviors identified as important for leadership are *task-oriented behavior* and *people-oriented behavior*. These two *metacategories*, or broadly defined behavior categories, were found to be applicable to effective leadership in a variety of situations and time periods.[20] Although they are not the only important leadership behaviors, concern for tasks and concern for people must be shown at some reasonable level. Thus, many approaches to understanding leadership use these metacategories as a basis for study and comparison. Important research programs on leadership behavior were conducted at Ohio State University, the University of Michigan, and the University of Texas.

© DENESE IZZARD-FERRIS/DENESE IZZARD-FERRIS PHOTOGRAPHY

Linda St. Clair (right) has been both an artistic-director of theater productions and a personnel manager for a technology firm. Her interactive leadership style worked equally well in both settings. As a theater director, she articulated a clear overarching vision, supported individual artists, encouraged collaborative relationships—and then let the creative process take its course. The job of a manager isn't very different. "When I was at my best in the corporation," she recalls, "I helped people get what they needed to be effectively creative." Good leaders, St. Clair believes, know how to build relationships and act not as commanders but as coaches, guides, and mentors.

········> CONCEPT CONNECTION <········

EXHIBIT 12.3
Personal Characteristics of Leaders

Physical Characteristics	Personality	Work-Related Characteristics
Energy	Self-confidence	Achievement drive, desire to excel
Physical stamina	Honesty and integrity	Conscientiousness in pursuit of goals
	Enthusiasm	Persistence against obstacles, tenacity
	Desire to lead	
	Independence	
Intelligence and Ability	**Social Characteristics**	**Social Background**
Intelligence, cognitive ability	Sociability, interpersonal skills	Education
Knowledge	Cooperativeness	Mobility
Judgment, decisiveness	Ability to enlist cooperation	
	Tact, diplomacy	

SOURCES: Based on Bernard M. Bass, *Bass & Stogdill's Handbook of Leadership: Theory, Research, and Managerial Applications*, 3rd ed. (New York: The Free Press, 1990): 80–81; and S. A. Kirkpatrick and E. A. Locke, "Leadership: Do Traits Matter?" *Academy of Management Executive* 5(2) (1991): 48–60.

OHIO STATE STUDIES

Researchers at Ohio State University surveyed leaders to study hundreds of dimensions of leader behavior.[21] They identified two major behaviors: consideration and initiating structure.

Consideration falls in the category of people-oriented behavior and is the extent to which the leader is mindful of subordinates, respects their ideas and feelings, and establishes mutual trust. Considerate leaders are friendly, provide open communication, develop teamwork, and are oriented toward their subordinates' welfare.

Initiating structure is the degree of task behavior—that is, the extent to which the leader is task oriented and directs subordinate work activities toward goal attainment. Leaders with this style typically give instructions, spend time planning, emphasize deadlines, and provide explicit schedules of work activities.

Consideration and initiating structure are independent of each other, which means that a leader with a high degree of consideration may be either high or low on initiating structure. A leader may have any of four styles: high initiating structure–low consideration, high initiating structure–high consideration, low initiating structure–low consideration, or low initiating structure–high consideration. The Ohio State research found that the high consideration–high initiating structure style achieved better performance and greater satisfaction than the other leader styles. The value of the high–high style is illustrated by Bob LaDouceur, the coach of an extraordinary high school football team.

As a manager, work to have both consideration and structure to achieve a balance.

THE DE LA SALLE SPARTANS

The De La Salle Spartans football team pulled off a 151-game winning streak that lasted for a decade—despite the fact that many of the players had previously been derided as "under-sized" and "untalented." Year after year, competing against bigger schools and tougher players, the De La Salle Spartans just kept on winning.

Years ago, coach Bob LaDouceur sized up his team of demoralized players and made a decision. He was going to teach these guys what it takes to win and then make it a day-today process. LaDouceur directs close attention to the tasks needed to accomplish the goal of winning. He keeps his players on a year-round strength and conditioning program. Each practice is methodical, and LaDouceur tells his players to leave every practice just a little bit better than they were when it started.

However, the coach hasn't just institutionalized the process of drills, workouts, and practices. He has also institutionalized a process of building bonds and intimacy among his players. "If a team has no soul," LaDouceur says, "you're just wasting your time." Tasks are important, but for LaDouceur, people always come first. "It's not about how we're getting better physically, it's about how we're getting better as people," he says. During the off season, players go camping and rafting together and volunteer for community service. When the season starts, the team attends chapel together for readings and songs. After every practice, a dinner is held at a player's home. As tensions build during the season, players are encouraged to speak their hearts, to confess their fears and shortcomings, and to talk about their commitments and expectations of themselves for the next game.[22]

consideration
A type of behavior that describes the extent to which the leader is sensitive to subordinates, respects their ideas and feelings, and establishes mutual trust.

initiating structure
A type of leader behavior that describes the extent to which the leader is task oriented and directs subordinate work activities toward goal attainment.

The high–high leadership style of coach Bob LaDouceur has accomplished remarkable results, yet research indicates that the high–high style is not always necessarily the best. Studies suggest that effective leaders may be high on consideration and low on initiating structure or low on consideration and high on initiating structure, depending on the situation.[23]

MICHIGAN STUDIES

Studies at the University of Michigan at about the same time took a different approach by comparing the behavior of effective and ineffective supervisors.[24] The most effective supervisors were those who focused on the subordinates' human needs to "build effective work groups with high performance goals." The Michigan researchers used the term *employee-centered leaders* for leaders who established high performance goals and displayed

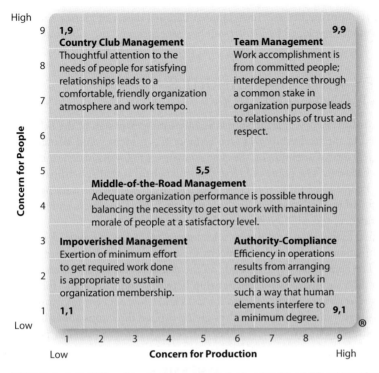

SOURCE: The Leadership Grid figure, Paternalism figure, and Opportunism figure from Robert R. Blake and Anne Adams McCanse, *Leadership Dilemmas-Grid Solutions* (formerly the *Managerial Grid* by Robert R. Blake and Jane S. Mouton) (Houston: Gulf Publishing Company, 1991). Grid figure, p. 29; Paternalism figure, p. 30; Opportunism figure, p. 31. Copyright © 1991 by Blake and Mouton, and Scientific Methods, Inc. Reproduced by permission of the owners.

EXHIBIT 12.4
The Leadership Grid Figure

supportive behavior toward subordinates. The less-effective leaders were called *job-centered leaders*; these leaders tended to be less concerned with goal achievement and human needs in favor of meeting schedules, keeping costs low, and achieving production efficiency.

THE LEADERSHIP GRID

Building on the work of the Ohio State and Michigan studies, Blake and Mouton of the University of Texas proposed a two-dimensional theory called the managerial grid, which was later restated by Blake and McCanse as the **leadership grid**.[25] The model and five of its seven major management styles are depicted in Exhibit 12.4. Each axis on the grid is a 9-point scale, with 1 meaning low concern and 9 meaning high concern.

Team management (9, 9) often is considered the most effective style and is recommended for leaders because organization members work together to accomplish tasks. *Country club management* (1, 9) occurs when primary emphasis is given to people rather than to work outputs. *Authority-compliance management* (9, 1) occurs when efficiency in operations is the dominant orientation. *Middle-of-the-road management* (5, 5) reflects a moderate amount of concern for both people and production. *Impoverished management* (1, 1) means the absence of a management philosophy; managers exert little effort toward interpersonal relationships or work accomplishment.

Contingency Approaches

How can two people with widely different styles both be effective leaders? The next group of theories builds on the leader–follower relationship of behavioral approaches to explore how the organizational situation influences leader effectiveness. These theories are termed

As a new manager, come to realize that both task-oriented behavior and people-oriented behavior are important, although some situations call for a greater degree of one over the other.

leadership grid
A two-dimensional leadership theory that measures the leader's concern for people and for production.

contingency approach
A model of leadership that describes the relationship between leadership styles and specific organizational situations.

situational theory
A contingency approach to leadership that links the leader's behavioral style with the task readiness of subordinates.

contingency approaches and include the situational theory of Hersey and Blanchard, the leadership model developed by Fiedler and his associates, and the substitutes-for-leadership concept.

HERSEY AND BLANCHARD'S SITUATIONAL THEORY

The **situational theory** of leadership is an interesting extension of the behavioral theories summarized in the leadership grid (see Exhibit 12.4). Hersey and Blanchard's approach focuses a great deal of attention on the characteristics of followers in determining appropriate leadership behavior. The point of Hersey and Blanchard is that subordinates vary in readiness level. People low in task readiness—because of little ability or training or insecurity—need a different leadership style than those who are high in readiness and have good ability, skills, confidence, and willingness to work.[26]

According to the situational theory, a leader can adopt one of four leadership styles based on a combination of relationship (concern for people) and task (concern for production) behavior. The appropriate style depends on the readiness level of followers.

Exhibit 12.5 summarizes the relationship between leader style and follower readiness. The *telling style* reflects a high concern for tasks and a low concern for people and relationships. This highly directive style involves giving explicit directions about how tasks should be accomplished. The *selling style* is based on a high concern for both people and tasks.

EXHIBIT 12.5

Hersey and Blanchard's Situational Theory of Leadership

- - - - - - - - - - - -

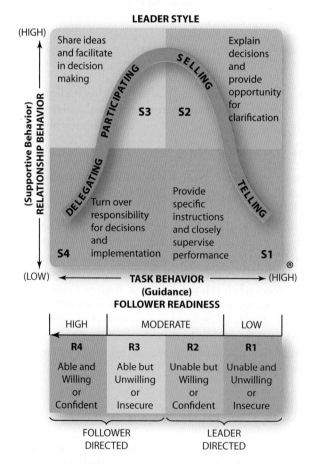

With this approach, the leader explains decisions and gives subordinates a chance to ask questions, and gain clarity and understanding about work tasks. The next leader behavior style, the *participating style*, is based on a combination of high concern for people and relationships and low concern for production tasks. The leader shares ideas with subordinates, gives them a chance to participate, and facilitates decision making. The fourth style, the *delegating style*, reflects a low concern for both relationships and tasks. This leader style provides little direction and little support because the leader turns over responsibility for decisions and their implementation to subordinates.

The bell-shaped curve in Exhibit 12.5 is called a *prescriptive* curve because it indicates when each leader style should be used. The readiness level of followers is indicated in the lower part of the exhibit. R1 is low readiness, and R4 represents high readiness. The telling style is for low-readiness followers because people are unable or unwilling—because of poor ability and skills, little experience, or insecurity—to take responsibility for their own task behavior. The leader is specific, telling people exactly what to do, how to do it, and when. The selling and participating styles work for followers at moderate readiness levels. For example, followers might lack some education and experience for the job but have high confidence, interest, and willingness to learn. As shown in the exhibit, the selling style is effective in this situation because it involves giving direction but also includes seeking input from others and clarifying tasks rather than simply instructing that they be performed. When followers have the necessary skills and experience but are somewhat insecure in their abilities or lack high willingness, the participating style enables the leader to guide followers' development and act as a resource for advice and assistance. When followers demonstrate high readiness—that is, they have high levels of education, experience, and readiness to accept responsibility for their own task behavior—the delegating style can effectively be used. Because of the high readiness level of followers, the leader can delegate responsibility for decisions and their implementation to subordinates who have the skills, abilities, and positive attitudes to follow through. The leader provides a general goal and sufficient authority to do the task as followers see fit.

To apply the Hersey and Blanchard model, the leader diagnoses the readiness level of followers and adopts the appropriate style—telling, selling, participating, or delegating. Using the incorrect style can hurt morale and performance. Consider what happened when Lawrence Summers, former president of Harvard University, tried to use a primarily telling style with followers who were at high readiness levels. Summers employed an assertive top-down style with followers who think of themselves not as employees but as partners in an academic enterprise. Faculty members at most universities have long been accustomed to decentralized, democratic decision making and having a say in matters such as department mergers or new programs of study. Summers made many decisions on his own that followers thought should be put to a faculty vote. Summers's leadership approach led to serious conflicts with some faculty members and demands for his ouster. Eventually, a vote of no confidence from faculty convinced Summers to resign with many of his goals and plans for the university unrealized.[27]

As a leader, only use the delegating style if the group has enough training, education, and experience; otherwise its use can be a disaster.

FIEDLER'S CONTINGENCY THEORY

Whereas Hersey and Blanchard focused on the characteristics of followers, Fiedler and his associates looked at some other elements of the organizational situation to assess when one leadership style is more effective than another.[28] The starting point for Fiedler's theory is the extent to which the leader's style is task oriented or relationship (people) oriented. Fiedler considered a person's leadership style to be relatively fixed and difficult to change; therefore, the basic idea is to match the leader's style with the situation most favorable for his or her effectiveness. By diagnosing leadership style and the organizational situation, the correct fit can be arranged.

Situation: Favorable or Unfavorable? The suitability of a person's leadership style is determined by whether the situation is favorable or unfavorable to the leader. The favorability of a leadership situation can be analyzed in terms of three elements: the quality of relationships between leader and followers, the degree of task structure, and the extent to which the leader has formal authority over followers.[29]

A situation would be considered *highly favorable* to the leader when leader–member relationships are positive, tasks are highly structured, and the leader has formal authority over followers. In this situation, followers trust, respect, and have confidence in the leader. The group's tasks are clearly defined, involve specific procedures, and have clear, explicit goals. In addition, the leader has formal authority to direct and evaluate followers, along with the power to reward or punish. A situation would be considered *highly unfavorable* to the leader when leader–member relationships are poor, tasks are highly unstructured, and the leader has little formal authority. In a highly unfavorable situation, followers have little respect for or confidence and trust in the leader. Tasks are vague and ill-defined and lacking in clear-cut procedures and guidelines. The leader has little formal authority to direct subordinates and does not have the power to issue rewards or punishments.

MATCHING LEADER STYLE TO THE SITUATION

Combining the three situational characteristics yields a variety of leadership situations, ranging from highly favorable to highly unfavorable. When Fiedler examined the relationships among leadership style and situational favorability, he found the pattern shown in Exhibit 12.6. Task-oriented leaders are more effective when the situation is either highly favorable or highly unfavorable. Relationship-oriented leaders are more effective in situations of moderate favorability.

The task-oriented leader excels in the favorable situation because everyone gets along, the task is clear, and the leader has power; all that is needed is for someone to lead the charge and provide direction. Similarly, if the situation is highly unfavorable to the leader, a great deal of structure and task direction is needed. A strong leader will define task structure and establish authority over subordinates. Because leader–member relations are poor anyway, a strong task orientation will make no difference in the leader's popularity. For example, researchers at the University of Chicago looked at CEOs of companies in turnaround

EXHIBIT 12.6
How Leader Style Fits the Situation

- - - - - - - - - - -

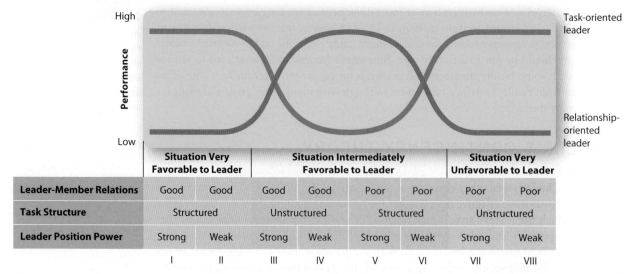

	Situation Very Favorable to Leader		Situation Intermediately Favorable to Leader				Situation Very Unfavorable to Leader	
Leader-Member Relations	Good	Good	Good	Good	Poor	Poor	Poor	Poor
Task Structure	Structured		Unstructured		Structured		Unstructured	
Leader Position Power	Strong	Weak	Strong	Weak	Strong	Weak	Strong	Weak
	I	II	III	IV	V	VI	VII	VIII

SOURCE: Based on Fred E. Fiedler, "The Effects of Leadership Training and Experience: A Contingency Model Interpretation," *Administrative Science Quarterly* 17 (1972): 455.

situations—where companies typically have high debt loads and a need to improve results in a hurry—and found that tough-minded, task-focused characteristics such as analytical skills, a focus on efficiency, and setting high standards were more valuable leader qualities than were relationships skills such as good communication, listening, and teamwork.[30]

The relationship-oriented leader performs better in situations of intermediate favorability because human-relations skills are important in achieving high group performance. In these situations, the leader may be moderately well liked, have some power, and supervise jobs that contain some ambiguity. A leader with good interpersonal skills can create a positive group atmosphere that will improve relationships, clarify task structure, and establish position power.

A leader, then, needs to know two things to use Fiedler's contingency theory. First, the leader should know whether he or she has a relationship- or task-oriented style. Second, the leader should diagnose the situation and determine whether leader–member relations, task structure, and position power are favorable or unfavorable.

Fiedler believed fitting leader style to the situation can yield big dividends in profits and efficiency.[31] On the other hand, the model has also been criticized.[32] For one thing, some researchers have challenged the idea that leaders cannot adjust their styles as situational characteristics change. Despite criticisms, Fiedler's model has continued to influence leadership studies. Fiedler's research called attention to the importance of finding the correct fit between leadership style and the situation.

SUBSTITUTES FOR LEADERSHIP

The contingency leadership approaches considered so far focus on the leaders' style, the subordinates' nature, and the situation's characteristics. The final contingency approach suggests that situational variables can be so powerful that they actually substitute for or neutralize the need for leadership.[33] This approach outlines those organizational settings in which a leadership style is unimportant or unnecessary.

Exhibit 12.7 shows the situational variables that tend to substitute for or neutralize leadership characteristics. A **substitute** for leadership makes the leadership style unnecessary or redundant. For example, highly professional subordinates who know how to do their tasks do not need a leader who initiates structure for them and tells them what to do. A **neutralizer** counteracts the leadership style and prevents the leader from displaying certain behaviors. For example, if a leader has absolutely no position power or is physically removed from subordinates, then the leader's ability to give directions to subordinates is greatly reduced.

As a new manager, remember that different situations and different followers may require different approaches to leadership.

substitute
A situational variable that makes a leadership style unnecessary or redundant.

neutralizer
A situational variable that counteracts a leadership style and prevents the leader from displaying certain behaviors.

EXHIBIT 12.7
Substitutes and Neutralizers for Leadership

Variable		Task-Oriented Leadership	People-Oriented Leadership
Organizational variables	Group cohesiveness	Substitutes for	Substitutes for
	Formalization	Substitutes for	No effect on
	Inflexibility	Neutralizes	No effect on
	Low position power	Neutralizes	Neutralizes
	Physical separation	Neutralizes	Neutralizes
Task characteristics	Highly structured task	Substitutes for	No effect on
	Automatic feedback	Substitutes for	No effect on
	Intrinsic satisfaction	No effect on	Substitutes for
Group characteristics	Professionalism	Substitutes for	Substitutes for
	Training and experience	Substitutes for	No effect on

2 Good leaders are participative, engaged, and supportive.

ANSWER: It all depends on the situation. Some circumstances call for a more authoritarian leader, and others call for more participation. Part of a leader's job is to monitor the situation and make judgments on which style is better for each situation.

As a new manager, avoid leadership overkill. Don't use a task-oriented style if the job already provides clear structure and direction. Concentrate instead on people and relationships. Remember that professional employees typically need less leadership.

charismatic leader
A leader who has the ability to motivate subordinates to transcend their expected performance.

Situational variables in Exhibit 12.7 include characteristics of the group, the task, and the organization itself. When followers are highly professional and experienced, both leadership styles are less important. People do not need much direction or consideration. With respect to task characteristics, highly structured tasks substitute for a task-oriented style, and a satisfying task substitutes for a people-oriented style. With respect to the organization itself, group cohesiveness substitutes for both leader styles. Formalized rules and procedures substitute for leader task orientation. Physical separation of leader and subordinate neutralizes both leadership styles.

The value of the situations described in Exhibit 12.7 is that they help leaders avoid leadership overkill. Leaders should adopt a style with which to complement the organizational situation. Consider the work situation for bank tellers. A bank teller performs highly structured tasks, follows clear written rules and procedures, and has little flexibility in terms of how to do the work. The head teller should not adopt a task-oriented style because the organization already provides structure and direction. The head teller should concentrate on a people-oriented style to provide a more pleasant work environment. In other organizations, if group cohesiveness or intrinsic satisfaction meets employees' social needs, then the leader is free to concentrate on task-oriented behaviors. The leader can adopt a style complementary to the organizational situation to ensure that both task needs and people needs of the work group will be met.

Leon Gorman stepped up to save the family business when his grandfather L.L. Bean died in 1967. Demonstrating visionary leadership, Gorman preserved the identity of the Maine-based outdoor clothing and supplies business while turning it into a successful multichannel billion-dollar enterprise. He improved employee morale and customer service by introducing stakeholder values that link success to customers, employees, stockholders, communities, and the environment. Employees are encouraged to provide feedback on products after testing them on tax-deductible field trips. The U.S. Department of Labor recognized L.L. Bean in its *Trendsetter Report* for avoiding overseas manufacturers that use "sweatshop" labor.

> CONCEPT CONNECTION <

Charismatic and Transformational Leadership

Research has also looked at how leadership can inspire and motivate people beyond their normal levels of performance. Some leadership approaches are more effective than others for bringing about high levels of commitment and enthusiasm. Two types with a substantial impact are *charismatic* and *transformational*.

Wendy Kopp's visionary leadership led to the initiation and growth of Teach for America, as described in the Benchmarking box.

CHARISMATIC AND VISIONARY LEADERSHIP

Charisma has been referred to as "a fire that ignites followers' energy and commitment, producing results above and beyond the call of duty."[34] The **charismatic leader** has the

BENCH-MARKING

Teach for America

Something like the word *no* has never stopped Wendy Kopp from marching ahead, even when one of her Princeton professors gave her some icy feedback when she proposed starting a sort of Peace Corps for teachers. "My dear Ms. Kopp," he responded, "you are quite evidently deranged."

Good thing she didn't listen to him, because Teach for America (TFA) has become one of the most respected educational programs in the United States, with applications from 11 percent of Ivy League seniors and 16 percent of Yale's graduating class. TFA only selects one out of every eight candidates. And results? In various studies, principals see TFA members as more effective than other beginning teachers, and TFA teachers were found to get higher math scores than peers.

Kopp never aspired to be running a huge corporation. All she wanted to do was reform public education. When she got to Princeton, she started to see the failures in the educational system and began organizing conferences on educational reform. It became so important to her that she wrote her senior thesis on the subject "A Plan and Argument for the Creation of a National Teacher Corps," followed by a letter to then President George H. W. Bush, asking him to start a national teacher corps, which elicited an impersonal rejection letter.

Like we said, "no" never stops Kopp. Despite her shyness, she drummed up enough courage to get on the phone, garnering support from various CEO's for her vision. Here she was, a lone young woman making cold calls to strangers. And they gave her money! The first year's budget was $2.5 million, enough to get 500 teachers started. Several years later, the start-up grants dried up and TFA was "near death." Most people would have thrown in the towel. Not Kopp. She got her executive team together and developed a new plan, cutting the budget and laying off 60 people. They had to strengthen the management team, set priorities, and diversify funding. The turn-around year was 1996 when some billionaires got interested. TFA raised $25 million in four months. And now the extended plan is for the 14,000 alumni to move into leadership positions in schools. The budget for 2010 is an astounding $160 million. All because Wendy Kopp had a dream and wouldn't give up. Says one major donor, "I'm bowled over by Wendy's absolute belief that TFA can change the world."

SOURCE: Roxanne Hai, personal communication, June 2009; Thomas L. Friedman, "Swimming Without a Suit," *New York Times*, Apr. 22, 2009, p. A27; Patricia Sellers, "The Recruiter," *Fortune*, Nov. 27, 2006, 87–90.

ability to inspire and motivate people to do more than they would normally do, despite obstacles and personal sacrifice. Followers are willing to put aside their own interests for the sake of the team, department, or organization. The impact of charismatic leaders is normally from (1) stating a lofty vision of an imagined future that employees identify with, (2) displaying an ability to understand and empathize with followers, and (3) empowering and trusting subordinates to accomplish results.[35] Charismatic leaders tend to be less predictable because they create an atmosphere of change, and they may be obsessed by visionary ideas that excite, stimulate, and drive other people to work hard.

Charismatic leaders include Mother Theresa, Sam Walton, Alexander the Great, Steve Jobs, David Koresh, Oprah Winfrey, Martin Luther King Jr., and Osama bin Laden. Charisma can be used for positive outcomes that benefit the group, but it can also be used for self-serving purposes that lead to deception, manipulation, and exploitation of others. When charismatic leaders respond to organizational problems in terms of the needs of the entire group rather than their own emotional needs, they can have a powerful, positive influence on organizational performance.[36]

Charismatic leaders are skilled in the art of *visionary leadership*. A **vision** is an attractive, ideal future that is credible yet not readily attainable. Vision is an important component of both charismatic and transformational leadership. Visionary leaders speak to the hearts of employees, letting them be part of something bigger than themselves. Where others see obstacles or failures, they see possibility and hope.

Whenever possible, take the high road and be an inspiration to your colleagues and followers.

As a leader, strive to help create a compelling vision and bring others along to follow the vision.

vision
An attractive, ideal future that is credible yet not readily attainable.

Charismatic leaders typically have a strong vision for the future, almost an obsession, and they can motivate others to help realize it.[37] These leaders have an emotional impact on subordinates because they strongly believe in the vision and can communicate it to others in a way that makes the vision real, personal, and meaningful. This chapter's Spotlight on Skills provides a short quiz to help you determine whether you have the potential to be a charismatic leader.

TRANSFORMATIONAL VERSUS TRANSACTIONAL LEADERSHIP

Transformational leaders are similar to charismatic leaders, but they are distinguished by their special ability to bring about innovation and change by recognizing followers' needs and concerns, helping them look at old problems in new ways, and encouraging them to question the status quo. Transformational leaders inspire followers not just to believe in the leader personally but to believe in their own potential to imagine and create a better future for the organization. Transformational leaders create significant change in both followers and the organization.[38]

Transformational leadership can be better understood in comparison to *transactional leadership*.[39] **Transactional leaders** clarify the role and task requirements of subordinates, initiate structure, provide appropriate rewards, and try to be considerate to and meet the social needs of subordinates. The transactional leader's ability to satisfy subordinates may improve productivity. Transactional leaders excel at management functions. They are hardworking, tolerant, and fair-minded. They take pride in keeping things running smoothly and efficiently. Transactional leaders often stress the impersonal aspects of performance such as plans, schedules, and budgets. They have a sense of commitment to the organization and conform to organizational norms and values. Transactional leadership is important to all organizations, but leading change requires a different approach.

Transformational leaders have the ability to lead changes in the organization's mission, strategy, structure, and culture, as well as to promote innovation in products and technologies. Transformational leaders do not rely solely on tangible rules and incentives to control specific transactions with followers. They focus on intangible qualities such as vision, shared values, and ideas to build relationships, give larger meaning to diverse activities, and find common ground to enlist followers in the change process.[40]

A recent study confirmed that transformational leadership has a positive effect on follower development and follower performance. Moreover, transformational leadership skills can be learned and are not ingrained personality characteristics.[41] However, some personality traits may make it easier for a leader to display transformational leadership behaviors. For example, studies of transformational leadership have found that the trait of agreeableness, as discussed in the previous chapter, is positively associated with transformational leaders.[42] In addition, transformational leaders are typically emotionally stable and positively engaged with the world around them, and they have a strong ability to recognize and understand others' emotions.[43] These characteristics are not surprising when we consider that these leaders accomplish change by building networks of positive relationships.

Always be fair-minded and hardworking as a leader.

transformational leader
A leader distinguished by a special ability to bring about innovation and change.

transactional leader
A leader who clarifies subordinates' role and task requirements, initiates structure, provides rewards, and displays consideration for subordinates.

Followership

No discussion of leadership is complete without a consideration of followership. Leadership matters, but without effective followers no organization can survive. Leaders can develop an understanding of their followers and how to help them be most effective.[44] Many of the qualities that define a good leader are the same qualities as those possessed by a good

SPOTLIGHT ON SKILLS

Are You a Charismatic Leader?

If you were the head of a major department in a corporation, how important would each of the following activities be to you? Answer Yes or No to indicate whether you would strive to perform each activity.

	YES	NO
1. Help subordinates clarify goals and how to reach them.	_____	_____
2. Give people a sense of mission and overall purpose.	_____	_____
3. Help get jobs out on time.	_____	_____
4. Look for the new product or service opportunities.	_____	_____
5. Use policies and procedures as guides for problem solving.	_____	_____
6. Promote unconventional beliefs and values.	_____	_____
7. Give monetary rewards in exchange for high performance from subordinates.	_____	_____
8. Command respect from everyone in the department.	_____	_____
9. Work alone to accomplish important tasks.	_____	_____
10. Suggest new and unique ways of doing things	_____	_____
11. Give credit to people who do their jobs well.	_____	_____
12. Inspire loyalty to yourself and to the organization.	_____	_____
13. Establish procedures to help the department operate smoothly.	_____	_____
14. Use ideas to motivate others.	_____	_____
15. Set reasonable limits on new approaches.	_____	_____
16. Demonstrate social nonconformity.	_____	_____

The even-numbered items represent behaviors and activities of charismatic leaders. Charismatic leaders are personally involved in shaping ideas, goals, and direction of change. They use an intuitive approach to develop fresh ideas for old problems and seek new directions for the department or organization. The odd-numbered items are considered more traditional management activities, or what would be called *transactional leadership*. Managers respond to organizational problems in an impersonal way, make rational decisions, and coordinate and facilitate the work of others. If you answered yes to more even-numbered than odd-numbered items, you may be a potential charismatic leader.

SOURCES: Based on the "Have You Got It?" quiz that appeared in Patricia Sellers, "What Exactly Is Charisma?" *Fortune* (Jan. 15, 1996): 68–75; Bernard M. Bass, *Leadership and Performance Beyond Expectations* (New York: Free Press, 1985); and Lawton R. Burns and Selwyn W. Becker, "Leadership and Managership," in S. Shortell and A. Kaluzny (Eds.), *Health Care Management* (New York: Wiley, 1986).

EXHIBIT 12.8
Styles of
Followership
– – – – – – – – – –

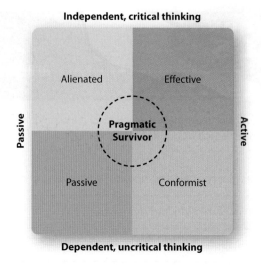

SOURCE: From *The Power of Followership* by Robert E. Kelley, p. 97, copyright © 1992 by Consultants to Executives and Organizations, Ltd. Used by permission of Doubleday, a division of Random House, Inc.

follower. Understanding differences in followers can improve one's effectiveness as both a follower and a leader. One model of followership is illustrated in Exhibit 12.8. Robert E. Kelley conducted extensive interviews with managers and their subordinates and came up with five *follower styles*, which are categorized according to two dimensions, as shown in the exhibit.[45]

The first dimension is the quality of independent **critical thinking** versus dependent **uncritical thinking**. Independent critical thinkers are mindful of the effects of their own and others' behavior on achieving organizational goals. They can weigh the impact of their boss's and their own decisions and offer constructive criticism, creativity, and innovation. Conversely, a dependent, uncritical thinker does not consider possibilities beyond what he or she is told, does not contribute to the cultivation of the organization, and accepts the supervisor's ideas without thinking.

The second dimension of follower style is *active* versus *passive* behavior. An active follower participates fully in the organization, engages in behavior that is beyond the limits of the job, demonstrates a sense of ownership, and initiates problem solving and decision making. A passive follower, by contrast, is characterized by a need for constant supervision and prodding by superiors. Passivity is often regarded as laziness; a passive person does nothing that is not required and avoids added responsibility.

The extent to which an individual is active or passive and is a critical independent thinker or a dependent uncritical thinker determines whether the person will be an alienated follower, a passive follower, a conformist, a pragmatic survivor, or an effective follower, as illustrated in Exhibit 12.8:

1. The **alienated follower** is a passive, yet independent critical thinker. Alienated employees are often effective followers who have experienced setbacks and obstacles, perhaps promises broken by their superiors. Thus, they are capable, but they focus exclusively on the shortcomings of their boss. Often cynical, alienated followers are able to think independently, but they do not participate in developing solutions to the problems or deficiencies they see. These people waste valuable time complaining about their boss without offering constructive feedback.

2. The **conformist** participates actively in a relationship with the boss but doesn't use critical thinking skills. In other words, a conformist typically carries out any and all orders regardless of the nature of the request. The conformist participates willingly but without

As a follower, see things through your own eyes and not through the eyes of others.

critical thinking
Thinking independently and being mindful of the effect of one's behavior on achieving goals.

uncritical thinking
Failing to consider the possibilities beyond what one is told; accepting others' ideas without thinking.

alienated follower
A person who is an independent, critical thinker but is passive in the organization.

conformist
A follower who participates actively in the organization but does not use critical thinking skills.

considering the consequences of what he or she is being asked to do—even at the risk of contributing to a harmful endeavor. A conformist is concerned only with avoiding conflict. This follower style might reflect an individual's overdependent attitude toward authority, yet it can also result from rigid rules and authoritarian environments that create a culture of conformity.

3. The **pragmatic survivor** has qualities of all four extremes—depending on which style fits with the prevalent situation. This type of person uses whatever style best benefits his or her own position and minimizes risk. Pragmatic survivors often emerge when an organization is going through desperate times, and managers find themselves doing whatever is needed to get themselves through the difficulty. Within any given company, some 25 percent to 35 percent of people tend to be pragmatic survivors, avoiding risks and fostering the status quo.[46]

4. The **passive follower** exhibits neither critical independent thinking nor active participation. Being passive and uncritical, these people show neither initiative nor a sense of responsibility. Their activity is limited to what they are told to do, and they accomplish things only with a great deal of supervision. Passive followers leave the thinking to the boss. Often this style is the result of a micromanaging boss who encourages passive behavior. People learn that to show initiative, accept responsibility, or think creatively is not rewarded and may even be punished by the boss, so they grow increasingly passive.

5. The **effective follower** is both a critical independent thinker and active in the organization. Effective followers behave the same toward everyone, regardless of their position in the organization. They develop an equitable relationship with their leaders and do not try to avoid risk or conflict. These people are capable of self-management, they discern strengths and weaknesses in themselves and their bosses, they are committed to something bigger than themselves, and they work toward competency, solutions, and positive impact. Effective followers recognize that they have power in their relationships with superiors; thus, they have the courage to manage upward, to initiate change, and to put themselves at risk or in conflict with the boss if they believe it serves the best interest of the team or organization.

Avoid being the complainer who never does anything; such a person is not generally valued.

Power and Influence

Both followers and leaders use power and influence to get things done in organizations.

 Power is the potential ability to influence the behavior of others.[47] Sometimes the terms *power* and *influence* are used synonymously, but there are distinctions between the two. Basically, **influence** is the effect a person's actions have on the attitudes, values, beliefs, or behavior of others. Whereas power is the capacity to cause a change in a person, influence may be thought of as the degree of actual change.

 Power results from an interaction of leader and followers. Some power comes from an individual's position in the organization. Power may also come from personal sources, such as an individual's personal interests, goals, and values, as well as from sources such as access to information or important relationships. Followers as well as leaders can tap into a variety of power sources.

POSITION POWER

The traditional manager's power comes from the organization. The manager's position gives him or her the power to reward or punish subordinates to influence their behavior. Legitimate power, reward power, and coercive power are all forms of position power used by managers to change employee behavior.

pragmatic survivor
A follower who has qualities of all four follower styles, depending on which fits the prevalent situation.

passive follower
A person who exhibits neither critical independent thinking nor active participation.

effective follower
A critical, independent thinker who actively participates in the organization.

power
The potential ability to influence others' behavior.

influence
The effect a person's actions have on the attitudes, values, beliefs, or behavior of others.

Legitimate Power. Power coming from a formal management position in an organization and the authority granted to it is called **legitimate power**. Once a person has been selected as a supervisor, most employees understand that they are obligated to follow his or her direction with respect to work activities. Subordinates accept this source of power as legitimate, which is why they comply.

Reward Power. Another kind of power, **reward power**, stems from the authority to bestow rewards on other people. Managers may have access to formal rewards such as pay increases or promotions. They also have at their disposal such rewards as praise, attention, and recognition. Managers can use rewards to influence subordinates' behavior.

Coercive Power. The opposite of reward power is **coercive power**. It refers to the authority to punish or recommend punishment. Managers have coercive power when they have the right to fire or demote employees, criticize, or withdraw pay increases. If an employee does not perform as expected, the manager has the coercive power to reprimand him, put a negative letter in his file, deny him a raise, and hurt his chances for a promotion.

PERSONAL POWER

In contrast to the external sources of position power, personal power most often comes from internal sources, such as an individual's special knowledge or personal characteristics. Personal power is the primary tool of the leader, and it is becoming increasingly important as more businesses are run by teams of workers who are less tolerant of authoritarian management.[48] Two types of personal power are *expert power* and *referent power*.

Expert Power. Power resulting from a person's special knowledge or skill regarding the tasks being performed is referred to as **expert power**. When someone is a true expert, others go along with recommendations because of his or her superior knowledge. Followers as well as leaders can possess expert power. For example, some managers lead teams in which members have expertise that the leader lacks. Some leaders at top management levels may lack expert power because subordinates know more about technical details than they do.

Referent Power. **Referent power** comes from an individual's personal characteristics, which so command others' identification, respect, and admiration that they wish to emulate that individual. Referent power does not depend on a formal title or position. When employees admire a supervisor because of the way she deals with them, the influence is based on referent power. Referent power is most visible in the area of charismatic leadership. In social and religious movements, we often see charismatic leaders who emerge and gain a tremendous following based solely on their personal power.

OTHER SOURCES OF POWER

There are additional sources of power that are not linked to a particular person or position but rather to the role an individual plays in the overall functioning of the organization. These important sources include personal effort, relationships with others, and information.

Personal Effort. People who show initiative, work beyond what is expected of them, take on undesirable but important projects, and show interest in learning about the organization and industry often gain power as a result. Managers come to depend on particular subordinates, for instance, whom they know they can count on to take on a disagreeable job or put forth extra effort when it's necessary. However, these people aren't pushovers. Related to personal effort is the individual's willingness to be assertive in asking for what she wants and needs from superiors.

legitimate power
Power that stems from a formal management position in an organization and the authority granted to it.

reward power
Power that results from the authority to bestow rewards on other people.

coercive power
Power that stems from the authority to punish or recommend punishment.

expert power
Power that stems from special knowledge of or skill in the tasks performed by subordinates.

referent power
Power that results from characteristics that command subordinates' identification with, respect and admiration for, and desire to emulate the leader.

3 Leaders should amass as much power as they can; it helps them get things done.

ANSWER: Leaders do need power, but all types, not just position or coercive power, which is too often what new leaders go after. Increasing expert and referent power are very important.

Assess Your Answer

Network of Relationships. People who are enmeshed in a network of relationships have greater power. A leader or employee with many relationships knows what's going on in the organization and industry, whereas one who has few interpersonal connections is often in the dark about important activities or changes. Developing positive associations with superiors or other powerful people is a good way to gain power, but people with the greatest power are those who cultivate relationships with individuals at all levels, both inside and outside the organization.

To increase your influence, increase your network.

Information. Information is a primary business resource, and people who have access to information and control over how and to whom it is distributed are typically powerful. To some extent, access to information is determined by a person's position in the organization. Top managers typically have access to more information than middle managers, who in turn have access to more information than lower-level supervisors or frontline employees.

INTERPERSONAL INFLUENCE TACTICS

The next question is how leaders use their power to implement decisions and facilitate change. Leaders often use a combination of influence strategies, and people who are perceived as having greater power and influence typically are those who use a wider variety of tactics. One survey of a few hundred leaders identified more than 4,000 different techniques these people used to influence others.[49]

However, these tactics fall into basic categories that rely on understanding the principles that cause people to change their behavior and attitudes. Exhibit 12.9 lists seven principles for asserting influence. Notice that most of these involve the use of personal power rather than relying solely on position power or the use of rewards and punishments.[50]

1. *Use rational persuasion.* The most frequently used influence strategy is to use facts, data, and logical argument to persuade others that a proposed idea, request, or decision is appropriate. Using rational persuasion can often be highly effective because most people have faith in facts and analysis.[51] Rational persuasion is most successful when a leader has technical knowledge and expertise related to the issue at hand (expert power), although

1. Use rational persuasion.
2. Make people like you.
3. Rely on the rule of reciprocity.
4. Develop allies.
5. Be assertive—ask for what you want.
6. Make use of higher authority.
7. Reward the behaviors you want.

EXHIBIT 12.9

Seven Interpersonal Influence Tactics for Leaders

referent power is also used. In other words, in addition to facts and figures, people also have to believe in the leader's credibility.

2. *Make people like you.* Recall our discussion of *likability* from the previous chapter. People would rather say yes to someone they like than to someone they don't. Effective leaders strive to create goodwill and favorable impressions. When a leader shows consideration and respect, treats people fairly, and demonstrates trust in others, people are more likely to want to help and support the leader by doing what he or she asks. In addition, most people like a leader who makes them feel good about themselves, so leaders should never underestimate the power of praise.

Work to be seen as a "good citizen" at work, not as a "taker."

3. *Rely on the rule of reciprocity.* Leaders can influence others through the exchange of benefits and favors. Leaders share what they have—whether it is time, resources, services, or emotional support. The feeling among people is nearly universal that others should be paid back for what they do in one form or another. This unwritten "rule of reciprocity" means that leaders who do favors for others can expect that others will do favors for them in return.[52]

4. *Develop allies.* Effective leaders develop networks of allies, people who can help the leader accomplish his or her goals. Leaders talk with followers and others outside of formal meetings to understand their needs and concerns as well as to explain problems and describe the leader's point of view. They strive to reach a meeting of minds with others about the best approach to a problem or decision.[53]

5. *Ask for what you want.* Another way to influence others is to make a direct and personal request. Leaders have to be explicit about what they want or they aren't likely to get it. An explicit proposal is sometimes accepted simply because others have no better alternative. Also, a clear proposal or alternative will often receive support if other options are less well defined.

6. *Make use of higher authority.* Sometimes to get things done, leaders have to use their formal authority, as well as gain the support of people at higher levels to back them up. However, research has found that the key to successful use of formal authority is to be knowledgeable, credible, and trustworthy—that is, to demonstrate expert and referent power as well as legitimate power. Managers who become known for their expertise, who are honest and straightforward with others, and who inspire trust can exert greater influence than those who simply issue orders.[54]

7. *Reward the behaviors you want.* Leaders can also use organizational rewards and punishments to influence others' behavior. The use of punishment in organizations is controversial, but negative consequences almost always occur for inappropriate or undesirable behavior. Leaders should not rely solely on reward and punishment as a means for influencing others, but rewards can be highly effective when combined with other tactics that involve the use of personal power.

Research indicates that people rate leaders as "more effective" when they are perceived to be using a variety of influence tactics. But not all managers use influence in the same way. Studies have found that leaders in human resources, for example, tend to use softer, more subtle approaches such as building goodwill, using favors, and developing allies, whereas those in finance are inclined to use harder, more direct tactics such as formal authority and assertiveness.[55]

Leadership as Service

To close this chapter, let's look at two timeless leadership approaches that are gaining renewed attention in today's environment of ethical scandals and weakened employee trust. Characteristics of servant leadership and moral leadership can be successfully used by leaders in all situations to make a positive difference.

SERVANT LEADERSHIP

Some leaders operate from the assumption that work exists for the development of the worker as much as the worker exists to do the work.[56] The concept of servant leadership, first described by Robert Greenleaf in 1970, has gained renewed interest in recent years as companies recover from ethical scandals and compete to attract and retain the best human talent.[57]

Such leaders operate on two levels: to fulfill their subordinates' goals and needs and to realize their organization's larger purpose or mission. **Servant leaders** give things away—power, ideas, information, recognition, credit for accomplishments, even money. Harry Stine, founder of Stine Seed Company in Adel, Iowa, casually announced to his employees at the company's annual postharvest luncheon that they would each receive $1,000 for each year they had worked at the company.[58] For some loyal workers, that amounted to a $20,000 bonus.[59] Or even more stunning was Miami banker Leonard Abess, who gave $60 million of his own money to 399 employees (including 72 former and retired employees), some of whom received $100,000 each.[60] Servant leaders truly value other people. They are trustworthy, and they trust others. They encourage participation, share power, enhance others' self-worth, and unleash people's creativity, full commitment, and natural impulse to learn and contribute. Servant leaders can bring their followers' higher motives to the work and connect their hearts to the organizational mission and goals.

Servant leaders often work in the nonprofit world because it offers a natural way to apply their leadership drive and skills to serve others. But servant leaders also succeed in business. Ari Weinzweig and Paul Saginaw, cofounders of Zingerman's Community of Businesses, built a $30 million food, restaurant, and training company using servant leadership principles. The leaders are continually asking employees, *What can I do for you?* "People give me assignments all the time," Weinzweig says. "Sometimes I'm the note-taker. . . . Sometimes I'm on my hands and knees wiping up what people spilled. We have to learn to be good followers."[61] Not being a servant leader can have negative consequences, as described in this chapter's Business Blooper.

As a leader, see yourself as serving your employees; you are there to meet their needs.

servant leader
A leader who works to fulfill subordinates' needs and goals as well as to achieve the organization's larger mission.

BUSINESS BLOOPER

General Motors

Despite a 95-percent collapse of stock price (from $70 to $4) during his nine years as CEO of General Motors (GM), Rick Wagoner remained the eternal optimist and continued to believe he could revitalize the company into the powerhouse it once was—that is, until President Obama asked him to step down. GM's first mistake was probably hiring Wagoner as top leader because he lacked the typical background of manufacturing, design, and marketing that the most successful auto executives have. GM lost its way in the 1970s but didn't realize it for 20 years; nor did Wagoner understand what kind of black hole he was about to step into. GM was undone also by its strong and disciplined culture (which helped perfect the assembly line), something that had become impervious to change. Rather than listen to the auto-buying consumer, GM chose to blame its problems on the unions, health care, government intervention, environmentalists, and so on. And in recent years, the penchant for separating executives from workers (through location, pay, etc.) allowed Wagoner to remain clueless. He presided over some of the biggest losses in company history, including $82 billion in four years, and the company's eclipse as the world's largest automaker by Toyota.

SOURCE: Richard S. Tedlow, "GM and the World We Have Lost," *Boston Globe*, June 3, 2009, p. A17; Micheline Maynard, "The Steadfast Optimist Who Oversaw GM's Long Decline," *New York Times*, Mar. 30, 2009, pp. B1, B8.

Fifty years ago, D. J. De Pree created environmental sustainability programs at Herman Miller, which designs and manufactures office furnishings. De Pree displayed moral leadership by acting on his belief that businesses should be careful stewards of natural resources. His innovative directives—such as that all employees should be able to look out a window from no more than 75 feet and that 50 percent of company-developed land should be green space—are still followed. Today, the company benefits from lower energy expenses by harvesting natural daylight. The Design Yard, located in Holland, Michigan, received Leadership in Energy and Environmental Design Gold recognition.

© HERMAN MILLER

⋯⋯⋯⋯⋯⋯⟩ CONCEPT CONNECTION ⟨⋯⋯⋯⋯⋯⋯

When in a moral dilemma, think of what is the right thing to do, rather than only the most financially beneficial action.

moral leadership
Distinguishing right from wrong and choosing to do right in the practice of leadership.

courage
The ability to step forward through fear and act on one's values and conscience.

MORAL LEADERSHIP

Because leadership can be used for good or evil, to help or to harm others, all leadership has a moral component. Leaders carry a tremendous responsibility to use their power wisely and ethically. Sadly, in recent years, too many have chosen to act from self-interest and greed rather than behaving in ways that serve and uplift others. The disheartening ethical climate in American business has led to a renewed interest in moral leadership. **Moral leadership** is about distinguishing right from wrong and choosing to do right. It means seeking the just, the honest, the good, and the decent behavior in the practice of leadership.[62] Moral leaders remember that business is about values, not just economic performance.

Distinguishing the right thing to do is not always easy, and doing it is sometimes even harder. Leaders are often faced with right-versus-right decisions, in which several responsibilities conflict with one another.[63] Commitments to superiors, for example, may mean a leader feels the need to hide unpleasant news about pending layoffs from followers. Moral leaders strive to find the moral answer or compromise rather than take the easy way out. Consider Katherine Graham, the long-time leader of *The Washington Post*, when she was confronted with a decision in 1971 about what to do with the Pentagon Papers, a leaked defense department study that showed the Johnson and Nixon administrations' deceptions about the Vietnam War. Graham admitted she was terrified; she knew she was risking the whole company on the decision, possibly inviting prosecution under the Espionage Act, and jeopardizing thousands of employees' jobs. She decided to go ahead with the story, and reporters Bob Woodward and Carl Bernstein made Watergate—and the *Washington Post*—a household name.[64]

Clearly, moral leadership requires **courage**, the ability to step forward through fear and act on one's values and conscience. As we discussed in Chapter 4, leaders often behave unethically simply because they lack courage. Most people want to be liked, and it is easy to do the wrong thing in order to fit in or impress others. One example might be a leader who holds his tongue in order to "fit in with the guys" when colleagues are telling sexually or racially offensive jokes. Moral leaders summon the fortitude to do the right thing even if it is unpopular. Standing up for what is right is the primary way in which leaders create an environment of honesty, trust, and integrity in the organization.

Summary

This chapter covered several important ideas about leadership. The concept of leadership continues to evolve and change with the times. Of particular interest in today's turbulent environment is a postheroic leadership approach. Two significant concepts in line with the postheroic approach are level-five leadership and interactive leadership, which is common among women leaders. Level-five leaders are characterized by personal humility combined with a strong determination to build a great organization that will thrive beyond the leader's direct influence. Interactive leadership emphasizes relationships and helping others develop to their highest potential and may be particularly well suited to today's workplace.

The early research on leadership focused on personal traits such as intelligence, energy, and appearance. Later, research attention shifted to leadership behaviors that are appropriate to the organizational situation. Behavioral approaches dominated the early work in this area; task-oriented behavior and people-oriented behavior were suggested as essential behaviors that lead work groups toward high performance. The Ohio State and Michigan approaches and the managerial grid are in this category. Contingency approaches include Hersey and Blanchard's situational theory, Fiedler's theory, and the substitutes-for-leadership concept.

Leadership concepts have evolved from the transactional approach to charismatic and transformational leadership behaviors. Charismatic leadership is the ability to articulate a vision and motivate followers to make it a reality. Transformational leadership extends charismatic qualities to guide and foster dramatic organizational change.

Being a good follower is an important component of being a good leader because effective leaders and effective followers share similar characteristics. An effective follower is both independent and active in the organization. Being an effective follower depends on not becoming alienated, conforming, or passive.

Leadership involves the use of power to influence others. Sources of power are both position-based (legitimate, reward, and coercive) and person-based (expert and referent). Other important sources of power in organizations are personal effort, a network of relationships, and access to information. Leaders rely more on personal power than position power, and they use a variety of interpersonal influence tactics to implement decisions and accomplish goals.

Two enduring approaches that reflect the idea of leadership as service are servant leadership and moral leadership. Servant leaders facilitate the growth, goals, and development of others to liberate their best qualities in pursuing the organization's mission. Moral leadership means seeking to do the honest and decent thing in the practice of leadership. Leaders can make a positive difference by applying characteristics of servant and moral leadership.

Discussion Questions

1. Do you think leadership style is fixed and unchangeable for a leader or flexible and adaptable? Discuss.

2. Suggest some personal traits that you believe would be useful to a business leader today. Are these traits more valuable in some situations than in others? As a potential new manager, are these the same traits you would want in a follower?

3. What is the difference between trait theories and behavioral theories of leadership?

4. Suggest the sources of power that would be available to a leader of a student government organization. What sources of power may not be available? To be effective, should student leaders keep power to themselves or delegate power to other students?

5. What skills and abilities does a manager need in order to lead effectively in a virtual environment? Do you believe a leader with a consideration style or an initiating-structure style would be more successful as a virtual leader? Explain your answer.

6. What is transformational leadership? Give examples of organizational situations that would call for transformational, transactional, or charismatic leadership.

7. How does level-five leadership differ from the concept of servant leadership? Do you believe anyone has the potential to become a level-five leader? Discuss.

8. Why do you think so little attention is given to followership compared to leadership in organizations? Discuss how the role of an effective follower is similar to the role of a leader.

9. Do you think leadership is more or less important in today's flatter, team-based organizations? Are some leadership styles better suited to such organizations as opposed to traditional hierarchical organizations? Explain.

10. Consider the leadership position of a senior partner in a law firm. What task, subordinate, and organizational factors might serve as substitutes for leadership in this situation?

11. Do you see yourself as having more leader qualities or manager qualities? Do you think you will become a better leader or manager by developing the characteristics you already have or by trying to develop the characteristics you don't have? Discuss.

Self Learning

What Is the Impact of Leadership?

What are your beliefs and understandings about how top leaders influence organizational performance? To learn about your beliefs, please answer whether each item below is Mostly True or Mostly False based on your personal beliefs.

	MOSTLY TRUE	MOSTLY FALSE
1. The quality of leadership is the most important influence on the performance of an organization.	_____	_____
2. People in top-level leadership positions have the power to make or break an organization.	_____	_____
3. Most activities in an organization have little to do with the decisions or activities of the top leaders.	_____	_____
4. Even in a bad economy, a good leader can prevent a company from doing poorly.	_____	_____
5. A company cannot do well unless it has high-quality leadership at the top.	_____	_____
6. High- versus low-quality leadership has a bigger impact on a firm's performance than the business environment.	_____	_____
7. Poor organizational performance is often due to factors beyond the control of even the best leaders.	_____	_____
8. Eventually, bad leadership at the top will trigger poor organizational performance.	_____	_____
9. Leaders typically should not be held responsible for a firm's poor performance.	_____	_____

Scoring and Interpretation This scale is about the "romance" of leadership, which is the romantic view that leaders are very responsible for organizational performance while other factors such as economic conditions are ignored. Company performance is difficult to control and is an outcome of complex forces. Attributing too much responsibility to leaders is a simplification shaped by our own mental construction more than by the reality and complexity of organizational performance. Top leaders are not heroes, but they are important as one of several key factors that can shape organizational performance.

Scoring: Give yourself 1 point for each item 1, 2, 4, 5, 6, and 8 marked as Mostly True and each item 3, 7, and 9 marked as Mostly False. A score of 7 or higher suggests a belief in the romance of leadership—that leaders have more control over performance outcomes than is actually the case.

If you scored 3 or less, then you may underestimate the impact of top leaders, a somewhat skeptical view. A score of 4 to 6 suggests a balanced view of leadership.

In Class: Sit with a student partner and explain your scores to each other. What are your beliefs about leadership? What is the basis for your beliefs? The teacher can ask for a show of hands concerning the number of high, medium, and low scores on the questionnaire. Discuss the following questions: Do you believe that presidents, top executives, and heads of not-for-profit organizations act alone and hence are largely responsible for performance? What is the evidence for this belief? What other forces will affect an organization? What is a realistic view of top leader influence in a large organization?

SOURCE: Adapted from Birgit Schyns, James R. Meindl, and Marcel A. Croon, "The Romance of Leadership Scale: Cross-Cultural Testing and Refinement," *Leadership* 3, no. 1 (2007): 29–46.

Group Learning

Assumptions About Leaders

Individually complete the sentences below.

1. A leader must always . . .
2. Leaders should never . . .
3. The best leader I ever had did . . .
4. The worst leader I ever had did . . .
5. When I am doing a good job as a leader, I . . .
6. I am afraid of leaders who . . .
7. I would follow a leader who . . .
8. I am repelled by leaders who . . .
9. Some people think they are good leaders, but they are not because they . . .
10. I want to be the kind of leader who . . .

In groups of four to six students, discuss the following:

A. What did you learn about your own assumptions about leadership?
B. Trace those assumptions back to theories on leadership in this chapter.
C. What were common themes in your group?

Copyright 2000 by Dorothy Marcic.

Action Learning

1. Find three people who have had bosses or CEOs who were either charismatic or transformational.
2. Ask them to describe what the leader was like; what were the values? the behaviors?
3. Ask them to contrast those charismatic or transformational leaders with an ineffective boss or CEO they worked with.
4. What were the differences in behavior? How did the behavior of the ineffective leaders affect the organization?
5. Ask them to give a few sentences on how they would compare the transformational or charismatic leader to the ineffective one.
6. Your instructor may ask you to write a paper on this subject or bring this information to class. Be prepared to discuss it.
7. What did you learn about transformational and charismatic leadership from this assignment? Did it agree with what the textbook described?

Ethical Dilemma

Too Much of a Good Thing?

Not long ago, Jessica Armstrong, vice president of administration for Delaware Valley Chemical Inc., a New Jersey-based multinational company, made a point of stopping by department head Darius Harris's office to lavishly praise him for his volunteer work with an after-school program for disadvantaged children in a nearby urban neighborhood. Now she was about to summon him to her office so she could take him to task for dedication to the same volunteer work.

It was Carolyn Clark, Harris's secretary, who'd alerted her to the problem. "Darius told the community center he'd take responsibility for a fund-raising mass mailing. And then he asked me to edit the letter he'd drafted, make all the copies, stuff the envelopes, and get it into the mail—most of this on my own time," she reported, still obviously indignant. "When I told him, 'I'm sorry, but that's not my job,'

he looked me straight in the eye and asked when I'd like to schedule my upcoming performance appraisal."

Several of Harris's subordinates also volunteered with the program. After chatting with them, Armstrong concluded most were volunteering out of a desire to stay on the boss's good side. It was time to talk to Harris.

"Oh, come on," responded Harris impatiently when Armstrong confronted him. "Yes, I asked for her help as a personal favor to me. But I only brought up the appraisal because I was going out of town, and we needed to set some time aside to do the evaluation." Harris went on to talk about how important working for the after-school program was to him personally. "I grew up in that neighborhood, and if it hadn't been for the people at the center, I wouldn't be here today," he said. Besides, even if he had pressured employees to help out—and he wasn't saying he had—didn't all the emphasis the company was putting on employee volunteerism make it okay to use employees' time and company resources?

After Harris left, Armstrong thought about the conversation. There was no question Delaware Valley actively encouraged employee volunteerism—and not just because it was the right thing to do. It was a chemical company with a couple of unfortunate accidental spills in its recent past that caused environmental damage and community anger.

Volunteering had the potential to help employees acquire new skills, create a sense of camaraderie, and play a role in recruiting and retaining talented people. But most of all, it gave a badly needed boost to the company's public image. Recently, Delaware Valley took every opportunity to publicize its employees' extracurricular community work on its Web site and in company publications. And the company created the annual Delaware Prize, which granted cash awards ranging from $1,000 to $5,000 to outstanding volunteers.

So now that Armstrong had talked with everyone concerned, just what was she going to do about the dispute between Darius Harris and Carolyn Clark?

What Would You Do?

1. Tell Carolyn Clark that employee volunteerism is important to the company and that while her performance evaluation will not be affected by her decision, she should consider helping Harris because it is an opportunity to help a worthy community project.

2. Tell Darius Harris that the employee volunteer program is just that: a volunteer program. Even though the company sees volunteerism as an important piece of its campaign to repair its tarnished image, employees must be free to choose whether to volunteer. He should not ask for help with the after-school program from his direct subordinates.

3. Discipline Darius Harris for coercing his subordinates to spend their own time on his volunteer work at the community after-school program. This action will send a signal that coercing employees is a clear violation of leadership authority.

13 Chapter Thirteen

Motivating Employees

LEARNING OBJECTIVES

After studying this chapter, you should be able to:

1 Define *motivation* and explain the difference between intrinsic and extrinsic rewards.

2 Identify and describe content theories of motivation based on employee needs.

3 Identify and explain process theories of motivation.

4 Describe the reinforcement perspective and how it can be used to motivate employees.

5 Discuss major approaches to job design and how job design influences motivation.

6 Explain how empowerment heightens employee motivation.

7 Describe ways in which managers can create a sense of meaning and importance through employee engagement.

New Manager's Questions

Please circle your opinion below each of the following statements.

1 Money is the most important motivator for employees.

STRONGLY AGREE < < <   > > > STRONGLY DISAGREE

| 1 | 2 | 3 | 4 | 5 |

2 A strong need for power is necessary to develop your career.

STRONGLY AGREE < < <   > > > STRONGLY DISAGREE

| 1 | 2 | 3 | 4 | 5 |

3 Too much feedback can be harmful to workers' productivity.

STRONGLY AGREE < < <   > > > STRONGLY DISAGREE

| 1 | 2 | 3 | 4 | 5 |

Most people begin a new job with energy and enthusiasm, but employees can lose their drive if managers fail in their role as motivators. It can be a problem for even the most successful of organizations and the most admired of managers when experienced, valuable employees lose the motivation and commitment they once felt, causing a decline in their performance. One secret for success in organizations is motivated and engaged employees.

Motivation is a challenge for managers because motivation arises from within employees and typically differs for each person. For example, Janice Rennie makes $350,000 a year selling residential real estate in Toronto; she attributes her success to the fact that she likes to listen carefully to clients and then find houses to meet their needs. Greg Storey is a skilled machinist who is challenged by writing programs for numerically controlled machines. After dropping out of college, he swept floors in a machine shop and was motivated to learn to run the machines. Frances Blais sells educational books and software. She is a top salesperson, but she doesn't care about the $50,000 plus commissions: "I'm not even thinking money when I'm selling. I'm really on a crusade to help children read well." In stark contrast, Rob Michaels gets sick to his stomach before he goes to work. Rob is a telephone salesperson who spends all day trying to get people to buy products they do not need, and the rejections are painful. His motivation is money; he earned $120,000 in the past year and cannot make nearly that much doing anything else.[1]

Rob is motivated by money, Janice by her love of listening and problem solving, Frances by the desire to help children read, and Greg by the challenge of mastering numerically controlled machinery. Each person is motivated to perform, yet each has different reasons for performing. With such diverse motivations among individuals, how do managers find the right way to motivate employees toward common organizational goals?

This chapter reviews several approaches to employee motivation. We begin by defining motivation and the types of rewards managers use. Then we examine several models that describe the employee needs and processes associated with motivation. We also look at the use of reinforcement for motivation, as well as examine how job design—changing the structure of the work itself—can affect employee satisfaction and productivity. Finally, we discuss the trend of empowerment and look at how managers imbue work with a sense of meaning by fostering employee engagement.

As a manager, always learn what motivates each individual who works for you, remembering that different people have different motivators.

motivation
The arousal, direction, and persistence of behavior.

The Container Store has the motto that one great person equals three good people. Here, an employee and Elfa storage system designer works with a couple to design a custom storage plan. Getting hired is quite competitive because the retailer has been on *Fortune* magazine's list of 100 Best Companies to Work for in America year after year since 2000. Employees get intrinsic rewards from knowing they were selected to work for this winning company. The Container Store also puts its money where its motto is—providing the extrinsic rewards of entry-level pay that is 50 percent to 100 percent higher than average retail pay, a 40-percent merchandise discount, and health insurance for both part-time and full-time employees.

PHOTO COURTESY OF THE CONTAINER STORE

••••••••••••> CONCEPT CONNECTION <••••••••••••

The Concept of Motivation

Most of us get up in the morning, go to school or work, and behave in ways that are predictably our own. We respond to our environment and the people in it with little thought as to why we work hard, enjoy certain classes, or find some recreational activities so much fun. Yet all these behaviors are motivated by something. **Motivation** refers to the forces either within or external to a person that arouse enthusiasm and persistence to pursue a certain course of action. Employee motivation affects productivity, and part of

| NEED Creates desire to fulfill needs (food, friendship, recognition, achievement) | → | BEHAVIOR Results in actions to fulfill needs | → | REWARDS Satisfy needs; intrinsic or extrinsic rewards |

FEEDBACK Reward informs person whether behavior was appropriate and should be used again.

a manager's job is to channel motivation toward the accomplishment of organizational goals.[2] The study of motivation helps managers understand what prompts people to initiate action, what influences their choice of action, and why they persist in that action over time.

A simple model of human motivation is illustrated in Exhibit 13.1. People have *needs*—such as for recognition, achievement, or monetary gain—that translate into an internal tension that motivates specific behaviors that seek to fulfill the need. To the extent that the behavior is successful, the person is rewarded in the sense that the need is satisfied. The reward also informs the person that the behavior was appropriate and can be used again in the future. When people have an excessive need for financial gain, they are prime targets of conmen, as illustrated in this chapter's Business Blooper.

Rewards are of two types: intrinsic and extrinsic. **Intrinsic rewards** are the satisfactions a person receives in the process of performing a particular action. The completion of a complex task may bestow a pleasant feeling of accomplishment, or solving a problem that benefits others may fulfill a personal mission. Frances Blais sells educational materials for the intrinsic reward of helping children read well. **Extrinsic rewards** are given by another person, typically a manager, and include promotions, pay increases, and bonuses. They originate externally and as a result of pleasing others. Rob Michaels, who hates his sales job, nevertheless is motivated by the extrinsic reward of high pay. Although extrinsic rewards are important, good managers strive to help people achieve intrinsic rewards as well. The most talented and innovative employees are rarely motivated exclusively by rewards such as money and benefits or even by praise and recognition. Instead, they seek satisfaction from the work itself.[3] For example, at Google, people are motivated by an idealistic goal of providing "automated universal transference," which basically means unifying data and information around the world and totally obliterating language barriers

Know yourself well enough to understand if you are more motivated by intrinsic or extrinsic rewards.

intrinsic reward
The satisfaction received in the process of performing an action.

extrinsic reward
A reward given by another person.

BUSINESS BLOOPER

Bernard L. Madoff

People thought of him as a charismatic, generous financial genius who would make them very, very rich. His returns were unlike anything else they'd ever seen. Did your grandmother ever tell you that when something is too good to be true, it probably is? That's the lesson here. Texan Bernie Madoff stole $50 billion from some very wealthy and savvy investors, as well as from retirement funds and a few nonprofits that ended up going out of business. He was the ultimate con man, manipulating and swindling people—feeding into their greed and using money from newer investors to pay off older investors in a huge Ponzi scheme or scam. Even Madoff himself knew it couldn't last forever, but he fooled a lot of people who should have known better. Even though he was 70 years old and was allowed house arrest in his penthouse while awaiting sentencing, he finally went to prison for what will surely be the rest of his life.

SOURCE: Julie Creswell and Landon Thomas, Jr., "The Talented Mr. Madoff," *New York Times*, Jan. 24, 2009, p. B1.

via the Internet. People are energized by the psychic rewards they get from working on intellectually stimulating and challenging technical problems, as well as by the potentially beneficial global impact of their work.[4]

The importance of motivation as illustrated in Exhibit 13.1 is that it can lead to behaviors that reflect high performance within organizations. Studies have found that high employee motivation goes hand in hand with high organizational performance and profits.[5] It is the responsibility of managers to find the right combination of motivational techniques and rewards to satisfy employees' needs and simultaneously encourage high work performance.

Some ideas about motivation, referred to as *content theories*, stress the analysis of underlying human needs and how needs can be satisfied in the workplace. *Process theories* concern the thought processes that influence behavior. They focus on how people seek rewards in work circumstances. *Reinforcement theories* focus on employee learning of desired work behaviors. In Exhibit 13.1, content theories focus on the concepts in the first box, process theories on those in the second, and reinforcement theories on those in the third.

NEW MANAGER'S SELF-TEST

Are You Engaged or Disengaged?[6]

The term *employee engagement* is becoming popular in the corporate world. To learn what engagement means, answer the following questions twice: (1) once for a course you enjoyed and performed well in and (2) a second time for a course you did not enjoy and performed poorly in. For the course you enjoyed and performed well in, write "1" to indicate whether each item is Mostly True or Mostly False. For the course you did not enjoy and performed poorly in, write "2" to indicate whether each item is Mostly True or Mostly False.

	MOSTLY TRUE	MOSTLY FALSE
1. I made sure to study on a regular basis.	_____	_____
2. I put forth effort.	_____	_____
3. I found ways to make the course material relevant to my life.	_____	_____
4. I found ways to make the course interesting to me.	_____	_____
5. I raised my hand in class.	_____	_____
6. I had fun in class.	_____	_____
7. I participated actively in small group discussions.	_____	_____
8. I helped fellow students.	_____	_____

SCORING AND INTERPRETATION: Engagement means that people involve and express themselves in their work, going beyond the minimum effort required. Engagement typically has a positive relationship with both personal satisfaction and performance. If this relationship was true for your classes, then the number of 1s in the Mostly True column will be higher than the number of 2s. You might expect a score of 6 or higher for a course in which you were engaged, and possibly 3 or lower if you were disengaged.

The challenge for a new manager is to learn to engage subordinates in the same way your instructors in your favorite classes were able to engage you. Teaching is similar to managing. What techniques did your instructors use to engage students? Which techniques can you use to engage people when you become a new manager?

Content Perspectives on Motivation

Content theories emphasize the needs that motivate people. At any point in time, people have a variety of needs. These needs translate into an internal drive that motivates specific behaviors in an attempt to fulfill the needs. In other words, our needs are like a hidden catalog of the things we want and will work to get. To the extent that managers understand employees' needs, they can design reward systems to meet them and direct employees' energies and priorities toward attaining organizational goals.

THE HIERARCHY OF NEEDS

Probably the most famous content theory was developed by Abraham Maslow.[7] Maslow's **hierarchy of needs theory** proposes that people are motivated by multiple needs and that these needs exist in a hierarchical order as illustrated in Exhibit 13.2. Maslow identified five general types of motivating needs in order of ascendance:

1. *Physiological needs.* These most basic human physical needs include food, water, and oxygen. In the organizational setting, they are reflected in the needs for adequate heat, air, and base salary to ensure survival.

2. *Safety needs.* These needs include a safe and secure physical and emotional environment and freedom from threats—that is, for freedom from violence and for an orderly society. In an organizational workplace, safety needs reflect the needs for safe jobs, fringe benefits, and job security.

3. *Belongingness needs.* These needs reflect the desire to be accepted by one's peers, have friendships, be part of a group, and be loved. In the organization, these needs influence the desire for good relationships with co-workers, participation in a work group, and a positive relationship with supervisors.

4. *Esteem needs.* These needs relate to the desire for a positive self-image and to receive attention, recognition, and appreciation from others. Within organizations, esteem needs reflect a motivation for recognition, an increase in responsibility, high status, and credit for contributions to the organization.

5. *Self-actualization needs.* These needs include the need for self-fulfillment, which is the highest need category. They concern developing one's full potential, increasing one's competence, and becoming a better person. Self-actualization needs can be met in the organization by providing people with opportunities to grow, be creative, and acquire training for challenging assignments and advancement.

content theories
A group of theories that emphasize the needs that motivate people.

hierarchy of needs theory
A content theory that proposes that people are motivated by five categories of needs—physiological, safety, belongingness, esteem, and self-actualization—that exist in a hierarchical order.

EXHIBIT 13.2
Maslow's Hierarchy of Needs
– – – – – – – – – –

Fulfillment off the Job	Need Hierarchy	Fulfillment on the Job
Education, religion, hobbies, personal growth	Self-Actualization Needs	Opportunities for training, advancement, growth, and creativity
Approval of family, friends, community	Esteem Needs	Recognition, high status, increased responsibilities
Family, friends, community groups	Belongingness Needs	Work groups, clients, coworkers, supervisors
Freedom from war, pollution, violence	Safety Needs	Safe work, fringe benefits, job security
Food, water, oxygen	Physiological Needs	Heat, air, base salary

SOURCE: Abraham F. Maslow, "A Theory of Human Motivation," *Psychological Review* 50 (1943): 370-396.

SPOTLIGHT ON SKILLS

Franzblau Media

Broadway musicals take the same planning and hard work as any other new venture. Producer Bill Franzblau creates a tight system to deliver a quality product (the musical) and give backers a comfortable return on their financial investment, such as he did in 2008 when box office records were broken with his newest musical, *Little House on the Prairie*.

A successful show requires a strong team, and Franzblau starts by hiring people who are better than he is in their jobs. "He pulls together not-necessarily-team-playing creative people and fosters an environment where they become valuable contributors," says frequent collaborator New York public relations executive Bill Hoffstetter. By gaining confidence through listening without ego and by honoring talent while not having to take credit, Franzblau inspires dedication and excellent results. Anyone's ideas are given consideration, but if it doesn't work, he says so. "He's that rare person in theater who says what he feels," notes Tony Award–winning playwright and composer Rupert Holmes, Franzblau's collaborator on the award-winning Broadway hit *Say Goodnight Gracie*. "He doesn't employ spin," he states. "While others embellish or cover up, Bill uses the unorthodox tactic of telling the kind truth." Tony-winning director and choreographer Hinton Battle elaborates further, "If he says he will do it, he will do it. He doesn't talk out of the side of his mouth and that is worth a *lot*."

Franzblau knows chemistry is important in building a team and is wary of hiring divas. His finely tuned sense of justice never lets temperamental members create situations of blatant unfairness, says Holmes. By not giving into outrageous demands, no matter how big the star, people learn to treat one another with respect.

Still, problems do erupt, and Franzblau handles them right away. "If ignored, business problems only fester and get worse, costing more financially and emotionally," he says. Crises often occur in shows, notes Battle, who worked with Franzblau on *Evil Dead: The Musical* and *RESPECT* and says, "The difference is Bill knows how to put out fires and still keep people interested. This is not a skill many producers have."

One of Franzblau's cardinal rules: You must lead by example. If the producer or leader is wild and crazy, others follow suit. So he remains calm, saving any sharpness in tone for those rare every-four-years-or-so extreme situations. And he never takes anything personally. "Look," he says, "what we do is make people laugh. We are about singing and dancing and telling jokes. We aren't opening up anyone's chest cavity for open-heart surgery, nor are we curing cancer. At the end of the day, we are entertainers, and we need to remember that. It helps maintain balance and a sense of proportion."

"Bill's a real gentleman," says Hofstetter. "We would do anything for him." Battle concurs. "He's one of the good ones."

SOURCES: Bill Franzblau, personal interview, June 2009; Hinton Battle, personal interview, July 2007; Bill Hofstetter, personal interview, July 2007; Rupert Holmes, personal interview, July 2007.

TAKE ACTION

As a new manager, recognize that some people are motivated primarily to satisfy lower-level physiological and safety needs, while others want to satisfy higher-level needs. Learn which lower- and higher-level needs motivate you by completing the Self Learning exercise on page 436.

Bill Franzblau keeps high levels of self-actualization by fostering team spirit and allowing people to be creative, as described in the Spotlight on Skills box.

According to Maslow's theory, low-order needs take priority—they must be satisfied before higher-order needs are activated. The needs are satisfied in sequence: Physiological needs come before safety needs, safety needs before social needs, and so on. A person desiring physical safety will devote his or her efforts to securing a safer environment and will not be concerned with esteem needs or self-actualization needs. Once a need is satisfied, it declines in importance and the next higher need is activated.

A study of employees in the manufacturing department of a major health-care company in the United Kingdom provides some support for Maslow's theory. Most line workers emphasized that they worked at the company primarily because of the good pay, benefits, and job security. Thus, employees' lower-level physiological and safety needs were being met. When questioned about their motivation, employees indicated the importance of positive social relationships with both peers and supervisors (belongingness needs) and a desire for greater respect and recognition from management (esteem needs).[8]

ERG THEORY

Clayton Alderfer proposed a modification of Maslow's theory in an effort to simplify it and respond to criticisms of its lack of empirical verification.[9] His **ERG theory** identified three categories of needs:

1. *existence needs*, or the needs for physical well-being;

2. *relatedness needs*, or the needs for satisfactory relationships with others; and

3. *growth needs*, or the needs that focus on the development of human potential and the desire for personal growth and increased competence.

The ERG model and Maslow's need hierarchy are similar because both are in hierarchical form and presume that individuals move up the hierarchy one step at a time. However, Alderfer reduced the number of need categories to three and proposed that movement up the hierarchy is more complex, reflecting a **frustration–regression principle**, namely, that failure to meet a high-order need may trigger a regression to an already fulfilled lower-order need. Thus, a worker who cannot fulfill a need for personal growth may revert to a lower-order need and redirect his or her efforts toward making a lot of money. The ERG model therefore is less rigid than Maslow's need hierarchy, suggesting that individuals may move down as well as up the hierarchy, depending on their ability to satisfy needs.

Need hierarchy theory helps explain why organizations find ways to recognize employees, encourage their participation in decision making, and give them opportunities to make significant contributions to the organization and society. At Sterling Bank, with headquarters in Houston, Texas, there are no *bank tellers*. These positions are now frontline managers who have the opportunity to make decisions and contribute ideas for improving the business.[10] USAA, which offers insurance, mutual funds, and banking services to 5 million current and former members of the military and their families, provides another example.

> **ERG theory**
> A modification of the needs hierarchy theory that proposes three categories of needs: existence, relatedness, and growth.
>
> **frustration–regression principle**
> The idea that failure to meet a high-order need may cause a regression to an already satisfied lower-order need.

USAA

USAA's customer-service agents are on the front lines in helping families challenged by war and overseas deployment manage their financial responsibilities. Managers recognize that the most important factor in the company's success is the relationship between USAA members and these frontline employees.

To make sure that the relationship is a good one, USAA treats customer-service reps, often considered the lowest rung on the corporate ladder, as valued professionals. People have a real sense that they're making life just a little easier for military members and their families, which gives them a feeling of pride and importance. Employees are organized into small, tightly knit "expert teams" and are encouraged to suggest changes that will benefit customers. Service reps don't have scripts to follow, and calls aren't timed. Employees know they can take whatever time they need to give the customer the best possible service.

Giving people the opportunity to make genuine contributions has paid off. In a study by Forrester Research, 81 percent of USAA customers said they believe the company does what's best for them rather than what's best for the bottom line. Compare that to about 20 percent of customers for other financial services firms.[11]

1 Money is the most important motivator for employees.

ANSWER: Though money is an important motivator, higher-level needs are vital for long-term motivation. Recognition, interesting work, and good co-workers—all these are important, too.

Assess Your Answer

Commitment Score

8.7

7.3

Burnout Score

4.0

1.7

Employees who have control over their work schedules

Employees who lack control over their work schedules

SOURCE: WFD Consulting data, as reported in Karol Rose, "Work-Life Effectiveness," *Fortune* (Sept. 29, 2003): S1–S17. Copyright WFD Consulting.

A recent survey found that employees who contribute ideas at work, such as customer-service reps at USAA, are more likely to feel valued, committed, and motivated. In addition, when employees' ideas are implemented and recognized, a motivational effect often ripples throughout the workforce.[12]

Many companies are finding that creating a humane work environment that allows people to achieve a balance between work and personal life is also a great high-level motivator. Flexibility in the workplace, including options such as telecommuting, flexible hours, and job sharing, is highly valued by today's employees because it enables them to manage their work and personal responsibilities. Flexibility is good for organizations, too. Employees who have control over their work schedules are significantly less likely to suffer job burnout and are more highly committed to their employers, as shown in Exhibit 13.3. This idea was supported by a survey conducted at Deloitte, which found that client-service professionals cited workplace flexibility as a strong reason for wanting to stay with the firm. Another study at Prudential Insurance found that work–life satisfaction and work flexibility directly correlated to job satisfaction, organizational commitment, and employee retention.[13]

A TWO-FACTOR APPROACH TO MOTIVATION

As a manager, remember that some people are motivated by money and others by interesting work and recognition.

hygiene factors
Factors that involve the presence or absence of job dissatisfiers, including working conditions, pay, company policies, and interpersonal relationships.

Frederick Herzberg developed another popular theory of motivation called the *two-factor theory*.[14] Herzberg interviewed hundreds of workers about times when they were highly motivated to work and other times when they were dissatisfied and unmotivated. His findings suggested that the work characteristics associated with dissatisfaction were quite different from those pertaining to satisfaction, which prompted the notion that two factors influence work motivation.

The two-factor theory is illustrated in Exhibit 13.4. The center of the scale is neutral, meaning that workers are neither satisfied nor dissatisfied. Herzberg believed that two entirely separate dimensions contribute to an employee's behavior at work. The first, called **hygiene factors**, involves the presence or absence of job dissatisfiers, such as working conditions, pay, company policies, and interpersonal relationships. When hygiene factors are poor, work is dissatisfying. However, good hygiene factors simply remove the dissatisfaction; they do not in themselves cause people to become highly satisfied and motivated in their work.

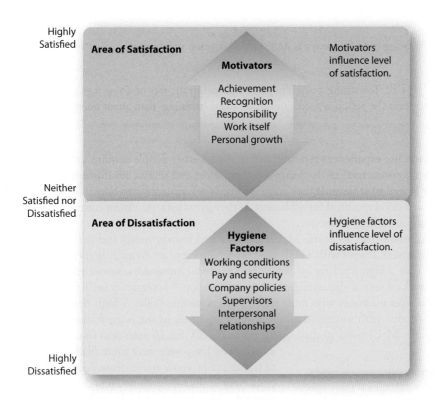

EXHIBIT 13.4
Herzberg's Two-
Factor Theory

The second set of factors does influence job satisfaction. **Motivators** focus on high-level needs and include achievement, recognition, responsibility, and opportunity for growth. Herzberg believed that when motivators are absent, workers are neutral toward work, but when motivators are present, workers are highly motivated and satisfied. Thus, hygiene factors and motivators represent two distinct factors that influence motivation. Hygiene factors work only in the area of dissatisfaction. Unsafe working conditions or a noisy work environment will cause people to be dissatisfied, but their correction will not lead to a high level of motivation and satisfaction. Motivators such as challenge, responsibility, and recognition must be in place before employees will be highly motivated to excel at their work.

The implication of the two-factor theory for managers is clear. On one hand, providing hygiene factors will eliminate employee dissatisfaction but will not motivate workers to high achievement levels. On the other hand, recognition, challenge, and opportunities for personal growth are powerful motivators and will promote high satisfaction and performance. The manager's role is to remove dissatisfiers—that is, to provide hygiene factors sufficient to meet basic needs—and then to use motivators to meet higher-level needs and propel employees toward greater achievement and satisfaction.

ACQUIRED NEEDS

The *acquired needs theory*, developed by David McClelland, proposes that certain types of needs are acquired during the individual's lifetime. In other words, people are not born with these needs but may learn them through their life experiences.[15] The three needs most frequently studied are these:

1. *need for achievement*—the desire to accomplish something difficult, attain a high standard of success, master complex tasks, and surpass others;

2. *need for affiliation*—the desire to form close personal relationships, avoid conflict, and establish warm friendships; and

3. *need for power*—the desire to influence or control others, be responsible for others, and have authority over others.

motivators
Factors that influence job satisfaction based on fulfillment of high-level needs such as achievement, recognition, responsibility, and opportunity for growth.

2 A strong need for power is necessary to develop your career.

ANSWER: Too strong a need for power can get in the way of doing a good job because it often means the person is more concerned about "winning" than about doing the best job.

Early life experiences typically determine whether people acquire these needs. If children are encouraged to do things for themselves and receive reinforcement, they will acquire a need to achieve. If they are reinforced for forming warm human relationships, then they will develop a need for affiliation. If they get satisfaction from controlling others, they will acquire a need for power.

For more than 20 years, McClelland studied human needs and their implications for management. People with a high need for achievement are frequently entrepreneurs. People who have a high need for *affiliation* are successful integrators, whose job is to coordinate the work of several departments in an organization.[16] Integrators include brand managers and project managers who must have excellent people skills. A high need for *power* often is associated with successful attainment of top levels in the organizational hierarchy. For example, McClelland studied managers at AT&T for 16 years and found that those with a high need for power were more likely to follow a path of continued promotion over time. More than half of the employees at the top levels had a high need for power. In contrast, managers with a high need for achievement but a low need for power tended to peak earlier in their careers and at a lower level. The reason is that achievement needs can be met through the task itself, but power needs can be met only by ascending to a level at which a person has power over others.

In summary, content theories focus on people's underlying needs and label those particular needs that motivate behavior. The hierarchy of needs theory, the ERG theory, the two-factor theory, and the acquired needs theory all help managers understand what motivates people. In this way, managers can design work to meet needs and hence elicit appropriate and successful work behaviors.

process theories
A group of theories that explain how employees select behaviors with which to meet their needs and determine whether their choices were successful.

At Computerized Facility Integration (CFI), clear, specific goals enhance employee motivation and commitment. CFI's turnover is 4 percent, dramatically lower than the industry average of 30 percent. Every employee—from clerical help to senior management—receives a monthly bonus for meeting established targets. "It varies by role, of course, but we clearly state what everyone should be achieving, and we reward people accordingly," says founder and chief executive officer (CEO) Robert Verdun. "One of the big advantages of this bonus system is that it obliges us to keep communicating." The Southfield, Michigan, company installs and services technology systems in office buildings and factories.

© ALISON ALIANO

>> CONCEPT CONNECTION <<

Process Perspectives on Motivation

Process theories explain how people select behavioral actions to meet their needs and determine whether their choices were successful. Important perspectives in this area include goal setting, equity theory, and expectancy theory.

GOAL SETTING

Recall from Chapter 5 our discussion of the importance and purposes of goals. Numerous studies have shown that specific, challenging targets significantly enhance people's motivation and performance levels.[17] You have probably noticed in your own life that you are more motivated when you have a specific goal such as making an A on a final exam, losing 10 pounds before spring break, or earning enough money during the summer to buy a used car.

Goal-setting theory, described by Edwin Locke and Gary Latham, proposes that managers can increase motivation and enhance performance by setting specific, challenging goals, and then helping people track their progress toward goal achievement by providing timely feedback. Key components of goal-setting theory include the following:[18]

- *Goal specificity* refers to the degree to which goals are concrete and unambiguous. Specific goals such as "visit one new customer each day," or "sell $1,000 worth of merchandise a week" are more motivating than vague goals such as "keep in touch with new customers" or "increase merchandise sales." For example, a lack of clear, specific goals is cited as a major cause of the failure of pay-for-performance incentive plans in many organizations.[19] Vague goals can be frustrating for employees.

- In terms of *goal difficulty*, hard goals are more motivating than easy ones. Easy goals provide little challenge for employees and don't require them to increase their output. Highly ambitious but achievable goals ask people to stretch their abilities and provide a basis for greater feelings of accomplishment and personal effectiveness. A study in Germany found that, over a three-year period, only employees who perceived their goals as difficult reported increases in positive emotions and feelings of job satisfaction and success.[20]

- *Goal acceptance* means that employees have to "buy into" the goals and be committed to them. Having people participate in setting goals is a good way to increase acceptance and commitment. At Aluminio del Caroni, a state-owned aluminum company in southeastern Venezuela, plant workers felt a renewed sense of commitment when top leaders implemented a *co-management* initiative that has managers and lower-level employees working together to set budgets, determine goals, and make decisions. "The managers and the workers are running this business together," said one employee who spends his days shoveling molten aluminum down a channel from an industrial oven to a cast. "It gives us the motivation to work hard."[21]

- Finally, the component of *feedback* means that people get information about how well they are doing in progressing toward goal achievement. It is important for managers to provide performance feedback on a regular, ongoing basis. However, self-feedback, where people are able to monitor their own progress toward a goal, has been found to be an even stronger motivator than external feedback.[22]

Why does goal setting increase motivation? For one thing, it enables people to focus their energies in the right direction. People know what to work toward, so they can direct their efforts toward the most important activities to accomplish the goals. Goals also energize behavior because people feel compelled to develop plans and strategies that keep them focused on achieving the target. Specific, difficult goals provide a challenge and encourage people to put forth high levels of effort. In addition, when goals are achieved, pride and satisfaction increase, contributing to higher motivation and morale.[23]

As a manager, give regular and meaningful feedback to employees.

To keep employees focused, use specific, challenging goals that team members help set.

goal-setting theory
A motivation theory in which specific, challenging goals increase motivation and performance when the goals are accepted by subordinates and these subordinates receive feedback to indicate their progress toward goal achievement.

3 Too much feedback can be harmful to workers' productivity.

ANSWER: Honest, matter-of-fact feedback helps workers know when they are doing well or not making the mark. Too much feedback is only a problem if it is given in a negative, punitive manner.

Assess
Your
Answer ?

EQUITY THEORY

Equity theory focuses on individuals' perceptions of how fairly they are treated compared with others. Developed by J. Stacy Adams, equity theory proposes that people are motivated to seek social equity in the rewards they expect for performance.[24]

According to equity theory, if people perceive their compensation as equal to what others receive for similar contributions, then they will believe that their treatment is fair and equitable. People evaluate equity by a ratio of inputs to outcomes. Inputs to a job include education, experience, effort, and ability. Outcomes from a job include pay, recognition, benefits, and promotions. The input-to-outcome ratio may be compared to another person in the work group or to a perceived group average. A state of **equity** exists whenever the ratio of one person's outcomes to inputs equals the ratio of another's outcomes to inputs.

Inequity occurs when the input-to-outcome ratios are out of balance, such as when a new, inexperienced employee receives the same salary as a person with a high level of education or experience. Interestingly, perceived inequity also occurs in the other direction. Thus, if an employee discovers she is making more money than other people who contribute the same inputs to the company, she may feel the need to correct the inequity by working harder, getting more education, or considering lower pay. Studies of the brain have shown that people get less satisfaction from money they receive without having to earn it than they do from money they work to receive.[25] Perceived inequity creates tensions within individuals that motivate them to bring equity into balance.[26]

The most common methods for reducing a perceived inequity are these:

- *Change work effort.* A person may choose to increase or decrease his or her inputs to the organization. Individuals who believe they are underpaid may reduce their level of effort or increase their absenteeism. Overpaid people may increase effort on the job.

- *Change outcomes.* A person may change his or her outcomes. An underpaid person may request a salary increase or a bigger office. A union may try to improve wages and working conditions to be consistent with a comparable union whose members make more money.

- *Change perceptions.* Research suggests that people may change perceptions of equity if they are unable to change inputs or outcomes. They may artificially increase the status attached to their jobs or distort others' perceived rewards to bring equity into balance.

- *Leave the job.* People who feel inequitably treated may decide to leave their jobs rather than suffer the inequity of being under- or overpaid. In their new jobs, they expect to find a more favorable balance of rewards.

The implication of equity theory for managers is that employees indeed evaluate the perceived equity of their own compared to others' rewards. Inequitable pay puts pressure on employees that is sometimes almost too great to bear. They attempt to change their work habits, try to change the system, or leave the job.[27] Consider Deb Allen, who went into the office on a weekend to catch up on work and found a document accidentally left on the copy machine. When she saw that some new hires were earning $200,000 more than their counterparts with more experience and that "a noted screw-up" was making more than highly competent people, Allen began questioning why she was working on weekends for less pay than many others were receiving. Allen became so demoralized by the inequity that she quit her job three months later.[28]

EXPECTANCY THEORY

Expectancy theory suggests that motivation depends on individuals' expectations about their ability to perform tasks and receive desired rewards. Expectancy theory is associated with the work of Victor Vroom, although a number of scholars have made contributions in this area.[29]

Expectancy theory is concerned not with identifying types of needs but with the thinking process that individuals use to achieve rewards. Consider Amy Huang, a university student

As a new manager, be alert to feelings of inequity among your team members. Don't play favorites such as regularly praising some members while overlooking others who are making similar contributions.

Remember, if you believe that hard work will help you achieve your goals, you will be more likely to work hard.

equity theory
A process theory that focuses on individuals' perceptions of how fairly they are treated relative to others.

equity
A situation that exists when the ratio of one person's outcomes to inputs equals that of another's.

expectancy theory
A process theory that proposes that motivation depends on individuals' expectations about their ability to perform tasks and receive desired rewards.

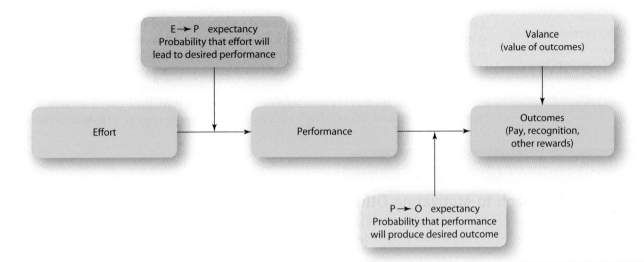

EXHIBIT 13.5
Major Elements of
Expectancy Theory

with a strong desire for a B in her accounting course. Amy has a C+ average and one more exam to take. Amy's motivation to study for that last exam will be influenced by: (1) the expectation that hard study will lead to an A on the exam and (2) the expectation that an A on the exam will result in a B for the course. If Amy believes she cannot get an A on the exam or that receiving an A will not lead to a B for the course, then she will not be motivated to study exceptionally hard.

Expectancy theory is based on the relationship among the individual's *effort*, the individual's *performance*, and the desirability of *outcomes* associated with high performance. These elements and the relationships among them are illustrated in Exhibit 13.5. The keys to expectancy theory are the expectancies for the relationships among effort, performance, and the value of the outcomes to the individual.

E → P expectancy involves determining whether putting effort into a task will lead to high performance. For this expectancy to be high, the individual must have the ability, previous experience, and necessary equipment, tools, and opportunity to perform. Let's consider a simple sales example. If Carlos, a salesperson at the Diamond Gift Shop, believes that increased selling effort will lead to higher personal sales, we can say that he has a high E → P expectancy. However, if Carlos believes he has neither the ability nor the opportunity to achieve high performance, both expectancy and motivation will be low.

P → O expectancy involves determining whether successful performance will lead to the desired outcome or reward. If the P → O expectancy is high, then the individual will be more highly motivated. If the expectancy is that high performance will not produce the desired outcome, motivation will be lower. If Carlos believes that higher personal sales will lead to a pay increase, we can say that he has a high P → O expectancy. He might be aware that raises are coming up for consideration, so he might choose to talk with his supervisor or other employees to see if increased sales will help him earn a better raise. If not, he will be less motivated to work hard.

Valence is the value of outcomes, or attraction to outcomes, for the individual. If the outcomes that are available from high effort and good performance are not valued by employees, then motivation will be low. Likewise, if outcomes have a high value, motivation will be higher. If Carlos places a high value on the pay raise, valence is high and he will have a high motivational force. On the other hand, if the money has low valence for Carlos, the overall motivational force will be low. For an employee to be highly motivated, all three factors in the expectancy model must be high.[30]

Expectancy theory attempts not to define specific types of needs or rewards but only to establish that they exist and may be different for every individual. One employee might

As a new manager, how would you manage expectations and use rewards to motivate subordinates to perform well? Complete the New Manager's Self-Test (page 424) to learn more about your approach to motivating others.

E → P expectancy
Expectancy that putting effort into a given task will lead to high performance.

P → O expectancy
Expectancy that successful performance of a task will lead to the desired outcome.

valence
The value or attraction an individual has for an outcome.

reinforcement theory
A motivation theory based on the relationship between a given behavior and its consequences.

want to be promoted to a position of increased responsibility, and another might have high valence for good relationships with peers. Consequently, the first person will be motivated to work hard for a promotion and the second for the opportunity of a team position that will keep him or her associated with a group. Recent studies substantiate the idea that rewards need to be individualized to be motivating. A recent finding from the U.S. Department of Labor shows that the number-one reason people leave their jobs is because they "don't feel appreciated." Yet Gallup's analysis of 10,000 workgroups in 30 industries found

NEW MANAGER'S SELF-TEST

Your Approach to Motivating Others

Think about situations in which you were in a student group or organization. Think about your informal approach as a leader and answer the questions below. Indicate whether each of the following items is Mostly False or Mostly True for you.

	MOSTLY TRUE	MOSTLY FALSE
1. I ask the other person what rewards he or she values for high performance.	_____	_____
2. I only reward people if their performance is up to standard.	_____	_____
3. I find out if the person has the ability to do what needs to be done.	_____	_____
4. I use a variety of rewards (treats, recognition) to reinforce exceptional performance.	_____	_____
5. I explain exactly what needs to be done for the person I'm trying to motivate.	_____	_____
6. I generously and publicly praise people who perform well.	_____	_____
7. Before giving somebody a reward, I find out what would appeal to that person.	_____	_____
8. I promptly commend others when they do a better-than-average job.	_____	_____

SCORING AND INTERPRETATION: The questions above represent two related aspects of motivation theory. For the aspect of *expectancy theory*, sum the points for Mostly True to the odd-numbered questions. For the aspect of *reinforcement theory*, sum the points for Mostly True for the even-numbered questions.

The scores for my approach to motivation are:

My use of expectancy theory _____
My use of reinforcement theory _____

These two scores represent how you apply the motivational concepts of expectancy and reinforcement in your role as an informal leader. Three or more points on *expectancy theory* means you motivate people by managing expectations. You understand how a person's effort leads to performance and make sure that high performance leads to valued rewards. Three or more points for *reinforcement theory* means that you attempt to modify people's behavior in a positive direction with frequent and prompt positive reinforcement. New managers often learn to use reinforcements first, and as they gain more experience are able to apply expectancy theory.

SOURCES: These questions are based on D. Whetten and K. Cameron, *Developing Management Skills*, 5th ed. (Upper Saddle River, NJ: Prentice-Hall, 2002): 302–303; and P. M. Podsakoff, S. B. Mackenzie, R. H. Moorman, and R. Fetter, "Transformational Leader Behaviors and Their Effects on Followers' Trust in Leader, Satisfaction, and Organizational Citizenship Behaviors," *Leadership Quarterly* 1(2) (1990): 107–142.

that making people feel appreciated depends on finding the right kind of reward for each individual. Some people prefer tangible rewards or gifts, while others place high value on words of recognition. In addition, some want public recognition while others prefer to be quietly praised by someone they admire and respect.[31]

Reinforcement Perspective on Motivation

The reinforcement approach to employee motivation sidesteps the issues of employee needs and thinking processes described in the content and process theories. **Reinforcement theory** simply looks at the relationship between behavior and its consequences. It focuses on changing or modifying employees' on-the-job behavior through the appropriate use of immediate rewards and punishments.

Behavior modification is the name given to the set of techniques by which reinforcement theory is used to modify human behavior.[32] The basic assumption underlying behavior modification is the **law of effect**, which states that behavior that is positively reinforced tends to be repeated, and behavior that is not reinforced tends not to be repeated. **Reinforcement** is defined as anything that causes a certain behavior to be repeated or inhibited. The four reinforcement tools are positive reinforcement, avoidance learning, punishment, and extinction, as summarized in Exhibit 13.6.

- **Positive reinforcement** is the administration of a pleasant and rewarding consequence following a desired behavior, such as praise for an employee who arrives on time or does a little extra work. Research shows that positive reinforcement does help to improve performance. Moreover, nonfinancial reinforcements such as positive feedback, social recognition, and attention are just as effective as financial incentives.[33] One study of employees at fast-food drive-through windows, for example, found that performance feedback and supervisor recognition had a significant effect on increasing the incidence of "up-selling," or

behavior modification
The set of techniques by which reinforcement theory is used to modify human behavior.

law of effect
The assumption that positively reinforced behavior tends to be repeated, and unreinforced or negatively reinforced behavior tends to be inhibited.

reinforcement
Anything that causes a given behavior to be repeated or inhibited.

positive reinforcement
The administration of a pleasant and rewarding consequence following a desired behavior.

EXHIBIT 13.6
Changing Behavior with Reinforcement
- - - - - - - - - - -

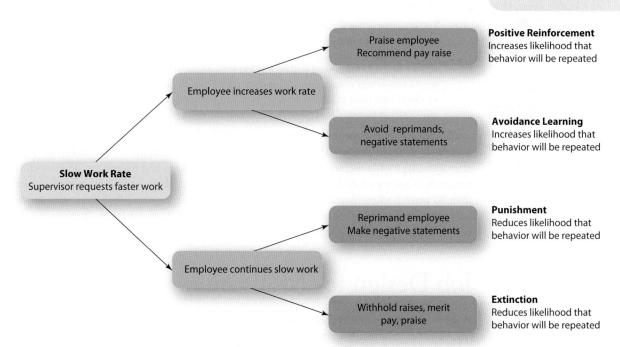

SOURCE: Based on Richard L. Daft and Richard M. Steers, *Organizations: A Micro/Macro Approach* (Glenview, IL: Scott, Foresman, 1986): 109.

Farm managers apply positive reinforcement by basing a fruit or vegetable picker's pay on the amount he or she harvests. A variation on this individual piece-rate system is a relative incentive plan that bases each worker's pay on the ratio of the individual's productivity to average productivity among all co-workers. A study of Eastern and Central European pickers in the United Kingdom found that workers' productivity declined under the relative plan. Researchers theorized that fast workers didn't want to hurt their slower colleagues, so they reduced their efforts. The study authors suggested that a team-based scheme—where everyone's pay increased if the team did well—would be more effective.

························> CONCEPT CONNECTION <·······················

As a leader, give positive feedback and other rewards for behaviors that you want to be repeated.

Remember: Reward and punishment are limited motivational tools that focus only on extrinsic rewards and lower-level needs. Use intrinsic rewards to meet higher level needs.

avoidance learning
The removal of an unpleasant consequence when an undesirable behavior is corrected.

getting customers to increase their orders.[34] Indeed, many people value factors other than money. Nelson Motivation Inc. conducted a survey of 750 employees across various industries to assess the value they placed on various rewards. Cash and other monetary awards came in dead last. The most valued rewards involved praise and manager support and involvement.[35]

- **Avoidance learning** is the removal of an unpleasant consequence following a desired behavior. Avoidance learning is sometimes called *negative reinforcement*. Employees learn to do the right thing by avoiding unpleasant situations. Avoidance learning occurs when a supervisor stops criticizing or reprimanding an employee once the incorrect behavior has stopped.

- **Punishment** is the imposition of unpleasant outcomes on an employee. Punishment typically occurs following undesirable behavior. For example, a supervisor may berate an employee for performing a task incorrectly. The supervisor expects that the negative outcome will serve as a punishment and reduce the likelihood of the behavior recurring. The use of punishment in organizations is controversial and often criticized because it fails to indicate the correct behavior. However, almost all managers report that they find it necessary to occasionally impose forms of punishment ranging from verbal reprimands to employee suspensions or firings.[36]

- **Extinction** is the withdrawal of a positive reward. Whereas with punishment, the supervisor imposes an unpleasant outcome such as a reprimand, extinction involves withholding pay raises, bonuses, praise, or other positive outcomes. The idea is that behavior that is not positively reinforced will be less likely to occur in the future. A good example of the use of extinction comes from Cheektowaga (New York) Central Middle School, where students with poor grades or bad attitudes are excluded from extracurricular activities such as athletic contests, dances, crafts, or ice-cream socials.[37]

Reward and punishment motivational practices dominate organizations. According to the Society for Human Resource Management, 84 percent of all companies in the United States offer some type of monetary or nonmonetary reward system, and 69 percent offer incentive pay, such as bonuses, based on an employee's performance.[38] However, in other studies, more than 80 percent of employers with incentive programs have reported that their programs are only somewhat successful or not working at all.[39] Despite the testimonies of organizations that enjoy successful incentive programs, criticism of these "carrot-and-stick" methods is growing.

Job Design for Motivation

A *job* in an organization is a unit of work that a single employee is responsible for performing. A job could include writing tickets for parking violators in New York City, performing MRI scans at Salt Lake Regional Medical Center, reading meters for Pacific Gas and Electric, or doing long-range planning for the WB television network. Jobs are an important consideration for motivation because performing their components may provide rewards that meet employees' needs. Managers need to know what aspects of a job provide motivation as well as how to compensate for routine tasks that have little inherent satisfaction. **Job design** is the application of motivational theories to the structure of work for improving productivity and satisfaction. Approaches to job design are generally classified as job simplification, job rotation, job enlargement, and job enrichment.

JOB SIMPLIFICATION

Job simplification pursues task efficiency by reducing the number of tasks one person must do. Job simplification is based on principles drawn from scientific management and industrial engineering. Tasks are designed to be simple, repetitive, and standardized. As complexity is stripped from a job, the worker has more time to concentrate on doing more of the same routine task. Workers with low skill levels can perform the job, and the organization achieves a high level of efficiency. Indeed, workers are interchangeable because they need little training or skill and exercise little judgment. As a motivational technique, however, job simplification has failed. People dislike routine and boring jobs and react in a number of negative ways, including sabotage, absenteeism, and unionization. Job simplification is compared with job rotation and job enlargement in Exhibit 13.7.

JOB ROTATION

Job rotation systematically moves employees from one job to another, thereby increasing the number of different tasks an employee performs without increasing the complexity of any one job. For example, an autoworker might install windshields one week and front bumpers the next. Job rotation still takes advantage of engineering efficiencies, but it provides variety and stimulation for employees. Although employees might find the new job interesting at first, the novelty soon wears off as the repetitive work is mastered.

Companies such as Home Depot, Motorola, 1-800-Flowers, and Dayton Hudson have built on the notion of job rotation to train a flexible workforce. As companies break away from ossified job categories, workers can perform several jobs, thereby reducing labor costs and giving people opportunities to develop new skills. At Home Depot, for example, workers scattered throughout the company's vast chain of stores can get a taste of the corporate climate by working at in-store support centers, while associate managers can dirty their hands out on the sales floor.[40] Job rotation also gives companies greater flexibility. One production worker might shift among the jobs of drill operator, punch operator, and assembler, depending on the company's need at the moment. Some unions have resisted the idea, but many now go along, realizing that it helps the company be more competitive.[41]

punishment
The imposition of an unpleasant outcome following undesirable behavior.

extinction
The withdrawal of a positive reward.

job design
The application of motivational theories to the structure of work for improving productivity and satisfaction.

job simplification
A job design whose purpose is to improve task efficiency by reducing the number of tasks a single person must do.

job rotation
A job design that systematically moves employees from one job to another to provide them with variety and stimulation.

EXHIBIT 13.7
Types of Job Design
- - - - - - - - - -

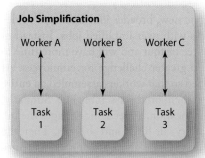

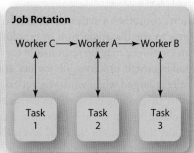

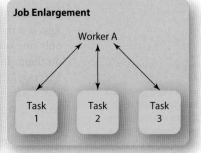

Job Simplification

Worker A Worker B Worker C

Task 1 Task 2 Task 3

Job Rotation

Worker C → Worker A → Worker B

Task 1 Task 2 Task 3

Job Enlargement

Worker A

Task 1 Task 2 Task 3

SPOTLIGHT ON SKILLS

The Carrot-and-Stick Controversy

Everybody thought Rob Rodin was crazy when he decided to wipe out all individual incentives for his sales force at Marshall Industries, a large distributor of electronic components based in El Monte, California. He did away with all bonuses, commissions, vacations, and other awards and rewards. All salespeople would receive a base salary plus the opportunity for profit sharing, which would be the same percent of salary for everyone, based on the entire company's performance. Six years later, Rodin says productivity per person has tripled at the company, but still he gets questions and criticism about his decision.

Rodin is standing right in the middle of a big controversy in modern management. Do financial and other rewards really motivate the kind of behavior organizations want and need? A growing number of critics say no, arguing that carrot-and-stick approaches are a holdover from the Industrial Age and are inappropriate and ineffective in today's economy. Today's workplace demands innovation and creativity from everyone—behaviors that rarely are inspired by money or other financial incentives. Reasons for criticism of carrot-and-stick approaches include the following:

1. *Extrinsic rewards diminish intrinsic rewards.* When people are motivated to seek an extrinsic reward—whether a bonus, an award, or the approval of a supervisor—they generally focus on the reward rather than on the work they do to achieve it. Thus, the intrinsic satisfaction people receive from performing their jobs actually declines. When people lack intrinsic rewards in their work, their performance stays just adequate to achieve the reward offered. In the worst case, employees may cover up mistakes or cheat to achieve the reward. One study, for example, found that teachers who were rewarded for increasing test scores frequently used various forms of cheating.

2. *Extrinsic rewards are temporary.* Offering outside incentives may ensure short-term success, but not long-term high performance. When employees are focused only on the reward, they lose interest in their work. Without personal interest, the potential for exploration, creativity, and innovation disappears. Although the current deadline or goal may be met, better ways of working and serving customers will not be discovered and the company's long-term success will be affected.

3. *Extrinsic rewards assume people are driven by lower-level needs.* Rewards such as bonuses, pay increases, and even praise presume that the primary reason people initiate and persist in behavior is to satisfy lower-level needs. However, behavior also is based on yearnings for self-expression and on feelings of self-esteem and self-worth. Typical individual incentive programs don't reflect and encourage the myriad behaviors that are motivated by people's need to express themselves and realize their higher needs for growth and fulfillment.

Today's organizations need employees who are motivated to think, experiment, and continuously search for ways to solve new problems. Alfie Kohn, one of the most vocal critics of carrot-and-stick approaches, offers the following advice to managers regarding how to pay employees: "Pay well, pay fairly, and then do everything you can to get money off people's minds." Indeed some evidence indicates that money is not primarily what people work for. Managers should understand the limits of extrinsic motivators and work to satisfy employees' higher, as well as lower, needs. To be motivated, employees need jobs that offer self-satisfaction in addition to a yearly pay raise.

SOURCES: Alfie Kohn, "Incentives Can Be Bad for Business," *Inc.* (Jan. 1998): 93–94; A. J. Vogl, "Carrots, Sticks, and Self-Deception" (an interview with Alfie Kohn), *Across the Board* (Jan. 1994): 39–44; Geoffrey Colvin, "What Money Makes You Do," *Fortune* (Aug. 17, 1998): 213–214; and Jeffrey Pfeffer, "Sins of Commission," *Business 2.0* (May 2004): 56.

JOB ENLARGEMENT

job enlargement
A job design that combines a series of tasks into one new, broader job to give employees variety and challenge.

Job enlargement combines a series of tasks into one new, broader job. This type of design is a response to the dissatisfaction of employees with oversimplified jobs. Instead of only one job, an employee may be responsible for three or four and will have more time to do them. Job enlargement provides job variety and a greater challenge for employees. At Maytag, jobs were enlarged when work was redesigned so that workers assembled an entire water pump rather than doing each part as it reached them on the assembly line. Similarly, rather than just changing the oil at a Precision Tune location, a mechanic changes the oil, greases the car, airs the tires, checks fluid levels, battery, air filter, and so forth. Then the same employee is responsible for consulting with the customer about routine maintenance or any problems he or she sees with the vehicle.

JOB ENRICHMENT

Recall the discussion of Maslow's need hierarchy and Herzberg's two-factor theory. Rather than just changing the number and frequency of tasks a worker performs, **job enrichment** incorporates high-level motivators into the work, including job responsibility, recognition, and opportunities for growth, learning, and achievement. In an enriched job, employees have control over the resources necessary for performing it, make decisions on how to do the work, experience personal growth, and set their own work pace. Research shows that when jobs are designed to be controlled more by employees than by managers, people typically feel a greater sense of involvement, commitment, and motivation, which in turn contributes to higher morale, lower turnover, and stronger organizational performance.[42]

Many companies have undertaken job-enrichment programs to increase employees' involvement, motivation, and job satisfaction. At Ralcorp's cereal manufacturing plant in Sparks, Nevada, for example, assembly-line employees screen, interview, and train all new hires. These employees are responsible for managing the production flow to and from their upstream and downstream partners, making daily decisions that affect their work, managing quality, and contributing to continuous improvement. Enriched jobs have improved employee motivation and satisfaction, and the company has benefited from higher long-term productivity, reduced costs, and happier, more motivated employees.[43]

JOB-CHARACTERISTICS MODEL

One significant approach to job design is the job-characteristics model developed by Richard Hackman and Greg Oldham.[44] Hackman and Oldham's research concerned **work redesign**, which is defined as altering jobs to increase both the quality of employees' work experience and their productivity. Hackman and Oldham's research into the design of hundreds of jobs yielded the **job-characteristics model**, which is illustrated in Exhibit 13.8. The model consists of three major parts: core job dimensions, critical psychological states, and employee growth-need strength.

Core Job Dimensions. Hackman and Oldham identified five dimensions that determine a job's motivational potential:

1. *Skill variety*—the number of diverse activities that compose a job and the number of skills used to perform it. A routine, repetitive assembly-line job is low in variety, whereas

job enrichment
A job design that incorporates achievement, recognition, and other high-level motivators into the work.

work redesign
The altering of jobs to increase both the quality of employees' work experience and their productivity.

job-characteristics model
A model of job design that comprises core job dimensions, critical psychological states, and employee growth-need strength.

EXHIBIT 13.8
The Job-Characteristics Model

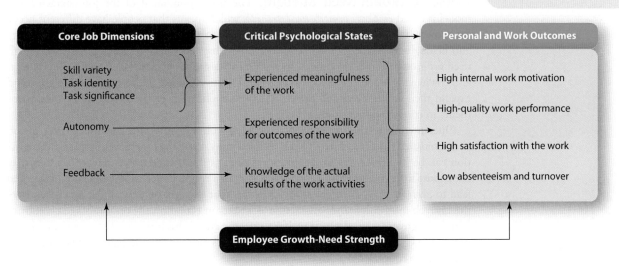

an applied research position that entails working on new problems every day is high in variety.

2. *Task identity*—the degree to which an employee performs a total job with a recognizable beginning and ending. A chef who prepares an entire meal has more task identity than a worker on a cafeteria line who ladles mashed potatoes.

3. *Task significance*—the degree to which the job is perceived as important and having impact on the company or consumers. People who distribute penicillin and other medical supplies during times of emergencies would feel they have significant jobs.

4. *Autonomy*—the degree to which the worker has freedom, discretion, and self-determination in planning and carrying out tasks. A house painter can determine how to paint the house; a paint sprayer on an assembly line has little autonomy.

5. *Feedback*—the extent to which doing the job provides information back to the employee about his or her performance. Jobs vary in their ability to let workers see the outcomes of their efforts. A football coach knows whether the team won or lost, but a basic research scientist may have to wait years to learn whether a research project was successful.

The job-characteristics model says that the more these five core characteristics can be designed into the job, the more the employees will be motivated and the higher will be performance, quality, and satisfaction.

Critical Psychological States. The model posits that core job dimensions are more rewarding when individuals experience three psychological states in response to job design. In Exhibit 13.8, skill variety, task identity, and task significance tend to influence the employee's psychological state of *experienced meaningfulness of work*. The work itself is satisfying and provides intrinsic rewards for the worker. The job characteristic of autonomy influences the worker's *experienced responsibility*. The job characteristic of feedback provides the worker with *knowledge of actual results*. The employee thus knows how he or she is doing and can change work performance to increase desired outcomes.

Personal and Work Outcomes. The impact of the five job characteristics on the psychological states of experienced meaningfulness, responsibility, and knowledge of actual results leads to the personal and work outcomes of high work motivation, high work performance, high satisfaction, and low absenteeism and turnover.

Employee Growth-Need Strength. The final component of the job-characteristics model is called *employee growth-need strength*, which means that people have different needs for growth and development. If a person wants to satisfy low-level needs such as safety and belongingness, the job-characteristics model has less effect. When a person has a high need for growth and development, including the desire for personal challenge, achievement, and challenging work, the model is especially effective. People with a high need to grow and expand their abilities respond favorably to the application of the model and to improvements in core job dimensions.

One interesting finding concerns the cross-cultural differences in the impact of job characteristics. Intrinsic factors such as autonomy, challenge, achievement, and recognition can be highly motivating in countries such as the United States. However, they may contribute little to motivation and satisfaction in a country such as Nigeria and might even lead to *demotivation*. A recent study indicates that the link between intrinsic characteristics and job motivation and satisfaction is weaker in economically disadvantaged countries with poor governmental social welfare systems and in high power distance countries as defined in Chapter 3.[45] Thus, the job-characteristics model would be expected to be less effective in these countries.

Innovative Ideas for Motivating

Despite the controversy over carrot-and-stick motivational practices discussed earlier in this chapter, organizations are increasingly using various types of incentive compensation as a way to motivate employees to higher levels of performance. Exhibit 13.9 summarizes several popular methods of incentive pay.

Variable compensation and forms of "at-risk" pay are key motivational tools that are becoming more common than fixed salaries at many companies. These programs can be effective if they are used appropriately and combined with motivational ideas that also provide employees with intrinsic rewards and meet higher-level needs. Effective managers don't use incentive plans as the sole basis of motivation. The most effective motivational programs typically involve much more than money or other external rewards. Two recent motivational trends are empowering employees and framing work to have greater meaning.

Go to the Ethical Dilemma on page 437 that pertains to the use of incentive compensation as a motivational tool.

EMPOWERING PEOPLE TO MEET HIGHER NEEDS

One significant way managers can meet higher motivational needs is to shift power down from the top of the organization and share it with employees to enable them to achieve goals. **Empowerment** is power sharing, the delegation of power or authority to subordinates in an organization.[46] Increasing employee power heightens motivation for task accomplishment because people improve their own effectiveness, choosing how to do a task and using their creativity.[47] Research indicates that most people have a need for *self-efficacy*, which is the capacity to produce results or outcomes, to feel that they are effective.[48]

Empowering employees involves giving them four elements that enable them to act more freely to accomplish their jobs: information, knowledge, power, and rewards.[49]

1. *Employees receive information about company performance.* In companies where employees are fully empowered, all employees have access to all financial and operational information.

As a leader, remember most people want to do well and to improve, so give them chances to learn and become more proficient.

empowerment
The delegation of power and authority to subordinates.

Program	Purpose
Pay for performance	Rewards individual employees in proportion to their performance contributions. Also called *merit pay*.
Gain sharing	Rewards all employees and managers within a business unit when predetermined performance targets are met. Encourages teamwork.
Employee stock ownership plan (ESOP)	Gives employees part ownership of the organization, enabling them to share in improved profit performance.
Lump-sum bonuses	Rewards employees with a one-time cash payment based on performance.
Pay for knowledge	Links employee salary with the number of task skills acquired. Workers are motivated to learn the skills for many jobs, thus increasing company flexibility and efficiency.
Flexible work schedule	*Flextime* allows workers to set their own hours. *Job sharing* allows two or more part-time workers to jointly cover one job. *Telecommuting*, sometimes called *flex-place*, allows employees to work from home or an alternative workplace.
Team-based compensation	Rewards employees for behavior and activities that benefit the team, such as cooperation, listening, and empowering others.
Lifestyle awards	Rewards employees for meeting ambitious goals with luxury items, such as high-definition televisions, tickets to big-name sporting events, and exotic travel.

EXHIBIT 13.9
New Motivational Compensation Programs

2. *Employees have knowledge and skills to contribute to company goals.* Companies use training programs and other development tools to help employees acquire the knowledge and skills they need to contribute to organizational performance.

3. *Employees have the power to make substantive decisions.* Empowered employees have the authority to directly influence work procedures and organizational performance such as through quality circles or self-directed work teams.

4. *Employees are rewarded based on company performance.* Organizations that empower workers often reward them based on the results shown in the company's bottom line. Organizations may also use other motivational compensation programs described in Exhibit 13.9 to tie employee efforts to company performance.

Many of today's organizations are implementing empowerment programs, but they are empowering workers to varying degrees. At some companies, empowerment means encouraging workers' ideas while managers retain final authority for decisions; at other companies it means giving employees almost complete freedom and power to make decisions and exercise initiative and imagination.[50] Current methods of empowerment fall along a continuum, as illustrated in Exhibit 13.10. The continuum runs from a situation

engagement
A situation in which employees enjoy their work, contribute enthusiastically to meeting goals, and feel a sense of belonging and commitment to the organization.

EXHIBIT 13.10
A Continuum of Empowerment

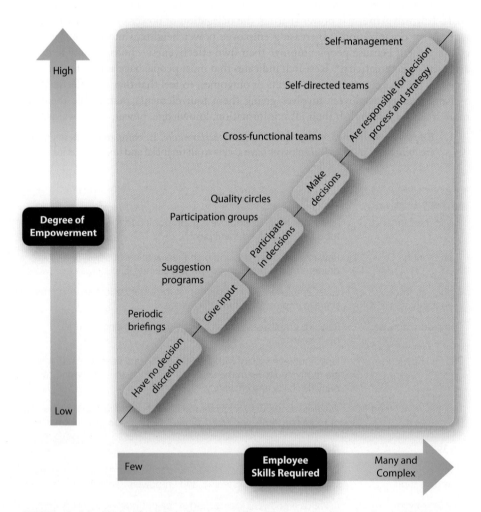

SOURCES: Based on Robert C. Ford and Myron D. Fottler, "Empowerment: A Matter of Degree," *Academy of Management Executive* 9(3) (1995): 21–31; Lawrence Holpp, "Applied Empowerment," *Training* (Feb. 1994): 39–44; and David P. McCaffrey, Sue R. Faerman, and David W. Hart, "The Appeal and Difficulties of Participative Systems," *Organization Science* 6(6) (Nov.–Dec. 1995): 603–627.

in which frontline workers have almost no discretion, such as on a traditional assembly line, to full empowerment, where workers even participate in formulating organizational strategy.

GIVING MEANING TO WORK THROUGH ENGAGEMENT

Another way to meet higher-level motivational needs and help people get intrinsic rewards from their work is to instill a sense of importance and meaningfulness. In recent years, managers have focused on employee engagement, which puts less emphasis on extrinsic rewards such as pay and more emphasis on fostering an environment in which people feel valued and effective. Employee **engagement** means that people enjoy their jobs and are satisfied with their work conditions, contribute enthusiastically to meeting team and organizational goals, and feel a sense of belonging and commitment to the orga-

nization. Fully engaged employees care deeply about the organization and actively seek out ways to serve the mission,[51] such as those at Patagonia, Inc., which is described in this chapter's Benchmarking box on page 434.

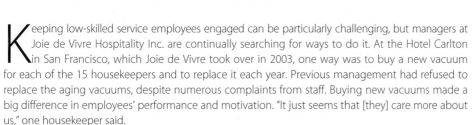

Brad Inman (center), chairman and founder of TurnHere, Inc. of Emeryville, California, gathers his staff every day at 3 p.m. to kick around ideas, see works in progress, talk about the financial status of the company, and discuss how to meet revenue goals. "At first people thought I was crazy when I said we should all get together every day," says Inman, founder of the company that is a leading platform for online video production and provides studio-quality Internet video advertising for clients. But Inman believes involving and listening to employees is critical to employee engagement. "The key to retention is for people to feel they are contributing to building something, not just showing up," says Inman.

··············**>** CONCEPT CONNECTION **<**········

How do managers develop engaged employees? Not by controlling and ordering them around but by organizing the workplace in such a way that each person can learn, contribute, and grow. Good managers channel employee motivation toward the accomplishment of organizational goals by tapping into each individual's unique set of talents, skills, interests, attitudes, and needs. By treating each employee as an individual, good managers can put people in the right jobs and provide intrinsic rewards to every employee every day. Then managers make sure people have what they need to perform, clearly define the desired outcomes, and get out of the way. At the Hotel Carlton in San Francisco, something as simple as buying new vacuum cleaners enhances employee engagement.

Try creating a work environment where people can learn, contribute, and grow.

Keeping low-skilled service employees engaged can be particularly challenging, but managers at Joie de Vivre Hospitality Inc. are continually searching for ways to do it. At the Hotel Carlton in San Francisco, which Joie de Vivre took over in 2003, one way was to buy a new vacuum for each of the 15 housekeepers and to replace it each year. Previous management had refused to replace the aging vacuums, despite numerous complaints from staff. Buying new vacuums made a big difference in employees' performance and motivation. "It just seems that [they] care more about us," one housekeeper said.

Caring about employees and helping them see their jobs as valuable and fun are top priorities for Joie de Vivre CEO Chip Conley. The company sponsors employee parties and awards, arranges annual employee retreats, and offers free classes on a variety of topics, including English as a second language. Most importantly, it pushes managers to seek and act on feedback from employees, to make the workplace feel like a community of caring, and to find ways to help people see how their jobs make a difference. It is essential, Conley says to "focus on the impact they're making rather than just on the task of cleaning the toilet."[52]

HOTEL CARLTON, JOIE DE VIVRE HOSPITALITY INC.

Even with two master's of business administration degrees and a coveted internship in Europe, when Californian Scott Robinson returned from France, he rejected chances for well-paying corporate jobs and instead *begged* for a job as a stock handler at outdoor-clothing and equipment manufacturer Patagonia, Inc. "I wanted to work for a company that's driven by values," he said simply. When he got back home, he read *Let My People Go Surfing*, part memoir, part manifesto, by Patagonia's founder Yvon Chouinard, whose goal for the company is "to produce the highest-quality products while doing the least possible harm to the environment." This mission is a constant inspiration for all of Patagonia's 1,274 employees, all the way from Chouinard to the headquarters receptionist, a guy who wears flip-flops. The mission guides every decision and management practice. Says the founder, "Most people want to do good things but don't. At Patagonia, it's an essential part of your life." In 2008, the company started a program to map the carbon footprint of every single product and to publish the information, whether good or bad.

Rather than being fear-based or mainly making employees feel good, Patagonia embraces a fourth way: stressing continuous improvement to become much better than the competition, as well as making employees feel comfortable. In Patagonia's 39 stores (in seven countries) and its headquarters, it offers on-site day care, full health insurance even to part-timers. And when the surf is up, Chouinard encourages people to hit the beach. People get fired who aren't up to the task. Chouinard sees outdoor activities as essential for employees because they are either testing equipment or coming up with improvements. Yet the company also demands creativity, collaboration, hard work, and results.

No one works there for the money: Pay rates are just barely above market rate. One of the best rewards, though, is a full-pay program that allows employees to take two months off to work for environmental groups. The culture is a magnet for top talent, and they get about 900 resumes for each job opening. The reason is simple, as described by one worker: "It's easy to go to work when you get paid to do what you love to do."

SOURCE: Alissa Walker, "Measuring Footprints," *Fast Company*, Apr. 2008, p. 59–60; Steve Hamm, "A Passion for the Plan," *BusinessWeek*, Aug. 21/28, 2006, pp. 92–94.

One way to evaluate how well a manager or a company is engaging employees is to use a metric developed by Gallup Organization researchers called the Q12. This list of 12 questions provides a way to assess how managers are doing in creating an environment that helps employees thrive in the workplace. The Q12 includes questions such as whether employees know what is expected of them, whether they have the resources they need to perform well, whether they feel appreciated and recognized for doing good work, whether they believe managers value their opinions, and whether they believe they have opportunities to learn and grow. The full list of 12 questions can be found in the book *First Break All the Rules* by researchers Marcus Cunningham and Curt Coffman.[53] When a majority of employees can answer the Q12 questions positively, the organization enjoys a highly motivated, engaged, and productive workforce.

Results of the Gallup study show that organizations where employees give high marks on the Q12 have less turnover, are more productive and profitable, and enjoy greater employee and customer loyalty.[54] Many companies have used the Q12 to pinpoint problems with motivation in the organization and find ways to solve them.

There also is a growing recognition that it is the behavior of managers that makes the biggest difference in whether people feel engaged at work.[55] Gallup Organization research conducted over 25 years indicates that the single most important variable in whether employees feel good about their work is the relationship they have with their direct supervisor.[56] Managers are responsible for keeping employees engaged and motivated so that they—and their organizations—thrive.

Summary

This chapter introduced a number of important ideas about the motivation of people in organizations. Rewards are of two types: intrinsic rewards that result from the satisfactions a person receives in the process of performing a job, and extrinsic rewards such as promotions that are given by another person. Managers work to help employees receive both intrinsic and extrinsic rewards from their jobs.

The content theories of motivation focus on the nature of underlying employee needs. Maslow's hierarchy of needs, Alderfer's ERG theory, Herzberg's two-factor theory, and McClelland's acquired needs theory all suggest that people are motivated to meet a range of needs.

Process theories examine how people go about selecting rewards with which to meet needs. Goal-setting theory indicates that employees are more motivated if they have clear, specific goals and receive regular feedback concerning their progress toward meeting goals. Equity theory says that people compare their contributions and outcomes with those of other people and are motivated to maintain a feeling of equity. Expectancy theory suggests that people calculate the probability of achieving certain outcomes. Still another

motivational approach is reinforcement theory, which says that employees learn to behave in certain ways based on the use of reinforcements.

The application of motivational ideas is illustrated in job design and other motivational programs. Job design approaches include job simplification, job rotation, job enlargement, job enrichment, and the job-characteristics model. Managers can change the structure of work to meet employees' high-level needs. The recent trend toward empowerment motivates by giving employees more information and authority to make decisions in their work while connecting compensation to the results.

Employee engagement has become one of the hottest topics in management. By engaging employees, managers can instill employees with a sense of importance and meaningfulness, helping them reap intrinsic rewards and meet higher-level needs. One way to measure the factors that determine whether people have high levels of engagement and motivation is the Q12, a list of 12 questions about the day-to-day realities of a person's job and workplace relationships.

Discussion Questions

1. In response to security threats in today's world, the U.S. government federalized airport security workers. Many people argued that simply making screeners federal workers would not solve the root problem: bored, low-paid, and poorly trained security workers have little motivation to be vigilant. How might these employees be motivated to provide the security that travel threats now demand?

2. One small company recognizes an employee of the month, who is given a parking spot next to the president's space near the front door. What theories would explain the positive motivation associated with this policy?

3. Using Hackman and Oldham's core job dimensions, compare and contrast the jobs of these two state employees: (1) Jared, who spends much of his time researching and debating energy policy to make recommendations that will eventually be presented to the state legislature, and (2) Anise, who spends her days planting and caring for the flower gardens and grounds surrounding the state capitol building.

4. If an experienced secretary discovered that she made less money than a newly hired janitor, how do you think she would react? What inputs and outcomes might she evaluate to make this comparison?

5. Would you rather work for a supervisor who has high need for achievement, for affiliation, or for power? Why? What are the advantages and disadvantages of each?

6. In one Florida school district, students are rewarded for good grades and attendance with Happy Meals from McDonald's. Do you believe this type of reinforcement can help improve student grades and attendance? What might be some potential problems with this approach?

7. A survey of teachers found that two of the most important rewards were the belief that their work was important and a feeling of accomplishment. According to Maslow's theory, what needs do these rewards meet?

8. The teachers in question 7 also reported that pay and benefits were poor, yet they continue to teach. Use Herzberg's two-factor theory to explain this finding.

9. What theories explain why employees who score high on the Q12 questionnaire are typically highly motivated and productive?

10. How can empowerment lead to higher motivation of employees? Could a manager's empowerment efforts sometimes contribute to demotivation as well? Discuss.

Self Learning

What Motivates You?

Indicate how important each characteristic is to you. Answer according to your feelings about the most recent job you had or about the job you currently hold. Circle the number on the scale that represents your feeling—1 (very unimportant) to 7 (very important).

1. The feeling of self-esteem a person gets from being in that job.
   1 2 3 4 5 6 7

2. The opportunity for personal growth and development in that job.
   1 2 3 4 5 6 7

3. The prestige of the job inside the company (i.e., regard received from others in the company).
   1 2 3 4 5 6 7

4. The opportunity for independent thought and action in that job.
   1 2 3 4 5 6 7

5. The feeling of security in that job.
   1 2 3 4 5 6 7

6. The feeling of self-fulfillment a person gets from being in that position (i.e., the feeling of being able to use one's own unique capabilities, realizing one's potential).
   1 2 3 4 5 6 7

7. The prestige of the job outside the company (i.e., the regard received from others not in the company).
   1 2 3 4 5 6 7

8. The feeling of worthwhile accomplishment in that job.
   1 2 3 4 5 6 7

9. The opportunity in that job to give help to other people.
   1 2 3 4 5 6 7

10. The opportunity in that job for participation in the setting of goals.
    1 2 3 4 5 6 7

11. The opportunity in that job for participation in the determination of methods and procedures.
    1 2 3 4 5 6 7

12. The authority connected with the job.
    1 2 3 4 5 6 7

13. The opportunity to develop close friendships in the job.
    1 2 3 4 5 6 7

Scoring and Interpretation

Score the exercise as follows to determine what motivates you:

Rating for question 5 = _____.

Divide by 1 = _____ security.

Rating for questions 9 and 13 = _____.

Divide by 2 = _____ social.

Rating for questions 1, 3, and 7 = _____.

Divide by 3 = _____ esteem.

Rating for questions 4, 10, 11, and 12 = _____.

Divide by 4 = _____ autonomy.

Rating for questions 2, 6, and 8 = _____.

Divide by 3 = _____ self-actualization.

Your instructor has national norm scores for presidents, vice presidents, and three managerial levels (upper middle, lower middle, and lower-level) that you can compare your mean importance scores with. How do your scores compare with the scores of managers working in organizations?

SOURCE: Lyman W. Porter, *Organizational Patterns of Managerial Job Attitudes* (New York: American Foundation for Management Research, 1964): 17, 19. Used with permission.

Group Learning

Work Versus Play

1. Form groups of three to four members. Answer this question: What drives you to expend energy on a play activity? For leisure, why do you choose the activities you do? (Don't discuss the particular activities but rather why you choose them.) Select one of your group members as presenter.

2. Each group presents its main points to the class. The instructor will draw on the board a table, similar to the following, based on information from the class presentations.

Activities	Outcome 1	Outcome 2	Outcome 3	Outcome 4	Outcome 5	Outcome 6
Example 1: Soccer	high-energy	team-bonding	fitness			
2						
3						
4						

3. Questions for class discussion:

    a. How can you build some of these motives for play into a work environment?

    b. What prevents you from making work more intrinsically motivating as play is?

    c. Which motivation theories are relevant here?

Developed by Phil Anderson, University of St. Thomas, Minneapolis. Used with permission.

Action Learning

1. Interview four people who've had at least three jobs (maybe part-time) in their lives.

2. Ask them which jobs they liked the best and which ones they worked the hardest at. Why did they like that job, and why did they work harder?

3. Try to find patterns in the answers of the four people. Compare your outcomes to the motivation theories in this chapter. Which theories are confirmed or disconfirmed based on your interviews?

4. Your instructor may ask you to write a report on your findings or meet in small groups to discuss patterns among all the interviewees. You would then be asked to either present your findings in class or write a group report.

Ethical Dilemma

To Renege or Not to Renege?

Federico Garcia, vice president of sales for Puget Sound Building Materials, a company based in Tacoma, Washington, wasn't all that surprised by what company president Michael Otto and chief financial officer (CFO) James Wilson had to say during their meeting that morning.

Last year, launching a major expansion made sense to everyone at Puget, a well-established company that provided building materials as well as manufacturing and installation services to residential builders in the Washington and Oregon markets. Puget looked at the record new housing starts and decided it was time to move into the California and Arizona markets, especially concentrating on San Diego and Phoenix, two of the hottest housing markets in the country. Federico carefully hired promising new sales representatives and offered them hefty bonuses if they reached the goals set for the new territory over the next 12 months. All of the representatives had performed well, and three

of them had exceeded Puget's goal—and then some. The incentive system he'd put in place had worked well. The sales reps were expecting handsome bonuses for their hard work.

Early on, however, it became all too clear that Puget had seriously underestimated the time it took to build new business relationships and the costs associated with the expansion, a mistake that was already eating into profit margins. Even more distressing were the most recent figures for new housing starts, which were heading in the wrong direction. As Michael said, "Granted, it's too early to tell if this is just a pause or the start of a real long-term downturn. But I'm worried. If things get worse, Puget could be in real trouble."

James looked at Federico and said, "Our lawyers built enough contingency clauses into the sales reps' contracts that we're not really obligated to pay those bonuses you promised. What would you think about not paying them?" Federico turned to the president, who said, "Why don't you think about it, and get back to us with a recommendation?"

Federico felt torn. On the one hand, he knew the CFO was correct. Puget wasn't, strictly speaking, under any legal obligation to pay out the bonuses, and the eroding profit margins were a genuine cause for concern. The president clearly did not want to pay the bonuses. But Federico had created a first-rate sales force that had done exactly what he'd asked them to do. He prided himself on being a man of his word, someone others could trust. Could he go back on his promises?

What Would You Do?

1. Recommend to the president that a meeting be arranged with the sales representatives entitled to a bonus and tell them that their checks were going to be delayed until the Puget's financial picture clarified. The sales reps would be told that the company had a legal right to delay payment and that it may not be able to pay the bonuses if its financial situation continues to deteriorate.

2. Recommend a meeting with the sales representatives entitled to a bonus and tell them the company's deteriorating financial situation triggers one of the contingency clauses in their contract so that the company won't be issuing their bonus checks. Puget will just have to deal with the negative impact on sales rep motivation.

3. Recommend strongly to the president that Puget pay the bonuses as promised. The legal contracts and financial situation don't matter. Be prepared to resign if the bonuses are not paid as you promised. Your word and a motivated sales team mean everything to you.

SOURCES: Based on Doug Wallace, "The Company Simply Refused to Pay," *Business Ethics* (Mar.–Apr. 2000): 18; and Adam Shell, "Overheated Housing Market Is Cooling," *USA Today*, Nov. 2, 2005 (www. usatoday.com/money/economy/housing/2005-11-01-real-estate-usat_x.htm).

14 Chapter Fourteen

Managing Communication

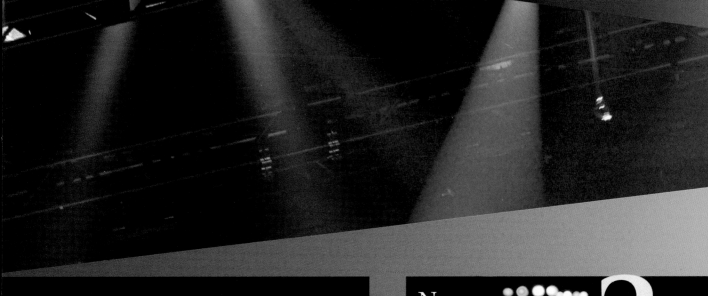

LEARNING OBJECTIVES

After studying this chapter, you should be able to:

1 Explain why communication is essential for effective management, and describe the communication process.

2 Describe the concept of channel richness, and explain how communication channels influence the quality of communication.

3 Understand how gender differences, nonverbal communication, and listening affect the effectiveness of communication.

4 Explain the difference between formal and informal organizational communications and the importance of each for organization management.

5 Identify how structure influences team communication outcomes.

6 Appreciate the role of personal communication channels in enhancing organizational communication.

7 Recognize the manager's role in creating dialogue, managing crisis communication, offering feedback, and creating a climate of trust.

Please circle your opinion below each of the following statements.

1 Good communication is really just common sense.

STRONGLY AGREE < < <   > > > STRONGLY DISAGREE

| 1 | 2 | 3 | 4 | 5 |

2 E-mailing is an efficient and effective tool for communication.

STRONGLY AGREE < < <   > > > STRONGLY DISAGREE

| 1 | 2 | 3 | 4 | 5 |

3 People are generally good listeners.

STRONGLY AGREE < < <   > > > STRONGLY DISAGREE

| 1 | 2 | 3 | 4 | 5 |

Personal networking is an important skill for managers because it enables them to get things done more smoothly and rapidly than they could do in isolation. Networking builds social, work, and career relationships that facilitate mutual benefit. How do managers build a personal network that includes a broad range of professional and social relationships? One key is knowing how to communicate effectively. In fact, communication is a vital factor in every aspect of the manager's job.

Organizations in today's complex business environment depend on effective communication to ensure business success. This is especially true in the competitive world of retailing. Target, ranked 33rd on the *Fortune* 500, banks on a steady stream of bold new product ideas to stay competitive against Walmart and its low-price strategy. Yet Target managers know employee enthusiasm and knowledge is just as important as the products. Target educates employees with frequent communication about the company's vision, values, and strategic goals. Before trendsetting new products are launched in stores, for example, top managers thoroughly educate more than 150 marketing managers, public relations representatives, and even the training staff on the marketing strategy behind each product. "We take the time to communicate to our broad organization what they do, why they're doing it, and how it fits the whole," explains chief executive officer (CEO) Gregg Steinhafel.[1]

Target's managers know that effective organizational communication leads to business success and impressive financial gains. A study by Watson Wyatt Worldwide found that companies with the most effective communication programs provided a 47 percent higher total return to shareholders from 2002 to 2006 when compared with companies that had less effective communication.[2]

As a manager, keep in touch with all your employees, find out what's going on, and learn to listen.

Not only does effective communication lead to better bottom-line results but also much of a manager's time is spent communicating. Managers spend at least 80 percent of every working day in direct communication with others. In other words, 48 minutes of every hour is spent in meetings, on the telephone, communicating online, or talking informally while walking around. The other 20 percent of a typical manager's time is spent doing desk work, most of which is also communication in the form of reading and writing.[3]

This chapter explains why managers should make effective communication a priority. We begin by examining communication as a crucial part of the manager's job and describe a model of the communication process. Next we consider the interpersonal aspects of communication, including communication channels, persuasion, gender differences, listening skills, and nonverbal communication that affect managers' ability to communicate. Then we look at the organization as a whole and consider formal upward, downward, and horizontal communications as well as personal networks and informal communications. Finally, we describe the manager's role in creating dialogue, managing crisis communication, using feedback and learning to improve employee performance, and creating a climate of trust and openness.

Communication Is the Manager's Job

strategic conversation
Dialogue across boundaries and hierarchical levels about the team or organization's vision, critical strategic themes, and the values that help achieve important goals.

Exhibit 14.1 illustrates the crucial role of managers as communication champions. Managers gather important information from both inside and outside the organization and then distribute appropriate information to others who need it. Managers' communication is *purpose directed* in that it directs everyone's attention toward the vision, values, and desired goals of the team or organization and influences people to act in a way to achieve the goals. Managers facilitate *strategic conversations* by using open communication, actively listening to others, applying the practice of dialogue, and using feedback for learning and change. **Strategic conversation** refers to people talking across boundaries and hierarchical levels

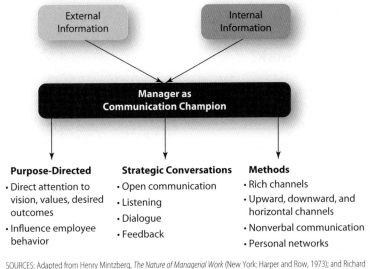

EXHIBIT 14.1

The Manager as Communication Champion

SOURCES: Adapted from Henry Mintzberg, *The Nature of Managerial Work* (New York: Harper and Row, 1973); and Richard L. Daft, *The Leadership Experience*, 3rd ed. (Cincinnati: South-Western, 2005): 346.

about the team or organization's vision, critical strategic themes, and the values that help achieve important goals.[4] For example, at Royal Philips Electronics, president Gerald Kleisterlee defined four strategic technology themes that he believes should define Philips's future in the industry: display, storage, connectivity, and digital video processing. These themes intentionally cross technology boundaries, which require that people communicate and collaborate across departments and divisions to accomplish goals.[5]

Communication permeates every management function described in Chapter 1.[6] For example, when managers perform the planning function, they gather information; write letters, memos, and reports; and meet with other managers to formulate the plan. When managers lead, they communicate to share a vision of what the organization can be and motivate employees to help achieve it. When managers organize, they gather information about the state of the organization and communicate a new structure to others. Communication skills are a fundamental part of every managerial activity.

As a manager, make it a point to talk to people who aren't in your group, finding out what's happening in other departments, and how they see the situation; don't stay in your own clique.

WHAT IS COMMUNICATION?

A professor at Harvard once asked a class to define communication by drawing pictures. Most students drew a manager speaking or typing on a computer keyboard. Some placed "speech balloons" next to their characters; others showed pages flying from a printer. "No," the professor told the class, "none of you has captured the essence of communication." He went on to explain that communication means "to share," not "to speak" or "to write."

As communication champion for Marriott International, CEO Bill Marriott gathers information and communicates the vision, values, and goals of the company. Here he stops to congratulate employees on the opening of a new Renaissance Grand Hotel in downtown St. Louis. In his blog, *Marriott on the Move* at www.blogs.marriott.com, the CEO opens communication with Marriott customers and employees and shares his views on current events and how they affect the company's mission.

········> CONCEPT CONNECTION <········

Are You Building a Personal Network?

How much effort do you put into developing connections with other people? Personal networks may help a new manager in the workplace. To learn something about your networking skills, answer the questions below. Please indicate whether each item is Mostly True or Mostly False for you in school or at work.

	MOSTLY TRUE	MOSTLY FALSE
1. I learn early on about changes going on in the organization and how they might affect me or my position.	_____	_____
2. I network as much to help other people solve problems as to help myself.	_____	_____
3. I am fascinated by other people and what they do.	_____	_____
4. I frequently use lunches to meet and network with new people.	_____	_____
5. I regularly participate in charitable causes.	_____	_____
6. I maintain a list of friends and colleagues to whom I send holiday greeting cards.	_____	_____
7. I maintain contact with people from previous organizations and school groups.	_____	_____
8. I actively give information to subordinates, peers, and my boss.	_____	_____

SCORING AND INTERPRETATION: Give yourself 1 point for each item marked as Mostly True. A score of 6 or higher suggests active networking and a solid foundation on which to begin your career as a new manager. When you create a personal network, you become well connected to get things done through a variety of relationships. Having sources of information and support helps a new manager gain career traction. If you scored 3 or less, you may want to focus more on building relationships if you are serious about a career as a manager. People with active networks tend to be more effective managers and have broader impact on the organization.

Communication is the process by which information is exchanged and understood by two or more people, usually with the intent to motivate or influence behavior. Communication is not just sending information. Honoring this distinction between *sharing* and *proclaiming* is crucial for successful management. A manager who does not listen is like a used-car salesperson who claims, "I sold a car—they just did not buy it." Management communication is a two-way street that includes listening and other forms of feedback. Effective communication, in the words of one expert, occurs as follows:

> When two people interact, they put themselves into each other's shoes, try to perceive the world as the other person perceives it, and try to predict how the other will respond. Interaction involves reciprocal role taking, the mutual employment of empathetic skills. The goal of interaction is the merger of self and other, a complete ability to anticipate, predict, and behave in accordance with the joint needs of self and other.[7]

communication
The process by which information is exchanged and understood by two or more people, usually with the intent to motivate or influence behavior.

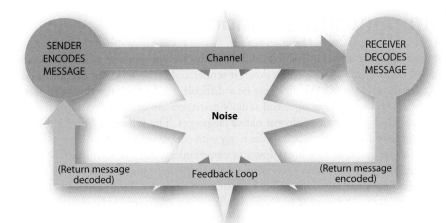

EXHIBIT 14.2
A Model of the Communication Process
– – – – – – – – – – –

It is the desire to share understanding that motivates executives to visit employees on the shop floor, hold small informal meetings, or eat with employees in the company cafeteria. The information that managers gather from direct communication with employees shapes their understanding of the organization.

THE COMMUNICATION PROCESS

Many people think communication is simple. After all, we communicate every day without even thinking about it. However, communication usually is complex, and the opportunities for sending or receiving the wrong messages are innumerable. No doubt you have heard someone say, "But that's not what I meant!" Have you ever received directions you thought were clear and yet still got lost? How often have you wasted time on misunderstood instructions?

To better understand the complexity of the communication process, note the key elements outlined in Exhibit 14.2. Two essential elements in every communication situation are the sender and the receiver. The *sender* is anyone who wishes to convey an idea or concept to others, seek information, or express a thought or emotion. The *receiver* is the person to whom the message is sent. The sender **encodes** the idea by selecting symbols with which to compose a message. The **message** is the tangible formulation of the idea that is sent to the receiver. The message is sent through a **channel**, which is the communication carrier. The channel can be a formal report, a telephone call, an e-mail message, or a face-to-face meeting. The receiver **decodes** the symbols to interpret the meaning of the message. Encoding and decoding are potential sources for communication errors because knowledge, attitudes, and background act as filters and create *noise* when translating from symbols to meaning. Finally, **feedback** occurs when the receiver responds to the sender's communication with a return message. Without feedback, the communication is *one-way*; with feedback, it is *two-way*. Feedback is a powerful aid to communication effectiveness, because it enables the sender to determine whether the receiver correctly interpreted the message.

As a new manager, become a communication champion by communicating across boundaries, actively listening to others, and using feedback to make improvements.

encode
To select symbols with which to compose a message.

message
The tangible formulation of an idea to be sent to a receiver.

channel
The carrier of a communication.

decode
To translate the symbols used in a message for the purpose of interpreting its meaning.

feedback
A response by the receiver to the sender's communication.

1 Good communication is really just common sense.

ANSWER: Communication *seems* simple and mostly common sense, but it is far more complicated—which is why we keep saying, "That's not what I meant." Effective communication requires sensitivity to the speaker, the ability to truly listen and give feedback, among other essentials.

Communicating Among People

The communication model in Exhibit 14.2 illustrates the components of effective communication. Communications can break down if sender and receiver do not encode or decode language in the same way.[8] We all know how difficult it is to communicate with someone who does not speak our language, and today's managers are often trying to communicate with people who speak many different native languages. The following Spotlight on Skills offers suggestions for communicating effectively with people who speak a different language.

Many factors can lead to a breakdown in communications. For example, the selection of communication channel can determine whether the message is distorted by noise and interference. The listening skills of both parties and attention to nonverbal behavior can determine whether a message is truly shared. Thus, for managers to be effective communicators, they must understand how factors such as communication channels, the ability to persuade, gender differences, nonverbal behavior, and listening all work to enhance or detract from communication.

SPOTLIGHT ON SKILLS

Breaking Down Language Barriers

In today's global business environment, odds are good you'll find yourself conversing with an employee, a colleague, or a customer who has limited skills in your native language. Here are some guidelines that will help you speak—and listen—more effectively.

1. *Keep your message simple.* Be clear about what you want to communicate and keep to the point. Avoid slang. Using too many culturally narrow expressions, idioms, and colloquialisms and too much humor can cause your message to be totally lost in translation.

2. *Select your words with care.* Don't try to dazzle with your vocabulary. Choose simple words and look for opportunities to use cognates—that is, words that resemble words in your listener's language. For example, *banco* in Spanish means "bank" in English. Assemble those simple words into equally simple phrases and short sentences. And be sure to avoid idioms, slang, jargon, and vague terminology such as *soon*, *often*, or *several*.

3. *Pay close attention to nonverbal messages.* Don't cover your mouth with your hand. Being able to see your lips helps your listener decipher what you are saying.

4. *Speak slowly and carefully.* In particular, avoid running words together. "Howyadoin?" won't make any sense to someone still struggling with the English language, for example.

5. *Allow for pauses.* If you're an American, your culture has taught you to avoid silence whenever possible. However, pauses give your listener time to take in what you have said, ask a question, or formulate a response.

6. *Fight the urge to shout.* Speaking louder doesn't make it any easier for someone to understand you. It also tends to be intimidating and could give the impression that you are angry.

7. *Pay attention to facial expressions and body language, but keep in mind that the meaning of such cues can vary significantly from culture to culture.* For example, Americans may view eye contact as a sign you're giving someone your full attention, but the Japanese consider prolonged eye contact rude.

8. *Check for comprehension frequently and invite feedback.* Stop from time to time and make sure you're being understood, especially if the other person laughs inappropriately, never asks a question, or continually nods and smiles politely. Ask the listener to repeat what you've said in his or her own words. If you find the other person hasn't understood you, restate the information in a different way instead of simply repeating yourself. Similarly, listen carefully when the non-native speaks and offer feedback so the person can check your understanding of his or her message.

Effective multicultural communication isn't easy, but a small investment in clear communication will result in trust and improved productivity.

SOURCES: Marshall Goldsmith, "Crossing the Cultural Chasm," BusinessWeek.com, May 30, 2007, (www.businessweek.com/careers/content/may2007/ca20070530_521679.htm?chan=search) (accessed Apr. 8, 2008); "How to Communicate with a Non Native English Speaker," wikiHow (www.wikihow.com/Communicate-With-a-Non-Native-English-Speaker); Sondra Thiederman, "Language Barriers: Bridging the Gap" (www.thiederman.com/articles_detail.php?id=39); and "Communicating with Non-Native Speakers," Magellan Health Services (www.magellanassist.com/mem/library/default.asp?TopicId=95&CategoryId=0&ArticleId=5).

COMMUNICATION CHANNELS

Managers have a choice of many channels through which to communicate to other managers or employees. A manager may discuss a problem face to face, make a telephone call, use instant messaging, send an e-mail, write a memo or letter, or post an entry to a company blog, depending on the nature of the message. Research has attempted to explain how managers select communication channels to enhance communication effectiveness.[9] The research has found that channels differ in their capacity to convey information. Just as a pipeline's physical characteristics limit the kind and amount of liquid that can be pumped through it, a communication channel's physical characteristics limit the kind and amount of information that can be conveyed through it. The channels available to managers can be classified into a hierarchy based on information richness.

The Hierarchy of Channel Richness. **Channel richness** is the amount of information that can be transmitted during a communication episode. The hierarchy of channel richness is illustrated in Exhibit 14.3. The capacity of an information channel is influenced by three characteristics: (1) the ability to handle multiple cues simultaneously; (2) the ability to facilitate rapid, two-way feedback; and (3) the ability to establish a personal focus for the communication. Face-to-face discussion is the richest medium because it permits direct experience, multiple information cues, immediate feedback, and personal focus. Face-to-face discussions facilitate the assimilation of broad cues and deep, emotional understanding of the situation. Telephone conversations are next in the richness hierarchy. Although eye contact, posture, and other body language cues are missing, the human voice can still carry a tremendous amount of emotional information. P. Diddy has learned that face-to-face and direct communication is necessary for business success as shown in the Benchmarking box on page 448.

Electronic messaging, such as e-mail and instant messaging, is increasingly being used for messages that were once handled via the telephone. However, in a survey by researchers at Ohio State University, most respondents said they preferred the telephone or face-to-face conversation for communicating difficult news, giving advice, or expressing affection.[10] Because e-mail messages lack both visual and verbal cues and don't allow for interaction and feedback, messages can sometimes be misunderstood. Using e-mail to discuss disputes, for example, can lead to an escalation rather than a resolution of conflict.[11] Studies have found that e-mail messages tend to be much more blunt than other forms of communication, even other written communications. This bluntness can cause real problems when communicating cross-culturally, because some cultures consider directness rude or insulting.[12] Instant messaging alleviates the problem of miscommunication to some extent by allowing

channel richness
The amount of information that can be transmitted during a communication episode.

EXHIBIT 14.3
A Continuum of Channel Richness

- - - - - - - - - - -

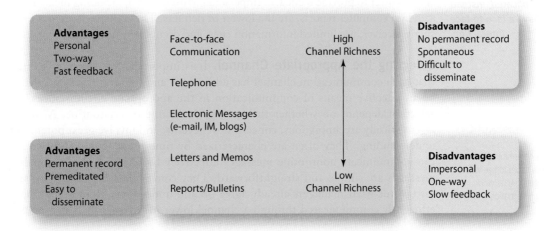

Advantages		Disadvantages
Personal	Face-to-face Communication — High Channel Richness	No permanent record
Two-way		Spontaneous
Fast feedback	Telephone	Difficult to disseminate
	Electronic Messages (e-mail, IM, blogs)	
Advantages	Letters and Memos	**Disadvantages**
Permanent record		Impersonal
Premeditated	Reports/Bulletins — Low Channel Richness	One-way
Easy to disseminate		Slow feedback

BENCH-MARKING

Sean John

Sean "Diddy" Combs debuted his Sean John clothing line in 1999 with the goal of finding some integrative solution between high-end clothing and clothes with a certain sense of street smarts. Ten years and $800 million later and with a Fifth Avenue boutique, Combs believes he has brought the two styles together.

"Because people knew that I was a hip-hop artist and I owned the brand, they thought the brand was going to just embody the stereotype of what they think hip-hop is, just baggy jeans and oversized T-shirts. It was important for me to push the limits and push the boundaries," said Combs.

Other hip-hop artists have ventured into the fashion field. Among them are Beyonce and Snoop Dog, but even years ago analysts said Combs had the greatest chance of success, partly because he had learned a lot about management and strategy and partly because he keeps control of his own company, being engaged in day-to-day operations. Unlike many other companies, Sean John makes 70 percent of its own clothing. Combs has learned the hard way: both from flat clothing sales as the urban look has peaked, and from being distracted running an empire that includes restaurants and music publishing. To address these issues, he fired long-time business associate and friend, Jeffrey Tweedy, putting in his stead former Joseph Aboud Apparel CEO Robert J. Wichser. Combs vowed at the recent meeting with his closely directed designers that he would focus more on the clothing line.

Because of his celebrity, he's able to gain more attention in the marketplace than many other brands. But this "personality muscle" doesn't help much in human relations or the boardroom. "You have to invest in executive talent in order to one day own or be part of a Fortune 500 company," he said, thinking. "I'm more mature now. I understand. It's all right to need people."

SOURCE: Nedra Rhone, "Style Done Diddy's Way at Macy's," *Atlanta Constitution*, Oct. 9, 2008, p. E1; Patricia Hurtado, "The Rap on Puffy," *New York Times*, July 24, 2005, pp. A1, A3.

for immediate feedback. **Instant messaging (IM)** allows users to see who is connected to a network and share shorthand messages or documents with them instantly. A growing number of managers are using IM, indicating that it helps people get responses faster and collaborate more smoothly.[13] Overreliance on e-mail and IM can damage company communications, however, because people stop talking to one another in a rich way that builds solid interpersonal relationships. Some research, though, indicates that electronic messaging can enable reasonably rich communication if the technology is used appropriately.[14] Organizations are also using videoconferencing, which offers video capabilities to provide visual cues and greater channel richness.

Don't use e-mail when you need to send a message that is emotionally charged or complicated; instead have a face-to-face interaction.

Still lower on the hierarchy of channel richness are written letters and memos. Written communication can be personally focused, but it conveys only the cues written on paper and is slower to provide feedback. Impersonal written media, including fliers, bulletins, and standard computer reports, are the lowest in richness. These channels are not focused on a single receiver, use limited information cues, and do not permit feedback.

Selecting the Appropriate Channel. It is important for managers to understand that each communication channel has advantages and disadvantages and that each can be an effective means of communication in the appropriate circumstances.[15] Channel selection depends on whether the message is routine or nonroutine. *Nonroutine messages* typically are ambiguous, concern novel events, and involve great potential for misunderstanding. They often are characterized by time pressure and surprise. Managers can communicate nonroutine messages effectively by selecting rich channels. *Routine* messages are simple and straightforward. They convey data or statistics or simply put into words what managers already agree on and understand. Routine messages can be efficiently communicated through a channel lower in richness such as e-mail. Written

instant messaging (IM)

Electronic communication that allows users to see who is connected to a network and share information instantly.

2 E-mailing is an efficient and effective tool for communication.

ANSWER: E-mail is best used for more routine, unambiguous, and nonemotional messages. When there is uncertainty, fear, danger of being misunderstood, or any emotional component, then talking directly (face to face or over the telephone) is preferable.

communications should also be used when the communication is official and a permanent record is required.[16]

Consider the alert to consumers issued by the federal Food and Drug Administration following a widespread *E. coli* outbreak in September 2006. Tainted bagged spinach sickened 199 people in at least 26 states and resulted in one death. Grocers immediately pulled the product from shelves, and widespread news coverage warned the public not to consume any bagged spinach until the cause of the contamination could be identified. An immediate response was critical. This type of nonroutine communication forces a rich information exchange. The group facing such a communication challenge will meet face to face, brainstorm ideas, and provide rapid feedback to resolve the situation and convey the correct information. If, in contrast, an agency director is preparing a press release about a routine matter such as a policy change or new department members, less information capacity is needed. The director and public relations people might begin developing the press release with an exchange of memos, telephone calls, and e-mail messages.

The key is to select a channel to fit the message. During a major acquisition, one firm decided to send top executives to all of the acquired company's major work sites, where most of the workers met the managers in person, heard about their plans for the company, and had a chance to ask questions. The results were well worth the time and expense of the personal face-to-face meetings because the acquired workforce saw the new managers as understanding, open, and willing to listen.[17] Communicating their nonroutine message about the acquisition in person prevented damaging rumors and misunderstandings. The choice of a communication channel can also convey a symbolic meaning to the receiver; in a sense, the medium becomes the message. The firm's decision to communicate face to face with the acquired workforce signaled to employees that managers cared about them as individuals. Some people have to learn the hard way that electronic communication may not be the most appropriate for some situations, as described in this chapter's Business Blooper.

BUSINESS BLOOPER

"Overtexed" Here

Tory Johnson interviewed a promising candidate for an internship in her small recruiting firm. Her mind was made up—that is, until she got a so-called thank you note, including "words" such as *hiya* and *thanx* and ending with three exclamation points and a smiley face. "The e-mail just ruined it for me," said Johnson, who is president of Women For Hire Inc.

Another job candidate sent a "friend" request to Wendi Friedman Tush right after an interview. Responded Friedman Tush: "I'm not his friend. I'm not even his employer. I was somebody who interviewed him. They are called social-networking sites for a reason."

SOURCE: Sarah E. Needleman, "Ths for the IView! I Wud Luv to Work 4U!!:)," *Wall Street Journal,* July 29, 2008, p. D1.

COMMUNICATING TO PERSUADE AND INFLUENCE OTHERS

Communication is not just for conveying information; it's also used to persuade and influence people. Although communication skills have always been important to managers, the ability to persuade and influence others is even more critical today. Businesses are run largely by cross-functional teams that are actively involved in making decisions. Issuing directives is no longer an appropriate or effective way to get things done.[18]

Go to the Self Learning exercise on page 466, which pertains to your level of communication apprehension.

To persuade and influence, managers have to communicate frequently and easily with others. Yet some people find interpersonal communication experiences unrewarding or difficult and thus tend to avoid situations where communication is required. The term **communication apprehension** describes this avoidance behavior and is defined as "an individual's level of fear or anxiety associated with either real or anticipated communication." With training and practice, managers can overcome their communication apprehension and become more effective communicators.

Effective persuasion doesn't mean telling people what you want them to do; instead, it involves listening, learning about others' interests and needs, and leading people to a shared solution.[19] Managers who forget that communication means *sharing*, as described earlier, aren't likely to be as effective at influencing or persuading others, as the founder and president of the executive coaching firm Valuedance learned the hard way.

VALUEDANCE

When Susan Cramm was asked by a client to help persuade the client's boss to support an initiative she wanted to launch, Cramm readily agreed. They scheduled a meeting with the boss, then held a series of planning sessions in which the two discussed the current situation at the client's firm, weighed the options, and decided on the best approach for launching the initiative. Filled with enthusiasm and armed with a PowerPoint presentation, Cramm was sure the client's boss would see things their way.

An agonizing 15 minutes later, she was out the door, PowerPoint deck and all, having just had a lesson about the art of persuasion. What went wrong? Cramm had focused on the hard, rational matters and ignored the soft skills of relationship building, listening, and negotiating that are so crucial to persuading others. "Never did we consider the boss's views," Cramm said later about the planning sessions she and her client held to prepare for the meeting. "Like founding members of the 'It's all about me' club, we fell upon our swords, believing that our impeccable logic, persistence, and enthusiasm would carry the day."

With that approach, the meeting was over before it even began. The formal presentation shut down communications because it implied that Cramm had all the answers and the boss was just there to listen and agree.[20]

As this example shows, people stop listening to someone when that individual isn't listening to them. By failing to show interest in and respect for the boss's point of view, Cramm and her client lost the boss's interest from the beginning, no matter how suitable the ideas they were presenting. To effectively influence and persuade others, managers have to show they care about how the other person feels. Persuasion requires tapping into people's emotions, which can only be done on a personal, rather than a rational, impersonal level.

GENDER DIFFERENCES IN COMMUNICATION

As a new manager, you will undoubtedly encounter a variety of different communication styles in the workplace. Class, race, ethnicity, and gender are all factors that influence how people communicate. Managers should work hard to shed any innate or rigid opinions about a person's communication style so these beliefs don't hinder understanding or adversely affect such personnel decisions as hiring or promoting. It is much more productive to recognize and appreciate differences in communication styles, thereby reducing some of

communication apprehension
An individual's level of fear or anxiety associated with interpersonal communications.

nonverbal communication
A communication transmitted through actions and behaviors rather than through words.

the problems that naturally occur when a sender and receiver do not encode or decode language in the same way.

One difference managers encounter frequently relates to gender. How does gender affect communication style? For most women, although certainly not all, talking means *conversation* and is primarily a language of rapport, a way to establish connections and negotiate relationships. Women use their unique conversational style to show involvement, connection, and participation, such as by seeking similarities and matching experiences with others. They tend to interrupt less than men do and work hard to keep a conversation going. For most men, on the other hand, talk is primarily a means to preserve independence and negotiate and maintain status in a hierarchy. Men tend to use verbal language to exhibit knowledge and skill such as by telling stories, joking, or passing on information.[21] Another notable difference related to communication in the workplace is how women and men claim credit for work accomplished. Because women typically seek to build rapport, they are inclined to downplay their expertise and accomplishments rather than display them. Men, on the other hand, tend to value their position at center stage, enjoy demonstrating their knowledge, and more easily take credit for their accomplishments.[22] When managers understand this gender difference, they can make an extra effort to encourage women to take credit when it is deserved.

Women and men also display differences in body language. Women tend to use more submissive gestures when communicating with men: using less body space, pulling in their body, tilting their heads while talking or listening, putting their hands in their laps more often, and lowering their eyes. Men tend to stare more, point more, take up more space, keep their heads straight, sit in a more outstretched position, and use larger, more sweeping gestures.[23] Grasping the different communication styles of men and women may help managers maximize every employee's talents and encourage both men and women to contribute more fully to the organization.

© BOB DAEMMRICH/THE IMAGE WORKS

Rosa and Jorrick Battles, a successful entrepreneurial couple, manage gender differences in communication to plan their schedules and run their business. Women tend to build rapport and relationships in their communications by sharing information. Men tend to negotiate hierarchy and gather information to make decisions. Researchers show that women typically read more nonverbal cues to enrich their understanding. They also use questions that solicit participation. These differences can enhance or hinder communications in the workplace and in personal experiences. Communication problems send couples into therapy more than any other relationship issue.

····· **>> CONCEPT CONNECTION** <······

Start noticing gender differences in communications and make sure women are fully included in discussions.

NONVERBAL COMMUNICATION

Body language is one aspect of nonverbal communication. **Nonverbal communication** refers to messages sent through human actions and behaviors rather than through words.[24] Managers are watched, and their behavior, appearance, actions, and attitudes are symbolic of what they value and expect of others.

Most of us have heard the saying "Actions speak louder than words." Indeed, we communicate without words all the time, whether we realize it or not. Most managers are astonished to learn that words themselves carry little meaning. A significant portion of the shared understanding from communication comes from the nonverbal messages of facial expression, voice, mannerisms, posture, and dress. Without these cues, miscommunication may occur.

© ARTIGA PHOTO/CORBIS

Communication is conveyed not only by *what* is said but also *how* it is said as well as by the facial expressions and body language of the people involved. Face-to-face communication is the richest channel of communication because it facilitates these nonverbal cues and allows for immediate feedback. Important issues should be discussed face to face, such as in this meeting between two businesswomen.

····· **>> CONCEPT CONNECTION** <······

Use communication to tap into people's imagination and emotions. When influencing or persuading, first listen—noting nonverbal cues—and strive to understand the other person's point of view.

Nonverbal communication occurs mostly face to face. One researcher found three sources of communication cues during face-to-face communication: the *verbal*, which are the actual spoken words; the *vocal*, which include the pitch, tone, and timbre of a person's voice; and *facial expressions*. According to this study, the relative weights of these three factors in message interpretation are verbal impact, 7 percent; vocal impact, 38 percent; and facial impact, 55 percent.[25] To some extent, we are all natural *face readers*, but facial expressions can be misinterpreted, suggesting that managers need to ask questions to make sure they're getting the right message. Managers can hone their skills at reading facial expressions and improve their ability to connect with and influence followers. Studies indicate that managers who seem responsive to the unspoken emotions of employees are more effective and successful in the workplace.[26]

Tuning in to the nonverbal messages of customers also has its benefits. In an effort to better serve customers during busy store hours, Ace Hardware turned employees into "customer quarterbacks" whose job was to read nonverbal messages of customers as they entered the store. Based on nonverbal cues, each customer was classified as a browser, a mission shopper with no time to talk, or someone starting a new project. Customer quarterbacks would then interpret their nonverbal cues to determine how best to serve them.[27]

Improve your ability to communicate with others by noticing facial expressions.

LISTENING

One of the most important tools of manager communication is listening to both employees and customers. Most managers now recognize that important information flows from the bottom up, not the top down, and managers had better be tuned in.[28] Some organizations use innovative techniques for finding out what's on employees' and customers' minds. When Intuit's president and CEO Stephen M. Bennett took over, the company instituted an annual employee survey that gives managers an opportunity to listen to employees' feelings on a range of company practices. During the year, managers are then encouraged to meet with subordinates to gather more feedback. Since instituting these listening strategies, turnover at Intuit has dropped from 24 percent to 12 percent. "Employees know that we are serious about asking for their feedback, and we listen and do something about it," Bennett says.[29]

As a new manager, your social disposition gives others glimpses into your managerial style. Are you friendly and approachable? A good listener? Goal oriented? Take the New Manager's Self-Test on page 454 to learn more about your social disposition.

Managers are also tapping into the interactive nature of blogs to stay in touch with employees and customers. Blogs—running Web logs that allow people to post opinions, ideas, and information—provide a low-cost, always-fresh, real-time link between organizations and customers, employees, news media, and investors.[30] One estimate is that 11 percent of *Fortune* 500 companies use blogs to keep in touch with stakeholders.[31] One of the most active and successful bloggers is Jonathan Schwartz, CEO of Sun Microsystems.

SUN MICROSYSTEMS

"One of the wonderful things about blogs is that I don't have to walk through campus to figure out what's on people's minds. I just go to blogs.sun.com, and I read what they're thinking," says Jonathan Schwartz, CEO of Sun Microsystems. Schwartz has his own blog that allows him to communicate efficiently to a large number and variety of stakeholders. "My number one priority is ensuring my communications are broadly received. Blogging to me has become the most efficient form of communication. When I blog, I'm talking to the world," says Schwartz.

Blogs not only give organizations a human voice but also enable companies to influence opinion, tap into the expertise and ideas of core constituents, and treat employees and customers like friends rather than foes. Schwartz's blog is written in an informational, conversational style that keeps people coming back for more. Topics include updates on the company's mission, new product announcements, personal insights about his job as CEO, and responses to employee questions and concerns.

Although the number of top executives using blogs is relatively small today, Schwartz says, "In ten years, most of us will communicate directly with customers, employees, and the broader business community through blogs. For executives, having a blog is not going to be a matter of choice, any more than e-mail is today."[32]

3 People are generally good listeners.

ANSWER: Most people don't listen well enough, which leads to many communication errors. Learning to listen effectively can be a long struggle for many of us, but it is a very worthwhile endeavor.

Through his blog, Schwartz has gained access to volumes of feedback from customers and employees. He recognizes the value of listening to this feedback and responding with appropriate actions and information. Done correctly, listening is a vital link in the communication process shown in Exhibit 14.2 (page 445).

Listening involves the skill of grasping both facts and feelings to interpret a message's genuine meaning. Only then can the manager provide the appropriate response. Listening requires attention, energy, and skill. Although about 75 percent of effective communication is listening, most people spend only 30 to 40 percent of their time listening, which leads to many communication errors.[33] One of the secrets of highly successful salespeople is that they spend 60 percent to 70 percent of a sales call letting the customer talk.[34] However, listening involves much more than just not talking. Many people do not know how to listen effectively. They concentrate on formulating what they are going to say next rather than on what is being said to them. Our listening efficiency, as measured by the amount of material understood and remembered by subjects 48 hours after listening to a 10-minute message, is no better than 25 percent on average.[35]

What constitutes good listening? Exhibit 14.4 gives 10 keys to effective listening and illustrates a number of ways to distinguish a bad listener from a good listener. A good listener

listening
The skill of receiving messages to accurately grasp facts and feelings to interpret the genuine meaning.

EXHIBIT 14.4
Ten Keys to Effective Listening

Keys to Effective Listening	Poor Listener	Good Listener
1. Listen actively.	Is passive, laid back	Asks questions, paraphrases what is said
2. Find areas of interest.	Tunes out dry subjects	Looks for new learning
3. Resist distractions.	Is easily distracted; answers phone or sends text messages	Gives full attention, fights distractions, maintains concentration
4. Capitalize on the fact that thought is faster.	Tends to daydream	Mentally summarizes; weighs the evidence
5. Be responsive.	Avoids eye contact; is minimally involved	Nods and shows interest
6. Judge content, not delivery.	Tunes out if delivery is poor	Judges content; skips over delivery errors
7. Avoid premature judgment.	Has preconceptions	Does not judge until comprehension is complete
8. Listen for ideas.	Listens for facts	Listens to central themes
9. Work at listening.	Shows no energy; forgets what the speaker says	Works hard; exhibits active body state and eye contact
10. Exercise one's mind.	Resists difficult material in favor of light, recreational material	Uses heavier material as exercise for the mind

SOURCES: Adapted from Diann Daniel, "Seven Deadly Sins of (Not) Listening" (www.cio.com/article/print/134801) (accessed Apr. 8, 2008); Sherman K. Okum, "How to Be a Better Listener," *Nation's Business* (Aug. 1975): 62; and Philip Morgan and Kent Baker, "Building a Professional Image: Improving Listening Behavior," *Supervisory Management* (Nov. 1985): 34–38.

NEW MANAGER'S SELF-TEST

What Is Your Social Disposition?

How do you come across to others? What is your social disposition? To find out, please mark whether each item below is Mostly True or Mostly False for you.

	MOSTLY TRUE	MOSTLY FALSE
1. I want to climb the corporate ladder as high as I can.	_____	_____
2. I confront people when I sense a conflict.	_____	_____
3. People consider me cooperative and easy to work with.	_____	_____
4. I like to get right to the point.	_____	_____
5. I make quick decisions, usually without consulting others.	_____	_____
6. I make a real effort to understand other peoples' point of view.	_____	_____
7. I enjoy competing and winning.	_____	_____
8. I like to get to the bottom line.	_____	_____
9. I take a personal interest in people.	_____	_____

SCORING AND INTERPRETATION: Give yourself 1 point for items 1, 2, 4, 5, 7, and 8 that you marked Mostly True and 1 point for items 3, 6, and 9 that you marked Mostly False. The questions pertain to whether your social disposition is one of being focused and driven toward personal success or whether you tend to come across as affable and friendly. If you scored 7 or higher, then you are probably ambitious and goal oriented. A score of 3 or less would mean that you probably are empathic, ask questions, and enjoy collaborating with others.

A person with a driven disposition may be promoted to manager but may not be a good listener, fail to pick up on body language, or take time to engage in dialogue. A manager has to get things done through other people, and it helps to slow down, listen, build relationships, and take the time to communicate. Too much focus on your personal achievement may come across as uncaring. A new manager with a friendly disposition is often a good listener, makes inquiries, and experiences fewer communication mistakes.

SOURCE: Based on "Social Styles," in Paula J. Caproni, *Management Skills for Everyday Life: The Practical Coach*, 2nd ed. (Upper Saddle River, NJ: Prentice-Hall, 2005): 200–203.

finds areas of interest, is flexible, works hard at listening, and uses thought speed to mentally summarize, weigh, and anticipate what the speaker says. Good listening means shifting from thinking about self to empathizing with the other person, so it requires a high degree of emotional intelligence, as described in Chapter 11.

Organizational Communication

Another aspect of management communication concerns the organization as a whole. Communications throughout an organization typically flow in three directions—downward, upward, and horizontally. Managers are responsible for establishing and maintaining formal channels of communication in these three directions. Managers also use informal channels, which means they get out of their offices and mingle with employees.

FORMAL COMMUNICATION CHANNELS

Formal communication channels are those that flow within the chain of command or task responsibility defined by the organization. The three formal channels and the types of information conveyed in each are illustrated in Exhibit 14.5.[36] Downward and upward communications are the primary forms of communication used in most traditional, vertically organized companies. However, many of today's organizations emphasize horizontal communication, with people continuously sharing information across departments and levels.

Electronic communication such as e-mail and instant messaging have made it easier than ever for information to flow in all directions. For example, the U.S. Army is using technology to rapidly transmit communications about weather conditions and the latest intelligence on the insurgency to lieutenants in the field in Iraq. Similarly, the U.S. Navy uses instant messaging to communicate within ships, across navy divisions, and even back to the Pentagon in Washington. "Instant messaging has allowed us to keep our crew members on the same page at the same time," says Lieutenant Commander Mike Houston, who oversees the Navy's communications program. "Lives are at stake in real time, and we're seeing a new level of communication and readiness."[37]

Downward Communication. The most familiar and obvious flow of formal communication, **downward communication**, refers to the messages and information sent from top management to subordinates in a downward direction.

Managers can communicate downward to employees in many ways. Some of the most common are through speeches, messages in company newsletters, e-mail, information leaflets tucked into pay envelopes, material on bulletin boards, and policy and procedures manuals. Managers sometimes use creative approaches to downward communication to make sure employees get the message.

formal communication channel
A communication channel that flows within the chain of command or task responsibility defined by the organization.

downward communication
Messages sent from top management down to subordinates.

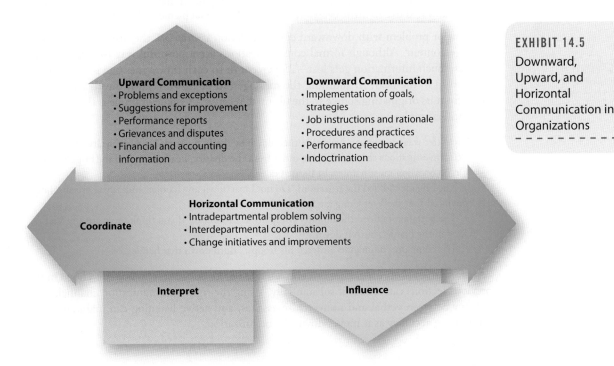

EXHIBIT 14.5
Downward, Upward, and Horizontal Communication in Organizations

Managers also have to decide what to communicate about. It is impossible for managers to communicate with employees about everything that goes on in the organization, so they have to make choices about the important information to communicate.[38] Unfortunately, many U.S. managers could do a better job of effective downward communication. The results of one survey found that employees want open and honest communication about both the good and the bad aspects of the organization's performance. But when asked to rate their company's communication effectiveness on a scale of 0 to 100, the survey respondents' score averaged 69. In addition, a study of 1,500 managers, mostly at first and second management levels, found that 84 percent of these leaders perceive communication as one of their most important tasks, yet only 38 percent believe they have adequate communications skills.[39]

Managers can do a better job of downward communication by focusing on specific areas that require regular communication. Recall our discussion of purpose-directed communication from early in this chapter. Downward communication usually encompasses these five topics:

1. *Implementation of goals and strategies.* Communicating new strategies and goals provides information about specific targets and expected behaviors. It gives direction for lower levels of the organization. *Example*: "The new quality campaign is for real. We must improve product quality if we are to survive."

2. *Job instructions and rationale.* These directives indicate how to do a specific task and how the job relates to other organizational activities. *Example*: "Purchasing should order the bricks now so the work crew can begin construction of the building in two weeks."

3. *Procedures and practices.* These messages define the organization's policies, rules, regulations, benefits, and structural arrangements. *Example*: "After your first 90 days of employment, you are eligible to enroll in our company-sponsored savings plan."

4. *Performance feedback.* These messages appraise how well individuals and departments are doing their jobs. *Example*: "Joe, your work on the computer network has greatly improved the efficiency of our ordering process."

5. *Indoctrination.* These messages are designed to motivate employees to adopt the company's mission and cultural values and to participate in special ceremonies, such as picnics and United Way campaigns. *Example*: "The company thinks of its employees as family and would like to invite everyone to attend the annual picnic and fair on March 3."

A major problem with downward communication is *drop-off*, the distortion or loss of message content. Although formal communications are a powerful way to reach all employees, much information gets lost—25 percent or so each time a message is passed from one person to the next. In addition, the message can be distorted if it travels a great distance from its originating source to the ultimate receiver. A tragic example is the following historical example.

> A reporter was present at a hamlet burned down by the U.S. Army 1st Air Cavalry Division in 1967. Investigations showed that the order from the division headquarters to the brigade was: "On no occasion must hamlets be burned down."
> The brigade radioed the battalion: "Do not burn down any hamlets unless you are absolutely convinced that the Viet Cong are in them."
> The battalion radioed the infantry company at the scene: "If you think there are any Viet Cong in the hamlet, burn it down."
> The company commander ordered his troops: "Burn down that hamlet."[40]

Information drop-off cannot be completely avoided, but the techniques described in the previous sections can reduce it substantially. Using the right communication channel, consistency between verbal and nonverbal messages, and active listening can maintain communication accuracy as it moves down the organization.

Upward Communication. Formal **upward communication** includes messages that flow from the lower to the higher levels in the organization's hierarchy. Most organizations take pains to build in healthy channels for upward communication. Employees need to air grievances, report progress, and provide feedback on management initiatives. Coupling a healthy flow of upward and downward communication ensures that the communication circuit between managers and employees is complete.[41] Five types of information communicated upward are the following:

1. *Problems and exceptions.* These messages describe serious problems with and exceptions to routine performance to make senior managers aware of difficulties. *Example*: "The printer has been out of operation for two days, and it will be at least a week before a new one arrives."

2. *Suggestions for improvement.* These messages are ideas for improving task-related procedures to increase quality or efficiency. *Example*: "I think we should eliminate step 2 in the audit procedure because it takes a lot of time and produces no results."

3. *Performance reports.* These messages include periodic reports that inform management how individuals and departments are performing. *Example*: "We completed the audit report for Smith & Smith on schedule but are one week behind on the Jackson report."

4. *Grievances and disputes.* These messages are employee complaints and conflicts that travel up the hierarchy for a hearing and possible resolution. *Example*: "The manager of operations research cannot get the cooperation of the Lincoln plant for the study of machine utilization."

5. *Financial and accounting information.* These messages pertain to costs, accounts receivable, sales volume, anticipated profits, return on investment, and other matters of interest to senior managers. *Example*: "Costs are 2 percent over budget, but sales are 10 percent ahead of target, so the profit picture for the third quarter is excellent."

Many organizations make a great effort to facilitate upward communication. Mechanisms include suggestion boxes, employee surveys, open-door policies, management information system reports, and face-to-face conversations between workers and executives.

Horizontal Communication. **Horizontal communication** is the lateral or diagonal exchange of messages among peers or co-workers. It may occur within or across departments. The purpose of horizontal communication is both to inform and request support and coordinate activities. Horizontal communication falls into one of three categories:

1. *Intradepartmental problem solving.* These messages take place among members of the same department and concern task accomplishment. *Example*: "Kelly, can you help us figure out how to complete this medical expense report form?"

2. *Interdepartmental coordination.* Interdepartmental messages facilitate the accomplishment of joint projects or tasks. *Example*: "Bob, please contact marketing and production and arrange a meeting to discuss the specifications for the new subassembly. It looks like we might not be able to meet their requirements."

3. *Change initiatives and improvements.* These messages are designed to share information among teams and departments that can help the organization change, grow, and improve. *Example*: "We are streamlining the company travel procedures and would like to discuss them with your department."

Recall from Chapter 7 that many organizations build in horizontal communications in the form of task forces, committees, or even a matrix or horizontal structure to encourage coordination. At Chicago's Northwestern Memorial Hospital, two doctors created a horizontal task force to reduce the incidence of hospital-borne infections. The infection epidemic that kills nearly 100,000 people a year is growing worse worldwide, but

upward communication
Messages transmitted from the lower to the higher levels in the organization's hierarchy.

horizontal communication
The lateral or diagonal exchange of messages among peers or co-workers.

Northwestern reversed the trend by breaking down communication barriers. Infectious-disease specialists Lance Peterson and Gary Noskin launched a regular Monday morning meeting involving doctors and nurses, lab technicians, pharmacists, computer technicians, admissions representatives, and even the maintenance staff. The enhanced communication paid off. Over a three-year period, North-western's rate of hospital-borne infections plunged 22 percent and was roughly half the national average.[42]

TEAM COMMUNICATION CHANNELS

A special type of horizontal communication is communicating in teams. At W. L. Gore, the chemical company best known for Gore-Tex, the core operating units are small, self-managing teams.[43] Its team members work together to accomplish tasks, and the team's communication structure influences both team performance and employee satisfaction.

Research into team communication has focused on two characteristics: the extent to which team communications are centralized and the nature of the team's task.[44] The relationship between these characteristics is illustrated in Exhibit 14.6. In a **centralized network**, team members must communicate through one individual to solve problems or make decisions. In a **decentralized network**, individuals can communicate freely with other team members. Members process information equally among themselves until all agree on a decision.[45]

In laboratory experiments, centralized communication networks achieved faster solutions for simple problems. Members could simply pass relevant information to a central person for a decision. Decentralized communications were slower for simple problems because information was passed among individuals until someone finally put the pieces together and solved the problem. However, for more complex problems, the decentralized communication network was faster. Because all necessary information was not restricted to one person, a pooling of information through widespread communications provided greater input into the decision. Similarly, the accuracy of problem solving was related to problem complexity. The centralized networks made fewer errors on simple problems but more errors on complex ones. Decentralized networks were less accurate for simple problems but more accurate for complex ones.[46]

The implication for organizations is as follows: In a highly competitive global environment, organizations typically use teams to deal with complex problems. When team activities are complex and difficult, all members should share information in a decentralized

If you have a complex task, make sure members of the team can all communicate easily to one another.

centralized network
A team communication structure in which team members communicate through a single individual to solve problems or make decisions.

decentralized network
A team communication structure in which team members freely communicate with one another and arrive at decisions together.

EXHIBIT 14.6
Effectiveness of Team Communication Networks

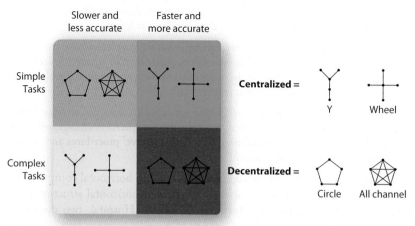

SOURCES: Adapted from A. Bavelas and D. Barrett, "An Experimental Approach to Organization Communication," *Personnel* 27 (1951): 366–371; M. E. Shaw, *Group Dynamics: The Psychology of Small Group Behavior* (New York: McGraw–Hill, 1976); and E. M. Rogers and R. A. Rogers, *Communication in Organizations* (New York: Free Press, 1976).

structure to solve problems. Teams need a free flow of communication in all directions.[47] Teams that perform routine tasks spend less time processing information, and thus communications can be centralized. Data can be channeled to a supervisor for decisions, freeing workers to spend a greater percentage of time on task activities.

PERSONAL COMMUNICATION CHANNELS

Personal communication channels exist outside the formally authorized channels. These informal communications coexist with formal channels but may skip hierarchical levels, cutting across vertical chains of command to connect virtually anyone in the organization. In most organizations, these informal channels are the primary way information spreads and work gets accomplished. Three important types of personal communication channels are *personal networks*, the *grapevine*, and *written communication*.

Developing Personal Communication Networks. **Personal networking** refers to the acquisition and cultivation of personal relationships that cross departmental, hierarchical, and even organizational boundaries.[48] Smart managers consciously develop personal communication networks and encourage others to do so. In a communication network, people share information across boundaries and reach out to anyone who can further the goals of the team and organization. Exhibit 14.7 illustrates a communication network. Some people are central to the network while others play only a peripheral role. The key is that relationships are built across functional and hierarchical boundaries.

The value of personal networks for managers is that people who have more contacts have greater influence in the organization and get more accomplished. For example, in Exhibit 14.7, Sharon has a well-developed personal communication network, sharing information and assistance with many people across the marketing, manufacturing, and engineering departments. Contrast Sharon's contacts with those of Mike or Jasmine. Who do you think is likely to have greater access to resources and more influence in the organization? Here are a few tips from one expert networker for building a personal communication network:[49]

1. *Build it before you need it.* Smart managers don't wait until they need something to start building a network of personal relationships—by then, it's too late. Instead, they show genuine interest in others and develop honest connections.

As a manager, solicit bad information from below, so you can avoid problems erupting.

personal communication channels
Communication channels that exist outside the formally authorized channels and do not adhere to the organization's hierarchy of authority.

personal networking
The acquisition and cultivation of personal relationships that cross departmental, hierarchical, and even organizational boundaries.

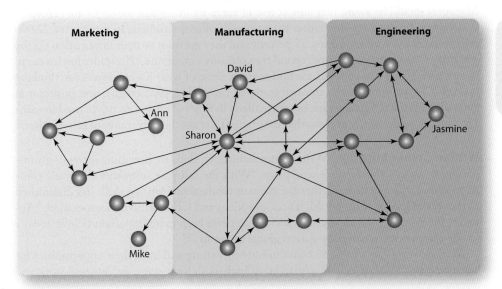

EXHIBIT 14.7

An Organizational Communication Network

Use your lunches and break times to develop closer relationships and communications with colleagues.

As a new manager, it is essential to build and nurture a personal communication network. Refer back to the New Manager's Self-Test on page 444 to determine the effectiveness of your networking skills. Networking plugs you into the grapevine and supplements formal communication channels.

2. *Never eat lunch alone.* People who excel at networking make an effort to be visible and connect with as many people as possible. Master networkers keep their social, business conference, and event calendars full.

3. *Make it win–win.* Successful networking isn't just about getting what *you* want; it's also about making sure other people in the network get what *they* want.

4. *Focus on diversity.* The broader your base of contacts, the broader your range of influence. Build connections with people from as many different areas of interest as possible (both within and outside the organization).

Most of us know from personal experience that "who you know" sometimes counts for more than what you know. By cultivating a broad network of contacts, managers can significantly extend their influence and accomplish greater results.

The Grapevine. Although the word *gossip* has a negative connotation, it may actually be good for a company, especially during times of change, such as layoffs and downsizing. In fact, gossip can be an invaluable tool for managers who may be able to keep a better pulse on what's happening in the workplace by relying on information from employees who are known for spreading and knowing office gossip.[50] Gossip typically travels along the **grapevine**, an informal, person-to-person communication network that is not officially sanctioned by the organization.[51] The grapevine links employees in all directions, ranging from the CEO through middle management, support staff, and line employees. The grapevine will always exist in an organization, but it can become a dominant force when formal channels are closed. In such cases, the grapevine is actually a service because the information it provides helps makes sense of an unclear or uncertain situation. Employees use grapevine rumors to fill in information gaps and clarify management decisions. One estimate is that as much as 70 percent of all communication in a firm is carried out through its grapevine.[52] The grapevine tends to be more active during periods of change, excitement, anxiety, and sagging economic conditions. For example, a survey by professional employment services firm Randstad found that about half of all employees reported first hearing of major company changes through the grapevine.[53]

Surprising aspects of the grapevine are its accuracy and its relevance to the organization. About 80 percent of grapevine communications pertain to business-related topics rather than personal gossip. Moreover, from 70 percent to 90 percent of the details passed through a grapevine are accurate.[54] Many managers would like the grapevine to be destroyed because they consider its rumors to be untrue, malicious, and harmful, which typically is not the case. Managers should be aware that almost five of every six important messages are carried to some extent by the grapevine rather than through official channels. In a survey of 22,000 shift workers in varied industries, 55 percent said they get most of their information via the grapevine.[55] Smart managers understand the company's grapevine. "If a leader has his ear to the ground, gossip can be a way for him to get a sense of what his employees are thinking or feeling," says Mitch Kusy, an organizational consultant, psychologist, and professor at Antioch University.[56] In all cases, but particularly in times of crisis, executives need to manage communications effectively so that the grapevine is not the only source of information.[57]

Written Communication. Written communication skills are becoming increasingly important in today's collaborative workplace. "With the fast pace of today's electronic communications, one might think that the value of fundamental writing skills has diminished in the workplace," said Joseph M. Tucci, president and CEO of EMC Corporation. "Actually, the need to write clearly and quickly has never been more important than in today's highly competitive, technology-driven global economy."[58]

Managers who are unable to communicate in writing will limit their opportunities for advancement. "Writing is both a 'marker' of high-skill, high-wage, professional work and

grapevine
An informal, person-to-person communication network of employees that is not officially sanctioned by the organization.

a 'gatekeeper' with clear equity implications," says Bob Kerrey, president of New School University in New York and chair of the National Commission on Writing. Managers can improve their writing skills by following these guidelines:[59]

Figure out the main point before you start writing. Reread to make sure you have stated it clearly and concisely.

- *Respect the reader.* The reader's time is valuable; don't waste it with a rambling, confusing memo or e-mail that has to be read several times to try to make sense of it. Pay attention to your grammar and spelling. Sloppy writing indicates that you think your time is more important than that of your readers. You'll lose their interest—and their respect.

- *Know your point and get to it.* What is the key piece of information that you want the reader to remember? Many people just sit and write, without clarifying in their own mind what it is they're trying to say. To write effectively, know what your central point is and write to support it.

- *Write clearly rather than impressively.* Don't use pretentious or inflated language and avoid jargon. The goal of good writing for business is to be understood the first time through. State your message as simply and as clearly as possible.

- *Get a second opinion.* When the communication is highly important, such as a formal memo to the department or organization, ask someone you consider to be a good writer to read it before you send it. Don't be too proud to take their advice. In all cases, read and revise the memo or e-mail a second and third time before you hit the send button.

A former manager of communication services at consulting firm Arthur D. Little Inc. has estimated that around 30 percent of all business memos and e-mails are written simply to get clarification about an earlier written communication that didn't make sense to the reader.[60] By following these guidelines, you can get your message across the first time.

Innovations in Organizational Communication

As a manager, you can develop a climate of trust by becoming more trustworthy.

Organizations with a high level of communication effectiveness develop strategies to encourage dialogue, manage crisis communication, use feedback to develop employees, and create a climate of trust and openness.

DIALOGUE

Dialogue is a group communication process in which people together create a stream of meaning that enables them to understand each other and share a view of the world.[61] People may start out at polar opposites, but by talking openly they discover common ground, common issues, and common goals on which they can build a better future. Dialogue is never superficial; it is always a shared inquiry where the participants seek a greater understanding of each other. To build and maintain strong relationships, managers need to develop the ability to engage in dialogue. When Whole Foods CEO John Mackey was heckled by an animal rights activist at an annual meeting, he agreed to a personal dialogue with the activist. Through careful listening and willingness to learn, he discovered some weaknesses in his company's policies on animal products and became a firm proponent of many of the activist's positions. Because of his ability to create a successful dialogue, he also converted the opponent into a vocal advocate for Whole Foods.[62]

A useful way to describe dialogue is to contrast it with discussion. The differences between dialogue and discussion are shown in Exhibit 14.8 (on page 462). The intent of discussion, generally, is to deliver one's point of view and persuade others to adopt it. A discussion is often resolved by logic or "beating down" opponents. Dialogue, by contrast, asks that participants suspend their attachments to a particular viewpoint so that a deeper level of listening, synthesis, and meaning can evolve from the group. A dialogue's focus is to reveal feelings and

dialogue
A group communication process aimed at creating a culture based on collaboration, fluidity, trust, and commitment to shared goals.

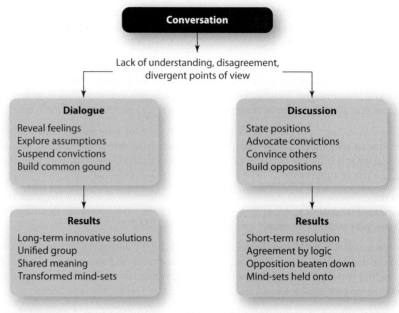

Conversation

Lack of understanding, disagreement,
divergent points of view

Dialogue
Reveal feelings
Explore assumptions
Suspend convictions
Build common gound

Discussion
State positions
Advocate convictions
Convince others
Build oppositions

Results
Long-term innovative solutions
Unified group
Shared meaning
Transformed mind-sets

Results
Short-term resolution
Agreement by logic
Opposition beaten down
Mind-sets held onto

SOURCE: Adapted from Edgar Schein, "On Dialogue, Culture, and Organizational Learning," *Organizational Dynamics* (Autumn 1993): 46.

When an extortionist claimed to have placed seven pesticide-contaminated candy bars in Sydney area stores, manufacturer MasterFoods Australia/New Zealand's response was a textbook example of effective crisis communication. President Andy Weston-Webb announced, "It's not safe to eat Mars or Snickers bars" and immediately activated recall plans. MasterFoods launched a public relations campaign that included interviews with Weston-Webb, full-page newspaper ads, a company hotline, and media access to the burial of 3 million candy bars in a deep pit. The two-month absence of the popular snacks cost MasterFoods more than $10 million, but the company emerged with its reputation intact. During the first week of the products' return, sales surged 300 percent.

> CONCEPT CONNECTION <

build common ground. Both forms of communication—dialogue and discussion—can result in change. However, the result of discussion is limited to the topic being deliberated, whereas the result of dialogue is characterized by group unity, shared meaning, and transformed mind-sets. As new and deeper solutions are developed, a trusting relationship is built among team members.[63]

CRISIS COMMUNICATION

Over the past few years, the sheer number and scope of crises have made communication a more demanding job for managers. Organizations face small crises every day, whether charges of racial discrimination, a factory fire, or a flu epidemic. Moreover, acts of intentional evil such as bombings and kidnappings continue to increase, causing serious repercussions for people and organizations.[64] Crises are like fires, and effective communications are the best way to douse them. The slower the response, the faster the crisis grows, fueled by misinformation, rumors, and fears. Prompt and thoughtful communications can counter confusion and replace it with confidence in the organization's leaders.[65] Managers can develop four primary skills for communicating in a crisis.[66]

- *Maintain your focus.* Good crisis communicators don't allow themselves to be overwhelmed by the situation. Calmness and listening become more important than ever. Managers also learn to tailor their communications to reflect hope and optimism at the same time they acknowledge the current difficulties.

- *Be visible.* Many managers underestimate just how important their presence is during a crisis.[67] A manager's job is to step out immediately to both reassure employees and respond to public concerns. Face-to-face communication with employees is crucial for letting people know that managers care about them and what they're going through.

- *Get the awful truth out.*[68] Effective managers gather as much information as they can, do their best to determine the facts, and tell the truth to employees and the public as soon as possible. Getting the truth out quickly prevents rumors and misunderstandings.

- *Communicate a vision for the future.* People need to feel that they have something to work for and look forward to. Moments of crisis present opportunities for managers to communicate a vision of a better future and unite people toward common goals.

FEEDBACK AND LEARNING

Feedback occurs when managers use evaluation and communication to help individuals and the organization learn and improve. It enables managers to determine whether they have been successful in communicating with others. Recall from Exhibit 14.2 (page 445) that feedback is an important part of the communication process. However, despite its importance, feedback is often neglected. Giving and receiving feedback is typically difficult for both managers and employees. Yet, by avoiding feedback, people miss a valuable opportunity to help one another learn, develop, and improve.[69]

When someone gives you negative feedback, rather than defend yourself and prove the person wrong, just listen quietly and say, "thank you for the information" and nothing more.

Successful managers focus their feedback to help develop the capabilities of subordinates, and they encourage critical feedback from employees. When managers enlist the whole organization in reviewing the outcomes of activities, they can quickly learn what does and does not work and use that information to improve the organization. Consider how the U.S. Army's feedback system promotes whole-system learning. The Spotlight on Skills box describes how the Army is learning by communicating feedback about the consequences of field operations and simulated battles.

SPOTLIGHT ON SKILLS

U.S. Army

At the National Training Center just south of Death Valley, U.S. Army troops engage in a simulated battle. The "enemy" has sent unmanned aerial vehicles (UAVs) to gather targeting data. When the troops fire on the UAVs, they reveal their location to attack helicopters hovering just behind a nearby ridge. After the exercise, unit members and their superiors hold an *after-action review* to review battle plans, discuss what worked and what didn't, and talk about how to do things better. General William Hertzog suggests that inexpensive decoy UAVs might be just the thing to make a distracted enemy reveal its location. The observation became a "lesson learned" for the entire army, and UAVs became an important part of battle operations in Iraq.

Many researchers attribute the transformation of the army from a demoralized, dysfunctional organization following the Vietnam War into an elite force capable of effectively completing Operation Iraqi Freedom to this unique feedback and learning system. In the U.S. Army, after-action reviews take just 15 minutes, and they occur after every identifiable event—large or small, simulated or real. The review involves asking four simple questions: What was supposed to happen? What actually happened? What accounts for any difference? What

can we learn? It is a process of identifying mistakes, innovating, and continually learning from experience.

The lessons are based not only on simulated battles but also on real-life experiences of soldiers in the field. The Center for Army Lessons Learned (CALL) sends experts into the field to observe after-action reviews, interview soldiers, and compile intelligence reports. Leaders in all army divisions are currently engaged in a detailed analysis of lessons learned during Operation Iraqi Freedom and Operation Enduring Freedom. The lessons will be used to train soldiers and develop action plans for resolving problems in future conflicts. For example, many of the problems and issues from a similar process following Operation Desert Storm had been resolved by the time of Operation Iraqi Freedom. A primary focus for current leaders is to improve training regarding the difficult shift from offensive operations to humanitarian and relief efforts.

SOURCE: Thomas E. Ricks, "Army Devises System to Decide What Does, and Does Not, Work," *Wall Street Journal*, May 23, 1997; Stephanie Watts Sussman, "CALL: A Model for Effective Organizational Learning," *Strategy* (Summer 1999): 14–15; John O'Shea, "Army: The Leader as Learner-in-Chief," *The Officer* (June 2003): 31; Michael D. Maples, "Fires First in Combat—Train the Way We Fight," *Field Artillery* (July–Aug. 2003): 1; Thomas E. Ricks, "Intelligence Problems in Iraq Are Detailed," *Washington Post*, Oct. 25, 2003; and Richard W. Koenig, "Forging Our Future: Using Operation Iraqi Freedom Phase IV Lessons Learned," *Engineer* (Jan.–Mar. 2004): 21–22.

CLIMATE OF TRUST AND OPENNESS

Perhaps the most important thing managers can do to enhance organizational communication is to create a *climate of trust and openness*. Open communication and dialogue can encourage people to communicate honestly with one another. Subordinates will feel free to transmit negative as well as positive messages without fear of retribution. Efforts to develop interpersonal skills among employees can also foster openness, honesty, and trust. Building trust is not one of the top goals of many bloggers, as shown in the Spotlight on Ethics box.

Second, managers should develop and use *formal communication channels* in all directions. Scandinavian Design uses two newsletters to reach employees. Dana Corporation has developed innovative programs such as the "Here's a Thought" board—called a *HAT rack*—to get ideas and feedback from workers. Other techniques include direct mail, bulletin boards, blogs, and employee surveys.

Third, managers should encourage the use of *multiple channels*, including both formal and informal communications. Multiple communication channels include written directives, face-to-face discussions, and the grapevine. For example, managers at GM's Packard Electric plant use multimedia, including a monthly newspaper, frequent meetings of employee teams, and an electronic news display in the cafeteria. Sending messages through multiple channels increases the likelihood that they will be properly received.

Fourth, the structure should *fit communication needs*. An organization can be designed to use teams, task forces, project managers, or a matrix structure as needed to facilitate the horizontal flow of information for coordination and problem solving. Structure should also reflect information needs. When team or department tasks are difficult, a decentralized structure should be implemented to encourage discussion and participation.

TAKE ACTION

As a manager, remember that organizational secrets don't often remain that way; therefore, tell the truth and be open from the beginning.

SPOTLIGHT ON SKILLS

Gawker and TechCrunch

New York's Gossip site Gawker flashed this headline in May 2009: "Could Apple Buy Twitter?" What followed was a story about a Silicon Valley deal maker who'd been recruited by Apple to seal the acquisition. Within hours, reputable Silicon Valley sites were carrying the same story. Hundreds of viewer comments were posted, and the original Gawker page was viewed 22,000 times in the first 12 hours. Problem was, no one was able to verify the facts. Not that this surprised the original writers, who knew it could all be just an empty rumor. Even TechCrunch noted that it had "checked with other sources who claim to know nothing about any Apple negotiations." Was anyone contrite? On the contrary, TechCrunch author Michael Arrington noted, "I don't ever want to lose the rawness of blogging." Such ideas are not unusual in the blogging world. And this truth-be-damned method doesn't seem too far off from an earlier era of journalism immortalized in Orson Welles's classic movie *Citizen Kane* in which the publisher (modeled after William Randolph Hearst) is told that a reporter sent to Cuba was having trouble finding the war. The response? "You provide the prose poems. I'll provide the war." It was a freewheeling time of what became knows as "yellow journalism" when newspapers competed for the limited readership by printing the most outrageous stories. Gradually, most newspapers embraced credibility and truth seeking as core values.

Bloggers aren't constrained by the truth and see their role as writing about the scuttlebutt and what people are talking about. Few of them have training as journalists. Because funds for staffing are small and competition is so fierce, bloggers at Gawker, TechCrunch, and others go for compelling stories. Says Arrington, "Getting it right is expensive. Getting it first is cheap."

SOURCE: Damon Darlin, "Get the Tech Scuttlebutt! (It Might Even Be True)," *New York Times*, June 7, 2009, p. B3.

Summary

A manager's communication is purpose directed in that it unites people around a shared vision and goals and directs attention to the values and behaviors that achieve goals. Managers facilitate strategic conversations by using open communication, actively listening to others, applying the practice of dialogue, and using feedback for learning and change.

Communication is the process in which information is exchanged and understood by two or more people. Two essential elements in every communication situation are the sender and the receiver. The sender encodes the idea by selecting symbols with which to compose a message and selecting a communication channel. The receiver decodes the symbols to interpret the meaning of the message. Feedback occurs when the receiver responds to the sender's communication with a return message.

Communication among people can be affected by communication channels, gender differences, nonverbal communication, and listening skills. An important aspect of management communication is persuasion. The ability to persuade others to behave in ways that help accomplish the vision and goals is crucial to good management.

Organization-wide communication typically flows in three directions: downward, upward, and horizontally. Managers are responsible for maintaining formal channels of communication in all three directions. Teams with complex tasks need to communicate successfully in all directions through a decentralized communication network.

Personal communication channels exist outside formally authorized channels and include personal networks, the grapevine, and written communication. Managers with more contacts in their personal network have greater influence in the organization. The grapevine carries workplace gossip, a dominant force in organization communication when formal channels are closed. The ability to write clearly and quickly is increasingly important in today's collaborative work environment.

To enhance organizational communication, managers should understand how to engage in dialogue, manage crisis communication, use feedback and learning to improve employee performance, and create a climate of trust and openness.

Discussion Questions

1. Lee's Garage is an internal Walmart Web site that CEO H. Lee Scott uses to communicate with the company's 1.5 million U.S. employees. A public relations associate screens employee questions, and Scott dictates his responses to an aide, who then posts them on the Web. What would you predict are the advantages and potential problems to this method of upper-level management connection with employees?

2. Describe the elements of the communication process. Give an example of each part of the model as it exists in the classroom during communication between teacher and students.

3. What communication channel would you select if you had to give an employee feedback about the way he mismanaged a call with a key customer? What channel would you use to announce to all employees the deadline for selecting new health-care plans? Why?

4. What are the characteristics of an effective listener? How would you rate yourself on those characteristics?

5. What are techniques for reducing the risk of *drop-off*, the distortion of a message being sent from top management to subordinates?

6. Try to recall an incident at school or work when information was passed primarily through the grapevine. How accurate were the rumors, and how did people react to them? How can managers control information that is processed through the grapevine?

7. What is the difference between a discussion and a dialogue? What steps might managers take to transform a discussion into a constructive dialogue?

8. How does a climate of trust and openness improve organizational communication?

9. Some senior managers believe they should rely on written information and computer reports because these yield more accurate data than face-to-face communications. Do you agree? Why or why not?

10. Assume that you have been asked to design a training program to help managers become better communicators. What would you include in the program?

Self Learning

Personal Assessment of Communication Apprehension

The following questions are about your feelings toward communication with other people. Indicate the degree to which each statement applies to you by marking 3 (Agree), 2 (Undecided), 1 (Disagree). There are no right or wrong answers. Many of the statements are similar to other statements. Do not be concerned about their similarities. Work quickly and record your first impressions.

	DISAGREE	UNDECIDED	AGREE
1. When talking in a small group of acquaintances, I am tense and nervous.	1	2	3
2. When presenting a talk to a group of strangers, I am tense and nervous.	1	2	3
3. When conversing with a friend or colleague, I am calm and relaxed.	1	2	3
4. When talking in a large meeting of acquaintances, I am calm and relaxed.	1	2	3
5. When presenting a talk to a group of friends or colleagues, I am tense and nervous.	1	2	3
6. When conversing with an acquaintance or colleague, I am calm and relaxed.	1	2	3
7. When talking in a large meeting of strangers, I am tense and nervous.	1	2	3
8. When talking in a small group of strangers, I am tense and nervous.	1	2	3
9. When talking in a small group of friends and colleagues, I am calm and relaxed.	1	2	3
10. When presenting a talk to a group of acquaintances, I am calm and relaxed.	1	2	3
11. When I am conversing with a stranger, I am calm and relaxed.	1	2	3
12. When talking in a large meeting of friends, I am tense and nervous.	1	2	3
13. When presenting a talk to a group of strangers, I am calm and relaxed.	1	2	3
14. When conversing with a friend or colleague, I am tense and nervous.	1	2	3
15. When talking in a large meeting of acquaintances, I am tense and nervous.	1	2	3
16. When talking in a small group of acquaintances, I am calm and relaxed.	1	2	3
17. When talking in a small group of strangers, I am calm and relaxed.	1	2	3
18. When presenting a talk to a group of friends, I am calm and relaxed.	1	2	3
19. When conversing with an acquaintance or colleague, I am tense and nervous.	1	2	3
20. When talking in a large meeting of strangers, I am calm and relaxed.	1	2	3
21. When presenting a talk to a group of acquaintances, I am tense and nervous.	1	2	3
22. When conversing with a stranger, I am tense and nervous.	1	2	3

23. When talking in a large meeting of friends or colleagues, I am calm and relaxed. _____   _____   _____

- -

24. When talking in a small group of friends or colleagues, I am tense and nervous. _____   _____   _____

- -

Scoring and Interpretation This questionnaire permits computation of four subscores and one total score. Subscores relate to communication apprehension in four common situations—public speaking, meetings, group discussions, and interpersonal conversations. To compute your scores, add or subtract your scores for each item as indicated next.

Subscore Scoring Formula. For each subscore, start with 18 points. Then add the scores for the plus (+) items and subtract the scores for the minus (−) items.

Public Speaking
18 + scores for items 2, 5, and 21; −scores for items 10, 13, and 18. Score = _____

Meetings
18 + scores for items 7, 12, and 15; −scores for items 4, 20, and 23. Score = _____

Group Discussions
18 + scores for items 1, 8, and 24; −scores for items 9, 16, and 17. Score = _____

Interpersonal Conversations
18 + scores for items 14, 19, and 22; −scores for items 3, 6, and 11. Score = _____

Total Score
Sum the four subscores for Total Score: _____

This personal assessment provides an indication of how much apprehension (fear or anxiety) you feel in a variety of communication settings. Total scores may range from 24 to 120. Scores above 72 indicate that you are more apprehensive about communication than the average person. Scores above 85 indicate a high level of communication apprehension. Scores below 59 indicate a low level of apprehension. These extreme scores (below 59 and above 85) are generally outside the norm. They suggest that the degree of apprehension you may experience in any given situation may not be associated with a realistic response to that communication situation.

Scores on the subscales can range from a low of 6 to a high of 30. Any score above 18 indicates some degree of apprehension. For example, if you score above 18 for the public speaking context, then you are like the overwhelming majority of people.

To be an effective communication champion, you should work to overcome communication anxiety. The interpersonal conversations create the least apprehension for most people, followed by group discussions, larger meetings, and then public speaking. Compare your scores with another student. What aspect of communication creates the most apprehension for you? How do you plan to improve it?

SOURCES: J. C. McCroskey, "Measures of Communication-Bound Anxiety," *Speech Monographs* 37 (1970): 269–277; J. C. McCroskey and V. P. Richmond, "Validity of the PRCA as an Index of Oral Communication Apprehension," *Communication Monographs* 45 (1978): 192–203; J. C. McCroskey and V. P. Richmond, "The Impact of Communication Apprehension on Individuals in Organizations," *Communication Quarterly* 27 (1979): 55–61; and J. C. McCroskey, *An Introduction to Rhetorical Communication* (Englewood Cliffs, NJ: Prentice Hall, 1982).

Group Learning

The following exercise will help you understand how "Yes, but" statements are so familiar and how "Yes, and" statements keep a dialogue or conversation going more effectively.

1. Form into pairs.

2. One person starts with a yes–no question relating to an "untrue" fact, asking about something that can be seen.

3. The other person affirms this statement (even if it is not actually true and might be ridiculous) and adds another yes–no question. You must be careful *not* to respond with a "Yes, but" answer.

4. Go through the questions and statements as quickly as you can.

5. The instructor will call time after several minutes.

6. The instructor will lead a discussion. How difficult was it to avoid the "Yes, but" statements? What was the effect of responding "Yes, and" continually?

Example of a possible dialogue:
"Is your hair green?"

"Yes, and yesterday it was blue. Do you change the color of your hair on a daily basis?"

"Yes, and I change my shirt daily. Did you tear a hole in your shirt at lunch today?

"Yes, and it was very large. Did everyone notice?"

"Yes, and I was very pleased with myself that I managed not to laugh. Are you going to buy a new shirt?

"Yes, and I'm going to that new mall on the moon to do it. Do you go to the moon often?"

"Yes, and sometimes Mars as well. Can you breathe in the vacuum on the moon?"

"Yes, and under water as well. Do you know how to breathe liquid nitrogen?"

SOURCES: Adapted by Steven S. Taylor (2007) from the work of Keith Johnstone, *Improvisation and the Theatre* (New York: Theater Arts Book Publisher, 1987). Used with permission.

Action Learning

1. Pair up with another student. You will be studying organizational communications at your university (or another company, which one of you may or may not work at).

2. Go to page 454 and the section on "Organizational Communication," especially referring to the sections on downward and upward communication. Become familiar with the two lists of communication channels in both upward and downward communication.

3. Go to the university (or company) Web site and find the places relevant to faculty and students. Look for examples of upward and downward communication. Write them down.

4. What is the purpose of each of these communications? What, in reality, do you expect the actual consequence of each communication to be?

5. The instructor may ask you to either bring your findings to class for a discussion or to hand in a written report.

Ethical Dilemma

On Trial

When Werner and Thompson, a Los Angeles business and financial management firm, offered Iranian-born Firoz Bahmani a position as an accountant assistant one spring day in 2007, Bahmani felt a sense of genuine relief, but his relief was short-lived.

With his degree in accounting from a top-notch American university, he knew he was more than a little overqualified for the job. But time after time, he'd been rejected for suitable positions. His language difficulties were the reason most often given for his unsuccessful candidacy. Although the young man had grown up speaking both Farsi and French in his native land, he'd only begun to pick up English shortly before his arrival in the United States a few years ago. Impressed by his educational credentials and his quiet, courtly manner, managing partner Beatrice Werner overlooked his heavy accent and actively recruited him for the position, the only one available at the time. During his interview, she assured him he would advance in time.

It was clear to Beatrice that Firoz was committed to succeeding at all costs. But it soon also became apparent that Firoz and his immediate supervisor, Cathy Putnam, were at odds. Cathy was a seasoned account manager who had just transferred to Los Angeles from the New York office. Saddled with an enormous workload, she let Firoz know right from the start, speaking in her rapid-fire Brooklyn accent, that he'd need to get up to speed as quickly as possible.

Shortly before Cathy was to give Firoz his three-month probationary review, she came to Beatrice, expressed her frustration with Firoz's performance, and suggested that he be let go. "His bank reconciliations and financial report preparations are first-rate," Cathy admitted, "but his communication skills leave a lot to be desired. In the first place, I simply don't have the time to keep repeating the same directions over and over again when I'm trying to teach him his responsibilities. Then there's the fact that public contact is part of his written job description. Typically, he puts off making phone calls to dispute credit-card charges or ask a client's staff for the information he needs. When he does finally pick up the phone . . . well, let's just say I've had more than one client mention how hard it is to understand what he's trying to say. Some of them are getting pretty exasperated."

"You know, some firms feel it's their corporate responsibility to help foreign-born employees learn English," Beatrice began. "Maybe we should help him find an English-as-a-second-language course and pay for it."

"With all due respect, I don't think that's our job," Cathy replied, with barely concealed irritation. "If you come to the United States, you should learn our language. That's what my mom's parents did when they came over from Italy. They certainly didn't expect anyone to hold their hands. Besides," she added, almost inaudibly, "Firoz's lucky we let him into this country."

Beatrice had mixed feelings. On one hand, she recognized that Werner and Thompson had every right to require someone in Firoz's position be capable of carrying out his public contract duties. Perhaps she had made a mistake in hiring him, but as the daughter of German immigrants herself, she knew firsthand both how daunting language and cultural barriers could be and that they could be overcome in time. Perhaps in part because of her family background, she had a passionate commitment to the firm's stated goals of creating a diverse workforce and a caring, supportive culture. Besides she felt a personal sense of obligation to help a hard-working, promising employee realize his potential. What will she advise Cathy to do now that Firoz's probationary period is drawing to a close?

What Would You Do?

1. Agree with Cathy Putnam. Despite your personal feelings, accept that Firoz Bahmani is not capable of carrying out the accountant assistant's responsibilities. Make the break now and give him his notice on the grounds

that he cannot carry out one of the key stated job requirements. Advise him that a position that primarily involves paperwork would be a better fit for him.

2. Place Firoz with a more sympathetic account manager who is open to finding ways to help him improve his English and has the time to help him develop his assertiveness and telephone skills. Send Cathy Putnam to diversity awareness training.

3. Create a new position at the firm that will allow Firoz to do the reports and reconciliations for several account managers, freeing the account assistants to concentrate on public contact work. Make it clear that he will have little chance of future promotion unless his English improves markedly.

SOURCES: Mary Gillis, "Iranian Americans," *Multicultural America* (www.everyculture.com/multi/Ha-La/Iranian-Americans.html) (accessed Sept. 19, 2006); and Charlene Marmer Solomon, "Managing Today's Immigrants," *Personnel Journal* 72(3) (Feb. 1993): 56–65.

15 Chapter Fifteen

Leading Teams

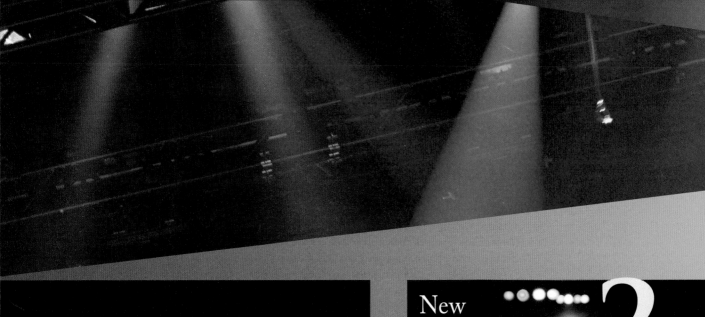

LEARNING OBJECTIVES

After studying this chapter, you should be able to:

1 Identify the types of teams in organizations.

2 Discuss some of the problems and challenges of teamwork.

3 Identify roles within teams and the type of role you could play to help a team be effective.

4 Explain the general stages of team development.

5 Identify ways in which team size and diversity of membership affect team performance.

6 Explain the concepts of team cohesiveness and team norms and their relationship to team performance.

7 Understand the causes of conflict within and among teams and how to reduce conflict.

8 Define the outcomes of effective teams and how managers can enhance team effectiveness.

New Manager's Questions

Please circle your opinion below each of the following statements.

1 *Team* is just another word for group.

STRONGLY AGREE < < <   > > > STRONGLY DISAGREE

| 1 | 2 | 3 | 4 | 5 |

2 It's better if team members are in the same location.

STRONGLY AGREE < < <   > > > STRONGLY DISAGREE

| 1 | 2 | 3 | 4 | 5 |

3 The best team members are those who encourage other members.

STRONGLY AGREE < < <   > > > STRONGLY DISAGREE

| 1 | 2 | 3 | 4 | 5 |

Many people get their first management experience in a team setting, and you will probably sometimes have to work in a team as a new manager. Teams have become the primary way in which many companies accomplish their work, from the assembly line to the executive suite. Teams have real advantages, but it can sometimes be tough to work in a team. You may have already experienced the challenges of teamwork as a student, when you've had to give up some of your independence and rely on the team to perform well in order to earn a good grade.

Good teams can be highly productive, but teams aren't always successful. In a survey of manufacturing organizations, about 80 percent of respondents said they used some kind of teams, but only 14 percent of those companies rated their teaming efforts as highly effective. Slightly more than half of the respondents said their efforts were only "somewhat effective," and 15 percent considered their efforts not effective at all.[1]

This chapter focuses on teams and their applications within organizations. We look at why organizations use teams, discuss the dilemma of teamwork, and provide an overview of what makes an effective team. We define various types of teams, explore the stages of team development, and examine how characteristics such as size, cohesiveness, diversity, and norms influence team effectiveness. We also discuss how individuals can make contributions to teams, look at techniques for managing team conflict, and describe how negotiation can facilitate cooperation and teamwork. The final section of the chapter focuses on the outcomes of effective work teams within organizations. Teams are a central aspect of organizational life, and the ability to manage them is a vital component of manager and organization success.

Remember that it takes work to turn a group of people into a team.

team
A unit of two or more people who interact and coordinate their work to accomplish a specific goal.

Why Teams at Work?

Why aren't organizations just collections of individuals going their own way and doing their own thing? Clearly, teamwork provides benefits; if it didn't, companies wouldn't continue to use this structural mechanism. Organizations are by their very nature made up of various individuals and groups that have to work together and coordinate their activities to accomplish objectives. Much work in organizations is *interdependent*, which means that individuals and departments rely on other individuals and departments for information or resources to accomplish their work. When tasks are highly interdependent, a team can be the best approach to ensuring the level of coordination, information sharing, and exchange of materials necessary for successful task accomplishment.

WHAT IS A TEAM?

A **team** is a unit of two or more people who interact and coordinate their work to accomplish a specific goal.[2] At Cirque du Soleil, the chief executive officer (CEO), chief operating officer, chief financial officer, and vice president of creation function as a top management team to develop, coordinate, and oversee acrobatic troupes that travel to approximately 100 cities on four continents a year. Google assembles teams of three or four employees to assess new ideas and recommend whether they should be implemented. And at the Ralston Foods plant in Sparks,

The power of effective teamwork is illustrated by Lance Armstrong's record-breaking accomplishment in winning the Tour de France seven consecutive years from 1999 to 2005. Armstrong, shown here in the yellow jersey with teammates during the 92nd Tour de France, succeeded not just as an individual but as part of a team. Members of the Discovery Channel Team (previously the U.S. Postal Service Cycling Team) united around a shared purpose of helping Armstrong win the 21-day competition, pacing his ride, and protecting him from other cyclists and spectators.

© JOEL SAGET/AFP/GETTY IMAGES

> CONCEPT CONNECTION <

1 *Team* is just another word for group.

ANSWER: A group is not necessarily a team, which generally has a shared purpose and collective responsibility.

Nevada, teams of production workers handle all team hiring, scheduling, quality, budgeting, and disciplinary issues.[3]

The definition of a team has three components. First, two or more people are required. Second, people in a team have regular interaction. People who do not interact, such as those standing in line at a lunch counter or riding in an elevator, do not compose a team. Third, people in a team share a performance goal, whether to design a new handheld computing device, build an engine, or complete a class project.

Although a team is a group of people, the two terms are not interchangeable. An employer, a teacher, or a coach can put together a *group* of people and never build a *team*. The team concept implies a sense of shared mission and collective responsibility. Exhibit 15.1 lists the primary differences between groups and teams. One example of a true team comes from the military, where U.S. Navy surgeons, nurses, anesthesiologists, and technicians make up eight-person forward surgical teams that operated for the first time ever in combat during Operation Iraqi Freedom. These teams were scattered over Iraq and were able to move to new locations and be set up within an hour. With a goal of saving the 15 percent to 20 percent of wounded soldiers and civilians who will die unless they receive critical care within 24 hours, members of these teams smoothly coordinated their activities to accomplish a critical shared mission.[4]

THE DILEMMA OF TEAMS

If you've been in a class where the instructor announced that part of the grade would be based on a team project, you probably heard a few groans. The same thing happens in organizations. Some people love the idea of teamwork, others hate it, and many people have both positive and negative emotions about working as part of a team. There are three primary reasons teams present a dilemma for most people:

- *We have to give up our independence.* When people become part of a team, their success depends on the team's success; therefore, they are dependent on how well other people perform, not just on their own individual initiative and actions. Most people are comfortable with the idea of making sacrifices to achieve their own individual success, yet teamwork

Group	Team
• Has a designated strong leader	• Shares or rotates leadership roles
• Holds individuals accountable	• Holds team accountable to each other
• Sets identical purpose for group and organization	• Sets specific team vision or purpose
• Has individual work products	• Has collective work products
• Runs efficient meetings	• Runs meetings that encourage open-ended discussion and problem solving
• Measures effectiveness indirectly by influence on business (such as financial performance)	• Measures effectiveness directly by assessing collective work
• Discusses, decides, delegates work to individuals	• Discusses, decides, shares work

EXHIBIT 15.1

Differences Between Groups and Teams

SOURCE: Adapted from Jon R. Katzenbach and Douglas K. Smith, "The Discipline of Teams," *Harvard Business Review* (Mar.–Apr. 1995): 111–120.

How Do You Like To Work?[5]

Your approach to your job or schoolwork may indicate whether you thrive on a team. Answer the questions below about your work preferences. Please answer whether each item below is Mostly True or Mostly False for you.

	MOSTLY TRUE	MOSTLY FALSE
1. I prefer to work on a team rather than do individual tasks.	_____	_____
2. Given a choice, I try to work by myself rather than face hassles of group work.	_____	_____
3. I enjoy the personal interaction when working with others.	_____	_____
4. I prefer to do my own work and let others do theirs.	_____	_____
5. I get more satisfaction from a group victory than an individual victory.	_____	_____
6. Teamwork is not worthwhile when people do not do their share.	_____	_____
7. I feel good when I work with others even when we disagree.	_____	_____
8. I prefer to rely on myself, rather than others, to do an assignment.	_____	_____

SCORING AND INTERPRETATION: Give yourself 1 point for each odd-numbered item you marked as Mostly True and 1 point for each even-numbered item you marked Mostly False. An important part of a new manager's job is to be both part of a team and to work alone. These items measure your preference for group work. Teamwork can be both frustrating and motivating. If you scored 2 or fewer points, then you definitely prefer individual work. A score of 7 or above suggests that you prefer working in teams. A score of 3 to 6 indicates comfort working alone and in a team. A new manager needs to do both.

TAKE ACTION

Be aware of the dilemma teamwork creates. Some will be energized and excited by working as part of a team, while others will be apprehensive, cynical, or annoyed. Be alert to the possibility of free riding, and make sure work activities are distributed equitably.

free rider
A person who benefits from team membership but does not make a proportionate contribution to the team's work.

demands that they make sacrifices for *group* success.[6] The idea is that each person should put the team first, even if at times it hurts the individual. Many employees, particularly in individualistic cultures such as the United States, have a hard time appreciating and accepting that concept. Some cultures, such as Japan, have had greater success with teams because traditional Japanese culture values the group over the individual.

- *We have to put up with free riders.* Teams are sometimes made up of people who have different work ethics. The term **free rider** refers to a team member who attains benefits from team membership but does not actively participate in and contribute to the team's work. You might have experienced this frustration in a student project team, where one member put little effort into the group project but benefited from the hard work of others when grades were handed out. Free riding is sometimes called *social loafing* because some members do not exert equal effort.[7]

- *Teams are sometimes dysfunctional.* Some companies have had great success with teams, but there are also numerous examples of how teams in organizations fail spectacularly.[8] A great deal of research and team experience over the past few decades has produced significant insights into what causes teams to succeed or fail. The evidence shows that how teams are managed plays the most critical role in determining how well they function.[9] Exhibit 15.2 lists five dysfunctions that are common in teams and describes the contrasting desirable characteristics that effective team leaders develop.

Dysfunction	Effective Team Characteristics
Lack of Trust—People don't feel safe to reveal mistakes, share concerns, or express ideas.	**Trust**—Members trust one another on a deep emotional level; feel comfortable being vulnerable with one another.
Fear of Conflict—People go along with others for the sake of harmony; don't express conflicting opinions.	**Healthy Conflict**—Members feel comfortable disagreeing and challenging one another in the interest of finding the best solution.
Lack of Commitment—If people are afraid to express their true opinions, it's difficult to gain their true commitment to decisions.	**Commitment**—Because all ideas are put on the table, people can eventually achieve genuine buy-in around important goals and decisions.
Avoidance of Accountability—People don't accept responsibility for outcomes; engage in finger-pointing when things go wrong.	**Accountability**—Members hold one another accountable rather than relying on managers as the source of accountability.
Inattention to Results—Members put personal ambition or the needs of their individual departments ahead of collective results.	**Results Orientation**—Individual members set aside personal agendas; focus on what's best for the team. Collective results define success.

EXHIBIT 15.2
Five Common Dysfunctions of Teams

SOURCE: Based on Patrick Lencioni, *The Five Dysfunctions of a Team* (New York: John Wiley & Sons, 2002).

How to Make Teams Effective

Smoothly functioning teams don't just happen. Stanford sociologist Elizabeth Cohen studied group work among young school children and found that only when teachers took the time to define roles, establish norms, and set goals did the groups function effectively as a team.[10] In organizations, effective teams are built by managers who take specific actions to help people come together and perform well as a team.

Some of the factors associated with team effectiveness are illustrated in Exhibit 15.3. Work-team effectiveness is based on three outcomes—productive output, personal satisfaction, and the capacity to adapt and learn.[11] *Satisfaction* pertains to the team's ability to meet the personal needs of its members and hence maintain their membership and commitment. *Productive output* pertains to the quality and quantity of task outputs as defined by team goals. *Capacity to adapt and learn* refers to the ability of teams to bring greater knowledge and skills to job tasks and enhance the potential of the organization to respond to new threats or opportunities in the environment.

EXHIBIT 15.3
Work-Team Effectiveness Model

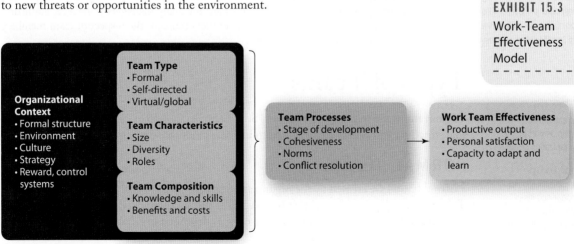

Organizational Context
• Formal structure
• Environment
• Culture
• Strategy
• Reward, control systems

Team Type
• Formal
• Self-directed
• Virtual/global

Team Characteristics
• Size
• Diversity
• Roles

Team Composition
• Knowledge and skills
• Benefits and costs

Team Processes
• Stage of development
• Cohesiveness
• Norms
• Conflict resolution

Work Team Effectiveness
• Productive output
• Personal satisfaction
• Capacity to adapt and learn

MODEL OF TEAM EFFECTIVENESS

The model of team effectiveness in Exhibit 15.3 provides a structure for the remainder of this chapter. The factors that influence team effectiveness begin with the organizational context.[12] The organizational context in which the team operates is described in other chapters and includes such matters as structure, strategy, environment, culture, and reward systems. Within that context, managers define teams. Important team characteristics are the type of team, the team structure, and team composition. Managers must decide when to create permanent teams within the formal structure and when to use a temporary task team. The diversity of the team in terms of task-related knowledge and skills can have a tremendous impact on team processes and effectiveness. In addition, diversity in terms of gender and race affect a team's performance.[13] Team size and roles also are important.

These team characteristics influence processes internal to the team, which, in turn, affect output, satisfaction, and the team's contribution to organizational adaptability. Good team leaders understand and manage stages of team development, cohesiveness, norms, and conflict to build an effective team. These processes are influenced by team and organizational characteristics and by the ability of members and leaders to direct these processes in a positive manner.

EFFECTIVE TEAM LEADERSHIP

Team leaders play an important role in shaping team effectiveness. In addition to managing internal processes, there are three specific ways in which leaders contribute to team success:[14]

- *Rally people around a compelling purpose.* It is the leader's responsibility to articulate a clear, compelling purpose and direction, one of the key elements of effective teams. This ensures that everyone is moving in the same direction rather than floundering around wondering why the team was created and where it's supposed to be going. Indie band Dirty Projectors has a leader who knows how to move the members towards his vision of excellence, as described in this chapter's Benchmarking box.

- *Share power.* Good team leaders embrace the concept of teamwork in deeds as well as in words. This means sharing power, information, and responsibility. It means letting team members who do the work have a say in how to do it. It requires that the leader have faith that team members will make good decisions, even if those decisions might not be the ones the leader would make.

- *Admit ignorance.* Often, people appointed to lead teams find that they don't know nearly as much as their teammates know. Good team leaders aren't afraid to admit their ignorance and ask for help. This serves as a *fallibility model* that lets people know that lack of knowledge, problems, concerns, and mistakes can be discussed openly without fear of appearing incompetent. Although it's hard for many managers to believe, admitting ignorance and being willing to learn from others can earn the respect of team members faster than almost any other behavior.

Go to the Self Learning exercise on page 496 that pertains to effective versus ineffective teams.

Types of Teams

Organizations use many types of teams. Some are created as part of the organization's formal structure, and others are designed to increase employee participation.

FORMAL TEAMS

Formal teams are created by the organization as part of the formal organization structure. Two common types of formal teams are vertical and horizontal, which typically represent vertical and horizontal structural relationships, as described in Chapter 7. These two types of teams are illustrated in Exhibit 15.4.

formal team
A team created by the organization as part of the formal organization structure.

vertical team
A formal team composed of a manager and his or her subordinates in the organization's formal chain of command.

BENCH-MARKING

Dirty Projectors

Being a rock star, with a small *s*, in an indie band might seem like a dream life of parties and performances, but Dirty Projectors leader and front man 27-year-old David Longstreth has a frenetic and disciplined schedule of long hours. In between finalizing the bands most current album, *Bitte Orca*, he squeezes in music video production and rehearsals for a performance with David Byrne at Radio City Music Hall, and he even managed to write a complicated seven-part vocal suite—from scratch—in a mere 10 days. Admired for his out-of-the-box creativity, Longstreth notes, "You can have outlandish ideas, but if you don't work at them, they just remain outlandish ideas. Anyone can have an idea. Work is transformative." Longstreth was always immersed in music, starting with his parents' vast record collection, through Beatles addiction in high school and mastering classical music in college.

Dirty Projectors music doesn't follow some mainstream formula, for the songs skillfully balance catchy melodies and razor-sharp harmonies with abstract formal experimentation. Longstreth plays guitar, sings, and is the group's visionary leader. Though Longstreth is seen by some as a mad genius, band members speak of him with deference and are comfortable with him as boss and musical director. Longstreth has difficult goals for the group because, as he even admits, his music is difficult for people to comprehend. "The people I really admire, like William Blake and John Coltrane and Richard Wagner, had these ridiculously full universes that took their entire lives to describe. So from one album to the next it's been hard for people to see the way they're all related, but the whole thing makes sense to me." More than any other indie band, Dirty Projectors have devoted themselves to intense and dazzling musical technique with irregular rhythms and extremely intricate vocals that take more than one listening to fully appreciate. Such complication is difficult to perform, and Longstreth helps the group achieve perfection by requiring long and painstaking rehearsals. Yet the group willingly participates in the marathon sessions. "Dave pushes you beyond where you thought you could go," says band member Amber Coffman, 24. "He pushes and pushes and sometimes you feel like you're going to have a breakdown. But at the end of it you are realizing a new level of capability within yourself."

SOURCE: Ben Sisario, "The Experimental, Led by the Obsessive," *New York Times*, June 7, 2009, pp. AR21, AR27.

Vertical Team. A **vertical team** is composed of a manager and his or her subordinates in the formal chain of command. Sometimes called a *functional team* or a *command team*, the vertical team may in some cases include three or four levels of hierarchy within a functional department. Typically, the vertical team includes a single department in an organization. The third-shift nursing team on the second floor of St. Luke's Hospital is a vertical team

EXHIBIT 15.4
Horizontal and Vertical Teams in an Organization

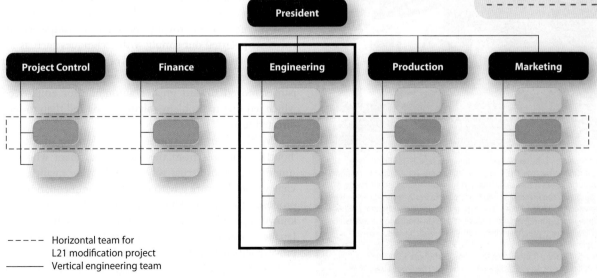

President

| Project Control | Finance | Engineering | Production | Marketing |

- - - - - Horizontal team for L21 modification project
——— Vertical engineering team

that includes nurses and a supervisor. A financial analysis department, a quality control department, an accounting department, and a human-resource department are all vertical or command teams. Each is created by the organization to attain specific goals through members' joint activities and interactions.

As a manager, make sure you periodically form cross-functional teams so that you have new people in the conversations; otherwise, you will likely have the same outcome with the same people.

Horizontal Team. A **horizontal team** is composed of employees from about the same hierarchical level but from different areas of expertise.[15] A horizontal team is drawn from several departments, is given a specific task, and may be disbanded after the task is completed. Horizontal teams include cross-functional teams, committees, and special-purpose teams.

As described in Chapter 7, a *cross-functional team* is a group of employees from different departments formed to deal with a specific activity; the group exists only until the task is completed. Sometimes called a *task force*, the team might be used to create a new product in a manufacturing organization or a new history curriculum in a university. When several departments are involved, and many views have to be considered, tasks are best served with a horizontal, cross-functional team.

As a manager, make sure you allow self-directed teams to be truly self-directed, but make sure they have enough management support to achieve their goals.

A **committee** generally is long-lived and may be a permanent part of the organization's structure. Membership is often decided by a person's title or position rather than by personal expertise. A committee needs official representation, compared with selection for a cross-functional team, which is based on personal qualifications for solving a problem. Committees typically are formed to deal with tasks that recur regularly. For example, a grievance committee handles employee grievances; an advisory committee makes recommendations in the areas of employee compensation and work practices; a worker–management committee may be concerned with work rules, job design changes, and suggestions for work improvement.[16]

Special-purpose teams, sometimes called *project teams*, are created outside the formal organization structure to undertake a project of special importance or creativity.[17] Examples include the team that developed the first IBM ThinkPad and the project team for the Motorola RAZR cell phone. A special-purpose team still is part of the formal organization and has its own reporting structure, but members perceive themselves as a separate entity.[18]

horizontal team
A formal team composed of employees from about the same hierarchical level but from different areas of expertise.

At Lucasfilm Ltd., teams form around projects. To facilitate these self-directed teams, the company responsible for the *Star Wars* and *Indiana Jones* franchises moved its formerly separate divisions to a campus in the Presidio of San Francisco. An easily reconfigurable work environment encourages the sharing of ideas and technology between Industrial Light & Magic, the visual-effects division, and LucasArts, the video game company. Project teams also work on visual effects for other films, like the visual effects for *Transformers* and the *Pirates of the Caribbean* franchise. In this photo, producer Julio Torres reviews work on LucasArts' video game *Star Wars: The Force Unleashed*.

SELF-DIRECTED TEAMS

Some teams are designed to increase the participation of workers in decision making and the conduct of their jobs, with the goal of improving performance. Employee involvement started out simply with techniques such as information sharing with employees or asking employees for suggestions about improving the work. Gradually, companies moved toward greater autonomy for employees, which led first to problem-solving teams and then to self-directed teams.[19]

Problem-solving teams typically consist of 5 to 12 hourly employees from the same department who voluntarily meet to discuss ways of improving quality, efficiency, and the work environment. Recommendations are proposed to management for approval. The most widely known application is *quality circles*, which were first used by Japanese companies to let employees focus on ways to improve quality in the production process. International Paper Company's Texarkana mill instituted a work systems team

© RICHARD MORGENSTEIN

to focus on solving and preventing snafus in the logistically complex process of producing 1,800 to 1,900 tons of bleached board a day for packaging, milk cartons, drinking cups, and folding cartons. This problem-solving team has played a significant role in helping the mill thrive amid brutal market conditions and stiff competition.[20]

As a company matures, problem-solving teams can gradually evolve into self-directed teams, which represent a fundamental change in how work is organized. **Self-directed teams** typically consist of 5 to 20 multiskilled workers who rotate jobs to produce an entire product or service or at least one complete aspect or portion of a product or service (e.g., engine assembly, insurance claim processing). The central idea is that the teams themselves, rather than managers or supervisors, take responsibility for their work, make decisions, monitor their own performance, and alter their work behavior as needed to solve problems, meet goals, and adapt to changing conditions.[21]

Self-directed teams are permanent teams that typically include the following elements:

- The team includes employees with several skills and functions, and the combined skills are sufficient to perform a major organizational task. A team may include members from the foundry, machining, grinding, fabrication, and sales departments, with members cross-trained to perform one another's jobs. The team eliminates barriers among departments, enabling excellent coordination to produce a product or service.

- The team is given access to resources such as information, equipment, machinery, and supplies needed to perform the complete task.

- The team is empowered with decision-making authority, which means that members have the freedom to select new members, solve problems, spend money, monitor results, and plan for the future.[22] Self-directed teams can enable employees to feel challenged, find their work meaningful, and develop a stronger sense of identity with the organization.

Innovative Uses of Teams

Some exciting new approaches to teamwork have resulted from advances in information technology, shifting employee expectations, and the globalization of business. Two types of teams that are increasingly being used are virtual teams and global teams.

VIRTUAL TEAMS

A **virtual team** is made up of geographically or organizationally dispersed members who are linked primarily through advanced information and telecommunications technologies.[23] Although some virtual teams are made up of only organizational members, virtual teams often include contingent workers, members of partner organizations, customers, suppliers, consultants, or other outsiders. Team members use e-mail, instant messaging, telephone and text messaging, wikis and blogs, videoconferencing, and other technology tools to collaborate and perform their work, although they might also sometimes meet face to face. Many virtual teams are cross-functional teams that emphasize solving customer problems or completing specific projects. Others are permanent self-directed teams.

With virtual teams, team membership may change fairly quickly, depending on the tasks to be performed.[24] One of the primary advantages of virtual teams is the ability to rapidly assemble the most appropriate group of people to complete a complex project, solve a particular problem, or exploit a specific strategic opportunity. Virtual teams present unique challenges. Exhibit 15.5 (on page 480) lists some critical areas managers should address when leading virtual teams. Each area is discussed in more detail below:[25]

- *Using technology to build relationships* is crucial for effective virtual teamwork. Leaders first select people who have the right mix of technical, interpersonal, and communication skills to work in a virtual environment, and then they make sure they have opportunities

committee
A long-lasting, sometimes permanent team in the organization structure created to deal with tasks that recur regularly.

special-purpose team
A team created outside the formal organization to undertake a project of special importance or creativity.

problem-solving team
Typically 5 to 12 hourly employees from the same department who meet to discuss ways of improving quality, efficiency, and the work environment.

self-directed team
A team consisting of 5 to 20 multiskilled workers who rotate jobs to produce an entire product or service, often supervised by an elected member.

virtual team
A team made up of members who are geographically or organizationally dispersed, rarely meet face to face, and do their work using advanced information technologies.

EXHIBIT 15.5
What Effective
Virtual Team
Leaders Do
- - - - - - - - - -

Practice	How It's Done
Use Technology to Build Relationships	• Bring attention to and appreciate diverse skills and opinions • Use technology to enhance communication and trust • Ensure timely responses online • Manage online socialization
Shape Culture Through Technology	• Create a psychologically safe virtual culture • Share members' special experiences/strengths • Engage members from cultures where they may be hesitant to share ideas
Monitor Progress and Rewards	• Scrutinize electronic communication patterns • Post targets and scorecards in virtual work space • Reward people through online ceremonies, recognition

SOURCE: Based on Table 1, "Practices of Effective Virtual Team Leaders," in Arvind Malhotra, Ann Majchrzak, and Benson Rosen, "Leading Virtual Teams," *Academy of Management Perspectives* 21(1) (Feb. 2007): 60–69; and Table 2, "'Best Practices' Solutions for Overcoming Barriers to Knowledge Sharing in Virtual Teams," in Benson Rosen, Stacie Furst, and Richard Blackburn, "Overcoming Barriers to Knowledge Sharing in Virtual Teams," *Organizational Dynamics* 36(3) (2007): 259–273.

to know one another and establish trusting relationships. Encouraging online social networking, where people can share photos and personal biographies, is one key to virtual team success. Leaders also build trust by making everyone's roles, responsibilities, and authority clear from the beginning, by shaping norms of full disclosure and respectful interaction, and by providing a way for everyone to stay up-to-date. In a study of which technologies make virtual teams successful, researchers found that round-the-clock virtual work spaces—where team members can access the latest versions of files, keep track of deadlines and timelines, monitor one another's progress, and carry on discussions between formal meetings—got top marks.[26] Today, many virtual teams use wikis to facilitate this kind of regular collaboration and open information sharing.

• *Shaping culture through technology* involves creating a virtual environment in which people feel safe to express concerns, admit mistakes, share ideas, acknowledge fears, or ask for help. Leaders reinforce a norm of sharing all forms of knowledge, and they encourage people to express "off-the-wall" ideas and ask for help when it's needed. Team leaders set the example by their own behavior. Leaders also make sure they bring diversity issues into the open and educate members early on regarding possible cultural differences that could cause communication problems or misunderstandings in a virtual environment.

• *Monitoring progress and rewarding members* means that leaders stay on top of the project's development and make sure everyone knows how the team is progressing toward meeting goals. Posting targets, measurements, and milestones in the virtual workspace can make progress explicit. Leaders also provide regular feedback, and they reward both individual and team accomplishments through such avenues as virtual award ceremonies and recognition at virtual meetings. They are liberal with praise and congratulations, but criticism or reprimands are handled individually rather than in the virtual presence of the team.

Assess
Your
Answer

2 It's better if team members are in the same location.

ANSWER: A growing trend in organization is virtual teams, some members of which actually never meet face to face because they are in far-flung locations. Virtual teams can be very effective if managed properly.

As the use of virtual teams grows, there is growing understanding of what makes them successful. Some experts suggest that managers solicit volunteers as much as possible for virtual teams, and interviews with virtual team members and leaders support the idea that members who truly want to work as a virtual team are more effective.[27] At Nokia, a significant portion of its virtual teams are made up of people who volunteered for the task.

In a study of 52 virtual teams in 15 leading multinational companies, London Business School researchers found that Nokia's teams were among the most effective, even though they were made up of people working in several different countries, across time zones and cultures. What makes Nokia's teams so successful?

Nokia managers are careful to select people who have a collaborative mind-set, and they form many teams with volunteers who are highly committed to the task or project. The company also tries to make sure some members of a team have worked together before, providing a base for trusting relationships. Making the best use of technology is critical. In addition to a virtual work space that team members can access 24 hours a day, Nokia provides an online resource where virtual workers are encouraged to post photos and share personal information. With the inability of members to get to know each another one of the biggest barriers to effective virtual teamwork, encouraging and supporting social networking has paid off for Nokia.[28]

GLOBAL TEAMS

As the example of Nokia shows, virtual teams are also sometimes **global teams**. *Global teams* are cross-border work teams made up of members of different nationalities whose activities span multiple countries.[29] Some global teams are made up of members who come from different countries or cultures and meet face to face, but many are virtual global teams whose members remain in separate locations around the world and conduct their work electronically.[30] For example, global teams of software developers at Tandem Services Corporation coordinate their work electronically so that the team is productive around the clock. Team members in London code a project and transmit the code each evening to members in the United States for testing. U.S. team members then forward the code they've tested to Tokyo for debugging. The next morning, the London team members pick up the code debugged by their Tokyo colleagues, and another cycle begins.[31]

global team
A work team made up of members of different nationalities whose activities span multiple countries; may operate as a virtual team or meet face to face.

Global teams present enormous challenges for team leaders, who have to bridge gaps of time, distance, and culture.[32] In some cases, members speak different languages, use different technologies, and have different beliefs about authority, communication, decision making, and time orientation. For example, in some cultures, such as the United States, communication is explicit and direct, whereas in many other cultures meaning is embedded in the way the message is presented. U.S.-based team members are also typically highly focused on "clock time" and tend to follow rigid schedules, whereas many other cultures have a more relaxed, cyclical concept of time. These different cultural attitudes can affect work pacing, team communications, decision making, the perception of deadlines, and other issues, all of it providing rich soil for misunderstandings. No wonder then that when the executive council of *CIO* magazine asked global chief information officers to rank their greatest challenges, managing virtual global teams ranked as the most pressing issue.[33]

© MARK LEONG/REDUX

For Lotus Symphony, a package of PC software applications, IBM assigned the project to teams in Beijing, China; Austin, Texas; Raleigh, North Carolina; and Boeblingen, Germany. Leading the project, the Beijing group—shown here with Michael Karasick (center), who runs the Beijing lab, and lead developer Yue Ma (right)—navigated the global team through the programming challenges. To help bridge the distance gap, IBM uses Beehive, a corporate social network similar to Facebook, where employees create profiles, list their interests, and post photos.

········> CONCEPT CONNECTION <········

Organizations using global teams invest the time and resources to adequately educate employees, such as Accenture, which trains all consultants and most of its services workers in how to effectively collaborate with international colleagues.[34] Managers working with global teams make sure all team members appreciate and understand cultural differences, are focused on clear goals, and understand their roles and responsibilities. For a global team to be effective, all team members must be willing to deviate somewhat from their own values and norms and establish new norms for the team.[35] As with virtual teams, carefully selecting team members, building trust, and sharing information are critical to success.

Team Characteristics

After deciding the type of team to use, the next issue of concern to managers is designing the team for greatest effectiveness. Team characteristics of particular concern are size, diversity, and member roles.

SIZE

Remember—smaller teams are more nimble and tend to function more effectively.

More than 30 years ago, psychologist Ivan Steiner examined what happened each time the size of a team increased, and he proposed that team performance and productivity peaked at about five members—a quite small number. He found that adding additional members beyond that caused a decrease in motivation, an increase in coordination problems, and a general decline in performance.[36] Since then, numerous studies have found that smaller teams perform better, although most researchers say it's impossible to specify an optimal team size. One recent investigation of team size based on data from 58 software-development teams found that the five best-performing teams ranged in size from three to six members.[37] Results of a recent Gallup poll in the United States show that 82 percent of employees agree that small teams are more productive.[38]

Teams need to be large enough to incorporate the diverse skills needed to complete a task, enable members to express good and bad feelings, and aggressively solve problems.

However, they should also be small enough to permit members to feel an intimate part of the team and to communicate effectively and efficiently. In general, as a team increases in size, it becomes harder for each member to interact with and influence the others. Subgroups often form in larger teams and conflicts among them can occur. Turnover and absenteeism are higher because members feel less like an important part of the team.[39] Large projects can be split into components and assigned to several smaller teams to keep the benefits of small size. At Amazon.com, CEO Jeff Bezos established a "two-pizza rule." If a team gets so large that members can't be fed with two pizzas, then it should be split into smaller teams.[40]

DIVERSITY

As a new manager, remember that team effectiveness depends on selecting the right type of team for the task, balancing the team's size and diversity, and ensuring that both task and social needs are met.

Because teams require a variety of skills, knowledge, and experience, it seems likely that heterogeneous teams would be more effective than homogeneous ones. In general, research supports this idea, showing that diverse teams produce more innovative solutions to problems.[41] Diversity in terms of functional area and skills, thinking styles, and personal characteristics is often a source of creativity. In addition, diversity may contribute to a healthy level of disagreement that leads to better decision making.

Research studies have confirmed that both functional diversity and gender diversity can have a positive impact on work-team performance.[42] Racial, national, and ethnic diversity can also be good for teams, but in the short term these differences might hinder team interaction and performance. Teams made up of racially and culturally diverse members tend to have more difficulty learning to work well together, but the problems do fade over time with effective leadership.[43]

MEMBER ROLES

For a team to be successful over the long run, it must be structured so as to both maintain its members' social well-being and accomplish its task. In successful teams, the requirements for task performance and social satisfaction are met by the emergence of two types of roles: task specialist and socioemotional.[44]

People who play the **task specialist role** spend time and energy helping the team reach its goal. They often display the following behaviors:

- *initiate ideas*—proposing new solutions to team problems;

- *giving opinions*—offering opinions on task solutions and giving candid feedback on others' suggestions;

- *seeking information*—asking for task-relevant facts;

- *summarizing*—relating various ideas to the problem at hand and pulling ideas together into a summary perspective; and

- *energizing*—stimulating the team into action when interest drops.[45]

People who adopt a **socioemotional role** support team members' emotional needs and help strengthen the social entity. They display the following behaviors:

- *encouraging*—being warm and receptive to others' ideas and praising and encouraging others to draw forth their contributions;

- *harmonizing*—reconciling group conflicts and helping parties in disagreement reach agreement;

- *reducing tension*—telling jokes or in other ways drawing off emotions when the group atmosphere is tense;

- *following*—going along with the team and agreeing to other team members' ideas; and

- *compromising*—shifting own opinions to maintain team harmony.[46]

Teams with mostly socioemotional roles can be satisfying, but they also can be unproductive. At the other extreme, a team made up primarily of task specialists will tend to have a singular concern for task accomplishment. This team will be effective for a short period of time but will not be satisfying for members over the long run. Effective teams have people in both task specialist and socioemotional roles. A well-balanced team will do best over the long term because it will be personally satisfying for team members as well as permit the accomplishment of team tasks.

Team Processes

Now we turn our attention to internal team processes. Team processes pertain to those dynamics that change over time and can be influenced by team leaders. In this section, we discuss stages of development, cohesiveness, and norms. The fourth type of team process, conflict, will be covered in the next section.

task specialist role
A role in which the individual devotes personal time and energy to helping the team accomplish its task.

socioemotional role
A role in which the individual provides support for team members' emotional needs and social unity.

3 The best team members are those who encourage other members.

ANSWER: Though encouragement is important, other skills are needed as well, such as seeking information, giving opinions, initiating idea, energizing the group, reducing tensions, and compromising, among others.

Assess Your Answer

STAGES OF TEAM DEVELOPMENT

After a team has been created, it develops through distinct stages.[47] New teams are different from mature teams. Recall a time when you were a member of a new team such as a fraternity or sorority pledge class, a committee, or a small team formed to do a class assignment. Over time, the team changed. In the beginning, team members had to get to know one another, establish roles and norms, divide the labor, and clarify the team's task. In this way, each member became part of a smoothly operating team. The challenge for leaders is to understand the stages of development and then take action that will lead to smooth functioning.

Research findings suggest that team development is not random but evolves over definitive stages. One useful model for describing these stages is shown in Exhibit 15.6. Each stage confronts team leaders and members with unique problems and challenges.[48]

Forming. The **forming** stage of development is a period of orientation and getting acquainted. Members break the ice and test one another for friendship possibilities and task orientation. Uncertainty is high during this stage, and members usually accept whatever power or authority is offered by either formal or informal leaders. During this initial stage, members are concerned about such things as "What is expected of me?" "What behavior is acceptable?"

forming
The stage of team development characterized by orientation and acquaintance.

storming
The stage of team development in which individual personalities and roles emerge along with resulting conflicts.

EXHIBIT 15.6

Five Stages of Team Development

- - - - - - - - - - - -

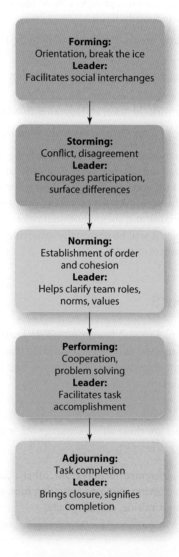

"Will I fit in?" During the forming stage, the team leader should provide time for members to get acquainted with one another and encourage them to engage in informal social discussions.

Storming. During the **storming** stage, individual personalities emerge. People become more assertive in clarifying their roles and what is expected of them. This stage is marked by conflict and disagreement. People may disagree over their perceptions of the team's goals or how to achieve them. Members may jockey for position, and coalitions or subgroups based on common interests may form. Unless teams can successfully move beyond this stage, they may get bogged down and never achieve high performance. During the storming stage, the team leader should encourage participation by each team member. Members should propose ideas, disagree with one another, and work through the uncertainties and conflicting perceptions about team tasks and goals.

Norming. During the **norming** stage, conflict is resolved, and team harmony and unity emerge. Consensus develops on who has the power, who the leaders are, and what the members' roles are. Members come to accept and understand one another. Differences are resolved, and members develop a sense of team cohesion. During the norming stage, the team leader should emphasize unity within the team and help to clarify team norms and values.

Performing. During the **performing** stage, the major emphasis is on problem solving and accomplishing the assigned task. Members are committed to the team's mission. They are coordinated with one another and handle disagreements in a mature way. They confront and resolve problems in the interest of task accomplishment. They interact frequently and direct their discussions and influence toward achieving team goals. During this stage, the leader should concentrate on managing high task performance. Both socioemotional and task specialists contribute to the team's functioning. Some teams, however, may never fully get to the performing stage because the organization has too much chaos, as described in this chapter's Business Blooper (on page 486).

Adjourning. The **adjourning** stage occurs in committees and teams that have a limited task to perform and are disbanded afterward. During this stage, the emphasis is on wrapping up and gearing down. Task performance is no longer a top priority. Members may feel heightened emotionality, strong cohesiveness, and depression or regret over the team's disbandment. At this point, the leader may wish to signify the team's disbanding with a ritual or ceremony, perhaps giving out plaques and awards to signify closure and completeness.

These five stages typically occur in sequence, but they may occur quite rapidly in teams that are under time pressure. The stages may also be accelerated for virtual teams. For example, at McDevitt Street Bovis, a large construction-management firm, bringing

Remember—when you are on a team that is having conflicts in the early stages, that is a normal part of the developmental process.

norming
The stage of team development in which conflicts developed during the storming stage are resolved and team harmony and unity emerge.

performing
The stage of team development in which members focus on problem solving and accomplishing the team's assigned task.

adjourning
The stage of team development in which members prepare for the team's disbandment.

MERCURY PHOENIX WNBA TEAM PHOTO

To accomplish their goals—whether in the business world or on the basketball court—teams have to successfully advance to the performing stage of team development. The WNBA's Phoenix Mercury teammates shown here blend their talents and energies so effortlessly that they play the game not like separate people but like a coordinated piece of a whole. Phoenix recently began using psychological testing as part of the appraisal of new coaches and potential draft picks. Managers think testing gives them another tool for building a high-performance team. As part-owner Anne Mariucci puts it, "If a person isn't dotting the I's and crossing the T's, we know why, and we can surround that person with people who complement that. . . ."

CONCEPT CONNECTION

BUSINESS BLOOPER

Yahoo

For a year and a half, cofounder and CEO Jerry Yang tried to resuscitate Yahoo by rallying top executives to get along better, but his inability to make tough decisions diminished his efforts to get Yahoo out of the ditch. So in November 2008 Yang resigned as CEO; company stocks briefly went up as the board searched for a new CEO who would be different—the anti-Jerry. When Carol Bartz was named CEO in early 2009, she immediately did yet another corporate shake-up, the sixth in two years, in hopes of bringing the company out of darkness. By August 2009, Yahoo announced it had increased earnings by 8 percent—but only by reducing operating expenses by $150 million, which included layoffs. Yahoo had 9 percent fewer employees in 2009 than in 2008.

SOURCE: Stephen Manning, "Companies Stay Afloat by Cutting Way Back," *Charleston Sunday Gazette-Mail*, Aug, 2, 2009, p. C 5; Miguel Helft, "Yahoo Chief Rearranges Managers Once Again," *New York Times*, Feb. 27, 2009, p. B5.

people together for a couple of days of team building helps teams move rapidly through the forming and storming stages.

MCDEVITT STREET BOVIS

Rather than having its typical construction project be characterized by conflicts, frantic scheduling, and poor communications, McDevitt Street Bovis wants its collection of contractors, designers, suppliers, and other partners to function like a true team—putting the success of the project ahead of their own individual interests.

The team-building process at Bovis is designed to take teams to the performing stage as quickly as possible by giving everyone an opportunity to get to know one another, explore the ground rules, and clarify roles, responsibilities, and expectations. The team is first divided into separate groups that may have competing objectives—such as the clients in one group, suppliers in another, engineers and architects in a third, and so forth—and asked to come up with a list of their goals for the project. Although interests sometimes vary widely in purely accounting terms, common themes almost always emerge. By talking about conflicting goals and interests, as well as what all the groups share, facilitators help the team gradually come together around a common purpose and begin to develop shared values that will guide the project. After jointly writing a mission statement for the team, each party says what it expects from the others so that roles and responsibilities can be clarified. The intensive team-building session helps take members quickly through the forming and storming stages of development. "We prevent conflicts from happening," says facilitator Monica Bennett. Leaders at McDevitt Street Bovis believe building better teams builds better buildings.[49]

TEAM COHESIVENESS

Another important aspect of the team process is cohesiveness. **Team cohesiveness** is defined as the extent to which members are attracted to the team and motivated to remain in it.[50] Members of highly cohesive teams are committed to team activities, attend meetings, and are happy when the team succeeds. Members of less-cohesive teams are less concerned about the team's welfare. High cohesiveness is normally considered an attractive feature of teams.

Determinants of Team Cohesiveness. Several characteristics of team structure and context influence cohesiveness. First is *team interaction*. When team members have frequent contact, they get to know one another, consider themselves a unit, and become more committed to the team.[51] Second is the concept of *shared goals*. If team members agree on purpose and direction, then they will be more cohesive. Third is *personal attraction to the team*, meaning that members have similar attitudes and values and enjoy being together.

team cohesiveness
The extent to which team members are attracted to the team and motivated to remain in it.

Two factors in the team's context also influence group cohesiveness. The first is the *presence of competition*. When a team is in moderate competition with other teams, its cohesiveness increases as it strives to win. Finally, *team success* and the favorable evaluation of the team by outsiders add to cohesiveness. When a team succeeds in its task and others in the organization recognize the success, then members feel good and their commitment to the team will be high.

Consequences of Team Cohesiveness. The outcome of team cohesiveness can fall into two categories—morale and productivity. As a general rule, morale is higher in cohesive teams because of increased communication among members, a friendly team climate, maintenance of membership because of commitment to the team, loyalty, and member participation in team decisions and activities. High cohesiveness has almost uniformly good effects on the satisfaction and morale of team members.[52]

With respect to the productivity of the team as a whole, research findings suggest that cohesive teams have the potential to be productive, but the degree of productivity depends on the relationship between management and the working team. One study surveyed more than 200 work teams and correlated job performance with their cohesiveness.[53] Highly cohesive teams were more productive when team members felt management support and less productive when they sensed management hostility and negativism.

TEAM NORMS

A **team norm** is an informal standard of conduct that is shared by team members and guides their behavior.[54] Norms are valuable because they provide a frame of reference for what is expected and acceptable.

Norms begin to develop in the first interactions among members of a new team.[55] Exhibit 15.7 illustrates four common ways in which norms develop. Sometimes, the first behaviors that occur in a team set a precedent. For example, at one company, a team leader began his first meeting by raising an issue and then "leading" team members until he got the solution he wanted. The pattern became ingrained so quickly into an unproductive team norm that members dubbed meetings the "Guess What I Think" game.[56] Other influences on team norms include critical events in the team's history, as well as behaviors, attitudes, and norms that members bring with them from outside the team.

As a team leader, build a cohesive team by focusing people on shared goals, giving team members time to know one another, and doing what you can to help people enjoy being together as a team.

team norm
A standard of conduct that is shared by team members and guides their behavior.

EXHIBIT 15.7
Four Ways Team Norms Develop

Critical events in team's history

Primacy: first-behavior precedents

Team Norms

Explicit statements from leader or member

Carryover from other experiences

As a manager, consider developing a list of values and norms and sharing those with the group and new members as they join the group.

Team leaders play an important role in shaping norms that will help the team be effective. For example, research shows that when leaders have high expectations for collaborative problem solving, teams develop strong collaborative norms.[57] Making explicit statements about desired team behaviors is a powerful way in which leaders influence norms. Explicit statements symbolize what counts and thus have considerable impact. Ameritech CEO Bill Weiss established a norm of cooperation and mutual support among his top leadership team by bluntly telling team members that if he caught anyone trying to undermine the others, the guilty party would be fired.[58]

Managing Team Conflict

The final characteristic of team process is conflict. Conflict can arise among members within a team or between one team and another. **Conflict** refers to antagonistic interactions in which one party attempts to block the intentions or goals of another.[59] Competition, which is rivalry among individuals or teams, can have a healthy impact because it energizes people toward higher performance.[60]

Whenever people work together in teams, some conflict is inevitable. Bringing conflicts out into the open and effectively resolving them is one of the team leader's most challenging, yet most important, jobs. For example, studies of virtual teams indicate that how they handle internal conflicts is critical to their success, yet conflict within virtual teams tends to occur more frequently and take longer to resolve because people are separated by space, time, and cultural differences. Moreover, people in virtual teams tend to engage in more inconsiderate behaviors such as name-calling and insults than do people who work face to face.[61]

BALANCING CONFLICT AND COOPERATION

Mild conflict can actually be beneficial to teams.[62] A healthy level of conflict helps to prevent **groupthink**, the phenomenon that occurs when people are so committed to a cohesive team that they are reluctant to express contrary opinions. Author and scholar Jerry Harvey tells a story of how members of his extended family in Texas decided to drive 40 miles to Abilene on a hot day when the car's air conditioning didn't work. Everyone was miserable. Each person later admitted that he or she had not wanted to go but went along to please the others. Harvey used the term *Abilene paradox* to describe this tendency to go along with others for the sake of avoiding conflict.[63] Similarly, when people in work teams go along simply for the sake of harmony, problems typically result. Thus, a degree of conflict leads to better decision making because multiple viewpoints are expressed. Among top management teams, for example, low levels of conflict have been found to be associated with poor decision making.[64]

As a manager, keep the right balance between conflict and cooperation; too much conflict is harmful, but too little squelches ideas and creativity.

However, conflict that is too strong, that is focused on personal rather than work issues, or that is not managed appropriately can be damaging to the team's morale and productivity. Too much conflict can be destructive, tear relationships apart, and interfere with the healthy exchange of ideas and information.[65] Team leaders have to find the right balance between conflict and cooperation, as illustrated in Exhibit 15.8. Too little conflict can decrease team performance because the team doesn't benefit from a mix of opinions and ideas—even disagreements—that might lead to better solutions or prevent the team from making mistakes. At the other end of the spectrum, too much conflict outweighs the team's cooperative efforts and leads to a decrease in employee satisfaction and commitment, hurting team performance. A moderate amount of conflict that is managed appropriately typically results in the highest levels of team performance.

Day Star Coffee is exploring new ways of collaboration, new ways to resolve conflicts, as described in the Spotlight on Skills box.

conflict
Antagonistic interaction in which one party attempts to thwart the intentions or goals of another.

groupthink
The tendency for people to be so committed to a cohesive team that they are reluctant to express contrary opinions.

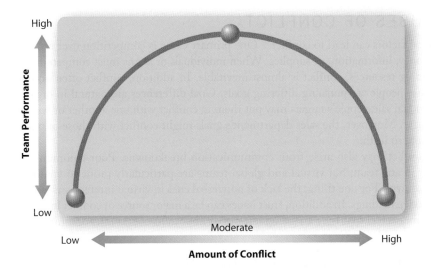

EXHIBIT 15.8
Balancing Conflict
and Cooperation

SPOTLIGHT ON SKILLS

Day Star Coffee

odd Khozein was going to be a Flamenco dancer, but a knee injury at age 20 stole that dream. So he studied economics, but then family pressure found him in medical school. After he graduated, he realized he wanted to start a business that would be based on a model of collaboration that would help build a more collaborative world of commerce. That's when he crossed paths with recently widowed Linda Assaf, who had, with her late husband, built up a small empire of coffee kiosks in convention centers. The couple was making millions of dollars when Hurricanes Katrina and then Rita hit. Not only did they lose their sites in New Orleans, but the flood of evacuees into Houston and Austin overtook those convention centers. After her husband's sudden death, she managed to keep the business going. She had, after all, her reputation as honest, hard-working, and capable. Growing the business was another story. When she met Khozein at a conference, she realized he had the necessary skills to help her develop her coffee empire even further.

They spent nine days reading and strategizing. Both had strong spiritual foundations as members of the Bahá'í Faith and deeply believed in working to improve the world. So they redesigned the coffee kiosk firm, calling it Day Star Coffee and started getting it placed in new convention centers. People remembered Assaf and how honestly she had always run her business. "Our success as we reemerged was because of relationships," she said. But that was only the beginning. They wanted to prove that it was possible to run a business without profit maximization as the prime motive, so they decided to test whether they could design a human-resource-driven organization—that is, one operated on the basis of courtesy, joy, and happiness—that could be successful. After two years, they have found their turnover rates are much lower than other vendors, their customer lines are much longer, and their cost of doing business is less because of low turnover and a committed and focused workforce of 70 employees.

Assaf and Khozein brought in two other partners and started what is now a successful consulting company, specializing in—you guessed it—collaboration. Plus they've recently started a financial services firm. Their ultimate goal is to revolutionize business, help bring about larger collaboration, and reduce the redundancies of heavy competition. "We are basically operating our companies on a model of 13th-century European monarchies, with kings and queens (CEOs), knights (managers) and serfs (workers). Hasn't society come past this by now?" Khozein asked.

If Assaf and Khozein have their way, Day Star Coffee and their other companies will prove that having goals larger than individual wealth is what is needed now. "We've seen whole industries collapse recently because of an outdated business model," said Khozein. "We've got to come up with something new that works and is sustainable."

SOURCES: Linda Assaf, personal communication, June 2009; Todd Khozein, personal communication, June 2009.

CAUSES OF CONFLICT

Go to the Ethical Dilemma on page 497 that pertains to team cohesiveness and conflict.

Several factors can lead to conflict.[66] One primary cause is competition over resources such as money, information, or supplies. When individuals or teams must compete for scarce or declining resources, conflict is almost inevitable. In addition, conflict often occurs simply because people are pursuing differing goals. Goal differences are natural in organizations. Individual salespeople's targets may put them in conflict with one another or with the sales manager. Moreover, the sales department's goals might conflict with those of manufacturing, and so forth.

Conflict may also arise from communication breakdowns. Poor communication can occur in any team, but virtual and global teams are particularly prone to communication breakdowns. For one thing, the lack of nonverbal cues in virtual interactions leads to more misunderstandings. In addition, trust issues can be a major source of conflict in virtual teams if members feel that they are being left out of important communication interactions.[67]

As a manager, make sure team members know each other's responsibilities; this can be done through written roles and plenty of conversations among members to discuss assumptions.

STYLES TO HANDLE CONFLICT

Teams as well as individuals develop specific styles for dealing with conflict based on the desire to satisfy their own concern versus the other party's concern. A model that describes five styles of handling conflict is in Exhibit 15.9. The two major dimensions are the extent to which an individual is assertive or cooperative in his or her approach to conflict.[68]

1. The *competing style* reflects assertiveness to get one's own way. It should be used when quick, decisive action is vital on important issues or unpopular actions, such as during emergencies or urgent cost cutting.

2. The *avoiding style* reflects neither assertiveness nor cooperativeness. It is appropriate when an issue is trivial, when there is no chance of winning, when a delay to gather more information is needed, or when a disruption would be costly.

3. The *compromising style* reflects a moderate amount of both assertiveness and cooperativeness. It is appropriate when the goals on both sides are equally important, when opponents

EXHIBIT 15.9
A Model of Styles to Handle Conflict

	Uncooperative	Cooperative
Assertive	Competing	Collaborating
Assertiveness (Attempting to satisfy one's own concerns)		Compromising
Unassertive	Avoiding	Accommodating

Cooperativeness
(Attempting to satisfy the other party's concerns)

SOURCE: Adapted from Kenneth Thomas, "Conflict and Conflict Management," in M. D. Dunnette (Ed.) *Handbook of Industrial and Organizational Behavior* (New York: John Wiley, 1976): 900.

have equal power and both sides want to split the difference, or when people need to arrive at temporary or expedient solutions under time pressure.

4. The *accommodating style* reflects a high degree of cooperativeness, which works best when people realize that they are wrong, when an issue is more important to others than to oneself, when building social credits for use in later discussions, and when maintaining harmony is especially important.

5. The *collaborating style* reflects both a high degree of assertiveness and cooperativeness. The collaborating style enables both parties to win, although it may require substantial bargaining and negotiation. The collaborating style is important when both sets of concerns are too important to be compromised, when insights from different people need to be merged into an overall solution, and when the commitment of both sides is needed for a consensus.

Effective team members vary their style to fit the specific situation. Each of the five styles is appropriate in certain cases. These styles of handling conflict are especially useful when an individual disagrees with others. But what does a manager or team leader do when a conflict erupts among others within a team or among teams for which the manager is responsible?

Research suggests the use of superordinate goals, mediation, and negotiation for resolving conflicts among people or departments:

*   *Superordinate goals.* The larger objective that cannot be attained by a single party is identified as a **superordinate goal**.[69] It is similar to the concept of vision. A powerful vision often compels people to overcome conflicts and cooperate for the greater good. Similarly, to be achieved, a superordinate goal requires the cooperation of conflicting team members. People must pull together. To the extent that employees can be focused on team or organization goals, the conflict will decrease because they see the big picture and realize they must work together to achieve it.

*   *Mediation.* Using a third party to settle a dispute is referred to as **mediation**. A mediator could be a supervisor, a higher-level manager, an outside consultant, or someone from the human-resource department. The mediator can discuss the conflict with each party and work toward a solution. If a solution satisfactory to both sides cannot be reached, the parties might be willing to turn the conflict over to the mediator and abide by his or her solution.

NEGOTIATION

One distinctive type of conflict management is **negotiation**, whereby people engage in give-and-take discussions and consider various alternatives to reach a joint decision that is acceptable to both parties. Negotiation is used when a conflict is formalized, such as between a union and management.

Types of Negotiation. Conflicting parties may embark on negotiation from different perspectives and with different intentions, reflecting either an *integrative* approach or a *distributive* approach.

Integrative negotiation is based on a win–win assumption in that all parties want to come up with a creative solution that can benefit both sides. Rather than viewing the conflict as a win–lose situation, people look at the issues from multiple angles, consider trade-offs, and try to "expand the pie" rather than divide it. With integrative negotiation, conflicts are managed through cooperation and compromise, which fosters trust and positive long-term relationships. **Distributive negotiation**, on the other hand, assumes the size of the pie is fixed, and each party attempts to get as much of it as it can. One side wants to win, which means the other side must lose. With this win–lose approach, distributive negotiation is competitive and adversarial rather than collaborative, and it does not typically lead to positive long-term relationships.[70]

As a new manager, appreciate that some conflict can be healthy, but don't let conflict reduce the team's effectiveness and well-being. Take the New Manager's Self-Test on page 492 to learn about your personal style for handling conflict.

superordinate goal
A goal that cannot be reached by a single party.

mediation
The process of using a third party to settle a dispute.

negotiation
A conflict-management strategy whereby people engage in give-and-take discussions and consider various alternatives to reach a joint decision that is acceptable to both parties.

integrative negotiation
A collaborative approach to negotiation that is based on a win–win assumption, whereby the parties want to come up with a creative solution that benefits both sides of the conflict.

distributive negotiation
A competitive and adversarial negotiation approach in which each party strives to get as much as it can, usually at the expense of the other party.

Most experts emphasize the value of integrative negotiation for today's collaborative business environment. That is, the key to effectiveness is to see negotiation not as a zero-sum game but as a process for reaching a creative solution that benefits everyone.[71]

Rules for Reaching a Win–Win Solution. Achieving a win–win solution through integrative negotiation is based on four key strategies:[72]

1. *Separate the people from the problem.* For successful integrative negotiation, people stay focused on the problem and the source of conflict rather than attacking or attempting to discredit each other.

NEW MANAGER'S SELF-TEST

Managing Conflict

Conflicting opinions and perspectives occur in every team. The ability to handle conflict and disagreement is one mark of a successful new manager. To understand your approach to managing conflict, think about disagreements you have had with people on student teams or in other situations, then answer each of the following items as Mostly True or Mostly False for you.

	MOSTLY TRUE	MOSTLY FALSE
1. I typically assert my opinion to win a disagreement.	_____	_____
2. I often suggest solutions that combine others' points of view.	_____	_____
3. I prefer to not argue with team members.	_____	_____
4. I raise my voice to get other people to accept my position.	_____	_____
5. I am quick to agree when someone makes a good point.	_____	_____
6. I tend to keep quiet rather than argue with other people.	_____	_____
7. I stand firm in expressing my viewpoints during a disagreement.	_____	_____
8. I try to include other people's ideas to create a solution they will accept.	_____	_____
9. I like to smooth over disagreements so people get along.	_____	_____

SCORING AND INTERPRETATION: Three categories of conflict-handling strategies are measured in this instrument: competing, accommodating, and collaborating. By comparing your scores, you can see your preferred conflict-handling strategy.

Give yourself one point for each item marked Mostly True.
Competing: Items 1, 4, 7
Accommodating: Items 2, 5, 8
Collaborating: Items 3, 6, 9

For which conflict-handling strategy do you score highest? New managers may initially be accommodating to get along with people until they size up the situation. A competing style that is too strong may prevent subordinates from having a say in important matters. The collaborating style tries for a win–win solution and has the long-run potential to build a constructive team. How would your strategy differ if the other people involved in a disagreement were family members, friends, subordinates, or bosses?

2. *Focus on interests, not current demands.* Demands are what each person wants from the negotiation, whereas interests are why they want them. Consider two sisters arguing over the last orange in the fruit bowl. Each insists she should get the orange and refuses to give up (demands). Then the girls' aunt walks in and asks each girl *why* she wants the orange (interests). As it turns out, one wants to eat the orange, and the other wants the peel to use for a class project. By focusing on the interests, the sisters arrive at a solution that gives each girl what she wants.[73] *Demands* create yes-or-no obstacles to effective negotiation, whereas *interests* present problems that can be solved creatively.

3. *Generate many alternatives for mutual gain.* Both parties in an integrative negotiation come up with a variety of options for solving the problem and engage in give-and-take discussions about which alternatives can get each side what it wants.

4. *Insist that results be based on objective standards.* Each party in a negotiation has its own interests and would naturally like to maximize its outcomes. Successful negotiation requires focusing on objective criteria and maintaining standards of fairness rather than using subjective judgments about the best solution.

Always try first to find the win–win solution.

Work-Team Effectiveness

Teams are the building blocks of today's organizations, but teams do not always live up to their potential or to the dreams that managers have for them. In this section, we look at the positive outcomes of effective teams. By assessing teams in terms of productive output, personal satisfaction, and the capacity to adapt and learn, managers can better identify actions that will enhance work-team effectiveness.[74]

PRODUCTIVE OUTPUT

One aspect of effectiveness relates to whether the team's output (such as decisions, products, or services) meets the requirements of customers or clients in terms of quality, quantity, and timeliness. An IBM team made up of members in the United States, Germany, and the United Kingdom, for example, used collaboration software as a virtual meeting room to solve a client's technical problem resulting from Hurricane Katrina within the space of just a few days.[75] Whether online or in physical space, effective meetings are essential to effective teamwork. The Spotlight on Skills on page 494 gives some tips for running a great meeting.

Effective teams can unleash enormous energy and creativity from employees. **Social facilitation** refers to the tendency for the presence of others to enhance one's motivation and performance. Simply being in the presence of other people has an energizing effect.[76] This benefit of teams is often lost in virtual and global teams because people are working in isolation from their teammates. Good virtual team leaders build in communication mechanisms that keep people interacting.

SATISFACTION OF MEMBERS

Another important question is whether the team experience contributes to the well-being, personal satisfaction, and development of its members. Effective teams provide multiple opportunities for people to satisfy their individual needs and to develop both personally and professionally.[77] As described in Chapter 13, employees have needs for belongingness and affiliation, and working in teams can help meet these needs. Participative teams can also reduce boredom, increase individuals' feeling of dignity and self-worth, and contribute to skill development because the whole person is employed. For example, at Radius, a Boston restaurant,

social facilitation
The tendency for the presence of others to influence an individual's motivation and performance.

SPOTLIGHT ON SKILLS

How to Run a Great Meeting

A recent survey in the United States and Britain found that people spend an average of 5.6 hours a week in meetings, yet 69 percent of respondents considered most of that time wasted. Meetings can be excellent avenues to solving problems, sharing information, and achieving shared goals, but good meetings don't just happen. Here are some tips on how to make meetings worthwhile and productive:

Prepare in Advance

Advance preparation is the single most important tool for running an efficient, productive meeting.

- *Define the purpose.* Is the meeting's purpose to share information, draw on participants' expertise and skills, elicit their commitment to a project, or coordinate the efforts required to accomplish a specific task? The leader needs to be clear about what the purpose is. If a meeting isn't essential, don't have it.
- *Invite the right people.* Meetings fail when too many, too few, or the wrong people are involved. Don't let the meeting get too big, but make sure everyone with a contribution to make or a stake in the topic is represented.
- *Prepare an agenda and identify the expected outcome.* Distributing a simple list of the topics to be discussed lets people know what to expect. If the meeting is for exploration only, say so. A lack of decision making can be frustrating if participants expect action to be taken.

Bring Out the Best During the Meeting

During the meeting, certain techniques will bring out the best in people and ensure a productive session:

- *Start on time, state the purpose, and review the agenda.* Starting on time has symbolic value because it tells people

that the topic is important and that the leader values their time. Begin by stating the meeting's explicit purpose and clarifying what should be accomplished by its conclusion.

- *Establish ground rules.* Outlawing cell phones, PDAs, and laptops can make sure people aren't distracted. Other rules concern how people should interact such as emphasizing equal participation and respectful listening.
- *Create involvement.* Good leaders draw out the silent and control the talkative so that the meeting isn't dominated by one or two assertive people. In addition, they encourage a free flow of ideas, provoke discussion with open-ended questions, and make sure everyone feels heard.
- *Keep it moving.* Allowing participants to waste time by getting into discussions of issues not on the agenda is a primary reason people hate meetings. Move the meeting along as needed to meet time constraints.

Attend to the End as Much as the Beginning

Review and follow-up are important to summarize and implement agreed-upon points.

- *End with a call to action.* Summarize the discussion, review any decisions made, and make sure everyone understands his or her assignments.
- *Follow up swiftly.* Send a short memo to summarize the meeting's key accomplishments, outline agreed-upon activities, and suggest schedules for implementation.

SOURCES: Based on Suzanne Bates, "Learning to Lead: Five Steps to Pain Free, Productive Meetings," *Supervision* (Aug. 2006): 18–19; Beth Bratkovic, "Running an Effective Meeting," *Government Finance Review* (Apr. 2007): 58–60; Phred Dvorak, "Corporate Meetings Go Through a Makeover," *Wall Street Journal*, Mar. 6, 2006; Antoney Jay, "How to Run a Meeting," *Harvard Business Review* (Mar.–Apr. 1976): 120–134; and Richard Axelrod, Emily M. Axelrod, Julie Beedon, and Robert Jacobs, "Creating Dynamic, Energy-Producing Meetings," *Leader to Leader* (Spring 2005): 53–58.

As a manager, use participative teams whenever it is practical to increase productivity and reduce boredom.

two-person kitchen teams have full responsibility for their part of a meal, which gives them a greater sense of accomplishment and importance and enables them to expand their culinary and organizational skills.[78] People who have a satisfying team environment cope better with stress, enjoy their jobs, and have a higher level of organizational commitment.

CAPACITY TO ADAPT AND LEARN

A professor of management at Santa Clara University analyzed 14 years of National Basketball Association results and found that teams who had members who had played together longer won more games. Members had learned to anticipate their teammates' moves and adapt their own behavior to defeat the competition.[79] The same thing happens in effective work teams, where members can anticipate one another's actions and respond appropriately. A good example is the emergency room trauma team at Massachusetts General Hospital, which functions so smoothly that the team switches leaders seamlessly depending on the crisis at hand. With each new emergency, direction may come from a doctor, nurse, intern, or technician—whoever is particularly experienced with the problem.[80] Over time, effective teams learn from experience and use that learning to revitalize and regenerate themselves, smoothly adapting to shifting organizational and competitive demands.[81]

Summary

Several important concepts about teams were described in this chapter. Teams can be effective in providing the coordination and information sharing needed to accomplish interdependent tasks. However, teams present a dilemma for many people. Individuals have to give up their independence and sometimes make sacrifices for the good of the team. Other potential problems are free riders and dysfunctional teams.

Some teams are part of the formal structure, while others are designed to increase employee involvement and participation. Formal teams include vertical teams along the chain of command and horizontal teams such as cross-functional teams, committees, and special-purpose teams. Employee involvement via teams brings lower-level employees into decision processes to improve quality, efficiency, and job satisfaction. Companies typically start with problem-solving teams, which may evolve into self-directed teams that take on responsibility for manage-

ment activities. Innovative approaches to teamwork include virtual teams and global teams, which place new demands on team leaders.

Most teams go through systematic stages of development: forming, storming, norming, performing, and adjourning. Team characteristics that influence organizational effectiveness are size, diversity, cohesiveness, norms, and members' roles.

All teams experience some conflict because of scarce resources, ambiguous responsibilities, communication breakdown, or goal conflicts. Some conflict is beneficial, but too much can hurt the team and the organization. Techniques for managing and resolving conflicts include superordinate goals, mediation, and negotiation.

To identify ways to improve work-team effectiveness, managers can assess teams in terms of productive output, personal satisfaction, and the capacity to adapt and learn.

Discussion Questions

1. Volvo went to self-directed teams to assemble cars because of the need to attract and keep workers in Sweden, where pay raises are not a motivator (high taxes) and many other jobs are available. Are these factors good reasons for using a team approach? Discuss.

2. Discuss how the dilemmas of teamwork might be intensified in a virtual team. What dilemmas do you feel when you have to do class assignments as part of a team? Discuss.

3. Suppose you are the leader of a team that has just been created to develop a new registration process at your college or university. How can you use an understanding of the stages of team development to improve your team's effectiveness?

4. Imagine yourself as a potential member of a team responsible for designing a new package for a breakfast cereal. Do you think interpersonal skills would be equally important if the team is organized face to face versus a virtual team? Why or why not? Might different types of interpersonal skills be required for the two types of teams? Be specific.

5. If you were the leader of a special-purpose team developing a new computer game and conflicts arose related to power and status differences among team members, what would you do? How might you use the various conflict-resolution techniques described in the chapter?

6. Experts say that for teams to function well, members have to get to know one another in some depth. What specifically would you do to facilitate this in a one-location team? What about in a global virtual team?

7. When you are a member of a team, do you adopt a task specialist or a socioemotional role? Which role is more important for a team's effectiveness?

8. Some people argue that the presence of an outside threat correlates with a high degree of team cohesion. Would you agree or disagree? Explain your answer.

9. Do you believe that admitting ignorance is a good way for a team leader to earn respect? Would this cause some people to disrespect the leader and question his or her suitability for team leadership? Discuss.

10. In one company, 40 percent of workers and 20 percent of managers resigned during the first year after they had been reorganized into teams. What might account for this dramatic turnover? How might managers ensure a smooth transition to teams?

Self Learning

This and That: Best Team—Worst Team

Think of two teams of which you were a member—the best and the worst in terms of personal satisfaction and team performance. These teams could come from any area in your experience—for example, athletic team, student club, class team, work team, project team, church committee, or volunteer organization. List below the specific behaviors of the teams that made them the best and worst for you.

Best team behaviors: _____

_____

Worst team behaviors: _____

_____

In class: (1) Sit in a small group of three to five students. Each student tells the brief story of his or her best and worst team experiences. (2) After all stories are heard, one team member writes on a flipchart (or blackboard) two headings—"More of This" and "Less of That." Under "This," write team member suggestions for positive behaviors that make for effective teamwork. Under "That," write team member suggestions for negative behaviors that prevent effective teamwork. (3) After brainstorming items, each group condenses each list to five key behaviors the group considers most important. (4) After the lists are finalized, students can walk around the classroom and review all lists. (5) Discuss answers to the questions below either in your group or as a class.

1. What is the most important behavior for This and for That?

2. What factors influence the presence of This or That behaviors on a team?

3. What personal changes would you need to make as a team member to demonstrate more of This?

4. What personal changes would you need to make as a team member to demonstrate less of That?

5. How might a team leader be able to attain more of This on a team and less of That?

SOURCE: Based on James W. Kinneer, "This and That: Improving Team Performance," in *The 1997 Annual: Volume 2, Consulting* (San Francisco: Pfeiffer, 1997): 55–58.

Group Learning

Grandma's Bakery Case Study

A graduate class in management consulting has received permission to study Grandma's Bakery. The employees of the bakery identify with the company, and things always seem to work well. Most of the staff members have been with the company for more than 10 years. The owner is very supportive of his employees. He has an equalitarian attitude and respects the workers as individuals. He continually refers to his staff as "my family." From the employee's perspective, Grandma's Bakery is an ideal small business.

The class assignment is to observe the bakery operation and suggest any noted recommendations for improvement. In one area, the class notes that the task of bagging assorted cookies seems inefficient. The job involves eight staff members. Each member stands in front of cartons filled with assorted cookies. A bag is held in the left hand. The right hand has to make an extended reach to pick up the cookies and place them in the bag. The staff works at a relaxed, informal pace. The tasks do not align with principles of motion economy. For example, the staff members do not use both hands simultaneously, and each hand works in opposite directions. In addition, they do not have materials prepositioned for ease of reach.

When the graduate students suggest highly structured changes to accommodate efficiency, the owner graciously rejects their recommendations. The students are confused by his reaction.

1. Form groups and answer the following questions:

   Why did the owner reject the recommendations?

   What elements regarding team motivation were overlooked in the study?

   What steps would you take as a group if you were studying Grandma's Bakery?

2. With the whole class, discuss the answers of each group. What did you learn about team effectiveness?

Action Learning

Teams on TV

1. Form into groups of three to five members. As a group, choose a TV show in which teams are central to the plot. Examples include *The Office*, *Law & Order* (any version), *CSI*, *Boston Legal*, and *Friends*, among others. Make sure the instructor agrees with your choice of TV show.

2. Watch several shows (make sure group members watch the same shows) and study team behavior. Use the information under "Member Roles" (page 483) and "Stages of Team Development" (page 484). Take notes on which characters perform which roles and which stages of development the group is in during a particular show.

3. As a group, come to an agreement on which roles and stages were present in those shows.

4. Your instructor will tell you whether to prepare either a group presentation or group paper on your findings.

5. What did you learn about teams from this assignment? Were there any surprises?

Ethical Dilemma

One for All and All for One?

Melinda Asbel watched as three of her classmates filed out of the conference room. Then she turned back to the large wooden table and faced her fellow members (a student and three faculty members) of the university's judiciary committee.

The three students—Joe Eastridge, Brad Hamil, and Lisa Baghetti—had just concluded their appeal against a plagiarism conviction stemming from a group project for an international marketing course. Melinda, who happened to be in the class with the students on trial, remembered the day the professor, Hank Zierden, had asked Joe, Brad, and Lisa, along with the group's leader, Paul Colgan, to stay after class. She happened to walk by the classroom a half hour later to see four glum students emerge. Even though Paul had a chagrined expression on his face, Joe was the one who looked completely shattered. It didn't take long for word to spread along the ever-active grapevine that Paul had admitted to plagiarizing his part of the group paper.

At the hearing, the students recounted how they'd quickly and unanimously settled on Paul to lead the group. He was by far the most able student among them, someone who managed to maintain a stellar GPA even while taking a full course load and holding down a part-time job. After the group worked together for weeks analyzing the problem and devising a marketing plan, Paul assigned a section of the final paper to each member. With the pressure of all those end-of-the-semester deadlines bearing down on them, everyone was delighted when Paul volunteered to write the company and industry background, the section that typically took the most time to produce. Paul gathered in everyone's contributions, assembled them into a paper, and handed out the final draft to the other members. They each gave it a quick read. They liked what they saw and thought they had a good chance for an A.

Unfortunately, as Paul readily admitted when Professor Zierden confronted them, he had pulled the section he'd contributed directly off the Internet. Pointing out the written policy he had distributed at the beginning of the semester stating that each group member was equally responsible for the final product, the professor gave all four students a zero for the project. The group project and presentation counted for 30 percent of the course grade.

Joe, Brad, and Lisa maintained they were completely unaware that Paul had cheated. "It just never occurred to us Paul would ever need to cheat," Brad said. They were innocent bystanders, the students argued. Why should they be penalized? Besides, the consequences weren't going to fall on each of them equally. Although Paul was suffering the embarrassment of public exposure, the failing group project grade would only put a dent in his solid GPA. Joe, on the other hand, was already on academic probation.

A zero probably meant he wouldn't make the 2.5 GPA he needed to stay in the business program.

At least one of the faculty members of the judiciary committee supported Professor Zierden's actions. "We're assigning more and more group projects because increasingly that's the way these students are going to find themselves working when they get real jobs in the real world," he said. "And the fact of the matter is that if someone obtains information illegally while on the job, it's going to put the whole corporation at risk for being sued or worse."

Even though she could see merit to both sides, Melinda was going to have to choose. If you were Melinda, how would you vote?

What Would You Do?

1. Vote to exonerate the three group project members who didn't cheat. You're convinced they had no reason to suspect Paul Colgan of dishonesty. Exonerating them is the right thing to do.

2. Vote in support of Hank Zierden's decision to hold each individual member accountable for the entire project. The professor clearly stated his policy at the beginning of the semester, and the students should have been more vigilant. The committee should not undercut a professor's explicit policy.

3. Vote to reduce each of the three students' penalties. Instead of a zero, each student will receive only half of the possible total points for the project, which would be an F. You're still holding students responsible for the group project, but you are not imposing catastrophic punishment. This compromise both undercuts the professor's policy and punishes "innocent" team members to some extent, but not as severely.

SOURCE: Based on Ellen R. Stapleton, "College to Expand Policy on Plagiarism," *The Ithacan Online* (Apr. 12, 2001) (www.ithaca.edu/ithacan/articles/0104/12/news/0college_to_e.htm).

Chapter 1: Case for Critical Analysis

Elektra Products, Inc.

Barbara Russell, a manufacturing vice president, walked into the monthly companywide meeting with a light step and a hopefulness she hadn't felt in a long time. The company's new, dynamic CEO was going to announce a new era of employee involvement and empowerment at Elektra Products, an 80-year-old, publicly held company that had once been a leading manufacturer and retailer of electrical products and supplies. In recent years, the company had experienced a host of problems: market share was declining in the face of increased foreign and domestic competition, new product ideas were few and far between, departments such as manufacturing and sales barely spoke to one another, morale was at an all-time low, and many employees were actively seeking other jobs. Everyone needed a dose of hope.

Martin Griffin, who had been hired to revive the failing company, briskly opened the meeting with a challenge: "As we face increasing competition, we need new ideas, new energy, new spirit to make this company great. And the source for this change is you—each one of you." He then went on to explain that under the new empowerment campaign, employees would be getting more information about how the company was run and would be able to work with their fellow employees in new and creative ways. Martin proclaimed a new era of trust and cooperation at Elektra Products. Barbara felt the excitement stirring within her; but as she looked around the room, she saw many of the other employees, including her friend Simon, rolling their eyes. "Just another pile of corporate crap," Simon said later. "One minute they try downsizing, the next reengineering. Then they dabble in restructuring. Now Martin wants to push empowerment. Garbage like empowerment isn't a substitute for hard work and a little faith in the people who have been with this company for years. We made it great once, and we can do it again. Just get out of our way." Simon had been a manufacturing engineer with Elektra Products for more than 20 years. Barbara knew he was extremely loyal to the company, but he and a lot of others like him were going to be obstacles to the empowerment efforts.

Top management assigned selected managers to several problem-solving teams to come up with ideas for implementing the empowerment campaign. Barbara loved her assignment as team leader of the manufacturing team, working on ideas to improve how retail stores got the merchandise they needed when they needed it. The team thrived, and trust blossomed among the members. They even spent nights and weekends working to complete their report. They were proud of their ideas, which they believed were innovative but easily achievable: permit a manager to follow a product from design through sales to customers, allow salespeople to refund up to $500 worth of merchandise on the spot, make information available to salespeople about future products, and swap sales and manufacturing personnel for short periods to let them get to know one another's jobs.

When the team presented its report to department heads, Martin Griffin was enthusiastic. But shortly into the meeting he had to excuse himself because of a late-breaking deal with a major hardware store chain. With Martin absent, the department heads rapidly formed a wall of resistance. The director of human resources complained that the ideas for personnel changes would destroy the carefully crafted job categories that had just been completed. The finance department argued that allowing salespeople to make $500 refunds would create a gold mine for unethical customers and salespeople. The legal department warned that providing information to salespeople about future products would invite industrial spying.

The team members were stunned. As Barbara mulled over the latest turn of events, she considered her options: keep her mouth shut, take a chance and confront Martin about her sincerity in making empowerment work, push slowly for reform and work for gradual support from the other teams, or look for another job and leave a company she really cares about. Barbara realized she was looking at no easy choices and no easy answers.

Questions

1. How might top management have done a better job changing Elektra Products into a new kind of organization? What might it do now to get the empowerment process back on track?

2. Can you think of ways Barbara could have avoided the problems her team faced in the meeting with department heads?

3. If you were Barbara Russell, what would you do now? Why?

SOURCE: Based on Lawrence R. Rothstein, "The Empowerment Effort That Came Undone," *Harvard Business Review* (Jan.–Feb. 1995): 20–31.

Chapter 2: Case for Critical Analysis

Rio Grande Supply Company

Jasper Hennings, president of Rio Grande Supply Company, knew full well that a company's top executives were largely responsible for determining a firm's corporate culture. That's why he took such personal pride in the culture of his Texas-based wholesale plumbing supply company. It didn't just pay lip service to the values it espoused: integrity, honesty, and a respect for each individual employee. His management team set a good example by living those principles. At least that's what he'd believed until the other day.

The importance Jasper attached to respecting each individual was apparent in the company's Internet use policy. It was abundantly clear that employees weren't to use Rio Grande's computers for anything but business-related activities. However, Jasper himself had vetoed the inclusion of what was becoming a standard provision in such policies that management had the right to access and review anything employees created, stored, sent, or received on company equipment. He cut short any talk of installing software filters that would prevent abuse of the corporate computer system. Still, the company reserved the right to take disciplinary action, including possible termination, and to press criminal charges if an employee was found to have violated the policy.

So how was Jasper to square his cherished assumptions about his management team with what he'd just discovered? Henry Darger, his hard-working chief of operations and a member of his church, had summarily fired a female employee for having accessed another worker's e-mail surreptitiously. She hadn't taken her dismissal well. "Just ask Darger what he's up to when he shuts his office door," she snarled as she stormed out of Jasper's office. She made what Jasper hoped was an idle threat to hire a lawyer.

When Jasper asked Henry what the fired employee could possibly have meant, tears began to roll down the operations chief's face. He admitted that ever since a young nephew had committed suicide the year before and a business he'd helped his wife start had failed, he'd increasingly been seeking escape from his troubles by logging onto adult pornography sites. At first, he'd indulged at home, but of late he'd found himself spending hours at work visiting pornographic sites, the more explicit the better. Jasper was stunned. After a few speechless minutes, he told Henry to take the rest of the day off, go home, and think things over.

The president himself needed the afternoon to gather his wits. How should he handle this turn of events? On the one hand, Henry's immediate dismissal of the woman who'd tapped into another employee's e-mail when the operations chief was violating the Internet policy himself was hypocritical, to say the least. The person charged with enforcing that policy needed to be held to the highest standards. On the other hand, Jasper knew that Rio Grande employees routinely used computers at their desks to check personal e-mail, do banking transactions, check the weather, or make vacation arrangements. The company had turned a blind eye because it didn't seem worth the effort of enforcing the hard-and-fast policy for such minor infractions. Besides, Henry was a valued, if clearly troubled, employee. Replacing him would be costly and difficult. If Jasper decided to keep him on, the president clearly had no choice but to cross the line and get involved in Henry's private life, and he would be treating Darger differently from the treatment the female employee received.

When he met with Henry again first thing in the morning, he needed to have a plan of action.

Questions

1. What environmental factors have helped to create the situation Jasper Hennings faces? What factors does Jasper need to consider when deciding on his course of action?

2. Analyze Rio Grande's culture. In addition to the expressed cultural values and beliefs, what other subconscious values and beliefs do you detect? Are conflicting values present? When values are in conflict, how would you decide which ones take precedence?

3. Assume you are Jasper. What are the first two action steps you would take to handle the Henry Darger situation? How would your role as a cultural leader influence your decision? What message will your solution send to the other managers and rank-and-file employees?

SOURCES: Based on Willard P. Green, "Pornography at Work," *Business Ethics* (Summer 2003): 19; Patrick Marley, "Porn-Viewing Parole Agent Regains Job," *Milwaukee Journal Sentinel* (Jan. 24, 2006) (www.jsonline.com/story/idex.aspx?id=387492); "Sample Internet Policies for Businesses and Organizations," *Websense* (www.websense-sales.com/internet-access-policy.html); and Art Lambert, "Technology in the Workplace: A Recipe for Legal Trouble," *Workforce* (Feb. 14, 2005) (www.workforce.com/archive/article/23/95/08.php).

Chapter 3: Case for Critical Analysis

Shui Fabrics

Ray Betzell, general manager for the past five years of a joint venture between Ohio-based Rocky River Industries and Shanghai Fabric Ltd., was feeling caught in the middle these days.

As he looked out over Shanghai's modern gleaming skyline from his corner office, Ray knew his Chinese deputy general manager, Chiu Wai, couldn't be more pleased with the way things were going. Ten years ago, Rocky River had launched Shui Fabrics, a 50–50 joint venture between the U.S. textile manufacturer and the Chinese company, to produce, dye, and coat fabric for sale to both Chinese and international sportswear manufacturers. After many obstacles, considerable red tape, and several money-losing years, the joint venture was fulfilling Chiu Wai's expectations—and those of the local government and party officials who were keeping careful tabs on the enterprise—much more quickly than he'd anticipated. By providing jobs to close to 3,000 people, Shui was making a real contribution to the local economy. Job creation was no small accomplishment in a country where outside experts estimated that the actual (as opposed to the official) unemployment rate routinely hovered around 20 percent.

From Chiu Wai's point of view, Shui was generating just the right level of profit—not too little and, just as importantly, not too much. With so many U.S.–Chinese joint ventures still operating in the red, Chiu Wai saw no reason why Ray's American bosses shouldn't be more than satisfied with their 5 percent annual return on investment. Those earnings also weren't going to land him in hot water with local authorities, many of whom still viewed profits made by Western companies on Chinese soil as just one more instance of exploitation in a long history of foreign attempts at domination.

If Chiu Wai had been eavesdropping on the conversation Ray had just had with Rocky River president Paul Danvers, however, the Chinese manager would have certainly been dismayed. Ray, who'd thoroughly enjoyed his time in China, was painfully aware of the quiet frustration in his boss's voice as it traveled over the phone lines from the other side of the world. To be sure, Paul conceded, Shui had cut Rocky River's labor costs, given the company access to the potentially huge Chinese market, and helped inoculate the firm against the uncertainty surrounding the periodic, often contentious U.S.–Chinese textile trade negotiations. Current U.S. tariffs and quotas could change at any time.

"But a 5 percent ROI [return on investment] is just pathetic," Paul complained. "And we've been stuck there for three years now. At this point, I'd expected to be looking at something more on the order of 20 percent." He pointed out that greater efficiency plus incorporating more sophisti-

cated technology would allow Shui to reduce its workforce substantially and put it on the road to a more acceptable ROI. "I'm well aware of the fact that the Chinese work for a fraction of what we'd have to pay American workers, and I do appreciate the pressure the government is putting on you guys. But still, it doesn't make any sense for us to hire more workers than we would in a comparable U.S. plant."

After an uncomfortable silence, during which Ray tried and failed to picture broaching the subject of possible layoffs to his Chinese counterparts, he heard Paul ask the question he'd been dreading: "I'm beginning to think it's time to pull the plug on Shui. Is there any way you can see to turn this around, Ray, or should we start thinking about other options? Staying in China is a given, but there has to be a better way to do it."

Questions

1. How would you characterize the main economic, legal–political, and sociocultural differences influencing the relationship between the partners in Shui Fabrics? What GLOBE Project dimensions would help you understand the differences in Chinese and American perspectives illustrated in the case?

2. How would you define Shui's core problem? Are sociocultural differences the main underlying cause of this problem? Why or why not? How would you handle the conflict with your boss back in the United States?

3. If you were Ray Betzell, what other options to the 50–50 joint venture would you consider for manufacturing textiles in China? Make the argument that one of these options is more likely to meet Rocky River's expectations than the partnership already in place.

SOURCES: Based on Katherine Xin and Vladimir Pucik, "Trouble in Paradise," *Harvard Business Review* (August 2003): 27–35; Lillian McClanaghan and Rosalie Tung, "Summary of 'Negotiating and Building Effective Working Relationships with People in China,'" presentation by Sidney Rittenberg, Pacific Region Forum on Business and Management Communication, Simon Fraser University, Harbour Centre, Vancouver, B.C., March 21, 1991 (http://www.cic.sfu.ca/forum/rittenbe.html); and Charles Wolfe Jr., "China's Rising Unemployment Challenge," *Asian Wall Street Journal*, July 7, 2004 (available at RAND Corporation Web page, http://www.rand.org/commentary/2004/07/07/AWSJ.html).

Chapter 4: Case for Critical Analysis

Empress Luxury Lines

From what computer technician Kevin Pfeiffer just told him, it looked to Antonio Melendez as if top management at Empress Luxury Lines finally found a way to fund the computer system upgrade he'd been requesting ever since he'd taken the job two years ago.

It all began innocently enough, Kevin said. When he reported to the luxury cruise line's corporate headquarters, his supervisor Phil Bailey informed him that the computer system had been hit by a power surge during the fierce

thunderstorms that rolled through southern Florida the night before. "Check out the damage and report directly back to me," Phil instructed.

When Kevin delivered what he thought would be good news—the damaged underground wires and computer circuits could be repaired to the tune of about $15,000—he couldn't understand why Phil looked so deflated. "Go out to the reception area. I've got to call Roger," Phil snapped, referring to Empress's CFO—and Antonio's boss. In a few minutes, Phil called Kevin back into the office and instructed him to dig up nearly all the underground wire and cable and then haul it all off before the insurance adjustor appeared. If Kevin carried out Phil's orders, he knew the costs would balloon astronomically to about a half-million dollars, a tidy sum that would go a long way toward covering the costs of a computer system upgrade, as Phil pointed out.

Kevin took a deep breath and refused, even though as a new hire he was still on probation. When Antonio congratulated Kevin on his integrity, the technician shook his head. "Didn't really matter," he said. "On my way back to my cubicle, Matt passed me on his way to do the deed."

Antonio could guess at the motivation behind the scam. During the 1990s, Empress increased its fleet of ships in response to the healthy demand for its luxury cruises during the stock market bubble. But the bubble burst, the nation was traumatized by September 11, and some of the vacationers who did venture onto cruises were felled by an outbreak of the Norwalk virus. Bookings fell off precipitously. To top it all off, the 2005 hurricanes hit, forcing Empress to write piles of refund checks for its Caribbean and Gulf of Mexico cruises while coping with steep increases in fuel costs. Seriously sagging earnings explained why Antonio's requests for that system upgrade went unheeded.

He could also guess at the likely consequences if he chose to do the right thing. Since taking the job, he'd heard rumors that Empress successfully defrauded insurance companies before he arrived.

He dismissed them at the time, but now he wasn't so sure. No confidential mechanism was in place for employees to report wrongdoing internally, and no protections were available for whistle-blowers. Shaken, Antonio wasn't feeling at all confident that, even if he bypassed the CFO, he would find upper-level management all that eager to thwart the scheme. He had a hunch that the person most likely to be penalized was the whistle-blower.

"I debated about just calling the insurance company," Kevin said, "but I decided to come to you first." So what should Antonio do? Should he advise Kevin to go ahead and report Empress to the insurance company? Or should he treat Kevin's communication as confidential and deal with the situation himself, in effect putting only his own job in jeopardy? And considering the high degree of personal risk and the low probability that the problem would actually be addressed, shouldn't he just sweep the problem under the rug?

Questions

1. When determining what his obligations are to his subordinate, Kevin Pfeiffer, what decision would Antonio Melendez most likely reach if he applied the utilitarian approach to decision making? What conclusions would probably result if he employed the individualism approach?

2. Put yourself in Antonio's position and decide realistically what you would do. Is your response at a preconventional, conventional, or postconventional level of moral development? How do you feel about your response?

3. If Antonio or Kevin were fired because they reported Empress's fraud, would they be justified in removing all traces of their employment at the cruise line from their resumes so they don't have to explain to a prospective employer why they were fired? Why or why not?

SOURCES: Based on Don Soeken, "On Witnessing a Fraud," *Business Ethics* (Summer 2004): 14; Amy Tao, "Have Cruise Lines Weathered the Storm?" *BusinessWeek Online* (Sept. 11, 2003) (www.businessweek.com/bwdaily/dnflash/sep2003/nf20030911_6693_db014.htm); and Joan Dubinsky, "A Word to the Whistle-Blower," *Workforce* (July 2002): 28.

Chapter 5: Case for Critical Analysis

Nielsen Media Research

David Calhoun left a job he loved as a star executive at General Electric to step into a mess as CEO of the ACNielsen Corporation. His immediate challenge: The media research unit, which is under heavy fire from television clients such as NBC and CBS for chronic delays in reporting television ratings. Nielsen held a conference call with major clients acknowledging the delays and promising to do better, but the following Monday, the company again failed to report any ratings at all for the previous day. Nielson was not delivering data to customers as promised.

What's the big deal? Calhoun and chief of research Susan Whiting know that about $70 billion a year in advertising revenues for the television industry depends on Nielsen ratings. Viewers might think TV networks are in the business of providing entertainment, but management's primary goal is providing eyeballs for advertisers. When television managers and advertisers don't get timely, accurate data from Nielsen, they're shooting in the dark with decisions about how to allocate resources. Daily meetings at some companies are scheduled based on getting the information from Nielsen when promised. "There is so much revenue involved over which we have no quality control," said Alan Wurtzel, president of research for NBC. "We don't just use this data for analytical purposes. This is the currency of the business."

Calhoun and other top managers are analyzing what went wrong at Nielsen. Established in 1923 to perform surveys of the production of industrial equipment, Nielsen became a household name when it launched its television ratings system in 1950. More than 60 years later, Nielsen still functions as a near monopoly in the ratings business. Yet the company could be facing a serious threat from cable and satellite companies that are working on a way to get set-top boxes to provide real-time TV viewing data to rival Nielsen's.

Managers see several factors involved in the problems at Nielsen, but the biggest one is that the amount of data the company processes doubled in a year, overloading computer servers and straining the company's human systems. The increase has come both because of changes in how people are watching television, such as over the Internet and other digital devices, and in the amount of information networks want. As the television business gets cut into thinner slices, clients need even more precise data to make good decisions. Nielsen is pursuing a strategy it calls "Anytime, Anywhere Media Measurement" to stay relevant and address new competition, but it has to get its quality problems fixed fast.

Clients understand the strain, but they have little sympathy. They want to know why Nielsen managers didn't anticipate the spike in data demands and plan accordingly.

Questions

1. Where do you think the problems lie at Nielsen? For example, are they primarily with the company's strategic goals and plans, tactical goals and plans, or operational goals and plans? With alignment of goals and plans?

2. Do you think developing a strategy map would be a good idea for Nielsen? Why or why not?

3. If you were David Calhoun, what kind of planning processes might you implement right now to fix this problem?

SOURCE: Based on Bill Carter, "Nielsen Tells TV Clients It Is Working on Ending Delays in Ratings," *New York Times*, Feb. 9, 2008, p. C3; Richard Siklos, "Made to Measure," *Fortune* (Mar. 3, 2008): 68–74; and Louise Story, "Nielsen Tests Limits of Wider Tracking," *International Herald Tribune*, Feb. 28, 2008, p. 13.

Chapter 6: Case for Critical Analysis

Pinnacle Machine Tool Company

Don Anglos had to decide whether to trust his gut or his head, and he had to make that decision by next week's board meeting. Either way, he knew he was bound to make at least a member or two of his senior management team unhappy.

The question at hand was whether Pinnacle Company, the small, publicly held Indiana-based machine tool company he led as CEO, should attempt to acquire Hoilman Inc. Hoilman was a company known for the cutting-edge sensor technology and communications software it had developed to monitor robotics equipment. Anglos had just heard a credible rumor that one of Pinnacle's chief competitors was planning a hostile takeover of the company. Coincidentally, Don Anglos knew Hoilman well because he had recently held exploratory talks about the possibility of a joint venture designed to develop similar technology capable of monitoring a broad range of manufacturing equipment. The joint venture did not work out. But now, by acquiring Hoilman, Pinnacle could develop software that transmitted real-time information on its customers' equipment, enabling it to set itself apart by providing top-notch service far more sophisticated than its current standard maintenance and service contracts.

Don, a hard-charging 48-year-old, firmly believed that bigger was better. It was a premise that had served his Greek immigrant father well as he built a multimillion-dollar business from nothing by acquiring one commercial laundry after another. The CEO had to admit, however, that getting bigger in the machine tool industry, currently a slow-growing sector that faced increasing competition from low-priced foreign manufacturers, was going to be a challenge. Still, he had been convinced to sign on as Pinnacle's CEO four years ago not only because the company had

relatively healthy earnings but also because his sixth sense told him the company had growth potential. He hadn't been entirely sure where that potential lay, but he was a problem solver with a proven track record of successfully spotting new market opportunities. In the past, he acted on hunches, which had paid off handsomely.

So far, Anglos had managed to modestly nudge Pinnacle's revenue growth and increase its market share through aggressive pricing that successfully kept customers from switching to several potential foreign rivals. But those moves inevitably chipped away at the company's healthy profit margins. In any case, he recognized he'd taken the company down that road as far as he could. It was time for a real change in strategy. Instead of concentrating on manufacturing, he wanted to transform Pinnacle into a high-tech service company. Such a drastic metamorphosis was going to require a new, service-oriented corporate culture, he admitted, but it was the only way he could see achieving the growth and profitability he envisioned. Acquiring Hoilman looked like a good place to start, but this option would be gone if Hoilman sold out to another firm.

Jennifer Banks, services division head, was enthusiastic about both the acquisition and the new strategy. "Acquiring Hoilman is the chance of a lifetime," she crowed. Not all the senior managers agreed. In particular, Sam Lodge, the chief financial officer (CFO), advanced arguments against the acquisition that were hard to dismiss. The timing was wrong, he insisted. Pinnacle's recent drop in profitability hadn't escaped Wall Street's attention, and the further negative impact on earnings that would result from the Hoilman acquisition wasn't likely to make already wary investors feel any better. But then Sam shocked Don by offering an even more fundamental critique. "Getting into the service business is a mistake, Don. It's what everybody's doing right now. Just look at the number of our competitors who've already taken steps to break into the services market. What makes you think we'll come out on top? And when I look at our customers, I just don't see any evidence that even if they wanted to, they could afford to buy any add-on services any time soon."

With such a big decision, Don's head had to agree with Lodge's position that was based on his usual CFO thoroughness with number crunching, but his gut wasn't so sure. Sometimes, he thought, you just have to go with your instincts. And his instincts were champing at the bit to go after Hoilman.

Questions

1. What steps in the decision-making process have Don Anglos and Pinnacle taken? Which ones have they not completed?

2. Which decision-making style best describes Don's approach: directive, analytical, conceptual, or behavioral? Which style best describes Sam Lodge's approach?

3. Would you recommend that Pinnacle attempt to acquire Hoilman? If so, why? If not, what alternatives would you suggest?

SOURCE: Based on Paul Hemp, "Growing for Broke," *Harvard Business Review* (Sept. 2002): 27–37.

Chapter 7: Case for Critical Analysis

FMB&T

Marshall Pinkard, president and CEO of FMB&T, a growing California-based regional commercial and consumer retail bank, clicked on an e-mail from Ayishia Coles. Ayishia was the bright, hardworking, self-confident woman who'd recently come on board as the bank's executive vice president and chief information officer. The fact that the person in Coles's position in the company's traditional vertical organization now reported directly to him and was a full-fledged member of the executive committee reflected FMB&T's recognition of just how important information technology was to all aspects of its increasingly competitive business. The successful, leading-edge banks were the ones using information technology not only to operate efficiently but also to help them focus more effectively on customer needs. Marshall settled back to read what he expected would be a report on how she was settling in. He was sadly mistaken.

After a few months on the job, Ayishia Coles was frustrated. What she needed from him, she wrote, was a clear statement of her responsibilities and authority. The way Ayishia saw it, the relationship between information technology and the bank's other business units was muddled, often causing considerable confusion, friction, and inefficiency. Typically, someone from retail banking or marketing, for example, came to her department with a poorly defined problem, such as how to link up checking account records with investment records, and they always expected a solution the same day. What made the situation even more vexing was that more often than not, the problem crossed organizational lines. She found that the more work units the problem affected generally, the less likely it was that any single unit took responsibility for defining exactly what it wanted IT to do. Who exactly was supposed to be getting all these units together and coordinating requests? When she tried to step into the breach and act as a facilitator, unit managers usually didn't welcome her efforts.

Despite the vagueness of their requests, the work units still expected IT to come up with a solution—and come up with it quickly. All these expectations seemed almost calculated to drive the methodical IT folks mad. Before taking on a problem, they wanted to make sure they thoroughly understood all of its dimensions so that the solution would fit seamlessly into the existing systems. This coordination took time that other parts of the bank weren't willing to give IT.

In addition, Ayishia knew the IT staff was increasingly feeling underused. The staff wanted to identify opportunities for dazzling new IT developments to contribute to business strategies, but it found itself limited to applications work. Ayishia's greatest concern was the president of a large regional branch who was actively campaigning to locate decentralized IT departments in each large branch under branch authority so that work would be completed faster to meet branch needs. He said it would be better to let work units coordinate their own IT departments rather than run everything through corporate IT. Under that scenario, Ayishia Coles's department could end up half its current size.

Marshall leaned back in his high-backed executive chair and sighed. At the very least, he needed to clarify Ayishia's authority and responsibilities as she had asked him to do. But he recognized that the new vice president was talking about a much larger can of worms. Was it time to rethink the bank's entire organizational structure?

Questions

1. What are the main organizational causes of the frustration that Ayishia Coles feels?

2. If you were Marshall Pinkard, how would you address both Ayishia's request for clarification about her authority and responsibilities and the underlying problems her e-mail brings to his attention? Can the problems be addressed with minor adjustments, or would

you need to consider a drastic overhaul of the bank's organizational structure? What environmental and technological factors would influence your decision?

3. Sketch a general chart for the type of organization that you think would work best for IT at FMB&T.

SOURCES: Based on Perry Glasser, "In CIOs We Trust," *CIO Enterprise* (June 15, 1999): 34–44; Stephanie Overby, "What Really Matters: Staying in the Game," *CIO Magazine* (October 1, 2004) (www.cio.com/archive/100104/role.html); and Alenka Grealish, "Banking Trends in 2005 That Will Make A Difference," *Bank Systems & Technology* (December 14, 2004) (www.banktech.com/news/showarticle.html?articleid=55301770).

Chapter 8: Case for Critical Analysis

Southern Discomfort

Jim Malesckowski remembers the call of two weeks ago as if he just put down the telephone receiver. "I just read your analysis, and I want you to get down to Mexico right away," Jack Ripon, his boss and chief executive officer, had blurted in his ear. "You know we can't make the plant in Oconomo work anymore—the costs are just too high. So go down there, check out what our operational costs would be if we move, and report back to me in a week."

At that moment, Jim felt as if a shiv had been stuck in his side, just below the rib cage. As president of the Wisconsin Specialty Products Division of Lamprey, Inc., he knew quite well the challenge of dealing with high-cost labor in a third-generation, unionized U.S. manufacturing plant. And although he had done the analysis that led to his boss's knee-jerk response, the call still stunned him. There were 520 people who made a living at Lamprey's Oconomo facility, and if it closed, most of them wouldn't have a journeyman's prayer of finding another job in the town of 9,000 people.

Instead of the $16-per-hour average wage paid at the Oconomo plant, the wages paid to the Mexican workers—who lived in a town without sanitation and with an unbelievably toxic effluent from industrial pollution—would amount to about $1.60 an hour on average. That's a savings of nearly $15 million a year for Lamprey that would be offset in part by increased costs for training, transportation, and other matters.

After two days of talking with Mexican government representatives and managers of other companies in the town, Jim had enough information to develop a set of comparative figures of production and shipping costs. On the way home, he started to outline the report, knowing full well that unless some miracle occurred, he would be ushering in a blizzard of pink slips for people he had come to appreciate.

The plant in Oconomo had been in operation since 1921, making special apparel for persons suffering injuries and other medical conditions. Jim had often talked with employees who would recount stories about their fathers or grandfathers working in the same Lamprey company plant—the last of the original manufacturing operations in town.

But friendship aside, competitors had already edged past Lamprey in terms of price and were dangerously close to overtaking it in product quality. Although both Jim and the plant manager had tried to convince the union to accept lower wages, union leaders resisted. In fact, on one occasion when Jim and the plant manager tried to discuss a cell manufacturing approach, which would cross-train employees to perform as many as three different jobs, local union leaders could barely restrain their anger. Yet probing beyond the fray, Jim sensed the fear that lurked under the union reps' gruff exteriors. He sensed their vulnerability but could not break through the reactionary bark that protected it.

A week has passed and Jim just submitted his report to his boss. Although he didn't specifically bring up the point, it was apparent that Lamprey could put its investment dollars in a bank and receive a better return than what its Oconomo operation is currently producing.

Tomorrow, he'll discuss the report with the CEO. Jim doesn't want to be responsible for the plant's dismantling, an act he personally believes would be wrong as long as there's a chance its costs can be lowered. "But Ripon's right," he said to himself. "The costs are too high, the union's unwilling to cooperate, and the company needs to make a better return on its investment if it's to continue at all. It sounds right but feels wrong. What should I do?"

Questions

1. What forces for change are evident at the Oconomo plant?

2. What is the primary type of change needed— changing "things" or changing the "people and culture?" Can the Wisconsin plant be saved by changing things alone, by changing people and culture, or must both be changed? Explain your answer.

3. What do you think is the major underlying cause of the union leaders' resistance to change? If you were Jim Malesckowski, what implementation tactics would you use to try to convince union members to change to save the Wisconsin plant?

SOURCE: Doug Wallace, "What Would You Do?" *Business Ethics* (Mar.–Apr. 1996): 52–53. Copyright 1996 by New Mountain Media LLC. Reproduced with permission of New Mountain Media LLC.

Chapter 9: Case for Critical Analysis

Draper Manufacturing

"You see what I'm up against?" asked Ralph Draper wearily as he escorted Ted Hanrahan, a diversity consultant, into his modest office on a rainy October day. Ralph was the new CEO of Draper Manufacturing, a small mattress manufacturer. He'd recently moved back to Portland, Oregon, his hometown, to take over the reins of the family-owned company from his ailing father. Ralph and Ted had just come from a contentious meeting of Draper's top managers that vividly illustrated the festering racial tensions Ralph wanted Ted to help alleviate.

It hadn't taken long for sales manager Brent Myers to confront shipping and receiving department head Adam Fox, an African American and the only nonwhite manager. "Why can't your boys get orders shipped out on time?" Brent demanded. "Isn't there some way you can get them to pay a little less attention to their bling and a little more to their responsibilities?" Adam Fox shot back angrily, "If you tightwads actually hired enough people to get the job done, there wouldn't be any problem." The other managers sat by silently, looking acutely uncomfortable, until the quality control head worked in a joke about his wife. Most laughed loudly, and Ralph took the opportunity to steer the conversation to other agenda topics.

The main challenge Draper faces is the price of oil, which had passed $100 per barrel mark that summer. In addition to powering the Draper operations and shipping, petroleum is an essential raw material for many mattress components from polyester and thread to foam. In addition, the Gulf hurricanes caused severe shortages of TDI, the chemical used to make polyurethane foam, a key component. So far, the company had passed its cost increases on to the consumer, but with increased competition from low-priced Asian imports, no one knew how long that strategy would work. To survive in mattress manufacturing, Draper needs to find ways to lower costs and increase productivity. Ralph completely understands why Brent is pressuring Adam to ship orders out more quickly.

The current workforce reflects Draper's determination to keep labor costs low. It employs 90 people full-time, the majority of whom are Asian and Hispanic immigrants and African Americans. Although women make up 75 percent of the workforce, nearly all of the shipping department employees are young African American men. Instead of adding to its permanent workforce, the company hires part-time workers from time to time, mostly Hispanic females. It tends to engage Asians as mechanics and machine operators because human-resources head Teresa Burns believes they have superior technical skills. The result is a diverse but polarized workforce. "This is a time everyone needs to pull together," said Ralph. "But what's happening is that each minority group sticks to itself. The African Americans and Asians rarely mix, and most of the Mexicans stay to themselves and speak only in Spanish."

When two of the older white shipping employees retired last year, Ralph didn't replace them, hoping to improve efficiency by cutting salary costs. "It seems to me that some of our workers are just downright lazy sometimes," said Ralph. "I myself have talked to Adam about pushing his kids to develop a work ethic. But he insists on blaming the company for the department's problems. You can see why we want your help."

Questions

1. How would a cultural audit help Draper Manufacturing assess its diversity issues? What questions do you suggest be included in the cultural audit?

2. If you were the shipping and receiving or human-resources manager, how do you think you would feel about working at Draper? What are some of the challenges you might face at this company?

3. If you were Ted Hanrahan, what suggestions would you make to Draper's managers to help them move toward successfully managing diversity issues?

Source: Based on "Northern Industries," a case prepared by Rae Andre of Northeastern University; "Interesting Times Indeed. Let's Review, Shall We?" *BedTimes* (Dec. 2005) (www.sleepproducts. org/Content/ContentGroups/BEDtimes1/20052/December6/Interesting_ times_indeed.htm); and Jacqueline A. Gilbert, Norma Carr-Rufino, John M. Ivancevich, and Millicent Lownes-Jackson, "An Empirical Examination of Inter-Ethnic Stereotypes: Comparing Asian American and African American Employees," *Public Personnel Management* (Summer 2003): 251–266.

Chapter 10: Case for Critical Analysis

Lincoln Electric

Imagine having a management system that is so successful people refer to it with capital letters—the Lincoln Management System—and other businesses benchmark their own systems by it. That is the situation of Ohio-based Lincoln Electric. For a number of years, other companies have tried to figure out Lincoln Electric's secret: how management coaxes maximum productivity and quality from its workers, even during difficult financial times. Lately, however, Lincoln Electric has been trying to solve a mystery of its own: Why is the company having such difficulty exporting a management system abroad that has worked so well at home?

Lincoln Electric is a leading manufacturer of welding products, welding equipment, and electric motors, with more than $1 billion in sales and 6,000 workers worldwide. The company's products are used for cutting, manufacturing, and repairing other metal products. Although it is now a publicly traded company, members of the Lincoln family still own more than 60 percent of the stock.

Lincoln uses a diverse control approach. Tasks are precisely defined, and individual employees must exceed strict performance goals to achieve top pay. The incentive and control system is powerful. Production workers are paid on a piece-rate basis, plus merit pay based on performance. Employees also are eligible for annual bonuses, which fluctuate according to the company's profits, and they participate in stock purchase plans. A worker's bonus is based on four factors: work productivity, work quality, dependability, and cooperation with others. Some factory workers at Lincoln have earned more than $100,000 a year.

However, the Lincoln system succeeds largely because of an organizational culture based on openness and trust, shared control, and an egalitarian spirit. To begin with, the company has earned employee trust with its no layoff policy. In fact, the last time it laid off anyone was in 1951. Although the line between managers and workers at Lincoln is firmly drawn, managers respect the expertise of production workers and value their contributions to many aspects of the business. The company has an open-door policy for all top executives, middle managers, and production workers, and regular face-to-face communication is encouraged. Workers are expected to challenge management if they believe practices or compensation rates are unfair. Most workers are hired right out of high school and then trained and cross-trained to perform different jobs. Some eventually are promoted to executive positions because Lincoln believes in promoting from within. Many Lincoln workers stay with the company for life.

One of Lincoln's founders felt that organizations should be based on certain values, including honesty, trustworthiness, openness, self-management, loyalty, accountability, and cooperativeness. These values continue to form the core of Lincoln's culture, and management regularly rewards employees who manifest them. Because Lincoln so effectively socializes employees, they exercise a great degree of self-control on the job. Each supervisor oversees 100 workers, and less-tangible rewards complement the piece-rate incentive system. Pride of workmanship and feelings of involvement, contribution, and esprit de corps are intrinsic rewards that flourish at Lincoln Electric. Cross-functional teams are empowered to make decisions, and they take responsibility for product planning, development, and marketing. Information about the company's operations and financial performance is openly shared with workers throughout the company.

Lincoln emphasizes anticipating and solving customer problems. Sales representatives are given the technical training they need to understand customer needs, help customers understand and use Lincoln's products, and solve problems. This customer focus is backed by attention to the production process through the use of strict accountability standards and formal measurements for productivity, quality, and innovation for all employees. In addition, a software program called Rhythm helps streamline the flow of goods and materials in the production process.

Lincoln's system worked so well in the United States that senior executives decided to extend it overseas. Lincoln built or purchased 11 plants in Japan, South America, and Europe, with plans to run the plants from the United States using Lincoln's expertise with management-control systems. Managers saw the opportunity to beat local competition by applying manufacturing control incentive systems to reduce costs and raise production in plants around the world. The results were abysmal and nearly sunk the company. Managers at international plants failed to meet their production and financial goals every year—they exaggerated the goals sent to Lincoln's managers to receive more resources, especially during the recession in Europe and South America. Many overseas managers had no innate desire to increase sales, and workers were found sleeping on benches because not enough work was available. The European labor culture was hostile to the piece-work and bonus-control system. The huge losses in the international plants, which couldn't seem to adopt Lincoln's vaunted control systems, meant the company would have to borrow money to pay U.S. workers' bonuses or forgo bonuses for the first time in Lincoln's history. Top managers began to wonder: Had they simply done a poor job of applying the Lincoln Management System to other cultures, or was it possible that it simply wasn't going to work abroad?

Questions

1. Does Lincoln follow a hierarchical or decentralized approach to management? Explain your answer and give examples.

2. Based on what you've just read, what do you think makes the Lincoln System so successful in the United States?

3. What is the problem with transporting Lincoln's control systems to other national cultures? What suggestions would you make to Lincoln's managers to make future international manufacturing plants more successful?

4. Should Lincoln borrow money and pay bonuses to avoid breaking trust with its U.S. workers? Why or why not?

Sources: Based on Herb Greenberg, "Why Investors May Do Well with Firms That Avoid Layoffs," *Wall Street Journal*, Sept. 9, 2006; Mark Gottlieb, "Feeding the Dragon," *Industry Week* 251(1) (Feb. 2002): 54–55; Donald Hastings, "Lincoln Electric's Harsh Lessons from International Expansion," *Harvard Business Review* (May–June, 1999): 3–11; and Joseph Maciariello, "A Pattern of Success: Can This Company Be Duplicated?" *Drucker Management* 1(1) (Spring 1997): 7–11.

Chapter 11: Case for Critical Analysis

Reflex Systems

As the plane took off from the L.A. airport for Chicago and home, Henry Rankin tried to unwind, something that didn't come naturally to the Reflex Systems software engineer. He needed time to think, and the flight from Los Angeles was a welcome relief. He went to Los Angeles to help two members of his project team solve technical glitches in software. Rankin had been pushing himself and his team hard for three months now, and he didn't know when they would get a break. Rankin was responsible for the technical implementation of the new customer-relationship management (CRM) software being installed for western and eastern sales offices in Los Angeles and Chicago. The software was badly needed to improve follow-up sales for his company, Reflex Systems. Reflex sold exercise equipment to high schools and colleges through a national force of 310 salespeople. The company also sold products to small and medium-sized businesses for their recreation centers.

Rankin knew CEO Mike Frazer saw the new CRM software as the answer to one of the exercise equipment manufacturer's most persistent problems. Even though Reflex's low prices generated healthy sales, follow-up service was spotty. Consequently, getting repeat business from customers—high schools, colleges, and corporate recreation centers—was an uphill battle. Excited by the prospect of finally removing this major roadblock, Frazer ordered the CRM software installed in just 10 weeks, a goal Rankin privately thought was unrealistic. He also felt the project budget wasn't adequate. Rankin thought about meeting the next day with his three Chicago team members and about the status update he would give his boss, Nicole Dyer, the senior vice president for information technology. Rankin remembered that Dyer had scheduled 10 weeks for the CRM project. He had always been a top performer by driving himself hard and had been in his management position three years now. He was good with technology, but he was frustrated when members of his five-person team didn't seem as committed. Dyer told him last week that she didn't feel a sense of urgency from his team. How could she think that? Rankin requested that team members work evenings and weekends because the budget was too tight to fill a vacant position. They agreed to put in the hours, although they didn't seem enthusiastic.

Still, Frazer was the boss, so if he wanted the job done in 10 weeks, Rankin would do everything in his power to deliver, even if it meant the entire team worked nights and weekends. He wasn't asking any more of his subordinates than he was asking of himself, as he frequently reminded them when they came to him with bloodshot eyes and complained about the hours. Rankin thought back to a flight one month ago when he returned to Chicago from Los Angeles. Sally Phillips sat next to him. Phillips was on one of five members on Rankin's team and told him she had an offer from a well-known competitor. The money was less, but she was interested in the quality-of-life aspect of the company. Phillips asked for feedback on how she was doing and about her career prospects at Reflex. Rankin said he didn't want her to leave, but what more could he say? She got along well with people, but she wasn't as technically gifted as some on the team. Rankin needed her help to finish the project, and he told her so. Two weeks later, she turned in her letter of resignation, and now the team was shorthanded. Rankin was also aware that his own possible promotion in two years, when Nicole Dyer was eligible for retirement, depended on his success with this project. He would just take up the slack himself. He loved studying, analyzing, and solving technical problems when he could get time alone.

Henry Rankin knew that Nicole Dyer had noticed a lack of commitment on the part of the team members. He wondered whether she had discussed the team's performance with Frazer as well. Rankin hadn't noticed any other problems, but he recalled his partner on the project, Sam Matheny, saying that two Chicago team members, Bob Finley and Lynne Johnston, were avoiding each other. How did Sam know that? Matheny was in charge of nontechnical sales implementation of the CRM project, which meant training salespeople, redesigning sales procedures, updating customer records, and so forth. Rankin called Finley and Johnston to his office and said he expected them to get along for the good of the project. Finley said he had overreacted to Johnston from lack of sleep and wondered when the project would be over. Rankin wasn't certain because of all the problems with both software and hardware, but he said the project shouldn't last more than another month.

As the plane taxied to the gate, an exhausted Rankin couldn't quell his growing fears that as the deadline fast approached, the project team was crumbling. How could he meet that deadline? As the plane taxied to the gate at Chicago, Rankin wondered about the project's success. Was there more to managing this team than working hard and pushing others hard? Even he was tired. Maybe he would ask his wife when he got home. He hadn't seen her or the kids for a week, but they had not complained.

Questions

1. What personality and behavior characteristics does Henry Rankin exhibit? Do you think these traits contribute to a good person–job fit for him? If you were an executive coach hired to help Rankin be a better manager, what would you say to him? Why?

2. Does Rankin display Type A or Type B behavior? What are the causes of stress for his team?

3. If you were Rankin, how would you have handled your team members (Sally Phillips, Bob Finley, and Lynne Johnston)? Be specific. What insights or behaviors would make Rankin a better manager?

Chapter 12: Case for Critical Analysis

Mountain West Health Plans, Inc.

"Be careful what you wish for," thought Martin Quinn, senior vice president for service and operations for Mountain West Health Plans, Inc., a Denver-based health insurance company. When there was an opening for a new director of customer service last year due to Evelyn Gustafson's retirement, Quinn had seen it as the perfect opportunity to bring someone in to control the ever-increasing costs of the labor-intensive department. He'd been certain he had found just the person in Erik Rasmussen, a young man in his late 20s with a shiny new bachelor's degree in business administration.

A tall, unflappable woman, Evelyn Gustafson consistently showed warmth and concern toward her mostly female, nonunionized employees as they sat in their noisy cubicles, fielding call after call about Mountain West's products, benefits, eligibility, and claims. Because she had worked her way up from a customer-service representative position herself, she could look her subordinates right in the eye after they'd fielded a string of stressful calls and tell them she knew exactly how they felt. She did her best to offset the low pay by accommodating the women's needs with flexible scheduling, giving them frequent breaks, and offering plenty of training opportunities that kept them up-to-date in the health company's changing products and in the latest problem-solving and customer-service techniques.

Her motto was "Always put yourself in the subscriber's shoes." She urged representatives to take the time necessary to thoroughly understand the subscriber's problem and do their best to see that it was completely resolved by the call's completion. Their job was important, she told them. Subscribers counted on them to help them negotiate the often Byzantine complexities of their coverage. Evelyn's subordinates adored her, as demonstrated by the 10-percent turnover rate compared to the typical 25- to 45-percent rate for customer-service representatives. Mountain West subscribers were generally satisfied, although Quinn did hear some occasional grumbling about the length of time customers spent on hold.

However, whatever her virtues, Gustafson firmly resisted all attempts to increase efficiency and lower costs in a department where salaries accounted for close to 70 percent of the budget. That's where Erik Rasmussen came in. Upper-level management charged him with the task of bringing costs under control. Eager to do well in his first management position, the hard-working, no-nonsense young man made it a priority to increase the number of calls per hour that each representative handled. For the first time ever, the company measured the representatives' performance against statistical standards that emphasized speed, recorded the customer-service calls, and used software that generated automated work schedules based on historical information and projected need. Efficient, not flexible, scheduling was the goal. In addition, the company cut back on training.

The results, Martin Quinn had to admit, were mixed. With more efficient scheduling and clear performance standards in place, calls per hour increased dramatically, and subscribers spent far less time on hold. The department's costs were finally heading downward, but department morale was spiraling downward as well, with the turnover rate currently at 30 percent and climbing. And Quinn was beginning to hear more complaints from subscribers who'd received inaccurate information from inexperienced representatives or representatives who sounded rushed.

It was time for Rasmussen's first performance review. Quinn knew the young manager was about to walk into his office ready to proudly recite the facts and figures that documented the department's increased efficiency. What kind of an evaluation was he going to give Rasmussen? Should he recommend some midcourse corrections?

Questions

1. How would you describe Evelyn Gustafson's leadership style? What were its strengths and weaknesses? What were the sources of her influence?

2. How would you describe Erik Rasmussen's leadership style as he tried to effect change? What are its strengths and weaknesses? What are the sources of his influence?

3. If you were Martin Quinn, would you recommend modifications in Erik Rasmussen's leadership style that you would like him to adopt? Do you think it will be possible for Rasmussen to make the necessary changes? If not, why not? If you do think change is possible, how would you recommend the desired changes be facilitated?

SOURCES: Based on Gary Yukl, *Leadership in Organizations*, 4th ed. (Englewood Cliffs, NJ: Prentice Hall, 1998): 66–67; and "Telephone Call Centers: The Factory Floors of the 21st Century," *Knowledge @ Wharton* (April 10, 2002) (http://knowledge.wharton.upenn.edu/index.cfm?fa=viewArticle&ID=540).

Chapter 13: Case for Critical Analysis

Kimbel's Department Store

Frances Patterson, Kimbel's CEO, looked at the latest "Sales by Manager" figures on her daily Web-based sales report. What did these up-to-the-minute numbers tell her about the results of Kimbel's trial of straight commission pay for its salespeople?

A regional chain of upscale department stores based in St. Louis, Kimbel's faces the challenge shared by most department stores these days: how to stop losing share of overall retail sales to discount store chains. A key component of the strategy the company formulated to counter this long-term trend is the revival of great customer service on the floor, once a hallmark of upscale stores. Frances knows Kimbel's has its work cut out for it. When she dropped in on several stores incognito a few years ago, she was dismayed to discover that finding a salesperson actively engaged with a customer was rare. In fact, finding a salesperson when a customer wanted to pay for an item was often difficult.

About a year and a half ago, the CEO read about a quiet revolution sweeping department store retailing. At stores such as Bloomingdale's and Bergdorf Goodman, managers put all salespeople on straight commission. Frances decided to give the system a year-long try in two area stores.

Such a plan, she reasoned, would be good for Kimbel's if it lived up to its promise of attracting better salespeople, improving their motivation, and making them more customer-oriented. It could also potentially be good for employees. Salespeople in departments such as electronics, appliances, and jewelry, where expertise and highly personalized services paid off, had long worked solely on commission. But the majority of employees earned an hourly wage plus a meager 0.5 percent commission on total sales. Under the new scheme, all employees would earn a 7-percent commission on sales. When she compared the two systems, she saw that a new salesclerk in women's wear would earn $35,000 on $500,000 in sales, as opposed to only $18,000 under the old scheme.

With the trial period about to end, Frances notes that while overall sales in the two stores have increased modestly, so also has employee turnover. When the CEO examined the sales-by-manager figures, it was obvious that some associates had thrived and others had not. Most fell somewhere in the middle.

For example, Juan Santore is enthusiastic about the change—and for good reason. He works in women's designer shoes and handbags, where a single item can cost upward of $1,000. Motivated largely by the desire to make lots of money, he's a personable, outgoing individual with an entrepreneurial streak. Ever since the straight commission plan took effect, he has put even more time and effort into cultivating relationships with wealthy customers, and it shows. His pay has increased an average of $150 per week.

It's a different story in the lingerie department, where even luxury items have more modest price tags. The lingerie department head, Gladys Weinholtz, said salespeople in her department are demoralized. Several valued employees had quit, and most miss the security of a salary. No matter how hard they work, they cannot match their previous earnings. "Yes, they're paying more attention to customers," conceded Gladys, "but they're so anxious about making ends meet, they tend to pounce on the poor women who wander into the department." Furthermore, lingerie sales associates are giving short shrift to duties such as handling complaints or returns that don't immediately translate into sales. "And boy, do they ever resent the sales superstars in the other departments," said Gladys.

The year is nearly up. It's time to decide. Should Frances declare the straight commission experiment a success on the whole and roll it out across the chain over the next six months?

Questions

1. What theories about motivation underlie the switch from salary to commission pay?

2. What needs are met under the commission system? Are they the same needs in the shoes and handbag department as they are in lingerie? Explain.

3. If you were Frances Patterson, would you go back to the previous compensation system, implement the straight commission plan in all Kimbel's stores, or devise and test some other compensation method? If you decided to test another system, what would it look like?

SOURCES: Based on Cynthia Kyle, "Commissions question—to pay . . . or not to pay?" *Michigan Retailer* (March 2003) (www.retailers.com/news/retailers/03mar/mr0303commissions.html); "Opinion: Effective Retail Sales Compensation," *Furniture World Magazine* (March 7, 2006) (www.furninfo.com/absolutenm/templates/NewsFeed.asp?articleid=6017); Terry Pristin, "Retailing's Elite Keep the Armani Moving Off the Racks," *New York Times*, Dec. 22, 2001; Francine Schwadel, "Chain Finds Incentives a Hard Sell," *Wall Street Journal*, July 5, 1990; and Amy Dunkin, "Now Salespeople Really Must Sell for Their Supper," *BusinessWeek* (July 31, 1989): 50–52.

Chapter 14: Case for Critical Analysis

Hunter-Worth

Christmas was fast approaching. Just a short while ago, Chuck Moore, national sales manager for Hunter-Worth, a New York–based multinational toy manufacturer, was confident the coming holiday was going to be one of the company's best in years. At a recent toy expo, Hunter-Worth had unveiled a new interactive plush toy that was cuddly, high-tech, and tied into a major holiday motion picture expected to be a smash hit. Chuck had thought the toy would do well, but frankly, the level of interest took him by surprise. The buyers at the toy fair raved, and the subsequent preorder volume was extremely encouraging. It had all looked so promising, but now he couldn't shake a sense of impending doom.

The problem in a nutshell was that the Mexican subsidiary that manufactured the toy couldn't seem to meet a deadline. Not only were all the shipments late so far but also they fell well short of the quantities ordered. Chuck decided to e-mail Vicente Ruiz, the plant manager, about the situation before he found himself in the middle of the Christmas season with parents clamoring for a toy he couldn't lay his hands on.

In a thoroughly professional e-mail that started with a friendly "Dear Vicente," Chuck inquired about the status of the latest order, asked for a production schedule for pending orders, and requested a specific explanation as to why the Mexican plant seemed to be having such difficulty shipping orders out on time. The reply appeared within the hour, but to his utter astonishment, it was a short message from Vicente's secretary. She acknowledged the receipt of his e-mail and assured him the Mexican plant would be shipping the order, already a week late, in the next 10 days.

"That's it," Chuck fumed. "Time to take this to Sato." He prefaced his original e-mail and the secretary's reply with a terse note expressing his growing concern over the availability of what could well be this season's must-have toy. "Just what do I have to do to light a fire under Vicente?" he wrote. He then forwarded it all to his supervisor and friend, Michael Sato, the executive vice president for sales and marketing.

Next thing he knew, he was on the phone with Vicente—and the plant manager was furious. "Signor Moore, how dare you go over my head and say such things about me to my boss?" he sputtered, sounding both angry and slightly panicked. It seemed that Michael had forwarded Chuck's e-mail to Hunter-Worth's vice president of operations, who had sent it on to the Mexican subsidiary's president.

That turn of events was unfortunate, but Chuck wasn't feeling all that apologetic. "You could have prevented all this if you'd just answered the questions I e-mailed you last week," he pointed out. "I deserved more than a form letter—and from your secretary, no less."

"My secretary always answers my e-mails," replied Vicente. "She figures that if the problem is really urgent, you would pick up the phone and talk to me directly. Contrary to what you guys north of the border might think, we do take deadlines seriously here. There's only so much we can do with the supply problems we're having, but I doubt you're interested in hearing about those." And Vicente hung up the phone without waiting for a response.

Chuck was confused and disheartened. Things were only getting worse. How could he turn the situation around?

Questions

1. Based on Vicente Ruiz's actions and his conversation with Chuck Moore, what differences do you detect in cultural attitudes toward communications in Mexico as compared with the United States? Is understanding these differences important? Explain.

2. What was the main purpose of Chuck's communication to Vicente? To Michael Sato? What factors should he have considered when choosing a channel for his communication to Vicente? Are they the same factors he should have considered when communicating with Michael Sato?

3. If you were Chuck, what would you have done differently? What steps would you take at this point to make sure the supply of the popular new toy is sufficient to meet the anticipated demand?

SOURCES: Based on Harry W. Lane, *Charles Foster Sends an E-Mail* (London, Ontario: Ivey Publishing, 2005); Frank Unger and Roger Frankel, *Doing Business in Mexico: A Practical Guide on How to Break into the Market* (Barton, Australia: Council on Australia Latin America Relations and the Department of Foreign Affairs and Trade, 2002): 24–27; and Ignacio Hernandez, "Doing Business in Mexico—Business Etiquette—Understanding U.S.–Mexico Cultural Differences," MexGrocer.com (www.mexgrocer.com/business-in-mexico.html) (accessed Sept. 18, 2006).

Chapter 15: Case for Critical Analysis

Calgary Oil Shale Technologies, Inc.

When Martin Bouchard took over as president and CEO of Calgary Oil Shale Technologies, Inc. (COST), one of his top goals was to introduce teams as a way of solving the morale and productivity problems at the company's Alberta field operations site. COST is a subsidiary of an international oilfield services company. The subsidiary specializes in supplying technology and data management to optimize the recovery of oil from oil shale formations in Alberta, Colorado, and Utah. Oil shale is sedimentary rock containing a high proportion of organic matter that can be converted into crude oil or natural gas. With the price of crude oil skyrocketing and world supplies limited, energy companies in Canada and the United States were making a big push to recover hydrocarbons trapped in oil shale and slow-forming oil formations. Through its proprietary logging technology, COST could distinguish oil-bearing rock layers and help energy companies gain higher productivity from oil shale production.

COST used highly trained professionals such as geologists, geophysicists, and engineers to handle the sophisticated technology. They also used skilled and semiskilled labor to run the company's field operations. The two groups regularly clashed, and when one engineer's prank sent a couple of operations workers to the emergency room, the local press had a field day publishing articles about the conflict. The company hired Algoma Howard, a First Nations (American Indian) descendant, to develop a teamwork program to improve productivity and morale at the Calgary facility. She previously had great success using teams as a way to bring people together, enable them to understand one another's problems and challenges, and coordinate their efforts toward a common goal. The idea was to implement the program at other COST locations after the pilot project.

In Alberta, Howard had a stroke of luck in the form of Carlos Debrito, a long-time COST employee who was highly respected at the Alberta office and was looking for one final challenging project before he retired. Debrito had served in just about every possible line and staff position at COST over his 26-year career, and he understood the problems workers faced on both the technical and field sides of the business. Howard was pleased when Debrito agreed to serve as leader for the Alberta pilot program.

The three functional groups at the Alberta site included operations, made up primarily of hourly workers who operated and maintained the logging equipment; the "below ground" group, consisting of engineers, geologists, and geophysicists who determined where and how to dig or drill; and a group of equipment maintenance people who were on call. Howard and Debrito decided the first step was to get these different groups talking to one another and sharing ideas. They instituted monthly "fireside chats," optional meetings to which all employees were invited. The chats were held in the cafeteria during late afternoon, and people could have free coffee or tea and snacks brought by Howard and Debrito. The idea was to give employees a chance to discuss difficult issues and unresolved problems in a relaxed, informal setting. The only people who showed up at the first meeting were a couple of engineers who happened to wander by the cafeteria and see the snack table. Debrito opened the meeting by folding out a cardboard "fireplace" and pulling four chairs around it for the small group to talk. Word quickly spread of the silly "fireplace" incident (and the free food), and more and more people gradually began to attend the meetings. Early sessions focused primarily on talking about what the various participants saw

as "their" group's needs, as well as the problems they experienced in working with the "other" groups. One session almost came to fisticuffs until Debrito loudly announced that someone needed to go out and get another log for the fire, breaking the tension and moving things along. During the next session, Debrito and Howard worked with the group to come up with "rules of engagement," including such guidelines as "focus on the issue, not the person," "lose the words *us* and *them*," and "if you bring it up, you have to help solve it."

Within about six months, the fireside chats had evolved into lively problem-solving discussions focused on issues that all three groups found important. For example, a maintenance worker complained that a standard piece of equipment failed repeatedly due to cold weather and sand contamination. Debrito listened carefully and then drew a maintenance engineer into the discussion. The engineer came up with a new configuration better suited to the conditions, and downtime virtually disappeared.

The next step for Howard and Debrito was to introduce official "problem-busting" teams. These temporary teams included members from each of the three functional areas and from various hierarchical levels, and each was assigned a team leader, which was typically a respected first-line supervisor. Team leaders were carefully trained in team-building, shared-leadership, and creative problem-solving techniques. The teams were asked to evaluate a specific problem identified in a fireside chat and then craft and implement a solution. The teams were disbanded when the problem was solved. CEO Martin Bouchard authorized the teams to address problems within certain cost guidelines without seeking management approval.

Despite the camaraderie that had developed during the fireside chats, some delicate moments occurred when engineers resented working with field personnel and vice versa. In addition, some managers felt disempowered by the introduction of problem-busting teams. They had seen their role as that of problem solver. Now they were asked to share responsibility and support decisions that might come from the lowest-level workers in the company. Building commitment and trust among lower-level employees wasn't easy either. Howard suggested to Debrito that they use a "connection ladder" that she had observed used in a hospital nursing team. The idea is for the leader to identify where each team member is in terms of connection/disconnection with the process to determine what approach can help move the person from indifference toward commitment. Over time, and with Debrito's and Howard's continuing guidance, the problem-busting teams eventually began to come together and focus on a number of chronic problems that had long been ignored.

About a year and a half into the team-building program, the entire workforce in Alberta was organized into permanent cross-functional teams that were empowered to make their own decisions and elect their own leaders. By this time, just about everyone was feeling comfortable working cross-functionally, and within a few months, things were really humming. The professional and hourly workers got along so well that they decided to continue the fireside chat sessions after work, either in the cafeteria with snacks provided by volunteers or at a local bar. Some tensions between the groups remained, of course, and at one of the chats an operations worker jokingly suggested that the team members should duke it out once a week to get rid of the tensions so they could focus all their energy on their jobs. Several others joined in the joking, and eventually the group decided to square off in a weekly hockey game. For the opening game, Howard served as goalie on one side and Debrito as goalie on the other. Implementation of teams at the Alberta facility was deemed by management to be a clear success. Productivity and morale were soaring and costs continued to decline.

The company identified the Colorado office as the next facility where Algoma Howard and her leadership team needed to introduce the cross-functional teams that had proven so successful in Alberta. Howard's team felt immense pressure from top management to get the team-based productivity project up and running smoothly and quickly in Colorado. Top executives believed the lessons learned in Alberta would make implementing the program at other sites less costly and time-consuming. However, when Howard and her team attempted to implement the program at the Colorado facility, things did not go well. Because people were not showing up for the fireside chats, Howard's team, feeling pressed for time, made attendance mandatory. Ground rules were set by the leadership team at the beginning, based on the guidelines developed in Alberta, and the team introduced specific issues for discussion, again using the information it had gleaned from the early freewheeling Alberta sessions as a basis. However, the meetings still produced few valuable ideas or suggestions.

When it came time to form problem-busting teams, Howard thought it might be a good idea to let the groups select their own leaders as a way to encourage greater involvement and commitment among the Colorado workers. The leaders were given the same training that had been provided in Alberta. However, although a few of the problem-busting teams solved important problems, none of them showed the

kind of commitment and enthusiasm Howard had seen in Alberta. In addition, the Colorado workers refused to participate in softball games and other team-building exercises that her team developed for them. Howard finally convinced some workers to join in a softball game by bribing them with free food and beer, but the first game ended with a fight between two operations workers and a group of engineers.

"If I just had a Carlos Debrito in Colorado, things would go a lot more smoothly," Howard thought. "These workers don't trust us the way workers in Alberta trusted him." It seemed that no matter how hard Howard and her team tried to make the project work in Colorado, morale continued to decline and conflicts between the different groups of workers actually seemed to increase.

Questions

1. Algoma Howard and Carlos Debrito phased in permanent cross-functional teams in Alberta. What types of teams are the fireside chats and problem-busting teams? Through what stage or stages of team development did these groups evolve?

2. What role did Carlos Debrito play in the success of the Alberta team-based productivity project? What leadership approach did he employ to help reduce conflict between labor and the professionals? Do you agree with Algoma Howard that if she just had a Carlos Debrito in Colorado, the project would have succeeded? Explain your answer.

3. What advice would you give Algoma Howard and her team for improving the employee-involvement climate, containing costs, and meeting production goals at the Colorado facility?

SOURCES: Based on Michael C. Beers, "The Strategy That Wouldn't Travel," *Harvard Business Review* (Nov.–Dec. 1996): 18–31; Cathy Olofson, "Can We Talk? Put Another Log on the Fire," *Fast Company* (Dec. 19, 2007) (www.fastcompany.com/magazine/28/minm.html) (accessed Sept. 3, 2008); Karen Blount, "How to Build Teams in the Midst of Change," *Nursing Management* (Aug. 1998): 27–29; and Erin White, "How a Company Made Everyone a Team Player," *Wall Street Journal*, Aug. 13, 2007.

Appendix A Case for Critical Analysis

Emma's Parlor

Emma Lathbury's shoulders sagged as she flipped the cardboard sign hanging in the window of her tearoom's front door from "Open" to "Closed." The normally indefatigable 52-year-old owner of Emma's Parlor was bone tired. Any doubts she'd harbored about the wisdom of seriously considering some major changes in her business were fast disappearing.

She hadn't felt this weary since she'd left nursing in the early 1990s. After years of working as an intensive care nurse—with its grueling hours, emotionally draining work,

and lack of both respect and autonomy—she'd developed a bad case of burnout. At the time, she was convinced she could walk away from a secure, if difficult, profession and figure out a way of making a living that suited her high-energy, outgoing personality. Then one day, she noticed an 1870s-vintage Gothic Revival cottage for sale in the small Illinois farming community near where she'd grown up, and the answer to her dilemma came to her with a startling clarity. She'd get the financing, buy the house, and open up a cozy Victorian tearoom. Emma was certain she could make it work.

And she had. Her success was due in part to her unintentionally perfect timing. Specialty teas had taken off during the 1990s, with no end in sight to their current double-digit annual growth rate. But the solid performance of Emma's Parlor also owed a good deal to its owner's hard work and all those 60- and 70-hour weeks she'd put in, which was more fun when she worked for herself. She'd personally chosen the precise shades of purple and plum for the cottage's exterior, hung the lace curtains, selected the fresh flowers that graced the small circular tables, hired the staff, and tracked down and tested recipes for the finger sandwiches, scones, jams, and Battenburg cake that earned her glowing reviews in numerous guidebooks and a national reputation. Quickly realizing that special events were key to attracting customers, she organized and publicized fanciful gatherings that drew everyone from children toting their favorite stuffed animals to an Alice-in-Wonderland affair to women dressed in their best outfits, complete with big floppy hats, to a Midwest version of a royal garden party. The tearoom, which now employed about 20 people, was nearly always completely booked.

Most of all, the former nurse developed a real expertise when it came to teas, becoming particularly fascinated by the medicinal benefits of herbal teas. She started by conducting evening workshops on the efficacy of organic teas in treating everything from a simple upset stomach to menopausal distress. Eventually, she began blending her own Emma's Parlor Organic Teas and selling them to retail stores, restaurants, and individuals over the Web. As more and more publicity pointed to the benefits of tea, her Web-based business flourished, generating slightly less revenue than she was realizing from the tearoom. The profit margins were higher.

Despite the fulfillment she found in running her own business, it was getting too big for her to handle. Emma was beginning to experience the all-too-familiar symptoms of burnout. After she locked the front door, she made herself a soothing cup of rosebud tea, kicked off her sensible shoes, and sat down to review her options. Maybe she could drop the tearoom and focus on the Internet business or vice versa. She could try to master the fine art of delegation and turn Emma's Parlor over to an experienced restaurant manager, or she could take herself out of the picture by selling the tearoom outright. Then again, she could simply close the restaurant or the Internet business.

Questions

1. At what business stage is Emma's Parlor? At what stage is her Web-based organic tea business? What synergies exist between the two businesses? How critical do you think those synergies are to the success of each business?

2. How does Emma Lathbury fit the profile of the typical entrepreneur? Which of those traits are likely to continue to serve her well, and which might be counterproductive at this stage of her business?

3. After listing the pros and cons for each of Emma's options and considering her personality, which course of action would you recommend?

SOURCES: Based on Alison Stein Wellner, "Business Was Booming But the Richardsons Were Seriously Burned Out," *Inc. Magazine* (April 2006): 52–54; Mark Blumenthal, "Total Tea Sales in U.S. Forecast for $10 Billion in 2010," *HerbalGram* (2004): 61–62; and TeaMap Tearoom Directory (www.teamap.com).

Chapter 1: On the Job Video Case

Innovative Management for Turbulent Times

NUMI ORGANIC TEA

When Danielle Oviedo showed up for her first day as the manager of the Distribution Center at Numi Organic Tea in Oakland, California, her new direct reports were not happy about the change. They loved Oviedo's predecessor, who was more like a friend to them. Numi's director of operations, Brian Durkee, was looking for someone with specific skills and experience when he hired Danielle; popularity wasn't on the list. Durkee hired Danielle because of her effectiveness and success as a manager in previous positions. She also had experience leading much bigger teams in similar departments. Growing 180 percent in one year can wreak havoc at a small company like Numi; Durkee needed managers who could respond to the demands of rapid expansion, minimize the bumps along the way, and grow with the organization.

Prior to Danielle's arrival, lead times for customer orders were far from competitive, and Numi's inability to process orders efficiently had caught up with the company. Most of Numi's food service customers sell Numi teas exclusively in their cafes, restaurants, or hotels. Although loyal customers love Numi's products, some were considering taking their business elsewhere because inventory receipt was unpredictable.

Danielle quickly observed that each employee in the distribution center tended to perform his or her task in isolation with little attention to anything else. To solve this problem, she trained all the distribution center employees in every critical task and process, explaining how all the pieces fit together. In the future, everyone on her staff would perform multiple tasks, depending on what pressing deadlines loomed. A great example of today's new manager, Danielle helped team members understand their jobs on a conceptual level so they could see how their work and success linked directly to Numi's larger goals and success.

Turning this very different group of workers into a well-oiled team that felt invested in the future of the company didn't happen overnight. Some people resisted and resented the added responsibility; they weren't used to the flexibility or increased communication required by this new way of working.

Eventually Danielle's team started to click. Its newfound effectiveness, combined with her planning and organizing skills, as well as some key innovations, made a huge impact on lead times. With additional tweaks and time to practice the new distribution center regime, Danielle's team cut lead times for international orders by about 75 percent—from 15 to 5 days. Lead times for domestic orders historically averaged 3 to 5 days. Since Danielle has gotten things under control, orders often ship the same day or within a maximum of 2 to 3 days.

Numi's customer service manager, Cindy Graffort, is thrilled about Danielle's achievements and said none of these changes were possible before Danielle arrived, even though serious attempts had been made previously to address inefficiencies. According to Cindy, the dramatic changes were a direct result of Danielle's ability to come up with innovative solutions to the problems plaguing the distribution center. When asked for more insight into Danielle's managerial success, Cindy can't say enough about Danielle's impressive human skills. Unlike old-school managers, who would hide in their warehouse offices and manage employees from afar, Danielle usually can be found out on the floor "working with her teammates to ensure they understand the process and being supportive."

According to Durkee, Danielle is a "calm and assertive leader [who people] grab on to . . . and follow." No matter how crazy things get in the warehouse with huge, time-sensitive orders coming in and going out, Danielle keeps a "calm, cool head," which helps her team stay calm and focused. She inspires confidence that everything will get done—and it does.

As for Danielle's take on her management style, she thinks her practice of asking team members for their suggestions yields amazing results. While she implements many of their ideas, the real coup is that her team members come to work every day knowing anything is possible.

Discussion Questions

1. What are some drawbacks of Danielle's predecessor's tendency to treat her employees like friends?

2. How likely is Danielle to become a candidate for top management someday?

3. Can conceptual skills be cultivated easily? Explain.

Chapter 2: On the Job Video Case

The Environment and Corporate Culture

PRESERVE

Ever since green became the new black, U.S. companies have been scrambling to change their products, packaging, and energy consumption to stay in the game. Thanks to Eric Hudson's perceptive scanning of the external environment in the mid-1990s, he saw an opportunity others missed when the eco craze hit.

At a sociocultural level, Hudson observed that an increasing number of consumers were actively engaged in their local recycling programs, and recycled materials were plentiful. Even though consumers made the effort to recycle, they never saw what happened to their recycling after it left the curb. A self-congratulatory pat on the back was their only reward. How satisfying could it be for recycling zealots to purchase something—anything—made with recycled materials?

Hudson broke into the natural product arena with an innovative toothbrush made from recycled materials—a bold decision in 1996.

Hudson named his first product the Preserve Toothbrush, and a company called Recycline was born. (The company has since been rebranded "Preserve," with the "Recycline" name stepping into the background as the parent company.) The Preserve Toothbrush, with nylon bristles and a 100 percent recycled-plastic, reverse-curved, ergonomic handle, was a hit with eco-conscious consumers. The buzz grew and new converts flocked to it.

Energetic and full of ideas, Hudson gradually added other sleek and stylish products to his developing venture. Preserve's current product line features razors, colanders, cutting boards, tableware, and more. It also formed a strategic partnership with Whole Foods, which provided an ideal opportunity to expand its line and customer base. Preserve's latest joint venture with Target will bring its products to the masses.

Although Preserve doubled its business every year for the last three years, Hudson and his senior management team need to stay attuned to different dimensions of the external environment to ensure they don't miss important news that could affect the company. Not surprisingly, advances in the plastics technologies are always on their radar. Both Hudson and Preserve's director of marketing, C. A. Webb, are anticipating future competition from big corporate players who enter the green market determined to make a profit. The possibility of a green backlash in the United States also concerns Hudson.

Webb believes that customers can sense if a company has integrity and are getting wise to the "green-washing effect" in which businesses cultivate a superficial green image without enough substance to back it up. A close look at Preserve's internal culture confirms that this company is eco conscious and has been from the start.

After working at Fidelity Investments for six years, Hudson wanted to run his own business and do something for the planet. Eager to shed the stiff shackles of corporate America, he craved a culture that was both casual and effective. He knew his company needed to strike a balance between being process driven and agile. The vice president of sales, John Turcott, thinks Preserve's small size—14 employees—makes collaboration critical to its culture. Everything at Preserve, even collaboration, happens at high speed, so everyone has to be driven, creative, and adaptable. "The entrepreneurial slant is, 'We gotta get these things done *today*.' So our decision-making process is quicker. We pull together the resources we need to solve a problem, we get it done and move on to the next thing." Anyone interested in taking on a new initiative is encouraged to do so, regardless of position.

As Preserve's cultural leader, Hudson practices what he preaches. When he isn't pedaling 22 miles to and from work on his bicycle, he's cruising in a Volkswagen that has been converted to run on french-fry grease—an emerging symbol of the modern-day eco hero. Everyone at Preserve tries to do right by the natural environment, whether it's composting, conserving energy, using eco-friendly cleaning products, or anything else that makes a difference. Many take the commuter rail to work, even if it would be faster and much more convenient to drive.

Discussion Questions

1. Which of the following best describes Preserve's culture: adaptable, consistent, successful, collaborative, or high performing? Explain.

2. In the future, to whom should Hudson pay close attention and why: customers or competitors?

3. Explain what other aspects of the general environment are relevant to Preserve.

Chapter 3: On the Job Video Case

Managing in a Global Environment

EVO

The Internet is an inherently global market, so regardless of a company's intended target market, it may find customers around the world. Evo, a Seattle-based online retailer of all ski-, snowboard-, wake-, and skate-related items, serves customers who live in places as exotic as Bahrain, Turkey, and Bali. Ultimately, founder Bryce Phillips is happy and successful. For the foreseeable future, however, Evo's global prospects are limited by territory-specific licensing and distribution agreements with manufacturers.

International customers who want to purchase something from Evo cannot complete their transactions online due to complexities, including exchange rates and shipping regulations. Therefore, they must call Evo customer-service representatives (CSRs) directly to discuss their order. Although Evo has CSRs staffing the phones for extended hours to accommodate calls from distant time zones, the modest volume of international orders does not justify funding a 24-hour customer-service line.

In spite of these challenges, 5 percent of Evo's business is nondomestic, with Canada accounting for most of this. Canada also represents the biggest potential for expanding global sales because many of Evo's licensing agreements allow for distribution within North America. British and German citizens place their share of orders, too. Phillips is confident his company will be able to expand its global reach as licensing practices change to reflect the boundary-free world of e-commerce and Evo becomes more established as a global brand.

Everyone who works in customer service at Evo has a collection of stories about interesting and challenging interactions with international customers. For starters, callers often are disappointed to learn they cannot order the particular snowboard they had been dreaming of. Sometimes, CSRs are able to find comparable items available in a customer's region. Language barriers arise as well, but Evo reps usually figure out what customers with limited English-language skills are trying to say. In addition, French- or Spanish-speaking employees serve as translators when necessary.

It's unlikely that Evo will need to set up operations abroad because its shipping partners are already everywhere they need to be. Most overseas manufacturers from whom Evo sources products have U.S. offices or representatives, so Evo buyers rarely need to leave Seattle. Even when travel is required, the East Coast is typically the farthest that buyers need to go for big industry trade shows.

The majority of Evo's international transactions are relatively seamless, but day-to-day operations can still be affected by global events. "Manufacturers overseas can impact us," noted Molly Hawkins, whose playful title is *Strategery*. "There was a lock at all the ports in China and we couldn't import any of their products. Therefore, a lot of soft goods like jackets and pants couldn't be shipped."

Although the world tends to come to Evo, Phillips wanted to share his favorite global travel destinations with customers. Now evoTRIP offers extreme ski, snowboarding, and surf expeditions to South America, Japan, Indonesia, and Switzerland, and the company has plans to offer future trips to more places. "The reason I get so excited about this concept is that it is near and dear to what all of us value," said Phillips. "It's getting out there, learning more about different cultures, doing the activities in different parts of the world, and seeing beautiful locations you've never seen before."

Logistics for evoTRIP are outsourced through JustFares.com, which specializes in international travel. To offer the richest, most authentic cultural experience, evoTRIP always uses local guides. Professional athletes from each country travel with the groups, too, so evoTrippers can experience the culturally specific nuances within seemingly universal sports.

Although evoTRIP focuses on serving up global fun and excitement to participating travelers, Phillips sees every trip as an opportunity for Evo's "ambassadors" to connect with potential customers in every country they visit. There is no virtual translation, and there are no time-zone differences or boundaries.

Discussion Questions

1. Why should Evo avoid setting up operations in other countries if possible?

2. What political and economic challenges could evoTRIP encounter when conducting business in other countries?

3. What cultural differences should Evo and evoTRIP participants pay attention to when traveling abroad?

Chapter 4: On the Job Video Case

Ethics and Social Responsibility
CITY OF GREENSBURG, KANSAS

May 4, 2007, started out like any day for the 1,500 residents of Greensburg, Kansas. Weather forecasters predicted afternoon storms, but few residents paid much attention. Folks in this rural community had seen their share of storms and knew the drill.

By 6 P.M., the National Weather Service issued a tornado warning for Kiowa County. Still, tornadoes are hit or miss. Around 9:20 P.M., storm sirens sounded, and residents took cover in bathrooms and basements. When they emerged from their shelters, their lives would be changed forever.

"My town is gone," announced the city administrator, Steve Hewitt, in the first press conference on May 5. "I believe 95 percent of the homes are gone. Downtown buildings are gone, my home is gone, and we've got to find a way to make this work and get this town back on its feet." Even with 700 homes to rebuild, the residents were prepared to start with a clean slate. Although the tornado was devastating, the town viewed it as a blessing in disguise. Both Hewitt and Mayor Lonnie McCollum rallied the people and vowed to rebuild a green town.

Although both Hewitt and McCollum believed Greensburg should be rebuilt in a socially responsible way using sustainable practices, designs, and materials, they faced some ethical dilemmas. Hewitt frequently explained his broader view of the stakeholders affected by their choices: "We're making 100-year decisions that will affect our children and our children's children." Although Hewitt wouldn't describe it that way, he and McCollum took a utilitarian approach to these big decisions. For them, reducing Greensburg's impact on the environment felt like the right or ethical thing to do, especially when considering the well-being of future generations.

Living in trailers provided by the Federal Emergency Management Agency (FEMA), some residents struggled to embrace a long-term view. They knew it would take longer to build green because of the education, research, and fund-raising required. Many residents felt impatient and had trouble thinking beyond their immediate needs as individuals. Greensburg upped the ante and the costs of rebuilding when the city council approved an ordinance declaring all municipal buildings would be built to the highest Leadership in Energy and Environmental Design (LEED) green building rating for sustainability: LEED Platinum.

LEED is a third-party certification program. It has become the nationally accepted benchmark for the design, construction, and operation of green buildings. LEED gives building owners the tools they need to have a measurable and immediate impact on their buildings' performance. LEED promotes a whole-building approach to sustainability by recognizing performance in five key areas of human and environmental health: materials selection, sustainable site development, energy efficiency, water savings, and indoor environmental quality.

In Hewitt's mind, Greensburg had an economic responsibility to construct buildings that achieved maximum energy efficiency. So even if it cost more initially to build LEED-Platinum facilities, the town's energy costs as well as its operating costs would be significantly lower in the future.

While Hewitt worked hard to manage and raise funds for Greensburg's reconstruction projects, others were doing their part to help. The husband-and-wife team of executive director Daniel Wallach and Catherine Hart, coordinator of educational services, worked together to launch Greensburg GreenTown, a 501(c)(3) not-for-profit organization, which was designed to provide Greensburg with the information, support, and resources it needed to rebuild the town as a green community.

One of Wallach's favorite projects was BTI Greensburg, the local John Deere dealership. With Wallach's encouragement, owners Mike and Kelly Estes decided to build a state-of-the art green facility. By using radiant heat, passive cooling, solar and wind power, and recycling their used oil, BTI Greensburg reduced its utility costs by hundreds of dollars every month. With the corporate support of John Deere, BTI Greensburg became the flagship green shop for John Deere dealerships around the world. As the biggest business in Greensburg, BTI is a major stakeholder. When Mike Estes publicly states, repeatedly, that rebuilding green "is the right thing to do," people listen.

Discussion Questions

1. What are the potential consequences of rebuilding Greensburg without concern for green practices?

2. Besides lowering energy costs, how else might Greensburg benefit from becoming a green town?

3. At what stage of moral development are Hewitt and McCollum—preconventional, conventional, or postconventional? Please explain.

Chapter 5: On the Job Video Case

Planning and Goal Setting
FLIGHT 001

"We came up with this concept out of need," said Brad John, cofounder of Flight 001. John and fellow cofounder John Sencion had, until the late 90s, been working in different aspects of the fashion industry in New York. Both traveled often between the United States, Europe, and Japan for work. No matter how many times they began a trip, they spent the days and hours before they left racing all over town picking up last-minute essentials. By the time they got to the airport, they were sweaty, stressed, and miserable—not living the glamorous existence they envisioned when they got into the fashion industry.

On a 1998 flight from New York to Paris, the weary travelers came up with an idea for a one-stop travel shop targeted at fashion-forward globe-trotters like themselves. Flight 001 sells guidebooks, cosmetics, laptop bags, luggage, electronics and gadgets, passport covers, and other personal consumer products. Sencion summed up their mission: "We're trying to bring a little fun and glamour back into travel."

When asked who does the planning at Flight 001, John automatically replied, "John Sencion." When pressed, he admitted that it's really more of a decentralized approach, with everyone contributing within his or her area of expertise and experience. At the top, John focused on financial forecasts, planning for expansion, and retailing issues. Sencion focused on new products and design. At the retail level, John also sought input from store managers to provide a three-dimensional perspective on his purchasing plans and sales data.

One of John's current strategic goals is expansion. The company, now in its tenth year, has seven stores in the United States and one boutique in Harvey Nichols, an upscale department store in the United Arab Emirates. It wants to be in every major city in the United States, Europe, and Asia. In total, John hopes to open 20 to 30 shops worldwide at a rate of 5 to 10 per year. Confident in his ability to open individual stores, his new challenge will be opening multiple stores simultaneously. Location, start-up costs, and cash flow are currently the biggest hurdles. "In retail, as soon as you sign that lease, money starts going out, so you need to get that store open quickly," John said. Managing human resources plays an important role in getting up to speed. New stores are staffed with employees from existing Flight 001 shops to save time and money in training. Plus, the company reduces its risk by hiring employees it knows.

Financial planning is another tricky aspect of any business, especially during economic downturns when consumers curtail spending and sales fall short of forecasts. "We had planned to do a certain amount of business in 2008," John explained, "but because of the current economy, we're falling short of our sales goals." As a result, Flight 001 had to cut unnecessary spending. Until consumer confidence improves, John will carefully control inventory and hiring.

Also integral to the strategic plan is a transition from boutique to brand. The company recently began work on an exclusive product line designed and manufactured by Flight 001. This goal works to support its expansion plans as Flight 001 strives to differentiate itself and add value to the brand in a retail space dominated by larger, one-stop shopping outlets such as Target and online retailers offering the convenience of 24/7 shopping.

With all the talk about expansion and new product lines, it will be increasingly important for Flight 001 to not become distracted from what makes it special in the first place: location, design, and an impeccable product line.

Discussion Questions

1. How was the concept of Flight 001 created?

2. In what ways might the introduction of the Flight 001 brand of products be considered a stretch goal?

3. What external factors might trigger the need for contingency planning at small specialty retailers such as Flight 001?

Chapter 6: On the Job Video Case

Decision Making
GREENSBURG, KANSAS

It's almost impossible to assign credit or blame to any one person for Greensburg's decision to rebuild the small Kansas town as a model green community after a tornado decimated 95 percent of its buildings. Many folks in Greensburg would assert that whoever made the decision made a good one. Other residents make a different case. It's complicated.

Former mayor Lonnie McCollum expressed interest in exploring the possibilities of running Greensburg's municipal buildings on solar and wind power well before the EF5 tornado hit in May 2004. After the storm, he saw the tragedy as an opportunity to reinvent the dying town and put it back on the map. But McCollum was not the sole decision maker. He was the leader of a small community facing endless uncertainties. He wanted to give people a sense of direction; something to live for. He made a decision to lead and assert his ideas. Ultimately, the Greensburg City Council would have to vote on this matter.

Some questioned whether McCollum had spent any time coalition building. However, Greensburg was in crisis after the storm, and the timing wasn't right for coalition building. McCollum had not engaged in rational forms of the decision-making process regarding the benefits of turning his town green. Before the tornado, he may have thoughtfully weighed the pros and cons, but in the end, this wasn't a programmed decision. McCollum wasn't operating from a logical place after the tornado hit. He was using his intuition—his gut; he was passionate about his vision for Greensburg.

While McCollum may not have built a coalition, he had cultivated a fierce ally in Steve Hewitt, Greensburg's city administrator. Hewitt took McCollum's vision and expanded it. Like McCollum, Hewitt believed, without a doubt, that Greensburg had an opportunity to become a thriving town again with green as its theme. The real work was convincing Greensburg's residents and council members to implement the proposed plan.

After multiple rounds of community meetings in which residents engaged in rigorous debate, the Greensburg' City Council voted in favor of rebuilding the town using green methods and materials. And when the council members voted on the specifics of implementation, they decided to build all municipal buildings to the Leadership in Energy and Environmental Design (LEED) Platinum standard, which is the highest nationally accepted benchmark for the design, construction, and operation of high-performance green buildings.

Greensburg resident Janice Haney didn't think the community meetings allowed enough space for true debate. Instead, she was convinced the meetings were token gestures toward community involvement. Questions were raised asking if Haney was playing devil's advocate after the fact or if there was an atmosphere of conformity cultivated so residents were afraid to voice their true opinions. Some residents questioned whether Hewitt and the city council saw what they wanted to see and heard what they wanted to hear. Were some residents influenced by their initial impressions that McCollum made a passionate, solo decision?

Considering this decision involved an entire town, residents clearly had very different propensities for risk. Many people were probably more risk averse than usual because they had just lost their homes and businesses. And while there's plenty of rational information regarding the benefits of green building, the decision still involves a degree of uncertainty and ambiguity. No one can predict the exact costs of fossil fuels in the future, nor can they calculate precisely how much Greensburg will save through its use of solar and wind power. Whether or not Greensburg will be able to raise all the funds needed to rebuild according to LEED Platinum standards is also uncertain.

There is no way to convince every Greensburg resident that going green was a good decision. Perhaps all Hewitt and the city council can hope for is support from a majority of residents. In their minds, what were the alternatives? The town was dying. Today, Greensburg is rebuilding thanks to generous corporate sponsorships and government grants. The town also stars in a TV show on Planet Green. The TV show is aptly named *Greensburg*.

Discussion Questions

1. What ideas support the argument that McCollum, Hewitt, and the city council made good decisions?

2. What insights might come out of analyzing Greensburg's decision-making process after the fact?

3. Were Hewitt and McCollum overconfident in offering their solution for the town? Explain.

Chapter 7: On the Job Video Case

Designing Adaptive Organizations

EVO

When Bryce Phillips started selling ski and snowboard equipment on eBay, he managed everything—customer care, supply chain, technology, buying, and finance—all from his apartment. Eight years later, Phillips's company, Evo, runs a hugely successful e-commerce site, employs more than 60 people, manages its Seattle flagship store, and operates a 40,000-square-foot distribution center. Evo has grown at least 70 percent every year and recently hit $10 million in sales. To effectively lead this rapidly expanding venture, Phillips continually looks for ways to delegate responsibilities to the capable managers around him.

As a pretty straightforward business, Evo is well served by its flat, functional structure. A recent company-wide meeting showcased this ever-morphing structure. Department heads introduced themselves and their staffs and explained the function of their departments so new employees and the whole company would have a better understanding of how all the pieces of the company fit together. Nathan Decker, the director of e-commerce, explained how the new creative services team would operate. Phillips gave the latest details on his current passion, a new adventure travel offering called evoTRIP.

Beyond its formal structure, Evo works within a set of core values called the "Great 8," which provides another important operating framework. The Great 8 includes authenticity, balanced ambition, credibility, style, leadership, respect, communication, and evolución. On Evo's Web site, Phillips explained, "Even with all of the changes, many things have remained constant, and we are where we are because we have stayed true to the Great 8. We established the Great 8 to guide us through the decisions, big and small, that we make every day. Decisions from how we set up a new display in the store, to what investment we take on, and who we decide to work with to lead this company are scrutinized using the Great 8 as the final sounding board. We don't take this lightly."

In 2004, when Evo employed only six people, flexibility was a way of life. Everyone wore multiple hats and did everything necessary to get the job done. As the number of employees on payroll approached 50 and 60, it was time to make sure the people who dealt directly with customers possessed the authority and flexibility to deliver excellent service. This organizational soul-searching yielded the new customer care policy: "Just Say YES!" Now, customer-service representatives (CSRs) make their own decisions about how to make customers happy. Reps no longer use the phrases "Could you please hold while I talk to my manager?" or "I'm afraid we'll have to get back to you on that." If free shipping is likely to guarantee a return customer, then free shipping it is. If throwing in free ski poles means winning a lifelong customer, CSRs can authorize free ski poles.

Recently, Evo's organizational adaptability was put to the test. Delivering packages to customers on time is essential to running a successful e-commerce company, so Evo decided to stop outsourcing its distribution when the company realized it couldn't control quality. Beyond the massive task of building out the physical plant, setting up the distribution center (DC) involved hiring a dozen people and creating defined roles and responsibilities for these new positions. The DC was easily incorporated into the supply-chain department thanks to its broadly defined function.

Midway through construction of the new DC, Evo faced the unexpected loss of an employee. Evo's head buyer became ill suddenly and died within two months. Her husband was in charge of launching the DC, but he had to take a leave of absence to care for his wife. Down two department heads, Evo faced an organizational crisis and had to adapt quickly. Because the responsibilities and authority of both positions were clearly defined, two people, one step down the chain of command, were able to jump into their former bosses' shoes with relatively few glitches.

Phillips was last overheard discussing ways Evo could adapt to the troubled U.S. economy. Luckily, tackling monster moguls on the ski slopes had prepared him for almost anything.

Discussion Questions

1. Given Evo's current structure and pace of growth, what organizational challenges might arise in the future?

2. Is Evo a centralized or decentralized company? Explain.

3. Imagine it is 20 years from now and Evo is organized into divisions. What are they?

Chapter 8: On the Job Video Case

Change and Innovation

SCHOLFIELD HONDA

Not long ago, the phrase "hybrid SUV" would have been considered an oxymoron, but almost overnight, hybrid cars of all shapes and sizes became mainstream. As gas prices soared and concerns about the environment deepened, many people were looking for innovative solutions to energy problems and wondering about the cars of the future.

Enter Lee Lindquist, alternative fuels specialist at Scholfield Honda in Wichita, Kansas. Lindquist loves technology, is a passionate environmentalist, and has found the perfect way to make a difference at work. While researching

alternative fuel vehicles for his upcoming presentation at the local Sierra Club, he learned Honda had been selling a natural gas vehicle in New York and California since 1998, where it was marketed as a way for municipalities and fleet customers to address air quality issues. He also discovered that the Honda Civic GX was the greenest model currently available for sale in the United States.

Lindquist couldn't believe Honda's most innovative car had been on the market for 10 years and still hadn't been embraced by Honda dealerships or consumers. One challenge of offering the Civic GX to the public was the lack of natural gas fueling stations and the high cost of purchasing and installing individual fueling stations for home use. With any new technology, a critical mass of early adopters helped lay groundwork for others. In the case of the Civic GX, Honda dealerships weren't adopting *or* promoting the new technology, and Lindquist viewed this lack of entrepreneurship as unacceptable.

Rising fuel prices provided the perfect opportunity to introduce cost-conscious and green-minded customers to the Civic GX. When Lindquist brought the Civic GX idea to his boss, owner Roger Scholfield was skeptical. He had long been promoting the Honda brand as fuel efficient and didn't want to confuse customers with the "new" vehicle. Nevertheless, he eventually warmed to the idea and, with Lindquist's help, he started marketing the car to corporate and government customers.

When the infamous tornado hit Greensburg in 2007, going green at Scholfield Honda took on new meaning. Emboldened after top management implemented his first recommendation to stock the Civic GX, Lindquist saw an amazing chance to promote the Civic GX and position Scholfield Honda as the regional leader in green-vehicle technology. Scholfield, a long-time supporter of local communities, already was planning to make a generous contribution to Greensburg, but he envisioned something fairly different from his young, determined employee. However, Lindquist urged Scholfield to donate a Civic GX and a fueling station to Greensburg GreenTown, the organization set up to educate the town's residents about green building methods and products.

Well aware of the media attention surrounding Greensburg, Scholfield was open to Lindquist's idea. Greensburg residents, along with folks across the entire region and country, would learn about Honda's cutting-edge alternative. Scholfield questioned his decision to donate the car even as he was driving to Greensburg to present the expensive gift, but ultimately he knew investing in change was the right thing to do.

Since the donation, Scholfield's customers have shown more interest in alternative fuel vehicles and recognize the dealership's contribution to the green transformation occurring nationwide. Honda U.S.A. also has applauded Scholfield's efforts.

Anyone interested in buying a Civic GX today needs to get in line because dealerships can't keep the cars in stock. While waiting, sip coffee from a compostable corn-based cup, toss old soda cans from your back seat into a recycling bin, and grab a free reusable green shopping bag on your way out. The dealership might even be giving away small trees on the day you stop by. Lindquist recognized that Scholfield Honda's culture also needed to change, so he convinced Scholfield to form a "Green Team" that meets monthly to identify what's next at this ever-changing workplace.

Discussion Questions

1. Beyond fueling issues, what might explain dealers' failure to promote the Civic GX?

2. How might Scholfield Honda expand on the changes put into motion by Lindquist?

3. How could the Honda Corporation capitalize on innovation at the dealership level?

Chapter 9: On the Job Video Case

Human Resource Management

MAINE MEDIA WORKSHOPS

Since 1973, the Maine Media Workshops have seen some of the most talented filmmakers, photographers, and writers pass through its doors. The program started as a summer camp of sorts for amateurs and professionals alike wanting to hone their skills while enjoying a week along the beautiful coast of Rockport, Maine. Over the years, students have had the opportunity to work with and learn from Hollywood's heavy hitters: Vilmos Zsigmond, Oscar-winning cinematographer on *Close Encounters of the Third Kind*, *The Black Dahlia*, and *The Deer Hunter*; Alan Myerson, Emmy-winning director of everything from *The Love Boat* to *The Larry Saunders Show*, *Boston Public*, and *Lizzie McGuire*; and even Gene Wilder. The names are impressive, but what has always set the work-

shops apart is the intensity and quality of the program. The family-style lobster dinner at the end is an added bonus.

Selection has always been a big job at the Maine Media Workshops. From January through November, the organization needs instructors to teach weeklong classes in the 500 or so courses they offer. For any small company, doing that kind of staffing blitz year after year would be challenging. For the staff at the Maine Media Workshops, there's an added degree of HR difficulty. With the exception of the skeleton crew of full-timers, the organization is entirely served by week-to-week temporary workers. In the time it takes most new hires to get their employee handbook and complete their W2 forms, the instructors at the Maine Media Workshops are already moving on.

"Just because somebody is good at making images doesn't make him or her a good teacher," explained

Elizabeth Greenburg, director of education. "What makes a good teacher is someone who is generous enough and open enough to share her life, her experience, her career and her knowledge 24/7 with students." The Maine Media Workshops have a very specific culture, and that is part of what attracts students. The instructors become mentors and coaches who are expected to dine with students, participate in social events, and be available to students to discuss an assignment or just to "pick their brains."

Selecting a perfect balance of professional experience, leadership, and generosity isn't something you can do in an interview. The best way a potential employer can do a background check (vetting) and assess someone's performance is through personal recommendations. That, of course, requires a lot of scouting and many contacts. With no time or budget for on-the-job training, the HR department likes to reach out to people who, like Greenburg, were once students so the potential new hire truly understands what it takes to perform to the Maine Media Workshops' standard. In addition to personal referrals, the program directors are always looking for places to connect new people with the school. Festivals such as Sundance are perfect places to recruit like-minded talent.

Compensation is surprisingly not an issue for the big guys and everyday professionals alike. Although the Maine Media Workshops pay a fair wage, the real compensation doesn't come in a check. "No one comes here for the money," said Mimi Edmunds, film program manager. "They come here because they love it."

Discussion Questions

1. Why might the instructors at the Maine Media Workshops be vetted very carefully if they are teaching only for one week?

2. The Maine Media Workshops recently expanded its Web site to serve the needs of an increasingly global audience for the school. Would e-cruiting be an appropriate recruiting tool for the Maine Media Workshops? Why or why not?

3. Complete a job analysis for one of the courses at the Maine Media Workshops. Then create a job posting for that position. Include a full job description, qualifications, and a realistic preview of the job for the applicant.

Chapter 10: On the Job Video Case

Managing Quality Control and Performance

PRESERVE

When John Lively, director of operations at Preserve, arrived for his first day on the job 10 years ago, there wasn't much to see. The company, which makes housewares and personal care products from recycled plastics, was just getting started. Three or four people in one room would do whatever it took to get the company off the ground. It's hard to believe, but in 1999 the whole idea of an IT department and all the organizational tools to which we've grown accustomed was still new. Larger companies certainly had systems in place, but those tools were merely something a four-person start-up company hoped to acquire someday.

"My original mandate for Preserve was to come in and look at their customer relationship management database," Lively recalled. His charge was not to manage customers but to look at the data the company had accumulated and come up with a way to use it to improve efficiency. It was not an easy task. At the end of six or seven months, however, he had trained the staff to print shipping labels.

Just when everyone started to get acclimated to Lively's newly efficient system, Walmart called. "Growth happens," Lively said. "But you're always hedging, saying, 'I'm not really sure that's gonna happen; maybe we won't get that big account.'" That year Preserve experienced a remarkable 75 percent growth in revenue, yet Lively was running the entire administrative part of the company with only a few eager, but inexperienced, office mates. Instead of anticipating staffing and infrastructure needs as it should have been doing, Preserve was hiring folks to recover from the large influx of business. "Looking at it and saying, 'How could we have done better?' has definitely resulted in some hierarchy of management," Lively admitted. Up to this point, Preserve had been a very flat organization. It was time for some real reporting structure.

IT systems and accounting continue to be the most important factors in improving Preserve's organizational performance. Lively is constantly working with his crew to forecast and project sales, profit, and expenses. Making each department accountable for its day-to-day spending ensures accurate balance sheets and profit and loss statements. "It's a large undertaking to understand where we need to be and look around process-wise to get those actuals in the books quicker," Lively lamented. Preserve now employs two controllers, freeing Lively to work on the big picture.

Forecasts show sales aren't going down anytime soon, and Preserve has reacted by asking more from its vendors and manufacturing partners. The factory responsible for manufacturing its most popular product, the Preserve Toothbrush, now handles all the inventory management and shipping on behalf of Preserve. When it comes to quality control, the factory implements its own systems and standards. Preserve works with them initially to set the standards, then it steps back unless problems arise.

The choice to outsource adds value in the form of reduced cycle time and improved service to the customer.

Preserve's total quality management approach results in cost savings and improvement in accuracy and efficiency in all aspects of Preserve's business. As the company grows, even stricter financial and manufacturing controls will no doubt result in a more hierarchical structure. Although this poses some threat to Preserve's casual and open culture, all recognize that it is a necessary part of growth. A smoothly run organization means the folks at Preserve can get back to doing what they do best—creating innovative, Earth-friendly products.

Discussion Questions

1. Do you think Preserve would benefit from employing an activity-based costing system? Explain.

2. Do you think implementing a formal corporate governance policy is appropriate for Preserve? Why or why not?

Chapter 11: On the Job Video Case

Dynamics of Behavior in Organizations

NUMI ORGANIC TEA

Getting a job offer from Numi Organic Tea is kind of like getting accepted into a big Mafia family, minus the illegal activities and violence. Fierce loyalty is critical for survival. A willingness to work long and strange hours is non-negotiable. Reminiscent of beloved patriarchs, Ahmed Rahim, cofounder and CEO, still interviews nearly every serious prospect. And once you're in, other family members will keep an eye on you until you have earned their trust.

When asked about his and cofounder sister Rheem's hands-on involvement with hiring, Rahim explained their philosophy that, "People are everything for a company. You can have a great product and great mission, but without the right people, you don't have the right formula."

In spite of the rigorous, time-consuming vetting process, Numi hasn't had much trouble finding and retaining talent. Fifty people currently work for this progressive Oakland-based company. Given the pace of growth, Numi can't afford to lose the time and energy resulting from hasty hiring decisions and the inevitable turnover. The company would rather make sure each person it hires has the desired skills and experience, fits well with the culture, and can serve as a Numi ambassador everywhere he or she goes.

Jen Mullin, vice president of marketing, recently hired an assistant for the public relations (PR) team to focus on connecting with customers through social-networking sites such as MySpace and Facebook. Duties also include drumming up business on Numi's blog and attending industry events, which are often held on nights and weekends. Flexibility ranks high on the list of traits Mullin sought in a new assistant because people's roles change constantly and work hours are rarely 9 to 5.

She was also looking for someone who was passionate about Numi tea and shared the organizational commitment to organics, sustainability, and fair trade so this person could effectively represent Numi in any context. (Numi cohorts have been known to spend Friday nights attending talks on the latest organic breakthroughs.) For the optimal person–job fit, Mullin needed someone with a can-do attitude and the ability to take initiative, work, and solve problems independently. She was also looking for someone who was trustworthy, positive, upbeat, and willing to do whatever it took to get the job done.

Beyond having the right personality, the new PR assistant needed to be a savvy MySpace and Facebook user so she or he could have authentic interactions with people on behalf of Numi. Constant communication with customers requires a high level of emotional intelligence.

Mullin said it's pretty clear after 60 days whether or not someone is going to work out. And in the case of the new PR assistant, Numi scored. When asked to help with a marketing research project, new assistant Tish went above and beyond the call of duty. She put together a visually engaging and informative PowerPoint presentation of her insightful analysis and confidently shared it with the entire company.

Regardless of how many people join the staff, Numi's growth makes it difficult for anyone to feel on top of his or her workload. To get rid of stress, many employees take breaks in the company's tea garden, where they sip tea and cultivate an inner calm. Mullin's team meets weekly to prioritize and, if necessary, change project due dates so people don't feel continuously behind and overwhelmed. Flextime helps a lot of Numi folks manage their daily stress, too.

Most Numi employees come across as ambitious and hardworking, and yet the place seems to be populated by high-achieving and high-performing Type B personalities. Further investigation would probably unearth some Type A personalities, too, but the vibe is definitely Type B.

Discussion Questions

1. Are Numi's expectations for organizational citizenship realistic? Explain.

2. How is Numi susceptible to hiring the wrong people in spite of its efforts?

3. What qualities are hardest to assess given the limited contact possible through interviews? What are some possible solutions to this challenge?

Chapter 12: On the Job Video Case

Leadership

CITY OF GREENSBURG, KANSAS

After working in Oklahoma City as a parks director, Steve Hewitt wanted to run an entire town. A smaller community seemed the perfect place to get hands-on leadership experience before tackling a bigger city, so Hewitt took the city administrator position in his hometown of Greensburg, Kansas (population 1,500). Standing in the remains of his kitchen, looking up at the dark sky on May 4, 2007, he realized that he got more than he'd bargained for.

Across town, Mayor Lonnie McCollum and his wife clung to a mattress as their dream home was ravaged. McCollum, a beloved long-time resident, had been the write-in candidate for mayor in the last election and won unanimously. Midwesterners value humility, and as traits go McCollum was as humble as they come. His quiet, referent power, bestowed on him by the residents, had little to do with formal position. In McCollum's mind, he'd been drafted to serve, and his job was to revive the dying town.

McCollum's visionary idea was to transform Greensburg into a city run on wind and solar power. He convinced the city it needed a full-time administrator to make big changes. Intense and fast-talking, Hewitt provided the perfect complement to McCollum's slow, measured demeanor. Hewitt was excited to help McCollum improve the town. Neither could foresee how these plans would come into play after the tornado.

Hewitt headed straight for command central that ominous night to begin coordinating search and rescue efforts. McCollum knew Hewitt could lead in this crisis, so he stayed with his injured wife.

By morning, everyone knew Greensburg was gone. At a press conference, McCollum announced that the town would rebuild as a model green community. Although the world cheered him on, residents had mixed feelings. McCollum explained, "It's a real feeling to not have a place to keep you warm and dry . . . they were impatient and they were afraid." Ultimately, the stress of the tornado took its toll on McCollum, and he decided to resign. "They didn't need me; they had good leadership," said McCollum, referring to younger, tougher-skinned Hewitt.

Daniel Wallach, executive director of Greensburg GreenTown, described Hewitt as the kind of guy "you want taking the last shot in a basketball game. . . . He has incredible capacity and endurance and that's what has suited him perfectly for the role in this community . . . to help bring it back." While McCollum provided the vision for rebuilding Greensburg, Hewitt's charismatic and transformational leadership ensured that the former mayor's vision became a reality.

Three different mayors have held office since McCollum resigned. To ensure no one impedes the town's progress, Hewitt found himself taking a crash course on interpersonal influence tactics and rational persuasion. "It is what it is, but I have to work with these people and we're gonna get it done," he said. And he has done just that. Hewitt increased his staff from 20 to 35 people and established full-time fire, planning, and community-development departments. To keep Greensburg on the map, he spent hours doing weekly interviews with media from all over the world. At quitting time, he would go to the Federal Emergency Management Agency trailer he shared with his wife and young son. "You know you gotta not just be that team leader, you gotta be that counselor, that friend, and you also gotta be the boss," said Hewitt, a true servant leader, underlining the importance of simultaneously being people- and task-oriented.

"He's has been very open as far as information," said recovery coordinator Kim Alderfer. "He's very good about delegating authority. He gives you the authority to do your job. He doesn't have time to micromanage."

Hewitt wasn't afraid to ruffle feathers. When people opposed the new building codes, Hewitt found the courage, through moral leadership, to say, "No. You're going to build it right and you're going to do it to code." He claimed, "I'm dumb enough not to care what people say, and young enough to have the energy to get through it."

Discussion Questions

1. Would Steve Hewitt be considered a level-five leader? Explain.

2. How does having two distinct leadership roles, mayor and city administrator, create a challenging environment for effective leadership?

3. Is Hewitt a high- or low-dominance leader? Why?

Chapter 13: On the Job Video Case

Motivating Employees

FLIGHT 001

All retail jobs are not created equal. Just ask Amanda Shank. At a previous job, a storeowner bluntly told her, "You're just a number. You can be replaced at any time." Shank said, "When you're told something like that, why would you want to put any effort in?" That sort of callous treatment is hardly an incentive. Luckily, after landing a job at Flight 001, Shank started to feel motivated again.

Flight 001 cofounder Brad John frequently visits his New York stores to talk with staff about what's happening. While visiting Amanda Shank's Brooklyn store, where she had recently been promoted to assistant store manager, John asked if customers were shopping differently after the airlines had added new fees for checked luggage. Shank confirmed John's suspicions and gave him a full report along with recommendations for how they might make adjustments in inventory and merchandising.

Shank is thrilled to have found a place where she can make a contribution and be challenged. "At this company they make an effort to show you you're appreciated; you have a say in what goes on. You're given compliments and feedback about what you could be better at," she explained. Instead of dooming her to dissatisfaction, Flight 001's hygiene factors helped set the stage for her to feel motivated on multiple levels. Working in an environment in which her ideas are valued and put into action meets her needs for recognition, respect, growth, and self-fulfillment. Shank also benefits from a sense of "task significance" because the owners genuinely reinforce the perception that her job is important and has a direct effect on customers and Flight 001's success.

Although opportunities for job enrichment might seem limited in retail, store leader Claire Rainwater involves her crew members in projects that use their strengths. If someone excels at organization and operations, she asks that person to identify and implement an improvement that excites him or her. She gives visually talented associates free reign to create new merchandising displays. Rainwater could easily provide direction on how to approach these tasks, but as a good manager she allows her crew members the autonomy to determine how they want to approach and execute tasks, which ultimately creates a greater sense of empowerment and engagement. If Rainwater merely gave her crew members more variety (job enlargement), they wouldn't learn as much or experience the same degree of achievement.

On the debate about intrinsic versus extrinsic rewards, Rainwater is the first to admit that both rewards would be *more* than satisfactory in an ideal world. She concedes that liking where you work and the people with whom you work engenders a sense of belonging that can offset a less than thrilling paycheck. In general, retail isn't known for generous entry-level compensation. To show up and make an effort, workers need a sense of equity, which probably comes from feeling they're paid fairly in the context of retail. Promotions, which usually involve taking on additional management responsibilities, are the answer for those who seek greater financial rewards. High-end retail also tends to pay better because it requires employees with the skills and competence needed to deliver sophisticated customer service and helpful product information.

A big factor in retail compensation is that, historically, the industry has employed a temporary workforce. Flight 001's head of crew development, Emily Griffin, confirmed that "retail is temporary for a lot of people." Most associates just want to make some money while pursuing other interests such as being students, photographers, musicians, and so on. A career in retail interests only a handful of people. According to Griffin, "There's room for everybody in retail." Customers love the variety of people who work at Flight 001. When visiting a store, customers want to talk to someone interesting and, as Griffin put it, "They don't just want somebody chewing gum behind the register."

Usually, Griffin can tell which associates are passing through and who might stick around. What is interesting is that when she started at Flight 001, Griffin thought *she* was passing through.

Discussion Questions

1. According to Maslow's hierarchy, which basic needs did Shank's old boss fail to meet?

2. How might feeling underpaid affect the work of a Flight 001 associate?

3. Speculate about the possible reasons why Griffin stayed at Flight 001 to pursue a career.

Chapter 14: On the Job Video Case

Communication

GREENSBURG PUBLIC SCHOOLS

Greensburg superintendent Darrin Headrick was driving home the night the tornado hit town. He stopped at Greensburg High School principal Randy Fulton's house to take cover. He soon discovered the entire school system was wiped out. Every building was gone. Textbooks were scattered all over town, and computers were destroyed. Only the bleachers behind the football field remained.

Headrick had some tough decisions to make. To help families feel like it was worth coming back to Greensburg, he had to reassure them school would be back in session by fall. Headrick knew he could turn this tragedy into an opportunity and make the Greensburg schools better than ever.

Along with 95 percent of the town's 1,500 residents, Headrick was homeless. With only four months to restore Greensburg Unified School District 422, Headrick went to work. All he had to work with was his laptop and cell phone, so he got in his truck and started looking for a wireless signal.

For the first three months after the tornado, no one could live in Greensburg. Because the tornado had affected telephone service, no one had a home telephone (landline); people were either in shelters or staying with friends and family out of town. Everyone was eager to reconnect and get information. The Federal Emergency Management Agency provided primary crisis communications by distributing flyers at checkpoints on the edges of town with important updates, but residents had to come to town to get them. Although flyers wouldn't usually be considered a rich channel, they were invaluable under these circumstances.

Unable to access the school's normal communication channels, Headrick took a lesson from his students, who preferred to communicate via text messaging because of its capacity for rapid exchange. Headrick realized text messaging was the perfect new channel for disseminating formal school communications. Few people had computers or landlines, but most folks had cell phones. Those who didn't own cell phones quickly acquired them. Headrick set up a centralized network in which families were able to subscribe to a text service and receive important updates instantly wherever they were.

Once the text service was up and running, Headrick was struck by its efficiency. He also observed students' text messaging habits to see what else he could learn. Even though it wasn't appropriate for the school administration to use the informal shorthand used by students (r u there?), he appreciated students' mastery of the art of keeping messages simple. The school focused on creating clear messages that conveyed the essential information people needed without the usual filler. This new streamlined approach was liberating.

When things stabilized, Headrick set up forums at which students, parents, and teachers could participate in two-way, face-to-face communication. The text service was fabulous, but it didn't allow for real feedback or personal dialogue. Left to its own devices, the school grapevine would surely spread false information.

The community had experienced a traumatic event, and people needed to spend time together to heal. Headrick wanted to check in and make sure everyone understood school really *would* begin as usual. The only way he could be sure people were truly receiving this message was to look them in the eyes, read their body language, and provide other nonverbal reassurances if their facial expressions revealed doubts. He also wanted to listen to students' and teachers' concerns and stories.

Rebuilding will take several years, but thanks to a temporary campus of trailers, the Greensburg schools started on time that fall. Communications within the school have continued to change. Every Greensburg High student now has a laptop and hands in assignments via e-mail. Teachers provide instant feedback on homework through instant messaging. Students can download notes when they miss class. And rather than spending hours trying to track down parents over the phone, teachers use e-mail whenever possible.

The administration, teachers, students, and parents of Greensburg schools still talk to each other in person when it makes sense. The rest of the time, they happily communicate using the latest technologies.

Discussion Questions

1. Describe the advantages and disadvantages of text messaging as the preferred communication channel in Greensburg after the tornado.

2. What lessons can corporate managers take from this story?

3. What was Headrick's vision for Greensburg schools? Why was it important for him to have a vision?

Chapter 15: On the Job Video Case

Teamwork

EVO

Evo had supported a sports team of hard-core athletes for years, but it only recently attempted the experiment of launching a formal workplace team. Like many companies, the online retailer of snowboard, ski, skate, and wake gear had been in the habit of sloppily throwing around team metaphors to describe anything involving random groups of employees. Evo finally got serious about the team concept when the company formed a creative services team.

Evo's creative services team is composed of three full-time members: Tre Dauenhauer, staff photographer; Pubs One, graphic designer; and Sunny Fenton, copywriter. Together they produce magazine ads, all the content for Evo's Web site, and more.

Before being appointed to the team, Dauenhauer realized he and One needed to coordinate their efforts more effectively. One came by Dauenhauer's desk one afternoon to ask if he had any cool photos of fashionable skiers sitting around a picnic table. When Dauenhauer asked when he needed the photo, One responded, "Today." Dauenhauer knew he couldn't find this kind of photo at an online stock agency; he would have to shoot it. Given One's last-minute request, there wasn't enough time for Dauenhauer to help him.

The team's individual roles are far from interchangeable, even though Dauenhauer might dabble in design, One may write a few lines of copy, and Fenton might snap photos on occasion. Their projects require the individual contribution of all three: cool pictures, clever words, and a visually compelling design that brings everything together on the page. They're committed to their common purpose and excited about what they can do together.

When the team first launched, the members moved into their own space, away from Evo's chaotic, open-plan work areas. Being together every day enabled the team members to become better acquainted and move through the "forming" stage more quickly.

Dauenhauer, One, and Fenton needed help navigating the conflict-ridden, storming stage of their team's development. Before joining the team, they functioned individually and weren't used to making decisions as a group or sharing power. Creative types are often independent and opinionated; in art school, most students focus on developing and expressing their creative voices, which can make for a very competitive atmosphere where team assignments are essentially nonexistent.

So to help the team members learn to work together, Nathan Decker, director of e-commerce, became their team leader. The bottom line is that Decker is the boss. He makes sure this talented trio delivers the goods and steers clear of dysfunction. Initially, Evo planned to hire an experienced creative director with knowledge of photography and design to lead the team, but it couldn't comfortably fund the position.

With Decker's skillful negotiation of conflicts, Dauenhauer, One, and Fenton are learning how to communicate with each other in ways that are less likely to escalate into conflict. Having a leader to facilitate difficult conversations has helped build team cohesiveness.

After the creative services team finishes each project, Decker brings everyone together for a postmortem to go over what they learned and how they could do things differently. They also identify new routines and rituals to incorporate into their process.

To work better as a team, Dauenhauer said they're figuring out how to speak a common language. Instead of making vague and confusing comments such as, "The message needs to be bigger," Dauenhauer tries to find more specific feedback, such as "I think the text needs to pop off the page more," or "the message isn't reading well."

Eventually, Dauenhauer thinks they'll need a leader with a creative background, but for now, Decker will keep everyone on the express train from storming to performing.

Discussion Questions

1. What style did the team use to handle conflicts initially? What style(s) are they learning to use?

2. What type of conflict negotiation is Decker using: integrative or distributive?

3. How can Decker effectively lead when the team starts "norming"?

4. How might the team benefit from having a leader with a creative background?

Chapter 1: Biz Flix Video Case

In Good Company

A corporate takeover brings star advertising executive Dan Foreman (Dennis Quaid) a new boss who is half his age. Carter Duryea (Topher Grace), Dan's new boss, wants to prove his worth as the new marketing chief at *Sports America*, Waterman Publishing's flagship magazine. Carter applies his unique approaches while dating Dan's daughter, Alex (Scarlett Johansson).

Management Behavior This sequence starts with Carter Duryea entering Dan Foreman's office. It follows Foreman's interaction with Teddy K. (Malcolm McDowell), Globecom CEO, after Teddy K.'s speech. Carter Duryea enters while saying, "Oh, my God, Dan. Oh, my God." Mark Steckle (Clark Gregg) soon follows. The sequence ends with Carter asking, "Any ideas?" Dan Forman says, "One." The film cuts to the two of them arriving at Eugene Kalb's (Philip Baker Hall) office building.

What to Watch for and Ask Yourself

- Which management skills discussed in this chapter does Mark Steckle possess? Which does he lack?

- The sequence shows three people who represent different hierarchical levels in the company. Which hierarchical levels do you attribute to Carter Duryea, Dan Foreman, and Mark Steckle?

- Critique the behavior shown in the sequence. What are the positive and negative aspects of the behavior shown?

Chapter 2: Biz Flix Video Case

Charlie Wilson's War

Democratic Congressman Charlie Wilson (Tom Hanks) from East Texas lives a reckless life that includes heavy drinking and chasing attractive women. The film focuses on the Afghanistan rebellion against the Soviet occupies in the 1980s. Wilson becomes the unlikely champion of the Afghan cause through his role in two major congressional committees that deal with foreign policy and covert operations. Houston socialite Joanne Herring (Julia Roberts) strongly urges the intervention. CIA agent Gust Avrakotos (Philip Seymour Hoffman) helps with some details.

Organizational Culture Observations This sequence appears early in the film after a scene showing the characters drinking and partying in a hot tub. It opens with a shot of the Capitol building. Congressman Charlie Wilson talks to his assistant Bonnie (Amy Adams) while walking to chambers for a vote. The sequence ends after Wilson enters the chambers. The film cuts to Wilson's office, where Larry Liddle (Peter Gerety) and his daughter Jane (Emily Blunt) wait for Wilson to arrive.

What to Watch for and Ask Yourself

- This chapter discussed organizational culture as having three levels of visibility. Visible artifacts are at the first level and are the easiest to see. Which visible artifacts did you observe in this sequence?

- Values appear at the next level of organizational culture. You can infer a culture's values from the behavior of organizational members. Which values appear in this sequence?

- Organizational members will unconsciously behave according to the basic assumptions of an organization's culture. You also infer these from observed behavior. Which basic assumptions appear in this sequence?

Chapter 3: Biz Flix Video Case

Lost in Translation

Jet lag conspires with culture shock to force the meeting of Charlotte (Scarlett Johansson) and Bob Harris (Bill Murray). Neither can sleep after their Tokyo arrival. They meet in their luxury hotel's bar, forging an enduring relationship as they experience Tokyo's wonders, strangeness, and complexity. Based on director Sophia Coppola's Academy Award–winning screenplay, this film was shot entirely on location in Japan. It offers extraordinary views of various parts of Japanese culture that are not available without visiting.

Cross-Cultural Observations This sequence is an edited composite taken from different parts of *Lost in Translation*. It shows selected aspects of Tokyo and Kyoto,

Japan. Charlotte has her first experience with the complex, busy Tokyo train system. She later takes the train to Kyoto, Japan's original capital city for more than ten centuries.

What to Watch for and Ask Yourself

- While watching this scene, pretend you have arrived in Tokyo and are experiencing what you are seeing. Do you understand everything you see?

- Is Charlotte bewildered by her experiences? Is she experiencing some culture shock?

- What aspects of Japanese culture appear in this scene? What do you see as important values of Japanese culture?

Chapter 4: Biz Flix Video Case

The Emperor's Club

William Hundert (Kevin Kline), a professor at the exclusive Saint Benedict's Academy for Boys, believes in teaching his students about living a principled life. He also wants them to learn his beloved classical literature. A new student, Sedgewick Bell (Emile Hirsch), challenges Hundert's principled ways. Bell's behavior during the 73rd annual Mr. Julius Caesar Contest causes Hundert to suspect that Bell leads a less-than-principled life, a suspicion confirmed years later during a reenactment of the competition.

Ethics and Ethical Behavior Mr. Hundert is the honored guest of his former student Sedgewick Bell (Joel Gretsch) at Bell's estate. Depaak Mehta (Rahul Khanna), Bell, and Louis Masoudi (Patrick Dempsey) compete in a reenactment of the Julius Caesar competition. Bell wins the competition, but Hundert notices that Bell is wearing an earpiece. Earlier in the film, Hundert had suspected that

young Bell wore an earpiece during the competition, but Headmaster Woodbridge (Edward Herrmann) urged him to ignore his suspicion.

This scene appears at the end of the film. It is an edited version of the competition reenactment. Bell announced his candidacy for the U.S. Senate just before he spoke with Hundert in the bathroom. In his announcement, he carefully described his commitment to specific values he would pursue if elected.

What to Watch for and Ask Yourself

- Does William Hundert describe a specific type of life that one should lead? If so, what are its elements?

- Does Sedgewick Bell lead that type of life? Is he committed to any specific view or theory of ethics?

- What consequences or effects do you predict for Sedgewick Bell because of the way he chooses to live his life?

Chapter 5: Biz Flix Video Case

Inside Man

New York City detective Keith Frazier (Denzel Washington) leads an effort to remove Dalton Russell (Clive Owen) and his armed gang from the Manhattan Trust Bank building. Complexities set in when bank chairman Arthur Case (Christopher Plummer) seeks the help of power broker Madeline White (Jodie Foster) to prevent the thieves from getting a particular safe deposit box. This fast-paced action film goes in many directions to reach its unexpected ending.

Planning This scene starts as Captain John Darius (Willem Dafoe) approaches the diner. Detectives Keith

Frazier and Bill Mitchell (Chiwetlel Ejiofor) leave the diner to join Captain Darius. The scene ends after the three men enter the New York Police Department command post after Captain Darius says, "Your call." The film cuts to Madeline White and Arthur Case walking along a river.

What to Watch for and Ask Yourself

- Does this scene show strategic or tactical planning?
- What pieces of the planning type does it specifically show? Give examples from the scene.
- Do you expect this plan to succeed? Why or why not?

Chapter 6: Biz Flix Video Case

Failure to Launch

Meet Tripp (Matthew McConaughey), 35 years old, nice car, loves sailing, and lives in a nice home: his parents' house. Tripp's attachment to his family usually annoys any woman with whom he becomes serious. Mother Sue (Kathy Bates) and father Al (Terry Bradshaw) hire Paula (Sarah Jessica Parker). She specializes in detaching people like Tripp from their families. The term *failure to launch* refers to the failure to move out of the family home at an earlier age.

The Bird Problem: Fast Decision Making! This fast-moving sequence begins with the sound of a bird chirping as it perches on a tree limb. Kit (Zooey Deschanel) and Ace (Justin Bartha) have waited patiently for the bird's arrival. This bird has annoyed Kit for many days.

Ace believes that Kit only pumped the shotgun twice. The sequence ends after the bird leaves the house. The film continues with Kit and Ace embracing and then cuts to a baseball game.

What to Watch for and Ask Yourself

- Does "the bird problem" present Kit and Ace with a programmed or nonprogrammed decision? What features of their decision problem led to your choice?
- Assess the degree of certainty or uncertainty that Kit and Ace face in this decision problem. What factors set the degree of certainty or uncertainty?
- Review the earlier section describing the decision-making steps. Which of those steps appears in "the bird problem?" Note the examples of each step that you see.

Chapter 7: Biz Flix Video Case

Rendition

U.S. government operatives suddenly whisk Anwar el-Ibrahimi (Omar Metwally) from his flight from Cape Town, South Africa, after it arrives in Washington, D.C. He is a suspected terrorist whom the government sends to North Africa for torture and interrogation (extraordinary rendition). Douglas Freeman (Jake Gyllenhaal), a CIA analyst, becomes involved. He reacts negatively to the torture techniques and urges el-Ibrahimi's release. The story has other complications in the form of el-Ibrahimi's pregnant wife at home, who desperately works for her husband's safe return.

Organizational Structure This scene opens with a night shot of the Washington monument. It follows a discussion between Kahlid (Moa Khouas) and Hamadi (Hassam Ghancy), the leader of the terrorist bomb group. Congressional aide Alan Smith's (Peter Sarsgaard) voice-over asks, "She called you?" The scene ends after Senator Hawkins (Alan Arkin) tells Alan to back off. The film cuts to a panning shot of a market area and Douglas Freeman drinking.

Alan Smith's question, "She called you?" refers to Corrine Whitman (Meryl Streep), head of U.S. intelligence. She authorized the extraordinary rendition of el-Ibrahimi. Alan Smith, earlier in the film, pressed her for el-Ibrahimi's release and his return to the United States. Whitman lied about el-Ibrahimi's existence. This scene does not explicitly discuss organizational structure, but you can infer several aspects of structure from the scene.

What to Watch for and Ask Yourself

- What formal tasks does this scene imply? What reporting relationships does it show?
- Can you sense the division of labor represented by Senator Hawkins and Alan Smith? Corrine Whitman does not appear in this scene but is also part of a division of labor.
- Does the scene show line authority or staff authority? Does it imply a functional or divisional structure? Give some examples from the scene.

Chapter 8: Biz Flix Video Case

Field of Dreams

Ray Kinsella (Kevin Costner) hears a voice while working in his Iowa cornfield that says, "If you build it, he will come." Ray concludes that "he" is the legendary "Shoeless Joe" Jackson (Ray Liotta), a 1919 Chicago White Sox player suspended for supposedly taking part in "throwing" the 1919 World Series. With the support of his wife, Annie (Amy Madigan), Ray jeopardizes his farm by replacing some cornfields with a modern baseball diamond. Shoeless Joe soon arrives, followed by the rest of the suspended players. This charming fantasy film, based on W. P. Kinsellas's novel *Shoeless Joe*, shows the rewards of pursuing a dream.

Forces for Change This scene is part of the "People Will Come" sequence toward the end of the film. By this time in the story, Ray has met Terrence Mann (James Earl Jones). They have traveled together from Boston to Minnesota to find A. W. "Moonlight" Graham (Burt Lancaster). At this point, the three are at Ray's Iowa farm.

This scene follows Mark's (Timothy Busfield) arrival to discuss the foreclosure of Ray and Annie's mortgage. Mark, who is Annie's brother, cannot see the players on the field. Karin (Gaby Hoffman), Ray and Annie's daughter, has proposed that people will come to Iowa City and buy tickets to watch a baseball game. Mark does not understand her proposal. The film continues to its end.

What to Watch for and Ask Yourself

- Who is the target of change in this scene?
- What are the forces for change? Are the forces for change internal or external to the change target?
- Does the scene show the role of leadership in organizational change? If it does, who is the leader? What does this person do to get desired change?

Chapter 9: Biz Flix Video Case

Played

Ray Burns (Mick Rossi) does prison time for a crime he did not commit. After his release, he focuses on getting even with his enemies. This fast-moving film peers deeply into London's criminal world, which includes some crooked London police, especially Detective Brice (Vinnie Jones). The film's unusual ending reviews all major parts of the plot.

Recruitment These scenes begin with a close-up of a photograph of an ape that Riley (Patrick Bergin) carefully examines. We follow Detective Brice's order to Riley to kill the person who will not give them money. Riley shoots him in a pub. The scenes end after Ray Burns accepts Riley's offer. He walks away saying, "All right. Let's rock and roll, man. All right. Thanks, Riley." Riley says, "Thank you, Ray."

The film cuts to Terry (Trevor Nugent) talking to Nikki (Meridith Ostrom) before Ray's arrival.

What to Watch for and Ask Yourself

- This chapter emphasized a strategic approach to human-resource management. Detective Brice outlines a strategy in the opening of these scenes for the job he describes to Riley. What are the key parts of that strategy? What are the human-resource implications of the strategy?

- Riley's next step is to recruit Ray Burns. Which recruitment guidelines and activities does he follow? Give examples from that portion of the film scenes.

- Does Riley give Ray a "realistic job preview"? Use examples from the film scenes to support your answer.

Chapter 10: Biz Flix Video Case

In Bruges

Hit man Ray (Colin Farrell) botches the simple job of murdering a priest in a confessional. The "botch" occurs when a bullet passes through the priest's body into a young boy's head. Deeply troubled, Ray and fellow hit man Ken (Brendan Gleeson) go to the beautiful medieval Flemish city of Bruges, Belgium. Ken engages in tourist activities, which Ray finds highly boring. Various characters, such as an American dwarf actor and a beautiful woman selling drugs on a film set, add color and interest to this film.

Customer Focus This sequence has two parts that are separated by a title slide that reads "And another interaction for the ticket seller." Watch Part I up to the title slide and pause the film. Answer the first two questions. Restart the film sequence and play to the end. Answer the third question.

Part I. This sequence starts as Ken enters the tower to buy a ticket. It ends after he asks the ticket seller (Rudy Blomme) whether he is happy. This sequence follows the discussion about the city of Bruges between Ken and Ray.

Part II. This sequence begins as Ken and Harry Waters (Ralph Fiennes) approach the bell tower. It follows their discussion over beers about where Harry should shoot Ken. The ticket seller tells Ken that the tower is closed because a visitor had a heart attack. This sequence ends after Harry's interaction with the ticker seller. The film continues with various scenes based on the plaza.

What to Watch for and Ask Yourself

- Ken is the customer, and the ticket seller responds to him as a customer. Do you perceive the ticket seller as having a customer focus as emphasized in this chapter? Why or why not?

- The ticket seller will interact with Ken and Harry Waters in Part II of this film sequence. Do you predict that the ticket seller's customer approach could result in negative results for him? Why or why not?

- Part II offers a lesson in customer focus. What did the ticket seller fail to understand about his customers?

Chapter 11: Biz Flix Video Case

Because I Said So

Meet Daphne Wilder (Diane Keaton)—your typical meddling, overprotective, and divorced mother of three daughters. Two of her three beautiful daughters have married. That leaves Millie (Mandy Moore) as the focus of Daphne's undivided attention and compulsive behavior to find Millie a mate. Daphne places some online advertising, screens the applicants, and submits those she approves to Millie. Along the way, Daphne meets Joe (Stephen Collins), the father of one applicant. Romance emerges, and the film comes to a delightful, though expected, conclusion.

Personality Assessment This scene starts after Daphne answers her cell phone and says the person has the wrong number. It follows the frantic rearrangement of the sofa, which ends up in the same place it started. The film cuts to Millie and Jason (Tom Everett Scott) dining at his place.

What to Watch for and Ask Yourself

- Which Big Five personality traits best describe Daphne? Give examples of behavior from the film scene to support your observations.
- Which Big Five personality traits best describe Millie? Give examples of behavior from the film scene to support your observations.
- Review the discussion of emotional intelligence earlier in this chapter. Assess both Daphne and Millie on the four parts of emotional intelligence.

Chapter 12: Biz Flix Video Case

Doomsday

The Reaper virus strikes Glasgow, Scotland, on April 3, 2008. It spreads and devastates the population throughout Scotland. Authorities seal off the borders and do not allow anyone to enter or leave the country. No aircraft flyovers are permitted. Social decay spreads, and cannibalistic behavior develops among the few remaining survivors. Eventually, no one is left alive in the quarantined area. The Reaper virus reemerges in 2032, this time in London, England. Classified satellite images show life in Glasgow and Edinburgh. Prime Minister John Hatcher (Alexander Siddig) and his assistant Michael Canaris (David O'Hara) assign the task of finding the cure to Security Chief Bill Nelson (Bob Hoskins).

Leadership This sequence starts at the beginning of DVD Chapter 4, "No Rules, No Backup" with a shot of the Department of Domestic Security emblem. The film cuts to Major Eden Sinclair (Rhona Mitra) standing in the rain smoking a cigarette while waiting for Chief Nelson. The sequence ends after Michael Canaris leaves the helicopter while saying to Sinclair, "Then you needn't bother coming back." He closes the helicopter's door. Major Sinclair blows her hair from her face while pondering his last statement. The film cuts to the helicopter lifting off the tarmac.

What to Watch for and Ask Yourself

- Assess the behavior of both Major Sinclair and Michael Canaris. Which leadership traits discussed earlier and shown in Exhibit 12.3 (page 387) does their behavior show?
- Apply the behavioral approaches to leadership discussed earlier in this chapter. Which parts apply to Sinclair and Canaris's behavior? Draw specific examples from the film sequence.
- Does this film sequence show any aspects of charismatic and transformational leadership? Draw some examples from the sequence.

Chapter 13: Biz Flix Video Case

Friday Night Lights (I)

The Odessa, Texas, passion for Friday night high school football comes through clearly in this cinematic treatment of H. G. (Buzz) Bissinger's well-regarded book of the same title.[57] Coach Gary Gaines (Billy Bob Thornton) leads the Permian High Panthers to the 1988 semifinals where it must compete against a team of much larger players. Fast-moving pace in the football sequences and a slower pace in the serious, introspective sequences give this film many fine moments.

Motivation This sequence starts with a panning shot of the Winchell's house. Coach Gaines says to Mike Winchell (Lucas Black), "Can you get the job done, Mike?" The sequence follows a harsh practice and Mike talking to his brother or sister from a telephone booth. The film continues with the Odessa-Permian versus Cooper football game.

What to Watch for and Ask Yourself

- This chapter defined motivation as "the forces either within or external to a person that arouse enthusiasm and persistence to pursue a certain course of action." Does Mike Winchell show the characteristics of this definition early in the sequence? Do you expect him to show any of the characteristics after the sequence ends and he returns to the team?

- Which needs discussed earlier in this chapter does Mike appear focused on early in the sequence? Which needs can become his focus later in the sequence? See the hierarchy of needs theory and ERG theory sections earlier in the chapter for some suggestions.

- Apply the various parts of goal-setting theory to this sequence. Which parts of that theory appear in this sequence?

Chapter 14: Biz Flix Video Case

Friday Night Lights (II)

The Odessa, Texas, passion for Friday night high school football comes through clearly in this cinematic treatment of H. G. (Buzz) Bissinger's well-regarded book of the same title.[70] Coach Gary Gaines (Billy Bob Thornton) leads the Permian High Panthers to the 1988 semifinals where it must compete against a team of much larger players. A fast-moving pace in the football sequences and a slower pace in the serious, introspective sequences give this film many fine moments.

Communication This sequence[71] begins with a shot of Coach Gaines and the team gathered around him during the half-time break. He starts his speech to the team by saying, "Well, it's real simple. You got two more quarters and that's it." It ends after Gaines says, "Boys, my heart is full. My heart's full."

What to Watch for and Ask Yourself

- This chapter emphasized the speaker and the listener(s) in the communication process. Coach Gaines is the speaker, and team members and assistant coaches are listeners. Only Gaines spoke. Did he still meet the basic requirements of effective communication? Draw examples from his speech to support your conclusions.

- This chapter distinguished between purpose-directed communication and strategic conversation. Which of these communication types best fits this sequence? Draw examples from the sequence to make your point.

- Assess the effectiveness of this communication event. How do you expect team members and the assistant coaches to react in the second half of the game?

Chapter 15: Biz Flix Video Case

Welcome Home, Roscoe Jenkins

Hollywood talk-show host Roscoe Jenkins (Martin Lawrence) returns to his Georgia home for his parents' 50th wedding anniversary. Cultures clash between the big-city Roscoe and other family members. The culture clash becomes even more severe because of the presence of his upper-class fiancée, Bianca Kittles (Joy Bryant), who does not understand this family and feels superior to them.

Conflict: It Can Sneak Up on You This sequence starts with Roscoe and his brother, Sheriff Otis Jenkins (Michael Clarke Duncan), carrying a tub of fish and ice from Monty's butcher shop to Sheriff Jenkins's pickup truck. It follows the baseball game during which Roscoe hit a ball that struck Mama Jenkins (Margaret Avery) in the head. This sequence ends after Sheriff Jenkins knocks out his brother. The film continues with Roscoe walking down a dirt road. Betty (Mo'Nique) approaches in her car.

What to Watch for and Ask Yourself

- Based on your understanding of a team as described in this chapter, do Roscoe Jenkins and his brother, Sheriff Otis Jenkins, form a team in this film sequence? Why or why not?

- This chapter defined conflict as "antagonistic interaction in which one party attempts to block the intentions or goals of another." Does the interaction in this film sequence show this definition in action? Give examples from the sequence.

- Which conflict-handling style best fits the behavior shown in this film sequence? Give some examples from the sequence.

Welcome Home, Roscoe Jenkins

Managing Small Business Start-ups
Do You Think Like an Entrepreneur?[1]

An entrepreneur faces many demands. Do you have the proclivity to start and build your own business? To find out, consider the extent to which each of the following statements characterizes your behavior. Please answer each of the following items as Mostly True or Mostly False for you.

	MOSTLY TRUE	MOSTLY FALSE
1. Give me a little information and I can come up with a lot of ideas.	_____	_____
2. I like pressure in order to focus.	_____	_____
3. I don't easily get frustrated when things don't go my way.	_____	_____
4. I identify how resources can be recombined to produce novel outcomes.	_____	_____
5. I enjoy competing against the clock to meet deadlines.	_____	_____
6. People in my life have to accept that nothing is more important than the achievement of my school, my sport, or my career goals.	_____	_____
7. I serve as a role model for creativity.	_____	_____
8. I think "on my feet" when carrying out tasks.	_____	_____
9. I am determined and action-oriented.	_____	_____

SCORING AND INTERPRETATION: Each question pertains to some aspect of improvisation, which is a correlate of entrepreneurial intentions. Entrepreneurial improvisation consists of three elements. Questions 1, 4, and 7 pertain to creativity or ingenuity, the ability to produce novel solutions under constrained conditions. Questions 2, 5, and 8 pertain to working under pressure or stress, the ability to excel under pressure-filled circumstances. Questions 3, 6, and 9 pertain to action or persistence, the determination to achieve goals and solve problems in the moment. If you answered Mostly True to at least two of three questions for each subscale or six of nine for all the questions, then consider yourself an entrepreneur in the making with the potential to manage your own business. If you scored one or fewer Mostly True on each subscale or three or fewer for all nine questions, then you might want to consider becoming a manager by working for someone else.

Many people dream of starting their own business. Some decide to start a business because they're inspired by a great idea or want the flexibility that comes from being self-employed. Others decide to go into business for themselves after they get laid off or find their opportunities limited in big companies. Interest in entrepreneurship and small business is at an all-time high. At college campuses across the United States, ambitious courses, programs, and centers teach the fundamentals of starting a small business. Entrepreneurs have access to business incubators, support networks, and online training courses. The enormous growth of franchising gives beginners an escorted route into a new business. In addition, the Internet opens new avenues for small business formation.

Today, the fastest-growing segment of small business in both the United States and Canada is in one-owner operations, or *sole proprietorships*.[2] Sole proprietorships in the United States reached an all-time high of 19.5 million in 2004, the most recent year with statistics available.[3] After the crash of the dot-com boom, many of these entrepreneurs are finding opportunities in low-tech businesses such as landscaping, child care, and janitorial services. Overall, since the 1970s, the number of businesses in the United States economy has been growing faster than the labor force.[4]

However, running a small business is difficult and risky. The U.S. Small Business Administration (SBA) reports that about 30 percent of small businesses fail within two years of opening, and 56 percent fold after four years.[5] For high-tech businesses, the failure rate is even higher. Research indicates that the chances are only 6 in 1 million that an idea for a high-tech business eventually turns into a successful public company.[6] Despite these risks, people are entering the world of entrepreneurship at an unprecedented rate. In 2006, an estimated 649,700 new businesses were established in the United States, while an estimated 564,700 closed their doors for good.[7] Small-business formation is the primary process by which an economy recreates and reinvents itself,[8] and the turbulence in the small-business environment is evidence of a shifting but thriving U.S. economy.

What Is Entrepreneurship?

Entrepreneurship is the process of initiating a business venture, organizing the necessary resources, and assuming the associated risks and rewards.[9] An **entrepreneur** is someone who engages in entrepreneurship. An entrepreneur recognizes a viable idea for a business product or service and carries it out by finding and assembling the necessary resources—money, people, machinery, location—to undertake the business venture. Entrepreneurs also assume the risks and reap the rewards of the business. They assume the financial and legal risks of ownership and receive the business's profits.

A good example of entrepreneurship is Jeff Fluhr, who dropped out of Stanford during his first year of graduate school to launch StubHub, a leading Internet player in the burgeoning market of ticket reselling, an industry that may be doing as much as $10 billion a year in volume. Hardworking and persistent, Fluhr struggled to raise money during the early days of the business, a time when many investors had been stung by the dot-com crash. His tenacity paid off as he convinced executives from Viacom Inc., Home Box Office, and Madison Square Garden to invest in his plan to reinvent the online ticket-resale industry. StubHub gives consumers access to high-demand concert, theater, and

entrepreneurship
The process of initiating a business venture, organizing the necessary resources, and assuming the associated risks and rewards.

entrepreneur
Someone who recognizes a viable idea for a business product or service and carries it out.

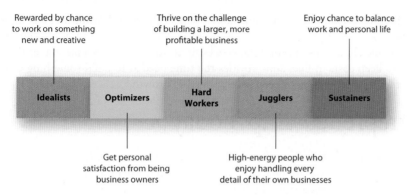

SOURCE: Based on a study conducted by Yankelovich Partners for Pitney Bowes in Mark Henricks, "Type-Cast," *Entrepreneur* (Mar. 2000): 14–16.

EXHIBIT A.1
Five Types of Small-Business Owners

sporting events that are usually unavailable because promoters now reserve large blocks of tickets for fan-club members, season-ticket holders, and sponsors. StubHub allows sellers to list tickets at StubHub—free of charge—and sell them either by auction or at a fixed price. The company's two call centers receive approximately 2,500 calls a day and sell more than $200 million worth of tickets annually.[10] Fluhr, who comes from a family of entrepreneurs, was willing to take the risks and is now reaping the rewards of entrepreneurship.

Successful entrepreneurs have many different motivations, and they measure rewards in different ways. One study classified small-business owners in five different categories, as illustrated in Exhibit A.1. Some people are *idealists*, who like the idea of working on something that is new, creative, or personally meaningful. *Optimizers* are rewarded by the personal satisfaction of being business owners. Entrepreneurs in the *sustainer* category like the chance to balance work and personal life and often don't want the business to grow too large, while *hard workers* enjoy putting in the long hours and dedication to build a larger, more profitable business. The *juggler* category includes entrepreneurs who like the chance a small business gives them to handle everything themselves. These high-energy people thrive on the pressure of paying bills, meeting deadlines, and making payroll.[11]

Compare the motivation of Paula Turpin to that of Greg Littlefield. Turpin borrowed a few thousand dollars to start a hair salon, Truly Blessed Styles, in Shirley, New York. She does all the cutting, styling, and coloring herself, while her mother helps schedule appointments and keeps the books. Turpin likes the flexibility and freedom of working for herself. Although she hopes to expand by adding beauty supplies, she doesn't want the headaches of managing a large business. Greg Littlefield quit his management job and started a cleaning service because he reasoned that it would never lack customers. From the beginning, when he was working two part-time jobs and cleaning buildings by himself at night, Littlefield had plans for expansion. Within a decade, Littlefield's firm, Professional Facilities Management, grew into a 900-employee company providing a range of services including housekeeping, landscaping, minor maintenance, and security services.[12] Greg Littlefield reflects the motivation of a *hard worker*, whereas Paula Turpin's motivation is more that of a *sustainer*.

Sometimes people start new businesses when they lose their jobs due to corporate downsizing. The major layoffs in the early 2000s provided just the push some latent entrepreneurs needed to strike out on their own. Some experts think an economic downturn is actually the best time to start a business. For one thing, a downturn opens up lots of opportunities because people are looking for lower costs and better ways of doing things. The economic climate also enables the new business to hire good people, forces the entrepreneur to keep costs in line, and provides the time needed to build something of lasting value rather than struggling to keep pace with rapid growth.[13]

Entrepreneurship Today

Not so long ago, scholars and policy makers worried about the potential of small business to survive. The turbulence in the technology sector and the demise of many dot-com start-ups heightened concerns about whether small companies can compete with big business. However, entrepreneurship and small business, including high-tech start-ups, are vital, dynamic, and increasingly important parts of the U.S. economy. Small businesses represent 99.7 percent of all firms and employ about half of all private-sector employees. In addition, small businesses have generated 60 percent to 80 percent of new jobs annually over the last decade.[14]

Entrepreneurship in other countries is also booming. The list of entrepreneurial countries around the world, shown in Exhibit A.2, is intriguing. A project monitoring entrepreneurial activity around the world reports that an estimated 47.4 percent of adults age 18

EXHIBIT A.2
Entrepreneurial Countries Around the World

Country	Percentage of Individuals Age 18 to 64 Active in Starting or Managing a New Business, 2007
Thailand	47.4
Peru	39.0
Colombia	33.6
Venezuela	24.9
China	24.6
Argentina	24.1
Dominican Republic	23.2
Brazil	22.4
Chile	21.4
Iceland	19.8
Greece	18.7
Uruguay	18.5
Ireland	16.8
Portugal	15.4
Hong Kong	15.0

SOURCE: Table 1, "Prevalence Rates of Entrepreneurial Activity Across Countries, 2007," in Niels Bosma, Kent Jones, Erkko Autio, and Jonathan Levie, *Global Entrepreneurship Monitor 2007 Executive Report* (Babson College and the London Business School), March 14, 2008. Permission to reproduce this table has been kindly granted by the copyright holders. The GEM is an international consortium comprising 42 countries in 2007. Our thanks go to the authors, researchers, funding bodies and other contributors who have made this possible.

to 64 in Thailand are either starting up or managing new enterprises. The percentage in Peru is 39 percent; in Colombia, 33.6 percent. China and Argentina also show higher rates of entrepreneurial activity than the U.S. rate of 14.1 percent. China's boost in entrepreneurial activity continues to increase due to the rapid expansion of the Chinese economy, especially in the big cities.[15]

DEFINITION OF SMALL BUSINESS

The U.S. Small Business Administration defines a small business as "one that is independently owned and operated and which is not dominant in its field of operation."[16] Exhibit A.3 gives a few examples of how the SBA defines small business for a sample of industries.

However, the definition of small business is currently under revision in response to concerns from small-business owners. After nationwide public hearings, the SBA determined that standards should be changed in light of shifting economic and industry conditions. Redefining small-business size standards is a daunting task, but SBA leaders agree that the standards need to be more flexible in today's world. The SBA's definition has been revised a number of times over the years to reflect changing economic conditions.[17]

Exhibit A.3 also illustrates general categories of businesses most entrepreneurs start: manufacturing, retail, and Internet services. Additional categories of small businesses are construction, hospitality, communications, finance, and real estate.

IMPACT OF ENTREPRENEURIAL COMPANIES

The impact of entrepreneurial companies on the U.S. economy is astonishing. According to the Small Business Administration, businesses with fewer than 500 employees represent 99.7 percent of all firms with employees in the United States, employ more than 50 percent of the nation's nonfarm private sector workers, and generate more than 50 percent of the

Manufacturing	
Soft-drink manufacturing	Number of employees does not exceed 500
Electronic computer manufacturing	Number of employees does not exceed 1,000
Prerecorded CD, tape, and record producing	Number of employees does not exceed 750
Retail (Store and Nonstore)	
Sporting goods stores	Average annual receipts do not exceed $6.5 million
Electronic auctions	Average annual receipts do not exceed $23.0 million
Convenience stores	Average annual receipts do not exceed $6.5 million
Miscellaneous Internet Services	
Internet service providers	Average annual receipts do not exceed $23.0 million
Web search portals	Average annual receipts do not exceed $6.5 million
Internet publishing and broadcasting	Number of employees does not exceed 500

EXHIBIT A.3
Examples of SBA Definitions of Small Business

SOURCE: U.S. Small Business Administration, *Table of Small-Business Size Standards Matched to North American Industry Classification System Codes* (www.sba.gov/idc/groups/public/documents/sba_homepage/serv_sstd_tablepdf.pdf) (accessed June 23, 2008).

nation's nonfarm gross domestic product. In addition, small businesses represent 97 percent of America's exporters and produce 28.6 percent of all export value.[18] In 2000, the status of the SBA administrator was elevated to a cabinet-level position in recognition of the importance of small business in the U.S. economy.[19]

Inspired by the growth of companies such as eBay, Google, and Amazon.com, entrepreneurs are still flocking to the Internet to start new businesses. In addition, demographic and lifestyle trends create new opportunities in areas such as environmental services, lawn care, computer maintenance, children's markets, fitness, and home health care. Entrepreneurship and small business in the United States is an engine for job creation and innovation.

- **Job Creation**. Researchers disagree over what percentage of new jobs is created by small business. Research indicates that the *age* of a company, more than its size, determines the number of jobs it creates. In other words, virtually *all* new jobs in recent years have come from new companies, which include not only small companies but also new branches of huge, multinational organizations.[20] However, small companies still are thought to create a large percentage of new jobs in the United States. The SBA reports that small businesses create 65 percent or more of America's new jobs. Jobs created by small businesses give the United States an economic vitality no other country can claim. However, as reflected in Exhibit A.2 earlier in this appendix (page 542), entrepreneurial economic activity is dramatically expanding in other countries as well.

- **Innovation**. According to Cognetics, Inc., a research firm run by David Birch that traces the employment and sales records of some 9 million companies, new and smaller firms have been responsible for 55 percent of the innovations in 362 different industries and 95 percent of all radical innovations. In addition, fast-growing businesses, which Birch calls *gazelles*, produce twice as many product innovations per employee as do larger firms. Small firms that file for patents typically produce 13 to 14 times more patents per employee than large patenting firms.[21] Among the notable products for which small businesses can be credited are WD-40, the jet engine, and the shopping cart.

Who Are Entrepreneurs?

The heroes of American business—Henry Ford, Steve Jobs, Sam Walton, Bill Gates, Oprah Winfrey, Larry Page, Sergey Brin—are almost always entrepreneurs. Entrepreneurs start with a vision. Often they are unhappy with their current jobs and see an opportunity to bring together the resources needed for a new venture. However, the image of entrepreneurs as bold pioneers probably is overly romantic. A survey of the CEOs of the nation's fastest-growing small firms found that these entrepreneurs could be best characterized as hardworking and practical, with great familiarity with their market and industry.[22] For example, Jason Goldberg, T-Mobile USA's former strategic-planning director, grew frustrated with the flood of unqualified candidates he received from popular job boards so he created Jobster as a new approach to online recruiting. Jobster takes advantage of the referring power of a social network, meaning that every job candidate is recommended by a trusted reference. Job recruiters reduce their risk of hiring an unknown candidate when they hire someone who comes with a referral. Striking a nerve with the hiring community, Jobster has signed 475 corporate clients since its launch in 2005, and its roster of clients is growing 30 percent every year.[23]

DIVERSITY OF ENTREPRENEURS

Entrepreneurs often have backgrounds and demographic characteristics that distinguish them from other people. Entrepreneurs are more likely to be the first-born within their families, and their parents are more likely to have been entrepreneurs. In addition, immigrants are more likely to start small businesses than native-born Americans.[24] Consider former veterinarian Salvador Guzman, who moved from Mexico to become a busboy in a friend's Mexican restaurant in Nashville, Tennessee. Energized by the opportunities to succeed in the United States as an entrepreneur, Guzman started his own restaurant with three partners and a savings of $18,000, joining more than 2.4 million self-employed immigrants in the United States. Now he owns 14 restaurants and the first Spanish-language radio station in Tennessee.[25]

Entrepreneurship offers opportunities for individuals who may feel blocked in established corporations. Women-owned and minority-owned businesses may be the emerging growth companies of the next decade. In 2005, women owned 6.5 million U.S. businesses that generated $950.6 billion in revenues and employed more than 7 million workers. In Canada as well, women entrepreneurs are thriving. Since 1989, the rate of small businesses started by women in Canada grew 60 percent faster than the growth in the number of small businesses started by men.[26] Statistics for minorities in the United States are also impressive, with minorities owning 4.1 million firms that generated $694 billion in revenues and employed 4.8 million people.[27] The number of new firms launched by minorities is growing about 17 percent a year, with African American businesses growing at a rate of about 26 percent a year. African American males between the ages of 25 and 35 start more businesses than any other group in the country. Moreover, the face of entrepreneurship for the future will be increasingly diverse. When Junior Achievement (an organization that educates young people about business) conducted a poll of teenagers ages 13 to 18, it found a much greater interest among minorities than whites in starting a business, as shown in Exhibit A.4.[28]

The types of businesses launched by minority entrepreneurs are also increasingly sophisticated. The traditional minority-owned mom-and-pop retail store or restaurant is being

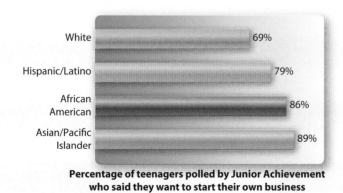

Percentage of teenagers polled by Junior Achievement who said they want to start their own business

White 69%
Hispanic/Latino 79%
African American 86%
Asian/Pacific Islander 89%

SOURCE: Junior Achievement Survey results reported in Cora Daniels, "Minority Rule," *FSB* (December 2003–January 2004): 65–66.

EXHIBIT A.4
A Glimpse of Tomorrow's Entrepreneurs

replaced by firms in industries such as financial services, insurance, and media. For example, Pat Winans, an African American who grew up in a Chicago ghetto, started Magna Securities, a successful institutional brokerage firm in New York City, with just $5,000. Ed Chin, a third-generation Chinese American, founded AIS Corporation to offer small and midsized companies the kind of sophisticated insurance packages usually available only to large companies. Chin originally found a niche by catering to the Asian marketplace, but word of mouth has helped his company expand beyond that market.[29]

PERSONALITY TRAITS

A number of studies have investigated the personality characteristics of entrepreneurs and how they differ from successful managers in established organizations. Some suggest that entrepreneurs in general want something different from life than do traditional managers. Entrepreneurs seem to place high importance on being free to achieve and maximize their potential. Some 40 traits are identified as being associated with entrepreneurship, but 6 have special importance.[30] These characteristics are illustrated in Exhibit A.5.

Internal Locus of Control. The task of starting and running a new business requires the belief that you can make things come out the way you want. The entrepreneur not only has a vision but also must be able to plan to achieve that vision and believe it will happen. An **internal locus of control** is the belief by individuals that their future is within their control and that external forces have little influence. For entrepreneurs, reaching the future is seen as being in the hands of the individual. Many people, however, feel that the world is highly uncertain and that they are unable to make things come out the way they want. An **external locus of control** is the belief by individuals that their future is not within their control but rather is influenced by external forces. Entrepreneurs are individuals who are convinced they can make the difference between success and failure; hence, they are motivated to take the steps needed to achieve the goal of setting up and running a new business.

internal locus of control
The belief by individuals that their future is within their control and that external forces have little influence.

external locus of control
The belief by individuals that their future is not within their control but is influenced by external forces.

EXHIBIT A.5
Characteristics of Entrepreneurs

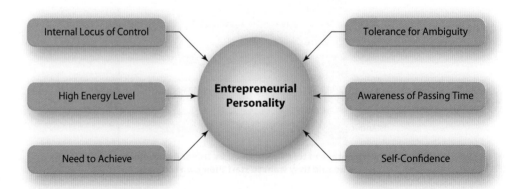

SOURCE: Adapted from Charles R. Kuehl and Peggy A. Lambing, *Small Business: Planning and Management* (Ft. Worth, TX: Dryden Press, 1994): 45.

High Energy Level. A business start-up requires great effort. Most entrepreneurs report struggle and hardship. They persist and work incredibly hard despite traumas and obstacles. A survey of business owners reported that half worked 60 hours or more per week. Another reported that entrepreneurs worked long hours, but that beyond 70 hours little benefit was gained. New business owners work long hours, with only 23 percent working fewer than 50 hours, which is close to a normal workweek for managers in established businesses.

Need to Achieve. Another human quality closely linked to entrepreneurship is the **need to achieve**, which means that people are motivated to excel and pick situations in which success is likely.[31] People who have high achievement needs like to set their own goals, which are moderately difficult. Easy goals present no challenge; unrealistically difficult goals cannot be achieved. Intermediate goals are challenging and provide great satisfaction when achieved. High achievers also like to pursue goals for which they can obtain feedback about their success.

Self-Confidence. People who start and run a business must act decisively. They need confidence about their ability to master the day-to-day tasks of the business. They must feel sure about their ability to win customers, handle the technical details, and keep the business moving. Entrepreneurs also have a general feeling of confidence that they can deal with anything in the future; complex, unanticipated problems can be handled as they arise.

Awareness of Passing Time. Entrepreneurs tend to be impatient; they feel a sense of urgency. They want things to progress as if there is no tomorrow. They want things moving immediately and seldom procrastinate. Entrepreneurs seize the moment.

Tolerance for Ambiguity. Many people need work situations characterized by clear structure, specific instructions, and complete information. **Tolerance for ambiguity** is the psychological characteristic that allows a person to be untroubled by disorder and uncertainty. This trait is important because few situations present more uncertainty than starting a new business. Decisions are made without clear understanding of options or certainty about which option will succeed.

These personality traits and the demographic characteristics discussed earlier offer an insightful but imprecise picture of the entrepreneur. Successful entrepreneurs come in all ages, from all backgrounds, and they may have a combination of personality traits. No one should be discouraged from starting a business because he or she doesn't fit a specific profile. One review of small business suggests that the three most important traits of successful entrepreneurs, particularly in a turbulent environment, are realism, flexibility, and passion. Even the most realistic entrepreneurs tend to underestimate the difficulties of building a business, so they need flexibility and a passion for their idea to survive the hurdles.[32]

Social Entrepreneurship: An Innovative Approach to Small Business

In today's shifting business and social environment, a new breed of entrepreneur has emerged—the **social entrepreneur**. Social entrepreneurs are leaders who are committed to both good business and positive social change. They create new business models that

need to achieve
A human quality linked to entrepreneurship in which people are motivated to excel and pick situations in which success is likely.

tolerance for ambiguity
The psychological characteristic that allows a person to be untroubled by disorder and uncertainty.

social entrepreneur
Entrepreneurial leaders who are committed to both good business and changing the world for the better.

meet critical human needs and solve important problems that remain unsolved by current economic and social institutions.[33] Consider Earl Martin Phalen, who founded Building Educated Leaders for Life (BELL) out of his Boston living room in 1992 to provide after-school and summer support services to low-income students in grades K–6. As an African American growing up in the state's foster-care system, Phalen understood firsthand how the right kind of support can change lives and communities. "To know that [somebody] supported me, and all of a sudden, it took my life from going to jail to going to Yale," he says of his motivation to start BELL. All 20 students in BELL's first class went on to college.[34]

Social entrepreneurship combines the creativity, business smarts, passion, and hard work of the traditional entrepreneur with a mission to change the world for the better. One writer referred to this new breed as a cross between Richard Branson, the high-powered CEO of Virgin Airlines, and Mother Teresa, a Catholic nun who dedicated her life to serving the poor.[35] Social entrepreneurs have a primary goal of improving society rather than maximizing profits, but they also emphasize solid business results, high performance standards, and accountability for results. The organizations created by social entrepreneurs may or may not make a profit, but the bottom line for these companies is always social betterment rather than economic return. For entrepreneur Peter Thum, founder of Ethos Water, the purpose of his business was to sell expensive bottled water in the West in stores like Starbucks and donate part of the profits to clean-water initiatives in developing countries such as Honduras and Kenya. By 2010, Ethos will give more than $10 million a year to nonprofits that fund safe-water projects.[36]

Social entrepreneurship is not new, but the phenomenon has blossomed over the past 20 or so years. Exact figures for the number of social entrepreneurs are difficult to verify, but estimates number in the tens of thousands working around the world. The innovative organizations created by social entrepreneurs are defying the traditional boundaries between business and welfare.[37] One good illustration is Homeboy Industries, a company that started 12 years ago in a converted warehouse in Los Angeles. With 18 employees, Homeboy emphasizes rehabilitation of former gang members over revenue. The silk-screening part of the business generated $1.1 million in 2008, and the bakery produced another $3 million in revenue. Jesuit priest and founder Reverend Gregory Boyle explains that the "cash-producing part of the business brings in enough to pay for the free services." These services include therapy for former gang members, housing assistance, job development, counseling, and tattoo-removal treatments. Boyle's goal is to hire and train the neighborhood's young men to break the cycle of gangs, crime, and imprisonment.[38]

Launching an Entrepreneurial Start-Up

Whether one starts a socially oriented company or a traditional for-profit small business, the first step in pursuing an entrepreneurial dream is to come up with a viable idea and then plan like crazy. Once someone has a new idea in mind, a business plan must be drawn and decisions must be made about legal structure, financing, and basic tactics, such as whether to start the business from scratch and whether to pursue international opportunities from the start.

Reasons for Starting a Business

41% Joined Family Business
36% To Control My Future
27% To Be My Own Boss
25% To Fulfill a Dream
5% Downsized/Laid Off

Source of New Business Ideas

37% In-Depth Understanding of Industry/Profession
36% Market Niche Spotted
7% Brainstorming
4% Copying Someone Else
4% Hobby
11% Other

SOURCES: *1994 Inc. 500 Founder's Survey.* Copyright 1994 and 2001 by Mansueto Ventures LLC. Reproduced with permission of Mansueto Ventures LLC in the format Textbook via Copyright Clearance Center.

STARTING WITH THE IDEA

To some people, the idea for a new business is the easy part. They do not even consider entrepreneurship until they are inspired by an exciting idea. Other people decide they want to run their own business and set about looking for an idea or opportunity. Exhibit A.6 shows the most important reasons that people start a new business and the source of new business ideas. Note that 37 percent of business founders got their idea from an in-depth understanding of the industry, primarily because of past job experience. Interestingly, almost as many—36 percent—spotted a market niche that wasn't being filled.[39] After Camille Young decided to develop a healthier lifestyle and diet, she became frustrated trying to find organic food in Jersey City. Young explains, "I had to go to Manhattan to find organic food. It was annoying that Jersey City didn't even have a juice bar. Then I started thinking, Why don't I open one?" To fill this market niche, she opened two BaGua Juice stores that sell a variety of nutritious smoothies to health-conscious consumers.[40]

The trick for entrepreneurs is to blend their own skills and experience with a need in the marketplace. Acting strictly on one's own skills may produce something no one wants to buy. On the other hand, finding a market niche that the entrepreneur does not have the ability to fill doesn't work either. Both personal skill and market need typically must be present.

WRITING THE BUSINESS PLAN

Once an entrepreneur is inspired by a new business idea, careful planning is crucial. A **business plan** is a document that specifies the business details prepared by an entrepreneur prior to opening a new business. Planning forces the entrepreneur to carefully think through the issues and problems associated with starting and developing the business. Most entrepreneurs have to borrow money, and a business plan is absolutely critical for persuading lenders and investors to participate in the business. Studies show that small businesses with a carefully thought-out, written business plan are much more likely to succeed than those without one.[41] To attract the interest of venture capitalists or other potential investors, the entrepreneur should keep the plan crisp and compelling.

EXHIBIT A.6
Sources of Entrepreneurial Motivation and New Business Ideas

business plan
A document specifying the business details prepared by an entrepreneur prior to opening a new business.

The details of a business plan may vary, but successful business plans generally share several characteristics.[42] They:

- demonstrate a clear, compelling vision that creates an air of excitement;

- provide clear and realistic financial projections;

- profile potential customers and the target market;

- include detailed information about the industry and competitors;

- provide evidence of an effective entrepreneurial management team;

- pay attention to good formatting and clear writing;

- are short—no more than 50 pages;

- highlight critical risks that may threaten business success;

- spell out the sources and uses of start-up funds and operating funds; and

- capture the reader's interest with a killer summary.

CHOOSING A LEGAL STRUCTURE

Before entrepreneurs begin a business, and perhaps again as it expands, they must choose an appropriate legal structure for the company. The three basic choices are proprietorship, partnership, or corporation.

Sole Proprietorship. A **sole proprietorship** is defined as an unincorporated business owned by an individual for profit. Proprietorships make up the majority of businesses in the United States. This form is popular because it is easy to start and has few legal requirements. A proprietor has total ownership and control of the company and can make all decisions without consulting anyone. However, this type of organization also has drawbacks. The owner has unlimited liability for the business, meaning that if someone sues, the owner's personal as well as business assets are at risk. Also, financing can be harder to obtain because business success rests on one person's shoulders.

Partnership. A **partnership** is an unincorporated business owned by two or more people. Partnerships, like proprietorships, are relatively easy to start. Two friends may reach an agreement to start a graphic arts company. To avoid misunderstandings and to make sure the business is well planned, it is wise to draw up and sign a formal partnership agreement with the help of an attorney. The agreement specifies how partners are to share responsibility and resources and how they will contribute their expertise. The disadvantages of partnerships are the unlimited liability of the partners and the disagreements that almost always occur among strong-minded people. A poll by *Inc.* magazine illustrated the volatility of partnerships. Fifty-nine percent of respondents considered partnerships a bad business move, citing reasons such as partner problems and conflicts. Partnerships often dissolve within five years. Respondents who liked partnerships pointed to the equality of partners (sharing of workload and emotional and financial burdens) as the key to a successful partnership.[43]

Corporation. A **corporation** is an artificial entity created by the state and existing apart from its owners. As a separate legal entity, the corporation is liable for its actions and must

sole proprietorship
An unincorporated business owned by an individual for profit.

partnership
An unincorporated business owned by two or more people.

corporation
An artificial entity created by the state and existing apart from its owners.

pay taxes on its income. Unlike other forms of ownership, the corporation has a legal life of its own; it continues to exist regardless of whether the owners live or die. And the corporation, not the owners, is sued in the case of liability. Thus, continuity and limits on owners' liability are two principal advantages of forming a corporation. For example, a physician can form a corporation so that liability for malpractice will not affect his or her personal assets. The major disadvantage of the corporation is that it is expensive and complex to do the paperwork required to incorporate the business and to keep the records required by law. When proprietorships and partnerships are successful and grow large, they often incorporate to limit liability and to raise funds through the sale of stock to investors.

ARRANGING FINANCING

Most entrepreneurs are particularly concerned with financing the business. A few types of businesses can still be started with a few thousand dollars, but starting a business usually requires coming up with a significant amount of initial funding. An investment is required to acquire labor and raw materials and perhaps a building and equipment. High-tech businesses, for example, typically need from $50,000 to $500,000 just to get through the first six months, even with the founder drawing no salary.[44]

Many entrepreneurs rely on their own resources for initial funding, but they often have to mortgage their homes, depend on credit cards, borrow money from a bank, or give part of the business to a venture capitalist.[45] Exhibit A.7 summarizes the most common sources of start-up capital for entrepreneurs. The financing decision initially involves two options—whether to obtain loans that must be repaid (debt financing) or whether to share ownership (equity financing).

Debt Financing. Borrowing money that has to be repaid at a later date to start a business is referred to as **debt financing**. One common source of debt financing for a start-up is to

debt financing
Borrowing money that has to be repaid at a later date in order to start a business.

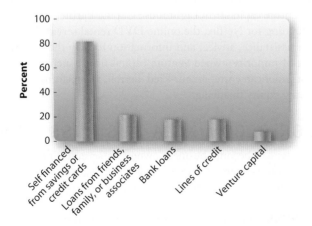

SOURCE: Jim Melloan, "The Inc. 5000," *Inc.* (September 1, 2006): 187. Copyright 2006 by Mansueto Ventures LLC. Reproduced with permission of Mansueto Ventures LLC in the format Textbook via Copyright Clearance Center.

EXHIBIT A.7
Sources of Start-Up Capital for Entrepreneurs

borrow from family and friends. Increasingly, entrepreneurs are using their personal credit cards as a form of debt financing. Another common source is a bank loan. Banks provide some 25 percent of all financing for small business. Sometimes entrepreneurs can obtain money from a finance company, wealthy individuals, or potential customers. A typical source of funds for businesses with high potential is through **angel financing**. Angels are wealthy individuals, typically with business experience and contacts, who believe in the idea for the start-up and are willing to invest their personal funds to help the business get started. Significantly, angels also provide advice and assistance as the entrepreneur is developing the company. The entrepreneur wants angels who can make business contacts, help find talented employees, and serve as all-around advisors.

Another form of loan financing is provided by the Small Business Association (SBA). Staples, which started with one office-supply store in Brighton, Massachusetts, in 1986, got its start toward rapid growth with the assistance of SBA financing. Today, Staples is North America's largest operator of office superstores, with 1,738 retail outlets in the United States and Canada, a thriving international presence in 27 countries, and $27 billion in sales.[46] SBA financing is especially helpful for people without substantial assets, providing an opportunity for single parents, minority-group members, and others with a good idea but who might be considered high risk by a traditional bank. The percentage of SBA loans to women, Hispanics, African Americans, and Asian Americans has increased significantly in recent years.[47]

Equity Financing. Any money invested by owners or by those who purchase stock in a corporation is considered equity funds. **Equity financing** consists of funds that are invested in exchange for ownership in the company.

A **venture capital firm** is a group of companies or individuals that invests money in new or expanding businesses for ownership and potential profits. This form of capital is a potential for businesses with high earning and growth possibilities. Venture capitalists are particularly interested in high-tech businesses such as biotechnology, innovative online ventures, or telecommunications because they have the potential for high rates of return on investment.[48] The venture capital firm Lighthouse Capital Partners, for example, provided some of the early funding for Netflix, the online DVD rental service.[49] Venture capitalists also usually provide assistance, advice, and information to help the entrepreneur prosper. A growing number of minority-owned venture capital firms, such as Provender Capital, founded by African American entrepreneur Fred Terrell, are ensuring that minorities have a fair shot at acquiring equity financing.[50]

TACTICS FOR BECOMING A BUSINESS OWNER

Aspiring entrepreneurs can become business owners in several different ways. They can start a new business from scratch, buy an existing business, or start a franchise. Another popular entrepreneurial tactic is to participate in a business incubator.

Start a New Business. One of the most common ways to become an entrepreneur is to start a new business from scratch. This approach is exciting because the entrepreneur sees a need for a product or service that has not been filled before and then sees the idea or dream become a reality. Ray Petro invested his $50,000 life savings and took out a $25,000 loan

angel financing
Financing provided by a wealthy individual who believes in the idea for a start-up and provides personal funds and advice to help the business get started.

equity financing
Financing that consists of funds that are invested in exchange for ownership in the company.

venture capital firm
A group of companies or individuals that invests money in new or expanding businesses for ownership and potential profits.

to launch Ray's Mountain Bike Indoor Park after learning from other mountain-biking enthusiasts of their frustration with not being able to ride during the winter months. Taryn Rose started her shoe company, Taryn Rose International, after searching for stylish shoes that wouldn't destroy her feet while working long hours as an orthopedic surgeon.[51] The advantage of starting a business is the ability to develop and design the business in the entrepreneur's own way. The entrepreneur is solely responsible for its success. A potential disadvantage is the long time it can take to get the business off the ground and make it profitable. The uphill battle is caused by the lack of established clientele and the many mistakes made by someone new to the business. Moreover, no matter how much planning is done, a start-up is risky, with no guarantee that the new idea will work. Some entrepreneurs, especially in high-risk industries, develop partnerships with established companies that can help the new company get established and grow. Others use the technique of outsourcing— having some activities handled by outside contractors—to minimize the costs and risks of doing everything in-house.[52] For example, Philip Chigos and Mary Domenico are building their children's pajama business from the basement of their two-bedroom apartment, using manufacturers in China and Mexico to produce the goods and partnering with a local firm to receive shipments, handle quality control, and distribute finished products.[53]

Buy an Existing Business. Because of the long start-up time and the inevitable mistakes, some entrepreneurs prefer to reduce risk by purchasing an existing business. This direction offers the advantage of a shorter time to get started and an existing track record. The entrepreneur may get a bargain price if the owner wishes to retire or has other family considerations. Moreover, a new business may overwhelm an entrepreneur with the amount of work to be done and procedures to be determined. An established business already has filing systems, a payroll tax system, and other operating procedures. Potential disadvantages are the need to pay for goodwill that the owner believes exists and the possible existence of ill will toward the business. In addition, the company may have bad habits and procedures or outdated technology, which may be why the business is for sale.

Buy a Franchise. Franchising is perhaps the most rapidly growing path to entrepreneurship. The International Franchise Association reports that the country's 909,253 franchise outlets account for about $2.3 trillion in annual sales and are the source of 21 million jobs, 15.3 percent of all U.S. private-sector jobs.[54] **Franchising** is an arrangement by which the owner of a product or service allows others to purchase the right to distribute the product or service with help from the owner. The franchisee invests his or her money and owns the business but does not have to develop a new product, create a new company, or test the market. Franchises exist for weight-loss clinics, pet-sitting services, sports photography, bakeries, janitorial services, auto-repair shops, real-estate offices, and numerous other types of businesses, in addition to the traditional fast-food outlets. Exhibit A.8 lists the top 10 fastest-growing franchises, including the type of business, the number of outlets, and the initial franchise costs. Initial franchise fees don't include the other start-up costs the entrepreneur will have to cover.

The powerful advantage of a franchise is that management help is provided by the owner. For example, Subway does not want a franchisee to fail. Subway has regional development agents who do the research to find good locations for Subway's sandwich outlets.

franchising
An arrangement by which the owner of a product or service allows others to purchase the right to distribute the product or service with help from the owner.

Franchise	Type of Business	Number of Outlets	Franchise Costs
7–11	Convenience store	5,580	Varies
Subway	Submarine sandwich restaurant	21,344	$15,000
Dunkin' Donuts	Doughnut shop	5,451	$40,000—80,000
Pizza Hut	Pizza restaurant	4,757	$25,000
McDonald's	Hamburger restaurant	11,772	$45,000
Sonic Drive-in Restaurant	Drive-in hamburger restaurant	2,655	$45,000
KFC Corp.	Fast food chicken restaurant	4,287	$25,000
Intercontinental Hotels	Middle market lodging	2,541	Varies
Dominos Pizza	Pizza delivery	4,571	$25,000
RE/MAX Int'l	Real estate agency	4,315	$12,500—25,000

SOURCE: Based on data 2008 Fastest-Growing Franchises, Entrepreneur.com, www.entrepreneur.com/franzone/fastestgrowing/index.html (accessed June 23, 2008).

The Subway franchisor also provides two weeks of training at company headquarters and ongoing operational and marketing support.[55] Franchisors provide an established name and national advertising to stimulate demand for the product or service. Potential disadvantages are the lack of control that occurs when franchisors want every business managed in exactly the same way. In some cases, franchisors require that franchise owners use certain contractors or suppliers that might cost more than others would. In addition, franchises can be expensive, and the high start-up costs are followed with monthly payments to the franchisor that can run from 2 percent to 15 percent of gross sales.[56]

Entrepreneurs who are considering buying a franchise should investigate the company thoroughly. The prospective franchisee is legally entitled to a copy of franchisor disclosure statements, which include information on 20 topics, including litigation and bankruptcy history, identities of the directors and executive officers, financial information, identification of any products the franchisee is required to buy, and from whom those purchases must be made. The entrepreneur also should talk with as many franchise owners as possible, because they are among the best sources of information about how the company really operates.[57] Exhibit A.9 (on page 555) lists some specific questions entrepreneurs should ask about themselves and the company when considering buying a franchise. Answering such questions can improve the chances for a successful career as a franchisee.

business incubator
An innovation that provides shared office space, management support services, and management advice to entrepreneurs.

Participate in a Business Incubator. An attractive option for entrepreneurs who want to start a business from scratch is to join a business incubator. A **business incubator** typically provides shared office space, management-support services, and management and legal advice to entrepreneurs. Incubators also give entrepreneurs a chance to share information with one another about local business, financial aid, and market opportunities.

Questions about the Entrepreneur	Questions about the Franchisor	Before Signing the Dotted Line
1. Will I enjoy the day-to-day work of the business?	1. What assistance does the company provide in terms of selection of location, setup costs, and securing credit; day-to-day technical assistance; marketing; and ongoing training and development?	1. Do I understand the risks associated with this business, and am I willing to assume them?
2. Do my background, experience, and goals make this opportunity a good choice for me?	2. How long does it take the typical franchise owner to start making a profit?	2. Have I had an advisor review the disclosure documents and franchise agreement?
3. Am I willing to work within the rules and guidelines established by the franchisor?	3. How many franchises changed ownership within the past year, and why?	3. Do I understand the contract?

SOURCES: Based on Thomas Love, "The Perfect Franchisee," *Nation's Business* (Apr. 1998): 59–65; and Roberta Maynard, "Choosing a Franchise," *Nation's Business* (Oct. 1996): 56–63.

A recent innovation is the *virtual incubator*, which does not require that people set up on-site. These virtual organizations connect entrepreneurs with a wide range of experts and mentors and offer lower overhead and cost savings for cash-strapped small-business owners. Christie Stone, cofounder of Ticobeans, a coffee distributor in New Orleans, likes the virtual approach because it gives her access to top-notch advice while allowing her to keep her office near her inventory.[58]

The concept of business incubators arose about two decades ago to nurture start-up companies. Business incubators have become a significant segment of the small-business economy, with approximately 1,400 in operation in North America and an estimated 5,000 worldwide.[59] The incubators that are thriving are primarily not-for-profits and those that cater to niches or focus on helping women or minority entrepreneurs. These incubators include those run by government agencies and universities to boost the viability of small business and spur job creation. The great value of an incubator is the expertise of a mentor, who serves as advisor, role model, and cheerleader, and ready access to a team of lawyers, accountants, and other advisors. Incubators also give budding entrepreneurs a chance to network and learn from one another.[60] "The really cool thing about a business incubator is that when you get entrepreneurial people in one place, there's a synergistic effect," said Tracy Kitts, vice president and chief operating officer of the national Business Incubation Association. "Not only do they learn from staff, they learn tons from each other, and this really contributes to their successes."[61]

STARTING AN ONLINE BUSINESS

Many entrepreneurs are turning to the Internet to expand their small businesses or launch a new venture. In fact, 12.1 percent of sole proprietors are engaging in e-commerce, up from 9.4 percent in 2005, according to a survey of 1,235 businesses.[62] Anyone with an idea, a personal computer, access to the Internet, and the tools to create a Web site can start an online business. These factors certainly fueled Ashley Qualls's desire to create a Web site that has become a destination for million of teenage girls. Starting at age 15, Ashley

EXHIBIT A.9

Sample Questions for Choosing a Franchise

launched Whateverlife.com with a clever Web site, an $8 domain name, and a vision to provide free designs (hearts, flowers, celebrities) for MySpace pages. Her hobby exploded into a successful business with advertising revenue of more than $1 million so far. Ashley's motivation to start Whateverlife.com was fueled by an opportunity to turn a rewarding hobby into a thriving online business.[63]

Additional incentives for starting an online business include low overhead and the ability to work from home or any location. These are some of the incentives that motivated Landy Ung to launch 8coupons.com, a business that sends discount coupons directly to users' mobile phones via text messages. She and her boyfriend, Wan His Yuan, run the business from their 500-square-foot studio apartment, meaning headquarters is, effectively, their couch. Ung and Yuan have put $30,000 into the business, and operating costs remain low. The business demands many hours of hard work and diligence, however, frequently keeping both up until 3 A.M.[64]

Entrepreneurs who aspire to start online businesses follow the usual steps required to start a traditional business: identify a profitable market niche, develop an inspiring business plan, choose a legal structure, and determine financial backing. Beyond that, they need to be unusually nimble, persistent in marketing, savvy with technology, and skillful at building online relationships. Several steps required to start an online business are highlighted here.

- **Find a market niche**. To succeed in the competitive online market, aspiring entrepreneurs need to identify a market niche that isn't being served by other companies. Online businesses experience success when they sell unique, customized, or narrowly focused products or services to a well-defined target audience.

- **Create a professional Web site**. Online shoppers have short attention spans, so a Web site should entice them to linger. To improve customers' online experience, Web sites should be easy to navigate, intuitive, and offer menus that are easy to read and understand. Even "small-time" sites need "big-time" designs and should avoid common mistakes such as typos, excessively large files that are slow to load, too much information, and sensory overload.[65] FragranceNet.com competes with big-time competitors with a Web site that clearly communicates its value proposition (designer brands at discount prices), easy navigation, and superior customer service.[66]

- **Choose a domain name**. A domain name gives a company an address on the Web and a unique identity. Domain names should be chosen carefully and be easy to remember, pronounce, and spell. How is a domain name selected? The options for creating a domain name are many and include (1) using the company name (dell.com), (2) creating a domain name that describes your product or service (1-800-Flowers.com), or (3) choosing a domain name that doesn't have a specific meaning and provides options for expanding (Google.com).[67]

- **Build online relationships**. In a storefront business, business owners develop loyal customer relationships through personal attention and friendly service. In the virtual business world, however, business owners connect with customers primarily through an online experience. Creating a positive, online relationship with customers requires time and resources, as Marla Cilley, owner of FlyLady.net, discovered. Cilley cultivated a cultlike following to her Internet business by sharing personal encouragement and housecleaning advice to middle-aged homemakers who call themselves FlyLadies. Her adoring customers send her nearly 5,000 grateful messages each day. She hired a team of six offsite readers to respond to each one. Through positive customer experiences and shared testimonials, Cilley continues to grow her self-help empire.[68] This demanding process of responding to thousands of e-mails helps FlyLady.com develop a loyal following and strong customer relationships.

Managing a Growing Business

Once an entrepreneurial business is up and running, how does the owner manage it? Often the traits of self-confidence, creativity, and internal locus of control lead to financial and personal grief as the enterprise grows. A hands-on entrepreneur who gave birth to the organization loves perfecting every detail. But after the start-up, continued growth requires a shift in management style. Those who fail to adjust to a growing business can be the cause of the problems rather than the solution.[69] In this section, we look at the stages through which entrepreneurial companies move and then consider how managers should carry out their planning, organizing, leading, and controlling.

STAGES OF GROWTH

Entrepreneurial businesses go through distinct stages of growth, with each stage requiring different management skills. The five stages are illustrated in Exhibit A.10.

1. *Start-up*. In this stage, the main problems are producing the product or service and obtaining customers. Several key issues facing managers are: Can we get enough customers? Will we survive? Do we have enough money? Burt's Bees was in the start-up stage

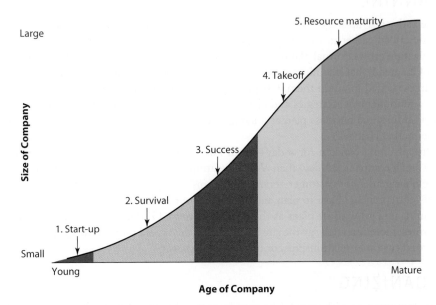

SOURCE: Based on Neil C. Churchill and Virginia L. Lewis, "The Five Stages of Small Business Growth," *Harvard Business Review* (May–June 1993): 30–50.

EXHIBIT A.10

Five Stages of Growth for an Entrepreneurial Company

- - - - - - - - - -

when Roxanne Quimby was making candles and personal care products by hand from the beeswax of Burt Shavitz's bees and selling them at craft fairs in Maine.

2. *Survival.* At this stage, the business demonstrates that it is a workable business entity. It produces a product or service and has sufficient customers. Concerns here involve finances—generating sufficient cash flow to run the business and making sure revenues exceed expenses. The organization will grow in size and profitability during this period. Burt's Bees reached $3 million in sales by 1993, and Quimby moved the business from Maine to North Carolina to take advantage of state policies that helped her keep costs in line.

3. *Success.* At this point, the company is solidly based and profitable. Systems and procedures are in place to allow the owner to slow down if desired. The owner can stay involved or consider turning the business over to professional managers. Quimby chose to stay closely involved with Burt's Bees, admitting that she's a bit of a control freak about the business.

4. *Takeoff.* Here the key problem is how to grow rapidly and finance that growth. The owner must learn to delegate, and the company must find sufficient capital to invest in major growth. This period is pivotal in an entrepreneurial company's life. Properly managed, the company can become a big business. However, another problem for companies at this stage is how to maintain the advantages of "smallness" as the company grows. In 2003, Quimby sold 80 percent of Burt's Bees to AEA Investors, a private equity firm, for more than $175 million. She continued as CEO and focuses on continuing to grow the business.

5. *Resource maturity.* At this stage, the company's substantial financial gains may come at the cost of losing its advantages of small size, including flexibility and the entrepreneurial spirit. A company in this stage has the staff and financial resources to begin acting like a mature company with detailed planning and control systems.

PLANNING

In the early start-up stage, formal planning tends to be nonexistent except for the business plan described earlier in this chapter. The primary goal is simply to remain alive. As the organization grows, formal planning usually is not instituted until the success stage. Recall from Chapter 1 that planning means defining goals and deciding on the tasks and use of resources needed to attain them. Chapters 5 and 6 describe how entrepreneurs can define goals and implement strategies and plans to meet them. It is important that entrepreneurs view their original business plan as a living document that evolves as the company grows or the market changes.

One planning concern for today's small businesses is the need to be Web savvy. For many small companies today, their Web operations are just as critical as traditional warehouse management or customer-service operations. The growing importance of e-business means entrepreneurs have to plan and allocate resources for Internet operations from the beginning and grow those plans as the company grows. Of the small companies that have Web sites, more than half say the site has broken even or paid for itself in greater efficiency, improved customer relationships, or increased business.[70]

ORGANIZING

In the first two stages of growth, the organization's structure is typically informal, with all employees reporting to the owner. Around the third stage—success—functional managers often are hired to take over duties performed by the owner. A functional organization structure will begin to evolve with managers in charge of finance, manufacturing, and marketing. Another organizational approach is to use outsourcing, as described earlier. Method, a company launched by two 20-something entrepreneurs to develop a line of non-toxic cleaning products in fresh scents and stylish packaging, contracted with an industrial designer for the unique dish-soap bottle and uses contract manufacturers in every region of the country to rapidly make products and get them to stores.[71]

During the latter stages of entrepreneurial growth, managers must learn to delegate and decentralize authority. If the business has multiple product lines, the owner may consider creating teams or divisions responsible for each line. The organization must hire competent managers and have sufficient management talent to handle fast growth and eliminate problems caused by increasing size. As an organization grows, it might also be characterized by greater use of rules, procedures, and written job descriptions. For example, Tara Cronbaugh started a small coffeehouse in a college town, but its success quickly led to the opening of three additional houses. With the rapid growth, Cronbaugh found that she needed a way to ensure consistency across operations. She put together an operations manual with detailed rules, procedures, and job descriptions so managers and employees at each coffeehouse would be following the same pattern.[72] Chapters 7 through 9 discuss organizing in detail.

CONTROLLING

Financial control is important in each stage of the entrepreneurial firm's growth. In the initial stages, control is exercised by simple accounting records and by personal supervision. By stage 3—success—operational budgets are in place, and the owner should start implementing more structured control systems. During the takeoff stage, the company will need to make greater use of budgets and standard cost systems and use computer systems to provide statistical reports. These control techniques will become more sophisticated during the resource maturity stage.

As Amazon.com grew and expanded internationally, for example, entrepreneur and CEO Jeff Bezos needed increasingly sophisticated control mechanisms. Bezos hired a computer-systems expert to develop a system to track and control all of the company's operations.[74] Control is discussed in Chapter 10.

LEADING

The driving force in the early stages of development is the leader's vision. This vision, combined with the leader's personality, shapes corporate culture. The leader can signal cultural values of service, efficiency, quality, or ethics. Often entrepreneurs do not have good people skills but do have excellent task skills in either manufacturing or marketing. By the success stage of growth, the owner must either learn to motivate employees or bring in managers who can. Rapid takeoff is not likely to happen without employee cooperation. The president of Foreign Candy Company of Hull, Iowa, saw his company grow rapidly when he concentrated more on employee needs and less on financial results. He made an effort to communicate with employees, conducted surveys to learn how they were feeling about the company, and found ways to involve them in decision making. His shift in leadership style allowed the company to enter the takeoff stage with the right corporate culture and employee attitudes to sustain rapid growth.

Leadership also is important because many small firms have a hard time hiring qualified employees. Labor shortages often hurt small firms that grow rapidly. A healthy corporate culture can help attract and retain good people.[73] Chapters 11 through 15 present the dynamics of leadership.

Summary

- *Entrepreneurship* is the process of initiating a business, organizing the necessary resources, and assuming the associated risks and rewards. Entrepreneurship plays an important role in the economy by stimulating job creation, innovation, and opportunities for minorities and women. An entrepreneur recognizes a viable idea for a business product or service and combines the necessary resources to carry it out. Entrepreneurs may be classified as *idealists*, *optimizers*, *sustainers*, *hard workers*, or *jugglers*.

- The Small Business Administration defines a *small business* as "one that is independently owned and operated and which is not dominant in its field of operation." The U.S. economy is ripe for entrepreneurial ventures, but entrepreneurial activity is also booming in other countries, with some of the highest rates in developing nations.

- Entrepreneurs place high importance on being free to achieve and maximize their potential. An entrepreneurial personality includes the traits of internal locus of control, high energy level, need to achieve, tolerance for ambiguity, awareness of passing time, and self-confidence.

- A new breed of entrepreneur, the *social entrepreneur*, is committed to both good business and positive social change. Social entrepreneurs sometime blur the line between business and social activism because they combine the creativity, business smarts, passion, and hard work of the traditional entrepreneur with a mission to improve the world.

- A business plan is a document specifying the business details prepared by an entrepreneur prior to opening a new business. Businesses with carefully written business plans are more likely to succeed than those without them. Small businesses may be organized as sole proprietorships, partnerships, or corporations. Initial funding for a small business may come from debt financing, borrowing money that has to be repaid, or equity financing, funds that are invested in exchange for ownership.

- Small businesses generally proceed through five stages of growth: start-up, survival, success, takeoff, and resource maturity. The management functions of planning, organizing, leading, and controlling should be tailored to each stage of growth.

Discussion Questions

1. You are interested in being your own boss and have the chance to buy a franchise office-supply store that is for sale in your city. You will need outside investors to help pay the franchise fees and other start-up costs. How will you determine if this is a good entrepreneurial opportunity and make your decision about buying the store?

2. Over the past 20 years, entrepreneurship has been the fastest-growing course of study on campuses throughout the country. However, debate continues about whether you can teach someone to be an entrepreneur. Do you think entrepreneurship can be taught? Why or why not?

3. Why would small-business ownership have great appeal to immigrants, women, and minorities?

4. Consider the six personality characteristics of entrepreneurs. Which two traits do you think are most like those of managers in large companies? Which two are least like those of managers in large companies?

5. How would you go about deciding whether you wanted to start a business from scratch, buy an existing business, or buy into a franchise? What information would you collect and analyze?

6. Many entrepreneurs say they did little planning, perhaps scratching notes on a legal pad. How is it possible for them to succeed?

7. What personal skills do you need to keep your financial backers feeling confident in your new business? Which skills are most useful when you're dealing with more informal sources such as family and friends versus receiving funds from stockholders, a bank, or a venture capital firm? Would these considerations affect your financing strategy?

8. Many people who are successful at the start-up stage of a business are not the right people to carry the venture forward. How do you decide whether you're better suited to be a serial entrepreneur (start the business and then move on to start another) or whether you can guide the venture as it grows and matures?

9. How does starting an online business differ from starting a small business such as a local auto-repair shop or delicatessen? Is it really possible for businesses that operate totally in cyberspace to build close customer relationships? Discuss.

10. Do you think entrepreneurs who launched new businesses on their own after deciding to leave jobs versus those who have been forced to leave jobs as a result of downsizing are likely to have different traits? Which group is more likely to succeed? Why?

Self Learning

What's Your Entrepreneurial IQ?

Rate yourself on the following 15 behaviors and characteristics, according to the following scale.

① = Strongly disagree

② = Disagree

③ = Agree

④ = Strongly agree

1. I am able to translate ideas into concrete tasks and outcomes.
   1 2 3 4

2. When I am interested in a project, I tend to need less sleep.
   1 2 3 4

3. I am willing to make sacrifices to gain long-term rewards.
   1 2 3 4

4. Growing up, I was more of a risk taker than a cautious child.
   1 2 3 4

5. I often see trends, connections, and patterns that are not obvious to others.
   1 2 3 4

6. I have always enjoyed spending much of my time alone.
   1 2 3 4

7. I have a reputation for being stubborn.
   1 2 3 4

8. I prefer working with a difficult but highly competent person to working with someone who is congenial but less competent.
   1 2 3 4

9. As a child, I had a paper route, a lemonade stand, or another small enterprise.
   1 2 3 4

10. I usually keep New Year's resolutions.
    1 2 3 4

11. I'm not easily discouraged, and I persist when faced with major obstacles.
    1 2 3 4

12. I recover quickly from emotional setbacks.
   1 2 3 4

13. I would be willing to dip deeply into my nest egg—and possibly lose all I had saved—to go it alone.
   1 2 3 4

14. I get tired of the same routine day in and day out.
   1 2 3 4

15. When I want something, I keep the goal clearly in mind.
   1 2 3 4

Scoring and Interpretation

Total your score for the 15 items. If you tallied 50–60 points, then you have a strong entrepreneurial IQ. A score of 30–50 indicates good entrepreneurial possibilities. Your chances of starting a successful entrepreneurial business are good if you have the desire and motivation. If you scored below 30, you probably do not have much entrepreneurial potential.

Go back over each question, thinking about changes you might make to become more or less entrepreneurial, depending on your career interests.

Ethical Dilemma

Closing the Deal

As the new, heavily recruited CEO of a high-technology start-up backed by several of Silicon Valley's leading venture capitalists, Chuck Campbell is flying high—great job, good salary, stock options, and a chance to be in on the ground floor and build one of the truly great 21st-century organizations. Just a few days into the job, Chuck participated in a presentation to a new group of potential investors for funding that could help the company expand marketing, improve its services, and invest in growth. By the end of the meeting, the investors had verbally committed $16 million in funding.

But things turned sour pretty fast. As Chuck was leaving about 9 P.M., the corporate controller, Betty Mars, who just returned from an extended leave, cornered him. He was surprised to find her working so late, but before he could even open his mouth, Betty blurted out her problem: The numbers Chuck had presented to the venture capitalists were flawed. "The assumptions behind the revenue growth plan are absolutely untenable," she said. "Not a chance of ever happening." Chuck was stunned. He told Betty to get on home and he'd stay and take a look at the figures.

At 11 P.M., Chuck was still sitting in his office wondering what to do. His research showed that the numbers were indeed grossly exaggerated, but most of them were at least statistically possible (however remote that possibility was). However, what really troubled him was that the renewal income figure was just flat-out false—and it was clear that one member of the management team who participated in the presentation knew it was incorrect all along. To make matters worse, it was the renewal income figure that ultimately made the investment so attractive to the venture capital firm. Chuck knew what was at stake—no less than the life or death of the company itself. If he told the truth about the deceptive numbers, the company's valuation would almost certainly be slashed and the $16 million possibly canceled.

What Would You Do?

1. Say nothing about the false numbers. Of course, the company will miss the projections and have to come up with a good explanation, but isn't that par for the course among fledgling high-tech companies? Chances are the whole thing will blow over without a problem.

2. Go ahead and close the deal, but come clean later. Explain that the controller had been on an extended leave of absence and, because you had been on the job only a few days, you had not had time to personally do an analysis of the numbers.

3. Take swift action to notify the venture capitalists of the truth of the situation—and start cleaning house to get rid of people who would knowingly lie to close a deal.

SOURCE: Adapted from Kent Weber, "The Truth Could Cost You $16 Million," *Business Ethics* (Mar.–Apr. 2001): 18.

Appendix B

Continuing Case

General Motors Celebrates 100 Years of Change and Innovation

Of the many important dates in automotive history, September 16, 2008, marks both the end of an era and a bold new beginning. On that historic Tuesday, eager crowds packed the Renaissance Center in Detroit, Michigan, to celebrate a once-in-a-lifetime event: the 100-year anniversary of General Motors (GM).

Following months of centennial-themed pageantry and parades, the American automaker's towering headquarters had taken on a museum-like aura. On the ground floor sat immaculate showroom classics from the company's fabled past: an orange 1963 Corvette Sting Ray, a pistachio 1952 Saab, a shiny black 1955 Chevrolet Bel Air coupe, and an apple-green 1973 Opel GT. Auto enthusiasts, reporters, and GM employees alike gazed nostalgically on the rows of vintage cars as the clock turned back to a glorious bygone era in America's history.

Despite the irresistible charm projected by these solid-steel visitors from GM's legendary past, it was a concept vehicle from the company's future that had the crowd's engines revving on the main floor. For years, GM's management had talked of introducing alternative-energy models that excite consumers and protect the environment. Now, at this momentous celebration, the talk was over, and GM pulled back the curtain on what it says is the future of the auto industry: the Chevy Volt.

With its aerodynamic design and 40 miles of emissions-free driving on a single electric charge, GM's first-ever plug-in electric vehicle is a far cry from the gas-guzzling trucks and SUVs that delivered the company's greatest financial successes in recent decades. Indeed, the Volt represents a sea change for the world's largest auto manufacturer. Unlike hybrids that use electric power to improve the mileage of their gasoline engines, the Volt uses a gasoline generator to assist the range of its battery-powered electric drive unit. According to GM, driving the Volt will save owners $1,500 annually in energy costs. It's no wonder company officials cite the concept as proof of GM's intention to lead the reinvention of the automobile.

But the arrival of the Volt comes at a pivotal moment in GM's history. Ripple effects from an international mortgage crisis in 2008 triggered the industry's worst sales slump since 9/11. Soaring energy prices in the same period forced management to abandon Hummer and other super-sized models that once represented hope for a financial recovery. But the list goes on. GM also faces slumping shares, stupefying quarterly losses, ballooning debt, steep competition from Toyota, precarious dealings with labor unions, and almost insurmountable fuel-efficiency regulations from the federal government.

If history is any indication, GM will tackle these challenges head on, displaying the same innovative spirit that gave the business its first 100 years of manufacturing excellence. Since its founding in 1908, the automaker has repeatedly demonstrated its strong capacity for innovation and change. From speedometers (1901 Oldsmobile) and electric headlights (1909 Cadillac) to automatic transmissions (1940 Oldsmobile) and mass-produced V-8 engines (1914 Cadillac), GM teams have given the world hundreds of innovative firsts.

Whether it's big-idea concepts that reshape the future or smaller innovations that improve existing products, Chief Executive Officer (CEO) Rick Wagoner and his management teams are developing the strategies that will guide the company successfully for the next 100 years. In his speech introducing the Volt's historic unveiling, Wagoner underscored the remarkable times in which we are living. "GM's centennial comes at an incredible time in our industry. The entire world is watching, hoping for a breakthrough in personal transportation that will address the very real energy and environmental challenges facing the globe."

The stakes have never been higher. If GM is to avoid becoming a museum of America's great automobile-manufacturing past, management must deliver breakthrough ideas that once again stoke consumers' passions. With the Chevy Volt in production and a large cache of renowned brands including Cadillac, Chevrolet, Pontiac, and Saturn, there is every reason to believe GM will succeed.

QUESTIONS

1. Which management functions and skills enabled GM's leaders to create a bold vision for reinventing the automobile around green technology?

2. Identify social, political, and economic forces that affect the auto industry and the practice of management at GM.

3. Which historical management perspective fueled GM's transformation into a manufacturing powerhouse in the early twentieth century?

SOURCES: Robert Snell, "GM Unveils Its Chevy Volt at Centennial Celebration," *Detroit News*, Sept. 16, 2008 (www.detnews.com) (accessed Oct. 8, 2008); Anita Lienert, "Aerodynamic Chevrolet Volt Electrifies GM's 100th-Anniversary Celebration," *Inside Line* (Sept. 16, 2008) (www.edmunds.com/insideline) (accessed Oct. 10, 2008); David Phillips, "Innovations Propel Success," *Detroit News*, Sept. 16, 2008 (www.detnews.com) (accessed Oct. 7, 2008); "GM Starts Its Next 100 Years with New Approach," *Bay City Times*, Sept. 28, 2008 (http://blog.mlive.com/bcopinion/2008/09/gm_starts_its_next_100_years_w.html) (accessed Oct. 11, 2008); and David Kiley, "J.D. Power: Retail Sales To Be 2 Million Lower in 2008," *BusinessWeek* online, Oct. 8, 2008 (www.businessweek.com/autos/autobeat/archives/2008/10/ jd_power_retail.html) (accessed Oct. 11, 2008).

The Volt: GM's Ultimate Green Machine

Imagine that you are one of millions of Americans whose commute to school or work is less than 40 miles round trip. Each morning, you hop in a sleek compact and drive off to your destination. At night, you park safely in the garage and plug your vehicle into a standard household electric socket for bedtime. After repeating this pattern for months, you never use a drop of gas or emit an ounce of emissions. Moreover, charging your vehicle costs you just 80 cents each day and consumes less energy annually than your own home refrigerator.

If you are one of the thousands of excited consumers lining up to purchase the 2010 Chevy Volt, this scenario is not fantasy—it's your future. In fact, it's the future that

General Motors envisions for each one of America's more than 200 million licensed drivers.

In a move to reinvent the automobile for the needs of the 21st century, GM unveiled its first electric car during the company's historic 2008 centennial celebration. The Volt, with its emissions-free driving and 2010 delivery date, promises to become the ultimate green machine for eco-minded consumers everywhere.

While the cost of operating the aerodynamic electric compact is roughly equivalent to the price of a cup of coffee, the driving experience is priceless. The electric drive unit delivers 150-horsepower, 0-to-60 acceleration in 9 seconds, and top speeds of 100 miles per hour. Drivers who make longer trips than the battery's 40-mile range get an automatic recharge from Volt's gas-powered generator. And although it runs on batteries, the Volt is no golf cart. The environmentally friendly four-door vehicle features a sporty-yet-sophisticated stance, aerodynamic design, closed front grille, and more. The futuristic cockpit takes cues from the latest in design trends; the metallic-white center control console could pass for a next-generation iPod.

How did GM go from being the world's largest manufacturer of gas-guzzling Hummers and Escalades to an electric-car company producing what one observer has called a "Viper for tree huggers"? The dramatic shift is related to multiple threats in the organization's external environment.

First, there's oil: Wildly fluctuating gas prices—such as the $5-per-gallon spike in 2008—have caused drivers to moderate driving habits and stay away from dealerships. Then, there's government regulation: The Democrat-controlled U.S. Congress overwhelmingly passed the Energy Independence and Security Act of 2007, which in addition to banning the use of ordinary incandescent light bulbs, raised corporate average fuel economy (CAFE) standards on automakers to a fleetwide average of 35 mpg. Next, there's the philosophy of sustainability: Many leaders in business and government see environmental "clean" technology as a way of striking a balance between today's economic development needs and those of future generations. Another pressure comes from lobbyists: Powerful voices are sounding the alarm on impending global catastrophe and have demanded that manufacturers put the brakes on industry to save the planet. Finally, there's the competition: *Green* is an important buzzword in business today, and vehicles such as the Toyota Prius and the Tesla Roadster that leave a small carbon footprint are putting pressure on GM to get out in front.

Whatever the economic, political, and social forces driving big changes at GM, leadership is determined to create a new culture of innovation and change. Whether it's the emissions-free promise of the Volt, the gravity-defying fuel efficiency of the Chevy Tahoe Hybrid, or the next-generation thinking of the hydrogen-powered Cadillac Provoq, the presence of exciting alternative-fuel vehicles sends a message to stakeholders that the future of the automobile is still in Detroit.

QUESTIONS

1. What management strategies might be most effective in helping GM adapt to uncertainty and change in its external environment?

2. What obstacles does GM face as it attempts to bring its corporate culture into alignment with the needs and challenges of the twenty-first century?

3. As GM continues its attempts to demonstrate good corporate citizenship, what complex issues and obstacles may frustrate its efforts?

SOURCES: Peter Fairley, "The New CAFE Standards—Fuel Standards Will Likely Be Achievable But Won't Encourage Innovation," *Technology Review*, Jan. 15, 2008 (www.technologyreview.com/ energy/20067) (accessed Oct. 11, 2008); Anita Lienert, "Aerodynamic Chevrolet Volt Electrifies GM's 100th-Anniversary Celebration," *Inside Line*, Sept. 16, 2008 (www.edmunds.com/insideline) (accessed Oct. 11, 2008); Robert Snell, "GM Enters Its Second Century by Finally Taking Wraps off Volt," *Detroit News*, Sept. 17, 2008 (www.detnews.com) (accessed Oct. 11, 2008); U.S. Department of Transportation, "Distribution of Licensed Drivers—2006," Federal Highway Administration, Highway Statistics 2006 Table DL-20 (www.fhwa.dot.gov/policy/ohim/hs06/htm/ dl20.htm); and David Welch, "GM Charges Up the Electric Chevy Volt—GM Introduces the Chevy Volt, a Sleek Electric Car Capable of 40 mpg on a Single Charge," *BusinessWeek*, Sept., 17, 2008 (www.businessweek.com/lifestyle/content/sep2008/bw20080916_356100.htm) (accessed Oct. 11, 2008).

The Moment of Decision: Can Management Fix GM's Financial Crisis?

In the months leading up to 2009, news leaked that General Motors was pitching a merger to other Big Three automakers. Although they are famous crosstown rivals, GM, Ford, and Chrysler are facing a brutal common enemy: global economic crisis. As the companies struggled to survive the worst sales slump in decades, an unexpected meltdown in the U.S. mortgage industry spawned an international credit crisis, freezing cash flows worldwide.

Unable to obtain money, and burning through $1 billion of its own reserves monthly, GM set out to find partners who might circle the wagons to stave off bankruptcy. Chairman Rick Wagoner and President Frederick Henderson met with Ford executives Alan Mulally and William Ford Jr. to propose merging their companies to survive the economic downturn. After numerous meetings, Mr. Mulally and Mr. Ford concluded that Ford Motor Company could reorganize better on its own. Not willing to give up on the idea, Wagoner took his pitch to Chrysler.

The past few years have been a moment of decision for GM. With the world's top automaker inching close to a financial precipice, senior executives have begun making tough choices and seeking out innovative solutions to rescue the organization.

Of the many possible options for saving GM, a merger strategy is perhaps the boldest. First, a merger could solidify GM's position as global sales leader over Japanese rival Toyota, which in recent years has challenged GM's status as the world's top automaker. Although its position as top automaker is not unimportant, the bigger problem is cash: GM doesn't have any. The company reported losses of $18.7 billion in the first half of 2008, and the ensuing plunge of shares to their lowest levels since 1950 left the company valued at just $3 billion. Against that backdrop, Chrysler's $11-billion cash horde looked especially inviting to former CEO Wagoner and his executive management teams.

Not surprisingly, analysts were divided about a merger option. Van Conway, a merger and acquisitions expert and partner at Conway & MacKenzie, cheered GM's survival instinct. "You want to be the last man standing here because the car market is going to come back." However, Erich Merkle, an analyst at the accounting firm Crowe Horwath, did not applaud the move. "If you put two auto companies together, both that are losing money, both that are losing market share, you've just got an auto company that's losing market share faster and losing more money."

Management has other options for performing what amounts to emergency bypass surgery on the 100-year-old company. For example, in July 2008, Wagoner announced a plan to cut $10 billion in costs while raising $5 billion through asset sales through the end of 2009. Within months, the iconic Hummer brand was up for sale. Next followed a steady drumbeat of plant closings throughout the Midwest—even the company's Detroit headquarters was rumored to be up for sale.

Among GM's most difficult decisions has been what to do about skyrocketing labor costs. The United Auto Workers Union, once a symbol of workforce stability and fairness, has become a financial albatross around GM's neck. GM spends as much as $1,635 on every vehicle sold to cover benefits for active and retired U.S. workers. In addition, with all compensation perks factored in, pay for GM workers adds up to $73 per hour. Toyota pays nothing for retirees and only $215 per vehicle to cover active-worker benefits. Management addressed the imbalance in 2006 by offering 126,000 employees as much as $140,000 to sever all ties with the company. The massive buyout was part of a four-point restructuring plan announced in 2005 to achieve $7 billion in cost reductions.

Yet of all the tricks GM has up its sleeve to manage its financial crisis, one option is reportedly off the table. In a written statement to the press, management acknowledged "unprecedented challenges" related to global financial markets. The statement firmly added, "But bankruptcy protection is not an option GM is considering. Bankruptcy would not be in the interests of our employees, stockholders, suppliers, or customers."

QUESTIONS

1. What planning approaches and methods might GM adopt to help manage its turbulent environment and respond effectively to global economic crisis?

2. In what way does a merger solution to GM's financial crisis represent strategic thinking and planning?

3. As GM's managers continue making decisions that affect the company's ultimate survival, what prevents them from making purely rational decisions, and what common decision-making errors must they guard against?

SOURCES: Jeff Green, "GM Is Said to Be in Preliminary Talks With Chrysler," Bloomberg, Oct. 11, 2008 (www.bloomberg.com) (accessed Oct. 12, 2008); Alex Taylor III, "Deepening Gloom at General Motors," Fortune (June 19, 2008) (http://money.cnn.com/2008/06/19/news/companies/taylor_gm.fortune/index.htm) (accessed Oct. 13, 2008); "Toyota Zooms Past GM," The Street.com, Apr. 24, 2007 (www.thestreet.com) (accessed Oct. 12, 2008); Bill Vlasic, "G.M. Said to Seek Merger with Ford Before Chrysler," New York Times, Oct. 11, 2008 (www.nytimes.com/2008/10/12/business/12auto.html) (accessed Oct. 15, 2008); "General Motors Could Sell Detroit Headquarters to Raise Cash," Boston Herald, Oct. 7, 2008 (www.bostonherald.com) (accessed Oct. 13, 2008); Alex Taylor III, "Behind Ford's Scary $12.7 Billion Loss—The Big Three Are Hemorrhaging Money, and Struggling to Stay Competitive with Foreign Rivals," Fortune (Jan. 26, 2007) (http://money.cnn.com/2007/01/26/news/companies/ pluggedin_taylor_ford.fortune/index.htm) (accessed Oct. 10, 2008); "Ford, GM Say They Won't File for Bankruptcy," MSNBC.com, Oct. 10, 2008 (www.msnbc.msn.com/id/27101859) (accessed Oct. 12, 2008); David Kiley, "Can GM Make It?" BusinessWeek Online, Oct. 9, 2008 (www.businessweek.com/lifestyle/content/oct2008/ bw2008109_718575.htm) (accessed Oct. 12, 2008); Tom Krisher, "General Motors Putting Hummer Brand and French Factory Up for Sale," Associated Press, Sept. 24, 2008 (www.canadaeast.com/article/article/425760) (accessed Oct. 12, 2008); Sharon Silke Carty, "GM Offers Buyouts to 126,000," USA Today, Mar. 27, 2006 (www.usatoday.com) (accessed Oct. 10, 2008); Tom Krisher, "Analysts: GM Would Need Cash to Acquire Chrysler," ABC News, Oct. 11, 2008 (http://abcnews.go.com/Business/wireStory?id=6009470) (accessed Oct. 14, 2008); Rick Haglund, "Why GM and Chrysler? You May Not Like the Answer," Mlive.com, Oct. 15, 2008 (www.mlive.com) (accessed Oct. 15, 2008); Alex Taylor III, "Gentlemen, Start Your Turnaround," Fortune (Jan. 8, 2008) (http://money.cnn.com/2008/01/07/news/companies/gm_turnaround.fortune/index.htm) (accessed Oct. 15, 2008); and "Global Auto Market May 'Collapse' in 2009—J.D. Power Points to Growing Concerns Around Credit Availability," MSNBC.com, Oct. 10, 2008 (www.msnbc.msn.com/id/27114183) (accessed Oct. 13, 2008).

Diversity Equals Opportunity at General Motors

William "Billy" Durant and Henry Ford are celebrated founders of the two greatest automobile companies in America's history: General Motors and Ford Motor Company. Ford was the famous inventor who introduced the Model T, the world's first affordable automobile. Durant was an entrepreneur whose Flint, Michigan, carriage business manufactured a variety of luxury models and farm wagons for diverse types of customers.

Although both were pioneers of the auto industry, their approaches could not have been more different. Whereas Ford remained focused on one brand and one vehicle, Durant dreamed of a whole family of car companies, each producing different models for different kinds of consumers and needs. Not satisfied owning only GM Buick in 1908, Durant proceeded to acquire Oldsmobile, Cadillac, and the Oakland Motor Car Company (Pontiac), among others, bringing them under one roof alongside Chevrolet, which he cofounded on the side.

The story of William Durant is a powerful metaphor for the spirit of diversity that infuses the work and culture of GM today. In the global marketplace, managers interact with people of different cultures, languages, beliefs, and values. Recognizing diversity, and the unique way people with different backgrounds interact and communicate, is key to success in the international arena.

As GM celebrates 100 years of auto-manufacturing greatness, its workforce is increasingly made up of people of all ethnicities and walks of life. The company is home to a variety of employee-resource groups, including the African Ancestry Network, the Hispanic Initiative Team, the Native American Cultural Network, the People with Disabilities Group, and the Veteran's Affinity Group. Employees who join these special support groups discover a wealth of resources for career and personal development.

By promoting a workforce that is as diverse as its customer base, GM brings a broad range of ideas and voices to bear on tough business challenges. "By valuing and respecting differences and similarities in the workplace, we will be in a better position to win in the marketplace," said Rod Gillum, vice president of corporate responsibility and diversity at GM. "It is our goal to recruit and retain diverse talent that reflects our global customers and to create an environment where everyone can fully contribute in creating great GM products and services."

The top automaker has made great strides toward Gillum's goal. *DiversityInc* magazine ranks GM among its Top 50 Companies for Diversity. The magazine writes that GM shows "unbiased retention" in hiring people of all races, ethnicities, and gender—and at all levels of the organization. To appear in the magazine's rankings, companies must demonstrate a commitment to diversity in four areas: CEO commitment, human capital, organizational communications, and supplier diversity.

Cultivating a broad multinational workforce means eliminating glass ceilings that discourage groups from participating fully in the company. Edward T. Welburn is GM's vice president of global design, heading up a multinational division with 11 design centers around the world. Appointed in 2005, Welburn is the sixth person to hold this position, and the first African American. Under his leadership, GM unified its design efforts worldwide by establishing coordinated collaboration among 1,900 designers in eight countries.

The results speak for themselves. Whether it's the sleek luxury of the Cadillac CTS or the retrospective cool of the 2010 Chevy Camaro, GM's most exciting new concepts are developing rapidly under Welburn's watchful eye. Hired by GM in 1972, Welburn appears to have been born for the job. "All I ever wanted to do was design cars," the design chief says.

Yet for any diversity initiative to thrive in an organization, it must have support all the way to the top. Former CEO Rick Wagoner understood the challenges of the new millennium as well as diversity's role in meeting those challenges. "At General Motors, we know that to succeed in today's global marketplace, we need a diverse workforce, one that brings together a wide range of talents, ideas, experiences, and perspectives."

QUESTIONS

1. What do you think are the most compelling advantages of diversity presented here?

2. What challenges do managers face in creating a diverse workplace, and how might they respond to these challenges?

3. Do you think that GM's encouragement of employee networks always leads to a culture of diversity and cooperation? Explain.

SOURCES: Bryce G. Hoffman, "Legendary Execs: 7 Notable Presidents Who Helped Shape GM," *Detroit News*, Aug. 30, 2008 (www.detnews.com) (accessed Oct. 13 2008); David Phillips, "Legacy of Innovation," *Detroit News*, Sept. 16, 2008 (www.detnews.com) (accessed Oct. 15, 2008); General Motors, "African Americans Take the Driver's Seat in GM Product Development," *The Inside Scoop*, vol. 1, no. 2 (February 2007), http://www.gmdynamic.com/newsletter/diversity/feb_07/feb-stry1.html (accessed October 14, 2008); Katie Merx, "GM Turns 100 with Focus on Future," *USA Today*, January 1, 2008, http://www.usatoday.com/money/autos/2008-01-01-gm-birthday_N.htm (accessed October 13, 2008); "2008 DiversityInc Top 50 Companies for Diversity: General Motors" *DiversityInc* (June 2, 2008), http://www.diversityinc.com/public/3335.cfm (accessed October 13, 2008); General Motors, "Leadership from a Design Perspective— GM Design Chief Addresses Entrepreneurs' Conference," *Inside Scoop*, 2(6) (June 2008) (www.gmdynamic.com/newsletter/diversity/june_08/story2.html) (accessed Oct. 14, 2008); and General Motors Web site, "Senior Leadership Group: Edward T. Welburn Jr., GM Vice President, Global Design" (www.gm.com/corporate/investor_information/corp_gov/bios/welburn.jsp) (accessed Oct. 14, 2008).

Blogs Take GM's Corporate Communication into Fast Lane

Whether it's the no-nonsense directness of legendary CEO Jack Welch, the point-by-point simplicity of financial guru Suze Orman, or the change-the-world idealism of Apple's Steve Jobs, effective communicators exhibit powerful mastery over their messages.

Yet in the age of new media and the Internet, getting one's point across requires mastery of both the message and medium. Thanks to blogs, texting, instant messaging, and social-networking Web sites, leaders have more options than ever before for reaching large audiences.

Who exactly are the grand communicators of the digital age? The pimple-faced founders of Facebook? The 30-something search-engine geniuses at Google? Try Bob Lutz, the 77-year-old vice chairman of global product development at General Motors. Lutz stunned the business community in 2005 when he ventured out into the blogosphere, exchanging his podium for podcasts and memoranda for message boards. Launched as the social media initiative of GM's Global Communications Group, Lutz's FastLane blog marked the first time an executive of a nontechnology Fortune 100 firm began blogging as a means of corporate communication.

Like other blogs, FastLane features commentary, product news, podcasts, video clips, photo galleries, user feedback, and twittering. Visitors to the blog—mostly car enthusiasts, members of the press, and GM employees—find information about auto shows, new vehicles, manufacturing breakthroughs, and more. With trademark informality, FastLane defines itself as "your source for the latest, greatest musings of GM leaders on topics relevant to the company, the industry and the global economy, and—most of all—to our customers."

Although the blogosphere is generally upbeat, blogs can become caldrons of conflict between adversarial groups. As a consequence of the blogosphere's reach and informal style, inartful comments may be published instantly on blogs and disseminated worldwide in seconds, creating severe headaches for public relations teams.

One such headache occurred in 2008 when off-the-cuff comments made during a closed-door session with journalists spread like wildfire across the blogosphere. Vice Chairman Lutz stated that hybrids didn't make "economic sense," adding that global warming was "a total crock." Critics seized on the moment to advance their crusade against the automaker. Lutz likewise took to his FastLane blog to respond.

"An offhand comment I made recently about the concept of global warming seems to have a lot of people heated, and it's spreading through the Internet like ragweed," wrote Lutz in his February 21, 2008, FastLane entry. "My opinions on the subject—like anyone's—are immaterial. General Motors is dedicated to the removal of cars and trucks from the environmental equation, period."

The vice chairman urged the public to ignore his personal musings and to focus instead on the company's push for clean transportation. "We're going to keep working on it—via E85, hybrids, hydrogen and fuel cells, and the electrification of the automobile." Lutz took the opportunity to praise GM's new electric car. "The Chevrolet Volt program is occurring under my personal watch, because I—and others in senior management—believe in it. I fully expect that it will revolutionize the automotive industry."

GM's ongoing support for FastLane shows that executives at the top automaker see blogging as a legitimate form of corporate communication. And no surprise: FastLane is an information center, marketing tool, crisis-management instrument, and customer-feedback system wrapped up in one. If Lutz is any indication, the corporate blog is here to stay. Where else could an outspoken vice chairman find so versatile a megaphone?

QUESTIONS

1. Visit FastLane online to identify the blog's various communication channels and their channel richness.

2. Is the information posted at FastLane appropriate for a blog? Why or why not?

3. What unique communication benefits do blogs offer to GM executives?

SOURCES: Glenn Hunter, "GM's Lutz On Hybrids, Global Warming and Cars As Art," *D magazine* (Jan. 30, 2008) (http://frontburner.dmagazine.com/2008/01/30/gms-lutz-on-hybrids-global-warming-and-cars-as-art) (accessed Oct. 17, 2008); Rob Kelley, "Tahoe Hybrid SUV named 'Green Car of Year,'" CNNMoney, Nov. 18, 2007 (http://money.cnn.com/2007/11/15/autos/green_car/index.htm) (accessed Oct. 17, 2008); Bob Lutz, "Talk About a Crock," FastLane Blog, Feb. 21, 2008 (http://fastlane.gmblogs.com/archives/2008/02/talk_about_a_cr.html) (accessed Oct. 17, 2008); "Welcome to Fastlane," FastLane Blog, Jan. 5, 2005 (http://fastlane.gmblogs.com/archives/2005/01/welcome_to_fast_1.html) (accessed Oct. 17, 2008); "Half of GM Plants to Be Landfill-Free By Late 2010," *GreenBiz*, Sept. 8, 2008 (www.greenbiz.com/news/2008/09/08/ half-gm-plants-be-landfill-free-by-late-2010) (accessed Oct. 17, 2008); and Kevin Krolicki, "GM Exec Stands by Calling Global Warming a 'Crock,'" Reuters, Feb. 22, 2008 (www.reuters.com) (accessed Oct. 17, 2008).

General Motors Gives Design Teams the Green Light

With all the bad news about layoffs, outsourcing, and plant closings at General Motors, it's not hard to guess what keeps many GM employees up at night. However, with the company's renewed mission to reinvent the automobile, and with a new $25-billion bailout from the federal government for automakers who invest in green technology, at least one group at GM is sleeping a little easier.

E-Flex Systems, the hybrid-vehicle task force behind the 2010 Chevy Volt, recently received the green light from senior management to design cleaner more energy-efficient vehicles. And now with a $25-billion credit line from the feds, GM's group of more than 600 engineers and designers is hard at work developing high-quality low-emissions vehicles for the future. In videotaped comments posted on the company's FastLane blog, Bob Lutz, GM's vice chairman of global product development, explained the automaker's perspective on quality. "If you ask me, 'Are we satisfied where we are in quality?' the answer has to be 'No.' Because until you're absolutely perfect, which no company will ever be, this is really an area where you strive."

Although quality may be a never-ending pursuit, getting it right may be more important than ever before in GM's history. In recent years, the company has overhauled design processes to make way for alternative-fuel vehicles such as the Chevy Tahoe hybrid, the hydrogen-powered Equinox SUV, and the battery-powered Volt. Such uncharted waters could prove treacherous if controls are not in place to measure performance and provide swift corrective action when problems arise.

In the case of the Chevy Volt, E-Flex teams are keeping a close eye on the car's plug-in electric-drive unit—especially the mission-critical lithium-ion batteries that deliver Volt's 40 miles of gas-free driving. As anyone with a laptop computer knows, battery technology is improving slowly. Drawbacks of batteries include limited storage capacity, cost of production, performance deterioration, and life cycle—and they're heavy, too. "It's the biggest challenge we have with this car," says Andrew Farah, chief engineer of the E-Flex Systems group. To ensure quality in Volt's state-of-the-art battery technology, engineers are testing batteries from Massachusetts-based supplier A123 Systems as well as packs from Compact Power, a subsidiary of LG Chem.

While not on par with the V-8 engines GM pioneered in the past, Volt's electric drive train produces plenty of pep. The unit delivers 150 horsepower, 273 pound-feet of torque, speeds of 100 miles per hour, and 0-to-60 acceleration in 9 seconds. "That doesn't sound like a golf cart to me," quipped Tony Posawatz, vehicle line director for the Volt. "It'll be fun to drive." But Volt's game-changing fuel efficiency also comes from its unique design. The Volt seats only four people, allowing integration of a six-foot T-shaped battery that sits economically under the center spine and rear seats. As Global Design Vice President Ed Welburn notes, "The battery is so integrated into the design that it's like, 'where is it?'" Precisely the point, according to chief engineer Farah. "The whole idea is to integrate it. You don't want to have a battery with some wheels."

GM product-development teams have more ordinary concerns as well. Although the Volt's electric motor is pivotal, Lutz notes that consumers are more likely to notice things like precise body fits and the radiance of the paint job. "These are things that people associate with quality," says the vice chairman. "They like to have an object that looks like it was put together with great care and by somebody that had a lot of respect for the ultimate customer." As Lutz sees it, the customer is always at the center of GM's commitment to quality. "We shoot not only for absence of problems, but we especially shoot for a joyous owner experience."

QUESTIONS

1. How might GM use organizational control to ensure that the Chevy Volt meets the expectations set for it during the vehicle's early planning stages?

2. Which total quality management techniques may not be applicable to GM as it pioneers next-generation alternative-fuel vehicles?

3. Would the partnership approach to supply chain management improve GM's procurement of materials for new energy-efficient vehicles? Why or why not?

SOURCES: Michael Kanellos, "Does GM Now Mean 'Green Motors'?" *CNET News*, Dec. 14, 2007 (http://news.cnet.com/Does-GMnow-mean-green-motors/2100-11389_3-6222853.html) (accessed Oct. 13, 2008); Robert Snell, "GM Enters Its Second Century by Finally Taking Wraps Off Volt," *Detroit News*, Sept. 17, 2008 (www.detnews.com) (accessed Oct. 11, 2008); "GM Starts Its Next 100 Years with New Approach," *Bay City Times*, Sept. 28, 2008 (http://blog.mlive.com/bcopinion/2008/09/gm_starts_its_next_100_years_w.html) (accessed Oct. 11, 2008); James Quinn, "GM Steers Towards Green Funding," *Telegraph*, Oct. 13, 2008 (www.telegraph.co.uk) (accessed Oct. 14, 2008); Chuck Squatriglia, "GM Dedicates Design Studio to Electric Vehicles," *Wired*, Dec. 11, 2007 (www.wired.com/cars/futuretransport/news/2007/12/eflex) (accessed Oct. 13, 2008); General Motors, "The Case for GM: Has GM Closed the Quality Gap?" (videotaped interview with Bob Lutz), GM FastLane Blog, Oct. 6, 2008 (http://fastlane.gmblogs.com) (accessed Oct. 13, 2008); and David Welch, "GM Charges Up the Electric Chevy Volt," *BusinessWeek Online*, Sept. 17, 2008 (www.businessweek.com/lifestyle/content/sep2008/ bw20080916_356100.htm) (accessed Oct. 13, 2008).

Appendix C

Solutions to Chapter 3's Group Learning

1. (1) China (1.3 billion)
   (2) India (1.0 billion)
   (3) United States (278 million)
   (4) Indonesia (228 million)
   (5) Brazil (174 million)
   (6) Russia (145 million)

2. (1) Mandarin (15.0%)   (2) English (5.5%)
   (3) Spanish (5.0%)   (4) Arabic (3.3%)
   (5) Hindi (3.2%)   (6) Bengali (3.0%)

3. c. 6,800

4. b. 203

5. 300 percent

6. 77 million

7. a. decreased—from 980 million in 1970 to 780 million in 2000

8. b. $1.2 trillion

9. 45 percent

10. 42nd in the world at 78.5 years.

11. b. 37th in the world according to the World Health Organization

12. c. 2/3

13. 66 percent

14. 50 percent

15. a. 1/10

16. b. 20 percent

17. c. 35 percent

18. Mexico City

19. $70.6 trillion

20. 1,308 percent (from 376,000 to 492 million)

21. South Africa with 29.1 percent, Swaziland with 25.9 percent, and Botswana with 23.9 percent. The greatest decreases were in Uganda, which went from 30 percent in 1992 to today's 5.4 percent, and Zimbabwe, which went from 124.6 percent in 2003 to 15 percent today because of aggressive public-health education programs.

22. 4.98

23. b. Cleaning his or her teeth with the tap running. According to the United Nations, in the world's 40 poorest countries, people only have access to an average of 30 liters or less per day each. The absolute minimum for well-being is considered to be 50 liters per day.

24. c. Poverty is the main reason for girls not attending school. In many communities daughters are valued less than sons, and their education is consequently considered a waste of time and money.

25. a. The United States gives the least aid as a proportion of GDP. Although the United States gives more foreign aid in absolute terms than any other country, it amounts to only 0.1 percent of its GDP. The United States gives $11 billion a year in aid and recently announced an increase of $5 billion over the next three years.

26. 60 percent would be Asian
    80 percent would be nonwhite
    67 percent would be non-Christian
    25 percent would live in substandard housing
    17 percent would be illiterate
    2 percent would have a college education
    4 percent would own a computer

27. False. All regions of the world are going through a profound transformation because the population is aging as mortality rates and fertility rates have fallen and life expectancy has increased.

28. b. 25 percent

29. a. Canada

30. c. 1 billion

31. c. Tokyo

32. c. $20 billion

SOURCES: *State of the World*, Worldwatch Institute, 2009; United Nations Web site, 2009; "What's Your Global IQ?" *Newsweek*, July 2–July 9, 2007, pp. 36–37; *World Economic and Social Survey 2007*, E/2007/50/Rev.1, United Nations, 2007; "State of the World Quiz," BBC News *This World*, Feb. 2, 2005.

Glossary

A

accountability The fact that the people with authority and responsibility are subject to reporting and justifying task outcomes to those above them in the chain of command.

achievement culture A results-oriented culture that values competitiveness, personal initiative, and achievement.

adaptability culture A culture characterized by values that support the company's ability to interpret and translate signals from the environment into new behavior responses.

adjourning The stage of team development in which members prepare for the team's disbandment.

administrative model A decision-making model that describes how managers actually make decisions in situations characterized by nonprogrammed decisions, uncertainty, and ambiguity.

administrative principles A subfield of the classical management perspective that focuses on the total organization rather than the individual worker, delineating the management functions of planning, organizing, commanding, coordinating, and controlling.

affirmative action A policy that requires employers to take positive steps to guarantee equal employment opportunities for people within protected groups.

alienated follower A person who is an independent, critical thinker but is passive in the organization.

ambidextrous approach Incorporating structures and processes that are appropriate for both the creative impulse and for the systematic implementation of innovations.

ambiguity A condition in which the goals to be achieved or the problem to be solved is unclear, alternatives are difficult to define, and information about outcomes is unavailable.

angel financing Financing provided by a wealthy individual who believes in the idea for a start-up and provides personal funds and advice to help the business get started.

application form A device for collecting information about an applicant's education, previous job experience, and other background characteristics.

assessment center A technique for selecting individuals with high managerial potential based on their performance on a series of simulated managerial tasks.

attitude A cognitive and affective evaluation that predisposes a person to act in a certain way.

attributions Judgments about what caused a person's behavior—either characteristics of the person or of the situation.

authoritarianism The belief that power and status differences should exist within the organization.

authority The formal and legitimate right of a manager to make decisions, issue orders, and allocate resources to achieve organizationally desired outcomes.

avoidance learning The removal of an unpleasant consequence when an undesirable behavior is corrected.

B

balanced scorecard A comprehensive management-control system that balances traditional financial measures with measures of customer service, internal business processes, and the organization's capacity for learning and growth.

balance sheet A financial statement that shows the firm's financial position with respect to assets and liabilities at a specific point in time.

behaviorally anchored rating scale (BARS) A rating technique that relates an employee's performance to specific job-related incidents.

behavioral sciences approach A subfield of the humanistic management perspective that applies social science in an organizational context and draws from economics, psychology, sociology, and other disciplines.

behavior modification The set of techniques by which reinforcement theory is used to modify human behavior.

benchmarking The continuous process of measuring products, services, and practices against major competitors or industry leaders.

Big Five personality factors Dimensions that describe an individual's extroversion, agreeableness, conscientiousness, emotional stability, and openness to experience.

blog Web log that allows individuals to post opinions and ideas.

bottom-of-the-pyramid (BOP) concept The idea that large corporations can both alleviate social problems and make a profit by selling goods and services to the world's poorest people.

bounded rationality The concept that people have the time and cognitive ability to process only a limited amount of information on which to base decisions.

brainstorming A technique that uses a face-to-face group to spontaneously suggest a broad range of alternatives for decision making.

bureaucratic organizations A subfield of the classical management perspective that emphasized management on an impersonal, rational basis through such elements as clearly defined authority and responsibility, formal record keeping, and separation of management and ownership.

business incubator An innovation that provides shared office space, management support services, and management advice to entrepreneurs.

business intelligence software Software that analyzes data from multiple sources and extracts useful insights, patterns, and relationships that might be significant.

business plan A document specifying the business details prepared by an entrepreneur prior to opening a new business.

C

centralization The location of decision authority near top organizational levels.

centralized network A team communication structure in which team members communicate through a single individual to solve problems or make decisions.

central planning department A group of planning specialists who develop plans for the organization as a whole and its major divisions and departments and typically report directly to the president or CEO.

ceremony A planned activity at a special event that is conducted for the benefit of an audience.

certainty The situation in which all the information the decision maker needs is fully available.

chain of command An unbroken line of authority that links all individuals in the organization and specifies who reports to whom.

change agent An organization development (OD) specialist who contracts with an organization to facilitate change.

changing The intervention stage of organization development in which individuals experiment with new workplace behavior.

channel The carrier of a communication.

channel richness The amount of information that can be transmitted during a communication episode.

charismatic leader A leader who has the ability to motivate subordinates to transcend their expected performance.

chief ethics officer A company executive who oversees ethics and legal compliance.

classical model A decision-making model based on the assumption that managers should make logical decisions that will be in the organization's best economic interests.

classical perspective A management perspective that emerged during the nineteenth and early 20th centuries that emphasized a rational, scientific approach to the study of management and sought to make organizations efficient operating machines.

coaching A method of directing, instructing, and training a person with the goal of developing specific management skills.

coalition An informal alliance among managers who support a specific goal.

code of ethics A formal statement of the organization's values regarding ethics and social issues.

coercive power Power that stems from the authority to punish or recommend punishment.

cognitive dissonance A condition in which two attitudes or a behavior and an attitude conflict.

collectivism A preference for a tightly knit social framework in which individuals look after one

another and organizations protect their members' interests.

committee A long-lasting, sometimes permanent team in the organization structure created to deal with tasks that recur regularly.

communication The process by which information is exchanged and understood by two or more people, usually with the intent to motivate or influence behavior.

communication apprehension An individual's level of fear or anxiety associated with interpersonal communications.

compensation Monetary payments (wages, salaries) and nonmonetary goods and commodities (benefits, vacations) used to reward employees.

compensatory justice The concept that individuals should be compensated for the cost of their injuries by the party responsible and also that individuals should not be held responsible for matters over which they have no control.

competitive advantage What sets the organization apart from others and provides it with a distinctive edge in the marketplace.

competitors Other organizations in the same industry or type of business that provide goods or services to the same set of customers.

conflict Antagonistic interaction in which one party attempts to thwart the intentions or goals of another.

conformist A follower who participates actively in the organization but does not use critical thinking skills.

consistency culture A culture that values and rewards a methodical, rational, orderly way of doing things.

consideration A type of behavior that describes the extent to which the leader is sensitive to subordinates, respects their ideas and feelings, and establishes mutual trust.

content theories A group of theories that emphasize the needs that motivate people.

contingency approach A model of leadership that describes the relationship between leadership styles and specific organizational situations.

contingency plans Plans that define company responses to specific situations such as emergencies, setbacks, and unexpected conditions.

contingent professionals People, mostly retirees, who bring needed expertise.

contingent workers People who work for an organization, but not on a permanent or full-time basis, including temporary placements, contracted professionals, and leased employees.

continuous improvement The implementation of a large number of small, incremental improvements in all areas of the organization on an ongoing basis.

coordination The quality of collaboration across departments.

core competence A business activity that an organization does particularly well in comparison to competitors.

corporate social responsibility (CSR) The obligation of organization management to make decisions and take actions that will enhance the welfare and interests of society as well as the organization.

corporate university An in-house training and education facility that offers broad-based learning opportunities for employees.

corporation An artificial entity created by the state and existing apart from its owners.

cost leadership A type of competitive strategy with which the organization aggressively seeks efficient facilities, cuts costs, and employs tight cost controls to be more efficient than competitors.

countertrade The barter of products for other products rather than their sale for currency.

courage The ability to step forward through fear and act on one's values and conscience.

creativity The generation of novel ideas that might meet perceived needs or offer opportunities for the organization.

critical thinking Thinking independently and being mindful of the effect of one's behavior on achieving goals.

cross-functional team A group of employees from various functional departments that meet as a team to resolve mutual problems.

culture change A major shift in the norms, values, attitudes, and mindset of the entire organization.

cultural intelligence (CQ) A person's ability to use reasoning and observation skills to interpret unfamiliar gestures and situations and devise appropriate behavioral responses.

cultural leader A manager who uses signals and symbols to influence corporate culture.

culture The set of key values, beliefs, understandings, and norms that members of an organization share.

customers People and organizations in the environment that acquire goods or services from the organization.

cycle time The steps taken to complete a company process.

D

data Raw, unsummarized, and unanalyzed facts and figures.

debt financing Borrowing money that has to be repaid at a later date in order to start a business.

decentralization The location of decision authority near lower organizational levels.

decentralized control The use of organizational culture, group norms, and a focus on goals rather than on rules and procedures to foster compliance with organizational goals.

decentralized network A team communication structure in which team members freely communicate with one another and arrive at decisions together.

decentralized planning Managers of divisions or departments work with planning experts to develop their own goals and plans.

decision A choice made from available alternatives.

decision making The process of identifying problems and opportunities and then resolving them.

decision styles Differences among people with respect to how they perceive problems and make decisions.

decode To translate the symbols used in a message for the purpose of interpreting its meaning.

delegation The process managers use to transfer authority and responsibility to positions below them in the hierarchy.

departmentalization The basis on which individuals are grouped into departments and departments into the total organization.

descriptive An approach that describes how managers actually make decisions rather than how they should make decisions according to a theoretical ideal.

devil's advocate A decision-making technique in which an individual is assigned the role of challenging the assumptions and assertions made by the group to prevent premature consensus.

diagnosis The step in the decision-making process in which managers analyze underlying causal factors associated with the decision situation.

dialogue A group communication process aimed at creating a culture based on collaboration, fluidity, trust, and commitment to shared goals.

differentiation A type of competitive strategy with which the organization seeks to distinguish its products or services from those of competitors.

discretionary responsibility Organizational responsibility that is voluntary and guided by the organization's desire to make social contributions not mandated by economics, law, or ethics.

discrimination The hiring or promoting of applicants based on criteria that are not job relevant; when people act out their prejudicial attitudes toward people who are the targets of their prejudice.

distributive justice The concept that different treatment of people should not be based on arbitrary characteristics. In the case of substantive differences, people should be treated differently in proportion to the differences among them.

distributive negotiation A competitive and adversarial negotiation approach in which each party strives to get as much as it can, usually at the expense of the other party.

diversity All the ways in which employees differ.

divisional structure An organization structure in which departments are grouped based on similar organizational outputs.

downward communication Messages sent from top management down to subordinates.

dynamic capabilities Leveraging and developing more from the firm's existing assets, capabilities, and core competencies in a way that will provide a sustained competitive advantage.

E

e-business Any business that takes place by digital processes over a computer network rather than in physical space.

e-commerce Business exchanges or transactions that occur electronically.

economic dimension The dimension of the general environment representing the overall economic health of the country or region in which the organization operates.

economic value–added (EVA) A control system that measures performance in terms of after-tax profits minus the cost of capital invested in tangible assets.

effective follower A critical, independent thinker who actively participates in the organization.

effectiveness The degree to which the organization achieves a stated goal.

efficiency The use of minimal resources—raw materials, money, and people—to produce a desired volume of output.

electronic brainstorming Bringing people together in an interactive group over a computer network to suggest alternatives; sometimes called *brainwriting*.

employment test A written or computer-based test designed to measure a particular attribute such as intelligence or aptitude.

empowerment The delegation of power and authority to subordinates.

encode To select symbols with which to compose a message.

engagement A situation in which employees enjoy their work, contribute enthusiastically to meeting goals, and feel a sense of belonging and commitment to the organization.

enterprise resource planning (ERP) system A networked information system that collects, processes, and provides information about an organization's entire enterprise from identification of customer needs and receipt of orders to distribution of products and receipt of payments.

entrepreneur Someone who recognizes a viable idea for a business product or service and carries it out.

entrepreneurship The process of initiating a business venture, organizing the necessary resources, and assuming the associated risks and rewards.

E → P expectancy Expectancy that putting effort into a given task will lead to high performance.

equity A situation that exists when the ratio of one person's outcomes to inputs equals that of another's.

equity financing Financing that consists of funds that are invested in exchange for ownership in the company.

equity theory A process theory that focuses on individuals' perceptions of how fairly they are treated relative to others.

ERG theory A modification of the needs hierarchy theory that proposes three categories of needs: existence, relatedness, and growth.

escalating commitment Continuing to invest time and resources in a failing decision.

ethical dilemma A situation that arises when all alternative choices or behaviors are deemed undesirable because of potentially negative consequences, making it difficult to distinguish right from wrong.

ethics The code of moral principles and values that governs the behaviors of a person or group with respect to what is right or wrong.

ethics committee A group of executives assigned to oversee an organization's ethics by ruling on questionable issues and disciplining violators.

ethics training Training programs to help employees deal with ethical questions and values.

ethnocentrism A cultural attitude marked by the tendency to regard one's own culture as superior to others; the belief that one's own group or subculture is inherently superior to other groups or cultures.

euro A single European currency that replaced the currencies of 15 European nations.

exit interview An interview conducted with departing employees to determine the reasons for their termination.

expatriates Employees who live and work in a country other than their own.

expectancy theory A process theory that proposes that motivation depends on individuals' expectations about their ability to perform tasks and receive desired rewards.

expert power Power that stems from special knowledge of or skill in the tasks performed by subordinates.

exporting An entry strategy in which the organization maintains its production facilities within its home country and transfers its products for sale in foreign countries.

external locus of control The belief by individuals that their future is not within their control but is influenced by external forces.

extinction The withdrawal of a positive reward.

extranet An external communications system that uses the Internet and is shared by two or more organizations.

extrinsic reward A reward given by another person.

F

fast-cycle team A multifunctional team that is provided with high levels of resources and empowerment to accomplish an accelerated product development project.

feedback A response by the receiver to the sender's communication.

flat structure A management structure characterized by an overall broad span of control and relatively few hierarchical levels.

focus A type of competitive strategy that emphasizes concentration on a specific regional market or buyer group.

force-field analysis The process of determining which forces drive and which resist a proposed change.

formal communication channel A communication channel that flows within the chain of command or task responsibility defined by the organization.

formal team A team created by the organization as part of the formal organization structure.

forming The stage of team development characterized by orientation and acquaintance.

franchising A form of licensing in which an organization provides its foreign franchisees with a complete package of materials and services; an arrangement by which the owner of a product or service allows others to purchase the right to distribute the product or service with help from the owner.

free rider A person who benefits from team membership but does not make a proportionate contribution to the team's work.

frustration–regression principle The idea that failure to meet a high-order need may cause a regression to an already satisfied lower-order need.

fundamental attribution error The tendency to underestimate the influence of external factors on another's behavior and to overestimate the influence of internal factors.

functional structure The grouping of positions into departments based on similar skills, expertise, and resource use.

G

general environment The layer of the external environment that affects the organization indirectly.

glass ceiling Invisible barrier that separates women and minorities from top management positions.

global outsourcing Engaging in the international division of labor so as to obtain the cheapest sources of labor and supplies regardless of country; also called *offshoring*.

global team A work team made up of members of different nationalities whose activities span multiple countries; may operate as a virtual team or meet face to face.

goal A desired future state that an organization attempts to realize.

goal-setting theory A motivation theory in which specific, challenging goals increase motivation and performance when the goals are accepted by subordinates and these subordinates receive feedback to indicate their progress toward goal achievement.

grapevine An informal, person-to-person communication network of employees that is not officially sanctioned by the organization.

groupthink The tendency of people in groups to suppress contrary opinions; the tendency for people to be so committed to a cohesive team that they are reluctant to express contrary opinions.

H

halo effect A type of rating error that occurs when an employee receives the same rating on all dimensions regardless of his or her performance on individual ones; an overall impression of a person or situation based on one characteristic, either favorable or unfavorable.

Hawthorne studies A series of experiments on worker productivity begun in 1924 at the Hawthorne plant of Western Electric Company in Illinois; attributed employees' increased output to managers' better treatment of them during the study.

hero A figure who exemplifies the deeds, character, and attributes of a strong corporate culture.

hierarchical control The use of rules, policies, hierarchy of authority, reward systems, and other formal devices to influence employee behavior and assess performance.

hierarchy of needs theory A content theory that proposes that people are motivated by five categories of needs—physiological, safety, belongingness, esteem, and self-actualization—that exist in a hierarchical order.

high-context culture A culture in which communication is used to enhance personal relationships.

high-performance culture A culture based on a solid organizational mission or purpose that uses shared adaptive values to guide decisions and business practices and to encourage individual employee ownership of both bottom-line results and the organization's cultural backbone.

horizontal communication The lateral or diagonal exchange of messages among peers or co-workers.

horizontal linkage model An approach to product change that emphasizes shared development of innovations among several departments.

horizontal team A formal team composed of employees from about the same hierarchical level but from different areas of expertise.

human capital The economic value of the knowledge, experience, skills, and capabilities of employees.

humanistic perspective A management perspective that emerged near the late nineteenth century and emphasized understanding human behavior, needs, and attitudes in the workplace.

human relations movement A movement in management thinking and practice that emphasizes satisfaction of employees' basic needs as the key to increased worker productivity.

human resource management (HRM) Activities undertaken to attract, develop, and maintain an effective workforce within an organization.

human resource planning The forecasting of human resource needs and the projected matching of individuals with expected job vacancies.

human resources perspective A management perspective that suggests jobs should be designed to meet higher-level needs by allowing workers to use their full potential.

humility Being unpretentious and modest rather than arrogant and prideful.

hygiene factors Factors that involve the presence or absence of job dissatisfiers, including working conditions, pay, company policies, and interpersonal relationships.

I

idea champion A person who sees the need for and champions productive change within the organization.

idea incubator An in-house program that provides a safe harbor where ideas from employees throughout the organization can be developed without interference from company bureaucracy or politics.

implementation The step in the decision-making process that involves using managerial, administrative, and persuasive abilities to translate the chosen alternative into action.

income statement A financial statement that summarizes the firm's financial performance for a given time interval; sometimes called a *profit-and-loss statement*.

individualism A preference for a loosely knit social framework in which individuals are expected to take care of themselves.

individualism approach The ethical concept that acts are moral when they promote an individual's best long-term interests.

influence The effect a person's actions have on the attitudes, values, beliefs, or behavior of others.

information Data that have been converted into a meaningful and useful context for the receiver.

information technology (IT) The hardware, software, telecommunications, database management, and other technologies used to store, process, and distribute information.

infrastructure A country's physical facilities that support economic activities.

initiating structure A type of leader behavior that describes the extent to which the leader is task oriented and directs subordinate work activities toward goal attainment.

instant messaging (IM) Electronic communication that allows users to see who is connected to a network and share information instantly.

integrative negotiation A collaborative approach to negotiation that is based on a win–win assumption, whereby the parties want to come up with a creative solution that benefits both sides of the conflict.

intelligence team A cross-functional group of managers and employees who work together to gain a deep understanding of a specific competitive issue and offer insight and recommendations for planning.

interactive leadership A leadership style characterized by values such as inclusion, collaboration, relationship building, and caring.

interim manager A manager who is not affiliated with a specific organization but works on a project-by-project basis or provides expertise to organizations in a specific area.

internal environment The environment that includes the elements within the organization's boundaries.

internal locus of control The belief by individuals that their future is within their control and that external forces have little influence.

international dimension The portion of the external environment that represents events originating in foreign countries as well as opportunities for U.S. companies in other countries.

international human resource management (IHRM) A subfield of human resource management that addresses the complexity that results from recruiting, selecting, developing, and maintaining a diverse workforce on a global scale.

international management The management of business operations conducted in more than one country.

intranet An internal communications system that uses the technology and standards of the Internet but is accessible only to people within the organization.

intrinsic reward The satisfaction received in the process of performing an action.

intuition The immediate comprehension of a decision situation based on past experience but without conscious thought.

involvement culture A culture that places high value on meeting the needs of employees and values cooperation and equality.

ISO 9000 standards A set of standards as outlined by the International Organization for Standardization that represent an international consensus of what constitutes effective quality management.

J

job analysis The systematic process of gathering and interpreting information about the essential duties, tasks, and responsibilities of a job.

job-characteristics model A model of job design that comprises core job dimensions, critical psychological states, and employee growth-need strength.

job design The application of motivational theories to the structure of work for improving productivity and satisfaction.

job description A concise summary of the specific tasks and responsibilities of a particular job.

job enlargement A job design that combines a series of tasks into one new, broader job to give employees variety and challenge.

job enrichment A job design that incorporates achievement, recognition, and other high-level motivators into the work.

job evaluation The process of determining the value of jobs within an organization through an examination of job content.

job rotation A job design that systematically moves employees from one job to another to provide them with variety and stimulation.

job satisfaction A positive attitude toward one's job.

job simplification A job design whose purpose is to improve task efficiency by reducing the number of tasks a single person must do.

job specification An outline of the knowledge, skills, education, and physical abilities needed to adequately perform a job.

joint venture A strategic alliance or program by two or more organizations.

justice approach The ethical concept that moral decisions must be based on standards of equity, fairness, and impartiality.

K

knowledge A conclusion drawn from information after it is linked to other information and compared to what is already known.

knowledge management The process of systematically gathering knowledge, making it widely available throughout the organization, and fostering a culture of learning.

knowledge management portal A single point of access for employees to multiple sources of information that provides personalized access on the corporate intranet.

L

labor market The people available for hire by the organization.

large-group intervention An approach that brings together participants from all parts of the organization (and may include key outside stakeholders as well) to discuss problems or opportunities and plan for major change.

law of effect The assumption that positively reinforced behavior tends to be repeated, and unreinforced or negatively reinforced behavior tends to be inhibited.

leadership The ability to influence people toward the attainment of organizational goals.

leadership grid A two-dimensional leadership theory that measures the leader's concern for people and for production.

learning A change in behavior or performance that occurs as the result of experience.

learning organization An organization in which everyone is engaged in identifying and solving problems, enabling the organization to continuously experiment, improve, and increase its capability.

legal–political dimension The dimension of the general environment that includes federal, state, and local government regulations and political activities designed to influence company behavior.

legitimate power Power that stems from a formal management position in an organization and the authority granted to it.

line authority A form of authority in which individuals in management positions have the formal power to direct and control immediate subordinates.

listening The skill of receiving messages to accurately grasp facts and feelings to interpret the genuine meaning.

locus of control The tendency to place the primary responsibility for one's success or failure either within oneself (internally) or on outside forces (externally).

long-term orientation A greater concern for the future and high value on thrift and perseverance.

low-context culture A culture in which communication is used to exchange facts and information.

M

Machiavellianism The tendency to direct much of one's behavior toward the acquisition of power and the manipulation of other people for personal gain.

management The attainment of organizational goals in an effective and efficient manner through planning, organizing, leading, and controlling organizational resources.

management by objectives (MBO) A method of management whereby managers and employees define goals for every department, project, and person and use them to monitor subsequent performance.

management information system (MIS) A computer-based system that provides information and support for effective managerial decision making.

management science perspective A management perspective that emerged after World War II and applied mathematics, statistics, and other quantitative techniques to managerial problems.

managing diversity Creating a climate in which the potential advantages of diversity for organizational or group performance are maximized while the potential disadvantages are minimized.

market-entry strategy An organizational strategy for entering a foreign market.

matching model An employee selection approach in which the organization and the applicant attempt to match each other's needs, interests, and values.

matrix approach An organization structure that uses functional and divisional chains of command simultaneously in the same part of the organization.

matrix boss The product or functional boss, responsible for one side of the matrix.

mediation The process of using a third party to settle a dispute.

mentor Higher-ranking organizational member who is committed to providing upward mobility and support to a protégé's professional career.

mentoring When an experienced employee guides and supports a less-experienced employee.

merger The combining of two or more organizations into one.

message The tangible formulation of an idea to be sent to a receiver.

mission The organization's reason for existence.

mission statement A broadly stated definition of the organization's basic business scope and operations that distinguish it from similar types of organizations.

modular approach The process by which a manufacturing company uses outside suppliers to provide large components of the product, which are then assembled into a final product by a few workers.

moral leadership Distinguishing right from wrong and choosing to do right in the practice of leadership.

moral-rights approach The ethical concept that moral decisions are those that best maintain the rights of those people affected by them.

motivation The arousal, direction, and persistence of behavior.

motivators Factors that influence job satisfaction based on fulfillment of high-level needs such as achievement, recognition, responsibility, and opportunity for growth.

Myers–Briggs Type Indicator (MBTI) Personality test that measures a person's preference for introversion versus extroversion, sensation versus intuition, thinking versus feeling, and judging versus perceiving.

N

natural dimension The dimension of the general environment that includes all elements that occur naturally on Earth, including plants, animals, rocks, and natural resources such as air, water, and climate.

need to achieve A human quality linked to entrepreneurship in which people are motivated to excel and pick situations in which success is likely.

negotiation A conflict-management strategy whereby people engage in give-and-take discussions and consider various alternatives to reach a joint decision that is acceptable to both parties.

neutralizer A situational variable that counteracts a leadership style and prevents the leader from displaying certain behaviors.

new-venture fund A fund providing resources from which individuals and groups can draw to develop new ideas, products, or businesses.

new-venture team A unit separate from the mainstream of the organization that is responsible for developing and initiating innovations.

nonprogrammed decision A decision made in response to a situation that is unique, is poorly defined and largely unstructured, and has important consequences for the organization.

nonverbal communication A communication transmitted through actions and behaviors rather than through words.

normative An approach that defines how a decision maker should make decisions and provides guidelines for reaching an ideal outcome for the organization.

norming The stage of team development in which conflicts developed during the storming stage are resolved and team harmony and unity emerge.

O

on-the-job training (OJT) A type of training in which an experienced employee "adopts" a new employee to teach him or her how to perform job duties.

open-book management Sharing financial information and results with all employees in the organization.

open innovation Extending the search for and commercialization of new ideas beyond the boundaries of the organization.

organization development (OD) The application of behavioral science techniques to improve an organization's health and effectiveness through its ability to cope with environmental changes, improve internal relationships, and increase learning and problem-solving capabilities.

operational goals Specific, measurable results expected from departments, work groups, and individuals within the organization.

operational plans Plans developed at the organization's lower levels that specify action steps toward achieving operational goals and that support tactical planning activities.

opportunity A situation in which managers see potential organizational accomplishments that exceed current goals.

organization A social entity that is goal directed and deliberately structured.

organizational behavior An interdisciplinary field dedicated to the study of how individuals and groups tend to act in organizations.

organizational citizenship Work behavior that goes beyond job requirements and contributes as needed to the organization's success.

organizational commitment Loyalty to and heavy involvement in one's organization.

organizational change The adoption of a new idea or behavior by an organization.

organizational control The systematic process through which managers regulate organizational activities to make them consistent with expectations established in plans, targets, and standards of performance.

organizational environment All elements existing outside the organization's boundaries that have the potential to affect the organization.

organization chart The visual representation of an organization's structure.

organization structure The framework in which the organization defines how tasks are divided, resources are deployed, and departments are coordinated.

organizing The deployment of organizational resources to achieve strategic goals.

P

partnership An unincorporated business owned by two or more people.

passive follower A person who exhibits neither critical independent thinking nor active participation.

pay for performance Incentive pay that ties at least part of compensation to employee effort and performance.

peer-to-peer file sharing File sharing that allows PCs to communicate directly with one another over the Internet, bypassing central databases, servers, control points, and Web pages.

people change A change in the attitudes and behaviors of a few employees in the organization.

perception The cognitive process people use to make sense out of the environment by selecting, organizing, and interpreting information.

perceptual defense The tendency of perceivers to protect themselves by disregarding ideas, objects, or people that are threatening to them.

perceptual distortions Errors in perceptual judgment that arise from inaccuracies in any part of the perceptual process.

perceptual selectivity The process by which individuals screen and select the various stimuli that vie for their attention.

performance The organization's ability to attain its goals by using resources in an efficient and effective manner.

performance appraisal The process of observing and evaluating an employee's performance, recording the assessment, and providing feedback to the employee.

performance gap A disparity between existing and desired performance levels.

performing The stage of team development in which members focus on problem solving and accomplishing the team's assigned task.

permanent teams A group of participants from several functions who are permanently assigned to solve ongoing problems of common interest.

personal communication channels Communication channels that exist outside the formally authorized channels and do not adhere to the organization's hierarchy of authority.

personal networking The acquisition and cultivation of personal relationships that cross departmental, hierarchical, and even organizational boundaries.

personality The set of characteristics that underlie a relatively stable pattern of behavior in response to ideas, objects, or people in the environment.

person–job fit The extent to which a person's ability and personality match the requirements of a job.

plan A blueprint specifying the resource allocations, schedules, and other actions necessary for attaining goals.

planning The act of determining the organization's goals and the means for achieving them.

P → O expectancy Expectancy that successful performance of a task will lead to the desired outcome.

point–counterpoint A decision-making technique in which people are assigned to express competing points of view.

political instability Events such as riots, revolutions, or government upheavals that affect the operations of an international company.

political risk A company's risk of loss of assets, earning power, or managerial control due to politically based events or actions by host governments.

positive reinforcement The administration of a pleasant and rewarding consequence following a desired behavior.

power The potential ability to influence others' behavior.

power distance The degree to which people accept inequality in power among institutions, organizations, and people.

pragmatic survivor A follower who has qualities of all four follower styles, depending on which fits the prevalent situation.

prejudice The tendency to view people who are different as being deficient.

pressure groups Interest groups that work within the legal–political framework to influence companies to behave in socially responsible ways.

problem A situation in which organizational accomplishments have failed to meet established goals.

problem-solving team Typically 5 to 12 hourly employees from the same department who meet to discuss ways of improving quality, efficiency, and the work environment.

procedural justice The concept that rules should be clearly stated and consistently and impartially enforced.

process An organized group of related tasks and activities that work together to transform inputs into outputs and create value.

process theories A group of theories that explain how employees select behaviors with which to meet their needs and determine whether their choices were successful.

product change A change in the organization's product or service outputs.

programmed decision A decision made in response to a situation that has occurred often enough to enable decision rules to be developed and applied in the future.

projection The tendency to see one's own personal traits in other people.

project manager A person responsible for coordinating the activities of several departments on a full-time basis for the completion of a specific project.

punishment The imposition of an unpleasant outcome following undesirable behavior.

Q

quality circle A group of 6 to 12 volunteer employees who meet regularly to discuss and solve problems that affect the quality of their work.

R

realistic job preview A recruiting approach that gives applicants all pertinent and realistic information about the job and the organization.

recruiting The activities or practices that define the desired characteristics of applicants for specific jobs.

reengineering The radical redesign of business processes to achieve dramatic improvements in cost, quality, service, and speed; also called *business process reengineering*.

referent power Power that results from characteristics that command subordinates' identification with, respect and admiration for, and desire to emulate the leader.

refreezing The reinforcement stage of organization development in which individuals acquire a desired new skill or attitude and are rewarded for it by the organization.

reinforcement Anything that causes a given behavior to be repeated or inhibited.

reinforcement theory A motivation theory based on the relationship between a given behavior and its consequences.

responsibility The duty to perform the task or activity an employee has been assigned.

responsibility center An organizational unit under the supervision of a single person who is responsible for its activity.

reward power Power that results from the authority to bestow rewards on other people.

rightsizing Intentionally reducing the company's workforce to the point where the number of employees is deemed to be right for the company's current situation.

risk A situation in which a decision has clear-cut goals and good information is available but the future outcomes associated with each alternative are subject to chance.

risk propensity The willingness to undertake risk with the opportunity of gaining an increased payoff.

role A set of expectations for one's behavior.

role ambiguity Uncertainty about what behaviors are expected of a person in a particular role.

role conflict Incompatible demands of different roles.

S

satisficing To choose the first solution alternative that satisfies minimal decision criteria, regardless of whether better solutions are presumed to exist.

scenario building Looking at trends and discontinuities and imagining possible alternative futures to build a framework within which unexpected future events can be managed.

scientific management A subfield of the classical management perspective that emphasized scientifically determined changes in management practices as the solution to improving labor productivity.

selection The process of determining the skills, abilities, and other attributes a person needs to perform a particular job.

self-directed team A team consisting of 5 to 20 multiskilled workers who rotate jobs to produce an entire product or service, often supervised by an elected member.

servant leader A leader who works to fulfill subordinates' needs and goals as well as to achieve the organization's larger mission.

self-serving bias The tendency to overestimate the contribution of internal factors to one's successes and the contribution of external factors to one's failures.

short-term orientation A concern with the past and present and a high value on meeting social obligations.

single-use plans Plans that are developed to achieve a set of goals that are unlikely to be repeated in the future.

situational theory A contingency approach to leadership that links the leader's behavioral style with the task readiness of subordinates.

Six Sigma A quality control approach that emphasizes a relentless pursuit of higher quality and lower costs.

skunkworks A separate, small, informal, highly autonomous, and often secretive group that focuses on breakthrough ideas for a business.

slogan A phrase or sentence that succinctly expresses a key corporate value.

social entrepreneur Entrepreneurial leaders who are committed to both good business and changing the world for the better.

social facilitation The tendency for the presence of others to influence an individual's motivation and performance.

social networking Online interaction in a community format where people share personal information and photos, produce and share all sorts of information and opinions, or unify activists and raise funds.

sociocultural dimension The dimension of the general environment representing the demographic characteristics, norms, customs, and values of the population within which the organization operates.

socioemotional role A role in which the individual provides support for team members' emotional needs and social unity.

sole proprietorship An unincorporated business owned by an individual for profit.

span of management The number of employees reporting to a supervisor; also called span of control.

special-purpose team A team created outside the formal organization to undertake a project of special importance or creativity.

staff authority A form of authority granted to staff specialists in their area of expertise.

stakeholder Any group within or outside the organization that has a stake in the organization's performance.

standing plans Ongoing plans that are used to provide guidance for tasks performed repeatedly within the organization.

stereotype threat A psychological experience of a person who, usually engaged in a task, is aware of a stereotype about his or her identify group that suggests he or she will not perform well on that task.

stereotyping Associating a rigid, exaggerated, and irrational belief with a particular group of people; placing an employee into a class or category based on one or a few traits or characteristics; the tendency to assign an individual to a group or broad category and then

attribute generalizations about the group to the individual.

storming The stage of team development in which individual personalities and roles emerge along with resulting conflicts.

story A narrative based on true events and repeated frequently and shared among organizational employees.

strategic conversation Dialogue across boundaries and hierarchical levels about the team or organization's vision, critical strategic themes, and the values that help achieve important goals.

strategic goals Broad statements of where the organization wants to be in the future; they pertain to the organization as a whole rather than to specific divisions or departments.

strategic management The set of decisions and actions used to formulate and implement strategies that will provide a competitively superior fit between the organization and its environment so as to achieve organizational goals.

strategic plans The action steps by which an organization intends to attain strategic goals.

strategy The plan of action that prescribes resource allocation and other activities for dealing with the environment, achieving a competitive advantage, and attaining organizational goals.

strategy execution The stage of strategic management that involves the use of managerial and organizational tools to direct resources toward achieving strategic outcomes.

strategy formulation The stage of strategic management that involves the planning and decision making that lead to the establishment of the organization's goals and of a specific strategic plan.

strategy map A visual representation of the key drivers of an organization's success that shows the cause-and-effect relationships among goals and plans.

stress A physiological and emotional response to stimuli that place physical or psychological demands on an individual.

stretch goal A reasonable yet highly ambitious and compelling goal that energizes people and inspires excellence.

substitute A situational variable that makes a leadership style unnecessary or redundant.

superordinate goal A goal that cannot be reached by a single party.

suppliers People and organizations that provide the raw materials the organization uses to produce its output.

survey feedback A type of organization development (OD) intervention in which questionnaires on organizational climate and other factors are distributed among employees and their results reported back to them by a change agent.

sustainability Economic development that generates wealth and meets the needs of the current population while preserving the environment for the needs of future generations.

SWOT analysis Analysis of the strengths, weaknesses, opportunities, and threats (SWOT) that affect organizational performance.

symbol An object, act, or event that conveys meaning to others.

synergy The condition that exists when the organization's parts interact to produce a joint effect that is greater than the sum of the parts acting alone.

T

tactical goals Goals that define the outcomes that major divisions and departments must achieve for the organization to reach its overall goals.

tactical plans Plans designed to help execute major strategic plans and to accomplish a specific part of the company's strategy.

tall structure A management structure characterized by an overall narrow span of management and a relatively large number of hierarchical levels.

task environment The layer of the external environment that directly influences the organization's operations and performance.

task force A temporary team or committee formed to solve a specific short-term problem involving several departments.

task specialist role A role in which the individual devotes personal time and energy to helping the team accomplish its task.

team A unit of two or more people who interact and coordinate their work to accomplish a specific goal.

team-based structure Structure in which the entire organization is made up of horizontal teams that coordinate their activities and work directly with customers to accomplish the organization's goals.

team building A type of organization development (OD) intervention that enhances the cohesiveness of departments by helping members learn to function as a team.

team cohesiveness The extent to which team members are attracted to the team and motivated to remain in it.

team norm A standard of conduct that is shared by team members and guides their behavior.

technological dimension The dimension of the general environment that includes scientific and technological advancements in the industry and society at large.

technology change A change that pertains to the organization's production process.

telecommuting Using computers and telecommunications equipment to perform work from home or another remote location.

360-degree feedback A process that uses multiple raters, including self-rating, to appraise employee performance and guide development.

tolerance for ambiguity The psychological characteristic that allows a person to be untroubled by disorder and uncertainty.

top leader The overseer of both the product and functional chains of command, responsible for the entire matrix.

total quality management (TQM) A concept that focuses on managing the total organization to deliver quality to customers; an organization-wide commitment to infusing quality into every activity through continuous improvement. Four significant elements of TQM are employee involvement, focus on the customer, benchmarking, and continuous improvement.

traits Distinguishing personal characteristics such as intelligence, values, and appearance.

transactional leader A leader who clarifies subordinates' role and task requirements, initiates structure, provides rewards, and displays consideration for subordinates.

transformational leader A leader distinguished by a special ability to bring about innovation and change.

two-boss employees Employees who report to two supervisors simultaneously.

Type A behavior Behavior pattern characterized by extreme competitiveness, impatience, aggressiveness, and devotion to work.

Type B behavior Behavior pattern that lacks Type A characteristics and includes a more balanced, relaxed lifestyle.

U

uncertainty The situation that occurs when managers know which goals they wish to achieve, but information about alternatives and future events is incomplete.

uncertainty avoidance A value characterized by people's intolerance for uncertainty and ambiguity and resulting support for beliefs that promise certainty and conformity.

uncritical thinking Failing to consider the possibilities beyond what one is told; accepting others' ideas without thinking.

unfreezing The stage of organization development in which participants are made aware of problems to increase their willingness to change their behavior.

upward communication Messages transmitted from the lower to the higher levels in the organization's hierarchy.

utilitarian approach The ethical concept that moral behaviors produce the greatest good for the greatest number.

V

valence The value or attraction an individual has for an outcome.

venture capital firm A group of companies or individuals that invests money in new or expanding businesses for ownership and potential profits.

vertical team A formal team composed of a manager and his or her subordinates in the organization's formal chain of command.

virtual network structure An organization structure that disaggregates major functions to separate companies that are brokered by a small headquarters organization.

virtual team A team made up of members who are geographically or organizationally dispersed, rarely meet face to face, and do their work using advanced information technologies.

vision An attractive, ideal future that is credible yet not readily attainable.

wage and salary surveys Surveys that show what other organizations pay incumbents in jobs that match a sample of "key" jobs selected by the organization.

whistle-blowing The disclosure by an employee of illegal, immoral, or illegitimate practices by an organization.

wiki A Web site that allows anyone with access, inside or outside the organization, to create, share, and edit content through a simple, browser-based user interface.

work redesign The altering of jobs to increase both the quality of employees' work experience and their productivity.

work specialization The degree to which organizational tasks are subdivided into individual jobs; also called *division of labor*.

Endnotes

CHAPTER 1

Innovation for Turbulent Times

1. Bruce Moeller, as told to Stephanie Clifford, "The Way I Work," *Inc. Magazine* (July 2007): 88–91.

2. Darrell Rigby and Barbara Bilodeau, "The Bain 2005 Management Tool Survey," *Strategy & Leadership* 33(4) (2005): 4–12.

3. Todd G. Buchholz, "The Right Stuff to Be CEO," *The Conference Review Board* (November–December 2007): 13.

4. Geoffrey Colvin, "What Makes GE Great?" *Fortune* (March 6, 2006): 90–96; and Betsy Morris, "The GE Mystique," *Fortune* (March 6, 2006): 98–104.

5. James A. F. Stoner and R. Edward Freeman, *Management,* 4th ed. (Englewood Cliffs, NJ: Prentice Hall, 1989).

6. Peter F. Drucker, *Management Tasks, Responsibilities, Practices* (New York: Harper & Row, 1974).

7. Jennifer Reingold, "Target's Inner Circle," *Fortune* (March 31, 2008): 74–86.

8. Robert L. Katz, "Skills of an Effective Administrator," *Harvard Business Review* 52 (September–October 1974): 90–102.

9. Charles Fishman, "Sweet Company," *Fast Company* (February 2001): 136–145.

10. A. I. Kraut, P. R. Pedigo, D. D. McKenna, and M. D. Dunnette, "The Role of the Manager: What's Really Important in Different Management Jobs," *Academy of Management Executive* 19(4) (2005): 122–129.

11. Christopher A. Bartlett and Sumantra Ghoshal, "Changing the Role of Top Management: Beyond Systems to People," *Harvard Business Review* (May–June 1995): 132–142; and Sumantra Ghoshal and Christopher A. Bartlett, "Changing the Role of Top Management: Beyond Structure to Processes," *Harvard Business Review* (January–February 1995): 86–96.

12. Clinton O. Longenecker, Mitchell J. Neubert, and Laurence S. Fink, "Causes and Consequences of Managerial Failure in Rapidly Changing Organizations," *Business Horizons* 50 (2007): 145–155.

13. Based on Sydney Finkelstein, "Seven Habits of Spectacularly Unsuccessful Executives," *Fast Company* (July 2003): 84–89; S. Finkelstein, *Why Smart Executives Fail* (New York: Portfolio, 2003); Ram Charan and Jerry Useem, "Why Companies Fail" *Fortune* (May 27, 2002): 50–59; and John W. Slocum Jr., Cass Ragan, and Albert Casey, "On Death and Dying: The Corporate Leadership Capacity of CEOs," *Organizational Dynamics* 30(3) (Spring 2002): 269–281.

14. Patricia Wallington, "Toxic!" *CIO* (April 15, 2006): 34–36.

15. Based on Longenecker et al., "Causes and Consequences"; Finkelstein, "Seven Habits"; Charan and Useem, "Why Companies Fail"; and Slocum et al., "On Death and Dying."

16. Alan Murray, "Behind Nardelli's Abrupt Exit; Executive's Fatal Flaw: Failing to Understand New Demands on CEOs," *Wall Street Journal,* January 4, 2007, p. A1; Brian Grow, "Out at Home Depot," *BusinessWeek* (January 15, 2007): 56–62.

17. Diane Brady, "'Being Mean Is So Last Millennium,'" *BusinessWeek* (January 15, 2007); and Murray, "Behind Nardelli's Abrupt Exit."

18. For a review of the problems faced by first-time managers, see Linda A. Hill, "Becoming the Boss," *Harvard Business Review* (January 2007): 49–56; Loren B. Belker and Gary S. Topchik, *The First-Time Manager: A Practical Guide to the Management of People,* 5th ed. (New York: AMACOM, 2005); J. W. Lorsch and P. F. Mathias, "When Professionals Have to Manage," *Harvard Business Review* (July–August 1987): 78–83; R. A. Webber, *Becoming a Courageous Manager: Overcoming Career Problems of New Managers* (Englewood Cliffs, NJ: Prentice Hall, 1991); D. E. Dougherty, *From Technical Professional to Corporate Manager: A Guide to Career Transition* (New York: Wiley, 1984); J. Falvey, "The Making of a Manager," *Sales and Marketing Management* (March 1989): 42–83; M. K. Badawy, *Developing Managerial Skills in Engineers and Scientists: Succeeding as a Technical Manager* (New York: Van Nostrand Reinhold, 1982); and M. London, *Developing Managers: A Guide to Motivating and Preparing People for Successful Managerial Careers* (San Francisco: Jossey-Bass, 1985).

19. Erin White, "Learning to Be the Boss; Trial and Error Is the Norm as New Managers Figure Out How to Relate to Former Peers," *Wall Street Journal,* November 21, 2005, p. B1.

20. This discussion is based on Linda A. Hill, *Becoming a Manager: How New Managers Master the Challenges of Leadership,* 2nd ed. (Boston: Harvard Business School Press, 2003): 6–8; and L. A. Hill, "Becoming the Boss," *Harvard Business Review* (January 2007): 49–56.

21. See also "Boss's First Steps," sidebar in White, "Learning to Be the Boss"; and Belker and Topchik, *The First-Time Manager.*

22. Jeanne Whalen, "Chance Turns a Teacher into a CEO; Religion Lecturer Leaves Academic Path and Learns to Run a Biotech Start-Up," *Wall Street Journal,* October 17, 2005, p. B4.

23. Erin White, "Learning to Be the Boss," *Wall Street Journal,* Nov. 21, 2005; Jared Sandberg, "Down Over Moving Up: Some New Bosses Find They Hate Their Jobs," *Wall Street Journal,* July 27, 2005; Heath Row, "Is Management for Me? That Is the Question," *Fast Company* (Feb.–Mar. 1998): 50–52; Timothy D. Schellhardt, "Want to Be a Manager? Many People Say No, Calling Job Miserable," *Wall Street Journal,* Apr. 4, 1997; and Matt Murray, "Managing Your Career—The Midcareer Crisis: Am I in This Business to Become a Manager?" *Wall Street Journal,* July 25, 2000.

24. This questionnaire is adapted from research findings reported in Linda A. Hill, *Becoming a Manager*; and John J. Gabarro, *The Dynamics of Taking Charge* (Boston: Harvard Business School Press, 1987).

25. Henry Mintzberg, "Managerial Work: Analysis from Observation," *Management Science* 18 (1971): B97–B110.

26. Based on Damien Cave, "A Tall Order for a Marine: Feeding the Hand That Bit You," *New York Times,* December 30, 2007, p. 4.3.

27. Mintzberg, "Managerial Work."

28. Matthew Boyle and Jia Lynn Yang, "All in a Day's Work," *Fortune* (March 20, 2006): 97–104.

29. Susan Spielberg, "The Cheesecake Factory: Heather Coin," *Nation's Restaurant News* 38(4) (January 26, 2004): 38–39.

30. Lance B. Kurke and Howard E. Aldrich, "Mintzberg Was Right! A Replication and Extension of *The Nature of Managerial Work*," *Management Science* 29 (1983): 975–984; Cynthia M. Pavett and Alan W. Lau, "Managerial Work: The Influence of Hierarchical Level and Functional Specialty," *Academy of Management Journal* 26 (1983): 170–177; and Colin P. Hales, "What Do Managers Do? A Critical Review of the Evidence," *Journal of Management Studies* 23 (1986): 88–115.

31. Mintzberg, "Rounding out the Manager's Job," *Sloan Management Review* (Fall 1994): 11–26.

32. Edward O. Welles, "There Are No Simple Businesses Anymore," *The State of Small Business* (1995): 66–79.

33. This section is based on Peter F. Drucker, *Managing the Nonprofit Organization: Principles and Practices* (New York: HarperBusiness, 1992); and Thomas Wolf, *Managing a Nonprofit Organization* (New York: Fireside/Simon & Schuster, 1990).

34. Christine W. Letts, William P. Ryan, and Allen Grossman, *High Performance Nonprofit Organizations* (New York: Wiley & Sons, 1999): 30–35.

35. Carol Hymowitz, "In Sarbanes-Oxley Era, Running a Nonprofit Is Only Getting Harder," *Wall Street Journal*, June 21, 2005; and Bill Birchard, "Nonprofits by the Numbers," *CFO* (June 2005): 50–55.

36. This section is based on "The New Organization: A Survey of the Company," *The Economist* (January 21, 2006); Harry G. Barkema, Joel A. C. Baum, and Elizabeth A. Mannix, "Management Challenges in a New Time," *Academy of Management Journal* 45(5) (2002): 916–930; Michael Harvey and M. Ronald Buckley, "Assessing the 'Conventional Wisdoms' of Management for the 21st Century Organization," *Organizational Dynamics* 30(4) (2002): 368–378; and Toby J. Tetenbaum, "Shifting Paradigms: From Newton to Chaos," *Organizational Dynamics* (Spring 1998): 21–32.

37. Caroline Ellis, "The Flattening Corporation," *MIT Sloan Management Review* (Summer 2003): 5.

38. Christopher Rhoads and Sara Silver, "Working at Home Gets Easier," *Wall Street Journal*, December 29, 2005, p. B4; Cliff Edwards, "Wherever You Go, You're on the Job," *Business-Week* (June 20, 2005): 87–90; and Kelley Holland, "When Work Time Isn't Face Time," *New York Times*, December 3, 2006, p. 3.3.

39. Kerr Inkson, Angela Heising, and Denise M. Rousseau, "The Interim Manager: Prototype of the 21st Century Worker," *Human Relations* 54(3) (2001): 259–284.

40. Keith H. Hammonds, "Smart, Determined, Ambitious, Cheap: The New Face of Global Competition," *Fast Company* (February 2003): 91–97.

41. Holland, "When Work Time Isn't Face Time."

42. Carla Johnson, "Managing Virtual Teams," *HR Magazine* (June 2002): 69–73; "The New Organisation," *The Economist* (January 21, 2006).

43. Holland, "When Work Time Isn't Face Time."

44. Bill Carter, "ABC Says It Was Outbid by NBC for Paris Hilton Interview," *New York Times,* June 22, 2007, pp. C1, C4.

45. This section is based on Loretta Ucelli, "The CEO's 'How to' Guide to Crisis Communications," *Strategy & Leadership* 30(2) (2002): 21–24; Eric Beaudan, "Leading in Turbulent Times," *Ivey Business Journal* (May–June 2002): 22–26; Christine Pearson, "A Blueprint for Crisis Management," *Ivey Business Journal* (January–February 2002): 68–73; Leslie Wayne and Leslie Kaufman, "Leadership, Put to a New Test," *New York Times* (September 16, 2001): section 3, 1, 4; Jerry Useem, "What It Takes," *Fortune* (November 12, 2001): 126–132; and Andy Bowen, "Crisis Procedures that Stand the Test of Time," *Public Relations Tactics* (August 2001): 16.

46. June Kronholz and Stefan Fatsis, "Obstacle Course: After Hurricane, Tulane University Struggles to Survive," *Wall Street Journal* (September 28, 2005): pp. A1, A8.

47. Beaudan, "Leading in Turbulent Times."

48. Ronald A. Heifetz and Donald L. Laurie, "The Leader as Teacher: Creating the Learning Organization," *Ivey Business Journal* (January–February 2003): 1–9.

49. Peter Senge, *The Fifth Discipline: The Art and Practice of Learning Organizations* (New York: Doubleday/Currency, 1990).

50. Copyright 2007 by Emerald Group Publishing Limited. Reproduced with permission of Emerald Group Publishing Limited in the format Textbook via Copyright Clearance Center.

51. See Keith Leslie, Mark A. Loch, and William Schaninger, "Managing Your Organization by the Evidence," *McKinsey Quarterly*, 3 (2006); Thomas H. Davenport, Laurence Prusak, and H. James Wilson, *What's the Big Idea? Creating and Capitalizing on the Best New Management Thinking* (Boston: Harvard Business School Press, 2003); Daniel James Rowley, "Resource Reviews," *Academy of Management Learning and Education* 2(3) (2003): 313–321; Jane Whitney Gibson, Dana V. Tesone, and Charles W. Blackwell, "Management Fads: Here Yesterday, Gone Today?" *SAM Advanced Management Journal* (Autumn 2003): 12–17; David Collins, *Management Fads and Buzzwords: Critical-Practices Perspective*, (London: Routledge, 2000); Timothy Clark, "Management Research on Fashion: A Review and Evaluation," *Human Relations* 54(12) (2001): 1650–1661; Brad Jackson, *Management Gurus and Management Fashions* (London: Routledge, 2001); Patrick Thomas, *Fashions in Management Research: An Empirical Analysis* (Aldershot, UK: Ashgate, 1999).

52. Daniel A. Wren, "Management History: Issues and Ideas for Teaching and Research," *Journal of Management* 13 (1987): 339–350.

53. Business historian Alfred D. Chandler, Jr., quoted in Jerry Useem, "Entrepreneur of the Century," *Inc.* (20th Anniversary Issue, 1999): 159–174.

54. Ibid.

55. The following is based on Daniel A. Wren, *The Evolution of Management Thought*, 4th ed. (New York: Wiley, 1994), Chapters 4, 5; and Claude S. George, Jr., *The History of Management Thought* (Englewood Cliffs, NJ: Prentice-Hall, 1968), Chapter 4.

56. Cynthia Crossen, "Early Industry Expert Soon Realized a Staff Has Its Own Efficiency," *Wall Street Journal*, November 6, 2006, p. B1.

57. Alan Farnham, "The Man Who Changed Work Forever," *Fortune* (July 21, 1997): 114; Charles D. Wrege and Ann Marie Stoka, "Cooke Creates a Classic: The Story Behind F. W. Taylor's Principles of Scientific Management," *Academy of Management Review* (October 1978): 736–749; Robert Kanigel, *The One Best Way: Frederick Winslow Taylor and the Enigma of Efficiency* (New York: Viking, 1997); and "The X and Y Factors: What Goes Around Comes Around," special section in "The New Organisation: A Survey of the Company," *The Economist* (January 21–27, 2006): 17–18.

58. Quoted in Ann Harrington, "The Big Ideas," *Fortune* (November 22, 1999): 152–154.

59. Wren, *Evolution of Management Thought*, 171; and George, *History of Management Thought*, 103–104.

60. Gary Hamel, "The Why, What, and How of Management Innovation," *Harvard Business Review* (February 2006): 72–84; Peter Coy, "Cog or Co-Worker?" *BusinessWeek* (August 20 & 27, 2007): 58–60.

61. Max Weber, *General Economic History* (Frank H. Knight, Trans.) (London: Allen & Unwin, 1927); Max Weber, *The Protestant Ethic and the Spirit of Capitalism* (Talcott Parsons, Ed.) (New York: Scribner, 1930); and Max Weber, *The Theory of Social and Economic Organizations* (A. M. Henderson and Talcott Parsons, Ed. and Trans.) (New York: Free Press, 1947).

62. Kelly Barron, "Logistics in Brown," *Forbes* (January 10, 2000): 78–83; Scott Kirsner, "Venture Vérité: United Parcel Service," *Wired* (September 1999): 83–96; "UPS," *Atlanta Journal and Constitution*, April 26, 1992; and Kathy Goode, Betty Hahn, and Cindy Seibert, "United Parcel Service: The Brown Giant" (unpublished manuscript, Texas A&M University, 1981).

63. Henri Fayol, *Industrial and General Administration* (J. A. Coubrough, Trans.) (Geneva: International Management Institute, 1930); Henri Fayol, *General and Industrial Management* (Constance Storrs, Trans.) (London: Pitman and Sons, 1949); and W. J. Arnold et al., *BusinessWeek, Milestones in Management* (New York: McGraw-Hill, vol. I, 1965; vol. II, 1966).

64. Mary Parker Follett, *The New State: Group Organization: The Solution of Popular Government* (London: Longmans, Green, 1918); and Mary Parker Follett, *Creative Experience* (London: Longmans, Green, 1924).

65. Henry C. Metcalf and Lyndall Urwick (Eds.), *Dynamic Administration: The Collected Papers of Mary Parker Follett* (New York: Harper & Row, 1940); Arnold, *Milestones in Management*.

66. Follett, *The New State;* Metcalf and Urwick, *Dynamic Administration* (London: Sir Isaac Pitman, 1941).

67. William B. Wolf, *How to Understand Management: An Introduction to Chester I. Barnard* (Los Angeles: Lucas Brothers, 1968); and David D. Van Fleet, "The Need-Hierarchy and Theories of Authority," *Human Relations* 9 (Spring 1982): 111–118.

68. Gregory M. Bounds, Gregory H. Dobbins, and Oscar S. Fowler, *Management: A Total Quality Perspective* (Cincinnati: South-Western Publishing, 1995): 52–53.

69. Curt Tausky, *Work Organizations: Major Theoretical Perspectives* (Itasca, IL: F. E. Peacock, 1978), p. 42.

70. Charles D. Wrege, "Solving Mayo's Mystery: The First Complete Account of the Origin of the Hawthorne Studies—The Forgotten Contributions of Charles E. Snow and Homer Hibarger." Paper presented to the Management History Division of the Academy of Management (August 1976).

71. Ronald G. Greenwood, Alfred A. Bolton, and Regina A. Greenwood, "Hawthorne a Half Century Later: Relay Assembly Participants Remember," *Journal of Management* 9 (Fall/Winter 1983): 217–231.

72. F. J. Roethlisberger, W. J. Dickson, and H. A. Wright, *Management and the Worker* (Cambridge, MA: Harvard University Press, 1939).

73. H. M. Parson, "What Happened at Hawthorne?" *Science* 183 (1974): 922–932; John G. Adair, "The Hawthorne Effect: A Reconsideration of the Methodological Artifact," *Journal of Applied Psychology* 69(2) (1984): 334–345; and Gordon Diaper, "The Hawthorne Effect: A Fresh Examination," *Educational Studies* 16(3) (1990): 261–268.

74. Greenwood, Bolton, and Greenwood, "Hawthorne a Half Century Later," 219–221.

75. Roethlisberger and Dickson, *Management and the Worker.*

76. Ramon J. Aldag and Timothy M. Stearns, *Management*, 2d ed. (Cincinnati: South-Western Publishing, 1991): 47–48.

77. Tausky, *Work Organizations*, 55.

78. Douglas McGregor, *The Human Side of Enterprise* (New York: McGraw-Hill, 1960): 16–18.

79. Jack Ewing, "No-Cubicle Culture," *BusinessWeek* (August 20 & 27, 2006): 60.

80. Wendell L. French and Cecil H. Bell Jr., "A History of Organizational Development," in Wendell L. French, Cecil H. Bell Jr., and Robert A. Zawacki, *Organization Development and Transformation: Managing Effective Change* (Burr Ridge, IL: Irwin McGraw-Hill, 2000): 20–42.

81. Samuel Greengard, "Twenty-Five Visionaries Who Shaped Today's Workplace," *Workforce* (January 1997): 50–59; and Ann Harrington, "The Big Ideas," *Fortune* (November 22, 1999): 152–154.

82. Mauro F. Guillen, "The Age of Eclecticism: Current Organizational Trends and the Evolution of Managerial Models," *Sloan Management Review* (Fall 1994): 75–86.

83. Jeremy Main, "How to Steal the Best Ideas Around," *Fortune* (October 19, 1992): 102–106.

84. Darrell Rigby and Barbara Bilodeau, "Bain's Global 2007 Management Tools and Trends Survey," *Strategy & Leadership* 35(5) (2007): 9–16.

85. Thomas H. Davenport and Laurence Prusak, with Jim Wilson, *What's the Big Idea? Creating and Capitalizing on the Best Management Thinking* (Boston: Harvard Business School Press, 2003). Also see Theodore Kinni, "Have We Run Out of Big Ideas?" *Across the Board* (March–April 2003): 16–21; and Joyce Thompson Heames and Michael Harvey, "The Evolution of the Concept of the Executive from the 20th Century Manager to the 21st Century Global Leader," *Journal of Leadership and Organizational Studies* 13(2) (2006): 29–41.

CHAPTER 2

The Environment and Corporate Culture

1. Christopher Palmeri, "What Went Wrong at Mattel" *Business-Week Online*, August 14, 2007 (www.businessweek.com/bwdaily/dnflash/content/aug2007/db20070814_154726_page_2.htm) (accessed February 5, 2008).

2. David Barboza and Louise Story, "Dancing Elmo Smackdown," *New York Times,* online edition, July 26, 2007 (www.nytimes.com/2007/07/26/business/26toy.html?_r=1&scp=1&sq=dancing+elmo+smackdown&st=nyt&oref=slog in) (accessed February 5, 2008).

3. This section is based on Richard L. Daft, *Organization Theory and Design*, 8th ed. (Cincinnati: South-Western, 2004): 136–140.

4. L. J. Bourgeois, "Strategy and Environment: A Conceptual Integration," *Academy of Management Review* 5 (1980): 25–39.

5. Google Web site. Retrieved February 7, 2008, from www.google.com.

6. Cliff Edwards, "Wherever You Go, You're On the Job," *BusinessWeek* (June 20, 2005): 87–90.

7. "Tools for Better Living," *Fortune* (December 11, 2006): 135.

8. Stephen Baker and Adam Astor, "The Business of Nanotech," *BusinessWeek* (February 14, 2005): 64–71.

9. William B. Johnston, "Global Work Force 2000: The New World Labor Market," *Harvard Business Review* (March–April 1991): 115–127.

10. U.S. Census Bureau, "The Face of Our Population," 2008 (http://factfinder.census.gov/jsp/saff/SAFFInfo.jsp?_pageId=tp9_race_ethnicity) (accessed January 28, 2008).

11. "You Raised Them, Now Manage Them," *Fortune* (May 28, 2007): 38–46.

12. U.S. Census (www.census.gov).

13. Sebastian Moffett, "Senior Moment: Fast-Aging Japan Keeps Its Elders on the Job Longer," *Wall Street Journal*, June 15, 2005, p. A1.

14. Samuel Loewenberg, "Europe Gets Tougher on U.S. Companies," *New York Times*, April 20, 2003.

15. Barney Gimbel, "Attack of the Wal-Martyrs," *Fortune* (December 11, 2006): 125.

16. Andrew Adam Newman, "Environmentalists Push, but Home Depot Refuses to Drop Ads on Fox News," *New York Times*, July 30, 2007 (www.nytimes.com/2007/07/30/business/media/30depot.html?scp=1&sq=Environmentalists+Push%2C+but+Home+Depot&st=nyt) (accessed July 30, 2007).

17. Dror Etzion, "Research on Organizations and the Natural Environment," *Journal of Management* 33 (August 2007): 637–654.

18. Bruce Horovitz, "Whole Foods Sacks Plastic Bags," *USA Today*, January 22, 2008, p. B1.

19. Stuart Birch, "Now Companies Are Going Green Right from the Start," *The Times* (United Kingdom), Green Motoring Focus Report 7, January 25, 2008, p. 7.

20. Matthew L. Wald, "What's Kind to Nature Can be Kind to Profits," *New York Times*, May 17, 2006 (www.nytimes.com/2006/05/17/business/ businessspecial2/17giant.html?scp=1&sq=What%27s+Kind+to+Nature+Can+Be+Kind+to+Profits&st=nyt) (accessed January 30, 2008).

21. Jessi Hempel, "The MySpace Generation," *BusinessWeek* (December 12, 2005): 86–94.

22. John Simons, "Stop Moaning about Gripe Sites and Log On," *Fortune* (April 2, 2001): 181–182.

23. Jon Swartz, "MySpace Cranks Up Heat in Turf War with Facebook," *USA Today*, December 21, 2007 (www.usatoday.com/tech/ webguide/2007-12-20-myspace_n.htm) (accessed December 21, 2007).

24. Gary Rivlin, "When Buying a Diamond Starts with a Mouse," *New York Times*, January 7, 2007 (www.nytimes.com/2007/01/07/business/yourmoney/07nile.html?_r=1&scp=1&sq=When+buying+a+diamond+starts+with+a+mouse&st=nyt&oref=slogin) (accessed January 15, 2007).

25. Paul Glader, "Steel-Price Rise Crimps Profits, Adds Uncertainty," *Wall Street Journal*, February 23, 2004.

26. John R. Wilke and Kathy Chen, "Planned Economy; As China's Trade Clout Grows, So Do Price-Fixing Accusations," *Wall Street Journal*, February 10, 2006.

27. Nortel Web site (www.nortel.com) (accessed February 2, 2008).

28. Ibid.

29. "China's Ministry of Railways Chooses Nortel Mobile Network to Enable High-Speed Railway to Run Smoother GSM-R Wireless Staff Communication and Signaling Optimize Train Performance," *M2 Press-wire*, January, 29, 2008, Business and Company Resource Center database (accessed February 11, 2008).

30. Acquired from Nortel Networks, *Corporate Backgrounder*, 1.

31. Ibid.

32. Roger O. Crockett, "Finally Good News From Nortel," *Business-Week* (November 6, 2007) (http://www.businessweek.com/technology/content/nov2007/tc2007116_384831.htm?chan=search) (accessed February 12, 2008).

33. Olga Kharif, "Nortel's New Lease on Life," *BusinessWeek Online*, January 26, 2006 (accessed February 3, 2008); Roger O.

Crockett, "Nortel: Desperately Seeking Credibility," *Business-Week* (January 17, 2005): 60–61; Bernard Simon, "A Bright New Day for the Telecom Industry, If the Public Will Go Along," *New York Times*, January 12, 2004; Mark Heinzl, "Nortel's Profit of $499 Million Exceeds Forecast," *Wall Street Journal*, January 30, 2004; Joseph Weber with Andy Reinhardt and Peter Burrows, "Racing Ahead at Nortel," *BusinessWeek* (November 8, 1999): 93–99; Ian Austen, "Hooked on the Net," *Canadian Business* (June 26–July 10, 1998): 95–103; "Nortel's Waffling Continues; First Job Cuts, Then Product Lines, and Now the CEO. What's Next?" *Telephony* (May 21, 2001): 12; Sara Silver and Joann S. Lublin, "Corporate News: Nortel CEO to Step Aside Soon—Zafirovski Took Firm Into Bankruptcy, Sold Assets After Failed Turnaround," *Wall Street Journal*, August 8, 2009, p. B5.

34. Robert B. Duncan, "Characteristics of Organizational Environment and Perceived Environmental Uncertainty," *Administrative Science Quarterly 17* (1972): 313–327; and Daft, *Organization Theory and Design*.

35. The self-test questions are based on ideas from R. L. Daft and R. M. Lengel, *Fusion Leadership* (San Francisco: Berrett Koehler, 2000): Chapter 4; B. Bass and B. Avolio, *Multifactor Leadership Questionnaire,* 2nd ed. (Menlo Park, CA: Mind Garden, 2004); and Karl E. Weick and Kathleen M. Sutcliffe, *Managing the Unexpected: Assuring High Performance in an Age of Complexity* (San Francisco: Jossey-Bass, 2001).

36. Sarah Moore, "On Your Markets," *Working Woman* (February 2001): 26; and John Simons, "Stop Moaning about Gripe Sites and Log On," *Fortune* (April 2, 2001): 181–182.

37. Tom Duffy, "Spying the Holy Grail," *Microsoft Executive Circle* (Winter 2004): 38–39.

38. Stephan M. Wagner and Roman Boutellier, "Capabilities for Managing a Portfolio of Supplier Relationships," *Business Horizons* (November–December 2002): 79–88; Peter Smith Ring and Andrew H. Van de Ven, "Developmental Processes of Corporate Interorganizational Relationships," *Academy of Management Review* 19 (1994): 90–118; Myron Magnet, "The New Golden Rule of Business," *Fortune* (February 21, 1994): 60–64; and Peter Grittner, "Four Elements of Successful Sourcing Strategies," *Management Review* (October 1996): 41–45.

39. Patricia Sellers, "The Business of Being Oprah," *Fortune* (April 1, 2002): 50–64.

40. Yoash Wiener, "Forms of Value Systems: A Focus on Organizational Effectiveness and Culture Change and Maintenance," *Academy of Management Review* 13 (1988): 534–545; V. Lynne Meek, "Organizational Culture: Origins and Weaknesses," *Organization Studies* 9 (1988): 453–473; John J. Sherwood, "Creating Work Cultures with Competitive Advantage," *Organizational Dynamics* (Winter 1988): 5–27; and Andrew D. Brown and Ken Starkey, "The Effect of Organizational Culture on Communication and Information," *Journal of Management Studies* 31(6) (November 1994): 807–828.

41. Joanne Martin, *Organizational Culture: Mapping the Terrain* (Thousand Oaks, CA: Sage Publications, 2002); Ralph H.

Kilmann, Mary J. Saxton, and Roy Serpa, "Issues in Understanding and Changing Culture," *California Management Review* 28 (Winter 1986): 87–94; and Linda Smircich, "Concepts of Culture and Organizational Analysis," *Administrative Science Quarterly* 28 (1983): 339–358.

42. Based on Edgar H. Schein, *Organizational Culture and Leadership*, 2nd ed. (San Francisco: Jossey-Bass, 1992): 3–27.

43. Michael G. Pratt and Anat Rafaeli, "Symbols as a Language of Organizational Relationships," *Research in Organizational Behavior* 23 (2001): 93–132.

44. Christine Canabou, "Here's the Drill," *Fast Company* (February 2001): 58.

45. Chip Jarnagin and John W. Slocum, Jr. "Creating Corporate Cultures through Mythopoetic Leadership," *Organizational Dynamics* 36(3) (2007): 288–302.

46. Robert E. Quinn and Gretchen M. Spreitzer, "The Road to Empowerment: Seven Questions Every Leader Should Consider," *Organizational Dynamics* (Autumn 1997): 37–49.

47. Toyota Web site (www.toyota.com) (accessed February 12, 2008).

48. Jarnagin and Slocum, "Creating Corporate Cultures."

49. Martin, *Organizational Culture*, pp. 71–72.

50. Terrence E. Deal and Allan A. Kennedy, *Corporate Cultures: The Rites and Rituals of Corporate Life* (Reading, MA: Addison-Wesley, 1982).

51. Arthur Yeung, "Setting People Up for Success: How the Portman Ritz-Carlton Hotel Gets the Best From Its People," *Human Resource Management* 45(2) (Summer 2006): 267–275.

52. Patricia Jones and Larry Kahaner, *Say It and Live It: Fifty Corporate Mission Statements That Hit the Mark* (New York: Currency Doubleday, 1995).

53. Harrison M. Trice and Janice M. Beyer, "Studying Organizational Cultures Through Rites and Ceremonials," *Academy of Management Review* 9 (1984): 653–669.

54. PRWeb, November 3, 2005 (www.prweb.com/releases/2005/11/prweb306461.php) (accessed February 7, 2008).

55. Jennifer A. Chatman and Karen A. Jehn, "Assessing the Relationship Between Industry Characteristics and Organizational Culture: How Different Can You Be?" *Academy of Management Journal* 37(3) (1994): 522–553.

56. John P. Kotter and James L. Heskett, *Corporate Culture and Performance* (New York: The Free Press, 1992).

57. This discussion is based on Paul McDonald and Jeffrey Gandz, "Getting Value from Shared Values," *Organizational Dynamics* 21(3) (Winter 1992): 64–76; Daniel R. Denison and Aneil K. Mishra, "Toward a Theory of Organizational Culture and Effectiveness," *Organization Science* 6(2) (March–April 1995): 204–223; and Richard L. Daft, *The Leadership Experience,* 3rd ed. (Cincinnati: South-Western, 2005), pp. 570–573.

58. Lucas Conley, "Rinse and Repeat," *Fast Company* (July 2005): 76–77.

59. Robert Hooijberg and Frank Petrock, "On Cultural Change: Using the Competing Values Framework to Help Leaders Execute a Transformational Strategy," *Human Resource Management* 32(1) (1993): 29–50.

60. Patrick Lencioni, "Make Your Values Mean Something," *Harvard Business Review* (July 2002): 113–117, and Melanie Warner, "Confessions of a Control Freak," *Fortune* (September 4, 2000): 130–140.

61. Tim Young, "Rewarding Work," *HR Management,* Issue 172 (2005) (www.hrmreport.com); and Janet Guyon, "The Soul of a Money-Making Machine," *Fortune* (October 3, 2005): 113–120.

62. Rekha Balu, "Pacific Edge Projects Itself," *Fast Company* (October 2000): 371–381.

63. Jeffrey Pfeffer, *The Human Equation: Building Profits by Putting People First* (Boston: Harvard Business School Press, 1998).

64. Jeremy Kahn, "What Makes a Company Great?" *Fortune* (October 26, 1998): 218; James C. Collins and Jerry I. Porras, *Built to Last: Successful Habits of Visionary Companies* (New York: HarperCollins, 1994); and James C. Collins, "Change Is Good— But First Know What Should Never Change," *Fortune* (May 29, 1995): 141.

65. Andrew Wahl, "Culture Shock," *Canadian Business* (October 10–23, 2005): 115–116.

66. Jennifer A. Chatman and Sandra Eunyoung Cha, "Leading by Leveraging Culture," *California Management Review* 45(4) (Summer 2003): 20–34.

67. This section is based on Jeff Rosenthal and Mary Ann Masarech, "High Performance Cultures: How Values Can Drive Business Results," *Journal of Organizational Excellence* (Spring 2003): 3–18.

68. Nelson D. Schwartz, "One Brick at a Time," *Fortune* (June 12, 2006): 45–46.

69. Katherine Mieszkowski, "Community Standards," *Fast Company* (September 2000): 368; Rosabeth Moss Kanter, "A More Perfect Union," *Inc.* (February 2001): 92–98; and Raizel Robin, "Net Gains segment of E-Biz That Works," *Canadian Business* (October 14–October 26, 2003): 107.

70. Reggie Van Lee, Lisa Fabish, and Nancy McGaw, "The Value of Corporate Values: A Booz Allen Hamilton/Aspen Institute Survey," *Strategy + Business* 39 (Spring 2005): 52–65.

71. Lucas Conley, "Cultural Phenomenon," *Fast Company* (April 2005): 76–77.

72. Rosenthal and Masarech, "High-Performance Cultures."

73. John P. Kotter and James L. Heskett, *Corporate Culture and Performance* (New York: The Free Press, 1992); Eric Flamholtz and Rangapriya Kannan-Narasimhan, "Differential Impact of Cultural Elements on Financial Performance," *European Management Journal* 23(1) (2005): 50–64. Also see J. M. Kouzes and B. Z. Posner, *The Leadership Challenge: How to Keep Getting Extraordinary Things Done in Organizations,* 3rd ed. (San Francisco: Jossey-Bass, 2002).

74. Micah R. Kee, "Corporate Culture Makes a Fiscal Difference," *Industrial Management* (November–December 2003): 16–20.

75. Rosenthal and Masarech, "High Performance Cultures"; Lencioni, "Make Your Values Mean Something"; and Thomas J. Peters and Robert H. Waterman, Jr., *In Search of Excellence* (New York: Warner, 1988).

76. Jarnagin and Slocum, "Creating Corporate Cultures."

77. Guyon, "The Soul of a Moneymaking Machine"; and Geoff Colvin, "The 100 Best Companies to Work for in 2006," *Fortune* (January 23, 2006).

CHAPTER 3

Managing in a Global Environment

1. Ted C. Fishman, "How China Will Change Your Business," *Inc. Magazine* (March 2005): 70–84; and Stephen Baker, "The Bridges Steel Is Building," *BusinessWeek* (June 2, 1997): 39.

2. Figures provided by CXO Media, reported in Steve Ulfelder, "All the Web's a Stage," *CIO* (October 1, 2000): 133–142; and Pete Engardio, "A New World Economy," *BusinessWeek* (August 22–29, 2005): 52–58.

3. Jason Dean, "Upgrade Plan: Long a Low-Tech Player, China Sets Its Sights on Chip Making," *Wall Street Journal*, February 17, 2004, p. A1.

4. Engardio, "A New World Economy."

5. Cassell Bryan-Low, "Criminal Network: To Catch Crooks in Cyberspace, FBI Goes Global," *Wall Street Journal*, November 21, 2006, p. A1.

6. Joseph B. White, "There Are No German or U.S. Companies, Only Successful Ones," *Wall Street Journal*, May 7, 1998, p. A1.

7. Ted C. Fishman, "Half a World Away, An Entrepreneur Grapples with (and Profits from) China's Boom." Special section in "How China Will Change Your Business," *Inc* (March 2005): 70–84.

8. Adapted from Cynthia Barnum and Natasha Wolniansky, "Why Americans Fail at Overseas Negotiations," *Management Review* (October 1989): 54–57.

9. Adam Lashinsky, "Intel Outside," and Patricia Sellers, "Blowing in the Wind." Special supplement, "Fortune 500: The World of Ideas," *Fortune* (July 25, 2005): 127–138.

10. Louise Story, "Seeking Leaders, U.S. Companies Think Globally," *New York Times*, December 12, 2007, p. A1.

11. Phred Dvorak and Merissa Marr, "In Surprise Move, Sony Plans to Hand Reins to a Foreigner," *Wall Street Journal*, March 7, 2005; Carol Hymowitz, "More American Chiefs Are Taking Top Posts at Overseas Concerns," *Wall Street Journal*, October 17, 2005, p. B1; and Justin Martin, "The Global CEO: Overseas Experience Is Becoming a Must on Top Executives' Resumes," *Chief Executive* (January–February 2004): 24.

12. Jean Kerr, "Export Strategies," *Small Business Reports* (May 1989): 20–25.

13. Fishman, "How China Will Change Your Business."

14. Jennifer Pellet, "The New Logic of Outsourcing: The Next Generation of Offshoring—Innovating and Engineering—Is at Hand (Roundtable)," *Chief Executive* (September 2007): 36–41.

15. Alison Stein Wellner, "Turning the Tables" *Inc.* (May 2006): 55–59.

16. Pellet, "The New Logic of Outsourcing."

17. Fishman, "How China Will Change Your Business."

18. Engardio, "A New World Economy."

19. Louise Story, "After Stumbling, Mattel Cracks Down in China," *New York Times*, August 29, 2007 (www.nytimes.com/2007/08/29/business/worldbusiness/29mattel.html?ref=business. . .) (accessed August 29, 2007).

20. James Flanigan, "Now, High-Tech Work Is Going Abroad," *New York Times*, November 17, 2005, p. C6.

21. Sheridan Prasso, "Google Goes to India," *Fortune* (October 29, 2007): 160–166.

22. Cited in Gary Ferraro, *Cultural Anthropology: An Applied Perspective*, 3rd ed. (Belmont, CA: West/Wadsworth, 1998): 68.

23. Jim Holt, "Gone Global?" *Management Review* (March 2000): 13.

24. Ibid.

25. "Slogans Often Lose Something in Translation," *The New Mexican*, (July 3, 1994).

26. Louis S. Richman, "Global Growth Is on a Tear," in Fred Maidment (Ed.), *International Business 97/98, Annual Editions* (Guilford, CT: Dushkin, 1997): 6–11.

27. "The Global Competitiveness Report 2007–2008," World Economic Forum, (www.gcr.weforum.org) (accessed April 30, 2008).

28. Andrew E. Serwer, "McDonald's Conquers the World," *Fortune* (October 17, 1994): 103–116.

29. David W. Conklin, "Analyzing and Managing Country Risks," *Ivey Business Journal* (January–February 2002): 37–41.

30. Bruce Kogut, "Designing Global Strategies: Profiting from Operational Flexibility," *Sloan Management Review* 27 (Fall 1985): 27–38.

31. Ian Bremmer, "Managing Risk in an Unstable World," *Harvard Business Review* (June 2005): 51–60; and Mark Fitzpatrick, "The Definition and Assessment of Political Risk in International Business: A Review of the Literature," *Academy of Management Review* 8 (1983): 249–254.

32. Jason Bush, "Business in Russia Just Got Riskier," *BusinessWeek* (April 23, 2007): 43.

33. Kevin Sullivan, "Kidnapping Is Growth Industry in Mexico; Businessmen Targeted in Climate of Routine Ransoms, Police Corruption," *Washington Post*, September 17, 2002, p. A01.

34. Conklin, "Analyzing and Managing Country Risks"; Nicolas Checa, John Maguire, and Jonathan Barney, "The New World Disorder," *Harvard Business Review* (August 2003): 71–79; and Jennifer Pellet, "Top 10 Enterprise Risks: What Potential Threats Keep CEOs Up at Night? (Roundtable)," *Chief Executive* (October–November 2007): 48–53.

35. See Conklin, "Analyzing and Managing Country Risks."

36. Barbara Whitaker, "The Web Makes Going Global Easy, Until You Try to Do It," *New York Times*, September 2000, p. H20.

37. Geert Hofstede, "The Interaction Between National and Organizational Value Systems," *Journal of Management Studies* 22 (1985): 347–357; and Geert Hofstede, "The Cultural Relativity of the Quality of Life Concept," *Academy of Management Review* 9 (1984): 389–398.

38. Geert Hofstede, "Cultural Constraints in Management Theory," *Academy of Management Executive* 7 (1993): 81–94; and G. Hofstede and M. H. Bond, "The Confucian Connection: From Cultural Roots to Economic Growth," *Organizational Dynamics* 16 (1988): 4–21.

39. For an overview of the research and publications related to Hofstede's dimensions, see "Retrospective: *Culture's Consequences*," a collection of articles focusing on Hofstede's work, in *The Academy of Management Executive* 18(1) (February 2004): 72–93. See also Michele J. Gelfand, D. P. S. Bhawuk, Lisa H. Nishii, and David J. Bechtold, "Individualism and Collectivism" in R. J. House, P. J. Hanges, M. Javidan, and P. Dorfman (Eds.), *Culture, Leadership and Organizations: The GLOBE Study of 62 Societies* (Thousand Oaks, CA: Sage, 2004).

40. Robert J. House, Paul J. Hanges, Mansour Javidan, and Peter W. Dorfman (Eds.), *Culture, Leadership, and Organizations: The GLOBE Study of 62 Societies* (Thousand Oaks, CA: Sage Publications, 2004); M. Javidan and R. J. House, "Cultural Acumen for the Global Manager: Lessons from Project GLOBE," *Organizational Dynamics* 29(4) (2001): 289–305; and R. J. House, M. Javidan, Paul Hanges, and Peter Dorfman, "Understanding Cultures and Implicit Leadership Theories Across the Globe: An Introduction to Project GLOBE," *Journal of World Business* 37 (2002): 3–10.

41. Chantell E. Nicholls, Henry W. Lane, and Mauricio Brehm Brechu, "Taking Self-Managed Teams to Mexico," *Academy of Management Executive* 13(2) (1999): 15–27; Carl F. Fey and Daniel R. Denison, "Organizational Culture and Effectiveness: Can American Theory Be Applied in Russia?" *Organization Science* 14(6) (November–December 2003): 686–706; and Ellen F. Jackofsky, John W. Slocum, Jr., and Sara J. McQuaid, "Cultural Values and the CEO: Alluring Companions?" *Academy of Management Executive* 2 (1988): 39–49.

42. J. Kennedy and A. Everest, "Put Diversity in Context," *Personnel Journal* (September 1991): 50–54.

43. Terence Jackson, "The Management of People Across Cultures: Valuing People Differently," *Human Resource Management* 41(4) (Winter 2002): 455–475.

44. Elizabeth Esfahani, "Thinking Locally, Succeeding Globally," *Business 2.0* (December 2005): 96–98.

45. This discussion is based on "For Richer, for Poorer," *The Economist* (December 1993): 66; Richard Harmsen, "The Uruguay Round: A Boon for the World Economy," *Finance & Development* (March 1995): 24–26; Salil S. Pitroda, "From GATT to WTO: The Institutionalization of World Trade," *Harvard International Review* (Spring 1995): 46–47, 66–67; and World Trade Organization (www.wto.org) (accessed February 11, 2008).

46. "The History of the European Union" (www.europa.eu.int/abc/history/index_en.htm) (accessed February 11, 2008).

47. European Commission Economic and Financial Affairs Web site (http://ec.europa.eu/economy_finance/the_euro/index_en.htm?cs_mid=2946) (accessed August 8, 2008).

48. Lynda Radosevich, "New Money," *CIO Enterprise*, section 2 (April 15, 1998): 54–58.

49. Tapan Munroe, "NAFTA Still a Work in Progress," *Knight Ridder/Tribune News Service* (January 9, 2004): 1; and J. S. McClenahan, "NAFTA Works," *IW* (January 10, 2000): 5–6.

50. Amy Barrett, "It's a Small (Business) World," *BusinessWeek* (April 17, 1995): 96–101.

51. Eric Alterman, "A Spectacular Success?" *The Nation* (February 2, 2004): 10; Jeff Faux, "NAFTA at 10: Where Do We Go From Here?" *The Nation* (February 2, 2004): 11; Geri Smith and Cristina Lindblad, "Mexico: Was NAFTA Worth It? A Tale of What Free Trade Can and Cannot Do," *BusinessWeek* (December 22, 2003): 66; Jeffrey Sparshott, "NAFTA Gets Mixed Reviews," *Washington Times*, December 18, 2003, p. C10; and Munroe, "NAFTA Still a Work in Progress."

52. Munroe, "NAFTA Still a Work in Progress"; Sparshott, "NAFTA Gets Mixed Reviews"; and Amy Borrus, "A Free-Trade Milestone, with Many More Miles to Go," *BusinessWeek* (August 24, 1992): 30–31.

53. Nina Easton, "Make the World Go Away," *Fortune* (February 4, 2008): 105–108.

54. Pete Engardio, Aaron Bernstein, and Manjeet Kripalani, "Is Your Job Next?" *BusinessWeek* (February 3, 2003): 50–60.

55. Jyoti Thottam, "Is Your Job Going Abroad?" *Time* (March 1, 2004): 26–36.

56. Easton, "Make the World Go Away."

57. Michael Schroeder and Timothy Aeppel, "Skilled Workers Mount Opposition to Free Trade, Swaying Politicians," *Wall Street Journal*, October 10, 2003, p. A1.

58. Alison Stein Wellner, "Turning the Tables," *Inc. Magazine* (May 2006): 55–59.

59. Easton, "Make the World Go Away."

60. William J. Holstein, "Haves and Have-Nots of Globalization," *New York Times*, July 8, 2007, p. BU4.

61. Christopher Bartlett, *Managing Across Borders*, 2nd ed. (Boston: Harvard Business School Press, 1998); and quote from Buss, "World Class: Non-American CEOs Are Having a Big Impact at Traditional U.S. Companies," *Chief Executive* (April 1, 2004): 44–47.

62. Morgan W. McCall, Jr., and George P. Hollenbeck, "Global Fatalities: When International Executives Derail," *Ivey Business Journal* (May–June 2002): 75–78.

63. The discussion of cultural intelligence is based on P. Christopher Earley and Elaine Mosakowski, "Cultural Intelligence," *Harvard Business Review* (October 2004): 139; Ilan Alon and James M. Higgins, "Global Leadership Success Through Emotional and Cultural Intelligence," *Business Horizons* 48 (2005): 501–512; P. C. Earley and Soon Ang, *Cultural Intelligence: Individual Actions Across Cultures* (Stanford, CA: Stanford Business Books); and David C. Thomas and Kerr Inkson, *Cultural Intelligence* (San Francisco: Berrett-Koehler, 2004).

64. Pat McGovern, "How to Be a Local, Anywhere," *Inc. Magazine* (April 2007): 113–114.

65. These components are from Earley and Mosakowski, "Cultural Intelligence."

66. Karl Moore, "Great Global Managers," *Across the Board* (May–June 2003): 40–43.

67. Richard E. Nisbett, *The Geography of Thought: How Asians and Westerners Think Differently . . . and Why* (New York: The Free Press, 2003), reported in Sharon Begley, "East vs. West: One Sees the Big Picture, The Other Is Focused," *Wall Street Journal*, March 28, 2003, p. B1.

68. Robert T. Moran and John R. Riesenberger, *The Global Challenge* (London: McGraw-Hill, 1994): 251–262.

69. Joann S. Lublin, "Companies Use Cross-Cultural Training to Help Their Employees Adjust Abroad," *Wall Street Journal*, August 4, 1992, p. 1.

70. Gilbert Fuchsberg, "As Costs of Overseas Assignments Climb, Firms Select Expatriates More Carefully," *Wall Street Journal*, January 9, 1992, p. 1.

71. Valerie Frazee, "Keeping Up on Chinese Culture," *Global Workforce* (October 1996): 16–17; and Jack Scarborough, "Comparing Chinese and Western Cultural Roots: Why 'East Is East and . . . ,'" *Business Horizons* (November–December 1998): 15–24.

72. Mansour Javidan and Ali Dastmalchian, "Culture and Leadership in Iran: The Land of Individual Achievers, Strong Family Ties, and Powerful Elite," *Academy of Management Executive* 17(4) (2003): 127–142.

73. Randall S. Schuler, Susan E. Jackson, Ellen Jackofsky, and John W. Slocum, Jr., "Managing Human Resources in Mexico: A Cultural Understanding," *Business Horizons* (May–June 1996): 55–61.

74. Towers Perrin data reported in "Workers Want . . ." sidebar in Peter Coy, "Cog or Co-Worker?" *Business-Week* (August 20 & 27, 2007): 58–60.

75. Xu Huang and Evert Van De Vliert, "Where Intrinsic Job Satisfaction Fails to Work: National Moderators of Intrinsic Motivation," *Journal of Organizational Behavior* 24 (2003): 159–179.

76. Shari Caudron, "Lessons from HR Overseas," *Personnel Journal* (February 1995): 88.

77. Reported in Begley, "East vs. West."

CHAPTER 4

Managerial Ethics and Corporate Social Responsibility

1. Bethany McLean, "Why Enron Went Bust," *Fortune* (December 24, 2001): 58–68; and survey results reported in Patricia Wallington, "Honestly?!" *CIO* (March 15, 2003): 41–42.

2. Mike Esterl, "Executive Derision: In Germany, Scandals Tarnish Business Elite," *Wall Street Journal*, March 4, 2008, p. A1.

3. Gordon F. Shea, *Practical Ethics* (New York: American Management Association, 1988); and Linda K. Treviño, "Ethical Decision Making in Organizations; A Person-Situation Interactionist Model," *Academy of Management Review* 11 (1986): 601–617.

4. Thomas M. Jones, "Ethical Decision Making by Individuals in Organizations: An Issue-Contingent Model," *Academy of Management Review* 16(1991): 366–395.

5. Shelby D. Hunt and Jared M. Hansen, "Understanding Ethical Diversity in Organizations," *Organizational Dynamics* 36(2) (2007): 202–216.

6. John R. Emshwiller and Alexei Barrionuevo, "U.S. Prosecutors File Indictment Against Skilling," *Wall Street Journal*, February 20, 2004, p. A1.

7. See Clinton W. McLemore, *Street-Smart Ethics: Succeeding in Business Without Selling Your Soul* (Louisville, KY: Westminster John Knox Press, 2003), for a cogent discussion of some ethical and legal issues associated with Enron's collapse.

8. Rushworth M. Kidder, "The Three Great Domains of Human Action," *Christian Science Monitor*, January 30, 1990, p. 13.

9. Linda K. Treviño and Katherine A. Nelson, *Managing Business Ethics: Straight Talk About How to Do It Right* (New York: John Wiley & Sons, 1995): 4.

10. Jones, "Ethical Decision Making by Individuals in Organizations."

11. Based on a question from a General Electric employee ethics guide, reported in Kathryn Kranhold, "U.S. Firms Raise Ethics Focus," *Wall Street Journal*, November 28, 2005, p. B4.

12. Based on information in Constance E. Bagley, "The Ethical Leader's Decision Tree," *Harvard Business Review* (February 2003): 18–19.

13. Based on information in Vadim Liberman, "Scoring on the Job," *Across the Board* (November– December 2003): 46–50.

14. From Jeffrey Kluger, "What Makes Us Moral? *Time* (December 3, 2007): 54–60.

15. "The Morality Quiz" at www.time.com/morality (accessed February 19, 2008).

16. This discussion is based on Gerald F. Cavanagh, Dennis J. Moberg, and Manuel Velasquez, "The Ethics of Organizational Politics," *Academy of Management Review* 6 (1981): 363–374; Justin G. Longenecker, Joseph A. McKinney, and Carlos W. Moore, "Egoism and Independence: Entrepreneurial Ethics," *Organizational Dynamics* (Winter 1988): 64–72; Carolyn Wiley, "The ABCs of Business Ethics: Definitions, Philosophies, and Implementation," *IM* (February 1995): 22–27; and Mark Mallinger, "Decisive Decision Making: An Exercise Using Ethical Frameworks," *Journal of Management Education* (August 1997): 411–417.

17. Michael J. McCarthy, "Now the Boss Knows Where You're Clicking," and "Virtual Morality: A New Workplace Quandary," *Wall Street Journal*, October 21, 1999, p. B1; and Jeffrey L. Seglin, "Who's Snooping on You?" *Business 2.0* (August 8, 2000): 202–203.

18. John Kekes, "Self-Direction: The Core of Ethical Individualism," in Konstanian Kolenda (Ed.), *Organizations and Ethical Individualism* (New York: Praeger, 1988): 1–18.

19. Tad Tulega, *Beyond the Bottom Line* (New York: Penguin Books, 1987).

20. L. Kohlberg, "Moral Stages and Moralization: The Cognitive-Developmental Approach," in T. Lickona (Ed.), *Moral Development and Behavior: Theory, Research, and Social Issues* (New York: Holt, Rinehart & Winston, 1976): 31–83; L. Kohlberg, "Stage and Sequence: The Cognitive-Developmental Approach to Socialization," in D. A. Goslin (Ed.), *Handbook of Socialization Theory and Research* (Chicago: Rand McNally, 1969); Linda K. Treviño, Gary R. Weaver, and Scott J. Reynolds, "Behavioral Ethics in Organizations: A Review," *Journal of Management* 32(6) (December 2006): 951–990; and Jill W. Graham, "Leadership, Moral Development, and Citizenship Behavior," *Business Ethics Quarterly* 5(1) (January 1995): 43–54.

21. See Thomas Donaldson and Thomas W. Dunfee, "When Ethics Travel: The Promise and Peril of Global Business Ethics," *California Management Review* 41(4) (Summer 1999): 45–63.

22. Transparency International, "The BPI 2006—The Ranking" (www.transparency.org/policy_research/ surveys_indices/bpi/ bpi_2006) (accessed February 18, 2007).

23. Eugene W. Szwajkowski, "The Myths and Realities of Research on Organizational Misconduct," in James E. Post (Ed.), *Research in Corporate Social Performance and Policy* (Greenwich, CT: JAI Press, 1986), 9:103–122; and Keith Davis, William C. Frederick, and Robert L. Blostrom, *Business and Society: Concepts and Policy Issues* (New York: McGraw-Hill, 1979).

24. Douglas S. Sherwin, "The Ethical Roots of the Business System," *Harvard Business Review* 61 (November–December 1983): 183–192.

25. Nancy C. Roberts and Paula J. King, "The Stakeholder Audit Goes Public," *Organizational Dynamics* (Winter 1989): 63–79; Thomas Donaldson and Lee E. Preston, "The Stakeholder Theory of the Corporation: Concepts, Evidence, and Implications," *Academy of Management Review* 20(1) (1995): 65–91; and Jeffrey S. Harrison and Caron H. St. John, "Managing and Partnering with External Stakeholders," *Academy of Management Executive* 10(2) (1996): 46–60.

26. Clay Chandler, "The Great Wal-Mart of China," *Fortune* (July 25, 2005): 104–116; and Charles Fishman, "The Wal-Mart You Don't Know—Why Low Prices Have a High Cost," *Fast Company* (December 2003): 68–80.

27. David Wheeler, Barry Colbert, and R. Edward Freeman, "Focusing on Value: Reconciling Corporate Social Responsibility, Sustainability, and a Stakeholder Approach in a Networked World," *Journal of General Management* 28(3) (Spring 2003): 1–28; James E. Post, Lee E. Preston, and Sybille Sachs, "Managing the Extended Enterprise: The New Stakeholder View," *California*

Management Review 45(1) (Fall 2002): 6–28; and Peter Fritsch and Timothy Mapes, "Seed Money; In Indonesia, A Tangle of Bribes Creates Trouble for Monsanto," *Wall Street Journal*, April 5, 2005, p. A1.

28. Max B. E. Clarkson, "A Stakeholder Framework for Analyzing and Evaluating Corporate Social Performance," *Academy of Management Review* 20(1) (1995): 92–117.

29. C. K. Prahalad and S. L. Hart, "The Fortune at the Bottom of the Pyramid," *Strategy + Business* 26 (2006): 54–67.

30. Rob Walker, "Cleaning Up," *New York Times Magazine* (June 10, 2007): 20.

31. Ibid.

32. This definition is based on Marc J. Epstein and Marie-Josée Roy, "Improving Sustainability Performance: Specifying, Implementing and Measuring Key Principles," *Journal of General Management* 29(1) (Autumn 2003): 15–31; World Commission on Economic Development, *Our Common Future* (Oxford, UK: Oxford University Press, 1987): and Marc Gunther, "Tree Huggers, Soy Lovers, and Profits," *Fortune* (June 23, 2003): 98–104.

33. Cornelia Dean, "Executive on a Mission: Saving the Planet," *New York Times*, May 22, 2007, p. F1.

34. John Carey, "Hugging the Tree Huggers," *BusinessWeek* (March 12, 2007): 66–68.

35. Reported in Kate O'Sullivan, "Virtue Rewarded," *CFO* (October 2006): 47–52.

36. Carey, "Hugging the Tree Huggers."

37. Mark Borden, Jeff Chu, Charles Fishman, Michael A. Prospero, and Danielle Sacks, "50 Ways to Green Your Business," *Fast Company* (November 2007): 90–98.

38. Mark S. Schwartz and Archie B. Carroll, "Corporate Social Responsibility: A Three-Domain Approach," *Business Ethics Quarterly* 13(4) (2003): 503–530; and Archie B. Carroll, "A Three-Dimensional Conceptual Model of Corporate Performance," *Academy of Management Review* 4 (1979): 497–505. For a discussion of various models for evaluating corporate social performance, also see Diane L. Swanson, "Addressing a Theoretical Problem by Reorienting the Corporate Social Performance Model," *Academy of Management Review* 20(1) (1995): 43–64.

39. Milton Friedman, *Capitalism and Freedom* (Chicago: University of Chicago Press, 1962): 133; and Milton Friedman and Rose Friedman, *Free to Choose* (New York: Harcourt Brace Jovanovich, 1979).

40. Eugene W. Szwajkowski, "Organizational Illegality: Theoretical Integration and Illustrative Application," *Academy of Management Review* 10 (1985): 558–567.

41. Reported in Ronald W. Clement, "Just How Unethical is American Business?" *Business Horizons* 49 (2006): 313–327.

42. David J. Fritzsche and Helmut Becker, "Linking Management Behavior to Ethical Philosophy—An Empirical Investigation," *Academy of Management Journal* 27 (1984): 165–175.

43. John Hechinger, "Financial-Aid Directors Received Payments from Preferred Lender; Student Loan Xpress Puts Three Managers on Leave Amid Multiple Inquiries," *Wall Street Journal*, April 10, 2007, p. A3; and Kathy Chu, "Three University Financial Aid Chiefs Suspended," *USA Today*, April 6, 2007 (www.usatoday.com/money/industries/ banking/2007-04-06-loans-usat_N .htm) (accessed April 6, 2007).

44. O'Sullivan, "Virtue Rewarded."

45. Katie Hafner and Claudi H. Deutsch, "When Good Will Is Also Good Business," *New York Times*, September 14, 2005, p. C1 (www.nytimes.com).

46. Saul W. Gellerman, "Managing Ethics from the Top Down," *Sloan Management Review* (Winter 1989): 73–79.

47. Michael E. Brown and Linda K. Treviño, "Ethical Leadership: A Review and Future Directions," *The Leadership Quarterly* 17 (2006): 595–616; Gary R. Weaver, Linda Klebe Treviño, and Bradley Agle, "'Somebody I Look Up To': Ethical Role Models in Organizations," *Organizational Dynamics* 34(4) (2005): 313–330; and L. K. Treviño, G. R. Weaver, David G. Gibson, and Barbara Ley Toffler, "Managing Ethics and Legal Compliance: What Works and What Hurts?" *California Management Review* 41(2) (Winter 1999): 131–151.

48. Ibid.

49. Treviño et al., "Managing Ethics and Legal Compliance."

50. Carolyn Wiley, "The ABC's of Business Ethics: Definitions, Philosophies, and Implementation," *IM* (January–February 1995): 22–27; Joseph L. Badaracco and Allen P. Webb, "Business Ethics: A View from the Trenches," *California Management Review* 37(2) (Winter 1995): 8–28; and Ronald B. Morgan, "Self- and Co-Worker Perceptions of Ethics and Their Relationships to Leadership and Salary," *Academy of Management Journal* 36(1) (February 1993): 200–214.

51. Journal Communications—Code of Ethics, from Codes of Ethics Online, The Center for the Study of Ethics in the Professions, Illinois Institute of Technology (www.iit.edu/ departments/csep/PublicWWW/codes/index.html).

52. Cheryl Rosen, "A Measure of Success? Ethics After Enron," *Business Ethics* (Summer 2006): 22–26.

53. Alan Yuspeh, "Do the Right Thing," *CIO* (August 1, 2000): 56–58.

54. Reported in Rosen, "A Measure of Success?"

55. Beverly Geber, "The Right and Wrong of Ethics Offices," *Training* (October 1995): 102–118.

56. Kranhold, "U.S. Firms Raise Ethics Focus"; and *Our Actions: GE 2005 Citizenship Report*, General Electric Company, 2005.

57. Amy Zipkin, "Getting Religion on Corporate Ethics: A Scourge of Scandals Leaves its Mark," *New York Times*, October 18, 2000, p. C1.

58. Marcia Parmarlee Miceli and Janet P. Near, "The Relationship Among Beliefs, Organizational Positions, and Whistle-Blowing Status: A Discriminant Analysis," *Academy of Management Journal* 27 (1984): 687–705.

59. Eugene Garaventa, "*An Enemy of the People* by Henrik Ibsen: The Politics of Whistle-Blowing," *Journal of Management Inquiry* 3(4) (December 1994): 369–374; and Marcia P. Miceli and Janet P. Near, "Whistleblowing: Reaping the Benefits," *Academy of Management Executive* 8(3) (1994): 65–74.

60. Reported in Rosen, "A Measure of Success?"

61. Jayne O'Donnell, "Blowing the Whistle Can Lead to Harsh Aftermath, Despite Law," *USA Today*, July 31, 2005 p. B1 (www.usatoday.com).

62. This example comes from Susan Pulliam, "Crossing the Line; At Center of Fraud, WorldCom Official Sees Life Unravel," *Wall Street Journal*, March 24, 2005, p. A1; and Susan Pulliam, "Over the Line: A Staffer Ordered to Commit Fraud Balked, Then Caved," *Wall Street Journal*, June 23, 2003, p. A1.

63. Homer H. Johnson, "Does It Pay to Be Good? Social Responsibility and Financial Performance," *Business Horizons* (November–December 2003): 34–40; Jennifer J. Griffin and John F. Mahon, "The Corporate Social Performance and Corporate Financial Performance Debate: Twenty-Five Years of Incomparable Research," *Business and Society* 36(1) (March 1997): 5–31; Bernadette M. Ruf, Krishnamurty Muralidar, Robert M. Brown, Jay J. Janney, and Karen Paul, "An Empirical Investigation of the Relationship Between Change in Corporate Social Performance and Financial Performance: A Stakeholder Theory Perspective," *Journal of Business Ethics* 32(2) (July 2001): 143; and Philip L. Cochran and Robert A. Wood, "Corporate Social Responsibility and Financial Performance," *Academy of Management Journal* 27 (1984): 42–56.

64. Paul C. Godfrey, "The Relationship Between Corporate Philanthropy and Shareholder Wealth: A Risk Management Perspective," *Academy of Management Review* 30(4) (2005): 777–798; Oliver Falck and Stephan Heblich, "Corporate Social Responsibility: Doing Well by Doing Good," *Business Horizons* 50 (2007): 247–254; J. A. Pearce II and J. P. Doh, "The High Impact of Collaborative Social Initiatives"; Curtis C. Verschoor and Elizabeth A. Murphy, "The Financial Performance of Large U.S. Firms and Those with Global Prominence: How Do the Best Corporate Citizens Rate?" *Business and Society Review* 107(3) (Fall 2002): 371–381; Johnson, "Does It Pay to Be Good?"; and Dale Kurschner, "Five Ways Ethical Business Creates Fatter Profits," *Business Ethics* (March–April 1996): 20–23. Also see studies reported in Lori Ioannou, "Corporate America's Social Conscience," *Fortune* (May 26, 2003): S1–S10.

65. Verschoor and Murphy, "The Financial Performance of Large U.S. Firms."

66. Phred Dvorak, "Finding the Best Measure of 'Corporate Citizenship,'" *Wall Street Journal*, July 2, 2007, p. B3.

67. Jean B. McGuire, Alison Sundgren, and Thomas Schneeweis, "Corporate Social Responsibility and Firm Financial Performance," *Academy of Management Journal* 31 (1988): 854–872; and Falck and Heblich, "Corporate Social Responsibility."

68. David Vogel, *Is There a Market for Virtue?* (Washington, DC: Brookings Institution Press, 2006).

69. Daniel W. Greening and Daniel B. Turban, "Corporate Social Performance as a Competitive Advantage in Attracting a Quality Workforce," *Business and Society* 39(3) (September 2000): 254; and O'Sullivan, "Virtue Rewarded."

70. "The Socially Correct Corporate Business," in Leslie Holstrom and Simon Brady, "The Changing Face of Global Business," *Fortune* (July 24, 2000): S1–S38.

CHAPTER 5

Managerial Planning and Goal Setting

1. Quoted in Oren Harari, "Good/Bad News About Strategy," *Management Review* (July 1995): 29–31.

2. Amitai Etzioni, *Modern Organizations* (Englewood Cliffs, NJ: Prentice Hall, 1984): 6.

3. Ibid.

4. Max D. Richards, *Setting Strategic Goals and Objectives*, 2nd ed. (St. Paul, MN: West, 1986).

5. C. Chet Miller and Laura B. Cardinal, "Strategic Planning and Firm Performance: A Synthesis of More Than Two Decades of Research," *Academy of Management Journal* 37(6) (1994): 1649–1685.

6. This discussion is based on Richard L. Daft and Richard M. Steers, *Organizations: A Micro/Macro Approach* (Glenview, IL: Scott, Foresman, 1986): 319–321; Herbert A. Simon, "On the Concept of Organizational Goals," *Administrative Science Quarterly* 9 (1964): 1–22; and Charles B. Saunders and Francis D. Tuggel, "Corporate Goals," *Journal of General Management* 5 (1980): 3–13.

7. Marc Gunther, "Tree Huggers, Soy Lovers, and Profits," *Fortune* (June 23, 2003): 98–104.

8. Paul Sloan, "The Sales Force That Rocks," *Business 2.0* (July 2005): 102–107.

9. Mary Klemm, Stuart Sanderson, and George Luffman, "Mission Statements: Selling Corporate Values to Employees," *Long-Range Planning* 24(3) (1991): 73–78; John A. Pearce II and Fred David, "Corporate Mission Statements: The Bottom Line," *Academy of Management Executive* (1987): 109–116; Jerome H. Want, "Corporate Mission: The Intangible Contributor to Performance," *Management Review* (August 1986): 46–50; and Forest R. David and Fred R. David, "It's Time to Redraft Your Mission Statement," *Journal of Business Strategy* (January–February 2003): 11–14.

10. "Tennessee News and Notes from State Farm," (State Farm Mutual Automobile Insurance Company, 2004).

11. Jeffrey A. Trachtenberg, "Borders Business Plan Gets a Rewrite; It Will Reopen Web Site, Give Up Most Stores Abroad, Close Many Waldenbooks," *Wall Street Journal*, March 22, 2007, p. B1.

12. Paul Meising and Joseph Wolfe, "The Art and Science of Planning at the Business Unit Level," *Management Science* 31 (1985): 773–781.

13. Based in part on information about 1-800-Flowers in Jenny C. McCune, "On the Train Gang," *Management Review* (October 1994): 57–60.

14. "Study: IRS Employees Often Steer Taxpayers Wrong on Law Questions," *Johnson City* [Tennessee] *Press*, September 4, 2003.

15. Geary A. Rummler and Kimberly Morrill, "The Results Chain," *TD* (February 2005): 27–35; and John C. Crotts, Duncan R. Dickson, and Robert C. Ford, "Aligning Organizational Processes with Mission: The Case of Service Excellence," *Academy of Management Executive* 19(3) (August 2005): 54–68.

16. This discussion is based on Robert S. Kaplan and David P. Norton, "Mastering the Management System," *Harvard Business Review* (January 2008): 63–77; and Robert S. Kaplan and David P. Norton, "Having Trouble with Your Strategy? Then Map It," *Harvard Business Review* (September–October 2000): 167–176.

17. Sayan Chatterjee, "Core Objectives: Clarity in Designing Strategy," *California Management Review* 47(2) (Winter 2005): 33–49.

18. Edwin A. Locke, Gary P. Latham, and Miriam Erez, "The Determinants of Goal Commitment," *Academy of Management Review* 13 (1988): 23–39.

19. Peter F. Drucker, *The Practice of Management* (New York: Harper & Row, 1954); and George S. Odiorne, "MBO: A Backward Glance," *Business Horizons* 21 (October 1978): 14–24.

20. Jan P. Muczyk and Bernard C. Reimann, "MBO as a Complement to Effective Leadership," *The Academy of Management Executive* 3 (1989): 131–138; and W. Giegold, *Objective Setting and the MBO Process*, vol. 2 (New York: McGraw-Hill, 1978).

21. John Ivancevich, J. Timothy McMahon, J. William Streidl, and Andrew D. Szilagyi, "Goal Setting: The Tenneco Approach to Personnel Development and Management Effectiveness," *Organizational Dynamics* (Winter 1978): 48–80.

22. Brigitte W. Schay, Mary Ellen Beach, Jacqueline A. Caldwell, and Christelle LaPolice, "Using Standardized Outcome Measures in the Federal Government," *Human Resource Management* 41(3) (Fall 2002): 355–368.

23. Eileen M. Van Aken and Garry D. Coleman, "Building Better Measurement," *Industrial Management* (July–August 2002): 28–33.

24. Edison Electric Institute, "E-Mail: The DNA of Office Crimes," *Electric Perspectives* 28(5) (September–October 2003): 4; Marcia Stepanek with Steve Hamm, "When the Devil Is in the E-Mails," *Business Week* (June 8, 1998): 72–74; Joseph McCafferty, "The Phantom Menace," *CFO* (June 1999): 89–91; "Many Company Internet and E-Mail Policies Are Worth Revising," *The Kiplinger Letter* (February 21, 2003): 1; and Carol Hymowitz, "Personal Boundaries Shrink as Companies Punish Bad Behavior," *Wall Street Journal*, June 18, 2007, p. B1.

25. Curtis W. Roney, "Planning for Strategic Contingencies," *Business Horizons* (March–April 2003): 35–42; and "Corporate Planning: Drafting a Blueprint for Success," *Small Business Report* (August 1987): 40–44.

26. Ellen Florian Kratz, "For FedEx, It Was Time to Deliver," *Fortune* (October 3, 2005): 83–84.

27. This section is based on Steven Schnaars and Paschalina Ziamou, "The Essentials of Scenario Writing," *Business Horizons* (July–August 2001): 25–31; Audrey Schriefer and Michael Sales, "Creating Strategic Advantage with Dynamic Scenarios," *Strategy & Leadership* 34(3) (2006): 31–42; Geoffrey Colvin, "An Executive Risk Handbook," *Fortune* (October 3, 2005): 69–70; and Syed H. Akhter, "Strategic Planning, Hypercompetition, and Knowledge Management," *Business Horizons* (January–February 2003): 19–24.

28. Peter Cornelius, Alexander Van de Putte, and Mattia Romani, "Three Decades of Scenario Planning in Shell," *California Management Review* 48(1) (Fall 2005); and Schnaars and Ziamou, "The Essentials of Scenario Writing."

29. Colvin, "An Executive Risk Handbook"; and Ian Wylie, "There Is No Alternative to . . . ," *Fast Company* (July 2002): 106–110.

30. Bain & Company Management Tools and Trends Survey, reported in Darrell Rigby and Barbara Bilodeau, "A Narrowing Focus on Preparedness," *Harvard Business Review* (July–August 2007): 21–22.

31. Ian Mitroff with Gus Anagnos, *Managing Crises Before They Happen* (New York: AMACOM, 2001); Ian Mitroff and Murat C. Alpaslan, "Preparing for Evil," *Harvard Business Review* (April 2003): 109–115.

32. This discussion is based largely on W. Timothy Coombs, *Ongoing Crisis Communication: Planning, Managing, and Responding* (Thousand Oaks, CA: Sage Publications, 1999).

33. Ian I. Mitroff, "Crisis Leadership," *Executive Excellence* (August 2001): 19; and Andy Bowen, "Crisis Procedures that Stand the Test of Time," *Public Relations Tactics* (August 2001): 16.

34. Christine Pearson, "A Blueprint for Crisis Management," *Ivey Business Journal* (January–February 2002): 69–73.

35. See Mitroff and Alpaslan, "Preparing for Evil," for a discussion of the "wheel of crises" that outlines the many different kinds of crises organizations may face.

36. Harari, "Good News/Bad News About Strategy."

37. James C. Collins and Jerry I. Porras, "Building Your Company's Vision," *Harvard Business Review* (September–October 1996): 65–77.

38. Steven Kerr and Steffan Landauer, "Using Stretch Goals to Promote Organizational Effectiveness and Personal Growth: General Electric and Goldman Sachs," *Academy of Management Executive* 18(4) (November 2004): 134–138.

39. See Kenneth R. Thompson, Wayne A. Hockwarter, and Nicholas J. Mathys, "Stretch Targets: What Makes Them Effective?" *Academy of Management Executive* 11(3) (August 1997): 48.

40. Doug Bartholomew, "Gauging Success," *CFO-IT* (Summer 2005): 17–19.

41. This section is based on Liam Fahey and Jan Herring, "Intelligence Teams," *Strategy & Leadership* 35(1) (2007): 13–20.

42. Chet Miller and Laura B. Cardinal, "Strategic Planning and Firm Performance: A Synthesis of More than Two Decades of Research," *Academy of Management Journal* 37(6) (1994): 1649–1665.

43. Renée Dye and Olivier Sibony, "How to Improve Strategic Planning," *McKinsey Quarterly*, 3 (2007).

44. Keith H. Hammonds, "Michael Porter's Big Ideas," *Fast Company* (March 2001): 150–156.

45. John E. Prescott, "Environments as Moderators of the Relationship between Strategy and Performance," *Academy of Management Journal* 29 (1986): 329–346; John A. Pearce II and Richard B. Robinson, Jr., *Strategic Management: Strategy, Formulation, and Implementation*, 2nd ed. (Homewood, IL: Irwin, 1985); and David J. Teece, "Economic Analysis and Strategic Management," *California Management Review* 26 (Spring 1984): 87–110.

46. Jack Welch, "It's All in the Sauce," excerpt from his book, *Winning*, in *Fortune* (April 18, 2005): 138–144; and Constantinos Markides, "Strategic Innovation," *Sloan Management Review* (Spring 1997): 9–23.

47. Michael E. Porter, "What Is Strategy?" *Harvard Business Review* (November–December 1996): 61–78.

48. Arthur A. Thompson, Jr., and A. J. Strickland III, *Strategic Management: Concepts and Cases*, 6th ed. (Homewood, IL: Irwin, 1992); and Briance Mascarenhas, Alok Baveja, and Mamnoon Jamil, "Dynamics of Core Competencies in Leading Multinational Companies," *California Management Review* 40(4) (Summer 1998): 117–132.

49. Michael V. Copeland, "Stitching Together an Apparel Powerhouse," *Business 2.0* (April 2005): 52–54.

50. "Gaylord Says Hotels Prosper by Becoming Destinations," *The Tennessean*, July 24, 2005 (www.tennessean.com).

51. Chris Woodyard, "Big Dreams for Small Choppers Paid Off," *USA Today*, September 11, 2005, p. B7.

52. Michael Goold and Andrew Campbell, "Desperately Seeking Synergy," *Harvard Business Review* (September–October 1998): 131–143.

53. Elizabeth Olson, "OMG! Cute Boys, Kissing Tips and Lots of Pics, as Magazines Find a Niche," *New York Times*, May 28, 2007, p. C1.

54. Janet Adamy, "Bare Essentials; To Find Growth, No-Frills Grocery Goes Where Other Chains Won't," *Wall Street Journal* (August 30, 2005): pp. A1, A8.

55. Milton Leontiades, "The Confusing Words of Business Policy," *Academy of Management Review* 7 (1982): 45–48.

56. Lawrence G. Hrebiniak and William F. Joyce, *Implementing Strategy* (New York: Macmillan, 1984).

57. David Kirkpatrick, "Facebook's Plan To Hook Up the World," *Fortune* (June 11, 2007): 127–130; Brad Stone, "Facebook Expands Into MySpace's Territory," *New York Times*, May 25, 2007; and Vauhini Vara, "Facebook CEO Seeks Help as Site Suffers Growing Pains," *Wall Street Journal*, March 5, 2008, p. A1.

58. Vara, "Facebook CEO Seeks Help."

59. Michael E. Porter, "The Five Competitive Forces That Shape Strategy," *Harvard Business Review* (January 2008): 79–93; Michael E. Porter, *Competitive Strategy* (New York: The Free Press, 1980): 36–46; Danny Miller, "Relating Porter's Business Strategies to Environment and Structure: Analysis and Performance Implementations," *Academy of Management Journal* 31 (1988): 280–308; and Michael E. Porter, "From Competitive Advantage to Corporate Strategy," *Harvard Business Review* (May–June 1987): 43–59.

60. Michael E. Porter, "Strategy and the Internet," *Harvard Business Review* (March 2001): 63–78.

61. Andrew Park and Peter Burrows, "Dell, the Conqueror," *BusinessWeek* (September 24, 2001): 92–102; and Thompson and Strickland, *Strategic Management*.

62. Richard Teitelbaum, "The Wal-Mart of Wall Street," *Fortune* (October 13, 1997): 128–130.

63. Joshua Rosenbaum, "Guitar Maker Looks for a New Key," *Wall Street Journal*, February 11, 1998.

64. Nitin Nohria, William Joyce, and Bruce Roberson, "What Really Works," *Harvard Business Review* (July 2003): 43–52.

65. This discussion is based on J. Bruce Harreld, Charles A. O'Reilly III, and Michael L. Tushman, "Dynamic Capabilities at IBM: Driving Strategy into Action," *California Management Review* 49(4) (2007).

66. Diane Brady, "The Immelt Revolution," *BusinessWeek* (March 28, 2005): 64–73.

67. Alice Dragoon, "A Travel Guide to Collaboration," *CIO* (November 15, 2004): 68–75.

68. Don Tapscott, "Rethinking Strategy in a Networked World," *Strategy & Business*, 24 (Third Quarter 2001): 34–41.

69. Lawrence G. Hrebiniak, "Obstacles to Effective Strategy Implementation," *Organizational Dynamics* 35(1) (2006): 12–31; Eric M. Olson, Stanley F. Slater, and G. Tomas M. Hult, "The Importance of Structure and Process to Strategy Implementation," *Business Horizons* 48 (2005): 47–54; L. J. Bourgeois III and David R. Brodwin, "Strategic Implementation: Five Approaches to an Elusive Phenomenon," *Strategic Management Journal* 5 (1984): 241–264; Anil K. Gupta and V. Govindarajan, "Business Unit Strategy, Managerial Characteristics, and Business Unit Effectiveness at Strategy Implementation," *Academy of Management Journal* (1984): 25–41; and Jeffrey G. Covin, Dennis P. Slevin, and Randall L. Schultz, "Implementing Strategic Missions: Effective Strategic, Structural, and Tactical Choices," *Journal of Management Studies* 31(4) (1994): 481–505.

70. Based on a statement by Louis Gerstner, quoted in Harreld et al., "Dynamic Capabilities at IBM."

71. Olson, Slater, and Hult, "The Importance of Structure and Process."

72. Jay R. Galbraith and Robert K. Kazanjian, *Strategy Implementation: Structure, Systems and Process*, 2nd ed. (St. Paul, MN: West, 1986); and Paul C. Nutt, "Selecting Tactics to Implement Strategic Plans," *Strategic Management Journal* 10 (1989): 145–161.

73. This questionnaire is adapted from Dorothy Marcic and Joe Seltzer, *Organizational Behavior: Experiences and Cases* (Cincinnati: South-Western, 1998), pp. 284–287, and William Miller, *Innovation Styles* (Dallas, TX: Global Creativity Corporation, 1997).

74. Spencer E. Ante, "The New Blue," *BusinessWeek* (March 17, 2003): 80–88.

75. Brooke Dobni, "Creating a Strategy Implementation Environment," *Business Horizons* (March–April 2003): 43–46; Michael K. Allio, "A Short Practical Guide to Implementing Strategy," *Journal of Business Strategy* (August 2005): 12–21; "Strategy Execution: Achieving Operational Excellence," *Economist Intelligence Unit* (November 2004); and Thomas W. Porter and Stephen C. Harper, "Tactical Implementation: The Devil Is in the Details," *Business Horizons* (January–February 2003): 53–60.

76. Survey results reported in Hrebiniak, "Obstacles to Effective Strategy Implementation."

77. Steve Hamm, "Beyond Blue," *BusinessWeek* (April 18, 2005): 68–76.

78. Gupta and Govindarajan, "Business Unit Strategy"; and Bourgeois and Brodwin, "Strategic Implementation."

79. Obasi Akan, Richard S. Allen, Marilyn M. Helms, and Samuel A. Spralls III, "Critical Tactics for Implementing Porter's Generic Strategies," *Journal of Business Strategy* 27(1) (2006): 43–53.

80. Nitin Nohria, William Joyce, and Bruce Roberson, "What Really Works," *Harvard Business Review* (July 2003): 43–52.

81. Akan et al., "Critical Tactics'."

82. Ibid.

CHAPTER 6

Managerial Decision Making

1. Betsy Morris, "What Makes Apple Golden?" *Fortune* (March 17, 2008): 68–74.

2. Michael V. Copeland and Owen Thomas, "Hits (& Misses)," *Business 2.0* (January–February 2004): 126.

3. Michael V. Copeland, "Stuck in the Spin Cycle," *Business 2.0* (May 2005): 74–75; and Adam Horowitz, Mark Athitakis, Mark Lasswell, and Owen Thomas, "101 Dumbest Moments in Business," *Business 2.0* (January–February 2004): 72–81.

4. Herbert A. Simon, *The New Science of Management Decision* (Englewood Cliffs, NJ: Prentice Hall, 1977): 47.

5. Samuel Eilon, "Structuring Unstructured Decisions," *Omega 13* (1985): 369–377; and Max H. Bazerman, *Judgment in Managerial Decision Making* (New York: Wiley, 1986).

6. James G. March and Zur Shapira, "Managerial Perspectives on Risk and Risk Taking," *Management Science* 33 (1987): 1404–1418; and Inga Skromme Baird and Howard Thomas, "Toward a Contingency Model of Strategic Risk Taking," *Academy of Management Review* 10 (1985): 230–243.

7. Hugh Courtney, "Decision-Driven Scenarios for Assessing Four Levels of Uncertainty," *Strategy & Leadership* 31(1) (2003): 14–22.

8. Reported in David Leonhardt, "This Fed Chief May Yet Get a Honeymoon," *New York Times*, August 23, 2006, p. C1.

9. Michael Masuch and Perry LaPotin, "Beyond Garbage Cans: An AI Model of Organizational Choice," *Administrative Science Quarterly* 34 (1989): 38–67; and Richard L. Daft and Robert H. Lengel, "Organizational Information Requirements, Media Richness and Structural Design," *Management Science* 32 (1986): 554–571.

10. Ben Worthen, "Cost Cutting Versus Innovation: Reconcilable Difference," *CIO* (October 1, 2004): 89–94.

11. David M. Schweiger, William R. Sandberg, and James W. Ragan, "Group Approaches for Improving Strategic Decision Making: A Comparative Analysis of Dialectical Inquiry, Devil's Advocacy, and Consensus," *Academy of Management Journal* 29 (1986): 51–71; and Richard O. Mason and Ian I. Mitroff, *Challenging Strategic Planning Assumptions* (New York: Wiley InterScience, 1981).

12. Michael Pacanowsky, "Team Tools for Wicked Problems," *Organizational Dynamics* 23(3) (Winter 1995): 36–51.

13. Thomas H. Davenport and Jeanne G. Harris, "Automated Decision Making Comes of Age," *MIT Sloan Management Review* (Summer 2005): 83–89; and Stacie McCullough, "On the Front Lines," *CIO* (October 15, 1999): 78–81.

14. Julie Schlosser, "Markdown Lowdown," *Fortune* (January 12, 2004): 40; and Srinivas Bollapragada, Prasanthi Ganti, Mark Osborn, James Quaile, and Kannan Ramanathan, "GE's Energy Rentals Business Automates Its Credit Assessment Process," *Interfaces* 33(5) (September–October 2003): 45–56.

15. Mitchell Waldrop, "Chaos, Inc.," *Red Herring* (January 2003): 38–40; Andy Serwer, "Southwest Airlines: The Hottest Thing in the Sky," *Fortune* (March 8, 2004): 86–106; Perry Flint, "The Darkest Hour," *Air Transport World* (December 2005): 52–53; *Southwest Airlines 2005 Annual Report* (www.southwest.com/investor_relations/swaar05.pdf); and John Heimlich, "State of the Industry Q&A," Air Transport Association of America, Inc. (April 11, 2006) (www.airlines.org/econ/d.aspx?nid=9630).

16. Herbert A. Simon, *The New Science of Management Decision* (New York: Harper & Row, 1960): 5–6; and Amitai Etzioni, "Humble Decision Making," *Harvard Business Review* (July–August 1989): 122–126.

17. James G. March and Herbert A. Simon, *Organizations* (New York: Wiley, 1958).

18. Herbert A. Simon, *Models of Man* (New York: Wiley, 1957): 196–205; and Herbert A. Simon, *Administrative Behavior*, 2nd ed. (New York: The Free Press, 1957).

19. Paul C. Nutt, "Expanding the Search for Alternatives During Strategic Decision Making," *Academy of Management Executive* 18(4) (2004): 13–28.

20. Weston H. Agor, "The Logic of Intuition: How Top Executives Make Important Decisions," *Organizational Dynamics* 14 (Winter 1986): 5–18; and Herbert A. Simon, "Making Management Decisions: The Role of Intuition and Emotion," *Academy of Management Executive* 1 (1987): 57–64. For a recent review of research, see Erik Dane and Michael G. Pratt, "Exploring Intuition and Its Role in Managerial Decision Making," *Academy of Management Review* 32(1) (2007): 33–54.

21. Study reported in C. Chet Miller and R. Duane Ireland, "Intuition in Strategic Decision Making: Friend or Foe in the Fast-Paced 21st Century?" *Academy of Management Executive* 19(1) (2005): 19–30.

22. See Gary Klein, *Intuition at Work: Why Developing Your Gut Instincts Will Make You Better at What You Do* (New York: Doubleday, 2002); Kurt Matzler, Franz Bailom, and Todd A. Mooradian, "Intuitive Decision Making," *MIT Sloan Management Review* 49(1) (Fall 2007): 13–15; Malcolm Gladwell, *Blink: The Power of Thinking Without Thinking* (New York: Little Brown, 2005); and Sharon Begley, "Follow Your Intuition: The Unconscious You May Be the Wiser Half," *Wall Street Journal*, August 30, 2002, p. A6.

23. Michel Pireu, "A Fickle Guide Likely to Lead to Disaster," *Business Day*, Oct. 2, 2008: 12; and Stephen Turner, "Intuition at Work: Why Developing Your Gut Instincts Will Make You Better at What You Do," *Library Journal* (February 1, 2003): 99.

24. Miller and Ireland, "Intuition in Strategic Decision Making"; and Eric Bonabeau, "Don't Trust Your Gut," *Harvard Business Review* (May 2003): 116ff.

25. Eugene Sadler-Smith and Erella Shefy, "The Intuitive Executive: Understanding and Applying 'Gut Feel' in Decision Making," *Academy of Management Executive* 18(4) (2004): 76–91; Simon, "Making Management Decisions"; and Ann Langley, "Between 'Paralysis by Analysis' and 'Extinction by Instinct,'" *Sloan Management Review* (Spring 1995): 63–76.

26. See Kenneth R. Brousseau, Michael L. Driver, Gary Hourihan, and Rikard Larsson, "The Seasoned Executive's Decision Making Style," *Harvard Business Review* (February 2006): 110ff, for a discussion of how decision-making behavior evolves as managers progress in their careers.

27. William B. Stevenson, Jon L. Pierce, and Lyman W. Porter, "The Concept of 'Coalition' in Organization Theory and Research," *Academy of Management Review* 10 (1985): 256–268.

28. George T. Doran and Jack Gunn, "Decision Making in High-Tech Firms: Perspectives of Three Executives," *Business Horizons* (November–December 2002): 7–16.

29. Stephanie N. Mehta and Fred Vogelstein, "AOL: The Relaunch," *Fortune* (November 14, 2005): 78–84.

30. James W. Fredrickson, "Effects of Decision Motive and Organizational Performance Level on Strategic Decision Processes," *Academy of Management Journal* 28 (1985): 821–843; James W. Fredrickson, "The Comprehensiveness of Strategic Decision Processes: Extension, Observations, Future Directions," *Academy of Management Journal* 27 (1984): 445–466; James W.

Dean, Jr., and Mark P. Sharfman, "Procedural Rationality in the Strategic Decision-Making Process," *Journal of Management Studies* 30(4) (July 1993): 587–610; Nandini Rajagopalan, Abdul M. A. Rasheed, and Deepak K. Datta, "Strategic Decision Processes: Critical Review and Future Directions," *Journal of Management* 19(2) (1993): 349–384; and Paul J. H. Schoemaker, "Strategic Decisions in Organizations: Rational and Behavioral Views," *Journal of Management Studies* 30(1) (January 1993): 107–129.

31. Marjorie A. Lyles and Howard Thomas, "Strategic Problem Formulation: Biases and Assumptions Embedded in Alternative Decision-Making Models," *Journal of Management Studies* 25 (1988): 131–145; and Susan E. Jackson and Jane E. Dutton, "Discerning Threats and Opportunities," *Administrative Science Quarterly* 33 (1988): 370–387.

32. Richard L. Daft, Juhani Sormumen, and Don Parks, "Chief Executive Scanning, Environmental Characteristics, and Company Performance: An Empirical Study" (unpublished manuscript, Texas A&M University, 1988).

33. Jena McGregor, "Gospels of Failure," *Fast Company* (February 2005): 62–67.

34. C. Kepner and B. Tregoe, *The Rational Manager* (New York: McGraw-Hill, 1965).

35. Nanette Byrnes, "Avon: More Than Cosmetic Changes," *BusinessWeek* (March 12, 2007): 62–63.

36. Paul C. Nutt, "Expanding the Search for Alternatives During Strategic Decision Making," *Academy of Management Executive* 18(4) (2004): 13–28; and P. C. Nutt, "Surprising but True: Half the Decisions in Organizations Fail," *Academy of Management Executive* 13(4) (1999): 75–90.

37. Pallavi Gogoi and Michael Arndt, "Hamburger Hell," *BusinessWeek* (March 3, 2003): 104.

38. Peter Mayer, "A Surprisingly Simple Way to Make Better Decisions," *Executive Female* (March–April 1995): 13–14; and Ralph L. Keeney, "Creativity in Decision Making with Value-Focused Thinking," *Sloan Management Review* (Summer 1994): 33–41.

39. Janet Guyon, "The Soul of a Money-making Machine," *Fortune* (October 3, 2005): 113–120; and Robert Levering and Milton Moskowitz, "And the Winners Are . . . (The 100 Best Companies to Work For)," *Fortune* (January 23, 2006): 89–108.

40. Mark McNeilly, "Gathering Information for Strategic Decisions, Routinely," *Strategy & Leadership* 30(5) (2002): 29–34.

41. Ibid.

42. Jenny C. McCune, "Making Lemonade," *Management Review* (June 1997): 49–53; and Douglas S. Barasch, "God and Toothpaste," *New York Times*, December 22, 1996, pp. 26–29.

43. Based on A. J. Rowe, J. D. Boulgaides, and M. R. McGrath, *Managerial Decision Making* (Chicago: Science Research Associates, 1984); and Alan J. Rowe and Richard O. Mason, *Managing with Style: A Guide to Understanding, Assessing, and Improving Your Decision Making* (San Francisco: Jossey-Bass, 1987).

44. Mark Gunther, "Jeff Zucker Faces Life Without *Friends*," *Fortune*, May 12, 2003 (http://money.cnn.com/magazines/fortune/fortune_archive/2003/05/12/342332/index.htm) (accessed August 13, 2008).

45. This section is based on John S. Hammond, Ralph L. Keeney, and Howard Raiffa, *Smart Choices: A Practical Guide to Making Better Decisions* (Boston: Harvard Business School Press, 1999); Max H. Bazerman and Dolly Chugh, "Decisions Without Blinders," *Harvard Business Review* (January 2006): 88–97; J. S. Hammond, R. L. Keeney, and H. Raiffa, "The Hidden Traps in Decision Making," *Harvard Business Review* (September–October 1998): 47–58; Oren Harari, "The Thomas Lawson Syndrome," *Management Review* (February 1994): 58–61; Dan Ariely, "Q&A: Why Good CIOs Make Bad Decisions," *CIO* (May 1, 2003): 83–87; Leigh Buchanan, "How to Take Risks in a Time of Anxiety," *Inc.* (May 2003): 76–81; and Max H. Bazerman, *Judgment in Managerial Decision Making*, 5th ed. (New York: John Wiley & Sons, 2002).

46. Kathleen M. Eisenhardt, "Strategy as Strategic Decision Making," *Sloan Management Review* (Spring 1999): 65–72.

47. R. B. Gallupe, W. H. Cooper, M. L. Grise, and L. M. Bastianutti, "Blocking Electronic Brainstorms," *Journal of Applied Psychology* 79 (1994): 77–86; R. B. Gallupe and W. H. Cooper, "Brainstorming Electronically," *Sloan Management Review* (Fall 1993): 27–36; and Alison Stein Wellner, "A Perfect Brainstorm," *Inc.* (October 2003): 31–35.

48. Wellner, "A Perfect Brainstorm"; Gallupe and Cooker, "Brainstorming Electronically."

49. Michael A. Roberto, "Making Difficult Decisions in Turbulent Times," *Ivey Business Journal* (May–June 2003): 1–7.

50. Eisenhardt, "Strategy as Strategic Decision Making"; and David A. Garvin and Michael A. Roberto, "What You Don't Know About Making Decisions," *Harvard Business Review* (September 2001): 108–116.

51. Roberto, "Making Difficult Decisions."

52. David M. Schweiger and William R. Sandberg, "The Utilization of Individual Capabilities in Group Approaches to Strategic Decision Making," *Strategic Management Journal* 10 (1989): 31–43; and "The Devil's Advocate," *Small Business Report* (December 1987): 38–41.

53. Doran and Gunn, "Decision Making in High-Tech Firms."

54. Eisenhardt, "Strategy as Strategic Decision Making."

55. Garvin and Roberto, "What You Don't Know About Making Decisions."

56. Irving L. Janis, *Groupthink: Psychological Studies of Policy Decisions and Fiascoes*, 2nd ed. (Boston: Houghton Mifflin, 1982).

57. Jerry B. Harvey, "The Abilene Paradox: The Management of Agreement," *Organizational Dynamics* (Summer 1988): 17–43.

58. Hans Wissema, "Driving Through Red Lights; How Warning Signals Are Missed or Ignored," *Long Range Planning* 35 (2002): 521–539.

59. Ibid.

60. Thomas L. Friedman, "It's a Flat World, After All," *New York Times Magazine* (April 3, 2005): 32–37.

61. Ibid.

62. Based on Andrew Mayo, "Memory Bankers," *People Management* (January 22, 1998): 34–38; William Miller, "Building the Ultimate Resource," *Management Review* (January 1999), 42–45; and Todd Datz, "How to Speak Geek," *CIO Enterprise*, Section 2 (April 15, 1999): 46–52.

63. Richard McDermott, "Why Information Technology Inspired but Cannot Deliver Knowledge Management," *California Management Review* 41(4) (Summer 1999): 103–117.

64. Thomas H. Davenport, Laurence Prusak, and Bruce Strong, "Business Insight (A Special Report): Organization; Putting Ideas to Work: Knowledge Management Can Make a Difference—But It Needs to Be More Pragmatic," *Wall Street Journal*, March 10, 2008, p. R6.

65. Meridith Levinson, "Business Intelligence: Not Just for Bosses Anymore," *CIO* (January 15, 2006): 82–88; and Alice Dragoon, "Business Intelligence Gets Smart," *CIO* (September 15, 2003): 84–91.

66. David Stires, "How the VA Healed Itself," *Fortune* (May 15, 2006): 130–136.

67. This discussion is based on Judy Sweeney and Simon Jacobson, "ERP Breaks," *Industry Week* (January 2007): 11a–13a; and Vincent A. Mabert, Ashok Soni, and M. A. Venkataramanan, "Enterprise Resource Planning: Common Myths Versus Evolving Reality," *Business Horizons* (May–June 2001): 69–76.

68. Sweeney and Jacobson, "ERP Breaks."

69. Adapted from Carolyn Hopper, *Practicing Management Skills* (New York: Houghton Mifflin, 2003); and Jacquelyn Wonder and Priscilla Donovan, "Mind Openers," *Self* (March 1984).

70. Derek Slater, "What Is ERP?" *CIO* Enterprise (May 15, 1999): 86.

71. Anya Kamenetz, "The Network Unbound," *Fast Company* (June 2006): 68ff; and Stephen Baker and Heather Green, "Blogs Will Change Your Business," *BusinessWeek* (May 2, 2005): 56–67.

72. Baker and Green, "Blogs Will Change Your Business."

73. Stanley Holmes, "Into the Wild Blog Yonder," *BusinessWeek* (May 22, 2006): 84–86; and Erin White, Joann S. Lublin, and David Kesmodel, "Executives Get the Blogging Bug," *Wall Street Journal*, July 13, 2007, p. B1.

74. Cindy Waxer, "Workers of the World—Collaborate," *FSB* (April 2005): 57–58.

75. Evelyn Nussenbaum, "Technology to Boost Teamwork," *Forbes Small Business* (February 2008): 51–54; and Russ Juskalian, "Wikinomics Could Change Everything As Concept of Sharing Spreads," *USA Today*, January 2, 2007 (www.usatoday.com) (accessed January 2, 2007).

76. This discussion of social networks is based on Kamenetz, "The Network Unbound."

77. Brad Stone, "Facebook Expands into MySpace's Territory," *New York Times*, May 25, 2007; and Heather Green, "The Water Cooler is Now on the Web," *BusinessWeek* (October 1, 2007), p. 78.

78. Spencer E. Ante with Amy Borrus and Robert D. Hof, "In Search of the Net's Next Big Thing," *BusinessWeek* (March 26, 2001): 140–141; and Amy Cortese, "Peer to Peer: P2P Taps the Power of Distant Computers in a Way that Could Transform Whole Industries," *BusinessWeek* 50 (supplement) (Spring 2001): 194–196.

79. Mark Roberti, "Peer-to-Peer Isn't Dead," *The Industry Standard* (April 23, 2001): 58–59.

80. Jim Turcotte, Bob Silveri, and Tom Jobson, "Are You Ready for the E-Supply Chain?" *APICS–The Performance Advantage* (August 1998): 56–59.

81. This discussion is based on Long W. Lam and L. Jean Harrison-Walker, "Toward an Objective-Based Typology of E-Business Models," *Business Horizons* (November–December 2003): 17–26; and Detmar Straub and Richard Klein, "E-Competitive Trans-formations," *Business Horizons* (May–June 2001): 3–12.

82. Tom Lowry, "In the Zone," *BusinessWeek* (October 17, 2005): 66–78; and Tom Lowry, "TV's New Parallel Universe," *Business-Week* (November 14, 2005): 72–74.

83. Robert Berner, "J. C. Penney Gets the Net," *BusinessWeek* (May 7, 2007): 70; and "Jcpenney.Com Celebrates 10th Anniversary of Online Shopping," *Business Wire* (November 8, 2004).

84. Nanette Byrnes, "More Clicks at the Bricks," *BusinessWeek* (December 17, 2007): 50–52.

85. "The Web Smart 50," *BusinessWeek* (November 21, 2005): 82–112.

86. Jonathan L. Willis, "What Impact Will E-Commerce Have on the U.S. Economy?" *Economic Review—Federal Reserve Bank of Kansas City* 89(2) (Second Quarter 2004): 53ff; and Timothy J. Mullaney with Heather Green, Michael Arndt, Robert D. Hof, and Linda Himelstein, "The E-Biz Surprise," *Business Week* (May 12, 2003): 60–68.

87. Straub and Klein, "E-Competitive Transformations."

88. "The Web Smart 50."

CHAPTER 7

Designing Adaptive Organizations

1. Carlos Ghosn, "Saving the Business Without Losing the Company," *Harvard Business Review* (January 2002): 37–45; Jay Greene, "Less Could Be More at Microsoft," *BusinessWeek* (October 3, 2005): 40; and Josée Valcourt, "Chrysler Begins Overhaul in Engineering," *Wall Street Journal*, February 19, 2008, p. A13.

2. John Child, *Organization: A Guide to Problems and Practice*, 2nd ed. (London: Harper & Row, 1984).

3. Adam Smith, *The Wealth of Nations* (New York: Modern Library, 1937).

4. This questionnaire is based on Richard M. Wielkiewicz, "The Leadership Attitudes and Beliefs Scale: An Instrument for Evaluating College Students' Thinking About Leadership and Organizations," *Journal of College Student Development* 41 (May–June 2000): 335–346.

5. This discussion is based on Richard L. Daft, *Organization Theory and Design*, 4th ed. (St. Paul, MN: West, 1992): 387–388.

6. C. I. Barnard, *The Functions of the Executive* (Cambridge, MA: Harvard University Press, 1938).

7. Thomas A. Stewart, "CEOs See Clout Shifting," *Fortune* (November 6, 1989): 66.

8. Michael G. O'Loughlin, "What Is Bureaucratic Accountability and How Can We Measure It?" *Administration & Society* 22(3) (November 1990): 275–302; and Brian Dive, "When Is an Organization Too Flat?" *Across the Board* (July–August 2003): 20–23.

9. Gary L. Neilson and Bruce A. Pasternack, "The Cat That Came Back," *Strategy + Business*, 40 (August 17, 2005): 32–45.

10. Carrie R. Leana, "Predictors and Consequences of Delegation," *Academy of Management Journal* 29 (1986): 754–774.

11. Curtis Sittenfeld, "Powered by the People," *Fast Company* (July–August 1999): 178–189.

12. Barbara Davison, "Management Span of Control: How Wide Is Too Wide?" *Journal of Business Strategy* 24(4) (2003): 22–29; Paul D. Collins and Frank Hull, "Technology and Span of Control: Woodward Revisited," *Journal of Management Studies* 23 (March 1986): 143–164; David D. Van Fleet and Arthur G. Bedeian, "A History of the Span of Management," *Academy of Manage-ment Review* 2 (1977): 356–372; and C. W. Barkdull, "Span of Control—A Method of Evaluation," *Michigan Business Review* 15 (May 1963): 25–32.

13. Gary Neilson, Bruce A. Pasternack, and Decio Mendes, "The Four Bases of Organizational DNA," *Strategy + Business*, 33 (December 10, 2003): 48–57.

14. Barbara Davison, "Management Span of Control"; Brian Dive, "When Is an Organization Too Flat?"; and Brian Dumaine, "What the Leaders of Tomorrow See," *Fortune* (July 3, 1989): 48–62; and Raghuram G. Rajan and Julie Wulf, "The Flatten-ing Firm: Evidence from Panel Data on the Changing Nature of Corporate Hierarchies," working paper, reported in Caroline Ellis, "The Flattening Corporation," *MIT Sloan Management Review* (Summer 2003): 5.

15. William G. Ouchi, "Power to the Principals: Decentralization in Three Large School Districts," *Organization Science* 17, (2) (March–April 2006): 298–307.

16. Dennis Cauchon, "The Little Company That Could," *USA Today*, October 9, 2005, p. B1.

17. William Neuman, "Management of Subways to Be Split," *New York Times*, December 6, 2007, p. B1.

18. Steffan M. Lauster and J. Neely, "The Core's Competence," *Strategy + Business*, 38 (April 15, 2005): 40–49.

19. Clay Chandler and Paul Ingrassia, "Just as U.S. Firms Try Japanese Management, Honda Is Centralizing," *Wall Street Journal*, April 11, 1991, p. A1.

20. The following discussion of structural alternatives draws from Jay R. Galbraith, *Designing Complex Organizations* (Reading, MA: Addison-Wesley, 1973); Jay R. Galbraith, *Organization Design* (Reading, MA: Addison-Wesley, 1977); Jay R. Galbraith, *Designing Dynamic Organizations* (New York: AMACOM, 2002); Robert Duncan, "What Is the Right Organization Structure?" *Organizational Dynamics* (Winter 1979): 59–80; N. Anand and Richard L. Daft, "What Is the Right Organization Design?" *Organizational Dynamics* 36(4) (2007): 329–344; and J. McCann and Jay R. Galbraith, "Interdepartmental Relations," in P. Nystrom and W. Starbuck (Eds.), *Handbook of Organizational Design* (New York: Oxford University Press, 1981): 60–84.

21. Based on the story of Blue Bell Creameries in Richard L. Daft, *Organization Theory and Design*, 9th ed. (Mason, OH: South-Western, 2007): 103.

22. Anand and Daft, "What Is the Right Organization Design?"

23. Eliza Newlin Carney, "Calm in the Storm," *Government Executive* (October 2003): 57–63; and Internal Revenue Service (www.irs.gov) (accessed April 20, 2004).

24. David Enrich and Carrick Mollenkamp, "Citi's Focus: Out with Old, In with Profit Drivers," *Wall Street Journal*, February 20, 2008, p. C3.

25. Robert J. Kramer, *Organizing for Global Competitiveness: The Geographic Design* (New York: The Conference Board, 1993): 29–31.

26. Maisie O'Flanagan and Lynn K. Taliento, "Nonprofits: Ensuring That Bigger Is Better," *McKinsey Quarterly,* 2 (2004): 112ff.

27. Lawton R. Burns, "Matrix Management in Hospitals: Testing Theories of Matrix Structure and Development," *Administrative Science Quarterly* 34 (1989): 349–368; Carol Hymowitz, "Managers Suddenly Have to Answer to a Crowd of Bosses," *Wall Street Journal*, August 12, 2003, p. B1.

28. Stanley M. Davis and Paul R. Lawrence, *Matrix* (Reading, MA: Addison-Wesley, 1977).

29. Alfred P. West, Jr., and Yoram (Jerry) Wind, "Putting the Organization on Wheels: Workplace Design at SEI," *California Management Review* 49(2) (Winter 2007): 138–153.

30. Melissa A. Schilling and H. Kevin Steensma, "The Use of Modular Organizational Forms: An Industry-Level Analysis," *Academy of Management Journal*, 44(6) (December 2001): 1149–1169.

31. Susan G. Cohen and Don Mankin, "Complex Collaborations for the New Global Economy," *Organizational Dynamics* 31(2) (2002): 117–133; David Lei and John W. Slocum Jr., "Organizational Designs to Renew Competitive Advantage," *Organizational Dynamics* 31(1) (2002): 1–18.

32. Raymond E. Miles and Charles C. Snow, "The New Network Firm: A Spherical Structure Built on a Human Investment Philosophy," *Organizational Dynamics* (Spring 1995): 5–18; and Raymond E. Miles, Charles C. Snow, John A. Matthews, Grant Miles, and Henry J. Coleman, Jr., "Organizing in the Knowledge Age: Anticipating the Cellular Form," *Academy of Management Executive* 11(4) (1997): 7–24.

33. Jena McGregor, with Michael Arndt, Robert Berner, Ian Rowley, Kenji Hall, Gail Edmondson, Steve Hamm, Moon Ihlwan, and Andy Reinhardt, "The World's Most Innovative Companies," *BusinessWeek* (April 24, 2006), p. 62.

34. Raymond E. Miles and Charles C. Snow, "Organizations: New Concepts for New Forms," *California Management Review* 28 (Spring 1986): 62–73; and "Now, The Post-Industrial Corporation," *BusinessWeek* (March 3, 1986): 64–74.

35. N. Anand, "Modular, Virtual, and Hollow Forms of Organization Design," working paper, London Business School (2000); Don Tapscott, "Rethinking Strategy in a Networked World," *Strategy & Business*, 24 (Third Quarter 2001): 34–41.

36. Malcolm Wheatley, "Cycle Company with a Virtual Spin," *MT* (September 2003): 78–81.

37. Gregory G. Dess, Abdul M. A. Rasheed, Kevin J. McLaughlin, and Richard L. Priem, "The New Corporate Architecture," *Academy of Management Executive* 9(3) (1995): 7–20.

38. Philip Siekman, "The Snap-Together Business Jet," *Fortune* (January 21, 2002): 104[A]–104[H].

39. Kathleen Kerwin, "GM: Modular Plants Won't Be a Snap," *BusinessWeek* (November 9, 1998): 168, 172.

40. Robert C. Ford and W. Alan Randolph, "Cross-Functional Structures: A Review and Integration of Matrix Organization and Project Management," *Journal of Management* 18(2) (1992): 267–294; and Paula Dwyer with Pete Engardio, Zachary Schiller, and Stanley Reed, "Tearing Up Today's Organization Chart," *BusinessWeek* (Twenty-First Century Capitalism, Special Issue): 80–90.

41. These disadvantages are based on Michael Goold and Andrew Campbell, "Making Matrix Structures Work: Creating Clarity on Unit Roles and Responsibilities," *European Management Journal* 21(3) (June 2003): 351–363; Hymowitz, "Managers Suddenly Have to Answer to a Crowd of Bosses"; and Dwyer et al., "Tearing Up Today's Organization Chart."

42. Geoff Keighley, "Massively Multinational Player," *Business 2.0* (September 2005): 64–66.

43. Dexter Filkins, "Profusion of Rebel Groups Helps Them Survive in Iraq," *New York Times*, December 2, 2005, p. A1 (www.nytimes.com).

44. Scott Shane and Neil A. Lewis, "At Sept. 11 Trial, Tale of Missteps and Mismanagement," *New York Times*, March 31, 2006, p. A1 (www.nytimes.com).

45. Raymond E. Miles, "Adapting to Technology and Competition: A New Industrial Relations System for the Twenty-First Century," *California Management Review* (Winter 1989): 9–28; and Miles and Snow, "The New Network Firm."

46. Dess et al., "The New Corporate Architecture"; Henry W. Chesbrough and David J. Teece, "Organizing for Innovation: When Is Virtual Virtuous?" *The Innovative Entrepreneur* (August 2002): 127–134;

N. Anand, "Modular, Virtual, and Hollow Forms"; and M. Lynne Markus, Brook Manville, and Carole E. Agres, "What Makes a Virtual Organization Work?" *Sloan Management Review* (Fall 2000): 13–26.

47. Anand and Daft, "What Is the Right Organization Design?"

48. Laurie P. O'Leary, "Curing the Monday Blues: A U.S. Navy Guide for Structuring Cross-Functional Teams," *National Productivity Review* (Spring 1996): 43–51; and Alan Hurwitz, "Organizational Structures for the 'New World Order,'" *Business Horizons* (May–June 1996): 5–14.

49. Jay Galbraith, Diane Downey, and Amy Kates, "Processes and Lateral Capability," Chapter 4 in *Designing Dynamic Organizations: A Hands On Guide for Leaders at All Levels* (New York: AMACOM, 2002).

50. Sara Lipka, "The Lawyer Is In," *Chronicle of Higher Education* (July 1, 2005): A19, A21.

51. Lee Iacocca with William Novak, *Iacocca: An Autobiography* (New York: Phantom Books, 1984): 152–153.

52. Miriam Jordan and Jonathan Karp, "Machines for the Masses," *Wall Street Journal*, December 9, 2003, p. A19.

53. William J. Altier, "Task Forces: An Effective Management Tool," *Management Review* (February 1987): 52–57.

54. "Task Forces Tackle Consolidation of Employment Services," *Shawmut News*, Shawmut National Corporation (May 3, 1989): 2.

55. Henry Mintzberg, *The Structure of Organizations* (Englewood Cliffs, NJ: Prentice Hall, 1979).

56. Paul R. Lawrence and Jay W. Lorsch, "New Managerial Job: The Integrator," *Harvard Business Review* (November–December 1967): 142–151.

57. Ronald N. Ashkenas and Suzanne C. Francis, "Integration Managers: Special Leaders for Special Times," *Harvard Business Review* (November–December 2000): 108–116.

58. This discussion is based on Michael Hammer and Steven Stanton, "How Process Enterprises *Really* Work," *Harvard Business Review* (November–December 1999): 108–118; Richard L. Daft, *Organization Theory and Design*, 5th ed. (Minneapolis, MN: West, 1995): 238; Raymond L. Manganelli and Mark M. Klein, "A Framework for Reengineering," *Management Review* (June 1994): 9–16; and Barbara Ettorre, "Reengineering Tales from the Front," *Management Review* (January 1995): 13–18.

59. Hammer and Stanton, "How Process Enterprises *Really* Work."

60. Michael Hammer, definition quoted in "The Process Starts Here," *CIO* (March 1, 2000): 144–156; and David A. Garvin, "The Processes of Organization and Management," *Sloan Management Review* (Summer 1998): 33–50.

61. Frank Ostroff, *The Horizontal Organization: What the Organization of the Future Looks Like and How It Delivers Value to Customers* (New York: Oxford University Press, 1999).

62. Dan Groszkiewicz and Brent Warren, "Alcoa's Michigan Casting Center Runs the Business from the Bottom Up," *Journal of Organizational Excellence* (Spring 2006): 13–23.

63. Erik Brynjolfsson, Amy Austin Renshaw, and Marshall Van Alstyne, "The Matrix of Change," *Sloan Management Review* (Winter 1997): 37–54.

64. Harold J. Leavitt, "Why Hierarchies Thrive," *Harvard Business Review* (March 2003): 96–102, provides a discussion of the benefits and problems of hierarchies. See Timothy Galpin, Rod Hilpirt, and Bruce Evans, "The Connected Enterprise: Beyond Division of Labor," *Journal of Business Strategy* 28(2) (2007): 38–47, for a discussion of the advantages of horizontal over vertical designs.

65. Eric M. Olson, Stanley F. Slater, and G. Tomas M. Hult, "The Importance of Structure and Process to Strategy Implementation," *Business Horizons* 48 (2005): 47–54.

66. Michael E. Porter, *Competitive Strategy* (New York: The Free Press, 1980): 36–46.

67. Tom Burns and G. M. Stalker, *The Management of Innovation* (London: Tavistock, 1961).

68. John A. Coutright, Gail T. Fairhurst, and L. Edna Rogers, "Interaction Patterns in Organic and Mechanistic Systems," *Academy of Management Journal* 32 (1989): 773–802.

CHAPTER 8

Managing Change and Innovation

1. Reported in "Ninety Years in Business," *The Conference Board Review* (September–October 2006): 30–39.

2. Mark Landler, "Nokia Pushes to Regain U.S. Sales in Spite of Apple and Google," *New York Times*, December 10, 2007.

3. Martin Fackler, "Electronics Company Aims to Create Break-Out Products," *New York Times*, April 25, 2006, p. C1; and Peter Lewis, "A Perpetual Crisis Machine," *Fortune* (September 19, 2005): 58–76.

4. Bruce Nussbaum, with Robert Berner and Diane Brady, "Get Creative," *BusinessWeek* (August 1, 2005): 60–68; and Jena McGregor, Michael Arndt, Robert Berner, Ian Rowley, Kenji Hall, Gail Edmondson, Steve Hamm, Moon Ihlwan, and Andy Reinhardt, "The World's Most Innovative Companies," *BusinessWeek* (April 24, 2006): 62 (www.businessweek.com).

5. Based on H. Thomas Hurt, Katherine Joseph, and Chester D. Cook, "Scales for the Measurement of Innovativeness," *Human Communication Research* 4(1) (1977): 58–65; and John E. Ettlie and Robert D. O'Keefe, "Innovative Attitudes, Values, and Intentions in Organizations," *Journal of Management Studies* 19(2) (1982): 163–182.

6. Keith Bradsher, "Newest Export Out of China: Inflation Fears," *New York Times*, April 16, 2004, p. A1.

7. Scott Kirsner, "Five Technologies That Will Change the World," *Fast Company* (September 2003): 93–98; Peter Grant and Amy Schatz, "Battle Lines; For Cable Giants, AT&T Deal Is One More Reason to Worry," *Wall Street Journal*, March 7, 2006, p. A1; Stuart F. Brown, "The Automaker's Big-Time Bet on Fuel Cells," *Fortune* (March 30, 1998): 122(B)–122(D); and Alex Taylor III, "Billion-Dollar Bets," *Fortune* (June 27, 2005): 138–154.

8. Kirsner, "Five Technologies."

9. David Henry, "Creativity Pays. Here's How Much," *BusinessWeek* (April 24, 2006): 76.

10. Richard L. Daft, "Bureaucratic vs. Nonbureaucratic Structure in the Process of Innovation and Change," in Samuel B. Bacharach (Ed.), *Perspectives in Organizational Sociology: Theory and Research* (Greenwich, CT: JAI Press, 1982): 129–166.

11. Charles A. O'Reilly III and Michael L. Tushman, "The Ambidextrous Organization," *Harvard Business Review* (April 2004): 74–81; and M. L. Tushman and C. A. O'Reilly III, "Building an Ambidextrous Organization: Forming Your Own 'Skunk Works,'" *Health Forum Journal* 42(2) (March–April 1999): 20–23.

12. C. Brooke Dobni, "The Innovation Blueprint," *Business Horizons* (2006): 329–339.

13. Glenn Rifkin, "Competing Through Innovation: The Case of Broderbund," *Strategy + Business* 11 (Second Quarter 1998): 48–58; and Deborah Dougherty and Cynthia Hardy, "Sustained Product Innovation in Large, Mature Organizations: Overcoming Innovation-to-Organization Problems," *Academy of Management Journal* 39(5) (1996): 1120–1153.

14. Adapted from Patrick Reinmoeller and Nicole van Baardwijk, "The Link Between Diversity and Resilience," *MIT Sloan Management Review* (Summer 2005): 61–65.

15. Teresa M. Amabile, "Motivating Creativity in Organizations: On Doing What You Love and Loving What You Do," *California Management Review* 40(1) (Fall 1997): 39–58; Brian Leavy, "Creativity: The New Imperative," *Journal of General Management* 28(1) (Autumn 2002): 70–85; and Timothy A. Matherly and Ronald E. Goldsmith, "The Two Faces of Creativity," *Business Horizons* (September–October 1985): 8.

16. Lee Gomes, "Our Columnist Judges a Brainstorming Bee, and Meets a Genius," *Wall Street Journal*, March 5, 2008, p. B1.

17. Gordon Vessels, "The Creative Process: An Open-Systems Conceptualization," *Journal of Creative Behavior* 16 (1982): 185–196.

18. Robert J. Sternberg, Linda A. O'Hara, and Todd I. Lubart, "Creativity as Investment," *California Management Review* 40(1) (Fall 1997): 8–21; Amabile, "Motivating Creativity in Organizations"; Leavy, "Creativity: The New Imperative"; and Ken Lizotte, "A Creative State of Mind," *Management Review* (May 1998): 15–17.

19. James Brian Quinn, "Managing Innovation: Controlled Chaos," *Harvard Business Review* 63 (May–June 1985): 73–84; Howard H. Stevenson and David E. Gumpert, "The Heart of Entrepreneurship," *Harvard Business Review* 63 (March–April 1985): 85–94; Marsha Sinetar, " Entrepreneurs, Chaos, and Creativity—Can Creative People Really Survive Large Company Structure?" *Sloan Management Review* 6 (Winter 1985): 57–62; and Constantine Andriopoulos, "Six Paradoxes in Managing Creativity: An Embracing Act," *Long Range Planning* 36 (2003): 375–388.

20. Cynthia Browne, "Jest for Success," *Moonbeams* (August 1989): 3–5; and Rosabeth Moss Kanter, *The Change Masters* (New York: Simon and Schuster, 1983).

21. Chuck Salter, "Google: The Faces and Voices of the World's Most Innovative Company," *Fast Company* (March 2008): 74–91.

22. Sherry Eng, "Hatching Schemes," *The Industry Standard* (November 27–December 4, 2000): 174–175.

23. Reena Jana, "Brickhouse: Yahoo's Hot Little Incubator," *IN* (November 2007): 14.

24. McGregor et al., "The World's Most Innovative Companies."

25. Barry Jaruzelski, Kevin Dehoff, and Rakesh Bordia, "Money Isn't Everything," *Strategy + Business*, 41 (December 5, 2005): 54–67; William L. Shanklin and John K. Ryans, Jr., "Organizing for High-Tech Marketing," *Harvard Business Review* 62 (November–December 1984): 164–171; and Arnold O. Putnam, "A Redesign for Engineering," *Harvard Business Review* 63 (May–June 1985): 139–144.

26. Rob Cross, Andrew Hargadon, Salvatore Parise, and Robert J. Thomas, "Business Insight" (A Special Report); "Together We Innovate: How Can Companies Come Up with New Ideas? By Getting Employees Working with One Another," *Wall Street Journal*, September 15, 2007, p. R6.

27. Andrew H. Van de Ven, "Central Problems in the Management of Innovation," *Management Science* 32 (1986): 590–607; Richard L. Daft, *Organization Theory and Design* (South-Western, 2007); and Science Policy Research Unit, University of Sussex, *Success and Failure in Industrial Innovation* (London: Centre for the Study of Industrial Innovation, 1972).

28. Daft, *Organization Theory*.

29. Brian Dumaine, "How Managers Can Succeed Through Speed," *Fortune* (February 13, 1989): 54–59; and George Stalk, Jr., "Time—The Next Source of Competitive Advantage," *Harvard Business Review* (July–August 1988): 41–51.

30. Steve Hamm, with Ian Rowley, "Speed Demons," *BusinessWeek* (March 27, 2006): 68–76; and John A. Pearce II, "Speed Merchants," *Organizational Dynamics* 30(3) (2002): 191–205.

31. V. K. Narayanan, Frank L. Douglas, Brock Guernsey, and John Charnes, "How Top Management Steers Fast Cycle Teams to Success," *Strategy & Leadership* 30(3) (2002): 19–27.

32. The discussion of open innovation is based on Henry Chesbrough, "The Era of Open Innovation," *MIT Sloan Management Review* (Spring 2003): 35–41; Julian Birkinshaw and Susan A. Hill, "Corporate Venturing Units: Vehicles for Strategic Success in the New Europe," *Organizational Dynamics* 34(3) (2005): 247–257; Amy Muller and Liisa Välikangas, "Extending the Boundary of Corporate Innovation," *Strategy & Leadership* 30(3) (2002): 4–9; Navi Radjou, "Networked Innovation Drives Profits," *Industrial Management* (January–February 2005): 14–21; Darrell Rigby and Barbara Bilodeau, "The Bain 2005 Management Tool Survey," *Strategy & Leadership* 33(4) (2005): 4–12; Ian Mount, "The Return of the Lone Inventor," *FSB (Fortune Small Business)* (March 2005): 18; McGregor et al., "The World's Most Innovative Companies;" and Henry Chesbrough, "The Logic of Open Innovation: Managing Intellectual Property," *California Management Review* 45(3) (Spring 2003): 33–58.

33. Reported in Jill Jusko, "A Team Effort," *Industry Week* (January 2007): 42, 45.

34. Larry Huston and Nabil Sakkab, "Connect and Develop; Inside Procter & Gamble's New Model for Innovation," *Harvard Business Review* (March 2006): 58–66; G. Gil Cloyd, "P&G's Secret: Innovating Innovation," *Industry Week* (December 2004): 26–34; Bettina von Stamm, "Collaboration with Other Firms and Customers: Innovation's Secret Weapon," *Strategy & Leadership* 32(3) (2004): 16–20; Robert Berner, "Why P&G's Smile Is So Bright," *BusinessWeek* (August 12, 2002): 58–60; Robert D. Hof, "Building an Idea Factory," *BusinessWeek* (October 11, 2004): 194–200; Patricia Sellers, "P&G: Teaching an Old Dog New Tricks," *Fortune* (May 31, 2004): 167–180; and Ellen Byron, "Bottle Curve; P&G's Push into Perfume Tests a Stodgy Marketer," *Wall Street Journal*, November 12, 2007, p. A1.

35. Daniel T. Holt, Matthew W. Rutherford, and Gretchen R. Clohessy, "Corporate Entrepreneurship: An Empirical Look at Individual Characteristics, Context, and Process," *Journal of Leadership and Organizational Studies* 13(4) (2007): 40–54.

36. Robert I. Sutton, "The Weird Rules of Creativity," *Harvard Business Review* (September 2001): 94–103.

37. Jane M. Howell, "The Right Stuff: Identifying and Developing Effective Champions of Innovation," *Academy of Management Executive* 19(2) (2005): 108–119.

38. Harold L. Angle and Andrew H. Van de Ven, "Suggestions for Managing the Innovation Journey," in A. H. Van de Ven, H. L. Angle, and Marshall Scott Poole (Eds.), *Research in the Management of Innovation: The Minnesota Studies* (Cambridge, MA: Ballinger/Harper & Row, 1989).

39. C. K. Bart, "New Venture Units: Use Them Wisely to Manage Innovation," *Sloan Management Review* (Summer 1988): 35–43; Michael Tushman and David Nadler, "Organizing for Innovation," *California Management Review* 28 (Spring 1986): 74–92; Peter F. Drucker, *Innovation and Entrepreneurship* (New York: Harper & Row, 1985); and Henry W. Chesbrough, "Making Sense of Corporate Venture Capital, *Harvard Business Review* 89(3) (March 2002): 90.

40. McGregor et al., "The World's Most Innovative Companies."

41. Christopher Hoenig, "Skunk Works Secrets," *CIO* (July 1, 2000): 74–76; and Tom Peters and Nancy Austin, *A Passion for Excellence: The Leadership Difference* (New York: Random House, 1985).

42. Hoenig, "Skunk Works Secrets."

43. Sutton, "The Weird Rules of Creativity."

44. Robert C. Wolcott and Michael J. Lippitz, "The Four Models of Corporate Entrepreneurship," *MIT Sloan Management Review* (Fall 2007): 75–82.

45. Wolcott and Lippitz, "The Four Models of Corporate Entrepreneurship"; Alan Deutschman, "Building a Better Skunkworks," *Fast Company* (March 2005): 69–73.

46. McGregor et al., "The World's Most Innovative Companies."

47. Wolcott and Lippitz, "The Four Models of Corporate Entrepreneurship."

48. E. H. Schein, "Organizational Culture," *American Psychologist* 45 (February 1990): 109–119; Eliza Newlin Carney, "Calm in the Storm," *Government Executive* 35(15) (October 2003): 57.

49. Rosabeth Moss Kanter, "Execution: The Un-Idea," sidebar in Art Kleiner, "Our 10 Most Enduring Ideas," *Strategy + Business* 41 (December 12, 2005): 36–41.

50. Michelle Conlin, "Tough Love for Techie Souls," *BusinessWeek* (November 29, 1999): 164–170.

51. M. Sashkin and W. W. Burke, "Organization Development in the 1980s," *General Management* 13 (1987): 393–417; and Richard Beckhard, "What Is Organization Development?" in Wendell L. French, Cecil H. Bell, Jr., and Robert A. Zawacki (Eds.), *Organization Development and Transformation: Managing Effective Change* (Burr Ridge, IL: Irwin McGraw-Hill, 2000): 16–19.

52. Wendell L. French and Cecil H. Bell, Jr., "A History of Organization Development," in French, Bell, and Zawacki, *Organization Development and Transformation*, pp. 20–42; and Christopher G. Worley and Ann E. Feyerherm, "Reflections on the Future of Organization Development," *Journal of Applied Behavioral Science* 39(1) (March 2003): 97–115.

53. Paul F. Buller, "For Successful Strategic Change: Blend OD Practices with Strategic Management," *Organizational Dynamics* (Winter 1988): 42–55; Robert M. Fulmer and Roderick Gilkey, "Blending Corporate Families: Management and Organization Development in a Postmerger Environment," *Academy of Management Executive* 2 (1988): 275–283; and Worley and Feyerherm, "Reflections on the Future of Organization Development."

54. W. Warner Burke, "The New Agenda for Organization Development," *Organizational Dynamics* (Summer 1997): 7–19.

55. This discussion is based on Kathleen D. Dannemiller and Robert W. Jacobs, "Changing the Way Organizations Change: A Revolution of Common Sense," *Journal of Applied Behavioral Science* 28(4) (December 1992): 480–498; and Barbara Benedict Bunker and Billie T. Alban, "Conclusion: What Makes Large Group Interventions Effective?" *Journal of Applied Behavioral Science* 28(4) (December 1992): 570–591.

56. B. B. Bunker and B. T. Alban, "Conclusion: What Makes Large Group Interventions Effective?" *Journal of Applied Behavioral Science* 28(4) (December 1992): 572–591.

57. Dave Ulrich, Steve Kerr, and Ron Ashkenas, with Debbie Burke and Patrice Murphy, *The GE Work-Out: How to Implement GE's Revolutionary Method for Busting Bureaucracy and Attacking Organizational Problems—Fast!* (New York: McGraw-Hill, 2002); J. Quinn, "What a Work-Out!" *Performance* (November 1994): 58–63; and Bunker and Alban, "Conclusion: What Makes Large Group Interventions Effective?"

58. Kurt Lewin, "Frontiers in Group Dynamics: Concepts, Method, and Reality in Social Science," *Human Relations* 1 (1947): 5–41; and E. F. Huse and T. G. Cummings, *Organization Development and Change*, 3rd ed. (St. Paul, MN: West, 1985).

59. Based on John Kotter's eight-step model of planned change, which is described in John Kotter, *Leading Change* (Boston: Harvard Business School Press, 1996): 20–25; and "Leading Change: Why Transformation Efforts Fail," *Harvard Business Review* (March–April, 1995): 59–67.

60. Pierre Loewe and Jennifer Dominiquini, "Overcoming the Barriers to Effective Innovation, *Strategy & Leadership* 34(1) (2006): 24–31; and Jennifer Robison, "Innovation the Right Way: A Case Study in How a Manufacturing Company Got Innovation Right," *Gallup Management Journal* (May 10, 2007).

61. Kotter, *Leading Change*; and "Leading Change: Why Transformation Efforts Fail," *Harvard Business Review* (March–April, 1995): 59–67.

62. J. P. Kotter and L. A. Schlesinger, "Choosing Strategies for Change," *Harvard Business Review* 57 (March–April 1979): 106–114.

63. Robison, "Innovation the Right Way."

64. G. Zaltman and Robert B. Duncan, *Strategies for Planned Change* (New York: Wiley InterScience, 1977).

65. Leonard M. Apcar, "Middle Managers and Supervisors Resist Moves to More Participatory Management," *Wall Street Journal*, September 16, 1985, p. 1.

66. Dorothy Leonard-Barton and Isabelle Deschamps, "Managerial Influence in the Implementation of New Technology," *Management Science* 34 (1988): 1252–1265.

67. Kurt Lewin, *Field Theory in Social Science: Selected Theoretical Papers* (New York: Harper & Brothers, 1951).

68. Paul C. Nutt, "Tactics of Implementation," *Academy of Management Journal* 29 (1986): 230–261; Kotter and Schlesinger, "Choosing Strategies"; R. L. Daft and S. Becker, *Innovation in Organizations: Innovation Adoption in School Organizations* (New York: Elsevier, 1978); and R. Beckhard, *Organization Development: Strategies and Models* (Reading, MA: Addison-Wesley, 1969).

69. Rob Muller, "Training for Change," *Canadian Business Review* (Spring 1995): 16–19.

70. Gerard H. Seijts and Grace O'Farrell, "Engage the Heart: Appealing to the Emotions Facilitates Change," *Ivey Business Journal* (January–February 2003): 1–5; John P. Kotter and Dan S. Cohen, *The Heart of Change: Real-Life Stories of How People Change Their Organizations* (Boston: Harvard Business School Press, 2002); and Shaul Fox and Yair Amichai Hamburger, "The Power of Emotional Appeals in Promoting Organizational Change Programs," *Academy of Management Executive* 15(4) (2001): 84–95.

71. Gina Burkhardt and Diane Gerard, "People: The Lever for Changing the Business Model at Learning Point Associates," *Journal of Organizational Excellence* (Autumn 2006): 31–43.

72. Henry Hornstein, "Using a Change Management Approach to Implement IT Programs," *Ivey Business Journal* (January–February 2008); Philip H. Mirvis, Amy L. Sales, and Edward J. Hackett, "The Implementation and Adoption of New Technology in Organizations: The Impact on Work, People, and Culture,"

Human Resource Management 30 (Spring 1991): 113–139; Arthur E. Wallach, "System Changes Begin in the Training Department," *Personnel Journal* 58 (1979): 846–848, 872; and Paul R. Lawrence, "How to Deal with Resistance to Change," *Harvard Business Review* 47 (January–February 1969): 4–12, 166–176.

73. Dean Foust with Gerry Khermouch, "Repairing the Coke Machine," *BusinessWeek* (March 19, 2001): 86–88.

74. Strategos survey results, reported in Loewe and Dominiquini, "Overcoming the Barriers to Effective Innovation."

75. Joy Persaud, "Strongest Links," *People Management* (May 29, 2003): 40–41.

76. By Jennie Carter Thomas and Harry N. Hollis, Belmont University. Used with permission.

CHAPTER 9

Managing Human Resources and Diversity

1. Results of a McKinsey Consulting survey, reported in Leigh Branham, "Planning to Become an Employer of Choice," *Journal of Organizational Excellence* (Summer 2005): 57–68.

2. Robert L. Mathis and John H. Jackson, *Human Resource Management: Essential Perspectives*, 2nd ed. (Cincinnati, OH: South-Western Publishing, 2002): 1.

3. See James C. Wimbush, "Spotlight on Human Resource Management," *Business Horizons* 48 (2005): 463–467; Jonathan Tompkins, "Strategic Human Resources Management in Government: Unresolved Issues," *Public Personnel Management* (Spring 2002): 95–110; Noel M. Tichy, Charles J. Fombrun, and Mary Anne Devanna, "Strategic Human Resource Management," *Sloan Management Review* 23 (Winter 1982): 47–61; Cynthia A. Lengnick-Hall and Mark L. Lengnick-Hall, "Strategic Human Resources Management: A Review of the Literature and a Proposed Typology," *Academy of Management Review* 13 (July 1988): 454–470; and Eugene B. McGregor, *Strategic Management of Human Knowledge, Skills, and Abilities*, (San Francisco: Jossey-Bass, 1991).

4. Edward E. Lawler III, "HR on Top," *Strategy + Business,* 35 (Second Quarter 2004): 21–25.

5. P. Wright, G. McMahan, and A. McWilliams, "Human Resources and Sustained Competitive Advantage: A Resource-Based Perspective," *International Journal of Human Resource Management* 5 (1994): 301–326; Tompkins, "Strategic Human Resource Management in Government: Unresolved Issues"; and Wimbush, "Spotlight on Human Resource Management."

6. B. Becker and M. Huselid, "High Performance Work Systems and Firm Performance: A Synthesis of Research and Managerial Implications," *Research in Personnel and Human Resources Management* 16 (1998): 53–101; S. Ramlall, "Measuring Human Resource Management's Effectiveness in Improving Performance," *Human Resource Planning* 26 (2003): 51; Mark A. Huselid, Susan E. Jackson, and Randall S. Schuler, "Technical and Strategic Human Resource Management Effectiveness as Determinants of Firm Performance," *Academy of Management Journal* 40(1)

(1997): 171–188; and John T. Delaney and Mark A. Huselid, "The Impact of Human Resource Management Practices on Perceptions of Organizational Performance," *Academy of Management Journal* 39(4) (1996): 949–969.

7. James N. Baron and David M. Kreps, "Consistent Human Resource Practices," *California Management Review* 41(3) (Spring 1999): 29–53.

8. Sunil J. Ramlall, "Strategic HR Management Creates Value at Target," *Journal of Organizational Excellence* (Spring 2006): 57–62.

9. Cynthia D. Fisher, "Current and Recurrent Challenges in HRM," *Journal of Management* 15 (1989): 157–180.

10. Floyd Kemske, "HR 2008: A Forecast Based on Our Exclusive Study," *Workforce* (January 1998): 46–60.

11. This definition and discussion is based on George Bollander, Scott Snell, and Arthur Sherman, *Managing Human Resources,* 12th ed. (Cincinnati, OH: South-Western, 2001): 13–15; and Harry Scarbrough, "Recipe for Success," *People Management* (January 23, 2003): 22–25.

12. Susan Cantrell, James M. Benton, Terry Laudal, and Robert J. Thomas, "Measuring the Value of Human Capital Investments: The SAP Case," *Strategy & Leadership* 34(2) (2006): 43–52.

13. Rich Wellins and Sheila Rioux, "The Growing Pains of Globalizing HR," *Training and Development* (May 2000): 79–85.

14. Helen DeCieri, Julie Wolfram Cox, and Marilyn S. Fenwick, "Think Global, Act Local: From Naive Comparison to Critical Participation in the Teaching of Strategic International Human Resource Management," *Tamara: Journal of Critical Postmodern Organization Science* 1(1) (2001): 68ff; S. Taylor, S. Beecher, and N. Napier, "Towards an Integrative Model of Strategic Human Resource Management," *Academy of Management Review* 21 (1996): 959–985; and Mary Ann Von Glinow, Ellen A. Drost, and Mary B. Teagarden, "Converging on IHRM Best Practices: Lessons Learned from a Globally Distributed Consortium on Theory and Practice," *Human Resource Management* 41(1) (Spring 2002): 123–140.

15. Von Glinow, Drost, and Teagarden, "Converging on IHRM Best Practices"; and Jennifer J. Laabs, "Must-Have Global HR Competencies," *Workforce* 4(2) (1999): 30–32.

16. Section 1604.1 of the EEOC Guidelines based on the Civil Rights Act of 1964, Title VII.

17. Reported in D. T. Hall and P. H. Mirvis, "The New Protean Career: Psychological Success and the Path with a Heart," in D. T. Hall & Associates (Eds.), *The Career is Dead—Long Live the Career: A Relational Approach to Careers* (San Francisco: Jossey-Bass, 1995): 15–45.

18. Based on Douglas T. Hall and Jonathan E. Moss, "The New Protean Career Contract: Helping Organizations and Employees Adapt," *Organizational Dynamics* (Winter 1998): 22–37; and M. V. Roehling, M. A. Cavanaugh, L. M. Moynihan, and W. R. Boswell, "The Nature of the New Employment Relationship: A Content Analysis of the Practitioner and Academic Literatures," *Human Resource Management* 39(4) (2000): 305–320.

19. A. S. Tsui, J. L. Pearce, L. W. Porter, and A. M. Tripoli, "Alternative Approaches to the Employee-Organization Relationship: Does Investment in Employees Pay Off?" *Academy of Management Journal* 40 (1997): 1089–1121; and D. Wang, A. S. Tsui, Y. Zhang, and L. Ma, "Employment Relationships and Firm Performance: Evidence from an Emerging Economy," *Journal of Organizational Behavior* 24 (2003): 511–535.

20. Based on Branham, "Planning to Become an Employer of Choice."

21. This discussion is based on Jaclyn Fierman, "The Contingency Workforce," *Fortune* (January 24, 1994): 30–31; Kris Maher, "More People Pushed Into Part-Time Work Force," *Wall Street Journal*, March 8, 2008; Marshall Goldsmith, "The Contingent Workforce," *BusinessWeek* (May 23, 2007) (www.businessweek.com/careers/content/may2007/ca20070523_580432.htm) (accessed April 8, 2008); and John Tagliabue, "Europe No Longer Shuns Part-Time and Temporary Jobs," *New York Times*, May 11, 2006, p. C1.

22. Goldsmith, "The Contingent Workforce."

23. Thomas Frank, "TSA Struggles to Reduce Persistent Turnover," *USA Today*, February 25, 2008, p. A4.

24. Ellen Gragg, "Are Telecommuting and Flextime Dead?" *Office Solutions* (January/February 2006): 28ff; and Stephen Barr, "Working from Home a Work in Progress," *Washington Post*, June 19, 2007, p. D4.

25. Gragg, "Are Telecommuting and Flextime Dead?"

26. John Challenger, "There Is No Future for the Workplace," *Public Management* (February 1999): 20–23; and Susan Caminiti, "Work-Life," *Fortune* (September 19, 2005): S1–S17.

27. Stephanie Armour, "Generation Y: They've Arrived at Work with a New Attitude," *USA Today*, November 6, 2005, pp. 92–98 (www.usatoday.com); Ellyn Spragins, "The Talent Pool," *FSB* (October 2005): 92–101; and Caminiti, "Work-Life."

28. James R. Morris, Wayne F. Cascio, and Clifford Young, "Downsizing After All These Years: Questions and Answers about Who Did It, How Many Did It, and Who Benefited From It," *Organizational Dynamics* (Winter 1999): 78–86; William McKinley, Carol M. Sanchez, and Allen G. Schick, "Organizational Downsizing: Constraining, Cloning, Learning," *Academy of Management Executive* 9(3) (1995): 32–42; and Brett C. Luthans and Steven M. Sommer, "The Impact of Downsizing on Workplace Attitudes," *Group and Organization Management* 2(1) (1999): 46–70.

29. Effective downsizing techniques are discussed in detail in Bob Nelson, "The Care of the Un-Downsized," *Training and Development* (April 1997): 40–43; Shari Caudron, "Teaching Downsizing Survivors How to Thrive," *Personnel Journal* (January 1996): 38; Joel Brockner, "Managing the Effects of Layoffs on Survivors," *California Management Review* (Winter 1992): 9–28; and Kim S. Cameron, "Strategies for Successful Organizational Downsizing," *Human Resource Management* 33(2) (Summer 1994): 189–211.

30. James G. March and Herbert A. Simon, *Organizations* (New York: Wiley, 1958).

31. Dennis J. Kravetz, *The Human Resources Revolution* (San Francisco: Jossey-Bass, 1989).

32. David E. Ripley, "How to Determine Future Workforce Needs," *Personnel Journal* (January 1995): 83–89.

33. J. W. Boudreau and S. L. Rynes, "Role of Recruitment in Staffing Utility Analysis," *Journal of Applied Psychology* 70 (1985): 354–366.

34. Megan Santosus, "The Human Capital Factor," *CFO-IT* (Fall 2005): 26–27.

35. Reported in Robert E. Ployhart, "Staffing in the 21st Century: New Challenges and Strategic Opportunities," *Journal of Management* 32(6) (December 2006): 868–897.

36. Brian Dumaine, "The New Art of Hiring Smart," *Fortune* (August 17, 1987): 78–81.

37. This discussion is based on Mathis and Jackson, *Human Resource Management*, Chapter 4, pp. 49–60.

38. Victoria Griffith, "When Only Internal Expertise Will Do," *CFO* (October 1998): 95–96, 102.

39. J. P. Wanous, *Organizational Entry* (Reading, MA: Addison-Wesley, 1980).

40. Samuel Greengard, "Technology Finally Advances HR," *Workforce* (January 2000): 38–41; and Scott Hays, "Hiring on the Web," *Workforce* (August 1999): 77–84.

41. Simona Covel, "Start-Up Lures Talent with Creative Pitch," *Wall Street Journal*, June 4, 2007, p. B4.

42. Kathryn Tyler, "Employees Can Help Recruit New Talent," *HR Magazine* (September 1996): 57–60.

43. Sarah E. Needleman, "If You Want to Stand Out, Join the Crowd," *Wall Street Journal*, August 14, 2007, p. B6.

44. Ron Stodghill, "Soul on Ice," *FSB* (October 2005): 129–134.

45. Miriam Jordan, "Bourbon, Baseball Bats, and Not the Bantu," *Wall Street Journal*, September 18, 2007, p. B1.

46. Milt Freudenheim, "More Help Wanted: Older Workers Please Apply," *New York Times*, March 23, 2005, p. A1.

47. "Bank of America to Hire 850 Ex-Welfare Recipients," *Johnson City* [Tennessee] *Press*, January 14, 2001; E. Blacharczyk, "Recruiters Challenged by Economy, Shortages, Unskilled," *HR News* (February 1990): B1; Victoria Rivkin, "Visa Relief," *Working Woman* (January 2001): 15.

48. Wimbush, "Spotlight on Human Resource Management."

49. P. W. Thayer, "Something's Old, Something's New," *Personnel Psychology* 30 (1977): 513–524.

50. J. Ledvinka, *Federal Regulation of Personnel and Human Resource Management* (Boston: Kent, 1982); and Civil Rights Act, Title VII, Section 2000e et seq., U.S. Code 42 (1964).

51. Reported in Stephanie Clifford, "The New Science of Hiring," *Inc. Magazine* (August 2006): 90–98.

52. George Bohlander, Scott Snell, and Arthur Sherman, *Managing Human Resources*, 12th ed. (Cincinnati, OH: South-Western, 2001): 202.

53. Ibid.

54. "Assessment Centers: Identifying Leadership through Testing," *Small Business Report* (June 1987): 22–24; and W. C. Byham, "Assessment Centers for Spotting Future Managers," *Harvard Business Review* (July–August 1970): 150–167.

55. Erin White, "Walking a Mile in Another's Shoes—Employers Champion Tests of Job Candidates to Gauge Skills at 'Real World' Tasks" (Theory and Practice column), *Wall Street Journal*, January 16, 2006, p. B3.

56. Mike Thatcher, "'Front-line' Staff Selected by Assessment Center," *Personnel Management* (November 1993): 83.

57. Alan Finder, "For Some, Online Persona Undermines a Resumé," *New York Times*, June 11, 2006, p. A1.

58. Bernard Keys and Joseph Wolfe, "Management Education and Development: Current Issues and Emerging Trends," *Journal of Management* 14 (1988): 205–229.

59. "2007 Industry Report," *Training* (November–December 2007): 8–24.

60. William J. Rothwell and H. C. Kazanas, *Improving On-the-Job Training: How to Establish and Operate a Comprehensive OJT Program* (San Francisco: Jossey-Bass, 1994).

61. Jeanne C. Meister, "The Brave New World of Corporate Education," *Chronicle of Higher Education* (February 9, 2001): B10; and Meryl Davids Landau, "Corporate Universities Crack Open Their Doors," *Journal of Business Strategy* (May–June 2000): 18–23.

62. Meister, "The Brave New World of Corporate Education"; Edward E. Gordon, "Bridging the Gap," *Training* (September 2003): 30; and John Byrne, "The Search for the Young and Gifted," *BusinessWeek* (October 4, 1999): 108–116.

63. Doug Bartholomew, "Taking the E-Train," *Industry Week* (June 2005): 34–37; and Joel Schettler, "Defense Acquisition University: Weapons of Mass Instruction," *Training* (February 2003): 20–27.

64. Jim Dow, "Spa Attraction," *People Management* (May 29, 2003): 34–35.

65. See C. H. Deutsch, "A New Kind of Whistle-Blower: Company Refines Principles of Coaching and Teamwork," *New York Times*, May 7, 1999; and B. Filipczak, "The Executive Coach: Helper or Healer?" *Training* (March 1998): 30–36.

66. Survey by HR consulting firm Watson Wyatt, reported in Kelley Holland, "Performance Reviews: Many Need Improvement," *New York Times*, September 10, 2006, p. 3.3.

67. Walter W. Tornow, "Editor's Note: Introduction to Special Issue on 360-Degree Feedback," *Human Resource Management* 32(2–3) (Summer–Fall 1993): 211–219; and Brian O'Reilly, "360 Feedback Can Change Your Life," *Fortune* (October 17, 1994): 93–100.

68. Kris Frieswick, "Truth and Consequences," *CFO* (June 2001): 56–63.

69. This discussion is based on Dick Grote, "Forced Ranking: Behind the Scenes," *Across the Board* (November–December 2002): 40–45; Matthew Boyle, "Performance Reviews: Perilous Curves Ahead," *Fortune* (May 28, 2001): 187–188; Carol Hymowitz, "Ranking Systems Gain Popularity but Have Many Staffers Riled," *Wall Street Journal*, May 15, 2001, p. B1; and Frieswick, "Truth and Consequences."

70. Reported in Jena McGregor, "The Struggle to Measure Performance," *BusinessWeek* (January 9, 2006): 26–28.

71. Ibid.

72. Erin White, "How to Reduce Turnover—Restaurant Chain Retains Workers Using Rankings and Rewards," *Wall Street Journal*, November 21, 2005, p. B5; and Lou Kaucic, "Finding Your Stars," *Microsoft Executive Circle* (Summer 2003): 14.

73. V. R. Buzzotta, "Improve Your Performance Appraisals," *Management Review* (August 1988): 40–43; and H. J. Bernardin and R. W. Beatty, *Performance Appraisal: Assessing Human Behavior at Work* (Boston: Kent, 1984).

74. Bernardin and Beatty, *Performance Appraisal.*

75. Richard I. Henderson, *Compensation Management: Rewarding Performance*, 4th ed. (Reston, VA: Reston, 1985).

76. L. R. Gomez-Mejia, "Structure and Process Diversification, Compensation Strategy, and Firm Performance," *Strategic Management Journal* 13 (1992): 381–397; and E. Montemayor, "Congruence Between Pay Policy and Competitive Strategy in High-Performing Firms," *Journal of Management* 22(6) (1996): 889–908.

77. Renée F. Broderick and George T. Milkovich, "Pay Planning, Organization Strategy, Structure and 'Fit': A Prescriptive Model of Pay," paper presented at the 45th Annual Meeting of the Academy of Management, San Diego, August 1985.

78. E. F. Lawler, III, *Strategic Pay: Aligning Organizational Strategies and Pay Systems* (San Francisco: Jossey-Bass, 1990); and R. J. Greene, "Person-Focused Pay: Should It Replace Job-Based Pay?" *Compensation and Benefits Management* 9(4) (1993): 46–55.

79. L. Wiener, "No New Skills? No Raise," *U.S. News and World Report* (October 26, 1992): 78.

80. Data from Hewitt Associates, Bureau of Labor Statistics, reported in Michelle Conlin and Peter Coy, with Ann Therese Palmer, and Gabrielle Saveri, "The Wild New Workforce," *BusinessWeek* (December 6, 1999): 39–44.

81. U.S. Chamber of Commerce, *2005 Employee Benefits Study* (Washington, DC: U.S. Chamber of Commerce, 2005) (www.uschamber.com/press/releases/2006/april/06-72.htm) (accessed April 11, 2008).

82. Frank E. Kuzmits, "Communicating Benefits: A Double-Click Away," *Compensation and Benefits Review* 30(5) (September–October 1998): 60–64; and Lynn Asinof, "Click and Shift: Workers Control Their Benefits Online," *Wall Street Journal*, November 27, 1997.

83. Robert S. Catapano-Friedman, "Cafeteria Plans: New Menu for the '90s," *Management Review* (November 1991): 25–29.

84. Society for Human Resource Management 2006 Talent Management Survey Report, reported in "Formal Findings," *Wall Street Journal*, June 4, 2007.

85. Scott Westcott, "Goodbye and Good Luck," *Inc. Magazine* (April 2006): 40–42.

86. Nanette Byrnes, "Star Search," *BusinessWeek* (October 10, 2005): 68–78.

87. Mike Brewster, "No Exit," *Fast Company* (April 2005): 93.

88. Russ Wiles, "Businesses Encourage Employees to Learn Spanish," *USA Today*, December 7, 2007 (www.usatoday.com/money/workplace/2007-12-08) (accessed March 17, 2008).

89. Susan Caminiti, "The Diversity Factor," *Fortune* (October 19, 2007): 95–105.

90. Gail Robinson and Kathleen Dechant, *Academy of Management Executive* 11(3) (1997): 26.

91. Michael L. Wheeler, "Diversity: The Performance Factor," *Harvard Business Review* (March 2005): S1–S7.

92. Ibid.

93. Caminiti, "The Diversity Factor."

94. M. Fine, F. Johnson, and M. S. Ryan, "Cultural Diversity in the Workforce," *Public Personnel Management* 19 (1990): 305–319.

95. Taylor H. Cox, "Managing Cultural Diversity: Implications for Organizational Competitiveness," *Academy of Management Executive* 5(3) (1991): 45–56; and Faye Rice, "How to Make Diversity Pay," *Fortune* (August 8, 1994): 78–86.

96. U.S. Department of Labor, Report of the Taskforce on the Aging of the American Workforce, February, 2008 (www.bls.gov) (accessed March 13, 2008).

97. The Bureau of Labor Statistics.

98. Ibid.

99. Kimberly L. Allers with Nadira A. Hira, "The Diversity List," *Fortune* (August 22, 2005); Elizabeth Wasserman, "A Race for Profits," *MBA Jungle* (March–April 2003): 40–41; and Amy Aronson, "Getting Results: Corporate Diversity, Integration, and Market Penetration," special advertising section, *BusinessWeek* (October 20, 2003).

100. Immigrant statistics from the U.S. Census Bureau reported in "Census Numbers Show Education Divide Among Immigrant Groups," *USA Today* (September 27, 2007) (www.cnn.com/2007/US/09/26/census.immigrants.ap/index.html?loc=interstitialskip) (accessed August 25, 2008).

101. Joseph Daniel McCool, "Diversity Pledges Ring Hollow," *BusinessWeek*, February 28, 2008 (http://search.businessweek.com/Search?searchTerm=diversity+pledges+ring+hollow&resultsPerPage=20) (accessed March 11, 2008).

102. "On Diversity, America Isn't Putting Its Money Where Its Mouth Is," *Wall Street Journal*, February 25, 2008, p. B1.

103. Helen Bloom, "Can the U.S. Export Diversity?" *Across the Board* (March–April 2002): 47–51.

104. Richard L. Daft, *The Leadership Experience,* (Cincinnati, OH: Cengage Learning, 2008): 340.

105. Honeywell Web site (www.honeywell.com) (accessed March 4, 2008).

106. Michael L. Wheeler, "Diversity: Business Rationale and Strategies," *The Conference Board,* Report No. 1130-95-RR, 1995, p. 14.

107. Ibid.

108. Anthony Oshiotse and Richard O'Leary, "Corning Creates an Inclusive Culture to Drive Technology Innovation and Performance," *Global Business and Organizational Excellence* (Wiley InterScience), 26(3) (March–April 2007): 10.

109. Elizabeth D. Macgillivray, H. Juanita M. Beecher, and Deirdre Golden, "Legal Developments—Religion at Work," *Wiley Inter-Science* (November–December 2007): 67.

110. UPS Web site (www.ups.com/pressroom/us/awards/citizenship) (accessed March 6, 2008).

111. Taylor Cox, Jr., and Ruby L. Beale, *Developing Competency to Manage Diversity* (San Francisco: Berrett-Koehler, 1997): 2.

112. Gail Robinson and Kathleen Dechant, "Building a Business Case for Diversity," *Academy of Management Executive* 11(3) (1997): 22.

113. Sonie Alleyne and Nicole Marie Richardson, "The 40 Best Companies for Diversity," *Black Enterprise* 36(12) (July 2006): 15.

114. Robinson and Dechant, "Building a Business Case for Diversity," 27.

115. Ibid., 22.

116. Carol Hymowitz, "Coaching Men on Mentoring Women Is Ernst & Young Partner's Mission," *Wall Street Journal Online* (www.wsj.com), June 14, 2007 (accessed July 9, 2007).

117. Kris Maher, "Lockheed Settles Racial-Discrimination Suits," *Wall Street Journal Online* (http://online.wsj.com/article_print/SB119932555019663957.html), January 3, 2008 (accessed March 11, 2008).

118. "Diversity in the Federal Government," report of a roundtable discussion on "Addressing Diversity Issues in the Government," July 10, 2003, moderated by Omar Wasow, executive director of BlackPlanet.com, reported in *New York Times Magazine* (September 14, 2003): 95–99.

119. Norma Carr-Ruffino, *Managing Diversity: People Skills for a Multicultural Workplace* (Tucson, AZ: Thomson Executive Press, 1996): 92.

120. Roy Harris, "The Illusion of Inclusion," *CFO* (May 2001): 42–50.

121. Stephanie N. Mehta, "What Minority Employees Really Want," *Fortune* (June 10, 2000): 181–186.

122. Vivek Wadhwa, "The True Cost of Discrimination," *Business-Week,* June 6, 2006 (www.businessweek.com/smallbiz/content/jun2006) (accessed March 7, 2008).

123. Carr-Ruffino, *Managing Diversity: People Skills for a Multicultural Workplace,* 98–99.

124. Cox and Beale, "Developing Competency to Manage Diversity," 79.

125. Ibid., 80–81.

126. Loriann Roberson and Carol T. Kulik, "Stereotype Threat at Work," *Academy of Management Perspectives* 21(2) (May 2007): 25–27.

127. Ibid., 26.

128. Robert Doktor, Rosalie Tung, and Mary Ann von Glinow, "Future Directions for Management Theory Development," *Academy of Management Review* 16 (1991): 362–365; and Mary Munter, "Cross-Cultural Communication for Managers," *Business Horizons* (May–June 1993): 69–78.

129. Jim Carlton, "Dig In," *Wall Street Journal* (November 14, 2005); Tony DiRomualdo, "Is Google's Cafeteria a Competitive Weapon?" *Wisconsin Technology Network* (August 30, 2005) (http://wistechnology.com/article.php?id=2190); Marc Ramirez, "Tray Chic: At Work, Cool Cafeterias, Imaginative Menus," *Seattle Times,* November 21, 2005, p. C1 (http://seattletimes.nwsource.com/html/living/2002634266_cafes21.html?pageid=display-in-thenews.module&pageregion=itnbody).

130. Marianne Bertrand and Sendhil Mullainathan, "Are Emily and Greg More Employable than Lakisha and Jamal?" National Bureau of Economic Research report, as reported in L. A. Johnson, "What's in a Name: When Emily Gets the Job Over Lakisha," *The Tennessean,* January 4, 2004; Marianne Bertrand and Sendhil Mullainathan, "Are Emily and Greg More Employable than Lakisha and Jamal? A Field Experiment on Labor Market Discrimination." *American Economic Review* 94(4) (September 2004): 991–1013.

131. Marie Valla, "France Seeks Path to Workplace Diversity," *Wall Street Journal,* January 3, 2007, p. 12.

132. Alice H. Eagly and Linda L. Carli, "Leadership," *Harvard Business Review* (September, 2007): 64.

133. Sheila Wellington, Marcia Brumit Kropf, and Paulette R. Gerkovich, "What's Holding Women Back?" *Harvard Business Review* (June 2003): 18–19.

134. Julie Amparano Lopez, "Study Says Women Face Glass Walls as Well as Ceilings," *Wall Street Journal,* March 3, 1992, p. B1; Ida L. Castro, "Q: Should Women Be Worried About the Glass Ceiling in the Workplace?" *Insight* (February 10, 1997): 24–27; Debra E. Meyerson and Joyce K. Fletcher, "A Modest Manifesto for Shattering the Glass Ceiling," *Harvard Business Review* (January–February 2000): 127–136; Wellington, Brumit Kropf, and Gerkovich, "What's Holding Women Back?"; and Annie Finnigan, "Different Strokes," *Working Woman* (April 2001): 42–48.

135. Catalyst survey results reported in Jason Forsythe, "Winning with Diversity," *New York Times Magazine* (March 28, 2004): 65–72.

136. Eagly and Carli, "Leadership," 64.

137. Jory Des Jardins, "I Am Woman (I Think)," *Fast Company* (May 2005): 25–26; Lisa Belkin, "The Opt-Out Revolution," *New York Times Magazine* (October 26, 2003): 43–47, 58; Finnigan, "Different Strokes," 42–48; and Meyerson and Fletcher, "A Modest Manifesto for Shattering the Glass Ceiling."

138. Statistics from the U.S. Census Bureau, Current Population Survey, 2004 Annual Social and Economic Supplement, as reported in "2003 Median Annual Earnings by Race and Sex" (www.infoplease.com/ipa/A0197814. html); and "The Economics of Gender and Race: Examining the Wage Gap in the United States," The Feminist Majority Foundation Choices Campus Campaign (www.feministcampus.org).

139. Cliff Edwards, "Coming Out in Corporate America," *Business-Week* (December 15, 2003): 64–72; and Belle Rose Ragins, John M. Cornwell, and Janice S. Miller, "Heterosexism in the Workplace: Do Race and Gender Matter?" *Group & Organization Management* 28(1) (March 2003): 45–74.

140. Melanie Trottman, "A Helping Hand," *Wall Street Journal,* November 14, 2005, p. R5; B. Ragins, "Barriers to Mentoring: The Female Manager's Dilemma," *Human Relations* 42(1) (1989): 1–22; and Belle Rose Ragins, Bickley Townsend, and Mary Mattis, "Gender Gap in the Executive Suite: CEOs and Female Executives Report on Breaking the Glass Ceiling," *Academy of Management Executive* 12(1) (1998): 28–42.

141. Trottman, "A Helping Hand."

142. David A. Thomas, "The Truth About Mentoring Minorities—Race Matters," *Harvard Business Review* (April 2001): 99–107.

143. Mary Zey, "A Mentor for All," *Personnel Journal* (January 1988): 46–51.

144. Sylvia Ann Hewlett and Carolyn Buck Luce, "Off-Ramps and On-Ramps; Keeping Talented Women on the Road to Success," *Harvard Business Review* (March 2005): 43–54.

145. Belkin, "The Opt-Out Revolution."

146. C. J. Prince, "Media Myths: The Truth About the Opt-Out Hype," *NAFE Magazine* (Second Quarter 2004): 14–18; and Patricia Sellers, "Power: Do Women Really Want It?" *Fortune* (October 13, 2003): 80–100.

147. Jia Lynn Yang, "Goodbye to All That," *Fortune* (November 14, 2005): 169–170.

148. Sheila Wellington, Marcia Brumit Kropf, and Paulette R. Gerkovich, "What's Holding Women Back?" *Harvard Business Review* (June 2003): 18–19.

149. The Leader's Edge/Executive Women Research 2002 survey, reported in "Why Women Leave," *Executive Female* (Summer 2003): 4.

150. Barbara Reinhold, "Smashing Glass Ceilings: Why Women Still Find It Tough to Advance to the Executive Suite," *Journal of Organizational Excellence* (Summer 2005): 43–55; Des Jardins, "I Am Woman (I Think)"; and Alice H. Eagly and Linda L. Carli, "The Female Leadership Advantage: An Evaluation of the Evidence," *Leadership Quarterly* 14 (2003): 807–834.

151. Claudia H. Deutsch, "Behind the Exodus of Executive Women: Boredom," *USA Today,* May 2, 2005, p. 3.4.

152. Eagly and Carli, "The Female Leadership Advantage"; Reinhold, "Smashing Glass Ceilings"; Sally Helgesen, *The Female Advantage: Women's Ways of Leadership* (New York: Doubleday

Currency, 1990); Rochelle Sharpe, "As Leaders, Women Rule: New Studies Find that Female Managers Outshine Their Male Counterparts in Almost Every Measure," *BusinessWeek* (November 20, 2000): 5ff; and Del Jones, "2003: Year of the Woman Among the Fortune 500?" (December 30, 2003): 1B.

153. Tamar Lewin, "At Colleges, Women Are Leaving Men in the Dust," *New York Times Online* (www.nytimes.com/2006/07/09/education/09college.html?_r=1&scp=1&sq=at%20colleges, %20women%20are%20leaving%20men%20in%20the%20dust &st=cse&oref=slogin), July 9, 2006 (accessed March 13, 2008).

154. Alex Kingsbury, "Admittedly Unequal," *U.S. News & World Report* (June 25, 2007): 50.

155. Michelle Conlin, "The New Gender Gap"; and Michelle Conlin, "A Better Education Equals Higher Pay," *BusinessWeek* (May 26, 2003): 74–82.

156. Quoted in Conlin, "The New Gender Gap."

157. Kathryn M. Bartol, David C. Martin, and Julie A. Kromkowski, "Leadership and the Glass Ceiling: Gender and Ethnic Group Influences on Leader Behaviors at Middle and Executive Managerial Levels," *Journal of Leadership and Organizational Studies* 9(3) (2003): 8–19; Bernard M. Bass and Bruce J. Avolio, "Shatter the Glass Ceiling: Women May Make Better Managers," *Human Resource Management* 33(4) (Winter 1994): 549–560; and Sharpe, "As Leaders, Women Rule," 75–84.

158. Dwight D. Frink, Robert K. Robinson, Brian Reithel, Michelle M. Arthur, Anthony P. Ammeter, Gerald R. Ferris, David M. Kaplan, and Hubert S. Morrisette, "Gender Demography and Organization Performance: A Two-Study Investigation with Convergence," *Group & Organization Management* 28(1) (March 2003): 127–147; Catalyst research project cited in Reinhold, "Smashing Glass Ceilings."

CHAPTER 10

Managing Quality and Performance

1. Sally B. Connelly, "Lean and Mean," Inside Business, *Time* (August, 2006): A4.

2. Yochi J. Dreazen, "More Katrina Woes: Incidents of Fraud at Red Cross Centers," *Wall Street Journal*, October 19, 2005.

3. Adapted from J. J. Ray, "Do Authoritarians Hold Authoritarian Attitudes?" *Human Relations* 29 (1976): 307–325; and Douglas S. Sherwin, "The Meaning of Control," *Dunn's Business Review* (January 1956).

4. Sherwin, "The Meaning of Control."

5. Russ Banham, "Nothin' But Net Gain," *eCFO* (Fall 2001): 32–33.

6. "On Balance," an interview with Robert Kaplan and David Norton, *CFO* (February 2001): 73–78; and Bill Birchard, "Intangible Assets + Hard Numbers=Soft Finance," *Fast Company* (October 1999): 316–336.

7. Andy Neely and Mohammed al Najjar, "Management Learning Not Management Control: The True Role of Performance

Measurement," *California Management Review* 48(3) (Spring 2006): 105.

8. This discussion is based on a review of the balanced scorecard in Richard L. Daft, *Organization Theory and Design*, 7th ed. (Cincinnati, OH: South-Western, 2001): 300–301.

9. Neely and al Najjar, 105, 112.

10. Robert Kaplan and David Norton, "The Balanced Scorecard: Measures That Drive Performance," *Harvard Business Review* (January–February 1992): 71–79; and Chee W. Chow, Kamal M. Haddad, and James E. Williamson, "Applying the Balanced Scorecard to Small Companies," *Management Accounting* 79(2) (August 1997): 21–27.

11. Based on Kaplan and Norton, "The Balanced Scorecard"; Chow, Haddad, and Williamson, "Applying the Balanced Scorecard"; and Cathy Lazere, "All Together Now," *CFO* (February 1998): 28–36.

12. Jessi Hempil, "Finding Cracks in Facebook," *Fortune* (May13, 2008) (http://money.cnn.com/2008/05/12/technology/cracks_facebook_hempel.fortune/index.htm?postversion=2008051308) (accessed May 14, 2008).

13. Geert J. M. Braam and Edwin J. Nijssen, "Performance Effects of Using the Balanced Scorecard: A Note on the Dutch Experience," *Long Range Planning* 37 (2004): 335–349; Kaplan and Norton, "The Balanced Scorecard"; and Cam Scholey, "Strategy Maps: A Step-by-Step Guide to Measuring, Managing, and Communicating the Plan," *Journal of Business Strategy* 26(3) (2005): 12–19.

14. Nils-Göran Olve, Carl-Johan Petri, Jan Roy, and Sofie Roy, "Twelve Years Later: Understanding and Realizing the Value of Balanced Scorecards," *Ivey Business Journal* (May–June2004); Eric M. Olson and Stanley F. Slater, "The Balanced Scorecard, Competitive Strategy, and Performance," *Business Horizons* (May–June 2002): 11–16; and Eric Berkman, "How to Use the Balanced Scorecard," *CIO* (May 15, 2002): 93–100.

15. Ibid.; and Brigitte W. Schay, Mary Ellen Beach, Jacqueline A. Caldwell, and Christelle LaPolice, "Using Standardized Outcome Measures in the Federal Government," *Human Resource Management* 41(3) (Fall 2002): 355–368.

16. Braam and Nijssen, "Performance Effects."

17. Olve et al., "Twelve Years Later."

18. Peter Valdes-Dapena, "Tiny Smart Car Gets Crash Test Kudos," *Fortune* (May 14, 2008) (http://money.cnn.com/2008/05/14/autos/smart_fortwo_iihs_crash_test/index.htm) (accessed May 14, 2008).

19. Richard E. Crandall, "Keys to Better Performance Measurement," *Industrial Management* (January–February 2002): 19–24; Christopher D. Ittner and David F. Larcker, "Coming Up Short on Nonfinancial Performance Measurement," *Harvard Business Review* (November 2003): 88–95.

20. Crandall, "Keys to Better Performance Measurement."

21. Frank Eltman, "Tracking Systems Help Cities Monitor Employees, Save," *The Tennessean*, November 16, 2007.

22. Charles Fishman, "No Satisfaction," *Fast Company* (December 2006–January 2007): 88.

23. Adam Lashinsky, "Meg and the Machine," *Fortune* (September 1, 2003): 68–78.

24. Sumantra Ghoshal, *Strategic Control* (St. Paul, MN: West, 1986), Chapter 4; and Robert N. Anthony, John Dearden, and Norton M. Bedford, *Management Control Systems*, 5th ed. (Homewood, IL: Irwin, 1984).

25. Bruce G. Posner, "How to Stop Worrying and Love the Next Recession," *Inc.* (April 1986): 89–95.

26. William G. Ouchi, "Markets, Bureaucracies, and Clans," *Administrative Science Quarterly* 25 (1980): 129–141; and B. R. Baligia and Alfred M. Jaeger, "Multinational Corporations: Control Systems and Delegation Issues," *Journal of International Business Studies* (Fall 1984): 25–40.

27. Sherwin, "The Meaning of Control."

28. Anna Wilde Mathews, "New Gadgets Track Truckers' Every Move," *Wall Street Journal*, July 14, 1997.

29. Perry Pascarella, "Open the Books to Unleash Your People," *Management Review* (May 1998): 58–60.

30. Nadine Heintz, "Everyone's a CFO," *Inc.* (September 2005): 42, 45.

31. Ibid.

32. Mel Mandell, "Accounting Challenges Overseas," *World Trade* (December 1, 2001).

33. John A. Parnell, C. W. Von Bergen, and Barlow Soper, "Profiting from Past Triumphs and Failures: Harnessing History for Future Success," *SAM Advanced Management Journal* (Spring 2005): 36–59.

34. A. V. Feigenbaum, *Total Quality Control: Engineering and Management* (New York: McGraw-Hill, 1961); John Lorinc, "Dr. Deming's Traveling Quality Show," *Canadian Business* (September 1990): 38–42; Mary Walton, *The Deming Management Method* (New York: Dodd-Meade & Co., 1986); and J. M. Juran and Frank M. Gryna (Eds.), *Juran's Quality Control Handbook*, 4th ed. (New York: McGraw-Hill, 1988).

35. Edward E. Lawler III and Susan A. Mohrman, "Quality Circles after the Fad," *Harvard Business Review* (January–February 1985): 65–71; and Philip C. Thompson, *Quality Circles: How to Make Them Work in America* (New York: AMACOM, 1982).

36. D. J. Ford, "Benchmarking HRD," *Training and Development* (July 1993): 37–41.

37. Tracy Mayor, "Six Sigma Comes to IT: Targeting Perfection," *CIO* (December 1, 2003): 62–70; Hal Plotkin, "Six Sigma: What It Is and How to Use It," *Harvard Management Update* (June 1999): 3–4; Tom Rancour and Mike McCracken, "Applying 6 Sigma Methods for Breakthrough Safety Performance," *Professional Safety* 45(10) (October 2000): 29–32; G. Hasek, "Merger Marries Quality Efforts," *Industry Week* (August 21, 2000): 89–92; and Lee Clifford, "Why You Can Safely Ignore Six Sigma," *Fortune* (January 22, 2001): 140.

38. Dick Smith and Jerry Blakeslee "The New Strategic Six Sigma," *Training & Development* (September 2002): 45–52; Michael

Hammer and Jeff Goding, "Putting Six Sigma in Perspective," *Quality* (October 2001): 58–62; and Mayor, "Six Sigma Comes to IT."

39. Plotkin, "Six Sigma: What It Is"; Timothy Aeppel, "Nicknamed 'Nag,' She's Just Doing Her Job," *Wall Street Journal*, May 14, 2002; and John S. McClenahen, "ITT's Value Champion," *IndustryWeek* (May 2002): 44–49.

40. "CEO Expects Good Things as Textron Does Six Sigma Right," *USA Today,* January 21, 2008.

41. Philip R. Thomas, Larry J. Gallace, and Kenneth R. Martin, *Quality Alone Is Not Enough* (New York: American Management Association,1992).

42. Kate Kane, "L.L. Bean Delivers the Goods," *Fast Company* (August–September 1997): 104–113.

43. George Taninecz, "Change for the Better," *Industry Week* (October 2004): 49–50; and "Dana Corporation Earns Record Sixth Industry Week 10 Best Plants Award," *PR Newswire* (September 27, 2004): 1.

44. Sholnn Freeman, "Auto Parts Maker Files Chapter 11; Rising Costs, Cuts in Detroit Prompt Move by Dana Corp.," *Washington Post*, March 4, 2006; and Doron Levin, "Dana's Bankruptcy Is Payback to Ford, Other Automakers," *Pittsburgh Post-Gazette*, March 9, 2006.

45. "Dana Holding Corporation Reports First-Quarter 2008 Results" (www.dana.mediaroom.com/index.php/press_releases/2144) (accessed May 15, 2008).

46. Clifford, "Why You Can Safely Ignore Six Sigma"; and Hammer and Goding, "Putting Six Sigma in Perspective."

47. Syed Hasan Jaffrey, "ISO 9001 Made Easy," *Quality Progress* 37(5) (May 2004): 104; Frank C. Barnes, "ISO 9000 Myth and Reality: A Reasonable Approach to ISO 9000," *SAM Advanced Management Journal* (Spring 1998): 23–30; and Thomas H. Stevenson and Frank C. Barnes, "Fourteen Years of ISO 9000: Impact, Criticisms, Costs, and Benefits," *Business Horizons* (May–June 2001): 45–51.

48. David Amari, Don James, and Cathy Marley, "ISO 9001 Takes On a New Role—Crime Fighter," *Quality Progress* 37(5) (May 2004): 57ff.

49. Don L. Bohl, Fred Luthans, John W. Slocum Jr., and Richard M. Hodgetts, "Ideas That Will Shape the Future of Management Practice," *Organizational Dynamics* (Summer 1996): 7–14.

50. John Berry, "How to Apply EVA to I.T.," *CIO* (January 15, 2003): 94–98.

CHAPTER 11

Dynamics of Behavior in Organizations

1. See Michael West, "Hope Springs," *People Management* (October 2005): 38ff ; and Mark C. Bolino, William H. Turnley, and James M. Bloodgood, "Citizenship Behaviors and the Creation of Social Capital in Organizations," *Academy of Management Review* 27(4) (2002): 505–522.

2. Reported in Del Jones, "Optimism Puts Rose-Colored Tint in Glasses of Top Execs," *USA Today*, December 15, 2005 (www.usatoday.com).

3. Jerry Krueger and Emily Killham, "At Work, Feeling Good Matters," *Gallup Management Journal* (December 8, 2005).

4. Jeffrey Zaslow, "Pursuits: Happiness, Inc.," *The Wall Street Journal*, March 18, 2006.

5. John W. Newstrom and Keith Davis, *Organizational Behavior: Human Behavior at Work,* 11th ed. (Burr Ridge, IL: McGraw-Hill Irwin, 2002): Chapter 9.

6. S. J. Breckler, "Empirical Validation of Affect, Behavior, and Cognition as Distinct Components of Attitude," *Journal of Personality and Social Psychology* (May 1984): 1191–1205; and J. M. Olson and M. P. Zanna, "Attitudes and Attitude Change," *Annual Review of Psychology* 44 (1993): 117–154.

7. M. T. Iaffaldano and P. M. Muchinsky, "Job Satisfaction and Job Performance: A Meta-Analysis," *Psychological Bulletin* (March 1985): 251–273; C. Ostroff, "The Relationship Between Satisfaction, Attitudes, and Performance: An Organizational Level Analysis," *Journal of Applied Psychology* (December 1992): 963–974; and M. M. Petty, G. W. McGee, and J. W. Cavender, "A Meta-Analysis of the Relationship Between Individual Job Satisfaction and Individual Performance," *Academy of Management Review* (October 1984): 712–721.

8. "Worried at Work: Generation Gap in Workplace Woes," International Survey Research (www.isrsurveys.com) (accessed May 19, 2004).

9. Tony Schwartz, "The Greatest Sources of Satisfaction in the Workplace Are Internal and Emotional," *Fast Company* (November 2000): 398–402.

10. William C. Symonds, "Where Paternalism Equals Good Business," *BusinessWeek* (July 20, 1998): 16E4, 16E6.

11. "Engaged Employees Drive the Bottom Line," Towers Perrin-International Survey Research (www.isrinsight.com/pdf/solutions/EngagementBrochureFinalUS.pdf) (accessed November 14, 2008).

12. "Closing the Engagement Gap: A Road Map for Driving Superior Business Performance" (Towers Perrin Global Workforce Study, 2007–2008) (http://links.mkt304.com/ctt?kn=1&m=1506453&r=MTUwMTY1NjAyNDkS1&b=2&j=NjE1NjYwMzQS1&mt=2&rj=NjE1MzQwMzcS1) (accessed on November 18, 2008).

13. W. Chan Kin and Renée Mauborgne, "Fair Process: Managing in the Knowledge Economy," *Harvard Business Review* (January 2003): 127–136.

14. Survey results reported in Del Jones, "Optimism Puts Rose-Colored Tint in Glasses of Top Execs," *USA Today* (December 15, 2005).

15. For a discussion of cognitive dissonance theory, see Leon A. Festinger, *Theory of Cognitive Dissonance* (Stanford, CA: Stanford University Press, 1957).

16. J. A. Deutsch, W. G. Young, and T. J. Kalogeris, "The Stomach Signals Satiety," *Science* (April 1978): 22–33.

17. Richard B. Chase and Sriram Dasu, "Want to Perfect Your Company's Service? Use Behavioral Science," *Harvard Business Review* (June 2001): 79–84.

18. H. H. Kelley, "Attribution in Social Interaction," in E. Jones et al. (Eds.), *Attribution: Perceiving the Causes of Behavior* (Morristown, NJ: General Learning Press, 1972).

19. See J. M. Digman, "Personality Structure: Emergence of the Five-Factor Model," *Annual Review of Psychology* 41 (1990): 417–440; M. R. Barrick and M. K. Mount, "Autonomy as a Moderator of the Relationships Between the Big Five Personality Dimensions and Job Performance," *Journal of Applied Psychology* (February 1993): 111–118; and J. S. Wiggins and A. L. Pincus, "Personality: Structure and Assessment," *Annual Review of Psychology* 43 (1992): 473–504.

20. Del Jones, "Not All Successful CEOs Are Extroverts," *USA Today*, June 6, 2006, p. B1.

21. Reported in Christopher Palmeri, "Putting Managers to the Test," *BusinessWeek* (November 20, 2006): 82.

22. Tim Sanders, *The Likeability Factor: How to Boost Your L-Factor and Achieve the Life of Your Dreams* (New York: Crown, 2005).

23. Lisa Takeuchi Cullen, "SATs for J-O-B-S," *Time* (April 3, 2006): 89.

24. Lori Gottlieb, "How Do I Love Thee?" *Atlantic Monthly* (March 2006): 58–70; Rachel Lehmann-Haupt, "Is the Right Chemistry a Click Nearer?" *New York Times*, February 12, 2006; and Christopher Palmeri, "Dr. Warren's Lonely Hearts Club," *BusinessWeek Online* (February 20, 2006) (www.businessweek.com/magazine/content/06_08/b3972111.htm).

25. Daniel Goleman, "Leadership That Gets Results," *Harvard Business Review* (March–April 2000): 79–90; Richard E. Boyatzis and Daniel Goleman, *The Emotional Competence Inventory–University Edition*, The Hay Group, 2001; and Daniel Goleman, *Emotional Intelligence: Why It Can Matter More than IQ* (New York: Bantam Books, 1995).

26. Alan Farnham, "Are You Smart Enough to Keep Your Job?" *Fortune* (January 15, 1996): 34–47.

27. Hendrie Weisinger, *Emotional Intelligence at Work* (San Francisco, CA: Jossey–Bass, 2000); D. C. McClelland, "Identifying Competencies with Behavioral-Event Interviews," *Psychological Science* (Spring 1999): 331–339; Daniel Goleman, "Leadership That Gets Results," *Harvard Business Review* (March–April 2000): 78–90; D. Goleman, *Working with Emotional Intelligence* (New York: Bantam Books, 1999); and Lorie Parch, "Testing . . . 1, 2, 3," *Working Woman* (October 1997): 74–78.

28. Cliff Edwards, "Death of a Pushy Salesman," *BusinessWeek* (July 3, 2006): 108–109.

29. J. B. Rotter, "Generalized Expectancies for Internal Versus External Control of Reinforcement," *Psychological Monographs* 80, (609) (1966).

30. See P. E. Spector, "Behavior in Organizations as a Function of Employee's Locus of Control," *Psychological Bulletin* (May 1982): 482–497.

31. T. W. Adorno, E. Frenkel-Brunswick, D. J. Levinson, and R. N. Sanford, *The Authoritarian Personality* (New York: Harper & Row, 1950).

32. Niccolo Machiavelli, *The Prince* (George Bull, Trans.) (Middlesex: Penguin, 1961).

33. Richard Christie and Florence Geis, *Studies in Machiavellianism* (New York: Academic Press, 1970).

34. R. G. Vleeming, "Machiavellianism: A Preliminary Review," *Psychological Reports* (February 1979): 295–310.

35. Christie and Geis, *Studies in Machiavellianism*.

36. Carl Jung, *Psychological Types* (London: Routledge and Kegan Paul, 1923).

37. Mary H. McCaulley, "Research on the MBTI and Leadership: Taking the Critical First Step," keynote address, The Myers–Briggs Type Indicator and Leadership: An International Research Conference, January 12–14, 1994.

38. Alison Overhold, "Are You a Polyolefin Optimizer? Take This Quiz!" *Fast Company* (April 2004): 37.

39. Reported in Cullen, "SATs for J-O-B-S."

40. Charles A. O'Reilly III, Jennifer Chatman, and David F. Caldwell, "People and Organizational Culture: A Profile Comparison Approach to Assessing Person-Organization Fit," *Academy of Management Journal* 34(3) (1991): 487–516.

41. Anna Muoio, "Should I Go .Com?" *Fast Company* (July 2000): 164–172.

42. Michelle Leder, "Is That Your Final Answer?" *Working Woman* (December–January 2001): 18.

43. David A. Kolb, "Management and the Learning Process," *California Management Review* 18(3) (Spring 1976): 21–31.

44. See David. A. Kolb, I. M. Rubin, and J. M. McIntyre, *Organizational Psychology: An Experimental Approach*, 3rd ed. (Englewood Cliffs, NJ: Prentice Hall, 1984): 27–54.

45. T. A. Beehr and R. S. Bhagat, *Human Stress and Cognition in Organizations: An Integrated Perspective* (New York: Wiley, 1985); and Bruce Cryer, Rollin McCraty, and Doc Childre, "Pull the Plug on Stress," *Harvard Business Review* (July 2003): 102–107.

46. Reported in Brian Nadel, "The Price of Pressure," special advertising feature, *Fortune* (December 11, 2006): 143–146.

47. Health and Safety Authority survey, reported in Joe Humphreys, "Stress Will Be Main Cause of Workplace Illness by 2020," *Irish Times*, July 27, 2005.

48. Don Mills, "Running on High Octane or Burning Out Big Time? Stress Flunkies," *National Post* [Toronto], April 8, 2006.

49. M. Friedman and R. Rosenman, *Type A Behavior and Your Heart* (New York: Knopf, 1974).

50. Reported in "Work Stress Is Costly," *Morning Call* [Allentown, PA], October 18, 2005.

51. Families and Work Institute survey, reported in "Reworking Work," *Time* (July 25, 2005): 50–55; Spherion survey, reported in Donna Callea, "Workers Feeling the Burn: Employee Burnout a

New Challenge to Productivity, Morale, Experts Say," *News Journal*, March 27, 2006); Mills, "Running on High Octane or Burning Out Big Time?"; Vani Doraisamy, "Young Techies Swell the Ranks of the Depressed," *The Hindu* (India), October 11, 2005.

52. Jenna Goudreau, "Dispatches from the War on Stress," *BusinessWeek* (August 6, 2007): 74–75.

53. Claire Sykes, "Say Yes to Less Stress," *Office Solutions* (July–August 2003): 26; and Andrea Higbie, "Quick Lessons in the Fine Old Art of Unwinding," *New York Times*, February 25, 2001.

54. Donalee Moulton, "Buckling Under the Pressure," *OH & S Canada* 19(8) (December 2003): 36.

55. Rosabeth Moss Kanter, "Balancing Work and Life," Knight-Ridder Tribune News Service, April 8, 2005.

56. Leslie Gross Klass, "Quiet Time at Work Helps Employee Stress," *Johnson City* [TN] *Press*, January 28, 2001.

57. Moulton, "Buckling Under the Pressure."

58. Goudreau, "Dispatches from the War on Stress."

59. David T. Gordon, "Balancing Act," *CIO* (October 15, 2001): 58–62.

CHAPTER 12

Leadership

1. Leigh Buchanan, "Pat McGovern . . . For Knowing the Power of Respect" in "25 Entrepreneurs We Love," *Inc Magazine* (April 2004): 110–147; Melanie Warner, "Confessions of a Control Freak," *Fortune* (September 4, 2000): 130–140.

2. Greg Jaffe, "Change of Command; A Marine Captain Trains Iraqi Colonel to Take Over Fight," *Wall Street Journal*, February 24, 2005; and Jackie Spinner, "Training a New Army from the Top Down; U.S. Military Struggles to 'Build Leaders,'" *Washington Post*, November 1, 2005.

3. Kevin Kelleher, "How To . . . Spot Great Chief Executives," *Business 2.0* (April 2005): 42.

4. Gary Yukl, "Managerial Leadership: A Review of Theory and Research," *Journal of Management* 15 (1989): 251–289.

5. James M. Kouzes and Barry Z. Posner, "The Credibility Factor: What Followers Expect from Their Leaders," *Management Review* (January 1990): 29–33.

6. Joseph L. Badaracco, Jr., "A Lesson for the Times: Learning From Quiet Leaders," *Ivey Business Journal* (January–February 2003): 1–6; and Matthew Gwyther, "Back to the Wall," *Management Today* (February 2003): 58–61.

7. See J. Andrew Morris, Céleste M. Brotheridge, and John C. Urbanski, "Bringing Humility to Leadership: Antecedents and Consequences of Leader Humility," *Human Relations* 58(10) (2005): 1323–1350; Linda Tischler, "The CEO's New Clothes," *Fast Company* (September 2005): 27–28; James C. Collins, *From Good to Great: Why Some Companies Make the Leap . . . And Others Don't* (New York: HarperCollins 2001); Charles A. O'Reilly III

and Jeffrey Pfeffer, *Hidden Value: How Great Companies Achieve Extraordinary Results with Ordinary People* (Boston: Harvard Business School Press, 2000); Rakesh Khurana, "The Curse of the Superstar CEO," *Harvard Business Review* (September 2002): 60–66, excerpted from his book, *Searching for a Corporate Savior: The Irrational Quest for Charismatic CEOs* (Princeton, NJ: Princeton University Press, 2002); and Joseph Badaracco, *Leading Quietly* (Boston: Harvard Business School Press, 2002).

8. Center for Creative Leadership study, reported in Andre Martin, "What Is Effective Leadership Today?" *Chief Executive* (July–August 2006): 24; and "The Demise of the Heroic Leader," *Leader to Leader* (Fall 2006): 55–56.

9. Jim Collins, "Level 5 Leadership: The Triumph of Humility and Fierce Resolve," *Harvard Business Review* (January 2001): 67–76; Jim Collins, "Good to Great," *Fast Company* (October 2001): 90–104; A. J. Vogl, "Onward and Upward" (an interview with Jim Collins), *Across the Board* (September–October 2001): 29–34; and Jerry Useem, "Conquering Vertical Limits," *Fortune* (February 19, 2001): 84–96.

10. Collins, "Level 5 Leadership."

11. Judy B. Rosener, *America's Competitive Secret: Utilizing Women as a Management Strategy* (New York: Oxford University Press, 1995): 129–135.

12. Rochelle Sharpe, "As Leaders, Women Rule," *BusinessWeek* (November 20, 2000): 75–84.

13. Alice H. Eagly and Linda L. Carli, "The Female Leadership Advantage: An Evaluation of the Evidence," *Leadership Quarterly* 14 (2003): 807–834; Rosener, *America's Competitive Secret;* Judy B. Rosener, "Ways Women Lead," *Harvard Business Review* (November–December 1990): 119–125; Sally Helgesen, *The Female Advantage: Women's Ways of Leadership* (New York: Currency/Doubleday, 1990); and Bernard M. Bass and Bruce J. Avolio, "Shatter the Glass Ceiling: Women May Make Better Managers," *Human Resource Management* 33(4) (Winter 1994): 549–560.

14. Sharpe, "As Leaders, Women Rule," 75–84.

15. Kevin S. Groves, "Gender Differences in Social and Emotional Skills and Charismatic Leadership," *Journal of Leadership and Organizational Studies* 11(3) (2005): 30ff.

16. Gary Yukl and Richard Lepsinger, "Why Integrating the Leading and Managing Roles Is Essential for Organizational Effectiveness," *Organizational Dynamics* 34(4) (2005): 361–375.

17. Miguel Helft, "Can She Turn Yahoo Into, Well, Google?" *New York Times*, July 1, 2007; and Miguel Helft, "Industry Insiders Praise Yahoo Choice for Key Post," *New York Times*, December 7, 2006.

18. G. A. Yukl, *Leadership in Organizations* (Englewood Cliffs, NJ: Prentice Hall, 1981); and S. C. Kohs and K. W. Irle, "Prophesying Army Promotion," *Journal of Applied Psychology* 4 (1920): 73–87.

19. R. Albanese and D. D. Van Fleet, *Organizational Behavior: A Managerial Viewpoint* (Hinsdale, IL: Dryden Press, 1983).

20. Gary Yukl, Angela Gordon, and Tom Taber, "A Hierarchical Taxonomy of Leadership Behavior: Integrating a Half Century

of Behavior Research," *Journal of Leadership and Organizational Studies* 9(1) (2002): 13–32.

21. C. A. Schriesheim and B. J. Bird, "Contributions of the Ohio State Studies to the Field of Leadership," *Journal of Management* 5 (1979): 135–145; and C. L. Shartle, "Early Years of the Ohio State University Leadership Studies," *Journal of Management* 5 (1979): 126–134.

22. Don Wallace, "The Soul of a Sports Machine," *Fast Company* (October 2003): 100–102; and Neil Hayes, *When the Game Stands Tall: The Story of the De La Salle Spartans and Football's Longest Winning Streak* (Berkeley, CA: Frog/North Atlantic Books, 2005).

23. P. C. Nystrom, "Managers and the High-High Leader Myth," *Academy of Management Journal* 21 (1978): 325–331; and L. L. Larson, J. G. Hunt, and Richard N. Osborn, "The Great High-High Leader Behavior Myth: A Lesson from Occam's Razor," *Academy of Management Journal* 19 (1976): 628–641.

24. R. Likert, "From Production- and Employee-Centeredness to Systems 1–4," *Journal of Management* 5 (1979): 147–156.

25. Robert R. Blake and Jane S. Mouton, *The Managerial Grid III* (Houston: Gulf, 1985).

26. Paul Hersey and Kenneth H. Blanchard, *Management of Organizational Behavior: Utilizing Human Resources*, 4th ed. (Englewood Cliffs, NJ: Prentice Hall, 1982).

27. Robert Tomsho and John Hechinger, "Crimson Blues; Harvard Clash Pits Brusque Leader Against Faculty," *Wall Street Journal*, February 18, 2005; and Ruth R. Wisse, "Cross Country; Coup d' Ecole," *Wall Street Journal*, February 23, 2006.

28. Fred E. Fiedler, "Assumed Similarity Measures as Predictors of Team Effectiveness," *Journal of Abnormal and Social Psychology* 49 (1954): 381–388; F. E. Fiedler, *Leader Attitudes and Group Effectiveness* (Urbana, IL: University of Illinois Press, 1958); and F. E. Fiedler, *A Theory of Leadership Effectiveness* (New York: McGraw-Hill, 1967).

29. Fred E. Fiedler and M. M. Chemers, *Leadership and Effective Management* (Glenview, IL: Scott, Foresman, 1974).

30. Reported in George Anders, "Theory and Practice: Tough CEOs Often Most Successful, a Study Finds," *Wall Street Journal*, November 19, 2007.

31. Fred E. Fiedler, "Engineer the Job to Fit the Manager," *Harvard Business Review* 43 (1965): 115–122; and F. E. Fiedler, M. M. Chemers, and L. Mahar, *Improving Leadership Effectiveness: The Leader Match Concept* (New York: Wiley, 1976).

32. R. Singh, "Leadership Style and Reward Allocation: Does Least Preferred Coworker Scale Measure Tasks and Relation Orientation?" *Organizational Behavior and Human Performance* 27 (1983): 178–197; and D. Hosking, "A Critical Evaluation of Fiedler's Contingency Hypotheses," *Progress in Applied Psychology* 1 (1981): 103–154.

33. S. Kerr and J. M. Jermier, "Substitutes for Leadership: Their Meaning and Measurement," *Organizational Behavior and Human Performance* 22 (1978): 375–403; and Jon P. Howell and Peter W. Dorfman, "Leadership and Substitutes for Leadership among Professional and Nonprofessional Workers," *Journal of Applied Behavioral Science* 22 (1986): 29–46.

34. Katherine J. Klein and Robert J. House, "On Fire: Charismatic Leadership and Levels of Analysis," *Leadership Quarterly* 6(2) (1995): 183–198.

35. Jay A. Conger and Rabindra N. Kanungo, "Toward a Behavioral Theory of Charismatic Leadership in Organizational Settings," *Academy of Management Review* 12 (1987): 637–647; Jaepil Choi, "A Motivational Theory of Charismatic Leadership: Envisioning, Empathy, and Empowerment," *Journal of Leadership and Organizational Studies* 13(1) (2006): 24ff; and William L. Gardner and Bruce J. Avolio, "The Charismatic Relationship: A Dramaturgical Perspective," *Academy of Management Review* 23(1) (1998): 32–58.

36. Robert J. House and Jane M. Howell, "Personality and Charismatic Leadership," *Leadership Quarterly* 3(2) (1992): 81–108; and Jennifer O'Connor, Michael D. Mumford, Timothy C. Clifton, Theodore O. Gessner, and Mary Shane Connelly, "Charismatic Leaders and Destructiveness: A Historiometric Study," *Leadership Quarterly* 6(4) (1995): 529–555.

37. Robert J. House, "Research Contrasting the Behavior and Effects of Reputed Charismatic vs. Reputed Non-Charismatic Leaders," paper presented as part of a symposium, "Charismatic Leadership: Theory and Evidence," Academy of Management, San Diego, 1985.

38. Bernard M. Bass, "Theory of Transformational Leadership Redux," *Leadership Quarterly* 6(4) (1995): 463–478; Noel M. Tichy and Mary Anne Devanna, *The Transformational Leader* (New York: John Wiley & Sons, 1986); and Badrinarayan Shankar Pawar and Kenneth K. Eastman, "The Nature and Implications of Contextual Influences on Transformational Leadership: A Conceptual Examination," *Academy of Management Review* 22(1) (1997) 80–109.

39. The terms *transactional* and *transformational* come from James M. Burns, *Leadership* (New York: Harper & Row, 1978); and Bernard M. Bass, "Leadership: Good, Better, Best," *Organizational Dynamics* 13 (Winter 1985): 26–40.

40. Richard L. Daft and Robert H. Lengel, *Fusion Leadership: Unlocking the Subtle Forces that Change People and Organizations* (San Francisco: Berrett-Koehler, 1998).

41. Taly Dvir, Dov Eden, Bruce J. Avolio, and Boas Shamir, "Impact of Transformational Leadership on Follower Development and Performance: A Field Experiment," *Academy of Management Journal* 45(4) (2002): 735–744.

42. Robert S. Rubin, David C. Munz, and William H. Bommer, "Leading from Within: The Effects of Emotion Recognition and Personality on Transformational Leadership Behavior," *Academy of Management Journal* 48(5) (2005): 845–858; and Timothy A. Judge and Joyce E. Bono, "Five-Factor Model of Personality and Transformational Leadership," *Journal of Applied Psychology* 85(5) (October 2000): 751ff.

43. Rubin, Munz, and Bommer, "Leading from Within."

44. Barbara Kellerman, "What Every Leader Needs to Know About Followers," *Harvard Business Review* (December 2007): 84–91.

45. Robert E. Kelley, *The Power of Followership* (New York: Doubleday, 1992).

46. Ibid., 117–118.

47. Henry Mintzberg, *Power In and Around Organizations* (Englewood Cliffs, NJ: Prentice Hall, 1983); and Jeffrey Pfeffer, *Power in Organizations* (Marshfield, MA: Pitman, 1981).

48. Jay A. Conger, "The Necessary Art of Persuasion," *Harvard Business Review* (May–June 1998): 84–95.

49. D. Kipnis, S. M. Schmidt, C. Swaffin-Smith, and I. Wilkinson, "Patterns of Managerial Influence: Shotgun Managers, Tacticians, and Politicians," *Organizational Dynamics* (Winter 1984): 58–67.

50. These tactics are based on Kipnis et al., "Patterns of Managerial Influence"; and Robert B. Cialdini, "Harnessing the Science of Persuasion," *Harvard Business Review* (October 2001): 72–79.

51. Kipnis et al., "Patterns of Managerial Influence"; and Jeffrey Pfeffer, *Managing with Power: Politics and Influence in Organizations* (Boston: Harvard Business School Press, 1992), Chapter 13.

52. Ibid.

53. V. Dallas Merrell, *Huddling: The Informal Way to Management Success* (New York: AMACOM, 1979).

54. Robert B. Cialdini, *Influence: Science and Practice*, 4th ed. (Boston: Pearson Allyn & Bacon, 2000).

55. Harvey G. Enns and Dean B. McFarlin, "When Executives Influence Peers, Does Function Matter?" *Human Resource Management* 4(2) (Summer 2003): 125–142.

56. Daft and Lengel, *Fusion Leadership*.

57. Leigh Buchanan, "In Praise of Selflessness: Why the Best Leaders Are Servants," *Inc. Magazine* (May 2007): 33–35.

58. Robert K. Greenleaf, *Servant Leadership: A Journey into the Nature of Legitimate Power and Greatness* (Mahwah, NJ: Paulist Press, 1977).

59. Anne Fitzgerald, "Christmas Bonus Stuns Employees," *Des Moines Register*, December 20, 2003 (www.desmoinesregister.com).

60. See www.mahalo.com/leonard-abess.

61. Buchanan, "In Praise of Selflessness."

62. Richard L. Daft, *The Leadership Experience*, 3rd ed. (Cincinnati, OH: South-Western, 2005), Chapter 6.

63. Badaracco, "A Lesson for the Times: Learning From Quiet Leaders."

64. Jim Collins, "The 10 Greatest CEOs of All Time," *Fortune* (July 21, 2003): 54–68.

CHAPTER 13

Motivating Employees

1. David Silburt, "Secrets of the Super Sellers," *Canadian Business* (January 1987): 54–59; "Meet the Savvy Supersalesmen," *Fortune* (February 4, 1985): 56–62; Michael Brody, "Meet Today's Young American Worker," *Fortune* (November 11, 1985): 90–98; and Tom Richman, "Meet the Masters. They Could Sell You Anything," *Inc.* (March 1985): 79–86.

2. Richard M. Steers and Lyman W. Porter (Eds.), *Motivation and Work Behavior*, 3rd ed. (New York: McGraw-Hill, 1983); Don Hellriegel, John W. Slocum, Jr., and Richard W. Woodman, *Organizational Behavior*, 7th ed. (St. Paul, MN: West, 1995): 170; and Jerry L. Gray and Frederick A. Starke, *Organizational Behavior: Concepts and Applications*, 4th ed. (New York: Macmillan, 1988): 104–105.

3. Carol Hymowitz, "Readers Tell Tales of Success and Failure Using Rating Systems," *Wall Street Journal*, May 29, 2001.

4. Alan Deutschman, "Can Google Stay Google?" *Fast Company* (August 2005): 62–68.

5. See Linda Grant, "Happy Workers, High Returns," *Fortune* (January 12, 1998): 81; Elizabeth J. Hawk and Garrett J. Sheridan, "The Right Stuff," *Management Review* (June 1999): 43–48; Michael West and Malcolm Patterson, "Profitable Personnel," *People Management* (January 8, 1998): 28–31; Anne Fisher, "Why Passion Pays," *FSB* (September 2002): 58; and Curt Coffman and Gabriel Gonzalez-Molina, *Follow This Path: How the World's Great Organizations Drive Growth By Unleashing Human Potential* (New York: Warner Books, 2002).

6. Questions based on Mitchell M. Handelsman, William L. Briggs, Nora Sullivan, and Annette Towler, "A Measure of College Student Course Engagement," *Journal of Educational Research* 98 (January–February 2005): 184–191.

7. Abraham F. Maslow, "A Theory of Human Motivation," *Psychological Review* 50 (1943): 370–396.

8. Sarah Pass, "On the Line," *People Management* (September 15, 2005): 38.

9. Clayton Alderfer, *Existence, Relatedness, and Growth* (New York: The Free Press, 1972).

10. Robert Levering and Milton Moskowitz, "2004 Special Report: The 100 Best Companies to Work For," *Fortune* (January 12, 2004): 56–78.

11. Jena McGregor, "Employee Innovator; Winner: USAA," *Fast Company* (October 2005): 57.

12. Jeff Barbian, "C'mon, Get Happy," *Training* (January 2001): 92–96.

13. Karol Rose, "Work-Life Effectiveness," *Fortune* (September 29, 2003): S1–S17.

14. Frederick Herzberg, "One More Time: How Do You Motivate Employees?" *Harvard Business Review* (January 2003): 87–96.

15. David C. McClelland, *Human Motivation* (Glenview, IL: Scott, Foresman, 1985).

16. David C. McClelland, "The Two Faces of Power," in D. A. Colb, I. M. Rubin, and J. M. McIntyre (Eds.), *Organizational Psychology* (Englewood Cliffs, NJ: Prentice Hall, 1971): 73–86.

17. See Gary P. Latham and Edwin A. Locke, "Enhancing the Benefits and Overcoming the Pitfalls of Goal Setting," *Organizational Dynamics* 35(4) (2006): 332–338; Edwin A. Locke

and Gary P. Latham, "Building a Practically Useful Theory of Goal Setting and Task Motivation: A 35-Year Odyssey," *American Psychologist* 57(9) (September 2002): 705ff; Gary P. Latham and Edwin A. Locke, "Self-Regulation through Goal Setting," *Organizational Behavior and Human Decision Processes* 50(2) (December, 1991): 212–247; G. P. Latham and G. H. Seijts, "The Effects of Proximal and Distal Goals on Performance of a Moderately Complex Task," *Journal of Organizational Behavior* 20(4) (1999): 421–428; P. C. Early, T. Connolly, and G. Ekegren, "Goals, Strategy Development, and Task Performance: Some Limits on the Efficacy of Goal Setting," *Journal of Applied Psychology* 74 (1989): 24–33; E. A. Locke, "Toward a Theory of Task Motivation and Incentives," *Organizational Behavior and Human Performance* 3 (1968): 157–189; and Gerard H. Seijts, Ree M. Meertens, and Gerjo Kok, "The Effects of Task Importance and Publicness on the Relation Between Goal Difficulty and Performance," *Canadian Journal of Behavioural Science* 29(1) (1997): 54ff.

18. Locke and Latham, "Building a Practically Useful Theory."

19. Edwin A. Locke, "Linking Goals to Monetary Incentives," *Academy of Management Executive* 18(4) (2005): 130–133.

20. Latham and Locke, "Enhancing the Benefits."

21. Brian Ellsworth, "Making a Place for Blue Collars in the Boardroom," *New York Times*, August 3, 2005.

22. J. M. Ivanecevich and J. T. McMahon, "The Effects of Goal Setting, External Feedback, and Self-Generated Feedback on Outcome Variables: A Field Experiment," *Academy of Management Journal* 25(2) (June 1982): 359–372; and G. P. Latham and E. A. Locke, "Self-Regulation Through Goal Setting," *Organizational Behavior and Human Decision Processes* 50(2) (1991): 212–247.

23. Gary P. Latham, "The Motivational Benefits of Goal-Setting," *Academy of Management Executive* 18(4) (2004): 126–129.

24. J. Stacy Adams, "Injustice in Social Exchange," in L. Berkowitz (Ed.), *Advances in Experimental Social Psychology*, 2nd ed. (New York: Academic Press, 1965); and J. Stacy Adams, "Toward an Understanding of Inequity," *Journal of Abnormal and Social Psychology* (November 1963): 422–436.

25. "Study: The Brain Prefers Working Over Getting Money for Nothing," TheJournalNews.com, May 14, 2004 (www.thejournalnews.com/apps/pbcs.dll/frontpage).

26. Ray V. Montagno, "The Effects of Comparison to Others and Primary Experience on Responses to Task Design," *Academy of Management Journal* 28 (1985): 491–498; and Robert P. Vecchio, "Predicting Worker Performance in Inequitable Settings," *Academy of Management Review* 7 (1982): 103–110.

27. James E. Martin and Melanie M. Peterson, "Two-Tier Wage Structures: Implications for Equity Theory," *Academy of Management Journal* 30 (1987): 297–315.

28. Jared Sandberg, "Why You May Regret Looking at Papers Left on the Office Copier," *Wall Street Journal*, June 20, 2006.

29. Victor H. Vroom, *Work and Motivation* (New York: Wiley, 1964); B. S. Gorgopoulos, G. M. Mahoney, and N. Jones, "A Path-Goal Approach to Productivity," *Journal of Applied Psychology* 41 (1957): 345–353; and E. E. Lawler III, *Pay and Organizational Effectiveness: A Psychological View* (New York: McGraw-Hill, 1981).

30. Richard L. Daft and Richard M. Steers, *Organizations: A Micro/Macro Approach* (Glenview, IL: Scott, Foresman, 1986).

31. Studies reported in Tom Rath, "The Best Way to Recognize Employees," *Gallup Management Journal* (December 9, 2004): 1–5; and Erin White, "Theory and Practice: Praise from Peers Goes a Long Way—Recognition Programs Help Companies Retain Workers as Pay Raises Get Smaller," *Wall Street Journal*, December 19, 2005.

32. Alexander D. Stajkovic and Fred Luthans, "A Meta-Analysis of the Effects of Organizational Behavior Modification on Task Performance, 1975–95," *Academy of Management Journal* (October 1997): 1122–1149; H. Richlin, *Modern Behaviorism* (San Francisco: Freeman, 1970); and B. F. Skinner, *Science and Human Behavior* (New York: Macmillan, 1953).

33. Stajkovic and Luthans, "Effects of Organizational Behavior Modification on Task Performance"; and Fred Luthans and Alexander D. Stajkovic, "Reinforce for Performance: The Need to Go Beyond Pay and Even Rewards," *Academy of Management Executive* 13(2) (1999): 49–57.

34. Daryl W. Wiesman, "The Effects of Performance Feedback and Social Reinforcement on Up-Selling at Fast-Food Restaurants," *Journal of Organizational Behavior Management* 26(4) (2006): 1–18.

35. Reported in Charlotte Garvey, "Meaningful Tokens of Appreciation," *HR Magazine* (August 2004): 101–105.

36. Kenneth D. Butterfield and Linda Klebe Treviño, "Punishment from the Manager's Perspective: A Grounded Investigation and Inductive Model," *Academy of Management Journal* 39(6) (December 1996): 1479–1512; and Andrea Casey, "Voices from the Firing Line: Managers Discuss Punishment in the Workplace," *Academy of Management Executive* 11(3) (1997): 93–94.

37. Winnie Hu, "School's New Rule for Pupils in Trouble: No Fun," *New York Times*, April 4, 2008.

38. Amy Joyce, "The Bonus Question; Some Managers Still Strive to Reward Merit," *Washington Post*, November 13, 2005.

39. Survey results from World at Work and Hewitt Associates reported in Karen Kroll, "Benefits: Paying for Performance," *Inc.* (November 2004): 46; and Kathy Chu, "Firms Report Lackluster Results from Pay-for-Performance Plans," *Wall Street Journal*, June 15, 2004.

40. Barbian, "C'mon, Get Happy."

41. Norm Alster, "What Flexible Workers Can Do," *Fortune* (February 13, 1989): 62–66.

42. Christine M. Riordan, Robert J. Vandenberg, and Hettie A. Richardson, "Employee Involvement Climate and Organizational

Effectiveness," *Human Resource Management* 44(4) (Winter 2005): 471–488.

43. Glenn L. Dalton, "The Collective Stretch," *Management Review* (December 1998): 54–59.

44. J. Richard Hackman and Greg R. Oldham, *Work Redesign* (Reading, MA: Addison-Wesley, 1980); and J. Richard Hackman and Greg Oldham, "Motivation through the Design of Work: Test of a Theory," *Organizational Behavior and Human Performance* 16 (1976): 250–279.

45. Xu Huang and Evert Van de Vliert, "Where Intrinsic Job Satisfaction Fails to Work: National Moderators of Intrinsic Motivation," *Journal of Organizational Behavior* 24 (2003): 157–179.

46. Edwin P. Hollander and Lynn R. Offermann, "Power and Leadership in Organizations," *American Psychologist* 45 (February 1990): 179–189.

47. Jay A. Conger and Rabindra N. Kanungo, "The Empowerment Process: Integrating Theory and Practice," *Academy of Management Review* 13 (1988): 471–482.

48. Ibid.

49. David E. Bowen and Edward E. Lawler III, "The Empowerment of Service Workers: What, Why, How, and When," *Sloan Management Review* (Spring 1992): 31–39; and Ray W. Coye and James A. Belohav, "An Exploratory Analysis of Employee Participation," *Group and Organization Management* 20(1) (March 1995): 4–17.

50. This discussion is based on Robert C. Ford and Myron D. Fottler, "Empowerment: A Matter of Degree," *Academy of Management Executive* 9(3) (1995): 21–31.

51. This definition is based on Mercer Human Resource Consulting's Employee Engagement Model as described in Paul Sanchez and Dan McCauley, "Measuring and Managing Engagement in a Cross-Cultural Workforce: New Insights for Global Companies," *Global Business and Organizational Excellence* (November–December 2006): 41–50.

52. Phred Dvorak, "Hotelier Finds Happiness Keeps Staff Checked In" (Theory & Practice column), *Wall Street Journal*, December 17, 2007.

53. Marcus Buckingham and Curt Coffman, *First, Break All the Rules: What the World's Greatest Managers Do Differently* (New York: Simon & Schuster, 1999).

54. Curt Coffman and Gabriel Gonzalez-Molina, *Follow This Path: How the World's Greatest Organizations Drive Growth by Unleashing Human Potential* (New York: Warner Books, 2002), as reported in Anne Fisher, "Why Passion Pays," *FSB* (September 2002): 58.

55. Theresa M. Welbourne, "Employee Engagement: Beyond the Fad and Into the Executive Suite, " *Leader to Leader* (Spring 2007): 45–51.

56. This discussion is based on Tony Schwartz, "The Greatest Sources of Satisfaction in the Workplace are Internal and Emotional," *Fast Company* (November 2000): 398–402; Marcus Buckingham and Curt Coffman, *First, Break All the Rules: What the World's Greatest Managers Do Differently* (New York: Simon and Schuster, 1999); and Jerry Krueger and Emily Killham, "At Work, Feeling Good Matters," *Gallup Management Journal* (December 8, 2005).

57. J. Craddock (Ed.), *VideoHound's Golden Movie Retriever* (Detroit, MI: Gale Cengage Learning, 2008): 368.

CHAPTER 14

Managing Communication

1. Jennifer Reingold, "Target's Inner Circle," *Fortune* (March 31, 2008): 76–86.

2. "Effective Communication Strategy Impacts Bottom Line," *Executive's Tax & Management Report* (January 2008): 15.

3. Henry Mintzberg, *The Nature of Managerial Work* (New York: Harper & Row, 1973).

4. Phillip G. Clampitt, Laurey Berk, and M. Lee Williams, "Leaders as Strategic Communicators," *Ivey Business Journal* (May–June 2002): 51–55.

5. Ian Wylie, "Can Philips Learn to Walk the Talk?" *Fast Company* (January 2003): 44–45.

6. Fred Luthans and Janet K. Larsen, "How Managers Really Communicate," *Human Relations* 39 (1986): 161–178; and Larry E. Penley and Brian Hawkins, "Studying Interpersonal Communication in Organizations: A Leadership Application," *Academy of Management Journal* 28 (1985): 309–326.

7. D. K. Berlo, *The Process of Communication* (New York: Holt, Rinehart and Winston, 1960): 24.

8. Bruce K. Blaylock, "Cognitive Style and the Usefulness of Information," *Decision Sciences* 15 (Winter 1984): 74–91.

9. Robert H. Lengel and Richard L. Daft, "The Selection of Communication Media as an Executive Skill," *Academy of Management Executive* 2 (August 1988): 225–232; Richard L. Daft and Robert H. Lengel, "Organizational Information Requirements, Media Richness and Structural Design," *Managerial Science* 32 (May 1986): 554–572; and Jane Webster and Linda Klebe Treviño, "Rational and Social Theories as Complementary Explanations of Communication Media Choices: Two Policy-Capturing Studies," *Academy of Management Journal* 38(6) (1995): 1544–1572.

10. Research reported in "E-mail Can't Mimic Phone Calls," *Johnson City* [TN] *Press*, September 17, 2000.

11. Raymond E. Friedman and Steven C. Currall, "E-Mail Escalation: Dispute Exacerbating Elements of Electronic Communication (www.mba.vanderbilt.edu/ray.friedman/pdf/emailescalation.pdf); Lauren Keller Johnson, "Does E-Mail Escalate Conflict?" *MIT Sloan Management Review* (Fall 2002): 14–15; and Alison Stein Wellner, "Lost in Translation," *Inc. Magazine* (September 2005): 37–38.

12. Wellner, "Lost in Translation"; Nick Easen, "Don't Send the Wrong Message; When E-Mail Crosses Borders, a Faux Pas Could Be Just a Click Away," *Business 2.0* (August 2005): 102.

13. Scott Kirsner, "IM Is Here. RU Prepared?" *Darwin Magazine* (February 2002): 22–24.

14. John R. Carlson and Robert W. Smud, "Channel Expansion Theory and the Experiential Nature of Media Richness Perceptions," *Academy of Management Journal* 42(2) (1999): 153–170; R. Rice and G. Love, "Electronic Emotion," *Communication Research* 14 (1987): 85–108.

15. Ronald E. Rice, "Task Analyzability, Use of New Media, and Effectiveness: A Multi-Site Exploration of Media Richness," *Organizational Science* 3(4) (November 1992): 475–500; and M. Lynne Markus, "Electronic Mail as the Medium of Managerial Choice," *Organizational Science* 5(4) (November 1994): 502–527.

16. Richard L. Daft, Robert H. Lengel, and Linda Klebe Treviño, "Message Equivocality, Media Selection and Manager Performance: Implication for Information Systems," *MIS Quarterly* 11 (1987): 355–368.

17. Mary Young and James E. Post, "Managing to Communicate, Communicating to Manage: How Leading Companies Communicate with Employees," *Organizational Dynamics* (Summer 1993): 31–43.

18. Jay A. Conger, "The Necessary Art of Persuasion," *Harvard Business Review* (May–June 1998): 84–95.

19. Ibid.

20. Susan Cramm, "The Heart of Persuasion," *CIO* (July 1, 2005): 28–30.

21. Deborah Tannen, *You Just Don't Understand: Women and Men in Conversation* (New York: Ballantine Books, 1991): 77.

22. Ibid, 125.

23. Rosalind Barnett and Caryl Rivers, *Same Difference: How Gender Myths Are Hurting Our Relationships, Our Children, and Our Jobs* (New York: Perseus Books Group, 2004): 133.

24. I. Thomas Sheppard, "Silent Signals," *Supervisory Management* (March 1986): 31–33.

25. Albert Mehrabian, *Silent Messages* (Belmont, CA: Wadsworth, 1971); and Albert Mehrabian, "Communicating without Words," *Psychology Today* (September 1968): 53–55.

26. Meridith Levinson, "How to Be a Mind Reader," *CIO* (December 1, 2004): 72–76; Mac Fulfer, "Nonverbal Communication: How to Read What's Plain as the Nose . . . ," *Journal of Organizational Excellence* (Spring 2001): 19–27; and Paul Ekman, *Emotions Revealed: Recognizing Faces and Feelings to Improve Communication and Emotional Life* (New York: Time Books, 2003).

27. Aili McConnon, "Ace Hardware: Calling the Right Play for Each Customer," *BusinessWeek* online (February 21, 2008) (www.businessweek.com/magazine/content/08_09/b4073050445440.htm) (accessed March 28, 2008).

28. C. Glenn Pearce, "Doing Something about Your Listening Ability," *Supervisory Management* (March 1989): 29–34; and Tom Peters, "Learning to Listen," *Hyatt Magazine* (Spring 1988): 16–21.

29. Kelley Holland, "Under New Management; The Silent May Have Something to Say," *New York Times,* November 5, 2006 (www.nytimes.com) (accessed December 4, 2006).

30. Debbie Weil, *The Corporate Blogging Book* (New York: Penguin Group, 2006): 3.

31. Fortune 500 Business Blogging Wiki (www.socialtext.net/bizblogs/index.cgi) (accessed April 9, 2008).

32. Interview by Oliver Ryan, "Blogger in Chief," *Fortune* (November 13, 2006): 51.

33. M. P. Nichols, *The Lost Art of Listening* (New York: Guilford Publishing, 1995).

34. "Benchmarking the Sales Function," a report based on a study of 100 salespeople from small, medium, and large businesses conducted by Ron Volper Group Inc. Sales Consulting and Training, White Plains, New York (1996), as reported in "Nine Habits of Highly Successful Salespeople," *Inc. Small Business Success.*

35. Gerald M. Goldhaber, *Organizational Communication*, 4th ed. (Dubuque, IA: Brown, 1980), p. 189.

36. Richard L. Daft and Richard M. Steers, *Organizations: A Micro/Macro Approach* (New York: Harper Collins, 1986); and Daniel Katz and Robert Kahn, *The Social Psychology of Organizations*, 2nd ed. (New York: Wiley, 1978).

37. Greg Jaffe, "Tug of War: In the New Military, Technology May Alter Chain of Command," *Wall Street Journal*, March 30, 2001; and Aaron Pressman, "Business Gets the Message," *Industry Standard* (February 26, 2001): 58–59.

38. Phillip G. Clampitt, Robert J. DeKoch, and Thomas Cashman, "A Strategy for Communicating about Uncertainty," *Academy of Management Executive* 14(4) (2000): 41–57.

39. Reported in Louise van der Does and Stephen J. Caldeira, "Effective Leaders Champion Communication Skills," *Nation's Restaurant News* (March 27, 2006): 20.

40. J. G. Miller, "Living Systems: The Organization," *Behavioral Science* 17 (1972): 69.

41. Michael J. Glauser, "Upward Information Flow in Organizations: Review and Conceptual Analysis," *Human Relations* 37 (1984): 613–643; and "Upward/Downward Communication: Critical Information Channels," *Small Business Report* (October 1985): 85–88.

42. Thomas Petzinger, "A Hospital Applies Teamwork to Thwart An Insidious Enemy," *Wall Street Journal*, May 8, 1998.

43. Gary Hamel, "What Google, Whole Foods Do Best," *Fortune* (October 1, 2007): 124.

44. E. M. Rogers and R. A. Rogers, *Communication in Organizations* (New York: The Free Press, 1976); and A. Bavelas and D. Barrett, "An Experimental Approach to Organization Communication," *Personnel* 27 (1951): 366–371.

45. This discussion is based on Daft and Steers, *Organizations.*

46. Bavelas and Barrett, "An Experimental Approach"; and M. E. Shaw, *Group Dynamics: The Psychology of Small Group Behavior* (New York: McGraw-Hill, 1976).

47. Richard L. Daft and Norman B. Macintosh, "A Tentative Exploration into the Amount and Equivocality of Information Processing in Organizational Work Units," *Administrative Science Quarterly* 26 (1981): 207–224.

48. This discussion of informal networks is based on Rob Cross, Nitin Nohria, and Andrew Parker, "Six Myths About Informal Networks," *MIT Sloan Management Review* (Spring 2002): 67–75; and Rob Cross and Laurence Prusak, "The People Who Make Organizations Go—or Stop," *Harvard Business Review* (June 2002): 105–112.

49. Tahl Raz, "The 10 Secrets of a Master Networker," *Inc.* (January 2003).

50. Stephanie Armour, "Office Gossip Has Never Traveled Faster, Thanks to Tech," *USA Today*, November 1, 2007 (www.usatoday.com/tech/webguide/internetlife/2007-09-09-office-gossip-technology_n.htm) (accessed March 28, 2008).

51. Keith Davis and John W. Newstrom, *Human Behavior at Work: Organizational Behavior*, 7th ed. (New York: McGraw-Hill, 1985).

52. Suzanne M. Crampton, John W. Hodge, and Jitendra M. Mishra, "The Informal Communication Network: Factors Influencing Grapevine Activity," *Public Personnel Management* 27(4) (Winter 1998): 569–584.

53. Survey results reported in Jared Sandberg, "Ruthless Rumors and the Managers Who Enable Them," *Wall Street Journal*, October 29, 2003.

54. Donald B. Simmons, "The Nature of the Organizational Grapevine," *Supervisory Management* (November 1985): 39–42; and Davis and Newstrom, *Human Behavior*.

55. Barbara Ettorre, "Hellooo. Anybody Listening?" *Management Review* (November 1997): 9.

56. Eilene Zimmerman, "Gossip Is Information by Another Name," *New York Times*, February 3, 2008, p. BU15.

57. Lisa A. Burke and Jessica Morris Wise, "The Effective Care, Handling, and Pruning of the Office Grapevine," *Business Horizons* (May–June 2003): 71–74; "They Hear It Through the Grapevine," cited in Michael Warshaw, "The Good Guy's Guide to Office Politics," *Fast Company* (April–May 1998): 157–178; and Carol Hildebrand, "Mapping the Invisible Workplace," *CIO Enterprise*, section 2 (July 15, 1998): 18–20.

58. The National Commission on Writing, "Writing Skills Necessary for Employment, Says Big Business," September 14, 2004 (www.writingcommission.org/pr/writing_for_employ.html) (accessed April 8, 2008).

59. Based on Michael Fitzgerald, "How to Write a Memorable Memo," *CIO* (October 15, 2005): 85–87; and Jonathan Hershberg, "It's Not Just What You Say," *Training* (May 2005): 50.

60. Mary Anne Donovan, "E-Mail Exposes the Literacy Gap," *Workforce* (November 2002): 15.

61. David Bohm, *On Dialogue* (Ojai, CA: David Bohm Seminars, 1989).

62. George Kohlrieser, "The Power of Authentic Dialogue," *Leader to Leader* (Fall 2006): 37.

63. This discussion is based on Glenna Gerard and Linda Teurfs, "Dialogue and Organizational Transformation," in Kazinierz Gozdz (Ed.), *Community Building: Renewing Spirit and Learning in Business* (Santa Barbara, PA: New Leaders, 1995): 142–153; and Edgar H. Schein, "On Dialogue, Culture, and Organizational Learning," *Organizational Dynamics* (Autumn 1993): 40–51.

64. Ian I. Mitroff and Murat C. Alpaslan, "Preparing for Evil," *Harvard Business Review* (April 2003): 109–115.

65. Brad Ritter and Janet Ritter, "Crisis Communication: Taking Center Stage With Confidence," *Government Finance Review* 23(6) (December, 2007): 51.

66. This section is based on Leslie Wayne and Leslie Kaufman, "Leadership, Put to a New Test," *New York Times*, September 16, 2001; Ian I. Mitroff, "Crisis Leadership," *Executive Excellence* (August 2001): 19; Jerry Useem, "What It Takes," *Fortune* (November 12, 2001): 126–132; Andy Bowen, "Crisis Procedures That Stand the Test of Time," *Public Relations Tactics* (August 2001): 16; and Matthew Boyle, "Nothing Really Matters," *Fortune* (October 15, 2001): 261–264.

67. Stephen Bernhut, "Leadership, with Michael Useem," *Ivey Business Journal* (January–February 2002): 42–43.

68. Mitroff, "Crisis Leadership."

69. Jay M. Jackman and Myra H. Strober, "Fear of Feedback," *Harvard Business Review* (April 2003): 101–108; and Dennis Tourish, "Critical Upward Communication: Ten Commandments for Improving Strategy and Decision Making," *Long Range Planning* 38 (2005): 485–503.

70. J. Craddock (Ed.), *VideoHound's Golden Movie Retriever* (Detroit: Gale, Cengage Learning, 2008): 368.

71. This sequence is heavily based on DVD Chapter 27, "Half-Time." However, we edited in scenes from other parts of the film to reduce the number of identifiable talent to whom we must pay a fee. If you have seen this film, then you will know that this exact sequence does not exist at any point in the film.

CHAPTER 15

Leading Teams

1. Industry Week/Manufacturing Performance Institute's Census of Manufacturers for 2004, reported in Traci Purdum, "Teaming, Take 2," *Industry Week* (May 2005): 41–43.

2. Carl E. Larson and Frank M. J. LaFasto, *TeamWork* (Newbury Park, CA: Sage, 1989).

3. Telis Demos, "Cirque du Balancing Act," *Fortune* (June 12, 2006): 114; Erin White, "How a Company Made Everyone a Team Player," *Wall Street Journal*, August 13, 2007; David Kirkpatrick, "Inside Sam's $100 Billion Growth Machine," *Fortune* (June 14, 2004): 80–98; Daniel R. Kibbe and Jill

Casner-Lotto, "Ralston Foods: From Greenfield to Maturity in a Team-Based Plant, *Journal of Organizational Excellence* (Summer 2002): 57–67.

4. "'Golden Hour' Crucial Time for Surgeons on Front Line," *Johnson City* [TN] *Press*, April 1, 2003.

5. Based on Eric M. Stark, Jason D. Shaw, and Michelle K. Duffy, "Preference for Group Work, Winning Orientation, and Social Loafing Behavior in Groups," *Group & Organization Management* 32(6) (December 2007): 699–723.

6. Study by G. Clotaire Rapaille, reported in Karen Bernowski, "What Makes American Teams Tick?" *Quality Progress* 28(1) (January 1995): 39–42.

7. Robert Albanese and David D. Van Fleet, "Rational Behavior in Groups: The Free-Riding Tendency," *Academy of Management Review* 10 (1985): 244–255.

8. David H. Freedman, "The Idiocy of Crowds" ("What's Next" column), *Inc. Magazine* (September 2006): 61–62.

9. "Why Some Teams Succeed (and So Many Don't)," *Harvard Management Update* (October 2006): 3–4.

10. Reported in Jerry Useem, "What's That Spell? Teamwork!" *Fortune* (June 12, 2006): 65–66.

11. Eric Sundstrom, Kenneth P. DeMeuse, and David Futrell, "Work Teams," *American Psychologist* 45 (February 1990): 120–133.

12. Deborah L. Gladstein, "Groups in Context: A Model of Task Group Effectiveness," *Administrative Science Quarterly* 29 (1984): 499–517.

13. Sujin K. Horwitz and Irwin B. Horwitz, "The Effects of Team Diversity on Team Outcomes: A Meta-Analytic Review of Team Demography," *Journal of Management* 33(6) (December 2007): 987–1015; and Dora C. Lau and J. Keith Murnighan, "Demographic Diversity and Faultlines: The Compositional Dynamics of Organizational Groups," *Academy of Management Review* 23(2) (1998): 325–340.

14. Based on J. Richard Hackman, *Leading Teams: Setting the Stage for Great Performances* (Boston: Harvard Business School Press, 2002): 62. Susan Caminiti, "What Team Leaders Need to Know," *Fortune* (February 20, 1995): 93–100; J. Thomas Buck, "The Rocky Road to Team-Based Management," *Training & Development* (April 1995): 35–38; and Lee G. Bolman and Terrence E. Deal, "What Makes a Team Work?" *Organizational Dynamics* (August 1992): 34–44; Amy Edmondson, Richard Bohmer, and Gary Pisano, "Speeding Up Team Learning," *Harvard Business Review* (October 2001): 125–132; and Jeanne M. Wilson, Jill George, and Richard S. Wellings, with William C. Byham, *Leadership Trapeze: Strategies for Leadership in Team-Based Organizations* (San Francisco: Jossey-Bass, 1994): 14.

15. Thomas Owens, "Business Teams," *Small Business Report* (January 1989): 50–58.

16. "Participation Teams," *Small Business Report* (September 1987): 38–41.

17. Susanne G. Scott and Walter O. Einstein, "Strategic Performance Appraisal in Team-Based Organizations: One Size Does Not Fit All," *Academy of Management Executive* 15(2) (2001): 107–116.

18. Larson and LaFasto, *TeamWork*.

19. James H. Shonk, *Team-Based Organizations* (Homewood, IL: Business One Irwin, 1992); and John Hoerr, "The Payoff from Teamwork," *BusinessWeek* (July 10, 1989): 56–62.

20. Jennifer Robison, "An International Paper Mill Saves Itself," *Gallup Management Journal* (December 14, 2006) (http://gmj.gallup.com) (accessed May 20, 2008).

21. Ruth Wageman, "Critical Success Factors for Creating Superb Self-Managing Teams," *Organizational Dynamics* (Summer 1997): 49–61.

22. Thomas Owens, "The Self-Managing Work Team," *Small Business Report* (February 1991): 53–65.

23. The discussion of virtual teams is based on Wayne F. Cascio and Stan Shurygailo, "E-Leadership and Virtual Teams," *Organizational Dynamics* 31(4) (2002): 362–376; Anthony M. Townsend, Samuel M. DeMarie, and Anthony R. Hendrickson, "Virtual Teams: Technology and the Workplace of the Future," *Academy of Management Executive* 12(3) (August 1998): 17–29; and Deborah L. Duarte and Nancy Tennant Snyder, *Mastering Virtual Teams* (San Francisco: Jossey-Bass, 1999).

24. Jessica Lipnack and Jeffrey Stamps, "Virtual Teams: The New Way to Work," *Strategy & Leadership* (January–February 1999): 14–19.

25. This discussion is based on Arvind Malhotra, Ann Majchrzak, and Benson Rosen, "Leading Virtual Teams," *Academy of Management Perspectives* 21(1) (February 2007): 60–69; Benson Rosen, Stacie Furst, and Richard Blackburn, "Overcoming Barriers to Knowledge Sharing in Virtual Teams," *Organizational Dynamics* 36(3) (2007): 259–273; Marshall Goldsmith, "Crossing the Cultural Chasm; Keeping Communication Clear and Consistent with Team Members from Other Countries Isn't Easy, Says Author Maya Hu-Chan," *BusinessWeek* online (May 31, 2007) (www.businessweek.com/careers/content/may2007/ca20070530_521679.htm) (accessed August 24, 2007); and Bradley L. Kirkman, Benson Rosen, Cristina B. Gibson, Paul E. Tesluk, and Simon O. McPherson, "Five Challenges to Virtual Team Success: Lessons from Sabre, Inc.," *Academy of Management Executive* 16(3) (2002): 67–79.

26. Ann Majchrzak, Arvind Malhotra, Jeffrey Stamps, and Jessica Lipnack, "Can Absence Make a Team Grow Stronger?" *Harvard Business Review* 82(5) (May 2004): 131.

27. Lynda Gratton, "Working Together . . . When Apart," *Wall Street Journal*, June 18, 2007; Kirkman et al., "Five Challenges to Virtual Team Success."

28. Pete Engardio, "A Guide for Multinationals: One of the Greatest Challenges for a Multinational Is Learning How to Build a Productive Global Team," *BusinessWeek* (August 20, 2007): 48–51; and Gratton, "Working Together . . . When Apart."

29. Vijay Govindarajan and Anil K. Gupta, "Building an Effective Global Business Team," *MIT Sloan Management Review* 42(4) (Summer 2001): 63–71.

30. Charlene Marmer Solomon, "Building Teams Across Borders," *Global Workforce* (November 1998): 12–17.

31. Carol Saunders, Craig Van Slyke, and Douglas R. Vogel, "My Time or Yours? Managing Time Visions in Global Virtual Teams," *Academy of Management Executive* 18(1) (2004): 19–31.

32. This discussion is based on Jeanne Brett, Kristin Behfar, and Mary C. Kern, "Managing Multicultural Teams," *Harvard Business Review* (November 2006): 84–91; and Saunders, Van Slyke, and Vogel, "My Time or Yours?"

33. Richard Pastore, "Global Team Management: It's a Small World After All," *CIO* (January 23, 2008) (www.cio.com/article/174750/Global_Team_Management_It_s_a_Small_World_After_All) (accessed May 20, 2008).

34. Engardio, "A Guide for Multinationals."

35. Sylvia Odenwald, "Global Work Teams," *Training and Development* (February 1996): 54–57; and Debby Young, "Team Heat," *CIO* (September1, 1998): 43–51.

36. Reported in Jia Lynn Yang, "The Power of Number 4.6," part of a special series, "Secrets of Greatness: Teamwork," *Fortune* (June 12, 2006): 122.

37. Martin Hoegl, "Smaller Teams—Better Teamwork: How to Keep Project Teams Small," *Business Horizons* 48 (2005): 209–214.

38. Reported in "Vive La Difference" box in Julie Connelly, "All Together Now," *Gallup Management Journal* (Spring 2002): 13–18.

39. For research findings on group size, see M. E. Shaw, *Group Dynamics*, 3rd ed. (New York, NY: McGraw-Hill, 1981); G. Manners, "Another Look at Group Size, Group Problem-Solving and Member Consensus," *Academy of Management Journal* 18 (1975): 715–724; and Martin Hoegl, "Smaller Teams—Better Teamwork: How to Keep Project Teams Small," *Business Horizons* 48 (2005): 209–214.

40. Yang, "The Power of Number 4.6."

41. Warren E. Watson, Kamalesh Kumar, and Larry K. Michaelsen, "Cultural Diversity's Impact on Interaction Process and Performance: Comparing Homogeneous and Diverse Task Groups," *Academy of Management Journal* 36 (1993): 590–602; Gail Robinson and Kathleen Dechant, "Building a Business Case for Diversity," *Academy of Management Executive* 11(3) (1997): 21–31; and David A. Thomas and Robin J. Ely, "Making Differences Matter: A New Paradigm for Managing Diversity," *Harvard Business Review* (September–October 1996): 79–90.

42. J. Stuart Bunderson and Kathleen M. Sutcliffe, "Comparing Alternative Conceptualizations of Functional Diversity in Management Teams: Process and Performance Effects," *Academy of Management Journal* 45(5) (2002): 875–893; and Marc Orlitzky and John D. Benjamin, "The Effects of Sex Composition on Small Group Performance in a Business School Case Competition," *Academy of Management Learning and Education* 2(2) (2003): 128–138.

43. Watson, Kumar, and Michaelsen, "Cultural Diversity's Impact."

44. George Prince, "Recognizing Genuine Teamwork," *Supervisory Management* (April 1989): 25–36; K. D. Benne and P. Sheats, "Functional Roles of Group Members," *Journal of Social Issues* 4 (1948): 41–49; and R.F. Bales, *SYMOLOG* (Case Study Kit) (New York: Free Press, 1980).

45. Robert A. Baron, *Behavior in Organizations*, 2nd ed. (Boston, MA: Allyn & Bacon, 1986).

46. Ibid.

47. Kenneth G. Koehler, "Effective Team Management," *Small Business Report* (July 19, 1989): 14–16; and Connie J. G. Gersick, "Time and Transition in Work Teams: Toward a New Model of Group Development," *Academy of Management Journal* 31 (1988): 9–41.

48. Bruce W. Tuckman and Mary Ann C. Jensen, "Stages of Small-Group Development Revisited," *Group and Organizational Studies* 2 (1977): 419–427; and Bruce W. Tuckman, "Developmental Sequences in Small Groups," *Psychological Bulletin* 63 (1965): 384–399. See also Linda N. Jewell and H. Joseph Reitz, *Group Effectiveness in Organizations* (Glenview, IL: Scott, Foresman,1981).

49. Thomas Petzinger Jr., "Bovis Team Helps Builders Construct a Solid Foundation," *Wall Street Journal*, March 21, 1997.

50. Shaw, *Group Dynamics*.

51. Daniel C. Feldman and Hugh J. Arnold, *Managing Individual and Group Behavior in Organizations* (New York: McGraw-Hill, 1983).

52. Dorwin Cartwright and Alvin Zander, *Group Dynamics: Research and Theory*, 3rd ed. (New York: Harper & Row, 1968); and Elliot Aronson, *The Social Animal* (San Francisco: W. H. Freeman, 1976).

53. Stanley E. Seashore, *Group Cohesiveness in the Industrial Work Group* (Ann Arbor, MI: Institute for Social Research, 1954).

54. J. Richard Hackman, "Group Influences on Individuals," in M. Dunnette (Ed.), *Handbook of Industrial and Organizational Psychology* (Chicago: Rand McNally, 1976).

55. The following discussion is based on Daniel C. Feldman, "The Development and Enforcement of Group Norms," *Academy of Management Review* 9 (1984): 47–53.

56. Wilson et al., *Leadership Trapeze*, p. 12.

57. Simon Taggar and Robert Ellis, "The Role of Leaders in Shaping Formal Team Norms," *The Leadership Quarterly* 18 (2007): 105–120.

58. Geoffrey Colvin, "Why Dream Teams Fail," *Fortune* (June 12, 2006): 87–92.

59. Stephen P. Robbins, *Managing Organizational Conflict: A Nontraditional Approach* (Englewood Cliffs, NJ: Prentice Hall, 1974).

60. Daniel Robey, Dana L. Farrow, and Charles R. Franz, "Group Process and Conflict in System Development," *Management Science* 35 (1989): 1172–1191.

61. Yuhyung Shin, "Conflict Resolution in Virtual Teams," *Organizational Dynamics* 34(4) (2005): 331–345.

62. Dean Tjosvold, Chun Hui, Daniel Z. Ding, and Junchen Hu, "Conflict Values and Team Relationships: Conflict's Contribution to Team Effectiveness and Citizenship in China," *Journal of Organizational Behavior* 24 (2003): 69–88; C. De Dreu and E. Van de Vliert, *Using Conflict in Organizations* (Beverly Hills, CA: Sage, 1997); and Kathleen M. Eisenhardt, Jean L. Kahwajy, and L. J. Bourgeois III, "Conflict and Strategic Choice: How Top Management Teams Disagree," *California Management Review* 39(2) (Winter 1997): 42–62.

63. Jerry B. Harvey, "The Abilene Paradox: The Management of Agreement," *Organizational Dynamics* (Summer 1988): 17–43.

64. Eisenhardt, Kahwajy, and Bourgeois, "Conflict and Strategic Choice."

65. Koehler, "Effective Team Management"; and Dean Tjosvold, "Making Conflict Productive," *Personnel Administrator* 29 (June 1984): 121.

66. This discussion is based in part on Richard L. Daft, *Organization Theory and Design* (St. Paul, MN: West, 1992), Chapter 13; and Paul M. Terry, "Conflict Management," *Journal of Leadership Studies* 3(2) (1996): 3–21.

67. Shin, "Conflict Resolution in Virtual Teams."

68. This discussion is based on K. W. Thomas, "Towards Multidimensional Values in Teaching: The Example of Conflict Behaviors," *Academy of Management Review* 2 (1977): 487.

69. Robbins, *Managing Organizational Conflict.*

70. La Piana Associates Inc., "The Negotiation Process: The Difference Between Integrative and Distributive Negotiation" (www.lapiana.org/resources/tips/negotiations).

71. Rob Walker, "Take It or Leave It: The Only Guide to Negotiating You Will Ever Need," *Inc.* (August 2003): 75–82.

72. Based on Roger Fisher and William Ury, *Getting to Yes: Negotiating Agreement Without Giving In* (New York, NY: Penguin, 1983).

73. This familiar story was reported in La Piana Associates, "The Negotiation Process."

74. Based in part on "A Note for Analyzing Work Groups," prepared by Linda A. Hill, Harvard Business School Publishing (www.hbsp.harvard.edu).

75. "Big and No Longer Blue," *The Economist* (January 21–27, 2006) (www.economist.com).

76. R. B. Zajonc, "Social Facilitation," *Science* 149 (1965): 269–274; and Miriam Erez and Anit Somech, "Is Group Productivity Loss the Rule or the Exception? Effects of Culture and Group-Based Motivation," *Academy of Management Journal* 39(6) (1996): 1513–1537.

77. Claire M. Mason and Mark A. Griffin, "Group Task Satisfaction; The Group's Shared Attitude to Its Task and Work Environment," *Group and Organizational Management* 30(6) (2005): 625–652.

78. Gina Imperato, "Their Specialty? Teamwork," *Fast Company* (January–February 2000): 54–56.

79. Reported in Scott Thurm, "Theory and Practice: Teamwork Raises Everyone's Game—Having Employees Bond Benefits Companies More Than Promoting 'Stars,'" *Wall Street Journal*, November 7, 2005.

80. Kenneth Labich, "Elite Teams Get the Job Done," *Fortune* (February 19, 1996): 90–99.

81. Linda A. Hill, *A Note for Analyzing Effective Work Groups* (Cambridge, MA: Harvard Business School Publishing) (www.hbsp.harvard.edu).

APPENDIX A

Managing Small Business Start-ups

1. Based on Keith M. Hmieleski and Andrew C. Corbett, "Proclivity for Improvisation as a Predictor of Entrepreneurial Intentions," *Journal of Small Business Management* 44(1) (January 2006): 45–63; and "Do You Have an Entrepreneurial Mind?" *Inc.com* (October 19, 2005).

2. Elizabeth Olson, "They May Be Mundane, But Low-Tech Businesses Are Booming," *New York Times*, April 28, 2005 (www.nytimes.com/2005/04/28/business/28sbiz.html?_r=1&scp=1&sq=They%20May%20Be%20Mundane,%20But%20Low-Tech%20Businesses%20Are%20Booming&st=cse&oref=slogin); and "CIBC Report Predicts Canada Will Be Home to One Million Women Entrepreneurs By 2010," *Canada NewsWire* (June 28, 2005): 1.

3. U.S. Small Business Administration (www.sba.gov).

4. John Case, "Where We Are Now," *Inc.* (May 29, 2001): 18–19.

5. Amy E. Knaup, "Survival and Longevity in the Business Employment Dynamics Database," *Monthly Labor Review*, 128(5) (May 2005): 50–56; and Brian Headd, "Redefining Business Success: Distinguishing Between Closure and Failure," *Small Business Economics,* 21(1) (August 2003): 51–61.

6. Reported in "Did You Know?" in J. Neil Weintraut, "Told Any Good Stories Lately?" *Business 2.0* (March 2000): 139–140.

7. U.S. Small Business Administration (www.sba.gov).

8. John Case, "Who's Looking at Start-Ups?" *Inc.* (May 29, 2001): 60.

9. Donald F. Kuratko and Richard M. Hodgetts, *Entrepreneurship: A Contemporary Approach,* 4th ed. (Fort Worth, TX: Dryden Press, 1998): 30.

10. Steve Stecklow, "StubHub's Ticket to Ride," *Wall Street Journal*, January, 17, 2006.

11. Study conducted by Yankelovich Partners, reported in Mark Henricks, "Type-Cast," *Entrepreneur* (March 2000): 14–16.

12. Olson, "Low-Tech Businesses Are Booming."

13. Norm Brodsky, "Street Smarts: Opportunity Knocks," *Inc.* (February 2002): 44–46; and Hilary Stout, "Start Low," *Wall Street Journal*, May 14, 2001.

14. U.S. Small Business Administration (www.sba.gov).

15. Global Entrepreneurship Monitor, "Table 2: Prevalence Rates of Entrepreneurial Activity Across Countries, 2007," *2007 GEM Tables and Figures,* Babson College and the London Business School, March 14, 2008 (www.gemconsortium.org/about.aspx?page=pub_gem_global_reports).

16. U.S. Small Business Administration (www.sba.gov).

17. Thuy-Doan Le Bee, "How Small Is Small? SBA Holds Hearings to Decide," *Sacramento Bee*, June 29, 2005.

18. U.S. Small Business Administration (www.sba.gov).

19. Barbara Benham, "Big Government, Small Business," *Working Woman* (February 2001): 24.

20. Research and statistics reported in "The Job Factory," *Inc.* (May 29, 2001): 40–43.

21. Ian Mount, "The Return of the Lone Inventor," *FSB* (March 2005): 18; Office of Advocacy, U.S. Small Business Administration (www.sba.gov/advo).

22. John Case, "The Origins of Entrepreneurship," *Inc.* (June 1989): 51–53.

23. Jeanette Borzo, "Taking on the Recruiting Monster," *Business 2.0* (January–February 2007): 44.

24. Kauffman Foundation (www.kauffman.org).

25. "Small Business Ambassador," *FSB* (February 2007): 28.

26. U.S. Small Business Administration (www.sba.gov); "CIBC Report Predicts Canada Will Be Home to One Million Women Entrepreneurs by 2010," *Canada NewsWire* (June 28, 2005): 1.

27. U.S. Small Business Administration (www.sba.gov).

28. Statistics reported in Cora Daniels, "Minority Rule," *FSB* (December 2003–January 2004): 65–66; Elizabeth Olson, "New Help for the Black Entrepreneur," *New York Times*, December 23, 2004; and David J. Dent, "The Next Black Power Movement," *FSB* (May 2003): 10–13.

29. Ellyn Spragins, "Pat Winans" profile, and Cora Daniels, "Ed Chin" profile, in "The New Color of Money," *FSB* (December 2003–January 2004): 74–87.

30. This discussion is based on Charles R. Kuehl and Peggy A. Lambing, *Small Business: Planning and Management,* 3rd ed. (Ft. Worth, TX: Dryden Press, 1994).

31. David C. McClelland, *The Achieving Society* (New York: Van Nostrand, 1961).

32. Paulette Thomas, "Entrepreneurs' Biggest Problems—and How They Solve Them," *Wall Street Journal* (March 17, 2003).

33. Definition based on Albert R. Hunt, "Social Entrepreneurs: Compassionate and Tough-Minded," *Wall Street Journal* (July 13, 2000); David Puttnam, "Hearts Before Pockets," *New Statesman* (February 9, 2004): 26; and Christian Seelos and Johanna Mair, "Social Entrepreneurship: Creating New Business Models to Serve the Poor," *Business Horizons* 48 (2005): 241–246.

34. Cheryl Dahle, "Filling the Void: The 2006 Social Capitalist Award Winners," *Fast Company* (January–February 2006): 50–61.

35. Puttnam, "Hearts Before Pockets."

36. Jessica Harris, "Ethics in a Bottle," *FSB* (November 2007): 44.

37. Cheryl Dahle, "The Change Masters," *Fast Company* (January 2005): 47–58; David Bornstein, *How to Change the World: Social Entrepreneurs and the Power of New Ideas* (Oxford: Oxford University Press, 2004).

38. James Flanigan, "Small Businesses Offer Alternatives to Gang Life," *New York Times*, March 20, 2008 (www.nytimes.com/2008/03/20/business/smallbusiness/20edge.html) (accessed June 23, 2008).

39. Leslie Brokaw, "How to Start an *Inc.* 500 Company," *Inc.* 500 (1994): 51–65.

40. Interview with Phaedra Hise, "A Chance to Prove My Worth," *FSB* (February 2007): 26.

41. Paul Reynolds, "The Truth About Start-Ups," *Inc.* (February 1995): 23; Brian O'Reilly, "The New Face of Small Businesses," *Fortune* (May 2, 1994): 82–88.

42. Based on Ellyn E. Spragins, "How to Write a Business Plan That Will Get You in the Door," *Small Business Success* (November 1990); Linda Elkins, "Tips for Preparing a Business Plan," *Nation's Business* (June 1996): 60R–61R; Carolyn M. Brown, "The Do's and Don'ts of Writing a Winning Business Plan," *Black Enterprise* (April 1996): 114–116; and Kuratko and Hodgetts, *Entrepreneurship,* 295–397. For a clear, thorough, step-by-step guide to writing an effective business plan, see Linda Pinson and Jerry Jinnett, *Anatomy of a Business Plan,* 5th ed. (Virginia Beach, VA: Dearborn, 2001).

43. The INC. FAXPOLL, *Inc.* (February 1992): 24.

44. Duncan MacVicar, "Ten Steps to a High-Tech Start-Up," *Industrial Physicist* (October 1999): 27–31.

45. "Venture Capitalists' Criteria" *Management Review* (November 1985): 7–8.

46. "Staples Makes Big Business from Helping Small Businesses," *SBA Success Stories* (www.sba.gov/successstories.html) (accessed on March 12, 2004); Staples (www.staples.com/sbd/content/about/media/overview.html) (accessed July 16, 2008).

47. Elizabeth Olson, "From One Business to 23 Million," *New York Times*, March 7, 2004 (http://query.nytimes.com/gst/fullpage.html?res=9C03E6D6113FF934A35750C0A9629CB63) (accessed July 16, 2008).

48. "Where the Venture Money Is Going," *Business 2.0* (January–February 2004): 98.

49. Gary Rivlin, "Does the Kid Stay in the Picture?" *New York Times*, February 22, 2005.

50. Dent, "The Next Black Power Movement."

51. Kristen Hampshire, "Roll With It," *FSB* (November 2005): 108–112; Jennifer Maxwell profile in Betsy Wiesendanger, "Labors of Love," *Working Woman* (May 1999): 43–56; Jena McGregor, Taryn Rose profile in "25 Top Women Business Builders," *Fast Company* (May 2005): 67–75.

52. Wendy Lea, "Dancing with a Partner," *Fast Company* (March 2000): 159–161.

53. Matt Richtel, "Outsourced All the Way," *New York Times*, June 21, 2005 (www.nytimes.com).

54. International Franchise Association (www.franchise.org/) (accessed June 23, 2008).

55. Quinne Bryant, "Who Owns 20+ Subway Franchises?" *Business Journal of Tri-Cities Tennessee/Virginia* (August 2003): 42–43.

56. For a current discussion of the risks and disadvantages of owning a franchise, see Anne Fisher, "Risk Reward," *FSB* (December 2005–January 2006): 44.

57. Anne Field, "Your Ticket to a New Career? Franchising Can Put Your Skills to Work in Your Own Business," in *Business Week Investor: Small Business* section, *BusinessWeek* (May 12, 2003): 100+; and Roberta Maynard, "Choosing a Franchise," *Nation's Business* (October 1996): 56–63.

58. Darren Dahl, "Getting Started: Percolating Profits." *Inc.* (February 2005): 38.

59. 2006 figures from the National Business Incubation Association (www.nbia.org/resource_center/bus_inc_facts/index.php/) (accessed July 16, 2008).

60. Oringel, "Sowing Success."

61. Laura Novak, "For Women, a Recipe to Create a Successful Business," *New York Times*, June 23, 2007 (www.nytimes.com/2007/06/23/business/smallbusiness/23cocina.html?_r=1&sq =Laura%20Novak,%20â€œFor%20Women,%20a%20Recipe%20to%20Create%20a%20Successful%20Business&st=cse&adxnnl=1&oref=slogin&scp=1&adxnnlx=1225894278=APkyZ4kswGDrm3QtejIg6A) (accessed June 23, 2008).

62. Sue Shellenbarger, "The Job That Follows You Wherever You May Roam," *Wall Street Journal* online (http://online.wsj.com/public/us) (accessed July 10, 2008).

63. Chuck Salter, "Girl Power," *Fast Company* (September, 2007): 104.

64. Ellen Simon, "Starting Simple," *Miami Herald*, November 13, 2007.

65. Jason R. Rich, *Unofficial Guide to Starting a Business Online*, 2nd ed. (New York: Wiley, 2006): 116.

66. Ellen Reid Smith, *e-loyalty: How to Keep Customers Coming Back to Your Website* (New York: HarperCollins, 2000): 19.

67. Ibid, 127.

68. Susan G. Hauser, "Nagging for Dollars," *FSB* (September 2007): 76.

69. Carrie Dolan, "Entrepreneurs Often Fail as Managers," *Wall Street Journal*, May 15, 1989.

70. George Mannes, "Don't Give Up on the Web," *Fortune* (March 5, 2001): 184B–184L.

71. Bridgett Finn, "Selling Cool in a Bottle," *Business 2.0* (December 1, 2003) (http://money.cnn.com/magazines/business2/business2_archive/2003/12/01/354202/index.htm) (accessed November 5, 2008).

72. Amanda Walmac, "Full of Beans," *Working Woman* (February 1999): 38–40.

73. Udayan Gupta and Jeffery A. Tannenbaum, "Labor Shortages Force Changes at Small Firms," *Wall Street Journal*, May 22, 1989; "Harnessing Employee Productivity," *Small Business Report* (November 1987): 46–49; and Molly Kilmas, "How to Recruit a Smart Team," *Nation's Business* (May 1995): 26–27.

74. Saul Hansell, "Listen Up! It's Time for a Profit: A Front Row Seat as Amazon Gets Serious," *New York Times*, May 20, 2001.

Name Index

A

Abdul, Paula, 155
Abess, Leonard, 403
Adams, J. Stacy, 422
Adamy, Janet, 154
Adler, Nancy J., 76
Alban, Billie T., 259
Alderfer, Clayton, 417
Alexander, Francine, 292
Anderson, Mitch, 353
Anderson, Ray, 118
Andre, Rae, 505
Andrews, Edmund, 49
Ang, Soon, 96
Angle, Harold L., 255
Ante, Spencer E., 198
Antonellis, Dominic, 11
Armstrong, Lance, 472
Arpey, Gerald, 123
Arrington, Michael, 436
Arvey, R.D., 292
Ashford, S.J., 68
Assaf, Linda, 489
Athitakis, Mark, 82
Austen, I., 53
Axelrod, Emily M., 494
Axelrod, Richard, 494
Axtell, R., 88
Ayers, Charlie, 304

B

Baig, Edward C., 45
Baker, Dianne, 12
Baker, Kent, 425
Barbaro, Michael, 342
Barbaroza, David, 22
Barnard, Chester I., 28–29
Barnes, Brooks, 151, 355
Barrett, D., 430
Barrios, Sergio, 331
Bartholomew, Doug, 198
Bartz, Carol, 486
Bass, Bernard M., 387, 397
Bass, Steedman, 229
Bates, Suzanne, 494
Battista, Judy, 195
Battle, Hinton, 416
Battles, Rosa and Jorrick, 423
Bavega, Alok, 329
Bavelas, A., 430
Beale, Ruby L., 303
Becker, Selwyn W., 397
Beedon, Julie, 494
Beers, Michael C., 499
Begley, Thomas M., 163
Bell, Bob, 149

Bennet, Bill, 229
Bennett, Amanda, 299
Bennett, Monica, 486
Bennett, Stephen, 249, 424
Benson, Ray, 6
Bentham, Jeremy, 109
Benton, James M., 274
Berner, Mary, 222
Bernstein, Carl, 404
Betts, Paul, 79
Betzell, Ray, 501–502
Bezos, Jeff, 41, 482
Blais, Frances, 412, 413
Blanchard, Ken, 390–391
Blount, Karen, 499
Blow-Mitchell, Pamela, 306
Bohlander, George, 286
Boren, Suzanne A., 329
Boutin, Paul, 506
Bovée. C.L., 88
Boyd, David P., 163
Bratkovic, Beth, 494
Brin, Sergey, 253
Brown, Chris, 107
Brown, Michael, 121
Bruce, Reginald A., 267
Bubbeo, Daniel, 382
Bunker, Barbara Benedict, 259
Burger, J.M., 364
Buri, John R., 238
Burns, Lawton R., 397
Burrows, P., 53

C

Calhoun, David, 503
Callea, Donna, 370
Cameron, K., 424
Cameron, Kim S., 64
Campbell, J.P., 292
Campbell, Lewis, 335
Cannell, Kelly, 14
Cantrell, Susan, 274
Capell, Kerry, 250
Capowski, Genevieve, 386
Caproni, Paula J., 426
Caramanica, Jon, 261
Carr, David, 149, 232
Carroll, Archie B., 119
Carr-Rufino, Norma, 505
Carter, Bill, 504
Castagna, Vanessa, 307
Chandrasekar, N. Anand, 94
Chappell, Tom, 187
Childs, Ted, 295–296
Choo, Jimmy, 324
Chouinard, Yvon, 434

Chow, Chee W., 322
Cleveland, Joseph, 306
Clifford, Stephanie, 289
Coffin, Charles, 8
Coffman, Curt, 434
Cohen, Elizabeth, 475
Cohen, Rob, 285
Cohl, Michael, 226
Coin, Heather, 16
Colbert, B., 116
Collins, James, 149
Collins, Jim, 383
Colvin, Geoffrey, 428
Conley, Chip, 433
Conley, Lucas, 382
Constantine, Mark, 62
Convis, Gary, 337
Cook, John D., 352
Cook, Scott, 249
Coombs, W. Timothy, 147
Coulter, Mary, 299
Cowell, Simon, 155
Cowen, Scott, 21
Cox, Taylor Jr., 303
Coy, P., 53
Cramm, Susan, 422
Creswell, Julie, 413
Croon, Marcel A., 406
Crouse, Karen, 280
Cullen, John B., 127
Cullman, Joseph F., 383
Cunningham, Marcus, 434
Curtis, Kent, 311

D

Daft, Richard L., 425, 415
Daley, Kevin, 113
Daniel, Diann, 425
Darlin, Damon, 436
Davis, Keith, 99
de Mestral, George, 249
De Pree, D.J., 404
DeAngelis, David, 362
Decker, Susan, 386
DeCocinis, Mark, 59
Dee, Jonathan, 220
Deming, W. Edwards, 33
Denison, Daniel R., 352
Denison, D.R., 61
Dharchaudhuri, Indira, 287
Diesel, Vin, 285
DioGuardia, Kara, 261
Dowd, Maureen, 179
Down, John, 78
Drakerman, Lisa, 13
Drucker, Peter, 8, 143, 161

John, Brad, 519, 525
Johnson, David W., 385
Johnson, Dwayne, 355
Johnson, Frank P., 385
Johnson, M. Eric, 44
Johnson, Magic, 177
Johnson, Tori, 421
Johnstone, Keith, 439
Jones, Charisse, 107
Jones, George, 139
Jung, Andrea, 185
Jung, Carl, 364

K

Kaluzny, A., 397
Kanter, Rosabeth Moss, 250
Kantor, Mickey, 93
Kaplan, Michael, 288
Kaplan, Robert S., 137, 141, 322
Kaser, Joyce, 308
Katzenbach, Jon R., 473
Kauffman, Stuart, 178
Kawamoto, Nobuhiko, 220
Kazin, Michael, 49
Kelly, Robert E., 398
Kennedy, J., 89
Kepler, Nick, 257
Kern, Mark, 284
Kerrey, Bob, 433
Khatri, Naresh, 329
Khozein, Todd, 489
Kimble, Linda, 124
Kinneer, James W., 496
Kiper, Mel and Kim, 195
Kirby, Mike, 318
Kirkpatrick, S.A., 387
Klam, Danny, 321
Klam, Rock, 321
Klein, Gary, 180–181
Kleisterlee, Gerald, 415
Knight, Chuck, 191
Knowles, Beyoncé, 304
Knudstorp, Jorgen Vig, 64
Koenig, Richard W., 435
Koh, Christine, 96
Kohlberg, L., 111
Kohn, Alfie, 428
Kolata, Gina, 102
Kolind, Lars, 31
Kopp, Wendy, 362, 395
Koren, Yehuda, 149
Kotter, John P., 61, 262, 264
Krebs, Erc, 176
Kuhse, Patrick, 123

Kurtz, Kevin, 11
Kurtzman, Joel, 333
Kusy, Mitch, 432
Kyle, Cynthia, 510

L

Lade, Diane C., 22
LaDouceur, Bob, 388
Lafley, A.G., 254
Lahive, Ross, 115
Lambert, Art, 320
Lamy, Pascal, 93
Land, Edwin, 249
Lane, Harry W., 510
Langer, Amy, 371
Lasswell, Mark, 82
Latham, Gary, 421
Laudal, Terry, 274
Le Jeune, Michael, 261
Leahy, Tad, 198
Levine, Andrew, 331
Levine, J.B., 53
Lewin, Kurt, 263
Lickona, T., 111
Light, Alan, 160
Lindquist, Lee, 522
Liu, Ada, 79
Lively, John, 528
Locke, E.A., 387
Locke, Edwin, 421
Locklear, Dr. Lynn, 138
Loh, Zaneta, 321
Longstreth, David, 477
Lownes-Jackson, Millicent, 505
Lowry, Adam, 50
Loyalka, Michelle Dammon, 48

M

Machiavelli, Niccolo, 364
Maciariello, Joseph, 514
Mackenzie, S.B., 424
Mackey, John, 66, 433
Madoff, Bernard L., 21, 413
Magner, Marge, 307
Maher, Kris, 320
Mammo, Abate, 329
Manning, George, 311
Manning, Stephen, 486
Maples, Michael D., 435
Marcic, Dorothy, 37, 85, 205, 311, 379, 407
Marggraff, Jim, 45
Mariucci, Anne, 485
Marley, Patrick, 501
Marriott, Bill, 415

Masarech, Mary Ann, 65
Maslow, Abraham, 30, 415
Mason, Richard O., 204
Mathis, Robert L., 286
Maynard, Micheline, 403
Mayo, Elton, 29
McCaffrey, David P., 432
McClanaghan, Lillian, 502
McClelland, David, 419
McCollum, Lonnie, 518, 519, 527
McCroskey, J.C., 439
McFayden, Shannon, 362
McGovern, Pat, 94, 380, 385
McGrath, Joe, 79
McGregor, Douglas, 30
McKeever, Jeffrey, 191
McKinstry, Nancy, 76, 297
McMillen, Steve, 311
McNelis, John, 330
McNerney, Jim, 11
McShane, Steven L., 88
Mead, R., 88
Meindl, James R., 406
Mellon, Tamara, 324
Michaels, Rob, 412, 413
Middelhoff. Thomas, 74
Milken, Michael, 45
Mill, John Stuart, 109
Miller, Capt. Sean, 16
Miller, Jonathan, 183
Miller, Naomi, 311
Millett, Tim, 363
Milliott, Jim, 45
Mills, Don, 370
Mintzberg, Henry, 16, 17, 19, 415
Mishra, A.K., 61
Misra, Punit, 117–118
Moeller, Bruce, 6
Monforton, Lisa, 82
Moore, Diane, 113
Moorman, R.H., 424
Moran, Bill, 154
Morgan, Philip, 425
Morrison, Elizabeth W., 256
Morrison, E.W., 68
Mosakowski, Elaine, 96
Moss, Jonathan E., 278
Moss, Michael, 252
Mullin, Jen, 526
Myers, David, 124

N

Nardelli, Bob, 11, 212
Needleman, Sarah E., 421

Company Index

Subject Index

360-degree feedback, 291

A

Abilene paradox, 192, 428
acceptance theory of authority, 29, 214
accomodator learning style, 338
accountability, 214–215
achievement culture, 63
acquired needs theory, 385–386
acquisitions, 257
adaptability culture, 61–62
adapting to environment, 55–56
adaptive cultures, 60–61
adjourning stage of team development, 425
administrative model of decision-making, 178, 179–181
administrative principles, 28
affective component of attitudes, 320
affirmative action, 275, 283
Age Discrimination in Employment Act, 303
aging workforce, 296
alienated followers, 364
ambidextrous approach, 248
ambiguity and decision making, 177
American Idol, 155, 261
Americans with Disabilities Act, 283, 303
analytical decision styles, 188
application form, 286
assertiveness, 86
assessment center, 288
assimilator learning style, 338
attitudes
    components, 320–321
    conflicts, 323–324
    definition, 319
    high-performance, 321–323
attributions, 326–328
authoritarianism, 333
authority, 214
avoidance learning, 392

B

bad decisions, 188–190
balance sheets, 481
balanced scorecard, 475
bargaining power of buyers and suppliers, 158
BARS (behaviorally anchored rating scale), 292–293
base of the pyramid, 117
Because I Said So, 535
behavior modification, 391

behavioral approaches to understanding leadership
    leadership grid, 355
    Ohio State studies, 354
    task-oriented and people-oriented behavior, 353
    University of Michigan studies, 354–355
behavioral component of attitudes, 320
behavioral decision styles, 188
behavioral sciences approach, 33
behaviorally anchored rating scale (BARS), 292–293
benchmarking, 33–34, 488
benefits, 294
bias
    ethnocentrism, 304–305
    prejudice, discrimination, stereotypes, 302–304
Big Five personality factors, 328–329
big hairy audacious goal (BHAG), 149
blogs, 199, 390, 402
bottom-of-the-pyramid (BOP) concept, 117–118
boundary-spanning activities, 55–56
bounded rationality, 179
brainstorming, 191
brainwriting, 191
bribery, 112–113
budgetary control, 480–481
bureaucracy, 27
bureaucratic organizations, 26–27
business intelligence, 55
business intelligence software, 194
business performance dashboards, 150–151, 198
business process aspect of balanced scorecard, 476
business process reengineering, 235
business-level strategy, 157–161
buyers and bargaining power, 158

C

cafeteria-plan benefits packages, 294
Canada
    cultural intelligence, 94
    NAFTA, 91–92
careers
    changing nature, 276–280
    women's careers, 305–309
    see also HRM
central planning departments, 148
centralization, 218–220
centralized network, 396
ceremonies and corporate culture, 60

certainty and decision making, 176
chain of command, 214–217
change
    agent, 260
    changing nature of careers, 276–280
    changing people and culture, 256–260
    changing social contract, 276–278
    coercion, 265
    communication and education, 264
    culture change, 257, 259
    force-field analysis, 263–264
    implementation tactics, 264–265
    management support, 265
    need, 260–261
    negotiation, 265
    participation, 265
    people change, 256
    product change, 248
    resistance, 261–263
    technology change, 248
    training and development, 257
    see also innovation
changing as OD step, 260
changing social contract, 276–278
    see also HRM
channels of communication
    appropriate channels, 386–387
    channel definition, 383
    channel richness, 385–386
    communication channels, 385–387
    see also communication; organizational communication
charismatic leadership, 360–362
Charlie Wilson's War, 529
chief accounting officer, 122
chief ethics officer, 122
China
    business relationships, 48, 89
    international business, 46–47, 80
    lead paint, 22, 80
    vitamin supplies, 51–52
CIL (Committee on Industrial Lighting), 29
Civil Rights Act of 1964, 275, 303
Civil Rights Act of 1991, 307
classical model of decision-making, 178
classical perspective
    administrative principles, 28–29
    background, 24–25
    bureaucratic organizations, 26–27
    definition, 24
    scientific management, 25–26
CMP (crisis-management plans), 148
coaching, 290
coalition building, 181
coalitions, 181

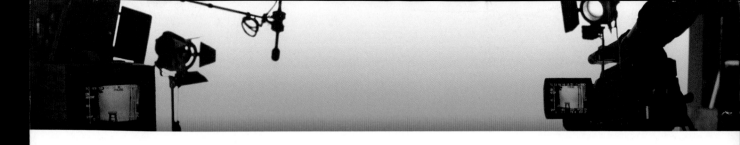